THE LAW OF PROPERTY
IN SCOTLAND

THE LAW OF PROPERTY IN SCOTLAND

Kenneth G C Reid MA, LLB, Solicitor
Professor of Property Law in the University of Edinburgh
Member of the Scottish Law Commission

with

FEUDAL SYSTEM by
George L Gretton BA, LLB, WS, NP
Lord President Reid Professor of Law in the University of Edinburgh

SERVITUDES and PUBLIC RIGHTS OF WAY by
A G M Duncan MA, LLB, WS
Formerly Senior Lecturer in Scots Law in the University of Edinburgh

CORPOREAL MOVEABLE PROPERTY by
William M Gordon MA, LLB, PHD
Douglas Professor of Civil Law in the University of Glasgow

SALE OF GOODS by
Alan J Gamble LLB, LLM, Advocate
Full-Time Chairman, Independent Tribunal Service

The Law Society of Scotland
Butterworths
Edinburgh   1996

The Law Society of Scotland
The Law Society's Hall, 26 Drumsheugh Gardens, EDINBURGH EH3 7YR

Butterworths United Kingdom	Butterworths, a Division of Reed Elsevier (UK) Ltd, 4 Hill Street, EDINBURGH EH2 3JZ and Halsbury House, 35 Chancery Lane, LONDON WC2A 1EL
Australia	Butterworths, Sydney, Melbourne, Brisbane, Adelaide, Perth, Canberra and Hobart
Canada	Butterworths Canada Ltd, Toronto and Vancouver
Ireland	Butterworth (Ireland) Ltd, Dublin
Malaysia	Malayan Law Journal Sdn Bhd, Kuala Lumpur
New Zealand	Butterworths of New Zealand Ltd, Wellington and Auckland
Singapore	Reed Elsevier (Singapore) Pte Ltd, Singapore
South Africa	Butterworths Publishers (Pty) Ltd, Durban
USA	Michie, Charlottesville, Virginia

First published 1996

A CIP Catalogue record for this book is
available from the British Library

ISBN 0 406 999 171

ISBN 0-406-99917-1

9 780406 999177

Typeset by Phoenix Photosetting, Chatham, Kent
Printed in Great Britain by
Antony Rowe Ltd, Chippenham, Wiltshire

Visit us on our website: http://www.butterworths.co.uk

Preface

This book is in essence a reprint of volume 18 of the *Laws of Scotland: Stair Memorial Encyclopaedia* but omitting the section on intellectual property. Volume 18 was published in 1993, but in this reprint it has been possible to incorporate all major changes and developments up to 1 August 1996. For later developments recourse may be had to the Updating Service of the *Encyclopaedia*.

Volume 18 took many years to write, and I am indebted to a number of people for help given in various ways. Here, however, I mention only one. My colleague Professor George Gretton has debated issues of property law with me since we were undergraduates together. To these discussions, which still continue, this book owes a special debt.

Kenneth G C Reid
Edinburgh
Lammas 1996

Authorship of this work

RIGHTS AND THINGS; CO-OWNERSHIP

Professor Kenneth G C Reid

FEUDAL SYSTEM

Professor George L Gretton

POSSESSION; LANDOWNERSHIP; WATER; REAL CONDITIONS;
REAL BURDENS

Professor Kenneth G C Reid

SERVITUDES

A G M Duncan

PUBLIC RIGHTS OVER LAND AND WATER

Paragraphs 494–513
Professor Kenneth G C Reid

Paragraphs 514–529
A G M Duncan

CORPOREAL MOVEABLE PROPERTY

Professor William M Gordon

ACCESSION

Paragraphs 570–587; 592–596
Professor Kenneth G C Reid

Paragraphs 588–591
Professor William M Gordon

TRANSFER OF OWNERSHIP

Paragraphs 597–607; 610–614; 640–670; 672–679; 684–719
Professor Kenneth G C Reid

Paragraphs 608–609; 615–623
Professor William M Gordon

Paragraphs 624–639; 671; 680–683
Alan J Gamble

Contents

NOTE: Throughout this work there are cross references to titles in the *Laws of Scotland: Stair Memorial Encyclopaedia*. These references comprise the title name in small capitals, usually followed by the volume number and sometimes followed by paragraph numbers, for example: 'WILLS AND SUCCESSION, vol 25, para 682.'

Table of Statutes

1

Table of Orders, Rules and Regulations

Table of Cases

A

References are to paragraphs

15

References are to paragraphs

B

References are to paragraphs

References are to paragraphs

C

References are to paragraphs

References are to paragraphs

References are to paragraphs

References are to paragraphs

References are to paragraphs

E

F

References are to paragraphs

G

References are to paragraphs

References are to paragraphs

H

References are to paragraphs

References are to paragraphs

References are to paragraphs

K

L

References are to paragraphs

References are to paragraphs

M

References are to paragraphs

References are to paragraphs

References are to paragraphs

References are to paragraphs

N

O

References are to paragraphs

References are to paragraphs

Q

R

References are to paragraphs

S

References are to paragraphs

References are to paragraphs

References are to paragraphs

T

References are to paragraphs

U

References are to paragraphs

References are to paragraphs

Y

References are to paragraphs

Z

References are to paragraphs

Abbreviations

AC	Law Reports, Appeal Cases (House of Lords and Privy Council) 1890–
AD	Appellate Division (S Africa) 1910–46
AD	Annual Digest and Reports of Public International Law Cases 1919–1949
AFDI	*Annuaires français de droit international* (1955–)
A-G	Attorney-General
AJCL	American Journal of Comparative Law
AJIL	American Journal of International Law (1907–)
ALR	Argus Law Reports (Australia) 1895–1973, and Australian Law Reports 1973–
AMS	Ancient Manuscripts of Scotland
APS	Acts of the Parliament of Scotland
AS	Act of Sederunt
AYIL	Australian Yearbook of International Law
Act of Adj	Act of Adjournal
Ad & El	Adolphus and Ellis's Reports (King's Bench and Queen's Bench) (England) 1834–42
Adam	Adam's Justiciary Reports 1894–1919
All ER	All England Law Reports 1936–
All ER Rev	All England Law Reports Annual Review 1982–
App Cas	Law Reports, Appeal Cases (House of Lords) 1875–90
App D	Appellate Division (S Africa) 1910–46
App Div	Appellate Division (New York Supreme Court) 1896–1955; 2d, 1955–
Arkley	Arkley's Justiciary Reports 1846–48
Arnot	Arnot's Criminal Trials 1536–1784
Asp MLC	Aspinall's Maritime Law Cases 1870–1943
ATC	Annotated Tax Cases 1922–
Aust	Australia
B & Ad	Barnewall and Adolphus's Reports (King's Bench) (England) 1830–34
B & Ald	Barnewall and Alderson's Reports (King's Bench) (England) 1817–22
B & C	Barnewall and Cresswell's Reports (King's Bench) (England) 1822–30
B & CR	Bankruptcy and Companies Winding up Reports 1918–41
B & S	Best and Smith's Reports (Queen's Bench) (England) 1861–70
BCC	British Company Cases (1983–)
BCLC	Butterworths Company Law Cases 1983–
BCR	British Columbia Reports 1867–1947
BILC	British International Law Cases
BTLC	Butterworths Trading Law Cases 1986–
BTR	British Tax Review 1956–
BYIL	British Yearbook of International Law 1920–
Beav	Beavan's Reports (Rolls Court) (England) 1838–66
Bell App	S S Bell's Scotch Appeals (House of Lords) 1842–50
Bell Fol Cas	P Bell's Folio Cases (Court of Session) 1794–95
Bell Oct Cas	P Bell's Octavo Cases (Court of Session) 1790–92
Bing	Bingham's Reports (Common Pleas) (England) 1822–34
Bing NC	Bingham's New Cases (Common Pleas) (England) 1834–40
Biss & Sm	Bisset and Smith's Digest (S Africa)

Bligh	Bligh's Reports (House of Lords) 1819–21
Bligh NS	Bligh's Reports, New Series (House of Lords) 1827–37
Bos & P	Bosanquet and Puller's Reports (Common Pleas) (England) 1796–1804
Bos & PNR	Bosanquet and Puller's New Reports (Common Pleas) (England) 1804–07
Bro Parl Cas	J Brown's Cases in Parliament, 8 vols, 1702–1800
Broun	Broun's Justiciary Reports 1842–45
Brown's Supp	Brown's Supplement to Morison's Dictionary of Decisions (Court of Session) 1622–1794
Brown's Syn	Brown's Synopsis of Decisions (Court of Session) 1532–1827
Bruce	Bruce's Decisions (Court of Session) 1714–15
Buchan	Buchanan's Reports (Court of Session) 1800–13
Burr	Burrow's Reports, King's Bench, 5 vols, 1756–1772
C	Command Papers 1833–99
CA	Court of Appeal
CAR	Commonwealth Arbitration Reports 1905–65
C & P	Carrington and Payne's Reports (Nisi Prius) (England) 1823–41
CB	Common Bench (England) 1845–56
CBNS	Common Bench, New Series (England) 1856–65
CCR	County Court Rules (England)
CDE	*Cahiers de Droit Européen* (1965–)
CFI	Court of First Instance
CL	Current Law 1947–
CLJ	Cambridge Law Journal
CLR	Commonwealth Law Reports (Australia) 1903–
CLY	Current Law Year Book 1947–
CMLR	Common Market Law Reports 1962–
CML Rev	Common Market Law Review (1963–)
CPD	Law Reports, Common Pleas Division (England) 1875–80
CYIL	Canadian Yearbook of International Law
Camb LJ	Cambridge Law Journal 1921–
Camp	Campbell's Reports (Nisi Prius) (England) 1807–16
Cas tep Talb	Cases in Equity temp Talbot
Cd	Command Papers 1900–18
Ch	Law Reports, Chancery Division (England) 1890–
Ch App	Law Reports, Chancery Appeals (England) 1865–75
Ch D	Law Reports, Chancery Division (England) 1875–90
Ch Rob	Christopher Robinson's Reports (Admiralty) (England) 1798–1808
Cl & Fin	Clark and Finnelly's Reports (House of Lords) 1831–46
Cm	Command Papers 1986–
C-MAC	Courts-Martial Appeal Court
Cmd	Command Papers 1919–56
Cmnd	Command Papers 1956–86
Com Cas	Commercial Cases 1895–1941
Com Dig	Comyn's Digest 1792 (England)
Com LR	Commercial Law Reports 1981–
Conv (NS)	Conveyancer and Property Lawyer
Conv Rev	Conveyancing Review 1957–1963
Cornell ILJ	Cornell International Law Journal
Coup	Couper's Justiciary Reports 1868–85
Cox CC	Cox's Criminal Cases (England) 1843–1941
Cr App Rep	Criminal Appeal Reports (England) 1908–
Crim LR	Criminal Law Review (England) 1954–

D	Dunlop's Session Cases 1838–62
DC	Divisional Court
D (HL)	House of Lords cases in Dunlop's Session Cases 1838–62
DLR	Dominion Law Reports (Canada) 1912–55; 2d, 1956–67; 3d, 1968–83; 4th 1984–
DNB	Dictionary of National Biography
Dalr	Dalrymple's Decisions (Court of Session) 1698–1718
Deas & And	Deas and Anderson's Decisions (Court of Session) 1829–32
De G	De Gex (Bankruptcy) (England) 1844–48
De G & J	De Gex and Jones's Reports (Chancery) (England) 1857–59
De G & Sm	De Gex and Smale's Reports (Chancery) (England) 1846–52
De G F & J	De Gex, Fisher and Jones's Reports (Chancery) (England) 1859–62
De G J & Sm	De Gex, Jones and Smith's Reports (Chancery) (England) 1862–65
De G M & G	De Gex, Macnaghten and Gordon's Reports (Chancery) (England) 1851–57
Dirl	Dirleton's Decisions (Court of Session) 1665–77
Dods	Dodson's Reports (Admiralty) (England) 1811–22
Dow	Dow's Reports (House of Lords) 1812–18
Dow & Cl	Dow and Clark's Reports (House of Lords) 1827–32
Durie	Durie's Decisions (Court of Session) 1621–42
EAT	Employment Appeal Tribunal
E & B	Ellis and Blackburn's Reports (Queen's Bench) (England) 1852–58
E & E	Ellis and Ellis's Reports (Queen's Bench) (England) 1858–61
E B & E	Ellis, Blackburn and Ellis's Reports (Queen's Bench) (England) 1858–60
EC	European Communities
ECHR	European Court of Human Rights
ECJ	European Court of Justice (Court of Justice of the European Communities)
ECR	European Court of Justice Reports 1954–
ECSC	European Coal and Steel Community
EEC	European Economic Community
EG	Estates Gazette 1858–
EGD	Estates Gazette Digest 1902–
EHD	English Historical Documents
EHR	Economic History Review
EHRR	European Human Rights Reports 1979–
EIPR	European Intellectual Property Review
ER	English Reports 1220–1865
Edgar	Edgar's Decisions (Court of Session) 1724–26
Elchies	Elchies' Decisions (Court of Session) 1733–54
Eng Judg	Decisions of English Judges during the Usurpation 1655–61
Eq Rep	Equity Reports (England) 1853–55
Esp	Espinasse's Nisi Prius Reports (England) 1793–1807
Euratom	European Atomic Energy Community
EuR	*Europarecht* (1966–)
Eur LR	European Law Review (1955–)
Eur YB	European Yearbook (1962–)
Ex D	Law Reports, Exchequer Division (England) 1875–80
Exch	Exchequer Reports (England) 1847–56
F	Fraser's Session Cases 1898–1906 (preceded by year and volume number); Federal Reporter (USA) 1880–1924; 2d, 1924– (preceded by volume number and followed by year)
FC	Faculty Collection (Court of Session) 1752–1825
F (HL)	House of Lords cases in Fraser's Session Cases 1898–1906

F (J)	Justiciary cases in Fraser's Session Cases 1898–1906
FLR	Family Law Reports (1980–)
FSR	Fleet Street Reports 1963–
F Supp	Federal Supplement (USA) 1932–
Falc	Falconer's Decisions (Court of Session) 1744–51
Fam	Law Reports, Family Division (England) 1972–
Ferg	Ferguson's Consistorial Decisions 1811–17
Forbes	Forbes' Journal of the Sessions 1705–13
Fount	Fountainhall's Decisions (Court of Session) 1678–1712
GA Resoln	General Assembly Resolution
GWD	Green's Weekly Digest 1986–
GYIL	German Yearbook of International Law
Gaz LR	Gazette Law Reports (New Zealand) 1898–1953
Gil & Fal	Gilmour's and Falconer's Decisions (Court of Session) 1661–66, 1681–86
Guth Sh Cas	Guthrie's Select Sheriff Court Cases
H & C	Hurlstone and Coltman's Reports (Exchequer) (England) 1862–66
H & N	Hurlstone and Norman's Reports (Exchequer) (England) 1856–62
HC	High Court
HL	House of Lords
HL Cas	House of Lords Cases 1847–66
HLR	Housing Law Reports 1981–
Hague Recueil	Hague Academy of International Law Recueil de Cours
Hailes	Hailes' Decisions (Court of Session) 1766–91
Hale PC	Hale's Pleas of the Crown 1678
Harc	Harcarse's Decisions (Court of Session) 1681–91
Hawk PC	Hawkin's Pleas of the Crown
Home	Clerk Home's Decisions (Court of Session) 1735–44
Hume	Hume's Decisions (Court of Session) 1781–1822
ICJ	International Court of Justice
ICJR	International Court of Justice Reports
ICLQ	International and Comparative Law Quarterly (1952–)
ICLQR	International and Comparative Law Quarterly Review 1952–
ICR	Industrial Cases Reports (England) 1972–
IH	Inner House
IL	The International Lawyer
ILJ	Industrial Law Journal
ILM	International Legal Materials
ILR	Irish Law Reports 1838–50
ILT	Irish Law Times 1867–
ILT Jo	Irish Law Times Journal 1867–
IR	Irish Reports 1893–
IRLR	Industrial Relations Law Reports 1972–
ITR	Industrial Tribunal Reports 1966–78
Imm AR	Immigration Appeal Reports 1972–
Ind JIL	Indian Journal of International Law (1960–)
Int Aff	International Affairs (1922–)
Int LR	International Law Reports
Irv	Irvine's Justiciary Reports 1851–68
J	Justice
JBL	Journal of Business Law
JC	Justiciary Cases 1917–
JCMS	Journal of Common Market Studies (1962–)

JDI	*Journal de Droit International* (1915–)
J Juris	Journal of Jurisprudence 1857–91
JLSS	Journal of the Law Society of Scotland 1956–
JO CECA	*Journal Officiel de la Communauté Européen du Charbon et de l'Acier* (1952–58)
JP	Justice of the Peace Reports (England) 1837–
JP Jo	Justice of the Peace and Local Government Review (England) 1837–
JPL	Journal of Planning Law 1948–53; Journal of Planning and Property Law 1954–72; and Journal of Planning and Environment Law 1973–
J Shaw	J Shaw's Justiciary Reports 1848–51
JR	Juridical Review 1889–
JSPTL	Journal of the Society of Public Teachers of Law
Jur Soc P	Juridical Society Papers 1858–74
JWTL	Journal of World Trade Law (1967–)
KB	Law Reports, King's Bench Division (England) 1900–52
KIR	Knight's Industrial Reports (England) 1966–75
K & J	Kay and Johnson's Reports (Chancery) (England) 1853–58
K & W Dic	Kames' and Woodhouselee's Dictionary of Decisions (Court of Session) 1540–1796
Kames Rem Dec	Kames' Remarkable Decisions (Court of Session) 1716–28
Kames Sel Dec	Kames' Select Decisions (Court of Session) 1752–68
Kilk	Kilkerran's Decisions (Court of Session) 1738–52
LA	Lord Advocate
LC	Lord Chancellor
LCJ	Lord Chief Justice
L Ed	Lawyer's Edition, United States Supreme Court Reports, 1754–1956
L Ed 2d	Lawyer's Edition, United States Supreme Court Reports, Second Series, 1956–(current)
LGR	Knight's Local Government Reports 1902–
LIEI	Legal Issues of European Integration (1974–)
LJ	Law Journal newspaper (England) 1866–1965; Lord Justice
L J-C	Lord Justice-Clerk
LJ Ch	Law Journal, Chancery (England) 1831–1946
LJ Ex	Law Journal, Exchequer (England) 1831–75
L J-G	Lord Justice-General
LJKB	Law Journal, King's Bench (England) 1900–52
LJP	Law Journal, Probate, Divorce and Admiralty (England) 1875–1946
LJPC	Law Journal, Privy Council 1865–1946
LJQB	Law Journal, Queen's Bench Division (England) 1831–1900
LJR	Law Journal Reports (England) 1947–49
LQR	Law Quarterly Review 1885–
LR A & E	Law Reports, Admiralty and Ecclesiastical (England) 1865–75
LRCCR	Law Reports, Crown Cases Reserved (England) 1865–75
LRCP	Law Reports, Common Pleas (England) 1865–75
LR Eq	Law Reports, Equity (England) 1865–75
LR Exch	Law Reports, Exchequer (England) 1865–75
LRHL	Law Reports, House of Lords (England and Ireland) 1866–75
LR Ir	Law Reports, Ireland 1877–93
LR P & D	Law Reports, Probate and Divorce (England) 1865–75
LRPC	Law Reports, Privy Council 1865–75
LRQB	Law Reports, Queen's Bench (England) 1865–75
LRRP	Law Reports, Restrictive Practices 1957–
LR Sc & Div	Law Reports, House of Lords (Scotch and Divorce) 1866–75
LS Gaz	Law Society's Gazette (England) 1903–
LT	Law Times Reports (England) 1859–1947

LT Jo	Law Times newspaper (England) 1843–1947
LTOS	Law Times Reports, Old Series (England) 1843–59
LVAC	Lands Valuation Appeal Court
Land Ct	Scottish Land Court
Law Com	Law Commission (England)
Ll L Rep	Lloyd's List Law Reports 1919–50
Lloyd's Rep	Lloyd's List Law Reports 1951–67; Lloyd's Law Reports 1968–
LoNJ	League of Nations Journal
LoNTS	League of Nations Treaty Series
Lyon Ct	Court of the Lord Lyon
M	Macpherson's Session Cases 1862–73
M (HL)	House of Lords cases in Macpherson's Session Cases 1862–73
M & S	Maule and Selwyn's Reports (King's Bench) (England) 1813–17
M & W	Meeson and Welsby (England) 1836–47
MLR	Modern Law Review 1937–
MR	Master of the Rolls
Mac & G	Macnaghten and Gordon's Reports (Chancery) (England) 1849–52
MacF	MacFarlane's Jury Trials (Court of Session) 1838–39
MacG Cop Cas	MacGillivray's Copyright Cases, 9 vols, 1901–1949
Macl & R	Maclean and Robinson's Scotch Appeals (House of Lords) 1839
Maclaurin	Maclaurin's Arguments and Decisions 1670–1770
Macq	Macqueen's House of Lords Reports 1851–65
Macr	Macrory's Patent Cases, 2 parts, 1847–1856
Mer	Merivale's Reports (Chancery) (England) 1815–17
Misc	New York Miscellaneous Reports 1892–1955; 2d, 1955–
Moo PCC	Moore's Privy Council Cases 1836–63
Moo PCCNS	Moore's Privy Council Cases, New Series 1862–1973
Mood & M	Moody and Malkin's Nisi Prius Reports (England) 1826–30
Moore Int Arb	Moore's History and Digest of International Arbitrations
Mor	Morison's Dictionary of Decisions (Court of Session) 1540–1808
Mun LR	Municipal Law Reports 1903–13
Murr	Murray's Jury Court Cases 1815–30
NI	Northern Ireland Law Reports 1925–
NJW	*Niue Juristische Wochenschrift* (1947–)
NLJ	New Law Journal (England) 1965–
NMS	National Manuscripts of Scotland
NY	New York Court of Appeals Reports 1847–1955; 2d, 1956–
NYS	New York Supplement 1888–1937; 2d, 1938–
NZ	New Zealand
NZLR	New Zealand Law Reports 1883–
NZULR	New Zealand University Law Review 1963–
OCR	Ordinary Cause Rules
OH	Outer House
OJ	Official Journal of the European Communities; C, Information; L, Legislation
OJEPO	Official Journal of the European Patent Office
OJLS	Oxford Journal of Legal Studies (1981–)
OLR	Ontario Law Reports 1901–30
OR	Ontario Reports 1931–73; 2d, 1974–
P	Law Reports, Probate, Divorce and Admiralty Division (England) 1890–1971
P & CR	Planning and Compensation Reports 1949–67; Property and Compensation Reports 1968– (England)
PC	Judicial Committee of the Privy Council

PCIJ	Permanent Court of International Justice Reports
PD	Law Reports, Probate, Divorce and Admiralty Division (England) 1875–90
PE Debs	European Parliament Debates
PL	Public Law
Pat	Paton's House of Lords Appeal Cases 1726–1821
Paters	Paterson's House of Lords Appeals 1851–73
Pitc	Pitcairn's Criminal Trials 1488–1624
Pol Q	Political Quarterly
QB	Queen's Bench Reports (England) 1841–52 (volume number precedes)
QB	Law Reports, Queen's Bench Division (England) 1891–1901, 1952– (year precedes)
QBD	Law Reports, Queen's Bench Division (England) 1875–90
QC	Queen's Counsel
R	Rettie's Session Cases 1873–98
RA	Rating Appeals 1965–
RBDI	*Revue belge de droit international* (1965–)
RC	Rules of the Court of Session
RdC	*Recueil des Cours* (Hague Recueil) (1923–)
RDE	*Revista di diritto europeo* (1961–)
RDI	*Revista di diritto internazionale* (1896–)
RFSP	*Revue française des sciences politiques*
RGDIP	*Revue général de droit international public* (1896–)
RGS	Register of the Great Seal of Scotland
RHDI	*Revue hellenique de droit international* (1948–)
R (HL)	House of Lords cases in Rettie's Session Cases 1873–98
RICS	Royal Institution of Chartered Surveyors, Scottish Lands Valuation Appeal Reports
R (J)	Justiciary cases in Rettie's Session Cases 1873–98
RMC	*Revue du Marché Commun* (1958–)
RPC	Reports of Patents, Designs and Trade Marks Cases 1884–; Restrictive Practices Court
RRC	Ryde's Rating Cases (England) 1956–
RSC	Rules of the Supreme Court (England)
RTDE	*Revue trimestrielle de droit européen* (1965–)
RTR	Road Traffic Reports 1970–
RVR	Rating and Valuation Reports (England) 1960–
Robert	Robertson's Scotch Appeals (House of Lords) 1707–27
Robin	Robinson's Scotch Appeals (House of Lords) 1840–41
Rose	Rose's Reports (Bankruptcy) (England) 1810–16
Ross LC	G Ross's Leading Cases in the Law of Scotland (Land Rights) 1638–1849
S	P Shaw's Session Cases 1821–38 (NE indicates New Edition)
SA	South African Law Reports 1947–
SALJ	South African Law Journal
SAL Rev	South African Law Review
SAR	South African Supreme Court Reports 1881–92
S & D Just	Shaw and Dunlop's Justiciary Cases 1819–31
SC	Session Cases 1907–; Supreme Court
SCCR	Scottish Criminal Case Reports 1981–
SCCR Supp	Scottish Criminal Case Reports Supplement 1950–80
SC (HL)	House of Lords cases in Session Cases 1907–
SC (J)	Justiciary Cases in Session Cases 1907–16
SCLR	Scottish Civil Law Reports 1987–

SCOLAG	The journal of the Scottish Legal Action Group
SCR	Summary Cause Rules
SC Resoln	Security Council Resolution
Sel Cas Ch	Select Cases in Chancery (England) 1724–33
SHLN	Scottish Housing Law News
SI	Statutory Instruments
SJ	Scottish Jurist 1829–73
SLCR	Scottish Land Court Reports in Scottish Law Review (1913–63) (preceded by year and volume number), and Scottish Land Court Reports 1982– (preceded by year)
SLCR App	Appendix to the annual reports of the Scottish Land Court 1963–
SLG	Scottish Law Gazette 1933–
SLJ	Scottish Law Journal and Sheriff Court Record 1858–61
SLM	Scottish Law Magazine and Sheriff Court Reporter 1862–67
SLPQ	Scottish Law and Practice Quarterly 1995–
SLR	Scottish Law Reporter 1865–1925
SL Rev	Scottish Law Review and Sheriff Court Reporter 1885–1963
SLT	Scots Law Times 1893–1908 (preceded by year and volume number), and 1909– (preceded by year)
SLT (ECCN)	Scots Law Times European Court Case Notes (1984–)
SLT (Land Ct)	Scottish Land Court Reports in Scots Law Times 1964–
SLT (Lands Trib)	Lands Tribunal for Scotland Reports in Scots Law Times 1971–
SLT (Lyon Ct)	Lyon Court Reports in Scots Law Times 1950–
SLT (Notes)	Notes of Recent Decisions in Scots Law Times 1946–1981
SLT (Sh Ct)	Sheriff Court Reports in Scots Law Times 1893–
SN	Session Notes 1925–48
SO	Standing Orders
SPD	State Papers Domestic
SPLP	Scottish Planning Law and Practice 1980–
SR & O	Statutory Rules and Orders
SRR	Scots Revised Reports 1707–1873, 1898–1908
STC	Simon's Tax Cases 1973–
Scot Law Com	Scottish Law Commission
Scot Hist Rev	Scottish Historical Review
Sh & Macl	P Shaw and Maclean's House of Lords Appeal Cases 1835–38
Sh App	P Shaw's Scotch Appeals (House of Lords) 1821–26
Sh Ct Rep	Sheriff Court Reports in Scottish Law Review 1885–1963
Shaw Just	P Shaw's Justiciary Reports 1819–31
Shaw Teind	P Shaw's Teind Court Decisions 1821–31
Sim	Simon's Reports (Chancery) (England) 1826–52
Sim & St	Simon & Stuart's Reports (Chancery) (England) 1822–26
Sim NS	Simon's Reports, New Series (Chancery) (England) 1850–52
Smith LC	Smith's Leading Cases (England)
Sol Jo	Solicitors' Journal (England) 1856–
Stair Rep	Stair's Reports (Court of Session) 1661–81
Stair Soc	Stair Society
State Tr	State Trials 1163–1820
State Tr NS	State Trials, New Series 1820–58
Stuart	Stuart, Milne and Peddie's Reports (Court of Session) 1851–53
Swan	Swanston's Reports (Chancery) (England) 1818–21
Swin	Swinton's Justiciary Reports 1835–41
Syme	Syme's Justiciary Reports 1826–29
TC	Tax Cases 1875–
TLR	Times Law Reports (England) 1884–1952
TR	Taxation Reports 1939–
TS	United Kingdom Treaty Series
Taunt	Taunton's Reports (Common Pleas) (England) 1807–19

Term Rep	Term Reports (England) 1785–1800
Tul LR	Tulane Law Review (1929–)
UNRIAA	United Nations Reports of International Arbitral Awards
UNTS	United Nations Treaty Series
US	United States Supreme Court Reports 1754–
VATTR	Value Added Tax Tribunal Reports 1973–
V-C	Vice-Chancellor
VLR	Victorian Law Reports 1875–1956
VR	Victorian Reports 1870–72, and 1957–
Ves	Vesey Junior's Reports (Chancery) (England) 1789–1817
Ves Sen	Vesey Senior's Reports (Chancery) (England) 1747–56
WALR	West Australian Law Reports 1898–1959
WAR	Western Australian Reports 1960–
W & S	Wilson and Shaw's House of Lords Cases 1825–34
WLR	Weekly Law Reports (England) 1953–
WN	Law Reports, Weekly Notes (England) 1866–1952
WR	Weekly Reporter (England) 1852–1906
WS	Writer to the Signet
WWR	Western Weekly Reports (Canada) 1911–1950, and 1955–
West	West's House of Lords Reports 1839–41
White	White's Justiciary Reports 1885–93
WuW	*Wirtschaft und Wettbewerb* (1951–)
YB	Year Books
YBILC	Yearbook of the International Law Commission
YBWA	Yearbook of World Affairs
YEL	Yearbook of European Law (1981–)
ZaöRV	*Zeitschrift für ausländisches öffentliches Recht und Völkerrecht* (1929–)

Contents

1. RIGHTS AND THINGS

(1) INTRODUCTION

1. A unitary law of property? The law of property, on one view, is no more than a collective name for three essentially different sets of rules which have developed in the different contexts of land, corporeal moveables, and incorporeal property. In Scotland this is the view which has tended to prevail in modern times. Such a view denies, or at least plays down, the number of common principles which are shared by property of all types. The approach adopted in this book is different. Its starting point is the thesis that the law of property is unitary in nature. There is only one set of rules and not three, although subject to local variations in particular cases. Of course this is not a new approach, but a very old one. It was perfectly familiar to the institutional writers, whose systematic exposition of the law involved the provision of separate books for the law of obligations and for the law of property[1]. It was familiar, too, from the *Institutes* of Justinian, the influence of which on the institutional writers was both extensive and profound[2].

So far as property law is concerned, the most extended attempt to present a unified treatment of the law is to be found, not in the traditional canon of institutional writings, but in the lectures of David Hume delivered to the students of the University of Edinburgh between 1786 and 1822[3]. The Stair Society has published these lectures in the form in which they were given in 1821–22, which was Hume's final year in office as Professor of Scots law[4]. The lectures are divided into five parts — Persons, Obligations, Property (two parts) and Actions — which is an expansion of the traditional tripartite classification of the Roman law (Persons, Things and Actions)[5]. Property is allocated two parts in recognition of the special nature of land law and of the feudal law on which it is based[6]. In the first part Hume sets out those rules which are of general applicability to both heritable and moveable property[7]. In the second part he expounds the feudal law. In both parts, but especially in the first, Hume's analysis is distinguished by its brilliance, originality and absolute clarity. No writer, either before or since, has made a more significant contribution to the literature of the law of property; even today Hume's *Lectures* remain a source of exceptional importance.

After Hume, the approach to property law changed. Hume's successor in the chair of Scots Law at Edinburgh University was George Joseph Bell, who had been his pupil, having attended his lectures in 1787–88. The present writer has in his possession a manuscript copy of notes made by a student who attended Bell's lectures during the session 1825–26. Superficially, they follow the same pattern as Hume's lectures, although the order now is Obligations, Property, Persons and Actions. But the treatment of property law is very different. As with Hume, the treatment is in two parts, but whereas Hume's division is into general principles and land law, Bell's division is into heritable property and moveable property. In Bell's lectures, the law of heritable property is treated as an entirely different subject from the law of moveable property, and no attempt is made to offer a general theory of property law[8]. Precisely the same pattern appears from Bell's *Principles*, the first edition of which appeared in 1829 and which was based on his lectures. The section on property law begins by noting the differences between heritable and moveable property, and the importance of feudal law for the former. It then continues:

> 'These different systems it may be proper to consider separately; taking first into view the jurisprudence of Land rights, and proceeding afterwards to the doctrines of property in Moveables'[9].

Probably one reason for the approach adopted by Bell was the establishment, in 1825, of a separate chair of conveyancing at Edinburgh University, and increasingly the intricacies of land law came to be seen as belonging more properly to lectures on conveyancing than to lectures on Scots law[10]. And so it was that, in the curriculum of Edinburgh University, and of the other Scottish universities also[11], the law of heritable property came to be severed from the law of moveable property; and, just as damagingly, the law of heritable property came to be seen as an appendix to the law of conveyancing, rather than, as might have been expected, the other way around[12].

It may be mistaken to place too much weight on the curricular organisation of universities. No doubt there were other factors at work also. But, whatever the causes, the result was that, after Hume, property law ceased to be viewed as a single integrated subject. There is no modern work giving a systematic and unitary exposition of the law of property, and in its absence the general principles of the subject have tended to be lost sight of, where they have not been disregarded altogether.

In this work an attempt is made to treat property law as a unitary subject, insofar as it is possible and useful to do so. The qualification is of course important. It would be idle to deny that in some areas of the law the rules are so different in relation to property of different types that an attempt at a unified treatment would be doomed to failure. As might be expected, the difficulty was anticipated by Hume:

> '[I]f we should examine at once the several articles of Real Right in their whole extent and application and should attempt alternately at each step of our progress, to illustrate two classes of rules, we should disjoint the members of each description, and be in no small risk of failing to gain a distinct notion of either'[13].

But there are many areas in which the rules are similar, or even identical, across the full spectrum of property. This is so in relation to topics as diverse as co-ownership, possession, accession, and the transfer of ownership. In cases such as these there can truly be said to be a general theory of property law, and it is one of the objects of the present work to attempt to identify that theory and to expound it.

1 Property law is treated in Book II and the opening titles of Book III of Stair's *Institutions*, and in Book II of Erskine's *Institutes*. Bankton's *Institutes* follows the same order as Stair but with the addition of a general discussion of the law in title 3 of Book I. Bankton calls his first Book 'Personal Rights' and his second 'Rights Real'. For Bell's *Principles*, see text and notes 8, 9, below.

2 Property law is the subject of Book II of Justinian's *Institutes*.

3 Hume was a pupil of John Millar, who was professor at Glasgow University from 1761 to 1801. There are some traces of Millar's influence in Hume's overall structure, but Millar's lecture course was very much shorter than Hume's, only fourteen lectures (out of fifty-one) being given to the law of property.

4 Ie Hume *Lectures* vols I–VI (Stair Soc vols 5 (1939), 13 (1949), 15 (1952), 17 (1955), 18 (1957) and 19 (1958), ed G C H Paton).

5 The tripartite classification is first found in Gaius *Institutes* I,8. See also Justinian *Institutes* I,2,12. Obligations were classified as part of Things.

6 Hume explains his organisation thus — 'It seems to be desirable to bestow on the doctrine of Real Rights a twofold discussion — one according to common and natural principles, so far as our practice has received these, and the other according to our feudal notions . . .': vol I (Stair Soc vol 5) p 11.

7 The most important section of this first part will be found at *Hume* vol III (Stair Soc vol 15) pp 202–261.

8 This is not, of course, to lay blame on Bell. Bell was a brilliant jurist but his interests lay elsewhere. Apart from his work on common property, which is of considerable importance and authority (see para 23 below), his contribution to the law of property is slight, at least by his own high standards.

9 Bell *Principles* s 636.

10 Of modern textbooks, W M Gloag and R C Henderson's *Introduction to the Law of Scotland*, now in its ninth edn (1987), most clearly illustrates the division of private law into Scots law and conveyancing. Gloag and Henderson is a book about Scots law. Thus it covers servitudes but not real burdens, pledge but not standard securities, and sale of goods but not sale of land.

11 The chair of conveyancing at Glasgow University was not established until 1861, but separate lectures on conveyancing had been instituted by the Faculty of Procurators much earlier, in 1817.

12 Conveyancing is part of the law of property, and not the other way about. In the *Stair Memorial Encyclopaedia* the general principles of property law are given in vol 18, while the detailed mechanics of conveyancing are given separately, in vol 6.

13 *Hume* vol 1 (Stair Soc vol 5) p 11.

2. Sources of property law. In Scotland, as in many other countries of Western Europe, the traditional sources of the law of property were Roman law and feudal law[1]. The modern position is different. Feudalism has long been in serious decline and may soon be abolished altogether[2]. Its role today is confined to the technical byways of land tenure, which are properly understood by an ever-diminishing band of lawyers[3]. Feudalism has long ceased to exercise a general influence over the development of the law of property in Scotland and, if the example of other countries is any guide, its eventual abolition is likely to leave few traces behind.

The position of Roman law is otherwise. The modern law of property in Scotland is laid on the foundations of the Roman law[4]. Many of the general concepts of the modern law, such as *dominium* or real rights or *traditio* or possession or *accessio*, are Roman concepts, and indeed the Roman name is often retained. Much of the content of the law is also Roman in origin, although it may have been substantially altered and developed in matters of detail. The influence of Roman law is at its most direct in the law of corporeal moveables, but it is strongly felt in the law of heritable property also, both at the level of general principles and also in relation to specific doctrines, such as servitudes and liferents[5]. Thus, so far as property law is concerned, modern Scots law may be classified along with the civilian legal systems of Western Europe, such as France and Germany, and with other 'mixed' legal systems such as Louisiana and the legal systems of southern Africa. Conversely, it has little in common with English law, and with other Anglo-American systems, except in relation to those few topics, such as easements (servitudes) and accession, where English law has drawn on Roman law. A lawyer trained in Scotland can without difficulty (other than linguistic difficulty) read and understand a book about the law of property in Germany or, indeed, in Japan (where the law is based on German law). But he is likely to be perplexed and bewildered by a book on the law of property in England.

1 SOURCES OF LAW (GENERAL AND HISTORICAL), vol 22, paras 548 ff. Thus Bell *Principles* s 636: 'A double system of jurisprudence, in relation to the subjects of property, has thus arisen in Scotland, as in most European nations; — the one regulating Land and its accessories according to the spirit and arrangements of the feudal system; the other regulating the rights to Moveables according to the principles of Roman jurisprudence which prevailed before the establishment of feus'. Bell, however, underestimates the influence of Roman law on land law.

2 Abolition has been the declared goal of a number of governments, and government bodies, since at least the 1960s. See *Land Tenure Reform in Scotland — A Plan for Reform* (1969) (Cmnd 4099); *Land Tenure Reform in Scotland* (Scottish Home and Health Department Green Paper, 1972); and *Abolition of the Feudal System* (Scot Law Com Discussion Paper no. 93) (1991).

3 See generally paras 41 ff below.

4 For a general discussion, see P Stein 'The Influence of Roman Law on the Law of Scotland' 1963 JR 205 at 226–231.

5 For the influence of Roman law on Craig's *Jus Feudale*, see P Stein 'The Influence of Roman Law on the Law of Scotland' 1963 JR 205 at 218, 219.

3. Rights in things: real rights. Property law is the law of things (*res*)[1]; but a thing is of significance to the law only insofar as it gives rise to rights which can be held by persons. Thus Bankton:

'Natural philosophy examines things according to their properties and qualities, in order to discover their powers; physick considers them with respect to their medicinal virtues, and other arts and sciences in the respective views proper to them; and positive law regards them as the subject of rights; for only rights are the object of laws'[2].

Property law, therefore, is concerned with rights in things, otherwise known as real rights. Rights in things are contrasted with rights against persons, or personal rights, which are the province of the law of obligations. The distinction between real rights and personal rights is of the first importance in legal systems based upon Roman law[3]. A real right or right in a thing (*jus in rem* or *jus in re*) is a right held directly in a thing. The real rights recognised in Scots law include ownership (*dominium*), lease and security[4]. So if A owns a car, his legal position may be analysed by saying that he has a real right (of ownership) in a thing (the car). The content of a real right depends both upon the type of right and also, in some cases, upon the type of thing. A personal right (*jus in personam*) is a right against another person or against a determinate, and usually small, number of other persons. The person against whom the right is held is under a direct obligation to the holder of the right, and obligation is the counterpart of right[5]. Among the personal rights recognised in Scots law are contractual rights and rights arising under the law of delict. So if B owes £1,000 to C, C has a personal right against B (to receive £1,000) and B has a correlative obligation to C (to pay £1,000). One way of characterising the difference between real rights and personal rights is to say that, while in general a real right is a right to use, or to prevent others from using, a thing, a personal right is a right to make a person perform some act, or alternatively to prevent him from performing some act.

Real rights are usually considered as better, or stronger, than personal rights, on the basis that things are more reliable than persons. Hume, for example, describes personal rights as having a 'feebler and more limited and uncertain operation'[6]. But this will not always be the case, and it is self-evident that a (personal) right against a solvent and willing debtor is a more valuable asset than a (real) right in respect of an ephemeral and deteriorating thing.

Of course, even real rights are ultimately enforceable only against persons. But this does not lead to the collapse of the distinction between real and personal rights.

A personal right is enforceable against a particular person or persons. A real right is enforceable against any person who challenges its existence, such as a person who seizes possession of the thing or who otherwise engages in unlawful interference. As Hume observes, in real rights there is

'an obligation upon all the world — not upon this or 'tother individual, but upon every man—to respect that right of his, and abstain from troubling him in the use and enjoyment of that thing ... If, therefore, it should so happen that this right of his is infringed, and that the thing is violently, surreptitiously or even casually taken from him, the title to vindicate and recover it attaches upon and follows the thing itself, go where it may ...'[7].

1 In English, 'thing' does not seem a sufficiently dignified word to carry the burden of having its own law. So the usual term is the law of 'property'. But 'thing' is more accurate, and 'property' has the disadvantage that it is also sometimes used to mean the principal right that can exist in a thing, ie ownership. See eg the Sale of Goods Act 1979 (c 54), s 17. In Germany, property law is called thing law (*Sachenrecht*), and the same is true in South Africa (in Afrikaans *Sakereg*).
2 Bankton *Institute* I,3,1. See also Stair *Institutions* I,1,22 and 23.
3 See generally: Stair I,1,22; *Bankton* II,1,1; Erskine *Institute* III,1,2; Hume *Lectures* vol I (Stair Soc vol 5, 1939 ed G C H Paton) p 10, and vol II (Stair Soc vol 13, 1949 ed G C H Paton) pp 2, 3; Bell *Principles* s 3. See also GENERAL LEGAL CONCEPTS, vol 11, paras 1099 ff.
4 For a complete list of real rights, see paras 4 ff below.
5 In real rights there is no obligant and hence no correlative obligation.
6 *Hume* vol II, p 3.
7 *Hume* vol II, p 2. See also *Stair* I,1,22 ('dominion is called a real right, because it respecteth things directly, but persons, as they have meddled with these things'), and *Bankton* II,1,1 ('a Right is termed Real, because it affects things; and persons only as possessors of them').

(2) THE REAL RIGHTS

4. What are the real rights? A definitive list of the real rights recognised in Scots law has never been attempted. Yet such a list seems an almost indispensable requirement of a study of the law of property.

Hume[1] quotes Heineccius to the effect that '*species juris in re sint quatuor ... Dominium, Hereditas, Servitus, Pignus*'[2]. It is thought that all modern civilian legal systems would accept at least three out of Heineccius' four real rights, namely ownership (*dominium*), servitude (*servitus*), and security (*pignus*)[3]. In the case of Scotland, Stair gives all three as being real rights, and adds also community and possession[4]. By 'community' Stair means rights held by the public at large, for example, in relation to rivers and the sea; and 'servitude' is used in a wider sense than the modern usage, to include liferent and lease as well as servitude proper[5]. To this list Hume, in a view which is traceable back, through John Millar, to Adam Smith[6], adds the real right of 'exclusive privilege', by which is meant rights in intellectual property and other monopoly rights. However, neither Stair nor Hume offers a systematic account of the real rights available in Scots law.

1 Hume *Lectures* vol IV (Stair Soc vol 17, 1955 ed G C H Paton) p 38. The same fourfold classification is given in Adam Smith *Lectures on Jurisprudence* (1978, ed R L Meek, D D Raphael and P G Stein) p 10. See also H van den Brink *The Charm of Legal History* (1974) pp 151, 152.
2 G Heineccius *Elementa Juris Civilis Secundum Ordinem Institutionum* (1767) s 334.
3 For the fourth real right, inheritance (*hereditas*), see para 5, note 23, below.
4 Stair *Institutions* II,1,1; II,1,28. Bankton follows Stair: see Bankton *Institute* I,1,86.
5 *Stair* II,6 preamble; II,7 preamble. Stair also includes teinds, which in the modern law are usually classified as separate tenements. See para 211 below.

6 Hume was a pupil of Millar who was a pupil of Adam Smith. An account of exclusive privilege as a real right appears both in Millar's (unpublished) lectures on Scots law, and in Adam Smith's *Lectures on Jurisprudence* pp 81–85. The writer is indebted to Dr J W Cairns for drawing this to his attention.

5. The real rights listed. It appears that the real rights recognised in Scots law are the following[1]:

(1) *Ownership* (*dominium*, occasionally anglicised as dominion). Ownership, which Stair describes as 'the main real right'[2], is defined by Erskine, in a famous phrase, as 'the right of using and disposing of a subject as our own, except in so far as we are restrained by law or paction'[3]. In civilian systems the traditional definition of ownership is that it is the right of use, enjoyment, and abuse (*jus utendi, fruendi, abutendi*).

(2) *Right in security.* The right held by a creditor in property in security of a debt owed to him is a real right[4]. Scots law recognises a number of different rights in security, the appropriateness of which in any given case depending both on the type of property and, in one case (the floating charge[5]) on the type of debtor. Prominent examples of rights in security are pledge (corporeal moveables), standard security (heritable property), and floating charge (property of all kinds owned by a company)[6].

(3) *Proper liferent.* Liferent corresponds to the *ususfructus* of Roman law. It is the right to the use or income of property for the duration of the holder's life[7]. Only a proper liferent is a real right. In an improper, or trust, liferent, the property is held by trustees and the liferenter's right is no more than the right of a beneficiary under a trust, which is a personal right[8].

(4) *Servitude.* A servitude, in the sense in which the word is used in the modern law, is a right held by one person in his capacity as owner of land in respect of other land which is not in his ownership[9]. The right has a number of different possible contents, such as a right of passage or a right to prevent building works[10].

(5) *Lease.* A lease is a right to possess land in exchange for a recurrent payment known as rent[11]. It is frequently emphasised that at common law a lease is a personal right only and not a real right[12]. However, the statute which effected the change in status was passed in 1449[13] and sufficient time has now elapsed for leases to be fully assimilated to other real rights. In some other countries leases are not recognised as real rights, and indeed in Scotland the hire of moveables confers a personal right only and so may be defeated by the creditors or alienees of the person whose property is being hired[14].

(6) *Possession.* The bare fact of possession of property confers the right not to be dispossessed except by consent or by the order of a court[15]. This real right exists independently of ownership or lease or other right giving specific entitlement to the property, and it may be exercised by a person, such as a squatter, whose possession is unlawful[16].

(7) *Rights held by the public.* Stair includes among the real rights, 'commonty, which all men have of things, which cannot be appropriated'[17]. The most important rights included under this heading are public rights of way[18], and public rights in the sea, rivers, lochs and the foreshore in respect of matters such as navigation and fishing[19]. Stair also makes mention of the right to air, which is 'common to all men, because it can have no limits or bounds, and because all men every where must necessarily breathe it', and of the right to acquire ownerless property, such as wild animals, by the doctrine of *occupatio*[20].

(8) *Exclusive privilege.* Hume, following Adam Smith, includes among the real rights 'exclusive privilege', by which is meant an exclusive, and valuable, right to do something and, hence, to stop others from doing the same thing[21]. Two main examples are given by Hume. One is the traditional rights of royal burghs and their merchant guilds in relation to trade and manufacture. The other is

rights of intellectual property, such as copyright and patent[22]. Hume's view cannot be accepted without a certain amount of damage to the core idea of real rights. For a real right is a right in a thing, and in the case of exclusive privilege it is not clear that there is a separate thing in respect of which a right can arise[23]. Nonetheless there are obvious points of resemblance between intellectual property rights and real rights in the traditional sense, in particular the fact that both types of right are enforceable against the world at large, and it is plain that intellectual property rights cannot be classified as personal rights. Consequently, unless they form a third category of right *sui generis*, as in some legal systems[24], it may be that Hume's classification ought to be accepted[25].

1 The possibility that other real rights exist cannot be entirely excluded. But the rights listed are certainly the main ones and may also be the only ones.
2 Stair *Institutions* II,1,28.
3 Erskine *Institute* II,1,1. For the content of ownership, see paras 193 ff and 531 ff below. The standard modern analysis of ownership is A Honore *Making Law Bind* (1987) pp 161 ff.
4 Stair *Institutions* II,5 preamble; II,10 preamble; Bankton *Institute* II,5,1; Erskine *Institute* II,1,1; Hume *Lectures* vol IV (Stair Soc vol 17, 1955 ed G C H Paton) p 2.
5 A floating charge is not, however, a real right until it attaches.
6 See further RIGHTS IN SECURITY, vol 20.
7 See further LIFERENT AND FEE, vol 13.
8 For the rights of beneficiaries, see para 10, head (1), below.
9 *Erskine* II,1,1; *Stair* II,1,1. There is a possible argument that real burdens, at least where they take the form of restrictions, are also real rights in the strict sense of the term: see para 413 below.
10 See further paras 439 ff below.
11 See further LANDLORD AND TENANT, vol 13.
12 Thus statute has bestowed on a lease 'the foreign and extrinsic character of a real right in land': *Hume* vol II (Stair Soc vol 13, 1949 ed G C H Paton) p 56. Hume treats of leases twice, once as personal rights (vol II, pp 56 ff) and then again as real rights (vol IV, pp 73 ff). See also *Stair* II,6 preamble; *Bankton* II,9,1; *Erskine* II,6,23. Adam Smith asserts that all real rights (other, presumably, than ownership), have their origins in contracts and were originally no more than personal rights. See Adam Smith *Lectures on Jurisprudence* (1978, ed R L Meek, D D Raphael and P G Stein) p 85.
13 Leases Act 1449 (c 6). See now also the Registration of Leases (Scotland) Act 1857 (c 26), s 2.
14 *Stair* I,15,4; *Erskine* III,3,14. See LOCATION, vol 14.
15 *Stair* II,1,1 and 18. See also D L Carey Miller *Corporeal Moveables in Scots Law* (1991) para 10.23.
16 See further paras 115 and 161 ff below.
17 *Stair* II,1,5.
18 See paras 495 ff below.
19 See paras 514 ff below.
20 *Stair* II,1,5. See also the rights discussed in J Rankine *The Law of Land-ownership in Scotland* (4th edn, 1909) ch 20.
21 *Hume* vol IV, pp 38–71. See also *Adam Smith* pp 81–85.
22 *Adam Smith* p 82 gives a third, namely the right of a hunter not to be interfered with when in pursuit of a wild animal. A modern example of this principle is *R v Mafohla* 1958 (2) SA 373.
23 Following Adam Smith, Hume seeks to assimilate this right to *Hereditas*, the right of the heir of a deceased person to accept his inheritance, which was said to be a real right in Roman law. But even if it could be said that the right of an heir is a real right in Scots law, which seems doubtful, the analogy is forced and unconvincing.
24 Eg, in Germany, where intellectual property rights (*Immaterialgüterrechte*) are classified separately.
25 Intellectual property forms the second part of this volume. See paras 801 ff below.

6. *Dominium* and the *jurae in re aliena*.

More than one real right may exist in respect of the same thing at the same time[1]. So land which is owned by A may be subject to a standard security held by B, a liferent held by C, a lease held by D, and a servitude held by E. A traditional method of classifying real rights is to distinguish between ownership (*dominium*) on the one hand and the subordinate[2] real rights, such as lease and security, on the other. Ownership is, so to speak, a right in one's own property. The subordinate real rights are *jura in re aliena*, that is to say, rights in the property of another. One advantage of this division is that it draws attention to the distinctive characteristics of ownership as a permanent and residual right. For usually the subordinate real rights are temporary in nature. They are burdens on the ownership of another, and if and when they come to an end, the residual right of ownership may be enjoyed unfettered. A right in security will come to an end when all the debts which it secures are paid. A lease will come to an end at the stipulated ish unless there is some reason for its continuation, such as the operation of tacit relocation. A liferent will come to end on the death of the liferenter. Only a servitude does not have a fixed term, although servitudes too can be extinguished in a number of different ways[3]. Ownership, by contrast, does not have a fixed term, and nor can the right usually be extinguished without the consent of the owner[4]. So if A owns a thing, then in the usual course of events he will continue to own it for as long as he chooses to do so.

The division of real rights into the right of ownership and the subordinate rights is not completely satisfactory. It fails to accommodate the, admittedly difficult, case of intellectual property. It also fails fully to accommodate the real right of possession, because possessors are frequently also owners and an owner with the real right of possession has a real right in his own property and not a real right in the property of another[5].

It has been stated that different real rights may co-exist in respect of the same thing at the same time. But this rule is subject to certain limitations. No difficulty arises where the real rights are different in type. The fact that A owns a thing does not of itself prevent B from having a right in security over it. But where real rights are of the same type, co-existence of rights is not always possible. The precise position varies from right to right. Thus if the real right of ownership in a thing is held by C, then it cannot also be the case that it is held by D. Two real rights of ownership cannot co-exist in respect of the same thing at the same time[6], although it is possible for the single right of ownership to be shared, as in the case of common property[7]. Hence if C owns, then it necessarily follows that D does not own. What is true of ownership is also true of liferent, of lease, and of possession[8]. But it is not 'true of security and servitude. More than one creditor may have a right in security in respect of the same thing, and in that case their respective entitlements to the thing are controlled by the rules of ranking; and it is commonplace for a number of servitude rights to co-exist in respect of the same land.

1 Stair *Institutions* II,1,28 and 42; Bankton *Institute* I,3,10; Erskine *Institute* II,1,1.
2 *Erskine* II,1,1, uses the term 'inferior real rights'.
3 For the ways in which servitudes can be extinguished, see paras 470 ff below.
4 But there are exceptions: see paras 9 and 663 ff below.
5 One way of dealing with this difficulty would be to modify the traditional classification so that rights are either in one's own property (ownership and, in certain cases, possession) or in the property of another (all other real rights).
6 *Erskine* II,1,1: '. . . it be a rule founded in common sense that two different persons cannot have, each of them, the full property of the same thing at the same time'. To this rule, the divided *dominium* of feudalism is a partial exception.
7 For shared ownership, see paras 17 ff below.
8 For possession, see para 118 below.

7. Classification by reference to holder of the right. Real rights may also be classified by reference to the type of person or persons who may hold the right. Three classes of right emerge:

(1) *Rights which may be held without restriction.* In general, real rights may be held by any natural or juristic person and without restriction. Thus this is much the largest of the three classes. It contains the following rights: ownership, right in security, lease, proper liferent, possession and intellectual property rights.

(2) *Rights held in one piece of land by persons in their capacity as owners of another piece of land.* The institutional writers distinguish between 'real' or 'praedial' servitudes on the one hand and 'personal' servitudes on the other[1]. A personal servitude is simply a right in a thing held by a person, that is to say, any of the rights listed at (1) above. The adjective 'personal' relates to the holder of the

right and is not intended to signify that the right itself is personal[2]. This is contrasted with a real or praedial servitude, which is a right in one piece of land, known as the servient tenement, which is held by a person in his capacity as owner of another piece of land, known as the dominant tenement. This is 'servitude' in the sense familiar to the modern law. The right to enforce the servitude is attached to the dominant tenement and passes with that tenement to successive owners. A real or praedial servitude is in turn part of a larger grouping of rights which may be termed 'real conditions'. A real condition is a right, such as a servitude or real burden or right of common interest, which is held by a person in his capacity as proprietor of property and enforceable in relation to some other property of which he is not the proprietor. As before, the adjective 'real' relates only to the holder of the right and signifies that the right attaches to the ownership of a dominant tenement. In fact, most real conditions are not real rights in the strictest sense of the term, although servitude is a real right. A full analysis of real conditions appears later in this volume[3].

(3) *Rights held by the public at large*. Some real rights are held by the public at large and may be exercised by any member of the public. These include public rights of way, and rights of fishing and navigation in the sea and other tidal waters[4].

1 Stair *Institutions* II,7 preamble; Erskine *Institute* II,9,5.
2 Personal servitudes are, of course, real rights. Thus *Stair* II,7 preamble: 'Servitudes are distinguished in real and personal, though neither of them be personal rights'.
3 See paras 344 ff below.
4 Strictly, the latter are held by the Crown in trust for the public, although nothing turns on this and the rights are directly enforceable by individual members of the public. See para 514 below.

8. Creation of real rights. Many real rights originate in contract, but the creation of the right itself is a process entirely distinct from the contract[1]. Except in the case of corporeal moveables, where writing is not usually required, there will almost always be a written deed granting the right which is executed by the granter and delivered to the grantee. Common examples are dispositions, standard securities and assignations. Delivery of the deed is then followed by some act which serves to publicise its existence, such as registration in a public register[2] or its formal intimation to a third party[3] or the taking of possession of the property to which the right relates[4]. Usually the real right comes into existence on the completion of registration or other public act, but in the case of floating charges the right remains personal even after registration in the Register of Charges and becomes real only if the charge attaches following the appointment of a receiver or a liquidator[5].

1 For the distinction between contract and the creation of the right, see further paras 606 ff below.
2 Thus dispositions, standard securities and long leases are registered in the Register of Sasines or Land Register. Transfers of shares are registered in the company's register of members.
3 As in the case of the assignation of personal rights, where intimation must be made to the debtor in the right being assigned.
4 As in lease, positive servitude, and pledge.
5 Companies Act 1985 (c 6), s 463(1); Insolvency Act 1986 (c 45), s 53(7).

9. Extinction of real rights. It would be impossible to give an exhaustive list of the circumstances under which a real right might come to be extinguished. The sheer variety of real rights, and of circumstances and combinations of circumstances which might arise, make that task impractical. But the important cases of extinction appear to be the following:

(1) *Expiry of term*. Some real rights endure only for a fixed term. This is true, for example, of leases and of many intellectual property rights. On the expiry of the term the right is extinguished, although in the case of leases an appropriate notice must be served by either the landlord or the tenant if the lease is not to continue from year to year by tacit relocation.

(2) *Negative prescription*. Although the actual terms are not found in the legislation, the Prescription and Limitation (Scotland) Act 1973 is drafted in such a way as to make separate provision for real rights and for personal rights. Personal rights prescribe negatively under sections 6 and 7 of the Act after either five years or twenty years respectively. Real rights prescribe after twenty years under section 8 of the Act[1]. A real right is extinguished by prescription if the right has subsisted for a continuous period of twenty years unexercised or unenforced, and without any relevant claim in relation to it having been made[2]. A relevant claim is a claim made in a court of competent jurisdiction in Scotland or in an arbitration by or on behalf of the holder of the right, either to establish the right or to contest any claim to a right inconsistent therewith[3]. Two real rights are declared imprescriptible by the Act, namely ownership of land and the right of a tenant under a lease which has been registered in the Register of Sasines or the Land Register[4]. Further, although ownership of corporeal moveables is prescriptible under section 8, there is an exception for ownership of stolen property in any question with the thief or other person privy to the theft[5].

(3) *Positive prescription*. The ownership of land can be acquired by positive prescription[6]; and since two rights of ownership cannot exist concurrently in the same thing, it follows that the acquisition of ownership on the part of one person is accompanied by the extinction of the right held by the person who was owner immediately prior to the expiry of the prescriptive period[7]. The rule is the same for leases, which can also be acquired by positive prescription[8]. Similar principles also operate in certain other cases of original acquisition of ownership[9].

(4) *Renunciation*. The holder of a real right may renounce or discharge that right, either expressly or by implication. Express discharges are commonplace in the case of rights in security, and are also found in relation to leases and certain other rights. The right of ownership of corporeal moveables is renounced by the physical abandonment of the property coupled with the intention to abandon[10], but it is unclear whether ownership of land can also be lost by abandonment. Where the right of ownership is renounced or abandoned, the right falls to the Crown on the principle *quod nullius est fit domini regis*[11]. Renunciation of other real rights results in their complete extinction.

(5) *Irritancy*. Feudal *dominium* and the right of a lessee under a lease may both be lost by irritancy, led by, respectively, the feudal superior and the landlord[12]. Irritancy requires a court action. Its effect is to extinguish the right.

(6) *Confusion*. If any of the *jurae in re aliena* come to be held by the owner of the thing in which the right subsists the right is extinguished by confusion. *Res sua nemini servit*[13]. An owner cannot have a right in security or a lease over his own property[14]. In the case of servitudes it has sometimes been argued that the right revives if the thing and the right come to be held again by separate hands[15], but the authorities are inconclusive[16].

(7) *Destruction of the thing*. If the thing perishes, so must the right. In the case of incorporeal property destruction means legal destruction and not physical destruction. So a standard security held over a lease will fall if the lease falls, for example by irritancy.

1 The Prescription and Limitation (Scotland) Act 1973 (c 52), s 8, applies to any right relating to property, whether heritable or moveable, not being a right falling within s 6 or s 7: s 8(2). Sections 6 and 7 provide for the prescription of obligations and (by s 15(2)) of correlative rights. A real right is a right in a thing and not a right correlative to an obligation owed by a person. Accordingly, real rights prescribe under s 8 and not under ss 6 and 7.
2 Ibid, s 8(1).
3 Ibid, ss 9(2), (4), 4(2).
4 Ibid, s 8(2), Sch 3(a), (b).
5 Ibid, Sch 3(g).

6 Ibid, s 1.
7 This is original acquisition, and hence a true case of extinction of the previous title. The person relying on prescription receives a new statutory title and not the title of the person who was owner immediately prior to the expiry of the prescriptive period.
8 Prescription and Limitation (Scotland) Act 1973, s 1 (registered leases), and s 2 (unregistered leases).
9 See further paras 673 ff below.
10 *Lord Advocate v Aberdeen University and Budge* 1963 SC 533, 1963 SLT 361; *Mackenzie v Maclean* 1981 SLT (Sh Ct) 40.
11 That which is ownerless belongs to the Crown. See Bankton *Institute* I,3,16; Erskine *Institute* II,1,12; Bell *Principles* s 1287. See generally paras 547 ff below.
12 See further paras 85 and 424 below (feudal *dominium*), and LANDLORD AND TENANT, vol 13, paras 423 ff.
13 No one can have a servitude over his own property.
14 *Lord Blantyre v Dunn* (1858) 20 D 1188. For some possible specialities, see W M Gloag *The Law of Contract* (2nd edn, 1929) p 727 and D J Cusine (ed) *The Conveyancing Opinions of J M Halliday* (1992) pp 377–381.
15 Or, to put the same thing in another way, if the dominant and servient tenements are separated once more.
16 *Erskine* II,9,37; Bell s 997; *Walton Bros v Glasgow Magistrates* (1876) 3 R 1130 at 1133, per Lord President Inglis. See also paras 453, 476, below.

10. Rights resembling real rights. Finally, mention may be made of a number of rights which, while sharing certain characteristics of real rights, are not real rights in the strict sense of the term.

(1) *Right of a beneficiary under a trust.* In a trust, ownership of the property is in the trustee or trustees, but subject to the right of the beneficiary or beneficiaries to ensure the proper implementation of the trust purposes. At first sight the right of a beneficiary might seem to be a real right. Thus the right prevails in a question with the creditors of the trustee, who are unable to attach trust property[1]. At common law it prevails also against transferees or other parties taking real rights in the property from the trustee, at least where they are in bad faith or have not given value for their grant[2]; but this common law rule has now been substantially modified by statute[3]. Nonetheless the right of the beneficiary is plainly personal and not real[4]. In principle a real right, as a right in a thing, burdens the thing no matter into whose hands it may fall. Considerations of good and bad faith are wholly irrelevant[5]. The right of a trust beneficiary, while generally stronger than the typical personal right, does not burden the property and, except in certain limited cases, does not affect the property in the hands of third parties.

(2) *Occupancy rights of a non-entitled spouse.* In terms of the Matrimonial Homes (Family Protection) (Scotland) Act 1981 occupancy rights arise where one party to a marriage owns, leases or otherwise has the right to occupy the matrimonial home[6] and the other party has no such right. The Act confers occupancy rights on the party (known as the non-entitled spouse) who would otherwise have no right to occupy. As originally drafted, the occupancy rights so conferred seemed to be an uneasy mixture of real and personal rights. On the one hand, there was a right, if in occupation, not to be excluded from the matrimonial home by the other party to the marriage (known as the entitled spouse). On the other hand there was a right, if not already in occupation, to enter and occupy the matrimonial home[7]. The former right was enforceable only against the entitled spouse whereas the latter right was enforceable against anyone. Subsequently the relevant provisions were brought into balance by also allowing the right not to be excluded to be enforced against anyone[8]. In its amended form, the Act thus gives substantial rights to the non-entitled spouse in relation to the matrimonial home. But these rights are not true rights in a thing because they

do not cover all cases where the matrimonial home passes out of the ownership[9] of the entitled spouse. The relevant rules here are complex and not entirely logical. Thus occupancy rights survive the transfer of the property by gift[10], but they may not survive the transfer of the property by sale[11]. Further, the rights do not prevail against creditors of the entitled spouse, so that an adjudging creditor or a trustee in sequestration will take the property free of the occupancy rights[12].

(3) *Incorporeal separate tenements.* Certain rights in land are treated as (incorporeal) separate tenements rather than as individual real rights. The reasons for this are historical and cannot be explored further here. Today the only important example is the right to fish for salmon[13]. In principle, a separate tenement is quite different from a real right in land. The latter is a right in land. The former is considered to be land itself, in which other people are capable of having rights. A separate tenement is thus a thing and not a right[14], and to say that a person holds the right of salmon fishings is, more accurately, to say that he has the *dominium utile* of the relevant (incorporeal) separate tenement. So *dominium utile* of salmon fishings is held in precisely the same way as *dominium utile* of bare land; and salmon fishings can be leased or granted in security or made the subject of other subordinate real rights in the same way as any other land. The differences in practice are less striking. Two seem important. First, and unlike real rights, the right of salmon fishings can be held concurrently by the owner of the river in which the right is exerciseable without the right being extinguished by confusion. This is because the right of salmon fishings is not regarded as a *jus in re aliena*, a mere right in the river, but as an independent piece of property on its own account. Secondly, the right of salmon fishings cannot be lost by negative prescription[15].

1 *Heritable Reversionary Co Ltd v Millar* (1892) 19 R(HL) 43. On this case, see further para 694 below. As far as sequestration is concerned, the rule is now statutory: Bankruptcy (Scotland) Act 1985 (c 66), s 33(1)(b).
2 Stair *Institutions* I,13,7; *Redfearn v Somervail* (1813) 1 Dow 50, 5 Pat 707, HL.
3 Trusts (Scotland) Act 1961 (c 57), s 2, discussed further at para 691 below.
4 See TRUSTS, TRUSTEES AND JUDICIAL FACTORS, vol 24, para 49.
5 The fact that at common law a trust right prevailed only against a transferee who was in bad faith discloses its true nature as a personal right. The common law rule was merely an application of the rule against 'offside goals' which applies also to a number of other rights, all of them personal.
6 For the meaning of 'matrimonial home', see the Matrimonial Homes (Family Protection) (Scotland) Act 1981 (c 59), s 22. As to occupancy rights under the Act generally, see further FAMILY LAW, vol 11, paras 854 ff.
7 Ibid, s 1(1) (as originally enacted). This meant that while the non-entitled spouse could not be prevented from entering the matrimonial home by a third party, there was nothing to stop that third party from promptly ejecting the spouse once entry had been effected. The whole process could then start all over again.
8 Ibid, s 1(1) (amended by the Law Reform (Miscellaneous Provisions) (Scotland) Act 1985 (c 73), s 13(2)).
9 Or right of lease, or as the case may be.
10 Matrimonial Homes (Family Protection) (Scotland) Act 1981, s 6(1)(a).
11 This is because in the case of sale, ibid, s 6(1)(a), does not apply where a bona fide purchaser receives either an affidavit or a renunciation as specified in s 6(3)(e).
12 But limited protection is conferred by ibid, s 12, and the Bankruptcy (Scotland) Act 1985 (c 66), s 41.
13 See further paras 207 ff below.
14 Of course, since rights, viewed from another aspect, are incorporeal property, it is true to say that all rights (other than ownership) are things. See para 16 below.
15 The right of salmon fishings is a real right of ownership in land and hence is imprescriptible in terms of the Prescription and Limitation (Scotland) Act 1973 (c 52), s 8(2), Sch 3(a).

(3) THINGS

11. Classification. Property law is the law of things, and of rights in things (real rights). Accordingly, a consideration of rights[1] leads on naturally to a consideration of things.

In Scots law, as in Roman law[2], things (*res*) are classified in two different ways. In the first place, all things are either corporeal or incorporeal; and in the second place, all things are either heritable or moveable. Corporeal things are things with a *corpus* or body, or in other words tangible things. Incorporeal things are rights, and have no physical presence[3]. So a book is corporeal and a right in contract or in delict is incorporeal[4]. The distinction between heritable things and moveable things is more complex and requires fuller discussion[5]. But, expressed broadly, the distinction is between land on the one hand and non-land on the other. So a field is heritable property, whereas a tractor is moveable property.

The use of the word 'heritable' rather than 'immoveable' discloses the historical importance of the distinction between heritable and moveable property in succession law. By the rules of intestate succession which were in force until 1964, heritable property was the property which was inherited by the heir-at-law, who was usually the eldest son, while moveable property was inherited by the other children, or by other relatives, and was administered and distributed on their behalf by an executor. This system, which incorporated a form of primogeniture, was dismantled by the Succession (Scotland) Act 1964. Under the modern law of succession no distinction is made between heritable and moveable property except in relation to legal rights, which continue to be taken only from the moveable estate of the deceased[6]. Further, both heritable and moveable property are now administered and distributed by an executor[7]. But the term 'heritable' remains[8].

The effect of classifying things in two different ways is to create four separate classes of property, namely corporeal heritable, corporeal moveable, incorporeal heritable, and incorporeal moveable. The distinction between corporeal property and incorporeal property reflects the obvious physical difference between, on the one hand, a tangible thing, and on the other hand, a right; and physical difference necessitates a difference in legal treatment[9]. So far as corporeal property is concerned, the further subdivision into moveable and heritable property is also based on physical differences, and it seems self-evident that, at least to some degree, land must be governed by rules which are different from the rules for corporeal moveable property. In the case of incorporeal property, however, the subdivision into heritable property and moveable property is largely artificial and in this work will often be disregarded. Indeed a more fruitful subdivision of incorporeal property is often into real rights and personal rights. The truth is that for many purposes property law works with three classes only, namely corporeal heritable property, corporeal moveable property and incorporeal property[10]; and the further subdivision of incorporeal property into incorporeal heritable and incorporeal moveable is important mainly in relation to choice of diligence and to the calculation of legal rights in the law of succession.

1 See paras 4 ff above.
2 Gaius *Institutes* II,12–14; Justinian *Institutes* II,2,1–3; Erskine *Institute* II,2,1 and 2.
3 Bankton *Institute* I,3,20: '[T]hings are most properly divided in the civil law into *corporeal* and *incorporeal*. Corporeal are such as fall under the senses, may be seen or felt, as the *ipsa corpora*, or species of things moveable and immoveable. Incorporeal are things not subject to the senses, but which have their existence in law, as rights of all kinds, the rights of property, obligation, succession etc.' See also *Erskine* II,2,1, and Bell *Commentaries* II,1.
4 Thus a right is an incorporeal thing. But a thing is itself the object of rights. From this it follows that with incorporeal property one holds a right in a right. See further para 16 below.
5 See paras 12–14 below.

6 Succession (Scotland) Act 1964 (c 41), ss 1, 10(2). For this reason the financial provision given as a prior right to the surviving spouse on intestacy requires to be drawn rateably from heritable and moveable property: s 9(3). Section 1 is subject to s 37(1)(a) which preserves the rule whereby titles and coats of arms transmit to the heir-at-law. As to the modern law of intestate succession, see further WILLS AND SUCCESSION, vol 25, paras 688 ff.

7 Ibid, s14.

8 The Scottish Law Commission has called for its replacement by the word 'immoveable'. See *Corporeal Moveables: Some Problems of Classification* (Scot Law Com Consultative Memorandum no. 26) (1976) paras 31, 32. 'Immoveable' is the normal term for the purposes of private international law.

9 *Bell* I,1: 'This is a division consistent with nature, and which ought not to be discarded'.

10 Eg in relation to the transfer of ownership.

12. Corporeal property: heritable or moveable?

Corporeal heritable property comprises land, and anything which is part of land[1]. Thus the component ingredients of land, such as soil, rock and minerals, are heritable. Also heritable is anything which has become part of the land by accession, for example a building, or a tree or a plant[2]. But industrial growing crops, that is to say, crops requiring annual seed and labour, do not accede and are not heritable[3]. Just as attachment to the land can make a moveable thing heritable, by the law of accession, so severance from the land has the effect of making a heritable thing moveable. So coal in the seam and trees in the ground are heritable, but mined coal and felled timber are moveable.

Necessarily, all corporeal property which is not heritable is classified as moveable property. Traditionally, moveable property is described as being property which either moves by itself or which can be moved by others. Thus Bell:

> 'Whatever moves, or is capable of being moved from place to place without injury or change of nature in itself, or in the subject with which it is connected, is moveable'[4].

But this is a description rather than a definition. Some moveable property is so substantial that in practice it is never moved[5], while, as Stair points out, the fact that soil is capable of being dug up and moved, or that 'the sea . . . hath its agitation by ebbing and flowing' does not prevent both from being classified as heritable[6].

1 See generally Stair *Institutions* II,1,2; Bankton *Institute* I,3,17–19; II,1,36–39; Erskine *Institute* II,2,2–4; Hume *Lectures* vol IV (Stair Soc vol 17, 1955 ed G C H Paton) pp 557 ff; Bell *Commentaries* II,1–3; Bell *Principles* ss 1471–1475.

2 For accession, see paras 570 ff below.

3 See para 595 below.

4 Bell *Principles* s 1472.

5 As in the case of 'mobile' homes. Some mobile homes, however, are considered to be heritable: see para 584 below.

6 *Stair* II,1,2.

13. Incorporeal property: heritable or moveable?

At one time the question of whether incorporeal property was heritable or moveable arose frequently and was keenly disputed. Usually the context was the law of intestate succession, and the dispute arose between the heir-at-law, who was entitled to the heritable property of the deceased, and the executor, who was entitled to the moveable property[1]. The modern law of succession is different, and little now turns on the distinction between heritable and moveable property, except that legal rights may be taken from moveable property only[2]. So far as incorporeal property is concerned, the principal significance of the heritable/moveable distinction in the modern law is in relation to choice of diligence. Thus, as a general rule, poinding and arrestment are the appropriate diligences for moveable property, and inhibition and adjudication for heritable property. In particular, all heritable rights are subject to inhibition and adjudication[3].

The rules which have developed for the attribution of heritable or moveable status to incorporeal property are complex, illogical, and, in many cases, of little or no contemporary importance. Only a brief treatment will be attempted here. Two general rules may be identified. In the first place, a right is heritable if it stands in some direct relation to land. Thus, real rights in land are heritable. Secondly, a right is also heritable if it will yield periodical profits in the future but without reference to a capital sum. 'Such rights are heritable, though they should have no connection with land . . . because by the annual profits arising from them they have a degree of resemblance to feudal rights'[4]. Heritable on this principle are annuities and pensions. Rights not falling within these two general rules are moveable, and moveable rights make up by far the larger part of incorporeal property.

An exhaustive list of heritable rights cannot be given. But the most important are listed below.

1 On behalf of the heirs *in mobilibus*, to whom it fell to be distributed.
2 See para 11 above.
3 Provided always that they are capable of voluntary alienation. See DILIGENCE, vol 8, paras 155, 197.
4 Erskine *Institute* II,2,6.

14. The heritable rights. The principal heritable rights are the following:
(1) *Real rights in land.* All real rights in land are heritable[1]. Thus a lease is heritable[2], as is a servitude and a right in security over land[3]. However, by statute[4], rights in security are declared moveable as regards the succession of the creditor except for the purposes of legal rights, an exception which leaves little content for the rule[5]. Arrears of interest on a secured loan are treated as moveable property, as are arrears of rent in a lease and arrears of feuduty[6]. A claim for damages in respect of breach of a security or a lease would also be moveable[7].
(2) *Uncompleted real rights in land.* Where a real right in land has been granted but title has not been completed by the grantee, the grantee's right is considered to be heritable[8]. The grantee must be in a position to complete the real right without some further act of the granter. The typical case for the application of this principle is where a deed, such as a disposition or standard security, has been delivered but not yet registered in the Register of Sasines or Land Register.
(3) *Personal rights to real rights in land.* A personal right to acquire ownership or other real right in land is probably itself classified as a heritable right. Of course, there is no direct right in the land[9], but there is a right to obtain such a direct right. There are two main examples. First, the interest of a beneficiary in a trust is heritable where it consists of a right to a conveyance of heritable property[10]; and this is so even where the heritable property is not yet acquired by the trustees provided that they are taken bound by the trust to acquire it[11]. Conversely, the interest of a beneficiary is moveable if it amounts merely to a right to demand payment of a sum of money or a share of a general trust fund[12].

The other example is, or may be, the right of a purchaser under missives of sale of heritable property. If A concludes missives to sell land to B, A has a contractual right to the price and B has a contractual right to a conveyance of the land. It has long been settled that the right of the seller to the price is moveable. Thus the price can be arrested in the hands of the purchaser[13], and it is available for the satisfaction of legal rights if the seller should die before the conveyancing is completed[14]. From this it might appear to follow that the corresponding right of the purchaser to a conveyance of the land is heritable[15], and it has been so held in the context of succession law[16]. But there is modern Outer House authority to the effect that the right of a purchaser under missives is moveable in questions involving diligence[17].
(4) *Personal bonds.* At common law the interest of a creditor in a personal bond was moveable before the term of payment but heritable thereafter if the bond contained an express provision for the payment of interest. This was because, like land, such a bond would yield future profits[18]. The rule was changed by the Bonds Act 1661[19] and, subject to minor exceptions contained in that Act, all of

which are now obsolete[20], personal bonds are moveable. However, a personal bond which is secured on land is heritable: thus the right of a creditor in a standard security is heritable both as to the security itself and also as to the personal bond[21].

(5) *Rights with a tract of future time.* Rights which have a *tractus futuri temporis* are heritable. Erskine's definition has been judicially approved[22]: '[t]hese are rights of such a nature that they cannot be at once paid or fulfilled by the debtor, but continue for a number of years, and carry a yearly profit to the creditor while they subsist, without relation to any capital sum or stock'[23]. The two established cases are annuities and pensions. Hume and Bell speculate as to whether patents and copyright are heritable on this principle[24], but it is now settled that intellectual property rights are moveable[25].

(6) *Goodwill.* The right to goodwill can be heritable or moveable, or it can be both in proportions. Goodwill is heritable to the extent that it is due to the premises in which the business is conducted. Conversely, it is moveable if it is attributable to the name and the reputation of the business. Much of the case law has concerned pubs, from which it appears that the goodwill of a pub is more likely to be heritable in a town or city than in the country[26], but that even in the former case some of the goodwill is usually considered moveable[27].

(7) *Titles of honour.* Titles of honour are heritable[28]. At common law they are inherited by the heir, and this rule has not been disturbed by the Succession (Scotland) Act 1964[29].

1 Erskine *Institute* II,2,5; Hume *Lectures* vol IV (Stair Soc vol 17, 1955 ed G C H Paton) p 557; Bell *Commentaries* II,3; Bell *Principles* s 1478.

2 *Hume* vol IV, p 564.

3 Ownership, although a heritable right, is not itself a thing capable of being owned. See para 16 below. Thus ownership, alone among the real rights, is not incorporeal property.

4 Titles to Land Consolidation (Scotland) Act 1868 (c 101), s 117 (amended by the Succession (Scotland) Act 1964 (c 41), s 34(1), (2), Sch 2, para 4, Sch 3). Section 117 of the 1868 Act is applied to standard securities by the Conveyancing and Feudal Reform (Scotland) Act 1970 (c 35), s 32, and to pecuniary real burdens by the Conveyancing (Scotland) Act 1874 (c 94), s 30 (amended by the Succession (Scotland) Act 1964, s 34(2), Sch 3).

5 This is because legal rights may be claimed only out of moveable property; and apart from legal rights the distinction between heritable and moveable property is of little importance in modern succession law. See para 11 above. However, an express bequest of moveable property would carry heritable securities: see *Hughes' Trustees v Corsane* (1890) 18 R 299.

6 This is because 'they are already payable, and yield no annual profits to the creditor by being unpaid': *Erskine* II,2,7. See also Bankton *Institute* II,1,36; *Hume* vol IV, p 572; Bell *Commentaries* II,7 and 8; Bell *Principles* ss 1479, 1484, 1496 ff, 1505.

7 *Fairlie's Trustees v Fairlie's Curator Bonis* 1932 SC 216, 1932 SLT 174.

8 Stair *Institutions* II,1,3; *Erskine* II,2,5; *Hume* vol IV, pp 557, 558; Bell *Commentaries* II,4; Bell *Principles* s 1485.

9 *Margie Holdings Ltd v Customs and Excise Comrs* 1991 SCLR 473, 1991 SLT 38.

10 Bell *Commentaries* II,4 and 5; Bell *Principles* ss 1482, 1996; *Learmonts v Shearer* (1866) 4 M 540; *Watson v Wilson* (1868) 6 M 258.

11 This is because the right of the beneficiary is still a right to heritable property. See generally J McLaren *Law of Wills and Succession as administered in Scotland* (3rd edn, 1894) ch XI; W A Wilson and A G M Duncan *Trusts, Trustees and Executors* (1975) pp 123 ff. Sometimes, and under the influence of English law, this situation is analysed as being constructive conversion by the trustees of moveable property into heritable property.

12 For the same reason, shares in a company or the right of partners in the property of the partnership are moveable even although the general fund may also contain heritable property. See *Erskine* II,2,8; Bell *Principles* s 1479. See also the Partnership Act 1890 (c 39), s 22.

13 See DILIGENCE, vol 8, para 275.

14 *Bankton* II,1,3; *Erskine* II,2,17; *Hume* vol IV, p 567; Bell *Commentaries* II,6; Bell *Principles* s 1479; *Chiesley v Chiesley* (1704) Mor 5531; *Heron v Espie* (1856) 18 D 917. The executor of the seller would be bound by the contract. Any specific legatee of the land is entitled to the price (*Pollok's Trustees v Anderson* (1902) 4 F 455, (1902) 9 SLT 393; *M'Arthur's Executors v Guild* 1908 SC 743, 15 SLT 1023),

and it may be that the same rule would apply in relation to a claim for prior rights made under s 8(1) of the Succession (Scotland) Act 1964.
15 That is not, however, a necessary consequence. The approach of the law seems to be that rights are moveable unless special cause can be shown to the contrary.
16 *Hume* vol IV, p 558; *Clayton v Lowthian* (1826) 2 W & S 40 at 50, per Lord Gifford; *Ramsay v Ramsay* (1887) 15 R 25. The price is then a moveable debt. It is thought that this rule does not depend on peculiarities of the law of succession, and in particular that it is not an example of property otherwise moveable becoming heritable by destination: see para 15 below.
17 *Leeds Permanent Building Society v Aitken Malone and Mackay* 1986 SLT 338, OH. This decision has been questioned: see G L Gretton *The Law of Inhibition and Adjudication* (1987) p 50.
18 *Erskine* II,2, 9–13; Bell *Commentaries* II,7; Bell *Principles* s 1495. Such a bond is distinguished from a right with a tract of future time (which is also heritable) by the fact that the payments of interest can be brought to an end at any time by the debtor repaying the debt.
19 The Bonds Act 1661 (c 32) re-enacted the Act of 1641 (c 57).
20 The most important in practice was where the bond contained a destination excluding executors. See para 15, note 11, below.
21 *Erskine* II,2,14; Bell *Commentaries* II,5; Bell *Principles* ss 1478, 1488. But this is subject to the rule that heritable securities are moveable for certain purposes: see the text, head (1), above.
22 *Hill v Hill* (1872) 11 M 247.
23 *Erskine* II,2,6. See also *Stair* II,1,4; *Hume* vol IV, pp 564, 565; Bell *Commentaries* II,4; Bell *Principles* s 1480.
24 *Hume* vol IV, pp 564, 565; Bell *Principles* s 1480.
25 *Advocate-General v Oswald* (1848) 10 D 969. Frequently this is provided for expressly by statute. See eg the Patents Act 1977 (c 37), s 31(2); the Copyright, Designs and Patents Act 1988 (c 48), s 90(1); and the Trade Marks Act 1994 (c 26), s 22.
26 *Graham v Graham's Trustees* (1904) 6 F 1015, 12 SLT 262; *Muirhead's Trustees v Muirhead* (1905) 7 F 496, 12 SLT 749.
27 *Murray's Trustee v M'Intyre* (1904) 6 F 588, 11 SLT 759; *Coles Executors v Inland Revenue* 1973 SLT (Lands Trib) 24.
28 *Erskine* II,2,6; Bell *Commentaries* I,120; Bell *Principles* s 1481.
29 Succession (Scotland) Act 1964, s 37(1)(a).

15. Things heritable by destination. In certain limited circumstances moveable property can be made heritable by an act of will on the part of the owner; but it seems that, at least in the modern law, heritable property cannot be made moveable by this method. The rule is set out by Erskine thus:

'Rights originally moveable may become heritable . . . by destination of the proprietor or creditor, who hath the right of settling any part of his estate in whatever manner he pleases, provided he shall properly discover his intention'[1].

The conversion from moveable to heritable property is effective only for the purposes of the law of succession, and the property remains moveable for all other purposes[2], including the law of diligence[3] and private international law[4]. Historically, destination was a device whereby the owner could increase the size of the estate to be inherited by his heir. In the modern law of succession, however, little now turns on the distinction between heritable and moveable property and destination is of much reduced significance.

The precise scope of destination in the modern law is uncertain. At one time the doctrine was undoubtedly a wide one. For example, destination was thought to explain the rule that the right of a purchaser of land holding under missives of sale is heritable, for 'the deceased by his contract, has in substance declared his will . . . to turn his money into land'[5]. But this view of a purchaser's right is probably inconsistent with the whole court decision in *Heron v Espie*[6], and the rule, although still recognised, can more readily be explained on other grounds[7]. In another case, where a person died while in the course of building a house, it was held that the sum required to complete the house was heritable by destination even although the deceased had been under no contractual obligation to expend this sum[8], but this decision has since been doubted, and in the modern law it seems that even a contractual obligation to expend money on improving heritage will not be sufficient to make that money heritable[9].

Destination requires a declaration of intention on the part of the deceased, and in principle that declaration may either be express[10] or implied. But while it is doubtful to what extent the law would now give effect to an express declaration of intention[11], the following cases of implied destination seem to be established. First, building materials are heritable by destination where the owner of the materials dies while the building work is still in progress and the materials have not become heritable by accession[12]. Secondly, individual parts of a building which have become temporarily detached, for example slates falling off a roof, are viewed as heritable provided that the deceased owner had intended that they should be re-attached[13]. Finally, Hume gives as examples of destination the loose parts of a steam engine in a colliery, fish in a pond, and pigeons in a dovecote[14]. In the first two cases destination is seeking to achieve what would have been achieved by accession if the owner had survived, while the third case is almost indistinguishable from the doctrine of constructive fixtures[15].

1 Erskine *Institute* II,2,14. That the deceased could do as he please with his property is emphasised again at II,2,19, where Erskine refers to the case where 'the creditor, who is absolute master of his own property, destines a moveable sum for his heir'.
2 *Stewart v Watson's Hospital* (1862) 24 D 256.
3 *Forbes v Drummond* (1772) 5 Brown's Supp 583; Bell *Principles* s 1475; J Graham Stewart *The Law of Diligence* (1898) pp 68, 69. But see note 11 below.
4 A E Anton *Private International Law* (2nd edn, 1990) pp 597–601.
5 Hume *Lectures* vol IV (Stair Soc vol 17, 1955 ed G C H Paton) p 558.
6 *Heron v Espie* (1856) 18 D 917. This concerned the right of the seller and not the right of the purchaser. The right was held to be moveable. It was emphasised that this result was not brought about by an act of intention on the part of the seller, and indeed the sale had proceeded by compulsory purchase. The account of the reasoning in *Heron v Espie* given in *M'Arthur's Executors v Guild* 1908 SC 743 at 747, 748, 15 SLT 1023 at 1025, 1026, per Lord President Dunedin, is not accurate.
7 And on grounds which are not confined to the law of succession. See para 14, head (3), above.
8 *Malloch v M'Lean* (1867) 5 M 335, OH.
9 *Fairlie's Trustees v Fairlie's Curator Bonis* 1932 SC 216, 1932 SLT 174.
10 As Hume points out, an express declaration of intention is practically a testamentary writing: see *Hume* vol IV, p 565. The relationship between an express destination in this sense and an express survivorship destination has never been explored.
11 The standard example given by the institutional writers was of a personal bond which expressly excluded executors, thus indicating that the bond was to go to the heir. See *Erskine* II,2,12; *Hume* vol IV, p 565; Bell *Commentaries* I,7; Bell *Principles* s 1491. In fact, bonds expressed in these terms were also heritable by statute (Bonds Act 1661 (c 32): see para 14, head (4), above), which may explain why, contrary to the usual rule for things heritable by destination, they were considered heritable for the purposes of diligence. See *Hume* vol IV, p 431, and *Graham Stewart* pp 549, 600, 601. The 1661 Act remains in force but it is thought that destinations in this form are now unknown. For other examples of express destination, see *Erskine* II,2,14, and J McLaren *Law of Wills and Succession as administered in Scotland* (3rd edn, 1894) para 378.
12 *Johnston v Dobie* (1783) Mor 5443; *Gordon v Gordon* (1806) Hume 188. On the same principle, dung which has not yet been applied to the land is heritable *destinatione*: see *Reid's Executors v Reid* (1890) 17 R 519.
13 *Erskine* II,2,14; Bell *Commentaries* II,2.
14 *Hume* vol IV, pp 565, 566.
15 *Fisher v Dixon* (1843) 5 D 775 at 808–810, per Lord Moncreiff (dissenting); *Fairlie's Trustees v Fairlie's Curator Bonis* 1932 SC 216 at 221, 222, 1932 SLT 174 at 177, per Lord President Clyde. For constructive fixtures, see para 576 below.

16. Rights in rights. Two propositions are clearly established. In the first place, property law is the law of rights in things, otherwise known as real rights[1]. In the second place, things can be both corporeal and also incorporeal, 'incorporeal things' being another name for rights[2]. From these two propositions a third follows. This is that there can be rights in incorporeal things, which is to say that there can be rights in rights. In this respect, as in so many other respects in relation to the law of property, Scots law follows Roman law. Gaius's celebrated division of private law was into Persons, Things, and Actions[3], and Things included both *res corporales* and *res incorporales*[4]. *Res incorporales* contained personal rights as well as real rights, so that the law of obligations was subsumed in the law of property. In Scotland the institutional writers render *res incorporales* as 'incorporeal things'[5] or 'incorporeal subjects'[6], and the framework of Gaius's scheme is adopted[7].

The result of this approach to the classification of rights may be explained by an example. Suppose that A owns a car, takes the lease of a plot of land, and lends B £1,000. The car is a corporeal thing. The lease and the debt are incorporeal things, the former being a real right and the latter a personal right. All three are A's property, and accordingly it can be said that A owns the car, the lease, and the debt. This method of describing A's position can be and has been criticised[8]. Thus it has been argued that it is artificial and misleading to speak of ownership of rights, or at least (in one version of this argument) of personal rights. On this view, a better way of describing A's position would be to say that he owns the car, leases the land, and has a claim against B for £1,000. It has been further argued that, if ownership of rights is accepted, then it must follow that ownership itself can be owned. Thus, the statement that 'A owns a car' could be given as 'A owns the ownership of a car' or even as 'A owns the ownership of the ownership of a car'[9]. The answer to this second argument is that in Scots law, as in Roman law[10], ownership itself cannot be owned. Ownership is a right, but, unlike other rights, it is not also a thing. The answer to the first argument is that both methods of describing A's position are correct. They are not in conflict with one another, and which is chosen will depend upon which right (that is, the right-right or the thing-right) it is intended to emphasise. This important point requires further exposition.

Consider, for example, A's real right, the right of lease. If we wish to focus on the relationship between A on the one hand and the right of lease on the other, then it is both correct and helpful to say that 'A has the real right of ownership of the real right of lease' or, more simply, that 'A owns the lease'[11]. If, on the other hand, we wish to focus on the relationship between A and the land, then it is equally correct, and helpful, to say that 'A has a real right of lease in the land'. The same point can be made in the case of the debt of £1,000. Thus A's relationship to the debt is brought into focus by saying that 'A owns the debt', while A's relationship with B is brought into focus by saying that 'A has a contractual right against B'. Naturally, property law is not much concerned with the relationship of A to B. That is a matter for the law of obligations[12]. Personal rights are usually of interest to property law only where they are being transferred or burdened[13]. But so far as (subordinate) real rights are concerned, such as a right of lease, property law is interested both in the relationship between A and the lease and in the relationship between A and the land. Both relationships are defined by real rights.

The conceptual advantages of characterising the relationship between a right and its holder as a relationship of ownership are considerable and manifest. In the first place, such a characterisation facilitates a proper analysis of the transfer of rights. Thus if A contracts to assign his debt to a third party, C, the legal position of the parties can be explained by saying that C has a personal right against A to the transfer of A's personal right against B; and, when the transfer is completed, by intimated assignation, that C has the real right of ownership to the personal right against B. The end result of the transaction is that A has transferred his right of ownership in the thing to C[14]. The analysis would be precisely the same if A had transferred, not an incorporeal thing (the debt), but a corporeal thing (the car).

A second advantage of this approach is that it allows a proper analysis of the legal issues which arise when subordinate real rights are granted in respect of an incorporeal thing. For example, it is difficult to explain how A can grant a standard security over the lease[15] if it is not accepted that his relationship to the lease is one of ownership. For no one can burden that which is not his. And the end result of the security transaction is that there are two rights over the incorporeal thing, namely A's real right of ownership and the heritable creditor's real right in security[16].

A final advantage of treating rights as things is that it draws attention to the unitary nature of the law of property by emphasising the rules which are common to both corporeal and incorporeal things. The unity of the law of property is one of the major themes of the present work[17].

1 See para 3 above.
2 See para 11 above.
3 Gaius *Institutes* I,8; Justinian *Institutes* I,2,12.
4 *Gaius* II,12–14; *Justinian* II,2,1–3.
5 Bankton *Institute* I,3,20; Erskine *Institute* II,2,1 and 2; Bell *Commentaries* II,1.
6 Bell *Principles* s 1476.
7 For an account of how other codified civilian systems have dealt with this issue, see M Kaser 'The Concept of Roman Ownership' (1964) 27 Tydskrif vir Hedendaagse Romeins-Hollandse Reg 5 at 16–18. As Kaser indicates, the later Codes have tended to abandon the idea that rights can be owned. See eg the peremptory statement in the Bürgerlicher Gesetzbuch (BGB) s 90 that 'Sachen im Sinne des Gesetzes sind nur körperliche Gegenstände' (Only corporeal property is a thing in the sense of the law).
8 Eg B Nicholas *An Introduction to Roman Law* (1962) p 107.
9 D Lloyd *The Idea of Law* (1973) pp 320–321.
10 J A C Thomas *Textbook of Roman Law* (1976) p 127.
11 To say simply that A 'has' the lease discloses nothing about the nature of A's relationship to the lease. Thus P B H Birks 'The Roman Law Concept of Dominium and the Idea of Absolute Ownership' 1985 Acta Juridica 1 at 26: 'Common lawyers prefer to say that a man owns his car but "has" — this is clearly evasive — a lease of an office'.
12 In the language of Bell (*Commentaries* I,302) property law is concerned with manners *extra corpus juris* and not with matters *in corpore juris*.
13 See paras 652 ff below.
14 *Erskine* III,5,1: Assignation is 'a written deed of conveyance by the proprietor to another of any subject not properly feudal'.
15 A standard security may be granted over a lease in terms of the Conveyancing and Feudal Reform (Scotland) Act 1970 (c 35), s 9(2), (8)(b).
16 It has been argued that what is really burdened by the security is not the lease but rather the land itself, but within the limits set by the lease. See H Silberberg and J Schoeman *The Law of Property* (2nd edn, 1983) pp 12, 13. But this does not seem an adequate explanation of what is actually taking place.
17 See para 1 above.

2. CO-OWNERSHIP

(1) INTRODUCTION

17. Terminology. The terminology which is now used with regard to co-ownership did not become fully established until the decision of the Second Division in *Banff Magistrates v Ruthin Castle Ltd*[1] in 1944. That terminology follows the vocabulary of English law in acknowledging two distinct types of co-ownership, namely common property and joint property[2]. Together common property and joint property make up the available categories of what is known as *pro indiviso*[3], or undivided, ownership[4]. The defining characteristic of *pro indiviso* ownership is that a single thing is held by two or more people as an undivided whole, and without particular physical parts of the thing being individually attributed. So if A and B own a house *pro indiviso*, A does not own all the rooms on one floor and B all the rooms on another, but rather each has an even share in the whole house.

Earlier terminology was imprecise in the extreme. The terms 'conjunct property'[5] and 'part ownership'[6] were often used and, perhaps, not always very carefully. More seriously (given the terminology which has now been adopted by the modern law) 'common property' and 'joint property' were used more or less interchangeably. Thus Erskine:

'The common property arising from commixtion is an undivided right: what formerly belonged to each of the different proprietors, becomes, by the act of mixing, the joint property of them all *pro indiviso*'[7].

Or again Bell, in the course of a passage which is generally regarded as the foundation of the modern law:

'Common property is a right of ownership vested *pro indiviso* in two or more persons . . . Although the whole subject cannot be disposed of otherwise than by mutual consent, each joint owner may sell his own *pro indiviso* right. . . '[8].

Both Erskine and Bell wrote before the binary structure of the modern law was established, which was not until the middle of the nineteenth century[9]. However, once it came to be accepted that there were two distinct categories of *pro indiviso* ownership, the continued freedom in the use of the terms 'joint' and 'common' was unhelpful and hindered the development of the law[10]. To some extent the terminological confusion continues even today, so that land held as common property is often referred to as a case of title in 'joint' names.

1 *Banff Magistrates v Ruthin Castle Ltd* 1944 SC 36 at 68, 1944 SLT 373 at 387, 388, per Lord Justice-Clerk Cooper, adopting W M Gloag and R C Henderson *Introduction to the Law of Scotland* (3rd edn, 1939) pp 489, 490 ((9th edn, 1987) para 40.13).
2 The vocabulary of English law, but not its content is followed: see para 20 below. 'Property' is used here in the sense of ownership.
3 In French law this is called ownership *par indivision*.
4 We are not concerned here with common interest, although traditionally, following Bell *Principles* s 1071, common interest is treated together with common property. In fact the two are very different. Common property is a right of *dominium*. Common interest is a type of real condition and so a burden on the *dominium* of another. For common interest, see further paras 354 ff below.
5 Eg Erskine *Institute* III,8,34 ff.
6 Eg Bell *Commentaries* II,544.
7 *Erskine* II,1,17.
8 Bell *Principles* ss 1072, 1073. At s 1083 Bell writes of 'joint property'.
9 See para 19 below.
10 See eg *Murray v Johnstone* (1896) 23 R 981, 4 SLT 81.

18. The early law. Although *pro indiviso* ownership seems always to have been recognised in Scots law[1], in the same way as much earlier it had been recognised in Roman law[2], there is little evidence of a general theory of such ownership before the nineteenth century. Instead, the tendency of the early law was to identify a number of situations in which *pro indiviso* ownership occurred, and then to develop specific rules for these situations[3]. Doubtless one reason for this approach was that at that time co-ownership was comparatively rare. The main cases of *pro indiviso* ownership identified were partnership property, conjunct fees of land, commonty, ships, heirs portioners, trusts, and certain parts of tenement buildings, most notably the common passage and stair. The institutional writers paid particular attention to partnership property[4], which is not now regarded as a case of *pro indiviso* ownership at all following acceptance of the view that a partnership is a separate legal person capable of holding property in its own name[5].

One result of this piecemeal approach might have been to suggest that there was no unified law at all and that each situation was governed by its own peculiar rules. However, that was not the view adopted by Bell who, with the publication of his *Principles*, became the first writer to offer a systematic exposition of *pro indiviso* ownership[6]. Quite properly, Bell's analysis has played a major part in the development of the modern law[7], but it is not certain whether Bell intended his remarks to cover all cases of *pro indiviso* ownership or whether he meant to exclude what in the modern law is known as joint property. Certainly there is no indication in Bell's analysis of the binary structure of joint and common property which only a few years later was to be established as the modern law[8].

1 Eg Craig *Jus Feudale* 2,8,35.
2 W W Buckland *Textbook of Roman Law* (3rd edn, 1963 by P Stein) pp 539, 540.
3 Stair *Institutions* I,7,15; I,16,1 ff; Bankton *Institute* I,8,36 and 40; Erskine *Institute* II,1,17; II,6,53; III,3,56; III,8,35. The one subject of general applicability which was discussed was the right to division, which was adapted from the *actio communi dividundo* of Roman law.
4 Corporate property was also sometimes regarded as held *pro indiviso*.
5 Thus partnership property is usually owned by the partnership and not by the individual partners. See G L Gretton 'Who Owns Partnership Property?' 1987 JR 163. This appears to have been overlooked in *McCallum* 1990 SCLR 399, 1990 SLT (Sh Ct) 90. The main property which partnerships do not own is feudal land, the title to which is taken in the name of trustees for behoof of the partnership (the trustees' ownership being an example of what in the modern law is called joint property). Bell, who was a forceful proponent of the view that partnerships have a separate legal *persona*, was nonetheless able to advance the apparently inconsistent view that partnership property is held *pro indiviso* by all the partners. See Bell *Principles* ss 353, 357.
6. Bell ss 1071 ff.
7 See *Grant v Heriot's Trust* (1906) 8 F 647 at 658, 13 SLT 986 at 991, per Lord President Dunedin who stated: '[B]efore the days of Mr George Joseph Bell the law of Scotland upon the law of common property, common interest, and joint property as distinguishable from each other was not very accurately understood, and it is the fact — as indeed our attention is called to the fact by Mr Bell himself — that the institutional writers treated these subjects somewhat inadequately'. The influence of Bell is manifest in cases such as *Murray v Johnstone* (1896) 23 R 981, 4 SLT 81.
8 See also para 19, note 1, below.

19. A binary law: joint property and common property. The first judicial suggestion[1] that there might be two distinct categories of *pro indiviso* ownership was made by Lord Moncreiff in *Cargill v Muir*[2], a case decided in 1837. The case was concerned with whether heirs portioners could hold a superiority of land, and Lord Moncreiff's analysis was little more than an adaptation of a distinction already well established in English law:

> 'Heirs-portioners are not *joint* proprietors, but as their name imports, *part-owners* or portioners. They hold *pro indiviso*, while the subject is undivided. But each has a title in herself to her own *part* or *share*, which she may alienate or burden by her own separate act. The condition of two *joint-proprietors* in the fee is very different; they have no separate estates, but only one estate vested in both, not merely *pro indiviso* in respect of possession, but altogether *pro indiviso* in respect of the *right*. The distinction is the same which the Lord Ordinary believes is expressed by English lawyers, by the terms *joint-tenants* and *tenants in common*'[2].

From this time on, the binary structure of the law seems never to have been in doubt[3]. In Scotland, as in England, it came to be accepted that there were two distinct classes of *pro indiviso* property[4]. But, what remained unclear for more than 100 years after *Cargill v Muir* was the precise content of each class. In *Cargill*, Lord Moncreiff had seemed to suggest that joint property was the larger of the two classes and that common property ('part ownership') was an unusual and privileged form of holding. The years immediately following *Cargill* saw a considerable body of case law on the question of trust property, from which it soon became plain that trust ownership was a form of joint property[5]. Nevertheless, apart from this, the division between joint and common property remained controversial and a number of different views were expressed, sometimes within the same case[6]. The law was still unsettled as late as *Schaw v Black*[7], which was decided in 1889. That case concerned the *pro indiviso* ownership of land by private individuals, which in the modern law would be classified as a clear example of common property. However, the court was unable to agree on its classification. Lord Kinnear was strongly of the view that the holding was an example of joint property and stated that:

> 'The assumption upon which ... the summons is framed, is that the defender is a part owner, having right to two definite fifth parts or shares of the subjects ... But a *pro*

indiviso proprietor is not a part owner but a joint owner. The distinction is very clearly brought out in Lord Moncreiff's judgment in the case of *Cargill v Muir*[8].

On the other hand, Lord Shand felt that the holding was common property and said:

> 'An instance in our law of joint proprietorship, in the sense of the joint ownership in the law of England, is that of trustees holding a conveyance in ordinary terms for trust purposes. In joint ownership the property is vested in A and B and the survivor. On the death of one of them his right goes necessarily to his survivor. A tenancy in common (as it is called in England), on the other hand, seems to arise where each of the *pro indiviso* proprietors has a certain share or right in the property, which he may himself dispose of as he thinks fit by a deed granted by himself. It appears to me that the right here held by ... each of the *pro indiviso* proprietors is a right of this latter kind, because each of the proprietors may dispose of his own share of the estate, and upon his death there is no vesting of his share in the surviving *pro indiviso* proprietors'[9].

Schaw v Black was ultimately decided on a different point, and the majority of the court reserved its view on the question of the boundary between joint and common property. It was more than fifty years later before the issue came before a court again, but on this occasion the law was finally settled beyond doubt. The facts of *Banff Magistrates v Ruthin Castle Ltd*[10] were that land was conveyed to A and B 'jointly and to their joint assignees'. It was held by the Second Division that, notwithstanding the use of the words 'jointly' and 'joint', the holding was common property and not joint property. The judgment by Lord Justice-Clerk Cooper is the leading modern statement of the law of *pro indiviso* ownership. Lord Cooper distinguishes joint and common property, and concludes that common property is the principal class, joint property being confined to a small number of special cases, most notably trusts and unincorporated associations:

> 'The distinctive feature of ... common property (derived from the fact that each co-owner has a separate and separable share) is the absolute right of every co-owner to terminate the community at will ... Joint property, on the other hand, has received little doctrinal exposition as a mode of holding property, probably because its attributes are not so much the incidents of the joint right as the consequences flowing from the relationship existing between the persons who alone can have such a joint right. So far as has been traced, there is no instance of a joint right in the strict sense having been held to exist except in persons who were inter-related by virtue of some trust, contractual or quasi-contractual bond — partnership or membership of an unincorporated association being common examples — and it seems to me that such an independent relationship is the indispensable basis of every joint right'[11].

Strictly, Lord Cooper's remarks were *obiter*, and they were not adopted by the rest of the court[12]. Nonetheless, they have been widely accepted, and may be accepted here, as an accurate statement of the modern law[13]. Three things in particular may be said in their favour. First, they are clear. Secondly, and unlike English law, they confine joint property, which is a highly restrictive form of holding, to a marginal position in the law of *pro indiviso* ownership. Finally, they provide a rational basis for the distinction between joint and common property by restricting the former to those cases where there is title without any accompanying beneficial interest.

1 The first suggestion by a Scots lawyer at all was probably by Bell. In the 4th edition of his *Commentaries*, published in 1821, Bell writes of ships that they can be held in part ownership, 'which corresponds with the English doctrine of tenancy in common, as contradistinguished from joint tenancy': II,636. Bell's source is a standard English work of the time, C Abbott (Lord Tenterden) *A Treatise of the Law relative to Merchant Ships and Seamen* (4th edn, 1812) pp 89 ff, where it says (at p 89): '[T]he several part-owners thereby become tenants in common with each other of their respective shares: each having a distinct, although undivided, interest in the whole; and upon the death of any one, his share goes to his own personal representatives, and does not accrue to others by survivorship'. In the 5th edition of his *Commentaries* (1826), the last for which he was responsible,

Bell no longer expressly limits his account of part owners to ships, although he comments that it is 'chiefly useful in relation to ships': II,655. The passage is unchanged in the standard modern edition, the 7th of 1870 (II,544). However, while Bell concedes the existence of what in modern terminology would be called common property, he does not concede the existence of joint property and the wording of the (later) general account of *pro indiviso* ownership in Bell *Principles* ss 1071 ff does not suggest that Bell thought that the binary structure of English law was part of the law of Scotland.

2 *Cargill v Muir* (1837) 15 S 408 at 409, OH (affd (1837) 15 S 408, IH).

3 Lord Moncreiff himself returned to the subject in *Lawson v Leith and Newcastle Steam-Packet Co* (1850) 13 D 175 at 180, 181, in the context of ships, commenting of an earlier case decided in 1830 that 'at that period, the distinction between the case of *joint*-owners and *part*-owners was very imperfectly understood'.

4 In *Gillespie and Paterson v City of Glasgow Bank* (1879) 6 R (HL) 104 an attempt was made to apply the same, or a similar, distinction to the question of liability for debts. The 'joint' liability of co-debtors such as trustees is contrasted with the '*pro indiviso*' liability of other debtors.

5 Eg *Dalgleish v Land Feuing Co Ltd* (1885) 13 R 223. See further para 34 below. A number of the cases on the question of trust property arose out of the collapse of the City of Glasgow Bank in 1878.

6 *McNeight v Lockhart* (1843) 6 D 128 at 136, per Lord Justice-Clerk Hope; *Johnston v Craufurd* (1855) 17 D 1023 (cf the views of Lord Ardmillan, the Lord Ordinary, at 1024, OH, with those of Lord Curriehill at 1025, 1026, IH); *Murray v Johnstone* (1896) 23 R 981, 4 SLT 81.

7 *Schaw v Black* (1889) 16 R 336.

8 (1889) 16 R 336 at 337, OH (revsd (1889) 16 R 336, IH). Lord Kinnear was to reassert the same view many years later: see *Grant v Heriot's Trust* (1906) 8 F 647 at 668, 13 SLT 986 at 997.

9 *Schaw v Black* (1889) 16 R 336 at 340, 341, IH.

10 *Banff Magistrates v Ruthin Castle Ltd* 1944 SC 36, 1944 SLT 373.

11 1944 SC 36 at 68, 1944 SLT 373 at 388.

12 Indeed Lord Mackay disputed the very existence of a binary law. See 1944 SC 36 at 55, 1944 SLT 373 at 382: 'I have from the first had considerable difficulty in appreciating that our Scottish law of conveyancing made any such absolute and unpassable cleavage between the two classes of common [ie *pro indiviso*] property. The incidents which were by the argument assigned to joint property in heritage would certainly make me pause long before I agreed to the distinction as a general one'. However, by 1944 it was far too late for views of this kind.

13 See eg T B Smith *A Short Commentary on the Law of Scotland* (1962) pp 479 ff; W M Gordon *Scottish Land Law* (1989) paras 15-09 ff; *Steele v Caldwell* 1979 SLT 228, OH.

20. Joint property and common property distinguished. In the modern law, common property is the dominant form of *pro indiviso* ownership, and joint property is probably confined to the two cases of trust ownership and ownership by unincorporated associations. Thus in the standard contemporary example of *pro indiviso* ownership, which is ownership of a matrimonial home and other matrimonial property[1] by a husband and wife, ownership is common and not joint[2].

The defining characteristics of joint and common property were originally borrowed from English law where an equivalent distinction is made between joint tenancies and tenancies in common[3], but modern Scots law does not follow English law in detail and is probably more Roman than English[4]. In common property each co-owner has a share in the *pro indiviso* whole which is separate in a legal, although not in a physical, sense from other shares held by other co-owners. In joint property there are no separate shares but only a single title to the thing which is held by the trustees for the time being or, as the case may be, by the members of the unincorporated association. From this initial difference stem most of the other differences between joint and common property. Thus the existence of a separate share gives an owner in common something which may be sold, or bequeathed, or burdened by the grant of a right in security, or again made subject to a survivorship destination. Conversely, the unity of title found in joint property means that there is no separate share which can be alienated or burdened. Ownership of joint property continues only for as long as the owner remains a trustee or a member of the unincorporated association, and on resignation or death all rights pass to the remaining trustees or, as the case may be, to the remaining members of the association. An express survivorship destination is not required, and indeed in the absence of distinct shares it is inappropriate to view the effect of the death of a trustee or an association member as an example of the operation of a special destination. A number of special rules exist in the case of common property only, of which the most important are the right of each co-owner to prevent changes to the property and the right to pursue for division and sale. A detailed account of the rules of common property and joint property is given below[5].

1 It is provided by the Family Law (Scotland) Act 1985 (c 37), s 25, that each party to the marriage is presumed to have 'an equal share' in household goods.
2 This is so even where title to a house is subject to a survivorship clause: see para 34 below.
3 For the English law, see 39 *Halsbury's Laws of England* (4th edn) paras 525 ff.
4 For a striking illustration of the continuing influence of Roman law, see *Scrimgeour v Scrimgeour* 1988 SLT 590, OH. See also G MacCormack 'The *Actio Communi Dividundo* in Roman and Scots Law' in A D E Lewis and D J Ibbetson (ed) *The Roman Law Tradition* (1993).
5 For the rules of common property, see paras 22–33 below, and for the rules of joint property, see paras 34–36 below.

21. Other cases of concurrently held rights. There are a small number of other cases where rights in property are held concurrently in such a way that the final result is, or at least resembles, co-ownership. These are considered later[1].

1 See paras 37 ff below.

(2) COMMON PROPERTY

22. Constitution. Common property (ownership in common) may be acquired either originally or derivatively, although the former is rare in practice and is not discussed further here[1]. So far as derivative acquisition is concerned, ownership in common is acquired in the same manner as other forms of ownership, the precise method depending upon the type of property in question[2]. However, a number of specialities require to be mentioned. If ownership is expressly granted to two or more people the result is always common property unless the grantees are taking as trustees or as members of an unincorporated association, in which case the result is joint property. It is thought that not even the most express words can create joint property if grantees are taking as ordinary persons and not as trustees or members of an association[3]. In some cases it may not be clear whether ownership is being conferred or some lesser right, and this difficulty arises particularly where, as with the common parts in a housing development, the common right is ancillary to a grant of full ownership of some other property (in the example given, a dwelling house). In such a case common ownership is effectively created by a grant, in the parts and pertinents clause, of 'common property' or of 'a *pro indiviso* share', but doubt has been expressed about the effect of a bare grant of a 'right in common', which has sometimes been interpreted as conferring, not common property but common interest[4]. However, common interest arises by operation of law and it is not clear that it is capable of being expressly created[5]. It is perhaps of significance that in the only modern case on this subject 'right in common' is interpreted as conferring a right of common property[6].

In view of the fact that common property may be held in shares of different sizes, a well-drawn grant will indicate the respective sizes of the shares being conferred on the grantees. Where the grant is silent, there is a presumption of equality of shares, so that a conveyance of a house 'to A and B' will, in the absence of any indications to the contrary, confer on each of A and B a one half *pro indiviso* share. In large housing developments, where rights of common property are to be conferred in respect of certain common areas, the developer may face the difficulty of not knowing at the time when the first houses are sold how many houses the development will ultimately contain. In this situation it is particularly important to specify the size of the shares of common property which are being granted, even if the final result is that proprietors receive shares of different sizes[7], and a disposition which takes refuge in an unspecified grant of common property may fail *quoad* the common parts on the grounds that the granter did not know the size of the share he was conferring and thus lacked the necessary intention to transfer ownership[8].

1 The main cases of original acquisition of common property are (1) by accession, if the principal was itself owned in common (para 574 below); (2) by specification, if there were two or more workmen (paras 559 ff below); (3) by commixtion of solids or confusion of liquids, where common property is the invariable result (para 564 below); and (4) by positive prescription, if both title and possession were held *pro indiviso*.

2 See generally paras 597 ff below.

3 See para 34 below.

4 *Johnston v White* (1877) 4 R 721; *George Watson's Hospital Governors v Cormack* (1883) 11 R 320; *McCallum v Gunn* 1955 SLT (Sh Ct) 85.

5 See para 358 below.

6 *WVS Office Premises Ltd v Currie* 1969 SC 170, 1969 SLT 254.

7 Thus suppose a developer imagines that he may build 400 houses. He dispones the first 200 conferring on each a 1/400 share of the common areas. Later he decides to build only 300 houses, with the result that the final 100 houses are granted a 1/200 share each. In such a case no practical difference arises from the difference in the size of the shares (see para 24 below), and each *pro indiviso* proprietor may make full use of the common areas.

8 As to the necessity for intention, see para 613 below. A different, but related problem, may arise where a developer embarks on an adjacent development, or on a second phase of the original development. Depending on the wording of the conveyances used in the original development, the developer may have disponed 100 per cent of the common parts and hence have no title to grant *pro indiviso* rights to houseowners in the second development.

23. Management: general principles. The first attempt to formulate a set of general rules for the management of common property was made by Bell in his *Principles*[1]. Bell's exposition has been closely followed by the courts and is of the highest authority. Unfortunately, it is not without its difficulties. Bell begins his analysis by adopting the rule of Roman law that management requires the consent of all *pro indiviso* owners, so that any one co-owner may prevent a decision with which he does not agree. This rule is expressed in the maxim *in re communi melior est conditio prohibentis*: in common property the objector is in the better position[2]. However, Bell then goes on to give the apparently different rule that:

> 'Where parties cannot agree, either the will of the majority rules, or the ordinary state must be continued'[3].

This is not very clearly expressed, but what it appears to mean is that, if a majority view can be obtained, that view will rule, but if no majority can be obtained, the course of action which has been proposed cannot be followed and matters must continue as they are. If this interpretation is correct, Bell's two rules cannot easily be reconciled. The first rule states that decisions must be made unanimously; the second rule states that they may be made by a majority[4]. However, since the second rule does not appear to have been noticed by the courts, while the first rule has been frequently affirmed[5], one possible approach is to disregard the second rule entirely. The universal rule then becomes the requirement of unanimity. Alternatively, an attempt can be made to reconcile the two rules, perhaps along the following lines. Bell expressly applies the first (unanimity) rule to three different situations, namely to court actions against third parties, to the granting of leases, and to alterations and repairs to the property[6]. There can be no doubt as to the first two of these, because on first principles court actions and the granting of leases are acts which follow from ownership, and in common property all are owners. The third (as to alterations and repairs) was the express rule of Roman law[7], and it may even be that the Roman rule on unanimity was confined to cases such as this. However, there is also a fourth situation which Bell does not expressly mention. This is the use made of the property by the co-proprietors, and if Bell's second (majority) rule applies at all, then it appears to apply here. Such a result is not without its attractions. It would mean, for example, that if the majority of proprietors in a tenement building agreed that the common passage could be used for parking push chairs, that use would be lawful[8]. It would also mean that some reasonable arrangement about use could not be prevented by a person who happened to hold a one-hundredth (or smaller) *pro indiviso* share in the property. It may also be argued that questions of use will not usually affect the fundamental interests of individual proprietors and that this is a case for whch decision by majority is appropriate. The issue of majority decisions as to use[9] has never been tested in the courts and it seems that no firm choice can be made between Bell's two rules.

In practice, questions of management usually involve either the use which can be made of the property or its physical alteration and repair, and these two subjects are considered separately below[10]. In the case of heritable property, the common law rules are sometimes altered or supplemented by real conditions such as real burdens and servitudes[11]. The rules of management have developed almost entirely in the context of corporeal property, and it is not clear that they would apply in precisely the same way in the case of incorporeal property. If co-owners are unable to reach agreement in matters of management, they can seek judicial regulation[12] or the appointment of a judicial factor[13]. Alternatively, and in practice very much more commonly, they may end their association with the property altogether, either by alienating their *pro indiviso* share[14] or by an action of division or division and sale[15]. Special rules for matrimonial homes are provided for by the Matrimonial Homes (Family Protection) (Scotland) Act 1981 (c 59) (as amended)[16].

1 Bell *Principles* s 1072 ff.
2 *Bell* ss 1072, 1075.
3 *Bell* s 1077.
4 It is not entirely clear what is meant by a majority. If there are four owners each with a one-quarter *pro indiviso* share, then a majority is three. But if one owner has a five-eighth share and the other three owners each have a one-eighth share, it is thought that the one owner with the five-eighth share constitutes a majority on his own while the three owners each with a one-eighth share do not.
5 Eg *Johnston v Craufurd* (1855) 17 D 1023 at 1025, per Lord Ivory; *Murray v Johnstone* (1896) 23 R 981 at 990, per Lord Moncreiff.
6 *Bell* s 1075. All three situations are considered separately below.
7 *Digest* 8, 2, 27; 8, 5, 11; 10, 3, 28.
8 Such a use would otherwise not be lawful: *Carmichael v Simpson* 1932 SLT (Sh Ct) 16.
9 Contrast here the position of physical alterations, where the first (unanimity) rule is firmly established. See para 25 below.
10 See paras 24, 25, below.
11 See para 26 below.
12 See para 30 below.
13 See para 31 below.
14 See para 28 below.
15 See paras 32, 33, below.
16 See para 27 below.

24. Use. Co-owners may come to an agreement[1] about the nature and extent of the use to be made of the property held in common, although, depending on its terms, such an agreement may be terminable at will. In the absence of such agreement, or of special provision made by real burdens and other real conditions[2], there are three main principles of use. First, each co-proprietor is entitled to make use, as it has been expressed, of 'every inch' of the property[3], and he is entitled to a rateable share of all profits which the property may produce[4]. So if land is tenanted, each co-owner is entitled to a share of the rents. It follows from this first principle that no co-owner may take exclusive possession of all or of any part of the property[5];

and the position is not altered even where, in breach of this rule, exclusive possession has been taken and maintained for twenty years, there being no recognised servitude of exclusive possession[6].

The second principle is that 'ordinary' uses only are permitted[7]. The dividing line between 'ordinary' use, which is allowed, and 'extraordinary' use, which is not, will depend partly on the nature of the property[8], and partly also on its recent history, because a use which begins its life as 'extraordinary' may, by passage of time, come to be accepted as 'ordinary'[9]. In one case the defender was interdicted from keeping a bath chair in an entrance hallway to a flatted building on the basis that the proper use of a hallway was for passage[10]. In another case the defender was prevented from using a common passageway for storing crates, but he was allowed to use it as the site of a dungheap, apparently on the basis of long prior use[11]. There are no other reported decisions on this question.

The final principle of use has been expressed as being that 'one proprietor must not obtain an excessive benefit at the expense of his co-proprietors'[12]. Whether a particular use or benefit is 'excessive' will depend partly on the number of other co-proprietors whose interests need to be safeguarded, and partly also, it has been suggested, in circumstances where the *pro indiviso* shares are uneven, on the size of the individual proprietor's share[13]. Thus, at least in cases where the common property is subject to heavy use, a person holding a nine-tenth share is probably entitled to make greater use of the property than a person holding the remaining one-tenth share. In principle a co-owner can communicate his right of use to others[14]. So the common passage and stair in a tenement building may be used by whole families, and their guests, to gain access to individual flats and not merely by the small number of actual co-owners. However, a co-owner cannot permit others to do that which he could not lawfully do himself, and the measure of the right of use conferred on non-owners is the right as held by the granter. In one reported case, where a right of salmon fishings was held in equal *pro indiviso* shares by the pursuers and the defenders, and where an agreement had been made between them for one year only which allowed fishing on alternate weeks, it was held that the defenders could not enter into timeshare agreements with third parties which purported to give fishing rights in perpetuity[15].

Difficult issues arise where, in breach of the first of the three principles identified above, exclusive possession is taken by one *pro indiviso* owner without the agreement of the other owner or owners. If the property is tenanted, so that the possession taken is civil, one owner collecting all the rents without accounting to the others, there is authority that this is a suitable case for the appointment of a judicial factor[16]. If, as more usually, the possession taken is natural possession, the question then arises as to whether the co-owner in breach can be forced to relinquish his exclusive control of the property. In one case it was doubted whether a *pro indiviso* proprietor can bring an action of ejection against another *pro indiviso* proprietor, on the basis that neither party is entitled to exclusive possession and that the title of the defender is as good, or as bad, as the title of the pursuer[17]. However, since the policy of the law is to discourage the use of self help[18], it is thought that there ought to be some judicial method of forcing a defender to share possession with the pursuer[19], and it may be that interdict is the appropriate remedy[20]. A co-owner who has maintained exclusive possession of common property without the consent of his fellow owners must account to them for the (ordinary) profits of the period of unlawful possession[21]. Ordinary profits include rents, if the property was tenanted[22], and agricultural produce in the case of farms. It has been held in the Outer House that a co-owner has no liability for rent in respect of natural possession held unlawfully[23], but there are difficulties with this decision[24] and it seems that the law cannot be regarded as settled beyond doubt.

1 As to whether the agreement must be unanimous or by simple majority, see para 23 above.
2 For special rules created by real conditions, see para 26 below.

3 Erskine *Institute* II,6,53.
4 *Erskine* III,3,56; Bell *Principles* s 1072.
5 *Bailey v Scott* (1860) 22 D 1105 at 1109, per Lord Benholme.
6 *Leck v Chalmers* (1859) 21 D 408.
7 *Bell* s 1075.
8 So eg a common drying green cannot be used as a market garden.
9 *Forster v Fryer* (1944) 60 Sh Ct Rep 39.
10 *Carmichael v Simpson* 1932 SLT (Sh Ct) 16.
11 *Wilson v Pattie* (1829) 7 S 316.
12 *George Watson's Hospital Governors v Cormack* (1883) 11 R 320 at 323, OH, per Lord M'Laren (affd (1883) 11 R 320, IH).
13 *Menzies v Macdonald* (1856) 2 Macq 463 at 473, HL, per Lord Cranworth LC. However, the opposite view was expressed by Lord Deas in the course of a dissenting opinion in the Court of Session: see *Menzies v Macdonald* (1854) 16 D 827 at 856 (affd (1856) 2 Macq 463, HL) and by Lord Kinnear in the sequel, *Menzies v Wentworth* (1901) 3 F 941 at 959, 9 SLT 107 at 110, 111.
14 *George Watson's Hospital Governors v Cormack* (1883) 11 R 320 at 323, OH, per Lord M'Laren (affd (1883) 11 R 320, IH). But he cannot grant a lease, because this implies exclusive possession of the whole property: see para 28 below.
15 *Bailey's Executors v Upper Crathes Fishing Ltd* 1987 SLT 405, OH.
16 *Bailey v Scott* (1860) 22 D 1105. As to the appointment of a judicial factor, see para 31 below.
17 *Price v Watson* 1951 SC 359, 1951 SLT 266, followed in *Reith v Paterson* 1993 SCLR 921, Sh Ct, and *Langstane (SP) Housing Association Ltd v Davie* 1994 SCLR 158, Sh Ct. See also the Matrimonial Homes (Family Protection) (Scotland) Act 1981 (c 59), s 4(7).
18 Self help will often amount to spuilzie: see paras 161 ff below.
19 It does not seem entirely satisfactory to say, as was said in *Price v Watson*, that the pursuer has his remedy in division and sale. The pursuer may wish to continue with the property and it seems unreasonable that he should be unable to do so merely on account of the unlawful behaviour of the defender.
20 For the use of interdict for the regulation of possession, see paras 155, 159, below.
21 For ordinary profits, see further para 168 below. If the defender obtained his possession vitiously, violent profits are due: para 169 below. However, a bona fide possessor is liable for neither ordinary nor violent profits: see para 171 below.
22 *Bailey v Scott* (1860) 22 D 1105.
23 *Denholm's Trustees v Denholm* 1984 SLT 319, OH.
24 These difficulties arise principally from the view, apparently held by the court, that in cases of disputes between *pro indiviso* proprietors the only remedies available are division and sale and the appointment of a judicial factor. With respect, this appears to confuse the proposition that these two remedies are always available, which is substantially true, with the proposition that these are the only two remedies which are available, which is false and contrary to many reported decisions before and, indeed, since. For an example of the latter, see *Bailey's Executors v Upper Crathes Fishing Ltd* 1987 SLT 405, OH. On the general question of rent for unlawful possession, see further para 168 below.

25. Alterations and repairs. No alterations can be made to common property without the consent of each *pro indiviso* proprietor. This rule is given by Bell[1], and it has frequently been applied by the courts[2]. It may be taken that any consent thus given will bind successors[3]. The rule is subject to the *de minimis* principle, so that in one case a proprietor was allowed to put a brass name plate on a gate which was owned in common[4]. Breaches of the rule can be prevented by interdict[5], but where an alteration is completed before a complaint is made the other co-proprietors may be personally barred from insisting on the restoration of the *status quo*, at least where they knew of the alteration and where it involved a substantial expenditure of money[6]. An alteration which remains in place will usually satisfy the rules of accession and so become part of the common property[7]. Sometimes, of course, an alteration is of benefit to the property, but a person who carries out such an alteration has no claim for a share of the cost, except in the unusual case of where he genuinely but mistakenly believed the thing to be his sole property[8].

There is an exception to the requirement of unanimity. In a passage which has been judicially approved[9], Bell states that 'necessary operations in rebuilding, repairing, etc, are not to be stopped by the opposition of any of the joint owners'[10]. This appears to mean that any one proprietor can instruct necessary repairs[11]; and if he does so, it is settled that the cost can be recovered from his fellow owners[12], presumably in proportion to the size of their respective shares[13]. Since the right to repair is unilateral, prior consultation is not necessary[14], but may be prudent if disputes are to be avoided later on as to whether the repairs were 'necessary' in the first place and whether the work was carried out at reasonable cost. In some cases the question of repairs is regulated by real burdens[15]. Bell's rule contemplates 'rebuilding' as well as 'repairing', but if a building comes to be completely destroyed, it is not clear either that a *pro indiviso* owner could rebuild solely on his own initiative or that he would be able to recover a share of the cost of so doing[16].

1 Bell *Principles* s 1075.
2 Eg *Anderson v Dalrymple* (1799) Mor 12831; *Reid v Nicol* (1799) Mor 'Property' App No 1; *Taylor v Dunlop* (1872) 11 M 25.
3 This is because the effect of consent is to convert the act from an unlawful one to a lawful one within the special rules of common property. Cf the position of consent to encroachment on property which belongs wholly to someone else.
4 *Barkley v Scott* (1893) 10 Sh Ct Rep 23. More precisely, he was allowed a plate which disclosed his name and profession, but not one which advertised his company.
5 *Riddell v Morisetti* 1994 GWD 38-2238, OH.
6 See para 176 below.
7 Bell s 1076.
8 *Allan v Macpherson* (1928) 44 Sh Ct Rep 63. See further para 173 below.
9 *Deans v Woolfson* 1922 SC 221, 1922 SLT 165.
10 Bell s 1075.
11 However, see *Murray v Johnstone* (1896) 23 R 981 at 990, per Lord Moncreiff, where it is said that a majority must concur in necessary repairs. It must be conceded that Bell is not entirely clear.
12 *Rennie v McGill* (1885) 1 Sh Ct Rep 158; *Miller v Crichton* (1893) 1 SLT 262, OH; W M Gloag *The Law of Contract* (2nd edn, 1929) p 323.
13 Bell s 1078. However, sometimes the matter will be regulated by real burdens.
14 *Rennie v McGill* (1885) 1 Sh Ct Rep 158.
15 See para 26 below.
16 *Deans v Woolfson* 1922 SC 221, 1922 SLT 165.

26. Special rules created by real conditions. In the case of land, the normal rules of common property may be amplified or altered by real conditions, that is to say, by real burdens, servitudes and common interest. The standard case for the application of real conditions is where an area of common property, such as a garden or, in a tenement building, a common passage and stair, is owned and used by the proprietors of other property which is held in individual ownership. The real conditions then serve to regulate use in a more precise way than is possible under the general law.

In practice, the most useful type of condition for this purpose is a real burden, and, particularly in the case of tenement property, it is normal for the common parts to be subject to regulation in relation to use and maintenance[1]. This is often achieved by means of a deed of conditions[2]. There are technical problems, considered elsewhere in this title[3], about the true identity of the dominant and the servient tenements, but in many cases the servient tenements are the individual *pro indiviso* shares[4] while the dominant tenements, carrying the right to enforce, are the neighbouring properties which are served by the common property[5].

Servitudes are less useful in this respect than real burdens and are found much less frequently. Since positive servitudes involve possessory rights, the servient tenement must be the common property as a whole and not individual shares in that property. This means that if a grant of servitude is not to fail as granted *a non domino* it must either be made before the property is divided into *pro indiviso* shares, or it must be granted by all of the *pro indiviso* owners. Neither may be easy to achieve in practice[6].

Unlike the other real conditions, common interest arises by implication of law and indeed probably cannot be expressly created[7]. Common interest appears to be present in all cases of common property within tenement buildings[8], in shared gardens such as the formal gardens found in some Georgian and Victorian building developments[9], and in other like cases[10]. Common interest controls the use to which the common property can be put but its precise content depends upon the type of property in question. For common property within tenements, the particular rules are part of the elaborate framework of the law of the tenement and are considered further in that context[11]. For shared gardens, common interest preserves the property for horticultural and recreational use and, probably, prevents recourse to division and sale by any of its owners[12]. Like real burdens, but unlike servitudes, the servient tenements in common interest are the individual *pro indiviso* shares in the common property and the dominant tenements, carrying enforcement rights, are the neighbouring houses or other properties which are served by the common property[13].

1   Eg *Wells v New House Purchasers Ltd* 1964 SLT (Sh Ct) 2; *McNally and Miller Property Co v Mallinson* 1977 SLT (Sh Ct) 33.
2   For deeds of conditions, see para 388 below.
3   See para 411 below.
4   This is certainly the case for those burdens which impose restrictions as to use.
5   The individual *pro indiviso* shares may possibly also be dominant tenements in a question with each other, although this would only become important if ownership of the common property came to be separated from ownership of the individual properties which are served by it.
6   *Grant v Heriot's Trust* (1906) 8 F 647, 13 SLT 986; *Fearnan Partnership v Grindlay* 1990 SLT 704, affd 1992 SLT 460, HL. See further para 28 below.
7   See para 358 below.
8   See para 232 below.
9   *Grant v Heriot's Trust* (1906) 8 F 647, 13 SLT 986; *Forster v Fryer* (1944) 60 Sh Ct Rep 39.
10   Eg it has been suggested, that it is present in common grazings: see *Fearnan Partnership v Grindlay* 1992 SLT 460, HL.
11   See paras 232 ff below.
12   In *Grant v Heriot's Trust* (1906) 8 F 647 at 665, 13 SLT 986 at 995, Lord M'Laren refers to the garden being 'maintained in perpetuity for the benefit of all'. See also Lord President Dunedin at 658, 991.
13   In *Grant v Heriot's Trust* (1906) 8 F 647 at 665, 13 SLT 986 at 995, Lord M'Laren stated that the right of common interest 'belonged to all the proprietors of the houses in the Square'.

27. Matrimonial homes. Important changes to the common law rules of management are made by the Matrimonial Homes (Family Protection) (Scotland) Act 1981 (as amended) in respect of matrimonial homes co-owned by a husband and wife[1]. 'Matrimonial home' is defined by the Act as meaning any house, caravan, houseboat or other structure which has been provided or has been made available by one or both of the spouses as, or has become a family residence, and it includes any garden or other ground or building attached to, and usually occupied with, or otherwise required for the amenity or convenience of, the house, caravan, houseboat or other structure[2]. Excluded from the definition is a residence provided or made available by one spouse for that spouse to reside in, whether with any child of the family or not, separately from the other spouse[2]. Except for the particular section[3] which deals with division and sale, the provisions of the Act discussed below apply not only to matrimonial homes which are owned in common by the spouses, but also to matrimonial homes owned by the spouses in common with one or more third parties[4].

So far as ownership in common is concerned, the main provisions of the Act are the following. Contrary to the rule of the common law[5], either spouse is entitled without the consent of the other to carry out such non-essential repairs or improvements to the matrimonial home as may be authorised by an order of the court[6], being such repairs or improvements as the court considers to be appropriate for the reasonable enjoyment of the spouse's occupancy rights[7]. Improvements include alterations and enlargement[8]. The court may apportion the expenditure thus incurred, having regard in particular to the respective financial circumstances of the spouses[9]. Either spouse may apply to the court for an order regulating the exercise of occupancy rights[10], and, in appropriate cases, an order may be obtained excluding the other spouse completely from the matrimonial home[11]. If one spouse conveys his or her *pro indiviso* share to a third party without the written consent of the other spouse[12], the third party acquires no right to occupy the matrimonial home[13]. The same rule applies in respect of grants of standard securities and other dealings[14] in relation to a *pro indiviso* share.

Finally, the Act gives the court discretion to refuse what at common law is an absolute right to division and sale[15]. Alternatively the court may postpone the granting of decree for such period as it may consider reasonable in the circumstances, which may include a period occurring after the marriage has been ended by divorce[16], or again it may grant decree subject to such conditions as it may prescribe. In the exercise of its discretion the court is directed to have regard to all the circumstances of the case, including in particular (1) the conduct of the spouses in relation to each other and otherwise; (2) the respective needs and financial resources of the spouses; (3) the needs of any child of the family; (4) the extent (if any) to which the matrimonial home is used in connection with a trade, business or profession of either spouse; and (5) whether the spouse bringing the action of division and sale offers or has offered to make available to the other spouse any suitable alternative accommodation[17]. No consensus has so far emerged as to how the discretion conferred by the Act should be exercised. On one view a *pro indiviso* proprietor is entitled to at least as much protection as a spouse whose only right in the house is a statutory occupancy right; and since the occupancy right of the latter can be taken away by the court only where his or her consent to a proposed sale was unreasonably withheld[18], so similar principles ought to be invoked in relation to the *pro indiviso* right of the former[19]. Another view emphasises the primacy of a co-owner's right to division and sale, and suggests that the discretion under the Act should be exercised only where there are strong reasons for doing so[20]. Whichever view is adopted, two things at least seem clear. First, the only circumstances which are relevant to the exercise of the court's discretion are those which relate directly to the matrimonial home. A court is not concerned with the history of the marriage or with the reasons for its breakdown[20]. Secondly, the discretion will be exercised in favour of a defender who can satisfy the court that he or she has a special need for occupation of the matrimonial home which would not be adequately provided for by payment of a share of its capital value[21].

1 As to the Matrimonial Homes (Family Protection) (Scotland) Act 1981 (c 59) generally, see FAMILY LAW, vol 10, paras 854 ff.
2 Ibid, s 22 (amended by the Law Reform (Miscellaneous Provisions) (Scotland) Act 1985 (c 73), s 13(10)).
3 Ie the Matrimonial Homes (Family Protection) (Scotland) Act 1981, s 19.
4 The usual expression used in the Matrimonial Homes (Family Protection) (Scotland) Act 1981 is 'where both spouses are entitled to occupy a matrimonial home'. However, s 19 applies to 'a matrimonial home which the spouses own in common'.
5 For the rule of the common law, see para 25 above.
6 Ie either the Court of Session or the sheriff court: Matrimonial Homes (Family Protection) (Scotland) Act 1981, s 22.
7 Ibid, s 2(4)(a). 'Occupancy rights' are defined as (1) the right, if in occupation of the matrimonial home, to continue in occupation and (2) the right, if not in occupation, to enter into and occupy the matrimonial home: ibid, s 22 (applying s 1(1), (4), as amended by the Law Reform (Miscellaneous Provisions) (Scotland) Act 1985, s 13(2))).
8 Matrimonial Homes (Family Protection) (Scotland) Act 1981, s 2(9).
9 Ibid, s 2(4)(b).
10 Ibid, s 3(1)(d). See further FAMILY LAW, vol 10, para 861. For common law rights to seek judicial regulation, see para 30 below.
11 Ibid, s 4 (amended by the Law Reform (Miscellaneous Provisions) (Scotland) Act 1985, s 13(5)). See further FAMILY LAW, vol 10, paras 863, 864.

12 Matrimonial Homes (Family Protection) (Scotland) Act 1981, s 6(3)(a)(i), applied by s 9(2). For the
   form of consent, see the Matrimonial Homes (Form of Consent) (Scotland) Regulations 1982,
   SI 1982/971. The Matrimonial Homes (Family Protection) (Scotland) Act 1981, s 6(3)(a)(ii),
   provides the alternative of a renunciation of occupancy rights, but it is not clear that a *pro indiviso*
   proprietor can renounce such rights, at least in a manner which could be enforced by third parties.
   Consent may be dispensed with by the court under s 7 (applied by s 9(2) and amended by the Family
   Law (Scotland) Act 1985 (c 37), s 28(2), Sch 2, and the Age of Legal Capacity (Scotland) Act 1991
   (c 50), s 10(1), Sch 1, para 37).
13 Matrimonial Homes (Family Protection) (Scotland) Act 1981, s 9(1)(b).
14 For the meaning of 'dealing', see ibid, s 6(2) (applied by s 9(2)).
15 Ibid, s 19. For the common law rules, see para 32 below, and *Dickson v Dickson* 1982 SLT 128, OH.
   The early law may have been different: see Bell *Principles* s 1079.
16 *Crow v Crow* 1986 SLT 270, OH. Nevertheless, the order under the Matrimonial Homes (Family
   Protection) (Scotland) Act 1981, s 19, must be made while the marriage still subsists.
17 Matrimonial Homes (Family Protection) (Scotland) Act 1981, s 19 (applying s 3(3)(a)–(d)).
18 Ibid, s 7 (as amended: see note 12 above). This provision has no application to an action of division
   and sale by one spouse against the other: *Dunsmore v Dunsmore* 1986 SLT (Sh Ct) 9.
19 *Hall v Hall* 1987 SCLR 38, 1987 SLT (Sh Ct) 15. The parallel is, however, inexact. A non-entitled
   spouse who loses his or her statutory occupancy rights is left with nothing. A *pro indiviso* owner who
   fails to gain the benefit of the 'section 19 discretion' receives, on sale, the capital value of his or her
   share in the house, which may be sufficient to fund the purchase of another house.
20 *Berry v Berry* 1988 SCLR 296, 1988 SLT 650, OH.
21 *Rae v Rae* 1991 SCLR 188, 1991 SLT 454.

28. Juristic acts. In common property each proprietor has a separate *pro indiviso*
share, which may be dealt with in much the same way as any other property. So a *pro
indiviso* share may be transferred *inter vivos*, whether gratuitously or for consideration[1]. It may be bequeathed by will, except where there is a survivorship destination which the proprietor is contractually bound not to evacuate[2]. Again, it may
be made the subject of a non-possessory right in security, such as a standard
security[3]. It may be attached by creditors of the proprietor by means of diligence[4],
and it forms part of his estate for the purposes of bankruptcy[5]. Finally, a proprietor is
able to subdivide his *pro indiviso* share, apparently without limit[6], and to dispose of
the subdivided parts.

This final point was settled by a majority of the whole court in *Menzies v
Macdonald* [7], a decision subsequently upheld in the House of Lords. However, there
are obvious difficulties in the idea of unlimited subdivision. If A, being the owner of
property to the extent of a one-half *pro indiviso* share, subdivides his share into 100
separate parts and sells 99, keeping the final part for himself, it is difficult to say that
there is no prejudice to B, the owner of the remaining one-half *pro indiviso* share.
Before the subdivision there were two owners, A and B, each with a one-half share.
After the subdivision there are 101 owners, one (B) with a one-half share, and the
remaining 100 with a one two-hundredth share each. B must now share possession,
not with one but with 100 others, and each must be consulted before management
decisions can be taken. This argument was made forcibly by Lord Deas, who was in
the minority in *Menzies*:

> 'Hitherto his [B's] right has been to possess and enjoy the whole and every part of the
> subject with one. Now his right is to be, to possess and enjoy the whole and every part of
> it with many. Strowan's [A's] concurrence has hitherto been sufficient for everything.
> But now there is to be a power of multiplication of proprietors, the exercise of which
> will render it hopeless to expect concurrence in anything'[8].

Lord Justice-Clerk Hope, who was also in the minority in *Menzies*, pointed to the
apparent paradox that A is able to sell important and substantial rights and yet remain
entitled to use the property in just the same manner as before:

> 'It will be a case . . . in which, while the conveyance is said to dispone a very great and
> valuable heritable right, yet in the granter the very same right will remain wholly
> unimpaired and undiminished in extent or exercise, and two proprietors will then

exercise, to the full extent of this universal right, the right of common property with Menzies [B]'[9].

The majority of the court in *Menzies* was not convinced by these practical worries, arguing that the holders of the subdivided shares would have in total no greater right of use of the property than that formerly held by their author, that accordingly the position of the other co-proprietor had not been worsened, except perhaps in respect of a certain loss of solitude, and that in the event of a dispute judicial regulation could be sought. Even solitude, according to Lord Cockburn, was not to everyone's taste, at least not in the case of Loch Rannoch[10], which was the subject of the dispute in *Menzies*:

'[T]hey [that is, the arguments against subdivision] seem all to proceed on the assumption that solitude is the only value of a Highland lake. This may be the opinion of some people; but it is certainly not the opinion of everybody. There are many to whom a lake is never so beautiful or interesting as when it is crowded with boats, engaged either in business or in pleasure ... The pursuer's [B's] interests (solitude excepted) are left untouched although a thousand other persons be admitted to the enjoyment of the water. Their sailing or floating, "or exercising all acts of property thereupon", ie upon the water, do not prevent him from doing the same'[11].

The arguments for the majority in *Menzies* do not readily convince, and it seems clear that, at least with some types of property and depending on the scale of the subdivision employed, subdivision by one *pro indiviso* proprietor is bound to have an adverse effect on the position of the other *pro indiviso* proprietors[12]. However, the law is now settled beyond doubt to the effect that subdivision is permitted.

Certain juristic acts are beyond the powers of a single *pro indiviso* owner[13]. Thus a single owner is unable to grant a lease which would be binding on successors[14], or a positive servitude[15], or a possessory right in security such as a pledge. Nor can he transfer any more than his own *pro indiviso* share, and a purported conveyance of the whole property is effective only *quoad* that share[16]. These limitations on the power of an owner acting alone are sometimes explained on the basis of the rule which requires unanimity in matters of management[17]. However, a more fundamental reason is that the excluded juristic acts confer possessory rights and so affect the whole property. Accordingly, they can be granted only by the owner of the whole property, that is to say, by all the owners in common acting together. In effect this is an application of the familiar rule *nemo dat quod non habet*: since a single *pro indiviso* owner does not 'have', therefore he cannot 'give'[18].

A question which has caused some difficulty is whether all owners in common can lease property to one of their own number. It has been held that such a lease breaches the rule that the same person cannot be both debtor and creditor in the same obligation[19]. Nevertheless, it is submitted that if all the co-owners acting together are able to grant a lease to a third party, then, equally, they are able to grant a lease to one of their own number. Properly analysed, such a lease is an agreement between, on the one hand, the parties who, acting together, alone have a right of exclusive possession and, on the other hand, a party who by himself has no such right. The debtor and the creditor are not the same[20].

1 Bell *Principles* s 1073.
2 On survivorship destinations generally, see G L Gretton 'Destinations' (1989) 34 JLSS 299. Express obligations not to evacuate are almost unknown. However, such an obligation is implied where either a property is bought by husband and wife, both contributing to the price, or where a property (or relevant share therein) was the subject of a gift. See *Perrett's Trustees v Perrett* 1909 SC 522, 1909 1 SLT 302; *Brown's Trustees v Brown* 1943 SC 488, 1944 SLT 215; *Hay's Trustee v Hay's Trustees* 1951 SC 329, 1951 SLT 170. A survivorship clause has no effect on the right of a *pro indiviso* proprietor to dispose of the property *inter vivos*: see *Steele v Caldwell* 1979 SLT 228, OH; *Smith v MacKintosh* 1989 SCLR 83, 1989 SLT 148, OH. Nor does it affect the right to seek a division and sale: *Dunsmore v Dunsmore* 1986 SLT (Sh Ct) 9. Cf *Allan v Macpherson* (1928) 44 Sh Ct Rep 63, which appears to be wrongly decided.

3 *Schaw v Black* (1889) 16 R 336; *McLeod v Cedar Holdings Ltd* 1989 SLT 620 at 623, per Lord Justice-Clerk Ross. For possessory securities such as pledge, see the text to notes 14–18 below. It is suggested in *Grant v Heriot's Trust* (1906) 8 F 647 at 663, 13 SLT 986 at 994, per Lord President Dunedin, that, following an action of division and sale, a heritable security 'which began life by sticking to the *pro indiviso* right, may go on with the same reason to stick to the right which the person gets instead of the *pro indiviso* right, namely, the right to a certain separate share of the property'. However, it is thought that this is not correct and that a right in security, as a real right, would continue to attach to a one-half share of the whole property until it was discharged. On this subject, see also *Morrison v Kirk* 1912 SC 44 at 48, 1911 2 SLT 355 at 356, per Lord Salvesen.

4 For adjudication, see Bell *Principles* s 1073 and G L Gretton *The Law of Inhibition and Adjudication* (2nd edn, 1996) p 216. For poinding, see the Debtors (Scotland) Act 1987 (c 18), s 41, and *Kinloch v Barclay's Bank plc* 1995 SCLR 975, Sh Ct. At common law the position with regard to poinding appears to have been otherwise: see *Fleming v Twaddle* (1828) 7 S 92. For arrestment, see DILIGENCE, vol 8, paras 267, 272.

5 Bankruptcy (Scotland) Act 1985 (c 66), s 31(1). However, see further s 31(6).

6 *Menzies v Macdonald* (1854) 16 D 827 at 846, 855, per Lord Rutherford and Lord Deas (affd (1856) 2 Macq 463, HL).

7 *Menzies v Macdonald* (1854) 16 D 827 (affd (1856) 2 Macq 463, HL).

8 *Menzies v Macdonald* (1854) 16 D 827 at 856.

9 (1854) 16 D 827 at 836.

10 At this time non-tidal lochs were often regarded as common property of the 'surrounding proprietors. The modern view is that there is several ownership *ad medium filum*: see para 305 below.

11 *Menzies v Macdonald* (1854) 16 D 827 at 840.

12 The sequel to *Menzies v Macdonald* demonstrates this: see *Menzies v Wentworth* (1901) 3 F 941, 9 SLT 107, discussed at para 30 below.

13 Hume *Lectures* vol IV (Stair Soc vol 17, 1955 ed G C H Paton) p 328; *Grant v Heriot's Trust* (1906) 8 F 647 at 662, 13 SLT 986 at 993, 994, per Lord President Dunedin.

14 *Campbell and Stewart v Campbell* 24 January 1809 FC; *Morrison* (1857) 20 D 276; *Bell's Executors v Inland Revenue* 1987 SLT 625. The question of a purely contractual right to possession was touched on in para 24 above. So far as the real right of lease is concerned there may possibly be a different rule where the common property is ancillary to some other piece of land of which the lessor is the exclusive owner. So if A leases his tenement flat to B, there is a certain awkwardness in saying that the lease is effective *quoad* the flat but ineffective *quoad* the lessor's *pro indiviso* right in the common passage and stair.

15 *Grant v Heriot's Trust* (1906) 8 F 647, 13 SLT 986; *WVS Office Premises Ltd v Currie* 1969 SC 170, 1969 SLT 254; *Feaman Partnership v Grindlay* 1990 SLT 704 (affd on other grounds, 1992 SLT 460, HL). The position of negative servitudes (which do not confer possessory rights) is unclear.

16 *McLeod v Cedar Holdings Ltd* 1989 SLT 620.

17 See para 23 above.

18 For the rule *nemo dat quod non habet*, see paras 669 ff below.

19 *Barclay v Penman* 1984 SLT 376, OH; *Bell's Executors v Inland Revenue* 1987 SLT 625; *Clydesdale Bank plc v Davidson* 1996 SCLR 119, 1996 SLT 437.

20 *Higgins v Lanarkshire Assessor* 1911 1 SLT 135, LVAC; *Pinkerton v Pinkerton* 1986 SLT 672, OH. Cf *Lord Blantyre v Dunn* (1858) 20 D 1188. See also W M Gordon *Scottish Land Law* (1989) para 15-15.

29. Title to sue.

As a general rule, actions affecting an individual *pro indiviso* share only may be raised by the owner of that share[1] while actions affecting the whole property must be raised by all the owners acting together[2]. However, the rule is easier to express than to apply. Thus it has been held that a single *pro indiviso* owner may sue in delict for recovery of a pro rata share of damage to the common property[3]. He may also defend or recover possession of the property in a question with a person who has no title, such as a squatter, or a neighbour whose building has encroached[4]. However, it appears that he cannot sue for a share of rent from a tenant[5]. The latter decision may be based on the related rule that all the creditors in a contract must join together in its enforcement[6]. Therefore, in the case of incorporeal property, each co-holder of the right must concur in its enforcement against the defender. Similarly, where land is leased, all co-owners must join in an action of removing against a tenant[7].

1 Thus eg one *pro indiviso* proprietor has title to sue in respect of a breach of the rules of management of common property by another *pro indiviso* proprietor.
2 Eg *Millar v Cathcart* (1861) 23 D 743.

3 *Lawson v Newcastle Steam-Packet Co* (1850) 13 D 175.
4 *Johnston v Craufurd* (1855) 17 D 1023; *Lade v Largs Baking Co Ltd* (1863) 2 M 17; *Laird v Reid* (1871) 9 M 699. See further para 141 below.
5 *Schaw v Black* (1889) 16 R 336.
6 W M Gloag *The Law of Contract* (2nd edn, 1929) pp 202–204.
7 Erskine *Institute* II,6,53; *Murdoch v Inglis* (1679) 3 Brown's Supp 297; *Johnston v Craufurd* (1855) 17 D 1023. However, if the lease was granted by one *pro indiviso* owner only, acting with the authority of the others, it has been suggested that the granter would then be able to lead a removing: *Crozier v Downie* (1871) 9 M 826.

30. Judicial regulation. One possible solution for managerial deadlock is to seek judicial regulation of the common property[1]. But while the availability of judicial regulation has often been asserted[2], there appears to be no reported case in which it has actually been granted, and serious doubts have been expressed as to its practicability:

> '[P]ermanent judicial regulation . . . if competent at all, must be competent to fix and regulate every act of administration and management, a supposition which seems to me inconsistent with the very notion of property . . . No permanent regulation could be laid down which would not become inapplicable on every change of circumstances, — such as an increase or diminution in the number of joint proprietors. A regulation which was to be varied from time to time, at the instance of any party interested, according to the varying views of judges, would be arbitrary, if not intolerable. Besides, what would this be but to make the Court permanent managers for the proprietors?'[3]

In only one reported case has an application for judicial regulation been made[4]. The pursuer was a *pro indiviso* owner of Loch Rannoch who, in an earlier litigation[5], had unsuccessfully attempted to prevent the then other *pro indiviso* owner from subdividing and selling his share. As a result, there were now six *pro indiviso* proprietors and the loch was in danger of being overfished. The pursuer proposed a scheme for the regulation of the fishing which would allocate a certain number of boats to each proprietor. He was unsuccessful. It was said that regulation would be introduced only where there was an 'abuse of the joint right' of a 'manifest and palpable kind'[6] by 'destroying or materially diminishing the subject-matter of the right'[7]. A heavy onus was said to rest on the pursuer, and this had not been discharged[8]. The court also indicated that it would not proceed to compulsory regulation if an attempt had not first been made at achieving voluntary regulation[9].

1 This paragraph is concerned with regulation in the strict sense of the term. For regulation by judicial factory, see para 31 below.
2 Eg *Menzies v Macdonald* (1854) 16 D 827, affd (1856) 2 Macq 463, HL; *Fearnan Partnership v Grindlay* 1992 SLT 460 at 465, HL, per Lord Jauncey. See also para 329 below.
3 *Menzies v Macdonald* (1854) 16 D 827 at 856, 857, per Lord Deas. In *Menzies v Wentworth* (1901) 3 F 941 at 949, OH (affd (1901) 3 F 941, 9 SLT 107, IH), Lord Stormonth-Darling commented on this passage, saying: 'It may be that Lord Deas magnified a little the difficulties of regulation, in order to enforce the view that Struan [the defender] could not subdivide his rights at all. But being now face to face with the difficulties which he anticipated, I confess that I strongly sympathise with these observations'.
4 *Menzies v Wentworth* (1901) 3 F 941, 9 SLT 107.
5 *Menzies v Macdonald* (1854) 16 D 827, affd (1856) 2 Macq 463, HL, discussed at para 28 above.
6 *Menzies v Wentworth* (1901) 3 F 941 at 953, OH, per Lord Stormonth-Darling.
7 *Menzies v Wentworth* (1901) 3 F 941 at 959, 9 SLT 107 at 110, IH, per Lord Kinnear. However, Lord M'Laren (at 958, 110) expressed the view that a proprietor is not bound to wait until he can prove actual injury before he seeks judicial regulation, and that apprehended injury is sufficient.
8 *Menzies v Wentworth* (1901) 3 F 941 at 954, OH, per Lord Stormonth-Darling.
9 (1901) 3 F 941 at 953, OH, per Lord Stormonth-Darling.

31. Appointment of a judicial factor. A second possible method of resolving disagreement among co-proprietors is by the appointment of a judicial factor[1] However, a court will appoint a factor only in exceptional circumstances, where no other method of managing the property seems possible[2]. Appointments are very rare in practice, and are found mainly in cases where property has been let and where the task of the factor is to collect and distribute the rents and to manage the leases[3].

1 See generally TRUSTS, TRUSTEES AND JUDICIAL FACTORS, vol 24, para 278, and N M L Walker *Judicial Factors* (1974) p 60.
2 *Allan* (1898) 6 SLT 106, OH, affd (1898) 6 SLT 152.
3 Eg *Mackintosh* (1849) 11 D 1029; *Morrison* (1857) 20 D 276; *Bailey v Scott* (1860) 22 D 1105.

32. Division and sale: entitlement. Any one co-owner is entitled to realise his share by having the property divided up rateably or, if physical division is impracticable, by having the property sold and the proceeds divided[1]. The rule applies to all common property, whether heritable or moveable, corporeal or incorporeal, although the reported cases are exclusively concerned with land[2]. The appropriate action is one for division, or, as in practice almost always, for division and[3] sale. Subject to the limited exceptions mentioned below, the right to division and sale is an absolute right to which no defence will be entertained[4]. Thus it does not matter that a ready market exists for the pursuer's *pro indiviso* share, so that he could have sold it without disturbing the shares of others. Nor does it matter that the share of the pursuer is small compared to the shares of the remaining *pro indiviso* proprietors. The reason for the rule is, or at least was[5], public policy[6]. Traditionally, the law did not look favourably on ownership in common, Bankton, for example, referring to 'the great inconveniency of possessing in common, whereby the subject is for most part neglected'[7]. Accordingly, a co-owner who wished to end the community of ownership ought to be entitled to do so. It might seem that an absolute right to division and sale is in breach of the rule that no person is to be deprived of property without his consent[8], but Stair's view was rather that division restores to the individual owners that which is their own, that is to say, a distinct physical share of the former common property[9].

There are four circumstances where division and sale is not, or may not be, available. First, it is not available where the parties have contracted to that effect[10]. Such a contract will not bind successors[11], and there seems to be no other mechanism by which successors can be bound[12]. Secondly, a proprietor may be personally barred from insisting on division and sale[13]. Thirdly, Bell states that division and sale is not available in respect of 'a thing of common and indispensable use, as a stair case or vestibule' to which may presumably be added a common garden and a common access road and, no doubt, a number of other examples[14]. Finally, there are special statutory rules for matrimonial homes which restrict, but do not exclude, the right to division and sale[15].

1 Craig *Jus Feudale* II,8,35,41; Stair *Institutions* I,7,15; Bankton *Institute* I,8,36,40; Erskine *Institute* III,3,56; Bell *Principles* ss 1079–1082; Bell *Commentaries* I,62. Traditionally, the obligation to divide is classified as an obligation of restitution, a view which may be traced to Justinian *Institutes* III,27,3. It seems likely that the right to division and sale developed separately for different types of property, such as ships or commonties or property held by heirs-portioners, and that the universal right was an invention of the later law. See also para 18 above. For the relationship between Roman law and Scots law, see G MacCormack 'The *Actio Communi Dividundo* in Roman and Scots Law' in A D E Lewis and D J Ibbetson (ed) *The Roman Law Tradition* (1993).
2 Thus the institutional writers make frequent references to ships. See also *Robertson's Trustee v Roberts* 1982 SLT 22, OH, which concerns incorporeal property (a lease).
3 'And' is sometimes given as 'or'.
4 *Upper Crathes Fishings Ltd v Bailey's Executors* 1991 SCLR 151, 1991 SLT 747.
5 The law cannot be said to be hostile to the principal modern example of common ownership, which is co-ownership of matrimonial property: see eg the Family Law (Scotland) Act 1985 (c 37),

s 25. Perhaps for this reason division and sale of matrimonial homes is now subject to statutory restrictions: see para 27 above.

6 Eg *Brock v Hamilton* (1857) 19 D 701 at 703, OH, per Lord Rutherford (reported as a note to *Anderson v Anderson* (1857) 19 D 700); *Banff Magistrates v Ruthin Castle Ltd* 1944 SC 36 at 68, 1944 SLT 373 at 388, per Lord Justice-Clerk Cooper.

7 *Bankton* I,8,36. As Craig points out (*Craig* 2,8,35), arguments of this kind can be found in Roman law, where the rule is substantially the same.

8 See para 613 below.

9 *Stair* I,7,15.

10 Bell *Commentaries* I,62; *Morrison v Kirk* 1912 SC 44, 1911 2 SLT 355; *Williams v Schellenberg* 1988 GWD 29-1254, OH. It is thought that division and sale is not prevented by a survivorship clause in which evacuation is contractually excluded: see para 28, note 2, above.

11 However, depending on the wording used, a person who has since disposed of his *pro indiviso* share may still be able to enforce the contract against a person who has not: see *Williams v Cleveland and Highland Holdings Ltd* 1989 GWD 33-1530, OH, affd 1990 GWD 30-1764.

12 Such a restriction cannot be imposed in the form of a real burden, although this is perhaps more a rule of real burdens than a rule of common property. See *Grant v Heriot's Trust* (1906) 8 F 647 at 658, 13 SLT 986 at 991, per Lord President Dunedin, and para 391 below.

13 *Upper Crathes Fishings Ltd v Bailey's Executors* 1991 SCLR 151 at 152, 1991 SLT 747 at 749, per Lord President Hope.

14 Bell *Principles* s 1082. One possible way of analysing this exception is to regard it as a restriction born of common interest: see para 26 above.

15 See para 27 above.

33. Division and sale: procedure. An action of division and sale may be raised either in the sheriff court or the Court of Session[1]. In the case of land, the pursuer probably need not be infeft provided that he holds under a delivered conveyance, and it appears that a beneficiary in a bare trust has a title to sue notwithstanding that the property is formally held by a trustee[2]. The action usually concludes for division of the common subjects, or, in the event of its being found that they are indivisible, for sale under authority of the court and division of the price[3]. Sale is available only where the property is considered to be indivisible and, unless this is admitted by the defender[4], the normal practice is to remit the question of divisibility to a person of skill[5]. A remittance is also necessary in undefended actions[6]. Once a person of skill has reported, a note of objections may be lodged by either party, but a reporter will be asked to reconsider his report only where the objections are cogent and articulate, or where there is some issue of principle identifiable *ex facie* from the report[7].

The question of the criteria to be applied in determining the physical divisibility of property was examined in the leading case of *Thom v Macbeth*[8]. There it was pointed out that:

'Physically, almost everything, every subject, whether heritable or moveable, is divisible, if all considerations of expense of division and of deterioration or possible destruction of the subject are to be disregarded. For example, it is physically possible to divide even a mansion-house, and to convert it into two or more dwellings. But considerations of expediency, of expense, and of deterioration cannot be left out of view, and in most cases it is just upon these considerations that the question depends whether a subject shall be specifically divided, or whether it shall be sold, and the price distributed'[9].

And again:

'[W]hen division is not reasonably practicable without sacrificing to an appreciable extent the interests of some or all of the parties the only resort is a sale and division of the price'[10].

In practice, the main criteria which have been used are, first, whether it is possible to divide the property in such a way as to give each co-proprietor a pro rata physical share, and, secondly, whether such a division would adversely affect the value of the property. Often the first is unattainable, and even where it can be attained this is usually at the cost of a material diminution in overall value. As a result, in the typical case common property is not divisible[11]. In some cases opposition to a sale, and hence support for division, is based upon what the courts have characterised as 'sentimental' reasons, that is to say, upon personal attachment to the property, but it is settled that such reasons cannot be allowed to prevail, at least where the result would be to cause pecuniary loss to the other proprietor or proprietors[12].

Where property is indivisible, the court will order it to be sold, and the proceeds are then divided rateably, subject to any special agreement which may have been reached by the parties[13]. Following the sale, a conveyance to the purchaser is granted by the co-proprietors, and, in the event of a co-proprietor refusing to sign, the court can authorise a signature on his behalf by the clerk of court[14]. The sale is usually by private bargain[15], replacing the earlier practice of sale by roup (auction); but there is no fixed rule that the one should be used in preference to the other, and the method of sale selected will be the one which is likely to yield the highest price[16].

In addition to sale by roup and sale by private bargain, there may also be a third possibility. Certainly this was the view of the institutional writers. Thus, for example, Bell, whose views on matters concerning common property are of particular authority:

> 'If the subject be not naturally divisible, the object of the application is, to enforce one or other of the following alternatives:- Either that the defenders should dispose of their shares at a certain price, or take the pursuer's share at the same rate; or that the whole should be exposed to sale, and converted into the divisible form of a price or sum of money'[17].

Like some other aspects of *pro indiviso* ownership[18], this rule seems first to have developed in the context of ships, but Bell gives the rule as a universal one, and it appears to have been applied in *Milligan v Barnhill*[19], which was a case involving heritable property[20]. The rule has since been pled in a modern Outer House case, *Scrimgeour v Scrimgeour*[21]. In that case the pursuer raised an action of division and sale in respect of a house which she owned in common with the defender. The pursuer concluded for warrant to purchase the defender's one-half share at the open market price fixed by a reporter. The action was undefended and decree was granted[22]. *Scrimgeour* was not followed in a subsequent Outer House case where the action was defended[23]. It is suggested, however, that the law is as stated by the institutional writers and as applied by the Lord Ordinary in *Scrimgeour*[24]. Nevertheless, some aspects of that law are unclear. Since the object of a sale is to realise the highest possible price, it appears that one owner will not be able to buy the share of another if the evidence is that a higher price might be obtained on the open market[25]. Further, an obvious difficulty arises if both parties wish to buy the share of the other, and it may be that this difficulty could only be resolved by a sale on the open market[26].

1 Sheriff Courts (Scotland) Act 1907 (c 51), s 5(3). See generally I D Macphail *Sheriff Court Practice* (1988) paras 23–37 ff.
2 *Bailey v Scott* (1860) 22 D 1105; *Johnston v MacFarlane* 1987 SCLR 104, 1987 SLT 593. However, cf *Allan* (1898) 6 SLT 152. A bare trust is one in which the trustee holds the property to the order of the beneficiary. Where the beneficial interest in a trust is itself held in common, then division and sale is presumably available in respect of that interest, except where the terms of the trust can be read as excluding the right.
3 Eg *Brock v Hamilton* (1857) 19 D 701, OH (reported as a note to *Anderson v Anderson* (1857) 19 D 700). See 3 *Encyclopaedia of Scottish Legal Styles* (1954) pp 65 ff, and W J Dobie *Styles for Use in the Sheriff Courts in Scotland* (1951) pp 84–86.
4 As in *Brock v Hamilton* (1857) 19 D 701, OH.
5 Eg *Anderson v Anderson* (1857) 19 D 700; *Morrison v Kirk* 1912 SC 44, 1911 2 SLT 355; *Upper Crathes Fishings Ltd v Bailey's Executors* 1991 SCLR 151, 1991 SLT 747. Alternatively, there can be a proof,

as in *Bryden v Gibson* (1837) 15 S 486. In *Thom v Macbeth* (1875) 3 R 161 at 165, per Lord Gifford, it was said that 'this question is in general, and certainly, in a case like the present, far better decided upon a remit to a person of skill and experience than by allowing the parties a general proof'.

6 *Bryden v Gibson* (1837) 15 S 486; *Scrimgeour v Scrimgeour* 1988 SLT 590, OH.

7 *Thom v Macbeth* (1875) 3 R 161; *Williams v Cleveland and Highland Holdings Ltd* 1993 SLT 398, OH. However, a reporter is constrained by the terms of his remit, and his report cannot be objected to on the grounds that it fails to cover matters not provided for in his remit.

8 *Thom v Macbeth* (1875) 3 R 161.

9 (1875) 3 R 161 at 165, per Lord Gifford.

10 (1875) 3 R 161 at 164, per Lord Justice-Clerk Moncreiff.

11 However, for a case where property was found to be divisible, see *Morrison v Kirk* 1912 SC 44, 1911 2 SLT 355. The conveyancing procedure in such cases is laid down in the Conveyancing (Scotland) Act 1874 (c 94), s 35.

12 *Thom v Macbeth* (1875) 3 R 161 at 164, 165, per Lord Ormidale; *Williams v Cleveland and Highland Holdings Ltd* 1993 SLT 398, OH.

13 *Tweedie v Ritchie* 1992 GWD 34-2008, Sh Ct; *Ralston v Jackson* 1994 SLT 771; *Johnston v Robson* 1995 SLT (Sh Ct) 26.

14 *Whyte v Whyte* 1913 2 SLT 85, OH. See also para 664, note 1, below.

15 *Campbells v Murray* 1972 SC 310, 1972 SLT 249.

16 *The Miller Group Ltd v Tasker* 1993 SLT 207. However, cf *Berry v Berry (No 2)* 1989 SLT 292, OH. The reporter may make a recommendation as to the method of sale.

17 Bell *Commentaries* I,62. See also Stair *Institutions* I,16,4; Bankton *Institute* I,8,40; Erskine *Institute* III,3,56.

18 See paras 18 and 19, note 1, above.

19 *Milligan v Barnhill* (1782) Mor 2486, 2 Hailes 897.

20 In *Stewart v Simpson* (1835) 14 S 72 at 73 the defender sought to resist the sale of the property by arguing, on the basis of *Milligan v Barnhill*, that 'before one of two joint-proprietors demanding a division could insist on the common property being brought to sale, he was bound to fix a value at which he would agree either to take the other half, or part with his own, and that it was only failing this option being consented to that he was entitled to insist for a sale'. To this the pursuer replied that (at 73, 74) 'whatever might be the rule as to the ordinary case of joint property, there could be no doubt that, as to company property, the regular and legal course which every partner was entitled to insist for was a sale of the property'. The pursuer was successful, but the court indicated that its decision turned on specialities of partnership law. *Milligan v Barnhill* was also a partnership case, although the title to the property was held *pro indiviso* by the partners. The form in which the title was held in *Stewart v Simpson* does not appear from the report. For partnership property, see further para 18, note 5, above.

21 *Scrimgeour v Scrimgeour* 1988 SLT 590, OH.

22 The case is remarkable for its copious citation of Roman and other civilian authority.

23 *Berry v Berry (No 2)* 1989 SLT 292, OH, where, somewhat surprisingly, Lord Cowie, the Lord Ordinary, expressed the view that (at 293): 'I do not regard the case of *Scrimgeour v Scrimgeour* as providing any assistance in the present case. The circumstances there were very special and do not support the general proposition that I have a wide discretion enabling me to lay down, in the absence of agreement between the parties, how the subjects should be disposed of'.

24 *Gray v Kerner* 1996 SCLR 331, Sh Ct. For an unsuccessful attempt to require a conveyance on the basis of the *condictio causa data causa non secuta*, see *Grieve v Morrison* 1993 SLT 852, OH.

25 1989 SLT 292 at 293, OH, per Lord Cowie.

26 However, see the remarks in *Scrimgeour v Scrimgeour* 1988 SLT 590 at 593, OH, per Lord McCluskey, about the Roman practice of a closed auction among the co-owners.

(3) JOINT PROPERTY

34. Examples of joint property. For many years the distinction between joint property and common property was not clearly drawn, but in modern times it has come to be accepted that the two form separate and distinctive categories of *pro indiviso* ownership, and that joint property is much the smaller category[1]. In the modern law probably only two examples of joint property are recognised, namely ownership by trustees and ownership by members of a club or other unincorporated association[2]. Thus Lord Justice-Clerk Cooper, in the leading case of *Banff Magistrates v Ruthin Castle Ltd*:

'So far as has been traced, there is no instance of a joint right in the strict sense having been held to exist except in persons who were inter-related by virtue of some trust, contractual or quasi-contractual bond — partnership[3] or membership of an unincorporated association being common examples — and it seems to me that such an independent relationship is the indispensable basis of every joint right'[4].

So far as trustees are concerned, the view that trust assets are held as joint property was already established in the nineteenth century and has never been seriously disputed[5]. The position of unincorporated associations is less clear and has been canvassed in only one reported decision, *Murray v Johnstone*[6], which was decided in 1896, before the modern distinction between joint and common property was properly established. In *Murray*, which was a decision of the Second Division, Lord Moncreiff was of the view that club property was common property, albeit subject to important specialities[7] while Lord Young was strongly of the view that it was not common property at all, commenting that:

'[T]he law of common property is almost ridiculously inapplicable. The idea of the law of common property applying to the money or the furniture in possession of the officers of a club is, I think, extravagant on the face of it. No club could be carried on on such a footing. This club, I suppose, has no property except the annual subscription of half-a-crown from each of its members. I suppose it would be contended that in accordance with the maxim [of common property] *melior est conditio prohibentis* if one member objects no use can be made of these half-crowns — that not one penny of them could be spent if a single member objects, because of the law of common property and the maxim *melior est conditio prohibentis*'[8].

The other two judges in the Division did not offer firm views on the type of holding. The actual decision in *Murray v Johnstone*, which was that a cup won by the club could not be given away by a majority vote and against the wishes of a minority of members, can be supported equally well whether the cup is classified as joint property or as common property[9]. In *Banff Magistrates* Lord Justice-Clerk Cooper was in no doubt that the assets of unincorporated associations are held by its members as joint property, and it is suggested that this must now be accepted as the modern law[10]. Of course where land is involved, and in some other cases also, club property is held by trustees for behoof of the club members, and in such cases the existence of the trust will of itself result in joint property.

With trusts, and also with unincorporated associations, the title to the property does not fully reflect economic reality. In economic reality the property belongs to the trust or, as the case may be, to the unincorporated association; but since neither is recognised in law as a separate legal person, some other solution must be found for formal ownership. The solution adopted is for the property to be held by trustees in the first case and by members of the unincorporated association in the second. However, their title is purely formal and the property cannot simply be applied for their own benefit.

In *Banff Magistrates* Lord Justice-Clerk Cooper expressed the view that the existence of an independent, contractual or quasi-contractual relationship between the parties 'is the indispensable basis of every joint right'[11]. Nonetheless, it is probably not open to parties to bring about a holding of joint property, at least in the normal course of events. Lord Cooper's dictum is not to be taken as meaning that the mere existence of a contract will convert common property into joint property. Therefore, where co-owners contract not to seek division and sale the result remains common property and not joint property[12]. The position is the same where co-ownership is subject to a contractual survivorship clause which cannot be evacuated[13]. Indeed it is thought that even if parties express in the clearest possible terms their intention to create a holding of joint property, the result remains common property nonetheless, for the rules of property law cannot be altered by contract, and the rule of *pro indiviso* ownership appears to be that only trustees and members of unincorporated associations are capable of holding subjects in the highly restrictive form of joint property[14].

The question of whether common property can be converted into joint property by contract is different from the question of whether the incidents of common property can be so altered by contract that the holding takes on a resemblance to joint property[15]. The second is obviously possible, at least to some degree. Thus co-owners may take title to land on the basis of a contractual survivorship destination, and may further agree that no one is to alienate or burden his share *inter vivos*, that no one will pursue for division and sale, and that all management decisions will be reached by a majority vote. However, a contract cannot achieve everything. It cannot, for example, provide for the *inter vivos* accretion which operates in joint property every time a proprietor resigns from the joint relationship[16]. Nor can it affect successors in circumstances where one *pro indiviso* owner sells in breach of the agreement[17]. The rights of creditors remain unaffected[18]. More importantly, however much the superficial characteristics of common property are altered by agreement, the fact that each proprietor continues to hold a separate *pro indiviso* share in the property makes the two forms of holding fundamentally distinct[19].

1 See paras 17 ff above.
2 There may possibly be others. Eg in certain corporations, not incorporated under the Companies Acts, there may be an argument that the rights of the corporators are held as joint property.
3 Some partnership property, notably land, is owned by trustees for behoof of the partnership. Otherwise partnership property is owned by the partnership itself, which is a separate legal person. Only the first is joint property. Indeed the second is not *pro indiviso* ownership at all: see para 18, note 5, above.
4 *Banff Magistrates v Ruthin Castle Ltd* 1944 SC 36 at 68, 1944 SLT 373 at 388.
5 Eg *Dalgleish v Land Feuing Co Ltd* (1885) 13 R 223. See further TRUSTS, TRUSTEES AND JUDICIAL FACTORS, vol 24, para 162, and W A Wilson and A G M Duncan *Trusts, Trustees and Executors* (1975) p 19.
6 *Murray v Johnstone* (1896) 23 R 981, 4 SLT 81.
7 These involved importing most of what are now recognised as the characteristics of joint property.
8 *Murray v Johnstone* (1896) 23 R 981 at 987. Lord Young did not state in terms that club property is joint property, but he commented that with clubs 'you are in an entirely different department and region from that which is regulated by the law of common property'.
9 On the basis that club property is joint property, unanimity is required before assets can be alienated in breach of the rules of the club. See para 36 below.
10 However, the position is different for proprietary clubs, for which see ASSOCIATIONS AND CLUBS, vol 2, paras 826 ff.
11 *Banff Magistrates v Ruthin Castle Ltd* 1944 SC 36 at 68, 1944 SLT 373 at 388.
12 Eg *Williams v Cleveland and Highland Holdings Ltd* 1989 GWD 33-1530, OH, affd 1990 GWD 30-1764. See also *Farquharson v Farquharson* 1991 GWD 5-271, Sh Ct (agreement not to sell).
13 Bell *Commentaries* I,62; *Steele v Caldwell* 1979 SLT 228, OH. Cf *Munro v Munro* 1972 SLT (Sh Ct) 6, which appears to be wrongly decided. As to this latter case, see K G C Reid 'Common Property: Clarification and Confusion' 1985 SLT (News) 57 at 58–60.
14 In *Banff Magistrates v Ruthin Castle Ltd* 1944 SC 36, 1944 SLT 373, where land was conveyed to A and B 'jointly and to their joint assignees' the property was said to be common property and not joint property, and the court indicated that it was not disposed to extend the existing examples of joint property, which it regarded as a very restrictive form of holding.
15 1944 SC 36 at 69, 1944 SLT 373 at 388, per Lord Justice-Clerk Cooper: '[I]t is unnecessary to determine the wider question whether it is impossible by any conveyancing device to create an indissoluble bond between co-owners who are not in the full sense joint proprietors, or — to put the question differently — whether it is possible in this respect to create a class of right midway between common property and joint property'. This is the second question.
16 See para 35 below.
17 A bona fide purchaser would receive a good title and would not be affected by the agreement entered into by his author: see paras 688 and 698, head (4), below.
18 Except, it has been held, in the case of survivorship clauses, which defeat a claim against the *pro indiviso* share by the creditor of a deceased debtor: *Barclays Bank Ltd v McGreish* 1983 SLT 344, OH. However, this decision has been criticised. See M Morton 'Special Destinations as Testamentary Instructions' 1984 SLT (News) 133; J M Halliday 'Special Destinations' 1984 SLT (News) 180;

G L Gretton 'Death and Debt' 1984 SLT (News) 299; D J Cusine 'Of Debts and Destinations' (1984) 29 JLSS 154.
19 See para 20 above.

35. Characteristics. In joint property there are no severable *pro indiviso* shares but rather a single title held jointly by all co-proprietors. As has been said of the case of trusts:

> 'There is no such thing as a separate but *pro indiviso* right . . . in each trustee. Each has the full title along with the other[s] . . . and if they die, his title carries the whole right, to the exclusion of any others'[1].

From this fundamental characteristic, all the other characteristics of joint property flow.

The unitary title held by the proprietors of joint property has been described, not inappropriately, as 'elastic'[2]. For the property belongs to those persons who for the time being are trustees or, as the case may be, members of the unincorporated association. When a trustee or a member dies, the slack in the title is taken up by the remaining trustees or members, and this is achieved without a survivorship destination or an express conveyance[3]. Similarly, when a person resigns as a trustee or as an association member, he takes nothing with him and the property is held by the remaining trustees or members without the need for a conveyance[4]. The position where new trustees or new members are assumed is less clear. In principle, the elasticity of the title should mean that assumption confers ownership; for title is held by the trustees or association members for the time being and, following assumption, the new trustee or member falls within the class of trustees or members[5]. This view has been asserted in the case law[6], and seems to be accepted, at least in the case of unincorporated associations, so that a person becomes owner of club property simply by joining the club[7]. However, the rule for trusts may be different. Modern trust legislation provides a model deed of assumption of new trustees which includes an express conveyance of the trust property[8]. While the model deed is not mandatory, it seems to be universally taken as the law that an assumed trustee is not owner of heritable property unless a conveyance in his favour has been registered in the Register of Sasines or Land Register[9]. Certainly the modern practice is always to use an express conveyance of trust property in the deed of assumption of new trustees.

It has been seen that in common property there is a separate *pro indiviso* share which can be transferred, or bequeathed, or made the subject of diligence[10]. In joint property there is no separate share, and hence no possibility of any of these juristic acts. Thus a purported conveyance by one joint proprietor of his 'share' in the property carries nothing[11]. In joint property there is no entitlement to division and sale[12]. Joint ownership comes to an end only when the property is alienated or destroyed, or when the number of trustees or association members is reduced to one, or on the winding up of the trust or association.

1 *Gordon's Trustees v Eglinton* (1851) 13 D 1381 at 1385, per Lord Justice-Clerk Hope.
2 *Dalgleish v Land Feuing Co Ltd* (1885) 13 R 223 at 230, 231, per Lord Shand.
3 *Gordon's Trustees v Eglinton* (1851) 13 D 1381; *Findlay* (1855) 17 D 1014; *Oswald's Trustees v City of Glasgow Bank* (1879) 6 R 461; *Murray v Johnstone* (1896) 23 R 981, 4 SLT 81. However, the statutory style of deed of assumption for new trustees includes an express survivorship destination: see the Trusts (Scotland) Act 1921 (c 58), s 21, Sch B.
4 *Dalgleish v Land Feuing Co Ltd* (1885) 13 R 223; *Murray v Johnstone* (1896) 23 R 981, 4 SLT 81. For trusts this rule is statutory: see the Trusts (Scotland) Act 1921, s 20.
5 However, it is possible to distinguish between the case of resignation and the case of assumption. There are no separate shares in joint property, so that in the case of resignation there is nothing for a

resigning proprietor to convey. But in the case of assumption it is possible to convey the whole property to the new and the surviving members, and this is what is always done in the case of trusts.

6 *Bell v City of Glasgow Bank* (1879) 6 R 548 especially at 553, per Lord President Inglis (affd (1879) 6 R(HL) 55); *Dalgleish v Land Feuing Co Ltd* (1885) 13 R 223 at 228, 229, per Lord Mure and Lord Shand. In these cases the context was trustees holding shares.

7 *Murray v Johnstone* (1896) 23 R 981, 4 SLT 81.

8 Trusts (Scotland) Act 1921, s 21, Sch B.

9 Eg W M Gordon *Scottish Land Law* (1989) para 16-26; J M Halliday *Conveyancing Law and Practice* vol IV (1990) para 53-08; *The Conveyancing Opinions of J M Halliday* (ed D J Cusine, 1992) pp 672, 673. The difference may matter. Thus suppose that A, the sole surviving trustee, assumes B and C as trustees and that the new title is not registered. Who is infeft? On the usual view of the law, only A is infeft, and so A can grant a disposition of the property. On the other hand, if it is the case that assumption by itself confers ownership, then all three are infeft. It is thought that the second view would not now be accepted as correct, at least in the case of heritable property, where registration has a special status.

10 See para 28 above.

11 *Livingstone v Allan* (1900) 3 F 233.

12 This follows as a matter of course from the absence of beneficial interest.

36. Management. Whereas in common property there are no fixed rules of management and individual decisions must usually be taken unanimously[1], in joint property rules of management are provided by the deed of trust or, as the case may be, by the rules of the association, as supplemented in both cases by the general law. A deed of trust will specify what is to happen to the trust property and may also list the powers which may be exercised by the trustees[2]. The rules of an unincorporated association may likewise provide for the administration of the association's property[3]. In both cases decisions which are taken within the terms of the deed of trust or, as the case may be, the rules of the association, may be taken by a simple majority of the co-owners, or by a smaller number if the power of decision-making has been delegated[4]. However, decisions which are in breach of the deed of trust or rules of association can be taken only with the unanimous consent of all those holding a beneficial interest in the property. In the case of trusts, the beneficial interest is held by the beneficiaries nominated by the deed of trust[5]. In the case of unincorporated associations it is held by all the members of the association. Thus in one reported decision, where a majority of members of a club wished to give a cup to one of its members, it was held that alienation of club property was not permitted by the ordinary club rules and that accordingly the consent of all the members was required[6].

There is a distinction between the making of a decision in relation to joint property and its implementation by juristic act. While decisions can usually be made by a simple majority, it does not necessarily follow that a simple majority suffices for the juristic act. In common property the rule is all co-owners must take part in the transfer of the thing or in the grant of a subordinate real right such as a right in security. Therefore, if land belongs to A, B and C in common, and if a disposition of that land is executed by A and B only, the effect is to transfer the *pro indiviso* shares of A and B, but not the share of C. *Nemo dat quod non habet*[7]. In joint property there is only a single title, and the question is, not whether each *pro indiviso* proprietor has transferred his individual share, but rather whether or not the single title has been transferred. Thus in joint property there are two possibilities only: either all the necessary parties have participated in the transfer, in which case the full title passes, or all the necessary parties have not participated, in which case no title passes. The difficulty lies in knowing which has occurred, for the rules are not clear. It is possible to read certain provisions of the Trusts (Scotland) Act 1921 as indicating that, in the case of trusts, a juristic act is effectively performed if it is performed by a majority of the trustees — or perhaps even, in relation to land, by a majority of the infeft ‚trustees[8]. Therefore, on this view a disposition of land will pass ownership if it is executed by a majority of trustees. However, the law cannot be regarded as settled[9], and in practice a purchaser or other grantee is likely to insist on execution by all of the trustees or association members, or by an agent validly appointed for the purpose of executing deeds.

1 See para 23 above.
2 In addition, certain powers are implied by law, or may be acquired by authority of the court: see the Trusts (Scotland) Act 1921 (c 58), ss 4, 5. See also TRUSTS, TRUSTEES AND JUDICIAL FACTORS, vol 24, para 202.
3 See further ASSOCIATIONS AND CLUBS, vol 2, para 804.
4 For trusts, see TRUSTS, TRUSTEES AND JUDICIAL FACTORS, vol 24, para 192, and A J P Menzies *The Law of Scotland affecting Trustees* (2nd edn, 1913) pp 86 ff. For unincorporated associations, see *Hopwood v O'Neill* 1971 SLT (Notes) 53, OH.
5 If it is a private trust, and if the beneficiaries are named in the deed of trust, there is no difficulty in identifying the beneficiaries. The position is much more difficult in the case of discretionary or of public trusts. The Trusts (Scotland) Act 1961 (c 57), s 1(1) (amended by the Age of Legal Capacity (Scotland) Act 1991 (c 50), s 10(1), Sch 1, para 27) makes provision for obtaining consent on behalf of beneficiaries not yet born, beneficiaries incapable of giving consent by reason of nonage or other incapacity, and persons who may become beneficiaries in the future.
6 *Murray v Johnstone* (1896) 23 R 981. Thus Lord Moncreiff at 990 said: 'The test whether in any particular case the disposal of club property by a committee or by a majority of members is or is not *ultra vires* is to inquire whether the proposed use or disposal of the article or fund is incidental to the purposes and proper management of the association. If it is not, a resolution so to dispose of it will not be sustained. In the present case if they had merely resolved that the cup should be held for the club by the defender as long as he remained a member, the resolution might have been justified as a reasonable act of management. But what is proposed is to alienate the club's property, and this I think cannot be done by the vote of the majority'. However, Lord Moncreiff's earlier attempt to assimilate this rule to the rule of common property, which distinguishes between necessary repairs and extraordinary use, is not convincing.
7 No one can give that which he does not have. See *McLeod v Cedar Holdings Ltd* 1989 SLT 620 and para 28 above.
8 See in particular the Trusts (Scotland) Act 1921, ss 7, 21. The true meaning and effect of s 7 is problematic. It provides that 'any deed bearing to be granted by the trustees under any trust, and in fact executed by a quorum of such trustees in favour of any person other than a beneficiary or a co-trustee under the trust where such person has dealt onerously and in good faith shall not be void or challengeable on' various grounds mainly, or perhaps entirely, connected with procedural irregularity. A quorum is usually a bare majority: see s 3(c). If s 7 is interpreted as concerned with procedural irregularity only, then it may be said to presuppose that a majority of trustees can convey trust property. In other words, good faith is required to cure, not absence of title (because, on this view, there is none), but irregularity of procedure. But if s 7 is interpreted as extending also to questions of title, then it may be said to presuppose that a majority of trustees cannot normally convey trust property, but that a bona fide third party falling within s 7 will be protected.
9 Cf the views of Lord Ormidale (the Lord Ordinary) and of the First Division in *Harland Engineering Co v Stark's Trustees* 1913 2 SLT 448, OH, 1914 2 SLT 292, a case decided prior to the Trusts (Scotland) Act 1921.

(4) OTHER CASES OF CONCURRENTLY HELD RIGHTS

37. Commonty. Commonty is, or, perhaps more accurately, was, a form of shared ownership of land for the purposes of grazing cattle or cutting peats[1]. Its origins go back at least to medieval times and very probably to much earlier, but it became rare in the modern period and it is not known whether any examples still survive[2]. It will be treated only briefly[3].

Commonty was a distinctive right of use of land which long pre-dates the modern law of common property, although in the later period it was increasingly assimilated to common property[4]. However, even in its later form commonty had a number of features which set it apart from the normal case of common property. One was that, like a servitude, a right of commonty was held as an inseparable pertinent of adjoining land. The system was that rights of use in the commonty were held by a number of separate plots of land, and the right of use could not be separated from ownership of the plot. Another distinctive feature was that there was no right of division at common law and when division was finally introduced, by an Act of 1695[5], it operated in a different fashion from the normal case of common property[6].

1 For common grazings in crofting tenure, see AGRICULTURE, vol I, paras 821, 822, and D J MacCuish and D̂ Flyn *Crofting Law* (1990) ch 8. Such common grazings involve common ownership of a crofting tenancy, held as a pertinent to other land also held on crofting tenure.
2 J Rankine *The Law of Land-ownership in Scotland* (4th edn, 1909) p 600.
3 For a fuller modern treatment, see W M Gordon *Scottish Land Law* (1989) pp 451 ff. See also I H Adams *Directory of Former Scottish Commonties* (1971). The only modern case is *Macandrew v Crerar* 1929 SC 699, 1929 SLT 540, where the decision was that the holding was common property and not commonty.
4 In the nineteenth century there was a certain amount of debate as to whether commonty was merely a form of common property or a properly distinctive holding. See eg *Menzies v Macdonald* (1854) 16 D 827, affd (1856) 2 Macq 463, HL. In his authoritative analysis of *pro indiviso* ownership, Bell took the latter view: see Bell *Principles* s 1087.
5 Division of Commonties Act 1695 (c 69).
6 See I H Adams 'Division of the Commonty of Hassendean 1761–1763' in *Miscellany I* (Stair Society vol 26, 1971) p 171.

38. Feudal ownership. According to the theory of feudalism which has come to be accepted in Scotland, every individual piece of feudal land is co-owned by the Crown, by the subject superior or superiors, and by the ultimate vassal[1]. Each has a distinctive share in *dominium*, whether *dominium utile*, *dominium directum* or, as the case of the Crown, *dominium eminens*. The economic reality is of course otherwise, and for practical purposes the person who has *dominium utile* is often treated as the sole owner[2]. The divided *dominium* of the feudal law may be contrasted with the shared *dominium* of *pro indiviso* ownership. Whereas in the feudal law each co-owner has a different interest in the same thing, in *pro indiviso* ownership *dominium* is shared, not divided, and there is a single interest of *dominium*. In practice the two types of co-ownership are frequently found together. So A and B may have a right in common to the *dominium utile*, or to the superiority[3], of land, as in the familiar instance of (the *dominium utile* of) a house being co-owned by a husband and a wife.

1 See paras 49 ff below.
2 See para 193 below.
3 *Cargill v Muir* (1837) 15 S 408.

39. Timeshares. Timeshares are found in Scotland, as in many other countries of the world. In a timeshare a number of different people are given the right to occupy and use land, typically a holiday complex, for a different, and fixed, period every year, usually in perpetuity. Timeshares may be created by various legal devices, although none involve co-ownership in the strict sense of the term[1]. The standard method of creating a timeshare is for the land to be held by a company or other body corporate, such as a bank. The right to occupy for the stipulated period each year takes the form of a personal right against the owner of the land, which may either be an ordinary contract or a right in trust. In both cases the holder of the timeshare right runs the risk of the owner of the land becoming insolvent, or selling to a third party who would not be bound by the contractual or trust right[2]. Another method sometimes found is for the land to be held by a company in which the timeshare holders are then allocated shares. The Timeshare Act 1992 provides for a cooling off period of fourteen days in relation to the formation of timeshare agreements and related loan agreements (timeshare credit agreements)[3].

1 Common property is not a suitable vehicle for a timeshare in respect that (1) the right to division and sale could not be excluded and (2) any agreement made between the *pro indiviso* proprietors, eg as to weeks of occupation, would not be binding on successors.

2 See paras 688 ff below.
3 Timeshare Act 1992 (c 35), ss 2, 3. See also the Timeshare (Cancellation Notices) Order 1992, SI 1992/1942.

40. Trusts. On at least one view of the English law of trusts, ownership is divided between trustee and beneficiary, the former holding the legal ownership of the trust property and the latter the beneficial or equitable ownership. However, while English law has been an important influence on the development of the law of trusts in Scotland, the idea of divided ownership has not been adopted. The position in Scots law is that full and undivided ownership of trust property is held by the trustee or trustees, and that the right of the beneficiary is simply a personal right to require implementation of the purposes of the trust[1].

1 See TRUSTS, TRUSTEES AND JUDICIAL FACTORS, vol 24, para 49, and W A Wilson and A G M Duncan *Trusts, Trustees and Executors* (2nd edn, 1995) pp 15–17.

3. THE FEUDAL SYSTEM

The Author is indebted to Dr H L MacQueen and Mr W D H Sellar for their valuable comments and suggestions.

(1) THE NATURE AND HISTORY OF FEUDAL LAW

41. Introductory. The law's past can be approached in two ways. The first is that of the legal historian, who approaches the law like any other topic of historical research. The second is that of the lawyer, for whom the law's past is the background to the present law. For the lawyer, therefore, feudal land law is what our land law would now be if all statutes were repealed. But what that state of affairs would be is determined not so much by examination of the reality of the medieval period as by consideration of almost exclusively post-medieval cases and juristic texts. Thus if a nineteenth-century decision of the Whole Court states that such-and-such was the feudal law, that statement is true for the lawyer, even though the historian may doubt it. Naturally, the extent of the discrepancy between the two approaches will vary according to which period is in question, and in general the later the period the smaller the discrepancy. Again, to the historian all is change, so that the feudalism of the twelfth century is not the feudalism of the fourteenth[1]. But to the lawyer the past is static, except to the extent that it has been changed by statute. To the lawyer the past is a two-dimensional picture, lacking in depth, for the common law, conceived as what the law would be if all statutes were repealed, is a fixed thing, incapable of alteration, and subject to development only in the sense of the working out of points of detail. The lawyer's history is thus a historical[2], but nonetheless a necessary conception. In what follows we shall consider feudalism both historically and legally. In the space available, only an outline is possible[3]. The end of Scots feudalism, which has had such dominance in our law for so many centuries, is rapidly approaching, and so the following survey is perhaps fitting, as a sort of obituary, the end of ane auld sang.

1 'The history of feudal law is the history of a series of changes which leave unchanged little that is of any real importance': F Pollock and F W Maitland *History of English Law* (2nd edn, 1899) vol 1, p 67. This, however, must be regarded as an overstatement.
2 It may be added that the modern Scots lawyer does have one advantage over the historian, which is that he speaks the language of feudalism as his native tongue, however attenuated or debased, whereas the historian, even if of the genius of a Maitland, must learn it as a foreign language.
3 A full treatment of Scots feudal law would require a whole treatise. Some attempt has been made to provide, in the footnotes, suggestions for further reading. In addition some aspects of feudal law are dealt with elsewhere in this volume, and also in the title on CONVEYANCING, vol 6.

42. What is feudalism? Feudalism is notoriously hard to define, and indeed historians have recently shown a tendency to abandon the concept altogether[1], an option obviously not open to the lawyer. For the modern lawyer feudalism is a system of land tenure, but in its origins it was far more than that. The great master of legal historians wrote:

'We may describe feudalism as a state of society in which all or a great part of public rights and duties are inextricably interwoven with the tenure of land, in which the whole governmental system — financial, military, judicial — is part of the law of private property'[2].

Ganshof wrote:

'Feudalism may be conceived of as a ... development pushed to extremes of the element of personal dependence in society, with a specialised military class occupying the higher levels in the social scale; an extreme subdivision of the rights of real property; a graded system of rights over land created by this subdivision and corresponding in broad outline to the grades of personal dependence just referred to; and a dispersal of political authority amongst a hierarchy of persons who exercise in their own interest powers normally attributed to the state'[3].

Thus in feudalism landownership and sovereignty coincided, so that the Crown's sovereignty over Scotland and its *dominium eminens*, its ultimate tenurial superiority, were the same thing, were identical concepts[4]. Since sovereignty involved jurisdiction, landownership implied jurisdiction, so that the royal courts could dispense justice because the Crown was the ultimate superior, and every subordinate owner of land likewise had the right to hold courts, and in fact did so[5]. Taxation was likewise raised by the Crown as superior rather than as sovereign, though more accurately it should be said that to the feudal mind no such distinction could be conceived. Land tenure penetrated every institution; land was not so much an asset, to be bought and sold, as today, but rather a focus of social relations. Even religion was feudalised. The Crown held Scotland as the vassal of God, and in prayer the act of holding the hands together was adopted from the feudal ceremony of homage, the *immixtio manuum*, so that the worshipper was binding himself as the vassal of God.

Two themes of feudalism require particular notice. The first is that the distinction between public law and private law, a distinction instrinsic to the law of the Roman Empire and to modern legal systems, was absent in feudalism. Feudalism involves a systematic denial of the distinction, as will be apparent from what has already been said. The other point is that ownership of land, something taken for granted by the Romans as by the moderns, did not exist under feudalism. Feudalism involves the absolute denial that land can be owned. Indeed, the very concept of a real right can hardly be said to exist under feudalism. Land rights are personal, not real. Land is not owned, but held in tenure, and tenure means a personal relationship with other people, the superior and the oversuperior, with the vassals and tenants. For the same reason land cannot, in the pure feudal conception, be sold or bequeathed. The power of sale and bequest go close to the heart of ownership, but no one can sell or bequeath what he does not own, and no one could own land. It is true that today we speak of *dominium utile* and *dominium directum*, and of course *dominium* means ownership. But these terms are not feudal, but result from the attempt made in the later middle ages, when feudalism was declining, to reconstruct it in accordance with civilian concepts. More will be said of this later.

---

1 Historiography is subject to passing fashions, of which this tendency may be one. One of the problems is how to distinguish western European feudalism from other systems with which it shares common features, such as ancient Japan. See *Les Liens de Vassalité* (Société Jean Bodin, 2nd edn, Brussels, 1958).

2 F W Maitland *Constitutional Law of England* (1st edn, 1900) pp 23, 24.
3 F L Ganshof *Qu'est-ce que la Féodalité?* (1944, in English as *Feudalism*), Introduction. This is a classic study of the subject, and more legal in its approach than the other classic study, M Bloch *La Société Féodale* (1939/40, in English as *Feudal Society*). Ganshof includes an extensive bibliography. See also D Herlihy *History of Feudalism* (1970). English feudalism was a major influence in Scotland. The literature on it is very large. See in particular S F C Milsom *Legal Framework of English Feudalism* (1976). Scots literature will be mentioned later.
4 We still have a relic of this in the rule that the Crown cannot dispone but only feu, for to dispone would, in the feudal scheme of things, be to alienate not only land but also sovereignty.
5 There were certain exceptions.

43. Origin of feudalism. The traditional opinion was that feudalism emerged in the fifth century, on the fall of the Roman Empire in the west, but this is now known to be inaccurate. Thus we have a conveyancing styles book by one Marculfus, written at Paris about 660, which does not indicate the existence of feudalism[1]. There is no real trace of feudalism in the *Edicta* of the Lombard kings such as Rothair (issued in 643) or Liutprand (issued 713–735). It seems that it emerged in the eighth century, in the Kingdom of the Franks[2]. Its social and economic causes cannot be traced here, and are perhaps not fully traceable, though the centuries following the fall of the Empire were a time of violence and famine, when early death by bloodshed or by starvation was common, when the population of western Europe was falling, when both life and property were at perpetual risk to the next wave of invaders, and had to be protected by the sword rather than by the law.

But the formal origin of feudalism can be identified[3]. It arose from the merger of two already existing institutions, benefice (*beneficium*) and vassalage. Benefice needs no explanation, being, with minor changes[4], merely a new name for the old Roman institution of *usufructus*. It appears that at this period much land was held in this way. Vassalage[5] we now think of as a part of feudal land tenure, but at this early period it had no connection with land. It was a personal compact between two men, binding each to support and protect the other. Its utility in those troubled times needs no explanation[6]. The relation was asymmetrical, one party, the lord, being the superior, and the other, the vassal, being the inferior, but the obligations of support and protection were reciprocal. One lord would typically have many vassals, and each party could call on the other in case of need. Vassalage at that time involved low status, and was in some ways like slavery, an institution then still common, but nonetheless there was a clear distinction between the vassal and the slave. The vassal was a free man. Thus he could marry, and acquire and dispose of property, without the consent of his lord, and the condition of vassalage, though lifelong, was not hereditary. In the eighth century — the process being well under way before the death of Charles Martel[7] — these two institutions of benefice and vassalage began to merge, so that those holding benefices became vassals to the owners, and personal vassals were given land in benefice[8]. Landowners thus became lords to their usufructuaries, and the new system was found so attractive that landowners themselves surrendered their land to the Crown, taking it back in usufructuary vassalage. From these beginnings feudalism[9] developed steadily, reaching its classical period in the eleventh and twelfth centuries.

Although the feu or fief was in origin a species of usufruct, it rapidly developed into a more substantial right, becoming, for example, hereditary, and as we shall see in the thirteenth century it began to be considered as a species of *dominium* or ownership.

1 *Marculfi Formulae*. This was not printed until 1613, so came just too late for Craig to take account of it in his *Jus Feudale*.
2 Ie France, the Low Countries, and western Germany.
3 The following account is based on the researches of F L Ganshof (see para 42, note 3, above), which have won general acceptance. Feudalism was not an evolution of the late Roman *emphyteusis*,

which by the time of the German conquest had effectively become ownership, at least in the western Empire: see further E Levy *Vulgar Roman Law — The Law of Property* (1951). Some influence arising from *emphyteusis* cannot, however, be ruled out, and of course later lawyers were very much aware of the parallel. Thus for instance Craig uses *emphyteusis* to mean 'feufarm'. The idea that feudalism evolved out of the ancient Germanic ideas of land tenure is also not one favoured by modern scholarship, though again some degree of influence cannot be ruled out.

4 *Beneficium* ended not only on the death of the usufructuary but also on the death of the owner. In early feudalism it was accordingly necessary to renew the investiture on the lord's death, as well as on the vassal's. Examples of such renewals can be found in Scottish medieval practice, but were probably used for a different reason, namely where for some particular cause the earlier grant might be voidable by the successor.

5 'Vassal' comes from *gwas*, a word from the old Celtic language of Gaul, meaning a servant or young man. The same word, with the same meaning, is to be found in the long poem *Gododdin*, the oldest surviving Scottish literary text, written in or near Edinburgh about AD 600, by the bard Aneirin in the Brythonic form of Celtic. *Gwas* is used in modern Welsh with the same meaning.

6 *The Formulary of Tours (Formulae Turonenses*, first half of the eighth century, quoted by Ganshof) gives a vassalage bond which narrates '*Dum et omnibus habetur percognitum, qualiter ego minime habeo, unde me pascere vel vestire debeam . . .*' ('Inasmuch as it is known to all and sundry that I lack the wherewithal to feed and clothe myself . . .').

7 Charles Martel, grandfather of the Emperor Charlemagne, died in 741. His successful resistance to the attempt of the Arabs to conquer France has always been regarded as one of the turning-points of European history.

8 However, it may be that personal vassalage did to some extent continue. We find it in late medieval Scotland under the name of 'manrent', though no continuity with the earlier period can be demonstrated: see J Wormald *Lords and Men in Scotland* (1985).

9 The derivation of the group of words 'fee', 'infeft', 'feu', 'fief', 'feudal' etc has been the subject of interminable debate by numerous authors over many centuries. There has even been a whole book on the subject: H Krawinkel *Feudum: Jugend eines Wortes* (Weimar, 1938). The word is certainly German, as Craig correctly surmised (*Jus Feudale* 1,9,1 ff).

44. Spread of feudalism. From the Frankish Kingdom, feudalism spread to Italy and, following the *reconquista*, to the Iberian peninsula. From western Germany it spread to the rest of Germany and to parts (though not all) of central Europe, but it did not penetrate to eastern Europe, nor to the Scandinavian peninsula, which is the reason for udal (allodial) ownership in Orkney and Shetland[1]. It spread with the crusades to Palestine. It was introduced to England in the eleventh century, and into Scotland in the reign of David I (1124–1153)[2]. 'Early Scottish feudalism, far from appearing undeveloped or only half formed, seems remarkably cut and dried, almost a copybook version of the feudalism of north-west Europe'[3].

By the time of Columbus, feudalism was much decayed, but some elements did find their way to the New World. For instance, the Charter of Maryland of 1632 granted the colony to Lord Baltimore:

'To hold of Us our Heirs and Successors, Kings of England . . . in free and common Soccage, by Fealty only for all Services, and not in Capite, nor Knight's Service, yielding therefore unto Us, our Heirs and Successors, Two Indian Arrows of these Parts, to be delivered to the said castle of Windsor, every Year, on Tuesday in Easter Week . . .'[4].

After independence in 1776, the Crown superiority vested in each state, and thereafter state legislation declared land to be allodial[5]. The English manorial system existed in parts of New York State, though eventually, in the nineteenth century, it was declared to have been unlawful *ab initio*[6]. More importantly, the full vigour of post-medieval French feudalism was introduced in the seventeenth century to the Province of Quebec, with land being granted *en fief* by the French Crown to *seigneurs* who then subinfeudated. The vassals paid feuduty in money and kind, called *cens et rentes*, to the *seigneur* each Martinmas, as with us, and on change of vassal a casualty was payable, the *lods et ventes*, and the superior had other rights and powers in addition. This system of seignories survived the British conquest, but came to an end with the Abolition of Feudal Rights and Duties in Lower Canada Act 1854, which converted the holdings of the vassals into *franc-alleu*, that is, allodial own-ership[7].

It must not be thought that feudalism was the same in all places and at all times. It varied from country to country, and from locality to locality, and from one century to the next. About the middle of the twelfth century an Italian jurist, Obertus de Orto, composed at Milan the *Consuetudines Feudales*, or *Libri Feudorum*, the *Books of the Feus*[8]. This work stated the feudal law of Lombardy at that period, but gradually became accepted by lawyers as a code of feudal law, and it became common to include it as an appendix to editions of the *Corpus Juris Civilis*, for, like the *Corpus*, it came to be conceived of as a part of the *jus commune europaeum*[9]. To the historian, the value of this work is limited, being merely one author's opinion of the law of one province at one period, but by lawyers it became accepted as the definitive statement of what may be called the common law of feudalism, which therefore must be presumed to apply everywhere, except in so far as derogated from by local custom or abrogated by municipal legislation. Thus Craig wrote of the *Books of the Feus*:

'*Sunt ergo hi libri authentici, ut nunc forum et doctores loquuntur; vimque legum, et auctoritatem juris sibi merito ex consensu pene omnium gentium compararunt*'[10].

However, the *Books of the Feus* are of persuasive rather than binding authority, much like the *Corpus Juris Civilis* itself, though less consulted than the compilation of Justinian. After the publication of Craig's *Jus Feudale* in 1655, Scots lawyers tended to take their feudal law from him, rather than looking behind him to the *Books of the Feus*[11]. Craig's study of feudal law, completed about 1606 though not put into print until 1655, is not only a leading work of Scots legal literature, but one of the most important studies of its subject from any country. Of all Scots lawyers, Craig probably achieved the widest reputation abroad, his book being accepted as a major work on feudal law throughout Europe. Indeed, it has never been entirely super-seded even by modern scholarship. Ross criticised Craig as being better versed in the civil law and the continental feudal law than in the older municipal law of Scotland[12], but the justness of this criticism is arguable[13].

1 Orkney and Shetland were part of Norway until 1468–69: see UDAL LAW, vol 24, para 302. See also G Donaldson 'Problems of Sovereignty and Law in Orkney and Shetland' in *Miscellany II* (Stair Soc vol 35, 1984 ed D Sellar) pp 13 ff. There seem to have been some other places in western Europe to which feudalism did not spread, such as Sardinia.
2 CONVEYANCING, vol 6, para 403, dates the introduction a little earlier, to the reign of Malcolm III (Malcolm Canmore), but it is doubtful whether there is any sound evidence for this. Formerly it was believed that it was introduced even earlier, in the reign of Malcolm II (Malcolm MacKenneth): see eg Craig *Jus Feudale* 1,8,1. For instance, there is a statute, now considered spurious, dated 1004, narrating that Malcolm II feued to his barons the whole of Scotland except for the moot hill at Scone. Sir John Skene prints this statute in his edition of *Regiam Majestatem* in 1609. Malcolm II in fact only came to the throne in 1005. For medieval Scots feudalism, see A A M Duncan *Scotland: The Making of the Kingdom* (1975), the same author's introduction to his edition of *The Acts of Robert I (Regesta Regum Scottorum*, vol V (1986)), and the following works by G W S Barrow: *Feudal Britain* (1956), *The Kingdom of the Scots* (1973), and *Anglo-Norman Era in Scottish History* (1980). See also H L MacQueen *Common Law and Feudal Society in Medieval Scotland* (1993).
3 G W S Barrow *Anglo-Norman Era in Scottish History* (1980) p 132.
4 Francis N Thorpe (ed) *Federal and State Constitutions, Colonial Charters, and Other Organic Laws* (Washington DC, 1909).
5 See J Kent *Commentaries on American Law*, the classical legal text of the United States, first published in 1826.
6 See eg D H Flaherty (ed) *Essays in the History of Early American Law* (1969) p 256.
7 To what extent elements of feudalism may have been introduced to Latin America the present writer has not been able to discover.
8 Obertus de Orto wrote the first draft of it to help his son who was studying law at Bologna University: see O F Robinson, T D Fergus and W M Gordon *Introduction to European Legal History* (1985) p 65. An English translation is appended to J A Clyde's translation of Thomas Craig's *Jus Feudale* (1934).

9 Medieval lawyers wrote commentaries on the *Libri Feudorum* in much the same way as on the *Corpus Juris*. Examples are Accursius, Revigny and Baldus.

10 Craig *Jus Feudale* 1,6,10. Clyde translates this: 'The *Books of the Feus* now take rank as an institutional work, as judges and lawyers say, entitled on their own merits to the authority they enjoy in all lands'. The rendering of '*authentici*' as 'institutional' is illustrative of Clyde's style of translation.

11 This issue would perhaps merit further research. A rare work, *Summary View of the Feudal Law with the Differences of the Scots law from it, together with a Dictionary of the select Terms of the Scots and English Law* (anon, Edinburgh, 1710), shows that as late as 1710 some lawyers at least were still reading the *Books of the Feus* themselves, and treating them as persuasive authority. It may also be asked whether Scots lawyers prior to Craig were really familiar with the *Books of the Feus*. The answer is probably affirmative, since before the Reformation it was common for young Scots lawyers to study at Orleans, a centre of feudal learning. The case of *Bishop of Aberdeen v Crab* (1382) *Registrum Episcopatus Aberdonensis*, vol 1, p 143 (Spalding and Maitland Clubs, 1845) shows that the *Libri Feudorum* were familiar to the fourteenth-century Scots lawyer. On this case, see R M Maxtone Graham 'Showing the Holding' 1957 JR 251, and P Stein 'Roman Law in Scotland' in *Ius Romanum Medii Aevi* Pars V, 13b (Milan, 1968). The action of 'showing the holding' was one whereby the superior could compel his vassal to produce his title deeds.

12 W Ross *Lectures on the History and Practice of the Law of Scotland relative to Conveyancing and Legal Diligence* (2nd edn, 1822) pp 61 ff. This is a work of considerable value. Its influence can be traced in later conveyancing works, and some of Ross's antiquarian researches have not yet been superseded even by modern scholarship.

13 See J W Cairns 'The *Breve Testatum* and Craig's *Jus Feudale*' (1988) 56 Leg Hist Rev 311. This has useful material on Craig's work, as does J W Cairns, T D Fergus and H L MacQueen 'Legal Humanism in Renaissance Scotland' in J MacQueen (ed) *Humanism in Renaissance Scotland* (1990). On Craig, see also J G A Pocock *The Ancient Constitution and the Feudal Law* (1957).

45. Decline and fall of feudalism. The decline of feudalism was already in progress in the fourteenth century, but the process was slow. The system demonstrated a remarkable capacity for survival, the forms of feudalism often surviving even after the economic and social substance had vanished. Thus in Scotland the bond between the vassal and his lord still nominally exists, in a period when a superiority has long been nothing but a commercial interest, a suitable investment for family trusts or limited companies or the Church of Scotland. To the notary of the time of the Emperor Charlemagne, to the author of the *Books of the Feus*, or even to Craig, the current Scottish system would appear not feudal but anti-feudal. Heritable proprietors are no longer bound to appear in arms at the summons of their superior, nor to attend his courts and to submit to his judgments in legal disputes, nor do unmarried owners find themselves faced with the choice either to accept the wife selected for them by their lord or to pay compensation if they are so ungrateful as to refuse. Properties may safely be offered for sale without fear of incurring the casualty of recognition, or even the casualty of composition, nor do law students have to master the casualties of relief, purpresture, non-entry, escheat, or disclamation. We complain that the law grows ever more complex, but sometimes we should recollect how much law has been consigned to a deserved and perpetual oblivion. Nonetheless, the Scottish system is still feudal, though most of the forms of feudalism have been abolished by statute, or have been abrogated by desuetude, and though the social and economic reality of feudalism has long since vanished.

It should perhaps be mentioned that the commercialisation of feudal institutions is older than might be imagined. Thus it is clear that even in the high middle ages wardships were bought and sold as investments. Even Craig felt that the feudalism of his day had so declined as hardly to deserve the name, and indeed he was right:

'*Post senescentibus seculis . . . militares operae negligi coeperunt, et Martia illa feudi natura inquinata, et corrupta est; ut hodie feudum in feudo vix agnoscamus, et hoc feudorum senium dici potest*'[1].

On the continent, as in Scotland, the decline was gradual, but the process was completed abruptly in the revolutionary period. On 4 August 1789 the French National Assembly enacted the final abolition of feudalism[2], and this abolition was carried by the victories of French arms to most of western continental Europe[3].

Only in some of the states of Germany did it survive this period, but the survival was not long continued. Prussia abolished the remains of feudalism in 1852, and in the few other German states where it still existed it was abolished soon thereafter[4], and, as we have seen, it was being abolished in the Province of Quebec at the same time[5]. We speak here of the final legal abolition: the economic and social content had long rotted away.

In England, the statute *Quia Emptores* of 1290 (18 Edw 1 st 1) provided that henceforth land could not be subinfeudated, but could be freely transferred without the consent of the lord. In a legal sense this was the beginning of the decline[6]. Freedom of alienation is an anti-feudal conception. Moreover, anyone claiming a seignory[7] had to show that the seignory had already existed in 1290. As the centuries passed, fewer and fewer such seignories could be established, so more and more landowners held direct from the Crown. Most of what remained of feudalism was abolished by Cromwell, and the abolition was ratified on the Restoration by the Tenures Abolition Act 1660 (c 24). After this the only real remains of feudalism were the lords of the manor and their vassals, the copyholders. Copyhold was abolished by the Law of Property Act 1922[8]. Lordships of the manor still nominally exist, to which some vestigial rights are still attached. They are bought and sold at London auctions, purchased by Americans, and by others who, from the respectable motives of antiquarianism, or from the baser motives of vanity, aspire to the empty status of a feudal lord, the prices attained often depending on the ocular attractiveness of the title deeds (Scots baronies have a similar market). In England, the Crown remains nominally the feudal superior, but it is a superiority devoid of content. Only in one country in the world does feudalism survive in any real sense, albeit attenuated to an extreme degree. That country is Scotland[9].

1 Craig *Jus Feudale* 1,9,19 ('But as the centuries passed, the military aspects began to be neglected and the martial nature of the feu became rotten and corrupt, and today it is hardly possible to recognise the feudal nature of the "feu", and one can speak of the senility of feudalism'). It must not be supposed that the decline of Scots feudalism proceeded upon a constant gradient. For example, just after Craig had finished his *Jus Feudale* there was a partial restoration of feudal rights by the Feuing of Wardlands Act 1606 (c 11; 12mo c 12) (APS IV, 287). See also the Ward Holding Act 1633 (c 1633; 12mo c 16) (APS V, 33).
2 This was the celebrated *nuit du 4 août*. The law (*arrêté*) itself was passed on 11 August. Section 1 begins uncompromisingly: '*L'assemblée nationale détruit entièrement le régime féodal*' (The National Assembly wholly abolishes the feudal system). Of course this could not be done overnight, and subsequent sections provide for a phased dismantling. Feuduties and other feudal prestations were made subject to a system of compulsory redemption (s 6).
3 For instance, feudalism was abolished in the Netherlands in 1798. But it seems already to have largely disappeared in any case before that time. Ulric Huber in his *Heedensdaegse Rechtsgeleertheyt* (1686) Bk 2, ch 36, mentions that in his time only two areas of land in Friesland were still feudal.
4 See R Huebner *Grundzüge des deutschen Privatsrechts* (2nd edn, 1913, in English as *History of Germanic Private Law*) Bk II, ch VII, s 48. However, in certain localities such as Mecklenburg feudal tenure was still in existence at the time of Huebner's book.
5 See para 44 above.
6 Maitland even says that English feudalism died with the Statute of Marlborough 1267 (52 Hen 3):' *Equity* (1909 edn) p 336. This part of the work is omitted in some later editions, being published separately as *Forms of Action at Common Law*, where the passage is found at p 34 of the 1968 edition.
7 'Seignory' is the English term, borrowed from the French, for a superiority.
8 Law of Property Act 1922 (c 16), s 128 (repealed).
9 Traces can be found elsewhere. In Sark there is a hereditary seigneur, who is vassal of the Queen (as Duchess of Normandy) and superior of the island, and he does have certain rights, including membership of the island's legislature, the *Chef Plaids*. More generally, the surviving monarchs of Europe are feudal, and the House of Lords is a feudal institution. These are traces of feudalism in public law: here we are concerned chiefly with feudalism in private law.

46. Survival of feudalism in Scotland.
Why did feudalism survive in Scotland? The answer is that true feudalism did not survive, for it was abolished in the eighteenth century[1]. What did survive was a commercial tenure, non-feudal in

spirit, engrafted on to the stock of feudalism. Feudalism survived in Scotland only by ceasing to be feudal. Feufarm was, and is, pseudo-feudal. As Stair says, it is in substance merely a 'perpetual location'[2] or perpetual lease. When in England an owner might grant a lease for 99 or 999 years, in Scotland he would feu. Functionally there was little difference. Feudalism had evolved into a means of reserving a sort of groundrent coupled with development controls. Indeed, one can almost speak of a rebirth of feudalism in the nineteenth century, as the fortuitous legal externality of urban and industrial growth. The subtext of much nineteenth-century litigation on feudal law is the question of to what extent the old rules of real feudalism were to be applied to this new pseudo-feudalism, to what extent factories and shops and warehouses and suburban housing estates were to be controlled by the *consuetudines* of medieval Lombardy and by the *constitutiones* of the Holy Roman Emperors[3].

1 See the Highland Services Act 1715 (c 54) (often known as the Clan Act 1715), and the Tenures Abolition Act 1746 (c 50). Of course feudalism was already in decline by the eighteenth century, partly as a result of legislation (where the fifteenth-century statute book is very significant), and partly by changing *mores*. The considerable success of James VI (1567–1625) in bringing the feudal lords under control must also be mentioned.

2 See the discussion of feufarm in para 68 below.

3 'The reason or rule of the fourteenth century becomes the ridiculous fiction of the nineteenth. Our land rights are determined by a series of statutes which indicate the struggle between an oligarchy desirous of retaining the hosts of warlike retainers who gave them power on the one hand, and the commercial spirit on the other hand, which sought to emancipate itself from the trammels of feudalism': *Cassels v Lamb* (1885) 12 R 722 at 762, per Lord Fraser.

(2) FEUDAL OWNERSHIP

47. Feudal and allodial. Feudal tenure is contrasted with allodial ownership[1], which simply means ownership in the civilian sense, ownership of land in the same sense as ownership of goods[2]. A car is not held feudally of a superior, and neither is allodial land. The *dominium eminens* or ultimate superiority of the Crown is allodial, because not held of a higher lord, except of God[3]. Other land is held feudally[4]. The term 'tenure' strictly implies feudality, but by an excusable inaccuracy is sometimes used of other rights to land. Thus the expression 'allodial tenure' is sometimes encountered. Originally a 'tenant' was a person who held in tenure[5], in other words as a vassal not as a lessee, but the original meaning has long since been reversed, so that in modern usage a 'tenant' is a lessee not a vassal[6]. But to this rule that all land is feudal there are certain exceptions. The first is udal land in Orkney and Shetland, which is, as the name indicates, allodial[7]. The second is the land occupied by the kirks and kirkyards of the Established Church[8]. But kirks are now by statute held by the Church of Scotland General Trustees as vassals of the Crown[9]. Kirkyards appear to remain allodial[10]. Although Erskine states that manses and glebes are allodial[11], the better view is that they are held of the Crown[12]. It is sometimes said that land which passes through the process of compulsory purchase thereby becomes allodial, but it is more accurate to say that, like manses and glebes, such land is allodial *de facto* but in theory still feudal[13]. In these various cases of nominal feudality, it would be difficult to specify the mode of tenure.

Ownership of land must be either allodial or feudal. Rights other than ownership cannot be allodial, for allodiality implies ownership, but rights other than ownership can be feudal or non-feudal. Leases and servitudes are examples of non-feudal rights. To what extent heritable securities may be considered feudal will be considered later[14].

1 'Allodial' is a word of Germanic origin, as Craig correctly surmises: *Jus Feudale* 1,9,24. The word 'udal' is cognate with it, so that udal land is allodial land.

2 '*Mobilia autem omnia allodialia sunt*' (All moveables are allodial): Craig *Jus Feudale* 1,9,25.
3 In Germany the estate at the top of the feudal chain was called, in a striking image, *Sonnenlehn* (feu of the sun).
4 The principle that all land, subject to minor exceptions, is held ultimately of the Crown was probably adopted from England. On the continent, at least in many places, there seems to have been a widespread survival of allodial ownership right through the middle ages.
5 In England an owner of land is still technically called a tenant in fee simple.
6 The explanation seems to be that lessees were once considered as vassals. One can find examples in the sixteenth century of infeftment being given for leases. In England, a lessee appears to be still regarded in theory as a vassal: see C F Kolbert and N A M Mackay *History of Scots and English Land Law* (1977) pp 83 ff. This work, based on Charles Farran's *Principles of Scots and English Land Law* (1958), is valuable but not always reliable.
7 For udal land, see *Lord Advocate v Aberdeen University and Budge* 1963 SC 533, 1963 SLT 361, and UDAL LAW, vol 24, especially para 324.
8 Stair *Institutions* II,3,4.
9 Church of Scotland (Property and Endowments) Act 1925 (c 33), Pt III (ss 26–33).
10 W M Gordon *Scottish Land Law* (1989) para 3–12 traces the legislation on kirkyards, which does not appear to feudalise the tenure.
11 Erskine *Institute* II,3,8.
12 Stair II,3,40; *Gordon* para 3–14. As Stair says, they are allodial for most purposes.
13 Much has been written on this, and there is a good deal of relevant case law: see generally *Gordon* paras 3–18 ff. The Lands Clauses Consolidation (Scotland) Act 1845 (c 19), s 80, says in terms that such land is feudal.
14 See para 112 below.

48. Sasine of the Crown.

Subject to the above exceptions[1], the Crown is deemed to be seised of the whole land of Scotland, without infeftment. The reason why no infeftment is necessary, or even possible, is that in feudal law to be infeft means to enter as vassal of a superior, and the Crown has no feudal superior, except God alone. Because no infeftment is required, the title of the Crown does not appear in the Sasine Register or the Land Register of Scotland. Hence where no infeftment of another party can be shown to exist, the land in question belongs to the Crown, not as a caduciary right, but by virtue of the doctrine of abiding supreme allodial sasine. In 1976, a Mr Gardner wished to record a title to the Island of Rockall on the footing that there existed no recorded title to it[2], but when he sought to do so a title was immediately recorded in favour of the Crown. This latter act was unnecessary since the Crown already had deemed sasine at common law[3].

The Crown's right as *ultimus haeres* is problematic[4], but whatever its basis may be, it is doubtful whether it is a feudal right, for it applies equally to moveable property and to allodial land, and also to feudal land held of a subject superior.

1 See para 47 above.
2 D L Gardner 'Legal Storm Clouds over Rockall' 1976 SLT (News) 257.
3 In any event Mr Gardner could have acquired no right (except by Crown grant) without possessing the barren island for ten years.
4 Since Scots law (unlike many other legal systems) recognises no limit to remoteness of inheritance, no one can die without heirs. In the eye of the common law we all share a common forefather in Adam, and therefore are all cousins, and the doctrine of an ultimate kinship of blood appears also to be that of modern genetic science. To assert that the Crown succeeds on failure of heirs is thus to assert what is impossible. The whole subject is obscure. Stair struggles with the theory at *Institutions* III,3,47, but does not give much light, and the same may be said of A R G McMillan *Law of Bona Vacantia in Scotland* (1936).

49. *Dominium utile* and *dominium directum*.

As we have seen, in feudalism, land was not considered as being capable of ownership or *dominium*. But when the night of barbarism yielded to dawn, and the study of Roman jurisprudence revived, lawyers felt that feudalism must be Romanised. But where was *dominium* to be located? Roman law demanded an undivided ownership[1], which was precisely what feudalism made impossible. A compromise was adopted, at some violence both to feudal and to civilian principles, by saying that feudal land was in multiple ownership, the superior having ownership of one sort, to which the name *dominium directum* was given, and the vassal ownership of another sort, *dominium utile*. These terms were the invention of the Glossators[2], and were adopted throughout Europe, including, of course, Scotland. *Utile* does not here mean 'useful'. The terminology was adopted from the two *actiones*, the *actio directa* and the *actio utilis*, the reference being to the Civil law, under which in addition to the *vindicatio civilis*, one of the *actiones directae*, there was also by praetorian authority the *vindicatio honoraria*, an *actio utilis*. The background idea here is that the ownership of the vassal is a sort of equitable ownership. But whilst Scotland adopted the terminology, we made no procedural distinction as to the vindicatory protection of these rights, so that with us the distinction between *directum* and *utile* is one of terminological convenience only[3].

Where there were more than two parties in the feudal chain, the terminology was inconvenient. Some theorists held that mid-superiors also held a *dominium utile* but the usage that has prevailed here is that *dominium utile* is ascribed only to the person at the foot of the feudal ladder, all those above him having *dominium directum*. The superiority of the Crown is commonly called the *dominium eminens*[4]. The term *dominium plenum* means full ownership, in other words allodial ownership. But by an inaccuracy sanctioned by usage, it is sometimes used to mean the right created by the merger, or consolidation, of two feudal estates. Thus if an owner acquires his superiority and consolidates it, he is sometimes said to have the *dominium plenum*, though of course he is still a vassal and has the *dominium utile*.

1 To what extent this is strictly true is of course a matter of controversy. There is for instance the celebrated passage in Gaius *Institutes* I,54, about *duplex dominium*.
2 They were traditionally attributed to Accursius, but in fact used earlier by Pillius (or Pilius) who held a chair at the University of Bologna in the 1170s. The literature on the whole subject is extensive, chiefly by continental scholars such as G Phillips, K Lautz and E Meynial. The leading modern study is Robert Feenstra's essay '*Les origines du Dominium Utile chez les Glosateurs*' in his *Fata Iuris Romani* (1974). See also A J van der Walt and D G Kleyn '*Duplex Dominium*: The History and Significance of the Concept of Divided Ownership' in D P Visser (ed) *Essays on the History of Law* (1989), a valuable study which contains extensive citation of the medieval and post-medieval literature.
3 'Nor has our law ever recognised anything similar to the distinction between the *actio directa* and the *actio utilis* or *in factum* of the Roman law': Æ J G Mackay *The Practice of the Court of Session* (1877) vol I, p 371.
4 In the United States the term 'eminent domain' survives, meaning the right, based on sovereignty, of each state, or of the United States, to acquire land compulsorily.

50. *Dominium*: the post-medieval position. In post-classical (late medieval) feudal law, both superior and vassal were considered as having ownership, and accordingly neither right was a burden on the other, each right being *dominium* and not *onus*. In the sixteenth century, Cujacius (Cujas) argued against this solution, and in favour of the view that the right of the vassal is (as it originally had been) a species of usufruct and hence a burden on the right of the superior. This view involves the conclusion that no one can own land except the Crown. We shall see in the next paragraph the contemporary Scottish response to Cujacius's view, but on the continent it seems to have had few adherents. Thus in France itself, in the next century, Domat was prepared to settle for divided ownership[1], while later still, in the eighteenth century, Pothier, while adhering to the terminology of *domaine direct* and *domaine utile*, observed of the former that: '*Cette espèce de domaine n'est point le domaine de propriété qui doit faire la matière du present traité; on doit plutôt l'appeller domaine de superiorité . . . C'est, à l'égard des héritages, le domaine utile qui s'appelle domaine de propriété*'[2]. This is very like our own manner of speaking, for we contrast the 'property' with the 'superiority', thereby implying that the latter is not really 'property' in the ordinary sense of landownership[3]. Indeed it may be that this passage influenced our own usage, for Pothier was once regarded by Scots lawyers as a jurist of high authority. In Germany, the theory of Cujacius fared no better. The Germans adhered with consistency to the theory of divided ownership, and indeed the preliminary paragraphs of the old Prussian Code dealing with feudal law were significantly headed '*vom Getheilten Eigenthume*'[4], an expression of which Craig would have approved. *Dominium directum* and *dominium utile* become in German *Obereigenthum* and *nutzbare Eigenthum* respectively.

1 Jean Domat *Les Loix Civiles dans leur Ordre Naturel* (1689) Pt I, Bk 1, Tit 4, Sect 10, para 6.
2 'This kind of estate is not the estate of ownership with which the present work is concerned. Instead one should call it an estate of superiority. As far as heritage is concerned, it is the *dominium utile* which is called the estate of ownership' ('*Domaine*' is a slippery word, not easy to translate). The passage can be found near the beginning of Pothier's *Traité du Droit de Domaine de Propriété*. Pothier in fact does not discuss feudalism in detail. In pre-revolutionary France, each province had its own feudalism, embodied in its *Coutumes*, whereas Pothier was seeking to restate French law as *droit commun*.
3 This usage expresses the practical truth that the superiority is a mere burden on the *dominium utile*, but as will be observed in the next paragraph Scots law in theory regards both as being owners.
4 'Of Divided Ownership': *Allgemeines Landrecht für die Preussischen Staaten* (Prussian Civil Code) (1794), *Erster Theil, Achtzehner Titel* (Pt I, Tit 18). This *Titel* contains a remarkable and lengthy codification of German, or rather Prussian, feudalism. Old German spelling is used in the text and in this note.

51. *Dominium:* Scotland. In Scotland, Craig discussed the views of Cujacius in great detail[1] and rejected them, maintaining the late medieval view that both superior and vassal have ownership or *dominium*. Thus Scots law, like that of Germany and France, remained true to the medieval analysis. Craig's treatment of this fundamental issue settled the matter. Thus Stair wrote:

'There must remain a right in the superior, which is called *dominium directum*; and withal a right in the vassal, called *dominium utile*; the reason of the distinction and terms thereof is, because it can hardly be determined, whether the right of property is in the superior or the vassal alone, so that the other should have only a servitude upon it; though some have thought superiority but a servitude, the property being in the vassal, and others have thought the fee itself to be but a servitude, to wit, the perpetual use and fruit; yet the reconciliation and satisfaction of both, have been well found out in this distinction, whereby neither's interest is called a servitude'[2].

The matter was thus settled. But in the eighteenth century Lord Kames revived the idea that the feu was a mere burden on the superiority[3]. It need hardly be said that Kames was a speculative writer, often brilliant but as often unsound. His contemporaries did not accept his suggestion[4]. But errors often assume a life of their own, and Kames was quoted with approval on at least one occasion in the nineteenth century[5], and it was doubtless to him that Lord Dunedin was referring when he said:

'If you had asked a Scottish lawyer of the eighteenth century if the superiority was a burden on the *dominium utile* he would infallibly have answered, that so far from being the case, the *dominium utile* was rather in the nature of a burden on the superior's title'[6].

The opposite position was adopted by Lord President Robertson:

'A superior, although an owner of heritage, is not an owner of land in the physical and corporeal sense of that term'[7].

This latter view would diminish a superiority into a mere incorporeal interest[8], leaving only the holder of the *dominium utile* as the owner of land. The true position is, as it has been since the late middle ages, half way between the error of Lord Dunedin and the error of Lord Robertson. Strictly feudalism is a form of multiple ownership, being a third type, additional to joint ownership and common ownership. Lord Fraser summed the matter up correctly:

'The vassal's right is not a burden on the superior's, but is a fee[9] in itself'[10].

It is because of this that the right of both the vassal and the superior are called *dominium*, that is, ownership, that both are classified as corporeal not incorporeal, and that both are conveyed by disposition not by assignation.

1 Craig *Jus Feudale* 1,9,9 ff. For the background, see J W Cairns 'Craig, Cujus, and the Definition of a Feudum: Is a Feu a Usufruct?' in P Birks (ed) *New Perspectives in the Roman law of Property: Essays in Honour of Barry Nicholas* (1989).
2 Stair *Institutions* II,3,7.
3 Henry Home, Lord Kames, *Elucidations* (1777) art 11. The passage is brief and not well argued, and elsewhere in his writings Kames steered well clear of this idea.
4 See eg W Ross *Lectures on the History and Practice of the Law of Scotland relative to Conveyancing and Legal Diligence* (1792) (2nd edn, 1822) II,222,223. Kames's chief argument was that a *dominium utile* can be extinguished by simple renunciation, from which he inferred that it must be a burden. But this was a mistake. As Ross observes, 'A simple renunciation is as insufficient to divest the vassal in favour of the superior, as it would be to divest the superior in favour of the vassal'.
5 *Sandeman v Scottish Property Investment Co* (1883) 10 R 614 at 632, per Lord Rutherford Clark, revsd (1885) 12 R (HL) 67.
6 *Heriot's Trust v Caledonian Rly Co* 1915 SC (HL) 52 at 60, 1915 1 SLT 347 at 352. Why the eighteenth-century lawyer is supposed to have had some insight into feudalism not revealed to jurists of earlier or later centuries, or why infallibility should be ascribed to his hypothetical utterances, should perhaps not be inquired into. Moreoever, had Lord Dunedin attempted to verify his assertion by the use of a time machine, he would soon have found himself disabused.
7 *Strathblane Heritors v Glasgow Corpn* (1899) 1 F 523 at 531, sub nom *M'Ewan v Glasgow Corpn* (1899) 6 SLT 302 at 303.
8 Just as Lord Dunedin's view that *dominium utile* is not really *dominium* but *onus* (burden) would make the vassal's estate incorporeal. Of course in Scots law *dominium* is corporeal whereas *onus* is incorporeal. Hence it is that both *dominium directum* and *dominium utile* are corporeal. In England a seignory is (or was) incorporeal. Pothier seems not to commit himself on this question, but there seems to be no suggestion that the *domaine de superiorité* was anything other than a *chose corporelle*.
9 'Fee' originally meant simply feu. When a feu became *dominium*, fee assumed the same sense. Fee thus now means ownership; hence its use as the term contrasting to liferent. A further shift of sense has occurred in improper, or trust, liferents, when the interest of the beneficiary entitled to the capital is described as a fee. This usage is convenient, though of course the beneficiary in a trust does not have ownership. See generally LIFERENT AND FEE, vol 13, paras 1601 ff.
10 *Cassels v Lamb* (1885) 12 R 722 at 759. This case (a decision of the Whole Court) contains a great deal of valuable feudal learning. Lord Fraser was in the minority. The decision of the majority, followed by the House of Lords in *Sandeman v Scottish Property Investment Co* (1885) 12 R (HL) 67, is arguably favourable to the view that the feu is a burden. But the House of Lords did not discuss the point, and indeed Lord Watson opined that the learning displayed in *Cassels v Lamb* was not necessary to the decision. The truth is that the question for decision in the *Cassels* and *Sandeman* cases was at that time still an open one, and the result finally arrived at, correctly or incorrectly, is consistent with the traditional view. For these cases, see further para 85 below.

52. *Dominium*: further points. We have seen that in Scots law neither estate is a burden on the other, but rather that in theory ownership is divided. In practice, of course, the superiority is a burden on the *dominium utile*. It remains to observe that in certain respects the law departs from the theory and adopts the practical reality. A common law example is where something is severed from the land, for instance where timber is felled or a building demolished. The felled timber or the building stones become moveable by severance. To whom do they belong? To the owner of the land, but who is the owner? There is here a tension between feudalism and the essentially Roman nature of Scots property law. The rule is that such materials are owned by the vassal, the basis of the rule being that it is the vassal not the superior who is 'really' the owner of the land[1]. Likewise there are many statutes which deal in one way or another with the ownership of land, such as the legislation concerning the upkeep of buildings and the demolition of dangerous structures. Such statutes are always Romanist rather than feudal in their approach, taking it for granted that the only 'owner' of land is the vassal.

1 See para 587 below. Contrast the case where, for instance, timber is felled by a lessee. The felled timber belongs to his landlord unless the lease otherwise provides.

(3) FEALTY AND JURISDICTION

53. Fealty homage and the feudal bond. The vassal owed his lord fealty[1] and in some cases also homage[2]. The precise difference between the two has been much debated and need not concern us here[3], except to observe that homage was the more profound obligation, and thus included fealty. In both the core of the obligation was *auxilium et consilium*. The obligations were, however, reciprocal[4]. Thus Craig:

'*Perfecto et constituto per sasinam feudo, tum demum inter dominum et vassalum obligationes oriuntur, et mutua officiorum omnium (quaecunque ad utilitatem, sive commodum alterius spectant) communio, adeo ut quemadmodum vassalus domino obsequi, et ejus dignitati et commodis studere et inservire, nemine ei praeposito, debet, sic et dominus vassalum tueri, ejus res, bona, famam, nullo alterius respecto habito, promovere tenetur*'[5].

Among other points this passage indicates that the feudal bond would arise by virtue of investiture. This is noteworthy because the oath might not be taken until after investiture. The oath might take various forms. There are two forms in the *Books of the Feus*, the shorter of which runs:

'*Ego Titius juro super haec sancta Dei Evangelia quod ab hac hora inantea usque ad ultimum diem vitae meae ero fidelis tibi Cajo domino meo contra omnem hominem excepto Imperatore vel Rege*'[6].

Skene gives:

'I become your man, my liege King, in land, lith, life and limb, warldie honour, homage, fealtie, and lawzie, against all that live and die; zour counsell conceiland that ze schaw me; the best counsell schawand, gif ye charge me; zour skaith and dishonour not to hear and see, bot I sall let[7] it all my gudlie power and warn zou theirof; swa help me God'[8].

In homage, though not in fealty, the vassal knelt to his lord and placed his hands in his lord's hands and gave the oath. Homage was used only for true feus, in other words military feus, or wardholdings as we call them, and therefore homage was abolished with the abolition of wardholding under George II[9], though it seems by then to have been long in disuse[10]. It does not appear that the obligation to swear fealty has ever been formally abolished, but must be deemed abrogated by desuetude[11]. There is, however, one occasion on which fealty is still given, namely by some Crown vassals at coronations. Fealty was also due to all oversuperiors up to and including the Crown, but was sworn only to the immediate superior[12]. Fealty or homage had to be renewed by an incoming vassal, and in principle also if the superior changed, but the latter seems at some stage to have ceased in practice, with some exceptions, such as coronations, as has been said.

The doctrine of fealty explains the rule of common law that an alien cannot own land in Scotland. For ownership involves tenure, and tenure involves fealty to the Crown, but an alien cannot owe fealty to the Crown, because he is already bound in fealty to a foreign prince[13]. Statute now allows aliens to acquire land in Scotland without restriction[14].

A similar problem arose if one man held land of two or more lords within the same kingdom. But this began to be allowed from about 900[15].

1 'Fealty' comes from the Latin *fidelitas*.
2 'Homage' comes from the Latin *homo*, because the vassal was the lord's 'man'.

3 See eg F L Ganshof *Qu'est ce que la Féodalité?* (1944, in English *Feudalism*), and Craig *Jus Feudale* 1,11,10 and 2,12,20. It seems that in Scots practice homage was rare: see I A Milne 'Heritable Rights: The Early Feudal Tenures' in *An Introduction to Scottish Legal History* (Stair Soc vol 20, 1958) p 147 at p 150.

4 It may be that the doctrine of warrandice is partly feudal in origin, arising out of the lord's duty to protect his vassal (though of course the idea of a guarantee of title is older than feudalism, being found in Roman law and perhaps all legal systems): see P R Hyams 'Warranty and Good Lordship in Twelfth Century England' (1987) Law and Hist Rev 435.

5 Craig *Jus Feudale* 2,11,1. Clyde's translation: 'Once the feu has been constituted by a completed act of sasine, the obligations inherent in the relation of superior and vassal spring into being and bind the parties in a community of mutual duty with respect to all that concerns their respective welfare and advantage. The vassal's duty to respect his superior and to study and advance his dignity and interest before those of all others finds its counterpart in the superior's obligation to protect the vassal's person, property, possessions and good name, without regard to third parties'.

6 'I Titius swear on this holy Gospel of God that from this hour forth to the last day of my life I shall be faithful to you Gaius my lord against all men except the Emperor or King': *Libri Feudorum* 2,7. Note the clause *excepto Imperatore vel Rege*. Whether this clause was used in Scots practice is unclear. *Regiam Majestatem* II,62 suggests that it was, but the *Regiam* was heavily influenced by English law and here may not reflect Scots practice. The oath from Skene about to be quoted omits the clause.

7 'Let' here meaning not 'allow' but 'prevent', an obsolete meaning which still survives in the phrase 'without let or hindrance'.

8 Sir John Skene *De Verborum Significatione* (1597).

9 Tenures Abolition Act 1746 (c 50).

10 It was already in disuse by the time of Craig: *Jus Feudale* 2,12,20.

11 *Craig* at 2,12,22 says that the oath of fealty was arguably not due in feufarm, and this is probably correct, feufarm being in substance a non-feudal tenure grafted on to the feudal system.

12 *Craig* 2,12,21.

13 This at least is the conceptual basis of the rule. Social policy may suggest other reasons. Numerous countries round the world have restrictions of various sorts on the acquisition of land by aliens, some by absolute prohibition (as in many Arab states), some by making official permission a prerequisite, some by stating a maximum hectarage which can be owned by aliens, and so forth.

14 Naturalization Act 1870 (c 14) (repealed); Status of Aliens Act 1914 (c 17), s 17 (amended by the British Nationality Act 1948 (c 56), s 34(3), Sch 4, Pt II).

15 *Ganshof*, Pt III, Ch 1, sect XXII. In Scotland it seems that the superior to whom fealty had first been sworn had priority: *Regiam Majestatem* (Stair Soc vol 11, 1947 ed Lord Cooper) p 154.

54. Jurisdiction, regality, barony.

In feudal theory 'superiority carrieth the right of jurisdiction over the vassal's lands and inhabitants thereof'[1], provided that the title was a regality or barony, or if jurisdiction was expressly conferred in the infeftment. Subject superiors[2] might hold their land in barony or in regality or neither. This classification is separate from the classification of the different types of tenure to be discussed below[3]. A person holding in barony was a territorial baron (*baro minor*), but not necessarily a baron in the peerage (*baro major*). Of course, many were both. Regality gave a greater jurisdiction than barony, but in either case the scope of the jurisdiction was determined by the terms of the grant[4]. These heritable jurisdictions continued in vigour until the eighteenth century. Dallas gives an example of a regality grant by James VII, part of which runs:

'To administrate justice within the said regality, and haill bounds thereof, to all persons complaining and having interest; malefactors and transgressors of laws to apprehend, examine, prosecute and incarcerate, and to bring them to the knowledge of an assize, for crimes of whatsoever nature or quality competent, to be judged by his Majesty's laws of the said ancient Kingdom; and that by hanging up, beheading, whipping, dipping or drowning in water, dismembration, fining, imprisonment, banishment or extermination out of the said regality'[5].

This passage relates to criminal jurisdiction, but civil jurisdiction was also granted.

'The Jurisdiction of a Baron or Barony, properly comprehends only Courts of Blood, and Bloodwyte, and Theft being taken with the Fang, with Pit and Gallows effeirand thereto: And also the Courts and Plaints in civil Matters betwixt Party and Party, who are in the Baron's Power by Act of Parliament; and also the taking Order with Meat and Drink, Metts and Measures, taking of Wearers of Hagbutts'[6].

The baron or lord of regality could sit in person, and occasionally did so, but ordinarily the judge would be a 'bailie' appointed by him. Notwithstanding the rule *nemo judex in causa sua* these courts were competent to hear and determine disputes between the lord and his vassals, and indeed this was the normal forum for the recovery of feudal prestations. The barony was a basic social unit of medieval and early modern society[7].

In feudal theory each superior had jurisdiction, so that a vassal was subject to the concurrent jurisdiction of his superior, his oversuperior, and so forth, up to and including the Crown, or in other words the royal courts[8]. Moreoever, not only vassals were thus subject to the jurisdiction, but all persons, part of the feudal chain or not, who resided within the area.

The Stair Society and other antiquarian societies have published from manuscripts many volumes illustrating the proceedings of these courts[9], whose decline can be dated from the sixteenth century[10], although their legal powers remained unaffected until the rising of Prince Charles, the Young Pretender, in the aftermath of which they were largely abolished, being restricted in civil matters to suits of up to £2 and in criminal matters to fines of up to £1 or three hours in the stocks[11]. The business of these courts naturally declined thereafter, and soon many ceased to sit at all. But some were apparently still in existence as late as 1870, though since the barons in practice were also justices of the peace there seems to have been some uncertainty as to whether they were holding court as barons or as justices[12]. These courts have never been formally abolished[13].

A corollary of the jurisdictional right of the lord was a certain penal responsibility for the actions of those within his fief[14].

1 Stair *Institutions* II,4,9. Cf II,3,3.
2 'Subject superior' means any superior other than the Crown.
3 For a review of the authorities on barony titles, see *Spencer-Thomas of Buquhollie v Newell* 1992 SLT 973, OH.
4 It may be suspected that barony and regality were not sharply distinct. W Croft Dickinson 'Freehold in Scots Law' 1945 JR 135 cites an example of a grant '*in baroniam et in liberam regalitatem*'. And the 'Barony and Regality of Glasgow' is familiar. In some cases there would be a barony within a regality. Stair II,3,45, seems to suggest that 'barony' could be used as a generic term.
5 George Dallas of St Martins *System of Stiles* (1697) Pt IV, Branch II (1774 edn, vol 2, p 232), a valuable work.
6 Whatever all that may mean. (Thomas Hope *Minor Practicks*, written in the time of Charles I, published 1726, p 304 of 1734 edition.) See also Stair II,3,62.
7 For a picture of baronies in the immediate post-medieval period, see M H B Sanderson *Scottish Rural Society in the Sixteenth Century* (1982). The barony (manor) was in some parts of Europe a continuation of territorial units which had existed continuously since Roman times. 'The manor as an administrative and economic unit predated feudalism': O F Robinson, T D Fergus and W M Gordon, *Introduction to European Legal History* (1985) p 59.
8 However, this was subject to the terms by which any given superior held. Thus if a baron minor subinfeudated, the question whether his vassal would then obtain jurisdictional rights depended on whether the charter contained a clause *cum curiis*. For the jurisdiction of the Court of Session in heritage, see H L MacQueen 'Jurisdiction in Heritage and the Lords of Council and Session after 1532' in *Miscellany II* (Stair Soc vol 35, 1984) pp 61 ff.
9 See eg C A Malcolm 'Sheriff and other Local Court Records 1385–1935' in *Sources and Literature of Scots Law* (Stair Soc vol 1, 1936) pp 111 ff. For valuable commentaries on the jurisdictional system, see W Croft Dickinson *Sheriff Court Book of Fife 1515–1522* (1928); W Croft Dickinson (ed) *Court Book of the Barony of Carnwath 1523–1542* (1937); and J M Webster and A A M Duncan (eds) *Regality of Dumfermline Court Book 1531–1538* (1953).
10 See further *Sanderson*. It may be added that much scholarly work remains to be done on feudal jurisdictions. See also H L MacQueen's paper cited in note 8 above.
11 Heritable Jurisdictions (Scotland) Act 1746 (c 43).
12 See *Fourth Report of the Commissioners appointed to inquire into the Courts of Law of Scotland* (1870) p 39. For extensive details of these courts, see App II, No 18, to the Report. For the practice of these

courts in their later period, see A Brown *Judicial Proceedings before the Baron Bailie Courts* (1816). A few of these courts still meet for ceremonial purposes, but do not seek to exercise jurisdiction.
13 See a letter by Ainslie Nairn at (1992) 37 JLSS 476.
14 See eg APS ii, 332, declaring every superior answerable at justice ayres for the conduct of his vassals.

(4) TRANSMISSIBILITY OF THE FEU

55. Inheritability. Originally a fief was usufructuary and so in theory not inheritable, but from the beginning the practice was to regrant it to the heir, the lord being moved by the same reasons which had moved him to make the original grant. In 877 the *placitum* of the Emperor Charles (Karl) II at Quierzy-sur-Oise made fiefs hereditary. It appears that this was intended only as a temporary measure, but certainly in practice it encouraged inheritability at least *de facto*. In 1037, the Emperor Conrad II enacted that fiefs should be hereditary. By the beginning of the twelfth century, when feudal law was introduced to Scotland, inheritability was universally accepted in Europe. To avoid any doubt, it was the practice in Scotland, from the earliest times, to insert in charters the destination *et haeredibus suis*[1]. This (in English as 'and to his heirs') survived to 1964, and a memory of it exists in its replacement 'and to his executors'[2]. The clause is unnecessary, and effectively meaningless, but it illustrates the conservatism of conveyancers, being a relic of a time, a thousand years ago, when a feu was a mere benefice[3].

At common law, on the death of the vassal the feu would pass to the eldest son, who was called the heir-at-law, or heir-of-line. If there were only daughters, it would pass to the daughters equally, as heirs portioner[4]. The rules were completely altered by the Succession (Scotland) Act 1964.

At common law there was no power to test on heritage. This rule was conceived partly in favour of the heir, and to that extent was perhaps not strictly a feudal rule, but partly in favour of the superior, so that, for instance, a legatee could be rejected by the superior even if the heir consented. This rule was not formally abolished until 1868[5]. But very early a practice developed of conveying to the 'legatee' before death, with a reservation of liferent, which had much the same effect as a will, except that it was unalterable. In the early eighteenth century conveyancers developed this idea by leaving the conveyance undelivered prior to death, and it was soon accepted that in that case the 'legatee' could compel, by action, the heir and the superior to give effect to it. All that was necessary was that *de praesenti* words of conveyance be used, which meant in effect that it was possible to test on heritage provided that the legacy contained the word 'dispone'. Very soon the reservation of the liferent, now being pointless, was dropped[6].

1 See eg charter of David I to Walter Riddale, about 1150, quoted by Gordon Donaldson in 'Early Scottish Conveyancing' in *Formulary of Old Scots Legal Documents* (Stair Soc vol 36, 1985).
2 The change was made after the Succession (Scotland) Act 1964 (c 41), on the principle that by that Act heritage fell to the executor not to the heir, though it may be said that the change was not necessary since the clause itself is unnecessary.
3 Craig (*Jus Feudale* 1,10,7 and 2,3,38) opined that the *et haeredibus* clause was necessary, but here, as so often, he was being the feudal scholar rather than the lawyer.
4 The detailed rules need not be considered here. They are to be found in the standard sources, such as Stair and Erskine.
5 Titles to Land Consolidation (Scotland) Act 1868 (c 101), s 20.
6 Thus John Dalrymple *Essay towards a General History of Feudal Property in Great Britain* (1757) p 151: 'We are approaching so fast to the practice of devising lands, that at present a bare disposition with a clause dispensing with non [sic] delivery, found lying by a man at his death, though it had neither procuratory of resignation, nor precept of sasine, would bind his heir'. And would also bind the superior.

56. Heritage and conquest. We now use the word 'heritage' to mean that which is immoveable. But formerly there was a distinction between immoveables which were heritage and immoveables which were conquest. Heritage was immoveable property acquired by inheritance. (Heritage is arguably so called not because it will pass to the heir from the owner, but because it has passed to the owner as heir[1].) Conquest was immoveable property acquired by purchase or other singular title[2]. Slightly different rules applied to the succession to each, conquest passing to the heir of conquest, though the differences emerged only where the vassal died without direct issue[3]. Conquest was merged into heritage in 1874[4]. However, even before that date it was common for lawyers to use the word 'heritage' as we do today, covering both heritage in the narrow sense, and conquest. It may be mentioned that William I of England was called 'the Conqueror' not because he seized the Crown by force of arms, but because his tenure of the Crown was not by inheritance[5]. The epithet is one of feudal principle, not of military history.

1 But contrast Stair *Institutions* II,1,2, and Erskine *Institute* II,2,3.
2 The distinction will be found in the *Regiam Majestatem* and the *Quoniam Attachiamenta*. Thus in the latter, ch 97, we read: '*Item statutum est quod conquestus cujuslibet liberi hominis legitimi qui moritur de ipso saisitus sine herede de corpore suo, graditim usque ad primogenitum ascendit, hereditas vero descendit gradatim*'.
3 See the standard sources, such as Stair and Erskine.
4 Conveyancing (Scotland) Act 1874 (c 94), s 37.
5 This was observed by Sir William Blackstone in his *Commentaries* Bk II, ch XV.

57. Subinfeudation: introduction. Subinfeudation is where the vassal grants land to a subvassal, the granter thus becoming lord to the grantee, and the existing superior becoming oversuperior to the grantee. Thus all parties other than the Crown and the holder of the *dominium utile* are midsuperiors. In practice it is quite common for there to be four or five midsuperiors, in an ascending ladder or chain, up to the Crown. Thus, suppose that A holds ward of the Crown and B holds feu of A and C holds feu of B and D holds blench of C. Then the Crown, A, B and C are all superiors. A, B and C are all midsuperiors. A, B, C and D are all vassals, C is the Crown's sub-sub-vassal. A is B's immediate superior, C's over-superior and D's over-over-superior. And so forth. The system is rather like a family tree, whereby the same person is, depending on the viewpoint, mother, grandmother, daughter, and so on. A closer analogy would be with subleases, where the same person may be from one viewpoint a lessee but from another a lessor.

58. Subinfeudation: more detail. Subinfeudation, which is effected by a feu charter or feu disposition or feu contract[1], is a grant *de me*, to be contrasted with a conveyance *a me* which is effected by disposition, and which results in the disappearance of the granter from the feudal chain, substituting the grantee as the new vassal of the existing superior. In subinfeudation the midsuperior remains liable for the feudal prestations due to the oversuperior. Subinfeudation without the consent of the superior became permissible in the eleventh century on the continent[2], but in Scotland the position was by no means clear. Indeed, it is involved in great obscurity. In practice the consent of the superior was generally sought, and the consent was given by charter of confirmation[3]. The main problems arose where the granter held by wardholding[4]. Stair at one place states that subinfeudation of land held by wardholding could not be subinfeudated without the lord's consent[5], but the position was rather more complex. At common law, a vassal holding ward could, at least in the post-medieval period, subinfeudate up to half his estate without the consent of his lord, but clearly the grantee would wish to see the consent of the lord (his oversuperior) because of the danger that the half might have been exceeded. This rule about the half was involved in much complexity, which complexity was further increased by a patchwork of legislation[6], over a considerable period, and not by any means self-consistent, sometimes allowing subinfeudation and sometimes restricting it. It may be added that parallel problems existed for mortification. '*Notandum est quod nec episcopi nec abbates possunt de terris suis aliquam partem donare ad remanentiam sine assensu et confirmatione Domini Regis, quod eorum baroniae sunt de eleemosyna Domini Regis et antecessorum ejus*'[7]. The matter was further complicated by the fact that the Crown was prohibited from making grants of land if the land was 'annexed' to the Crown, unless with parliamentary approval. Yet another dimension is the possibility that a grant in feufarm, whether by the Crown, the Church, or anyone else, was not regarded as requiring any consent provided that no *grassum* was paid, the reason being that the feuduty represented the full value of the land, so that the capital value remained the same[8]. The whole subject would require a small monograph to elucidate, and it was only in the eighteenth century that the idea emerged that a vassal is always presumed to have the power to subinfeudate. The view sometimes expressed in modern legal writing that a superior cannot object to subinfeudation because his vassal remains the same is very much an oversimplification, and is correct only for modern law.

A vassal could be expressly forbidden by his charter to subinfeudate, even for tenures other than wardholding or burgage. The Tenures Abolition Act 1746 makes null any clause *de non alienando sine consensu superiorum*[9] and this was probably intended to allow free subinfeudation as well as freedom to dispone, but the contrary was eventually held[10], and such clauses were only expressly annulled by later legislation[11]. As a result of this legislation, and as a result of the merger of burgage into feufarm[12], all land may now be freely subinfeudated, except where there is a pre-emption clause. It may be added that the double manner of holding was eventually held not to be a breach of a prohibition of subinfeudation[13].

1 They all have the same effect, but the feu contract takes the form of a bilateral deed.
2 F L Ganshof *Qu'est ce que la Féodalité?* (1944, in English *Feudalism*),3,2,XV. But it may be doubted whether this is strictly true. Thus see the *Libri Feudorum* 1,13, and note the similarity of what is there said with our own law in the medieval and early modern periods.
3 This is not to be confused with the charter of confirmation of an *a me* transfer, for which see later. Charters confirming subinfeudation were sometimes called 'upper confirmations'. They fell into disuse about the middle of the eighteenth century. Thomas Hope thus distinguishes them: '*Carta confirmationis duplex est; aliquando enim dominus confirmat alienationem factum a vassalo de ipso vassalo tenendam, aliquando de se ut domino superiore*': *Major Practicks* (Stair Soc vol 3, 1937) p 153.
4 Burgage could not be subinfeudated.
5 Stair *Institutions* II,3,32.
6 Eg the Feuing Act 1457 (c 15; 12mo c 71) (APS ii, 49); the Feuing Crown Lands Act 1503 (c 36; 12mo c 90) (APS ii, 253); the Feuing of Wardlands Act 1606 (c 11; 12mo c 12) (APS iv, 287); and the Ward Holding Act 1633 (c 16; 12mo c 16) (APS V, 33). There is extensive discussion in Stair II,11,13 ff. See also Lord Fraser in *Cassels v Lamb* (1885) 12 R 722, and see *Cockburn Ross v George Heriot's Hospital Governors* 6 June 1815 FC. Of the Act of 1606, Lord Fraser says: 'The hand on the clock was stopped by this legislation for 142 years. Feudal law triumphed, and the commerce in land was put an end to': *Cassels v Lamb* (1885) 12 R 722 at 766.
7 'It should be noted that bishops and abbots cannot make an absolute disposition of any part of their lands without the consent and confirmation of the King, because such lands are held in free alms of the King and his ancestors': *Regiam Majestatem* 2,23 (translation of Lord Cooper in Stair Soc vol 11, 1947). See also Thomas Hope *Major Practicks* (Stair Soc vol 3, 1937) p 181. Some restrictions continued after the Reformation: see H M Conacher 'Land Tenure in Scotland in the Seventeenth Century' 1938 JR 18.
8 To what extent this was accepted as law is unclear. H M Conacher wrote: 'The growing use of the feudi firma as a tenure was due to the fact that it was the one way of alienating land owned by the Church or annexed to the Crown': 'Feudal Tenure in Scotland in the 15th and 16th Centuries' 1936 JR 189.
9 Tenures Abolition Act 1746 (c 50), s 10.
10 *Campbell v Dunn* (1828) 6 S 679, a majority of six to four of the Whole Court.
11 Conveyancing (Scotland) Act 1874 (c 94), s 22; Conveyancing Amendment (Scotland) Act 1938 (c 24), s 8.
12 Conveyancing (Scotland) Act 1874, s 25.
13 *Colquhoun v Walker* (1867) 5 M 773; *Inglis v Wilson* 1909 SC 1393, 1909 2 SLT 166. As to the double manner of holding, see para 100 below.

59. Power to dispone. Disposition is transfer *a me* so as to substitute the grantee as the new vassal, the granter disappearing from the feudal chain[1]. At common law 'fees are . . . unalienable without consent of the superior . . . and there is no oblige-ment upon the superior to receive any stranger, or singular successor, to be his vassal'[2] except in the case of burgage. Any such unauthorised disposition was not only void but could also trigger the irritancy of recognition, and the *Books of the Feus* even decree that the lawyer involved is to have his right hand cut off[3], though it does not seem that this last rule was ever received into Scots law. Matters began to change in 1469, when a statute provided that a creditor attaching the land could compel the superior to give him entry[4], and conveyancers soon pressed this into use for sales, for if the superior refused consent, the seller and purchaser would conduct collusive litigation to enable the purchaser to enter as creditor. This Act thus effectively allowed freedom of disposition. But the position was not regularised until the Tenures Abolition Act 1746, which enacted that a purchaser could compel entry[5]. Even then an unco-operative superior could be compelled only by liti-gation, and it was not until 1874 that a disponee could take entry without any act being necessary on the part of the superior[6]. No restriction in the infeftment of the power of disposition has been competent since the 1746 Act, except for pre-emption clauses[7].

About the middle of the thirteenth century charters began to include a desti-nation *et assignatis suis*, which was perhaps intended to operate as a consent in advance to disposition[8]. But legal practice, both of the conveyancers and of the courts, was to the opposite effect. The view which prevailed was that 'assignee' does not mean 'disponee', and that the word must be read literally, as meaning assignees before infeftment[9]. Indeed, had it been otherwise the 1746 Act would have been unnecessary in this respect[10].

The subject, however, is not free of difficulty. The 1746 Act not only enables a disponee to compel a renewal of investiture, but also annuls clauses *de non alienando sine consensu superiorum* which were sometimes imposed as burdens. Why, before 1746, were such clauses ever used? Why declare forbidden what the law in any case forbade? It has been suggested that the right of the superior to refuse entry to a singular successor applied only to some tenures, and not to feufarm, and that the clause mentioned was a new invention, at the time of Charles I, to control alienations of feus[11]. This would explain the wording of the 1746 Act, but the matter is obscure. Other constructions are possible, such as that the clause was mere verbiage, or that it was used to bar collusive alienations under the 1469 Act.

Finally, just as bequest could be objected to both by the superior and by the disappointed heir, so, originally, alienation could be objected to not only by the superior but also by the family of the seller. Or so at least it would appear from late medieval conveyancing practice, when alienations either were accompanied by the consent of the family, or proceeded on a narrative that the sale was necessary because of insolvency[12]. But this rule either never fully established itself, or was abandoned, probably by the sixteenth century.

1 The Crown could not and cannot dispone, but only subinfeudate, since it must retain the ultimate superiority.
2 Stair *Institutions* II,3,5.
3 *Libri Feudorum* 2,55.
4 Diligence Act 1469 (c 12; 12mo c 36) (APS ii, 96). The fifteenth-century statute book contains much legislation cutting down feudal rights.
5 Tenures Abolition Act 1746 (c 50), s 12 (repealed). Stair had already urged this reform: II,4,6. In the same section he also urged the abolition of subinfeudation, a reform which may soon at last be enacted.
6 Conveyancing (Scotland) Act 1874 (c 94), s 4.
7 See *Matheson v Tinney* 1989 SLT 535, where the whole subject and its history are reviewed. Pre-emption rights have however been restricted by the Conveyancing Amendment (Scotland)

Act 1938 (c 24), s 9, the Conveyancing and Feudal Reform (Scotland) Act 1970 (c 35), s 46, and the Land Tenure Reform (Scotland) Act 1974 (c 38), s 13.

8 This was Craig's view: *Jus Feudale* 3,3,31. See also A A M Duncan *Scotland: The Making of the Kingdom* (1975) p 398, who gives an example as early as 1210, and interprets in the same way as Craig.

9 *Lord Carnegy v Lady Cranburn* (1663) Mor 10375; *Ogilvie v Kinloch* (1673) Mor 10384; *Lockhart v Nicolson's Creditors* (1696) Mor 6411; *Salmon v Boyd* (1769) Mor 4181; *Inverkeithing Magistrates v Ross* (1874) 2 R 48; *Stair* II,3,5; Erskine *Institute* II,7,5; Bell *Principles* s 727. The contrary was held in *Christie v Jackson* (1898) 6 SLT 245, OH, but an Outer House case could hardly overrule the prior tract of authority, not to mention *Stair* II,3,5; *Erskine* II,7,5 and *Bell* s 727. The position prior to the seventeenth-century needs further research, especially in view of Craig's opinion cited above. In theory it is possible that what we have is a seventeenth-century reconstruction of the law. But it is much more likely that the term 'assignees' was a dead letter from the beginning, and the case law from 1663 merely confirmed this.

10 Lord Dunedin appears to err in this matter in *Maguire v Burges* 1909 SC 1283, 1909 2 SLT 219.

11 H B King *Short History of Feudalism in Scotland* (1914) ch XV. This is a curious polemic work, of much interest but sometimes doubtful scholarship, which among other things argues strongly that at common law vassals by feufarm can alienate without the consent of the superior. King's views, though unorthodox, would perhaps merit a modern examination. It is striking that the superior's veto, apparently in all tenures, disappeared in France and in Germany 'from the 12th century at latest' (F L Ganshof *Qu'est ce que la Féodalité?* (1944, in English *Feudalism*), 3, 2, XVI), while in England it disappeared by the statute *Quia Emptores* in 1290 (18 Edw 1 st 1). Why should Scotland differ? And might feufarms have been an exception?

12 See W Ross *Lectures on the History and Practice of the Law of Scotland relative to Conveyancing and Legal Diligence* (1792) (2nd edn, 1822) II, 248. The subject seems never to have been fully investigated.

60. Position of the superior. The superiority was and is transferable either *inter vivos* or *mortis causa* in exactly the same way as the *dominium utile*. Indeed superiorities were, and to a very limited extent still are, bought and sold as investments[1]. Logically the vassal should have had the right to object to an *inter vivos* transfer, because that would be to change the nature of his fealty without his consent, and indeed there are traces of such a right in early continental feudalism, but it does not seem that such a rule ever established itself in Scotland. In form a disposition of a superiority is a disposition of the land itself, and not of the superiority. The reason lies in the principle that lord and vassal are both owners of the land, neither estate being a burden (in the technical sense) on the other, so that just as the vassal dispones the land itself, so does the superior. In conveyancing practice dispositions of superiority can be distinguished chiefly by the form of the clause of warrandice, which excepts feus rights.

A superior cannot create a new estate intermediate between his estate and that of his vassal[2]. Nor can the superiority be divided if to do so would mean that a vassal thereby acquires two separate superiors, though this does not bar *pro indiviso* ownership of the superiority, nor division along the boundary between separate feus, and the objection can also be waived by the vassal[3].

It is common for the mineral rights to be reserved to the superior[4]. Where that happens, the minerals are, however, not held by him *qua* superior, for his right to them is one of *dominium utile*, and he can alienate the minerals either by disposition or by subinfeudation.

1 The value lay in the feuduty (being abolished), in the possibility of irritancy, in casualties (now abolished), and in occasional lump sums paid for minutes of waiver of real burdens.

2 Stair *Institutions* II,4,5; *Douglas v Torthorell* (1670) Mor 15012; *Archbishop of St Andrews v Marquis of Huntly* (1862) Mor 15015. See also an Act of Robert III in 1400 (APS i, 213). But 'interjection' is competent with the vassal's consent: *Hotchkis v Walker's Trustees* (1822) 2 S 70 (NE 65).

3 *Dreghorn v Hamilton* (1774) Mor 15015; *Duke of Montrose v Colquhoun* (1781) Mor 8822, affd (1782) 6 Pat 805, HL; *Lamont v Duke of Argyll* (1819) 6 Pat 410, HL; *Graham v Westenra* (1826) 4 S 615 (NE 623); *Cargill v Muir* (1837) 15 S 408.

4 Minerals form a *separatum tenementum* and the right is thus (perhaps surprisingly) not *onus* but *dominium*. See para 212 below.

61. Who could be a vassal? In general there was no bar to a fief being held by a woman. If it were a military fief the military duties could be performed by her husband. But there was a difficulty for corporations[1]. A corporation may endure indefinitely[2], with the result that the superior would lose the casualty of relief, while in a military fief a corporation would be useless, especially as most medieval corporations were ecclesiastical or at least, like the medieval universities, closely connected with the church. There was also, at least in the earlier period, the problem of how a corporation could swear fealty or give homage. The rule developed that a superior could give or refuse entry to a corporation at his option, notwithstanding the legislation in favour of singular successors[3]. The usual practice eventually came to be for corporations either to take entry through nominees or to agree to a periodic substitute for composition[4]. It does not seem that the superior's right of veto was ever expressly abolished, but the issue became a dead one with the advent of automatic entry and the abolition of casualties.

Parallel issues might have arisen for trustees as vassals, but in practice it came to be accepted that a superior could not refuse them entry. It seems that casualties would be due on the death of the last trustee (casualty of relief), or an assumption of a new trustee (casualty of composition). But in a feu direct to trustees, the practice was to stipulate for more than this[5].

Whereas a corporation could be a vassal, a partnership, despite being a juristic person in its own right, and despite being able to hold a lease in its own name, has never been considered capable of ownership of land, and this has always been explained as being a doctrine of feudal law. This seems open to question, and the true explanation may instead lie in conveyancing practicalities[6].

1 It was not, however, until the late middle ages that anything like the modern conception of a corporation emerged.
2 'Incorporations are perpetual and do not die': Stair *Institutions* II,3,41.
3 Diligence Act 1469 (c 12; 12mo c 36) (APS ii, 96); Tenures Abolition Act 1746 (c 50). See *Stair* II,3,41. The issue is considered in detail in *Hill v Merchant Co of Edinburgh* 17 January 1815 FC. See also *Learmonth v Trinity Hospital Governors* (1854) 16 D 580.
4 See *Campbell v Orphan Hospital* (1843) 5 D 1273, and thereafter the Conveyancing (Scotland) Act 1874 (c 94), s 5.
5 A M Bell *Lectures on Conveyancing* (3rd edn, 1882) vol 2, p 1146.
6 See S Styles 'Why Can't Partnerships Own Heritage?' (1989) 34 JLSS 414, and G Gretton 'Problems in Partnership Conveyancing' (1991) 36 JLSS 232.

62. Sanctions for breach. In addition to rules restraining alienation, there were also rules which punished the vassal for making any attempt at unlawful alienation. This was the doctrine of recognition, to be discussed below[1].

1 See para 82 below.

63. Tenure, *reddendo* and casualty. There existed different types of tenure[1], though the distinction between them was often blurred in practice[2]. They differed according to the nature of the *reddendo*, the obligation of the vassal to the superior, and according to the casualties exigible. The concept of a casualty[3], though a central one, is hardly capable of exact definition, for on the one hand it is not always easy to distinguish between casualty and *reddendo*, and on the other it is not always easy to distinguish between casualty and feudal remedies[4]. Broadly a casualty was a right which accrued to the superior on an occasional and irregular basis, as opposed to the regular and constant rights under the *reddendo*. In general, casualties were real rights, and imported no personal liability, though the details are complex. The casualties incident to wardholding disappeared with the abolition of that tenure, while the other casualties were abolished in 1874 and 1914[5].

1 The different types of tenure are discussed in paras 64 ff below. 'The main division of infeftments in relation to the holding, is in ward, blench, feu, burgage, and mortification': Stair *Institutions* II,3,31.

2 C F Kolbert and N A M Mackay *History of Scots and English Land Law* (1977) p 37 write that 'probably it was not until the time of Craig that the Scots tenures were finally classified under the modern headings'. This seems doubtful. The final classification seems to have been pretty firmly in place by the middle of the fifteenth century and probably earlier, and the changes in the medieval period should not be exaggerated. Moreover, the term 'modern headings' may be queried, for arguably there has been more change in the pattern of tenures since Craig than there ever was before him, as witness the abolition of wardholding and of burgage and the emasculation of feufarm.

3 'Casualty' comes from the Latin *casus*, adjective *casualis*: something which falls, or a fortuitous occasion.

4 Thus irritancy was commonly called a casualty, but is perhaps more truly a remedy; indeed, Lord Watson denied that it was a casualty: *Sandeman v Scottish Property Investment Co* (1885) 12 R (HL) 67 at 71. Several of the casualties, such as recognition and disclamation, were in fact species of irritancy. Erskine (*Institutes* II,2,51) in turn doubts whether disclamation is really a casualty.

5 Conveyancing (Scotland) Act 1874 (c 94), s 17 (amended by the Feudal Casualties (Scotland) Act 1914 (c 48), s 24, Sch E). There was a system of compensation to the superior.

(5) TENURES

64. Wardholding. Wardholding (*feudum militare*) was the true feudal tenure[1], being military, all others being non-military and so merely semi-feudal. This tenure was mainly from the Crown, but a sub-vassal could also hold by this tenure. The vassal owed to the superior the *reddendo* of 'hunting and hosting'. A M Bell summarised it well:

'These were called the services of hosting and hunting, being obligations to attend the superior in time of the King's wars, and of trouble and insurrection in the country; to ride or go with him . . . in help and defence of himself and his friends, their honour, life, lands, goods and gear, and to appear with him in good equipage on local state occasions; in other words, in wars and commotions, and at frays and followings'[2].

This tenure was subject to all the feudal casualties[3], and derived its name from one of them, the casualty of ward. Where this casualty was commuted into a money payment, the tenure was called taxed wardholding.

After the rising of the Old Pretender, Prince James, the obligations of service, so far as they were military, were made void by statute[4]. Wardholding was finally abolished after the rising of the Young Pretender, Prince Charles, being converted to blench[5].

1 'The most proper feudal right we have': Stair *Institutions* II,3,31.
2 A M Bell *Lectures on Conveyancing* (3rd edn, 1882) vol I, p 573.
3 As to casualties, see paras 75 ff below.
4 Highland Services Act 1715 (c 54) (commonly called the Clan Act).
5 Tenures Abolition Act 1746 (c 50).

65. Burgage and booking tenure. Feudalism arose in a non-urban society, and towns were to a considerable extent outside the system: *Stadtluft macht frei*. Burgh charters seem first to have been granted in the time of David I, at which time Aberdeen, Berwick, Crail, Dunfermline, Edinburgh, Elgin, Haddington, Inverkeithing, Linlithgow, Perth, Roxburgh and Stirling were granted burgh status, and probably also Peebles and Rutherglen, with many others, such as Brechin, Dunblane, Glasgow and St Andrews soon following. The land of a burgh was nominally feudal (*feudum burgale*, or tenure *more burgi*), being held of the burgh's superior, who in a royal burgh would be the Crown but otherwise might be a subject superior. The only substantial feudal right was that the burghers could be subject to the jurisdiction of the superior as well as that of the burgh court, though speaking generally the hallmark of the burgh was self-government and exemption from the general machinery of feudalism. Apart from that, burgh land was, though nominally feudal, substantively allodial. The superior's consent to transfer was not required. Subinfeudation was incompetent: 'A tenement within brugh cannot be disponed to be haulden of the giver bot most be resigned'[1]. The burgh corporation acted as agent for the superior in effecting transfers, which were done by resignation and new sasine. The corporation thus acted rather as if it were itself the superior, but in law it was only the superior's agent. It was for long a matter of dispute whether the burghers held of the Crown or other superior individually, as has just been described, or whether they held as vassals of the burgh, and subvassals of the Crown, or, yet again, whether the burgh was the vassal and the burghers held land as corporators[2]. However, in one burgh, Paisley, the burgh corporation was the superior of the burgh land, and this was sometimes classified as a separate tenure, called booking tenure in Paisley[3]. There was no *reddendo* in burgage, since it was effectively allodial, except the obligation to 'watch and ward'[4], which meant to assist in the keeping of the peace within the burgh. But this was scarcely a feudal prestation, since the benefit enured to the burghers themselves. Burgage was subject to no casualties[5]. In 1874 both burgage tenure and booking tenure in Paisley were merged into feufarm[6]. Unlike other tenures, there was no common law bar to free alienation[7].

1 Hope *Major Practicks* (Stair Soc vol 3, 1937) p 158. Here 'tenement' means immoveable property. Because feuduty was not possible in burghs, where a person wished to sell land and retain a perpetual income from it, the mechanism of ground annual was used, and this explains the existence of ground annual.

2 See A M Bell *Lectures on Conveyancing* (3rd edn, 1882) vol 2, p 793, where the conflicting authorities are collected. Curiously Bell contradicts himself at vol 1, p 623. For a good example of the confusion, see *Perth Magistrates v Stewart* (1830) 9 S 118, where burgage property was conveyed 'to be holden of the King in free burgage . . . and also to be holden of the Magistrates in feu farm . . .'. Thomas Hope *Minor Practicks* (written in the time of Charles I but first printed in 1726) on p 317 of the 1734 edition writes: 'The Magistrates of Burghs royal, are not Superiors of Burgage-lands; but, being the King's Bailiffs and Sheriffs, within the Burghs, are commissioned and impowered by their Erection to sease their Burgesses . . . For, in effect, the Community of the Burgesses, are the King's Vassals, and not the Individuality of every Burgess'. Prior to the nineteenth century the nature of corporate ownership was rather vague, often being considered as a sort of joint ownership by the corporators.

3 For the origins, see *Chalmers v Paisley Magistrates* (1829) 7 S 718. See also C F Kolbert and N A M Mackay *History of Scots and English Land Law* (1977) p 69.

4 See eg *Dixon v Lawther* (1823) 2 S 176 (NE 158), where the *reddendo* was 'scot lot watch and ward and giving suit and presence to the courts of the said burgh and obeying the acts and statutes thereof'.

5 This at least is the conventional view, but see W M Gordon *Scottish Land Law* (1989) para 2–11.

6 Conveyancing (Scotland) Act 1874 (c 94), s 25. For further material on burgage tenure generally, see W Croft Dickinson *Early Records of the Burgh of Aberdeen* (1957) and H L MacQueen and W J Windram 'Laws and Courts of the Burghs' in *The Scottish Medieval Town* (ed M Lynch, M Spearman and G Stell, 1988).

7 *Hay of Crimonmogat v Bailies of Aberdeen* (1634) Mor 15031. This case also raises, but does not appear to settle, the question of whether a non-burgess could hold burgage.

66. Mortification. Mortification[1] was the granting of land *de me* for religious or charitable purposes, the grantee being the kirk, or a corporation, or trustees. It is generally said that the *reddendo* was *preces et lacrimae* which in effect meant masses for the soul of the benefactor, but it may be doubted whether this was an essential. There were no casualties. After the Reformation such land generally fell into lay hands, by fair means or foul, and an Act of 1587 vested in the Crown all land held by the kirk (the kirklands), with certain exceptions[2]. This Act seemingly did not affect land held in mortification by persons other than the kirk. Thus strictly mortification was not abolished at this time. But in practice after the Reformation it was no longer considered as being a distinct tenure, but was classified as blench. Conveyances for charitable purposes continued to be called mortifications at least until the eighteenth century, and even now there exist some charitable trusts which are called mortifications. As Professor Gordon says, after the Reformation 'mortification for some specified end became a purpose of a grant rather than a form of tenure'[3]. Indeed, the same may have been true in the early period[4].

The kirklands were of enormous significance before the Reformation. At the height of the power of the old church possibly as much as half of Scotland was so held[5].

1 Mortification is also called 'tenure by alms'. The corresponding English term 'mortmain' is also occasionally used.
2 Annexation of Temporalities Act 1587 (c 8; 12mo c 29) (APS iii, 431). The legal history of kirklands is extremely complex.
3 W M Gordon *Scottish Land Law* (1989) para 2–14.
4 A A M Duncan, introduction to *The Acts of Robert I* (*Regesta Regum Scottorum*, vol V (1986)), p 38, expresses the view that at the beginning of the fourteenth century alms was not in fact a feudal tenure.
5 On the eve of the Reformation the kirklands were estimated for tax purposes at half the land of the nation: see I F Grant *Social and Economic Development of Scotland before 1603* (1930) p 223.

67. Blench. Blench tenure (*alba firma*) is defined by Stair as one 'whose *reddendo* is a small elusory rent as being rather an acknowledgement of, than profit to, the superior . . . as a rose, a penny money, or the like'[1]. The characteristic blenchduty was one penny Scots a year, 'if asked allenarly'[2], but there were many others, such as a pair of dog collars, a pound of Zingiber, a wild duck, a mirror, a garlic head, and a red mantle[3]. It seems likely that blench was used where the land was sold for full value, so that it would have been inappropriate to impose onerous annual duties. This could also be effected by disposition, rather than by subinfeudation, but disposition could pose problems with the superior. In addition, the Crown could not, and still cannot, dispone, so where the Crown sold for full value, blench was necessary. However, some blenchduties were far from nominal. In such cases it is not easy to distinguish blench from feufarm. Blench is subject to the same casualties as feufarm. Blenchduties are redeemable in the same way as feuduties[4], though it may be wondered how one is to calculate the redemption value of a pound of Zingiber. Blench still exists, and because duties in feufarm are now either nominal or redeemed, blench and feufarm are now effectively the same.

1 Stair *Institutions* II,3,33.
2 *Si petatur tantum.*
3 Cosmo Innes *Scotch Legal Antiquities* (1872) p 65. There is a traditional tale among conveyancers that somewhere there is a blench *reddendo* of a rose at midwinter and a snowball at midsummer, but the present writer has been unable to verify this. The anonymous *Summary View of the Feudal Law with the Differences of the Scots law from it, together with a Dictionary of the select Terms of the Scots and English Law* (1710) p 88, instances a snowball, but does not mention the season. The tale seems unlikely since feudal prestations were normally due at the term days, Whitsunday and Martinmas. See also C F Kolbert and N A M Mackay *History of Scots and English Land Law* (1977) p 62.
4 Land Tenure Reform (Scotland) Act 1974 (c 38), s 7(3).

68. Feufarm. Feufarm or feuferme (*feudi firma*[1]) and blench are the only surviving tenures[2], and as has been said they are now effectively the same. Feufarm is only a quasi-feudal tenure, in substance being, as Stair says, a 'perpetual location'[3], that is, a perpetual lease. 'Farm' means rent[4]. Earlier Scottish writers often called feufarm '*emphyteusis*', after the Roman institution of that name, with which it had much in common, though they were probably not historically connected. Since feufarm was not a true feudal tenure, but a commercial tenure engrafted on to the stock of feudal law, uncertainty long existed as to the extent to which feudal law applied to it. For instance it was long uncertain whether it was subject to the casualty of relief[5], or whether irritancy against the feuar's superior could affect the feu itself[6]. The same doubt existed about non-entry. Thus Thomas Hope, in his irresistible *admixtio linguarum*:

'Quidam sunt opinati that few lands could never fall in non-entry, and that seaseing given to the first receaver of few filled the lands for him and his airs; because the fewer non est wassalus sed colonus perpetuus allanerly, et emphiteusis est perpetua locatio'[7].

Feufarm seems to have existed from almost the beginning of Scots feudalism[8], but became prominent, at least to the eye of the lawyer, only in the fifteenth century, when statutory measures began to be taken to encourage it[9]. The process began with an Act of 1457:

'... Quhat prelat, baronne, or free-halder, that can accord with his tennent, upon setting of few-ferme of his awin land in all or in part, our soveraine lord sall ratifie and appreive the said assedation ...'[10].

The point of this was that at this period consent to subinfeudation by the lord was necessary, at least in practice (see above). The Act thus operated as a general consent by the king to his vassals in chief. Statutory permission to those not holding direct of the Crown to grant feufarms without consent was given later, in 1503[11]. Moreover, where land owned by the Crown was 'annexed' land, it could not be feued, until permission to do so was granted in the same year[12]. The legal complexities surrounding the feuing of the kirklands have already been mentioned. It will be observed that the Act assumes that the feu will be granted to a sitting tenant, and in the fifteenth and sixteenth centuries this was the norm. The triumphant rise of feufarm in this period took place largely by the conversion of tacks (leases) into feus[13]. If no *grassum* was paid, the feuduty was normally larger than the rent previously paid, because the ex-tenant was receiving the benefit of perpetual tenure and immunity from future increases. If the whole value of the property was given by *grassum*, the tenure would be blench rather than feufarm. 'Tenure by feufarm became, in the course of the sixteenth century, extremely common in the three great classes of heritable property — the lands of the Crown, annexed and unannexed, the lands of the Church, and the lands holden of the Crown in ward and blench ferm'[14].

1   The grant was *in feudifirma feodo et haereditate pro perpetuo*, or, as we now write it, 'in feufarm fee and heritage for ever'.
2   Ie with the possible exception of mortification and the somewhat innominate tenure (or tenures) which exists in a shadowy fashion for churches, manses, glebes and property which has passed through compulsory purchase.
3   Stair *Institutions* II,11,31.
4   Post-classical Latin *firma*.
5   See Erskine *Institute* II,5,48. The view eventually prevailed that relief was exigible.
6   This was finally determined in the affirmative by *Cassels v Lamb* (1885) 12 R 722, and *Sandeman v Scottish Property Investment Co* (1885) 12 R (HL) 67.
7   Hope *Major Practicks* (Stair Soc vol 3, 1937) p 263.
8   The earliest known example is from about 1150, land being granted in *liberum firmum feudum*. See the *Liber de Calchou* (Book of Kelso) i, No 102, cited by I A Milne in 'Heritable Rights: The Early Feudal Tenures' in *An Introduction to Scottish Legal History* (Stair Soc vol 20, 1958) p 147 at p 154. But terminology can mislead, and early feufarm seems to have been more truly feudal than its later form. For instance, it seems to have been subject to the casualty of ward. Feufarm in its modern sense probably dates from the fourteenth century.
9   It is impossible to read the fifteenth-century statute book without being impressed with the almost Benthamite spirit with which Parliament sought to improve the Scottish system of land law, especially with a view to giving farmers suitable forms of tenure. The object was the encouragement of agriculture. The Leases Act 1449 (c 6) is, of these measures, the one best remembered today.
10   Feuing Act 1457 (c 15; 12mo c 71). 'Assedation' means lease, illustrating the fact that in the medieval and early modern period there was no sharp distinction between lease and feufarm. At this period we also sometimes find sasine given on leases.
11   Feuing Lands Act 1503 (c 37; 12mo c 91).
12   Feuing Lands Act 1503. Crown land which was 'annexed' could not be alienated without parliamentary sanction.
13   On this and other aspects of the rise of feufarm, see M Sanderson *Scottish Rural Society in the 16th Century* (1982); I F Grant *Social and Economic Development of Scotland before 1603* (1930);

H M Conacher 'Feudal Tenures in Scotland in the 15th and 16th Centuries' 1936 JR 189; H M Conacher 'Land Tenure in Scotland in the Seventeenth Century' 1938 JR 18; R Nicholson 'Feudal Developments in late Mediaeval Scotland' 1973 JR 1.
14 Thomas Thomson *Memorial on Old Extent* (1816) (Stair Soc vol 10, 1946) p 245.

69. Feuduty. Feuduties were payable in money, or in kind, or in both. Feuduties in kind were not abolished until 1924[1], though by then they were rare. The feuar might also be bound by his charter to give personal service to the superior. Military service (improper to feufarm, but sometimes found) became void by the Clan Act of 1715[2], but non-military personal service, especially agricultural, remained competent until 1934[3]. In 1974 it became incompetent to impose new feuduties[4], and machinery was set up for the redemption of existing feudities[5]. Most feuduties have now been redeemed, and those that still exist have largely been rendered nominal by inflation.

Redemption of feuduty does not terminate the feudal relation: the proprietor is still in theory a vassal. But feudality is only a shadow of what once it was. Today most proprietors do not know the name of their superior[6]. Many do not even know that they have one. Sometimes the identity of a superior cannot now be established, and to determine, for any piece of land, the complete chain of feudal superiors up to the Crown would often be hardly possible.

If the *dominium utile* was divided, each feuar is jointly and severally liable for the feuduty. This is called an unallocated or *cumulo* feuduty. The agreement between the feuars *inter se* as to their contribution is called an agreement of apportionment. The superior may however agree to allocate, which means waiving his joint and several claim. The feuars may now compel an allocation[7].

Feuduty can be enforced by personal action not only against the feuar but also against subvassals and tenants[8], though action against anyone except the immediate feuar is obsolete in modern practice. It is also a *debitum fundi*, which is to say a debt which is a real security on the land, and as such can be enforced by the real diligences of poinding of the ground and adjudication on a *debitum fundi*, though these are not now used for this purpose in practice. Irritancy is also available[9].

1 Conveyancing (Scotland) Act 1924 (c 27), s 12.
2 Highland Services Act 1715 (c 54) ('the Clan Act'). For interpretation, see *Duke of Argyle v Tarbert's Creditors* (1726) Mor 14495. Here the vassal was bound to hold a castle for the Duke against his enemies, and also to provide a boat for him.
3 Conveyancing (Scotland) Act 1874 (c 94), s 20; Conveyancing (Scotland) Act 1924 (c 27), s 12(7).
4 Land Tenure Reform (Scotland) Act 1974 (c 38), s 1.
5 Ibid, ss 4–6.
6 Even the solicitor attending to the conveyancing may not know this, because there is often no need to know. Nothing could illustrate better the speed with which feudalism is hurrying to the grave. Even when the present writer began in practice, the solicitors involved in the conveyancing would generally know the identity of the superior.
7 Conveyancing and Feudal Reform (Scotland) Act 1970 (c 35), ss 3–5.
8 Bell *Principles* s 700.
9 See para 85 below.

70. Other tenures. Land which has passed through compulsory purchase is, as we have seen, nominally still feudal, but is functionally allodial, and it is not possible to state what species of tenure is applicable, for there is no *reddendo* and there are no casualties. The same is true of manses and glebes of the established kirk[1]. It should also be repeated that although the types of tenure were in theory distinct, in practice features appropriate to one tenure might be found in another. Thus we have seen that in some blenchholdings the *reddendo* was by no means nominal, thus blurring the distinction between blench and feufarm, and we have also seen how such tenures by mortification as survived the Reformation came to be considered as feufarms. The tenure called socage, or soccage, which eventually became the chief

English tenure, is occasionally to be found in the medieval period, but it never established for itself a permanent place among the Scots tenures[2].

1 See para 47 above.
2 It is mentioned in *Regiam Majestatem* at 2,21. ('*Si quis liberum soccagium habernit . . .*'). See also Erskine *Institute* I,1,35, and G W S Barrow *Anglo-Norman Era in Scottish History* (1980).

71. An illustration. The present writer has before him an instrument of sasine in favour of Angus Mackintosh recorded in the Register of Sasines for Inverness on 2 January 1838. The tenure is feufarm, but the feuar is bound to attend his superior, the Earl of Moray, in the latter's 'hostings, hawkings and huntings . . . in all places of this Kingdom of Scotland on the north side of the Water of Spey' and later there is an obligation of 'attending and serving the said Earl . . . against all mortals'. This is a military obligation: the obligation to fight for the Earl. The deed contains other features of pure feudalism, including a prohibition against transferring the feu to any person not a member of the Clan Chattan[1], an irritancy clause in the event that the feuar should ever rise in arms against the Earl, an obligation on the vassal to attend the Earl's court thrice a year, a right to the Earl to seize the feuar's goods without any judicial process, and so forth. This deed illustrates how tenures were not wholly distinct, for it relates to feufarm but includes much of wardholding. It also illustrates the conservatism of lawyers[2]. In the reign of Her Majesty Queen Victoria, in the age of steam locomotives, of the *Edinburgh Review*, of Royal Commissions and Benthamite legislation, in the year when Steinheil communicated to the Göttingen Academy of Sciences his new system of electrical telegraphy, the Earl of Moray no longer needed the military services of his assembled vassals, nor did he need fear that they might rise against him with fire and sword, nor did he need secure himself against the danger that members of hostile clans might violate his hereditary domains. As for attendance at his court, by 1838 it would no longer have been held. As for the military obligation, it had been void for 123 years[3], while the restriction on alienating to a non-clan member had been null for 92 years[4].

1 Clan Chattan was a confederacy of clans, including Clan Mackintosh. For a case dealing with a similar clause, see *MacGillivray v Souter* (1862) 24 D 759.
2 It should not be taken as meaning that true feudalism or the old clan system was still alive in 1838. The clauses would have been repeated from earlier deeds, in this case probably dating from the seventeenth century.
3 Ie since the Highland Services Act 1715 ('the Clan Act') (c 54).
4 Ie since the Tenures Abolition Act 1746 (c 50).

72. Kindly tenants and tenants-at-will. In the late medieval and early modern period perpetual tacks were sometimes granted, the holder being called a kindly tenant[1] or rentaller[2]. 'Kindly' here means hereditary[3]. Over time, these tenancies were gradually either given up, or converted into feufarm or blench, except in four villages (in this context called 'towns') in the parish of Lochmaben in Dumfriesshire, namely Hightae, Smallholm, Heck and Greenhill, where they survive to this day[4]. Their tenure has been described as 'not feudal and yet not truly allodial' but 'a right which amounts to full proprietorship'[5]. Ownership is registered in a register called the Rent Roll[6] kept by the Chamberlain of the Earl of Mansfield, that is, his factor. The modern practice is for dispositions and other writs to be recorded in the General Register of Sasines for Dumfriesshire in the ordinary way, with notice given by letter to the Earl's factor. Whether failure to do either would prejudice the title is unclear. When Dumfriesshire becomes an operational area in respect of registered land, completion of title will be exclusively by registration[7], which will, perhaps, largely end the distinctiveness of this tenure. Virtually all the rents have been redeemed[8].

A tenancy-at-will is similar to a kindly tenancy in that it is a perpetual lease which exists by virtue of ancient local custom. The two may share a common historical origin[9], but are regarded as distinct in modern law. A tenant-at-will may now compulsorily purchase the land[10].

1   Useful work on this tenure has been done by Margaret H B Sanderson in *Scottish Rural Society in the Sixteenth Century* (1982). In addition to this and the sources mentioned below, there is some material in Robert Hunter *Treatise on the Law of Landlord and Tenant* (4th edn, 1876): see index sv 'Rental Rights'.

2   Whether these two terms were absolutely synonymous is not clear.

3   C F Kolbert and N A M Mackay *History of Scots and English Land Law* (1977) p 80 regard the derivation as open to question, and suggest alternative theories, namely that the tenant paid in kind, or that the tenure was due to the kindness of the landlord. But the matter is beyond doubt. See further C S Lewis *Studies in Words* (1960). Note, however, that what was special about the kindly tenancy was that it was perpetual and alienable, rather than that it was inheritable, for even tacks of limited duration are inheritable at common law, in that they pass to the heir for the balance of the term.

4   See John Carmont 'The King's Kindlie Tenants of Lochmaben' (1909) 21 JR 323, and *Kolbert and Mackay*. J M Halliday *Conveyancing* para 16-17 speaks of this tenure in the past tense, but it still exists. According to old oral tradition, the kindly tenants (other than purchasers) are descendants of the personal servants of Robert I: Sir Walter Scott *Minstrelsy of the Scottish Border*, note to 'The Harper of Lochmaben'. Certain parallels exist between kindly tenancies and the English copyhold.

5   *Royal Four Towns Fishing Association v Dumfriesshire Assessor* 1956 SC 379 at 388, 1956 SLT 217 at 220, LVAC, per Lord Sorn. See also *Marquis of Queensberry v Wright* (1838) 16 S 439. With respect, the dictum can hardly be correct. Proprietorship of land can only be feudal or allodial: *tertius non datur*. The meaning of allodial ownership is ownership which is not feudal. *Kolbert and Mackay* p 82 are no doubt correct in describing the right as feudal. Whether the superior is the Crown, the Earl being his agent, or whether the Earl is superior and the Crown oversuperior, is unclear. An unpublished research paper of 1987 by Roderick Paisley at Aberdeen University argues for the latter position.

6   It slightly resembles the German *Grundbuch* in appearance.

7   Land Registration (Scotland) Act 1979 (c 33), s 3(3)(c).

8   The Land Tenure Reform (Scotland) Act 1974 (c 38), s 4(7), provides for the redemption not only of feuduty but also of 'any other perpetual periodical payment in respect of the tenure, occupancy or use of land'. Some of the information in this paragraph has been kindly provided by Stephen Williams of Messrs McJerrow Stevenson, Lockerbie, and by J B Farquhar, factor to the Earl of Mansfield, Scone Palace.

9   The history of tenants-at-will seems not to have been researched.

10   Land Registration (Scotland) Act 1979, s 20. Kindly tenants are expressly excluded from these provisions: s 20(8)(a)(ii).

73. *Liberum maritagium*. *Liberum maritagium* (not to be confused with the casualty of marriage) was not a separate tenure, but a form of wardholding whereby the vassal was for a period exempted from most feudal prestations[1]. It was granted to females by way of family provision. It seems not to have survived the middle ages.

1   See further A A M Duncan *Acts of Robert I (Regesta Regum Scottorum*, vol V (1986)).

74. Liferent. Liferent is not a tenure, but it is convenient to say something of it here[1]. Improper liferent need not detain us, since it is merely a beneficial interest under a trust. In an improper liferent of land, therefore, the liferenter has no direct legal connection with the land at all[2], title being held solely by the trustees. But proper liferent is one of the real rights. At first sight liferent is merely the Scots term for *usufructus*, and thus has no particular connection with feudalism. But in fact it appears that the equation of liferent with usufruct is a post-medieval Romanisation of an uncivilian institution, rather as the categorisation of the estate of the vassal as *dominium utile* was a medieval Romanisation of an uncivilian institution[3]. The process was never completed, and whilst proper liferents must be generally conceived as Scots usufructs and as subordinate real rights *minus quam dominium*, nevertheless they retain some odd features. Thus Erskine deals with liferents under the head of 'servitudes', which is a strongly civilian approach. But he then writes:

> 'A simple liferent, where the subject is heritable, requires a sasine duly registered to make the right effectual . . . for a liferent of lands, though it be doubtless a burden upon

the subjects liferented, is truly a feudal right, much resembling property, which constitutes the liferenter *interim dominus* or proprietor for life'[4].

The striking expression *interim dominus* well conveys the fact that the proper liferent was never wholly civilianised. Strictly speaking, under modern law, the liferenter is not *dominus*, even *ad interim*, but the right does certainly have some features of *dominium* which arise from its feudal background. Thus where a superiority was liferented by reservation[5], it was the liferenter, not the fiar, who renews the investiture of the vassals[6]. In any proper liferent of feufarm it is the liferenter who must pay the feuduty to the superior. In a liferented superiority, the curious rule was that feuduties fell to the liferenter but casualties to the fiar. It should be noted that the liferenter had to complete title by investiture[7]. Since the same was true of the fiar[8], the fiar and liferenter were thus vassals of the same superior for the same property at the same time, and indeed this is still the law for proper liferents of land[9]. Presumably both were bound in fealty. However, the 'legal liferents', namely terce and courtesy, required no new infeftment. Thus if a man died infeft, his heir would have to obtain a renewal of investiture, but the widow obtained her terce by the process of *kenning*, which required no infeftment to complete it[10].

1 See generally LIFERENT AND FEE, vol 13, paras 1601 ff.
2 The same is true of an improper fiar.
3 The subject is well handled in C F Kolbert and N A M Mackay *History of Scots and English Land Law* (1977), ch 13, to which the present paragraph is indebted. Their work was based on C D'Olivier Farran *Principles of Scots and English Land Law* (1958). Farran at p 105 writes of the 'general tendency among Scots lawyers to dress up feudal ideas and objects in the fine clothes of Roman legal language, in which their barbarian limbs wriggle somewhat uncomfortably'. There is some truth in this, but, as we have seen, the 'tendency' existed throughout Europe and had already begun as long ago as the twelfth century.
4 Erskine *Institute* II,9,41.
5 That is to say, A infeft and seised as of fee, conveys to B under reservation of a liferent to himself. This was very common, even in the medieval period. Commonly B would be A's son. The doctrine never applied to liferents by constitution, as where X, infeft of fee, grants a liferent to Y, reserving the fee to himself or granting it to Z. For late authority, see *Henderson v Mackenzie* (1836) 14 S 540.
6 As *Kolbert and Mackay* remark (p 128): 'Surely no more striking demonstration of his not being a mere encumbrancer could be imagined? Here he is giving real rights which may well outlast his own interest'. See also W Croft Dickinson 'Freehold in Scots Law' 1945 JR 135.
7 This in principle is still the case today for proper liferents of land, being done by recording or registration.
8 Ie the person holding the fee.
9 As we shall see, something similar could happen in heritable securities, though in practice they were usually holden *de me*. By contrast, liferents never seem to have been held by base infeftment.
10 *Erskine* II,9,50.

(6) CASUALTIES

75. Casualty of ward. Wardholding received its name from the casualty of ward, whereby if the vassal was a pupil or minor, he was given into the guardianship of the superior, who also took the lands, until majority, for his own benefit. If the vassal were a female, the ward ended when she reached the age of fourteen, not majority. The right of guardianship, curious to the modern mind, was natural to the feudal mind, for vassalage was a bond like kinship. The right to the land was natural because the vassal was not capable of giving military service. (If the heir were a girl, she would be expected to marry at fourteen, when her husband could render military service.) The right of guardianship fell into disuse after the end of the medieval period, but the right to the land continued to be exercised until the abolition of wardholding. However, if the wardholding was 'taxed', the superior did not have the right to the land itself, but only to a fixed yearly sum during the ward. Taxed ward was thus a commercialisation of feudalism. The right of ward was often sold, the purchaser being called the donatar of the ward. An important aspect of this casualty is that it took effect even as against subvassals. Thus suppose A held ward of the Crown and B held by feufarm of A, and A died leaving a pupil heir, then B would lose possession for the duration of the ward. 'The circumstance of an under-vassal ... is always the worse the farther he is distant from the prime superior; since, by the death of the superiors interjected between him and the lord paramount ... he may be shut out from the revenues of his feu, perhaps for a series of minorities together. And this suggests why we so much aim at getting rid of subaltern superiors, in order to hold of the Crown'[1]. The subvassal thus exposed was said to hold by black ward, or ward-upon-ward, but black ward could be excluded by an upper confirmation, that is, by a charter by the oversuperior, and this was commonly done in practice, and again in some cases the subvassal was protected by statute[2]. The casualty of ward disappeared with the abolition of wardholding itself.

1 *Treatise concerning the Origin and Progress of Fees* (2nd edn, 1761) p 6. The authorship of this work, first published in 1734, is uncertain. It has been attributed to John Spotiswood, and also to John Mackenzie: see W Rodgers *Feudal Forms of Scotland viewed Historically* (1857) p 182. The work is dedicated to the WS Society, suggesting that the author was a member, but the society's records do not disclose any member of those names for the appropriate period.
2 Eg the Feuing Act 1457 (c 15, 12mo c 71) (APS ii, 49, c 15) provided that if A held by feufarm of B who held ward of C, A was protected against ward in favour of C.

76. Avail of marriage. The casualty of marriage, or avail of marriage, was exigible only in wardholding. Whether it existed in all cases is unclear. At any rate it was common practice to have an express *cum maritagio* clause. Originally the rule was that where the vassal was unmarried, the superior could offer him a suitable bride, and if he accepted her, the dowry (tocher) which came with her was payable to the superior. This sum was called the single avail of marriage. If he refused her, which of course he was at liberty to do, he had to pay double avail, though how the value of this was calculated in earlier times is unclear. But double avail was payable only if the bride offered and rejected was a suitable one in terms of social status and personal qualities[1]. In the post-medieval period, single avail was calculated not by the tocher but as two years' rental value of the vassal's whole heritable estate (not merely the land held of that superior) while double avail was calculated at three years' rental[2]. This casualty disappeared with wardholding itself.

1 There should be no 'disparagement': see the *Quoniam Attachiamenta* ch 90–94.
2 Stair *Institutions* II,4,47, where he also observes that the Court of Session had never found double avail to be due since the establishment of the court in 1532. For a striking case, see *Drummond v Stuart* (1678) Mor 8541.

77. *Jus primae noctis*. In folk tradition the most conspicuous feature of feudalism is perhaps the *jus primae noctis*, the right of the superior to sleep with the bride of any vassal or tenant immediately after the wedding. Whilst this right is commonly supposed to have had widespread existence, it is most especially associated with Scotland[1]. Though there is no reliable evidence that such a right was ever sanctioned by law, it does, astonishingly, seem to have existed as a matter of practice in some parts of Scotland[2].

1 Eg Sir William Blackstone, *Commentaries* Bk II, Ch 6: 'I cannot learn that this custom prevailed in England, though it certainly did in Scotland (under the name of *mercheta* or *marchata*) till abolished by Malcolm III'.
2 See Hector McKechnie '*Jus Primae Noctis*' (1930) 42 JR 303. Lest McKechnie's conclusions be dismissed as fanciful, it must be observed that he was a scholar of unquestioned reputation.

78. Casualty of aid. A superior in wardholding could in certain cases call on his vassals for financial support, called 'aid'. It appears that this was never formally abolished, until the final end of wardholding itself, but it seems to have been in desuetude by the seventeenth century. The last evidence of its survival is probably the following passage in Balfour:

> 'It is leasum to the superior, or overlord, to ask ony ressonabill help or subsidie fra his tenant[1], gif his sone and appeirand air to be maid ane knicht, or gif he is to marie his eldest dochter with ony man'[2].

1 Ie vassal.
2 Balfour *Practicks* (1579, but not printed until 1754) (Stair Soc vol 21, 1962 ed P G B McNeill) p 125.

79. Relief. Relief (medieval Latin *relevium*) was the sum payable to the superior by the heir on taking up the succession. For wardholdings it was calculated nominally at one year's value of the land[1]. For feufarm it was fixed at one year's feuduty[2]. After it became competent to bequeath heritage, the rule was that composition, not relief, was payable when the subjects passed to a person other than the heir[3]. Relief was abolished by the Conveyancing (Scotland) Act 1874[4].

1 Erskine *Institute* II,5,49.
2 There was at first doubt as to whether relief was due in feufarm (*Erskine* II,5,48), yet another indication of the merely semi-feudal nature of that tenure.
3 *Lamont v Rankin's Trustees* (1879) 6 R 739; affd (1880) 7 R (HL) 10.
4 Conveyancing (Scotland) Act 1874 (c 94), ss 15–17 (amended by the Feudal Casualties (Scotland) Act 1914 (c 48), s 24, Sch E).

80. Composition. At common law alienation *a me* was incompetent without the superior's consent, and so the payment to the superior for such consent was a matter for agreement. But in practice the sum payable was one year's value of the land, and this was called 'composition'. When in 1469 legislation required the superior to give entry to a creditor, this was the sum stated to be payable to him[1]. As we have seen, a purchaser could always compel entry if necessary by a collusive action *qua* creditor, and so the Act of 1469 effectively settled the amount of composition in all cases. In practice the charter commonly fixed the composition at a definite figure, and this was called 'taxed composition'[2]. Composition was also payable by a legatee. But where the successor was himself the heir, the case was called 'propulsion of the fee', and the successor called the *alioquin successorus* (or *alioqui successurus*) and relief, not composition, was payable[3]. Composition was abolished by the Conveyancing (Scotland) Act 1874[4].

1 Diligence Act 1469 (c 12; 12mo c 36) (APS ii, 96, c 12).
2 As to the calculation of composition generally, see J Craigie *Scottish Law of Conveyancing — Heritable Rights* (3rd edn, 1899) p 192, and the leading case of *George Heriot's Trust Governors v Paton's Trustees* 1912 SC 1123, 1912 2 SLT 116. The question of composition is the chief subject of H B King *Short History of Feudalism in Scotland* (1914), a polemical work of great interest but doubtful scholarship.
3 *Mackintosh v Mackintosh* (1886) 13 R 692.
4 Conveyancing (Scotland) Act 1874 (c 94), ss 15–17 (amended by the Feudal Casualties (Scotland) Act 1914 (c 48), s 24, Sch E).

81. Non-entry. If on the death of the vassal the heir failed to enter and renew the investiture, the superior was entitled to take the land *ad interim* since there was no vassal. This was the casualty of non-entry. Its precise effect varied according to the type of tenure[1]. It did not apply to burgage[2]. It was abolished by the Conveyancing (Scotland) Act 1874[3].

1 A M Bell *Lectures on Conveyancing* (2nd edn, 1882) vol 1, p 623.
2 The reason always given was that the burgh corporation is the vassal, and so the fee is always full. But on burgage, see further para 65 above.
3 Conveyancing (Scotland) Act 1874 (c 94), s 4(4). This subsection is obscure and it is difficult to resist the conclusion that the draftsman did not understand what he was doing. The matter cannot,

however, be analysed here. The leading case on the subsection is *Lord Advocate v Moray* (1890) 17 R 945.

82. Recognition. The casualty of recognition[1] was applicable to wardholding only[2], and operated where the vassal alienated, or purported to alienate, more than one-half of his land without the consent of the superior. It was an irritancy, which took back to the superior the whole land, not only the half. There are two logical puzzles about this casualty. The first is that if the alienation was *a me* it would in any case be null by the general law unless confirmed by the superior. If on the other hand the alienation was *de me*, then either it would be null unless confirmed[3] or at least the vassal would still be vassal for the whole estate held ward. How these difficulties were handled in the earlier periods is unclear, but in the seventeenth century at least it was settled that recognition did indeed operate in both types of case[4]. This casualty disappeared with the abolition of wardholding, at least by name. It seems, however, that at one time the term 'recognition' could be used in a wide sense to mean what we now call irritancy, and of course irritancy is still with us.

1 *Books of the Feus* 2,55, declares alienations without the consent of the superior void, and makes the attempt a ground of forfeiture. In addition the lawyer involved is to have his hand cut off, though this latter never was the law in Scotland.
2 So it is said. It is, however, not clear that this is wholly true. Thus consider Balfour: 'Landis set in few to ony man and his airis, for payment of certane zeirlie few-maill, with expres provision contenit in the infeftment, that it sall not be leasum to the fewar ... to annalzie the saidis landis in quhole or in part, without consent and licence of the settar of the few ... gif thay mak alienatioune utherwayis, thay to tyne and fofault the few-farme': Balfour *Practicks* (Stair Soc vol 21, 1962 ed P G B McNeill) p 172. Balfour then describes this sanction as recognition. Much could be said on this complex subject.
3 As to when the superior's consent to subinfeudation was requisite, see para 58 above.
4 See the extensive discussion in Stair *Institutions* II,11,10 ff, and *Lord Carnegy v Lady Cranburn* (1663) Mor 7732 and 10375. It seems that recognition was not much in use after the medieval period. It appears that it was James I who began to use it after 1424 as a weapon against Crown vassals. On recognition and other casualties, see Craig Madden 'Royal Treatment of Feudal Casualties in Late Medieval Scotland' 1976 Scot Hist Rev 172.

83. Disclamation and purpresture. The casualty of disclamation was a forfeiture or irritancy incurred where, as the *Books of the Feus* say, 'a vassal who in full knowledge of the nature of his act disowns his feu or any part of it, or repudiates any of the conditions on which he holds it ... forfeits the feu by reason of such disowning or denial'[1]. Erskine gives as an example a vassal who takes sasine from a person who is not his true superior[2]. The feudal reason for this casualty was that the vassal was in breach of his fealty. Indeed any serious breach of faith by the vassal could have this result, such as falsely accusing the superior of a crime[3]. Purpresture was very similar, but more specific, in that it arose where the vassal encroached physically on the land of his superior. Indeed purpresture might even be considered a sub-type of disclamation. These casualties, seemingly common to all tenures, have never been abolished, but have long been in desuetude.

1 *Books of the Feus* 2,26,4.
2 Erskine *Institute* II,5,51.
3 Balfour *Practicks* (Stair Soc vol 21, 1962 ed P G B McNeill) p 126.

84. Escheat. Liferent escheat was the forfeiture of the feu to the superior if the vassal became an outlaw, which could happen either for a capital crime or by being put to the horn in a civil cause. The forfeiture was not permanent, but ended at the vassal's death, or sooner if he were 'relaxed'. It was abolished as an effect of horning in 1746[1]. It seems never to have been abolished as a consequence of a capital crime, but has fallen into desuetude, and in any case there are now no capital crimes except treason, piracy and firing the Queen's shipyards. Liferent escheat must not be confused with single escheat, which related to moveable, not heritable, property, and was in favour of the Crown, not the superior. Stair was of the view that 'liferent escheat doth not arise from the nature of feus, or from the general feudal customs, but from our particular statutes and customs'[2].

1 Tenures Abolition Act 1746 (c 50), s 1.
2 Stair *Institutions* IV,9,2.

85. Irritancy. Irritancy, or 'tinsel', is sometimes classified as a casualty, and sometimes merely as a remedy. It exists only in two cases in land law, namely in favour of superiors and of lessees. It operates as an extinction of a right in land, and so can be invoked only by a person infeft in the land, whose right would thus be enlarged by the operation of irritancy. Hence a real burden in a disposition probably cannot be protected by an irritancy clause[1].

Irritancies are either conventional, being expressly stated in the charter, or legal. There is only one legal irritancy for feus, namely the Feu-Duty Act 1597[2], which provides for irritancy for failure to pay feuduty for five years. Conventional irritancies are dealt with elsewhere[3], and the only matter requiring specific attention here is the effect of an irritancy on the subvassal, if any. If the subinfeudation had been confirmed by the superior, as was the general early practice, the law was clear that irritancy of the midsuperiority would not affect the subvassal[4]. But eventually such confirmations were discontinued in practice. It was finally held by the Whole Court that irritancy of a midsuperiority involves irritancy of subfeus, if these latter have not been confirmed[5].

1 *Nulla sasina, nulla terra.* See para 424 below. The Conveyancing (Scotland) Act 1924 (c 27), s 23, gave to the creditor in a ground annual a right which is often termed an irritancy but which in fact is (as the statute correctly says) a type of adjudication.
2 Feu-Duty Act 1597 (c 17; 12mo c 250) (APS iv, 133, c 17), which must now be read in conjunction with the Conveyancing (Scotland) Acts (1874 and 1879) Amendment Act 1887 (c 69), s 4, the Conveyancing Amendment (Scotland) Act 1938 (c 24), s 6, and the Land Tenure Reform (Scotland) Act 1974 (c 38), s 15.
3 As to irritancy generally, see CONVEYANCING, vol 6, paras 533, 534.
4 If this happened, the subvassal became immediate vassal, but his holding was then the same as the forfeited midsuperiority. Thus if A held by feufarm from B, and B held ward of C, and there was irritancy (of whatever sort, including for instance recognition), then the effect, if A's holding had been confirmed by C, was that A held ward of C. See eg W Ross *Lectures on the History and Practice of the Law of Scotland relative to Conveyancing and Legal Diligence* (2nd edn, 1822) II, p 253.
5 *Cassels v Lamb* (1885) 12 R 722. The court was divided, and the opposing camps seem to have held their positions with some degree of animosity. There were good arguments for both positions. The decision overruled *Sandeman v Scottish Property Investment Co* (1883) 10 R 614, but that case was also under appeal in the House of Lords, and the House followed the decision in *Cassels*: *Sandeman v Scottish Property Investment Co* (1885) 12 R (HL) 67.

86. Tinsel of superiority. There is some evidence that the idea of disclamation could work in reverse, so that a serious breach of faith by the superior to his vassal could cause tinsel of the superiority[1]. But the subject is obscure. A statutory irritancy of the superiority was introduced in 1474[2], where the superior refused or failed to renew the investiture of his vassal. The sanction was to 'tyne the tennent for his lifetime', but it was unclear whether the lifetime concerned was that of the superior or that of the vassal, the latter being eventually established as the correct view[3]. The issue cannot arise in modern law, since renewal of investiture no longer needs any act by the superior.

1 Balfour *Practicks* (Stair Soc vol 21, 1962 ed P G B McNeill) p 126.
2 Entry to Lands Act 1474 (c 13; 12mo c 57). For further provisions of this Act, see para 94 below.
3 *Dickson v Lord Elphinstone* (1802) Mor 15024; *Rossmore's Trustees v Brownlie* (1877) 5 R 201.

(7) SASINE AND INFEFTMENT

87. Feudal conveyancing. In what follows we shall look at the outlines of feudal conveyancing in its later form, that is to say from the sixteenth to the nineteenth centuries. Feudal conveyancing was almost entirely abolished in the period 1845 to 1874 by legislation in the utilitarian spirit. Feudal conveyancing had indeed become an anachronism. The subject abounded in technicalities, and in what follows only an outline will be given[1].

1 A study of post-medieval feudal conveyancing, of the greatest value, is William Rodger *Feudal Forms of Scotland viewed Historically* (1857). Also to be referred to are the standard texts such as Stair *Institutions*, Erskine *Institute*, A M Bell *Lectures on Conveyancing* (3rd edn, 1882), and A Menzies *Conveyancing according to the Law of Scotland* (4th edn, 1900, by J S Sturrock). Robert Bell (brother of George Joseph Bell) *Treatise on the Conveyance of Land to a Purchaser and on the Manner of Completing his Title* (2nd edn, 1828, commonly called *Bell on Completing Title*) was a standard text in its time, but in the present writer's opinion is not always perfectly sound. Alexander Duff *Treatise on the Deeds and Forms used in the Constitution, Transmission and Extinction of Feudal Rights* (1838, commonly called *Duff's Feudal Conveyancing*) is of great value. There are numerous sources of styles, such as George Dallas of St Martins *System of Stiles* (1697), and the *Collection of Styles* (commonly called the *Juridical Styles*) of the Juridical Society of Edinburgh (1st edn, 1787; numerous later editions).

88. The rule that the fee must be full. With certain inevitable exceptions, such as the transitional period caused by a death, the rule was and is that the fee must be full, that is, that there must always be an identifiable person infeft. The rule is usually expressed by saying that a fee cannot be *in pendente*. The rule is feudal in as much as the superior is entitled to an identifiable vassal, but could equally be justified on civilian principles.

Thus a disposition to A and B in conjunct liferent and in fee to the longest liver of them would be bad because while both live no fiar can be ascertained[1]. If the rule is broken, the law will normally create a constructive trust and make one of the parties a fiar in trust to carry out the beneficial intention: this is called the doctrine of the fiduciary fee[2].

1 However, a disposition to A and B and survivor is, of course, good, because at first they are fiars in common. Also competent is a disposition to A and B in conjunct liferent and fee, which means that both are fiars in common, and the share of each will pass to his or her estate on death, but subject to a liferent of that share in favour of the longest liver.
2 The leading cases are *Frog's Creditors v His Children* (1735) Mor 4262, and *Newlands v Newlands' Creditors* (1794) Mor 4289, *sub nom Smith v Newlands* 4 Pat 43, HL. Some modifications were enacted by the Trusts (Scotland) Act 1921 (c 58). See generally W A Wilson and A G M Duncan *Trusts, Trustees and Executors* (1975).

89. Sasine. 'Sasine'[1] meant the possession of land, civilly or naturally, or more narrowly the act of giving and taking possession of land[2]. It was, and in theory still is, indispensable for the constitution of the right of the vassal as a real right: *nulla sasina, nulla terra*. Thus Balfour writes that 'the chartour is of nane avail gif na sasine follow thairupoun'[3]. The giving of sasine was a formal ceremony, enacted on the land in question, in which the land was delivered by handing over earth and stone. The parties could do this personally, but in the post-medieval period it was done by agents, the agent for the grantor being called the 'bailie' or 'baillie' and that of the grantee being the 'procurator and attorney'. This ceremony continued to be necessary down to 1845[4], by which time it had long been something of a farce. We have an account of how it happened about the year 1812:

'Suddenly five human beings appeared in one of the fields, the leader and spokesman being a notary. Two of the band were his clerks, or at least could sign their names. The remaining two were anything, generally captured in the vicinity by the notary, only a few minutes previously, and of whom he knew nothing whatever. They might have been, and frequently were, whinstone-nappers on the highway, ditchers, packmen, cadgers, weavers, cobblers, herds, colliers, carters, rat-catchers, dog-breakers, sweeps — in fact anything... Women, however, were always, and Irishmen generally, excluded... The notary then, to the amazement of the parties, proceeded to dub, we shall say, a cadger, with the title of "procurator and attorney" and a ditcher with that of "bailie."... The notary next, with a pleased air, pulled from a gaping outside coat-pocket, with flaps as broad as the ears of an elephant, a thickish paper, which he caused the cadger to shuffle to the ditcher for a moment, uttering at the same time some words, to them perfectly unintelligible... The notary wildly requested the ditcher "*qua* bailie" to lift a handful of earth, with as many small stones in it as he could get, and to tear up another handful of grass and stubble; which two handfuls the ditcher was implored to present to the cadger, alias the "procurator and attorney." The latter gentle-man... received the dirt, the stones, the grass and the stubble into his half-closed palms... Suddenly the notary put a shilling into the cadger's hand, which the latter was in the act, most promptly and naturally, of burying in the recesses of his own corduroys, when the notary wildly snatched it from him, and coolly replaced it in his own pocket, saying, with a grim smile, that he was "taking instruments."... Lastly the notary, with great solemnity, implored the hitherto inactive clerks to bear well in their memories all these interesting circumstances; the ditcher and the cadger received each a shilling for their pains, and the notary bid them good day...'[5].

The sasine could proceed lawfully only upon a precept of the superior, which in later practice left blanks for the names of the bailie and the procurator, which explains the cadger and the ditcher. However, a sasine on a precept from a party other than the superior would be valid if later ratified by the superior, and this became the norm, as we shall see. Originally it seems that the precept of sasine was a separate document from the charter, but at an early period it became the practice to combine them in a single deed, though the precept remained a distinct clause[6]. The giving of sasine was also called 'investiture', and, when oaths of fealty were still sworn, was preceded by the oath.

Under the earlier law, possession under a charter was sufficient, even if there had been no ceremony of sasine[7], but eventually the ceremony itself was regarded as necessary. The practice developed of having a notary present to record the ceremony in a notarial instrument[8], and very rapidly this instrument ceased merely to be evidence of the ceremony and became part of it. As Stair says:

'After instruments of sasine became in use, they were not only sustained as the mean of probation, that possession or sasine was given or taken, but they were the necessary solemnities to accomplish the right, which could not be supplied by any other mean of probation; though the superior with a thousand witnesses should subscribe all the contents of a sasine, it would be of no effect to make a right real without the attest of a notary'[9].

1 'Sasine' is sometimes spelt 'seisin', which is the English spelling. But the English term, as well as being different in spelling and pronunciation ('see-zin' as opposed to the Scots 'say-zeen'), is also somewhat different in meaning. Every conveyancer will have come across countless instruments of sasine in old titles.

2 For the whole subject, see the essays on seisin by F W Maitland in his *Collected Papers*. See also Andreas Heusler *Die Gewere* (1872).

3 Balfour *Practicks* (Stair Soc vol 21, 1962) p 187. Craig is to the same effect: *Jus Feudale* 2,8,18.

4 Infeftment Act 1845 (c 35).

5 *Reminiscences in Connection with the Legal Profession in Glasgow* (1873), anonymous, perhaps by John Buchanan. See I S 'Infeftment — as it was' (1980) 25 JLSS 90. For legal accounts of the giving of sasine in its latter period, see A Menzies *Conveyancing according to the Law of Scotland* (1856) pp 541 ff (or 4th edn, 1900, by J S Sturrock, pp 538 ff); A M Bell *Lectures on Conveyancing* (3rd edn, 1882), pp 648 ff. These two works give a good account of the late feudal land law. See also J M Halliday 'The Tragedy of Sasine' 1965 JR 105. The 'tragedy' was, for Halliday, the rigidity of the system. Another account, from J Craigie and J Bartholomew *The Elements of Conveyancing: Heritable Rights* (1908) p 16 is quoted in CONVEYANCING, vol 6, para 402, together with a striking parallel of the practice of Israelite land transfer in *Jeremiah* 32: 9–16 (see, however, para 90, note 7, below).

6 Craig tells us that the practice of incorporating the precept in the charter began about 1560; *Jus Feudale* 2,3,1. However, precepts of sasine from the Crown continued to be separate until the Writs Act 1672 (c 16; 12mo c 7).

7 Stair *Institutions* II,3,16. This continued to be the law if the vassal had a Crown charter of confirmation: *Wallace v University Court of St Andrews* (1904) 6 F 1093, 12 SLT 240.

8 Traditionally this was thought to have begun after the return of James I in 1424, but it has long been known that such instruments were in use earlier (this was first proved by Erskine). See further G Donaldson 'Early Scottish Conveyancing' in *Formulary of Old Scots Legal Documents* (Stair Soc vol 36, 1985).

9 *Stair* II,3,16. Lawyers commonly used 'sasine' to mean the instrument.

90. Symbols of sasine.

In general what was delivered was earth and stone (*terra et lapis*), but in special cases different symbols were requisite. Practice varied with time and place, but the standard rules as eventually settled were as follows. For an annualrent[1], earth, stone and a coin. For fishings[2], net and coble. For mills[3], clap and happer. For burgage subjects, hasp and staple. For teinds, a sheaf, or a handful of grass and corn. For patronage, a psalter and the kirk keys. For jurisdictions, the court books. For right of ferry, an oar and some water. For resignations to the superior the symbol was staff and baston. Because of fear that the wrong symbols might have been given, it was usual to add a clause 'and all other symbols usual and requisite'[4]. The use of symbols is not exclusively associated with feudal conveyancing. Thus the styles book of Marculfus of the seventh century, referred to earlier[5], gives for land *herba et terra* or *herba et cespes*, for houses *ostium et anaticula*, for a vineyard *terra et vinea*. Or again, in Texas in the 1820s, a purchaser would formally pull up grass, drive in a stake, throw a stone, and shout[6]. But the symbolic taking of possession seems not to have been practised in the ancient world[7].

1 Annualrent was the ancestor of the heritable security.
2 Fishings can be separate tenements held feudally.
3 Grain mills formerly had a special position in property law. Thus mill thirlage was of great legal and economic importance. The use of special symbols, and the requirement (in some cases, but not all) that there be a separate sasine taken for a mill illustrate this special position. 'Mills are not carried as part and pertinent, because they are esteemed as *separata tenementa*, requiring a special sasine: Stair *Institutions* II,3,71. This rule was eroded by *Rose v Ramsay* (1777) Mor 9645. Today grain mills have no special legal status.
4 Failure to use the correct symbols would make the sasine null: see eg *Ker v Scot's Creditors* (1702) Mor 14310, and *Brechin Town-Council v Arbuthnot* (1840) 3 D 216.
5 See para 43 above.
6 This comes from a complete conveyancing transaction of 1824 given in T R Fehrenbach *Lone Star* (1968) ch 9. Until 1836 Texas was part of Mexico.
7 Many legal documents of a conveyancing nature have survived from antiquity, and have been published. Nor, generally speaking, do the conveyancing transactions in the Old Testament reveal symbolic delivery: see an article on the subject in 1922 SLT (News) 187 (D M G: 'Early Conveyancing').

91. Registration of sasines.

In 1617 the public registration of instruments of sasine was made compulsory[1]. The effect of an unregistered instrument was for long a matter of dispute, but in 1847 it was finally settled that such an instrument is of no effect[2]. The ceremony having become pointless, it was rendered unnecessary in 1845[3]. The instrument itself was an unnecessary complication, and so in 1858 it was dispensed with, so that thereafter the conveyance could be registered directly[4]. On the conveyance was to be written a warrant for registration, which was the substitute for the instrument of sasine[5]. But in principle even today a disponee could take sasine by ceremony, obtain a notarial instrument of sasine in the old manner, and record that, leaving his disposition unrecorded, except where the Land Register of Scotland is in operation. Even today, an owner of land is deemed to have obtained feudal sasine[6].

1 Registration Act 1617 (c 16). This Act is still in force, though since 1858 conveyances themselves are registered directly: see below. But the name, the Register of Sasines, continues. For a systematic

study of the history both before and after 1617, see L Ockrent *Land Rights: An Enquiry into the History of Registration for Publication in Scotland* (1942).

2 *Young v Leith* (1847) 9 D 932. It had already been settled by statute that, in a competition between two sasines, preference went by date of registration, not by date of sasine: Real Rights Act 1693 (c 22). This Act remains in force, its modern effect being to prefer a first recorded disposition over a second, even though the second bears an earlier date.

3 Infeftment Act 1845 (c 35). The Act abolished the need for sasine as a ceremony, substituting a deemed sasine by the instrument itself.

4 Titles to Land (Scotland) Act 1858 (c 76), whose provisions were later incorporated in the Titles to Land Consolidation (Scotland) Act 1868 (c 101): see s 15.

5 Ibid, s 15.

6 Ibid, s 15, which is applied to the Land Register of Scotland by the Land Registration (Scotland) Act 1979 (c 33), s 29(2). It is odd, however, that, given the application of section 15 of the 1868 Act, warrants of registration are not required by the Keeper in land registration cases.

92. Notarial instruments and notices of title. Notarial instruments and notices of title, which are effectively equivalent, are the creatures of statute[1] which are available to give the equivalent of sasine in cases where the disposition is general and not special, that is, where the conveyance does not identify the land conveyed. Examples of general conveyances are wills, interlocutors appointing certain types of judicial factor and trusts for creditors, though these may also, depending on their form, be special conveyances. At common law in such cases it was necessary either to obtain the co-operation of the owner, or in *mortis causa* cases the heir-at-law, or to obtain decree of implementary or declaratory adjudication followed by renewal of investiture from the superior. Under the new system it is possible simply to record a notarial instrument or notice of title identifying the subjects.

1 Titles to Land (Scotland) Act 1858 (c 76), s 12, replaced by the Titles to Land Consolidation (Scotland) Act 1868 (c 101), s 19, and the Conveyancing Act 1924 (c 27), s 4.

93. Some technical terms. 'Sasine' has already been explained as the symbolic giving of possession. 'Infeftment'[1] is sometimes glossed as having the same meaning, but is strictly a broader term, meaning the feudal entry of a vassal with his superior, a process in which sasine was an essential step[2]. Thus there might be sasine without infeftment, but no infeftment without sasine. 'Feudalisation of title', or 'completion of title', means the same as infeftment, but is used rather to refer to the completion of the process, rather than the process as a whole. 'Entry' has the same meaning as infeftment[3]. The odd expression 'infeftment without entry' is explained below[4]. 'Investiture' has the same meaning as infeftment. 'Conveyance *a me*' means a conveyance which is intended to substitute the grantee for the granter as vassal to the granter's superior. It is thus a disposition. A 'conveyance *de me*' is a subinfeudation, so that the grantee will hold as vassal to the granter, and as subvassal to the granter's superior. A 'public infeftment' is an infeftment on an *a me* conveyance, while a 'base infeftment' is an infeftment on a *de me* conveyance, though these terms were misleading, because every infeftment is in truth a public matter.

'Fee' means a feudal estate of *dominium*, whether of property or superiority. It is thus to be contrasted with other real rights in land such as servitude or lease. Where a right of property is burdened by a liferent[5], the right so burdened is called a 'fee', because it is *dominium* even though burdened, but, as explained, any feudal *dominium*, burdened or not, is a fee. In improper liferents, where the property is held by trustees, the fee is in feudal terms in the trustees alone. But by a permissible and inveterate extension of language, the beneficiary who is to take after the death of the beneficial liferenter is said to have the fee. This usage is not misleading so long as it is recollected that the fee here is a beneficial fee and not a feudal fee, the latter being held by the trustees. A person holding a fee is called a 'fiar'. 'Fiar' thus means owner.

1 The word 'infeftment' belongs to the same group as feu, fief etc, as does the word 'fee', mentioned below. Stair *Institutions* II,3,12, correctly glosses infeftment as *infeudatio*.

2 Infeftment is not, however, a necessary consequence of registration in the General Register of Sasines or the Land Register of Scotland. Thus the holder of a thousand-year registered lease is not infeft.
3 Feudal entry must not be confused with the word 'entry' as used in modern missives, which means the date when possession is to pass. 'Entry' in this modern sense seldom coincides with feudal entry.
4 See para 102 below.
5 See para 74 above.

(8) FEUDAL CONVEYANCING *INTER VIVOS*

94. Original charters and charters by progress. An original charter was a charter by which land was subinfeudated, in other words a feu charter, nowadays called a 'feu disposition' or a 'feu contract'. A charter by progress was a charter from the superior which renewed investiture . There were several types of charter by progress, namely the charter of resignation, the charter of confirmation, the charter of confirmation and resignation, the charter of *novodamus*, and the charter of adjudication. The precept of *clare constat* was in effect a charter by progress but was not so called. All are now abolished except the charter of *novodamus*[1]. All will be mentioned later, except for charters of *novodamus* and charters of adjudication, which will therefore be briefly described in the next paragraph. Charters were in Latin until the second half of the seventeenth century, though some eighteenth-century examples exist. But Crown charters continued to be in Latin until 1847[2].

If a superior was under an obligation to grant a charter by progress, that is, to renew the investiture, and failed or refused to do so, a remedy was introduced by statute in 1474[3] whereby the vassal could obtain such investiture from the over-superior.

1 Conveyancing (Scotland) Act 1874 (c 94), s 4(1).
2 Crown Charters (Scotland) Act 1847 (c 51), s 25 (repealed).
3 Entry to Lands Act 1474 (c 13; 12mo c 57), mentioned in para 86 above in connection with tinsel of the superiority.

95. Charters of *novodamus* and of adjudication. The charter of *novodamus*[1] was and is used when superior and vassal agree to vary the terms of the holding. It can be used to waive or modify feudal burdens[2]. It formerly contained a precept of sasine on which title had to be completed. Today it is simply recorded or registered. The charter of adjudication was required where land was adjudged from the vassal. The adjudger needed feudal entry, and this required the co-operation of the superior, even though the adjudger had already obtained decree of adjudication. The superior would issue to the adjudger a charter of adjudication, containing precept of sasine in the ordinary way. As we have seen, after 1469 a creditor could always compel a superior to issue such a charter.

1 *De novo damus* being the distinctive clause.
2 Such burdens can also be discharged by minute of waiver, a modern practice now sanctioned by the Land Registration (Scotland) Act 1979 (c 33), s 18.

96. Subinfeudation. Investiture[1] could be *propriis manibus* where the sasine was given by the superior himself. Originally sasine was given in the presence of the other vassals, the *pares curiae*. This was called 'proper investiture', and ceased to be the practice at an early period[2], except for sasines given by husband to wife, and eventually, by a curious trick of language, the term *propriis manibus* came to refer to such a conveyance, even though the husband did not in fact give sasine personally. Improper investiture was where sasine was given by an agent for the superior, and this became invariable practice. It has often been stated that there was once a writ called the *breve testatum* out of which the later system evolved[3], but this appears to be erroneous[4].

The feu charter which preceded the sasine[5] contained a clause called the 'precept of sasine' which authorised the superior's agent (whose name was latterly left blank in the deed, for convenience) to give sasine to the vassal or his agent. Originally the precept was a separate document but was merged into the charter about 1560[6]. Thus, in addition to any prior contract, subinfeudation involved four or five steps, namely (1) the feu charter, (2) the precept of sasine (latterly part of the charter), (3) sasine, (4) the instrument of sasine, and finally, after 1617, (5) the recording of the instrument. Observe that the feu charter was not recorded. Charters and dispositions could not be recorded in the Sasine Register until 1858[7], but only instruments of sasine, and certain other writs, such as reversions.

1 The meaning of 'investiture' is explained in para 93 above. It derives from the Latin *investire*, to clothe. For a discussion of this metaphor, see Craig *Jus Feudale* 2,2,2.
2 An example as late as 1564 is noted by Gordon Donaldson 'Early Scottish Conveyancing' in *Formulary of Old Scots Legal Documents* (Stair Soc vol 36, 1985) p 174.
3 See eg J M Halliday *Conveyancing Law and Practice in Scotland* vol 1 (1985) paras 16-18, 16-19.
4 J J Robertson 'The Illusory Breve Testatum' in G W S Barrow (ed) *The Scottish Tradition* (1974); J W Cairns 'The Breve Testatum and Craig's Jus Feudale' (1988) 56 Leg Hist Rev 311.
5 It may be that originally the sasine preceded the charter: see *Donaldson* p 166.
6 *Craig* 2,3,1.
7 Titles to Land (Scotland) Act 1858 (c 76) (repealed).

97. Resignation. Resignation was, and is, the name for a conveyance by the vassal to his superior. Resignation was of two kinds, resignation *ad remanentiam perpetuam*[1], which operated as an outright and permanent conveyance, and resignation *in favorem*[2], which was a temporary resignation so that the superior could then regrant the land to another person, as will be explained below, by a charter of resignation[3]. The transitory right thus held by the superior is described by Craig as a *fideicommissarium feudum*, though in later practice the view seems to have developed that the resigning vassal was not divested until the investiture of his disponee[4]. Either kind of resignation was effected by the vassal appearing before his superior and handing to him a 'staff and baston'[5], though in later practice this was done through agents. A notary then prepared an instrument of resignation recording the event. Resignation *ad rem* continues to exist in modern law under simpler forms[6].

1 In practice this was called resignation *ad rem*.
2 This was abolished as a result of the Conveyancing (Scotland) Act 1874 (c 94), s 4. For a discussion, see W Ross *Lectures on the History and Practice of the Law of Scotland relative to Conveyancing and Legal Diligence* (2nd edn, 1822) II, 280 ff.
3 Thus a charter of resignation would follow a resignation *in favorem*, but not a resignation *ad remanentiam perpetuam*. The charter of resignation would contain a clause (the '*quaequidem* clause') explaining the cause of grant.
4 William Rodger *Feudal Forms of Scotland viewed Historically* (1857) p 24.
5 Also called a baton, staff or rod. 'Staff and baton' was the common phrase, or, in Latin deeds, *per fustim et baculum*. This symbol can be found at an early period under the names of *baculum* and *virgula*. Thus in 787 Tassilo III resigned the Duchy of Bavaria to Charlemagne by handing over a *baculum*. (The physical object used in Scots practice was a quill: see A M Bell *Lectures on Conveyancing* (3rd edn, 1882), p 781.) The law was as rigid about this as it was about the correct symbols for sasine: see *Carnegy v Cruikshanks' Creditors* (1729) Mor 14316, and *Earl of Aberdeen v Duncan* (1742) Mor 14316; Act of Sederunt 11 February 1708.
6 The usual modern method, sanctioned by the Conveyancing (Scotland) Act 1924 (c 27), s 11(2), is simply to grant a disposition to the superior with the words 'and I resign the said subjects *ad perpetuam remanentiam*' added to the dispositive clause.

98. Consolidation. If the property and the immediate superiority (or indeed any two adjacent feudal *dominia*) come into the ownership of the same person, it was once commonly thought that they merged, or became consolidated, *ipso facto*, but since 1787 the contrary has been settled[1]. Consolidation occurs by prescription[2], or by disposition *ad remanentiam perpetuam*[3], or by recorded minute of consolidation[4] or by deed of relinquishment[5].

The effect of consolidation is to extinguish the existing *dominium utile* so that the superiority becomes the *dominium utile*[6], but any heritable security over the *dominium utile* is unaffected[7], and pertinents benefiting only the *dominium utile* title will also extend to the consolidated estate[8].

1 *Bald v Buchanan* (1787) Mor 15084. See the discussion in William Rodger *Feudal Forms of Scotland viewed Historically* (1857) ch XIV.
2 This is unless the destinations differ: *Zuille v Morrison* 4 March 1813 FC. In express consolidation, the superiority destination prevails: *Pattison v Henderson* (1868) 6 M (HL) 147.
3 For the current form, see the Conveyancing (Scotland) Act 1924 (c 27), s 11. The matter had also been regulated by earlier nineteenth-century statutes.
4 Conveyancing (Scotland) Act 1874 (c 94), s 6; Conveyancing (Scotland) Act 1924, s 11.
5 Titles to Land Consolidation (Scotland) Act 1868 (c 101), s 110.
6 *Park's Curator Bonis v Black* (1870) 8 M 671. *Aliter*, of course, if a superiority is consolidated with an oversuperiority, but the substance is the same: the lower estate is extinguished.
7 *Fraser v Wilson* (1824) 2 Sh App 162, HL.
8 *Earl of Zetland v Glover Incorpn of Perth* (1870) 8 M (HL) 144.

99. Disposition. A disposition[1] was, and is, a conveyance *a me*, substituting a new vassal, the disponee, in place of the old one, the disponer. In a conveyance *a me*, or more fully *a me de superiore meo*, sometimes called feudal substitution, the disponer in effect says 'I convey to you from me to hold of my superior, who shall henceforth be your superior'. (By contrast a conveyance *de me*, or more fully *de me et successoribus meis*, is a subinfeudation, in which the granter in effect says 'I convey to you to hold of me and my successors as my vassal'.) In an *a me* conveyance the disponer would thus drop out of the feudal chain. The feudal problem was that the consent of the superior was requisite. This was a matter of first principles, for a superior cannot, by the feudal law, acquire a new vassal without giving entry to that vassal, in other words investing him, which involved among other things the rigmarole of sasine. We have seen that after 1469 this consent could be compelled if necessary by a collusive litigation between disponer and disponee, and that after the Tenures Abolition Act 1746 (c 50) it could be compelled by a non-collusive action, but until the Conveyancing (Scotland) Act 1874 (c 94) it was still necessary as a conveyancing formality.

We will deal first with the simple disposition *a me* and thereafter with the more complex disposition *a me vel de me* which, probably from the sixteenth century, was the more usual approach. The disponee could obtain entry in two ways. The first was that the disponer would resign the land to the superior *in favorem*. In later practice the disposition itself would contain a clause appointing an agent to resign on behalf of the disponer, with the name left blank for convenience. This clause was called the 'procuratory of resignation'. The resignation (*in favorem*) having been done, the superior would then grant a new charter to the disponee. This was called a 'charter of resignation'. It contained a precept of sasine in the ordinary way, on which the disponee would take sasine, on which followed an instrument of sasine, which would then, after 1617, be recorded. Thus entry by resignation involved the following steps, in addition to any prior contract: (1) disposition with procuratory of resignation; (2) resignation; (3) instrument of resignation; (4) charter of resignation; (5) sasine; (6) instrument of sasine; (7) registration of the instrument of sasine, after 1617.

At his option, the disponee could obtain entry in another manner, namely by confirmation[2]. For the disposition would in practice contain not only a procuratory of resignation but also another clause, the precept of sasine. On this the disponee would take sasine, and, after 1617, record the instrument of sasine. But this of itself did not give him entry, for as has been said, entry could be given only by the act of the superior. That valid sasine can be given only by the superior is an axiom of the feudal law[3]. So the sasine given by the disponer, even though recorded, was, taken by itself, null. But the disponee would then obtain from the superior a charter of confirmation, by which the superior ratified and adopted the sasine. The existing sasine was thus validated, and the disponee had entry as soon as he received this charter. The charter of confirmation, unlike the charter of resignation, contained no precept of sasine, for sasine had already been taken, albeit invalidly, and it was this existing sasine which was being confirmed. Entry by confirmation thus involved the following steps, in addition to any preliminary contract: (a) disposition with precept of sasine; (b) sasine; (c) instrument of sasine; (d) recording of instrument, after 1617; (e) charter of confirmation. It may be added that in practice the disponee usually took entry by confirmation rather than by resignation, though if the hand of the superior had to be forced, resignation was the way in which it was done. Historically, confirmation seems to have been a relatively late development.

It may be observed that until the nineteenth-century reforms, charters were never registered, but only the instruments of sasine. Therefore if the disponee took entry by the route of confirmation, he obtained his real right not when he recorded his sasine, for at that stage his sasine was null, but by the later, and unrecorded, charter of confirmation.

1 A disposition is a conveyance of corporeal property. Incorporeal property is conveyed by assignation.
2 This is not to be confused with confirmation of executors. Nor is it to be confused with the charter confirming a subinfeudation, sometimes called an 'upper confirmation' (see para 58 above), which in earlier practice was sometimes requisite.
3 There were certain exceptional cases where sasine could be given by an oversuperior.

100. The disposition *a me vel de me*. The methods of feudal entry described above had a disadvantage for the disponee, in that he had no real right until either (1) infeft on the precept of sasine in the charter of resignation, or (2) infeft of the sasine in the disposition confirmed by charter of confirmation. And the obtaining of the real right, since it in both cases required the co-operation of the superior, could prove slow. During this interval the disponee was at risk, even though he had paid the price and taken possession, for in feudal terms he was not a vassal, for he was not entered, and not validly seised, for this could not happen without investiture at the hand of the superior, while in civilian terms the disponee had as yet no real right. Strictly therefore the disponer was still the vassal, and he alone had the real right. If something happened in this interval which blocked the disponee from completing title, such as the insolvency of the disponer, the right of the disponee might be partly or wholly defeated. Such an event, if it took place, was called a 'midimpediment'.

To circumvent this danger, a new form of disposition was developed, apparently in the sixteenth century[1], called the 'disposition *a me vel de me*'. Here again the disponee could complete title either by resignation or by confirmation. The difference was that the disposition operated simultaneously as a conveyance *a me de superiore meo* and as a conveyance *de me*. The disponee would in the first instance treat it as a conveyance *de me*, as a subinfeudation. To do this, all he had to do was to take sasine on the precept. He was then the vassal of the disponer, the tenure in practice always being blench. Since he had then the *dominium utile*, a real right, the disponer being his superior, he had nothing to fear from, for instance, the insolvency of the disponer, or any other midimpediment. Thus unlike sasine taken on a precept in a simple *a me* disposition, the sasine taken on a disposition *a me vel de me* was valid *ab initio*. But the disponee could then obtain from the disponer's superior (temporarily the disponee's oversuperior) a charter of confirmation, the basis of this being that the sasine already taken was treated as if it were a null sasine on a simple *a me* disposition. When the charter of confirmation was obtained, the temporary midsuperiority was extinguished, and the disponee held direct of the superior. This temporary midsuperiority was called a 'defeasible midsuperiority'[2]. It may be added that such dispositions also contained a procuratory of resignation in the ordinary form, and the disponee could, if he chose, take entry in this manner, but he would, naturally, be unlikely to do so.

There is no escaping the verdict that the disposition *a me vel de me* was a convoluted conception, which reflects well on the ingenuity of its unknown inventor, but poorly on the coherence of conveyancing as a logical system. For it involved a sort of doublethink, namely thinking of one and the same disposition as a disposition *de me* at one time but as a disposition *a me* at another time.

It remains to be said that the whole system of feudal conveyancing, though beautiful in its own way, was hardly adapted to a period when land had become, like goods, a commodity to be bought and sold. Today a single deed suffices, the disposition[3]. Formerly there were three, the disposition, the instrument of sasine, and the charter by progress, all drafted by lawyers. In addition there was the ceremony of sasine, personally conducted by a notary on the land. Moreover these deeds were lengthy, especially the disposition, which was itself virtually three deeds in one, namely disposition, precept, and procuratory. The only beneficiaries of this system were the lawyers, though it must not be supposed that the system was developed by them to increase their fee income. It was a legacy of a feudal past, and when it was swept away in the nineteenth century, there is no evidence that lawyers made any particular objection.

1 The history is traced with great scholarship in William Rodger *Feudal Forms of Scotland viewed Historically* (1857). The validity of the new system was upheld in a series of cases at the close of the seventeenth century: see W Ross *Lectures on the History and Practice of the Law of Scotland relative to Conveyancing and Legal Diligence* (2nd edn, 1822) II,272.
2 Sometimes it was said that the temporary midsuperiority disappeared, and sometimes that the temporary base fee disappeared. The effect was the same, whichever way it was described. Perhaps one should simply say that the two temporary fees were consolidated, and indeed it was sometimes expressed in precisely that way.
3 See paras 640 ff below ('Transfer of Ownership').

101. Precepts of sasine. A precept of sasine on which sasine had been given was called an 'exhausted precept'; otherwise it was called 'unexhausted'. A precept was called 'definite' if either it was a precept in a conveyance *de me* (a definite base precept) or if it was a precept in a conveyance *a me* (a definite public precept). It was called 'indefinite' if contained in a disposition *a me vel de me*[1]. As Bell says:

'The true criterion by which to determine whether a precept conceived in terms indefinite or ambiguous is public or base, is found in the obligation to infeft. If it be an obligation to infeft by two manners of holding, one to be held *de me*, the other *a me de superiore meo*, the precept is alternative. If it be only to be held *a me de superiore meo*, it is a public precept, and no sasine can proceed upon it that will be effectual without confirmation. If it be to hold *de me*, the precept is base, and cannot be confirmed to the effect of creating a public holding'[2].

1 'The precept, if itself indefinite, was controlled by the obligation to infeft. . . . The base precept was, of course, quite inapplicable to a disposition': J Burns *Handbook of Conveyancing* (5th edn, 1938) p 197.
2 Bell *Principles* s 820.

102. Infeftment without entry. The expression 'infeftment without entry' was strictly a self-contradiction, because infeftment means the feudalisation of a right, by feudal entry. But the term was used, conveniently if inaccurately, to mean the position of a disponee who had taken sasine (and after 1617, recorded it) on a conveyance *a me vel de me* but who had not entered with the disponer's superior.

The disponee was thus infeft (because entered feudally with the disponer) but unentered (because not infeft with the disponer's superior). As has been explained, in the typical case a disponee would be temporarily infeft without entry.

103. Charter of confirmation and resignation. Charters of confirmation and of resignation have already been explained. They, like instruments of sasine, are familiar by sight, if not by content, to every conveyancer. There is another charter which is often come across in old sets of deeds, the charter of confirmation and resignation. Suppose (a frequent case) that X's vassal, A, disponed to B *a me vel de me*, with precept and procuratory, and B took base infeftment, and then, without taking public entry, disponed to C also *a me vel de me*, with precept and procuratory, on the precept of which C procured himself base infeft. Now, X's vassal was still A, and B was A's vassal, and C was B's vassal. C could unscramble this mess by obtaining from X a charter of confirmation and resignation, whereby X would confirm the sasine taken by B on A's precept and accept the resignation *in favorem* in virtue of the procuratory given by B. The result was that A and B vanished from the feudal chain, leaving C as X's direct vassal. In principle it is difficult to see why in this type of case X might not, as an alternative, have issued a charter confirming all the base infeftments taken by the alternative manner of holding, and thereby produced the same result, but at all events the method used by conveyancers, at least in the later period, was combined confirmation and resignation.

104. Assignation of unfeudalised title. Sometimes a purchaser would resell without having obtained infeftment, either public or base; in other words the precept and procuratory were both unexecuted. He could do this by assigning to the new purchaser his personal right. Though strictly the deed was purely an assignation, it was in practice called a disposition and assignation. It gave to the new purchaser the right to make use of the existing unexecuted precept and procuratory in the disposition in favour of the first purchaser. In practice the new purchaser would usually take base entry followed by confirmation. The instrument of sasine would narrate both the original disposition and the subsequent disposition and assignation. Suppose that A disponed to B, and B, infeft neither publicly nor base, disponed and assigned to C, and C delayed to feudalise his title. In that case C's right would be defeasible by a midimpediment arising on A's account, such as an adjudication against A completed by infeftment. That much is perhaps obvious. Less obvious is the rule that C, prior to infeftment, was liable to be defeated by a midimpediment arising on B's account[1].

The assignation of unfeudalised[2] title was superseded in practice in 1924 by the system of deduction of title, which, though formally different, is in substance the same[3]. The procedure was finally abolished in 1970[4].

1 This rule was established by *Bell v Garthshore* (1737) Mor 2848.
2 'Unfeudalised' meant, and indeed still means, a heritable right not completed by infeftment.
3 Conveyancing (Scotland) Act 1924 (c 27), ss 3–5.
4 Conveyancing and Feudal Reform (Scotland) Act 1970 (c 35),s 48, Sch 11, Pt II. To be precise, these provisions repealed the *statutory* rules which had been introduced to modify the common law. The common law rules themselves would thus seem to survive, but the point is academic.

105. Crown specialities. In fees held immediately of the Crown, certain specialities existed, of astonishing complexity, and to some extent they still exist. Entry could be by resignation or confirmation. We will outline the system used in the former case only. The singular successor, after obtaining his disposition, next had a Writer to the Signet draft a signature of resignation (containing the dispositive, *quaequidem, tenendas* and *reddendo* clauses) which was endorsed by the Writer to the Signet, and submitted to the Presenter of Signatures in Exchequer, with a note for enrolling, which was followed by a brieve for revising, which was followed by a note for resigning, which was followed by revision first by a Baron of Exchequer and thereafter by the Judge Reviser, which was followed by payment of the composition to the Receiver General, which was followed by ceremony of resignation (by quill) into the hands of one of the Barons by the Macer on behalf of the resigner, which was followed by registration of the Signature in the Books of Exchequer which was effected by the King's Remembrancer, whence it was taken to the Office of the Great Seal, where it was stamped with the Cachet of the Sign-Manual, followed by an Official Stamp by the Keeper. The signature thus laboriously completed became the starting point for the next stage, which was the issue of a precept directed to the Keeper of the Great Seal authorising him and directing him to instruct the Director of Chancery to prepare a charter. This precept then required to receive the Signet. After signeting it was taken to the Keeper of the Privy Seal and thence to the Director of Chancery. The third stage now ensued. The Director of Chancery would then draw up a charter, and would subscribe it, whence it would go to the Keeper of the Great Seal, who would also subscribe, and would affix the Great Seal, whence it would once more return to Chancery for registration there. Finally came the fourth stage, the gallop home with sasine followed by instrument of sasine followed by registration of sasine.

The above is the merest outline[1]. That our economy did not entirely collapse under the burden of this and similar insane procedures is an enduring tribute to the stamina of the Scottish people. The system was eventually simplified to some extent[2], and in 1874 was largely abolished[3].

1 Indeed, it omits an entire step, the intermediate precept under the Privy Seal, abolished by the Public Records (Scotland) Act 1809 (c 42), s 13 (repealed). For some account of the whole system, see Thomas Hope *Minor Practicks* (written in the time of Charles I, and published 1726), and A Duff *Feudal Conveyancing* (1838).
2 Crown Charters (Scotland) Act 1847 (c 51) (repealed); Titles to Land Consolidation (Scotland) Act 1868 (c 101).
3 Conveyancing (Scotland) Act 1874 (c 94), s 59.

106. Abolition of renewal of investiture. The most important change made by the Conveyancing (Scotland) Act 1874 was the introduction of implied entry. As soon as the disponee records his disposition in the Sasine Register, he is deemed to be infeft and entered *a me* without any act of entry with the superior[1]. Charters of confirmation and charters of resignation thereby became unnecessary and were in fact abolished[2]. The same applied to adjudications. The adjudger now simply registers his decree of adjudication in the Sasine Register and is thereby infeft in his adjudication. The old charter of adjudication, like the other charters, was abolished as unnecessary. The same applied to heritable securities. Previously if a heritable security was granted *a me* (which was admittedly uncommon), a charter of confirmation was required, but this became unnecessary. The only concession to feudality in the 1874 Act was the system of the notice of change of ownership. Such a notice was to be sent to the superior[3]. The sanction for failure to do so was that the disponer would remain jointly and severally liable for the personal prestations of the feu holding. These notices have never been abolished, but they were largely abandoned in practice during the 1970s.

Section 4(1) of the 1874 Act refers in the side note to the abolition of renewal of investiture. This was correct in one sense, but strictly the Act abolished renewal of investiture as an *act* but not as a *doctrine*. In other words, since 1874 there has still been, on every disposition, a renewal of investiture, but this has happened *ipso facto* upon the recording of the disposition without the need for any overt act by the superior[4]. The same applies to land registration cases. When a new proprietor is entered into the title sheet, there is a deemed renewal of investiture.

1 Conveyancing (Scotland) Act 1874 (c 94), s 4(2).
2 Ibid, s 4(1).
3 Ibid, s 4(2) proviso, Sch A.
4 Hence the notion, sometimes encountered, that ownership passes on the delivery of a disposition is not only incorrect at common law, which goes without saying, but also equally untrue under modern law: see paras 643, 644, below.

107. To what extent may the old system still be used? It is sometimes supposed that the legislation from 1845 merely provides optional simplified alternatives to the old pre-1845 system, which could in theory still be used. This is only partly true. The details are complex, but in brief it remains true that a disponee or feu disponee does not have to record his disposition or feu disposition in the Sasine Register. He could still take sasine on the land, take a notarial instrument of sasine from a notary, and record that instrument. (For this to happen, however, the deed would presumably have to contain an old-style precept of sasine.) On the other hand, actual entry with the superior by confirmation or resignation is now incompetent as a result of the 1874 reforms mentioned above.

(9) FEUDAL CONVEYANCING *MORTIS CAUSA*

108. Death. Under the old feudal law, there could be no valid bequest of land, which therefore always passed to the heir-at-law, also called the heir-of-line, typically the eldest son, as heir-at-law, or heir-of-line, thus excluding his brothers and sisters, but if there were only daughters, then to the daughters equally between them, as heirs portioner. And this continued to be the law down to 1964[1] if an owner died intestate. Here we are not concerned with the identification of the heir but with the feudalisation of his title. It is necessary to understand that the maxim *mortuus sasit vivum*[2], which was received in some countries, has never applied in Scotland, so that on the death of a vassal active steps are needed to secure the renewal of the investiture. At common law this, inevitably, required renewed sasine from the superior, either through the *clare constat* procedure or by the service procedure.

1 Both types of heir are now abolished and confirmation has been extended to heritage: Succession (Scotland) Act 1964 (c 41), ss 1, 14, 34(1), Sch 2, paras 1–3: see WILLS AND SUCCESSION, vol 25.
2 'The dead man gives sasine to the living man.'

109. *Clare constat* and service. If the defunct held not of the Crown but of a subject superior, the heir applied to the superior for renewal of the investiture. The superior, on being satisfied of the right, issued to the heir a precept of *clare constat* incorporating a precept of sasine, on which the heir would be infeft. Often the deceased vassal would have been infeft on an indefinite precept[1], in which case title would be completed by a combined charter of confirmation and precept of *clare constat*[2]. Precepts of *clare constat* were changed to writs of *clare constat* in 1858[3] and were finally abolished in 1964[4]. For burgage tenure there was an equivalent process, entry of heirs *more burgi*, which disappeared when burgage was merged into feufarm.

If, however, the defunct was vassal to the Crown, this procedure was not competent[5], but instead the service procedure had to be used. Here the heir obtained[6] from Chancery[7], on behalf of the Crown as superior, a brief or brieve[8] directing a judge to conduct an inquest before a jury as to the validity of the claimant's title[9]. The verdict, if favourable, was then retoured (returned) to Chancery, whereupon an extract, called the 'retour', was issued to the heir. But he was still uninfeft. Armed with the retour, he could obtain from Chancery a Crown precept of sasine, and on this he could procure himself infeft. The procedure — more complex than can be indicated by a mere outline — was much altered by nineteeth-century statutes[10], and finally abolished in 1964[11]. Service was competent not only to Crown vassals but also, as an alternative, to *clare constat* to vassals of subject superiors, and after the reforms of 1847 service rapidly became the usual route, with *clare constat* becoming rare[12].

1 As to indefinite precepts, see para 101 above.
2 A Duff *Feudal Conveyancing* (1838), p 488.
3 Titles to Land (Scotland) Act 1858 (c 76), s 11 (repealed); Titles to Land Consolidation (Scotland) Act 1868 (c 101), s 101 (repealed).
4 Succession (Scotland) Act 1964 (c 41), s 34(2), Sch 3, repealing the Titles to Land Consolidation (Scotland) Act 1868, s 101.
5 However, an example of *clare constat* given by the king to the Duke of Rothesay is cited in Henry Homes, Lord Kames *Elucidations*, art 15.
6 'Purchased' was the technical term.
7 On the Chancery, see Stair *Institutions* IV,1,2; IV,3,5 ff.
8 *Breve de inquisitione*. For the system of brieves generally, see H McKechnie *Judicial Process upon Brieves* (1956), H L MacQueen 'The Brieve of Right in Scots Law' 1976 J Leg Hist 52, and H L MacQueen 'Dissasine and Mortancestor in Scots Law' in A Kiralfy and H L MacQueen (eds) *New Perspectives in Scottish Legal History* (1984). This volume has a useful bibliography.
9 One of the matters to be determined was whether the defunct had, at his death, been *ad fidem et pacem nostram*. If not, the fief would be forfeit by treason: see Erskine *Institute* III,8,66. For early seventeenth-century examples of service, see *Formulary of Old Scots Legal Documents* (Stair Soc vol 36, 1985), a volume which contains many valuable feudal syles.
10 Service of Heirs (Scotland) Act 1847 (c 47) (repealed), which ended the procedure of issuing brieves from Chancery. Further provisions were made in the Titles to Land Consolidation (Scotland) Act 1868 and the Conveyancing (Scotland) Act 1874 (c 94). For a useful summary, see J Burns *Handbook of Conveyancing* (5th edn, 1938).
11 Succession (Scotland) Act 1964, s 14, Sch 3, substituting confirmation for both service and *clare constat*. 'Confirmation' here means the process, previously applicable only to moveables, to vest the *haereditas jacens* in the executor. It should not be confused with feudal confirmation.
12 This was ostensibly contrary to the feudal rule that sasine can be obtained only from the superior, for where the defunct was not a Crown vassal, the heir was taking a precept from an oversuperior. But feudal law did allow investiture to be given by an oversuperior on some occasions, of which this was not the only one.

110. Terce and courtesy. On the death of a married man the right of his heir was burdened with the terce *(tertia)* of his widow, which was a liferent of one-third of the property in which he was infeft at his death[1], except superiorities. Infeftment was the test. Thus leases and personal rights were excluded. The third was not particularised, but was effectively a lifetime one-third *pro indiviso* right to the whole. The widow did not need investiture, for the investiture of her late husband sufficed, but she did have to establish her right by a process called 'kenning'[2].

On the death of a married woman her heritable estate passed to her heir in the same way as for a deceased male, but her widower had a legal liferent comparable to terce, called courtesy. It was more extensive than terce in that it extended to all the land, not a third, but less extensive in that it applied only if there had been issue of the marriage[3]. Unlike terce, no process of law was necessary to establish the liferent. As with terce, no new infeftment was needed.

Major changes in the law of terce and courtesy were effected in 1924[4]. Final abolition took place in 1964[5].

1 The original rule was apparently one-third of the land held by the husband at the date of the marriage, not at the date of his death: see Craig *Jus Feudale* 2,22,18, and *Regiam Majestatem* II,16.
2 Erskine *Institute* II,9,50.
3 It was not a requirement that the issue should have survived the wife. A baby who died an hour after birth would suffice. The test in such cases was whether or not the baby had been heard to cry. If not, it was deemed a stillbirth and, absent other issue, there would be no courtesy. See W D H Sellar 'Courtesy, Battle and the Brieve of Right, 1368' in *Miscellany II* (Stair Soc vol 34, 1984) p 1.

4 Conveyancing (Scotland) Act 1924 (c 27), s 21 (repealed).
5 Succession (Scotland) Act 1964 (c 41), ss 10(1), Sch 2, para 4.

111. Destinations and tailzies. It was, however, competent for a person to complete title with a clause, called a 'destination', altering the legal course of succession. Since this appeared in his infeftment, the superior was bound by it[1]. The successor called under such a destination was called the 'heir of provision' or 'heir of tailzie'[2]. Originally the proprietor could generally alter or annul the destination, which is called 'evacuation'. But during the seventeenth century, methods were devised whereby destinations could be rendered unevacuable and also perpetual, affecting not merely the next generation, but all future generations. The means of so doing were invented by Thomas Hope[3] and soon upheld in litigation[4]. The way having been thus opened, legislation in 1685 put tailzies on a statutory footing[5]. The term 'tailzie' thereafter became reserved for such unevacuable and perpetual destinations[6]. Eventually it came to be felt that such tailzies were contrary to the public interest[7], and legislation began to emasculate them. In particular in 1848 it became possible to evacuate tailzies[8], and after 1914 it became impossible to create new tailzies[9]. Today only a handful remain[10], and probably all the survivors relate only to superiorities.

1 However, the superior had to consent to its original creation. *'Talliari feuda ex jure nostra non possunt, nisi ex consensu domini sui superiori'*: Craig *Jus Feudale* 2,16,20. But, as Craig also says, the difficulty could be obviated by erecting the destination in a subinfeudation.
2 The 'z' is silent. The word is cognate with the English term 'entail', which, since the eighteenth century, has often been used in Scotland as well as 'tailzie'.
3 Thomas Hope was Lord Advocate in the time of Charles I.
4 This was in the famous case of *Viscount of Stormonth v Annandale's Creditors* (1662) Mor 13994, 15475. See also Stair *Institutions* II,3,58.
5 Entail Act 1685 (c 26).
6 The case law and literature on tailzies are vast. Craig devotes a whole title to the subject (*Jus Feudale* 2,16). See E D Sandford *Treatise on the History and Law of Entails in Scotland* (1822; 2nd edn 1842); R Burgess *Perpetuities in Scots Law* (Stair Soc vol 31, 1979); W M Gordon *Scottish Land Law* (1989), ch 18; A W B Simpson 'Entails and Perpetuities' 1979 JR 1. For comparative material, see E Cecil *Primogeniture* (1895).
7 There seems to have been a general agreement about this from about 1765, though legislation was slow to arrive.
8 Entail Amendment Act 1848 (c 36) (the 'Rutherford Act'). Further important changes were made by the Entail (Scotland) Act 1882 (c 53).
9 Entail (Scotland) Act 1914 (c 43).
10 How many is hard to say. See *Burgess*.

(10) HERITABLE SECURITIES

112. Heritable securities. The history of the Scots law of heritable security[1] is one of considerable complexity, and has been subject to little research. Here we can give only the briefest outline. Heritable security has two sources, the infeftment of annualrent and the wadset, both apparently medieval in origin. In both the creditor was infeft.

In the annualrent, the creditor was infeft in a real burden, an *onus reale*, giving him the right to a certain sum from the land each year, a right which he could enforce by real diligence. At first there was no personal obligation by the debtor, but this was later added, seemingly at the time of the Reformation, when the restrictions of the canon law against interest-bearing personal obligations were relaxed[2], and thereby the annualrent was converted into the 'heritable bond'[3]. The right was feudal, so the creditor had to enter as vassal. The conveyance could be *a me* or *de me* or, as it usually was, *a me vel de me*. The creditor could in theory enter *a me* with the apparent result that the superior had, at the same time and for the same property, two vassals[4]. But the usual practice was for the creditor to take base infeftment only, as the vassal of his debtor, the holding being blench[5]. For a heritable creditor to enter into the feudal structure was odd. Lord Kames called it, with some justification, 'hocus-pocus'[6]. In the eighteenth century the heritable bond was modified, so that the debtor conveyed to the creditor not only an annualrent, but also the land itself[7]. This enabled the creditor if necessary to take possession of the land without adjudication. This new deed was called the 'heritable bond and disposition in security'[8], a name from which the word 'heritable' was soon dropped in practice. Before the end of the eighteenth century conveyancers yet further modified this deed so as to add to it a power of attorney in favour of the creditor enabling him to sell the land in the event of default. Before this, the creditor could enforce only by court action. The bond and disposition in security was then put under a certain degree of statutory regulation[9].

If the holding was, as it usually was, *de me,* there was no particular problem from the point of view of property law. The only problem was whether on repayment the creditor had to extinguish his infeftment by resignation or whether a mere discharge would suffice. On this practice varied, as did the opinions of writers[10]. But if the holding was *a me* the odd situation resulted that the superior had two vassals, and the infeftment of the creditor could be extinguished only by resignation. The problem became more complex when the bond and disposition in security was introduced, especially if the holding were *a me* and it took some time for it to be settled that such a deed did not divest the debtor[11].

The wadset[12] was a conveyance on which either base or public entry would be taken. At certain periods it was in the form of an absolute conveyance, with the right of reversion contained in a separate deed, and at other times the right of reversion was expressed in the wadset itself. In a proper wadset the creditor (the wadsetter) took possession, and there was no personal obligation by the debtor (the reverser), so that the wadsetter would do well or otherwise according to the profits obtainable from the land. The proper wadset was thus not really a security for a loan, but rather a temporary swap of land for money. In the improper wadset the reverser retained possession, but was personally bound to repay. To ensure, where the holding was public, that the reverser would be able to obtain new feudal entry, a letter of regress was obtained from the superior at the outset. Thus in a wadset held *a me* the reverser was generally considered as being divested feudally. If the wadset was held *de me,* the same doubts existed, alluded to earlier, as to whether a mere discharge would extinguish the infeftment or whether a resignation was requisite. Bonds of reversion in favour of the reverser were declared real rights by an Act of 1469[13]. The wadset ceased to be used about the middle of the eighteenth century[14], but it would perhaps be more accurate to say that while it disappeared as such, it in fact continued to flourish in two different forms. For at the time when the wadset was disappearing, the clause of disposition was being added to the heritable bond, so that the bond and disposition in security would appear to be, in some measure, a marriage of the old heritable bond and the old wadset. In addition, at about the same time the new *ex facie* absolute disposition was beginning to appear, which was really just the wadset in a different guise[15]. All this took place in the second half of the eighteenth century, which was the most important period of change in this area of law[16]. Hardly had the bond and disposition in security been introduced than, well before 1800, a clause was added giving the creditor a power of extra-judicial sale[17].

The bond and disposition in security and the *ex facie* absolute disposition were both abolished in 1970 and replaced by the standard security[18], which, however, is in truth merely a modification of the old bond, with some features of the *ex facie* added. The legislation is silent on the feudal effect of the standard security[19]. It is possible that it should be construed as an infeftment *a me*. But the better view, it is submitted, is that the standard security is entirely non-feudal[20].

1 As to heritable securities, see generally RIGHTS IN SECURITY, vol 20, paras 108 ff.
2 See especially the Usury Act 1587 (c 35; 12mo c 52) (APS iii, 451), the Usury Act 1594 (c 32; 12mo c 222) (APS iv, 70), and the Usury Act 1597 (c 18; 12mo c 251) (APS iv, 133).
3 However, heritable bonds continued, sometimes to be called annualrents, well into the nineteenth century.
4 Compare proper liferents, discussed in para 74 above.
5 This was usual but not universal. For instance, some creditors regarded it as beneath their dignity to enter base: see H H Monteath 'Heritable Rights: From Early Times to the Twentieth Century' in *An Introduction to Scottish Legal History* (Stair Soc vol 20, 1958) p 185.
6 Henry Home, Lord Kames *Historical Law-Tracts,* Tract IV. It may be mentioned that at this very day the creditor in an English mortgage is a lessee of his debtor, a device to which the epithet of Lord Kames might, if it were not for the courtesy due to a different legal system, be equally applied.
7 This is another odd conception (due to conservatism), for if the land is conveyed, what can be the point of also constituting a burden on the land in favour of the same grantee?
8 As to bonds and dispositions in security, see RIGHTS IN SECURITY, vol 20, paras 113 ff.
9 Notably the Heritable Securities (Scotland) Act 1845 (c 31) (repealed), the Heritable Securities (Scotland) Act 1847 (c 50) (repealed), the Titles to Land Consolidation (Scotland) Act 1868 (c 101), the Heritable Securities (Scotland) Act 1894 (c 44), and the Conveyancing (Scotland) Act 1924 (c 27).
10 The point became irrelevant when statute (see above) introduced recorded discharges.
11 *Campbell v Bertram* (1865) 4 M 23. See G L Gretton 'Radical Rights and Radical Wrongs' 1986 JR 51, 192.
12 As to wadset, see RIGHTS IN SECURITY, vol 20, para 109.
13 Reversion Act 1469 (c 3; 12mo c 27) (APS ii, 94). The preamble says that wadsets were then a new invention. As a result of the Registration Act 1617 (c 16; 12mo c 16), reversions are merely personal rights, but become real rights if recorded in the Register of Sasines.
14 However, the word was used not only in the narrow sense to mean a particular kind of heritable security, but also in a wide sense as a synonym for heritable security itself, and in this sense references to wadsets will be found well into the nineteenth century. Such references have misled some writers not conscious of the ambiguity.
15 For the effect of the *ex facie* absolute disposition in terms of property, see the article by Gretton cited in note 11 above. To what is said in that article, it should be added that Lord Kinnear, who in *Ritchie v Scott* (1899) 1 F 728, 6 SLT 408, started the erroneous idea that the *ex facie*, if granted directly to the debtor, was non-divestitive, later recanted in *Inglis v Wilson* 1909 SC 1393, 1909 2 SLT 166, and returned to orthodoxy. But no one picked this up, and much confusion was thereby caused.
16 It is difficult not to discern, in this period of very rapid change, the influence of the industrial revolution, which tended to turn land into a commodity.
17 Before this, enforcement was by real diligence, or by an action of ranking and sale: see eg Bell *Commentaries* II,232–244. Wadsets could also be enforced in these ways, and sometimes also by irritancy: see Stair *Institutions* II,10,6.
18 Conveyancing and Feudal Reform (Scotland) Act 1970 (c 35), s 9. As to standard securities, see RIGHTS IN SECURITY, vol 20, paras 147 ff.
19 Ibid, s 11(1), does not imply *infeudatio,* nor does the fact that it is a real right, for there are many non-feudal real rights in land, such as servitudes. Nor does registration imply infeftment. Thus a recorded long lease does not give infeftment.
20 If the feudal aspect of heritable security was 'hocus-pocus' in the eighteenth century (see above), it would now be much more so.

(11) STATUTORY ABOLITION

113. Statutory abolition of feudal law. Most feudal law has now disappeared, and we have already mentioned most of the steps of abolition. The following is a summary of the main steps of statutory abolition.

After 1469 a purchaser could compel entry with the superior, even against the latter's will, by a collusive action[1], and after 1746 he could do so by direct action[2]. From about the middle of the eighteenth century it in effect became possible to leave heritage by will to a person other than the heir, and this was made expressly competent by statute in 1868[3]. After 1964 heritage no longer passed to the heir even in intestate cases[4]. Military obligations were abolished in 1715[5]. Wardholding was finally abolished in 1746[6]. Feudal jurisdiction was largely abolished at the same period[7]. Actual sasine was made unnecessary in 1845[8]. Instruments of sasine were made unnecessary in 1858[9] when direct recording of dispositions and feu dispositions became competent. Actual entry with the superior became unnecessary after 1874[10], when the recording of the disposition operated as deemed entry. Personal services by vassals were abolished in 1934[11]. Legislation of 1874 and 1914 brought the systems of casualties to an end[12]. Feuduties began to be phased out from 1974[13]. The last vestiges of feudalism are likely to disappear soon[14]. Finally it remains to be observed that during the Cromwellian Usurpation, legislation was passed abolishing feudal law[15]. This lapsed with the restoration of Charles II, and it is unclear to what extent effect was given to it during the brief period when it was in force.

1 Diligence Act 1469 (c 12; 12mo c 36) (APS ii, 96).
2 Tenures Abolition Act 1746 (c 50).
3 Titles to Land Consolidation (Scotland) Act 1868 (c 101), s 20.
4 Succession (Scotland) Act 1964 (c 41), ss 1, 2, 14, 34(1), Sch 2, paras 1, 2.
5 Highland Services Act 1715 (c 54) (the 'Clan Act').
6 Tenures Abolition Act 1746.
7 Heritable Jurisdictions (Scotland) Act 1746 (c 43).
8 Infeftment Act 1845 (c 35).
9 Titles to Land (Scotland) Act 1858 (c 76), s 1.
10 Conveyancing (Scotland) Act 1874 (c 94), s 4(2).
11 Conveyancing (Scotland) Act 1874; Conveyancing (Scotland) Act 1924 (c 27), s 12(7).
12 Conveyancing (Scotland) Act 1874, ss 15–17, 18 (amended by the Feudal Casualties (Scotland) Act 1914 (c 48), s 24, Sch E).
13 Land Tenure Reform (Scotland) Act 1974 (c 38), s 1.
14 *Abolition of the Feudal System* (Scot Law Com Discussion Paper no. 93) (1991).
15 Ordinance of 12 April 1654 (APS vi, pt ii, 816, 817). This was also the ordinance annexing Scotland to England.

4. POSSESSION

The author records his appreciation of assistance given by Professor W M Gordon in the preparation of part of the text on the law of possession.

(1) INTRODUCTION

114. The concept of possession. Scots law, following Roman law, makes a clear distinction between possession on the one hand and ownership on the other, although the distinction has become less clear in practice by accepting a presumption of ownership of corporeal moveables arising from possession[1]. The distinction between possession and ownership is sometimes expressed as being that, while possession is in some sense a matter of fact, and not law, ownership is a matter of law, and not fact[2]. This is, however, to express the position too simply. Possession in Scots law is not a matter of fact in the sense that a holder of property is automatically regarded as being the possessor of it, or in the sense that whether or not there is possession can be determined merely by looking at the physical facts. The institutional writers, quoting texts of Roman law, state that to qualify as possessor the holder must hold on his own account, so that a depositee, for example, is not possessor[3]. It is likewise for a court to determine what factual relationship will constitute possession and this is not just a question of fact, although discussions of possession commonly assume that it is[4].

Another point of distinction between ownership and possession is that, while the former carries with it important rights, the latter on the whole does not. An owner of property is entitled to exercise a large number of rights in virtue of that ownership. In contrast, a possessor of property has few such rights merely in virtue of his possession. Possession in Scots law does not confer even the right to possession, the *jus possidendi,* for the right to possession is held by the owner of property or by one, such as a tenant, who derives his title from the owner[5]. The distinction between rights arising out of ownership and rights arising out of possession, is naturally of greatest importance in those cases where possession and ownership are in different hands. So if A possesses property but B is its owner or tenant or other person entitled to possession, the respective positions of the parties are measured by setting the rights conferred by possession against the rights conferred by ownership (or as the case may be). The result of such a dispute, it need hardly be said, is that B, the person entitled to possession, can recover possession from A, the person who is not so entitled. Matters are different in the more usual case where possession and the right to possession coincide. If A is both possessor of property and its owner — if A's possession, in other words, is of right — then it may seem scarcely necessary to consider whether his admitted right to protect that possession derives from the fact of ownership or from the fact of possession. Even in this case, however, the distinction must be observed if only to determine whether A must prove ownership or possession in order to qualify for his remedy. In practice, as will be explained later[6], the remedy sought almost always derives from ownership and it is ownership which falls to be proved. Nonetheless, a number of rights are conferred by possession alone. They may be said to be of two kinds. In the first place there are those rights, the *jura possessionis,* which may be exercised by one who possesses simply in virtue of the fact of his possession; and there are in the second place those innumerable rights for the acquisition or exercise of which possession is a necessary but not a sufficient condition. For rights of the first kind, possession alone is sufficient; for rights of the second kind something in addition to possession is required. Both are considered below[7].

1 See para 130 below.
2 Stair *Institutions* II,1,8; Erskine *Institute* II,1,20. See also *Digest* 41,2,12,1; ht 23 preamble; ht 29.
3 *Stair* II,1,17; *Erskine* II,1,20. In Roman law even a tenant or hirer was not entitled to possessory remedies, nor was a usufructuary or servitude holder, although the usufructuary and servitude holder were protected in the exercise of their rights by extensions of the normal possessory remedies.
4 Eg a court might hold that a traveller was not criminally liable as being in possession of dangerous drugs found in his luggage if convinced that he was genuinely unaware of their presence. At the same time, a court might allow the traveller to recover from a thief his luggage and all its contents on the basis that he had possession of them.
5 For the right to possession, see paras 126 ff below. A bare possessor does not have a right to possession although he does have a right not to be dispossessed except by consent or judicial warrant. See paras 161 ff below.
6 See paras 140, 141, below.
7 See paras 115, 116, below.

115. Rights arising directly out of possession: the jura possessionis. Possession, according to Bankton, is 'a right . . . whereby one is intitled to hold what he is possessed of, till a better right in another appears'[1]. The principal right of the possessor is the right to protect his possession. Nor need that possession be lawful in the sense of founded on a right to possession. Insofar as the fact of possession confers rights at all, it does so indiscriminately, on squatters and owners alike. Unlawfulness of possession is relevant only in a question with the rightful possessor. Thus on the one hand a possessor is fully protected against dispossession. There can be no extrajudicial dispossession against his will, for *brevi manu* seizure, even by the rightful possessor, is a spuilzie giving entitlement to the immediate return of the thing seized[2]. Nor, subject to the special statutory rules for lost property[3], can there be judicial dispossession except at the instance of the lawful possessor[4]. Similarly, a possessor is protected against acts of trespass or encroachment, except at the hands of the lawful possessor[5].

1 Bankton *Institute* I,3,20.
2 See para 162 below. See also para 140 below.
3 Civic Government (Scotland) Act 1982 (c 45), s 67. See further paras 547 ff below.
4 See para 141 below.
5 *Watson v Shields* 1996 SCLR 81.

116. Rights for which possession is a prerequisite. Possession is a necessary, although insufficient, condition for the acquisition or exercise of a number of different rights. In such cases the fact of possession, when combined with certain other facts, gives rise to the right. The following list, which is not exhaustive, indicates the variety of situations in which possession may be important.

(1) *Acquisition of real rights.* Possession is often a prerequisite of the acquisition of ownership and of other real rights. There is a strong connection, both historically and practically, between ownership on the one hand and possession on the other. In the acquisition of rights possession may operate in one of two ways. In some cases an initial act of possession is by itself sufficient to complete the right, while in other cases no right is acquired unless and until the possession is sustained for a certain length of time. Cases of the second kind are all cases of acquisition by positive prescription[1]. Cases of the first kind are more numerous and more varied. Thus at common law *traditio*, the handing over of possession, completed the transfer of ownership and this rule survives still in areas unclaimed by statute such as donation of corporeal moveables. Possession of corporeal moveables continues even today to raise a presumption of ownership[2]. Similarly, the act of taking possession of property not previously owned confers ownership through the doctrine of occupancy[3]; and the act of taking possession of land by a tenant completes his real right under the lease[4]. A number of other examples exist.

(2) *Protection against rectification of the Land Register.* The general powers of the Keeper of the Registers of Scotland to rectify inaccuracies in the Land Register[5] are greatly restricted where such rectification would prejudice a proprietor in possession of a registered interest in land[6]. Possession in this context is thought to include civil possession[7].

(3) *Right to a possessory judgment.* One who has possessed land for seven years on a *prima facie* title is entitled to an award of interim possession without consideration of the merits of competing rights to possession. This is known as a possessory judgment[8]. There is no equivalent right in the case of moveable property. Possessory judgments are, however, unknown in contemporary practice.

(4) *Right to a claim in delict for pure economic loss.* Damages for pure economic loss, not usually recoverable in delict, may nonetheless be recovered where the cause of the loss was damage to property in the possession of the claimant[9]. The rule is not yet fully developed, but it appears that the possession must normally be founded on a real right to possession such as ownership, liferent, security or lease[10], although a contractual right may also be sufficient if it confers on the claimant, in a question between the parties, the substance of ownership or other real right[11].

1 Prescription and Limitation (Scotland) Act 1973 (c 52), ss 1–3 (amended by the Land Registration (Scotland) Act 1979 (c 33), s 10). See further PRESCRIPTION AND LIMITATION.
2 See para 130 below.
3 See paras 540 ff below.

4 Leases Act 1449 (c 6). But not in the case of a long lease in an area which is operational for the purposes of registration of title: Land Registration (Scotland) Act 1979, s 3(3).
5 Land Registration (Scotland) Act 1979, s 9(1).
6 Ibid, s 9(3).
7 That at least is the opinion of the Keeper of the Register of Sasines: see (1984) 29 JLSS 175 at 176.
8 For possessory judgments, see para 146 below.
9 *Wimpey Construction (UK) Ltd v Martin Black & Co (Wire Ropes) Ltd* 1982 SLT 239, OH; *Blackburn v Sinclair* 1984 SLT 368, OH; *Nacap Ltd v Moffat Plant Ltd* 1986 SLT 326, revsd 1987 SLT 221. See further OBLIGATIONS.
10 *Nacap Ltd v Moffat Plant Ltd* 1987 SLT 221. See para 126 below.
11 *North Scottish Helicopters Ltd v United Technologies Corpn Inc* 1988 SLT 77, OH; *Mull Shellfish Ltd v Golden Sea Produce Ltd* 1992 SLT 703.

(2) ACQUISITION OF POSSESSION

(a) Introduction

117. Animus and corpus. Much of the law on the acquisition of possession is to be found in the institutional writers and they in turn borrow heavily from the Roman texts for their discussion and illustrations. Following Roman law it is said that acquisition of possession requires both *animus* (mind) and *corpus* (body). There must be both an intention to take the thing and some act of a physical nature giving effect to that intention. One without the other is insufficient. 'Corporal possession alone, can neither begin [possession] nor continue it; and if any act of the mind were enough, possession would be very large and but imaginary . . .'[1]. The acts which are in law sufficient to constitute on the one hand *animus* and on the other hand *corpus* are discussed in detail below[2], but some preliminary remarks are necessary first. Whatever its appeal to the juristic mind, the distinction between acts of the mind and acts of the body is too fine and too artificial to be sustainable in all cases. The truth is that *animus* and *corpus* are inextricably linked. For acts of the mind are evidenced principally by acts of the body, so that it frequently happens in practice that an act constituting *corpus* must also be looked to as evidence of *animus*. The actual use of a piece of property is frequently the best, and sometimes the only, evidence of the intention with which that use took place. Indeed the existence of *corpus* gives rise in law to a presumption of *animus*. But if *animus* is influenced by *corpus*, so *corpus* is in turn influenced by *animus*. Acts which taken by themselves are equivocal and without apparent significance may be treated as good evidence of *corpus* in circumstances where the necessary *animus* is clearly present. One who buys, for example, will be required to show fewer acts of possession than one who finds, for in the first case there is evident *animus possidendi* while in the second there is not: the finder may not be taking for himself.

1 Stair *Institutions* II,1,18. See also Stair II,1,17; Bankton *Institute* II,1,26; Erskine *Institute* II,1,20; Bell *Principles* s 1311.
2 For *corpus*, see paras 119–122 below, and for *animus*, see paras 123–125 below.

118. Competing claims to possession. As a general rule only one person can be in possession of property at any one time, for exclusivity is of the essence of possession[1]. So when two parties have competing claims to possession, only one can be accounted possessor. If A possesses property then it must follow that B does not. If B subsequently attempts to dispossess A there are three possible results. If B is successful, B is possessor. If B is unsuccessful, A remains possessor. Finally, if the contest is inconclusive, neither is possessor and the property is unpossessed. Dual possession is however possible where the claims of the parties are complementary rather than antagonistic. There are two cases. One is where parties are *pro indiviso* holders of the same right to possession (*jus possidendi*). Co-owners and co-tenants are typical examples. The other is where parties, such as landlord and tenant or superior and vassal, hold different but complementary interests in the same property. In the first case the possession is shared. In the second case one party has civil possession[2] and the other natural possession.

  1 Stair *Institutions* II,1,20; Bankton *Institute* II,1,26; Erskine *Institute* II,1,21.
  2 For civil possession, see para 121 below.

(b) Act of the Body

119. Initial detention. Possession requires an initial act of detention of the thing sought to be possessed, and without such detention there can be no possession[1]. Necessarily, the nature of the act of detention depends upon the nature of the thing possessed[2]. The essential common factor is the requirement of exclusive physical control. With corporeal moveables few difficulties arise:

> 'The clearest possession is of moveables . . . the possession whereof is simple and plain; holding and detaining them for our proper use, and debarring others from them, either by detaining them in our hands, or upon our bodies, or keeping them under our view or power, and making use of them, or having them in fast places, to which others had no easy access'[3].

Heritable property is less compact and correspondingly less easy to possess. The general rule here is that where boundaries are well recognised, possession of a part is considered possession of the whole:

> '[H]e who possesseth a field, needs not go about it all, or touch every turf of it, by himself or his cattle, but by possessing a part, possesseth the whole, unless there were contrary possessory acts'[4].

Boundaries are well recognised in the sense meant here if either they are specified in the title of the property or if they are established by long prior possession. In application of this principle to minerals it has been held that a party who holds on an express title possesses minerals by possession of the surface alone, but that in the absence of an express title the minerals must actually be worked for possession to be gained[5].

A number of special rules, for example the possession of symbols as the possession of property, have developed in the context of *traditio* (the delivery of possession for the purpose of transferring ownership). Such rules ameliorate what might otherwise appear as the inflexibility of a system heavily reliant on the concept of delivery, but it is thought that they have no bearing on the subject presently under consideration[6].

  1 Stair *Institutions* II,1,18. See also para 117 above.
  2 *Young v North British Rly Co* (1887) 14 R (HL) 53.
  3 Stair II,1,11.
  4 Stair II,1,13.
  5 *Crawfurd v Bethune* (1821) 1 S 111 (NE 110); *Forbes v Livingstone* (1827) 6 S 167.
  6 Thus it could scarcely be maintained that the possession of eg a net and coble, which is the symbol for *traditio* of salmon fishings, is to be regarded as possession of the fishings themselves. Stair, however, treats symbolic possession alongside other types of possession: Stair II,1,15 and 16.

120. Incorporeal property. Incorporeal property, as opposed to documentation evidential or constitutive of that property, has no physical presence and so cannot be detained; and since detention is a requirement of possession it follows that incorporeal property cannot be possessed[1]. Possession is thus confined to corporeal property only. There is, however, a legal fiction, for the limited purposes of positive prescription and of registration of title, that certain types of incorporeal heritable property are capable of possession. In such cases the thing possessed is by the governing statutes expressed as being an 'interest in land'[2], and interests in land are defined as including such (incorporeal) rights as leases, servitudes, standard securities and the right to fish for salmon. It is clear that 'possession' in this context has a special meaning; and in the absence of authority it may be suggested that right is 'possessed' in the sense intended by the statutes when it is being exercised[3]. Such exercise may or may not involve actual possession of the land to which the right relates. Thus on this view leases and servitudes are possessed, for the purposes of prescription and registration of title, by actual possession of the land, while standard securities are possessed by enforcing the conditions of the security and without possession of the land. It will be seen that in the former case two different things are being possessed, namely the land itself and, *fictione juris*, the incorporeal interest in the land.

1 Thus Erskine (in *Institute* II,9,3) writes of servitudes: 'As servitudes are incorporeal rights affecting lands which belong to another proprietor, few of them are capable of proper possession. Thus, where one has acquired the servitude of a road through his neighbour's grounds, such right cannot be properly apprehended or possessed. The lands indeed which are charged with the servitude may be possessed, but it is the owner of the servient tenement who possesses these, and not he who claims the servitude'. See also Stair *Institutions* II,7,1; Bankton *Institute* II,1,28.
2 Prescription and Limitation (Scotland) Act 1973 (c 52), ss 1–3 (amended by the Land Registration (Scotland) Act 1979 (c 33), s 10); Land Registration (Scotland) Act 1979, s 9(3).
3 This is certainly the case with servitudes. 'The use . . . or exercise of the right is, in servitudes, what seisin is in a right of lands; which exercise we improperly call possession, and is in Roman law styled "*quasi* possession" ': Erskine II,9,3.

121. Civil possession. The act of the body need not in all cases be the act of the possessor himself for it is possible to possess through the physical detention of another. Possession through another is called civil possession, as opposed to natural possession which is possession through an act of one's own[1]. In law, civil possession is the equal of natural possession for all purposes including prescription[2]. Civil possession arises where the person detaining the property does so not, or at any rate not exclusively, for himself, but on behalf of some other person, who is known as the civil possessor. The arrangement is of frequent occurrence. Thus tenants detain on behalf of their landlords, vassals on behalf of their superiors, pledgees on behalf of their debtors, liferenters on behalf of their fiars, and custodiers on behalf of the owners of the goods entrusted to them. A body corporate possesses civilly through its employees[3]. Invariably detentor and possessor stand in a pre-existing legal relationship, the lawfulness of the former's detention resting on some superior right to possession, most typically ownership, held by the latter[4]; and the detentor holds on behalf of the possessor because to do otherwise would be to deny the lawfulness of his own detention. Civil possession does not therefore usually arise where either there is no legal relationship between the parties or where the lawfulness of the detention is independent of such a relationship. A squatter, for example, holds for no one but himself, while a vassal, although holding for his superior, on whom his lawful possession ultimately depends, does not hold for his heritable creditor or for the dominant proprietor in a servitude right of way over his land. The titles of the heritable creditor and the dominant proprietor are dependent on that of the vassal, and not the other way about. Detention may begin as being on behalf of some other person but then suffer subsequent inversion. For example, a tenant who ceases to pay rent thereby ceases to hold for his landlord and holds only for himself[5].

A detentor may hold for himself concurrently with holding for another. A pledgee for example holds both for the owner of the goods pledged and also for his own interest as pledgee. There is civil possession in the one and natural possession in the other. It is also possible to hold for more than one civil possessor. Thus a subtenant holds not only for himself as subtenant, and for his immediate landlord as tenant, but he holds also for the head landlord as proprietor of the *dominium utile* and for the superior as proprietor of the *dominium directum*. The subtenant is in natural possession and the others are in civil possession.

It may sometimes happen that the true identity of the landlord or superior or other potential civil possessor is itself in dispute. In such a case doubt may arise as to which of the competing aspirants for the title is to be credited with the possession of the detentor. Where one or both of the parties are seeking to rely on prescription the resolution of this doubt becomes of the first importance. The probable resolution is that possession is attributed to the person from whom the detentor derives his title or, if they are different, to the person whose claim he acknowledges by, for example, the payment of rent[6].

1 Stair *Institutions* II,1,10 and 14; Erskine *Institute* II,1,22; Bell *Principles* s 1312. Erskine also includes under civil possession, possession *animo solo*. In Roman law the terms natural possession and civil possession were used differently: see para 125, note 1, below.
2 Prescription and Limitation (Scotland) Act 1973 (c 52), s 15.
3 *Birrell Ltd v City of Edinburgh District Council* 1982 SLT 111 at 114, per Lord Maxwell.
4 'How far the possession of one party profits another, is a point that may be settled by this rule: That where one possesses *in the right of another*, his possession will profit that other person': Lord Kilkerran, in reporting *Clerk v Earl of Home* (1747) Kilk 11 at 14, 15.
5 M Napier *Commentaries on the Law of Prescription in Scotland* (1839) pp 181–185.
6 *Napier* p 178.

122. Continuing detention. Once acquired by an initial act of detention, possession may then continue without the need for further acts. In such a case, possession is said to have been retained *animo solo*, by act of the mind alone[1]. In the absence of contrary evidence, the necessary act of the mind is presumed from the mere fact of initial detention. So possession of one's house is retained during absence at work or on holiday[2]. Similarly, possession of a holiday cottage is retained during the times of the year when it is not in use. But if *animus* is lost, then possession is lost also, so that one who alienates or abandons property thereby ceases to possess it. Possession *animo solo* is also lost where the thing comes to be detained by one who does not recognise the right of the possessor. A holiday cottage continues to be possessed if it lies empty or is lent to friends, but it ceases to be possessed if it comes to be occupied by a squatter[3].

1 The main sources for possession *animo solo* are Stair *Institutions* II,1,19, and Erskine *Institute* II,1,21. Erskine treats it as an example of civil possession: II,1,22.
2 *Ross's Dairies Ltd v Glasgow Corpn* 1972 SLT (Sh Ct) 48.
3 Or, more accurately, it is possessed by the squatter instead of by the owner. In Roman law possession was not lost until the fact of squatting was made known to the owner and the squatter was still not ejected.

(c) Act of the Mind

123. Introduction. It has been explained above that physical detention is not by itself sufficient to constitute possession[1]. The act of the body (*corpus possidendi*) must also be accompanied by an act of the mind (*animus possidendi*), although, unless the detention is itself unlawful, *animus* is presumed from *corpus*[2]. The act of the mind necessary for possession may be said to comprise two distinct elements, and both must be present. The first is the intention to exercise exclusive physical control over the thing detained. The act of the body must thus be mirrored in the act of the mind. Control without intention is not possession. The second element is the intention to exercise control for the benefit of oneself. Control exercised solely for the benefit of another is custody and not possession. Both elements are explored further below[3]. Possession is also an important concept in criminal law where there are a number of crimes of possession, ranging from possession of controlled drugs to possession of offensive weapons. But it appears that possession in criminal law may have a different and wider meaning than in civil law and, in particular, that facts which would be treated as custody in civil law may sometimes be treated as possession in criminal law[4].

1 See para 117 above.
2 Stair *Institutions* II,1,17; Bankton *Institute* II,1,26; Erskine *Institute* II,1,20.
3 See paras 124, 125, below.
4 G H Gordon *The Criminal Law of Scotland* (2nd edn, 1978) paras 3–38, 8–25.

124. Intention to exercise control. The exercise of control over the thing detained must be intentional; and while in most cases intention is readily demonstrated, difficult questions arise where a person is in possession of one piece of property in which a second piece of property lies forgotten or concealed. Does possession of a container object amount in law to possession of every item which is there contained? The answer may depend upon the history of the individual item in question. Thus it seems clear that to possess a house is also to possess everything within that house which was placed there by or with the knowledge of the possessor. That the possessor has subsequently forgotten about the item seems hardly to matter, for the initial *animus possidendi* may reasonably be considered to continue. The position is different, however, where the presence of the item is completely unknown to the possessor of the house.

In England and Wales this question has assumed considerable importance in the context of property which has been lost or abandoned. Under English law the first person to possess lost or abandoned property is entitled to retain it as against anyone but the true owner[1], and in a number of cases the court has been asked to decide between the competing claims of the finder of lost property and the possessor of the ground on which the find was actually made. The issue does not arise in the same way in Scotland because such rights as the common law gives to the first possessor of lost or abandoned property are removed by the statutory requirement that the property be handed over to the police[2]. There is also a question of the extent to which a finder can truly be said to hold for himself and so qualify for possession as opposed to custody[3]. But even in Scotland the interest of a first possessor may not be entirely extinguished, for there remains the statutory possibility of a reward for finding[4]; and, in any case, it is of importance beyond the narrow issue of lost and abandoned property whether items of which there is no actual knowledge, for example a present left secretly by a bashful guest, are possessed by the possessor of the object in which they lie concealed. The earlier English cases on this question are not easy to reconcile but the law may be regarded as having been settled by the decision of the Court of Appeal in *Parker v British Airways Board*[5] in 1982. In *Parker* the first possession of a bracelet found in a departure lounge at Heathrow Airport was held to be in the plaintiff who picked it up and not in the defendants who owned the building but knew nothing of the bracelet. The court agreed that it was possible for the occupier of a building to possess items of which he had no knowledge 'provided that the occupier's intention to exercise control over anything which might be on the premises was manifest'[6]. Such intention would usually be shown by the degree of control exercised, and in the case of a house the standard would normally be met[7]. However, in a place such as an airport lounge to which the public at large has access the degree of control will often be insufficient. *Parker* and the other leading cases are concerned with buildings; but it appears that the same general principles apply to all container objects, so that objects concealed in furniture or articles of clothing are possessed by the person who has control of the furniture or clothing[8].

With one unimportant exception[9], there is no direct Scottish authority on the question of concealed objects. Decisions in cases such as *Parker* are vulnerable to the criticism in Scotland that they are too much concerned with establishing an equitable system for lost and abandoned property and so too little concerned with the development of the general law of possession. Nonetheless *Parker* is likely to be an important influence when the question is eventually tested in the Scottish courts[10].

1 He has special property and is a bailee.
2 Civic Government (Scotland) Act 1982 (c 45), s 67. At common law the position in Scotland appears to have been broadly similar to the current position in England and Wales.
3 See further para 125 below.
4 Civic Government (Scotland) Act 1982, s 70. The reward is made to the 'finder', who is defined in s 67(1) as 'any person taking possession of any property'. Two points arise. First, since a finder will often hold the property for the owner rather than for himself, 'possession' may have to be interpreted as including custody. Secondly, there is an argument that the occupier of a house in which lost property is found 'has' possession but does not 'take' possession. If this is correct, the 'finder' is not the first person to possess but the first person to seize the property.
5 *Parker v British Airways Board* [1982] 1 QB 1004, [1982] 1 All ER 834. *Parker* follows *Bridges v Hawkesworth* (1851) 21 LJQB 75; *Hannah v Peel* [1945] 1 KB 509, [1945] 2 All ER 288; and *Kowal v Ellis* (1977) 76 DLR (3d) 546.
6 *Parker v British Airways Board* [1982] 1 QB 1004 at 1014, [1982] 1 All ER 834 at 840, per Donaldson LJ.
7 Thus 'I would be inclined to say that the occupier of a house will almost invariably possess any lost article on the premises. He may not have taken any positive steps to demonstrate his *animus possidendi*, but so firm is his control that the *animus* can be seen to attach to it': [1982] 1 QB 1004 at 1020, [1982] 1 All ER 834 at 845, per Eveleigh LJ. See also [1982] 1 QB 1004 at 1021, [1982] 1 All ER 834 at 846, per Sir David Cairns.
8 *Grafstein v Holme* [1958] 12 DLR (2d) 727.
9 *Hogg v Armstrong and Mowat* (1874) 1 Guth Sh Cas 438, which on similar facts applied *Bridges v Hawkesworth* (1851) 21 LJQB 75.
10 The approach adopted by *Bridges v Hawkesworth* (1851) 21 LJQB 75 and now by *Parker v British Airways Board* [1982] 1 QB 1004, [1982] 1 All ER 834, is not without its critics. T B Smith, for example, argues that an occupier of premises should always be treated as the possessor of lost property within these premises: *A Short Commentary on the Law of Scotland* (1962) pp 463, 464.

125. Intention to hold as one's own. In Roman law the necessary mental act was in general possession as owner (*animo domini*)[1]. Neither tenants, hirers nor even usufructuaries[2] were considered to be capable of possession. In Scots law the rule is very much less restrictive. All that is required of a possessor is detention 'for our own use'[3]. The test is *animus sibi habendi* and not *animus domini*. A tenant or a hirer or even a thief[4] is as capable of possession as an owner[5]. A thing may be held both for oneself and, at the same time, on behalf of someone else, and in practice such dual holding is of frequent occurrence. A tenant, for example, holds for himself as tenant and for his landlord as owner with the result that there is natural possession in the one and civil possession in the other[6]. However, a thing held exclusively for another is not possessed: the detentor in such a case has custody and not possession[7].

1 However, this strict rule was extended to include a person holding *precario*, a pledgee, and an *emphyteuta* (tenant under a long lease). A person detaining *animo domini* was termed a possessor or civil possessor. A natural possessor was a person detaining without the necessary *animus*.
2 A usufructuary did, however, have special possessory remedies.
3 Stair *Institutions* II,1,17. But the stricter formulation of the Roman law can be found both in Erskine *Institute* II,1,20 and in Bell *Principles* s 1311. Compare on this point W M Gordon *Scottish Land Law* (1989) paras 14-03–14-06 with D L Carey Miller *Corporeal Moveables in Scots Law* (1991) para 1.13.
4 In Roman law a thief was a possessor also.
5 Thus the institutional writers contrast a tenant, who is a possessor, with a custodier, who is not: Stair II,1,14 and 17; *Erskine* II,1,20 and 22.
6 See para 121 above.
7 Stair II,1,17; *Erskine* II,1,20; *Bell* s 1311. Custody and possession are usefully distinguished in *Hamilton v Western Bank of Scotland* (1856) 19 D 152 at 161, per Lord Ivory, and in *Sim v Grant* (1862) 24 D 1033. But the distinction may be difficult to sustain in practice: see G H Gordon *The Criminal Law of Scotland* (2nd edn, 1978) para 14-03.

(3) THE RIGHT TO POSSESSION

(a) Real Rights and Personal Rights

126. Introduction. Possession is either as of right or without right. There are or appear to be two categories of rightful possession[1]. The first is possession by one, such as the owner of property or its tenant or liferenter who, by virtue of that ownership or other right, holds a right to possession in relation to that property. A right to possession is a real right, enforceable against all who seek to challenge it. It may authorise natural possession or civil possession or both. The second category is possession by one who, while not himself holding a real right to possession, has a personal right to possession as against a person who does. A convenient term for such a personal right to possession is a licence. A service occupancy[2] is a familiar example. The distinction here drawn, between a real right to possession and a personal licence, may be the same as the distinction developed by Lord Justice-Clerk Ross in a different context between a right of possession and a contractual right of use[3]. A person who holds neither a real right to possession nor a personal licence has no entitlement to possess and may be dispossessed by the rightful possessor or possessors by means of an appropriate court action[4].

1 The discussion here is confined to rights of continuous and exclusive possession. But it should be noted that public rights of way and certain positive servitudes confer rights of intermittent and non-exclusive possession. Such rights are real and may be enforced both against the servient proprietor and against third parties.
2 A service occupancy means employment related accommodation, eg accommodation provided for a caretaker. See further LANDLORD AND TENANT, vol 13, para 115.
3 *Nacap Ltd v Moffat Plant Ltd* 1987 SLT 221. The context is a claim in delict for damage to property in the possession of the pursuer. Lord Ross's distinction is blurred in a later case on the same subject where a purely contractual right (hire) in relation to a helicopter is characterised by Lord Davidson as 'a possessory right by reason of a contract *attaching to the chattel itself*': *North Scottish Helicopters Ltd v United Technologies Corpn Inc* 1988 SLT 77 at 81, OH (emphasis added).
4 See paras 151 ff below. However, he may not be dispossessed by force or otherwise against his will: see paras 161 ff below.

127. Real right: the right to possession. The concept of right to possession (*jus possidendi*) has received little analysis in Scots law. The neglect is unfortunate for in almost every case it is the right to possession rather than possession itself which determines the outcome of a possessory dispute[1]. The account which follows is a first and provisional attempt at such an analysis.

The right to possession is a real right. Its holder, the rightful possessor, can vindicate the right against all challengers. If he is out of possession, possession may be recovered[2]; and if he is in possession he may defend that possession against all who seek to infringe upon it[3]. But while the right to possession is a real right, it is not an autonomous right[4]. It cannot exist on its own but only as part of some other and more general right, such as the right of ownership. To this rule of dependence there is a single statutory exception in the occupancy right conferred on a non-entitled spouse by the Matrimonial Homes (Family Protection) (Scotland) Act 1981[5]. The class of general rights which include within them the real right to possession is not entirely settled. Ownership[6], liferent and lease are clearly members. So are certain kinds of right in security such as lien and pledge. A creditor in a standard security has a right to possession but only if his debtor is in default[7]. An adjudger also has a right to possession. Beyond this point it is difficult to proceed with confidence. The list already given is probably not exhaustive and yet it is uncertain how it may be completed. The difficulty lies in distinguishing the real right from the personal licence[8]. A hirer of moveables is probably the most marginal example and the hardest to classify[9].

Since a real right to possession is part of some other, more general, real right, it would appear to follow that the right does not come into being until the more general right of which it is part is perfected. Accordingly, in principle, one whose title to the general right is incomplete — for example, an uninfeft proprietor of land who has not proceeded to registration — can have no real right to possession. Nevertheless it appears now to have been accepted that for certain purposes in the protection of possession an uncompleted title is sufficient[10].

The real right to possession may relate to natural or to civil possession or to both; and while a number of different parties may simultaneously be in civil possession, the right to natural possession is indivisible and there cannot be two such rights in respect of the same property[11]. So if A is entitled to natural possession then it necessarily follows that B is not so entitled. The identity of the person entitled to natural possession at any given moment depends upon the extent to which the property in question is encumbered by liferent, security, lease or other similar rights. Where property is entirely unencumbered, the owner[12] is the person entitled to natural possession. But the addition of encumbrances may alter the location of the right. Thus if an owner of land makes a grant of a lease, his right to natural possession passes with the lease to the tenant. Thereafter he possesses civilly only and any further natural possession would be unlawful. If the tenant then proceeds to sublet, the right to natural possession passes to the subtenant. Finally, if the subtenant grants a standard security over his interest, the right to possession remains with him unless and until he defaults on his loan. Of course, at some point in the future, security, sublease and lease will all come to an end. If the sublease ends before the lease the right to natural possession will revert in the first instance to the head tenant before passing finally to the owner. During the currency of the lease and sublease, the owner and head tenant have civil possession coupled with a residual right to natural possession, and this is sufficient title to defend or recover possession in a question with strangers to the land[13].

1 See paras 114, 115, above.
2 See paras 152 ff below.
3 See paras 174 ff below.
4 For this reason it is not included in the list of real rights given in para 5 above.
5 Matrimonial Homes (Family Protection) (Scotland) Act 1981 (c 59), s 1(1) (amended by the Law Reform (Miscellaneous Provisions) (Scotland) Act 1985 (c 73), s 13(2)). As to whether this is a real right in the strict sense, see para 10 above.
6 In the case of feudal land, this means both *dominium directum* and *dominium utile*.
7 Conveyancing and Feudal Reform (Scotland) Act 1970 (c 35), Sch 3, condition 10(3).
8 For personal licences, see para 128 below.
9 Since the right of hire is itself only a personal right, there is an obvious difficulty in saying that it includes a subsidiary right which is real. In *McArthur v O'Donnell* 1969 SLT (Sh Ct) 24 the hirer of furniture successfully recovered possession from a third party. But the pursuer's title to sue for delivery was upheld only on an unconvincing analogy with title to sue in delict. See also *North Scottish Helicopters Ltd v United Technologies Corpn Inc* 1988 SLT 77, OH, and *Shell UK Ltd v McGillvray* 1991 SLT 667, OH.
10 See para 142 below.
11 Although the single right may of course be held by more than one person *pro indiviso*. The extent to which one *pro indiviso* proprietor may enforce his right without the participation of the other or others is considered at para 141 below.
12 In the case of feudal land this refers to *dominium utile*.
13 *Steuart v Stephen* (1877) 4 R 873; *Brocket Estates Ltd v M'Phee* 1949 SLT (Notes) 35, OH. The position of the superior is the same: see para 141 below. Since trespass and encroachment, if continued unchecked, may lead to the establishment of a right, the interest of the holder of the residual right in acting will be obvious.

128. The personal right: the licence to possession. A licence to possession is a personal right, usually although not perhaps invariably[1] contractual in nature, which is enforceable by the licensee against the licensor. The licensor will usually be the holder of the real right to natural possession[2]. In practice, licences to possession conform to one of two types. In the first place there are those rights (*jura ad rem*) which will in the course of time mature into real rights. Thus the grantee of a delivered but unregistered disposition has, once the stipulated date of entry has arrived, a licence to possession. But until the disposition is registered, ownership, and with it the real right to possession, remains with the granter[3]. In the second place, there are those rights which it is never intended should become real. Notable amongst them are service occupancies and other cases of contractual rights to possess land which for one reason or another do not satisfy the requirements of a lease[4]. A licence may be for a fixed term or it may be revocable at will by the licensor[5], and it may or may not involve the payment of rent. Possession on the basis of a licence revocable at will is sometimes referred to as possession *precario* (precarious possession)[6].

A licensee is a possessor as of right, but the real right to possession remains with the licensor. Four consequences follow. First, the licensee is a lawful possessor of the property[7]. For the duration of the licence he alone is entitled to natural possession. Secondly, his licence, as a personal right, is enforceable only against the licensor. Thirdly, if the licensor interferes with the possession, he may be judicially opposed, failing which he may be ejected[8]. Finally, if there is interference at the hand of some third party the licensor alone has a direct remedy, albeit a remedy which in terms of the licence he may be contractually bound to pursue.

1 Non-contractual personal rights may arise under the law of unjustified enrichment. Thus if A transfers ownership of property to B under error, it is thought that A has a *condictio indebiti* to recover the property.
2 For if he is not, the licence will be *a non domino* and confer no right to natural possession.
3 See para 127 above.
4 Such rights are often described as 'licences', a specific application of the generic usage adopted here. For licences in this specific sense, see LANDLORD AND TENANT, vol 13, para 120.
5 For examples of licences revocable at will, see *White v Stevenson* 1956 SC 84, 1956 SLT 194 (person still in occupation of house after sequestration); *Birrell Ltd v City of Edinburgh District Council* 1982 SLT 111 (person still in occupation of shop after compulsory purchase); *Scottish Residential Estates Development Co Ltd v Henderson* 1991 SLT 490 (rent-free right to occupy cottage).
6 Erskine *Institute* II,1,23: 'Where one possesseth at his own request, by the tolerance or bare license of the proprietor, it is called "possession *precario*" '.
7 The range of possible situations qualifying as a licence is very wide, and in the case of some licences the detentor will lack the necessary *animus possidendi*, of holding the property for his own use, which is required for possession in its strict sense. See *Erskine* II,1,23, and para 125 above.
8 For the ejection of licensors by licensees, see para 141 below.

129. Presumption of lawful possession.
The possession of corporeal moveables is, in the absence of proof to the contrary, presumed to be lawful possession[1]; and from this first presumption arises a second, namely that the possessor of corporeal moveables is taken to be their owner[2]. The second presumption is in practice of much greater importance than the first.

1 Stair *Institutions* IV,45,17 (VII). This includes 'lawful' in the sense that possession was not acquired vitiously, against the will of the previous possessor. Despite the generality of the rule as given by Stair, it is now settled that the presumption does not extend to heritable property: see para 130 below.
2 See para 130 below.

130. Presumption that possession signifies ownership.
Although possession and ownership are distinct concepts, the right to enjoy possession is one of the main benefits of ownership and the fact that a person has possession of corporeal moveable property is taken to be an indication of ownership. The possessor is in law presumed to be owner[1]. Why this should be so is easily explained. In most cases there is no register of ownership of corporeal moveables. Ownership may be, and usually is, transferred without recourse to writing. The exercise of possessory rights

is therefore the easiest, and sometimes the only, way of showing that ownership is held.

For the presumption of ownership to operate the property must first be possessed in the strict sense of the term. Mere custody is insufficient[2]. Possession here means natural possession[3]. The presumption of ownership is a rule of the law of evidence only and the substantive law of property is left untouched: ownership is presumed of the possessor but whether he is really owner continues to be determined by the normal rules of property law. The purpose of the presumption is to provide a simple and convenient rule of evidence in the event of a dispute arising as to ownership. When such a dispute does arise, the current possessor has the benefit of the presumption and it is then for others to discharge the evidential burden of showing that ownership lies elsewhere[4]. The strength of the presumption is not constant but varies with the length and nature of the possession held[5]. Hume gives as an example of a weakened presumption the case of a valuable jewel in the possession of a common beggar[6]. Moreover there can be little doubt that the presumption is today less strong than in earlier times[7]. Since 1894 ownership on sale has been transferable without the transfer of possession[8] and for this and for other reasons[9] there has been in recent times a marked decline in the coincidence of ownership and possession.

Where corporeal moveables are possessed by more than one person, the presumption is that each has an equal *pro indiviso* share. More specifically, it is provided by the Family Law (Scotland) Act 1985 that household goods obtained in prospect of or during marriage, other than by gift or succession from a third party, are presumed to belong to the spouses equally[10]. Household goods are defined as any goods, including decorative or ornamental goods, kept or used at any time during the marriage in any matrimonial home for the joint domestic purposes of the parties to the marriage. However, money, securities, domestic animals and motor cars, caravans and other road vehicles are excluded[11]. The presumption is rebuttable but is not to be rebutted by reason only that while the parties were married and living together the goods in question were purchased from a third party by either party alone or by both in unequal shares[12].

There is some suggestion in the older authorities that the presumption of ownership from possession extends to heritable property[13], but this is not, or in any event is no longer, the law[14].

1 Stair *Institutions* IV,45,17 (VIII); Bankton *Institute* II,1,34; Erskine *Institute* II,1,24.
2 But Bell *Commentaries* I,304, can be read as implying the contrary. For the distinction between possession and custody, see para 125 above.
3 Bell *Principles* s 1313.
4 See further paras 148 ff below.
5 *George Hopkinson Ltd v Napier & Son* 1953 SC 139 at 147, 1953 SLT 99 at 102, per Lord President Cooper.
6 Hume *Lectures* vol III (Stair Soc vol 15, 1952 ed G C H Paton) p 231. See also *Ebrahim v Deputy Sheriff* (1961) 4 SA 265 at 268, per Henning J.
7 As early as 1848 Lord Cockburn said that '[t]his is a presumption liable to be rebutted, and perhaps liable to be rebutted easily': *Anderson v Buchanan* (1848) 11 D 270 at 284.
8 The current legislation is the Sale of Goods Act 1979 (c 54), s 17.
9 Eg the growing popularity in consumer sales of hire purchase and in commercial sales of clauses of retention of title.
10 Family Law (Scotland) Act 1985 (c 37), s 25(1). See *Kinloch v Barclay's Bank plc* 1995 SCLR 975, Sh Ct.
11 Family Law (Scotland) Act 1985, s 25(3).
12 Ibid, s 25(2).
13 Stair IV,45,17 (VII); Erskine II,1,24.
14 Hume *Lectures* vol IV (Stair Soc vol 17, 1955 ed G C H Paton) p 268. Thus the pursuer in an action of eg trespass of heritage must prove his title despite the fact that he is in possession: see para 142 below.

(b) Bona Fide Possession

131. Introduction. A bona fide possessor is one who possesses property in the reasonable but mistaken belief that his possession is as of right. His possession is without right but is believed to be lawful[1]. The error must be one of fact and not one of law[2]; and in practice such an error may readily enough be made, at least in the case of corporeal moveables where title is not evidenced by writing.

The bona fides of a possessor is important only in the event of his ultimate dispossession. Like any other possessor without title, a bona fide possessor is vulnerable to dispossession at the instance of the holder of the right to possession; but while good faith is not a defence to such an action, it confers on the defender certain claims in relation to the period of bona fide possession. The content of these claims is considered below[3].

1 Erskine *Institute* II,1,25: 'A *bona fide* possessor is one who, though he be not truly proprietor of the subject which he possesses, yet believes himself proprietor upon probable grounds, and with a good conscience'. See also Stair *Institutions* II,1,24; Bankton *Institute* I,8,12. 'Proprietor' must not be read as excluding other kinds of rights to possession. One who believes himself a tenant is as much a bona fide possessor as one who believes himself owner. For cases of bona fide possession involving rights other than ownership, see *Moir v Glen* (1831) 9 S 744 (superiority); *Yellowlees v Alexander* (1882) 9 R 765 (personal right to ownership under missives of sale); *Newton v Newton* 1925 SC 715, 1925 SLT 476 (personal right to ownership under trust).
2 See para 135 below.
3 See para 171 below.

132. Meaning of good faith. Good faith may be approached either subjectively or objectively. A subjective approach is concerned with actual knowledge, with what a party did or did not know about the lawfulness of his possession. An objective approach discards evidence of actual knowledge in favour of constructive knowledge, the knowledge that a possessor is deemed to have had. The first seeks to inquire into the mind of the possessor, while the second assumes that he has the mind of the reasonable man. Scots law makes no clear choice between subjectivity and objectivity but takes something from both[1]. Thus, on the one hand, the law inquires into the actual state of mind of the possessor. Did the possessor know, or did he not know, that his possession was without right? But, on the other hand, the law is not always content with the answer which it receives. A possessor who is genuinely unaware of the unlawfulness of his title is not necessarily accounted a bona fide possessor. Instead, objectivity is allowed to manifest itself in two ways. For first, actual knowledge is in certain circumstances supplemented by constructive knowledge; and secondly, knowledge, whether actual or constructive, is deemed to be interpreted by the possessor in a manner which is in all the circumstances reasonable. Both points are considered in greater detail below[2].

1 The approach of South African law provides an illuminating comparison: see D L Carey Miller *The Acquisition and Protection of Ownership* (1986) pp 51, 52.
2 See paras 134, 135, below.

133. Actual knowledge. Absence of actual knowledge of lack of title is in almost every case an indispensable condition of bona fide possession. A person who knows that his possession is unlawful cannot be a bona fide possessor. How much knowledge is required before the benefit of good faith is forfeited may sometimes be a nice question. Certainly the whole history of the defect need not be known. A party is in bad faith if he knows that he is not the rightful possessor even if he does not know the identity of the person who is[1]. But, conversely, it appears that good faith is preserved where the knowledge is of an imaginary defect and the title suffers from a quite different defect of which the possessor is unaware[2].

To the general rule just stated there is one exception. A person who has obtained decree in a possessory judgment on the basis of seven years' possession of land[3] is, according to Stair[4], and regardless of his state of actual knowledge, conclusively deemed to be in good faith for the duration of his possession unless and until such time as his title is set aside by reduction or declarator; and it may even be, although the passage is not clearly expressed, that Stair considered the deeming to operate retrospectively to include possession enjoyed prior to the possessory judgment having been obtained[5]. In current practice possessory judgments are almost unknown.

1 'A *male fide* possessor ... knows ... or, which comes to the same account, may upon the smallest reflection know that he is not the rightful owner': Erskine *Institute* II,1,25.
2 This appears to be the result of *Yellowlees v Alexander* (1882) 9 R 765.
3 For the seven year possessory judgment, see para 146 below.
4 Stair *Institutions* IV,26,3.
5 The effect on possessors of a possessory judgment, according to Stair, is that 'they do not only secure the profits they have made as *bona fide possessores*, but may continue to enjoy the future profits, till they be put *in mala fide*, by judicial production of a better right, by way of reduction, declarator or competition': Stair IV,26,3. In the phrase 'as *bona fide possessores*' it is not clear whether the 'as' is to be taken as meaning 'as if they were' or merely 'if they were'. The former seems more likely.

134. Constructive knowledge. Actual knowledge is not always conclusive in questions of faith, and constructive knowledge may also have a role to play, although in the present state of the authorities no confident statement of that role may yet be made. There is only one certain occurrence of constructive knowledge in the context of bona fide possession, namely, the rule that a possessor is deemed, at the time when he first took possession, to have carried out inquiries as to the state of his title such as would be carried out by any prudent purchaser. There can be no bona fide possession, it has been said, in the absence of a colourable title[1]. In the case of moveable property, where there is no register and, usually, no writing, this rule has little substance in practice, but in the case of land it has assumed considerable importance and particularly in modern times. Until 1871 the Register of Sasines had no index by property, so that it was impossible to obtain a list of deeds affecting a particular property, and examination of title was necessarily unreliable and cursory. All deeds registered in the Register of Sasines since 1871 have been indexed by property through the use of separate search sheets for each interest in land, and the new Land Register is also indexed by property, through the use of title sheets[2]. The absence of modern authority makes it difficult to assess the effect of these changes, but it is suggested that today a possessor of land is under a duty to consult the Register of Sasines or Land Register[3]. Otherwise he has failed to exercise the same care as a prudent purchaser[4]. If he does not consult the Registers, his possession should be considered to be in bad faith if such consultation would have revealed the defect in title — and perhaps even if it would not[5]. If this is correct, then the overall result of these administrative changes is a marked decline in the incidence of bona fide possession of land, for in modern times the plea is available only in the comparatively unusual circumstance that the defect in title is latent and so not discoverable from the Register.

1 Stair *Institutions* II,1,24; Bankton *Institute* I,8,12; *Blair v Bruce-Stewart* (1783) Mor 1775.
2 As to the Register of Sasines and Land Register, see CONVEYANCING, vol 6, paras 453, 707 ff. For the Land Register there is also an index map: see vol 6, para 733.
3 It appears that in *Trade Development Bank v Warriner and Mason (Scotland) Ltd* 1980 SC 74, 1980 SLT 223, it was the failure to examine the Register of Sasines which made the possession of the defenders *mala fide*. This may have been the law even prior to 1871. In *Haldane v Ogilvy* (1871) 10 M 62 at 71, Lord Benholme asked: 'The question is this, whether he [the possessor] was ... entitled to be ignorant of a fact which was declared on the face of his most important titles — his investiture under the Crown ... accessible to him on record, if not contained in his charter chest ... No man seems entitled to be ignorant, in such a case, when that ignorance is to be made to affect the rights of

others'. See also Lord Cowan at 73: 'As to the defence of *bona fide* perception, I am of the opinion . . . that no heritor can plead that defence when the facts on which it is alleged to be based are at variance with the terms of the title-deeds by which he is invested in his estate'.

4 As to a prudent purchaser, see *Soues v Mill* (1903) 11 SLT 98 at 100, per Lord Kyllachy. In practice a possessor should examine, in the case of Sasine land, a search in the Personal and Property Registers and a prescriptive progress of titles, and, in the case of Land Register land, an updated land certificate.

5 On the basis that if he has not consulted the Registers at all then his optimism as to title has no rational basis and does not qualify as good faith.

135. Interpretation of knowledge. Knowledge acquired by, or imputed to, a possessor is deemed to have been interpreted by him in a manner which is in all the circumstances reasonable. In particular and as a general rule, a possessor is presumed to know the law relevant to the particular facts and to be able to apply that law correctly. Thus it constitutes bad faith to accept a title from a child who purports to act with the consent of his guardian if the signature of the guardian is missing from the deed[1]. Such a deed is 'void by the obvious and universally known rules of law'[2]. The result may be different where the applicable law is obscure or uncertain. Unfortunately there is little authority on this question considered generally[3]; but it is settled that where the terms of a particular deed give rise to a number of different but plausible interpretations, a party is not to be regarded as in bad faith by accepting an interpretation other than the one ultimately upheld by a court[4]. It has been suggested that in some circumstances there may be a duty to take the opinion of counsel or some other appropriate expert[5].

1 *Lady Cardross v Hamilton* (1711) Mor 1747.
2 Erskine *Institute* II,1,27. Equivalent expressions are found in Stair *Institutions* II,1,24, and Bankton *Institute* I,8,16.
3 For the equivalent but much more developed doctrine in South African law, see D L Carey Miller *The Acquisition and Protection of Ownership* (1986) pp 51, 52.
4 See eg *Menzies v Menzies* (1863) 1 M 1025.
5 *Waugh v More Nisbett* (1882) 19 SLR 427.

136. Gratuitous possessors. In some areas of law a person who holds property by virtue of gift is treated in the same way as a person who holds in bad faith. This is not the case in the law of possession. Further, there is no indication in the authorities that a party is more likely to be regarded as in bad faith merely on the basis that he gave no consideration for his possession[1].

1 Rankine's view to the contrary appears to be incorrect: see J Rankine *The Law of Land-ownership in Scotland* (4th edn, 1909) p 81. Although *Cockburn v Robertson* (1697) Mor 1732 suggests that donation might affect faith, this suggestion has not been adopted in subsequent cases.

137. Termination of good faith. A party is entitled to the privileges of a bona fide possessor only in respect of the period for which his good faith actually endures[1]. The good faith with which possession was initially taken up may be lost either by the emergence of new facts or as a result of litigation.

New facts may come to light during the course of possession whether by chance or as a result of a claim by some other party. If the facts are such as plainly show the true state of the title, good faith is lost at once and no court action is necessary, at any rate for this purpose[2]. If, on the other hand, the new facts are equivocal and capable of an interpretation favourable to the possessor, good faith is preserved unless or until the fragility of the possessor's title is established by litigation. In such a case there may be a question as to the precise moment at which good faith is lost. The rule in Roman law was that in the event of litigation good faith was lost at litiscontestation, that is, at the point in proceedings when defences are lodged[3]. There is no such fixed rule in Scots law, but on the assumption that the defender has a plausible defence — for if he has not, good faith is lost long before litigation commences — it appears that the relevant time in most cases will be on the award of decree by the court of first instance[4]. However, in cases of particular difficulty or importance, good faith may be considered to continue throughout the appeal process until the defender's position is finally rejected by an appellate court[5].

1 Erskine *Institute* II,1,28.
2 *Erskine* II,1,28. Erskine's authority is *Wolmet's Children v Douglas* (1662) Mor 1730. Rankine's view (J Rankine *The Law of Land-ownership in Scotland* (4th edn, 1909) p 81) that *Wolmet's Children* concerns initial rather than supervening bad faith, and that accordingly subsequent private knowledge is never by itself sufficient to induce bad faith, seems inconsistent with the court's rejection of the defender's argument that 'private knowledge infers not *mala fides*, unless it had been anterior to her possession'. Stair *Institutions* II,1,24, offers more support for Erskine's position than Erskine himself perhaps realised. See also *Clyne v Clyne's Trustees* (1839) 2 D 243, and the discussion in D L Carey Miller *Corporeal Moveables in Scots Law* (1991) pp 83, 84.
3 This rule has been received into Roman-Dutch law: D L Carey Miller *The Acquisition and Protection of Ownership* (1986) pp 56, 57. It has been argued that the rule ought to be the same, or similar, in Scots law: see D L Carey Miller *Corporeal Moveables in Scots Law* (1991) p 85.
4 Bankton *Institute* I,8,13. See also *Stair* II,1,24. Erskine's view, that good faith is lost at the commencement of the action (*Erskine* II,1,29), appears to be mistaken. For a full review of the case law, see *Rankine* pp 81–83.
5 See eg *Cleghorn v Eliott* (1842) 4 D 1389; *Menzies v Menzies* (1863) 1 M 1025; *Houldsworth v Brand's Trustees* (1876) 3 R 304.

(4) PROTECTION OF NATURAL POSSESSION: TITLE TO SUE

(a) Introduction

138. Classification of remedies by result sought. The law classifies remedies in relation to natural possession according to whether they are in defence of existing possession or for the recovery of possession which has been lost. In cases of the first kind, a pursuer already in possession of property seeks to defend that possession against the unfriendly acts of some other person or persons. The remedy most commonly sought is interdict. In cases of the second kind, a pursuer not, or no longer, in possession of property seeks to gain or to regain possession. The principal remedies used are, in the case of land, ejection or interdict, and, in the case of corporeal moveables, delivery. A detailed account of these remedies is given below[1].

1 For recovery of lost possession, see paras 151 ff below, and for defence of existing possession, see paras 174 ff below.

139. Classification of remedies by title to sue. A second method of classifying remedies is by reference to title to sue. Thus the institutional writers divided remedies according to whether they were 'petitory' or 'possessory'[1]. A petitory remedy required of the pursuer some right in respect of the property. A possessory remedy required the fact of his current or recent possession, sometimes with and sometimes without an accompanying right. To modern eyes such a division line seems drawn in the wrong place. The remedies are not distinguished, as might be expected, according to whether a right to the property must be shown; and nor, despite first appearances, are they distinguished according to whether possession is required, for even in the case of remedies classified as petitory, the pursuer may often be called upon to prove his title by possession for the period of positive prescription. The main continuing justification for a distinction between petitory remedies and possessory remedies is that the latter may regulate questions of possession without investigating questions of right, and that accordingly in a possessory action a squatter or other possessor without title may sometimes succeed even against one who holds the right to possession[2]. But even this justification is of greatly diminished importance in modern times, for with the relaxation of the rules as to proof of title[3] petitory actions may sometimes settle questions of possession without consideration of questions of right. In the present work the division between possessory and petitory remedies is not used. In its place a distinction is made between those remedies for which some right is required of the pursuer and those remedies for which bare possession is sufficient. This distinction is explained further below[4].

1 Stair *Institutions* IV,3,47; IV,21,1; IV,26,1–3; Bankton *Institute* IV,24,49; Erskine *Institute* IV,1,47. The principal remedies classified as possessory were (1) spuilzie and (2) the seven-year possessory judgment.
2 His victory will usually be shortlived, for the rightful possessor can then proceed to recover the property by means of a petitory action.
3 See paras 142 ff below.
4 See paras 140, 141, below.

140. Possession as title to sue. As a general rule bare possession is not a sufficient title to sue in Scots law. Some right in the property must always be shown. To this rule there appear to be two exceptions. First, where property has been spuilzied from its possessor, that is to say, seized vitiously and without his consent, a remedy arises even in the absence of a right in the property. The remedy given by spuilzie is redelivery in the case of moveable property and ejection of the spuilzier in the case of land, accompanied in both cases by a claim for violent profits. Spuilzie is considered in detail below[1]. Secondly, it has recently been held that possession may be a sufficient title, not only for the recovery of possession which has been lost, as in the case of spuilzie, but also for the defence of existing possession through an action of trespass or encroachment[2]. However, this result does not seem consistent with existing case law on title to sue for the defence of possession[3].

1 See paras 161 ff below.
2 *Watson v Shields* 1996 SCLR 81. See also J Rankine *The Law of Land-ownership in Scotland* (4th edn, 1909) pp 9, 10, and W M Gordon *Scottish Land Law* (1989) para 14-14 where a similar view is expressed.
3 The view expressed in the existing case law is that possession can never be defended unless the possessor has, at least, a prima facie right to possession. See paras 142, 143, below.

141. Right in the property as title to sue. Apart from the case of spuilzie discussed above[1], remedies for the protection of possession are available only to a person holding a right in relation to the property in question[2]; and this rule applies to all remedies, whether in defence of existing possession[3] or in recovery of possession formerly held but now lost[4].

In the usual case only a real right to possession (*jus possidendi*)[5] is a sufficient title to sue; and since the principal rights which carry with them the real right to possession are the rights of ownership, liferent and lease[6], the pursuer's task is in practice to show either that he is the owner of property or its liferenter or tenant. A real right which has been restricted to civil possession remains sufficient title in a question with anyone other than the holder of the right to natural possession, and so in a question with a stranger to the property an action may be raised by a superior as well as by a vassal, and by a landlord as well as by a tenant[7]. Where a right to possession is held in common, each *pro indiviso* proprietor must concur in any litigation[8] except, it has been suggested, where the defender has not and never has had a shadow of a title to the property[9]. A personal licence to possession[10], which in general is insufficient as a title, will found an action in a question with the person from whom the licence is derived[11].

Where an action is defended the pursuer must lead evidence of title, in the absence of an admission by the defender. Proof of right to possession is a matter of considerable complexity. Thus in some cases complete and conclusive evidence of title is required of the pursuer. In other cases, prima facie evidence is sufficient. And the rules are different depending upon whether the property is heritable or moveable, and in the case of heritable property upon whether the title is registered in the Land Register or the Register of Sasines. These different rules as to proof of right now fall to be considered in detail under three separate headings, namely (1) Sasine land[12], (2) Land Register land[13] and (3) corporeal moveables[14].

1 See para 140 above.
2 For possession as of right, see paras 126 ff above.
3 Ie the remedies of interdict of trespass, removal of encroachment, and self-help. See further paras 178, 179, 182–184, below.
4 Ie the remedies of removing, ejection, interdict, delivery and self-help. See further paras 152 ff below.
5 For real rights to possession, see para 127 above.
6 But the right to possession is also carried by a number of other rights, including the rights of lien, pledge, standard security and adjudication.
7 For superiors, see Stair *Institutions* II,4,3; Erskine *Institute* II,5,1; *Laird of Lagg v Grierson* (1624) Mor 13787; *Marquis of Breadalbane v Campbell* (1851) 13 D 647. For landlords, see *Steuart v Stephen* (1877) 4 R 873 and *Brocket Estates Ltd v M'Phee* 1949 SLT (Notes) 35, OH. Both cases on landlords' title to sue relate to trespass and it appears never to have been expressly decided that a landlord has title to raise an action of ejection against a squatter, although it is thought that this result follows from first principles.
8 *Millar v Cathcart* (1861) 23 D 743. And it seems to follow that one *pro indiviso* proprietor is unable to raise an action for protection of possession against a fellow owner: see *Price v Watson* 1951 SC 359, 1951 SLT 266.
9 *Lade v Largs Baking Co Ltd* (1863) 2 M 17. See further para 29 above.
10 For licences to possession, see para 128 above.
11 Thus the licensee of land can interdict his licensor from trespassing; but only the licensor can interdict the trespass of a third party, although failure to do so might be in breach of the licence.
12 See paras 142–146 below.
13 See para 147 below.
14 See paras 148–150 below.

(b) Proof of Right: Sasine Land

142. Introduction. In an action for the protection of possession of land[1] the pursuer must prove that he holds a right to possession (*jus possidendi*) in relation to that land. Except in the case of actions of removing and ejection[2], however, there is probably no requirement that his title be completed by registration or, as the case may be, by possession[3], and an action lies equally in one who is uninfeft, for example the grantee of a delivered disposition or an executor after confirmation to a deceased's estate. In the case of Sasine land[4] proof of right to possession may be arduous and expensive. Indeed, the effort involved may sometimes be disproportionate to the benefit being sought. The law tries to meet this problem by prescribing an elaborate formula for proof of title which attempts to balance the legitimate interests of both pursuer and defender. Its basis is the proposition that in defended actions for the protection of possession there is a conflict as to the location of the real right to possession. The pursuer maintains that the right[5] is in him. The defender denies the pursuer's claim and may also claim a right to possession for himself. The formula then proceeds to grade the pursuer's task as to proof by reference to the averments made by the defender[6]. Three classes of defence are distinguished:
(1) where the defender denies the pursuer's right to the land without, however, averring any right in himself;

(2) where the defender avers that he has a right to the land but one which derives from the pursuer; and

(3) where the defender avers that he has a right to the land independent of and preferable to any right in the pursuer.

The evidence required of the pursuer then varies according to the class into which the defence falls. Only with class (3) defences is the pursuer put to a full proof of title. With defences of classes (1) and (2) he need show no more than a prima facie title, that is to say, a deed running in his favour, such as a disposition or lease, which bears to confer the right in question. Actual possession, past or present, is not required. A deed granted *a non domino* is a good prima facie title, with the result that a squatter or other possessor without right who takes the trouble to register an *a non domino* disposition can protect his possession against anyone but a defender falling into the third class.

The detailed rules now fall to be considered.

1 Other than an action founded on spuilzie, for which see paras 161 ff below. But see *Watson v Shields* 1996 SCLR 81.
2 See further LANDLORD AND TENANT, vol 13, para 494. The Scottish Law Commission has recommended that the requirement of a completed title in removings and ejections be abolished: see *Report on Recovery of Possession of Heritable Property* (Scot Law Com no. 118 (1989)) paras 620 ff.
3 *Mackie's Trustees v Reekie* (1832) 11 S 157; *Traill v Traill* (1873) 1 R 61 at 65, per Lord Neaves. This rule appears in a more resolute form in the context of possessory judgments: see para 146 below.
4 Ie land held on a title registered in the Register of Sasines.
5 Or at any rate *a* right, for there may be more than one.
6 Stair *Institutions* IV,26,15, gives the rules as follows: '[A]ny infeftment may remove a naked possessor, but cannot remove a possessor by infeftment, though posterior, unless the pursuer instruct his right immediately, or by progress from the King; or at least, that it is perfected by prescription, or that it hath continued in possession for seven years, and so hath the privilege of a possessory judgment, whereby the possession must be continued'.

143. Class (1) defence: no right. Where no right in respect of the land is averred by the defender, the pursuer is excused from showing more than a prima facie title[1]. Only the immediate deed in his favour need be produced. Evidence as to prior titles or as to possession for the period of positive prescription is not required. In *Mather v Alexander*, the leading modern authority, Lord Hunter explained the law thus:

'Can a member of the public claiming no right under a competing title . . . maintain that the deed [produced by the pursuer] proceeded *a non domino*? So far as he is concerned, must it not be taken as a good *prima facie* title which he is not in a position effectively to challenge? There are cases where a pursuer without necessarily having a title good against the world may say to a defender, "You at all events, have no interest to dispute the title I produce and to put me to an expensive proof of its validity"'[2].

In *Mather* itself the pursuer was held not bound to lead evidence of possession in support of his title; and while that decision appeared at one time to have been unsettled by two later decisions[3], it may now be regarded as good law[4]. The position may, however, be different where the defender, while not averring a title in himself, avers a title in some named third party[5].

1 *Colquhoun v Paton* (1859) 21 D 996 at 1001, per Lord Cowan.
2 *Mather v Alexander* 1926 SC 139 at 148, 1926 SLT 51 at 56.
3 *Leith-Buchanan v Hogg* 1931 SC 204, 1931 SLT 164; *Marquess of Ailsa v Monteforte* 1937 SC 805, 1937 SLT 614. *Leith-Buchanan* proceeded on an unjustifiably narrow view of the ratio in *Mather v Alexander*. In *Marquess of Ailsa* the proof of prescriptive possession followed on from a concession by counsel for the pursuers; and in a subsequent case it was doubted 'whether the pursuers were bound to lead evidence of prescriptive possession in the light of *Mather*' (*Wills' Trustees v Cairngorm Canoeing and Sailing School Ltd* 1976 SC (HL) 30 at 38, OH, per Lord Maxwell (affd IH and affd 1976 SC (HL) 30, 1976 SLT 162)).
4 It was reaffirmed in *Wills' Trustees v Cairngorm Canoeing and Sailing School Ltd* 1976 SC (HL) 30 at 37, 38, OH, per Lord Maxwell. It was also settled law before *Mather*, for which see : *Paterson v Marquis of*

Ailsa (1846) 8 D 752; *Colquhoun v Paton* (1859) 21 D 996 at 1001, per Lord Cowan; *Pirie v Rose* (1884) 11 R 490; *London, Midland and Scottish Rly Co v M'Donald* 1924 SC 835, 1924 SLT 630. In the most recent case, *Drumalbyn Development Trust v Page* 1987 SLT 379, where the Second Division was divided on the question of whether the defence contained relevant averments of title, the minority view, that there were no relevant averments of title, was not thought to excuse the pursuer from a proof of his own title. But this position appears to have been adopted without citation of the relevant authorities.

5 *Lock v Taylor* 1976 SLT 238, OH.

144. Class (2) defence: derivative right. Where the defender avers a right to the land but one which derives from the pursuer, the pursuer is excused proof of title; for the validity of the title of the defender necessarily supposes the validity of the title of the pursuer. The example most frequently encountered in practice is in actions of removing by a landlord against a tenant holding under a lease granted by the pursuer[1]. Stair suggests that in such a case the pursuer need not show even a prima facie title[2], so placing a tenant in a weaker position even than a squatter[3]. Similar rules operate where the titles of defender and pursuer, while not deriving one from the other, share a common root, and in cases of this kind the pursuer need do no more than trace his title back to the common root[4]. So in an action of removing a successor of the original landlord is required to show no more than the immediate disposition in his favour[5].

1 See LANDLORD AND TENANT, vol 13, para 493.
2 Stair *Institutions* IV,26,8: '[i]f the possessor have been introduced by the pursuer he cannot require any title for the removing at the pursuer's instance'. This view appears to have been adopted by the *Encyclopaedia of Scottish Legal Styles*: compare vol 8 sv removings with vol 4 sv ejection.
3 For which see para 143 above.
4 Stair IV,26,15; *Luss Estates Co v BP Oil Grangemouth Refinery Ltd* 1981 SLT 97, OH.
5 See LANDLORD AND TENANT, vol 13, para 494.

145. Class (3) defence: independent right. Only where the defender avers that he holds an independent and preferable right to possession is the pursuer put to proof of his title[1]. The defender's averments must disclose a prima facie title to the right founded upon[2]. A right is independent in the sense meant here if it does not derive from the pursuer[3]; and a right is preferable if it excludes the pursuer's own claim as rightful possessor. Only a real right to possession (*jus possidendi*) satisfies both conditions, and neither a personal licence to possession nor, it has been held, such subordinate rights as a servitude or public right of way[4] will put the pursuer to proof of title.

On being confronted by a defence of independent right the pursuer has, at least in theory, a choice as to how to proceed. On the one hand he can elect for a complete proof of title. On the other hand he can choose the less strenuous route of a possessory judgment. For the former course a prescriptive progress of titles accompanied by possession for the ten years of positive prescription is required[5]; for the latter a prima facie title and seven years' possession is sufficient. Possessory judgments are considered below[6]. For as long as the sheriff court was denied full jurisdiction in questions of heritable title, they were in widespread use; but when jurisdiction was finally granted to the sheriff court in 1907[7] they fell rapidly out of practice[8]. Any continuing utility was largely removed by the reduction of the period of positive prescription in 1970 from twenty to ten years[9]. Possessory judgments suffer from the serious disadvantage of settling only the question of interim possession leaving untouched any underlying conflict of title[10]. Often this is unsatisfactory, for in most cases a defender who puts forward a title of his own is not, or at any rate does not believe himself to be, a squatter or trespasser. On the contrary, he believes that he has a right to the land which excludes the right of the pursuer. In practice, actions of this kind are often boundary disputes between neighbours; and since the real issue between the parties is title rather than possession, success in a possessory action is of limited value. In a possessory action the pursuer is entitled to an award of interim possession if he has previously possessed for seven years, but the result is not *res judicata* as to questions of title, and the defender is free to commence new proceedings in which he may ultimately be successful[11].

1 Stair *Institutions* IV,26,15; *Colquhoun v Paton* (1859) 21 D 996 at 1001, per Lord Cowan.
2 Thus the description in the deed relied upon must be sufficiently wide to include the subjects in question: *Drumalbyn Development Trust v Page* 1987 SLT 379.
3 'Independent' is here opposed to 'derivative', for which see para 144 above.
4 *Wills' Trustees v Cairngorm Canoeing and Sailing School Ltd* 1976 SC (HL) 30 at 38, OH (affd IH and affd 1976 SC (HL) 30, 1976 SLT 162). But for a contrary view, see *Lord Saltoun v Park* (1857) 20 D 89 at 92, per Lord Ardmillan.
5 Prescription and Limitation (Scotland) Act 1973 (c 52), s 1 (amended by the Land Registration (Scotland) Act 1979 (c 33), s 10). See eg *Leith-Buchanan v Hogg* 1931 SC 204, 1931 SLT 164.
6 See para 146 below.
7 Sheriff Court (Scotland) Act 1907 (c 51), s 5(4).
8 H Burn Murdoch *Interdict in the Law of Scotland* (1933) para 88.
9 Conveyancing and Feudal Reform (Scotland) Act 1970 (c 35), s 8 (repealed). See now the Prescription and Limitation (Scotland) Act 1973, s 1 (as amended: see note 5 above).
10 In any case, interim possession can often be obtained by the alternative device of interim interdict.
11 See para 146 below.

146. The seven-year possessory judgment. For reasons which have already been explained[1], the seven-year possessory judgment is almost unknown in contemporary practice. Only a brief account is given here[2].

In order to obtain a possessory judgment two requirements must be satisfied. First, the land must have been possessed for seven years; and secondly, the possession must follow on and be attributable to a title which, prima facie at least, confers a right to possession (*jus possidendi*) on the pursuer. The possession required is often said to be of the same quality as for positive prescription[3]. It must be continuous and as of right. It must not be acquired or retained by force. It need not, however, be in good faith[4]. Indeed, good faith is a consequence rather than a cause of a possessory judgment, for a party who has obtained a possessory judgment is deemed a bona fide possessor until such time as his title is judicially set aside[5]. The period of possession is seven years and may include the possession of authors. The possession need not immediately precede the raising of the action provided that the pursuer has not been out of possession for seven years or more[6]. It is thought that where the possession being vindicated is natural possession the possession founded upon must itself be natural[7].

The possession must follow on a prima facie title to the subjects. Typically this is a disposition or a lease granted in favour of the pursuer. In the case of the former it is not necessary that the title be completed by registration[8].

The privilege of a possessory judgment may be claimed not only by the pursuer in an action in relation to land but also by the defender. Indeed, at one time it was commonly so used. Thus if A seeks to recover land which has been in the possession of B for seven years on a prima facie title, B is entitled to a possessory judgment and A's claim is, for the moment at least, defeated[9].

The effect of a possessory judgment, whether obtained by the pursuer or by the defender, is an entitlement to remain in possession unless and until the prima facie title is judicially set aside by reduction or declarator[10]: the seven years' possession gives rise to a presumption of validity of title which it is for a challenger to rebut[11].

1 See para 145 above.
2 For a more extended treatment, see J Rankine *The Law of Land-ownership in Scotland* (4th edn, 1909) pp 9–13 and H Burn Murdoch *Interdict in the Law of Scotland* (1933) paras 87–95. For the use of possessory judgments in the context of servitudes, see para 461 below.
3 Stair *Institutions* IV,26,3, speaks of 'seven years' lawful and uninterrupted possession'. On the nature of the possession required, see further *Maxwel v Ferguson* (1673) Mor 10628; *Calder v Adam* (1870) 8 M 645; *M'Kerron v Gordon* (1876) 3 R 429.

4 *Countess of Dunfermline v Lord Pitmedden* (1698) Mor 10630, which appears to be an authority to the contrary, may be explained on the basis of inversion of possession.

5 Stair IV,26,3. See also para 133 above.

6 Stair IV,26,4; Erskine *Institute* IV,1,49.

7 Conversely, civil possession is sufficient for an action of maills and duties: *Erskine* IV,1,49.

8 *Knox v Brand* (1827) 5 S 714 (NE 666); *Liston v Galloway* (1835) 14 S 97. The rule is the same for petitory actions: see para 142 above.

9 See eg *Porterfield v M'Millan* (1847) 9 D 1424; *Calder v Adam* (1870) 8 M 645.

10 Stair IV,26,3; *Erskine* IV,1,50; *Ferrier v Walker* (1832) 10 S 317; *Irvine v Robertson* (1873) 11 M 298.

11 Bankton *Institute* II,1,33.

(c) Proof of Right: Land on the Land Register

147. Effect of registration of title. In principle, the elaborate rules as to proof of title developed in the context of land registered in the Register of Sasines[1], are available also for land registered in the Land Register. In practice, however, they will only rarely be invoked, because under registration of title complete proof of right is peculiarly easy. Once land has been registered in the Land Register, the question of who is owner or, as the case may be, liferenter or tenant, is immediately and conclusively shown by an examination of the relevant title sheet. In consequence, it is both a necessary and also a sufficient condition of success in an action for protection of possession that the name on the title sheet is that of the pursuer[2]. It is a necessary condition because the person named on the title sheet alone holds the right in question; and it is a sufficient condition because, even where indemnity has been excluded by the Keeper[3] — and even, indeed, where the defender maintains that the Register is inaccurate[4] and that his own name should appear there in place of the pursuer's — the pursuer nevertheless remains the holder of the right in question unless and until the Register is rectified against him[5]. The only course open to an aggrieved defender is to seek rectification of the Register, for as long as the name of the pursuer remains on the title sheet he has no stateable defence to the pursuer's claim[6].

Short leases, that is leases for twenty years or less, do not appear on the Land Register[7], and a pursuer whose right to possession derives from a short lease must prove his title in the same way as for land registered in the Register of Sasines.

1 See paras 142–146 above.

2 Except where he is uninfeft (see para 142 above), in which case he must hold a grant from the person named on the title sheet.

3 Land Registration (Scotland) Act 1979 (c 33), s 12(2).

4 Ibid, s 9(1).

5 Ibid, s 3(1)(a). See further para 673 below.

6 But if the pursuer is in possession, rectification may be barred: ibid, s 9(3).

7 Short leases are overriding interests for the purposes of registration of title: ibid, ss 6(4), 28(1).

(d) Proof of Right: Corporeal Moveables

148. Introduction. In an action for the protection of possession of corporeal moveables the pursuer must show a right to possession (*jus possidendi*)[1], in practice usually the right of ownership[2]; and, since there is a presumption that the possessor of corporeal moveables is owner[3], the means by which ownership is established will depend upon whether the pursuer is in or out of possession or, to put the matter another way, upon whether the action is one in defence of existing possession or for the recovery of possession once held but now lost. These two actions require separate treatment[4].

1 See para 141 above. This rule does not apply where the action is founded in spuilzie: see paras 161 ff below.
2 See para 127 above.
3 See para 130 above.
4 See paras 149, 150, below.

149. Actions in defence of possession. The standard action in defence of existing possession is interdict[1]. Here the pursuer need do no more than establish current possession. He is then presumed to be owner and the burden of challenging his title passes to the defender, if he chooses to take it up.

1 See paras 191, 192, below.

150. Actions for recovery of possession. The usual action for recovery of natural possession of corporeal moveables is an action of delivery[1]. The extent to which the pursuer in such an action is called upon to prove his title depends upon the pleadings of the defender. Thus if the defender avers that he holds the goods on hire or pledge or on some other subordinate title bearing to derive from the pursuer, proof of title is excused because the validity of the title of the defender presupposes the validity of the title of his author[2]. The issue between the parties then resolves into whether the admitted subordinate title still subsists or has come to an end[3]. If, however, the defender avers that he holds on an independent title, or if without averring any title in himself he challenges the title of the pursuer, proof of the pursuer's title becomes necessary. Usually, the real issue between the parties then resolves into a competition as to ownership, and here the defender is at a considerable advantage, for as possessor he is presumed to be owner[4]. This presumption of ownership from possession places a double burden on the pursuer. Not only must he prove his own ownership by showing his own earlier possession, since in doing so he is merely discharging the burden of proof which always rests on a pursuer[5]. He must also show that the possession of the defender is consistent with the continuing existence of that earlier right of ownership[6]. In particular, he must show that the defender came into possession as a result of hire or loan or theft or of some other ground which does net imply ownership of the property. This rule may appear unfair to the pursuer, but it can be justified as being necessary to protect the position of the defender in view of the frequency and lack of formality with which corporeal moveables may change hands. Hume illustrates the problem with the following example:

'[T]ake the case of a horse which has been bought five or six times. How unjust it would be if the first owner were entitled to recover it from the last purchaser, if the latter do not prove all the different bargains which may have taken place'[7].

As possessor, the last purchaser is relieved from such a proof and it is for the first owner to demonstrate that his original ownership continues to subsist.

1 See further para 158 below.
2 The rule is the same in the case of land: see para 144 above.
3 *Hariot v Cuningham* (1791) Mor 12405.
4 See para 130 above.
5 Thus in the case of land, where no presumption of ownership arises from possession, proof of ownership by the pursuer has the effect of shifting the evidential burden to the defender who must then demonstrate that the ownership of the pursuer has come to an end. See Hume *Lectures* vol III (Stair Soc vol 15, 1952 ed G C H Paton) p 239.
6 Stair *Institutions* II,1,42; III,2,7; IV,21,5; IV,30,9 and 10; IV,45,17(VIII); Bankton *Institute* I,8,41; II,1,34; Erskine *Institute* II,1,24; Bell *Principles* ss 1314, 1320. The rule is illustrated by a large number of cases eg *Russel v Campbell* (1699) 4 Brown's Supp 468; *Scot v Elliot* (1672) Mor 12727; *Forsyth v Kilpatrick* (1680) Mor 9120; *Prangnell-O'Neill v Lady Skiffington* 1984 SLT 282.
7 *Hume* vol III, p 229.

(5) PROTECTION OF NATURAL POSSESSION: RECOVERY OF POSSESSION

(a) Introduction

151. Overview. This section considers the methods by which natural possession of property may be obtained or recovered by a person who is out of possession. The methods by which existing possession may be defended are considered later[1].

The question of title to sue in actions for the recovery of possession has already been considered[2]. In summary the rule is that natural possession of property may always be recovered by the holder for the time being of a right to possession (*jus possidendi*). Ownership, lease and liferent are the principal rights conferring a right to possession. Possession may also be recovered by a person who was dispossessed 'vitiously', that is to say, dispossessed by force or otherwise against his will, and without judicial warrant. In such a case no title is required beyond the fact of vitious dispossession[3]. Where a claim to possession is based on ownership or on some other right in the pursuer, the judicial remedies available are, in the case of land, ejection, removing or interdict[4], and in the case of corporeal moveables, delivery[5]. Where the claim is based on the fact of vitious dispossession, the judicial remedy, both for corporeal moveables and for land, is an action of spuilzie[6]. Sometimes a pursuer may be able to bring a claim under both heads, although in modern practice claims based on spuilzie are virtually unknown.

A pursuer is entitled not merely to the return of his property but to an accounting for the fruits of possession in respect of the period during which possession was wrongfully withheld. Where the wrongful possession was vitiously acquired, violent profits are due[7], but in all other cases, the liability of the outgoing possessor is restricted to ordinary profits only[8]. The outgoing possessor may himself have a claim in recompense in respect of expenditure on maintenance or improvement of the property[9]. Good faith may occasionally be relevant in establishing which of two parties in dispute is the rightful possessor[10] but it is not otherwise a defence in an action for recovery of possession. 'No person, though he should possess *optima fide*, is entitled to retain a subject not his own after the true owner appears, and makes good his claim to it; for the strongest *bona fides* must give way to truth'[11]. But good faith is a defence to a claim for either ordinary or violent profits[12].

Self-help may sometimes be available as an alternative to judicial remedies[13].

1 See paras 174 ff below.
2 See paras 138 ff above.
3 See para 162 below.
4 See paras 152–155 below.
5 See para 158 below.
6 See paras 161 ff below.
7 See para 169 below.
8 See para 168 below.
9 See paras 172, 173, below.
10 Ie by conferring a statutory good title on one who would otherwise have no title. See further paras 680 ff below. Good faith in such a case may have a special meaning: eg for the purposes of the Sale of Goods Act 1979 (c 54) a person is in good faith where he has acted honestly even although he may have been negligent (s 61(3)).
11 Erskine *Institute* II,1,25.
12 See para 171 below.
13 See paras 156, 160, 163, below.

(b) Recovery of Land founded on Right to Possession

152. Introduction. A person who holds a right to possession may recover land from a person who does not. The question of title to sue has already been considered[1]. A number of different remedies are available. Of the judicial remedies, actions of removing and actions of ejection, or their summary cause equivalent, are by far the most commonly encountered in practice, although interdict[2], where competent, is also sometimes found. Self-help is also lawful in certain circumstances[3]. Finally, it may be observed that the seizure of another's land without his consent will usually be a criminal offence in terms of the Trespass (Scotland) Act 1865 (c 56)[4].

1 See paras 138 ff above.
2 See para 155 below.
3 See para 156 below.
4 See *Paterson v Robertson* 1944 JC 166.

153. Removings and ejections distinguished. Removing and ejection are the normal judicial remedies for the recovery of land. From a procedural point of view the two remedies are similar, with the important difference that in the case of removings a preliminary notice to the defender is required[1]. A pursuer is not, however, free to choose between them. Ejection is available only in a limited number of circumstances. Where these circumstances do not obtain, removing must be used[2], although it seems that removing is always competent even where ejection might have been used[3]. The enumeration of the circumstances in which ejection may and may not be a competent remedy is not free from difficulty, but the position has been greatly simplified in practice by the introduction in 1976 of the summary cause procedure for sheriff courts. Under the 1976 rules[4] all actions for recovery of possession of land are to be disposed of under the summary cause procedure, except where containing a crave for payment of sums exceeding £1,500. The summary cause procedure makes no distinction between removings and ejections and so relieves the pursuer of the burden of selection between them.

Even after 1976, however, the distinction between removings and ejections remains of some importance, for three main reasons. First, the summary cause procedure does not apply to every case of recovery of possession of land[5]. In some circumstances the independent actions of ejection or removing continue to be used. Secondly, even under the summary cause procedure the distinction does not disappear entirely, for an accelerated procedure is available at the discretion of the sheriff where an action is in substance an action of ejection[5]. Finally, it appears to be the case, although the dearth of authority makes this conclusion somewhat speculative, that the remedies of interdict and self-help are available only in circumstances in which an action of ejection would also be available[6].

The distinction between ejections and removings is sometimes said to lie in the title or absence of title of the defender. But this is misleading, for it is the basis of all actions for the recovery of possession[7] that the pursuer is the rightful possessor and that the defender is not. If the possession of the defender is found to be of right, then, necessarily, the action will be dismissed regardless of whether it is a removing or an ejection. A more accurate way of expressing the distinction is to say that, whereas in removings the defender once had a right to possession, which has now expired, in ejections the defender has never possessed as of right[8]. This is probably as close as it is possible to approach to a statement of general principle. Certainly it has the merit of distinguishing the two paradigm cases — the tenant for whom an action of removing is necessary[9] and the squatter for whom an action of ejection is sufficient[10]. But it is not wholly accurate. Thus where the defender possessed on the basis of a personal licence which has now come to an end, ejection is available in some cases, contrary to the general rule, but not in others[11]. Ejection is also available to a purchaser against a seller once the disposition in his favour has been delivered[12] but probably not before then[13]. In cases such as these it is difficult to discern any guiding principle.

In practice, actions of removing almost always involve the relationship of landlord and tenant and they are considered further in that context[14].

1 Where the defender is a tenant, the notice has the additional function of preventing tacit relocation.
2 *Robb v Brearton* (1895) 22 R 885, 3 SLT 81; *Lowe v Gardiner* 1921 SC 211, 1921 1 SLT 44.
3 *Nisbet v Aikman* (1866) 4 M 284; *Marquis of Breadalbane v Cameron* 1923 SLT (Sh Ct) 6; *Earl of Eglinton v M'Luckie* 1944 SLT (Sh Ct) 21.
4 Sheriff Courts (Scotland) Act 1971 (c 58), s 35(1)(c) (amended by the Sheriff Courts (Scotland) Act 1971 (Private Jurisdiction and Summary Cause) Order 1988, SI 1988/1993); AS (Summary Cause Rules, Sheriff Court) 1976, SI 1976/476 (as amended).
5 See para 154 below.
6 See paras 155, 156, below.
7 Ie apart from spuilzie.
8 *Lowe v Gardiner* 1921 SC 211 at 218, 1921 1 SLT 44 at 47, per Lord Cullen.
9 See eg *Walker v Kerr* 1917 SC 102, 1916 2 SLT 277. Tenant includes subtenant: *Robb v Brearton* (1895) 22 R 885, 1895 3 SLT 81. The decision to the contrary in *South West Farmers Ltd v Gray* 1950 SLT (Sh Ct) 10 is *per incuriam*.
10 *Mather v Alexander* 1926 SC 139, 1926 SLT 51.
11 Ejection was held to be available in *Cairns v Innes* 1942 SC 164, 1942 SLT 129 (service occupancy) and in *Wallace v Simmers* 1960 SC 255, 1961 SLT 34 (licence), but not in *Lowe v Gardiner* 1921 SC 211, 1921 1 SLT 44; *Christie's Trustees v Munroe* 1961 SLT (Sh Ct) 41; and *Cook v Wylie* 1963 SLT (Sh Ct) 29 (purchaser possessing on missives).
12 *White v Stevenson* 1956 SC 84, 1956 SLT 194.
13 *Scottish Property Investment Co Building Society v Horne* (1881) 8 R 737.
14 See LANDLORD AND TENANT, vol 13, paras 462 ff.

154. Ejections. The action of ejection is often stated as being available where the defender possesses *vi clam aut precario* (by force, stealthily or precariously)[1]. But this is scarcely accurate. To say that ejection is available against possession acquired *vi aut clam* (vitious possession) is to confuse ejection in the sense discussed here with ejection in the sense of spuilzie[2]. Ejection in the sense discussed here is concerned solely with the title, or lack of title, of the defender and pays no regard to the manner in which his possession was originally acquired. Nor is it wholly accurate to say that ejection is available in all cases of possession *precario* for it has already been seen that in certain cases of precarious possession removing and not ejection is the proper remedy[3]. A better way of expressing the law is to say that ejection is available against a possessor without right in all cases where removing is not the required remedy, and that ejection is not otherwise available.

The sheriff court appears to have exclusive jurisdiction in actions of ejection[4]. The pursuer must aver, not only his own title but also the lack of title in the defender[5], and so long as he does so the competency of the remedy is not challengeable even by an averment of title on the part of the defender[6]. There is probably no power to order caution for violent profits[7]. Ejections must usually be taken under the summary cause procedure except where combined with a crave for payment of sums exceeding £1,500[8] or with some other crave such as interdict[9]. There are special rules for heritable creditors seeking to eject their debtors in enforcement of a standard security[10]. In actions of ejection taken under the summary cause procedure the sheriff is empowered to shorten or dispense with any period of time provided anywhere in the summary cause rules[11], a power of which it has been said that

'[t]heoretically, at least, there is nothing to prevent a summons being issued without *induciae* followed by a decree in absence with immediate extract and execution of diligence forthwith, leaving the defender with minimal information and no time to prepare for removal'[12].

Once decree is obtained and extracted execution of diligence proceeds at once without the need for a preliminary charge[13].

1 See eg *Hally v Lang* (1867) 5 M 951; *Lowe v Gardiner* 1921 SC 211, 1921 1 SLT 44.
2 In spuilzie 'ejection' refers to the past ejection of the pursuer rather than to the forthcoming ejection of the defender. See further paras 161 ff below.
3 For a full discussion of the different uses of removings and ejections, see para 153 above. For possession *precario*, see para 128 above.
4 *Middleton v Booth* 1986 SLT 450, OH. But the rule may be different if the action is combined with other conclusions. The rule is also different for ejections in the sense of spuilzie: see para 165 below.
5 *Hally v Lang* (1867) 5 M 951; *Lowe v Gardiner* 1921 SC 211 at 215, 1921 1 SLT 44 at 45, per Lord President Clyde; *Cairns v Innes* 1942 SC 164 at 171, 1942 SLT 129 at 133, per Lord President Normand. This is because the court must be satisfied from the pleadings that this is not a case for which a removing is the appropriate remedy.
6 *Asher v Macleod* 1948 SC 55, 1948 SLT 227.
7 *Inglis' Trustees v Macpherson* 1910 SC 46, 1909 2 SLT 363; *Mackays v James Deas & Son Ltd* 1977 SLT (Sh Ct) 10. See further A G M Duncan *Research Paper on Actions of Ejection and Removing* (Scot Law Com) (1984) para 6.4. But compare *Middleton v Booth* 1986 SLT 450, OH, which may confuse ejection in the present sense with ejection in the sense of spuilzie, for which (see para 165 below) caution for violent profits must be given.
8 Sheriff Courts (Scotland) Act 1971 (c 58), s 35(1)(c) (amended by the Sheriff Courts (Scotland) Act 1971 (Privative Jurisdiction and Summary Cause) Order 1988, SI 1988/1993) (substitution of the figure of £1,500).
9 A G M Duncan *Research Paper on Actions of Ejection and Removing* (Scot Law Com) (1984) para 7.19. Despite the word 'recovery', it is thought that an action is not outside the summary cause procedure merely because neither the pursuer nor his authors were formerly in possession of the land: para 7.16. On this compare *Prestwick Investment Trust v Jones* 1981 SLT (Sh Ct) 55 with *Bradford and Bingley Building Society v Walker* 1988 SLT (Sh Ct) 33 at 36.
10 If the creditor has issued a calling up notice or notice of default which has not been complied with, he proceeds by action of ejection: Heritable Securities (Scotland) Act 1894 (c 44), s 5. If he makes an application under s 24 of the Conveyancing and Feudal Reform (Scotland) Act 1970 (c 35) without seeking ejection, he proceeds by summary application. Finally, if he wishes to combine an application under s 24 with a warrant to eject, he proceeds by ordinary action. See AS (Amendment of Sheriff Court Ordinary Cause, Summary Cause, and Small Claims, Rules) 1990, SI 1990/661. See further D J Cusine *Standard Securities* (1991) para 8.23.
11 SCR, r 68A (added by SI 1980/455).
12 *Duncan* para 7.6.
13 On execution see further: *Duncan* ch 8; G Maher and D J Cusine *The Law and Practice of Diligence* (1990) para 9.93.

155. Interdict. While possession of land will usually be recovered by ejection or removing, or by the summary cause action for the recovery of possession of heritable property, it appears that interdict may sometimes be a competent alternative remedy. Interdict is attractive because of the speed with which an interim order can be obtained, and in recent years it has been found particularly useful in the context of industrial sit-ins[1]. The competency of interdict as a remedy is not, however, beyond doubt. For while the normal purpose of interdict is to prevent acts which have not yet been completed, in actions for repossession the act complained of, namely the possession of the defender, has already taken place and the remedy is in substance an attempt to enforce a positive obligation[2]. It may be of significance in this context that in all modern reported cases of interdict the defender has never been in possession for more than a few days[3]. However, in *Borrows v Colquhoun*[4], the leading case from the nineteenth century, the possession of the defenders had continued undisturbed for some two years prior to the petition. It was stated in *Borrows* that interdict was competent only because the defenders were no better than squatters. If the possession had been supported by a title of some kind the appropriate remedy would have been an action of removing[5]. It may follow from this line of reasoning that interdict is competent only in circumstances where an action of ejection (as opposed to an action of removing) would also be competent[6].

In addition to its use as an independent remedy, interdict against re-occupation is often found as a subsidiary crave in an action of ejection[7].

1 *Plessey Co plc v Wilson* 1983 SLT 139; *Caterpillar (UK) Ltd* 1987 GWD 14-516, OH. Where, as often occurs, sit-ins operate on a rota basis with employees entering and leaving frequently, they are perhaps better classified as cases of multiple trespass.
2 H Burn-Murdoch *Interdict in the Law of Scotland* (1933) para 126; but see also para 103 of that work. For a full discussion of the issues, see N R Whitty 'Positive and Negative Interdicts' (1990) 35 JLSS 453 and 510, especially at 510, 511. Interdict is of course competent where possession has not yet been taken: *Colquhoun and Cameron v Mackenzie* (1894) 22 R 23.
3 *Middleton v Booth* 1986 SLT 450, OH, and the cases cited at note 1 above.
4 *Borrows v Colquhoun* (1852) 14 D 791 (revsd 1 Macq 691, HL, on the ground that the defenders were lessees).
5 So interdict cannot be used to remove tenants: *Rankin v M'Lachlan* (1864) 3 M 128; *Johnston v Thomson* (1877) 4 R 868; *Alongi v Alongi* 1987 GWD 1-27, OH. See further LANDLORD AND TENANT, vol 13, para 470.
6 For which, see para 153 above.
7 A G M Duncan *Research Paper on Actions of Ejection and Removing* (Scot Law Com) (1984) para 7.19.

156. Self-help. In general, the policy of the law is opposed to self-help. '[P]rivate parties cannot right themselves, but, in order to avoid tumults and riots, must apply for redress to the judges or magistrates'[1]. Nonetheless *brevi manu* repossession of land is permissible in certain circumstances. Although not usually so expressed, the rule appears to be that the lawfulness of extrajudicial dispossession is measured by whether the appropriate judicial remedy would have been removing or ejection[2]. If the circumstances are such that removing is the appropriate judicial remedy, then *brevi manu* repossession is unlawful and founds a claim in damages even in the absence of injury to persons or property[3]. But where the appropriate judicial remedy is ejection, then repossession by self-help is not in itself unlawful[4], although any attendant injury or damage is actionable on general principles of delict[5]. In the case of dwelling houses, however, and subject to some exceptions[6], self-help is not permitted against a person whose possession was originally based on a contractual licence which has since come to an end[7].

The rules just described were developed in the nineteenth century. Unfortunately they do not sit easily with the older doctrine of spuilzie, which indeed appears largely to have been overlooked[8]. The result is a certain amount of confusion. In many cases, self-help, while perfectly lawful in the sense indicated above, namely of not giving rise to a claim in damages, will nonetheless be unlawful as a spuilzie. This is because self-help implies vitious dispossession[9] and vitious dispossession is usually a spuilzie. Some measure of practical reconciliation between the two doctrines may be possible. Thus it is not a spuilzie to seize back property which was itself seized, provided that the repossession takes place immediately after the original seizure[10]. So if B dispossesses A without A's consent, then it is not spuilzie for A to employ self-help against B if this is done at once. This rule covers a number of cases in practice. Moreover, even where *brevi manu* repossession by A is a spuilzie, the fact that A is the rightful possessor excludes a claim in violent profits against him[11], which removes much of the substance from the illegality. Of course, as the party despoiled of possession in such a case, B is entitled to have his possession restored; but since A, as rightful possessor, can promptly reverse the result of such an action by leading an action of ejection, the remedy is unlikely to commend itself to B.

1 Bankton *Institute* I,10,144. See also Stair *Institutions* II,1,22; IV,28,2; Erskine *Institute* II,1,23. It has been said that self-help should not be viewed as a normal alternative to an action of ejection: *Sinclair v Tod* 1907 SC 1038 at 1044, 15 SLT 113 at 115, per Lord Ardwall.
2 For the distinction between removing and ejection, see para 153 above.
3 *Brash v Munro and Hall* (1903) 5 F 1102, 11 SLT 231; Rent (Scotland) Act 1984 (c 58), s 23(1) (lease of a dwelling house). See also LANDLORD AND TENANT, vol 13, para 471. In relation to residential occupation, repossession occurring during the currency of a lease or licence is both a criminal and

also a civil wrong: Rent (Scotland) Act 1984, s 22 (amended by the Housing (Scotland) Act 1988
   (c 43), s 38) (criminal wrong); Housing (Scotland) Act 1988, ss 36, 37 (civil wrong).
4 *Macdonald v Duchess of Leeds* (1860) 22 D 1075; *Scott v McMurdo* (1869) 6 SLR 301; *Macdonald v
   Watson* (1883) 10 R 1079; *Sinclair v Tod* 1907 SC 1038, 15 SLT 113.
5 *Macdonald v Watson* (1883) 10 R 1079 at 1082, per Lord President Inglis.
6 Rent (Scotland) Act 1984, s 23A (added by the Housing (Scotland) Act 1988, s 40).
7 Rent (Scotland) Act 1984, s 23 (amended by the Housing (Scotland) Act 1988, s 39). This provision
   is necessary because the appropriate remedy for some cases of contractual licences is ejection: see
   para 153 above.
8 By the nineteenth century spuilzie was dormant. It passes unmentioned in the case law on self-help.
   For spuilzie, see paras 161 ff below.
9 Ie dispossession by force, or otherwise against the will of the possessor.
10 See para 163 below.
11 See para 169 below.

157. Removal of buildings. The remedies considered so far are directed at the
removal of persons. But unlawful possession may sometimes be accompanied by
building work, and in such a case the pursuer is entitled not only to the return of his
land but also to the removal of all buildings unlawfully erected thereon. In practice
most cases of unlawful erection are cases of encroachment by one neighbour on the
land of another. Usually in such cases the actual dispossession is comparatively slight
and the real possessory issue is defence rather than recovery. The remedy of removal
of buildings is considered further in that context[1].

Where on recovery of the property the pursuer does not choose to have unlawful
buildings removed he may incur liability to the defender on the principle of
recompense[2].

1 See paras 178, 179, below.
2 See para 173 below.

(c) Recovery of Corporeal Moveables founded on Right to Possession

158. Action of delivery. The normal judicial remedy for recovery of possession
of corporeal moveables is an action of delivery. Title to sue has already been
considered[1]. Usually the action is founded on some real right in the pursuer,
whether the right of ownership or some other right, for example pledge, which
confers entitlement to possession[2]. But delivery is also available to a person whose
right to possession is personal, although only in a question with the obligant in the
right. An example is a purchaser of goods under a contract in terms of which
ownership has not yet passed. In an action founded on a real right, the pursuer is
entitled to recover the property from the person currently in possession without
regard to the history of that possession or to considerations of good faith[3]. 'The
nature of a proper *rei vindicatio*, or real action for recovery of property, is that it
attaches to and follows the thing as the possession shifts from hand to hand'[4]. The
defender must relinquish possession and, in appropriate cases, seek a remedy against
his author. Where a possessor dies or is sequestrated, an action of delivery is available
against his executor or trustee, but in their capacity as possessors rather than as
judicial successors in title[5].

The right of the pursuer to follow his property through successive changes of
possession has as its counterpart[6] the obligations of the current possessor to make
delivery to the pursuer[7]. Traditionally this obligation is classified as restitution, and
is said to distinguish the action of delivery from its Roman law ancestor, the action
known as *rei vindicatio*, for in a *rei vindicatio* the possessor's obligation was purely
negative, being restricted to not withholding possession[8]. Indeed, although the

Roman law term is frequently found in the earlier case law it appears that *rei vindicatio* in the strict sense has not been received into Scots law[9]. At common law, the obligation 'to make delivery' does not seem to have included an obligation to trace the person to whom delivery should be made. But by statute, a person who knows, or reasonably ought to know, that goods in his possession are not his own must without unreasonable delay deliver them, or notify the fact of his possession, either to the person entitled to possession or to the police[10]. Failure to do so is a statutory offence[11] and may also amount to theft at common law[12].

There are four defences to an action of delivery, namely (1) that the defender is not or is no longer in possession[13], (2) that the defender is entitled to possession and the pursuer is not[14], (3) that the title of the pursuer to possession is no better than the title of the defender[15], and (4) that, while the defender has no title to possess, the title of the pursuer is vitiated by illegality[16]. Of these only the first is not in all circumstances a complete defence. Thus a party who, in the knowledge of his own lack of title, relinquishes possession, whether by alienation or by destruction, remains bound in restitution for the value of the thing formerly possessed unless or until it is vindicated from a subsequent possessor[17]. It is thought that the sale proceeds, if traceable, are held in constructive trust for the owner, which gives him a preferential claim in the event of the party's insolvency[18]. Good faith excludes a claim in restitution[19] although not a claim in recompense for any profits of the alienation[20].

Both the sheriff court and the Court of Session have jurisdiction in actions of delivery. If the action is raised in the sheriff court it must proceed under the summary cause procedure unless there is an additional crave for payment of money exceeding £1,500[21]. The action is taken under the small claims branch of that procedure if there is a claim in the alternative for payment of a sum of money not exceeding £750[22]. The Consumer Credit Act 1974[23] contains a number of special provisions in relation to repossessions arising out of hire purchase, conditional sale and consumer hire agreements. The original compulsitor for failure to comply with a decree for delivery was civil imprisonment but, in an application for warrant for imprisonment, the court now has discretion to recall the decree on which the application proceeds and make an order for the payment of a specified sum or make such other order as appears to the court to be just and equitable in the circumstances including a warrant to officers of court to search any premises and to take possession of, and deliver to the applicant, the goods in respect of which the decree was granted[24].

1　See paras 138–141 and 148–150 above.
2　Stair *Institutions* IV,3,45.
3　See eg *Scottish Central Rly Co v Ferguson & Co* (1863) 1 M 750; *Todd v Armour* (1882) 9 R 901.
4　Hume *Lectures* vol III (Stair Soc vol 15, 1952 ed G C H Paton) p 235.
5　For since *ex hypothesi* the thing was not the property of the original possessor, it is excluded from the assets of the executry or, as the case may be, the sequestration. See the Succession (Scotland) Act 1964 (c 41), s 14(1), and the Bankruptcy (Scotland) Act 1985 (c 66), s 31(1).
6　The term 'counterpart' is used loosely. Strictly the counterpart of an obligation of restitution is the right to recover the property from the particular obligant in question. The counterpart of a personal obligation is thus a personal right. But the personal right is ancillary to the right to recover from all possessors, which is a right *in rem*.
7　Stair I,7,1–9; Bankton *Institute* I,8,1; Erskine *Institute* III,1,10; Bell *Principles* s 1320. It has been pointed out by the Scottish Law Commission that right and correlative obligation are affected differently by negative prescription. Thus the right, at least where founded on ownership, does not prescribe for twenty years whereas the obligation of restitution prescribes after only five. See *Corporeal Moveables: Remedies* (Scot Law Com Consultative Memorandum no. 31 (1976)) para 7. But it is thought that nothing turns on this difference, for the obligation of restitution, although extinguished after five years, is continuously renewed by the mere fact of unlawful possession. Thus suppose that B is in unlawful possession of goods belonging to A. If after the expiry of five years B gives the goods to C there can be no doubt that A is entitled to recover from C for C is an unlawful possessor and subject to the obligation of restitution. It is submitted that A cannot be in an inferior

position if B, instead of giving the goods to C, retains them for himself. No doubt the obligation of restitution which arose at the moment when B first possessed has now been extinguished by short negative prescription. But the obligation of restitution is constantly renewed by the mere fact of possession. B still possesses and consequently remains subject to the obligation. For the same conclusion arrived at by a different route, see also D L Carey Miller *Corporeal Moveables in Scots Law* (1991) para 10.13.

8 *Stair* I,7,2; IV,3,45; IV,21,5; IV,30,8. For the relationship between vindication and restitution, see *Carey Miller* paras 10.01 ff.

9 *Stair* IV,3,45.

10 Civic Government (Scotland) Act 1982 (c 45), s 67(1), (3). See further para 548 below.

11 Ibid, s 67(6).

12 G H Gordon *The Criminal Law of Scotland* (2nd edn, 1978) paras 14-17–14-23.

13 *Gorebridge Co-operative Society Ltd v Turnbull* 1952 SLT (Sh Ct) 91. Possession is not used here in its technical sense and includes custody.

14 Ie that the owner or other rightful possessor is the defender and not the pursuer.

15 Ie that neither the pursuer nor the defender are rightful possessors.

16 This is the principle *in turpi causa melior est conditio possidentis*: Stair I,7,8.

17 *Stair* I,7,2; *Bankton* I,8,11; *Erskine* III,1,10; *Bell Principles* s 1320. For the position where the thing is manufactured by the possessor into a new product, see paras 559 ff below. As to how a successful claim for the value of the thing against a *male fide* possessor affects subsequent vindication from a third party actually in possession, see *Carey Miller* para 10.09.

18 *Jopp v Johnston's Trustee* (1904) 6 F 1028. See also W J Stewart *The Law of Restitution in Scotland* (1992) paras 611 ff.

19 Even where, the property having been consumed or destroyed by the defender, it cannot then be vindicated from some third party: *International Banking Corpn v Ferguson Shaw & Sons* 1910 SC 182 at 193, 1909 2 SLT 377 at 383, per Lord Ardwall; *North West Securities Ltd v Barrhead Coachworks Ltd* 1976 SC 68, 1976 SLT 99, OH. But see contra *Oliver and Boyd v Marr Typefounding Co Ltd* 1901 9 SLT 170, OH.

20 *Stair* I,7,11; *Erskine* III,1,10.

21 Sheriff Courts (Scotland) Act 1971 (c 58), s 35(1)(c) (amended by the Sheriff Courts (Scotland) Act 1971 (Privative Jurisdiction and Summary Cause) Order 1988, SI 1988/1993).

22 Sheriff Courts (Scotland) Act 1971, s 35(2) (substituted by the Law Reform (Miscellaneous Provisions) (Scotland) Act 1985 (c 73), s 18(1)); Small Claims (Scotland) Order 1988, SI 1988/1999, art 2.

23 Consumer Credit Act 1974 (c 39), ss 129, 133, 134 (s 129 amended by the Debtors (Scotland) Act 1987 (c 18), s 108(1), Sch 6, para 17).

24 Law Reform (Miscellaneous Provisions) (Scotland) Act 1940 (c 42), s 1. See also the Debtors (Scotland) Act 1987, s 100. See further DILIGENCE, vol 8, paras 347 ff.

159. Interdict and other judicial remedies. In the case of ships, aircraft, oil platforms, caravans and other substantial moveable structures, the real interest of a pursuer may be in having the defenders relinquish their unlawful possession rather than in securing redelivery. From a functional point of view, and from the point of view of the remedies which are required, structures of this kind are closer in nature to heritable property than to moveable property of more modest dimensions. Whether ejection, the normal possessory remedy for heritable property, is also available for moveable property has never been decided[1]. In two modern cases interdict was granted against the continued occupation of shipping in furtherance of an industrial dispute[2], but interdict may not be an appropriate remedy against occupiers of longer standing[3].

1 For ejection, see para 154 above.

2 *Phestos Shipping Co Ltd v Kurmiawan* 1983 SC 165, 1983 SLT 388; *Shell UK Ltd v McGillvray* 1991 SLT 667, OH.

3 See para 155 above.

160. Self-help. Unlike the case of land[1], it appears that self-help to recover moveables is not in itself unlawful, at least in the sense of founding a claim in damages[2]. But this general rule must be taken subject to three important qualifications. First, where the property is in a private house or on land to which the public at large does not have lawful access, its repossession will amount to trespass except where consent to enter has been granted[3]. Taken as a whole, therefore, the act is unlawful; but since the fact of trespass does not in itself give rise to a claim in damages[4] this may not appear as a serious discouragement. It is provided by the Consumer Credit Act 1974 that in the case of goods subject to a hire-purchase agreement, conditional sale agreement or consumer hire agreement which is a regulated agreement within the meaning of the Act[5], the creditor or owner may not enter any premises to take possession of goods except under an order of the court[6]. The second qualification is that, where self-help is accompanied by force, the use of force may be actionable in delict. But a person who has been forcibly dispossessed may himself use force, not only in defence of his property but in seeking its recovery where he has acted immediately and without delay[7]. Finally, self-help may often amount to spuilzie[8]. The interaction of self-help with spuilzie is considered elsewhere[9].

Further provision is made in the Consumer Credit Act 1974 in relation to hire purchase and conditional sale agreements which are regulated agreements within the meaning of the Act[10]. Where in the case of such an agreement the debtor has paid one-third or more of the total price of the goods[11], the creditor is not entitled to recover the goods from the debtor except on an order of the court[12]. If goods are recovered in contravention of this provision the agreement is considered to terminate and the debtor is released from all liability thereunder and may recover from the creditor all sums paid under the agreement[13]. The provision does not apply, and self-help remains lawful, where either at the time of repossession the debtor gives his consent[14] or where the agreement has already been terminated by the debtor[15].

1 See para 156 above.
2 D M Walker *The Law of Civil Remedies in Scotland* (1974) pp 46, 262–264. However, the rule has not been the subject of express decision.
3 See paras 180, 181, below.
4 See para 185 below.
5 'Regulated agreement' means a consumer credit agreement or consumer hire agreement (1) where the amount of credit (or in the case of hire the total amount of hire payments) does not exceed £15,000 and (2) which is not an exempt agreement: Consumer Credit Act 1974 (c 39), s 189(1). For consumer credit agreements and consumer hire agreements, see ss 8, 15 (amended by the Consumer Credit (Increase of Monetary Limits) Order 1983, SI 1983/1878, art 4, Sch, Pt II) (substituting the figure of £15,000). For exempt agreements, see the Consumer Credit Act 1974, s 16.
6 Consumer Credit Act 1974, s 92.
7 Stair *Institutions* II,1,20; Bankton *Institute* II,1,31; Erskine *Institute* II,1,23. The Scottish Law Commission has argued that reasonable force should be permitted in the recovery of property lost by theft or fraud even after a lapse of time from the actual dispossession. See *Corporeal Moveables: Remedies* (Scot Law Com Consultative Memorandum no. 31 (1976)) para 4.
8 For spuilzie, see paras 161 ff below.
9 See para 156 above.
10 For the meaning of regulated agreements, see note 5 above.
11 For this purpose the price includes any installation charge: Consumer Credit Act 1974, s 90(2).
12 Ibid, s 90(1).
13 Ibid, s 91.
14 Ibid, s 173(3). But prior consent, eg in the agreement itself, is insufficient.
15 Ibid, s 90(5).

(d) Spuilzie: Recovery founded on Vitious Dispossession

161. Introduction. A person who has been dispossessed vitiously is entitled to immediate reinstatement in his possession. Dispossession is vitious where it occurs without the consent of the possessor and without judicial warrant[1]. The basis of the right to reinstatement is the remedy which is known generically as spuilzie, and specifically as ejection[2] in the case of heritable property and as spuilzie in the case of moveables[3]. The generic usage ('spuilzie') is adopted in the present work. It should be emphasised that ejection in the sense of spuilzie is quite distinct from the modern substantive action of ejection[4]. Indeed different parties are 'ejected': in spuilzie 'ejection' refers to the past dispossession of the pursuer; in the modern substantive action it refers to the future dispossession of the defender.

If the volume of case law may be taken as a reliable guide, the remedy of spuilzie appears to have reached its highest point of development during the course of the seventeenth century. Stair treats of spuilzie in considerable detail, Bankton in rather less detail, and Erskine in less detail still. By the end of the eighteenth century the doctrine was already in decline. By the end of the nineteenth century it had practically disappeared[5]; and despite some recent interest in spuilzie in the context of hire purchase[6], there appears to be no reported case within the last two hundred years in which spuilzie may properly be regarded as the ground of decision. The reasons for this decline are not entirely clear, although several may be suggested. One is that greater civic order reduced the incidence of violent dispossessions. Another is that increased certainty as to title to property, and in particular to heritable property[7], removed a frequent source of dispute. A third reason is that other remedies were available to achieve with equal ease what had formerly been achieved by spuilzie.

The place of spuilzie in the modern law is therefore problematic. If it is accepted that common law remedies cannot fall into desuetude[8], then spuilzie exists still and continues to be available to a dispossessed party. Its discussion in the present tense is justified. Moreover, there remain even today circumstances in which spuilzie is the most fruitful remedy, and others indeed in which it is the only remedy. But as against this it may be conceded that the modern law of recovery of possession by self-help is not easily reconcilable with the rules of spuilzie[9], and as a result some doubt is cast on the present role of the remedy.

1 See para 164 below.
2 On ejection, see generally Stair *Institutions* I,9,25–27; IV,28,1–9; Bankton *Institute* I,10,145–149; Erskine *Institute* III,7,16; IV,1,15.
3 On spuilzie, see generally *Stair* I,9,16–24; IV,30,1–6; *Bankton* I,10,124–144; *Erskine* III,7,16; IV,1,15.
4 *Nisbet v Aikman* (1866) 4 M 284 at 291, per Lord Neaves; *Hally v Lang* (1867) 5 M 951. But it has been said, perhaps not entirely accurately, that the one is the 'linear successor' of the other (see *Price v Watson* 1951 SC 359 at 363, 1951 SLT 266 at 268, per Lord President Cooper). For the modern substantive action, see paras 153, 154, above.
5 In *Dickson v Dickie* (1863) 1 M 1157 at 1161 it is mentioned by Lord Justice-Clerk Inglis as being the appropriate (but not requested) remedy on the facts of that case.
6 *FC Finance Ltd v Brown & Son* 1969 SLT (Sh Ct) 41; *Mercantile Credit Co Ltd v Townsley* 1971 SLT (Sh Ct) 37. See also para 164 below.
7 By the end of the seventeenth century the beneficial effect of the establishment of the Register of Sasines in 1617 was becoming manifest.
8 See SOURCES OF LAW (FORMAL), vol 22, para 376. See also *Corporeal Moveables: Remedies* (Scot Law Com Consultative Memorandum no. 31 (1976)) paras 19–23.
9 See para 156 above.

162. Title of the pursuer. The title required of the pursuer is not entirely free from controversy. There is division in the case law, some cases holding that bare possession is sufficient to found an action in spuilzie[1] while others insisting that the pursuer show a right of some kind to the property[2]. Rankine occupies the middle ground between these views by requiring a title of the pursuer only where a title can be produced by the defender[3], but this position may be criticised as according with neither vein in the case law. It seems, however, that the law may be taken as settled, for it is the unanimous view of the institutional writers that possession alone is sufficient[4]. Thus according to Bankton:

'The pursuer's title, in an action of spuilie, is Possession of the goods . . . and if the possession was peaceable, even the true owner, seizing the goods from the possessor, will be liable in a spuilie . . . The party that is violently deprived of the possession must be first restored, and then the question of property considered . . .'[5].

Spuilzie is thus a possessory action[6]. All that is required of the pursuer is that he possessed the property at the time of the dispossession. This was the rule of Roman law in respect of possessory interdicts, which spuilzie is generally taken to resemble, and it is also the rule of the comparable action *mandament van spolie* in modern South African law[7].

If entitlement to the property is irrelevant for the pursuer, then it is irrelevant also for the defender. Ownership or other title to possession is no answer to an action of spuilzie[8]. The defender must return the property. The rule is *spoliatus ante omnia restituendus:* he who is despoiled must first be restored to his possession. The action is concerned with possession and not with right. But spuilzie is not *res judicata* as to possession[9]. Its purpose is merely to discourage possession taken vitiously; and a defender in an action of spuilzie who has, or believes himself to have, a good right to possession may proceed to enforce that right by means of a separate action[10].

1　*Montgomery v Hamilton* (1548) Mor 14731; *Lady Renton v Her Son* (1629) Mor 14733; *Gadzeard v Sheriff of Ayr* (1781) Mor 14732.
2　*Wishart v Arbuthnot* (1573) Mor 3605; *Gib v Hamilton* (1583) Mor 16080; *Mudiall v Frissal* (1628) Mor 14749; *Strachan v Gordons* (1671) Mor 1819. In *A v B* (1677) Mor 14751 the court professed itself undecided on the point. One reason for the confusion may be the rule that possession in moveables presumes ownership. It appears that a title was required for the brieve of dissasine, which is sometimes regarded as an ancestor of spuilzie: see H L MacQueen *Common Law and Feudal Society in Medieval Scotland* (1993) ch 5.
3　J Rankine *The Law of Land-ownership in Scotland* (4th edn, 1909) pp 21, 22.
4　Stair *Institutions* I,9,17; IV,28,2; Bankton *Institute* I,10,126; Erskine *Institute* IV,1,15. Stair's statement (I,9,19) that spuilzie is elided 'if the defender meddle with goods by a title or warrand from any other party to whom they belonged' must be taken as eliding the claim for violent profits only: see para 169 below. See also D L Carey Miller *Corporeal Moveables in Scots Law* (1991) paras 10.23, 10.24.
5　Bankton I,10,126.
6　And moreover a possessory action of the kind which requires no title in the pursuer: *Stair* IV,26,2; *Erskine* IV,1,47. For possessory actions, see para 139 above.
7　H Silberberg and J Schoeman *Law of Property* (2nd edn, 1983) pp 135–146. See also T W Price *The Possessory Remedies in Roman-Dutch Law* (1947).
8　Nonetheless in practice self-help by an owner is a usual and justifiable remedy: see paras 156, 160, above.
9　Bankton I,10,126; Erskine IV,1,15.
10　See paras 152–155, 158, above.

163. Quality of pursuer's possession.

The property must be in the possession of the pursuer at the time when the spuilzie is alleged to have taken place. 'Possession' here is used strictly, and mere custody is not sufficient[1]. Nor is a right to possession which is not accompanied by actual possession[2]. But possession does not necessarily imply current physical detention, and possession *animo solo*[3] is sufficient. The spuilzie of land held *animo solo* is sometimes referred to as intrusion[4]. Typically the pursuer in an action of spuilzie was in natural possession at the time when the property was taken, but civil possession is also a sufficient title except in respect of a claim for violent profits[5].

In Roman law the possessory interdicts were not available to a person whose own possession was vitious in a question with the person now carrying out the act of dispossession. Thus if A stole from B, B could recover the property by self-help without incurring the risk that A might use the possessory interdicts against him. The rule in Scots law appears to be different, and self-help for the recovery of property is justified only when it is used immediately after the initial act of dispossession. Thus:

'[T]he possessor against whom the violence is used may also use force on his part to maintain his possession, in the same manner that he might in defence of his life. But after he has lost the possession, however unwarrantably, he cannot use force to recover it, unless he do it *ex continenti* . . ., but must apply to the judge, that he may be restored by the order of law. For society could not subsist if it were permitted to private men *jus sibi dicere,* to do themselves right by the methods of force'[6].

1 For the difference between possession and custody, see para 125 above. Carey Miller's narrow view of the meaning of possession leads him to a narrow view of the remedy of spuilzie as excluding those holding property on the basis of a contractual right: see D L Carey Miller *Corporeal Moveables in Scots Law* (1991) p 220.
2 A F Rodger 'Spuilzie in the Modern World' 1970 SLT (News) 33 at 35.
3 For possession *animo solo,* see para 122 above.
4 Stair *Institutions* I,9,25; IV,28,1; Erskine *Institute* II,7,16. See further W M Gordon *Scottish Land Law* (1989) para 14–24.
5 Stair I,9,26; IV,28,3; Bankton *Institute* I,10,146; *Bruce v Bruce* (1628) Mor 3609; *Steill v Hay* (1666) Mor 3611; *Campbell v Glenorchy* (1668) Mor 10604. See also *Mercantile Credit Co Ltd v Townsley* 1971 SLT (Sh Ct) 37.
6 Erskine II,1,23. See also Stair I,9,26; II,1,22; IV,28,2; *Bankton* I,10,147; Bell *Principles* s 1319. But cf Erskine IV,1,15, and J Rankine *The Law of Land-ownership in Scotland* (4th edn, 1909) p 22. For other limitations on the use of self-help, see paras 156, 160, above.

164. Vitious dispossession. The pursuer must have been dispossessed without his consent, with the result that the possession of the defender is 'vitious'. Vitious possession includes, but strictly is wider than, possession *vi aut clam*[1], for it is easy to envisage circumstances in which possession is taken openly and without violence and yet without the consent of the person dispossessed. The absence of consent refers to the taking and not to the retaining, and a person who takes with consent but subsequently declines to yield up possession lawfully demanded — a hirer of a car, for example, who refuses to return it — is not a vitious possessor. It may sometimes be a nice point as to whether consent has truly been given. Thus possession is probably by consent where a legally binding undertaking was given to yield possession, as for example in a contract of sale or hire, if the actual act of dispossession was not attended by violence[2]. But possession is not considered to be by consent if the consent was fraudulently obtained[3].

If property has both a natural and a civil possessor, it appears that consent by the natural possessor alone is sufficient to prevent a claim in spuilzie[4]. This is because the underlying basis of the remedy is that people should not take the law into their own hands, and this is not violated in circumstances where the defender was given possession by the person in physical control of the property. This seems to have been overlooked in two modern hire purchase cases the facts of which were said to amount to spuilzie[5]. Briefly, the facts were that A, the owner of a car, entered into a contract of hire purchase with B; B, who was in natural possession, defaulted in his hire instalments and sold the car to C, a motor dealer; and C then sold on to D, a private individual who gained a good statutory title in terms of section 27 of the Hire Purchase Act 1964[6]. In these circumstances it was argued that C had spuilzied the car from A who was the person in civil possession at the time when C took delivery. But this argument fails to notice that the delivery of the car to C was the voluntary act of B, the natural possessor[7].

Dispossession carried out under judicial warrant is not spuilzie, whether consent is given or not. So it is not spuilzie for a creditor to poind his debtor's goods or for a landlord to resume possession of his land following the award of the appropriate court decree.

1 Erskine *Institute* II,1,23: 'Possession is got *clam* when one, conscious that his right in the subject is disputable, and apprehending that he will not be suffered to take open possession, catches an

occasion of getting into it surreptitiously, or in a clandestine manner, without the knowledge of the owner . . . Violent possession is when one turns another masterfully, or by force, out of possession, and puts himself in his place'.

2 Stair *Institutions* IV,29,9.

3 *Erskine* II,1,27.

4 *Stair* I,9,20; IV,28,7.

5 *FC Finance Ltd v Brown & Son* 1969 SLT (Sh Ct) 41; *Mercantile Credit Co Ltd v Townsley* 1971 SLT (Sh Ct) 37. Spuilzie was not, however, the ground of the ultimate decisions in those cases.

6 Hire Purchase Act 1964 (c 53), s 27 (substituted by the Consumer Credit Act 1974 (c 39), s 192(3)(a), Sch 4, para 22, and amended by the Sale of Goods Act 1979 (c 54), s 63(1), Sch 2, para 4). See further para 683 below.

7 The court may have been misled by the unjustifiably wide definition of spuilzie, as any act which denies the pursuer's right to possession, which is adopted in D M Walker *The Law of Delict in Scotland* (2nd edn, 1981) pp 1002–1011. Another case in which spuilzie was mistakenly relied on is *Mackinnon v Avonside Homes Ltd* 1993 SCLR 976, OH.

165. Remedies. Two distinct remedies are available in an action founded on spuilzie[1]. First, the pursuer is entitled to the immediate return of his property. In the case of moveable property, but not apparently in the case of heritage[2], spuilzie constitutes a *vitium reale* so that property can be recovered even from purchasers in good faith[3]. Where the property cannot be restored, the entitlement is to its value. In the second place, the pursuer is in most cases[4] entitled to violent profits in respect of the period of wrongful possession. Violent profits are discussed below[5].

If the action is raised in the sheriff court the summary cause procedure must be used except where there is an additional crave for payment of money exceeding £1,500[6]. In the Court of Session the action may proceed by summary petition[7]. Where violent profits are sought, caution must be given by the defender[8].

1 Stair *Institutions* I,9,16; Erskine *Institute* III,7,16. For the form of an action of ejection, see Stair IV,29,5; 4 *Encyclopaedia of Scottish Legal Styles* (1936) p 353; W J Dobie *Styles for Use in the Sheriff Courts in Scotland* (1951) p 138.

2 *Stair* IV,30,3.

3 *Stair* I,9,16; IV,30,3. But this has been disputed: see D L Carey Miller *Corporeal Moveables in Scots Law* (1991) para 10.25.

4 But not where

  (1) the possession of the pursuer is civil only (see para 163 above),

  (2) the property was returned immediately by the defender (*Stair* I,9,23; IV,29,7; Bankton *Institute* I,10,140; *Erskine* IV,1,15), or

  (3) the defender has a right to possession, whether public or private (see para 169 below).

5 See para 169 below.

6 Sheriff Courts (Scotland) Act 1971 (c 58), s 35(1)(c) (amended by the Sheriff Courts (Scotland) Act 1971 (Privative Jurisdiction and Summary Cause) Order 1988, SI 1988/1993).

7 Court of Session Act 1988 (c 36), s 45.

8 Ejection Caution Act 1594 (c 27); *Stair* IV,28,8.

166. Place of spuilzie in modern law. In order to succeed in an action founded on spuilzie a pursuer need prove only two things, namely his own original possession and the subsequent and vitious act of dispossession by the defender[1]. Simplicity is indeed one of the main attractions of the remedy. Not only is spuilzie the only remedy open to a person whose original possession was not based on right[2], but it is also an additional and valuable remedy even for the rightful possessor. In practice the second is more important than the first, and spuilzie is much more likely to be used by an owner against a thief[3] than by a thief against an owner. The reasons are readily apparent. A thief who seeks judicial repossession from an owner on the ground of spuilzie will succeed[4], but his success will be shortlived. For, if he can prove his ownership, the owner is entitled to an order for immediate redelivery[5]. In contrast, an owner who seeks judicial repossession from a thief is not only afforded a permanent remedy, but is excused the task, which is a requirement of remedies based on right[6], of proving the fact of his ownership.

1 See para 162 above.
2 See paras 115, 140, above.
3 Or by an owner against a squatter.
4 It has been suggested, however, that the owner might be assoilzied if he set up his title in defence and proved it. See W M Gordon *Scottish Land Law* (1989) para 14-23.
5 See para 158 above.
6 See para 141 above.

(e) Claims Arising on Recovery of Possession

(A) CLAIMS OF THE PARTY RECOVERING POSSESSION

167. Introduction. The rightful possessor is entitled not merely to the return of his property but to an accounting for the income or other fruits of the period in which possession was wrongfully withheld. Usually only the income actually produced during that period ('ordinary profits') is due[1] but in a small number of cases there is entitlement to attributed income calculated at a penal rate ('violent profits')[2]. The two claims are juridically distinct, although both may be founded in unjustified enrichment[3]. Sometimes certain further claims may also arise[4]. Good faith on the part of the unlawful possessor is a defence to a claim for either ordinary or for violent profits[5].

1 See para 168 below.
2 See para 169 below.
3 Certainly this is often true of ordinary profits. But see para 168, note 9, below. For violent profits, see J W G Blackie 'Enrichment and Wrongs in Scots Law' 1992 Acta Juridica 23.
4 See para 170 below.
5 See para 171 below.

168. Ordinary profits. By ordinary profits is meant the income actually arising during the period of unlawful possession of property. Where the possession begins with the consent of the rightful possessor but that consent is later withdrawn[1], ordinary profits are due from the time when the withdrawal of consent is notified to the possessor[2]. Where the possession has never been of consent, ordinary profits are due for the full period of possession[3].

The claim for ordinary profits is measured by the extent to which the unlawful possessor has been enriched[4]. Familiar examples of ordinary profits include crops grown on land, the young of animals, honey from bees, and, where the possession enjoyed is civil rather than natural, rent[5] or feuduty[6]. Industrial growing crops[7] may be claimed despite the fact that they may have involved the possessor in both money and skill[8]. Where profits arise in a tangible form, as in the case of crops still growing or newly harvested, the obligation of the defender is to make delivery to the rightful possessor[9]. But where the profits are not, or are no longer, tangible the obligation resolves into one to make an accounting[10]. A defender must account for fruits which he did not trouble to collect and which are not now capable of collection[11].

Profits which are attributable less to the thing unlawfully possessed than to the skill and enterprise of the person possessing need not be accounted for. '[I]ndustrial and artificial profits, in so far as they arise from the haver's industry and not from the thing, fall not under restitution'[12]. Whether a product of skill is considered to come within the exclusion is a question of degree. Thus industrial growing crops, despite involving the application of skill, are viewed as more the product of the land possessed than of the person possessing and must be accounted for. But goods manufactured with an unlawfully possessed machine, or the proceeds of a tennis tournament won through the use of a stolen racket, would, it may be assumed, fall outside the definition of ordinary profits. Examples less easy to classify may readily be figured.

In practice the thing possessed may often fail to produce any income at all and yet the possessor has still been enriched, at least in the sense of enjoying possession. Thus a squatter who occupies a house or a thief who drives a stolen car is enriched not only by the thing itself (which he must return) but by the use made of the thing. The one is living rent free; the other has free use of a car. Gloag's view was that

> '[I]f property is used in the knowledge that its owner did not intend it to be used gratuitously, an obligation to pay for it will be inferred by law. Thus where land is occupied without any lease a sum equivalent to rent is due'[13].

It is thought that this view may now represent the law[14].

1 Eg a licence or other contractual right to possession. Payment for possession during the contractual period depends on the terms, express or implied, of the contract.
2 Or, in the case of a contractual right not terminable at will, when the contract comes to an end. But in the case of leases violent profits are due if the possessor then fails to remove, and there may be an argument that the same ought to be true in the case of contractual rights. See para 169, note 4, below.
3 If the person in right of possession was also the immediately previous possessor, the absence of consent will result in spuilzie and so in a claim for violent profits. See para 169 below.
4 Stair *Institutions* IV,30,7; Hume *Lecutures* vol III (Stair Soc vol 15, 1952 ed G C H Paton) p 240. From this it follows that expenditure of an income nature may be set off by the defender against a claim for profits: see para 172 below. But capital expenditure is as a general rule recoverable only by a bona fide possessor (who is not in any event liable for the profits of his possession): see para 173 below. It has, however, been said that a claim for profits attributable to capital improvements carried out by the possessor can only be made under deduction of the cost of the improvements: *Barbour v Halliday* (1840) 2 D 1279 at 1284, OH, per Lord Cuninghame.
5 See eg *Smith v Beaton* 6 Feb 1810 FC.
6 See eg *Moir v Glen* (1831) 9 S 744.
7 Industrial growing crops are such crops as require annual seed and cultivation: see para 595 below.
8 Erskine *Institutions* II,1,26.
9 Ie for tangible profits are the property of the lawful possessor, whether, as in the case of natural fruits, because of accession or, as in the case of industrial fruits, because the unlawfulness of the possession is considered to confer original ownership on the person entitled to possession. This is thus a vindicatory rather than an enrichment claim.
10 *Denholm's Trustees v Denholm* 1984 SLT 319, OH.
11 *Erskine* II,1,26; *Hume* vol III, p 240.
12 *Stair* I,7,10.
13 W M Gloag *The Law of Contract* (2nd edn, 1929) p 329.
14 *York Buildings Co v Mackenzie* (1795) 3 Pat 378, HL; *Earl of Fife v Wilson* (1864) 3 M 323; *Denholm's Trustees v Denholm* 1984 SLT 319, OH (for which see also para 24 above); *Rochester Poster Services Ltd v A G Barr plc* 1993 SCLR 588, 1994 SLT (Sh Ct) 2; *GTW Holdings Ltd v Toet* 1994 SLT (Sh Ct) 16. The first case may have been decided on the principle of breach of fiduciary duty rather than of unlawful possession.

169. Violent profits. In the usual case of unlawful possession, the liability of the possessor is for ordinary profits only. But violent profits are exigible where the possession was either obtained or retained vitiously[1]. 'Violent profits are so called, because they arise from violent attaining or retaining of possession, and are partly persecutory, partly penal'[2]. Possession is obtained vitiously where the initial act of possession amounts to spuilzie; and possession is retained vitiously, at least in the restricted sense meant here, where a tenant of land refuses to remove at the end of his lease[3], and perhaps in some other cases also[4]. Violent profits are not due in the former case where the spuilzie was committed by the owner of the property or other rightful possessor[5].

The quantum of violent profits is the amount which the property might be made to yield by the utmost industry[6]. Traditionally, this was said to be double rent for land[7] within burghs[8], and it may be that the rule now applies to all cases involving land[9]. Where property is of a kind that no profit can be made even by the utmost industry — Stair gives corn as an example[10] — then there is no liability for violent profits.

1 Stair *Institutions* I,9,16; IV,29,1; Erskine *Institute* III,7,16. For vitious possession, see para 164 above.
2 Stair IV,29,2.
3 Stair II,9,44; IV,29,4; *Erskine* II,6,54. See further LANDLORD AND TENANT, vol 13, paras 505 ff.
4 It has been said that violent profits are always due for possession without title (*Houldsworth v Brand's Trustees* (1876) 3 R 304 at 310, per Lord Justice-Clerk Moncreiff) but this seems too broadly stated and would undermine the distinction between ordinary profits and violent profits. See also *Inglis' Trustees v Macpherson* 1910 SC 46, 1909 2 SLT 363; *Scottish Parcel Services Ltd v Sherwood Business Centres (UK) Ltd* 1989 SCLR 321, Sh Ct. A modified version of the same view is that violent profits are due when a contractual right on which possession was based has come to an end and the possessor fails to relinquish the property. However, *Stair* IV,30,7, can be read as meaning that, in the case of moveables, violent profits are due only where possession was vitiously obtained and not where it was obtained with consent but retained vitiously.
5 Stair I,9,19; Bankton *Institute* I,10,134; *Erskine* IV,1,15.
6 Stair II,9,44; *Bankton* I,10,133.
7 Whether built upon or not: *Jute Industries Ltd v Wilson and Graham Ltd* 1955 SLT (Sh Ct) 46.
8 Stair I,9,27; II,9,44; *Bankton* I,10,147; *Erskine* II,6,54. Burghs were abolished in the local government reorganisation of 1973: Local Government (Scotland) Act 1973 (c 65), s 1(5).
9 Stair IV,29,3.
10 Stair I,9,16; IV,30,7.

170. Other claims. A person from whom possession has been unlawfully withheld may have a claim in delict in respect of consequential loss. Certainly this is so where the loss consists of physical injury to the thing unlawfully possessed, so that a defender who damages the property in his possession must meet the cost of its repair. In such a case the injury is pursued for not as an autonomous wrongful act, although it may also qualify on that account, but as loss directly consequent upon an earlier wrongful act, namely the taking or retaining of possession. In the result, liability is in effect strict[1]. Whether a claim is also competent in respect of economic loss — the hotel bills, for example, of a dispossessed landowner — is uncertain[2]. Where, as in the case of hire or lease, the relationship between the parties is regulated by contract, damages may additionally or alternatively be available under the head of breach of contract[3].

1 Good faith is probably irrelevant.
2 But see *Howard v Muir* (1870) 8 SLR 6; *Aarons & Co Ltd v Fraser* 1934 SC 137, 1934 SLT 125; *Saeed v Waheed* 1995 SCLR 504, 1996 SLT (Sh Ct) 39.
3 *Houldsworth v Brand's Trustees* (1876) 3 R 304; *Tod v Fraser* (1889) 17 R 226; *Scottish Parcel Services Ltd v Sherwood Business Centres (UK) Ltd* 1989 SCLR 321, Sh Ct.

171. Defence of bona fide possession. The meaning of bona fide possession has already been considered[1]. A typical case in practice is a boundary dispute or other competition of title between two parties both of whom consider themselves as owner but where the court ultimately finds in favour of the party who is not in possession. The possession of the unsuccessful party is then explained as having been without right but bona fide[2].

Good faith is a complete defence to a claim for violent profits and a partial defence to a claim for ordinary profits. The role of good faith in relation to violent profits is not discussed further here. It is sufficient to observe that a possessor vulnerable to a claim for violent profits will only rarely be in good faith and then usually in a question between landlord and tenant[3].

So far as ordinary profits are concerned, a bona fide possessor is entitled to keep all fruits to which his imagined title, if good, would have given right[4]. Although this rule is usually found expressed in the context of land it is equally applicable to corporeal moveables[5]. The policy of the law is that a person who possesses in good faith should not be asked to account for fruits by one whose tardiness in asserting his own right allowed their consumption or gathering to take place[6].

The extent to which fruits may be retained in any given case depends upon the nature of the title on which the possession was believed to proceed. A person who believed himself owner has a more extensive entitlement than a person who believed himself merely liferenter[7] or tenant[8]. Occasionally the nature of the supposed title may exclude entirely any claim to fruits. Thus a person hiring a horse for a pantomime has, it is suggested, no right to any foal which it may produce in the excitement of performance. Difficult questions may sometimes arise, for example with minerals or with trees, as to which products constitute the thing possessed (and so must be returned) and which the fruits of the thing (and so may be retained)[9]. In all cases fruits must be applied in the first instance for the maintenance of the property and for other necessary expenditure of an income nature: only net fruits may be retained[10].

Entitlement to fruits is lost with good faith[11] but the loss is not retrospective. A possessor remains entitled to the fruits of his bona fide possession. The rules for determining which fruits fall within the period of bona fide possession are complex and depend upon whether the fruits are industrial, natural or civil. For industrial growing crops[12] it is sufficient that the possessor was in good faith at the time of sowing. The rule is *messis sementem sequitur:* the crop follows the sower. One who sows in good faith is entitled to reap the crop in bad faith[13]. There appears to be no authority applying a similar rule to corporeal moveables but it might be argued that the young of animals should be treated in the same manner as industrial fruits, at least where the bona fide possessor owns the male or pays for the serving of the female. For natural fruits the rule is different but uncertain. Stair and Hume, following the rule of Roman law, require good faith at the time of consumption so that fruits not consumed or otherwise disposed of at the onset of bad faith must be returned to the rightful possessor[14]. Bankton and Erskine, however, require good faith only at the time of perception, so that only fruits not actually separated need be returned, and consumption is unnecessary[15]. A choice between these views has yet to be made by the courts, but modern writers have generally supported the second view[16]. Finally, the rule for civil fruits, such as rents or feuduty, is different again. Civil fruits are considered to accrue from day to day[17] and a possessor is accordingly entitled to those fruits accruing up to the day on which good faith is ultimately lost. Arrears may be sued for even after the loss of good faith[18].

1 See paras 131 ff above.
2 A typical case, but not the only case. See W M Gordon *Scottish Land Law* (1989) para 14–51; D L Carey Miller *Corporeal Moveables in Scots Law* (1991) para 6.06.
3 Typical is the case of a tenant whose lease has come to an end while genuinely and reasonably believing it to remain current. See further *Houldsworth v Brand's Trustees* (1876) 3 R 304, and LANDLORD AND TENANT, vol 13, para 511.
4 J Rankine's view (*The Law of Land-ownership in Scotland* (4th edn, 1909) pp 76, 77) that this is an application of the rule that possession presumes ownership appears to mistake a rule of evidence for a rule of substantive law.
5 *Carey Miller* paras 6.04 ff. The strictures of Bankton *Institute* I,8,19, notwithstanding, the case law has followed Erskine *Institute* II,1,26, in extending the rule to incorporeal property: see eg *Ferguson v Lord Advocate* 1906 14 SLT 52, OH.
6 Stair *Institutions* I,7,12; II,1,23; *Erskine* II,1,25.
7 In *Darling's Trustees v Darling's Trustees* 1909 SC 445, 1909 1 SLT 207, the First Division refused to apply the principle of bona fide perception to a liferenter on the basis that the income in such a case is not the fruit but rather the thing itself. But it is submitted that this decision is incorrect and that with a liferent, as with any other *jus possidendi*, the 'thing' is the corporeal object to which the *jus* relates and the income thereof is the fruit of that thing. See also *Gordon* para 14–49.
8 *Erskine* II,6,22.
9 Aid may be obtained here from the more extensive case law on liferent and fee where similar difficulties occur. See LIFERENT AND FEE, vol 13, para 1639. However, since a liferenter is bound by the principle of use *salva rei substantia*, the rules may not be identical: see *Carey Miller* paras 6.12b, 6.12c.
10 *Cleghorn v Eliott* (1842) 4 D 1389. See also *Anderson v Anderson* (1869) 8 M 157.
11 For the ways in which good faith may be lost, see para 137 above.
12 For the meaning of industrial growing crops, see para 595 below.
13 *Bankton* I,8,18; *Erskine* II,1,26.

14 *Stair* I,7,10; Hume *Lectures* vol III (Stair Soc vol 15, 1952 ed G C H Paton) pp 240, 241.
15 *Bankton* I,8,18; *Erskine* II,1,25.
16 *Gordon* para 14-48; *Carey Miller* para 6.07.
17 Apportionment Act 1870 (c 35), s 2 (amended by the Statute Law Revision (No 2) Act 1893 (c 54)).
18 *Bonny v Morris* (1760) Mor 1728.

(B) CLAIMS OF THE PARTY FROM WHOM POSSESSION IS RECOVERED

172. Maintenance. In Roman law the person relinquishing possession had a claim for expenditure incurred in respect of necessary acts of maintenance. Good faith was not required. Rankine supports the existence of a similar rule in Scots law[1]. Bankton would allow a claim to a bona fide possessor for 'Necessary expenses, *ie*, such as save the house from perishing or growing worse'[2]. The law cannot, however, be regarded as settled[3]. There falls to be deducted from any claim for maintenance all fruits actually received[4]. The claim is accompanied by a right of lien or retention[5].

1 J Rankine *The Law of Land-ownership in Scotland* (4th edn, 1909) pp 89, 90.
2 Bankton *Institute* I,9,42. But cf I,8,15.
3 *Binning v Brotherstones* (1676) Mor 13401.
4 *Bankton* I,8,15.
5 *Bankton* I,8,15 and I,9,42.

173. Improvements. One who possesses unlawfully but in good faith has, on relinquishing possession, a claim in recompense for any improvements that have been carried out to the property[1]. The meaning of possession in good faith has already been considered[2]. By improvements are meant such permanent additions to the property as have by the law of accession become a part thereof[3]. The amount due is the amount by which the party reclaiming possession has been enriched, but under deduction, it has been suggested, of all fruits actually received by the bona fide possessor, except insofar as attributable to the improvements[4]. The improvements themselves cannot be removed because they belong to the owner of the principal thing[5]. So if A in good faith builds a house on land belonging to B or fits a new engine to a car belonging to C, the house accedes to the land and the engine to the car and must be returned with them subject only to a claim in recompense.

Not all improvements give rise to a claim. Only those made in the belief that they will enure to the benefit of the maker in his imagined capacity as owner, tenant[6] or other lawful possessor come within the rule. He must have expected to benefit from the improvements, either permanently or at least for a substantial period of time, and to have been disappointed in that expectation. This excludes not only possession held in male fide[7], but also bona fide possession on an imagined title so transient[8], or with so short a term left to run, that donation to the owner must necessarily be presumed. According to Hume, another case excluding recompense is where the improvements are 'of a fanciful sort, or such as are suited only to the particular taste and humour of the late possessor'[9].

In security of the claim for improvements there is a right of retention of or lien in the subjects improved[10]. This right, which applies to land as well as to corporeal moveables, depends upon possession and is lost with it; but a court will not require possession to be given up until the claim for recompense is satisfied. Loss of the lien does not imply loss of the claim which it secures. It has been suggested that the lien may be personal and hence not binding on a party acquiring title to the property after the improvements have been carried out[11].

Recompense for improvements is not confined to cases of unlawful possession, and similar rules apply in two other cases. One is where possession was on a subsistent but voidable title which has subsequently been avoided[12]. The other is where possession on the basis of one right, such as a right of liferent, was believed to be on the basis of a higher right, such as a right of fee. Good faith is required in both cases.

1 Stair *Institutions* I,8,6; Bankton *Institute* I,8,15; Erskine *Institute* III,1,11; Bell *Principles* s 538.
2 See paras 131 ff above.
3 Additions which have not acceded remain the property of the possessor and can be removed.
4 *Bankton* I,8,15. This is also the rule in South African law: H Silberberg and J Schoeman *Law of Property* (2nd edn, 1983) p 153.
5 Ie by accession: *Stair* II,1,40; *Bankton* I,9,42. This was treated as an open question in *Barbour v Halliday* (1840) 2 D 1279 at 1284, per Lord Cuninghame (the Lord Ordinary), and in *Duke of Hamilton v Johnston* (1877) 14 SLR 298 at 299, per Lord President Inglis, but these decisions were made under the former rule, now displaced, which generally excluded accession in the case of temporary possessors. See para 582 below.
6 Contrast here the position of one who is indeed tenant or other temporary but lawful possessor. Such a person is deemed to carry out any improvements for his own benefit as lawful possessor and is denied a claim in recompense at all: see eg *Wallace v Braid* (1900) 2 F 754.
7 *Erskine* III,1,11; Bell *Principles* s 538; *Barbour v Halliday* (1840) 2 D 1279; *Buchanan v Stewart* (1874) 2 R 78; *Duke of Hamilton v Johnston* (1877) 14 SLR 298. The contrary view is expressed by *Stair* I,8,6; II,1,40.
8 Eg a lease for six months.
9 Hume *Lectures* vol III (Stair Soc vol 15, 1952 ed G C H Paton) p 171. See also *Bankton* I,9,42 ('Voluptuary expences laid out only for decorement').
10 *Bankton* I,9,42; II,9,68; *Binning v Brotherstones* (1676) Mor 13401; *Barbour v Halliday* (1840) 2 D 1279. In Roman law the right of retention was the basic right and no direct claim for improvement was possible.
11 *Beattie v Lord Napier* (1831) 9 S 639. But in *Beattie* the possession appears to have been in male fide.
12 *Binning v Brotherstones* (1676) Mor 13401; *Trade Development Bank v Warriner and Mason (Scotland) Ltd* 1980 SLT 49, affd 1980 SC 74, 1980 SLT 223.

(6) PROTECTION OF NATURAL POSSESSION: DEFENCE OF POSSESSION

(a) General

174. Overview. An earlier section considered the recovery of possession by one who is out of possession[1]. This section now considers the methods by which existing possession of property may be defended against challenge.

The question of title to sue in actions in defence of possession has already been discussed[2]. The rule, in summary, is that natural possession may always be defended by that person who is for the time being rightful possessor of the property under dispute. Ownership, lease and liferent are the principal rights conferring the right to possession (*jus possidendi*) and hence legitimising possession.

Defence of possession is based upon the principle of absolute exclusivity: an owner or other lawful possessor is entitled to the peaceful use of property free from intrusion by others[3]. The principle is unaffected by the fact that a particular use of the property is neglected by the owner or that the use proposed by the intruder is harmless in itself. As Bell expresses the rule, an owner

'may prevent others from coming on his land for taking fuel, however necessary to them, and however inexhaustible the supply; or from hunting on his land, or setting foot upon it, or encroaching, however inoffensively'[4].

Subject to the defences noted below[5], the use of another's property without his consent is a civil, and in some cases also a criminal, wrong. So far as land is concerned, the civil wrong is known as either trespass or encroachment, depending upon whether the threat to possession is temporary and transient (trespass) or permanent or quasi-permanent (encroachment). Trespass and encroachment are both part of the same legal family and the distinction between them has no strictly legal significance, but, since they give rise to different kinds of problems in practice, it is convenient to discuss them separately[6]. 'Trespass' in Scots law is a term confined to the law of heritable property and does not include, as it does in English law, assault and other acts against the person.

Most cases of defence of possession concern land. However, the issue may also arise in connection with corporeal moveables, when, it is thought, analogous rules apply[7].

1 See paras 151 ff above.
2 See paras 138 ff above.
3 Erskine *Institute* II,1,1.
4 Bell *Principles* s 943.
5 See paras 176, 177, 181, below.
6 For encroachment, see paras 175 ff below. For trespass, see paras 180 ff below.
7 See further paras 191, 192, below.

(b) Encroachment

175. Definition. Encroachment is the permanent or quasi-permanent intrusion into land which is owned or otherwise lawfully possessed by another person[1]. Encroachment is always by things, whether, as typically, by a building, or by property of some other kind. Permanent intrusion by a person is not encroachment and is subject to a different set of rules[2]. In practice, cases of encroachment are almost always cross-boundary disputes between immediate neighbours, the paradigm example being where one person constructs a building partly on his own land and partly on land belonging to his neighbour.

It has been said of encroachment that 'a proprietor is not entitled to encroach upon his neighbour's property even to the extent of driving a nail into it'[3]. In one case the projection of a cornice a few inches beyond the central line of a mutual gable was found sufficient to give rise to a remedy[4]. Nor does it matter that no harm, actual or prospective, results from the encroachment[5]. But while the extent of the encroachment and the degree of harm sustained are not relevant to the question of whether a wrong has been committed in the first place, they may be relevant to the question of remedy[6].

Many different and varied examples of encroachment have come before the courts. Some cases concern the building of a wall wholly or partially on land belonging to someone else[7]. Others deal with the projection of cornices[8]. Probably the most frequently litigated subject has been signposts, in which connection it has been repeatedly affirmed by the courts that there is no right to erect a signpost on a wall belonging to another, even where the wall is part of a close giving access to the property to which the sign relates[9]. Encroachment is not, however, confined to building works, and many other examples exist. It is, for example, encroachment to deposit or abandon goods on land belonging to another[10]. In one well-known case from the late eighteenth century the defender was ordained to prune branches from trees in his garden which protruded over the wall into the garden of his neighbour[11]. Equally, it is encroachment to grow plants and trees in such a way that their roots penetrate into the adjoining garden[12]. In the absence of the servitude of stillicide, it is the encroachment to build so close to the boundary that the rainwater from the roof falls into a neighbour's land[13].

1 Possession in this context means natural possession. So it is encroachment if a landlord builds on land leased to a tenant, although in practice such a case would normally be viewed as breach of contract (ie of the lease).

2 The issue involved in such a case is recovery of possession rather than its defence. See further paras 152 ff above.

3 *Leonard v Lindsay and Benzie* (1886) 13 R 958 at 964, per Lord Young.

4 *Miln v Mudie* (1828) 6 S 967.

5 *Hazle v Turner* (1840) 2 D 886.

6 See para 178 below.

7 *Sanderson v Geddes* (1874) 1 R 1198; *Jack v Begg* (1875) 3 R 35; *Brown v Baty* 1957 SC 351, 1957 SLT 336, OH.

8 *Miln v Mudie* (1828) 6 S 967; *Hazle v Turner* (1840) 2 D 886.

9 *Thomson v Crombie* (1776) Mor 'Public Police' App No. 1; *Lowrie v Drysdale* 13 May 1812 FC; *Buchanan v Carmichael* (1823) 2 S 526 (NE 460); *Alexander v Butchart* (1875) 3 R 156. But see *Murdoch v Dunbar* (1783) Mor 13184.

10 Hume *Lectures* vol III (Stair Soc vol 15, 1952 ed G C H Paton) pp 204, 205.

11 *Halkerston v Wedderburn* (1781) Mor 10495.

12 Bell *Principles* s 942.

13 Erskine *Institute* II,9,9; *Bell* s 941.

176. The defence of consent. Consent is a complete defence, for it is of the essence of encroachment that the intrusion should be without permission of the owner or other rightful possessor. Consent may be given expressly. Alternatively, it may be implied by actings amounting to acquiescence so that the owner becomes personally barred from asserting his ownership[1]. So in *Duke of Buccleuch v Edinburgh Magistrates*[2] the defenders were held barred from objecting to pillars in the front elevation of the Assembly Rooms in Edinburgh's George Street which had been positioned on ground belonging to them more than thirty years previously[3].

Consent, whether granted expressly or implied by actings, is personal to the party granting it. As a general rule, successors in the land are not bound by such consent and are free to object even to encroachments which have been in place for a number of years[4]. In practice, this means that a person wishing to build on a neighbour's land cannot rely on personal consent but must seek to obtain a real right in that land[5].

Two qualifications may be made to the rule that consent does not transmit against successors. First, it has been suggested that a successor may be bound by the acquiescence of a predecessor if either he had notice of the encroachment or if the encroachment was obvious[6], but the law is not settled beyond doubt[7]. Secondly, the fact that consent was given at the time when the encroachment was first made may lead the court to refuse an application for removal of the encroachment which is made at the instance of a successor; but in such a case a claim will still lie in damages[8]. However, even if the defender is entitled to maintain the encroachment, it is not clear that he is entitled, without some further right such as servitude, to make use of it[9], although this issue is only likely to be important in the case of substantial encroachments involving all, or a large part of, a building or other structure[10].

1 See generally W M Gloag *The Law of Contract* (2nd edn, 1929) pp 167–171.

2 *Duke of Buccleugh v Edinburgh Magistrates* (1865) 3 M 528.

3 For other examples, see *Sclater v Oddie* (1881) 18 SLR 495; *Wilson v Pottinger* 1908 SC 580, 15 SLT 941; *Strathclyde Regional Council v Persimmon Homes (Scotland) Ltd* 1996 SLT 176, OH.

4 See eg *Ross v Martin* (1888) 15 R 282.

5 See para 177, head (1), below.

6 *Gloag* pp 170, 171; *Brown v Baty* 1957 SC 351, 1957 SLT 336, OH. The authorities relied on by Gloag are not, however, cases involving encroachment.

7 J M Halliday 'Acquiescence, Singular Successors and the Baby Linnet' (1977) 22 JR 89 at 92, 93. The issue has arisen incidentally in a number of cases but without being fully argued. See *Macnair v Cathcart* (1802) Mor 12832; *Taylor & Co v Smellie* (1869) 6 SLR 677; *Sanderson v Geddes* (1874) 1 R 1198. Much the same issue arises with pipeline servitudes (aqueduct), although there the question is usually presented as being whether the defender has the right to exercise the servitude rather than whether he can insist on keeping the pipeline. See *Macgregor v Balfour* (1899) 2 F 345, 7 SLT 273; *Robson v Chalmers Property Investment Co Ltd* 1965 SLT 381, OH; *More v Boyle* 1967 SLT (Sh Ct) 38. See also para 462 below.

8 See para 178 below.

9 For accession will confer ownership on the pursuer: see para 179 below.

10 In the typical case the encroachment is only to the extent of a wall or part of a wall and the question of use does not really arise.

177. Other defences. Apart from the defence of consent, four other defences are available in reply to an action founded on encroachment. These are:

(1) *Exercise of a right.* The defender may hold some right in respect of the land in dispute which legitimises his encroachment. Indeed, the land may even turn out to belong to him, for disputes ostensibly about encroachment are sometimes really disputes as to the true boundary between two properties[1]. Even if the land was not the defender's at the time of the initial intrusion the effect of ten years' possession on a *habile* title will be to confer a good title by operation of positive prescription. Other possibilities are that the defender has a lease over the land, or perhaps a servitude[2] or other real condition[3], although in general real conditions are not apt to permit permanent possession of the servient tenement[4].

(2) *Act of Parliament.* Encroachment may be authorised by statute. An example is the right of a proprietor of a tenement flat to apply to the sheriff for warrant to install necessary pipes in other parts of the tenement building[5].

(3) *Common gables.* Where individual plots of ground in a town or city are sold off by a landowner for the purpose of building houses, and where it is agreed that the houses to be built are to form a single continuous line, then the proprietor of any one plot is entitled to build his gable wall one half on his own ground and one half on the ground belonging to his neighbour[6]. This is a rule which was determined by Victorian building practices and is of little importance today.

(4) *Negative prescription.* There is an argument that the right to object to encroachments prescribes after twenty years, although the point is not free from doubt[7]. There is further uncertainty as to whether prescription would be affected by changes in the ownership of the land encroached upon.

1 Eg *Hetherington v Galt* (1905) 7 F 706, 13 SLT 90.
2 The permanent use of land belonging to another is not a recognised servitude: *Alexander v Butchart* (1875) 3 R 156; *Mendelssohn v The Wee Pub Co Ltd* 1991 GWD 26-1518, Sh Ct. But such a right may arise as an incidental part of another servitude. Eg the servitude of aqueduct carries with it a right to install pipes and other structures on the servient tenement, while it has been held that a servitude of way through a close includes a right to attach a sign to the wall: see *Walker's Trustees v Learmonth & Co* (1824) 3 S 288 (NE 202); *Cunningham v Stewart* (1888) 4 Sh Ct Rep 255.
3 In *M'Arly v French's Trustees* (1883) 10 R 574 the right to place a sign-board partly on another's wall was regarded, rather unconvincingly, as a right of common interest explained by use for the prescriptive period. Of this case Rankine justly observes that 'the reasons given for the decision do not appear to bring the case within any known doctrine of the law of property': see J Rankine *The Law of Land-ownership in Scotland* (4th edn, 1909) p 136.
4 That, certainly, appears to be the rule in the case of real burdens: see para 391 below.
5 Civic Government (Scotland) Act 1982 (c 45), s 88.
6 See para 218 below.
7 Prescription and Limitation (Scotland) Act 1973 (c 52), s 7 (amended by the Prescription and Limitation (Scotland) Act 1984 (c 45), s 5(3), Sch 1, and the Consumer Protection Act 1987 (c 43), s 6, Sch 1, Pt II, para 8). Negative prescription applies in what might be considered the analogous case of nuisance: *Harvie v Robertson* (1903) 5 F 338, 10 SLT 581. The counter-argument is that the right to object to encroachments is one of the rights consequent on *dominium* and is *res merae facultatis* within Sch 3(c) of the Prescription and Limitation (Scotland) Act 1973.

178. Judicial remedies. Where a proprietor or other lawful possessor of land has reasonable grounds for supposing that encroachment is about to take place, interdict is available and will almost always be granted. The fact that building work has actually started does not preclude an interdict, provided that the petition is brought before the building is substantially completed. Demolition of buildings and any other steps necessary to restore the possessory right of the petitioner may competently be ordered by the Court of Session in the course of a petition for interdict[1].

Where an act of encroachment has been completed by the erection of a building or some other structure, the position of the parties is more complex. In principle, a party encroached upon is entitled to have the encroachment removed. In practice, the court has a discretion to withhold this remedy, a discretion which is quite frequently exercised. It may sometimes be possible to circumvent this discretion by proceeding extrajudicially[2]. The discretion invested in the court has been described thus:

'. . . there is an equitable power vested in the Court in virtue of which, when the exact restoration of things to their previous condition is either impossible or would be attended with unreasonable loss and expense, quite disproportionate to the advantage it would give to the successful party, the Court can award an equivalent, — in other words, they can say upon what equitable conditions the building should be allowed to remain where it is, although it has been placed there without legal right'[3].

The cases indicate that the court is unlikely to exercise its discretion unless the encroachment is slight and its perpetrator acted in the belief that it was unobjectionable[4]. Consent by the then owner of the land will be a factor in favour of the discretion in a question with successors[5] and so will the fact that some reasonable use of neighbouring property depends on the encroachment being allowed to remain in place[6]. The most recent case[7] gives some indication of the circumstances in which the discretion will be exercised. In the course of conversion of the defenders' premises for use as a fish and chip restaurant an external flue was attached to a gable wall which belonged to the pursuer. The wall was windowless and the flue could not be seen from the pursuer's property. The flue was essential for the extraction of fumes and smells from the restaurant and the court accepted that it was impractical for it to be located elsewhere. Without the flue the restaurant would be obliged to close, although no doubt the premises could be used for some other purpose. The flue had been in position for nine years and permission for its erection had been given by a predecessor in title of the pursuer. In these circumstances the First Division felt justified in exercising its discretion and refusing to order the removal of the flue.

In addition to, or — in cases where its discretion has been exercised — instead of, ordering the removal of an encroachment, the court may also make an award of damages[8].

1 Court of Session Act 1988 (c 36), s 46. On the predecessor of this provision, see *George Heriot's Trust v Carter* (1903) 10 SLT 514, OH; *Maersk Co Ltd v National Union of Seamen* 1988 SLT 828, OH; *Stirling Shipping Co Ltd v National Union of Seamen* 1988 SLT 832, OH.
2 See para 179 below.
3 *Jack v Begg* (1875) 3 R 35 at 43, per Lord Gifford, and approved in *Grahame v Kirkcaldy Magistrates* (1882) 9 R(HL) 91.
4 *Davidson v Thomson* (1890) 17 R 287 at 292, 293, per Lord M'Laren; *Wilson v Pottinger* 1908 SC 580, 15 SLT 941; *Forbes v Inverurie Picture House Ltd* (1936) 53 Sh Ct Rep 43; *Anderson v Brattisani's* 1978 SLT (Notes) 42; *Stockton Park (Leisure) Ltd v Border Oats Ltd* 1991 SLT 333, OH.
5 *Anderson v Brattisani's* 1978 SLT (Notes) 42.
6 It seems to be taken for granted in cases such as this that the defender will be entitled to make use of the encroaching structure, although why he is able to use a structure part or all of which may belong to the pursuer, by accession, is not explained. See further para 179 below.
7 *Anderson v Brattisani's* 1978 SLT (Notes) 42.
8 For quantum, see *Forbes v Inverurie Picture House Ltd* (1936) 53 Sh Ct Rep 43; *Alvis v Harrison* 1989 SLT 746 (revsd 1991 SLT 64, HL, where the defender's actions were held to be a valid exercise of his right of servitude); *Strathclyde Regional Council v Persimmon Homes (Scotland) Ltd* 1996 SLT 176, OH.

179. Extrajudicial remedies. The availability of extrajudicial remedies depends to a considerable extent on the ownership of the thing which is alleged to have encroached. However, ownership is not always easily determined. Where the thing encroaching is obviously moveable — machinery, for example, or industrial growing crops — then it continues to belong to the person responsible for the encroachment. But in many cases the thing, while originally moveable, has become heritable by accession[1]. The relevant law is then complex and not altogether certain. An initial distinction must be made between encroaching property which rests entirely on the land of the party encroached upon and property which straddles the boundary, resting partly on the land encroached upon and partly on the land of the encroacher. In the former case, the law seems clear. The encroaching property accedes to the land and so belongs to the party encroached upon. In the latter case, there is a dearth of authority and the applicable law may depend on the nature of the encroaching property.

In the case of trees and other natural fruits straddling a boundary, a clear rule is given both in Roman law[2] and in Roman-Dutch law[3]. The rule is that where the roots penetrate to a material extent both pieces of land, the tree is the common property of both owners. Otherwise, the tree belongs solely to the owner of the land in which the roots are situated. This rule was considered and rejected by the Court of Session in *Hetherington v Galt*[4]. Instead, the court preferred a rule based on the siting of the stem of the tree. Where the stem was on the boundary the tree was common property. Where the stem was on one side of the boundary it was the sole property of the owner on that side. The location of the roots was said to be of no greater significance than the location of the branches. This approach can be criticised for overlooking the fact that accession is brought about in the first place, not by the stem or the branches, but by the drawing of nourishment through the roots[5]. Accordingly the analogy drawn between roots and branches is not convincing, and it is difficult to see why the location of the stem should be regarded as of greater importance than the location of the roots.

There appears to be no authority dealing with buildings erected across a boundary. If the rule for trees is to be regarded as of general applicability, then such buildings will be the common property of the proprietors on both sides[6]. It seems unlikely, however, that this is the law. Such a rule might possibly be workable in respect of substantial encroachments, but it seems unreasonable that a building built only to a small extent on neighbouring property should then be the common property of both proprietors; and if a distinction were attempted between substantial encroachments and slight encroachments, it is not obvious where the dividing line should lie. It is suggested that the position is in fact governed by the normal rules of accession, with the consequence that each proprietor is sole owner of that part of the building erected on his own land[7].

The question of ownership largely determines the availability of extrajudicial remedies. There are, as has been observed, four possibilities. The thing encroaching may belong solely to the person encroached upon; or it may belong partly to the person encroached upon and partly to the encroacher; or it may belong to both parties together as common property; or, finally, it may belong solely to the encroacher.

If the thing belongs solely to the person encroached upon, he is free to do with it as he wishes, unless he consented to the encroachment or is taken to have acquiesced in it[8]. He can destroy it:

'[o]ne may *brevi manu*, or at his own hand, without public authority, destroy or demolish any thing built or done upon his ground without his consent, or a servitude, tho' he sustain no detriment thereby'[9].

Alternatively he can leave it standing and use it for his own purposes[10]. The encroacher has no right to make use of it, and can, if necessary, be restrained as a trespasser.

If the thing belongs partly to one party and partly to the other, the rule is probably the same so far as concerns the part owned solely by the person encroached upon. So if a person constructs a building partly on his own land and partly on the land of his neighbour, he has no rights over the building insofar as it is built on his neighbour's land. He cannot even object to its demolition, except where either the law implies an obligation of support[11] or where the demolition is such as to be actionable in delict[12]. If this is correct, it will be seen that the party encroached upon may be better served by extrajudicial than by judicial remedies. For if he asks that the defender be ordered to remove the encroachment, a court may, in the exercise of its discretionary powers, refuse the application[13]. If, however, he chooses to remove the encroachment himself he cannot, it seems, usually be prevented by the court[14].

Where the thing is the common property of both parties the position is regulated by the usual rules of common property[15]. These prevent alteration or destruction by one party without the consent of the other. Probably the only example of common property arising out of encroachment is trees or other natural fruits whose stem extends on both sides of the boundary. Such trees and fruits cannot be uprooted by one party acting without the consent of the other[16], and nor, arguably, can branches be removed beyond normal acts of pruning[17].

The final possibility is that the thing is owned solely by the encroacher. Sole ownership may come about in one of two ways: the thing may be moveable property, or alternatively the thing may be heritable property but with foundations wholly within the encroacher's own land, the encroachment being some part of the structure which projects beyond the foundations and across the common boundary. Since the thing belongs to the encroacher it cannot lawfully be destroyed by the party encroached upon. But where the thing is moveable there seems no reason why it should not be returned *brevi manu* to the encroacher. So far as heritable encroachments are concerned it is necessary to distinguish trees and plants from buildings. In the case of trees and plants there is authority that the person encroached upon is entitled both to cut off overhanging branches and to sever roots which have penetrated his soil[18]. However, branches and roots so severed are not his. In the case of buildings self-help is probably excluded[19]. This is because the removal of an overhanging section of a building inflicts permanent damage on the building itself. A court order must be sought instead.

1 For accession, see paras 570 ff below.
2 *Digest* 41,1,7,13; Justinian *Institutes* II,1,31.
3 H Silberberg and J Schoeman *The Law of Property* (2nd edn, 1983) p 215.
4 *Hetherington v Galt* (1905) 7 F 706, 13 SLT 90.
5 See para 595 below.
6 This is true both under the Roman law and Roman-Dutch rule and the rule adopted in *Hetherington v Galt* (1905) 7 F 706, 13 SLT 90.
7 Stair *Institutions* II,1,40; *Jack v Begg* (1875) 3 R 35 at 44, per Lord Gifford; *Crichton v Turnbull* 1946 SC 52, 1946 SLT 156. But cf *Duke of Buccleugh v Edinburgh Magistrates* (1865) 3 M 528.
8 For consent and acquiescence, see para 176 above.
9 Bankton *Institute* II,7,8. Bankton notes, under reference to *Hay v Feuars* (1667) Mor 1818, that there are special rules for mills and dams 'which it is not lawful to demolish without authority of a judge, the public benefit being therein concerned'. Whether this is another example of a special rule for mills, or whether it supports some broader exception for public buildings, is uncertain.
10 Whether the encroacher is then entitled to recompense depends on whether he acted in good faith: see para 173 above.
11 See para 272 below.
12 It is likely that in some circumstances demolition is actionable in delict. But in the present state of the law it does not seem possible to be more specific.
13 See para 178 above.
14 This is an unexpected result. If a court is entitled to refuse to order demolition by the party encroaching, it seems inconsistent that it cannot prevent demolition by the party encroached upon. In principle, however, the two remedies are distinct. In the first case a party is being asked to demolish at his own expense property which does not belong to him. In the second case a party is offering at his own expense to demolish his own property. It must be conceded, however, that the cases have not usually paid much attention to the question of who owns the thing which has encroached.
15 For common property, see para 25 above.
16 *Hetherington v Galt* (1905) 7 F 706, 13 SLT 90.

17 The rule, stated in the text to note 18 below, that overhanging branches can be removed by the person encroached upon, is probably confined to trees owned solely by the encroacher.
18 Hume *Lectures* vol III (Stair Soc vol 15, 1952 ed G C H Paton) p 203 and the unreported case of *Geddes v Hardie* 7 June 1806 there cited. Alternatively, the person encroached upon can ask the court to order the encroacher to perform the necessary cutting: *Halkerston v Wedderburn* (1781) Mor 10495.
19 *Bankton* II,7,8.

(c) Trespass

180. Definition. Trespass consists of temporary or transient intrusion into land owned or otherwise lawfully possessed[1] by someone else. For this purpose land includes rivers and lochs. It also includes the airspace above land, to such height at least as is necessary for its reasonable use and enjoyment, and probably even beyond that height[2]. The intrusion may be by persons, by animals, or by things. Usually it is by persons[3]: probably the paradigm case of trespass is that of the member of the public who takes a short-cut over a private field. Intrusion by animals is trespass only where the animals are tame or otherwise kept in confinement, the remedy being against the owner of the animal or other person responsible for its control[4]. Finally, the intrusion may also be by things, although where such intrusion is permanent or semi-permanent it is classified as encroachment and not as trespass[5]. An example of trespass by things arose in *Brown v Lee Constructions Ltd* where interdict was obtained against the operation of a tower crane in such a way that it passed over land belonging to the petitioner[6].

Even a slight intrusion qualifies as trespass. Nor does it matter whether there is injury to the land intruded upon[7]. But both factors may have a bearing on the availability of remedies.

1 Possession in this context means natural possession. See para 175, note 1, above.
2 *Bernstein v Skyviews and General Ltd* [1978] QB 479, [1977] 2 All ER 902. See para 198 below.
3 Eg *Earl of Breadalbane v Livingston* (1790) Mor 4999, affd (1791) 3 Pat 221, HL.
4 Eg *Robertson v Wright* (1885) 13 R 174.
5 See para 175 above.
6 *Brown v Lee Constructions Ltd* 1977 SLT (Notes) 61, OH. For an English case with similar facts, and decided in the same way, see *Anchor Brewhouse Developments Ltd v Berkley House (Docklands Developments) Ltd* [1987] 2 EGLR 173.
7 In Hume *Lectures* vol III (Stair Soc vol 15, 1952 ed G C H Paton) p 205 Hume observes that: '. . . in exercising this prohibitory power, the heritor is not obliged to shew the special or immediate damage that would ensue from what he complains of. 'Tis sufficient for him to say, that such is his Charter, which the Law of the Land has given him, because such interferences occasion him jealousy and disquiet . . .; — because there can be no accurate rule to distinguish one sort of encroachment from another; and because there is no interference how harmless soever in the single instance, but may prove troublesome by being communicated to a number of persons; or which even in the single instance may not be made the pretended occasion of farther usurpations and encroachments'.

181. Defences. The following are defences to a claim based on trespass:
(1) *Consent.* If the owner or other lawful possessor consents to the intrusion, there is no trespass[1]. Consent may be either express or implied. Thus a householder probably impliedly consents to access over his garden path for members of the public who have some legitimate purpose in ringing his doorbell. But there is no implied consent for the public to enter his house, and an express invitation is required. Even after consent has been given, it may be withdrawn at will unless the parties have entered into contractual relations to the contrary[2].
(2) *Exercise of a right.* Intrusion in exercise of some appropriate real right or real condition is not trespass. In practice, the rights most commonly justifying a

temporary intrusion are either servitude rights or public rights of way or navigation. Hume says that there is a right to use the land of a neighbour to rest a ladder or to erect scaffolding if the repair of one's own property would otherwise be impossible[3].

(3) *Act of Parliament*. Intrusion may be authorised by statute. The Civil Aviation Act 1982[4], for example, permits the flight of aircraft at a height which, having regard to wind, weather and all the circumstances of the case, is reasonable. Similarly, a number of statutes confer rights of entry on public officials[5].

(4) *Judicial warrant*. Intrusion may also be authorised by judicial warrant. So in the execution of a poinding sheriff officers are entitled to enter the premises of the debtor including, where necessary, by means of opening shut and lockfast places[6]. There are many other examples.

(5) *Public interest*. Trespass may sometimes be justified in the public interest. Recognised examples include the extinguishing of a fire, the pursuit of a criminal, and the repelling of an enemy invasion[7]. All share the characteristic of emergency. Where an element of emergency is not present, trespass is much less likely to be justifiable[8]. So the public interest does not justify trespass in furtherance of a trade dispute, whether in the course of picketing[9] or of a sit-in[10]. In a case from the late eighteenth century, however, farmers were held entitled to pursue foxes through neighbouring farms on the basis that foxes were a threat to their sheep[11]. The result would presumably have been different if the foxes had been pursued for sport[12].

1 Eg *Steuart v Stephen* (1877) 4 R 873.
2 *Love-Lee v Cameron of Lochiel* 1991 SCLR 61 at 68, per Sheriff Principal Ireland.
3 Hume *Lectures* vol III (Stair Soc vol 15, 1952 ed G C H Paton) p 207. The right may be based on common interest: see para 359, head (9), below.
4 Civil Aviation Act 1982 (c 16), s 76.
5 Eg Rights of Entry (Gas and Electricity Boards) Act 1954 (c 21) (as amended). Further examples are listed in S Scott Robinson *The Law of Interdict* (1987) pp 53, 54.
6 Debtors (Scotland) Act 1987 (c 18), s 87. Certain safeguards are contained in s 18.
7 *Hume* vol III, pp 205, 206; Bell *Principles* s 957.
8 To a large extent, of course, this removes the point of the defence, at least as far as interdict is concerned. For if there is an emergency then there will in practice be no opportunity for obtaining interdict and no need of the defence; and if there is no emergency then there is no defence. The defence may, however, have some relevance in the context of a claim for damages: see para 185 below.
9 *Merry and Cuninghame v Aitken* (1895) 22 R 247.
10 *Caterpillar (UK) Ltd* 1987 GWD 14-516, OH. Section 13(2) of the Trade Union and Labour Relations Act 1974 (c 52) was thought by some to confer limited immunity in the case of sit-ins: see *Plessey Co plc v Wilson* 1983 SLT 139. But the Trade Union and Labour Relations Act 1974, s 13(2), was repealed by the Employment Act 1982 (c 46), s 19(1).
11 *Colquhoun v Buchanan* (1785) Mor 4997.
12 *Hume* vol III, p 206.

182. Remedies. A number of different remedies against trespass are available to a landowner or other lawful possessor. Future trespass may be checked by interdict[1]. Current trespass may be brought to an end by self-help[2]. There may be recovery for damage caused by trespassers[3]. Finally, special remedies exist in the case of straying animals[4]. Nonetheless, in practice landowners are often left without a suitable remedy, as interdict is not always available or practicable. Self-help depends on intercepting the trespasser, and damages presuppose damage. A landowner subjected to, say, an isolated act of trespass not accompanied by damage has no remedy against the trespasser. Trespassers, despite the familiar notice to the contrary, are very rarely 'prosecuted'.

Trespass may also be a criminal offence, but there is no general rule by which trespass is a crime, and its criminality depends on a series of statutes dealing with particular kinds of intrusion. The most important are the Trespass (Scotland) Act

1865[5], which makes it an offence to lodge or encamp on private property, the Game (Scotland) Act 1832[6] and the Night Poaching Act 1828[7] which deal with trespass in pursuit of game, and the Criminal Justice and Public Order Act 1994 which contains provisions aimed mainly at New Age travellers and hunt saboteurs[8].

1 For interdict, see para 183 below.
2 For self-help, see para 184 below.
3 For damages, see para 185 below.
4 For straying animals, see para 186 below.
5 Trespass (Scotland) Act 1865 (c 56), s 3 (amended by the Statute Law Repeals Act 1973 (c 39), s 1(1), Sch 1, and the Roads (Scotland) Act 1984 (c 54), s 156(1), (3), Sch 9, para 5(3), Sch 11).
6 Game (Scotland) Act 1832 (c 68), s 1 (amended by the Game Laws (Scotland) Amendment Act 1877 (c 28), s 10, Sch 1; Statute Law Revision (No 2) Act 1890 (c 51); Protection of Birds Act 1954 (c 30), s 15(2), Sch 6; Deer (Scotland) Act 1959 (c 40), s 36, Sch 3; and the Criminal Justice Act 1967 (c 80), ss 92, 106(2), Sch 3, Pt I). See further GAME, vol 11, paras 817–819.
7 Night Poaching Act 1828 (c 69), s 1 (extended by the Night Poaching Act 1844 (c 29), s 1, and amended by the Criminal Law Act 1977 (c 45), s 63(1), Sch 11, para 11). See further GAME, vol 11, para 810.
8 Criminal Justice and Public Order Act 1994 (c 33), ss 61, 62, 68, 69.

183. Interdict. In principle, interdict may be awarded against future acts of trespass, but in practice the remedy is often unavailable. For this the reasons are mainly practical. How, for example, is it possible to know in advance that a particular person is likely to trespass? Even if he has trespassed before (which is often a precondition of an award of interdict), how is it possible to predict, and to satisfy the court, that he will trespass again? Clearly, interdict is much more suited to some cases than to others. It is suitable for the case of the persistent and known trespasser, a neighbour perhaps who habitually uses a particular short-cut. It is very much less suitable for trespass by members of the public at large. With public trespass there are often formidable difficulties in identifying the persons concerned in order that they may be interdicted, and in any event an interdict against persons who have trespassed on one occasion is no protection against different persons trespassing on another[1].

Even if the practical difficulties can be overcome, interdict will not always be granted, for the remedy is within the discretion of the court, and there is no absolute entitlement to an award. It is not possible to lay down general rules as to when interdict will and will not be granted. Much depends on the facts of the individual case, and on whether the interdict under consideration is interim or perpetual[2]. But it is possible to indicate four circumstances under which interdict will not usually be granted. These are:

(1) *No reasonable likelihood of trespass.* On first principles, if there is no reasonable likelihood of trespass then there is nothing for the court to interdict[3]. The best evidence of future trespass is proof of past trespass[4]. The pursuer's case is also strengthened by showing that past acts of trespass involved the deliberate assertion of a legal right, such as a public or a servitude right of way the existence of which is disputed by the pursuer[5]. In one case, however, interdict was refused where the assertion of a right was not accompanied either by past acts or by threats of future acts[6].

(2) *Other remedies not pursued.* Interdict may not be granted where the pursuer has failed to pursue other, more apparently suitable, remedies[7]. At the very least a landowner is expected to give warning to the trespasser, and to monitor its effect, before approaching the court for interdict[8].

(3) *Trespass too trivial.* Interdict will not be granted where the threatened trespass is considered too trivial to warrant the full weight of the law. There must be at the least an 'appreciable wrong' to the pursuer[9]. Since, by definition, trespass is always temporary, it may often be vulnerable to arguments based on triviality. Nonetheless, as Burn-Murdoch warns, even here 'the maxim *de minimis non*

curat lex must be applied with caution. A very small hurt may be so magnified by continuance, that interdict is the only apt remedy'[10].

The leading case on the issue of triviality is *Winans v Macrae*[11]. Here the pursuer sought to interdict the defender 'from putting any lamb, lambs, sheep, cattle, or other bestial' on his lands to graze. The pursuer tenanted 200,000 acres of unfenced rough grazing. The defender, a shoemaker, inhabited a cottage adjacent to the pursuer's land. The only animal which the defender was averred and proved to keep was a pet lamb. Interdict was refused by the Second Divison in a judgment in which scorn for the pursuer's stance was barely concealed[12].

The prospect of injury to the pursuer's property is perhaps the most obvious way of demonstrating 'appreciable wrong'[13]. But it is not the only way and interdict has frequently been granted without averments of injury[14].

(4) *Special rule for straying animals.* Special considerations apply in relation to straying animals, and interdict is often refused. This subject is considered below[15].

1 An example is *Stirling Crawfurd v Clyde Navigation Trustees* (1881) 8 R 826.
2 For a discussion of interim interdict in the context of possession, see R Sutherland 'Possession in Scots Law: A Comparative Response' in E Attwooll (ed) *Perspectives in Jurisprudence* (1977) p 123 at pp 126–134.
3 *Hay's Trustees v Young* (1877) 4 R 398.
4 *Warrand v Watson* (1905) 8 F 253, 13 SLT 727.
5 *Paterson v M'Pherson* (1916) 33 Sh Ct Rep 237.
6 *Inverurie Magistrates v Sorrie* 1956 SC 175, 1956 SLT (Notes) 17.
7 *Campbell v Mackay* 1959 SLT (Sh Ct) 34.
8 *Paterson v M'Pherson* (1916) 33 Sh Ct Rep 237.
9 *Winans v Macrae* (1885) 12 R 1051 at 1063, per Lord Young.
10 H Burn-Murdoch *Interdict in the Law of Scotland* (1933) para 96. See also Hume *Lectures* vol III (Stair Soc vol 15, 1952 ed G C H Paton) p 205.
11 *Winans v Macrae* (1885) 12 R 1051.
12 See also *Robertson v Wright* (1885) 13 R 174.
13 *Cameron v Carlaw* (1899) 34 Sh Ct Rep 286; *Tindal v Bisset* (1917) 34 Sh Ct Rep 292; *Wills' Trustees v Cairngorm Canoeing and Sailing School Ltd* 1976 SC (HL) 30, 1976 SLT 162.
14 Eg *Brown v Lee Constructions Ltd* 1977 SLT (Notes) 61, OH.
15 See para 187 below.

184. Self-help. Recourse to the courts in respect of trespass is unusual. A simpler and, often, more effective remedy is for the landowner or other rightful possessor to take measures of his own. In principle such acts of self-help are perfectly lawful, subject however, to certain limits set both by the civil and the criminal law. Acts of self-help fall broadly into one of two categories. First, there are those acts which are designed to prevent or discourage trespass from taking place; and secondly, there are those acts which are designed to bring a particular instance of trespass to an end.

A landowner may seek to prevent trespass in many different ways. He may build a high wall and fortify it with barbed wire. He may install an alarm system. He may keep a dog. He may put up a notice warning that the property is private. But since he owes a duty of care in delict even to a trespasser[1], he cannot adopt more active methods of protection, such as mantraps.

The Guard Dogs Act 1975 lays down special rules in respect of guard dogs. A dog is a guard dog within the meaning of the 1975 Act if it is being used to protect (1) premises, (2) property kept on the premises or (3) a person guarding the premises or such property[2]. The Act provides that no guard dog may be kept on premises unless a person who is capable of controlling the dog is also present there and the dog is under his control, except while it is secured so that it is not at liberty to go freely about[3]. A notice containing a warning that a guard dog is present must be clearly exhibited at each entrance to the premises[4]. Failure to comply with these provisions is a criminal offence[5]. If a dog injures a person or other animal, its keeper is, on general principles of delict, liable in damages, and liability is strict if the provisions of the Guard Dogs Act 1975 have not been complied with or the use of a guard dog was not in the circumstances reasonable[6].

Once an act of trespass is under way, self-help may be used to bring it to an end. The precise rules are in some doubt. On the one hand, it is lawful to persuade a trespasser to leave, even, in some circumstances, by means of force. But, on the other hand, the use of force may sometimes be a civil or a criminal wrong or indeed both. So far as the criminal law is concerned, it is unclear to what extent defence of property justifies the use of force, and there are no reported cases directly in point[7]. There is a small amount of authority on the position in the civil law although any account of the rules remains speculative. The civil law appears to make a distinction between trespass on land and trespass within a private house. Trespass in a private house can be resisted by force, especially where it takes place by night and with the evident intention of committing theft[8]. A bare trespass on land, however, does not always justify the use of force. Hume indeed thought that force could never be justified for such a trespass[9], but the modern view is different[10]. In the modern law, force may be used against a trespasser who himself threatens or uses violence whether to persons or, probably, to property. A peaceful trespasser should first be invited to leave of his own accord and force should only be used as a last resort. In all cases where force is justifiable, the degree of force used must be properly matched to the circumstances of the trespass. Only the minimum force required by the circumstances may be employed and excessive force is actionable in delict[11]. In *Bell v Shand*[12], the only case in which this subject has been properly canvassed, a landowner was said by the First Division to be justified in apprehending a fifteen-year-old boy who appeared to be poaching and dragging him for some distance by the scruff of the neck.

A number of special rules apply in the case of straying animals, and these are considered later[13].

1 Occupiers' Liability (Scotland) Act 1960 (c 30), s 1(1).
2 Guard Dogs Act 1975 (c 50), s 7.
3 Ibid, s 1(1).
4 Ibid, s 1(3).
5 Ibid, s 5.
6 Animals (Scotland) Act 1987 (c 9), s 1(3)(a), 2(1)(c), (2). As to damages, see para 190 below.
7 G H Gordon *The Criminal Law of Scotland* (2nd edn, 1978) paras 28-35, 29-37.
8 Bell *Principles* s 961.
9 Hume *Lectures* vol IV (Stair Soc vol 17, 1955 ed G C H Paton) p 266.
10 *Bell v Shand* (1870) 7 SLR 267; *Aitchison v Thorburn* (1870) 7 SLR 347; *Wood v North British Rly Co* (1899) 2 F 1, 7 SLT 183. It is thought that the rules are broadly similar to those in English law, for which see 45 *Halsbury's Laws of England* (4th edn) para 1400.
11 Eg *Macdonald v Robertson* (1910) 27 Sh Ct Rep 103.
12 *Bell v Shand* (1870) 7 SLR 267.
13 See paras 188, 189, below.

185. Damages. '[E]very encroachment'[1] according to Erskine[2], 'founds the proprietor in an action of damages', provided, it is necessary to add, that loss can be shown[3]. The act of trespass is itself a civil wrong, from which it follows that damage to another's property or person which might not be actionable if caused on one's own land may become actionable if caused while trespassing on land belonging to someone else[4]. The wrong founded on in such a case is the trespass and not the damage: the damage is viewed as a consequence of the trespass rather than as a discrete wrong in itself. Erskine's dictum might be taken as meaning that liability for trespass is strict, but while this is a possible view of the law it seems more likely that liability is not strict[5]. Strict liability is, however, imposed by statute in relation to damage caused by certain types of animals[6].

If a trespass is brought about through the fault of some third party, an action for damages lies against the party in question[7], and on this principle a golf club has been held liable for damage caused to private property by golfers trespassing in search of lost golf balls[8].

1 'Encroachment' in this context includes trespass.
2 Erskine *Institute* II,1,1.
3 *Grahame v M'Kenzie* (1810) Hume 641; *Hill v Merricks and Hay* (1813) Hume 397; *Graham v Duke of Hamilton* (1868) 6 M 695; *Waugh v More Nisbett* (1882) 19 SLR 427; *Lock v Taylor* 1976 SLT 238, OH. In English law nominal damages may be recovered even if there has been no loss: see 45 *Halsbury's Laws of England* (4th edn) para 1403.
4 *Gibson v Stewart* (1894) 21 R 437; *Lindsay v Somerville* (1902) 18 Sh Ct Rep 230.
5 *Harvie v Turner* (1910) 32 Sh Ct Rep 267.
6 See para 190 below.
7 *Scott's Trustees v Moss* (1889) 17 R 32.
8 *Ritchie v Dysart Golf Club* (1909) 26 Sh Ct Rep 30; *Buchanan v Alexandra Golf Club* (1915) 32 Sh Ct Rep 251. But cf *Allan v Calderbraes Golf Club* (1934) 50 Sh Ct Rep 86.

186. Straying animals. The issues arising out of trespass by animals are sufficiently different from those arising out of ordinary trespass as to require separate treatment, and to some extent trespass by animals is governed by special rules, both of the common law and of statute.

In the early law animals seem to have been allowed to wander freely except during 'hayning time, while the crops are upon the ground'[1]. This was presumably because land was then almost entirely unenclosed and trespass could scarcely be avoided. By the seventeenth century, at the latest, the law had changed and trespass had ceased to be lawful[2], a position fortified by the enactment of the Winter Herding Act in 1686[3]. The Winter Herding Act remained in force until 1987 when it was repealed and replaced by the Animals (Scotland) Act of that year[4], which is now the principal enactment regulating trespass by animals.

Trespass by animals raises four main legal issues, namely: the prevention of trespass by interdict[5]; the detention of straying animals[6]; the killing or injuring of straying animals[7]; and claims for damages[8].

1 Stair *Institutions* II,1,7; II,3,67.
2 Bankton *Institute* IV,41,16; Erskine *Institute* II,1,1; III,6,28.
3 On the Winter Herding Act 1686 (c 21), see further *Civil Liability in Relation to Animals* (Scot Law Com Consultative Memorandum no. 55 (1982)) paras 2.2–2.12 and *Obligations: Report on Civil Liability in Relation to Animals* (Scot Law Com no. 97 (1985)) paras 2.13–2.19.
4 Animals (Scotland) Act 1987 (c 9).
5 See para 187 below.
6 See para 188 below.
7 See para 189 below.
8 See para 190 below.

187. Interdict of straying animals. The general principles governing the award of interdict have already been discussed[1]. So far as animals are concerned, the courts have usually been reluctant to grant interdict. This is partly because of a view that the keeping of animals is in some sense a good in itself, or at any rate a reasonable use of land. Partly, too, it is because of the obvious practical difficulties involved in preventing animals from straying. However, the keeper of an animal is expected to take all reasonable steps to prevent trespass, and interdict may be granted if the court is not satisfied that such steps have indeed been taken and that the only further course open to the keeper is to cease altogether the activity of keeping animals. What constitutes reasonable steps depends partly on the nature of the land, and even more on the type of animal in question. In general, it may be said that the practice of the court has been to grant interdict against the straying of domestic fowl, which are easily confined[2], but to refuse it in the case of cattle and sheep[3]. Cattle and sheep can only be completely restrained by the extensive use of fencing and the court has been unwilling to impose the burden of fencing on the keeper. Indeed, it has been suggested that fencing may be more a matter for the owner of the land trespassed upon than for the keeper of the trespassing animals[4].

1 See para 183 above.
2 *Cameron v Carlaw* (1899) 34 Sh Ct Rep 286; *Tindal v Bisset* (1917) 34 Sh Ct Rep 292.
3 *Winans v Macrae* (1885) 12 R 1051; *Robertson v Wright* (1885) 13 R 174; *Paterson v M'Pherson* (1916) 33 Sh Ct Rep 237; *Campbell v Mackay* 1959 SLT (Sh Ct) 34.
4 Eg the comment of Lord Young in *Winans v Macrae* (1885) 12 R 1051 at 1064 (the pet lamb case) that: 'If a man wants to protect his lands from being invaded in this way — against children toddling on to the grass at the roadside, or a lamb going on to it, or a cat, or a kitten — I say, if he wants to exclude that he must do so by other means — by fencing the lands, for example — but not by applying to Her Majesty's Judges for interdict'.

188. Detention of straying animals. The Winter Herding Act 1686 (c 21), now repealed, conferred certain rights of detention in respect of straying cattle and sheep. Its replacement is the Animals (Scotland) Act 1987, which provides that where an animal strays on to any land and is not then under the control of any person, the occupier of the land may detain the animal for the purpose of preventing injury or damage by it[1]. Unlike the Winter Herding Act 1686, the right of detention is not limited to cattle and sheep, but presumably not all animals will qualify as threatening injury or damage.

Once an animal is detained under the 1987 Act, its ultimate disposal is governed by Part VI of the Civic Government (Scotland) Act 1982 which deals with lost and abandoned property[2]. The main provisions of Part VI as they apply here[3] may be summarised as follows. A person detaining an animal must, without unreasonable delay, deliver the animal or report the fact of its detention either to the owner or lawful possessor or to the police[4]. If the animal is delivered or reported to the police, the police must take reasonable steps to identify and notify the owner or person entitled to possession[5]. If the owner claims the animal the chief constable has a discretion to require payment of a reward to the original detentor[6]. The chief constable may award interim custody of the animal in such manner as he considers appropriate[7]. If custody is awarded to the original detentor, and the animal remains unclaimed, the detentor becomes its owner at the end of two months[8]. Alternatively, the chief constable may at the end of two months either sell the animal or give it to the detentor[9]. The transferee receives a good title[10], but within a year of the disposal the previous owner may claim either the net proceeds of sale[11] or, where the animal was not sold, the return of the animal from the detentor[12]. It appears, however, that the previous owner has no such rights where the animal became the property of the detentor as a result of an award of interim custody[13].

The rights of detention conferred by the Winter Herding Act 1686 were rarely used in modern times and it is anticipated that the same may be true of the new provisions in the 1987 Act[14]. This is because the person whose land is trespassed upon has the trouble of carrying out the act of detention and of complying with the various statutory provisions, without, in most cases, much prospect of financial gain. No doubt detention may have a certain nuisance value which might discourage future trespasses. It may also have the immediate benefit of preventing injury to the land or crops. Beyond this it is difficult to see why the remedy might appear attractive.

1 Animals (Scotland) Act 1987 (c 9), s 3(1).
2 Except in the case of stray dogs where the applicable provision is the Dogs Act 1906 (c 32), s 4 (substituted by the Dogs (Amendment) Act 1928 (c 21), s 2, and amended by the Civic Government (Scotland) Act 1982 (c 45), ss 75(b), 128(1)(b)): Animals (Scotland) Act 1987, s 3(2). The Civic Government (Scotland) Act 1982, Pt VI, comprises ss 67–79.
3 For a fuller account of the Civic Government (Scotland) Act 1982, Pt VI, in the context of lost and abandoned property, see paras 547 ff below.

4 Ibid, s 67(1), (3).
5 Ibid, s 68(3).
6 Ibid, s 70(1)(a), (2).
7 Ibid, s 68(2).
8 Ibid, s 74 (amended by the Animals (Scotland) Act 1987 (c 9), s 3(2)).
9 Civic Government (Scotland) Act 1982, s 68(4).
10 Provided that he is in good faith, by which presumably is meant that he does not know the identity of the owner: ibid, s 71(1).
11 Ibid, s 72.
12 Ibid, s 71(1).
13 This is because ibid, s 71(2), applies only to a 'disposal' of property under s 68 or s 70. The granting of interim custody, while it falls within s 68, is not a 'disposal'. This reading is supported by the fact that a separate provision (s 74) was thought necessary to confer a statutory good title which in the case of 'disposals' is conferred by s 71(1).
14 *Obligations: Civil Liability in Relation to Animals* (Scot Law Com no. 97 (1985)) para 4.28.

189. Self-help: killing or injuring straying animals. A trespassing animal may cause or threaten injury to the landowner or to one of his animals. In practice the problem is almost always that of stray dogs worrying sheep or cattle. A landowner has the right to act to protect his person or his livestock, but subject always to limits set by the civil and criminal law. So far as the civil law is concerned the principal rules are now to be found in section 4 of the Animals (Scotland) Act 1987.

Section 4 of the 1987 Act confers immunity from civil liability for killing or causing injury to an animal. Immunity is conferred by section 4 where the defender acted for the protection of livestock in respect of which he was either the keeper, the owner or occupier of the land where the livestock was present, or a person authorised to act for the protection of the livestock by either such person[1]. Livestock is defined, widely, to mean any animals of a domestic variety (including in particular sheep, cattle and horses) and, while they are in captivity, any other animals[2]. Only non-domestic animals not in captivity are excluded[3]. Immunity is also conferred where the defender acted either in self-defence or for the protection of another person[4]. In all cases the defender must have acted in the reasonable belief that there was no other practicable means of preventing or, as the case may be, of dealing with the attack[5]. It is a condition of obtaining the immunity that the defender notify the police within forty-eight hours of the killing or injury[6].

The killing or injuring of a dog or other animal may also attract criminal penalties. In particular, unjustifiable injury inflicted on an animal belonging to someone else is the crime of malicious mischief. It appears that injury is justifiable in the criminal law in broadly the same circumstances in which it is justifiable in the civil law. Thus it is justifiable to kill or injure an animal in defence of life or limb, whether of a person or of another animal[7], but it is probably not justifiable to kill or injure in defence of property[8].

1 Animals (Scotland) Act 1987 (c 9), s 4(1)(a)(iii), (3).
2 Ibid, s 4(6).
3 Eg game. An example is *Scott v White* (1886) 2 Guth Sh Cas 470.
4 Animals (Scotland) Act 1987, s 4(1)(a)(i), (ii).
5 Ibid, s 4(4).
6 Ibid, s 4(1)(b).
7 *Farrell v Marshall* 1962 SLT (Sh Ct) 65.
8 *Clark v Syme* 1957 JC 1, 1956 SLT (Notes) 62.

190. Damages in respect of straying animals. A straying animal may cause damage to the land on which it trespasses. The Animals (Scotland) Act 1987 imposes strict liability in respect of damage caused by animals in three types of circumstances.

Where these circumstances do not apply liability is not strict. The three circumstances are:
(1) Where land or the produce of land, whether harvested or not, is materially
    damaged as a result of foraging by one of the following animals, namely cattle,
    horses, asses, mules, hinnies, sheep, pigs, goats and deer[1].
(2) Where persons or animals are bitten, savaged, attacked or harried by dogs or by
    certain specified dangerous wild animals[2].
(3) Where damage or injury is caused by any other animal belonging to a species
    whose members generally are by virtue of their physical attributes or habits
    likely (unless controlled or restrained) to injure severely or kill persons or
    animals or to damage property to a material extent, but only in respect of
    damage or injury directly referable to such physical attributes or habits[3].
It will be observed that only the first of the three categories is concerned exclusively
with trespass[4]. Liability in terms of the Act falls on the 'keeper' of the animal[5], and
'keeper' is defined as meaning the owner of an animal or its possessor[6]. Ownership
and possession are themselves given an extended meaning under the Act[7]. If an
animal is possessed by a person other than its owner then both are keepers within the
definition and an injured party has a choice of persons to sue.

  1 Animals (Scotland) Act 1987 (c 9), s 1(1)(b), (3)(b). This provision replaces similar provisions in the
    Winter Herding Act 1686 (c 21): Animals (Scotland) Act 1987, s 1(8)(b). Like the 1686 Act it is
    confined to damage done to land.
  2 Animals (Scotland) Act 1987, s 1(1)(b), (3)(a). As to the kinds of dangerous wild animals, see the
    Dangerous Wild Animals Act 1976 (c 38), s 7(4), Schedule (substituted by the Dangerous Wild
    Animals Act 1976 (Modification) Order 1984, SI 1984/1111). Included are animals such as lions,
    tigers, bears and cobras.
  3 Animals (Scotland) Act 1987, s 1(1)(b), (c).
  4 For a fuller discussion of ibid, s 1, see ANIMALS, vol 2, para 166.
  5 Ibid, s 1(1)(a).
  6 Ibid, s 5(1)(a).
  7 Ibid, s 5(1)(b), (2).

(d) Corporeal Moveables

191. Introduction. The size and nature of most items of corporeal moveable
property dictate that the typical case of intrusion involves the complete dispossession of the owner or other rightful possessor. Thus if A unlawfully takes a hat
belonging to B, A gains possession and B loses it. The intruder, A, becomes the
(unlawful) possessor and the remedy of the owner, B, is to seek recovery of
possession by means of an action of delivery. The issue, in other words, is not
defence of possession but recovery following its loss.
    This section, however, is concerned with defence of possession[1]. Issues of
defence arise only where the action of the intruder has not resulted in the complete
dispossession of the owner or other current possessor. Either there is no dispossession at all, or such dispossession as there is is only partial in effect. In the case of
land, events of this kind are of commonplace occurrence and the law — on trespass
and encroachment — is comparatively well developed. But in the case of corporeal
moveables such events are rare. Only in two types of circumstances are issues of
defence of possession likely to arise. One is where the property in question is
sufficiently large (for example, a ship[2] or a caravan) for events analogous to trespass
or encroachment on land to take place. In such a case the possession seized by the
intruder is exercised at the same time as the existing possession of the owner or other
lawful possessor. The other case is where the property is taken into the exclusive
control of the intruder but on a temporary and occasional basis only. An example is
the person who habitually and without permission uses a lawnmower belonging to
his neighbour.

1 For recovery of possession of corporeal moveables, see paras 151 and 158 ff above.
2 *Phestos Shipping Co Ltd v Kurmiawan* 1983 SC 165, 1983 SLT 388; *Shell UK Ltd v McGillvray* 1991 SLT 667, OH. As to the recovery of ships etc, see para 159 above.

192. Applicable rules. There is almost a complete lack of authority on defence of possession in the context of corporeal moveables, but there is no reason to suppose that the rules are substantially different from those developed in the context of land[1]. Indeed, intrusion on moveables must often involve intrusion on land. Intrusion on moveables appears to have been considered by the courts on only two occasions, in *Wilson v Shepherd*[2] and again in *William Leitch & Co Ltd v Leydon*[3]. The facts of both cases are strikingly similar. The pursuers were in the business of selling aerated water to members of the public[4]. The water was sold in bottles embossed with the pursuers' name. In terms of the contract of sale, or so it was averred, the bottles remained the property of the pursuers and were to be returned to them once the water had been consumed. A deposit was payable on return of the bottles. Some members of the public reused the bottles to buy paraffin (*Wilson*) or aerated water (*Leitch & Co Ltd*) from the respective defenders. The pursuers then sought interdict against the defenders from refilling the bottles.

These facts fall within the second of the two types of case identified earlier (that is, intruder in exclusive control on a temporary basis)[5]. The pursuers own the bottles and, after sale, are in civil possession. The purchasers of the bottles are lawful natural possessors for as long as the contents remain unconsumed, when they are under a duty to return the bottles to the pursuers. The defenders become temporary custodiers[6] when the bottles are left with them for refilling, but their custody derives from people who no longer have a right to possession and so is itself unlawful. In short, they are intruders. In these circumstances the pursuers have a choice of remedies. They can seek the return of the bottles from the (now) unlawful possessors. Alternatively they can interdict the defenders as intruders. The second course is followed because it is the only practicable one.

The pursuers succeeded in *Wilson*, at least to the extent of being granted a proof, but failed in *Leitch & Co Ltd* after proof. In neither case were issues of property law satisfactorily distinguished from issues of contract law, and the court was clearly influenced by considerations of equity. Nonetheless it appears to have been accepted by the court that the actions of the defenders were broadly comparable to trespass in the case of land[7]. In principle, at least, the pursuers were entitled to have their ownership protected. But in *Leitch & Co Ltd* that principle was not given effect to for a number of reasons special to the particular facts of the case[8].

1 For defence of possession in relation to land, see paras 175–190 above.
2 *Wilson v Shepherd* 1913 SC 300, 1912 2 SLT 455.
3 *William Leitch & Co Ltd v Leydon* 1930 SC 41, 1930 SLT 8, affd 1931 SC (HL) 1, 1931 SLT 2.
4 In *William Leitch & Co Ltd v Leydon* 1930 SC 41, 1930 SLT 8, affd 1931 SC (HL) 1, 1931 SLT 2, at least, the sale was through the intermediary of retail grocers.
5 See para 191 above.
6 *William Leitch & Co Ltd v Leydon* 1930 SC 41 at 65, 1930 SLT 8 at 21, per Lord Morison.
7 Trespass cases were cited in argument in *Wilson v Shepherd* 1913 SC 300, 1912 2 SLT 455. But of course, as Viscount Dunedin observed in *William Leitch & Co Ltd* 1931 SC (HL) 1 at 8, 1931 SLT 2 at 3: 'Trespass as to a chattel in a Scottish lawyer's mouth is a perfectly unmeaning phrase'. In any event trespass as to a chattel in English law is concerned with recovery of possession.
8 Thus the pursuers in *William Leitch & Co Ltd* failed to prove that ownership of the bottles had remained with them in all cases. They also failed to show that the defenders knew, or might easily know, that the bottles were theirs. Finally, and unlike *Wilson*, no damage was done to the bottles, which on general principles of trespass law made the case for interdict weaker.

5. LANDOWNERSHIP

(1) INTRODUCTION

193. Ownership of land. Almost all land in Scotland is held on feudal tenure and is subject to the rules of the feudal system[1]. Feudal theory divides ownership (*dominium*) of land into a number of separate interests held by different parties. There is the *dominium utile* held by the vassal or feuar, who is the party entitled to possession of the land[2]. There is the *dominium directum* (or superiority) held by a subject superior; and indeed, since there is no limit on the number of permissible superiorities, there may be a chain of subject superiors and superiorities. Finally, there is the ultimate *dominium directum* or superiority[3] held by the Crown. Each party in this feudal procession — the vassal, the subject superiors, the Crown — has a form of *dominium* in the land. They are all owners. *Dominium* is fragmented.

In this treatment of landownership, however, the complexities of feudal law may largely be disregarded. For in the first place, while feudalism survives in Scotland as a theoretical construct, it has almost ceased to operate as a living system. Feudal theory and landowning practice are no longer closely related. In theory land is feudal; in practice it may be treated in most circumstances as allodial[4], with the proprietor of the *dominium utile* as absolute owner. In the second place the law of landownership is primarily concerned with the rights and obligations of the party entitled to possession of land. In Scots feudalism it is only the ultimate vassal, the proprietor of the *dominium utile*, who is entitled to possession. The subject of this section is therefore the estate of the vassal.

1 For a full account of the feudal system, see paras 41 ff above.
2 The proprietor of the *dominium utile* has the principal right to possession (*jus possidendi*) of land. This right may be exercised by natural possession, or civilly, through the natural possession of another such as a tenant. For possession, see paras 114 ff above.
3 The ultimate superiority of the Crown is also known as *dominium eminens*.
4 Allodial property is property owned outright, without reference to a feudal superior. Thus corporeal moveable property is allodial.

194. Ownership of the *dominium utile* of land. Land may be divided into land the title to which is registered in the Land Register, and land which is unregistered but the deeds relating to which are recorded in the Register of Sasines. The registration counties currently operational for the purposes of the Land Register are the counties of Renfrew, Dunbarton, Lanark, Glasgow, Clackmannan, Stirling, West Lothian, Fife, Aberdeen and Kincardine[1]. In all other parts of Scotland the Register of Sasines remains the working register[2]. Even in those counties which are operational for the purposes of registration of title, a significant amount of land continues to be held on a Sasine title and only gradually will the position change.

The rules for determining the ownership of the *dominium utile* depend upon whether the land in question is Sasine land or Land Register land. The owner of the *dominium utile* of Land Register land is the person entered as proprietor of that interest in land in the Register[3]. The appearance of his name there is conclusive of his ownership. The fact that the deed in respect of which his registration proceeded may be open to challenge does not affect his status as owner, although it may be a ground for subsequent rectification of the Register against him[4]. In the case of Sasine land the owner is the grantee of the most recent valid conveyance, voluntary or judicial, to have been recorded in the Register of Sasines[5]. A valid voluntary conveyance is a conveyance granted by a party who at the time of granting was[6], or who subsequently became[7], owner of the land, or alternatively any conveyance the recording of which has been followed by possession for the prescriptive period of ten years by the grantee and his successors in title[8].

1 See further para 643 below.
2 See further CONVEYANCING, vol 6, paras 703, 714 ff. The current projections for the extension of the Land Register to the rest of Scotland are set out at 1992 SLT (News) 230.
3 Land Registration (Scotland) Act 1979 (c 33), ss 3(1)(a), 6(1)(b). See further para 673 below.
4 Land Registration (Scotland) Act 1979, s 9.
5 Ownership does not pass to the grantee until the moment of recording of the deed, and an unrecorded deed does not transfer ownership. See further paras 643, 644, below.
6 The granter must usually be owner because of the rule *nemo dat quod non habet*. See further paras 669 ff below.
7 This is the doctrine of accretion. See para 677 below.
8 Prescription and Limitation (Scotland) Act 1973 (c 52), s 1. See para 674 below.

195. Rights of the landowner. By landowner here and throughout this section is meant the owner of the *dominium utile* of land.

Bell characterises landownership thus:

'The chief attribute of property is the right of deriving from land and its accessories all the uses or services of which they are capable. This right may be considered, in relation to others, as "exclusive"; or in relation merely to the subject as "absolute" '[1].

Above all an owner has the right to possession (*jus possidendi*) of his land; and in the exercise of this right he may cultivate the land, or build a house or factory on it, or, in appropriate cases, take game[2] or fish (although not salmon)[3]. As Bell indicates, the right to possession is an exclusive one, and if it is sub-granted to others for a period of years, as it may be by means of a lease, the sub-grantee takes the place of the owner and has an exclusive right in turn. Trespassers and others who interfere with the right of exclusive possession act unlawfully and may be restrained. Possession is considered further above[4].

The right of the landowner is absolute as well as exclusive; but, as Bell acknowledges, this proposition cannot now be asserted without serious qualification[5]. Innumerable restrictions exist, both at common law and in virtue of statute, on the exercise of ownership. A complete list cannot be attempted here[6], but some of the more important restrictions are discussed elsewhere in this work[7]. For the owner of ordinary domestic property the most significant restriction is probably the limitation on the freedom to build imposed by planning and building legislation[8]. Commercial property is subject to detailed regulation in respect, for example, of fire safety[9], pollution[10], health and safety at work[11], and so on.

In addition to restrictions imposed by law, an owner may choose to restrict his absolute right of use by the granting of subordinate real rights, such as leases, rights in security or servitudes, or by entering into some contractual arrangement such as a licence.

1 Bell *Principles* s 939.
2 For game, see GAME, vol 11. See also S Scott Robinson *The Law of Game, Salmon and Freshwater Fishing in Scotland* (1990) pp 3–66; W M Gordon *Scottish Land Law* (1989) pp 249–283. The taking of game is subject to detailed statutory regulation.
3 For fishing, see para 280 below and, more generally, see FISHERIES, vol 11. The right to fish for salmon is a separate tenement and is often held by someone other than the owner of the water in respect of which it may be exercised. See paras 319 ff below.
4 See paras 114 ff above. For trespass, see paras 180 ff above.
5 *Bell* s 939: '[T]he absolute use . . . may be restrained . . . where it tends to the injury or discomfort of the public'.
6 There is a convenient list in J M Halliday *Conveyancing Law and Practice in Scotland* vol II (1986) para 23–50.
7 See BUILDING CONTROLS; COMPULSORY ACQUISITION, vol 5; ENVIRONMENT, vol 9; NUISANCE, vol 14; PUBLIC HEALTH, vol 19; and TOWN AND COUNTRY PLANNING, vol 23.
8 Ie the Town and Country Planning (Scotland) Act 1972 (c 52) (as amended); the Building (Scotland) Act 1959 (c 24); and the Building (Scotland) Act 1970 (c 38).
9 See the Fire Precautions Act 1971 (c 40), and the Fire Safety and Safety of Places of Sport Act 1987 (c 27).

10 See the Control of Pollution Act 1974 (c 40) and the Environmental Protection Act 1990 (c 43).
11 See the Health and Safety at Work etc Act 1974 (c 37).

(2) THE ESTATE OWNED

(a) Physical Limits

196. Introduction. On a horizontal plane the limits of landownership are the boundaries expressed in the title or titles to the land[1]. On a vertical plane the limits are, at one extremity the centre of the earth and at the other extremity 'the heavens', for landownership is *a coelo usque ad centrum*[2]. All heritable property lying within these physical limits belongs to the owner of the estate. But moveable property does not belong to a landowner merely by virtue of the fact that it is situated on his land[3].

To the rules stated thus far three important qualifications fall to be made. First, a landowner may sometimes hold rights in respect of heritable property beyond his own boundaries. Rights of this kind are known as 'pertinents'[4]. Secondly, a landowner may not always own all heritable property even within his own boundaries. Heritable property capable of severance in this way is known collectively as 'separate tenements'[5]. But most heritable property is not capable of severance. Finally, special and separate rules regulate the position of the owner of flatted property[6] and of minerals[7].

1 As to horizontal limits, see para 197 below.
2 As to vertical limits, see para 198 below.
3 Civic Government (Scotland) Act 1982 (c 45), s 73. This was also the common law. Of course a moveable object situated on land may become part of that land by accession.
4 See paras 199–206 below.
5 See paras 207–213 below.
6 See para 227 ff below.
7 See paras 252 ff below.

197. Horizontal limits. For land registered in the Land Register the horizontal limits of ownership are the boundaries given in the relevant title sheet. Except in the case of flatted property, registered land is described by a plan based on the Ordnance Survey map[1], thus ensuring a bounding title[2].

The rules for Sasine land are more complex. The starting point is the deed in respect of which the owner is infeft. Where this deed contains a bounding description, whether expressly or by reference to an earlier deed[3], then, and on the assumption that the granter was *in titulo* to make the grant in the first place[4], these boundaries mark the extent of the land. A bounding description may be achieved by verbal description of the boundaries, by plan, by measurements or, typically, by a combination of all three[5].

Where the deed contains only a general description ('Number 43 High Street, Linlithgow'), so that the individual boundaries are not specified, recourse must be had to extrinsic evidence. As Erskine observes, 'where a charter, without referring to any boundary, describes the lands or baronies by special names or designations, it can only be known by the common opinion of the country which lands fall under the designations expressed in the charter, and by what limits those lands are circumscribed'[6]. A distinction may be made here between a break-off conveyance (that is, a conveyance in which the granter 'breaks off' an area of ground to the grantee but retains adjoining ground) and an ordinary conveyance (where the granter conveys his entire interest and the adjoining ground is held by third parties). In the first case the question of boundaries arises between granter and grantee and the extrinsic evidence is required to explicate the deed to which both are parties. In the second case the question is one between the grantee and a third party and the extrinsic evidence is required to explicate, not only the immediate titles of the grantee and the third party, but also, it may be, the earlier titles of both. In both cases the most satisfactory extrinsic evidence is evidence of possession; and where the possession has persisted for ten[7] years openly, peaceably and without judicial interruption, the landowner has by positive prescription an unchallengeable title to the boundaries as possessed, provided only that the deed[8] on which his possession proceeded can be read as encompassing these boundaries[9]. Where the possession is insufficient for prescription to run, whether in respect of length or of quality, it may still be used to explain the boundaries, either by itself or along with other extrinsic evidence[10].

Where the titles of adjoining properties disclose a discrepancy as to the common boundary, the proprietors affected may execute and register in the Register of Sasines or, as the case may be, in the Land Register a plan containing an agreed common boundary[11]. On registration of the plan[12] there is in effect a deemed excambion (exchange) of the lands to the extent necessary to bring the agreed boundary into operation. The rules as to the erection and maintenance of boundary walls and fences are considered separately[13].

Finally, and for the sake of completeness, brief mention should be made of former royal forests[14]. A royal forest is a tract of land for the keeping of deer, and it retains the status of forest even where the trees fail. The word 'royal' signifies that the forest is *inter regalia minora* and so reserved from Crown and other grants unless expressly conveyed. Not even a bounding description will include a former royal forest in the absence of express grant[15]. At one time the foreshore was also thought to be *inter regalia minora* but this view is no longer held[16].

1 Land Registration (Scotland) Act 1979 (c 33), s 6(1)(a); *Registration of Title Practice Book* (1981) para E.14. For flatted property the title plan shows only the *solum* of the whole building (and common green), the individual flat being distinguished only by verbal description. In theory, boundaries, like everything else in the title sheet, are subject to the possibility of rectification under s 9 of the Land Registration (Scotland) Act 1979, but in practice the risks are small.

2 A bounding title is a title in which each boundary is described individually. Where some boundaries are described but others are not, the title is bounding only as to the described boundaries. Sometimes a boundary is so inadequately described that it is difficult to say whether it is bounding or not: see W M Gordon *Scottish Land Law* (1989) para 4-06. Apart from convenience, the main significance of a bounding title is that it is impossible to acquire land beyond the boundary by prescription.

3 Ie by virtue of the Conveyancing (Scotland) Act 1874 (c 94), s 61.

4 Or that his absence of title has been cured by prescription.

5. See CONVEYANCING, vol 6, paras 484–488. There is a useful list of the meaning of certain physical boundary features in J M Halliday *Conveyancing Law and Practice in Scotland* vol II (1986) para 18-11.

6 Erskine *Institute* II,6,2. See *Cattanach's Trustee v Jamieson* (1884) 11 R 972; *Murray's Trustee v Wood* (1887) 14 R 856; *Brown v North British Rly Co* (1906) 8 F 534, 13 SLT 797.

7 But in a question with the Crown involving the foreshore or salmon fishings the period is twenty years: Prescription and Limitation (Scotland) Act 1973 (c 52), s 1(4).

8 The deed must have been recorded in the Register of Sasines and the possession must be subsequent to the date of recording.

9 Prescription and Limitation (Scotland) Act 1973, s 1. An example is *Suttie v Baird* 1992 SLT 133. See further para 674 below and PRESCRIPTION AND LIMITATION.

10 *Baird v Fortune* (1861) 4 Macq 127 at 149, HL, per Lord Wensleydale; *Fraser v Grant* (1866) 4 M 596 at 600, per Lord Benholme; *Agnew v Lord Advocate* (1873) 11 M 309. When the prescriptive period was forty years this doctrine was of much greater importance than it is today.

11 Land Registration (Scotland) Act 1979, s 19, discussed at para 220 below.

12 In the case of Sasine land, the agreement on which the plan proceeded must also be registered: see ibid, s 19(2).

13 See paras 214 ff below.

14 As to royal forests, see Stair *Institutions* II,3,67; Erskine II,6,14; Bell *Principles* s 670.

15 Forest is unusual in being *inter regalia minora* but not a separate tenement, ie the owner of a royal forest also owns the *solum*.

16 See para 314 below.

198. Vertical limits. In respect of the vertical limits of landownership

'a conveyance of any land in unqualified terms gives a right of property in the substance or solid contents of the land without any assignable limit. This is what is meant by a conveyance being *a coelo ad centrum*. There are no limits in the vertical direction except such as physical conditions impose'[1].

So in a downwards direction landownership encompasses the ground itself and all that is part of the ground (*pars soli*). This includes the constituent materials of the ground — soil, stones, minerals and the like — and also trees, plants, buildings and other objects which, although above the ground, have acceded to it[2].

In an upwards direction, the landowner owns the airspace, apparently without limit, although in international law national sovereignty is not claimed in respect of outer space[3]. In England, where the doctrine of vertical ownership is less strong, ownership *a coelo* has been criticised as 'leading to the absurdity of a trespass ... being committed by a satellite every time it passes over a suburban garden'[4]. In the case in which these remarks were made the plaintiff failed to recover damages in respect of an aeroplane overflying his house and taking photographs. The court was unwilling to accept ownership of airspace to 'the heavens'. According to Griffiths J:

'The problem is to balance the rights of an owner to enjoy the use of his land against the rights of the general public to take advantage of all that science now offers in the use of air space. This balance is in my judgment best struck in our present society by restricting the rights of an owner in the air space above his land to such height as is necessary for the ordinary use and enjoyment of his land and the structures upon it, and declaring that above that height he has no greater rights in the air space than any other member of the public'[5].

It is doubtful if this represents Scots law. The question in Scotland is one of *dominium*, not of the balancing of 'rights'; and the authorities are unanimous in asserting that *dominium* lies in the landowner and in him alone. In the only modern case, *Brown v Lee Constructions Ltd*[6], the court seemed untroubled in granting interdict to a landowner against the passage of the jib of a tower crane. If a court were to recognise rights for the general public in airspace — and so far no court has done so — these could only be in the nature of rights of use and passage, analogous to public rights of way over land. Such rights are indeed already supplied by statute in the case of aircraft, the Civil Aviation Act 1982 providing that no action is to lie in respect of trespass or nuisance by reason only of flight at a height above the ground which, having regard to wind, weather and all the circumstances of the case is reasonable[7].

Ownership *a coelo usque ad centrum* is subject to the qualification that minerals, tenement flats and certain other types of property may have been broken off into separate ownership as separate tenements[8]. But the ownership of a separate tenement is circumscribed by the boundaries of that tenement and it is the owner of the *solum* who has residual rights *a coelo usque ad centrum*[9].

1 *Glasgow City and District Rly Co v Macbrayne* (1883) 10 R 894 at 899, OH, per Lord M'Laren (affd (1883) 10 R 894, IH). That ownership is *a coelo usque ad centrum* is a proposition frequently asserted in institutional writings. See Stair *Institutions* II,3,59; II,7,7; Erskine *Institute* II,6,1; II,9,9; Bell *Principles* ss 737, 940. For the history of the rule, see F Lyall 'The maxim *cujus est solum* in Scots law' 1978 JR 147.
2 For accession, see paras 570 ff below.
3 See PUBLIC INTERNATIONAL LAW, vol 19, para 674. Activity in outer space by United Kingdom nationals requires a licence issued in terms of the Outer Space Act 1986 (c 38). 'Outer space' includes the moon and other celestial bodies: s 13(1).
4 *Bernstein v Skyviews and General Ltd* [1978] QB 479 at 487, [1977] 2 All ER 902 at 907, per Griffiths J.
5 [1978] QB 479 at 488, [1977] 2 All ER 902 at 907.
6 *Brown v Lee Constructions Ltd* 1977 SLT (Notes) 61, OH.
7 Civil Aviation Act 1982 (c 16), s 76. In *Bernstein v Skyviews and General Ltd* [1978] QB 479, [1977] 2 All ER 902, the defendants had taken photographs as well flying into the plaintiff's airspace.

8 As to separate tenements, see paras 207–213 below.
9 *Watt v Burgess' Trustee* (1891) 18 R 766.

(b) Pertinents

199. Parts and pertinents. The term 'parts and pertinents' is generic for heritable rights which pass to successive owners of land by implication. Nonetheless, until as late as the eighteenth century parts and pertinents were 'anxiously enumerated in the tenendas[1] [clause] of every charter'[2]. Craig gives the following example of an enumeration of parts and pertinents:

'... along with houses, buildings, woods, plains, muirs, marshes, ways, paths, rivers, streams, lakes, meadows, pastures, and pasturages, mills multures and the sequels thereof, fowlings, huntings, fishings, peat-mosses, turbaries, rabbits, rabbit-warrens, doves and dove-cots, gardens, orchards, smithies, malt-kilns and brew-houses, broom, woods, forests, and coppice, timber, quarries of stone and lime, courts and their suits, herezelds, bloodwites, and merchets of women, together also with grazings, free ish and entry, and all other liberties, conveniences, profits, easements, and pertinents whatsoever, named as well as unnamed, under the ground as well as above the same, pertaining, or which may in any manner whatsoever lawfully pertain in the future, to the foresaid lands, including the castle, mills, parts, pendicles, and pertinents thereof, freely, fully, quietly, wholly, honourably, happily and in peace, without any impediment, revocation, contradiction, or obstacle whatsoever'[3].

Modern conveyancing practice, perhaps uncharacteristically, exhibits greater restraint. Since parts and pertinents are simply those heritable rights which are implied into a grant of lands, it follows that 'a grant of the lands of A ... is as extensive as a grant of A with parts and pertinents'[4], and except in the case of a break-off conveyance, where new pertinents may be required[5], there is no need to make mention of parts and pertinents. The modern practice is that a bare grant of 'parts and pertinents' without enumeration of specific rights is included as a matter of style in conveyances of Sasine land[6]. In the case of land registered in the Land Register the officially recommended form of conveyance[7] omits a grant of parts and pertinents but by statute carries, on registration, 'any right, pertinent or servitude ... forming part of' the land[8].

1 This practice was somewhat undermined by the rule that the tenendas clause cannot add to the property carried by the dispositive clause. Nonetheless, the inclusion of a right in the tenendas clause may be evidential of its status as a part and pertinent.
2 Erskine *Institute* II,6,4.
3 Craig *Jus Feudale* 2,3,30 (Clyde's translation). Craig blames the excessive length of the clause on the influence of English practice. Note also the caustic observation by Walter Ross that 'in Britain, this part of the *tenendas* may be observed to grow in every succeeding reign, till at last the store of words was totally exhausted ... The moment a new term was invented by any body, and known, the ordinary list became immediately enriched by it; in so much, indeed, that in many charters we often find repetitions of the same thing, under different words; which proves that conveyancers were more attentive to the practice of each other, than to the sense of what they themselves were doing': W Ross *Lectures on the History and Practice of the Law of Conveyancing and Legal Diligence* (2nd edn, 1822) II, p 165.
4 *Gordon v Grant* (1850) 13 D 1 at 7, per Lord Justice-Clerk Hope. For Land Register land this rule is statutory: Land Registration (Scotland) Act 1979 (c 33), s 3(1)(a).
5 Eg a servitude over the reserved land.
6 See the model disposition set out at para 642 below.
7 *Registration of Title Practice Book* (1981) para G.3.22. In England the phrase 'with the appurtenances' was widely used until the introduction in 1881 of a statutory list of rights carried in the transfer of land. The current English provision is the Law of Property Act 1925 (c 20), s 62.
8 Land Registration (Scotland) Act 1979, s 3(1)(a).

200. General. In normal usage 'parts' and 'pertinents' are bracketed together without any attempt to distinguish one from the other. It appears, however, that the two words are not synonymous[1]. A 'pertinent' is a right which pertains to the land and which stands in a subordinate and ancillary relationship to that land. A 'part' does not stand in a subordinate relationship but rather is directly of the principal land. It is suggested, therefore, that the best usage is to reserve 'parts' for those rights which are exercised over the land itself, and 'pertinents' for those rights which are exercised in association with the land but beyond its boundaries. In cases where the boundaries of the principal land are unclear this distinction is easier to express than to apply, and it may be uncertain whether a particular area of ground is a 'part' lying within the boundaries or a 'pertinent' lying beyond them.

The concern here is with pertinents rather than with parts[2]; and pertinents in the sense used here comprise those rights, including in some cases rights of ownership, which are exercisable by a landowner by virtue of his landownership but beyond his boundaries. There is no fixed list. The particular rights which accompany land vary from one case to the next. But it is possible to divide heritable property into four distinct categories based on its potential availability as a pertinent. The four categories are: (1) invariable pertinents, (2) presumed pertinents, (3) possible pertinents, and (4) property unavailable as pertinents.

1 Bankton *Institute* II,3,170; Erskine *Institute* II,6,11; Bell *Principles* s 741; *Forsyth v Durie* (1632) Mor 9629.
2 'Parts' comprise (1) the principal land itself (see paras 196–198 above), (2) anything which by accession has become part of that land, eg a house (see paras 570 ff below), and (3) the rights exercisable in respect of that land by virtue of the right of ownership, eg the rights of use and disposal (see para 195 above).

201. Invariable pertinents: real conditions. A real condition is a right attaching to one's own land but exercisable over land belonging to another. The principal real conditions are servitudes, real burdens and common interest[1]. A real condition is an invariable pertinent, for not only does it pass with the dominant land by implication but it is actually incapable of severance. Thus if Blackmains has a servitude right of way over Whitemains, the right is exercisable by all successive owners of Blackmains against all successive owners of Whitemains. Looked at from Blackmains, the servitude is a pertinent[2]. The difficulty in practice, of course, lies in showing that a real condition exists in the first place.

1 For real conditions, see further paras 344 ff below.
2 Looked at from Whitemains, the servitude is a burden on ownership.

202. Presumed pertinents. In two cases a presumption arises that land lying beyond the boundaries of the owner's land is a pertinent of that land.
(1) *Alveus of non-tidal waters.* The *alveus* of non-tidal waters is presumed to belong to the adjacent dry land *ad medium filum* (to the mid-point)[1]. The presumption does not apply to the *alveus* of tidal waters[2], nor to the foreshore[3].
(2) *Common passage and stair.* In flatted property the common passage and stair is presumed to be the common property of the proprietors of the flats to which it gives access, as a pertinent of their individual proprietorship[4]. There is no equivalent presumption for other parts of the building.
In both cases the presumption may be rebutted, either by the terms of the landowner's own title, or by the existence of a good and adverse title in the hands of some other party.

1 See paras 278, 304, below.
2 Instead it is presumed to belong to the Crown: see para 309 below.
3 The foreshore is treated, in this respect at least, in the same way as ordinary dry land: see para 314 below.
4 See para 231 below.

203. Possible pertinents. Land which is contiguous to the principal land is more likely to be regarded as a pertinent than land which is discontiguous, although discontiguity is not treated as a complete bar[1]. Similarly, land which covers a small area is more likely to be regarded as subordinate to and so a pertinent of the principal land than land which covers a large area[2]. The point at which land is too discontiguous or too large to qualify as a pertinent has not yet been judicially determined. But even if land is both contiguous and small, it is unlikely to be considered a pertinent unless it has been so created either by express grant or by prescription, methods of creation considered separately below[3].

1 Stair *Institutions* II,3,59; Bankton *Institute* II,3,170; Erskine *Institute* II,6,3; Bell *Principles* s 739; *Forsyth v Durie* (1632) Mor 9629.
2 But size is relative: see *Dalrymple v Earl of Stair* (1841) 3 D 837.
3 See paras 204, 205, below.

204. Express grant. A break-off grant may nominate certain land[1] as a pertinent of the land principally conveyed[2]. In practice this occurs most frequently where a building is being subdivided. In such a case the disposition conveys not only the individual flatted unit but also, in the pertinents clause, certain additional parts of the building or surrounding ground[3]. This may include common ownership of garden ground, the *solum* of the building, and the roof, as well as sole ownership of a garage or a cellar.

Once expressly so created, a pertinent remains a pertinent in perpetuity, subject to the rule that, like any other land, it may be acquired separately by express grant or by positive prescription. For Land Register land, the title sheet lists all pertinents created by the break-off grant[4], and these pass by implication in subsequent transmissions[5]. For Sasine land subsequent transmissions will usually import by reference the description of pertinents contained in the original break-off writ; but even where this is omitted it appears that the subsidiary rights created by that writ pass by implication as pertinents of the principal subjects.

1 It may also create servitudes: see para 201 above.
2 If a grant of pertinents is not to be *a non domino*, it can only be made in a break-off conveyance, where the granter owns the surrounding land from which the pertinents are taken.
3 Sometimes the pertinents are listed in a separate deed of conditions, but the deed must then be expressly imported into the pertinents clause of the disposition. The Land Registration (Scotland) Act 1979 (c 33), s 17, which makes real burdens contained in deeds of conditions directly effective without express importation, does not apply to pertinents.
4 Land Registration (Scotland) Act 1979, s 6(1)(e). See *Registration of Title Practice Book* (1981) para E.14.
5 Land Registration (Scotland) Act 1979, s 3(1)(a).

205. Prescription. It is a familiar rule that a landowner may acquire land beyond his existing boundaries by positive prescription. Where the targeted land is contiguous with existing boundaries acquisition will usually proceed on the basis that the new land is truly a part of the existing land[1]. But where the new land is discontiguous the only basis for acquisition is that of pertinent[2]. In neither case is it a bar to prescriptive acquisition that another party is expressly infeft in the targeted land[3].

Prescriptive acquisition of land as a pertinent of other land requires that appropriate possession has followed on the recording or registration of an appropriate title.

(1) *Title: Sasine land.* Any *ex facie* valid title to land is an appropriate title for the prescriptive acquisition of other land[4], provided that the targeted property is capable of being a pertinent of the principal property in respect of which the title exists[5]. The deed constituting the title must be recorded in the Register of Sasines. A prescriptive title requires *ex facie* validity only and it is incompetent to look to earlier deeds[6]. No express grant of pertinents is required[7] but the title must not be overtly inconsistent with the acquisition of the pertinent in question[8]. It has been settled law since the time of Stair that a bounding title is inconsistent with and so precludes the acquisition of land[9] beyond the stipulated boundary even where the acquisition is as a pertinent[10]. This is a severe limitation on the practical usefulness of prescription in this context. Nor is it logical: the fact that the boundaries of the principal land are specified ought not to affect the acquisition of a pertinent which, by definition, lies beyond these boundaries[11]. The rule, however, is now beyond challenge. It is avoided by an express mention in the title of the pertinent sought to be acquired[12].

(2) *Title: Land Register land.* In land registered in the Land Register, only a title in respect of which indemnity has been excluded by the Keeper is available for prescription[13]. Moreover, most titles to registered land are bounding titles[14]. The result is that in the typical case of registered land, where the title is bounding and where indemnity is not excluded, there is no place for prescription. Indeed the only circumstance in which prescriptive acquisition is likely to be available in practice is where the deed inducing registration contains an express grant of particular land as a pertinent and where the Keeper, having included the pertinent in the title plan, proceeds to exclude indemnity.

(3) *Possession.* In both bases the pertinent must be possessed for a continuous period of ten[15] years, openly, peaceably and without judicial interruption[16]. The possession must be attributable to the title, which implies on the one hand that no other more plausible attribution should exist[17], and on the other that the possession is in association with and as a pertinent of the principal land[18].

1 This is because less emphatic possession is required to show that the new land is part of the present land than to show that it is a pertinent. Further, '[w]here a tenement of land is possessed by one barely as a pertinent, and by another in virtue of an express right, he who possesses under the express right is *in dubio* to be preferred to the other': Erskine *Institute* II,6,3.
2 See eg *Cooper's Trustees v Stark's Trustees* (1898) 25 R 1160.
3 Stair *Institutions* II,3,73; *Erskine* II,6,3; Bell *Principles* s 746.
4 Prescription and Limitation (Scotland) Act 1973 (c 52), s 1 (amended by the Land Registration (Scotland) Act 1979 (c 33), s 10).
5 See para 203 above and para 206 below.
6 *Lord Advocate v Hunt* (1865) 3 M 426, revsd (1867) 5 M (HL) 1, in which prior titles were inspected to exclude a particular interpretation of a grant of pertinents, is inconsistent both with *Auld v Hay* (1880) 7 R 663 and with the wording of s 1(1)(b) of the Prescription and Limitation (Scotland) Act 1973. See also *Cooper's Trustees v Stark's Trustees* (1898) 25 R 1160; *Duke of Argyll v Campbell* 1912 SC 458, 1912 1 SLT 316. The views expressed by Lord Kinnear in the second of these cases is supported neither by the rest of the court nor, it seems, by other authority.
7 Ie because a grant of pertinents is implied into every title: see para 199 above.
8 That was the case in *Brown v Allan* 1950 SLT (Sh Ct) 66 where an express mention in the pertinents clause of the west half of a garden was held to exclude prescriptive acquisition of the east half.
9 But not, of course, servitudes: *Beaumont v Lord Glenlyon* (1843) 5 D 1337; *Gordon v Grant* (1850) 13 D 1. See para 201 above.
10 Stair II,3,73; *Erskine* II,6,3; Bell s 739; *Young v Carmichael* (1671) Mor 9636; *Thomson v Grieve* (1688) 2 Brown's Supp 118; *Plewlands v Dundas* (1695) 4 Brown's Supp 236; *Gordon v Grant* (1850) 13 D 1.
11 *Cooper's Trustees v Stark's Trustees* (1898) 25 R 1160 at 1168, 1169, per Lord M'Laren. As that case illustrates, the rule may give rise to a strained interpretation of what constitutes a bounding title.
12 Bell s 739. See eg *Nisbett v Hogg* 1950 SLT 289.
13 Prescription and Limitation (Scotland) Act 1973, s 1 (as amended: see note 4 above).
14 Land Registration (Scotland) Act 1979, s 6(1)(a); *Registration of Title Practice Book* (1981) para E.14. But the title to flatted property is not usually bounding. On the subject of flatted property, see also *Cooper's Trustees v Stark's Trustees* (1898) 25 R 1160.

15 The period is twenty years where prescription is pled against the Crown in any question involving the foreshore: Prescription and Limitation (Scotland) Act 1973, s 1(4).
16 Prescription and Limitation (Scotland) Act 1973, s 1 (as amended: see note 4 above).
17 *Duke of Argyll v Campbell* 1912 SC 458, 1912 1 SLT 316.
18 *Lord Advocate v Hunt* (1865) 3 M 426, revsd (1867) 5 M (HL) 1. It appears that this requirement may not be difficult to satisfy — see *Cooper's Trustees v Stark's Trustees* (1898) 25 R 1160 at 1168, per Lord M'Laren: 'Without attempting a definition, I think that in the case of urban property, if the property which is in dispute, and is claimed by the title of part and pertinent, has been occupied as part of the same habitation, or as part of the same place of business in conjunction with the principal subject, the condition of fair construction is satisfied. In other words, the clause of parts and pertinents is "susceptible" of a meaning which is consistent with the actual possession'.

206. Property unavailable as pertinents. The right of salmon fishing and other legal separate tenements are unavailable either as parts or as pertinents. They can never pass with land by implication but require an express grant[1]. This exclusion does not apply to conventional separate tenements.

1 See para 209 below.

(c) Separate Tenements

207. Introduction. Sometimes the expression 'separate tenement' (*tenementum separatum*) is used to denote any piece of ground which is held in separate ownership. On this usage if A and B own adjacent fields, each field is said to be a separate tenement. More strictly, however, a 'separate tenement' is any heritable property which is owned separately from the *solum* of the ground, and this is the usage adopted in the present title.

Used in this restricted sense, separate tenements are recognised only sparingly in Scots law. The general principle is that the owner of the *solum* of land owns *a coelo usque ad centrum*; and since all heritable property from the heavens to the centre of the earth is his there can be no question of separate tenements. Nonetheless a limited number of separate tenements are recognised[1]. It is accepted for example that B may own the minerals under A's land. In such a case A still owns *a coelo usque ad centrum* but subject to B's separate ownership of minerals. Flatted buildings are in a similar position. Thus suppose that A builds a block of four flats on his land. He sells three of the flats to B, C and D respectively and retains the ground floor flat for himself. In such a case each of B, C and D owns as a separate tenement the stratum of airspace represented by his or her flat, while A continues to own the *solum* and has residual ownership *a coelo usque ad centrum*[2].

Both examples given above (minerals and flatted houses) are corporeal. But it has long been recognised that separate tenements may also be incorporeal. Almost all incorporeal separate tenements are regalian rights[3], which is to say, property originally vested in the Crown but now often in private ownership. The origins of regalian rights deserve brief mention. In medieval Scotland, as in many other feudal kingdoms, certain rights over land were considered of such value and significance that they were by implication reserved from grants of land made by the Crown. Of these the most important in practice was the right to fish for salmon. The method by which reservation was achieved is curious. Since the right to fish for salmon, and other like rights, are incorporeal, the obvious solution would have been to recognise them as special real rights, analogous to servitudes[4]. The Crown grantee would then have had ownership of the river or loch, but qualified by the Crown's real right of salmon fishing. This is not the method which was adopted in Scotland. Instead the reserved regalian rights were treated as themselves things capable of ownership. They were not burdens on land but, as it were, 'land' itself, not real rights but separate tenements. The significance of this distinction is explained later[5]. Its effect is that a Crown grantee of a river or loch received and receives unqualified ownership of the *alveus* (bed) but without ownership of the accompanying salmon fishings.

Regalian rights were originally held by the Crown but, as *regalia minora*, they are capable of alienation and in practice often have been alienated. Thus in a salmon river it is commonplace to find that the river itself is the property of one person and the salmon fishings the property, as a separate tenement, of someone else entirely. The first party owns the river but cannot fish for salmon; the second party may fish for salmon but has no further rights in respect of the river[6].

1 See further paras 210 ff below.
2 This is on the assumption that the common law of the tenement applies. 'Tenement' in the context of 'law of the tenement' means something quite different, namely a building which is physically divided into separate and self-contained units. In practice the titles to the building very often provide that the *solum* is the common property of all proprietors. See further paras 227 ff below.
3 But not all regalian rights are incorporeal, eg mines of gold and silver.
4 An example of this method is South Africa, where mineral rights confer, not ownership of the minerals themselves, but a real right to work them. See H Silberberg and J Schoeman *The Law of Property* (2nd edn, 1983) p 424.
5 See para 208 below. As to real rights, see para 10, head (3), above.
6 See further paras 320–330 below.

208. Characteristics. Whether corporeal or incorporeal, a separate tenement is treated as an independent thing (*res*) and so may be owned and made subject to other, ancillary real rights. Like other land, separate tenements are feudal: the original Crown grant is a grant in feu, and subsequent subinfeudation is permitted. Where a separate tenement is transferred outright the appropriate deed is a disposition even in cases such as salmon fishings where the property is incorporeal. A separate tenement may also be the subject of a lease[1], a standard security[2] or of other ancillary real rights. This may be contrasted with interests in land not recognised as separate tenements, which cannot be owned feudally, granted in security, or leased in such a way that a real right is conferred on the tenant[3].

For the purposes of the law of accession corporeal separate tenements are treated as distinct from the estate from which they are withdrawn, and accession cannot take place across the boundaries of a separate tenement. So if A adds parquet flooring to his top floor flat, the parquet tiles accede to his own flat but not to the flat underneath[4].

1 See LANDLORD AND TENANT, vol 13, paras 194 ff.
2 Conveyancing and Feudal Reform (Scotland) Act 1970 (c 35), s 9(2), (8)(b).
3 But there are two cases in which a real right of lease may now be granted in respect of rights which are not themselves separate tenements, namely:
　(1) trout fishings. See the Freshwater and Salmon Fisheries (Scotland) Act 1976 (c 22), s 4 (lease real under the Leases Act 1449 (c 6)); and
　(2) shootings (game leases). See *Palmer v Brown* 1988 SCLR 499, 1989 SLT 128, OH (lease real under the Registration of Leases (Scotland) Act 1857 (c 26)).
4 See para 585 below.

209. Legal and conventional tenements. Regalian rights are separate tenements by legal implication. So when the Crown feus land to A the regalian rights are automatically reserved and would pass to A only if expressly conferred[1]. Similarly, when B dispones land to C no regalian rights pass without express conveyance[2], for such rights are incapable of becoming pertinents[3]. Of course in most cases a landowner will not hold any of the regalian rights; but with salmon rivers the riparian proprietor may sometimes acquire the right to the fishings, and in such a case the fishings will not pass to a future purchaser in the absence of an express conveyance[4]. In land registered in the Land Register, salmon fishings or other separate tenements are included in the title sheet of the principal subjects[5], and it seems likely that they then pass by implication in any subsequent conveyance[6].

Regalian rights may be classified as 'legal' separate tenements, which is to say, as separate tenements arising by implication of law and incapable of reintegration, in a legal sense, with the land from which they are drawn. There are also other legal separate tenements, most notably coal and teinds[7].

Not all separate tenements, however, arise by law. Corporeal separate tenements falling within certain recognised categories may be created conventionally, either by grant or by reservation[8]. An example is minerals. So if A, the owner of land, dispones the minerals under that land to B, or, conversely, if he dispones the land itself but under reservation of the minerals, the minerals are held separately from the land as a 'conventional' separate tenement. But express reservation is required, not just at the point of origin, but in all future conveyances. So if C conveys land to D and the disposition makes no mention of minerals, the minerals are assumed to be carried[9]. If C actually owns the minerals they will therefore pass to D. But if the minerals are a separate tenement and not in C's ownership, C is liable to D in warrandice[10]. In practice, of course, C will usually take care to exclude the minerals from the disposition if he does not own them or intend them to pass[11]. For reasons which have never been satisfactorily articulated, a different rule applies to conveyances of superiorities, so that if a granter owns both the superiority of land and the *dominium utile* of the minerals beneath, and if he then conveys 'the land', the minerals are not carried unless the deed indicates otherwise[12].

A conventional separate tenement may become a pertinent of other land and so be carried by implication in any conveyance thereof[13]. A familiar example is the case of a cellar under the common stair in a tenement building, which is a separate tenement in relation to the stair but a pertinent in relation to the flat which it serves. As already seen, the position of legal separate tenements is otherwise.

1 Stair *Institutions* II,3,60; Erskine *Institute* II,6,13; Bell *Principles* s 737.
2 Stair II,3,30; Erskine II,6,13; Bell ss 737,748. The decision in *Earl of Breadalbane v Jamieson* (1875) 2 R 826, that royal mines are carried in a conveyance by implication, is *per incuriam*. It was decided on the basis of *Oughterlony v Earl of Selkirk* (1755) Mor 164, a case which, as Monboddo's report discloses (see 5 Brown's Supp 836) was concerned not with royal mines but with mines of lead and copper. See also *M'Adam v Cathcart* 1908 16 SLT 234, OH.
3 See para 206 above.
4 *McKendrick v Wilson* 1970 SLT (Sh Ct) 39.
5 Land Registration (Scotland) Act 1979 (c 33), s 6(1)(e).
6 Ibid, s 3(1)(a).
7 See para 211 below. They are subject to the same rules, eg, as to the requirement of express conveyance. For teinds, see Hume *Lectures* vol VI (Stair Soc vol 19, 1958 ed G C H Paton) p 182.
8 See para 212 below.
9 *Lady Bruce v Erskine* (1716) Mor 9642. The rule is the same in the contract of sale: see *Whyte v Lee* (1879) 6 R 699; *Crofts v Stewart's Trustees* 1927 SC(HL) 65, 1927 SLT 362; *Campbell v M'Cutcheon* 1963 SC 505, 1963 SLT 290.
10 Much, of course, depends on the wording of the disposition. The underlying principle is that a conveyance of land includes all conventional separate tenements (but not legal separate tenements) except insofar as expressly excluded. In practice this principle is avoided in the case of another prominent example of conventional separate tenements, namely individual flats within a flatted building, by conveying not the land itself but the individual flat only.
11 This is done by listing the deed containing the reservation of minerals in the burdens section of the dispositive clause. In missives of sale minerals are always expressly excluded.
12 *Fleeming v Howden* (1868) 6 M 782; *Orr v Mitchell* (1893) 20 R (HL) 27.
13 See para 206 above.

210. Legal separate tenements: the *regalia*. The following are both *inter regalia minora* and also legal separate tenements[1]. The category includes corporeal property as well as (incorporeal) rights:

(1) *The right to fish for salmon*[2].
(2) *The right to gather mussels and the right to gather oysters*[3].

(3) *The right of port and the right of ferry*[4].

(4) *The right to hold fairs and markets*[5]. At common law a landowner is not entitled to hold a fair or market without an express Crown grant[6]. Where granted, the right of fairs and markets includes a right to levy dues on stallholders. As a separate tenement the right may in theory be given to a person other than the landowner, but this does not appear to have happened in practice. Most grants in fact were to royal burghs, and the only reported decision in modern times concerns a right to hold an annual fair granted to the burgh of St Andrews by a Charter of James VI of 1620[7]. Today fairs and markets are regulated by statute[8] and the regalian right is of little more than antiquarian interest.

(5) *Mines of gold and silver*. Mines of gold and silver[9] are reserved from Crown grants by virtue of the Royal Mines Act 1424[10]. But landowners[11] have a statutory right[12] to obtain a separate Crown grant of the mines within their lands, subject to payment of one tenth of the value of all metal mined[13]. The Crown is also entitled to feu royal mines to third parties but only where the landowner has first declined the offer of a Crown grant[14]. It appears that gold and silver are the only metals affected by Crown rights[15].

(6) *Petroleum and natural gas*. Petroleum existing in its natural condition is reserved to the Crown by virtue of the Petroleum (Production) Act 1934[16]. Petroleum for this purpose includes mineral oil and relative hydrocarbon and natural gas existing in its natural condition in strata[17].

A number of other rights considered by some early authorities as *inter regalia minora* are not now so regarded. These include the right to fish for white fish[18], the right to hunt for deer[19], the right to kill swans[20], and fortalices and castles and the right to build fortalices and castles[21].

1 Not all *regalia minora* are separate tenements, ie involve ownership separate from the ownership of the *solum*. Thus the seabed is owned by the Crown but is not a separate tenement. There are also Crown rights in relation to moveables, most notably the right to abandoned property.

2 See paras 320–330 below.

3 See paras 331–333 below.

4 See paras 334–336 below.

5 See generally Bell *Principles* ss 664–666. There is no treatment in either Stair *Institutions* or Erskine *Institute*.

6 Or without a grant *a non domino* and fortified by positive prescription.

7 *Central Motors (St Andrews) Ltd v St Andrews Magistrates* 1961 SLT 290.

8 Local Government and Planning (Scotland) Act 1982 (c 43), s 27; Civic Government (Scotland) Act 1982 (c 45), ss 9, 40. As to the statutory regulation of markets, see LOCAL GOVERNMENT, vol 14, paras 549, 562, 695 and 696.

9 The Royal Mines Act 1424 (c 13) contains two conditions for silver to come within the Crown reservation, namely that it must be found in lead and that 'thre halfpennys of siluer may be fynit owt of the punde of leide'. The first condition is invariably satisfied, whilst currency depreciation has long since made the second irrelevant. For the value of three halfpennies of silver, see *Erskine* II,6,16.

10 As to mines of gold and silver, see *Stair* II,3,60; Bankton *Institute* II,3,109; *Erskine* II,6,16; Hume *Lectures* vol IV (Stair Soc vol 17, 1955 ed G C H Paton) pp 237, 238; *Bell* s 669.

11 Ie the proprietors of the *dominium utile*: see *Duke of Argyle v Murray* (1739) Mor 13526; *Erskine* II,6,16.

12 *Earl of Hopeton v Offices of State* (1750) Mor 13527.

13 Mines and Metals Act 1592 (c 31).

14 For the procedure, see the Mines and Metals Act 1592.

15 The inclusion of copper, lead and tin in the Mines and Metals Act 1592, but not in the Royal Mines Act 1424, is probably not sufficient to reserve them to the Crown: *Earl of Breadalbane v Jamieson* (1875) 2 R 826 at 830–832, per Lord Curriehill. Craig counts copper, lead and salt as *inter regalia: Jus Feudale* 2,8,21.

16 Petroleum (Production) Act 1934 (c 36), s 1(1), (2) (substituted by the Oil and Gas (Enterprise) Act 1982 (c 23), s 18(1)). As to petroleum and gas generally, see ENERGY, vol 9, paras 721 ff and 856 ff.

17 Petroleum (Production) Act 1934, s 1(4) (renumbered by the Oil and Gas (Enterprise) Act 1982, s 18(1)). 'Coal or bituminous shales or other stratified deposits from which oil can be extracted by destructive distillation' are expressly excluded.

18 See paras 280, 306, 521, below.
19 *Duke of Athole v Macinroy* (1862) 24 D 673, displacing the view expressed by Stair (see *Stair* II,3,30) and Bankton (see *Bankton* II,3,166). See also para 544, note 6, below.
20 *Erskine* II,6,15; *Duke of Athole v Macinroy* (1862) 24 D 673. The contrary view was expressed by Stair (see *Stair* II,3,60) and Bankton (see *Bankton* II,3,166).
21 *Bankton* II,3,91; *Erskine* II,6,18; *Bell* s 743. The earlier and contrary view may be found in *Stair* II,3,65,66. See also *Home v Home* (1612) Mor 9627.

211. Other legal separate tenements. Coal and teinds are also separate tenements by implication of law, but do not originate in a reservation by the Crown.
(1) *Coal.* Unmined coal is the property of the Coal Authority[1]. By coal is meant bituminous coal, cannel coal and anthracite[2].
(2) *Teinds.* Teinds[3] or tithes are the right of the church to a tenth part of the land and industry of the laity, although this has long since been converted into a monetary equivalent[4]. Originally teinds were paid directly to the clergy or to religious foundations, but the pre-Reformation church introduced the practice of alienating the right to teinds to members of the laity, known as titulars. Titulars paid a proportion of the teinds collected, known as stipend, to the church, and the balance, known as free teinds, they were allowed to retain.

The proprietor of land burdened by teinds was entitled to, and often did, buy his own teinds from the titular[5]. As separate tenements teinds were transferred by a conveyance accompanied, prior to the reforms of 1845, by the giving of sasine through the appropriate feudal symbol[6]. But even where teinds were not so acquired the practice, and eventually the law[7], became that stipend was paid directly by the proprietor to the church[8], and the balance, if any, was then paid to the titular as free teinds[9].

Since 1925 stipend has been secured as a real burden, known as standard charge, on the land from which payment falls to be made[10]. Standard charge may be redeemed on payment of a capitalised sum to the Church of Scotland General Trustees[11], and since 1974 redemption is compulsory on the sale of the burdened land[12].

The redemption of standard charge does not remove the obligation to pay free teinds to the titular in circumstances where the teinds are held separately from the land[13]; but since the amounts involved are, with inflation, very small, it may be doubted whether the obligation is ever now exacted. Even today, however, an express right to teinds continues to be found in some dispositions of land.

1 Coal Industry Act 1994 (c 21), s 7(3). Prior to 31 October 1994 unmined coal was the property of the British Coal Corporation (formerly the National Coal Board).
2 Ibid, s 65(1).
3 The standard work on teinds is W Buchanan *Treatise on the Law of Scotland on the subject of Teinds or Tithes* (1862). For a useful modern summary, see W M Gordon *Scottish Land Law* (1989) pp 304–313.
    Teinds were once better known than they are today. The author is indebted to Dr H L MacQueen for drawing his attention to the following passage from chapter 35 of Walter Scott's *The Antiquary* (1816): ' "... and if ye have ony household affairs to attend to, Mrs Griselda, never make a stranger of me — I can amuse myself very weel with the larger copy of Erskine's Institutes". And taking down from the window seat that amusing folio ... he opened it, as if instinctively, at the tenth title of Book Second, "of Teinds, or Tythes", and was presently deeply wrapped up in an abstruse discussion concerning the temporality of benefices'.
4 See now the Church of Scotland (Property and Endowments) Act 1925 (c 33), s 16, Sch 6.
5 Act of 1633 (c 17) (repealed by the Statute Law Revision (Scotland) Act 1964 (c 80)). See now the Church of Scotland (Property and Endowments) Act 1925, s 18.
6 The symbol was grass and corn.
7 Church of Scotland (Property and Endowments) Act 1925, ss 8(1), 12(2).
8 It is now paid to the Church of Scotland General Trustees.
9 Church of Scotland (Property and Endowments) Act 1925, s 17.
10 Ibid, s 12(1).

11 Ibid, s 12(3), (4).
12 Land Tenure Reform (Scotland) Act 1974 (c 38), s 5(12).
13 There is no provision for the redemption of teinds. They are expressly excluded from the Land
Tenure Reform (Scotland) Act 1974 by s 4(7) and s 5(12).

212. Conventional separate tenements. While legal separate tenements may be either corporeal or incorporeal, conventional separate tenements are restricted to corporeal property, and attempts to reserve from grants of land such (incorporeal) rights as the right of shooting game have not met with success in the courts[1]. Moreover, even in the case of corporeal property the law has been reluctant to accept the principle of conventional separate tenements. The present rules have evolved pragmatically, in response to two very different socio-economic factors, namely the presence in the soil of large deposits of minerals, and the predilection of the nation's inhabitants for building upwards rather than outwards. Thus it is clearly settled law that both minerals and individual tenement flats may be separated conventionally from the ownership of the *solum*. But in most other respects the law is neither clear nor coherent.

It is convenient to distinguish corporeal property according to whether it lies above or beneath the surface of the earth.

(1) *Property beneath the surface.* It appears that horizontal strata lying beneath the surface of the earth can be separated from ownership of the surface. With respect to strata containing coal or other minerals this rule was established in the seventeenth century[2], although it was not until the decision of the House of Lords in *Graham v Duke of Hamilton*[3] in 1871 that it was conclusively settled that a grant of minerals is a grant of a stratum of earth and not merely a grant of an incorporeal right to extract the minerals[4]. It appears that the rule is now a general one, and that grants, or reservations, of strata may be made even where they do not contain minerals[5].

(2) *Property above the surface.* It appears that horizontal strata lying above the surface of the earth cannot usually be constituted as separate tenements. Certainly it is the case that property which is heritable only by accession — trees or pipes, for example — cannot competently be separated from the land to which it has acceded[6]. But flatted buildings are an exception: buildings of more than a single storey may be divided up into separate tenements, with each storey in the ownership of a different proprietor or proprietors[7]. There is also a second, but now obsolete, exception for mills, which may be separated from the land on which they are built[8]. A conventional separate tenement may be created by statute[9].

It has never been decided whether a stratum of unoccupied airspace can be constituted as a separate tenement.

1 *Hemming v Duke of Athole* (1883) 11 R 93; *Marquis of Huntly v Nicol* (1896) 23 R 610, 3 SLT 297 (interpreting *Earl of Aboyne v Innes* 22 June 1813 FC, affd (1819) 6 Pat 444, HL). But see also *Earl of Aboyne v Farquharson* Nov 16 1814 FC; *Murray v Peddie* (1880) 7 R 804. Alternative, but no more successful, bases suggested for such rights have been as servitudes and as real burdens.
2 Craig *Jus Feudale* II,8,17; Stair *Institutions* II,3,74; *Lord Burly v Sime* (1662) Mor 9630, 10374. See also Erskine *Institute* II,6,5; Bell *Principles* s 740. The history is traced by Lord Deas in *Graham v Duke of Hamilton* (1869) 7 M 976 at 982–983. Coal is now a legal separate tenement owned by the British Coal Corporation: see para 211 above. As to minerals generally, see MINES AND QUARRIES, vol 14; CONVEYANCING, vol 6, paras 491–495; and W M Gordon *Scottish Land Law* (1989) ch 6.
3 *Graham v Duke of Hamilton* (1871) 9 M(HL) 98 (revsg (1869) 7 M 976). See also *Simson v Kerr* (1792) 3 Pat 238, HL.
4 At one time attempts were made to classify the right to minerals as a servitude (*Harvie v Stewart* (1870) 9 M 129, per Lord Kinloch dissenting) or as a real burden (*Bain v Duke of Hamilton* (1865) 3 M 821 especially at 827, per Lord Curriehill), but both appear to fail on the basis that minerals are not exclusively for the benefit of a notional dominant tenement. A more fruitful method of classifying an incorporeal right to minerals would be as an incorporeal separate tenement (like salmon fishings) or as a separate nominate real right. But it is too late for arguments of this kind, and it appears that

even grants expressed as a right to work coal will be read as full grants of a stratum of earth: see *Duke of Hamilton v Dunlop* (1884) 11 R 963, affd (1885) 12 R(HL) 65.

5 *Glasgow City and District Rly Co v MacBrayne* (1883) 10 R 894; *Dicksons and Laing v Hawick Burgh* (1885) 13 R 163.

6 *Paul v Cuthbertson* (1840) 2 D 1286 (trees); *Hilson v Scott* (1895) 23 R 241 (mill lade); *Crichton v Turnbull* 1946 SC 52, 1946 SLT 156 (surface water and pipes).

7 For flatted buildings, see paras 227 ff below.

8 *Erskine* II,6,5; *Bell* s 743; *Rose v Ramsay* (1777) Mor 'Part and Pertinent' App No 1. In earlier times mills were regarded as legal separate tenements: *Craig* I,16,41; *Stair* II,3,71; *Bankton Institute* II,3,94; *Fleming v Ross* (1566) Mor 8895.

9 *Glasgow and South-Western Rly Co v Caledonian Rly Co* (1882) 9 R 779.

213. Additional regalian rights: wreck. The rights considered so far are those which a landowner might reasonably expect to exercise over his own land, and indeed would be able to exercise but for the fact that they are separate tenements. But feudalism also gave rise to certain regalian rights additional to normal rights of landownership and, in some cases, only tenuously related to the ownership of land at all[1]. For the most part these rights have been abolished by statute (for example, the right of heritable jurisdiction[2]) or fallen into disuse (for example, the right of forestry[3]), and the only modern survivor appears to be the right of wreck or 'wrak'[4].

The Crown right to unclaimed wreck is merely one aspect of the general Crown right to abandoned property[5]. In the case of wreck the right is now statutory[6]. In certain parts of the coastline the Crown right has been feued to subject proprietors, who thus stand in the place of the Crown with respect to that coastline. A Crown grant of wreck carries the right to all unclaimed debris resulting from shipwreck, including both the wrecked vessel itself and any cargo which it was carrying. It is immaterial whether the debris remains at sea or has been swept up on the shore[7]. Debris remaining at sea is sometimes described, according to its nature, as jetsam, flotsam or as lagan[8]. Aircraft and hovercraft debris is not included within a Crown grant of wreck[9].

Detailed rules for the administration of wreck are contained in the Merchant Shipping Act 1995[10]. The administration of wreck is in the hands of local receivers of wreck, who are usually customs officers. The proprietor of a Crown grant of wreck is required to deliver to the receiver a statement containing the particulars of his title and an address to which notices may be sent[11]. Within forty-eight hours of taking possession of any wreck found at a place to which the statement and title refer, the receiver is required to send to the address delivered a description of the wreck and of any marks by which it is distinguished[12]. If at the end of a period of one year from the time when the wreck first came into the possession of the receiver no claim thereto has been established, the wreck will be delivered to the Crown grantee on payment of all expenses, costs, fees and salvage dues in respect thereof[13]. Delivery does not by itself confer a good title on the Crown grantee[14], who remains vulnerable until the title of the original owner is extinguished by the long negative prescription[15].

1 This distinction is made in Erskine *Institute* II,6,13.

2 This right was abolished by the Heritable Jurisdictions (Scotland) Act 1746 (c 43), s 1. On the right of jurisdiction, see para 54 above.

3 The right of forestry conferred a right to any cattle straying on the grantee's land. It was not confined to grantees of royal forests (for which see para 197 above). See further Stair *Institutions* II,3,67; *Erskine* II,6,14; *Bell Principles* s 670. The right presupposes a Crown entitlement to straying cattle which does not now exist.

4 The leading modern case is *Lord Advocate v Hebden* (1868) 6 M 489. See also *Marquess of Breadalbane v Smith* (1850) 12 D 602. See generally paras 554–557 below.

5 For abandoned property, see paras 547 ff below. But in the old law the right was more extensive and included all wrecked goods, whether abandoned or not, provided that no living creature was found on board or survived the wreck, subject, however, to the owner having a year and a day in which to vindicate his claim. For the displacement of this rule, see eg *Monteir v Agnew* (1725) Mor 16796.

6 Merchant Shipping Act 1995 (c 21), s 241. This is merely declaratory of the common law, for which see *Stair* III,3,27; *Erskine* II,1,13; *Bell* s 1292.

7 *Lord Advocate v Hebden* (1868) 6 M 489. The Merchant Shipping Act 1995, s 255(1), defines 'wreck' to include jetsam, flotsam, lagan, and derelict found in or on the shores of the sea or any tidal water. For jetsam, flotsam and lagan, see note 8 below. Derelict (or waith) is property abandoned at sea by those in charge without hope of recovery or intention of returning: 43 *Halsbury's Laws of England* (4th edn) para 1008.

8 According to Bankton *Institute* I,8,5, flotsam refers to goods floating on the sea, jetsam to goods thrown overboard to lighten a ship during a storm, and lagan to goods sunk to the bottom of the sea.

9 Aircraft (Wreck and Salvage) Order 1938, SR & O 1938/136, art 2(b); Hovercraft (Application of Enactments) Order 1972, SI 1972/971, art 8(1) (amended by SI 1995/1299). But wrecked aircraft and hovercraft are brought within the administrative arrangements provided for in the Merchant Shipping Act 1995 and, if unclaimed, fall to the Crown.

10 Although there is no express exclusion in Part VI (ss 67–79) of the Civic Government (Scotland) Act 1982, it may be assumed that the provisions of that Part as to the disposal of lost and abandoned property are not intended to apply in the case of wreck.

11 Merchant Shipping Act 1995, s 242(1).

12 Ibid, s 242(2).

13 Ibid, s 243.

14 Ibid, s 244.

15 Prescription and Limitation (Scotland) Act 1973 (c 52), s 8.

(3) BOUNDARY WALLS AND FENCES

(a) General

214. Introduction. Boundary walls and fences were little used in Scotland until the eighteenth century when the fashion for enclosure developed. In earlier times boundaries or 'marches' were set out with march stones or, sometimes, left completely unmarked. March stones could be moved and so were not entirely reliable. Stair records that 'when march-stones are solemnly set, boys use sometimes to be laid upon them and sharply whipt, whereby they will be able to remember, and be good witnesses as to those marches when they are old, that impression on their fancy lasting long'[1]. In recent times fencing has become widespread, although not universal, and the whipping of boys has correspondingly declined.

1 Stair *Institutions* IV,43,7.

(b) Construction

215. Wall within an estate. Sometimes a boundary wall or fence is constructed on the exact line of the common boundary; and sometimes it is constructed wholly within the boundaries of one of the two adjoining estates. In each case the governing principles are different[1].

A landowner is always free to erect a wall or fence where it is to lie wholly within his own boundaries. But, except where the March Dykes Act 1661 applies[2], the expense of the work must then be borne by him alone[3]. In principle the wall may be of a design, and of a height, of the landowner's choosing; but this is subject to the planning laws and to the possible existence of restrictive servitudes[4] and real burdens[5]. In *Dunlop v Robertson*[6] the defender, a solicitor from Ayr, erected a boundary wall sixteen feet in height which, although entirely on his own ground, was a mere three feet from a house belonging to the pursuer. This blocked out the supply of daylight to the first two floors of the house. The pursuer sought demolition of the wall on the principle of *aemulatio vicini* (spite)[7] but he was not successful, the court accepting that the wall was built in order to preserve the defender's privacy. If *Dunlop* is correct, as it appears to be[8], it may be doubted whether the erection of a boundary[9] wall can ever be regarded as *in aemulationem vicini*.

1 For walls and fences on the common boundary, see para 217 below.
2 As to the March Dykes Act 1661, see para 216 below.
3 *Ord v Wright* (1738) Mor 10479; *Duncan v Ramsay* (1906) 23 Sh Ct Rep 181. But see *Seaton v Seaton* (1679) Mor 10476.
   Hume states that 'if the [neighbouring] heritor does take the benefit of the fence, this will be held to prove his approbation of it, and he will be liable for a part of the expense of erecting it in so far as he is benefited by it, as if he had concurred from the first': Hume *Lectures* vol III (Stair Soc vol 15, 1952 ed G C H Paton) p 416. Since liability is stated to be *quantum lucratus*, the argument may be based on recompense. But even if Hume is right it is difficult to see how a neighbour can 'take the benefit of the fence'. In a sense all neighbours receive the benefit of a boundary fence. What must be done to attract liability? Is a neighbour with small children — or with sheep — liable, while a neighbour without dependencies prone to straying is not? And if so, what is the extent of his or her benefit? It is not easy to establish satisfactory principles.
4 In particular a (negative) servitude of light in favour of the neighbour.
5 For an unusual situation, where the fence being erected was wholly within the defender's land but was said to affect the stability of a pre-existing wall built on both sides of the boundary, see *Thom v Hetherington* 1988 SLT 724, OH.
6 *Dunlop v Robertson* (1803) Hume 515.
7 For *aemulatio vicini*, see NUISANCE, vol 14, paras 2033–2036.
8 *Glassford v Astley* (1808) Mor 'Property' App No 7 (boundary screens within one foot of neighbour's windows) is to similar effect. Commenting on this case, and on the case of *Dunlop*, Hume in *Decisions* at p 516 wrote: 'On the first view, one may incline to think that an owner's privilege ought to give way, where his interest to maintain it in the particular instance bears a very low proportion to the inconvenience he thus occasions to his neighbour. But there can be no precise or practicable rule of distinction between greater and less in such matters; and the attempt to establish exceptions of this sort would engage the judge in inextricable difficulties. Besides, regard must be had to the endless diversity of the tastes, humours, and habits of different men, which make the same thing an object of gratification to one man, which is quite worthless in the eyes of another ... The law, therefore, justly and wisely inclines to support an owner of land in the exercise of his powers *in suo*, in any instance where he assigns any intelligible and allowable, though perhaps inconsiderable, benefit to himself in what he does. It is fair, in these circumstances, to ascribe his proceedings to the desire of his own advantage, though minute in the general estimation, and not to the gratification of spleen or enmity to his neighbour'.
9 Cf *Ross v Baird* (1829) 7 S 361 where the wall was not a boundary wall.

216. The March Dykes Act 1661.
Where the 1661 March Dykes Act applies it allows the recovery from a neighbouring proprietor of one half of the cost of erecting a boundary wall or fence. The Act does not apply in towns or in cities, nor to any plot of land of less than five acres[1], but it is a useful provision nonetheless and one which deserves to be better known.

The operative part of the Act reads:

'wher inclosours fall to be vpon the border of any persons inheritance the next adjacent heritor shall be at equall paines and charges in building ditching and planting that dyk which parteth their inheritance'[2].

'Heritor' here means owner, so that the Act cannot be used by a tenant or, it has been held, by a crofter[3]; but on the other hand 'dyk' means a wall or fence of any kind[4]. A proprietor who wishes to build a boundary wall under the Act proceeds as follows. Prior to starting work he must obtain either the consent of his neighbour or the authority of the court. The Court of Session has concurrent jurisdiction with the sheriff court[5]. Usually the court will appoint an expert to report on the feasibility of the project. The main ground for refusal of applications is that the project is 'visionary or absurd'[6], the expense of construction being disproportionate to any benefit which the defender might receive. So in one case the defender argued that 'her property, though of large extent, was mountainous and barren, and yielded but a small rent, and, of course, that the expense of the proposed inclosure of lands . . . would, however little her more opulent neighbour might feel it, be a burden far too heavy for her circumstances to bear'[7]. This argument was successful. The opinion of the court 'was that this act of Parliament ought to be interpreted as respecting cases in which mutual, though not therefore equal advantages were to accrue to the conterminous tenements; and as in no instance authorising an act of oppression, or of injustice to any individual'[7].

If the application to the court is successful, the pursuer builds the wall or fence and recovers half the cost ('equall paines and charges') from the defender. The Act does not authorise encroachment and, unless agreement with the defender can be reached, the wall must be built entirely on the pursuer's land[8]. The defender's liability is personal and does not transmit against successors in title[9].

1 *Penman v Douglas and Cochrane* (1739) Mor 10481.
2 Part of the March Dykes Act 1661 (c 41) was repealed by the Statute Law Revision (Scotland) Act 1906 (c 38).
3 *McDonald v Dalgleish* (1894) 21 R 900.
4 *Scott v Duke of Argyll* (1907) 14 SLT 829.
5 *Pollock v Ewing* (1869) 7 M 815.
6 Hume *Lectures* vol III, (Stair Soc vol 15, 1952 ed G C H Paton) p 415. See also Erskine *Institute* II,6,4.
7 *Earl of Peterborough v Garioch* (1784) Mor 10497. For other examples of this principle, see *Earl of Cassillis v Paterson* 28 Feb 1809 FC; *Earl of Airlie v Farquharson* (1887) 24 SLR 761, OH; *Secker v Cameron* 1914 SC 354, 1914 1 SLT 214.
    One common ground for refusing an application is that the natural boundaries, eg a stream, are already sufficient. See *Earl of Crawford v Rig* (1669) Mor 10475; *Pollock v Ewing* (1869) 7 M 815; *Graham v Irving* (1899) 2 F 29, 7 SLT 182.
8 *Graham v Irving* (1899) 2 F 29 at 34, per Lord M'Laren.
9 Bankton *Institute* I,10,153. Contrast here the rule for common gables given in para 218 below.

217. Wall on the common boundary. Ideally a division wall or fence ought to be erected on the exact boundary between two properties. The wall will then lie in each property to the extent of one half of its thickness, with the centre line marking the boundary. Often, however, this ideal is not achieved, and even where a wall marks the boundary accurately for part of its length it may deviate from the line in another part or parts.

Except for the special case of common gables, which is considered separately below[1], a wall cannot be built on both sides of the boundary without the consent of both proprietors. It makes no difference that the wall has been authorised by the court for the purposes of the March Dykes Act 1661 (c 41)[2]. So if proprietor A builds across the boundary without the consent of proprietor B, he is encroaching on B's land and, depending on the circumstances, may be required to remove the wall to the extent of the encroachment[3].

In practice the position may be regulated by real burdens. Thus in the development of a housing estate it is often provided in the titles of each house that the garden is to be fenced, that the fence may be built to the extent of one half on the property of the adjoining house, and that the proprietor who builds the fence may recover half of the cost from the other proprietor[4]. Provisions of these kinds are not without their difficulties. The legal basis of a reserved right to build on another's land is uncertain. It does not appear to be a servitude[5], and if it is intended as a real burden its validity is not beyond doubt[6]. Further, the provisions are not always well drafted. An obligation to build a wall is not valid unless accompanied by a time limit by which the work must be completed[7], but in practice time limits are often omitted. There may also be failure to specify the kind of fence or wall required to be built. It has been held in the sheriff court that where one or both of the properties are in agricultural use there is an implied condition that the fence should be stockproof[8], but this decision seems open to question[9].

An agreement to build is often accompanied by an agreement that the cost should be borne by both parties. Real burdens, where they provide for building, also invariably provide for the apportionment of cost. But in the absence of any such agreement or apportionment the full cost must usually be borne by the party who instructs the work[10].

1 See para 218 below.
2 *Graham v Irving* (1899) 2 F 29 at 34, per Lord M'Laren.
3 See further paras 175 ff above.
4 See eg the burdens in *Thom v Hetherington* 1988 SLT 724, OH.
5 *Campbell's Trustees v Glasgow Corpn* (1902) 4 F 752, 10 SLT 9, especially at 758, 10, per Lord Kinnear.
6 In *Scottish Temperance Life Assurance Co v Law Union and Rock Insurance Co* 1917 SC 175, 1917 1 SLT 4, a disposition reserved to the disponer 'full power and liberty to erect a stable and gig-house' on part of the ground disponed. The burden failed for more than one reason, but Lord Dundas commented that '[N]o authority was cited to us for the creation of a future and contingent real burden or condition of this kind. I gravely doubt if such a burden or condition could be validly created': 1917 SC 175 at 183, 1917 1 SLT 4 at 6. But cf *B & C Group Management Ltd v Haren* (4 December 1992, unreported), OH, where a reserved right to form a road was upheld as a real burden.
   In these cases the burden was contained, properly, in the title of the servient property. But in building developments the equivalent burden sometimes appears in the title of the dominant property only, which is of course fatal to the burden's validity. See para 388 below.
7 *Gammell's Trustees v The Land Commission* 1970 SLT 254, OH. This case is overlooked in J M Halliday *Conveyancing Law and Practice in Scotland* vol II (1986) para 19-30, where a different rule is given.
8 *Church of Scotland General Trustees v Phin* 1987 SCLR 240, Sh Ct.
9 It is contrary to the rule that positive obligations cannot be imported into real burdens by implication (for which rule, see para 417 below).
10 Usually but not always. The main exception is where the March Dykes Act 1661 applies. There may also be a second exception where the neighbouring proprietor makes use of the fence. See paras 215, 216, above.

218. Common gables. Common (or mutual) gable is the name given to the shared division wall between two separate but connected buildings. Common gables are found in semi-detached and terraced houses and also in tenements.

The law of common gables occupies many pages of the nineteenth century law reports, a fact largely explained by Victorian building practice. In the nineteenth, and earlier, centuries, most building work in towns and cities was carried out on a small scale and by individual builders. An area marked for development would be feued plot by plot, often to different builders, so that it might be many years before the entire area was built upon. In order to preserve a continous building line, some provision had to be made for the sharing of gable walls, and the rule evolved that the first builder to begin work could erect a gable half on his own plot and half on the adjoining plot. When the adjoining plot came to be built upon, the gable could be used but on payment of half of the cost of the initial erection.

Modern building practice is different. Today an area being developed for housing is almost always controlled by a single builder; and to a large extent the law on the erection of common gables has become dead law. It need be treated only briefly here[1].

The rules about the erection of common gables apply only to land in a town or city, and only where it is clear from a plan or from other circumstances that the houses to be built are to form a continuous building line[2]. Where the rules apply, the proprietor of each individual building plot is entitled to build a gable wall partly on his own plot and partly, to the extent of one half of the thickness, on the plot adjoining[3]. When the adjoining proprietor then comes to build he is entitled to use the gable as one of his walls, but subject to payment of half of the cost. The legal mechanism by which this result is achieved is complex. The law implies into the title of each party a reciprocal real condition, founded presumably on common interest[4], by which the first proprietor is bound to allow the second proprietor, on payment, to make use of the gable, while the second proprietor is prohibited from using even that part of the gable built on his own ground without paying half of the cost of construction[5]. These conditions run with the land[6]. In practice there are often express provisions in the titles which, in the event of conflict, prevail over the provisions implied by law. The obligation to make payment arises if and only if the second proprietor uses the gable[7]. It is unclear whether the obligation is to pay half of the actual cost of construction or whether account should be taken of inflation[8]. Payment is due to the first proprietor or, where ownership has changed, to his successors as proprietors; and where, as frequently happens, the dominant property has been subdivided, payment is due to the proprietor whose part includes the gable[9].

A considerable period may elapse between the construction of the gable by the first proprietor and its use by the second. Opinion is divided about the ownership of the gable during this period. The view usually expressed gives the first proprietor sole ownership until the time of payment (or, in some versions, time of use) when both proprietors become owner[10]. But, as its proponents readily concede[11], this view has its difficulties. Since half of the gable is built on land belonging to the second proprietor, ownership can only remain with the first proprietor by ignoring the law of accession. Further, it is unclear how, in the absence of an express conveyance, the mere fact of payment can transmit ownership from the first to the second proprietor. An alternative and, it is submitted, more satisfactory view is that both parties own _ad medium filum_ (to the mid-way point) from the moment the gable is first erected, but that common interest prohibits use by the second proprietor until payment is made[12].

If a common gable is destroyed, either party is free to rebuild, but it appears that the other party need not contribute to the cost unless and until he makes use of the new gable[13].

1 For a fuller treatment, see W M Gordon 'Mutual Gable Walls' (1980) 25 JLSS 141 and W M Gordon _Scottish Land Law_ (1989) pp 68–71.

2 In _Jack v Begg_ (1875) 3 R 35, where the proprietor of ground in an Edinburgh suburb took down an old mutual garden wall and replaced it with a gable four storeys high, both preconditions were said to be lacking.

3 _Law v Monteith_ (1855) 18 D 125; _Sanderson v Geddes_ (1874) 1 R 1198.

4 Although the term 'common interest' is not actually used. In fact the formula of ownership _ad medium filum_ coupled with common interest beyond the mid-point reappears in the context of maintenance. See paras 223 ff below.

5 _Law v Monteith_ (1855) 18 D 125; _Rodger v Russell_ (1873) 11 M 671. If the plots are in the same ownership at the time of construction but subsequently come to be divided, the real conditions come into existence at the time of division. See _Glasgow Royal Infirmary v Wylie_ (1877) 4 R 894 and _Baird v Alexander_ (1898) 25 R (HL) 35, 6 SLT 34.

6 Thus a trustee in sequestration is as much bound as the bankrupt whose place he has taken, and the price of the gable is in effect a preferred debt. See _Wallace v Brown_ 21 June 1808 FC and _Rodger v Russell_ (1873) 11 M 671.

7 _Calder v Pope_ (1900) 8 SLT 149, OH. For the meaning of use, see eg _Sinclair v Brown Bros_ (1882) 10 R 45 (wooden shed barely connected to gable held not to be use).

8 W M Gordon 'Mutual Gable Walls' (1980) 25 JLSS 141. According to Professor Gordon the obligation is to pay for a share proportionate to the amount of use taken and not necessarily for a half of the whole gable: _Scottish Land Law_ para 4-42.

9 _White v Weir_ (1895) 2 SLT 453; _Roberts v Galloway_ (1898) 6 SLT 25, OH. But compare _Calder v Pope_ (1900) 8 SLT 149, OH.

10 _Earl of Moray v Aytoun_ (1858) 21 D 33; _Rodger v Russell_ (1873) 11 M 671. When both parties come to own the gable, ownership is presumably _ad medium filum_. See para 223 below.

11 See the views expressed by Lord Justice-Clerk Moncreiff in _Rodger v Russell_ (1873) 11 M 671 and in _Robertson v Scott_ (1886) 13 R 1127.

12 This view was first expressed by Lord Craighill and Lord Rutherfurd Clark in _Robertson v Scott_ (1886) 13 R 1127.

13 _Stark's Trustees v Cooper's Trustees_ (1900) 2 F 1257, 8 SLT 170; _Glasgow Trades House v Ferguson_ 1979 SLT 187.

(c) Alteration of Boundaries

219. Location of boundaries. For land registered in the Land Register, boundaries are indicated on the plan included in the title sheet; and subject to limitations of scaling[1], these boundaries are definitive and may be relied upon[2]. For Sasine titles, however, the position is far less satisfactory[3]. Sometimes there is neither a plan nor a verbal description of the boundaries; and even where plans exist they may not be accurate[4], while verbal descriptions are often impenetrable or refer to physical objects which have long since disappeared.

Walls and fences are of limited help in locating the boundary. For the wall may be built wholly on one side of the boundary, or it may wander from one side to the other, or, in the worst cases, it may be built some distance behind or beyond the true boundary[5]. In well-drawn titles the wall or fence is incorporated into the description of the boundaries and it is stated whether the boundary is the outer face[6], the mid-point[7] or the inner face of the wall[8]. Where such precise information is available to the Keeper of the Land Register it is included in the title plan by means of a system of black arrows[9].

In Sasine titles it is not uncommon for there to be a discrepancy between the legal boundaries (that is, the actual boundaries) and the occupational boundaries (that is, the boundaries as occupied by the owner and indicated, usually, by walls or fences). Usually this passes unnoticed until first registration in the Land Register when, if the discrepancy is substantial, it may be necessary for the proprietor to reach some accommodation with his neighbour[10].

1 Title plans use Ordnance Survey maps on one of three scales, namely: (1) 1:10,000 (mountain and moorland); (2) 1:2,500 (other rural areas); and (3) 1:1,250 (urban areas). On these the limitations on scaling are: (a) six feet; (b) one foot six inches; and (c) nine inches. See the *Registration of Title Practice Book* (1981) paras E.07, E.08. No indemnity is payable for errors attributable to these limitations: see the Land Registration (Scotland) Act 1979 (c 33), s 12(3)(d).
2 The effect of s 3(1)(a) of the Land Registration (Scotland) Act 1979 is to confer ownership in respect of the boundaries disclosed on the title plan. This is so even where indemnity has been excluded, in whole or in part. See para 673 below.
3 See the discussion at para 197 above.
4 Victorian deeds sometimes employ the phrase 'plan or sketch' and all to often the plan is truly no more than a rough sketch.
5 An example is *Readman v Ferrier* (1904) 11 SLT 799, OH.
6 Ie '. . . bounded on the north by the outer [or northern] face of a stone wall . . .'.
7 Ie '. . . bounded on the north by the centre line of a stone wall . . .'.
8 Ie '. . . bounded on the north by the inner [or southern] face of a stone wall . . .'.
9 The arrow indicates the relationship of the boundary to the wall. The code is as follows: (1) *outer face*: the arrow is drawn outside the wall and pointing towards it; (2) *mid-point*: the arrow is drawn through the wall; (3) *inner face*: the arrow is drawn on the property side of the wall and pointing towards it. If the Keeper has examined the titles of the adjoining properties and if these agree as to the location of the boundaries, a black bar is added to the arrow. See further the *Registration of Title Practice Book* paras E.20–E.22.
  The arrow system is not guaranteed — indemnity is expressly excluded in the land certificate — but, subject to the very remote possibility of rectification, the proprietor owns in accordance with the arrows. See the Land Registration (Scotland) Act 1979, s 3(1)(a).
10 For a discussion of this problem, see the *Registration of Title Practice Book* paras E.16–E.19 and E.30–E.35. The Ordnance Survey map shows the occupational boundaries only, and on first registration the Keeper will compare these with the legal boundaries as disclosed by the title deeds. In practice the Keeper is often asked to do this in advance of an application for registration by means of a Form P16 Report. Where the discrepancy is large, the preferred solution is for the affected parties to bring the legal boundaries into line with the occupational boundaries by means of s 19 of the Land Registration (Scotland) Act 1979, for which see para 220 below.

220. Alteration by agreement. Adjoining proprietors are always free to alter their mutual boundary by agreement. But the boundary is not altered merely by the act of building a new fence on the agreed line[1]. Either there must be a conveyance of the relevant strips of land, whether by two separate dispositions or by a (single) contract of excambion, or there must be an agreement and plan made under the simplified procedure introduced by section 19 of the Land Registration (Scotland) Act 1979.

Section 19 applies only 'where the titles to adjoining lands disclose a discrepancy as to the common boundary'[2]. Such a discrepancy arises where either the titles of both parties lay claim to the same strip of land, or where the titles, although in agreement, do not coincide with the positioning of the boundary wall or fence. In practice the second — where legal and occupational boundaries disagree — is much the more common[3]. The procedure under section 19 is that a written[4] agreement is prepared together with a plan of the proposed new boundary. Both must be executed by the parties[5]. The new boundary comes into operation on registration of the plan[6] or, in the case of a Sasine title or titles, of the agreement and the plan[7].

1 *Readman v Ferrier* (1904) 11 SLT 799, OH.
2 Land Registration (Scotland) Act 1979 (c 33), s 19(1).
3 See para 219 above.
4 Halliday states that in the case of registered land the agreement need not be in writing, but this seems to overlook the rule that contracts relating to land must be constituted in formal writing: *Conveyancing Law and Practice in Scotland* vol II (1986) para 18-84(ii). Halliday gives a suggested style of agreement at para 18-85.
5 The Land Registration (Scotland) Act 1979, s 19(1) provides only for the execution of the plan. But on general principles the agreement, as one of the *obligationes literis*, must also be executed.
6 Ibid, s 19(3). The plan must include a docquet executed by both parties and 'referring to the agreement'. *Halliday* vol II, para 18-86, offers a style of docquet, but this seems to constitute an agreement of new rather than refer to a pre-existing agreement.
7 Land Registration (Scotland) Act 1979, s 19(2).

221. Alteration by the court: the March Dykes Act 1669. The purpose of the March Dykes Act 1669 (c 17) is to produce a boundary suitable for enclosure[1]. Consequently it applies only where, there being no previous form of enclosure, a boundary wall or fence is now to be erected, and where the existing boundaries 'are uneven or otherways incapable of ditch or dike'. Like the March Dykes Act 1661 (c 41)[2], the 1669 Act is probably confined to rural estates[3]. Perhaps because of these various limitations, applications under the 1669 Act are now almost unknown.

Briefly, the procedure under the 1669 Act is as follows. The sheriff, who has exclusive jurisdiction, must make a personal visit to the site except where this is dispensed with by both parties[4]. On the basis of this inspection he alters the boundary by adjudging land from one (or both) proprietors to the other. Title is completed by registration of the extract decree in the Register of Sasines or Land Register. Considerable exchanges of land may be ordered provided that they bear a reasonable relation to the boundary as a whole[5]. Any imbalance in value is rectified by an award of compensation.

1 *Earl of Kintore v Earl of Kintore's Trustees* (1886) 13 R 997.
2 For which, see para 216 above.
3 Bell *Principles* s 959.
4 *Lord Advocate v Sinclair* (1872) 11 M 137.
5 Erskine *Institute* I,4,3; Hume *Lectures* vol III (Stair Soc vol 15, 1952 ed G C H Paton) p 416; Bell s 959; *Pew v Miller* (1754) Mor 10484.

(d) Ownership and Maintenance

222. Wall built on one side of the boundary only. Except where the titles provide otherwise[1], a wall or fence built entirely on one side of a boundary belongs to the proprietor of the land on which it is built. This is because the wall or fence accedes to the land[2].

1 When the rule may perhaps be different. See para 224 below.
2 *Strang v Steuart* (1864) 2 M 1015 (affd (1866) 4 M(HL) 5); *Sanderson v Geddes* (1874) 1 R 1198.

223. Wall built on both sides of the boundary. The rules of accession would suggest that a wall or fence built on both sides of a boundary belongs to each proprietor to the extent, but only to the extent, that it lies on his or her land. For a long time, however, this view was resisted. The overwhelming burden of judicial opinion in the nineteenth century was that walls bestraddling a boundary were owned by both proprietors as common property[1]. Even apart from the question of accession[2], however, this was a difficult doctrine to maintain. This is because the rights associated with common property — for example, the right of veto and the right to division — are plainly unsuited to a boundary wall[3]; and there is the further difficulty that anything attached to the wall by one proprietor would become, by accession, the property of both. The turning point was the case of *Robertson v Scott*[4], decided by the Second Division in 1886. Since *Robertson v Scott* it has come to be accepted that walls and fences accede to the land on which they are built and that accession determines ownership[5]. The modern law is not now in doubt[6]. Consequently, in the common situation of a wall being built on the precise line of the boundary, each proprietor owns *ad medium filum* (to the mid-point). It has also come to be accepted that the part not owned is subject to reciprocal common interest rights[7] in respect of alterations[8], of repairs[9], and, in the case of common gables only, of the cost of erection[10]. The question of whether it is competent to contract out of the rule just stated is considered below[11].

The Scottish Law Commission is currently considering whether statutory regulation of boundary walls and fences is required, and, if so, whether a statute should follow or should alter the existing rules of the common law as to ownership and maintenance[12].

1 See especially *Law v Monteith* (1855) 18 D 125 and *Rodger v Russell* (1873) 11 M 671. See also Hume *Lectures* vol III (Stair Soc vol 15, 1952 ed G C H Paton) p 416.
2 One way out of the difficulty was to say that the *solum* on which the wall was built was itself common property. But this did not explain how the *solum* came to be common property. Clearly the mere erection of the wall was not sufficient: as Lord M'Laren pointed out in *Cochran's Trustees v Caledonian Rly Co* (1898) 25 R 572 at 579, several (ie separate) ownership could be converted into ownership in common only by a duly registered disposition. In general the view that the *solum* is common property is not supported by authority. See *Stewart v Sangster* (1849) 11 D 1176 (incorrect rubric); *Rodger v Russell* (1873) 11 M 671; but cf *Wallace v Brown* 21 June 1808 FC.
3 This difficulty led Lord President Inglis into special pleading in *Lamont v Cumming* (1875) 2 R 784 at 787: 'a gable is the subject of common property in a somewhat different way from any other thing'. As to common property generally, see paras 22 ff above.
4 *Robertson v Scott* (1886) 13 R 1127.
5 This was the view adopted in *Robertson v Scott* (1886) 13 R 1127 by Lord Craighill and Lord Rutherfurd Clark, but not by Lord Justice-Clerk Moncreiff who maintained the traditional view.
6 *Berkeley v Baird* (1895) 22 R 372, 2 SLT 497; *Cochran's Trustees v Caledonian Rly Co* (1898) 25 R 572, 5 SLT 341; *Glasgow Trades House v Ferguson* 1979 SLT 187; *Thom v Hetherington* 1988 SLT 724, OH.
7 For common interest, see paras 354 ff below.
8 See para 225, head (2), below.
9 See para 226, head (3), below.
10 See para 218 above.
11 See para 224 below.
12 *Mutual Boundary Walls* (Scot Law Com Consultation Paper) (1992).

224. Contracting out. Although in at least one case on boundary walls the court was prepared to entertain the idea that parties could make their own rules[1], it must now be taken as settled that the rules of accession cannot be altered by contract[2] and, in particular, that an agreement making a boundary wall common property would be ineffectual to alter ownership of the wall[3]. The position might be different if the provision were contained in the titles. After all, it is recognised that, by conveyance or by reservation, tenement buildings may come to be owned separately from the ground on which they are erected, and there may be an argument that the same thing is possible in the case of boundary walls. However, the point never appears to have been the subject of decision.

If it is accepted that in some circumstances boundary walls may be separated from the ownership of the ground, then they are subject to the usual rules of conventional separate tenements[4]. In terms of these rules the status of separate tenement is won only by express grant or reservation. What is required is an express declaration in the break-off conveyance of the land that the wall is to be owned as common property[5]. The expression 'mutual wall', which is not a technical term and is consistent both with ownership *ad medium filum* and with common property, is not sufficient for this purpose[6].

1 *Cochran's Trustees v Caledonian Rly Co* (1898) 25 R 572. That at least was the view of Lord Adam and Lord Kinnear although not of Lord M'Laren.
2 *Shetland Islands Council v BP Petroleum Development Ltd* 1990 SCLR 48, 1990 SLT 82, OH. See para 572 below.
3 As Lord M'Laren pointed out in *Cochran's Trustees v Caledonian Rly Co* (1898) 25 R 572 at 580, only a conveyance could bring about a change in the ownership.
4 For these rules, see paras 209, 212, above. Accession does not operate through separate tenements.
5 An alternative interpretation of such a declaration is that *both* the wall and the ground on which it is built are to be regarded as common property. This avoids the problem of separate tenements.
6 *Thom v Hetherington* 1988 SLT 724, OH. In *Thom* it seems to have been assumed that 'mutual wall' and 'mutual property' were synonymous with ownership *ad medium filum*, whereas in fact (see eg *Cochran's Trustees v Caledonian Rly Co* (1898) 25 R 572, 5 SLT 341) they can refer equally to common property. For this reason the terms are best avoided.

225. Alteration and maintenance of boundary walls or fences. The right to perform acts of maintenance of or alteration to a boundary wall or fence without the consent of one's neighbour depends upon the ownership of the wall or fence. Here there are three possibilities.

(1) *Ownership by one proprietor only.* A person who has sole ownership of a boundary wall or fence may make whatever alterations he pleases[1]. He may even demolish the wall. Conversely, his neighbour, who does not own the wall or fence, has no entitlement to interfere with that which is not his.

(2) *Ownership by both proprietors ad medium filum.* The ownership of each party is subject to obligations in common interest[2] to maintain that part of the wall which is his[3] and to do nothing to impair the strength and stability of the wall as a whole[4]. Subject to these obligations each proprietor can make alterations on his own side of the wall. In *Thom v Hetherington*, the leading modern case, the defender was held entitled to erect a fence close to and along the length of a boundary wall although the fence posts interfered to some extent with the foundations of the wall and increased the wind loading. The test to be applied in cases of this kind was set out by Lord Jauncey as follows:

'The presence of the fence up against the wall would only have been actionable if such presence impaired the strength or interfered with the stability of the wall . . . Such impairment or interference must in my view be measurable and not merely negligible. It is beyond dispute that the owner of one side of a garden wall would be entitled to insert nails or rose ties into the mortar for the purpose of training roses up it. Theoretically every intrusion into the mortar must weaken the bond which it creates between the bricks, but it is equally clear that the court would not restrain an owner from so acting'[5].

In application of this principle it has been held that a proprietor may build up his own side of a boundary wall in order to support an extension to his house[6].

(3) *Ownership by both parties in common.* Here the usual rules of common property apply, so that alterations by one proprietor without the consent of the other are

unlawful[7]. To this rule there is an exception for necessary repairs[8], and, in the case of common gables only, for such alterations as may be required for the normal enjoyment of a gable[9].

The full cost of alterations falls to be met by the party who instructed them. Nothing can be recovered from the adjoining proprietor. But there are special rules for repairs[10] and for alterations which can be brought within the March Dykes Act 1661[11].

1 Subject, however, to the same restrictions, eg with respect to servitudes of light, which affected the initial building of the wall. See para 215 above.
2 For common interest generally, see paras 354 ff below.
3 For maintenance, see para 226 below.
4 *Cochran's Trustees v Caledonian Rly Co* (1898) 25 R 572 at 597, per Lord M'Laren; *Glasgow Trades House v Ferguson* 1979 SLT 187 at 191, per Lord Justice-Clerk Wheatley. There is a precise parallel in the law of the tenement (see para 233 below), where individual proprietors come under a common interest obligation to do nothing which interferes with the support given by their property to the rest of the building, and it is thought that the tests for breach of the obligation are the same in both cases.
5 *Thom v Hetherington* 1988 SLT 724 at 728. The case contains a useful review of the authorities, although one which does not take into account the fact (para 223 above) that in the nineteenth century boundary walls were regarded as common property by the courts.
6 *Gray v Macleod* 1979 SLT (Sh Ct) 17; *Gill v Mitchell* 1980 SLT (Sh Ct) 48.
7 *Warren v Marwick* (1835) 13 S 944; *Dow and Gordon v Harvey* (1869) 8 M 118. See para 25 above.
8 Bell *Principles* ss 1075, 1078.
9 *Lamont v Cumming* (1875) 2 R 784; *Faichney v Cameron* (1900) 16 Sh Ct Rep 283. In *Lamont* one of the proprietors was allowed to increase the height of the common gable by several feet and to insert joists, fireplaces and vents. Today common gables are usually regarded as owned *ad medium filum*, which largely avoids the difficulty: see para 218 above.
10 See para 226 below.
11 *Cadell v Wilson* (1865) I Guthrie's Sel Sh Ct Ca 450. For the March Dykes Act 1661 (c 41), see para 216 above.

226. Recovery of maintenance costs. The right to carry out acts of maintenance and repair has already been considered[1]. A party who, in exercise of that right, repairs a boundary wall or fence is able to recover a share of the cost from his neighbour if, and only if, one of the following applies:

(1) *Agreement.* It is not enough for the other party to agree to the work being carried out, for that may not of itself import an obligation to contribute part of the cost. Express agreement as to payment should also be obtained.

(2) *Real burden.* Frequently titles contain real burdens by which both parties are bound to contribute to maintenance equally or on some other equitable basis. Depending on how the burden is worded, there may be no requirement to show that the repairs are essential, as opposed to merely prudent or desirable.

(3) *Wall owned ad medium filum.* Where a boundary wall or fence is owned *ad medium filum* the ownership of each party is subject to a common interest obligation to preserve the overall stability of the wall[2]. It is thought (although the point has been expressly decided only in relation to common gables[3]) that this includes a positive obligation to carry out necessary acts of maintenance[4]. So if a boundary wall is endangered by the failure of one party to carry out essential acts of maintenance on the side of the wall which he owns, the other party can require that the work be undertaken[5]. Each party is solely responsible for meeting the cost of repairs to his own side of the wall.

(4) *Wall owned in common.* The usual rules of common property apply, by which either party may carry out necessary[6] repairs and look to the other party for a *pro rata* contribution to the cost[7].

(5) *March Dykes Act 1661.* The March Dykes Act 1661, as interpreted, provides special rules for walls and fences coming within its terms[8]. It has been held that the maintenance provisions of the Act apply:

(a) to walls or fences originally erected at joint expense by order of the court made under the Act,

(b) to walls and fences for which the Act was available but which were erected at joint expense by agreement, and

(c) to other walls and fences which have been treated from time immemorial as march fences within (a) and (b)[9].

Briefly, the provisions of the Act are as follows. Either proprietor may require his neighbour to meet half the cost of repairing or, where necessary, of rebuilding the wall[10]. Ownership of the wall is irrelevant. The same procedure must be followed as for the original construction, so that an application to the court is necessary[11]. The court will not authorise the repair where its cost is markedly disproportionate to any benefit to the defender[12].

(6) *Statutory powers of local authorities.* A local authority may, by notice in writing, require the owner or owners of any building to bring the building into a reasonable state of repair, regard being had to its age, type and location[13]. 'Building' is defined sufficiently widely to include a boundary wall or fence[14]. If the owners fail to comply with the statutory notice, the authority is empowered to carry out the work itself and to recover the cost[15].

1 See para 225 above.
2 See para 225, head (2), above.
3 *Crisp v McCutcheon* 1963 SLT (Sh Ct) 4; *Glasgow Trades House v Ferguson* 1979 SLT 187.
4 An analogy can be drawn with the law of the tenement, where the upper proprietor is under a positive obligation to provide shelter, and the lower proprietor under a positive obligation to provide support. See paras 233, 234, below.
5 What he cannot do, however, is to carry out the work himself, for the property is not his.
6 For the meaning of necessary repairs in this context, see para 25 above.
7 Bell *Principles* s 1078; *Maclean v Burton-Mackenzie's Trustees* (1913) 29 Sh Ct Rep 334.
8 See further para 216 above.
9 *Strang v Steuart* (1864) 2 M 1015 (affd (1866) 4 M(HL) 5). The fence under consideration in *Strang* originally divided two fields within the same estate and so did not come within heads (a) and (b), and it was held (Lord Benholme dissenting) that there was insufficient evidence of use to bring it within (c). *Lockhart v Seivewright* (1758) Mor 10488 may be an example of (c).
10 *Paterson v MacDonald* (1880) 7 R 958.
11 *Duncan v Ramsay* (1906) 23 Sh Ct Rep 181.
12 *Blackburn v Head* (1903) 11 SLT 521, OH.
13 Civic Government (Scotland) Act 1982 (c 45), s 87(1). 'Local authority' means the islands or district council, except that in the case of a district in the Highland, Borders or Dumfries and Galloway regions the regional council is the local authority: s 87(6).
14 Ibid, s 87(2).
15 Ibid, s 99.

(4) THE LAW OF THE TENEMENT

(a) General

227. Introduction. Tenements or 'lands' were in widespread use in Scotland as early as the sixteenth century[1]. But despite this long history they are little discussed by juristic writers before Hume and Bell and there are almost no reported cases earlier than 1800. Indeed, considered as a whole there are insufficient reported decisions on the law of the tenement and hence many gaps in the law. Most of the early decisions arise out of the feuing of the Edinburgh New Town, and thereafter a steady stream of litigation continues throughout the nineteenth century, tailing off gradually after 1900.

The most widely accepted definition of a 'tenement' is as 'a single or individual building, although containing several dwelling-houses, with, it may be, separate means of access, but under the same roof, and enclosed by the same gables or walls'[2]. A building is equally a tenement whether originally built as such or converted at some later stage from a single house to two or more separate dwellings[3]. The *law* of the tenement is the set of common law rules which governs the division of rights and obligations within a tenement building. Broadly speaking, these rules provide for individual ownership of each flat coupled with ownership in common of the entrance passage and stair; and in addition, each proprietor has a right of common interest in those parts of the building which he does not own. Some of these common law rules are inconvenient in practice and so are almost always altered in the titles of individual flats. Recently, the Scottish Law Commission has been engaged on a research project on the law of the tenement which may ultimately lead to legislation[4].

The law of the tenement is drawn mainly with the standard Victorian or Edwardian tenement in mind. But it applies very much more widely than that with the result that it is not always possible to reconcile the rules with the architecture. This is a particular problem with former villas converted into flats. In the event of a conflict it seems that the architecture ought to prevail:

'The case of a common tenement, or, as it is termed, a land, is peculiar in this respect, that the common subject is the result of human design. The building in that case is erected on the plan of being parcelled out among the several proprietors; and it appears to me ... that the intention of the builder, as in substance constituting the law of such a land, must be our guide in ascertaining the rights of the several parties ... If we can ascertain the design of the original builder, as indicated by the structure of the tenement, the Court will hold that the rights he gave out in the several parts of the building are all to be governed by that design'[5].

1 Frank Worsdall *The Tenement: A Way of Life* (1979) p 1.
2 *Scott v Dundee Police Comrs* (1841) 4 D 292 at 303, per Lord Fullerton.
3 *WVS Office Premises Ltd v Currie* 1969 SC 170 at 179, 1969 SLT 254 at 260, per Lord Cameron.
4 *Law of the Tenement* (Scot Law Com Discussion Paper no. 91) (1990).
5 *Gellatly v Arrol* (1863) 1 M 592 at 601, 602, per Lord Benholme. In the case of conversions our concern is presumably with the design of the architect who supervised the subdivision.

(b) Ownership

228. Solum. The *solum* is the soil or ground on which the building is erected, together with such adjoining ground as belongs to the tenement[1]. In principle, ownership of the *solum* is ownership *a coelo usque ad centrum* (from the heavens to the centre of the earth), so that whoever owns the *solum* owns everything[2]. When a tenement building is first erected it accedes to the *solum* and belongs to the owner thereof. But once the individual flats[3] are conveyed separately they become conventional separate tenements[4]; and while accession continues to operate within each flat it ceases to operate from one flat to its neighbour or to the *solum*. Ownership of the *solum* then ceases to carry ownership of the individual flats. But it remains the residuary ownership *a coelo usque ad centrum*, including not only the earth *ad centrum* but also all airspace above the surface which has not been enclosed within four walls and conveyed as individual flats[5].

Surprisingly, perhaps, the question of ownership of the *solum* was not finally settled until *Johnston v White* in 1877[6], where it was held that, once a tenement has been divided into separate flats in separate ownership, the *solum* belongs to the proprietor of the lowest flat in the building[7]. Depending on the building, the lowest flat is the ground floor flat or the basement. Where there is more than one ground (or basement) flat the rule is that each proprietor owns the land on which his flat is actually built, together with any part of the garden or other ground which is immediately adjacent[8]. So at common law the back green of a tenement is owned in sections by the ground floor (or basement) proprietors. The *solum* beneath the common passage and stair is the property of whoever owns the passage and stair[9].

In practice the titles of a tenement very often provide that the *solum* and back green are the common property of all proprietors in the building[10].

1 For the meaning of *solum* in the context of a commercial contract, see *Bredero Aberdeen Centre Ltd v City of Aberdeen District Council* 1993 GWD 3-191.
2 See further paras 196 ff above.
3 In modern usage 'flat' usually means an individual dwelling house within a tenement building and it is used in this sense here. But 'flat' can also be used as a synonym of 'storey' and this usage is often found in older title deeds.
4 For conventional separate tenements, see paras 207 ff above.
5 *Watt v Burgess' Trustee* (1891) 18 R 766.
6 *Johnston v White* (1877) 4 R 721. Earlier cases were far from clear. In *Stewart v Blackwood* (1829) 7 S 362, for example, the court remained undecided, while in *Gellatly v Arrol* (1863) 1 M 592 at 603, Lord Neaves declared that ownership was shared by all the proprietors.
7 See also *WVS Office Premises Ltd v Currie* 1969 SC 170, 1969 SLT 254.
8 This is on analogy with the rule for roofs, for which see para 230 below.
9 At common law the passage and stair are owned in common by all proprietors to whose flats they give access. See para 231 below.
10 See para 241 below.

229. Walls. The owner of a flat has ownership of a stratum of airspace bounded by walls, by ceilings and by floors. The ownership of these bounding features is as follows:

(1) *Internal walls within a flat*. These are the sole property of the owner of that flat.
(2) *Internal walls between flats*. There have been no reported cases and ownership is unclear. There is some support for the view that such walls are the common property of the proprietors whose flats they divide[1]. But common property of walls is always an unsatisfactory result[2], and a better view, and one consonant with the rule for boundary walls generally[3], is that each proprietor is sole owner *ad medium filum* (to the halfway point), to the extent that the wall bounds his flat, with a right of common interest in respect of the remainder of the wall.
(3) *External walls*. These are the front and rear elevations and, where the tenement is at the end of a block, the gable end. It never seems to have been seriously doubted that external walls are owned section by section by the proprietor whose flat they bound[4]. This was assumed in one of the first cases on the law of the tenement, decided in 1698[5], and was, much later, restated authoritatively by Bell in a well-known passage in the *Principles:*

'In the common wall of one of the large tenements of Edinburgh, consisting of many floors belonging to different proprietors, there is no common property among the owners of the several floors, but a combination of individual property with common interest'[6].

The walls include the chimney vents and probably also, by accession, any pipes affixed to the walls such as waste pipes and down pipes[7]. An alternative view is that pipes remain moveable property, in which case they are presumably owned in common by all those whose flats they serve.
(4) *Common gables*. Tenements are often built in rows, in which case, like terraced and semi-detached houses, they share a common gable with the neighbouring buildings on either side. Common gables are owned *ad medium filum* by the respective owners of each house[8]. In the case of tenements this means that the proprietor of each flat owns to the mid-point the section of common gable bounding his property. There is a right of common interest in the rest of the gable.
(5) *Floors/ceilings*. The boundary between two flats built one on top of the other is the centre line of the joists[9].

1 J Rankine *The Law of Land-ownership in Scotland* (4th edn, 1909) p 667; J G S Cameron 'The Law of the Tenement' (1960) 2 Conv Rev 102 at 105.
2 In particular, because of accession. See para 241 below.
3 See para 223 above. See also the rule for common gables at head (4) in the text.
4 But see the views of Lord Cowan and Lord Neaves in *Gellatly v Arrol* (1863) 1 M 592.
5 *Hall v Corbet* (1698) Mor 12775.
6 Bell *Principles* s 1086.
7 This receives support from the fact that rhone pipes are treated as acceding to the roof: see *Duncan Smith and MacLaren v Heatly* 1952 JC 61, 1952 SLT 254.
8 See para 218 above.
9 *Girdwood v Paterson* (1873) 11 M 647; *M'Arly v French's Trustees* (1883) 10 R 574.

230. Roof. Although implicit in a passage from Erskine's *Institutes*[1] and in some of the earlier cases[2], it was not until *Taylor v Dunlop* in 1872 that the rule was authoritatively stated to be that the top floor proprietor owns the roof and the intermediate roof-space. The reason for this rule, according to Lord Deas in *Taylor*, is that 'the roof is just the covering wall which keeps out the weather'[3]. Where there is more than one top flat, each top proprietor owns that section of the roof directly above his own flat[4]. Similarly, the roof above the common passage and stair is owned by the proprietors of the common stair[5]. By accession the roof includes the rhones[6] and possibly also the chimney stalks[7], although there is sheriff court authority to the effect that chimney stalks are the common property of the proprietors having vents therein, in proportion to the number of vents[8]. Chimney cans are presumably part of the stalk to which they are attached. Ownership of the roof does not include the airspace above the roof, and this is the property of the owner or owners of the *solum* as the residuary owners *a coelo usque ad centrum*[9].

In practice the common law rule is often varied in the titles so that the roof is the common property of all the proprietors in the building.

1 Erskine *Institute* II,9,11,
2 *Nicolson v Melvill* (1708) Mor 14516; *Scott v Home* (1808) (unreported) (noted in Hume's *Lectures* vol III (Stair Soc vol 15, 1952 ed G C H Paton) p 272).
3 *Taylor v Dunlop* (1872) 11 M 25 at 30.
4 *Sanderson's Trustees v Yule* (1897) 25 R 211.
5 At common law, the proprietors of the common stair are all the proprietors to whose flats the stair gives access. See para 231 below.
6 *Duncan Smith and MacLaren v Heatly* 1952 JC 61, 1952 SLT 254.
7 Alternatively, and depending on the building, the chimney stalks may be regarded as part of the wall.
8 *Whitmore v Stuart and Stuart* (1902) 10 SLT 290, Sh Ct. The decision was influenced by what was said to be the contemporary practice in Edinburgh. If chimney stalks are indeed owned separately from the roof — ie if they are heritable but yet do not accede to the roof — then they must be (conventional) separate tenements. See also *Pitoy v Steele* (1960) 76 Sh Ct Rep 79.

Even if *Whitmore* is wrong and stalks do accede to the roof the result is often the same in practice because in the titles of many tenements the roof is made common property.
9 *Watt v Burgess' Trustee* (1891) 18 R 766. For encroachment into the airspace, eg by dormer windows, see para 245 below.

231. Common passage and stair. The common passage and stair are owned by all the proprietors in a tenement to whose flat they give access[1], but in what proportions has never been decided. The simplest and, it is submitted, the best view is that each proprietor co-owns the entire passage and stair in equal shares. Sometimes indeed this is provided for expressly in the titles. But a possible alternative view gives each proprietor co-ownership only of that section of the passage and stair which gives access to his particular flat, so that a ground floor proprietor, for example, would not own the stair at all[2]. On either view proprietors

of main door flats are excluded from ownership of the passage and stair except
where they have a connecting door leading into the common passage.

Included in the common passage and stair is the *solum* on which it is built and the
roof overhead, including any cupola. Both are common property. Also included are
the external walls and the doors to the front and rear. The other two (internal) walls
present greater difficulty. They mark the boundary between the individual flats and
the passage and stair, and there is old authority to suggest that they are owned, in
sections, by the proprietors of the flats which they bound[3]. Another view sometimes expressed is that they are the common property of, respectively, the owners of
the passage and stair and the owners of the flats on the far side of the wall, although in
what proportions is not clear[4]. Probably neither view represents the modern law,
and the second view in particular is subject to a number of technical and practical
objections[5]. The modern law is probably that the internal walls of the passage and
stair are to be treated in the same way as the other internal walls in the building: an
imaginary line is drawn though the centre *(medium filum)*; on the common passage
side of the line the walls are owned as common property by all the proprietors in the
tenement; on the other side of the line the walls are owned in sections by those
proprietors whose flats they bound[6].

1 *Anderson v Dalrymple* (1799) Mor 12831; *WVS Office Premises Ltd v Currie* 1969 SC 170, 1969 SLT
   254. However, in *McCallum v Gunn* 1955 SLT (Sh Ct) 85, Sheriff C J D Shaw (later Lord
   Kilbrandon) was only willing to allow the parties a common interest in the passage, which
   apparently left the passage itself without an owner.
2 J Rankine *The Law of Land-ownership in Scotland* (4th edn, 1909) p 677; J G S Cameron 'The Law of
   the Tenement' (1960) 2 Conv Rev 102 at 106.
3 *Anderson v Dalrymple* (1799) Mor 12831; *Ritchie v Purdie* (1833) 11 S 771.
4 *Rankine* pp 667–669; J G S Cameron 'The Law of the Tenement' (1960) 2 Conv Rev 102 at 107.
5 See K G C Reid 'The Law of the Tenement' (1983) 28 JLSS 472 at 475, 476.
6 The same conclusion is reached in W M Gordon *Scottish Land Law* (1989) para 15-37.

(c) Common Interest

232. Introduction. In the law of the tenement ownership is fortified by common
interest[1]. For while each individual proprietor owns only a certain part or parts of
the building, he has over the remainder of the building a right of common interest.
Common interest rights are reciprocal. In respect of his own part of the building
each owner is a servient proprietor, bound in common interest to his neighbours,
who are the dominant proprietors in the obligation; but in respect of the rest of the
building he is one of the dominant proprietors.

Common interest is implied by law. Indeed, probably it cannot be expressly
created. Common interest operates within a tenement almost as if it were a model
deed of conditions. The close physical proximity of tenement flats makes some form
of regulation imperative, and the general law provides a model set of rules which the
parties may or may not choose to modify by additional real burdens.

This point was first made by Stair, in a famous passage:

'[W]hen divers owners have parts of the same tenement, it cannot be said to be a perfect
division, because the roof remaineth roof to both, and the ground supporteth both; and
therefore by the nature of communion, there are mutual obligations upon both, viz that
the owner of the lower tenement must uphold his tenement as a foundation to the
upper, and the owner of the upper tenement must uphold his tenement as a roof and
cover to the lower: both which, though they have the resemblance of servitudes, and
pass with the thing to singular successors; yet they are rather personal obligations, such
as pass in communion even to the singular successors of either party'[2].

In two important respects the scope of common interest was and remains
uncertain. First, it is unclear whether the right extends across the boundaries of

individual tenements. A tenement for this purpose may be taken as being a building comprising all flats which are served by the same passage and stair, but including also main door flats directly underneath. Within such a tenement all proprietors are bound together in a network of common interest rights and obligations. But in practice the state of the adjoining tenement, if there is one, may also be of great importance. Does common interest extend beyond the common gable, so that control may be exercised over the next building? The answer is probably that it does not so extend[3]. But there may be exceptions, for in at least one reported case the court seemed to accept that a flatowner had a right of common interest over the garden of the tenement immediately adjoining[4].

Secondly, there is uncertainty about the relationship of common interest with common property. The basic principle is that each proprietor has a right of common interest over those parts of the building which he does not himself own. But some parts of the building are held as common property of all the proprietors. At common law only the passage and stair is common property, but title deeds frequently add to this the roof, the *solum* and sometimes even the external walls. Does common interest exist over property held in common? At first sight there may seem a difficulty in the idea that the same person can be both dominant and servient proprietor in the same obligation. But he would be servient proprietor in conjunction with his fellow co-owners, and dominant proprietor on his own account only. There seems no reason of technical law why this model should not be possible[5], and such authority as there is seems favourably disposed to the idea[6]. Since the effect of the titles is often to make many parts of a tenement building common property, there are clear and obvious advantages in allowing the simultaneous existence of common interest.

The content of common interest is, deliberately, left vague. The law says that the proprietor of flat A has a right of common interest over area B, without, however, indicating the limits of that right; and while the core content may now be taken as settled, there seems nothing to prevent a court from recognising additional rights in circumstances where these appear to be appropriate.

No further general statement can be made about content. Different rights (and correlative obligations) exist over different parts of the building. Most are negative in nature, which is to say that the servient proprietor is restrained from carrying out some activity not otherwise unlawful. But the two rights mentioned by Stair in the passage quoted earlier, namely cover and support, impose positive obligations on the servient proprietor and it is with these important rights that this account begins.

1 For common interest generally, see paras 354 ff below.
2 Stair *Institutions* II,7,6.
3 It has never been suggested that there are common interest obligations in the comparable situation of terraced houses.
4 *Calder v Merchant Co of Edinburgh* (1886) 13 R 623. There are also common interest rights in respect of common gables, for which see para 229, head (4), above.
5 K G C Reid 'Common Property: Clarification and Confusion' 1985 SLT (News) 57 at 61. See also para 26 above.
6 *Grant v Heriot's Trust* (1906) 8 F 647, 13 SLT 986; *Forster v Fryer* (1944) 60 Sh Ct Rep 39; *Fearnan Partnership v Grindlay* 1992 SLT 460, HL.

233. Right of support. There are three principal sources of support within a tenement building, namely

(1) *Lower flats*. In a tenement the lower flats must bear the weight of the upper flats[1]. In relation to the common interest right of support the lower flats are the servient properties and the upper flats are the dominant properties. Intermediate flats, however, are both servient and also dominant properties, being bound to support the flats above but being entitled in turn to support from those below.

(2) *Solum.* It appears that there is no corresponding obligation on the *solum* to bear the weight of the building as a whole. So in general there is no liability for subsidence, except, in delict, for subsidence caused by positive act[2].

(3) *Common gable.* Where two adjoining tenements are connected by a common gable, the gable is owned *ad medium filum* (to the mid-point) by the individual proprietors whose property it bounds, but each is obliged to maintain his own section of gable to the extent necessary for the support of both tenements[3]. The position is the same in respect of walls separating individual flats within a single tenement.

The obligation of support, where it exists, has both a positive and a negative aspect. The positive aspect is the obligation to keep one's property in sufficient repair for adequate support to be maintained[4]. In one case where a lower proprietor refused to carry out repairs the court ordered that they be instructed forthwith 'in the most efficient manner, and without any regard to the expense which would thereby be incurred'[5]. The rule, however, is different where the building itself comes to be destroyed, in whole or in part, and the issues arising here are discussed below[6]. Failure of support by the servient property may cause injury to the dominant property itself and in that case damages are due, but liability is not strict and negligence must be shown[7]. Nuisance may be an alternative basis of liability in this situation but once again liability is not strict[8].

The negative aspect is the obligation to avoid improvements or other operations in one's own property to the extent that they endanger support to other parts of the building. In *Fergusson v Marjoribanks*[9], the earliest of a number of similar cases[10], the owner of the ground and basement flats in a tenement was prevented from adding new doors, lengthening existing windows, and carrying out a number of related operations. According to the court the dominant proprietor or proprietors could object 'to any material alterations in the fabric, which might occasion even the apprehension of danger'[11]. The onus is on the servient proprietor to show that the operations can be carried out safely[12]. There is a corresponding obligation on the dominant proprietor not to alter his property to the effect of making a material increase in the weight to be supported[13]. Both parties, in short, must maintain the *status quo.*

---

1 Stair *Institutions* II,7,6; Bankton *Institute* II,7,9; Erskine *Institute* II,9,11; Bell *Principles* s 1086.

2 See further paras 253 ff below. Liability is strict.

3 *Glasgow Trades House v Ferguson* 1979 SLT 187. See paras 218, 225, head (2), above.

4 This is usually said to distinguish the common interest rights of support from servitude rights of support, although it appears that, contrary to the rule that servitudes are *in patiendo* only, a servitude of support can impose a positive obligation of repair where this is expressly provided for. See Stair II,7,6; *Erskine* II,9,8; *Bell* s 1003. In practice the existence of common interest renders servitudes of support redundant, at least in tenement buildings.

5 *M'Nair v M'Lauchlan and M'Keand* (1826) 4 S 546 (NE 554). The rule is the same for the obligation to provide shelter: see *Luke v Dundass* (1695) 4 Brown's Supp 258.

6 See para 235 below.

7 *Thomson v St Cuthbert's Co-operative Association Ltd* 1958 SC 380, 1959 SLT 54; *Kerr v McGreevy* 1970 SLT (Sh Ct) 7; *Doran v Smith* 1971 SLT (Sh Ct) 46; *Baxter v Pritchard* 1992 GWD 24-1385, Sh Ct.

8 That negligence is required was settled by the House of Lords in *RHM Bakeries (Scotland) Ltd v Strathclyde Regional Council* 1985 SC (HL) 17, 1985 SLT 214. This closes the door which appeared to be opened by the decision in *Macnab v McDevitt* 1971 SLT (Sh Ct) 41. But see now *Kennedy v Glenbelle Ltd* 1996 SCLR 411.

9 *Fergusson v Marjoribanks* 12 Nov 1816 FC.

10 The most important are *Pirnie v M'Ritchie* 5 June 1819 FC; *Dennistoun v Bell and Brown* (1824) 2 S 784 (NE 649); and *Gray v Greig* (1825) 4 S 104 (NE 105).

11 Bell puts it this way (*Principles* s 1086): '[E]ach party may make alterations and changes in his own wall, notwithstanding the common interest which is vested in others, provided he does not endanger that common interest, or expose those who hold it to reasonable alarm'. For the comparable rule for boundary walls and fences, see *Thom v Hetherington* 1988 SLT 724, OH, and para 225, head (2), above.

12 *Taylor v Dunlop* (1872) 11 M 25 at 31, per Lord Ardmillan.
13 W M Gordon *Scottish Land Law* (1989) para 15-39. This is the equivalent of the rule for servitudes that the dominant proprietor must not increase the burden on the servient proprietor. See para 464 below.

234. Right to shelter. Common interest confers a right to shelter. In Stair's words 'the owner of the upper tenement must uphold his tenement as a roof and cover to the lower'[1]. In practice this resolves into the rule that the owner of the roof (at common law the top floor proprietor) must maintain that roof in a wind and watertight condition, an obligation directly enforceable by the lower proprietors. The full cost of roof maintenance is borne by the roof proprietor alone. So inequitable is this rule that it is almost always altered in the title deeds, either by making the roof common property or by a real burden declaring maintenance a common responsibility, or often by both methods together. For, as the report of a case decided in 1708 observes, 'if the uppermost stories were burdened with the maintenance and upholding of the roof alone, none would buy them'[2]. It remains the case today that top flats in which the common interest obligation of shelter remains unaltered are not readily marketable.

Where the building itself is destroyed, whether in whole or in part, the right to shelter is extinguished pending reconstruction[3].

1 Stair *Institutions* II,7,6. See *Luke v Dundass* (1695) 4 Brown's Supp 258.
2 *Nicolson v Melvill* (1708) Mor 14516.
3 See para 235 below.

235. The limits of shelter and support: destruction and reconstruction. The rights of shelter and support apply only for so long as the tenement remains as a going concern. If the building is destroyed or badly damaged, they fall into abeyance until such time as it is rebuilt, and if part only of the building is destroyed or badly damaged they fall into abeyance in respect of that part. This was decided in *Thomson v St Cuthbert's Co-operative Association Ltd*[1], a case which innovates on the previous law and which may be criticised on that, as well as on other, grounds[2]. The court in *Thomson* was concerned that proprietors should not remain bound in common interest in perpetuity and regardless of how ruinous a building had become. But in seeking to avoid that difficulty[3], the decision in *Thomson* has created several others. Thus suppose that a tenement is destroyed by fire. The top floor proprietor wishes to rebuild but the other proprietors do not. The titles are silent. What is the top floor proprietor to do? He cannot force the lower floor proprietors to rebuild, because the obligation of support is in abeyance. Nor is it certain that he is entitled to rebuild by himself, even if he is willing to bear the cost[4]. In effect he is left with a stratum of airspace which he cannot use. In practice of course his position will often be protected by fire insurance; but it is unsatisfactory that the law of the tenement is unable to provide an adequate solution for the utilisation of his property.

Thomson may also be criticised as placing too much weight on an uncertain distinction, namely the distinction between repair and reconstruction. Where damage to the walls or roof falls into the category of repair, the owner must carry out the work in implement of the obligation of support or, as the case may be, of shelter. But where it is sufficiently serious to amount to reconstruction, the common interest obligation ceases and the owner need do nothing. The distinction is not easily made. In *Thomson* itself a supporting beam fractured, resulting in the partial withdrawal of support and damage to one of the flats above. Surprisingly, perhaps, this was treated as reconstruction and, in the absence of negligence[5], no liability fell on the owner of the beam.

1 *Thomson v St Cuthbert's Co-operative Association Ltd* 1958 SC 380, 1959 SLT 54.
2 K G C Reid 'Common Interest' (1983) 28 JLSS 428 at 433–435.
3 The difficulty in any event seems exaggerated. In practice titles often impose the very obligation which *Thomson* refused to recognise, namely the obligation to rebuild in perpetuity.
4 According to Stair *Institutions* II,7,6, the servitude of support carries with it a right to repair, and it may be that an analogous right exists in common interest. But difficulties would then arise if a lower proprietor wished to use his property for some other purpose.
5 Where a tenement building is destroyed through the negligence of one of the proprietors, a claim will be available in delict.

236. Right to light. At common law the land surrounding a tenement is the property of the ground floor proprietor or proprietors[1]; and while this land may be built upon[2], it is subject to a right to light in favour of the other proprietors in the tenement and also, it has been suggested, in favour of proprietors in the tenements immediately adjoining[3]. Thus in *Heron v Gray*[4] the ground floor proprietor was required to remove a wooden screen which obstructed the windows of a neighbour. Similarly, in *Boswell v Magistrates of Edinburgh* building on a back green was permitted only on the court's being satisfied 'that there would be no substantial interference with the light and air of the flats above'[5]. In both cases the court attributed the limitation to an implied servitude of light, but as it is settled that negative servitudes cannot be created by implication[6], it seems that this is properly classified as common interest. Certainly this is the view taken by later cases[7].

Common interest protects light only. Building work which does not affect light but is injurious only to prospect[8] or indeed to general amenity[9] cannot be prevented. But where, as is usually the case, the back green is made common property in the title deeds, building work of any kind is prevented by the rules of common property[10] and without recourse being necessary to common interest.

1 See para 228 above.
2 *Arrol v Inches* (1887) 14 R 394; *Birrell v Lumley* (1905) 12 SLT 719, OH. *Urquhart v Melville* (1853) 16 D 307, which contains remarks to the effect that the land may not be owned *a coelo usque ad centrum*, is best explained on the basis that the titles seemed to convey the adjacent airspace to the upper proprietor.
3 *Calder v Merchant Co of Edinburgh* (1886) 13 R 623. The issue is not, however, properly focused.
4 *Heron v Gray* (1880) 8 R 155.
5 *Boswell v Edinburgh Magistrates* (1881) 8 R 986.
6 Erskine *Institute* II,9,35. See J Rankine *The Law of Land-ownership in Scotland* (4th edn, 1909) p 426 and also pp 439–440 where *Heron v Gray* (1880) 8 R 155 is criticised as a 'serious innovation in our law of servitudes'.
7 *Calder v Merchant Co of Edinburgh* (1886) 13 R 623; *Arrol v Inches* (1887) 14 R 394.
8 *Birrell v Lumley* (1905) 12 SLT 719, OH.
9 *Barclay v M'Ewen* (1880) 7 R 792; *Calder v Merchant Co of Edinburgh* (1886) 13 R 623.
10 See para 244 below.

237. Right to use chimney vents. The external walls of a tenement are owned, section by section, by the proprietors whose flats they respectively bound[1]. Ownership of the wall includes ownership of any chimney vents. But each proprietor whose flat is served by vents is entitled in common interest to use these vents for the discharge of smoke. Thus in the leading case of *Gellatly v Arrol*[2] the pursuer was able to insist on the removal of alterations to a wall belonging to the defender on the ground that they interfered with the pursuer's common interest in the vents. The offending alterations diverted the vents from their original course, thus making them harder to clean and increasing the risk of fire[3]. The common interest entitlement is to use the vents originally designed for the flat in question and there is no right either to create additional vents or to use vents originally designed for another flat[4]. It has been held in the sheriff court that a vent may be adapted to serve a fish and chip shop by the insertion of a 'grease liner'[5].

1 See para 229, head (3), above.
2 *Gellatly v Arrol* (1863) 1 M 592.
3 See also *Todd v Wilson* (1894) 22 R 172, 2 SLT 351, where alterations which were similar but which did not interfere with the vents were permitted.
4 *Walker v Braidwood* (1797) Hume 512; *Stewart v Blackwood* (1829) 7 S 362.
5 *Varese v Paisley Dean of Guild Court* 1969 SLT (Sh Ct) 27.

238. Additional rights. It is open to the courts to declare the existence of further common interest rights. No doubt the power will be used circumspectly. Indeed courts have in the past refused to recognise rights of amenity and of prospect[1].

Two possible common interest rights may be suggested here. One is a right to use the roof or the walls for television aerials and satellite dishes[2]. The other relates to down pipes and other pipes. It seems likely that pipes accede to the wall and so are owned section by section by the respective owners of the wall[3]. But if one proprietor fails to maintain the section belonging to him, the overall efficiency of the pipes is impaired. It is suggested, therefore, that ownership of pipes is accompanied by a common interest obligation of maintenance[4]. The same should presumably be true of rhone pipes, which accede to the roof and so at common law are the property of the top floor proprietor or proprietors.

1 See para 236 above.
2 In practice the roof is often common property, in which case such a use is, presumably, permitted.
3 See para 229, head (3), above.
4 W M Gordon *Scottish Land Law* (1989) para 15-43.

239. Right to install pipes or drains. At common law a proprietor cannot install pipes or drains beyond the boundaries of his own flat, but the position is now regulated by section 88 of the Civic Government (Scotland) Act 1982. In terms of that section the owner of part of a building may apply to the sheriff by summary application for warrant to install pipes or drains in other parts of the building, or on the outside surface of any external wall or roof of the building, or in, through or under any land pertaining to the building[1]. The provision applies to parts of the building owned in common as well as to parts in the sole ownership of another proprietor. The pipes and drains are restricted to those which are necessary for the purpose of water supply to, or the soil, waste or rainwater drainage or the ventilation in connection with such drainage of, the applicant's part of the building. The application must follow on from a voluntary approach to the owner or owners of the property in question which has not met with success, and in particular warrant will always be refused if a written approach was not made at least twenty-eight days prior to the court application[2]. The granting of a warrant is discretionary[3], and may be made subject to conditions[4], and the sheriff must be satisfied that the installation in question is reasonable[5].

Installation may trigger accession, with the result that the pipes or drains will belong to the owner or owners of the part of the building in which they are laid[6].

An application also lies under section 88 for access to pipes and drains for the purpose of maintenance and repair[7].

1 Civic Government (Scotland) Act 1982 (c 45), s 88(1).
2 Ibid, s 88(1), (2)(b).
3 Ibid, s 88(1).
4 Ibid, s 88(3)(a).
5 Ibid, s 88(2)(a).
6 *Crichton v Turnbull* 1946 SC 52, 1946 SLT 156.
7 Civic Government (Scotland) Act 1982, s 88(1)(c).

(d) Variation in Title Deeds

240. Method. The time for altering the common law of the tenement is when flats are being sold off as individual units for the first time. As owner of the entire building, the seller is in a position to make his own rules as to division of ownership and liability for maintenance. This he does partly by providing for common ownership of certain parts of the building and partly by imposing real burdens in relation to maintenance. These are contained in the break-off conveyances granted to purchasers, either directly, or nowadays more usually indirectly by means of a separate deed of conditions which is incorporated into the conveyances[1].

No limit is set on the extent to which the common law of the tenement may be altered, and the most common variations are given below. It is essential that the disponer own the whole building, or at least the relevant parts thereof[2]; and the deed must be worded clearly. The latter point is illustrated by *Johnston v White*[3] where the break-off conveyance of a ground floor flat granted a 'right in common with the other proprietors of the tenement' to the *solum*. This was regarded as insufficient to displace the rule of the common law that the ground floor proprietor has sole ownership of the *solum*, apparently on the basis that 'right in common' should be interpreted as referring to common interest and not to common property[4]. Presumably the difficulty would have been met if the deed had granted a 'right of common property', although an express reservation of the remaining shares in the *solum* would also be prudent[5].

1 The Land Registration (Scotland) Act 1979 (c 33), s 17, which makes express incorporation unnecessary for real burdens ('land obligations'), does not apply to common parts. In practice, deeds of conditions are usually mentioned twice, once in the parts and pertinents clause in respect of the common parts and again in the burdens clause in respect of the real burdens. Strictly, only the former is necessary.
2 In practice this is not always given sufficient thought. Developers sometimes grant servitudes over land which they parted with the week before, or confer rights of common property in respect of land which they failed to reserve from an earlier conveyance.
3 *Johnston v White* (1877) 4 R 721.
4 The expression 'right in common' received the same interpretation in *George Watson's Hospital Governors v Cormack* (1883) 11 R 320. But in *WVS Office Premises Ltd v Currie* 1969 SC 170, 1969 SLT 254, it was read as meaning common property. Lord President Clyde commented that 'I do not regard *Johnston's* case as giving a definitive meaning to these words which universally must apply. In every case it is necessary to consider the whole terms of the deed to see what the parties meant': 1969 SC 170 at 175, 1969 SLT 254 at 257.
5 Cf *Watt v Burgess' Trustee* (1891) 18 R 766 which can be read as suggesting that the common law rules apply only to the extent that they are expressly repeated in the break-off conveyances. If that were correct there would be no point in having common law rules. The facts were that a number of flats were sold off without mention of the *solum*. But despite the fact that these included part of the ground floor, which at common law carries the *solum*, Lord M'Laren stated at 770: 'there is no conveyance of the *solum* to the owners of the flats, and so far as it can be held to exist as a separate subject in this peculiar kind of position of property the *solum* would seem to remain untransferred in the persons of the heirs or singular successors of the original proprietors . . .'. On this whole question see further K G C Reid 'The Law of the Tenement: Three Problems' (1990) 35 JLSS 368.

241. Common variations. The following parts are usually made the common property of all the proprietors in the building in equal shares, namely the *solum*, the common passage and stair[1], the roof (but not the roof space[2]), rhones and down pipes, and the back green. The object is not the same in all cases. For the passage and stair and back green the main object is to allow equality of use[3]; for the roof and pipes it is to make maintenance a common responsibility[4]; and for the *solum* it is to give all proprietors equal rights in the event of the building being destroyed[5].

Some deeds go much further and make extravagant provision for *pro indiviso* ownership. It is possible to go too far. It is this writer's opinion that walls in particular should never be made common property, because of the risk that accession might operate. For suppose that the owner of a first floor flat attaches some valuable object — an Adam fireplace, perhaps, or some antique panelling — to his own side of an external wall. If the common law applies, he owns the wall and the object remains his. But if the wall has been made common property then, by accession, the valuable object becomes common property also[6] and his neighbours have a windfall profit. Other examples can easily be figured[7].

Usually the redistribution of ownership is accompanied by real burdens requiring mutual maintenance of the roof, the passage and stair and other common parts[8]. Care should be taken to ensure that there are reciprocal rights to enforce, a point which is sometimes overlooked[9]. In older titles maintenance costs are often apportioned by reference to feuduty[10]. Until the abolition of domestic rates in 1989 rateable value was also commonly used[11]. The simplest, if not always the fairest, method of apportionment is to require an equal contribution from each flat.

1　The common passage and stair is already common property at common law, although in uncertain shares. See para 231 above.
2　A direction that the 'roof' is to be common property does not include the roof space, any more than a direction as to 'walls' includes the living accommodation on the inside of the walls.
3　For use, see para 242 below.
4　See para 246 below.
5　See para 251 below.
6　Bell *Principles* s 1076: 'When anything is built or planted on the common subject, it accresces to the common right'.
7　Wallpaper is a more prosaic example. Like Adam fireplaces, wallpaper also accedes. Consequently if the flatowner tires of the present wallpaper and wishes to change it, in strict law he must first obtain the permission of all of his fellow co-owners.
8　All too often the 'other common parts' are not defined and their content remains in doubt. See eg *McNally and Miller Property Co v Mallinson* 1977 SLT (Sh Ct) 33. Depending on the context in which it is used, the expression may mean the parts owned in common, or the parts used in common, or again it may not be possible to find any clear meaning in which case the burden fails from uncertainty.
9　Otherwise the right to enforce will only be in the superior, or, if the land was disponed rather than feued, there may be no subsisting right to enforce. On rights to enforce real burdens, see paras 397 ff below.
10　Redemption does not prevent the use of the former feuduty for the purposes of apportioning repairs.
11　For deeds executed prior to 1 April 1989 in relation to domestic subjects it is provided that any real burden which apportions liability according to the assessed rental or, as the case may be, the gross annual, net annual or rateable value of the properties shall be construed as a reference to the figure appearing in the valuation roll immediately prior to 1 April 1989. Liability is frozen at that figure and there is no provision for having the valuation roll updated. See the Abolition of Domestic Rates Etc (Scotland) Act 1987 (c 47), s 5(1). The provision does not deal with deeds executed on or after 1 April 1989 but which, mistakenly, refer to rateable value.

(e) Use

242. Parts owned in common. The usual rules of common property apply[1] to parts owned in common. So each proprietor is entitled to make all ordinary uses of the common parts, but extraordinary uses are prohibited. In the case of a back green the ordinary use is for drying clothes and for recreation, while the ordinary use of a passage and stair is for access. It has been held in the sheriff court that a passage and stair cannot be used for the storage of bath chairs[2], a decision which, if correct, would also seem to exclude bicycles and pushchairs, both of which are commonly found in practice[3]. There is a statutory duty to keep the passage and stair and back green free from combustible substances[4] and from anything which might obstruct egress from or access to the property in the event of fire[5]. Enforcement is by statutory notice issued by the fire authority, and a failure to comply with a notice is a criminal offence punishable by fine[6].

Even an ordinary use of common property is unlawful where it is exercised in such a way as to exclude co-owners from part of the property. So it is not open to a proprietor to fence off part of the back green, where it is owned in common, in order to cultivate it as a private garden[7].

In principle, an owner in common can always end his association with his fellow owners either by alienating his *pro indiviso* share or by seeking physical division or division and sale[8] of the property. But according to Bell the remedy of division and sale does not apply 'where it is a thing of common and indispensable use, as a staircase or vestibule'[9], a description which would appear to include the usual common parts such as the roof, the passage and stair, the back green and, at least for as long as the building remains standing[10], the *solum* of the tenement.

1　See paras 23 ff above.
2　*Carmichael v Simpson* 1932 SLT (Sh Ct) 16.
3　Ie unless it can be argued that the storing of bicycles and pushchairs is now so common it must be regarded as an ordinary use.
4　For this purpose, 'combustible substance' means anything which is dangerously combustible in normal conditions and includes any container holding the combustible substance including any such container forming part of a motor vehicle but does not include anything forming part of any common property: Civic Government (Scotland) Act 1982 (c 45), s 93(1). So motor bikes cannot be kept in the common passage.
5　Ibid, s 93(2). The duty is laid on the 'occupier', defined in s 92(1) as the occupier or occupiers of lands or premises having a right of access by, or a right in common to, the common property.
6　Ibid, s 93(4)–(9).
7　In such a case his co-owners can resist his exclusive occupation, although by what means is not entirely clear. See *Price v Watson* 1951 SC 359, 1951 SLT 266, and the discussion at para 24 above.
8　Ie sale of the property and division of the proceeds.
9　Bell *Principles* s 1082.
10　It seems that division and sale of the *solum* is competent after the building is destroyed. See *McLean v City of Glasgow District Council* 1987 SLT (Lands Trib) 2.

243. Parts owned exclusively by individual proprietors. In general a proprietor is free to use his own flat, and any other part of the tenement which is in his sole ownership, in any manner that he pleases. But this is subject to the common interest of the other proprietors, for example in relation to support[1] and light[2], and also to servitudes, real burdens and to the law of nuisance. The close physical proximity of houses within a tenement makes nuisance particularly apt[3].

1　See para 233 above.
2　See para 236 above.
3　See eg *Watt v Jamieson* 1954 SC 56, 1954 SLT 56, OH. See further NUISANCE, vol 14.

(f) Alterations

244. Parts owned in common. Alterations to common property need the consent of every co-owner, regardless of the size of his or her share[1]. The principle is that any co-owner 'may ... prevent any operations on the common subject by which its condition is to be altered; as, in a common stair or passage, he whose property lies next adjoining is not, without the consent of the rest, entitled to break the wall, and strike out a door'[2]. Proposed alterations by individual co-owners may be prevented by interdict; and if building work has actually proceeded, a return to the status quo may be ordered[3]. But the rule is different for necessary repairs, which any one proprietor is entitled to instruct without consent[4]. In view of changes in building technology, repairs may often involve a degree of alteration, so that the distinction between the two is not always sustainable in practice.

1　See para 25 above.
2　Bell *Principles* s 1075.

3 Subject, however, to the defence of personal bar, for which see para 176 above.
4 See para 246 below.

245. Parts owned exclusively by individual proprietors: dormer windows.

An individual owner is always free to alter his own property. But in the case of property within tenement buildings he must do nothing to endanger support[1], shelter[2] and light[3], all of which are protected by common interest.

One of the problems most frequently encountered in practice is of the top floor proprietor who extends into the roof space above his flat. At common law the roof space is his and no objection can be taken to its utilisation. But the position is different where the extension involves the construction of a dormer window or windows. The airspace above the roof line is the property, not of the top proprietor, but of the owner of the *solum*, who at common law is the ground floor proprietor; and even where the common law is altered, as often it is, so that the *solum* is the common property of all the proprietors, the top proprietor lacks that exclusive ownership of the airspace which is required for a permanent encroachment. But while the building of a dormer window may thus be prevented by interdict as an unlawful encroachment[4], in practice dormers are routinely built without objection. Once they are in place personal bar may prevent subsequent objection[5]; and in any event the encroachment is cured by positive prescription or, in the case of Land Register titles, by the act of registration itself[6].

1 See para 233 above.
2 See para 234 above.
3 See para 236 above.
4 *Watt v Burgess' Trustee* (1891) 18 R 766. *Sanderson's Trustees v Yule* (1897) 25 R 211, which might seem to be an authority to the contrary, was decided without the encroachment argument being put to the court.
5 Since the encroachment is obvious, personal bar may also bind successors. See *Taylor & Co v Smellie* (1869) SLR 677; *Brown v Baty* 1957 SC 351, 1957 SLT 336, OH.
6 Land Registration (Scotland) Act 1979 (c 33), s 3(1)(a). For a fuller discussion, see K G C Reid 'The Law of the Tenement: Three Problems' (1990) 35 JLSS 368 at 369, 370.

(g) Repairs

246. Parts owned in common.

In relation to common property, any one co-proprietor may instruct 'necessary' repairs[1] and then look to fellow proprietors for a contribution towards the cost[2], probably in proportion to the size of their respective shares[3]. Common interest, if it is accepted that the doctrine applies to property owned in common[4], provides an alternative basis of recovery for certain kinds of repair[5]. It is unclear how dilapidated property must have become before repairs are 'necessary' within this rule; but in practice the difficulty is often avoided by express provision for maintenance in the titles, although this may create its own problems of interpretation[6].

In the case of some common parts of a tenement the common law is supplemented by a statutory regime contained in the Civic Government (Scotland) Act 1982. Two provisions of the Act are relevant[7]. A duty is imposed on the 'occupier' of certain common parts, including the common passage and stair and back green, to keep the property clean to the satisfaction of the district or islands council[8]. An 'occupier' is any person who occupies premises having a right of access by, or a right in common to, the common parts[9]. Enforcement is by statutory notice[10]. It is a criminal offence, punishable by fine, to drop or deposit litter on the common parts[11]. A duty is also imposed on the owner or owners of every open space which is in a populous place and set apart for use by the owners or occupiers of two or more separate properties to maintain the open space and any boundary walls or fences so as to prevent danger or nuisance to the public[12]. It seems that a back green or other shared garden is an open space within this provision. Enforcement is by statutory notice[13], and it is provided that the cost of complying with the statutory duty may be recovered in equal proportions from each person entitled to use the open space in question[14].

1 Bell *Principles* s 1075; *Deans v Woolfson* 1922 SC 221, 1922 SLT 165.
2 *Miller v Crichton* (1893) 1 SLT 262, OH; W M Gloag *The Law of Contract* (2nd edn, 1929) p 323. 'Unnecessary' repairs are unlawful and presumably the full cost must be borne by the party who instructed them.
3 *Bell* s 1078. For repairs to common property, see generally para 25 above.
4 See para 232 above.
5 Ie where the disrepair threatens shelter or support.
6 See eg *McNally and Miller Property Co v Mallinson* 1977 SLT (Sh Ct) 33.
7 For statutory notices, including notices affecting common parts, see para 248 below.
8 Civic Government (Scotland) Act 1982 (c 45), s 92(1), (2).
9 Ibid, s 92(1).
10 Ibid, s 92(4), (5).
11 Ibid, s 92(9).
12 Ibid, s 95(1).
13 Ibid, s 95(2). For enforcement of statutory notices, see para 248 below.
14 Ibid, s 95(3). In most cases those entitled to use the open space will also be the owners thereof, and here s 95(3) simply re-states the common law position.

247. Parts owned exclusively by individual proprietors. The right to neglect one's property, if one chooses, is part of the right of ownership itself. Consequently, and as a general rule, a proprietor is not bound to maintain his own flat or other property which is in his sole ownership. But within a tenement neglect by one proprietor may easily result in harm to others; and in order to meet at least some aspects of this problem, common interest imposes an obligation on all lower proprietors to provide support for those above, and a corresponding obligation on all upper proprietors, and in particular on the owner of the roof, to provide shelter for those below[1]. However, common interest does not apply in a case where a building is badly damaged or destroyed, whether in whole or in part[2].

Real burdens may impose additional repair obligations, enforceable by the superior or by neighbours or by both.

1 Stair *Institutions* II,7,6; Erskine *Institute* II,9,11. See further paras 233, 234, above.
2 *Thomson v St Cuthbert's Co-operative Association Ltd* 1958 SC 380, 1959 SLT 54. See para 235 above.

248. Statutory notices. The Civic Government (Scotland) Act 1982 empowers local authorities[1] to require that buildings be brought into a reasonable state of repair, regard being had to their age, type and location[2]. The procedure is by written notice served on the owner or owners of the building, which notice must contain adequate specification of the repairs that are to be carried out[3]. Parallel general powers are contained in the Housing (Scotland) Act 1987[4], and there are further specific powers in the 1982 Act in relation to the painting of the common passage and stair[5]. Although widely drafted, these various provisions are in practice used almost exclusively for tenement buildings; and indeed the threat of alerting the local authority to the state of the building is a common and often successful method of persuading one's neighbours to agree to repairs.

Where a statutory notice is served under the 1982 Act but not complied with the local authority is empowered to carry out the work itself, and, if it does so, to recover the cost from the owner or owners of the premises[6]. 'Owner' in this context means the current owner and not the person who was owner at the time of service of the notice[7]. Where, as in a tenement, there is more than one owner the local authority may apportion the costs among them[8]; but no method of apportionment is prescribed, and it has been said that the local authority is entitled to adopt any reasonable method even where a different method is prescribed in the title deeds[9]. A particular difficulty arises where repairs are carried out by the local authority, not to common parts, but to individual flats within the building. In that situation the authority may, and often does, serve the initial statutory notice on all of the proprietors in the building[10], but nonetheless it is thought that the cost of repairs may be recovered only from those whose property has actually been repaired[11].

1 Civic Government (Scotland) Act 1982 (c 45), s 87.
2 'Local authority' means the district or islands council, except that in the case of districts situated within the Highland, Borders or Dumfries and Galloway regions it means the regional council: ibid, s 87(6).
3 Ibid, s 105. See *Gardner v City of Edinburgh District Council* 1991 SCLR 855, 1992 SLT 1149.
4 Housing (Scotland) Act 1987 (c 26), s 108. See further HOUSING, vol 11, para 1993.
5 Civic Government (Scotland) Act 1982, s 92(6). The obligation to paint is laid, not on the owners of the passage and stair, but on the owners of such premises as have a right of access by the passage and stair.
6 Ibid, s 99(2), (4). If necessary the cost can be secured by a charging order under s 108.
7 *Purves v City of Edinburgh District Council* 1987 SLT 366.
8 Civic Government (Scotland) Act 1982, s 99(5).
9 *R S and D Elliot Ltd v City of Edinburgh District Council* (10 August 1988, unreported) Sh Ct. Here the pursuers, who owned a shop, appealed against an apportionment made on the basis of rateable value. Calculated by rateable value their liability for repairs to the tenement was 30 per cent. But the titles provided that liability should be by feuduty, and calculated on this basis liability was reduced to 19 per cent. The appeal was refused. See also *City of Edinburgh District Council v William McIntosh & Co* 1992 GWD 1–3, Sh Ct.
10 *Edinburgh University Court v City of Edinburgh District Council* 1987 SLT (Sh Ct) 103; *City of Edinburgh District Council v Gardner* 1990 SLT 600.
11 K G C Reid 'The Law of the Tenement: Three Problems' (1990) 35 JLSS 368 at 371, 372. A different rule may apply where the whole building has become unstable and the repairs, while carried out on one part of the building only, enure to the general benefit. See para 249 below.

(h) Destruction

249. Costs of demolition. All proprietors must share the cost of demolition of a tenement building; and, in the absence of express provision in the titles, each is liable in the proportion which his flat bears, in a physical sense, to the building as a whole, although in practice an equal division of costs may appear a better solution. Difficult questions arise where part only of the tenement requires to be demolished. The general rule is that the cost of demolition lies with the party whose property is being demolished[1], and no contribution can be demanded from other parties except in respect of any common parts which are included in the demolition. But a different rule may apply where, as in the well-known case of *Smith v Giuliani*[2], the building as a whoe was structurally unsound and demolition of part is employed simply as a means of saving the rest. In such a case it is not only the demolished part which was defective, because even the part which remains had failed in its common interest duty of support. Disentangling the true basis of liability in such a case may be impossible without the assistance of clairvoyance[3], and there is much to be said for the simple rule that each proprietor must pay an equal share.

In practice, demolition is often carried out under the direction of the local authority. Section 13 of the Building (Scotland) Act 1959[4] provides that where a building is dangerous either to persons or to adjacent buildings, the local authority may serve a notice on its owner or owners requiring such operations for repair, securing or demolition as are necessary to remove the danger. In the event of failure to comply the local authority may carry out the work itself and recover the cost[5].

The statute gives no indication as to how the cost of work undertaken by the local authority should be apportioned amongst proprietors of a tenement[6], but clearly the authority should follow so far as is possible the underlying common law liability. In *Smith v Giuliani*, where part only of a building was demolished, the House of Lords accepted that all proprietors should share the cost of the work. According to Lord Dunedin, this was because the proprietors of the surviving part had a right of common interest in the demolished part, and common interest

'is a right of a proprietary character. Accordingly, when I have to apply the word "proprietor" in section 381 [of the Glasgow Police Act 1866[7]] to this peculiar kind of property, I conceive the proprietor includes not only the actual owner of the flat in question but also the other persons who have a common interest therein. Proprietor would ordinarily mean exclusive owner, but in this property there is no such thing as an exclusive owner'[8].

This passage appears to proceed on a misunderstanding as to the nature of common interest[9], for in the law of the tenement there are indeed 'exclusive owners', and a right of common interest—like a right of servitude or a real burden—is not *dominium* but rather a burden on *dominium*. Lord Dunedin's analysis does not appear in the speeches of the other members of the court, and it has enjoyed only mixed fortunes since[10]. It does not deserve to prosper. Nor was it necessary for the decision in *Smith v Giuliani* itself because, as has been seen, partial demolition following on from overall instability is one of the cases where at common law an equal contribution may probably be demanded[11].

In practice, of course, demolition costs are often covered by insurance, but the question of underlying liability remains of interest to the insurers.

1 *Glasgow Trades House v Ferguson* 1979 SLT 187.
2 *Smith v Giuliani* 1925 SC (HL) 45, 1925 SLT 392.
3 It will depend on whether the structure has failed at one point or at several points, on whether the structural failure was negligent, and on whether the building was altered in such a way as to increase the burden of support.
4 Building (Scotland) Act 1959 (c 24), s 13 (amended by the Local Government (Scotland) Act 1973 (c 65), s 134(2), Sch 15, para 10).
5 Building (Scotland) Act 1959, s 13(5) (as so amended).
6 This may be contrasted with the Housing (Scotland) Act 1987 (c 26) which provides that for demolitions carried out under its provisions the tenement owners are to be given an opportunity to agree the correct apportionment of costs, which failing the matter is to be settled by an arbiter: s 123(3)(c). By s 115 a local authority has power to demolish a building under the 1987 Act only where the entire building comprises houses which are not of a tolerable standard. 'Tolerable standard' is defined in s 86(1).
7 Glasgow Police Act 1866 (repealed). It is similar in wording to s 13 of the Building (Scotland) Act 1959.
8 *Smith v Giuliani* 1925 SC (HL) 45 at 59, 1925 SLT 392 at 400, 401.
9 K G C Reid 'Common Interest' (1983) 28 JLSS 428 at 432, 433. See para 362 below.
10 In *Duncan Smith and MacLaren v Heatly* 1952 JC 61, 1952 SLT 254, a decision which is reconcilable with *Smith v Giuliani* but not, it is thought, with Lord Dunedin's views there, Lord Cooper emphasised that the House of Lords in *Smith v Giuliani* had been proceeding 'on a construction of a different section of a different Act, and with express reference to the circumstances of the case'. But Lord Dunedin's analysis is used in a subsidiary argument accepted in *City of Edinburgh District Council v Gardner* 1990 SLT 600. See also *Gardner v City of Edinburgh District Council* 1991 SCLR 855, 1992 SLT 1149.
11 The circumstances of *Smith v Giuliani* were rather unusual, as the court recognised. Thus the Lord Chancellor declined to lay down any general rule and emphasised instead 'the special circumstances of this case'.

250. Rebuilding. Once a tenement has been demolished a decision may be taken to rebuild, or alternatively the *solum* may be disposed of for redevelopment[1].

Rebuilding is sometimes required in terms of the title deeds. But in the absence of express provision there it is thought that rebuilding can proceed only with the consent of all of the affected proprietors[2]. The common interest obligation of support perishes with the tenement and cannot be used as a means of forcing its reconstruction[3].

Since each proprietor continues to own the airspace formerly occupied by his, now demolished, flat[4], a rebuilt tenement ought, strictly, to occupy the same airspace as the original. In practice, however, any deviation, and consequent encroachment, is likely to go unchallenged and will in any case be cured by registration in the Land Register[5] or, in the case of Sasine titles, by positive prescription[6].

1 As to disposal of the *solum*, see para 251 below.
2 Ie for each retains ownership of his airspace and can prevent its use against his will. Partial rebuilding requires the consent only of the proprietors of the relevant part, so that a decision may be taken to rebuild a tenement, eg, only to first floor level.
3 *Thomson v St Cuthbert's Co-operative Association Ltd* 1958 SC 380, 1959 SLT 54. See para 235 above.
4 *Barr v Bass Ltd* 1972 SLT (Lands Trib) 5.
5 Land Registration (Scotland) Act 1979 (c 33), s 3(1)(a), for which see para 673 below.
6 Prescription and Limitation (Scotland) Act 1973 (c 52), s 1, for which see para 674 below.

251. Disposal of the *solum*. In many cases titles provide that the *solum* is the common property of all the proprietors in the tenement[1]; but even where the titles are silent all the proprietors own at least the strip of *solum* underneath the common passage and stair, the remaining sections being the property of the owner or owners of the ground floor flats[2]. Thus disposal of the *solum* following destruction of the building is a matter in which all proprietors have a voice.

Where the *solum* is common property any one proprietor is entitled to insist on physical division, or where division is impractical, on division and sale[3]. Where, however, the common law rules apply unaltered, the ground floor proprietors are free to sell their own section of *solum* and only the *solum* underneath the passage and stair is subject to division and sale.

In the acquisition of the former *solum* of a tenement it must be borne in mind that the airspace formerly occupied by individual flats continues to belong to the proprietors thereof[4]. Consequently, if it is intended to build into this airspace, conveyances will have to be obtained from the relevant proprietors.

1 Sometimes purchasers of upper flats insist on obtaining common property in the *solum* and withdraw from the purchase if it turns out not to be available, but this is a practice which seems open to question. See K G C Reid 'The Law of the Tenement: Three Problems' (1990) 35 JLSS 368.
2 See para 228 above.
3 *McLean v City of Glasgow District Council* 1987 SLT (Lands Trib) 2. For division and sale, see para 33 above.
4 *Barr v Bass Ltd* 1972 SLT (Lands Trib) 5.

(5) SUPPORT

(a) General

252. Introduction. The most recent decision on the law of support characterises the subject as 'curiously obscure and undeveloped'[1]. The description is apt. Lying on the boundary between the law of delict and property, but peripheral to both, the law of support has received little serious attention, either from judges or from jurists. Indeed until the middle of the nineteenth century there was practically no case law, and the subject is not discussed by the institutional writers. What made the law of support suddenly important was the industrial revolution and the huge increase in the demand for coal which it prompted. By 1851 there were 48,000 people employed in the coal mining industry in Scotland, and the figure would more than double before the end of the century[2]. At first, however, methods of coal-mining were properly cautious and did not, in general, lead to subsidence. The most favoured method, known as 'stoop and room', avoided complete excavation of the coal by allowing substantial coal pillars or 'stoops' to be left in place to provide support once the mine had been worked. In the course of the nineteenth century stoop and room began to give way to the 'longwall' system of working which involved total excavation and hence, not infrequently, to subsidence[3]. Naturally, subsidence led to claims for compensation from the owners of the surface; but in many cases the value of the coal was such that mining companies were content to run the risk of subsidence, and compensation claims, in order to extract as much coal as possible[4].

With the severe contraction of the coal industry in recent years, the law of support has declined in importance. But mining continues today, and not just for coal, and subsidence may in any event result from old workings. Tunnelling gives rise to the same kind of problems as mining[5]. Nor is the law exclusively concerned with subterranean activity. Subsidence can be caused by normal building operations on an adjacent piece of land[6]; and, in a rather different sense, questions of support may also arise where a common wall is shared by two adjacent buildings, a separate subject which requires separate treatment[7]. Finally, the law of support, intractable and uninviting though it may at first appear, is of considerable interest as an example of how property law attempts to resolve the legitimate but opposed claims of neighbouring proprietors.

1 *Rogano Ltd v British Railways Board* 1979 SC 297 at 301, per Lord Maxwell.
2 A K Cairncross (ed) *The Scottish Economy* (1954) p 77, table 36.
3 For an interesting account of some of the mining methods used, see the opinion of Lord Benholme in *Andrew v Henderson and Dimmack* (1871) 9 M 554 at 564 ff (revsd *sub nom Buchanan v Andrew* (1873) 11 M (HL) 13).
4 See eg *Anderson v M'Cracken Bros* (1900) 2 F 780, 7 SLT 427.
5 *Rogano Ltd v British Railways Board* 1979 SC 297.
6 *Lord Advocate v Reo Stakis Organisation Ltd* 1980 SC 203, 1980 SLT 237, OH, affd 1981 SC 104, 1982 SLT 140.
7 See para 272 below.

(b) Support by Land to Land

(A) SUMMARY

253. The rule in summary. This section is concerned with the support of land by other land. Support of buildings by buildings raises substantially different issues and is treated separately[1].

If land is not to subside, it requires both adjacent (lateral) and subjacent support. Where, therefore, adjoining land or, as in the case of minerals held as a separate tenement[2], a subjacent stratum of the same land, is owned by someone else, the question arises as to the obligation of that other person to provide the required degree of support. The detail of the law is discussed later, but the general position may be summarised as follows. There is no positive obligation on an adjacent or subjacent proprietor to provide support. He need take no action to maintain existing levels of support, and if support fails—typically as a result of old mineral workings—there is neither liability in damages nor an obligation to restore the status quo. But while positive action is not required by the law, any positive act which the proprietor chooses to perform on his own land must be performed so as not to endanger existing support. In practice, of course, the positive act giving rise to problems has usually been mining and the dispute is between, on the one hand, the owner of the mineral rights and, on the other hand, the owner of the surface. If support appears to be at risk from a positive act, the act may be prevented by the neighbour whose land is threatened. If the act proceeds and subsidence occurs, damages are due. Liability is strict. The obligation, at least in the normal case, is not diminished by the presence of buildings on the neighbour's land and if withdrawal of support causes damage to buildings the loss is recoverable.

It is often said that a proprietor of land has a 'right of support' in respect of adjacent and subjacent land[3]. The term, however, is misleading. It suggests a right akin to the admitted right of support in the law of the tenement, which is a right founded in common interest and imposing a positive duty on the servient proprietor[4]. But in the present case there is no such positive duty; and if there is no obligation to give support it follows that there can be no correlative right to receive it. A more accurate characterisation of the law, therefore, is to say that, in the exercise of their rights of ownership, adjacent and subjacent proprietors must refrain from any act which damages such support as is currently provided to a neighbour. The obligation is a negative one and the neighbour's 'right' is no more than the counterpart of that negative obligation.

1 See paras 271, 272, below.
2 For separate tenements, see paras 207 ff above.
3 The expression 'right of support' appears frequently in textbooks and case reports. For an appearance in statute, see the Coal Industry Nationalisation Act 1946 (c 59), s 48(1)(a).
4 See para 233 above.

(B) THE LEGAL BASIS OF SUPPORT

254. Introduction. What is the legal basis of the obligation (and correlative right) of support? Usually the right is described as a 'natural right'[1], but this is an evasive term which means no more than that the right arises by operation of law and so does not have to be 'acquired', as is the case with servitudes or real burdens[2]. In fact the legal relationship seems better approached as an obligation than as a right. Viewed from this aspect, adjacent or subjacent proprietors are subject to a restriction in the use of their land. Unless the restriction is to be treated as *sui generis*, which seems an improbable solution[3], it requires to be fitted into one of the existing categories of restriction. Three are suggested in the case law, namely (1) common interest, (2) delict and (3) implied servitude, and these may now be considered in turn.

1 Ie at least insofar as it relates to support of land in its natural, unbuilt-on state. As will be explained later, there is a view that support of land encumbered by buildings is a servitude right and hence an acquired right.
2 J Rankine *The Law of Land-ownership in Scotland* (4th edn, 1909) pp 367, 384, 385. 'Natural rights of property, or natural restrictions on the use of property, are such as are inherent in the idea of ownership in a civilised community, accrue simultaneously with the acquisition of real property, and are regarded as necessary for the peaceful enjoyment of social life': *Rankine* pp 384, 385.
3 But would be perfectly plausible if the right to minerals was itself an (incorporeal) right *sui generis*, as it is in some countries, and not an ordinary (corporeal) separate tenement.

255. Common interest. The obligation of support of land to land is sometimes said to be like the obligation of support in the law of the tenement by which lower flats must support the flats above. In the law of the tenement the obligation of support is founded on common interest[1]. Thus Lord Neaves:

'In the case of parties proprietors of subterranean and superficial estates restraints arise which must be more incumbent on the proprietor of the subterranean than of the superficial estate, because the proprietor of the superficial estate cannot do so much injury to the estate below. The way in which the restraint operates is, that the minerals must be worked so that the land above may be used and enjoyed, not destroyed or seriously damaged. That is the universal rule in the case of all parties who stand in this anomolous position to one another, neither having an unlimited right to their estate. The limitation is sometimes compared to the rights of parties to flats of houses. The right to one flat must be enjoyed without injury to another, certainly without bringing it down'[2].

But while this view is also found in one or two other cases[3], it cannot be regarded as the dominant analysis of the nature of the obligation of support.

1 See para 233 above.
2 *Andrew v Henderson and Dimmack* (1871) 9 M 554 at 569 (revsd *sub nom Buchanan v Andrew* (1873) 11 M (HL) 13).
3 *Hamilton v Turner* (1867) 5 M 1086 at 1089, 1090, OH, per Lord Kinloch; *Neill's Trustees v William Dixon Ltd* (1880) 7 R 741 at 746, per Lord Ormidale. In the second case the analysis appears to be based on the arguments presented for the (unsuccessful) pursuer in *Dunlop's Trustees v Corbet and Macnair* June 20 1809 FC.

256. Delict. In *Buchanan v Andrew* the Lord Chancellor, Lord Selborne, expressed the view that the owner of minerals is subject to

'the general restriction which every owner of property is under, expressed in the maxim *Sic utere tuo ut alienum non laedas*. When one man's property stands in such a position to another man's that by certain modes of using it he might destroy the property of the other, his own rightful use over his own property is limited by the obligation which he is under not to destroy the property of his neighbour. Therefore, although he would have been at liberty to take away, if he could do so without injuring his neighbour, everything reserved to him, yet he was not at liberty in taking it away to injure his neighbour'[1].

Here the obligation not to disturb support is seen, not as part of some special arrangement peculiar to mining law and policed by common interest, but, more simply, as one aspect of the general rule that one must not injure the property of one's neighbour. On this analysis the obligation not to withdraw support from the land of one's neighbour is no different from the obligation not to aim footballs at his window. Both obligations are founded in delict, or alternatively — and which comes to very much the same thing in practice — in nuisance[2]. The view that the obligation of support arises *ex delicto* is one which has been frequently expressed in the reported cases[3].

1 *Buchanan v Andrew* (1873) 11 M (HL) 13 at 18.
2 In *Lord Advocate v Reo Stakis Organisation Ltd* 1980 SC 203, 1980 SLT 237, OH, affd 1981 SC 104, 1982 SLT 140, a building suffered structural damage as a result of piling operations carried out in an adjoining building site which produced subsidence. It was held that a relevant case had been made in nuisance. See NUISANCE, vol 14, para 2029.
3 *Hamilton v Turner* (1867) 5 M 1086; *Bain v Duke of Hamilton* (1867) 6 M 1; *Daniel Stewart's Hospital Governors v Waddell* (1890) 17 R 1077; *Bank of Scotland v Stewart* (1891) 18 R 957.

257. Implied servitude. In one of the leading early cases, *Caledonian Railway Co v Sprot*, the obligation of support was classified as an implied servitude[1]. On this view, when minerals are first separated from the surface, the conveyance is said to include an implied grant (or in cases where minerals were granted rather than reserved, an implied reservation) of support. But this approach has not generally been accepted, either in Scotland or England, for unlike rights founded in delict or in common interest, which are 'natural' rights, a servitude is an 'acquired' right; and it is now established beyond challenge that the obligation of support, at least in its basic form, is a natural right.

However, the matter does not end there. In England, in a doctrine particularly associated with the decision of the House of Lords in *Dalton v Angus*[2], the natural obligation of support is regarded as confined to support of land in its 'natural state', which is to say, to support of land which is unbuilt on[3]. Where buildings have been erected there is no natural obligation and hence no obligation at all in the absence of servitude (easement). If a building was in existence at the time when severance took place, a servitude of support is implied into the grant or, as the case may be, into the reservation. But if a building post-dates severance there is no servitude in the absence of an express grant or the running of acquisitive prescription[4]. Is this also the law in Scotland? In *Rogano Ltd v British Railways Board*, the most recent reported decision on support, Lord Maxwell appears to follow the English rule:

> 'Where . . . land is built upon, the right of support as a natural incident of land-ownership is superseded and anything in the nature of a right of support must be found in the creation of a servitude'[5].

A similar view can be found in Rankine's *The Law of Land-ownership in Scotland*[6] and in textbooks which have relied on Rankine[7]. Surprisingly, however, little or no support for this approach is found in any other reported decision of the Scottish courts and at least one modern writer has expressed doubts as to its soundness[8].

1 *Caledonian Rly Co v Sprot* (1856) 16 D 559, revsd (1856) 2 Macq 449, HL. For implied servitudes, see paras 452 ff below.
2 *Dalton v Angus* (1881) 6 App Cas 740, HL.
3 'Support to that which is artificially imposed upon land cannot exist *ex jure naturae*, because the thing supported does not itself so exist': (1881) 6 App Cas 740 at 792, HL, per Lord Selborne LC. But this proceeds on the assumption that 'natural' in the context of 'natural right' means the same as 'natural' in the context of 'natural state'.
4 14 *Halsbury's Laws of England* (4th edn) paras 168–184.
5 *Rogano Ltd v British Railways Board* 1979 SC 297 at 301.
6 J Rankine *The Law of Land-ownership in Scotland* (4th edn, 1909) p 496.
7 Eg D R Stewart *A Treatise on the Law relating to Mines, Quarries and Minerals* (1894) p 170; D M Walker *The Law of Delict in Scotland* (2nd edn, 1981) p 948; W M Gloag and R C Henderson *Introduction to the Law of Scotland* (9th edn, 1987) p 664.
8 W M Gordon *Scottish Land Law* (1989) para 6-91.

258. Evaluation. The obligation of support has been variously ascribed to common interest, to delict and to implied servitude. Which ascription is correct? The authorities, as has been seen, are not at one in this matter and it is impossible to reach a view which can be reconciled with all of them.

It is universally accepted, at least in respect of land in its 'natural' state, that the obligation of support is a 'natural' and not an 'acquired' right. Implied servitude is therefore excluded as an explanation leaving a choice to be made between common interest and delict. At first sight common interest is an attractive solution. Nonetheless, it seems that it must be rejected, for a number of reasons. First, common interest invariably involves reciprocity of right and obligation[1]. The owner of A is under an obligation to the owner of B; but this is matched by a parallel obligation of the owner of B to the owner of A. But here there is no reciprocal obligation. The subjacent or adjacent proprietor is bound, but the proprietor being supported has no corresponding obligation[2]. Secondly, common interest is 'open-textured': it has a broad and indefinite content[3]. Here the content is narrow and definite. Thirdly, like most other real conditions, common interest is enforceable only by owners and only against owners. It is inseparable from *dominium*[4]. But the right of support is available more widely and in particular it is enforceable by tenants[5] and against tenants[6]. Finally, if the other instances of the doctrine may be taken as a reliable guide, common interest is recognised only where the rights and obligations in question cannot otherwise be explained. In particular, common interest is often the explanation for obligations which are positive in nature so cannot be founded either in servitude or in delict. But the obligation of support is a negative obligation and can be founded in delict. Delict is also the most popular explanation in the reported cases. The conclusion seems inescapable.

There remains the difficulty of land which has been built upon. In English law[7] buildings are not included within the natural obligation of support, and in a case where subsidence would not have occurred but for the weight of a building no damages are recoverable unless a servitude (easement) can be shown to have been constituted. A servitude will be implied where the building existed, or at least was in prospect, at the time of severance of the alleged dominant and servient tenements. Otherwise there is no servitude of support until the building has been standing for the period of acquisitive prescription, which, in both Scotland and England, is twenty years[8]. In Scotland, however, the rule is different. There is clear authority to the effect that buildings erected after severance but before the expiry of the twenty-year period are included within the obligation of support[9]; and from this it seems almost necessarily to follow that, even in respect of land which has been built upon, the obligation of support is natural (delictual) and not acquired (founded on servitude). For the obligation of support does not distinguish between built and unbuilt land and the obligation in respect of the former could be regarded as founded on servitude only if it were accepted that, on severance, there is implied into every conveyance and under all circumstances a servitude of support in respect of future buildings. This is a contrived doctrine and one moreover entirely without utility[10]. There may still be a role for servitude as creating rights of support more extensive than the natural right, but that is a different matter[11].

1 See paras 360 ff below.
2 In a valiant attempt to meet this point it has been suggested that the reciprocal obligation of the upper proprietor is an obligation to build with restraint (*Neill's Trustees v William Dixon Ltd* (1880) 7 R 741 at 746, per Lord Ormidale) or even to pay compensation if his building programme sterilises the mineral estate by making excessive demands in respect of support (*White v Dixon* (1881) 9 R 375 at 393, per Lord Shand).
3 See para 361 below.
4 See para 363 below. The right of support is also sometimes said to be inseparable from ownership but, strictly, this is not the case.
5 *Daniel Stewart's Hospital Governors v Waddell* (1890) 17 R 1077.
6 *Aitken's Trustees v Rawyards Colliery Ltd* (1894) 22 R 201.
7 See para 257 above.
8 So for the first twenty years of a building's life the owner of adjacent or subjacent soil may 'with perfect legality dig that soil away, and allow his neighbour's house, if supported by it, to fall in ruins to the ground': *Dalton v Angus* (1881) 6 App Cas 740 at 804, HL, per Lord Penzance.
9 See para 260 below.
10 In English law, of course, there is utility; or, to put it in another way, English law follows the logic of an acquired right of support by denying protection to buildings built after severance but which have not been in position for twenty years. There is thus a clear distinction between support for land in its natural state and support for land with buildings. In Scotland there is no such distinction and hence no reason for classifying the one as natural and the other as acquired.
11 See para 269 below.

(C) THE 'NATURAL' OBLIGATION

259. Obligation not to withdraw support. It is a civil wrong, actionable in delict[1], to withdraw support from land belonging to, or under the legal control of[2], another person. The paradigm case is mining[3]. So if minerals are owned or leased by A while the surface belongs to B, and if A's operations cause subsidence to B's land, A is liable to B in damages. The subsidence need not follow immediately: so long as causation can be established a lapse of time between act and consequence does not prevent a claim[4]. But the act founded on must have occurred after separation of the two properties, so that if C sells land to D reserving the minerals, there is no liability in C for subsidence caused by workings carried out prior to the sale[5].

The party providing support must take the support as he finds it, a doctrine both favourable and also unfavourable to his position. The favourable aspect is that there is no obligation to improve existing support. If B's land subsides due to the inherent inadequacy of that support, there is no liability in A. There is no positive obligation laid on A to provide support, for such an obligation would be unduly onerous, and A's obligation is limited to refraining from acts which would withdraw support from B. If there is no act then there is no liability[6]. The unfavourable aspect is that if support is withdrawn, whether as a result of mining or of some other activity, the fact that the pre-existing level of support was abnormally weak is not a defence[7]. Nor does it matter that the support was artificial and not natural[8]. A must not interfere with B's support, however it is derived and at whatever level it is set, and if he cannot work without threatening that support then he cannot work at all.

1 See para 258 above.
2 Eg in virtue of a tenancy.
3 But not the only case. See para 263 below.
4 The long negative prescription, which will eventually extinguish a claim, does not begin to run until the damage occurs. See the Prescription and Limitation (Scotland) Act 1973 (c 52), s 11(1), (4).
5 *Rogano Ltd v British Railways Board* 1979 SC 297.
6 *Rogano Ltd v British Railways Board* 1979 SC 297. It is true that in *Rogano* support was treated as a servitude, so that the decision can be explained on the basis that servitudes are not *in faciendo*. But there has been no reported decision in which a positive obligation to maintain has been said to exist and the law is not in doubt.
7 *White's Trustees v Duke of Hamilton* (1887) 14 R 597.
8 *Bald's Trustees v Alloa Colliery Ltd* (1854) 16 D 870 (support provided by water which had penetrated a partially worked-out seam).

260. Buildings. In English law the 'natural' obligation of support is restricted to land which has not been built upon, and an obligation to support buildings exists only where it has been acquired independently, usually as an implied easement (servitude) on the original separation of the two properties[1]. A building not in place at the time of separation is excluded from the obligation[2]. In Scotland the position is different, and that despite the fact that the law of support is sometimes said to be the same in the two jurisdictions[3]. Scots law makes no distinction between bare land and land covered in buildings. Nor is there any requirement that the building be in place at the time of original separation provided that it is there when the act causing the withdrawal of support takes place[4]. Thus Lord Kinloch:

> 'When the minerals are constituted into a separate property from the surface, the proprietor of the surface is not thereby disabled from building houses, more than from any other legal use of his property. Every legitimate use of his property remains to him the same as before. It was only such a legitimate use when the pursuer built the houses in question. The houses were built before the minerals were wrought beneath them. The miners came to the houses: not the houses to a worked-out mine'[5].

It is sometimes suggested that the right to support is forfeited by excessive building. This is an attempt to balance the interests of subjacent and surface proprietors: on this view the surface proprietor should not be permitted to build if the effect of his building is to sterilise the mineral rights beneath[6]. But this principle has never been applied in a reported decision, and the courts seem to have had no difficulty in accepting that support is due to substantial buildings such as tenements[7]. Where the substantial cause of damage to a building or other structure is inadequate construction or insufficient maintenance, no liability attaches to a party whose mining or other operations is the occasion of its ultimate collapse[8]. That conclusion follows from general principles of the law of delict.

1 14 *Halsbury's Laws of England* (4th edn) paras 172, 176.

2 Except where its building is within the contemplation of the parties. See para 258 above. An easement of support for a new building may be acquired by prescription.

3 But only by the House of Lords in Victorian times. See *Caledonian Rly Co v Sprot* (1856) 2 Macq 449 at 461, HL, per Lord Cranworth LC; *Buchanan v Andrew* (1873) 11 M (HL) 13 at 16, per Lord Selborne LC; *White v William Dixon Ltd* (1883) 10 R (HL) 45 at 46, per Lord Blackburn.

4 *Hamilton v Turner* (1867) 5 M 1086; *Bain v Duke of Hamilton* (1867) 6 M 1; *Aitken's Trustees v Rawyards Colliery Co Ltd* (1894) 22 R 201; *Dryburgh v Fife Coal Co Ltd* (1905) 7 F 1083, 13 SLT 312. The rule is the same where the obligation of support is expressed in the titles: see *Neill's Trustees v William Dixon Ltd* (1880) 7 R 741.

5 *Hamilton v Turner* (1867) 5 M 1086 at 1091, OH, per Lord Kinloch.

6 The view is particularly associated with Lord President Inglis: see *Hamilton v Turner* (1867) 5 M 1086 at 1095, and *White v William Dixon Ltd* (1881) 9 R 375 at 388. See also *Neill's Trustees v William Dixon Ltd* (1880) 7 R 741.

7 *Aitken's Trustees v Rawyards Colliery Co Ltd* (1894) 22 R 201.

8 *M'Intosh v Scott* (1859) 21 D 363; *Campbell's Trustees v Henderson* (1884) 11 R 520.

261. Strict liability? At one time an award of damages was thought to depend on a finding of 'improper' working of the minerals. But no clear view emerged as to how the distinction between 'proper' and 'improper' working should be drawn. Did working achieve the status of 'proper' working merely by being the normal method of mineral extraction in the area in question? Or did it cease to be 'proper' if it in fact caused damage to the surface, an approach scarcely distinguishable from strict liability? Both views had their supporters[1]. By the beginning of the twentieth century, however, the rule had developed, perhaps under English influence, that liability was strict in the sense of not requiring negligence[2]; and at the same time the expression 'improper' working had re-appeared in a quite different context and with a quite different meaning[3].

1 *Hamilton v Turner* (1867) 5 M 1086; *Andrew v Henderson and Dimmack* (1871) 9 M 554 (revsd *sub nom Buchanan v Andrew* (1873) 11 M (HL) 13).

2 *Dryburgh v Fife Coal Co Ltd* (1905) 7 F 1083, 13 SLT 312; *Angus v National Coal Board* 1955 SC 175, 1955 SLT 245.

3 By then 'proper working' had come to mean any ordinary working of minerals, whether it produced subsidence or not; and 'improper working' meant extraordinary or negligent working. The new context was the interpretation of compensation clauses (for which see para 265 below). See *Buchanan v Andrew* (1873) 11 M (HL) 13 at 20, per Lord Selborne LC; *Anderson v M'Cracken Bros* (1900) 2 F 780, 7 SLT 427; *Dryburgh v Fife Coal Co Ltd* (1905) 7 F 1083, 13 SLT 312.

262. Remedies. The remedies most frequently sought in relation to withdrawal of support are interdict and damages, accompanied sometimes by a declarator that the defender is bound not to interfere with support provided for the pursuer[1]. Interdict, while a discretionary remedy, will not be refused merely because the disbenefit to the defender in having to cease working exceeds any possible benefit to the pursuer from being relieved of the risk of subsidence[2]. In the case of damages, liability is strict[3], but, according to Rankine, the amount awarded is restricted to reasonable indemnity for the harm done and does not extend to the cost of reinstatement[4].

Only the actual wrongdoer may be sued[5]. Where an interval elapses between the act which removes support and the occurrence of subsidence itself, and where, during that interval, the subjacent (or, as the case may be, adjacent) land has changed hands, no liability attaches to the new owner and only the party who performed the wrongful act may be sued[6]. This may be said to follow from first principles of delict. However, in the case of subsidence brought about by coal-mining, the current holder of the licence to work the coal or, if there is no current holder, the Coal Authority has overriding liability[7].

A similar, but more difficult, issue arises where the land withdrawing support is tenanted. Here the act causing subsidence is the act of the tenant alone. Against whom does a remedy arise? There seem three possible answers. Either the tenant alone is liable, or the landlord alone is liable, or both landlord and tenant are liable jointly and severally. Professor W M Gordon suggests that the natural obligation of support does not extend to tenants, that the liability of a tenant rests on ordinary delictual principles and is not strict, and that accordingly, in the absence of negligent workmanship, a claim can be made against the landlord only[8]. But while this is a possible view on the authorities, or at least on some of them[9], a simpler and, it is submitted, more convincing view is to say that the primary liability rests on the tenant, as the wrongdoer, and that that liability is strict. On this view subsidence caused by a tenant is in exactly the same position as subsidence caused by an owner: liability arises *ex delicto* and is strict[10]. The landlord will, however, also be liable[11] where either the method of working was authorised by the lease, whether expressly or by implication[12], or, it has been suggested, where the landlord has participated in or has knowledge of the working of his tenant[13]. Where both landlord and tenant are liable, liability is joint and several and the pursuer has a choice of defenders[14].

The rule just stated does not, it is thought, apply to the case of superiors and feuars and there seems no good reason why a superior should be held liable for the wrongous acts of his feuar[15].

It is common for the title deeds of the affected parties to make express provision about the nature and extent of remedies for subsidence, and the effectiveness of such provisions is considered below[16].

1 In *Mid and East Calder Gas-Light Co v Oakbank Oil Co Ltd* (1891) 18 R 788 the pursuers sought to have the defenders ordained to carry out repairs to property damaged by their mining operations.
2 *Bank of Scotland v Stewart* (1891) 18 R 957.
3 See para 261 above.
4 J Rankine *The Law of Land-ownership in Scotland* (4th edn, 1909) p 495.
5 *Dryburgh v Fife Coal Co Ltd* (1905) 7 F 1083 at 1098, 13 SLT 312 at 313, per Lord Kyllachy.
6 *Geddes' Trustees v Haldane* (1905) 14 SLT 328.
7 Coal Industry Act 1994 (c 21), s 43. See further para 267A below.
8 W M Gordon *Scottish Land Law* (1989) pp 143, 144.
9 The main authorities which can be read as supporting this view are *Hamilton v Turner* (1867) 5 M 1086 and *Mid and East Calder Gas-Light Co v Oakbank Oil Co Ltd* (1891) 18 R 788. But it is possible to explain these cases on the basis that strict liability for withdrawal of support was not established until the early twentieth century; and in the case of *Hamilton* the distinction made between the liability of the landlord and the liability of the tenant was based on the express provision for indemnity contained in the landlord's title, there being no suggestion that, in the absence of such express provision, the basis of liability would have been different as between the two defenders. On this last point, see also *Bain v Duke of Hamilton* (1867) 6 M 1. If *Hamilton* and *Mid and East Calder Gas-Light Co* are read as supporting Professor Gordon's analysis, they cannot be reconciled with *Dryburgh v Fife Coal Co Ltd* (1905) 7 F 1083, 13 SLT 312: see text and note 11 below.
10 *Dryburgh v Fife Coal Co Ltd* (1905) 7 F 1083, 13 SLT 312.
11 And, it appears, in actions of interdict as well as actions for damages: see *Andrew v Henderson and Dimmack* (1871) 9 M 554 at 559, OH, per Lord Ormidale (affd (1871) 9 M 554, IH; revsd *sub nom Buchanan v Andrew* (1873) 11 M (HL) 13).
12 *Hamilton v Turner* (1867) 5 M 1086 at 1090, 1092, OH, per Lord Kinloch. A comparable rule exists in the case of nuisances committed by tenants: see NUISANCE, vol 14, para 2140.
13 *Swanson v Burnbank and Grougar Coal Co* 1926 SN 77, OH.
14 *Highgate & Co v Paisley Magistrates* (1896) 23 R 992.
15 For the equivalent rule in nuisance, see NUISANCE, vol 14, para 2141. We are concerned here with the superior of the land which withdraws support. Of course very often the owner (of the *dominium utile*) of this land, who in relation to his own superior is a feuar, is also the superior of the land from which support is withdrawn. (This is because in practice minerals are often reserved by the superior when land is being feued.) But that is another matter and has no bearing on liability.
16 See paras 264 ff below.

263. Adjacent support. Although almost all the reported decisions on support are concerned with subjacent support, and in particular with subsidence caused by mining, it appears that the provision of adjacent support is governed by the same general principles. Thus Hume:

'[P]ut the case that the owner of an area of ground in a town is digging the foundation of a new building, or is digging for sand, or stone, or the like, within his own bounds: He must take care so to conduct his operations as not to endanger or bring down his neighbour's house, previously erected on the verge of the adjoining area. At his own charge, by a retaining wall, or otherwise, he must secure his neighbour's foundations; or, if this cannot be effectively done, he must keep at the necessary distance, and desist from his purpose'[1].

The case law is sparse. In two Victorian cases liability for withdrawal of lateral support was acknowledged as arising *ex delicto* but only where the defender had been negligent in his operations[2]; and in *Lord Advocate v Reo Stakis Organisation Ltd*[3], decided in 1981, a remedy was said to be available in nuisance, the defenders' liability being characterised as strict. Today these decisions appear to be the wrong way round. If provision of adjacent support is analogous to subjacent support, the rule now is that liability in delict is strict[4]; but conversely liability under the law of nuisance is regarded as based on fault[5].

1 Hume *Lectures* vol III (Stair Soc vol 15, 1952 ed G C H Paton) p 208.
2 *M'Intosh v Scott* (1859) 21 D 363; *Campbell's Trustees v Henderson* (1884) 11 R 520.
3 *Lord Advocate v Reo Stakis Organisation Ltd* 1981 SC 104, 1982 SLT 140.
4 See para 261 above.
5 *RHM Bakeries (Scotland) Ltd v Strathclyde Regional Council* 1985 SC (HL) 17, 1985 SLT 214.

(D) VARIATION IN THE TITLES AND BY STATUTE

264. Contracting in. In the case of minerals, but not in other cases, the break-off conveyance which effects the initial separation from the surface often makes special provision about support. The following is typical:

'. . . reserving to the Superiors and their successors the whole mines, metals and minerals (other than coal in terms of the Coal Industry Nationalisation Act 1946), with power to the Superiors and their foresaids to work, win and carry away the same but so as not to enter upon the surface of the ground hereby disponed, and providing that the Superiors and their foresaids shall be bound and obliged to satisfy and pay the whole damages which may be occasioned to the subjects hereby disponed or to the buildings thereon through or in consequence of their working the said mines, metals and minerals . . .'[1].

In addition to reserving the minerals, this clause contains three separate elements, namely (1) a right to work the minerals, (2) an obligation not to enter upon the surface and (3) an obligation to pay for damage occasioned to the surface or to buildings built upon it. In fact these do no more than re-state the position at common law. For at common law the owner of minerals is entitled to work the minerals, but must not enter or break open the surface for that purpose without express stipulation in the titles (which there sometimes is[2]); and if subsidence occurs damages are due to the surface owner, liability being strict[3]. But the clause, like almost all such clauses, contains one notable omission: there is no express prohibition on lowering the surface, which is to say, there is no express obligation of support. This is a potential trap for the unwary purchaser. On its face the clause contracts into the common law and reinforces that law by repeating its terms. That may appear to confer adequate protection on the owner of the surface. But there is authority, considered below[4], which argues that the omission of an express obligation of support is tantamount to the implied exclusion of such an obligation. On this view the mineral owner is perfectly entitled to withdraw support provided only that, as the clause quoted says, he pays compensation for any damage thereby inflicted. By contracting into some of the common law rules he is deemed to have contracted out of the rest[5].

1 For this clause, and for a treatment of minerals in general, see CONVEYANCING, vol 6, paras 491 ff. An analysis of other clauses will be found in R Rennie 'Non-oil Related Minerals and Reservation Clauses' The Law Society of Scotland PQLE Paper, April 1988.
2 See eg *Hamilton v Turner* (1867) 5 M 1086.
3 In *Hamilton v Turner* (1867) 5 M 1086 the view seems to have been taken that an express clause imposed strict liability whereas the common law obligation did not. But it is now settled that liability at common law is also strict.
4 See para 265 below.
5 The practical significance of this conclusion is reduced by the fact that in most cases the British Coal Corporation already has a statutory right to lower the surface in the course of mining coal. See the Coal Industry Act 1975 (c 56), s 2, and para 267 below.

265. Contracting out. There are two obligations which a proprietor of minerals might wish to avoid, namely the obligation not to withdraw support and the obligation to pay damages; and since these are distinct obligations which give rise to different remedies (respectively interdict and damages), it appears that one may sometimes be excluded without the other.

At first the courts approached exclusion clauses with a certain amount of hesitation. The turning point was *Buchanan v Andrew*[1], decided in 1873. Here the superior, in reserving the minerals, excluded liability

'for any damage that may happen to the said piece of ground, buildings thereon, or existing hereafter thereon, by or through the working of the coal, fire-clay, ironstone, freestone, or other metals or minerals in or under the same, or in the neighbourhood thereof, by longwall workings, or otherwise . . .'.

This clause divided the Second Division, but the majority of the court was not willing to treat it as effectually excluding liability. On appeal to the House of Lords a more robust view prevailed. Parties, it was said, were free to contract as they wished. If the clause was onerous then no doubt that fact was reflected in the price originally paid. So long as an exclusion clause was worded clearly — and the clause under consideration was perfectly clear — then there was no reason why it should not be enforced. Subsequent cases have followed this approach[2], with the qualification that exclusion clauses are treated as confined to damage caused by bona fide mining activity and do not excuse damage otherwise occurring[3]. Even a provision which is drafted in the form of a compensation clause may be read as an exclusion clause to the extent that its terms for compensation fall short of what would be provided by the general law[4].

Buchanan v Andrew was in fact a case, not of damages but of interdict; and it was held that the express exclusion of damages there must be read as including an implied exclusion of the obligation of support itself[5]. Interdict, accordingly, was refused and the superior was free to lower the surface. Surprisingly, perhaps, the same conclusion has been reached in the converse situation of, where a right to damages is expressly conferred. In *Anderson v M'Cracken Brothers*[6] the express provision of damages was said to confer a right to lower the surface on payment of the stipulated compensation. The proper remedy of the pursuer was damages and not interdict. The result is different if the compensation clause refers to surface damage or accidental damage and not to subsidence damage caused by ordinary working[7]. In *Bank of Scotland v Stewart*[8] an implied right to lower the surface was also said to arise from an express and unqualified right to work the minerals. But both here and in *Anderson* weight was given to the supposed knowledge of the original parties to the deed that the minerals could not be adequately worked without subsidence, a speciality which may not apply in other cases and which comes close to violating the rule against extrinsic evidence in the interpretation of written documents.

Contracting out has no effect on the overriding statutory obligation of the British Coal Corporation to carry out remedial works or pay compensation where subsidence is caused by coal-mining[9].

1 *Buchanan v Andrew* (1873) 11 M (HL) 13 (revsg *sub nom Andrew v Henderson and Dimmack* (1871) 9 M 554).
2 Eg *Dryburgh v Fife Coal Co Ltd* (1905) 7 F 1083, 13 SLT 312. Exclusion clauses are much more common in some areas of the country (eg Lanarkshire and West Lothian) than in others: see R Rennie 'Non-oil Related Minerals and Reservation Clauses' The Law Society of Scotland PQLE Paper, April 1988.
3 Ie occurring other than by 'proper working'. See *Anderson v M'Cracken Bros* (1900) 2 F 780, 7 SLT 427. For the distinction between 'proper' and 'improper' working, see para 261, note 3, above.
4 *Barr v Baird & Co* (1904) 6 F 524, (1904) 11 SLT 710.
5 *Buchanan v Andrew* (1873) 11 M (HL) 13 at 19, per Lord Selborne LC.
6 *Anderson v M'Cracken Bros* (1900) 2 F 780, 7 SLT 427, following *Aspden v Seddon* (1875) LR 10 Ch App 394.
7 *White v William Dixon Ltd* (1881) 9 R 375, affd (1883) 10 R (HL) 45.
8 *Bank of Scotland v Stewart* (1891) 18 R 957.
9 Coal Mining Subsidence Act 1991 (c 45). See further para 267 below.

266. Juridical basis of variation. No satisfactory juridical basis can be established for variations of the kind just discussed. An obligation (on the mineral owner) to pay compensation cannot be constituted as a servitude. Nor can an obligation (on the surface owner) not to claim the compensation which the law of delict would otherwise provide. Real burdens are less restrictive as to content than servitudes; but even if such obligations may in principle be constituted as real burdens[1], there remains the difficulty that in many cases the written obligation appears in the title of the dominant property and not, as required, in the title of the servient tenement[2]. The classificatory problem would be solved if Scotland, like some other countries, treated minerals not as a corporeal separate tenement but as an (incorporeal) right, whether a nominate and distinct real right[3] or, like salmon fishings, as an incorporeal separate tenement[4]; for in such a case ancillary obligations could be classified as part of the content of the principal right itself. But while Scots law may have considered this solution at one stage in its development, it is clear that it does not represent the modern law[5]. The normal classificatory process, then, appears to fail. All that can be said is that variations in the common law of support are lawful and effective, and that the rights and obligations thus created are *sui generis*.

1 In itself an uncertain proposition.
2 See para 388 below. A typical situation is where A conveys to B reserving the minerals and taking himself bound to pay compensation for subsidence. The obligation is in the title of B, the dominant proprietor, and not that of A, the servient proprietor. Where the conveyance is a feu disposition, as it often is, this does not matter because it is well recognised that burdens on the superiority can be created in this fashion. See *Hamilton v Turner* (1867) 5 M 1086 and para 394 below. But where, as in *Anderson v M'Cracken Bros* (1900) 2 F 780, 7 SLT 427, the conveyance is an ordinary disposition no valid burden is created.
3 As in South Africa. See H Silberberg and J Schoeman *The Law of Property* (2nd edn, 1983) p 424.
4 See para 207 above.
5 See para 212 above.

267. Variation by statute. In the absence of a right to lower the surface conferred by the titles[1], and where none can be obtained by agreement, a mineral owner may apply under the Mines (Working Facilities and Support) Act 1966 for such a right to be conferred by the Court of Session[2]. In considering an application under the Act the court is directed to balance the relative value of the minerals and of any buildings or land which would be affected by subsidence, and to consider whether the working of the minerals is more important in the national interest than the maintenance of support[3]. If the application is successful an order will be made for the payment of compensation[4].

1 See para 265 above.
2 Mines (Working Facilities and Support) Act 1966 (c 4), ss 1, 2(1)(a). It must be shown that agreement is impossible for one of the reasons set out in s 3(2). By s 10 any right granted does not

confer on the applicant any greater or other power than if it had actually been granted by a person legally entitled to grant the right.

3 Ibid, s 2(2). Further, by s 3(1) no right is to be granted unless the court is satisfied that the grant is expedient in the national interest.

4 Ibid, s 8.

267A. Special rules for coal mining. The coal mining industry was substantially reorganised by the Coal Industry Act 1994. Between 1946, when the nationalisation of coal was completed, and 31 October 1994[1], when the reorganisation came into effect, almost all coal mining was carried out by the British Coal Corporation (formerly called the National Coal Board) acting under an exclusive statutory right[2]. The 1994 Act swept this statutory monopoly away and provided for the privatisation of the coal industry[3]. Under the Act licences to work coal are issued to private operators by a new public body called the Coal Authority[4]. As well as being the regulatory body for the industry, the Coal Authority also has residual ownership of unworked coal[5].

A licensed operator under the 1994 Act is absolutely entitled to withdraw support from land so far as may be reasonably requisite for the working of coal and provided that the withdrawal is preceded by three month's notice, duly publicised in accordance with the Act[6]. But the operator will then be liable to compensate or reinstate in terms of the Coal Mining Subsidence Act 1991. The 1991 Act provides that where land or buildings or other structures sustain subsidence damage caused by the withdrawal of support from land in connection with lawful coal-mining operations[7], the licence holder[8] must execute remedial works[9] or make payment of the cost of remedial works[10]. Alternatively, if the cost of remedial works exceeds the depreciation in value of the damaged property by more than 20 per cent the licence holder may at its option pay the amount of that depreciation[11]. Depending on the circumstances, further amounts may also be due under Part III of the Act in respect of dispossession from dwelling houses, the unsuitability of agricultural land for agricultural uses following the subsidence, and a number of other matters[12]. Special provision is made for cases where further damage is anticipated[13], and there are powers in relation to preventive works where a building or structure, currently undamaged, seems likely to suffer subsidence damage in the future[14]. In order to initiate a claim under the 1991 Act the affected proprietor must first serve a damage notice on the licence holder[15]. A holder is also liable for damage which occurred before the licence was obtained[16], and there is nothing to prevent claims being made even in respect of Victorian mining[17].

1 Coal Industry (Restructuring Date) Order 1994, SI 1994/2553.

2 Coal Industry Nationalisation Act 1946 (c 59), s 1.

3 Coal Industry Act 1994 (c 21), s 7(2).

4 Ibid, Pt II (ss 25–36).

5 Ibid, s 7(3).

6 Ibid, ss 38, 39. But by s 40 this is subject to (1) any pre-existing agreement to the contrary, including, presumably, an agreement contained in the titles, and (2) the Mines (Working Facilities and Support) Act 1966 (c 4), s 7, which enables restrictions to be placed on the working of mines for the benefit of the surface owner (see para 270 below).

7 Coal Mining Subsidence Act 1991 (c 45), s 1. For operations on or after 31 October 1994, a new s 1(3) (meaning of 'lawful coal-mining operations') is substituted by the Coal Industry Act 1994, s 42(1), Withdrawal of support can be passive, as for example where there is movement in the infill in an abandoned shaft: see *British Coal Corpn v Netherlee Trust Trustees* 1995 SLT 1038.

8 Or, where there is no licence holder, the Coal Authority. See the Coal Industry Act 1994, s 43.

9 Coal Mining Subsidence Act 1991, ss 2(1), (2)(a), 7.

10 Ibid, ss 2(1), (2)(b), 8, 9.

11 Ibid, s 10. See also s 11 (obligatory depreciation payments).

12 Ibid, Pt III, comprises ss 22–32.

13 Ibid, ss 16, 17.

14 Ibid, s 33.

15 Ibid, s 3. Where there is no licence holder the notice is served on the Coal Authority.

16 Coal Industry Act 1994, s 43(4)–(6). And see also the definition of 'lawful coal-mining operations' mentioned in note 7.

17 An example is *British Coal Corpn v Netherlee Trust Trustees* 1995 SLT 1038. However, in terms of s 3(3) of the Coal Mining Subsidence Act 1991 a damage notice must be served within six years of having gained the knowledge needed for founding the claim.

(E) OBLIGATIONS OF SUPPORT OTHERWISE ARISING

268. Introduction. As well as the 'natural' obligation considered above, obligations of support may arise in other ways. The two most significant are (1) servitude and (2) obligations created under the Mines (Working Facilities and Support) Act 1966 (c 4), s 7.

269. Servitude. Support of land to land is capable of being made a servitude; and while there is no reported decision in which a servitude was expressly created, there has been held to be implied in conveyances of land (the minerals being reserved) 'such a measure of support subjacent and adjacent as is necessary for the land in its condition at the time of the grant, or in the state for the purpose of putting it into which the grant is made'[1]. That is a servitude of implied grant, but it may be assumed that similar principles operate where the dominant tenement is being reserved and not granted. If, as is often asserted, the servitude of support is positive in nature[2] then the servitude may also be created by positive prescription[3], although there may be difficulties in establishing possession of the requisite quality[4].

In practice there seems little place for servitudes of support. For where land is unbuilt on, a servitude adds nothing to the 'natural' obligation arising *ex delicto;* and even where buildings exist, the servitude, at least in its implied form, is confined to buildings already erected or in prospect at the time of the grant and is therefore very much less extensive than the 'natural' obligation. The position is otherwise in England where the 'natural' obligation applies only to land not built upon and support for buildings depends entirely on the law of easements[5]. Even in Scotland, however, an express grant of servitude is advantageous if it embraces buildings so extensive as to be beyond the 'natural' obligation or if, as is apparently competent[6], the grant includes a positive obligation on the servient tenement to provide and maintain support[7].

1 *Caledonian Rly Co v Sprot* (1856) 2 Macq 449, HL, per Lord Cranworth LC. See also *North British Rly Co v Turners Ltd* (1904) 6 F 900, 12 SLT 176, and *Rogano Ltd v British Railways Board* 1979 SC 297.

2 Eg J Rankine *The Law of Land-ownership in Scotland* (4th edn, 1909) p 496.

3 Prescription and Limitation (Scotland) Act 1973 (c 52), s 3.

4 *Rankine* pp 499, 500.

5 Thus in England a new building (ie one built after severance and so not included in the implied easement) is not entitled to support for the first twenty years of its life, until prescription has operated. See *Dalton v Angus* (1881) 6 App Cas 740, HL. See also paras 257, 258, above.

6 Stair *Institutions* II,7,6; Erskine *Institute* II,9,8; Bell *Principles* s 1003.

7 The 'natural' obligation is negative only: see para 253 above.

270. The Mines (Working Facilities and Support) Act 1966. Section 7 of the Mines (Working Facilities and Support) Act 1966 applies where there is no pre-existing right of support in respect of buildings or works erected or intended to be erected, an unusual situation which, in Scotland at least, comes about only where the 'natural' right of support has been excluded in the titles or by other means[1]. Where there is no pre-existing right of support, and where it is not reasonably practicable to obtain such a right by private arrangement[2], a landowner or other person having an interest in the land may apply to the Secretary of State for Industry under section 7 for restrictions to be imposed on the working of minerals sufficient to secure support to the buildings or works[3]. If the Secretary of State is satisfied that a prima facie case has been made out the matter is then referred to the Court of Session[4]. In deciding whether or not to impose restrictions the court must have regard to the value of the buildings or works or the cost of repairing damage likely to be caused to them by subsidence as compared to the value of the minerals, or to the importance in the national interest of the erection or preservation of the buildings or works as compared with the importance in the national interest of the working of the minerals[5]. Any restrictions imposed will be on such terms and subject to such conditions and for such period as the court may think just[6], and the applicant will be required to pay compensation to the person who is thus prevented from working the minerals[7].

1 See para 265 above.
2 The applicant must show that a private arrangement cannot be obtained for one of the four reasons set out in s 3(2) of the Mines (Working Facilities and Support) Act 1966 (c 4).
3 Ibid, s 7(1).
4 Ibid, s 7(3).
5 Ibid, s 7(7). By s 7(4) the court is empowered to impose restrictions only where it is expedient in the national interest to do so.
6 Ibid, s 7(4).
7 Ibid, s 7(5). In the absence of agreement compensation will be determined by the court in accordance with s 8.

(c) Support by Buildings to Buildings

271. Subjacent support. Where two separate buildings or tenement flats are built one on top of the other, the provision of support is regulated by the common law of the tenement. The subject is treated elsewhere in this title[1], but the rule in summary is that lower flats are under a positive obligation, founded on common interest, to provide adequate support for the flat or flats above.

1 See para 233 above.

272. Adjacent support. Where adjoining buildings (or other structures) are built so as to touch each other, two physical arrangements are possible. Either the buildings share a wall (which may belong to either or to both of the buildings) or there are two separate walls built one alongside the other. The rules as to support depend upon which physical solution is adopted.
(1) *Shared wall.* Usually a shared wall between two buildings is owned by each *ad medium filum*[1]. Common gables[2] are the paradigm example. In such a case there are reciprocal duties of support, founded on common interest, by which each proprietor must maintain his own part of the wall so as to support that part which belongs to the other[3].
  The position is different where the wall is built solely within the boundaries of one of the properties. Here ownership is in one party only[4], so that, in the absence of servitude, the other party has no right to use the wall whether for the insertion of joists or for other purposes. A servitude may be granted expressly or impliedly, but more usually it arises by positive prescription[5]. Unless expressly provided for in the grant[6], a servitude of support imposes no duty on the servient proprietor to maintain support at its existing level. But while neglect is permissible, positive act is not if the result of that act is to imperil the servitude[7], a rule already familiar from the 'natural' obligation of support discussed above.
(2) *Separate walls.* In the absence of servitude[8], there is no obligation on the wall of one building or structure to provide support for the wall of an adjacent building

or structure. But where walls actually touch, as in practice they often do, neither party can object to the modest support thus provided[9] unless, it has been suggested, one wall depends upon the other to a degree which in the circumstances is unreasonable[10].

1 See paras 223, 224, above. The rule appears to be the same for walls separating individual flats within a tenement: see para 229 above.
2 For common gables, see para 218 above.
3 See para 226, head (3), above.
4 As a necessary consequence of the principle of accession.
5 As in *Murray v Brownhill* (1715) Mor 14521. See now the Prescription and Limitation (Scotland) Act 1973 (c 52), s 3.
6 Stair *Institutions* II,7,6; Erskine *Institute* II,9,8; Bell *Principles* s 1003.
7 *Murray v Brownhill* (1715) Mor 14521; *Rogano Ltd v British Railways Board* 1979 SC 297.
8 Relying on English authority, Rankine doubts whether prescription can operate in a case like this on the basis that 'the leaning of the one wall on the other, and its incapability of standing alone, are clandestine, and therefore insufficient to infer prescriptive possession': J Rankine *The Law of Land-ownership in Scotland* (4th edn, 1909) p 510.
9 This rule presupposes that each wall is built on its own side of the boundary. If a wall crosses the boundary it can be attacked as an encroachment, for which see paras 175 ff above.
10 *Leonard v Lindsay and Benzie* (1886) 13 R 958.

6. WATER

(1) INTRODUCTION

(a) Ownership of Water

273. Heritable or moveable? Water in its natural state is moveable property. In certain circumstances, however, water in contact with land becomes part of the land and so heritable by accession. It is thought that accession can only operate on standing water, for it is self-evident that water which is actually moving must always be moveable[1]. Standing water beneath the surface of the earth seems clearly heritable by accession; and there may be an argument that water lying on the surface, for example in a loch or a pool, is also heritable although it is uncertain whether there is sufficient physical and functional subordination for accession to operate[2].

1 But cf *Crichton v Turnbull* 1946 SC 52, 1946 SLT 156, where it is suggested that percolating rainwater may be heritable by accession.
2 For accession, see paras 578 ff below.

274. Ownership. In determining the ownership of water, as opposed to the ownership of the *alveus* or bed in which water is found[1], Scots law adopts the Roman law distinction between running water and standing water. The rule, according to Stair, is that

'running waters are common to all men, because they can have no bounds; but water standing, and capable of bounds, is appropriated'[2].

Running water, at least when left to run in its natural state[3], is treated as ownerless. This is partly because of the evident impracticality of attributing ownership of individual molecules in a fast-running stream, and partly because water, like air and light, is regarded as a natural resource which should not be the property of any one person. The rule for standing water is less clear. As standing water is readily identifiable, it can be argued that such water is the property of the person in or on whose land it stands. Certainly this must always be the case where the water can be regarded as heritable by accession[4]. But it may also be argued, and with equal plausibility, that standing water is ownerless.

Ownerless water, whether running or standing, is, like other ownerless property, available for occupation; and hence the first person to isolate such water in a container becomes its owner[5].

1　For ownership of the *alveus*, see paras 275–277 below.
2　Stair *Institutions* II,1,5. See also Erskine *Institute* II,1,5; Bankton *Institute* I,3,2.
3　The principle may not apply to water which has been subject to artificial operations, eg water in a mill lade or in a tap.
4　See para 273 above.
5　For occupation, see paras 540 ff below.

(b) Ownership of *Alveus*

275. Crown ownership and private ownership. Water lying on the surface of the earth may or may not be contained within a definite channel. The present section is concerned solely with cases such as rivers and lochs where there is a definite channel. For water in a definite channel, certain presumptions arise as to the ownership of the *alveus* (channel-bed). The law distinguishes two classes of channel. For channels of one class the *alveus* is presumed to belong to the proprietor of the adjoining land as a pertinent of that land[1]; and for channels of the other class the *alveus* is presumed to belong to the Crown as *inter regalia minora*. In practice it is rare for the presumptions to be departed from. Which of the two classes a particular *alveus* or section of *alveus* falls into depends on the nature of the water contained in the channel. Until 1877, the rule was expressed as being that where the water was navigable the *alveus* fell into the second class and so was presumed to belong to the Crown; and conversely, where the water was not navigable the *alveus* fell into the first class and was presumed to belong to the adjacent proprietor[2]. In 1877, however, the test of navigability was abandoned by Lord President Inglis in the leading case of *Colquhoun's Trustees v Orr Ewing & Co*[3] in favour of a new test drawn from English law and based on whether or not the water was tidal. This remains the law today, so that the *alveus* of tidal waters is presumed to belong to the Crown, while the *alveus* of non-tidal waters is subject to the contrary presumption of private ownership. The reasons for the introduction of the new rule are unclear[4], but the rule itself is now well established[5].

1　See para 202 above.
2　Bankton *Institute* I,3,4; Erskine *Institute* II,1,5; II,6,17; Hume *Lectures* vol IV (Stair Soc vol 17, 1955 ed G C H Paton) pp 244, 245; Bell *Principles* ss 648–650. See eg *Lord Advocate v Clyde Trustees* (1849) 11 D 391, affd (1852) 1 Macq 46, HL.
3　*Colquhoun's Trustees v Orr Ewing & Co* (1877) 4 R 344 (revsd on a different point (1877) 4 R (HL) 116).
4　It is interesting that Lord Inglis was forced to disassociate himself from remarks which he had made ten years' earlier in *Duke of Buccleuch v Cowan* (1866) 5 M 214 in which he asserted the primacy of the navigability test.
5　*Bowie v Marquis of Ailsa* (1887) 14 R 649; *Grant v Henry* (1894) 21 R 358, 1 SLT 448; *Gay v Malloch* 1959 SC 110, 1959 SLT 132; *Wills' Trustees v Cairngorm Canoeing and Sailing School Ltd* 1976 SC (HL) 30, 1976 SLT 162.

276. Tidal and non-tidal waters. As has been seen, ownership of the *alveus* depends upon whether waters are tidal or non-tidal[1]; and in the case of waters which are tidal in some parts but non-tidal in others, it is consequently of importance to know where the dividing line occurs. The rule is that waters are tidal as far as the highest point reached by the flow of ordinary spring tides; thereafter they are non-tidal[2]. The meaning of the highest point of a tide in this context is not, however, entirely clear. In *Bowie v Marquis of Ailsa*[3], the only case in which this difficulty is discussed, a section of river with no material saline content and where the only effect of the tide was to raise the level of the water was held to be non-tidal.

1 See para 275 above.
2 J Ferguson *The Law of Water and Water Rights in Scotland* (1907), p 107. As with the delimitation of the foreshore, it is the extent of ordinary spring tides that matters.
3 *Bowie v Marquis of Ailsa* (1887) 14 R 649.

277. Public and private waters. Waters are sometimes classified as 'public' or as 'private' waters. This classification is avoided in the present title because 'a public river is capable of various meanings, and the dexterous use of the term "public" is apt to mislead'[1]. It is only necessary to say here that 'public' is usually used to indicate that the waters are navigable, and 'private' to indicate that they are not navigable.

1 *Montgomerie v Buchanan's Trustees* (1853) 15 D 853 at 858, per Lord President M'Neill.

(2) NON-TIDAL RIVERS

(a) Introduction

278. Ownership of *alveus*. This section applies to rivers and streams which are wholly non-tidal, and also to the non-tidal part of rivers which are also partly tidal. The meaning of 'river' is considered later[1].

The *alveus* of a non-tidal river or stream is, like other land, owned *a coelo usque ad centrum*[2]. In addition to the river-bed itself it includes any islands in the river other than islands formed by avulsion[3]. As a general rule, the *alveus* of a non-tidal river belongs to the proprietor or proprietors of the land through which it runs[4], but it is necessary to distinguish three different situations:

(1) *River within one estate.* The *alveus* of a river or stream running wholly within one estate belongs solely to the proprietor of that estate.

(2) *River within several consecutive estates.* The *alveus* of a river or stream which passes consecutively through several estates belongs in turn, section by section, to the proprietor of each successive estate.

(3) *River on the boundary between two estates.* 'If a stream separates properties A and B — *prima facie*, the owner of the land A, as to *his* land, on one side, and the owner of land B, as to *his* land, on the other, are each entitled to the soil of the stream, *usque ad mediam aquae* — that is, *prima facie* so. It may be rebutted'[5]. As a pertinent of his land each proprietor is presumed to own the *alveus* up to the *medium filum*. In marking the *medium filum* the baseline taken is the river when it is ordinarily full, disregarding seasonal variations[6]. The presumption of ownership to the *medium filum* may be rebutted by the titles of either party[7], and the principles to be applied here are well settled. Thus where the titles are silent the presumption of ownership *ad medium filum* applies. Where the titles of one of the proprietors states his property to be bounded by the river, the presumption also applies, displacing on this occasion the usual rule by which the bounding object is excluded from the property[8]. Where, finally, the titles contain a bounding description which clearly excludes the river from the property, for example by reference to a plan, the presumption is rebutted and no part of the *alveus* is owned[9].

A 'riparian proprietor' is one who owns the *alveus*, or part of the *alveus*, of a river or stream[10].

1 See para 286 below.
2 For ownership *a coelo usque ad centrum*, see paras 196 ff above.
3 For avulsion, see para 592 below.
4 See para 275 above.
5 *Wishart v Wyllie* (1853) 1 Macq 389 at 389, HL, per Lord Cranworth LC.
6 *Menzies v Breadalbane* (1901) 4 F 55, 9 SLT 218. See also WATER AND WATER RIGHTS, vol 25, para 317. The rule is the same for lochs: see para 303 below.
7 It may also be rebutted where it can be shown that the river has shifted course as a result of avulsion; but not, it is thought, where the change of course is a result of alluvion. See *Stirling v Bartlett* 1992 SCLR 994, OH. For the difference between alluvion and avulsion, see para 592 below.
8 *Fisher v Duke of Atholl's Trustees* (1836) 14 S 880; *M'Intyre's Trustees v Cupar-Fife Magistrates* (1867) 5 M 780; *Gibson v Bonnington Sugar Refining Co Ltd* (1869) 7 M 394.
9 *North British Rly Co v Hawick Magistrates* (1862) 1 M 200.
10 In almost every case this means that he will also own part of the bank. See also WATER AND WATER RIGHTS, vol 25, para 303.

279. Use of water. Running water is *res nullius* and does not belong to the proprietor of the *alveus*[1]. But, subject to certain limitations[2], a riparian proprietor has the right to make free use of such water as passes over his section of *alveus*. So he may sail on the water or catch fish in it[3]; or he may consume it for domestic, although not for industrial, purposes[4]. His right is generally[5] an exclusive one and cannot lawfully be intruded upon either by a neighbour or by a third party. It has been held that the rights of a riparian proprietor are not available to one who owns only an insignificantly small section of *alveus*[6].

1 See para 274 above.
2 See para 281 below.
3 For fishing rights, see para 280 below.
4 For the significance of the distinction, see paras 287, 288, below.
5 If, however, the river is navigable, it is subject to the public right of navigation: see para 523 below.
6 *Marquess of Breadalbane v West Highland Rly Line* (1895) 22 R 307, 2 SLT 451 (revsg (1895) 2 SLT 261, OH). See also *Menzies v Macdonald* (1854) 16 D 827 at 840, per Lord Cockburn (affd (1856) 2 Macq 463, HL).

280. Fishing rights. Fish, until caught, are *res nullius*. A riparian proprietor does not, therefore, own the fish present in his waters; but with one exception he has the exclusive right to catch them[1]. The exception is salmon. The right to fish for salmon is a legal separate tenement and must be independently acquired, either by express grant or by prescription on a habile title[2]. If, as is frequently the case, he has not acquired this additional right a riparian proprietor must exercise his own, lesser, fishing rights in a manner which does not cause material disturbance to the salmon fishings[3]. The fishing rights of a riparian proprietor are exclusive. Members of the general public have no more right to fish in a proprietor's river than they have to walk over his land. Both activities are equally trespass[4]. The rule remains the same even where the river is navigable, and so subject to the public right of navigation, or where it is accessible to the public in some other way, for example by means of a public right of way[5]. In general, a riparian proprietor may fish only his own part of the river; but where a river is owned to the mid-point by two *ex adverso* proprietors, it has been suggested that each may be entitled to cast his rod into the waters belonging to the other[6].

The fishing rights of a riparian proprietor, and in particular the right to fish for trout, are sometimes of commercial value. But this value is not always easily realised for, unlike salmon fishing, trout fishing is not a separate feudal tenement and cannot be conveyed separately from the river[7], and nor, probably[8], can it be conferred on some other party as a servitude[9] or as a real burden[10]. However, the Freshwater and Salmon Fisheries (Scotland) Act 1976 permits leases of trout fishing effective against successors of the landlord[11].

1 For the methods by which trout fishing may be exercised, see FISHERIES, vol 11, paras 47 ff.

2 See para 322 below.
3 See para 326 below.
4 *Fergusson v Shirreff* (1844) 6 D 1363 *Bowie v Marquis of Ailsa* (1887) 14 R 649. For trespass generally, see paras 180 ff above.
5 *Grant v Henry* (1894) 21 R 358, 1 SLT 448; *Lennox v Keith* 1993 GWD 30-1913, OH. Hume (*Lectures* vol IV (Stair Soc vol 17, 1955 ed G C H Paton) pp 243, 245) and Bell (*Principles* s 747) would allow the public to fish in all navigable rivers, but this is because at the time they were writing navigable rivers were not regarded as being in private ownership (see para 275 above).
6 *Arthur v Aird* 1907 SC 1170, 15 SLT 209. Similar rules exist for trout fishing in lochs (see para 306 below) and for salmon fishing (see para 329 below).
7 *Patrick v Napier* (1867) 5 M 683; *East Lothian Angling Association v Haddington Town Council* 1980 SLT 213. This was not always thought to be the case: see eg *Bell* s 747; *Carmichael v Colquhoun* (1787) Mor 9645; *Fergusson v Shirreff* (1844) 6 D 1363.
8 See, however, the discussion in W M Gordon *Scottish Land Law* (1989) pp 243–244.
9 *Patrick v Napier* (1867) 5 M 683.
10 *Harper v Flaws* 1940 SLT 150, OH.
11 Freshwater and Salmon Fisheries (Scotland) Act 1976 (c 22), s 4.

281. Restrictions on use. 'There is nothing the operation and action of which are more uncertain than running water. The smallest interference with the course of running water may be productive of effects which nobody can foresee or could have contemplated'[1]. It is familiar that the right to use property is accompanied by certain restrictions on use. For running water the precarious nature of the supply makes the restrictions on use of particular importance. The principal restrictions are listed below:

(1) *Common interest.* Riparian ownership is burdened by a number of common interest obligations enforceable by the other riparian proprietors[2], and by the proprietors of salmon fishings[3].

(2) *Servitudes.* Riparian ownership may be burdened by servitudes. The most important is the servitude of *aquaehaustus* which confers on the dominant tenement a right to draw water from the servient tenement[4].

(3) *Nuisance.* The general law of nuisance applies to rivers and is of particular importance in relation to pollution[5].

(4) *Public rights of navigation.* Where a non-tidal river is navigable, the general public may be entitled to use it for navigation, and in such a case the riparian proprietor is barred from any action which interrupts, or threatens to interrupt, the public right[6].

(5) *Statutory restrictions.* As a resource of national importance running water is subject to a large number of statutory restrictions. Most operate in favour of public bodies. Thus the Flood Prevention (Scotland) Act 1961 (c 41) confers on local authorities extensive powers in the management of rivers[7]. Water authorities and water development boards have compulsory powers under the Water (Scotland) Act 1980 in relation to the extraction of water from rivers and streams[8]. Under the Civic Government (Scotland) Act 1982 district and islands councils are empowered to make byelaws on certain matters relating to non-tidal rivers and their banks, although the consent of the proprietor or proprietors is required[9]. Finally, not all statutory restrictions operate in favour of public bodies. An example of a restriction in favour of private individuals is the provision in the Land Drainage (Scotland) Act 1930 by which any owner or occupier of agricultural land may require the owner or occupier of any other land to maintain the banks and to scour the channel of any watercourse in circumstances where failure to do so would injure the agricultural land[10].

1 *Morris v Bicket* (1864) 2 M 1082 at 1089, per Lord Justice-Clerk Inglis (affd (1866) 4 M (HL) 44).
2 See paras 282 ff below.
3 See para 330 below.
4 For *aquaehaustus*, see further para 295 below.
5 See paras 298–300 below.

6 See para 519 below.
7 See further WATER AND WATER RIGHTS, vol 25, paras 377, 378.
8 Water (Scotland) Act 1980 (c 45), s 17. See further vol 25, para 519.
9 Civic Government (Scotland) Act 1982 (c 45), s 121(4), (5).
10 Land Drainage (Scotland) Act 1930 (c 20), s 1.

(b) Common Interest

282. Development of the doctrine. The institutional writers group running water together with light and air as *res communes*, '[t]hings, the property of which belongs to no person, but the use to all'[1]. A characteristic which unites all three is vulnerability of supply to interference. In the use and enjoyment of the light, air and running water naturally present within his boundaries, a proprietor is peculiarly at the mercy of his neighbour. By building a wall or a factory a neighbour may block out the sunlight or pollute the air, just as by erecting a dam he may arrest the flow of water in a river. But while the law, within certain limits[2], permits a neighbour to interfere with sunlight and air, it was settled by the time of Stair that he could not interfere with running water[3]. For the use of running water is subject at common law to detailed rules, comprising what may be termed a 'special regime'. By contrast the use of light and air is not, and its protection rests instead on such doctrines of the general law as nuisance.

While, however, the existence of a special regime for water was early established, the legal basis of that regime remained for a long time unclear. As the protection was available only for water, it necessarily proceeded, not on some general doctrine, but on a network of specific rights and obligations connecting the separate ownership interests held by different riparian proprietors. The earliest attempts to give a name to the special regime for water referred to 'natural servitudes'[4], that is, servitudes arising, not by grant or by prescription, but by 'the natural situation of the ground' and which 'nature itself may be said to constitute'[5]. By natural servitude was meant what in the modern law is termed common interest[6]. The first use of the actual term 'common interest' in reference to riparian rights may have been by Kames in the third edition of *Principles of Equity*[7] published in 1778, and certainly by the end of the eighteenth century the term was becoming established[8]. A certain amount of confusion remained, however. Instead of being perceived, like a servitude, as a type of real condition and hence as a burden on ownership, common interest was sometimes treated as a type of ownership in itself. On this view, common interest was, not a restraint on the riparian ownership of others, but rather a right which all proprietors shared over running water[9]. This confusion was resolved, although not entirely eliminated, by the leading case of *Morris v Bicket*[10] in 1864. The judgment of Lord Neaves in that case remains the most important single contribution to the development of the law of riparian rights and deserves extensive quotation. In the passage which follows, Lord Neaves describes the position of *ex adverso* proprietors whose estates are separated by a non-tidal river:

> 'They are, in the first place, proprietors respectively of the *solum* of the *alveus* up to the middle of the stream as it naturally flows; there is no common property in the *solum*. They are conterminous proprietors, whose march lies in the *medium filum fluminis*, and accordingly, if anything can be done that does not affect the state of the water, it may be done by each; the minerals under it belong to each party respectively, and may be a most valuable estate. Second, besides this ordinary right of property, which is precisely the same when the river is there as if it were to disappear and the channel become dry, they have a common interest arising from another right, as they have each a right in the water, not of property — for certainly *aqua profluens* is not the subject of property as long as it is running . . . But each heritor, as it passes, has a right of an incorporeal kind to the usufruct of that stream for domestic purposes and for agricultural purposes, and, it may

be, also for other purposes, subject to certain restrictions. This right in the general current of the stream gives him an interest [that is, common interest] in the whole of the *alveus*, and for this obvious reason, that no operation can, by the nature of things, be performed upon one half of the *alveus*, that shall not affect the flow of the water in the whole. Thus, neither of the opposite proprietors can withdraw the water by a cut, unless, at least, it were merely a pipe for domestic uses ... In the same way, if any channel is attempted to be stopped up, that cannot be allowed ... Now the common interest, therefore, amounts to a right of preventing anything that shall palpably affect the water ...'[11].

In the modern law, common interest, like servitudes and real burdens, is a type of real condition; but, unlike servitudes and real burdens, common interest is implied by law[12].

1 Erskine *Institute* II,1,5. See also Stair *Institutions* II,1,5; Bankton *Institute* I,3,2.
2 Eg limits imposed by the law of nuisance or the requirements of planning consent.
3 *Stair* II,7,12.
4 *Kelso v Boyds* (1768) Mor 12807; *Cruikshanks and Bell v Henderson* (1791) Hume 506.
5 *Erskine* II,9,2.
6 See paras 355 ff below. The contemporaneous development of common interest in the law of the tenement affords an instructive parallel.
7 Kames *Principles of Equity* (3rd edn) p 50.
8 *Marquis of Abercorn v Jamieson* (1791) Hume 510; *Braid v Douglas* (1800) Mor 'Property' App No 2; *Lanark Twist Co v Edmonstone* (1810) Hume 520.
9 This view was often found in the early development of common interest, and is not confined to common interest rights in rivers. See paras 356 and 362 below.
10 *Morris v Bicket* (1864) 2 M 1082 (affd (1866) 4 M (HL) 44).
11 (1864) 2 M 1082 at 1092, 1093, per Lord Neaves.
12 See paras 358 ff below. For real conditions generally, see paras 344 ff below.

283. Dominant and servient proprietors. In the case of non-tidal rivers, each proprietor is connected to every other proprietor by the reciprocal rights and obligations of common interest. Each riparian proprietor is at the same time both a servient and a dominant proprietor in that interest. He is a servient proprietor because in the use of his own section of river he is restricted by certain common interest obligations which are owed to the other riparian proprietors. He is a dominant proprietor because he has equivalent common interest rights against the other proprietors in respect of the sections of the river which belong to them. A party who is proprietor of the bank of a river but not of the *alveus ex adverso* — a very unusual situation in practice — is also considered to be a servient proprietor for the purposes of common interest[1]; but, since his ownership of the bank confers no right to use the river, it appears that he is not also a dominant proprietor. As well as the common interest obligations already mentioned, which are reciprocally enforceable, riparian proprietors are under an additional and separate obligation to the proprietor or proprietors of the separate tenement of salmon fishings in the river to perform no act which threatens the free passage of salmon[2].

1 See para 297 below.
2 See para 330 below.

284. Scope. The scope of the reciprocal rights and obligations arising out of common interest has been the subject of a number of different formulations. Thus it has been said that 'the superior heritor must transmit to the inferior the water of the stream undiminished in quantity and undeteriorated in quality'[1]. The corresponding right of the dominant proprietor is 'a right of preventing anything that shall palpably affect the water'[2]. But while the natural flow of the river or stream is the principal object of protection, the protection is conceived entirely in negative terms. The obligation on the servient proprietor is to refrain from any act which might interfere with the natural flow of the river. There is no accompanying obligation on him to take positive measures to preserve the natural flow[3]. Thus, common interest merely 'restrains all the heritors from any act of violent alteration, or prejudicial disposal of the stream to the detriment of any of the others'[4]. The rule is that 'no proprietor of one side of a stream is entitled to alter the flow of the stream without the consent of the proprietor of the other side, or even of those below'[5]. This is an important limitation on the operation of common interest. There will be many occasions on which the flow of a river is altered other than by the act of a riparian proprietor; and on such occasions the affected proprietors, while free to restore matters to their former state[6], are not obliged to do so. In one case[7], for example, a riparian proprietor was able successfully to resist the demand of a proprietor further upstream that he clear the *alveus* of silt. It appears to follow from the rule as stated that a riparian proprietor is helpless in circumstances where a progressive alteration of course further upstream will have the eventual result of diverting the river from his land.

1 *Hunter and Aikenhead v Aitken* (1880) 7 R 510 at 514, per Lord President Inglis.
2 *Morris v Bicket* (1864) 2 M 1082 at 1093, per Lord Neaves (affd (1866) 4 M (HL) 44).
3 Except where there is a threat to free drainage, for which see para 339 below. Of course a positive obligation could be imposed as a real burden: see *Lothian Regional Council v Rennie* 1991 SCLR 709, 1991 SLT 465.
4 Hume *Lectures* vol III (Stair Soc vol 15, 1952 ed G C H Paton) p 217.
5 *Duke of Roxburghe v Waldie's Trustees* (1879) 6 R 663 at 669, per Lord Justice-Clerk Moncreiff.
6 See para 285 below.
7 *Hope v Heriot's Hospital Governors* (1878) 15 SLR 400. See also *Strachan v City of Aberdeen* (1905) 12 SLT 725, OH.

285. Meaning of 'natural flow'. Common interest protects only the natural flow of a river or stream. The natural flow of a river may be defined as that flow which, in respect of quantity, quality and direction, persists in ordinary circumstances. The natural flow necessarily encompasses normal seasonal variations by which the river is increased in winter and diminished in summer[1]. The flow produced by some exceptional and extraordinary flood or drought is not, however, regarded as natural and is not protected by common interest. Consequently, a riparian proprietor may, if he chooses, repair the consequences of an event of this kind[2]. He may, for example, restore a flooded river to its former channel. Where, however, the event has brought about a permanent change, and where no attempt is made to restore the previous position, the new flow is treated after a lapse of time as being the natural flow[3].

1 *Menzies v Earl of Breadalbane* (1828) 3 W & S 235, HL; *Jackson v Marshall* (1872) 10 M 913.
2 *Duke of Gordon v Duff* (1735) Mor 12778; *Town of Nairn v Brodie, Lord Lyon* (1738) Mor 12779.
3 *Aberdeen Magistrates v Menzies* (1748) Mor 12787.

286. Meaning of 'river'. Only rivers and streams are protected by common interest. Any flow of water which is perennial and which runs in a definite channel is a river or stream for the purposes of common interest[1], without regard to the actual quantity of water[2]. In addition, certain sources feeding rivers or streams are considered as part of the river or stream in question. Three types of source may be distinguished:
(1) *Water in a definite channel.* The rule here was laid down in 1768 in the case of *Linlithgow Magistrates v Elphinstone*[3], and depends upon whether the flow is perennial. A perennial feeder stream is considered to be part of the river or stream into which it runs and its flow therefore protected by common interest. Conversely, running water which is merely occasional is neither a stream in its own right, nor is it part of the river into which it runs. It is not governed by

common interest. In *Linlithgow Magistrates* a loch which overflowed into a river was held on the evidence to be a *stagnum*, that is, a loch from which there is no perennial overflow[4]. Accordingly, the proprietors of the loch could not be prevented from diverting the present sporadic overflow. It may be doubted whether underground water can ever be considered as part of a river or stream even where the flow is perennial[5].

(2) *Water outside a definite channel.* Rain and other water percolating on or through the soil and outside a definite channel does not form part of the river or stream which it may ultimately supply. Such water is not protected by common interest and may be freely intercepted[6].

(3) *Water artificially introduced.* Examples of artificial introduction include the pumping of water from a mine and the leading of water from one stream to another through an intermediate canal. The artificial introduction of water to a river or stream is a breach of the common interest right to the natural flow and may, if desired, be resisted by the other riparian proprietors[7]. But if the proprietors, finding the presence of additional water advantageous, do not object to it, they have no corresponding right to require that the supply be continued[8], unless possession for the prescriptive period of twenty years has established a servitude right[9].

1 *Kelso v Boyds* (1768) Mor 12807; *Cruikshanks and Bell v Henderson* (1791) Hume 506; *M'Nab v Robertson* (1896) 24 R (HL) 34, 4 SLT 207.
2 The remarks to the contrary by Lord Young in *Murdoch v Wallace* (1881) 8 R 855 at 861 mis-state the law.
3 *Linlithgow Magistrates v Elphinstone* (1768) Mor 12805. See also Hume *Lectures* vol III (Stair Soc vol 15, 1952 ed G C H Paton) p 225; Bell *Principles* ss 1109, 1110; *Ardrossan Burgh v Dickie* (1902) 14 SLT 349.
4 For *stagna*, see para 303 below.
5 *Cruikshanks and Bell v Henderson* (1791) Hume 506.
6 See paras 337 ff below.
7 *Young & Co v Bankier Distillery Co* (1893) 20 R (HL) 76, 1 SLT 204.
8 *Irving v Leadhills Mining Co* (1856) 18 D 833; *Blair v Hunter Finlay & Co* (1870) 9 M 204. See also W M Gordon *Scottish Land Law* (1989) para 7-15.
9 *Lord Blantyre v Dunn* (1848) 10 D 509; *Cowan v Lord Kinnaird* (1865) 4 M 236; *Buchanan v Coubrough* (1869) 7 SLR 88; *Heggie v Nairns* (1882) 9 R 704.

287. Consumption for primary purposes. The consumption of water from a river or stream is in the ordinary case one of the clearest examples of breach of common interest[1]. But by an exception to the general prohibition, which was of considerable importance before the introduction of a public system of water supply, riparian proprietors, members of their families and others on their property with their consent are permitted to consume water for 'primary' purposes. 'Primary' purposes are domestic purposes, and are opposed in what is all too evidently an eighteenth-century classification to such merely 'secondary' purposes as agriculture or industry[2]. 'The superior heritor has the full use of the water, in passing, for the primary use of drink for man or beast, and for the family purposes of cooking, washing, bleaching, brewing for domestic use'[3]. It was suggested in a case of 1878 that primary uses might not include the use of water to flush toilets[4], but it may be doubted whether this is the modern law.

There is no limit as to how much water may be consumed for primary purposes. 'The inferior heritor cannot complain though the consumption of water in the upper lands happen to increase to his prejudice, as for instance, if more cattle come to be kept there, of more people to dwell there, than formerly'[5]. Nor is there any objection to the use of a pipe or other mechanical means in the removal of the water[6]. If, however, more water is removed than is actually consumed, the surplus must be returned, and the onus of proof rests with the party removing the water to show that this has been done[7]. It is a condition of the removal of water that it is consumed either on the river itself or on land belonging to the proprietor which is immediately adjacent[8], and water cannot lawfully be removed for the benefit of more distant land except in exercise of the servitude of *aquaehaustus*.

1 See eg *Duke of Buccleuch v Gilmerton Coal Co* 1894 1 SLT 576. On general principles the prohibition extends at appropriate times of the year to the consumption of flood water: *M'Lean v Hamilton* (1857) 19 D 1006.
2 For secondary purposes, see para 288 below.
3 Bell *Principles* s 1105. See also Hume *Lectures* vol III (Stair Soc vol 15, 1952 ed G C H Paton) pp 217, 218. *Ritchie v Johnstone* 15 Feb 1822 FC appears to be an example of water consumed in the domestic manufacture of malt.
4 *Bonthrone v Downie* (1878) 6 R 324 at 331, per Lord Shand.
5 Hume, commenting on *Ogilvy v Kincaid* (1791) Hume 508. See also the observation in *Hood v Williamsons* (1861) 23 D 496 at 499, per Lord Kinloch, that 'if there be not enough of water for both the upper and lower heritor, the Lord Ordinary conceives it cannot be held that the lower heritor is entitled to demand from the upper that the rations, so to speak, of both should be reduced so as to give a participation to each'.
6 *Ogilvy v Kincaid* (1791) Hume 508.
7 *Hood v Williamsons* (1861) 23 D 496.
8 *Lord Melville v Denniston* (1842) 4 D 1231.

288. Consumption for secondary purposes. It is sometimes suggested[1] that the exception which permits consumption of water for primary purposes[2] may in certain circumstances be extended to permit consumption for secondary purposes such as agriculture and industry. But as any general licence to consume for secondary purposes would destroy the protection which common interest exists to provide, it is apparent that consumption of this kind, if permitted at all, is permitted only in limited circumstances and subject to strict controls. The secondary use which receives the clearest, although by no means conclusive, support from the authorities is consumption for irrigation[3]. According to Ferguson, 'probably a reasonable use for that purpose would be sustained, provided it was not excessive in view of the size of the stream, and of the needs of the lower heritors, and care was taken to return the whole surplus to the channel'[4]. The possibility that consumption for industrial purposes might also be recognised was left open in a dictum of Lord Kyllachy:

'It is said to be the law of Scotland that no water can be taken from a running stream, except for primary purposes. It is said, on the other hand, that the law of Scotland, while not perhaps going so far as the law of America, permits, like the law of England, abstraction for manufacturing uses to a reasonable extent — the question of reasonableness being one of degree, and the test being whether the domestic or other primary uses are materially abridged. I reserve my opinion on that question until it arises, as it some day must'[5].

But the better view appears to be that consumption for industrial purposes is not permitted[6], except where twenty-years' user has established the servitude of *aquaehaustus*[7]. Where, however, the amount of water consumed is small in relation to the size of the stream, the damage may not be sufficiently material to constitute a breach of common interest[8].

1 J Rankine *The Law of Land-ownership in Scotland* (4th edn, 1909) pp 555–558; J Ferguson *Law of Water and Water Rights in Scotland* (1907) pp 240–242.
2 See para 287 above.
3 *Kelso v Boyds* (1768) Mor 12807, as interpreted by *Rankine* p 556; *Murdoch v Wallace* (1881) 8 R 855. Spray irrigation is subject to statutory control: see WATER AND WATER RIGHTS, vol 25, para 331.
4 *Ferguson* p 241.
5 *Milton v Glen-Moray Glenlivet Distillery Co Ltd* (1898) 1 F 135 at 142, 143, OH (affd (1898) 1 F 135, IH).
6 *Stevenson v Hogganfield Bleaching Co* (1892) 30 SLR 86; *Duke of Buccleuch v Gilmerton Coal Co* 1894 1 SLT 576.

7 Prescription and Limitation (Scotland) Act 1973 (c 52), s 3; *Beaton v Ogilvie* (1670) Mor 10912; *Wallace v Morrison* (1761) Mor 14511. For *aquaehaustus*, see para 490 below.
8 See para 289 below.

289. Materiality of disturbance. Every act performed by a riparian proprietor on a river or stream interferes to some extent with the flow of the water. But not every act is a breach of common interest, for otherwise riparian ownership could never be exercised. The rule is that only such acts as effect a material disturbance in the natural flow of a river are treated as in breach of common interest. What is prohibited is 'any act of violent alteration'[1] which 'shall palpably affect the water'[2]. The standard of materiality imported by common interest is an objective one and does not depend on achieving a balance between the subjective, personal interests of the parties who are riparian proprietors for the time being. Whether or not the disturbance caused by a particular act is material will depend to a considerable extent on the size of the river or stream in question.

1 Hume *Lectures* vol III (Stair Soc vol 15, 1952 ed G C H Paton) p 217.
2 *Morris v Bicket* (1864) 2 M 1086 at 1093, per Lord Neaves (affd (1866) 4 M (HL) 44).

290. Enforcement. The principal remedies of the dominant proprietor in enforcement of common interest rights are interdict, specific implement and damages[1]. The remedies may be exercised by all or any of the proprietors of the affected part of the river. No special interest need be shown. Whatever the law may have been at one time[2], it is now no longer necessary for the dominant proprietor to establish that some specific use of the river, present or future, is imperilled. Instead, as was said in one case, 'it is enough to say that the diversion of the stream may in future have serious consequences, which it is impossible at present to foresee'[3]. More controversially, it was said in the same case that, 'even if such an operation did the pursuer good instead of hurting him . . . he would be entitled to object'[4]. Common interest is a real condition and it appears that in appropriate cases the servient proprietor is entitled to make application to the Lands Tribunal for its variation or discharge[5].

In the enforcement of common interest rights certain specialities result from the relative positions on the river of the dominant and the servient proprietors, and it will be convenient to consider separately questions arising between successive proprietors[6], and questions arising between opposite proprietors[7].

1 See para 366 below.
2 In *Bannatyne v Cranston* (1624) Mor 12769 the pursuer showed injury to amenity, and in *Hamilton v Edington* (1793) Mor 12824 the majority of the court is reported as having required at least 'the merest possibility of damage'. Erskine *Institute* II,9,13, refers to the need for 'real prejudice'.
3 *Duke of Roxburghe v Waldie's Trustees* (1879) 6 R 663 at 666, per Lord Curriehill. See also *Burgess v Brown* (1790) Hume 504; *Braid v Douglas* (1800) Mor 'Property' App No 2; *Baillie v Lady Saltoun* (1821) 1 S 227 (NE 216), Hume 523.
4 *Duke of Roxburghe v Waldie's Trustees* (1879) 6 R 663 at 671, per Lord Gifford. The contrary view has also been expressed: *Hunter and Aikenhead v Aitken* (1880) 7 R 510 at 515, per Lord President Inglis; *Murdoch v Wallace* (1881) 8 R 855 at 861, per Lord Justice-Clerk Moncreiff.
5 Conveyancing and Feudal Reform (Scotland) Act 1970 (c 35), s 1. See further para 374 below. Other possible methods by which common interest may be extinguished are discussed at paras 367 ff below.
6 See paras 291–293 below.
7 See paras 294–297 below.

(c) Successive Proprietors

291. Introduction. In a question with each other, successive riparian proprietors must avoid activities which cause or threaten to cause material disturbance to the natural flow of the river or stream[1]. 'The superior heritor must transmit to the inferior the water of the stream undiminished in quantity and undeteriorated in quality'[2], and, except in relation to the consumption of water for 'primary' (that is, domestic) purposes[3], a superior proprietor has no higher right than an inferior proprietor to the water of a river.

1 See generally paras 284 ff above.
2 *Hunter and Aikenhead v Aitken* (1880) 7 R 510 at 514, per Lord President Inglis. See also *Stirling v Bartlett* (1990) The Times, 1 November.
3 See para 287 above.

292. Temporary diversion. The question which has arisen most frequently in practice between successive proprietors concerns the legality of temporary diversions of all or part of the river or stream. Most of the case law concerns mill lades drawing off water to power a mill. The general rule is that a proprietor who owns the river the whole way across[1] is entitled to make a temporary diversion in the course of the river. But since such a diversion must not adversely affect the common interest of the other riparian proprietors, it is subject to two important limitations. The first limitation is that the water diverted must be returned to the river within the proprietor's own boundaries[2]. The second is that the manner of the diversion must not be such as materially to disrupt the natural flow of the river downstream. Thus in the use of a dam a proprietor must ensure that there is no regorging on the waters of another proprietor further upstream[3]; and he must not reintroduce the diverted water in such a way that the natural force of the current is substantially increased[4]. Both limitations may be overcome by adverse possession for twenty years sufficient to constitute a servitude[5].

1 Where he does not own the river the whole way across, diversion is not permissible at all: see para 295 below.
2 *Cunningham v Kennedy* (1713) Mor 8903; Hume *Lectures* vol III (Stair Soc vol 15, 1952 ed G C H Paton) pp 218, 219.
3 Hume vol III, pp 221–222; Bell *Principles* ss 969, 1108; *Fairly v Earl of Eglinton* (1744) Mor 12780; *Burgess v Brown* (1790) Hume 504; *Baillie v Lady Saltoun* (1821) 1 S 227 (NE 216), Hume 523.
4 *Bell* s 1108.
5 See further para 295 below.

293. Temporary detention. Diversion is sometimes accompanied by the temporary detention of the diverted water in reservoirs. In water mills this was in order that sufficient water was accumulated to drive machinery. In the absence of a servitude right[1], the legality of detention depends on the proportion the water detained bears to the volume of the stream. In many, perhaps even in most, cases detention causes a sufficiently material[2] interruption of the natural flow to constitute a breach of common interest[3]. Conversely, the temporary detention of a small amount of a large river appears to be permissible[4].

1 The existence of a servitude may be the true ground of decision in *Lady Willoughby de Eresby v Wood* (1884) 22 SLR 471, OH.
2 See para 289 above.
3 This, at least, has been the result of the reported cases: *Marquis of Abercorn v Jamieson* (1791) Hume 510; *Lord Glenlee v Gordon* (1804) Mor 12834; *Hunter and Aikenhead v Aitken* (1880) 7 R 510. See also Hume *Lectures* vol III (Stair Soc vol 15, 1952 ed G C H Paton) p 220.
4 The conclusion in J Rankine *The Law of Land-ownership in Scotland* (4th edn, 1909) p 550, that 'every case will turn on its special circumstances, and on the determination of the question "whether under

all the circumstances of the case the use is reasonable and consistent with a correspondent enjoyment of right by the other party" ', is founded on contemporary American authority and is far too wide. See also W M Gordon *Scottish Land Law* (1989) para 7-59.

(d) Opposite Proprietors

294. Introduction. Where the boundary between two estates is marked by a non-tidal river or stream, there is a presumption that the proprietor of each estate owns the *alveus* of the waters on his own side as far as, but no further than, the *medium filum*[1]. A proprietor in this postion, who owns a river only part of the way across, is in a weaker position than a neighbour who owns for the full width. For not only is such a proprietor bound in common interest to proprietors of the river upstream or downstream of his own position[2], but he is additionally bound in common interest to the proprietor opposite who owns the remainder of the width. It is true that in both cases the common interest obligation is the same, namely that the servient proprietor must avoid any act which causes material disturbance to the river as it flows over the *alveus* of the dominant proprietor[3]; but it will be apparent that many uses of water which have no significant effect on the progress of a river further upstream or downstream may have a marked effect on the progress of a river on the opposite side of the *medium filum*.

1 See para 278 above.
2 See paras 291–293 above.
3 For a general account of common interest as it affects non-tidal rivers, see paras 282 ff above. On one view of the law, the proprietor is further burdened by the right of the opposite proprietor to fish in his waters: see further para 280 above.

295. Temporary diversion. It is the rule that:

'[w]here a running water is the boundary which divides between two tenements belonging to different proprietors, the one cannot divert the course of it without consent of the other, though that other should not allege any prejudice by it to himself but the depriving him of the pleasure of trouting, and the chance that he may have occasion for the water at some future time'[1].

This rule, namely that the temporary diversion of water is a breach of common interest in a question with the opposite proprietor, was settled as early as a case of 1624 in which the defender was interdicted from diverting part of a river through an artificial lade in order to drive his mill[2]. The rule may, however, be avoided, and the right to divert water lawfully exercised, by the acquisition of the appropriate positive servitude[3]. Two servitudes are relevant here. The servitude of *aquaehaustus* confers the right to withdraw water from a river, whether permanently for consumption, or for some temporary purpose such as the driving of a water-mill[4]. The servitude of damhead confers the more specialised right of building a dam across the river and on to the land opposite, and of withdrawing the water thereby collected[5]. As in practice both servitudes invariably arise by prescription rather than by grant, they are subject to the rule *tantum praescriptum quantum possessum* (prescription is measured by possession)[6].

1 Erskine *Institute* II,9,13. See also Stair *Institutions* II,7,12; Bankton *Institute* II,7,29; Hume *Lectures* vol III (Stair Soc vol 15, 1952 ed G C H Paton) p 222; Bell *Principles* s 1101.
2 *Bannatyne v Cranston* (1624) Mor 12769. The same result was reached in later cases: see *Hamilton v Edington* (1793) Mor 12824; *Braid v Douglas* (1800) Mor 'Property' App No 2; *Bridges v Lord Saltoun* (1873) 11 M 588.
3 *Stair* II,7,12.
4 *Morris v Bicket* (1864) 2 M 1082 at 1093, per Lord Neaves (affd (1866) 4 M (HL) 44); *Bridges v Lord Saltoun* (1873) 11 M 588. See also para 490 below, and WATER AND WATER RIGHTS, vol 25, paras 348 ff.

5 *Erskine* II,9,13; *Gairlton v Stevenson* (1677) Mor 14535.
6 *J White & Sons v J and M White* (1905) 8 F (HL) 41, 13 SLT 655. In the case of damhead the rule has been interpreted with some flexibility: see *Erskine* II,9,4; *Lyon and Gray v Bakers of Glasgow* (1749) Mor 12789.

296. Building on the *alveus*. In a question with the opposite proprietor, the construction of a weir or a dam is always a breach of common interest except where it proceeds either by consent or in the exercise of a right of servitude[1]. The fact that the construction may lie wholly within the builder's own side of the *alveus* is no defence[2]. Other kinds of building work on the *alveus*, even although not deliberately constructed to arrest the progress of the river, will unavoidably disrupt its flow and are also in breach of common interest if the disruption is material[3]. In *Morris v Bicket*[4], the leading authority on building on the *alveus*, the court interdicted a proprietor from constructing a building in such a way that it extended into the *alveus*. That the building was entirely *in suo* did not help the defender because the flow of the river as a whole was disrupted; and indeed the fact that building works must almost always have this effect was said to place upon the defender in such cases the onus of showing that the disruption was not material[5]. The law as settled by *Morris v Bicket* was set out by Lord Gifford in a subsequent case to the following effect:

'. . . if it could be clearly and indubitably shown that the operation of a proprietor in his own half of the *alveus* was so trifling in its nature or so evanescent in its endurance that it could not possibly have any permanent or appreciable effect on the current, and could not possibly injure . . . the rights and interests of the opposite proprietor, I do not think that the judgment in *Bicket v Morris* . . . would extend to such a case. I think there must always be at least the possibility of injury to the opposite proprietor, and, if such injury is shown to be impossible (and the *onus* of showing this will always rest on the party who is doing anything *in alveo*), then . . . the general right of a proprietor to use his own property would apply'[6].

1 The appropriate servitude is the servitude of damhead: see para 295 above.
2 *Duke of Roxburghe v Waldie* (1821) Hume 524; *Duke of Roxburghe v Waldie's Trustees* (1879) 6 R 663.
3 See para 289 above.
4 *Morris v Bicket* (1864) 2 M 1082, affd (1866) 4 M (HL) 44.
5 (1864) 2 M 1082 at 1089, per Lord Justice-Clerk Inglis. See also *Colquhoun's Trustees v Orr Ewing & Co* (1877) 4 R 344, revsd (1877) 4 R (HL) 116; *Robertson v Foote & Co* (1879) 6 R 1290.
6 *Robertson v Foote & Co* (1879) 6 R 1290 at 1297.

297. Building and other work on the bank. In his use of the river bank, as in his use of the river itself, the riparian proprietor continues to be bound by common interest. But since most uses of the bank have no effect on the flow of the river, the restriction is here of diminished significance[1]. A question which has given rise to difficulty in practice concerns the right of a proprietor to fortify his bank against encroachment by the river. It seems clear that a proprietor may reinforce his existing bank to prevent it from being eroded by the action of the water[2]. He is also entitled to build an artificial barrier sufficiently distant from the river as to check extraordinary flooding only, and whether such flooding has already taken place or is merely anticipated[3]. In neither case is there interference with the 'natural flow'[4]; and if, in the second case, the property *ex adverso* is damaged as a result of the flood water being thrown back, such damage is thought not to be actionable[5]. What, however, the proprietor is not entitled to do is to build an artificial barrier against ordinary seasonal flooding, for that is part of the 'natural flow' of the river[6].

1 But see *Noble's Trustees v Economic Forestry (Scotland) Ltd* 1988 SLT 662, OH; *Logan v Wang (UK) Ltd* 1991 SLT 580 at 581, 582, OH. In contrast with the position for building on the *alveus*, the onus remains throughout with the dominant proprietor to show that common interest has been infringed: *Jackson v Marshall* (1872) 10 M 913 at 919, per Lord Benholme.

2 WATER AND WATER RIGHTS, vol 25, para 324.
3 Erskine *Institute* II,1,5; Bell *Principles* s 971; *Farquharson v Farquharson* (1741) Mor 12799. On the
   right to check flooding which has already taken place, see para 285 above.
4 'Natural flow' does not include extraordinary floods: see para 285 above.
5 Or at least not in common interest: Hume *Lectures* vol III (Stair Soc vol 15, 1952 ed G C H Paton)
   p 224. But see contra *Johnstone v Scott* (1835) 13 S 717.
6 *Menzies v Earl of Breadalbane* (1828) 3 W & S 235, HL; *Morris v Bicket* (1864) 2 M 1082 (affd (1866) 4
   M (HL) 44); *Jackson v Marshall* (1872) 10 M 913; *Murdoch v Wallace* (1881) 8 R 855. On one view of
   the law, the land which is covered at ordinary seasonal floods is in any case considered to be part of
   the *alveus*: J Rankine *The Law of Land-ownership in Scotland* (4th edn, 1909) p 541. But this sits
   uneasily with the rules for determining the *medium filum*: see para 278 above.

(e) Pollution

298. Nuisance. In general, river pollution is a matter of public law, monitored by
such public bodies as the river purification boards. The public law aspects of
pollution are discussed elsewhere in this work[1]. Pollution may also be actionable in
private law, usually under the heading of nuisance. In principle, the proprietors of a
non-tidal river or stream have a remedy in nuisance against anyone who pollutes
that river or stream[2]; and the remedy is also available to the proprietors of the salmon
fishings[3]. The degree of pollution which is necessary before it becomes actionable is,
however, unclear. The only general proposition which can be advanced with
confidence is that pollution is always actionable where its effect is to make a river
which was formerly fit for primary uses[4] no longer so fit[5]. The converse proposition
is not, however, apt, and a remedy will not necessarily be denied even in respect of
rivers which remain fit for primary uses or in respect of rivers which were all along
fit only for secondary uses[6].

1 See WATER AND WATER RIGHTS, vol 25, paras 394 ff.
2 *Miller v Stein* (1791) Mor 12823; *Dunn v Hamilton* (1837) 15 S 853, affd 3 S & M 356, HL; *Collins v
   Hamilton* (1837) 15 S 895; *Rigby and Beardmore v Downie* (1872) 10 M 568.
3 *Mayor of Berwick v Hayning* (1661) Mor 12772; *Seafield v Kemp* (1899) 1 F 402, 6 SLT 289. See also
   para 330 below.
4 For the difference between primary and secondary uses, see paras 287, 288, above.
5 *Miller v Stein* (1791) Mor 12823; *Montgomerie v Buchanan's Trustees* (1853) 15 D 853.
6 See NUISANCE, vol 14, para 2079.

299. Common interest. While most river pollution cases are disposed of on the
basis of nuisance, it is possible that pollution is also actionable on the alternative basis
of common interest[1]. Hume and Bell, for example, both expressly assimilate the
right of a riparian proprietor to unpolluted water to the other common interest
rights[2]. The riparian proprietor, it is said, is entitled to receive water of the same
quality as that bestowed by nature. The significance of a common interest remedy
supplementary to the established remedy in nuisance is that with common interest
the standard imposed on the defender may be higher; for, on analogy with other
common interest obligations, any material deterioration in the quality of the water
is an infringement of common interest. There is, however, only sparse support in
the case law for the idea of an independent obligation based on common interest,
and the argument is made more difficult by the failure of some of the reported cases
to distinguish common interest from nuisance, giving rise to uncertainty as to the
ground on which the decision was ultimately reached[3]. Two important cases do,
however, suggest the existence of an independent common interest remedy. The
first case, *Duke of Buccleuch v Cowan*[4], although apparently an action founded on
nuisance, contains a number of references to common interest, among them the
following passage by Lord Neaves:

'... when a party pollutes running water, of which each proprietor has only what may
be called a usufruct, he is not operating *in suo* — he is operating *in alieno* ... The water

that is passing the upper heritor's door is ticketed and kept sacred for the primary purposes of life to that lower heritor; and any use of it which goes beyond that is an encroachment on the rights of our neighbour. Therefore the wrongdoer is not operating *in suo*, for he is trespassing on rights which belong to one who has a common interest in the whole stream; and when you come to encroach upon that, your position is very different from that of a person who merely makes additional noise, or who has a chimney which gives forth a little more smoke than others, and where all the circumstances must be taken into view, because it depends on rights of a totally different kind'[5].

In the second case, *Bankier Distillery Co v Young & Co*[6], water discharged by the defenders into a stream, while not actually making the stream unfit for primary uses, interfered with the particular use which the pursuers, who were distillers, wished to make of it. The pursuers were successful in obtaining interdict. The case is of interest, partly because the facts are such as would not readily bring success to a pursuer in an action founded on nuisance, and partly because the judgments contain various references to common interest[7].

1 For common interest, see paras 282 ff above.
2 Hume *Lectures* vol III (Stair Soc vol 15, 1952 ed G C H Paton) p 220; Bell *Principles* s 1106.
3 Eg *M'Gavin v M'Intyre Bros* (1890) 17 R 818, affd (1893) 20 R (HL) 49, 1 SLT 110.
4 *Duke of Buccleuch v Cowan* (1866) 5 M 214.
5 (1866) 5 M 214 at 238.
6 *Bankier Distillery Co v Young & Co* (1892) 19 R 1083, affd (1893) 20 R (HL) 76, 1 SLT 204.
7 In the House of Lords, Lord Watson expressed his doubts as to whether 'in returning the water in a state fit for primary uses he [the defender] has any right to alter its natural character, and so make it unfit for uses to which it had been put or might be put by a riparian proprietor below': (1893) 20 R (HL) 76 at 77, (1893) 1 SLT 204 at 204.

300. Defences. It has been suggested that certain defences are available in an action for pollution. For example, at one time it was strongly argued that the pollution of a river was not actionable where it was caused by 'useful manufactory' or by the introduction of domestic sewerage[1]. More recent case law has, however, rejected this approach[2]. A second argument with some currency was that rivers of more than a certain size should be considered as 'public' in respect that they could be used freely to transport polluted substances to the sea[3]. This argument too has failed to win acceptance, and in the modern law the only significance accorded to size is that in large rivers pollution is more readily diluted and disposed of, and so less likely to be actionable[4]. The one defence to an action founded on pollution which is unquestionably available is negative prescription, a riparian proprietor losing his right to object to a nuisance if it has persisted for twenty years[5].

1 *Dunn v Hamilton* (1837) 15 S 853 (affd 3 S & M 356, HL).
2 *Montgomerie v Buchanan's Trustees* (1853) 15 D 853; *Caledonian Rly Co v Baird & Co* (1876) 3 R 839. In *Caledonian Rly Co v Baird & Co* (1876) 3 R 839 at 848, Lord Gifford observed that if a party 'cannot erect a village without polluting this stream . . . then he must let the village alone'. The rule for tidal rivers is otherwise: see eg *Moncreiffe v Perth Police Comrs* (1886) 13 R 921.
3 Bell *Principles* s 1106; *Mayor of Berwick v Hayning* (1661) Mor 12772; *Inverness Magistrates v Skinners of Inverness* (1804) Mor 13191; *Downie v Earl of Moray* (1825) 4 S 167 (NE 169). It is, however, possible that the last two cases were decided on the ground of negative prescription.
4 *Dunn v Hamilton* (1837) 15 S 853 at 860, 862, per Lord Gillies and Lord Corehouse.
5 Prescription and Limitation (Scotland) Act 1973 (c 52), s 7. See further NUISANCE, vol 14, paras 2123 ff.

(f) Underground Water and Water in an Artificial Channel

301. Underground water. Water in a definite channel but underground is said to be governed by the same rules as water in a definite channel and above ground. Rivers are therefore treated in the same way regardless of whether they are on or underneath the surface[1].

1 J Ferguson *Law of Water and Water Rights in Scotland* (1907) p 332.

302. Water in an artificial channel. It is thought that the special rules which regulate water flowing in a natural channel have no application to water flowing in an artificial channel. Thus where an artificial stream passes through the land of more than one proprietor, no special presumption arises as to the ownership of the channel; and even where the rule for natural streams is in fact followed so that the channel is owned in sections by successive proprietors, the use of the water is, in the absence of agreement or of a servitude right[1], unprotected so that a superior proprietor is at liberty to detain or consume the water without regard to the interests of the inferior proprietor or proprietors[2].

1 *Prestoun v Erskine* (1714) Mor 10919 (servitude by prescription); *Strachan v City of Aberdeen* (1905) 12 SLT 725, OH (express servitude). The rule is the same where the artificial stream runs into a natural stream: see para 286 above.
2 But it has been suggested that there may be a place for judicial regulation: see *M'Crone v Ramsay* (1901) 9 SLT 118, OH.

(3) NON-TIDAL LOCHS

303. Introduction. The *alveus* (or '*fundus*') of a loch extends to that area of land covered by water when the loch is 'in its ordinary state, neither swelled by floods, nor decreased by any unusual drought'[1]. All seasonal variations are disregarded. Land which is dry except during seasonal floods is not, therefore, treated as part of a loch, and nor is land where the level of water is so low for it to be no more than a marsh[2]. Like other land, the *alveus* of a loch is owned *a coelo usque ad centrum*[3], and it includes any islands which may have formed. A loch which is self-contained and from which there is no perennial overflow is termed a '*stagnum*'[4].

1 *Dick v Earl of Abercom* (1769) Mor 12813; *Baird v Robertson* (1839) 1 D 1051. The rule for non-tidal rivers is the same: see para 278 above.
2 *Waugh v Wylie* (1885) 23 SLR 152.
3 For ownership *a coelo usque ad centrum*, see para 198 above.
4 For *stagna*, see WATER AND WATER RIGHTS, vol 25, paras 340, 341.

304. Ownership. The usual general rule is that the *alveus* of a non-tidal loch belongs to the proprietor or proprietors of the lands which surround it. In contrast to tidal lochs, non-tidal lochs do not belong to the Crown[1]. More specifically, the rule is that a loch wholly within one estate is presumed to belong to the proprietor of that estate as a pertinent thereof; and that a loch bordering on more than one estate is presumed to be 'divided among the fiars whose lands front thereupon'[2], without regard to how slight that frontage might be[3]. Whether in the second case, ownership is common or several is a question which is considered in the immediately following paragraph. In both cases the presumption as to ownership operates unless and until rebutted, and does not require fortification by possession on the part of the proprietor or proprietors[4]. The presumption is rebutted if the titles of a property abutting a loch contain a bounding description which, for example by reference to a plan, clearly exclude the loch from the estate[5]. It is also rebutted if some other party is able to produce a good and adverse title to the loch[6]. The question of ownership of the water comprising a loch has not yet been judicially determined. Where the loch is a *stagnum*[7], there is an argument that the water is the property of the proprietor of the *alveus*, but in other cases it seems likely that the water is *res nullius*[8].

1 At one time all navigable lochs were thought to belong to the Crown: see Bell *Principles* s 651; *Macdonnell v Caledonian Canal Comrs* (1830) 8 S 881. But this is no longer the law: see further para 275 above.
2 Stair *Institutions* II,3,73.
3 *Menzies v Macdonald* (1854) 16 D 827, affd (1856) 2 Macq 463, HL.
4 *Scott v Lord Napier* (1869) 7 M (HL) 35 at 74, per Lord Hatherley LC.
5 It is arguable that, on analogy with the rule for non-tidal rivers (see para 278 above), the expression 'bounded by' a loch does not exclude the loch.
6 Whether by valid grant from the then owner, as in *Montgomery v Watson* (1861) 23 D 635, or by a grant *a non domino* but fortified by prescription, as in *Baird v Robertson* (1836) 14 S 396.
7 See para 303 above.
8 See para 274 above.

305. Common ownership or several ownership? The *alveus* of a non-tidal loch is presumed to belong to the proprietors of its banks[1], and two different views may be found in the authorities as to the nature of this shared ownership:

(1) *Common ownership.* On this view the *alveus* of a non-tidal loch is owned in common by the proprietors of its banks, the size of each *pro indiviso* share being determined by the relative size of the frontages. As owners in common, each co-proprietor is entitled to use the entire loch, subject however to the usual restrictions which affect *pro indiviso* ownership. It has been suggested that the remedies of division and sale may not be available[2].

(2) *Several ownership.* On this view the *alveus* of a non-tidal loch is divided into a number of discrete sections, each section being the subject of separate ownership. A riparian proprietor owns only that section of *alveus* extending from his own bank to the *medium filum* of the loch; but he has in addition the right, attributable to common interest, to make use of the water throughout the loch. Thus Lord Selborne:

'So far as relates to the *solum* or *fundus* of the lake, it is considered to belong in severalty to the several riparian proprietors, if more than one, the space enclosed by lines drawn from the boundaries of each property *usque ad medium filum aquae* being deemed appurtenant to the land of that proprietor, exactly as in the common case of a river. But, for reasons which may be pronounced to be founded in part, if not wholly, on the irregularity of configuration, frequent in lakes, this *ex adverso* rule is not extended by the law of Scotland to these rights (such as boating, fishing, and fowling) which are exercised in or upon the surface of lake waters. These are to be enjoyed over the whole water's face by all the riparian proprietors in common, subject (if need be) to judicial regulation'[3].

The first of these competing views (common property) was the earlier to become established. It is to be found in Bell[4] and in a number of cases decided around the middle of the nineteenth century[5], and it remained the dominant view until the decision of the House of Lords in 1878 in the leading case of *Mackenzie v Bankes*[6]. In *Mackenzie* the House of Lords adopted the second view, the view that a loch is held in several ownership; but since the Court of Session in the same case had followed the older, common property, view without attracting comment in the higher court, it may be doubted whether the House of Lords was aware of the significance of its own adopted stance. The cases since *Mackenzie* have, however, followed the House of Lords rather than the Court of Session[7], and the idea of several ownership may now be regarded as established.

1 See para 304 above.
2 Bell *Principles* s 1111.
3 *Mackenzie v Bankes* (1878) 5 R (HL) 192 at 202.
4 *Bell* s 1111.
5 *Menzies v Macdonald* (1854) 16 D 827 (affd (1856) 2 Macq 463, HL); *Montgomery v Watson* (1861) 23
   D 635; *Stewart's Trustees v Robertson* (1874) 1 R 334. But see *Cochrane v Earl of Minto* (1815) 6 Pat 139,
   HL.
6 *Mackenzie v Bankes* (1877) 5 R 278, affd (1878) 5 R (HL) 192.
7 *Leny v Linlithgow Magistrates* (1894) 2 SLT 294 (a case which turns on which of the two views is
   correct); *Meacher v Blair-Oliphant* 1913 SC 417, 1913 2 SLT 196; *Kilsyth Fish Protection Association v
   M'Farlane* 1937 SC 757, 1937 SLT 562. *Menzies v Wentworth* (1901) 3 F 941, 9 SLT 107, which is to
   contrary effect, is a sequel to *Menzies v Macdonald* (1854) 16 D 827 (affd (1856) 2 Macq 463, HL).

306. Use of loch. In the use which a riparian proprietor may make of a loch it is necessary to distinguish between two separate categories of right. The principal right of a riparian proprietor arises in relation to that section of *alveus* which is exclusively his. Subject to a number of important restrictions[1], he may exercise full proprietorial rights in respect both of that section of *alveus*[2] and also of the water above it. These rights, which in a question with the public at large are exclusive rights[3], include the right to sail a boat, the right to take all fish other than salmon[4], and the right to consume the water. In addition, a riparian proprietor has an ancillary right, based upon common interest, to make use of that part of the *alveus* which is not his for purposes such as fishing and sailing[5]. Indeed, it has been been said that where a loch has overflowed its legal boundaries, the riparian proprietors are entitled to follow the water on to the adjoining banks 'for the purposes of fishing and fowling'[6].

Where, as must often be the case, a number of different proprietors are entitled to fish the same loch, a danger of over-fishing may arise. But while it appears that the court has power to regulate fishing in such circumstances[7], the power will be exercised sparingly. In the only reported application for its exercise, *Menzies v Wentworth,* the application was refused, Lord President Balfour commenting that:

> 'It appears to me that the law does not require a community of proprietors ... to observe the same standard of preservation of fish, or even of moderation in fishing, as the owner of a private loch might think fit to practise in his own interest. The Court should not, in my judgment, interfere unless the fishing is carried on in such a manner, or to such excess, as either to destroy or materially injure the reasonable enjoyment of the right'[8].

1 See paras 307, 308, below.
2 *Cochrane v Earl of Minto* (1815) 6 Pat 139, HL.
3 *Montgomery v Watson* (1861) 23 D 635.
4 See para 280 above.
5 See para 305 above.
6 *Dick v Earl of Abercorn* (1769) Mor 12813.
7 *Mackenzie v Bankes* (1878) 5 R (HL) 192 at 202, per Lord Selborne.
8 *Menzies v Wentworth* (1901) 3 F 941 at 956, 9 SLT 107 at 109. This case proceeded on the basis that
   the loch was common property: see para 305, note 7, above. As to judicial regulation, see generally
   para 30 above.

307. Common interest. The most important check on freedom of use arises out of common interest. The proprietor of a non-tidal loch may be burdened by two distinct sets of common interest obligations:

(1) *Obligations in favour of fellow proprietors.* Lochs owned by more than one party are affected by a reciprocal network of common interest rights and obligations. The scope of these rights and obligations is, however, unclear. At the least, each proprietor is bound to allow fellow proprietors the use of his own section of loch for sailing and for fishing[1]; but it is arguable that the burden extends further to include the kind of common interest obligations found in non-tidal rivers,

such as a prohibition on any material disturbance of the natural condition of the water[2].

(2) *Obligations in favour of proprietors of an adjoining river.* A loch which is not a *stagnum*[3] is treated for certain purposes as part of the river or stream which flows from it[4]. In consequence, the proprietors of the loch are included within the same network of common interest rights and obligations which governs the proprietors of the river or stream. The principal common interest obligation is an obligation to refrain from any act causing material disturbance to the natural flow of the river or stream.

It will be apparent that a loch which is owned by more than one party and which is not a *stagnum* is subject to both sets of common interest rights and obligations; and conversely, that a *stagnum* which is owned by a single party is entirely free from common interest leaving the proprietor at liberty to drain the loch or otherwise deal with it in any manner that he pleases[5].

1 See para 305 above.
2 For common interest obligations in non-tidal rivers, see paras 282 ff above.
3 For *stagna*, see para 303 above.
4 See para 286 above.
5 Stair *Institutions* II,3,73; Bell *Principles* s 1110.

308. Other restrictions on use. In addition to restrictions arising from common interest, a number of other restrictions may affect the proprietors of a loch. Thus the general law of nuisance applies to lochs and is of particular importance in relation to pollution. A loch may also be burdened by one of the water servitudes, or, where the loch is navigable, by a public right of navigation[1]. The Civic Government (Scotland) Act 1982[2] empowers district and islands councils, acting with the consent of the proprietors, to make byelaws on certain specified matters relating to non-tidal lochs and their banks.

1 See para 490 below (servitudes), and para 523 below (navigation).
2 Civic Government (Scotland) Act 1982 (c 45), s 121(4).

(4) TIDAL WATERS

(a) Rivers, Lochs and the Sea

309. Presumption of Crown ownership. The territorial sea adjacent to the United Kingdom is fixed at twelve nautical miles by the Territorial Sea Act 1987[1]. Within these territorial boundaries three main examples of tidal waters are usually distinguished, namely (1) tidal rivers, (2) sea lochs, estuaries, bays and other waters *intra fauces terrae* (literally, within the jaws of the land), and (3) the open sea. Whatever the position may have been at one stage in the development of the law of Scotland[2], it is now settled that the rule as to ownership is the same in all three cases[3], namely that the *alveus* or bed of tidal waters is presumed to belong to the Crown[4]. The position may be contrasted with non-tidal waters where the corresponding presumption is of private ownership[5]. Thus the proprietor of a river-bank will own the river-bed itself only if the water is non-tidal.

1 Territorial Sea Act 1987 (c 49), s 1(1). For the baselines from which the twelve miles are measured, see SEA AND CONTINENTAL SHELF.
2 *Lord Advocate v Clyde Navigation Trustees* (1891) 19 R 174; *Cuninghame v Ayrshire Assessor* (1895) 22 R 596, 2 SLT 618.
3 *Lord Advocate v Wemyss* (1896) 24 R 216, 4 SLT 194, revsd (1899) 2 F (HL) 1, 7 SLT 172; *Crown Estate Comrs v Fairlie Yacht Slip Ltd* 1976 SC 161, 1977 SLT 19, OH, affd 1979 SC 156; *Shetland*

Salmon Farmers Association v Crown Estate Comrs 1990 SCLR 484 at 512, 1991 SLT 166 at 186, per Lord McCluskey.
4 See paras 275, 276, above.
5 See para 278 above.

310. The nature of Crown ownership. Considerable uncertainty has been expressed as to the nature of Crown ownership of tidal waters and until comparatively recently two competing views were maintained in answer to this '*questio vexata*'[1]. On one view of the law, the Crown had no beneficial entitlement but owned merely in trust for the public at large in order to protect such public rights as the right of navigation. The rights in tidal waters were thus seen as an example of *regalia majora*[2]. The other view allowed the Crown full beneficial ownership, that is to say, absolute *dominium*, but subject to various public rights. The rights in tidal waters were thus seen as an example of *regalia minora*, burdened by *regalia majora* rights held for the public at large[3]. The first view was largely accepted as correct until the middle years of the nineteenth century[4], and indeed encountered no authoritative challenge until the end of that century and the leading case of *Lord Advocate v Clyde Navigation Trustees*[5]. In that case the Lord Advocate, on behalf of the Crown, sought declarator and interdict to prevent the defenders from depositing dredgings in Loch Long, a tidal loch. The defenders challenged the Crown's title to sue. The Crown's right, it was asserted,

> 'is confined to a mere protectorate for the purposes of fishing and navigation, so that, except where the interest of fishing and navigation are concerned the Crown has no higher or better title to the water and bed of this inland loch than the defenders themselves'[6].

The Second Division rejected this argument and found for the pursuer. The Crown, it was said, had beneficial ownership of the loch. The same conclusion has since been reached in a modern case which involved similar facts[7] and the doctrine of full ownership of the seabed may now be regarded as established beyond doubt. More recently, the Second Division has considered the juridical basis of Crown ownership of the seabed and concluded that it derives from the royal prerogative and not from the Crown's position as ultimate feudal superior[8]. The case in question concerned rights to the seabed around the Shetland Islands, where the principal tenure is udal and not feudal, and the effect of deciding in favour of a feudal basis would have been to leave the Shetland seabed as *res nullius* and hence, presumably, available for acquisition by *occupatio*[9].

1 *Lord Advocate v Clyde Trustees* (1849) 11 D 391 at 403, per Lord Jeffrey (affd (1852) 1 Macq 46, HL).
2 See eg *Agnew v Lord Advocate* (1873) 11 M 309 at 322, per Lord Justice-Clerk Moncreiff. For *regalia majora* and *regalia minora*, see W M Gordon *Scottish Land Law* (1989) pp 862–864. Only rights falling into the latter class are capable of alienation by the Crown.
3 See eg *Duchess of Sutherland v Watson* (1868) 6 M 199 at 212, 213, per Lord Neaves.
4 See para 514 below.
5 *Lord Advocate v Clyde Navigation Trustees* (1891) 19 R 174.
6 As summarised by Lord Kyllachy at (1891) 19 R 174 at 176, OH (affd (1891) 19 R 174, IH).
7 *Crown Estate Comrs v Fairlie Yacht Slip Ltd* 1976 SC 161, 1977 SLT 19, OH, affd 1979 SC 156.
8 *Shetland Salmon Farmers Association v Crown Estate Comrs* 1990 SCLR 484, 1991 SLT 166. The case is notable for its extended treatment of the relevant authorities.
9 Udal tenure applies only in Orkney and Shetland. See UDAL LAW, vol 24. The rule for the foreshore in Orkney and Shetland is different: see para 317 below.

311. Alienation to subject proprietors. Uncertainty about the nature of Crown ownership has been accompanied by uncertainty about whether the Crown has power to alienate the *alveus* of tidal waters to subject proprietors. Naturally, those who held the view, now discarded, that Crown ownership was fiduciary in character concluded that alienation was not possible[1]. But even amongst those who regarded Crown ownership as beneficial there was no consensus. In the opinion of Lord Watson, for example, the existence of the various public rights over tidal waters limited, or perhaps even precluded, alienation[2].

The modern view, however, is that alienation is competent[3], and Crown practice reflects this view in, for example, the leasing of the seabed for fish farming and the exacting of payment in respect of dredging on the seabed for sand and gravel[4]. The public rights over tidal waters are unaffected by any alienation or lease at the hands of the Crown[5]. Like other Crown property, the seabed is administered by the Crown Estate Commissioners acting under the Crown Estate Act 1961 (c 55)[6].

1 See eg _Agnew v Lord Advocate_ (1873) 11 M 309 at 322, per Lord Justice-Clerk Moncreiff.
2 _Lord Advocate v Wemyss_ (1899) 2 F (HL) 1 at 9, 7 SLT 172 at 174. See also _Lord Advocate v Clyde Navigation Trustees_ (1891) 19 R 174 at 176, OH, per Lord Kyllachy (affd (1891) 19 R 174, IH).
3 _Crown Estate Comrs v Fairlie Yacht Slip Ltd_ 1976 SC 161, 1977 SLT 19, OH, affd 1979 SC 156; _Shetland Salmon Farmers Association v Crown Estate Comrs_ 1990 SCLR 484, 1991 SLT 166 (Lord Murray _dubitante_).
4 Geoffrey Marston _The Marginal Seabed_ (1981) ch VIII. Some indication of the extent of the Crown grants is given in _Shetland Salmon Farmers Association v Crown Estate Comrs_ 1991 SLT 166 at 175.
5 For public rights, see paras 515, 518–521, below. Some of the difficulties which may arise in practice are mentioned in _Shetland Salmon Farmers Association v Crown Estate Comrs_ 1991 SLT 166 at 182, per Lord Murray.
6 See further THE CROWN.

312. Rights of adjacent proprietors. The proprietors of the banks or foreshore immediately adjacent to tidal waters are sometimes referred to as 'riparian proprietors', but the usage is misleading, for in almost every case the _alveus_ of the waters remains in Crown ownership and the adjacent proprietor has no rights therein beyond those held by the public at large[1]. Thus, although the proprietor may fish the waters or sail in them, he may do so only in exercise of the public rights of fishing and navigation[2], and he has no title to object to pollution or other interference with the waters unless his own land is also affected. In _Gay v Malloch_[3] the proprietor of one bank of a tidal river successfully interdicted the proprietor of the opposite bank from removing large stones from the riverbed. The pursuer was able to establish that the defender's actions would alter the flow of the river and so threaten his bank with erosion, and it appears that he would not otherwise have been successful[4].

1 _Macbraire v Mather_ (1871) 9 M 913; _Moncreiffe v Perth Police Comrs_ (1886) 13 R 921.
2 For public rights, see paras 518–521 below.
3 _Gay v Malloch_ 1959 SC 110, 1959 SLT 132.
4 See also _Ross v Powrie and Pitcaithley_ (1891) 19 R 314. In both cases, however, dicta may be found to the effect that the rights of 'riparian proprietors' in tidal and non-tidal waters are indistinguishable.

(b) Foreshore

313. Meaning of 'foreshore'. The extent of the foreshore is determined by reference to ordinary spring tides. The foreshore is defined as that part of the shore which is wholly covered by the sea at high tide and wholly uncovered at low tide[1]. This rule is peculiar to Scotland: in England and Wales account is also taken of neap tides, extent being determined by averaging ordinary spring and ordinary neap tides[2]. The location of the foreshore may alter over time as a result of the permanent advance or permanent retreat of the sea[3]. 'Sea-greens', the name given to saltings or strips of pasture covered only by occasional tides, are not considered as part of the foreshore[4]. Equally, outcrops of rocks or sandbanks in the sea proper but close to shore are not part of the foreshore, although they may belong to the proprietor of the foreshore as a pertinent[5].

1 *Bowie v Marquis of Ailsa* (1887) 14 R 649 at 660, 661, per Lord Trayner; *Fisherrow Harbour Comrs v Musselburgh Real Estate Co Ltd* (1903) 5 F 387, 10 SLT 512, 549.

2 J Ferguson *The Law of Water and Water Rights in Scotland* (1907) pp 56–58. In *Fisherrow Harbour Comrs v Musselburgh Real Estate Co Ltd* (1903) 5 F 387 at 393, 394, 10 SLT 549 at 549, Lord Young asserted: 'I quite see the desirableness of uniformity in the law of England and the law of Scotland in defining the boundaries of the seashore. But such uniformity should be obtained by choosing the best definition. I regard the definition arrived at by our own law as the best, and I therefore consider that uniformity should be attained not by the Scottish authorities adopting the rule which has been determined in the law of England, but by the English authorities adopting the rule laid down in our own law'. This advice appears to have been heeded. See the Control of Pollution Act 1974 (c 40), ss 4(4), 56(1) (amended by the Water Act 1989 (c 15), s 169, Sch 23, para 3) (definition of 'controlled waters'); and the Environmental Protection Act 1990 (c 43), s 29(8).

3 See para 594, head (3), below.

4 Erskine *Institute* II,6,17; *Aitken's Trustees v Caledonian Rly Co* (1904) 6 F 465, 11 SLT 724.

5 Hume *Lectures* vol IV (Stair Soc vol 17, 1955 ed G C H Paton) p 256; Bell *Principles* s 644; *Innes v Downie* (1807) Hume 552.

314. Acquisition of ownership.

While in feudal theory the foreshore was originally the property of the Crown, it is capable of being acquired by subject proprietors and in this respect is no different from any other land in Scotland. For many years the proper method of acquisition by subject proprietors was controversial. At one time the foreshore seems to have been regarded as *inter regalia* in the sense of requiring an express Crown grant[1]. By the early nineteenth century, however, the radically different view prevailed, that the foreshore passed to the *ex adverso* proprietor by implication, as a part and pertinent of his land[2]. The foreshore was thus seen as belonging to the same category as the *alveus* of non-tidal waters[3]. This second view did not, however, survive the decision of the Second Division in *Agnew v Lord Advocate*[4] in 1873. *Agnew*, by adopting a position intermediate between the two earlier views, established what is now accepted as the modern law[5]. On the one hand the view that the foreshore could pass merely by implication was rejected, Lord Neaves explaining matters thus:

'I am inclined to hold that the shore would not by implication necessarily pass in a general grant of the adjoining land. I think that probably its liability to the public use would raise a presumption against the implied grant. It is rather to be implied that the Crown would retain such a subject altogether, unless it expressly gave it out . . .'[6].

But on the other hand there was no return to the still earlier doctrine. Under the modern law ownership of the foreshore may be acquired in one of two ways. One is by grant from the Crown or other owner, and the other is by prescriptive possession on a title *habile* to include the foreshore.

1 See eg Erskine *Institute* II,6,17.

2 *Macalister v Campbell* (1837) 15 S 490; *Paterson v Marquis of Ailsa* (1846) 8 D 752; *Hunter v Lord Advocate* (1869) 7 M 899.

3 See para 278 above.

4 *Agnew v Lord Advocate* (1873) 11 M 309.

5 *Lord Advocate v Lord Blantyre* (1879) 6 R (HL) 72; *Luss Estates Co v BP Oil Grangemouth Refinery Ltd* 1981 SLT 97, OH, affd 1982 SLT 457.

6 *Agnew v Lord Advocate* (1873) 11 M 309 at 332.

315. Acquisition from existing owner.

The simplest way to acquire ownership of the foreshore is by grant from the existing owner, whether that owner is the Crown or a subject proprietor. The grant need not make express mention of the foreshore, and it is sufficient if the foreshore is included within the boundaries of the grant, whether these boundaries are express or fall to be explained by possession[1]. Where the boundary is indicated by a line on a plan which coincides with the then location of the high watermark, and where the high watermark subsequently changes, the boundary is the line as originally drawn and not the new high watermark[2].

The expressions most frequently used to specify the seaward boundary of a property have been judicially considered on a number of occasions and, except where this does serious violence to the context[3], their meanings may be regarded as fixed. Thus where a property is described as bounded by 'the sea' or by a tidal 'river', the seaward boundary is taken as being the low watermark of ordinary spring tides, and the foreshore is included[4]. The same result is reached where the property is described as bounded by 'the sea-beach' or 'the seashore'[5], a result which is in opposition to the usual rule that the boundary feature lies outside the property being described. Finally, and conversely, a property described as bounded by 'the sea-flood' or 'the flood-mark' has as its seaward boundary the high watermark, and the foreshore is excluded[6].

It has sometimes been suggested that expressions used to describe the seaward boundary may not bear the same meaning in grants from subject proprietors as they do in grants from the Crown. A subject proprietor, it is argued, has no reason to retain the foreshore and grants should as far as possible be interpreted in favour of the grantee[7]. The cases relied on for this view all have in common an unsuccessful attempt by a subject proprietor to assert ownership of the foreshore in a question with his grantee; and it may be that they can more plausibly be explained on the basis that the granter's own title to the foreshore was deficient[8].

1　The possession need not be for the prescriptive period: see *Lord Advocate v Wemyss* (1899) 2 F (HL) 1 at 9, 10, 7 SLT 172 at 175, per Lord Watson. But see contra *Lord Advocate v Lord Blantyre* (1879) 6 R (HL) 72 at 82, per Lord Mure.

2　*Secretary of State for Scotland v Coombs* 1991 GWD 39-2404, OH.

3　*Musselburgh Magistrates v Musselburgh Real Estate Co Ltd* (1904) 7 F 308, 12 SLT 636; *Luss Estates Co v BP Oil Grangemouth Refinery Ltd* 1987 SLT 201.

4　*Culross Magistrates v Earl of Dundonald* (1769) Mor 12810; *Boucher v Crawford* 30 Nov 1814 FC; *Darling's Trustees v Caledonian Rly Co* (1903) 5 F 1001, 11 SLT 176.

5　*Culross Magistrates v Geddes* (1809) Hume 554; *Luss Estates Co v BP Oil Grangemouth Refinery Ltd* 1987 SLT 201. The doubts expressed by Lord Justice-Clerk Macdonald and by Lord Trayner in *Musselburgh Magistrates v Musselburgh Real Estate Co Ltd* (1904) 7 F 308, 12 SLT 636, appear to be ill founded.

6　*Berry v Holden* (1840) 3 D 205; *Keiller v Dundee Magistrates* (1886) 14 R 191. But see contra *Hunter v Lord Advocate* (1869) 7 M 899.

7　J Ferguson *The Law of Water and Water Rights in Scotland* (1907) pp 76, 88; J Rankine *The Law of Land-ownership in Scotland* (4th edn, 1909) p 108.

8　See eg *Montrose Magistrates v Commercial Bank of Scotland Ltd* (1886) 13 R 947.

316. Acquisition by positive prescription. Ownership of the foreshore may also be acquired by possession for the prescriptive period founded on a *habile* title. A title is *habile* in the sense required if it is capable of including the foreshore, and it is not necessary that the foreshore be expressly mentioned[1]. The prescriptive period is twenty years in a question with the Crown, but otherwise is ten years[2]. The nature of the possession required for prescription has been described by Lord Watson in the following terms:

'It is, in my opinion, practically impossible to lay down any precise rule in regard to the character and amount of possession necessary in order to give a riparian proprietor a prescriptive right to foreshore ... The beneficial enjoyment of which the foreshore admits, consistently with the rights of navigation and of the general public[3], is an exceedingly variable quantity. I think it may be safely affirmed that in cases where the seashore admits of an appreciable and reasonable amount of beneficial possession consistently with these rights the riparian proprietor must be held to have had possession ... if he has had all the beneficial uses of the foreshore which would naturally have been enjoyed by the direct grantee of the Crown. In estimating the character and extent of his possession it must always be kept in view that possession of the foreshore in its natural state can never be, in the strict sense of term, exclusive. The proprietor cannot exclude the public from it at any time, and it is practically impossible to prevent occasional encroachments on his right, because the cost of preventive measures would be altogether disproportionate to the value of the subject' [4].

Special provision is made for the foreshore under the system of registration of title. Where an applicant's title is *a non domino,* the Keeper's usual practice is to accept the application, register the title, but to exclude the state indemnity[5]. Exclusion of indemnity is in fact a prerequisite of the operation of positive prescription[6]. The applicant becomes owner at the moment of registration, but his title is vulnerable to rectification at the instance of the Crown or other holder of the underlying title to the foreshore within the years of positive prescription[7]. At the end of the prescriptive period, and provided that the title has remained unchallenged, state indemnity is restored and the possibility of rectification disappears[8]. If the original exclusion of indemnity was made against the express wishes of the applicant, the Keeper must notify the Crown Estate Commissioners of the application, so presenting the opportunity to assert Crown rights and interrupt prescription[9].

1 See para 315 above.
2 Prescription and Limitation (Scotland) Act 1973 (c 52), s 1.
3 For public rights, see paras 524–526 below.
4 *Young v North British Rly Co* (1887) 14 R (HL) 53 at 54. See also *Aitken's Trustees v Caledonian Rly Co* (1904) 6 F 465, 11 SLT 724.
5 Land Registration (Scotland) Act 1979 (c 33), s 12(2); *Registration of Title Practice Book* (1981) para H.1.08. See generally K G C Reid 'A Non Domino Conveyances and the Land Register' 1991 JR 79.
6 Prescription and Limitation (Scotland) Act 1973, s 1(1) (amended by the Land Registration (Scotland) Act 1979, s 10).
7 Land Registration (Scotland) Act 1979, ss 3(1)(a), 9(1), (3)(a)(iv). See paras 673, 674, below.
8 This is because the initial absence of title has been cured by prescription. See also ibid, s 9(3)(a), which provides special protection for proprietors in possession.
9 Ibid, s 14.

317. Ownership in Orkney and Shetland. Except where it has been feudalised by acceptance of a Crown charter, the foreshore in Orkney and Shetland is held on udal tenure. Udal tenure excludes the Crown's claim, good throughout the rest of Scotland, as original owner of all land. The foreshore in Orkney and Shetland is thus in private ownership, usually of the *ex adverso* proprietor[1].

1 *Smith v Lerwick Harbour Trustees* (1903) 5 F 680, 10 SLT 742. See further UDAL LAW, vol 24, para 314.

318. Use. Ownership of the foreshore is subject to a number of restrictions as to use. Thus the owner must not interfere with the various public rights over the foreshore, such as the rights of navigation and recreation[1]. His ownership may be burdened by servitude rights[2] in favour of adjoining proprietors. Historically, the most important and valuable servitude over the foreshore was wreck and ware, which confers the right to gather seaweed and other sea produce[3]. The Civic Government (Scotland) Act 1982 empowers district and islands councils to preserve the amenity of the foreshore by making byelaws and by executing works. The authority extends seawards below low watermark up to a distance of 1,000 metres. In all cases where he can be ascertained and contacted, the consent of the proprietor must first be obtained by the council[4].

Subject to these restrictions, the proprietor may use the foreshore as he pleases. As his ownership extends *a coelo usque ad centrum* it includes both the minerals underneath the surface and things attached to the surface by accession[5]. Salmon, oysters and mussels, however, are separate legal tenements and may not be taken without express title[6]. The proprietor of the foreshore is free to erect artificial barriers against the sea, whether in self-protection or with the purpose of gaining land from the sea by alluvion[7]. In a case where a sudden spate had caused a tidal river to change its course, it was held in a question between the proprietor past whose lands the river formerly ran and the proprietor past whose lands it now ran that the former was entitled to build a bulwark on his own land with the aim of restoring the river to its original course[8]. Damage caused to others as a result of the construction of artificial barriers may be actionable in delict or in nuisance[9].

1 See paras 524 ff below.
2 But may not be burdened by common interest rights. Common interest does not affect the foreshore.
3 *Fullerton v Adamton and Monkton* (1697) Mor 13524; *Earl of Morton v Covingtree* (1760) Mor 13528; J Rankine *The Law of Land-ownership in Scotland* (4th edn, 1909) pp 257–259. See also para 491 below.
4 Civic Government (Scotland) Act 1982 (c 45), ss 120–123.
5 Eg cockle shells: *Secretary of State for Scotland v Inverness-shire Assessor* 1948 SC 334, 1948 SLT 413, LVAC.
6 See paras 319 ff below.
7 See para 593 below.
8 *Town of Nairn v Brodie, Lord Lyon* (1738) Mor 12779. The rule for non-tidal waters is the same: see para 285 above. The suddenness of the change excludes the operation of alluvion.
9 *Lindsay v Thomson* (1866) 5 M 29. See also para 312 above.

(5) THE SEPARATE TENEMENTS

(a) General

319. Introduction. Three categories of right relating to water have the status of legal separate tenements and may be held independently from the ownership of the water and adjacent dry land[1]. The explanation for this special status is in the main historical and is now of little significance, but the rule remains. The three categories in question are (1) the right of salmon fishing, (2) the right to gather mussels and the right to gather oysters, and (3) the right of port and the right of ferry.

1 For separate tenements, see paras 207 ff above.

(b) The Right of Salmon Fishing

320. Nature. In their natural state salmon are *res nullius*. They are not royal fish[1] and do not belong to the Crown. As *res nullius,* they remain ownerless until caught when they become the property of the captor by the doctrine of occupation. Farmed salmon reared in cages are the property of the fish farmer. In general, therefore, salmon are governed by the same rules as any other fish, and such special rules as exist affect not salmon but salmon fishing.

1 For royal fish, see para 543 below.

321. Crown right of salmon fishing. In feudal theory the right to fish for salmon is, like many other heritable rights, vested originally in the Crown. The Crown right is an exclusive right to take salmon in all waters within territorial limits, and without regard to whether the waters are tidal or non-tidal[1]. Orkney and Shetland, however, are excluded[2]. It appears that the right to take salmon includes the right to farm salmon[3]. At one time it was thought that the Crown right did not include fishing by rod and line, which was said to be available to riparian proprietors in the case of non-tidal waters and to the public at large in the case of tidal waters[4]. This view dates from a period when rod fishing was of comparatively little commercial value. It is now settled, however, that the Crown right is an exclusive right to take salmon by all permitted methods, including fishing by rod and line[5].

1 *Woods and Forests Comrs v Gammell* (1851) 13 D 854, affd (1859) 3 Macq 419, HL; *Joseph Johnston & Son Ltd v Morrison* 1962 SLT 322, OH.
2 *Lord Advocate v Balfour* 1907 SC 1360, 15 SLT 7, OH. See further UDAL LAW, vol 24, para 315.
3 That at least appears to be the rule in the analogous case of mussels. See *Mull Shellfish Ltd v Golden Sea Produce Ltd* 1992 SLT 703.
4 Hume *Lectures* vol IV (Stair Soc vol 17, 1955 ed G C H Paton) p 245; Bell *Principles* s 1112.
5 *Anderson v Anderson* (1867) 6 M 117.

322. Acquisition by subject proprietors. The Crown right of salmon fishing may be communicated to subject proprietors and this has now happened in most waters where salmon are to be found. Owing to the high value placed on salmon fishings, the Crown right was from an early period classified as *inter regalia minora* and consequently as a legal separate tenement[1], and it continues as a separate tenement in the hands of subject proprietors. Accordingly, there is no necessary coincidence between the proprietor of a stretch of water on the one hand and the proprietor of the salmon fishings in that water on the other. The identity of the proprietors may be the same but it need not be.

A subject proprietor may acquire the right of salmon fishing by one of two different methods. The first method is by express grant from the owner, who may be the Crown but today is usually another subject proprietor. The right of salmon fishing must be expressly conveyed in the dispositive clause[2] of the deed, and, in the absence of such express conveyance, the salmon fishings are not carried[3]. This rule, which is the rule for all legal separate tenements, holds even where the granter of the deed is a subject proprietor, for the mere fact that a right of salmon fishings has been associated with a particular piece of land over a substantial period is not sufficient in law to make it a pertinent of that land and so carried by implication[4]. The other method by which a right of salmon fishing may be acquired is by prescriptive possession on a title which is *habile* to include the right. Both methods are now considered in turn.

1 For legal separate tenements, see paras 209 ff above.
2 J Rankine *The Law of Land-ownership in Scotland* (4th edn) p 306.
3 Stair *Institutions* II,3,69; Bankton *Institute* II,3,111; Erskine *Institute* II,6,15.
4 Erskine II,6,15; *McKendrick v Wilson* 1970 SLT (Sh Ct) 39. But the contrary has also been suggested: see *Duke of Queensberry v Viscount of Stormont* (1773) Mor 14251; *Lord Advocate v Sinclair* (1865) 3 M 981, affd (1867) 5 M (HL) 97; *Lord Advocate v M'Culloch* (1874) 2 R 27.

323. Acquisition by express grant. The right of salmon fishings is a legal separate tenement and passes only where it is expressly mentioned in the grant or, in the case of Land Register titles, where it is expressly mentioned in the title sheet by reference to which the grant is made[1]. But even where salmon fishings are expressly mentioned difficult questions may arise as to the extent of the fishings granted. A number of different possibilities may be distinguished:

(1) *Definite boundaries.* Where the boundaries of the fishings are specified clearly in the grant, all difficulties are avoided. '[T]he natural and explicit clause in the charter ... is a clause "*cum piscationibus salmonum*" with a specification subjoined, by natural marks, of the extent of water over which the grant is meant to be given'[2]. It is, however, relatively unusual for the boundaries of the grant to be specified in this way.

(2) *Indefinite boundaries: presumptions.* More usually, the boundaries of salmon fishings are left uncertain. Typically the conveyance does no more than convey 'the salmon fishings' in a named river or loch, or alternatively 'the salmon fishings' in a named river or loch 'effeiring to' a particular estate. Whichever

form is used, the extent of the grantee's right is left in a state of uncertainty; but the interpretation of a grant in the alternative form (where the salmon fishings are linked to a particular estate) is aided by two well-established rules of construction. In the first place, a grant in the alternative form is presumed to carry only the salmon fishings in that part of the river which runs through or beside the estate in question. No right is conveyed to the fishings further upstream or downstream[3]. And in the second place, the extent to which the grant carries the right to fish across the full width of the river depends upon the ownership of the banks. If the estate includes both banks, then the grantee's right of salmon fishing is presumed to extend the full width of the river; but if the estate includes one bank only, the grantee's right is presumed to stop at the *medium filum*[4]. Both rules of construction may, however, be displaced by the circumstances described at (3) and (4) below.

(3) *Indefinite boundaries: extrinsic evidence.* It is competent to use extrinsic evidence as an interpretative aid where the boundaries of the salmon fishings are not clear from the terms of the grant itself. A number of examples appear from the authorities. Thus evidence of possession, although for less than the full prescriptive period, may be treated as explicative of a grant[5]. Evidence as to the size of a river or loch may indicate whether the right conferred is intended to refer to the whole area or merely to a part[6]. Again, it may be shown that the particular words used 'have a certain definite and well-known signification, and had that signification at the time that the grant was made'[7]. Finally, evidence that the granter has made subsequent grants in the same waters may give some indication as to the intended scope of the original grant[8].

(4) *Indefinite boundaries: prescriptive possession.* The most conclusive, and most common, method of establishing the extent of indefinite boundaries is by possession for the prescriptive period. For prescription to operate the title must be *habile* to include the particular salmon fishings possessed. A title to the salmon fishings 'effeiring to' a particular estate is *habile* to include the fishings over the whole width of a river even where the estate includes only one of its banks[9]. Where, however, the title contains the express qualification that nets may be drawn on one bank of the river only, it is probably *inhabile* to prescribe a right beyond the *medium filum*[10].

1 Land Registration (Scotland) Act 1979 (c 33), s 3(1)(a).
2 Hume *Lectures* vol IV (Stair Soc vol 17, 1955 ed G C H Paton) p 246. See also *Mackenzie v Davidson* (1841) 3 D 646 at 656, 657, per Lord Moncreiff.
3 *Stuart v M'Barnet* (1868) 6 M (HL) 123. This presumption does not, of course, apply where estate and river are discontiguous.
4 *Earl of Zetland v Tennent's Trustees* (1873) 11 M 469 at 474, per Lord Cowan; *Fothringham v Passmore* 1984 SC (HL) 96, 1984 SLT 401.
5 *Fraser v Grant* (1866) 4 M 596 at 600, per Lord Benholme.
6 An example is *Mackenzie v Davidson* (1841) 3 D 646.
7 *Fraser v Grant* (1866) 4 M 596 at 598, per Lord Justice-Clerk Inglis.
8 *Mackenzie v Davidson* (1841) 3 D 646 at 651, per Lord Jeffrey.
9 *Earl of Zetland v Tennent's Trustees* (1873) 11 M 469; *Warrand's Trustees v Mackintosh* (1890) 17 R (HL) 13 at 19, per Lord Watson; *Fothringham v Passmore* 1984 SC (HL) 96, 1984 SLT 401.
10 But see *Forbes v Monymusk* (1623) Mor 10840, discussed in Stair *Institutions* II,3,69.

324. Acquisition by prescription: title. For a conveyance of salmon fishings to have immediate effect, it must contain in the dispositive clause the words 'salmon fishings' or at least the Latin equivalent[1]. But for a conveyance to serve merely as the foundation writ for positive prescription the law is less strict and the more general word 'fishings' suffices[2]. Indeed in the case of barony titles even 'fishings' is not essential[3]. The grant need not flow, or bear to flow, from the Crown[4]. The rules are presumably the same for Land Register titles, except that the required word or words must appear on the title sheet itself[5]. One surprising result of these rules is that the title required for an initially valid grant on the one hand and for a valid foundation writ on the other is not the same. This disparity is unknown in other kinds of heritable rights[6], and indeed Hume was prompted to deny its existence by arguing that a title merely with 'fishings' should also be regarded as a valid grant, a view which has not, however, been adopted in the modern law[7].

1 See para 322 above.
2 Stair *Institutions* II,3,69; Bankton *Institute* II,3,111; Erskine *Institute* II,6,15; Bell *Principles* s 1112. As to whether it is sufficient if 'fishings' appears in the *tenendas* clause of a grant in feu, see W M Gordon *Scottish Land Law* (1989) p 213.
3 *Bankton* II,3,111; *Erskine* II,6,18; *Nicol v Lord Advocate* (1868) 6 M 972; *Duke of Richmond v Earl of Seafield* (1870) 8 M 530. The view expressed in *Stair* II,3,61, that a barony title carries the right of salmon fishings *ab initio* and without prescription has not been followed.
4 *Gordon* at p 211 doubts whether in such a case the title acquired is good against the Crown, but if prescription operates at all it can only do so to the effect of conferring ownership. At the end of ten years the grantee either owns the right or he does not, and if he does own it his right is necessarily good against the Crown. It is expressly provided by s 24 of the Prescription and Limitation (Scotland) Act 1973 (c 52) that the Act binds the Crown.
5 Prescription and Limitation (Scotland) Act 1973, s 1(1) (amended by the Land Registration (Scotland) Act 1979 (c 33), s 10). Indemnity must have been excluded.
6 Except for the separate tenements of mussels and oysters (see para 332 below) and port and ferry (see para 334 below).
7 Hume *Lectures* vol IV (Stair Soc vol 17, 1955 ed G C H Paton) p 247. Indeed in the modern law the wording of s 1(1) of the Prescription and Limitation (Scotland) Act 1973 may prompt the opposite argument, namely that a title not containing the words 'salmon fishings' is not 'sufficient in respect of its terms to constitute . . . a title' and hence not sufficient to found prescription.

325. Acquisition by prescription: possession. The period of possession which must be shown by a party relying on prescription is ten years, except in a question with the Crown when it is twenty years[1]. The nature of the possession required has been summarised by Lord Kinnear in the following terms:

'To convert his title from a grant in its own nature defective, into a valid and effectual right, he must prove full and continuous possession by a method recognised by the law, and commonly known to be lawful. His possession must be of such a character as to show at once that it is not precarious or a thing to be tolerated, but is enjoyed as the exercise of an undoubted right; and therefore such as to lead to an immediate challenge as soon as it is exercised'[2].

In the open sea, fishing either by fixed nets or by net and coble is sufficient possession to establish prescription[3]. In inland waters, where the use of fixed nets is prohibited, net and coble fishing is regarded as the most satisfactory form of possession. Lord Kinnear explains further:

'The characteristics of net and coble which make it evidence of full possession as of right are perfectly clear. In the first place, it is the general and well-known method of exercising the right . . . And secondly . . . it involves the most complete and decided adverse possession of the bank of the river . . . For these reasons, it cannot be imputed to tolerance'[4].

Fishing by rod and line does not share these characteristics and at one time was regarded as insufficient to establish prescription[5]. It will be apparent that fishing by rod and line can more readily be imputed to tolerance; and since trout are also fished by this method there may be no open assertion of a right to salmon. The law, however, is now that fishing by rod and line will set up prescription provided it is the usual, or at any rate a usual, means of fishing the waters in question[6].

When possession proceeds by agreement, prescription is usually excluded, and it has been held that where *ex adverso* proprietors agree to share the fishing in particular waters in a particular way no prescriptive rights can be established from the possession following on from the agreement[7]. Prescriptive possession is governed by the rule _tantum praescriptum quantum possessum_ and, except in the case of barony titles, no rights are acquired over parts of the water not actually fished[8].

1 Prescription and Limitation (Scotland) Act 1973 (c 52), s 1(1), (4).
2 _Maxwell v Lamont_ (1903) 6 F 245 at 260, 11 SLT 531 at 536.
3 _M'Douall v Lord Advocate_ (1875) 2 R (HL) 49.
4 _Maxwell v Lamont_ (1903) 6 F 245 at 260, 261, 11 SLT 531 at 537. See also _Ramsay v Duke of Roxburghe_ (1848) 10 D 661 at 665, per Lord Justice-Clerk Hope.
5 _Chisholm v Fraser_ (1801) Mor 'Salmon fishing' App No 1; _Duke of Sutherland v Ross_ (1836) 14 S 960.
6 _Stuart v M'Barnet_ (1868) 6 M (HL) 123; _Duke of Richmond v Earl of Seafield_ (1870) 8 M 530; _Duke of Roxburghe v Waldie's Trustees_ (1879) 6 R 663; _Warrand's Trustees v Mackintosh_ (1890) 17 R (HL) 13. There are, however, special rules for the right of salmon fishing by cruives: see para 326 below.
7 _Milne v Smith_ (1850) 13 D 112; _Fothringham v Passmore_ 1984 SC (HL) 96, 1984 SLT 401.
8 See eg _Richardson v Hay_ (1862) 24 D 775. For barony titles, cf _Lord Advocate v Cathcart_ (1871) 9 M 744 with _Lord Advocate v Lord Lovat_ (1880) 7 R (HL) 122.

326. Exercise of salmon fishing rights. The proprietor of salmon fishings may fish the waters in respect of which his right subsists at all permitted times and by all permitted methods[1]. In inland waters[2] the only methods of fishing which are permitted are net and coble, rod and line and, exceptionally, cruive-fishing[3]. Fishing by net and coble involves the use of a moving net which is swept through the water[4]. Beyond estuary limits and in the open sea the use of fixed engines such as stake nets is also permitted[5]. The estuary limits of more than 200 salmon rivers were fixed in the nineteenth century by the Salmon Fishery Commissioners appointed under the Salmon Fisheries (Scotland) Act 1862[6]. Cruive-fishing, which is only permitted in inland waters which are also non-tidal, was at one time highly prized but is now obsolete[7]. A cruive (or zair) is a box placed in a dam designed to trap fish entering into it. Cruive-fishing was not carried by a normal grant of salmon fishings but required either a special grant or prescriptive possession[8]. There is both a weekly and an annual close time during which salmon may not be taken by any method[9].

The right to fish for salmon is an exclusive one and, as in other cases of trespass on proprietary rights, may be protected by interdict[10]. Fishing for salmon without title or permission is also a criminal offence[11].

It is thought that the right to salmon carries also the right to other fish such as trout. But the right to other fish is not an exclusive right and must be shared, in the case of non-tidal waters with the riparian proprietor or proprietors[12], and in the case of tidal waters with the public at large[13]. The right of trout fishing yields to the right of salmon fishing and must be exercised in such a way that the salmon fishing is not materially prejudiced[14].

The proprietor of salmon fishings is subject to a number of restrictions in the exercise of his right. He is, for example, burdened by a number of common interest obligations enforceable by the other holders of salmon fishings in the same waters[15]; and in non-tidal rivers there is an additional common interest obligation, enforceable by the riparian proprietors, to avoid any act which affects the natural flow of the river except for the act of fishing itself or anything reasonably incidental thereto[16]. In navigable waters there must be no interference with the public right of navigation[17]. Finally, there are a number of statutory restrictions which are policed by district salmon fishery boards[18].

The right of salmon fishing is not lost when waters alter their course but accompanies the waters to their new location[19]. Nor is the right lost _non utendo_ by the operation of negative prescription for, as a separate tenement commanding its own infeftment[20], it is classified as a 'real right of ownership in land' and is imprescriptible[21].

1 See generally FISHERIES, vol 11, paras 5 ff.
2 'Inland waters' include all rivers above estuary limits and their tributary streams, and all waters, watercourses and lochs whether natural or artificial draining into the sea: Salmon and Freshwater Fisheries (Protection) (Scotland) Act 1951 (c 26), s 24(1).

3 Ibid, s 2(1), Cruive fishing, although not specified, comes within the proviso for 'any right of fishing for salmon in existence at the commencement of this Act'.

4 See FISHERIES, vol 11, para 11. A coble is a small, flat-bottomed boat, and traditionally one end of the net was guided by a person who was in the coble.

5 *Earl of Kintore v Forbes* (1826) 4 S 641 (NE 648), affd (1828) 3 W & S 261, HL.

6 Salmon Fisheries (Scotland) Act 1862 (c 97), s 6(1) (repealed). A complete list is given in S Scott Robinson *The Law of Game, Salmon and Freshwater Fishing in Scotland* (1990) pp 203–215. It is provided by the Salmon Act 1986 (c 62), s 7(1), that 'the estuary limits of a river shall be the limits fixed by judicial decision or fixed and defined under s 6(1) of the Salmon Fisheries (Scotland) Act 1862'.

7 In 1965 the Hunter Committee found cruive-fishing in existence only in two or three places. See *Second Report of the Committee on Scottish Salmon and Trout Fisheries* (the 'Hunter Report') (Cmnd 2691) (1965).

8 On cruive fishing, see further: Hume *Lectures* vol IV (Stair Soc vol 17, 1955 ed G C H Paton) pp 248–252; J Rankine *The Law of Land-ownership in Scotland* (4th edn, 1909) p 321.

9 See FISHERIES, vol 11, paras 14 ff.

10 For trespass, see paras 180 ff above.

11 Salmon and Freshwater Fisheries (Protection) (Scotland) Act 1951, s 1 (amended by the Freshwater and Salmon Fisheries (Scotland) Act 1976 (c 22), Sch 2, and the Salmon Act 1986 (c 62), Sch 4, para 7).

12 See paras 280, 306, above.

13 See para 521 below.

14 For non-tidal waters see *Mackenzie v Rose* (1830) 8 S 816; *Somerville v Smith* (1859) 22 D 279. For tidal waters, see para 515 below.

15 See further para 330 below.

16 See paras 282 ff above.

17 See paras 519, 520, 523, below.

18 See further FISHERIES, VOL 11, PARAS 31 FF.

19 *Straiton v Fullarton and Scott* (1752) Mor 12797; *Brodie v Nairn Magistrates* (1796) Mor 12830.

20 See para 322 above.

21 Prescription and Limitation (Scotland) Act 1973 (c 52), s 8, Sch 3(a).

327. Ancillary rights: introduction. The immediately preceding paragraph sets out the rights of a proprietor of salmon fishings within his own waters. In many cases, however, salmon fishing would scarcely be possible unless the proprietor had a number of additional rights beyond his own boundaries. Three distinct sets of additional, ancillary rights are recognised by the law, namely (1) rights over adjacent dry land, (2) rights across the *medium filum*, and (3) rights to the free passage of salmon. The first two comprise positive rights which may most conveniently be classified as part of the content of the principal right of salmon fishing[1]. The third set of rights operates only negatively and is part of the intricate network of common interest rights and obligations which is found in rivers and lochs.

1 This attribution may receive some support from *Miller v Blair* (1825) 4 S 214 (NE 217) and from the observation by Lord Justice-Clerk Hope in *Berry v Wilson* (1841) 4 D 139 at 147, that salmon fishings being a right of property and not a right of servitude, its proprietor also owns 'the use of the shore' (although not the shore itself). Alternative attributions are unpromising. Thus it seems clear from the cases, and also for other reasons, that the ancillary rights cannot be explained on the basis of servitude; and the absence of positive obligations on the 'servient' proprietor, and of any reciprocal counter-obligations, makes common interest an unnecessary and unconvincing explanation.

328. Rights over adjacent dry land. Where the right of salmon fishings is separately owned from the dry land immediately adjacent to the waters, the proprietor of the former has certain rights of use in respect of the latter. These rights are distinct from, and in addition to, the right in the general public to use the foreshore for the purposes of fishing[1]. In general, a proprietor of salmon fishings is entitled to make all uses of the banks or foreshore adjacent to the waters as are reasonably required for the conduct of his fishing. Thus he may use the land for necessary access to the waters on foot, or even by car or other vehicle if this is required either by the type of fishings or by the distance to the waters[2]. On arrival he may continue the use as a base for fishing, for example for casting his line, for drawing his nets, and for carrying out repairs to his tackle[3]. The uses must, however, meet the criterion of reasonableness, a principle which has been held to exclude the construction of a hut[4] and of a towing path[5]; and they must be exercised in a manner as little detrimental to the proprietor of the ground as is consistent with a full beneficial use of the right of salmon fishing[6]. The rights implied by law may be extended by servitude, whether created by grant or by possession for the twenty years of positive prescription[7].

1 See para 525 below.
2 *Miller v Blair* (1825) 4 S 214 (NE 217); *Middletweed Ltd v Murray* 1989 SLT 11, OH. It was said in the *Middletweed* case (at 14) that no account can be taken of the fact that the person seeking access is disabled.
3 Erskine *Institute* II,6,15; Hume *Lectures* vol IV (Stair Soc vol 17, 1955 ed G C H Paton) p 246; Bell *Principles* s 1120; *Mathew v Blair* (1612) Mor 14263; *Monymusk v Forbes* (1623) Mor 10783, 10840; *Lord Advocate v Sharp* (1878) 6 R 108.
4 *Mackinnon v Ellis* (1878) 5 R 832.
5 *Forbes v Smith* (1824) 2 S 721 (NE 602).
6 *Miller v Blair* (1825) 4 S 214 (NE 217).
7 *Middletweed Ltd v Murray* 1989 SLT 11, OH.

329. Rights across the *medium filum*. It frequently happens that the width of a single river is subject to the salmon rights of different proprietors, fishing from opposite sides. The line dividing the rights of *ex adverso* proprietors in this situation may be fixed by the respective titles of the parties or by prescriptive possession, but in the absence of either it is the *medium filum* of the river[1]. Until the decision of the House of Lords in *Fothringham v Passmore*[2] in 1984 the rule was thought to be that neither proprietor could fish across the river beyond his own boundaries and into the territory of his neighbour[3]. *Fothringham* introduced a new rule, namely that 'the riparian proprietor of one bank of a river having the right of salmon fishing is entitled to fish over so much of the stream as he can reach from his own territory by any lawful method of fishing'[4]. On the basis of this rule each *ex adverso* proprietor may fish into the waters of his neighbour provided that he himself remains stationed on his own side of the dividing line. In practice, *ex adverso* proprietors do not usually insist on their rights and some arrangement is reached whereby each fishes the whole width of the river on alternate days or on some other equitable basis. In *Fothringham* it was said that if the proprietors cannot agree on an arrangement of this kind, 'and if their enjoyment of their respective rights is seriously prejudiced in consequence, it will be for the Court to regulate their rights'[5], but the regulatory jurisdiction of the court has been questioned[6].

1 See para 323, head (2), above.
2 *Fothringham v Passmore* 1984 SC (HL) 96, 1984 SLT 401. On this case see further, K G C Reid 'Salmon Fishing in Troubled Waters' 1985 SLT (News) 217; C F Forder 'Tales from the River Bank' 1986 JR 25.
3 *Gay v Malloch* 1959 SC 110, 1959 SLT 132.
4 *Fothringham v Passmore* 1984 SC (HL) 96 at 139, 1984 SLT 401 at 413, per Lord Keith.
5 1984 SC (HL) 96 at 130, 1984 SLT 401 at 408, per Lord Fraser.
6 J Rankine *The Law of Land-ownership in Scotland* (4th edn, 1909) pp 314, 315; 'Regulation?' 1984 SLT (News) 336. Rankine suggests that court regulation is confined to cases of *pro indiviso* ownership, for which see para 30 above.

330. Right to the free passage of salmon. 'Among the several grants [of salmon fishings] which may subsist in the same river, the peculiar migratory habits[1] of the fish confer on the successive grantees a common interest, like that in running water'[2]. Thus, within the confines of a salmon river or loch, each proprietor of fishings has a right of common interest, enforceable against the riparian proprietors[3] and the other holders of salmon rights[4] alike, to the free passage of salmon from other parts of the waters to his own. This right is in addition to any rights which may arise under the general law, for example the law of nuisance or delict[5]. The common interest right enables the proprietor of salmon fishings to complain of obstructions downstream of his own beat which hinder or prevent the progress of fish upstream; and it has been held that the proprietor is also entitled to complain of obstructions which are upstream and which can have no direct effect on his fishing[6]. The obligation imposed by common interest is purely negative in character. The servient proprietors are not obliged to promote the progress of salmon; their duty is simply to refrain from any positive act — other than the act of fishing itself — which obstructs that progress.

The meaning of obstruction was considered by Lord President Inglis in *West v Aberdeen Harbour Commissioners*:

'... what is an obstruction in the legal sense? An improvement in the means of fishing, by which the lower heritor increases the produce of his fishings, is no obstruction, unless there is something illegal or objectionable in the mode by which he effects it. There is in one sense no more fatal obstruction to the passage of a fish than catching it ... There must be an obstruction that will prevent the passage of the fish ...'[7].

An obstruction which does not prevent the passage of fish is not actionable by a holder of the right of salmon fishings[8]. The obstruction need not be a physical barrier. Illegal methods of fishing[9], actings leading to a material reduction in the flow of water[10], and pollution[11] are all obstructions in the sense of the common interest obligation. Certain obstructions may, however, be justified as in exercise of servitude rights[12], while the right to challenge others may be lost by the long negative prescription[13].

Although circumstances may be envisaged in which the salmon fishings in one river are adversely affected by the actings of parties in another river or in the open sea, it is unclear whether the reciprocal network of common interest extends beyond the confines of individual units of water so as to give a proprietor in one unit a remedy against a proprietor in another[14].

The Secretary of State is empowered by the Salmon Act 1986 to make regulations with respect inter alia to obstructions in rivers or estuaries to the passage of salmon[15].

1 For an account of the migratory habits of salmon, see S Scott Robinson *The Law of Game, Salmon and Freshwater Fishing in Scotland* (1990) pp 72–73.

2 Bell *Principles* s 1112. See also Bell s 1119 and Hume *Lectures* vol IV (Stair Soc vol 17, 1955 ed G C H Paton) p 252.

3 Eg *Earl of Kintore v Pirie & Sons Ltd* (1903) 5 F 818, 10 SLT 485, (1906) 8 F 1085, 13 SLT 131, affd (1906) 8 F (HL) 16, 14 SLT 215.

4 Eg *West v Aberdeen Harbour Comrs* (1876) 4 R 207.

5 *Clements v Shell UK Ltd* 1991 GWD 35–2153. Claims under the general law may also be made against parties other than riparian proprietors and proprietors of salmon fishings.

6 *Colquhoun v Duke of Montrose* (1804) Mor 14283.

7 *West v Aberdeen Harbour Comrs* (1876) 4 R 207 at 211, per Lord President Inglis.

8 *West v Aberdeen Harbour Comrs* (1876) 4 R 207; *Duke of Sutherland v Ross* (1877) 4 R 765 (affd (1878) 5 R (HL) 137). If, however, the proprietor of salmon fishings is also a riparian proprietor, it may be actionable as a breach of the common interest right to an uninterrupted flow of water: see paras 284 ff above.

9 *Colquhoun v Duke of Montrose* (1793) Mor 12827; *Colquhoun v Duke of Montrose* (1804) Mor 14283.

10 *Earl of Kintore v Pirie & Sons Ltd* (1903) 5 F 818, 10 SLT 485, (1906) 8 F 1058, 13 SLT 131, affd (1906) 8 F (HL) 16, 14 SLT 215.

11 *Moncreiffe v Perth Police Comrs* (1886) 13 R 921.

12 Notably the servitude of damhead, for which see para 295 above. *Robertson v M'Kenzie and Graham* (1750) Mor 14290 may be an example of a servitude.

13 Prescription and Limitation (Scotland) Act 1973 (c 52), s 7. And see *Earl of Kintore v Pirie & Sons Ltd* (1903) 5 F 818, (1903) 10 SLT 485.

14 See further *Munro v Ross* (1846) 8 D 1029; *Johnston v Mackenzie and Beattie* (1868, unreported) summarised in C Stewart *The Law of Scotland relating to Rights of Fishing* (2nd edn, 1892 by J C Shairp) pp 153–154.

15 Salmon Act 1986 (c 62), s 3(2)(e). This power has not yet been exercised.

(c) The Right to gather Mussels and Oysters

331. Ownership. The question of ownership involves consideration of the anterior question of whether mussels and oysters are heritable property or moveable property. Since mussel and oyster scalps are found on the seabed, on the foreshore and on rocks, it has often been suggested that they are heritable, by operation of accession. Thus Lord Neaves:

'With regard to mussel-scalps . . . I consider these to be *partes soli* from their nature . . . The mussel has powers and organs of locomotion, which it puts in operation particularly early in life; but when it has once settled down and fixed its domicile, it seems to do so *animo remanendi* and there it remains generally for the full period of its life, till dislodged by some violent means'[1].

If this view is accepted, mussels and oysters belong to the proprietor of the *solum* to which they accede. An alternative, and perhaps preferable, view is that the degree of attachment to the *solum* is insufficient for accession to operate; from which it would follow that mussels and oysters were moveable property, *res nullius* and available for acquisition by occupation, so that the first person to appropriate them, whether by gathering or by marking out for further cultivation, became owner by that act of appropriation[2]. A definitive choice between these competing views has yet to be made[3].

1 *Duchess of Sutherland v Watson* (1868) 6 M 199 at 211. See also *Lindsay v Robertson* (1867) 5 M 864 at 868, per Lord Benholme; *Secretary of State for Scotland v Inverness-shire Assessor* 1948 SC 334, 1948 SLT 413, LVAC, *Mull Shellfish Ltd v Golden Sea Produce Ltd* 1992 SLT 703.
2 *Wallace v Assessor for Wigtownshire* (1902) 4 F 515, 9 SLT 515; *Parker v Lord Advocate* (1902) 4 F 698, 9 SLT 306 (affd (1904) 6 F (HL) 37, 12 SLT 33).
3 The Sea Fisheries (Shellfish) Act 1967 (c 83), s 7(2), provides that
    (1) all shellfish in relation to a which a statutory grant of several fishery has been made in terms of s 1 of the Act, and
    (2) all oysters in or on a private oyster bed marked out or known as such,
    are the absolute property of the grantee or, as the case may be, of the owner of the oyster bed. But this provision adds little to the common law, because if mussels and oysters are heritable they belong to the owner of the bed to which they have acceded, and if they are moveable then, in the situations to which s 7(2) applies, they will usually have been acquired by the fisherman by *occupatio*.

332. Right to gather: private rights. There is no necessary connection between the right to gather on the one hand and the right of ownership on the other[1]; for the right to gather mussels and the separate right to gather oysters are, like the right to fish for salmon[2], both separate feudal tenements. But whereas in the case of salmon the status of separate tenement arises out of the intrinsic value of the fishings, in the case of mussels and oysters the reason is usually said to be the danger of exhaustion by indiscriminate fishing[3]. In the present state of the authorities it is impossible to determine with confidence whether the rights to mussels and oysters are legal separate tenements (that is, tenements automatically separate from ownership of the *solum*) or conventional separate tenements (that is, tenements capable of being severed by conveyance or reservation)[4]; but the analogies which are frequently drawn with salmon fishing suggest the former[5]. If this is correct, then mussel and oyster fishings are *inter regalia minora*, vested originally in the Crown, and capable of acquisition by subject proprietors by express grant or by possession for the prescriptive period[6] on a *habile* title. An express grant requires the mention of the shellfish by name, although this may be done by the incorporation of the terms of some other deed[7]; but a title is *habile* for the purposes of prescription if it contains a general grant of 'fishings'[8]. The Crown right may also be leased and this is sometimes done in connection with fish farming[9]. The right cannot pass by implication as a part and pertinent.

Fishing for mussels and oysters is regulated by various statutes, most notably by the Sea Fisheries (Shellfish) Act 1967[10]. In terms of the 1967 Act the Secretary of State is empowered to grant a right of 'several fishery' for oysters, mussels or certain other shellfish on any portion of the shore and bed of the sea or of an estuary or tidal river[11]. Such a grant confers on the grantee the exclusive right of depositing, propagating, dredging, fishing for and taking the shellfish in question[12]. This provides an alternative, statutory, method of acquiring a right to mussels and oysters.

1 If, however, mussels and oysters are heritable, then the right to gather is a privilege of ownership, and it is the shellfish (and not the right to gather) which is the separate tenement.
2 See para 322 above.
3 *Grant v Ross* (1764) Mor 12801, Kames Sel Dec 282; *Duke of Argyll v Robertson* (1859) 22 D 261 at 264, per Lord Mackenzie; *Lindsay v Robertson* (1867) 5 M 864 at 866, per Lord Justice-Clerk Patton.
4 For the distinction between legal and conventional separate tenements, see para 209 above.
5 The strongest authority is *Agnew v Stranraer Magistrates* (1822) 2 S 42 (NE 36). But see contra *Duchess of Sutherland v Watson* (1868) 6 M 199 at 213, 214, per Lord Neaves. If mussels and oysters are conventional separate tenements, then (until actually separated) the right to gather belongs to the proprietor of the waters in which they are found. For saltwater shellfish this will be the Crown, except in cases where the foreshore is in private ownership. But for freshwater shellfish this will be the private individuals who own the river in question. W M Gordon takes the view that freshwater mussels and oysters are in private ownership: *Scottish Land Law* (1989) para 8-26.
6 The prescriptive period is now ten years: Prescription and Limitation (Scotland) Act 1973 (c 52), s 1(1). Section 1(4) does not apply to mussels and oysters.
7 As will usually be the case for Land Register land, the terms of the title sheet being incorporated into the grant. See the Land Registration (Scotland) Act 1979 (c 33), s 15(1). For Sasine land, see the Conveyancing (Scotland) Act 1874 (c 94), s 61.
8 *Duke of Argyll v Robertson* (1859) 22 D 261; *Lindsay v Robertson* (1868) 7 M 239.
9 See *Mull Shellfish Ltd v Golden Sea Produce Ltd* 1992 SLT 703, although in that case the lease appears to have been of the seabed only.
10 See FISHERIES, vol 11, paras 121, 122, 155 ff.
11 Sea Fisheries (Shellfish) Act 1967 (c 83), s 1 (amended by the Sea Fisheries Act 1968 (c 77), s 15(1), (2), and the Fishing Limits Act 1976 (c 86), s 9(1), Sch 2, para 15).
12 Sea Fisheries (Shellfish) Act 1967, s 2.

333. Right to gather: public rights. At one time the general public may have been entitled to gather mussels and oysters in the sea, foreshore and tidal rivers, in the same way as they are still permitted to gather other shellfish such as limpets, cockles and shrimps[1]. Even with the establishment in the eighteenth century of the rule that exclusive grants of gathering could be made by the Crown[2], the public rights did not immediately disappear, and for some time the law adopted the intermediate position that, while mussel and oyster fishings granted out could only be exercised by the individual grantees, mussel and oyster fishings still held by the Crown could be exercised by everyone[3]. This position, however, did not survive the decision of the First Division and the House of Lords in *Parker v Lord Advocate*[4] in 1904. In that case the Crown, which had earlier leased the mussel fishings of a section of foreshore to a private individual, sought declarator and interdict against members of the public who were continuing to gather mussels. The action was successful, and the decision appears to mark the final assimilation of mussel and oyster fishings to salmon fishings.

1 Balfour *Practicks* (Stair Soc vol 22, 1963 ed P G B McNeill) p 626; *Hall v Whillis* (1852) 14 D 324. Other shellfish may not be gathered in non-tidal (ie private) waters, the right to gather being exclusive to the riparian proprietors.
2 See para 332 above.

3 *Grant v Ross* (1764) Mor 12801, Kames Sel Dec 282; *Duke of Argyll v Robertson* (1859) 22 D 261; *Lindsay v Robertson* (1868) 7 M 239.
4 *Parker v Lord Advocate* (1902) 4 F 698, 9 SLT 306, affd (1904) 6 F (HL) 37, 12 SLT 33.

(d) Port and Ferry

334. Form. The right of port (or harbour) and the separate right of ferry are, like the right to fish for salmon and the right to gather mussels and oysters[1], *inter regalia minora* and legal separate tenements[2]. The rights originate in the Crown and continue to be held by the Crown except where they have been transmitted to subject proprietors. In practice, however, the rights are never exercised by the Crown. Historically their special status is due mainly to the failure of royal power and resources to provide sufficient ports and ferries, and it was a common practice of the Crown to include grants of port and ferry in grants of land to royal burghs and in grants of barony. The rights of port and ferry are acquired either by express grant from the owner, whether the Crown or a subject proprietor, or by prescriptive possession on a *habile* title. As legal separate tenements the rights require to be expressly conveyed in the dispositive clause of the grant[3].

The rights of port and ferry are of little importance today. In most cases harbours, and such ferries as have not been replaced by bridges, are now regulated by private Acts of Parliament and no longer depend on feudal Crown grants[4]. Only a brief account of the law need be given here[5].

1 See paras 320–330 and 331–333 above respectively.
2 For separate tenements, see paras 207 ff above.
3 But a charter to a royal burgh or a barony title is also probably sufficient for the purposes of prescription. See *Duke of Montrose v Macintyre* (1848) 10 D 896; *Macpherson v Mackenzie* (1881) 8 R 706.
4 See HARBOURS, vol 11, paras 1301 ff, and LOCAL GOVERNMENT, vol 14, paras 441 ff.
5 See generally Bankton *Institute* I,3–5; Erskine *Institute* II,6,17; Hume *Lectures* vol IV (Stair Soc vol 17, 1955 ed G C H Paton) pp 238–243; Bell *Principles* ss 652–658. For a recent account, see W M Gordon *Scottish Land Law* (1989) pp 285 ff.

335. Content. Grants of port and ferry do not by themselves confer ownership of the land in respect of which the grant is to be exercised. In the typical case, however, ownership of the land is additionally conferred; and even where this is not done — and, since rights of port and ferry are separate tenements, it need not be done — certain ill-defined rights to use the land in connection with the grant are implied.

A grant of port or of ferry confers one principal right, which is balanced by one principal obligation. The right is the exclusive[1] right, within the physical limits of the grant, to provide for the use of the general public and in return for payment[2] a harbour or, as the case may be, a ferry for the transport of passengers and their luggage[3]. The obligation, which is due to the public at large and is technically part of the *regalia majora*, is 'an obligation to keep sufficient boats on the ferry for the use of travellers, or to maintain the port in a condition fit for receiving shipping'[4]. The obligation is not unlimited, however, for no more money need be expended than is earned in fees from the public[5].

1 See para 336 below.
2 Complicated and restrictive rules govern the amount of payment which can be exacted: see J Rankine *The Law of Land-ownership in Scotland* (4th edn, 1909) pp 290, 291, 302.
3 The right of ferry does not usually include the right to carry cargo.
4 Erskine *Institute* II,6,17.
5 *Officers of State v Christie* (1854) 16 D 454.

336. Monopoly rights. Grants of port or of ferry are often of considerable physical extent; and within the boundaries of a grant the holder has a monopoly on the provision of port or ferry facilities. More specifically, the monopoly means, in the case of a grant of port, that no other party is entitled to use the foreshore to load or unload goods without payment of the appropriate port dues, far less to construct a rival public harbour of his own[1]; and in the case of a grant of ferry it means that no other party is entitled to carry passengers, except for members of his family, guests and persons in his employment[2]. However, in places where grants of harbour or port do not exist, it appears that there is nothing to prevent the owners of the land from building their own private port or jetty, or from operating their own ferry, and appropriate charges may be made[3]. But where a jetty is built on the foreshore in such a way that it interferes with the public rights therein[4], the public cannot be prevented from using it and charges cannot be levied[5].

1 *Edinburgh Magistrates v Scot* (1836) 14 S 922.
2 *London Midland and Scottish Rly Co v M'Donald* 1924 SC 835, 1924 SLT 630.
3 1924 SC 835 at 842, 1924 SLT 630 at 633, per Lord Sands.
4 For which see paras 524–526 below.
5 *Earl of Stair v Austin* (1880) 8 R 183. But see contra *Colquhoun v Paton* (1853) 16 D 206, (1858) 21 D 996.

(6) WATER OUTSIDE A DEFINITE CHANNEL

(a) Introduction

337. Rights held by proprietor. Where water lies outside a definite channel, the proprietor of the land in which it is found has two principal rights, namely the right of free use[1] and the right of free drainage[2]. The rules are the same whether the water lies beneath or above the surface.

1 See para 338 below.
2 See para 339 below.

338. Free use. Water outside a definite channel may be freely used and disposed of by the proprietor of the land in which it is found. Indeed on one view of the law such water may be regarded as his property[1]. The complex regime of common interest rights and obligations which regulates water found within definite channels has no counterpart here. But this is subject to the doctrine of *aemulatio vicini,* and a proprietor must not intercept percolating water merely out of spite towards his neighbour[2].

1 See para 274 above.
2 Scots law does not follow the rule for England and Wales set out in *Bradford Corpn v Pickles* [1895] AC 587, HL. See NUISANCE, vol 14, paras 2034, 2035.

339. Free drainage. The proprietor of low-lying ground is under an obligation to receive such water as runs naturally off a superior neighbour's land[1]. He has no claim for damages in respect of such water but must protect his own land as best he can consistent with allowing the water to drain freely from the superior land[2]. If he fails to allow free drainage he will be liable in damages for flooding or any other injury caused to the superior land[3]. He need not, however, receive a greater quantity of water than arises in the course of nature, except where there is a separate obligation to do so constituted as a servitude.

But while the proprietor of superior land thus has a right of free drainage, it is not a right which he is bound to exercise. He may have other uses for the water. Equally the inferior proprietor cannot require that a subsisting pattern of drainage into his land be continued, except where a servitude right has been established[4].

1 *Campbell v Bryson* (1864) 3 M 254. This is a 'natural servitude' or alternatively a right founded on common interest. See para 359, head (5), below.
2 Bell *Principles* s 969.
3 *Plean Precast Ltd v National Coal Board* 1985 SC 77, 1986 SLT 78, OH. But it may be doubted whether the finding of strict liability survives the decision of the House of Lords in *RHM Bakeries (Scotland) Ltd v Strathclyde Regional Council* 1985 SC (HL) 17, 1985 SLT 214.
4 *Prestoun v Erskine* (1714) Mor 10919; *Milton v Glen-Moray Glenlivet Distillery Co Ltd* (1898) 1 F 135, 6 SLT 5, 206. For an unsuccessful attempt to show a servitude right, see *Anderson v Robertson* 1958 SC 367.

(b) Surface Water

340. Drainage rights under common law. Surface water may be defined as water which arises in the course of nature, whether from the sky or from neighbouring land, and which then lies on the surface of land without occupying any definite channel. The term includes *stagna*[1], bogs and mosses, but not streams or lochs. Since Scotland has a superfluity of surface water the development of the law has been concerned mainly with questions of drainage. On this matter the governing principle is the rule already described[2], namely that water outside a definite channel is permitted to drain with the natural inclinations of the land. The rule is described by Erskine thus:

'Where two contiguous fields belong to different proprietors, one of which stands upon higher grounds than the other, nature itself may be said to constitute a servitude on the inferior tenement, by which it is obliged to receive the water that falls from the superior'[3].

The water may drain so as to feed a stream or pool situated wholly or partly in the inferior land, or it may remain as surface water. In either case the legal principle is the same.

The proprietor of superior land is entitled to alter the drainage provided by nature by the construction of artificial drainage works or by other acts of construction which have an incidental effect on drainage[4]. The proprietor of inferior land is bound to receive the water drained by artificial works, but has no corresponding right to require that the works be maintained in their existing form[5]. There are, however, a number of constraints on the superior proprietor. The works must fall wholly within his own territory[6], and must not be contrary to existing servitude rights[7]. The construction must be in the course of the 'natural use of his property'[8], and agricultural use will be regarded more favourably than use for a building development[9]. Certainly there is no right, in the absence of the servitude of eavesdrop, to collect rainwater on the roof of a house thereafter allowing it to fall on the land of a neighbour. The works must drain only such water as arises naturally on the property, and in a direction which follows the natural lie of the land. It has been suggested, however, that water rising naturally to the surface as a result of mining operations — as opposed to water which has been artificially pumped — falls within the superior proprietor's right[10]. Finally, in the exercise of his right the superior proprietor must have regard to the possible injury to the lands of the inferior proprietor. 'But as this right may be overstretched in the use of it, without necessity, to the prejudice of the inferior grounds, the question, How far it may be extended under particular circumstances must be arbitrary'[11]. It has been held that the right of drainage is not 'overstretched' unless it can be shown both that there have been damaging consequences to the inferior proprietor and that the actions of the superior proprietor are open to criticism as being an undue pressing of his rights[12]. Damages are not due in the absence of fault[13].

1 A *stagnum* is a loch or pool which has no outlet except in wet weather. See further para 303 above.
2 See para 339 above.

3 Erskine *Institute* II,9,2. See also Bankton *Institute* II,7,30; *Erskine* II,1,2; Bell *Principles* ss 968, 969.
4 *Erskine* II,9,2; *Plean Precast Ltd v National Coal Board* 1985 SC 77, 1986 SLT 78, OH.
5 *Anderson v Robertson* 1958 SC 367.
6 But see para 341 below.
7 *Crichton v Turnbull* 1946 SC 52, 1946 SLT 156.
8 *Erskine* II,9,2.
9 *Logan v Wang (UK) Ltd* 1991 SLT 580 at 584, OH, per Lord Prosser. See also para 343 below.
10 *Young & Co v Bankier Distillery Co* (1893) 20 R (HL) 76, 1 SLT 204; *Bankton* II,7,30. See also para 343 below.
11 *Erskine* II,9,2.
12 *Logan v Wang (UK) Ltd* 1991 SLT 580, especially at 584, OH, per Lord Prosser. In the same passage it is suggested that the actions of the superior proprietor must amount to actings *in aemulationem vicini*, but this appears to set an unduly high standard. See also *Campbell v Bryson* (1864) 3 M 254 at 259, per Lord Justice-Clerk Inglis; *Alvis v Harrison* 1989 SLT 746 (revsd on a different point 1991 SLT 64, HL).
13 *Noble's Trustees v Economic Forestry (Scotland) Ltd* 1988 SLT 662, OH.

341. Drainage rights by statute. A substantial statutory overlay to the common law is contained in statutes such as the Land Drainage (Scotland) Acts of 1930 and 1958[1]. By section 2 of the 1930 Act, for example, the owner of agricultural land which is being injured, or in danger of being injured, through the refusal of a neighbour to allow underground drainage through his land, may apply to the sheriff for authority to carry out the work. Statutory drainage rights are considered more fully elsewhere in this work[2].

1 Land Drainage (Scotland) Acts 1930 (c 20) and 1958 (c 24).
2 WATER AND WATER RIGHTS, vol 25, paras 363 ff.

(c) Underground Water

342. General principles. Like surface water, underground water outside a definite channel[1] is governed by the two general principles set out at the beginning of this section[2]. Thus, in the first place, water lying under land as a result of natural percolation may be intercepted and extracted by the proprietor of that land. So long as the presence of the water is due to natural causes, it is no objection to extraction that the water is percolating towards, or has percolated from, a stream or field belonging to someone else[3]. But subject to the exception noted below[4], a proprietor may not undertake works designed to attract water from another's land against the course of nature. In the second place, insofar as the water is not intercepted and used by the proprietor of land, it must be received by the proprietor of any adjoining land into which it naturally percolates. The servient proprietor is not entitled to check the natural progress of underground water across his boundaries by the erection of a barrier or by other artificial means[5].

1 For underground water confined to a definite channel, see para 301 above.
2 See paras 338, 339, above.
3 *Milton v Glen-Moray Glenlivet Distillery Co Ltd* (1898) 1 F 135, 6 SLT 5, 206.
4 See para 343 below.
5 *Hope v Wauchope* (1779) Mor 14538, which is an authority to the contrary, seems unlikely to be followed today.

343. Mining operations. The two rules set out in the immediately preceding paragraph might appear to make mining operations unlawful, for, by destroying the natural subterranean stratification, mining serves both to attract water and also to send water away in a manner materially different from that provided by nature.

However, this difficulty is avoided by treating mining as a 'natural' use of land, and the consequences of mining conducted in the normal way as 'natural' consequences. The rules therefore remain unbreached, while at the same time permitting mining by normal methods[1].

1 In *Durham v Hood* (1871) 9 M 474 at 479, Lord President Inglis said: 'There can be no doubt . . . that the owner of a mine is entitled to work out the minerals without regard to the interests of his neighbour, so long as he confines his operations to his own grounds, and resorts to no extraordinary means of working; and if the effect of working out these minerals be to throw water down upon his neighbour who lies upon a lower level than himself, that is just the natural servitude which the lower heritor below ground must submit to, as the lower heritor above ground does'. See also *Blair v Hunter Finlay & Co* (1870) 9 M 204; *Harvey v Wardrop* (1824) 3 S 322 (NE 229); *Wilsons v Waddell* (1876) 3 R 288, affd (1876) 4 R (HL) 29. For proper and improper means of working, see para 261, note 3, above.

7. REAL CONDITIONS

(1) DEFINITION

344. Terminology. Servitudes, real burdens[1] and rights of common interest all belong to the same juridical family, a proposition which is both beyond doubt and yet is asserted less frequently than perhaps it ought to be[2]. Certain other rights are also family members[3]. No single name for this family of rights commands universal acceptance[4]. In this title the term 'real conditions' is used, but with the warning that the term 'real conditions' is sometimes employed by other writers in a narrower sense, namely as a synonym for real burdens[5]. This section considers real conditions as a general category, and also considers rights of common interest. Real burdens and servitudes are dealt with separately[6].

Real conditions, in the sense used in this title, are rights held by a person in his capacity as proprietor of property and enforceable in relation to some other property of which he is not the proprietor. Real conditions may be either *in rem* (in a thing) or *in personam* (against a person). A real condition *in rem*, for example a servitude, is a *jus in re aliena*, a right in property belonging to someone else. A real condition *in personam*[7], for example a real burden, is a right enforceable against some other person in his capacity as proprietor of other property. A fundamental feature of real conditions, whether *in rem* or *in personam*, is the existence of two separate pieces of property, namely a dominant property (or dominant tenement) to which the right of enforcement attaches, and a servient property (or servient tenement) in respect of which the right may be exercised[8]. Real conditions 'run with' the dominant and the servient property, a characteristic which is usually taken as justifying the epithet 'real', although strictly only real conditions *in rem* are real rights[9].

Real conditions are found both in heritable and in moveable property, but mainly in the former. They may be said to have three defining characteristics. First, the creditor in the condition derives his rights from the fact of ownership of the dominant property. Secondly, either the condition is held *in rem*, as a true real right over the servient property, or else it is enforceable against successive proprietors of that property. However, even in the case of conditions *in rem*, the person against whom enforcement is usually sought is the proprietor for the time being of the servient property. Thirdly, the condition observes certain rules as to content. In particular the condition burdens the servient property or, as the case may be, the servient proprietor in a manner which is of benefit to the dominant property. These three characteristics may now be considered in turn[10].

1 In this context 'real burdens' means conditions of title found in conveyances and does not refer to the, now obsolete, heritable security which was known by the same name: see para 375 below.
2 For a fuller discussion of many of the points mentioned here, see K G C Reid 'Defining Real Conditions' 1989 JR 69.
3 See paras 349 ff below.
4 Another name sometimes used, at least for conditions relating to land, is 'land obligations': see Conveyancing and Feudal Reform (Scotland) Act 1970 (c 35), s 1(2).
5 See para 375 below. See also CONVEYANCING, vol 6, para 496, which refers to a 'semantic jungle'. In the terminology used in this volume a real burden is a *type* of real condition. A further, statutory, use of the term 'real condition' is for conditions imposed in assignations of leases: see Law Reform (Miscellaneous Provisions) (Scotland) Act 1985 (c 73), s 3, and para 352 below.
6 See respectively paras 375 ff and 439 ff below.
7 At first sight is seems contradictory to talk of a 'real' condition as being *'in personam'*. However, as is explained at para 7, head (2), above, 'real' in the context of 'real condition' does not signify a real right *stricto sensu*.
8 The terms 'dominant tenement' and 'servient tenement' are those traditionally used in the context of servitudes. Possible alternative terms, which have the blessing of statute, are 'benefited proprietor' and 'burdened proprietor': see the Conveyancing and Feudal Reform (Scotland) Act 1970, s 1(2).
9 For real rights, see paras 3 ff above.
10 See paras 345–348 below.

345. Right to enforce derived from ownership of dominant property. The creditor in a real condition (the 'dominant proprietor') is the proprietor for the time being of that property which, in compliance with the rules of creation appropriate to the condition in question, has been identified as the dominant property[1]. No other person may enforce the condition and nor may it competently be assigned to a third party[2]. The right to enforce is carried by implication in a conveyance of the dominant property and no special assignation is required[3]. Ownership is therefore the sole determinant of right to enforce, and for real conditions in land it is thought that actual infeftment is required[4]. In the case of positive servitudes[5], and possibly in other cases also, third parties may sometimes make use of a particular right, such as a servitude right of way, where the permission of the dominant proprietor has been given, but they have no independent rights of enforcement.

Sometimes there is more than one dominant property in respect of the same real condition. Real burdens, for example, may be enforceable both by a superior and also by co-feuars. Subdivision of the original dominant property will usually bring about the same result[6], although in particular cases a subdivided part of the former whole may be too distant from the servient property to show benefit from the condition[7]. However, subdivision of the dominant property is not always competent[8]. Finally, where the dominant property comes to be owned by two or more people *pro indiviso*, each *pro indiviso* proprietor is a dominant proprietor but subject to the usual rules of joint or common property which require combined action in the enforcement of property rights[9].

1 Thus a servitude cannot be acquired by a mere tenant: see *Douglas v Crossflags (Motors) Ltd* 1989 GWD 22-941, Sh Ct. It is this feature of running with the dominant property which distinguishes servitudes from other subordinate real rights such as leases and rights in security: see Stair *Institutions* II, 7, preamble ('not being subservient directly to persons, but to things') and Erskine *Institute* II, 9, 5. See further para 7 above.
2 *Bannerman's Trustees v Howard and Wyndham* (1902) 10 SLT 2 at 3, per Lord Moncreiff; *J A Mactaggart & Co v Harrower* (1906) 8 F 1101 at 1106, 14 SLT 277 at 280, Dean of Guild Court. This refers to assignation of the creditor's interest in a real condition. However, where a particular breach of a condition has occurred giving rise to a claim in damages, there seems no reason why that specific claim should not be assignable: see *Stevenson v Steel Co of Scotland Ltd* (1899) 1 F (HL) 91.
3 See eg *Braid Hills Hotel Co Ltd v Manuels* 1909 SC 120, 16 SLT 523.

4 See paras 397, 406, below.
5 See para 464 below.
6 We are concerned here with physical subdivision. For feudal subdivision of the dominant property, see K G C Reid 'Defining Real Conditions' 1989 JR 69 at 77, 78.
7 See further para 409 below (real burdens) and para 465 below (servitudes).
8 A superiority cannot be divided without the consent of the vassal. See Erskine *Institute* II,3,12: 'the superior has no power to make his vassal's condition worse, by putting him to the expense of double entries, or by increasing the number of persons to whom the feudal services are due'. And see Hume *Lectures* vol IV (Stair Soc vol 17, 1955 ed G C H Paton) p 201. However, where A feus to B and B divides the *dominum utile* into four, disponing the quarters to C, D, E and F, there seems no reason why A cannot likewise divide the superiority into four provided that the quarters coincide.
9 See para 29 above (common property) and para 36 above (joint property).

346. Conditions *in personam*: a personal right against the proprietor of the servient property. Subject to the single and important exception of servitudes, it appears that real conditions are always rights *in personam*[1]. A real burden, therefore, is a personal right as is a right of common interest. As Stair observes in relation to common interest rights:

> 'though they have the resemblance of servitudes, and pass with the thing to singular successors; yet they are rather personal obligations, such as pass in communion even to the singular successors of either party'[2].

Real conditions *in personam* are enforceable by the proprietor for the time being of the dominant property against the proprietor for the time being of the servient property. The right is not in a thing (and hence against 'the world') but against a person. Of course, it is true that the person against whom the right is enforceable will change through time as ownership of the servient property changes. In that respect real conditions are unlike other personal rights. Nevertheless at any one time the right is enforceable against only one person or, at most, against a small and determinate group of persons, namely the proprietor (or proprietors) of the servient property (or properties). Such real conditions form a separate category of personal right, closest to contract but yet distinct from it. In fact, like real rights in the strict sense, real conditions are usually contractual in origin[3]. If A dispones to B imposing a real burden, the disposition forms a contract between the parties of which the real burden is a term[4]. However, in a question between successors there is no contract[5] so that the continuing liability of B's successors to A's successors depends on the real condition. Even between the original parties there is a distinction between the contract and the real condition, the former coming into being at the moment when delivery of the disposition is accepted by B, and the latter requiring the further step of registration[6].

While a real condition *in personam* is a right against a person rather than a right in a thing, the right against a person is in respect of a thing (the servient property) and it is held by virtue of ownership of another thing (the dominant property). The relationship of right to things may be indirect but it is not negligible. Unlike other personal rights, which belong to the law of obligations[7], real conditions are correctly classified as part of the law of property. Two important functions are given to 'things' in the context of real conditions. In the first place the 'things' determine the identity both of the debtor and of the creditor in the obligation. In the second place they determine the content of the obligation, since real conditions are a restriction on the servient property for the benefit of the dominant property[8].

1 It is long settled law that servitudes are real rights. There may possibly be an argument that real burdens which impose a restriction (as opposed to real burdens which impose a positive obligation) are also real rights, but the issue seems never to have been properly focused in a reported case. See also the discussion in paras 347 and 413 below.

2 Stair *Institutions* II,7,6.
3 Ie usually but not always. Thus real burdens, conditions in leases and (most) rights in security, all originate in contract. The same is often true of servitudes, although servitudes may also be created by positive prescription. On the other hand there is no contract in the case of common interest.
4 See para 392 below.
5 Ie except, at least on the traditional view of the law, in the case of real burdens created in feudal grants: see para 393 below.
6 This distinction appears to have been overlooked in *Watters v Motherwell District Council* 1991 SLT (Lands Trib) 2.
7 As to the law of obligations, see OBLIGATIONS.
8 See para 348 below.

347. Conditions *in rem*: a real right over the servient property. The significance of the distinction between real conditions *in rem* and real conditions *in personam* concerns the person or persons against whom enforcement can be made. A condition *in personam* is enforceable only against the proprietor of the servient tenement. A condition *in rem*, as a real right, is enforceable against anyone who challenges its exercise[1]. Of course, in most cases the challenger is likely to be the proprietor of the servient property, but it may also be a tenant or other possessor of the property or a heritable creditor[2]. A condition *in personam*, such as a real burden, is not enforceable against a tenant or other third party[3].

Following Roman law, and in common with other modern civilian legal systems, Scots law classifies servitudes as real rights[4], and it seems likely that this is the sole example of a real condition *in rem*. To some extent, therefore, servitudes are set apart from other real conditions. One explanation for this separation lies in content. Servitudes consist either of restrictions on the servient property (negative servitudes) or of rights to make some limited use of that property (positive servitudes)[5]. From the point of view of the servient property, both are passive obligations (obligations *in patiendo*) which may as readily and as justly be complied with by a tenant or other third party as by an owner. The very content of servitudes, therefore, allows the existence of the real right; or perhaps, and with greater historical accuracy, it might be said, with Hume, that the fact of the real right restricts the content:

> '[A servitude] does not bind the owner of the servient lands to any act or exertion towards support of the burden; but to suffer only what is done on the other part. This, indeed, is a proper and a natural consequence of the notion of servitude as a real right, which is exerted over an inert and passive subject'[6].

The position is different with other real conditions, such as real burdens or rights of common interest, which are capable of taking the form of active obligations (obligations *in faciendo*). An active obligation is almost necessarily personal to the proprietor of the servient property (and his successors as proprietor)[7], for it would be a surprising rule if the mere fact of possession of the servient property, whether as tenant, licensee or even as squatter, carried with it liability for such positive real burdens as an obligation to build a house or to maintain a wall[8].

1 See para 3 above. Of course this proposition cannot be made entirely without qualification: eg a servitude burdening the *dominium utile* of land does not affect a superior who has not consented to its grant.
2 *Bennett v Playfair* (1877) 4 R 321; *Taylor's Trustees v M'Gavigan* (1896) 23 R 945, 3 SLT 107.
3 See para 413 below.
4 Stair *Institutions* II,7, preamble; Erskine *Institute* III,1,2.
5 *Erskine* II,9,1; Bell *Principles* s 984.
6 Hume *Lectures* vol III (Stair Soc vol 15, 1952 ed G C H Paton) p 271. See also J Rankine *The Law of Land-ownership in Scotland* (4th edn, 1909) pp 414, 415.
7 Indeed it seems that the very nature of a real right excludes the idea of liability for performance of a positive obligation. See para 3 above.
8 One possible approach would be to classify all active obligations as personal rights and all passive obligations as real rights. On this view servitudes would always be real while real burdens and rights

of common interest would be real or personal depending on the content of the particular condition. For some of the difficulties with this approach, see K G C Reid 'Defining Real Conditions' 1989 JR 69 at 90. It is further discussed, in the context of real burdens, at para 413 below.

348. Rules as to content. Each separate type of real condition has its own rules as to content. Servitudes, for example, are limited to certain known types[1]; common interest, which, unlike other real conditions, cannot be expressly created and arises only by operation of law, is similarly restricted[2]; and of real burdens it has been said that they must demonstrate 'qualities of permanency, immediate connection with the estate, [and] natural relation to the objects of the grant'[3]. Nevertheless, whatever the individual variations as to content, all real conditions have in common the fact that they must regulate the servient property for the benefit of the dominant property. A condition not in conformity with this basic rule is not a real condition.

The rule as to content has two aspects. First, the condition must regulate the servient property in some way[4]. Typically a real condition imposes a restriction on the servient property (for example, that it concede a right of access or must not be used for business purposes), or it lays its proprietor under an obligation to perform some act in relation to the property (for example to maintain it).

The second aspect of the rule is that the regulation must be for the benefit of the dominant property. 'Neither does the law give them countenance unless they have some tendency to promote the advantage of the dominant tenement'[5]. The benefit must be praedial and not merely personal to the individual creditor. In *Aberdeen Varieties Ltd v James F Donald (Aberdeen Cinemas) Ltd*[6] the owner of two theatres disponed one of them subject to a purported real burden, in favour of the reserved theatre, that the disponed theatre should not be used to stage any play which required to be submitted to the Lord Chamberlain under the Theatres Act 1843 (c 68). In a question between successors of the original parties it was held by the Second Division that the burden conferred personal rather than praedial benefit and could not be enforced. It was not a real condition. The relevant law was set out by Lord Justice-Clerk Aitchison in the following terms:

'The law will recognise restraints upon the use of property as being consistent with ownership, although they necessarily involve some limitation of the full rights of the owner, provided it can be said that the restraints are . . . intended and designed for the benefit of some other legitimate property interest, or its protection, or the peaceable possession of property, or its proper enjoyment, or, to put it more generally, for the securing of the dominant owner's rights and interests of ownership in his own subjects . . . But, on the other hand, if the restriction is not intended to protect the dominant property as such, or its amenity, or any of the requisites of its proper enjoyment, but is simply devised and intended to create a monopoly, or to impose a restraint of trade in perpetuity for the benefit of a trading or commercial concern, it cannot, in my judgment, receive any effect, except as a personal contract between the original contracting parties, and it is not capable of being erected into a real right[7] so as to become an inherent condition of the title'[8].

One property cannot be said to benefit from a restriction imposed on another unless the two properties are reasonably close together. They need not however be contiguous[9]. One of the difficulties with the purported real burden in the *Aberdeen Varieties* case was that the two properties were separated by as much as half a mile.

1 See para 447 below.
2 See paras 358 ff below.
3 *Stewart v Duke of Montrose* (1860) 22 D 755 at 803, 804, per Lord Deas. See further para 391 below.
4 However, in the case of positive obligations, the property in question may be some other subjects adjacent to the servient property. A standard example is a real burden on a lower proprietor to maintain the roof of a tenement in circumstances where the roof is the sole property of the upper proprietor.
5 Erskine *Institute* II,9,33. These words were used in the context of servitudes.

6 *Aberdeen Varieties Ltd v James F Donald (Aberdeen Cinemas) Ltd* 1939 SC 788, 1940 SLT 58 (revsd 1940 SC (HL) 52, 1940 SLT 374).
7 By 'real right' in this context is meant real condition and not real right *stricto sensu*.
8 *Aberdeen Varieties Ltd v James F Donald (Aberdeen Cinemas) Ltd* 1939 SC 788 at 802, 1940 SLT 58 at 65. Similarly, an obligation to enter into a personal bond is not a real burden: *Corpn of Tailors of Aberdeen v Coutts* (1840) 1 Robin 296 at 325, 326, per Lord Corehouse. The distinction between this doctrine, of praedial benefit, and the doctrine of interest to enforce, while clear enough in principle, is frequently blurred in practice: see *Aberdeen Varieties Ltd v James F Donald (Aberdeen Cinemas) Ltd* 1940 SC (HL) 52, 1940 SLT 374, and para 407 below.
9 J Rankine *The Law of Land-ownership in Scotland* (4th edn, 1909) p 370.

(2) INCIDENCE

349. Introduction. While there seems no reason in principle why real conditions should not occur in property of other kinds, in practice they are almost unknown outside heritable property. This section on incidence, therefore, is concerned with land, although brief mention will be made at the end of the possible incidence of real conditions in moveable property[1].

Land is presumed free from perpetual burdens and the presumption is not lightly overcome[2]. In land law real conditions are acknowledged only where the relevant rules of constitution have been scrupulously observed[3]. Rules of constitution vary from one type of condition to another. Usually a public act of some kind is required, typically either registration of the condition in the Register of Sasines or Land Register, or its exercise or possession. By this means a purchaser of the servient property is alerted to the extent and nature of the obligations affecting the land. Failure to observe the rules of constitution is not remedied by the evident intention of the parties that the condition should be real[4].

The existence of a real condition presupposes the existence of a dominant and a servient property. Usually the servient property is land or, more correctly, the *dominium utile* of land, but it can also be a right of lease[5] or a right of sublease. If there is no servient property there can be no real condition at all, even where there is a potential dominant property[6]. Furthermore, condition and property must be properly distinct. Thus if A dispones land to B imposing real burdens or servitudes the condition of distinctness is satisfied. B has full *dominium* of the land, and the real burden or servitude is a purely extrinsic[7] restriction on that *dominium*. But if A leases land to B the position is different because a lease has no existence independent from the conditions which it contains. The conditions are an intrinsic part of the lease, and although they bind successive holders of the lease, they do so, not as real conditions, but by operation of the rule *assignatus utitur jure auctoris*[8].

The dominant property in a real condition is either a piece of land which is physically separate from the servient property or alternatively a second interest in respect of the same land. These are considered in more detail below[9]. In the first case, Whitemains is burdened in favour of Blackmains. In the second case, the *dominium utile* of Whitemains is burdened in favour of, for example, the *dominium directum* of Whitemains.

1 See para 353 below.
2 See eg J M Halliday *Conveyancing Law and Practice in Scotland* vol II (1986) para 19-31.
3 See eg *Anderson v Dickie* 1915 SC (HL) 79, 1915 1 SLT 393. See further para 392 below.
4 *Halliday* vol II para 20-36. However, compare *Inverlochy Castle Ltd v Lochaber Power Co* 1987 SLT 466, OH.
5 Eg when a lease is burdened by a standard security: see *Trade Development Bank v Warriner and Mason (Scotland) Ltd* 1980 SC 74, 1980 SLT 223. Conditions imposed in assignations of leases appear to be a second example: see para 352 below. However, as the text explains, a lease is not a servient property in respect of the conditions of the lease itself.
6 In this respect *Inverlochy Castle Ltd v Lochaber Power Co* 1987 SLT 466, OH appears to be wrongly decided: see K G C Reid 'Defining Real Conditions' 1989 JR 69 at 83–84.

7 For further discussion of the extrinsic/intrinsic distinction see Bell *Commentaries* I,302.
8 For this rule, see para 660 below. In fact the distinction rarely matters in practice. For a case where it did matter, see *Trade Development Bank v Warriner and Mason (Scotland) Ltd* 1980 SC 74, 1980 SLT 223. A detailed analysis of this important case will be found at 1983 SLT (News) 169 and 189.
9 See paras 350, 351, below.

350. Separate land as dominant property. In the paradigm case of real conditions the dominant property is an area of land separate from but neighbouring on the servient property. Four such real conditions are recognised, namely:
(1) servitudes[1],
(2) common interest[2],
(3) non-feudal real burdens[3], that is to say, real burdens created in a disposition and where the dominant property is either land reserved by the disponer or some other neighbouring area or areas of land[4], and
(4) real conditions in assignations of leases, which were introduced by statute in 1985[5].

Although sometimes found in isolation, real conditions of the kinds described above are more usually part of a network of interrelated rights and obligations. In the case of a flatted building, for example, the top flat of the building will be a servient property, and probably in respect of more than one type of real condition. Thus by the common law of the tenement the top flat is under a common interest obligation to provide cover. In addition it will probably be subject to a real burden or burdens to maintain common parts in the building. The dominant properties, in both obligations, will be the remaining flats of the building. However, as well as being a servient property the top flat will also be a dominant property. Thus it in turn has certain rights of common interest, for example for support, in respect of the other flats. It will have reciprocal rights in terms of the real burden of maintenance, and it may also have rights of servitude, for example a right of access over a pathway. What is true of the top flat is also true *mutatis mutandis* of the other flats in the building. While flatted buildings exhibit a particularly complex pattern of real conditions, similar if simpler patterns may often be found as between ordinary neighbouring properties.

1 For servitudes, see para 443 below.
2 For common interest, see para 363 below.
3 For non-feudal real burdens, see paras 403, 404, below.
4 Further, in feudal real burdens subject to co-feuars' rights, the rights of co-feuars are founded on ownership of neighbouring land.
5 Law Reform (Miscellaneous Provisions) (Scotland) Act 1985 (c 73), s 3. See further para 352 below.

351. Different interest in the same land as dominant tenement. In some real conditions the dominant property is no more than a second real right affecting the servient property, with the result that dominant and servient properties are different rights or interests in the same piece of land. The real condition then attaches to and runs with the dominant real right or interest and is enforceable against the holder of the servient real right or interest. The main, and perhaps the only, potential examples of dominant interests in land are superiority, lease and standard security[1]. In the case of superiorities the corresponding real conditions are (feudal) real burdens[2]. So if A feus to B imposing real burdens, the dominant property is the reserved superiority and the servient property the new *dominium utile*, the burdens then being enforceable by all successive superiors against all successive vassals[3]. With leases, the corresponding real conditions are those terms of the lease itself, express or implied, which are binding on the landlord[4]. Here the dominant property is the tenant's interest under the lease and the servient property is the landlord's interest, which is to say the *dominium utile* of land[5]. Finally, in the case of standard securities the real conditions are the statutory standard conditions, as augmented or varied by agreement between the parties[6]. The dominant property is the standard security and the servient property the *dominium utile* or other interest in land in respect of which the security was granted. It will be seen that with the two *jura in re aliena*, namely lease and standard security, the real conditions are part of the content of the real right itself with the result that real right and real condition are not properly distinct[7].

Real conditions falling into this category exhibit the same general characteristics as other real conditions *in personam*. There is both a dominant and a servient property; the conditions are enforceable by successive proprietors of the former against successive proprietors of the latter[8]; and the conditions are real only insofar as they regulate the servient property for the benefit of the dominant property. This final point is readily illustrated. Thus conditions in leases are real only where they are considered to be *inter naturalia* of the lease[9]. Conditions in standard securities must, it is thought, be of substantially the same kind as the model standard conditions[10]. Furthermore, real burdens in grants of feu, although apparently wider in scope, must also enure to the benefit of the superiority[11].

1 Possibly there may also be other examples, such as floating charges. As to floating charges, see COMPANIES, vol 4, paras 651 ff, and CONVEYANCING, vol 6, para 638.
2 For feudal real burdens, see para 398 below.
3 Where the positions are reversed, and the burden is on the superiority rather than on the *dominium utile*, the result is not a real burden but may be a real condition. See para 394 below.
4 At first sight this analysis may seem surprising. However, positive obligations of the kind which affect landlords cannot be real rights in the strict sense; and if they were only personal rights they would not bind successors. The conclusion that they are real conditions seems inescapable. Identical considerations apply in relation to the statutory standard conditions found in standard securities, as to which see note 6 below.
5 The same is true, *mutatis mutandis*, of subleases.
6 For the statutory standard conditions, see the Conveyancing and Feudal Reform (Scotland) Act 1970 (c 35), s 11(2), Sch 3 (amended by the Redemption of Standard Securities (Scotland) Act 1971 (c 45) s 1; the Insolvency Act 1985 (c 65), s 235(1), Sch 8, para 18; the Bankruptcy (Scotland) Act 1985 (c 66), s 75(1), Sch 7, para 8; and the Insolvency Act 1986 (c 45), s 439(2), Sch 14). See further *Trade Development Bank v Warriner and Mason (Scotland) Ltd* 1980 SC 74, 1980 SLT 223, and the comments on that case published at 1983 SLT (Notes) 169, 189.
7 Unlike the position for servient tenements (as to which see para 349 above) this is of no particular significance. So whereas conditions binding on a landlord in a lease are real conditions (because here the lease is the dominant property) conditions binding on a tenant are not (because a lease cannot be the servient property). In fact real right and real condition are distinct at least to the extent that a real condition can be enforced only against the servient proprietor.
8 Thus eg real conditions in a standard security are enforceable by the creditor for the time being in the standard security against the owner for the time being of the secured subjects. For the definition of 'debtor' as including 'proprietor', see the Conveyancing and Feudal Reform (Scotland) Act 1970, Sch 3 (as amended: see note 6 above).
9 See LANDLORD AND TENANT, vol 13, paras 240–242.
10 Ie the statutory standard conditions, as to which, see note 6 above. Of course a standard security will also contain a number of personal obligations which do not transmit against successors, most notably the obligation of the debtor to repay the loan.
11 See para 408 below.

352. Conditions in assignations of leases. Section 3 of the Law Reform (Miscellaneous Provisions) (Scotland) Act 1985, which has as its side-note 'Creation of real conditions in assignations of certain long leases', adds a number of subsections to section 3 of the Registration of Leases (Scotland) Act 1857. The new section 3(2) of the 1857 Act is the principal provision and provides as follows:

'. . . it shall be, and shall be deemed always to have been, competent in an assignation under this section to impose conditions and make stipulations which, upon the recording of such assignation or the registration under the Land Registration (Scotland) Act 1979 of the assignee's interest, shall be as effectual against any singular successor of the assignee in the subjects assigned as if such assignee had been a grantee of the lease and it had been duly recorded or, as the case may be, the grantee's interest had been so registered'.

Section 3(2) of the 1857 Act, therefore, permits, retrospectively, the imposition of conditions (real conditions according to the side-note[1]) in assignations of long leases. Alternatively, a separate deed of conditions may be used[2]. However, the effect of such conditions is not entirely clear. It is provided that conditions in assignations are 'as effectual against any singular successor of the assignee in the subjects assigned as if such assignee had been a grantee of the lease'[3]. Nevertheless, the fact that the assignee is a deemed grantee of the lease would seem to have no bearing on the enforceability of a condition unless the condition is itself declared to be a deemed term of the lease, which it is not; and even if the condition were so declared it would be enforceable, not by the cedent who created it, but by the landlord[4].

Commentators on section 3 of the Law Reform (Miscellaneous Provisions) (Scotland) Act 1985[5] have suggested that the provision deals with part disposals of leases, where conditions are imposed in the assignation for the benefit of the part of the tenancy retained by the cedent. The dominant property is the retained tenancy and the servient property is the assigned tenancy. The model is the part disposal of a *dominium utile* by disposition accompanied by the imposition of (non-feudal) real burdens[6]; and if section 3 of the 1985 Act can really be read in this sense (which perhaps is open to doubt) the conditions imposed by application of section 3 are a further example of real conditions *in personam*.

1 The Registration of Leases Act 1857 (c 26), s 3(5) (added by the Law Reform (Miscellaneous Provisions) (Scotland) Act 1985 (c 73), s 3) also refers to the conditions becoming 'real obligations affecting the land'.
2 Registration of Leases Act 1857, s 3(5) (as so added).
3 Ibid, s 3(2) (as so added).
4 In which case it would not be a real condition at all: see para 349 above.
5 J M Thomson *The Law Reform (Miscellaneous Provisions) (Scotland) Act 1985* (1986); J M Halliday *Conveyancing Law and Practice in Scotland* vol III (1987) p 224.
6 As to (non-feudal) real burdens, see para 403 below.

353. Moveable property. Real conditions are not usually found in moveable property although there seems no reason in principle why a security or other interest burdening moveable property, whether corporeal or incorporeal, should not be policed by real conditions in which the security or other interest forms the dominant property. Conditions in floating charges may perhaps be an example of this[1]. Furthermore, Gloag points out that[2]:

'The authorities ... though by no means conclusive, lend some countenance to the view that if A owns moveable property under an obligation to B not to use it in a particular way, purchasers from A, if at the time of purchase they have notice of this restriction, are bound to observe it, and may be interdicted by B if they disregard it'[3].

Nevertheless, even if the rule is as suggested by Gloag, which seems open to doubt, the absence of a potential dominant property excludes real conditions as a possible explanation, and the authorities themselves lay emphasis on equitable ideas of notice.

1 As to floating charges, see COMPANIES, vol 4, paras 651 ff, and CONVEYANCING, vol 6, para 638.
2 W M Gloag *The Law of Contract* (2nd edn, 1929) p 268.
3 There are two cases in favour of this view and one against. They are, respectively: *M'Cosh v Crow & Co* (1903) 5 F 670, 11 SLT 19, and *William Morton & Co v Muir Bros & Co* 1907 SC 1211, 15 SLT 252

(both of which are in favour of this view); and *Andrew Melrose & Co v Aitken, Melrose & Co* 1918 1 SLT 109 (which is against this view).

(3) COMMON INTEREST

(a) Origins and Development

354. Terminology. Although the doctrine itself can be traced back at least as far as the late seventeenth century it was not until a hundred years after that that the term 'common interest' came to be applied[1]. Indeed 'common interest' as a term must always be approached with caution: before it gained its current meaning it was used in a quite different sense, to describe the right of a *pro indiviso* proprietor to possession of the writs[2], and even today the term is not always used in its proper technical sense[3].

1 Kames *Principles of Equity* (3rd edn, 1778) I, 50 (but not earlier editions); *Marquis of Abercorn v Jamieson* (1791) Hume 510; *Braid v Douglas* 24 Jan 1800 FC, (1800) Mor 'Property' App No 2; *Lanark Twist Co v Edmonstone* (1810) Hume 520. For an account of the history of common interest, see *Smith v Giuliani* 1925 SC (HL) 45 at 56 ff, 1925 SLT 392 at 399 ff, per Lord Dunedin.
2 See Mor 'Common Interest'.
3 See eg *Donald & Sons v Esslemont and Macintosh* 1923 SC 122, 1922 SLT 650; *Stockton Park (Leisure) Ltd v Border Oats Ltd* 1991 SLT 333 at 335, OH.

355. Common interest as a 'natural' servitude. The early history of common interest is bound up with the law of the tenement on the one hand and with the law of riparian rights on the other. Both have in common the fact that a single thing (a tenement building or, as the case may be, a non-tidal river) is owned in separate units and by different people[1], so that the interests of one proprietor may be adversely affected by the activity or neglect of another. The point is an obvious one. If the owner of a lower tenement flat demolishes a load-bearing wall, the whole building is affected; likewise if an upper riparian proprietor diverts the course of a river the natural flow of the whole river is affected. By the end of the seventeenth century it had come to be accepted that special protection was required for riparian and for tenement proprietors over and above the protection provided by the general law. The new rule is found in Stair's *Institutions*[2]. According to Stair, in a tenement building there was an obligation of support on the lower proprietors and a corresponding obligation of shelter on the upper proprietors[3], while in a river the upper proprietors were taken bound not to interfere with the natural flow of the river. These new obligations presented obvious problems of classification. Of existing categories of obligation they were closest to servitudes, with the result that early common interest, like the early real burden[4], was often classified as a servitude[5]. However, in at least one respect servitude was not an adequate explanation. Servitudes require to be created either by grant or by positive prescription. With common interest there was no grant, and if prescription were to be required, the future servient proprietor would be free to withdraw support or, as the case may be, divert the river, until the then prescriptive period of forty years had passed. The solution adopted in the eighteenth century was to say that an obligation of this nature was a servitude but of a special kind known as a 'natural' servitude[6]. A 'natural' servitude was one which 'nature itself may be said to constitute'[7], and arose not by grant or prescription, but simply by force of law, by 'the natural situation of the ground'[7]. However, apart from method of constitution, common interest was regarded as indistinguishable from other servitudes.

1 Ie '... the owners of subjects possessed in separate portions, but still united by their common interest...': Bell *Principles* s 1086.

2 Stair *Institutions* II,7,6 and 12. It is not clear to what extent the rule was invented by Stair. Certainly no cases are cited except, in relation to rivers, *Bairdie v Scartsonse* (1624) Mor 14529, of which the report is only two lines long.

3 See also, following Stair, Bankton *Institute* II,7,9, and Erskine *Institute* II,9,11.

4 See para 381 below.

5 Eg *Hall v Corbet* (1698) Mor 12775. *Ritchie v Purdie* (1833) 11 S 771 seems to be the last case in which the servitude attribution was used.

6 *Luke v Dundass* (1695) 4 Brown's Supp 258; *Kelso v Boyds* (1768) Mor 12807; *Cruikshanks and Bell v Henderson* (1791) Hume 506.

7 *Erskine* II,9,2. See also para 442 below.

356. Common interest as common property. At the end of the eighteenth century and the beginning of the nineteenth an attempt was made to assimilate the 'natural' servitude to common property, itself at the time a concept of uncertain scope[1]. Since this development was contemporaneous with the gradual re-naming of the 'natural servitude' as 'common interest' it is tempting to treat it as a product of linguistic confusion. The attempted assimilation was most marked in the law of the tenement. Thus in *Robertson v Ranken* upper proprietors trying to prevent lower proprietors in the same building from building new doors and windows argued that:

> 'Wherever a tenement consists of several stories, belonging to different proprietors, it is implied in the right of each, that without his consent no material alteration that is not necessary, can be lawfully made on the plan of the building in general ... Thus the various owners come to have a mutual or common interest in all the different portions of the fabric; which, if it be not so extensive as the right of property, is not on that account the less entitled to protection'[2].

Although the phrase 'common interest' is used, the suggested right to preserve the *status quo* points towards common property and this seems borne out by the fact that the only Scots authority cited in support, a passage from Bankton[3], deals with common property. In the event the alterations were allowed, on what ground is not clear, but the same argument reappeared in a later case, *Cuddie v McKechnie*[4]. However, in this later case the action was abandoned before a decision could be reached. The most extended treatment of this view of common interest was given by Hume. Hume's conclusion was that:

> '... this principle goes the length of restraining each heritor generally from all such operations as materially change the condition — the aspect, or description — of the great tenement, or Land, in which they have all a certain interest'[5].

Most of the cases relied on by Hume are cases of common property.

1 See para 18 above.

2 *Robertson v Ranken* (1784) Mor 14534.

3 Bankton *Institute* II,7,11. Significantly Bankton's section on the obligation of cover and support, although a mere two paragraphs earlier (*Bankton* II,7,9), was not mentioned.

4 *Cuddie v McKechnie* (1804) Hume 516.

5 Hume *Lectures* vol III (Stair Soc vol 15, 1952 ed G C H Paton) pp 227, 228.

357. Common interest as an independent real condition. The choice between natural servitude and common property had, and continues to have, important implications for the nature of common interest. If common interest is truly a servitude it confers only limited and specific rights, such as the right of support and the right to shelter. However, if common interest can be classified as a type of common property it is both wider and less clearly defined, conferring on each individual proprietor a right to preserve the *status quo* and hence a potential veto on the activities of his neighbours. Until the second decade of the nineteenth century these opposing views of common interest appear to have developed largely in isolation, but they finally came together in two cases, *Fergusson v Marjoribanks*[1] and *Pirnie v M'Ritchie*[2], decided respectively in 1816 and 1819. The facts in both cases were substantially the same. Upper proprietors in a tenement objected to alterations proposed by the ground floor proprietor contending, on the familiar common property argument, that they were entitled to prevent 'any material alterations' in the building. They were successful but their argument was not. In the *Fergusson* case the court decided that objection could not be made to all material alterations, but only to such alterations as interfered with the specific right held by the pursuer, in this case the right of support:

> '[T]he right of the owner of a storey over the walls below him, was not properly either a servitude or a right of common property, but a common interest, such as to entitle him to object to any material alteration in the fabric, which might occasion even the apprehension of danger [to support]'[3].

In this passage both traditional explanations for common interest are rejected. The obligation of support in a tenement is said not to be founded on common property, but nor is it founded on servitude[4]. These two decisions mark the beginning of the emergence of common interest as an independent real condition[5], a process which may be regarded as completed with the publication in 1829 of Bell's authoritative definition in the first edition of his *Principles*:

> 'A species of right, differing from common property, takes place among the owners of subjects possessed in seperate portions, but still united by their common interest: It is recognised in law as COMMON INTEREST. It accompanies and is incorporated with the several rights of individual property . . . Thus, in the common wall of one of the large tenements of Edinburgh, consisting of many floors belonging to different proprietors, there is no common property among the owners of the several floors; but a combination of individual property with common interest. Each is proprietor of the wall of his own floor, and can prevent all encroachments upon it; but he is bound to the rest (having a common interest in it) to support it, and is not entitled to alter it, to such a degree as to encroach on or endanger the common interest. And so, 1. This common interest is distinguishable from *servitude*, in so far as each person concerned is bound by the common interest to maintain his own wall; which in mere servitude he would not be obliged to do. 2. It is distinguishable from *property*, in so far as no one having merely a common interest is entitled to break or touch the wall or space which belongs to another; but has only the right to prevent injury, and insist on support. And, 3. Each party may make alterations and changes on his own wall, notwithstanding the common interest which is vested in others, provided he does not endanger that common interest, or expose those who hold it to reasonable alarm: It is different in common property; no one common proprietor being entitled without the consent of all the rest to alter the state of the common subject'[6].

It will be seen that the view of common interest which finally prevailed was much closer to servitude than to common property. Like servitude, common interest is a real condition, a burden on the ownership of others rather than itself a type of ownership. However, the servitude model ultimately appeared unsatisfactory, for three reasons. First, as has already been seen[7], common interest did not conform to the rules of constitution prescribed for servitudes. Secondly, servitudes cannot, at least as a general rule, impose positive obligations on the servient proprietor, whereas the obligation of support considered in *Fergusson* and *Pirnie* was positive in nature. Finally, servitudes are restricted to certain known types, whereas one of the most important characteristics of common interest as it has developed is its flexibility as to content.

1 *Fergusson v Marjoribanks* 12 Nov 1816 FC.
2 *Pirnie v M'Ritchie* 5 June 1819 FC.
3 *Fergusson v Marjoribanks* 12 Nov 1816 FC, per Lord Glenlee, Lord Bannatyne and Lord Craigie.
4 In fact this conclusion was anticipated by Stair who wrote of the obligations of shelter and support in a tenement that 'though they have the resemblance of servitudes, and pass with the thing to singular

successors; yet they are rather personal obligations, such as pass in communion even to the singular successors of either party': Stair *Institutions* II,7,6. As Stair says, common interest rights, unlike servitudes, are personal and not real: see para 346 above.

5 For common interest in rivers the equivalent leading case is *Morris v Bicket* (1864) 2 M 1082 (affd (1866) 4 M (HL) 44).

6 Bell *Principles* s 1086. The text varies slightly from edition to edition. The version given here is taken from the fourth edition (1839), being the last for which Bell himself was responsible.

7 See para 355 above.

(b) Constitution and Content

358. Constitution. Common interest arises by implication of law[1]. Nothing appears in writing, far less on the Land Register or Register of Sasines, so that for the purposes of registration of title common interest is classified as an overriding interest[2]. The rule is explained by Bankton, in the context of law of the tenement as follows:

'[Common interest] arises from the communication or connection between the respective stories and the roof, more than a proper servitude, which is constituted by the deed of the party. Now this regulation takes place from the nature of the thing, and custom of borow [that is, burgh] alone'[3].

Nevertheless while, as Bankton observes, common interest owes its existence to the 'nature of the thing', it is only in relation to a small number of 'things' that common interest is admitted by the law, with the result that it is a much narrower category than real burdens and servitudes.

The fact that common interest is implied by law does not of itself mean that it cannot also be expressly created, and it has been suggested from time to time that express creation is competent[4]. However, it is submitted that these suggestions are unsound. Quite apart from any dogmatic objections, they face the practical difficulty that there are no acknowledged rules of constitution[5]. Furthermore, since common interest does nothing which is not capable of being done already by real burdens and servitudes, both of which have clear and strict rules of constitution, it is thought unlikely that these rules can be circumvented simply by asserting that the right sought to be created was a right of common interest rather than a servitude or a real burden.

1 Bell *Principles* s 1086: 'It accompanies and is incorporated with the several rights of individual property.'

2 Land Registration (Scotland) Act 1979 (c 33), s 28(1)(i) 'overriding interest'.

3 Bankton *Institute* II,7,9.

4 Most recently this has been suggested by Lord Jauncey in *Fearnan Partnership v Grindlay* 1992 SLT 460 at 463, HL. See also the cases discussed in para 362 below.

5 Although Professor W M Gordon accepts the view that common interest can be expressly created, no rules of constitution are given. See W M Gordon *Scottish Land Law* (1989) ch 15. This may be compared with his treatment of servitudes and real burdens where detailed rules are set out. As a minimum, in relation to the express creation of common interest, an answer to the following questions would be required:
   (1) In what kind of deeds can common interest competently be created?
   (2) Is registration required?
   (3) What restrictions are there as to content?
   (4) Is common interest available for heritable property of all types?
   (5) How specific need the grant be, and, in particular, is it sufficient to make a bare grant of 'common interest' leaving the law to imply the content?

359. Incidence. The following are the situations in which the law implies the existence of common interest. Almost all[1] share the fact of a single thing, such as a tenement building or a river, which is in the (several) ownership of two or more people and in which the role of common interest is to establish a basic set of rules for the welfare of the thing taken as a whole. As frequently happens in the case of tenement buildings, these rules can be displaced or augmented by agreement among the proprietors by the use of real burdens or servitudes:

(1) *Tenement buildings.* Each proprietor has a right of common interest in those parts of the building which he does not own. Common interest includes the right to support, the right to shelter and, in respect of any garden ground, the right to light[2].

(2) *Non-tidal rivers.* Each riparian proprietor has a common interest right as against the other proprietors to the effect that there is to be no interference with the natural flow of the river[3].

(3) *Non-tidal lochs.* Common interest confers on each proprietor a right of use for sailing, fishing and other purposes in respect of those parts of the loch which he does not himself own[4].

(4) *Salmon fishings.* A proprietor of salmon fishings has a right to the free passage of salmon, enforceable against riparian proprietors and other proprietors of salmon fishings in the same river[5].

(5) *Drainage.* A landowner has a right to use the natural lie of the land to drain water, whether surface or underground, on to the land of his neighbours[6].

(6) *'Mutual' walls.* Where boundary walls or mutual gables are owned by neighbouring proprietors *ad medium filum*, each has a common interest right of support in the part which is owned by the other[7].

(7) *Buildings on public roads.* In *Donald & Sons v Esslemont and Macintosh*[8] it was held by the First Division that where a building abuts a public[9] road there is a right to light from the street sufficient, in that case, to prevent the building of a bridge across it[10]. The rule is different for private roads[11].

(8) *Private gardens in common ownership.* Where private gardens serving two or more buildings are in common ownership, it has been suggested that the *pro indiviso* proprietors have additional and separate rights of common interest[12]. The rule may not be restricted to private gardens but may apply to certain other cases of common property[13].

(9) *Access for repair.* Hume states that:

> 'I think it may be maintained with respect to conterminous proprietors in a Burgh, which in many instances, owing to the crowded situation of the building, cannot be repaired without some temporary interference, as by resting ladders on the next area, or suspending a scaffold over the next area, that this slight and temporary inconvenience must be put up with, from the necessity of the case'[14].

There have been no reported decisions on this point.

1 Except perhaps (5) (drainage), (7) (right to light in a public road) and (9) (right of access for repair). Indeed if there is a sustainable distinction in the modern law between natural servitude and common interest, it may be that, as Erskine states (*Institute* II,9,2), drainage rights are truly an example of the former.
2 See further paras 232 ff above.
3 See further paras 282 ff above. The right may also extend to freedom from pollution: para 299 above.
4 See further para 307 above.
5 See further para 330 above.
6 See further paras 340, 342, above.
7 See further paras 225, 226, above.
8 *Donald & Sons v Esslemont and Macintosh* 1923 SC 122, 1922 SLT 650.
9 Lord Skerrington distinguishes such a public road from a road in which there is merely a public or servitude right of way: 1923 SC 122 at 135, 1922 SLT 650 at 658.
10 Lord President Clyde in his judgment said 'The defenders . . . point out that in no case has the right of the owner of a street-frontage to light from the street been positively affirmed after challenge; and I have not been able to discover any reasoned examination or formulation of the right in any of the books. The right is, in my opinion, one of the pertinents or qualities of property abutting on a public

street, inherent in and inseparable from its situation . . .': 1923 SC 122 at 130, 1922 SLT 650 at 655. The term 'common interest' is not used, although it is used, in a non-technical sense, in another part of the case.

11 See para 362 below.
12 *Grant v Heriot's Trust* (1906) 8 F 647, 13 SLT 986; *Forster v Fryer* (1944) 60 Sh Ct Rep 39.
13 See para 26 above.
14 Hume *Lectures* vol III (Stair Soc vol 15, 1952 ed G C H Paton) p 207. As to whether a wider right of access might exist in some circumstances, see para 457 below.

360. Reciprocity of obligation. Almost all cases of common interest involve a single thing *(res)*, such as a tenement building or a river, which is owned in separate parts by different proprietors; and the rule then is that each individual proprietor has a right of common interest in respect of those parts of the thing which he does not himself own[1]. It follows that common interest is characterised by reciprocity of obligation, for each individual proprietor is at the same time both a dominant and a servient proprietor, and the part of the thing which he owns is both a dominant and a servient tenement. Further, the rights and obligations making up a network of common interest are either identical or at least in some relationship of equivalence. Thus within a tenement building a lower proprietor must support the upper; but in return the upper proprietor must give shelter to the lower proprietor. Each is both a dominant and also a servient proprietor and the obligation on the one is the counterpart of the obligation on the other. In practice the network of common interest rights and obligations within a single building or other thing operates much like a model deed of conditions[2], but with the difference that common interest is implied by law so that its regulatory provisions are less detailed than in a typical deed of conditions.

1 This probably includes those parts owned in common: see para 232 above.
2 That is to say, a deed containing real burdens and prepared under the powers conferred by the Conveyancing (Scotland) Act 1874 (c 94), s 32, and the Land Registration (Scotland) Act 1979 (c 33), s 17.

361. Content. Like servitudes and real burdens today, common interest at one time seems to have consisted of a specific obligation or set of obligations. Stair, for example, refers to the obligations of support and shelter in a tenement and the obligation not to divert water in a river[1]. However, by the time of Bell common interest had grown more flexible, and while the obligations identified by Stair and others continued to be recognised, they were no longer regarded as exhaustive. Thus it became sufficient for the law to say that there was a right of common interest in a thing, without specifying precisely what that right consisted of, and indeed nineteenth-century definitions of common interest are often circular, the obligation on the servient proprietor being expressed as an obligation not to endanger the common interest[2]. So in a tenement building it was settled by the time of Stair that common interest included the rights of shelter and support. These rights have since been extended by the courts to include, for example, a right to light[3]. Bell expresses the view that 'the exercise and effect of the common interest must, when dissensions arise, be regulated by law or equity'[4] and there seems no reason why the content of common interest should not be further extended today where this is to the benefit of the property viewed as a whole.

1 Stair *Institutions* II,7,6,12.
2 Thus it is said that the servient proprietor may make alterations in his property 'provided he does not endanger that common interest': Bell *Principles* s 1086. See further *Taylor v Dunlop* (1872) 11 M 25 at 31, per Lord Ardmillan where he says: 'The existence of a common interest in the tenement imposes an equitable restriction on the owners. Each must use the subject of which each is owner so as to conserve that common interest . . .'
3 See paras 232 ff above.
4 *Bell* s 1086.

362. A right intermediate between servitude and common property? At one time there was doubt whether common interest should be classified as a real condition, or, like a right of common property, as a real right *stricto sensu*[1]; and while it has long been settled that common interest is a real condition only, the influence of the converse view has proved surprisingly persistent and has caused continuing confusion in the modern law. An example is Lord Dunedin's influential *dictum* in *Smith v Giuliani* that:

'. . . common interest is not a right of servitude nor of common property, but it is a right of a proprietary character'[2].

On one level there is nothing in this *dictum* to which objection can be taken, for it is beyond dispute both that common interest is neither servitude nor common property, and also that it is a right of a 'proprietary' character, at least in the sense that it is part of the law of property rather than the law of obligations. However, if common interest is 'proprietary' in this narrow sense, then so too are servitude and common property with which it is being contrasted, and it is difficult to avoid the feeling that the proper sense of Lord Dunedin's words is that common interest is to be regarded as a right intermediate between servitude and common property, that is to say something more than a real condition but less than a right of full *dominium,* in short a real right *sui generis.*

Considerations such as these may have influenced the court in *George Watson's Hospital Governors v Cormack*[3] where, in a decision which would surprise most conveyancers, a conveyance of 'a right and interest' in Edinburgh's George Square Gardens 'jointly and in common with the other proprietors' was held to confer, not a right of common property, but a right of common interest. This suggests a more powerful doctrine of common interest than is usually conceded, but the decision offends against the rule that a right of common interest cannot be expressly created[4] and it was not followed in a more recent case[5]. In a similar vein there have been several cases in which it was suggested that the relationship between a private lane and the houses served by it might be one of common interest[6], but the suggestions are tentative and the cases in question can be more satisfactorily explained as examples either of common property[7] or of servitude[8].

These are unusual cases. Taken as a whole there seems nothing in the reported case law since the middle of the nineteenth century to unsettle the proposition that common interest is a real condition and not a real right. However, it is an interesting survival of the earlier view that modern textbooks often treat common interest side by side with common property rather than with other real conditions such as servitudes or real burdens[9].

1 See paras 355 ff above.
2 *Smith v Giuliani* 1925 SC (HL) 45 at 59, 1925 SLT 392 at 400. See further para 249 above.
3 *George Watson's Hospital Governors v Cormack* (1883) 11 R 320. See also the earlier case of *Johnston v White* (1877) 4 R 721.
4 See para 358 above.
5 *WVS Office Premises Ltd v Currie* 1969 SC 170, 1969 SLT 254. Cf *McCallum v Gunn* 1955 SLT (Sh Ct) 85.
6 In fact if common interest were to be applied to lanes a more convincing analysis would be several ownership in the part of the lane *ex adverso* one's own house accompanied by common interest in the rest. The model is non-tidal rivers.
7 *Mackenzie v Carrick* (1869) 7 M 419; *Glasgow Jute Co v Carrick* (1869) 8 M 93. In *Mackenzie* Lord Justice-Clerk Patton seems to regard common interest as 'a right of property': (1869) 7 M 419 at 420; while in *Glasgow Jute Co* Lord Deas expressly decides the case on the basis of common property. In both cases (and unlike the cases referred to at note 8 below), there is the difficulty that if the lane is not common property it is left without an owner.
8 *Bennett v Playfair* (1877) 4 R 321; *Shiel v Young* (1895) 3 SLT 171, OH. See also *Taylor's Trustees v M'Gavigan* (1896) 23 R 945, 3 SLT 107 (involving the back green of a tenement) where,

notwithstanding the rubric, the case appears to have been decided on the basis of servitude. It is on the basis of these cases that the editor of the tenth edition of Bell *Principles* added the following passage to s 1086: 'Where neighbouring owners or tenants have a common interest in anything . . . [a]ny one of the community is entitled to maintain the existing state of possession against the others'. The passage is comprehensible only when it is realised that it contemplates, not a dispute between the dominant and the servient proprietors in common interest (which is the usual situation) but a dispute between fellow dominant proprietors.

9 For an example, see W M Gordon *Scottish Land Law* (1989) ch 15. The practice is probably traceable to Bell *Principles* s 1071 ff although, of course, one of Bell's concerns was precisely to distinguish between common property and common interest.

(c) Enforcement

363. Title and interest to enforce. Title to enforce rests in the proprietor for the time being of the dominant tenement[1]. Probably he must be infeft[2]. The right runs with the land and no separate assignation is required. A tenant or other person whose rights fall short of ownership does not have title to enforce[3]. Often there is more than one dominant tenement: in a flatted building, for example, all lower flats are dominant tenements in respect of the obligation of shelter, while all upper flats are dominant tenements in respect of the obligation of support.

Interest to enforce must be praedial, which is to say that the obligation on the servient tenement must confer benefit on the dominant tenement[4]; but since common interest arises by force of law, and since it is more or less confined to situations where both dominant and servient proprietors own different parts of the same thing, it is difficult to conceive of a situation where the test of praedial benefit would not be satisfied.

1 This is the very essence of the idea of a real condition: see para 345 above.
2 That, at least, is the rule for real burdens: see para 397 below.
3 See para 406 below.
4 See para 348 above. For the position in relation to real burdens, see para 407 below.

364. Liability in the obligation. Liability rests with the proprietor of the servient tenement for the time being[1] and there is no liability in tenants or in other holders of lesser rights[2]. It is uncertain whether infeftment determines liability or whether common interest follows the complex rules which have developed in the case of real burdens[3].

1 See para 346 above.
2 See para 413 below.
3 For these rules, see para 412 below.

365. Division of dominant or servient tenements. It is thought that common interest is unaffected by the physical division either of the dominant or of the servient tenement and that the right or, as the case may be, the obligation, will continue to attach to both parts of the former single tenement[1]. This is because common interest is conceived for the benefit of the tenement as a whole and cannot usually be attributed to one part rather than another. Thus if a ground floor flat is subdivided it seems clear that both subdivided parts are dominant tenements in the obligation of shelter, and equally that they are servient tenements in the obligation of support.

In the case of feudal division, which is to say, in the case of either tenement being subfeued, it is thought that the rights and obligations attach to the *dominium utile* only and not to the reserved superiority.

1 For the equivalent rule for real burdens, see paras 409, 414, below.

366. Remedies. The principal remedies available to a dominant proprietor are interdict[1], implement[2] and damages. Where breach of common interest results in damage to property owned by the dominant proprietor, so that the claim resembles a claim in delict, it has been held that liability is not strict and that negligence must be shown[3]. There is concurrent jurisdiction in the sheriff court[4] and the Court of Session.

1 Eg *Fergusson v Marjoribanks* 12 Nov 1816 FC; *Morris v Bicket* (1864) 2 M 1082 (affd (1866) 4 M (HL) 44).
2 Eg *M'Nair v M'Lauchlan and M'Keand* (1826) 4 S 546 (NE 554).
3 *Thomson v St Cuthbert's Co-operative Association Ltd* 1958 SC 380, 1959 SLT 54; *Kerr v McGreevy* 1970 SLT (Sh Ct) 7; *Doran v Smith* 1971 SLT (Sh Ct) 46. This may be contrasted with the right of support in respect of mines and other separate tenements beneath the ground where liability is strict: see para 261 above.
4 Sheriff Courts (Scotland) Act 1907 (c 51), s 5(4).

(d) Extinction

367. Introduction. Unless one accepts a resurrectionist view of common interest, by which the law not only creates the right in the first place but also re-creates it of new if it happens to be extinguished, it appears that, like other real conditions, common interest is capable of permanent extinction. On this aspect of common interest, as on a number of other aspects, there is a dearth of direct authority, but from first principles it appears that common interest may be extinguished in any one of the ways described in this section[1].

1 See paras 368 ff below.

368. Express consent. A dominant proprietor may agree to discharge a right of common interest, either in whole or in part. The terms of any deed registered in the Register of Sasines or Land Register whereby a 'land obligation' is varied or discharged is binding on the successors both of the dominant and of the servient tenements[1]. 'Land obligation' is defined, as it is in the provisions for variation and discharge by the Lands Tribunal discussed later[2], as:

> 'an obligation relating to land which is enforceable by a proprietor of an interest in land, by virtue of his being such proprietor, and which is binding upon a proprietor of another interest in that land, or of an interest in other land, by virtue of his being such proprietor'[3].

This definition is sufficiently wide to encompass all real conditions, including rights of common interest. Accordingly, it appears that rights of common interest, like real burdens[4], may be discharged by a minute of waiver[5]. Alternatively, common interest is in effect discharged by the creation of a real burden over the dominant tenement which is inconsistent with it: for example, a real burden on a ground floor flat to contribute to the maintenance of the roof restricts to that extent the obligation of shelter imposed by common interest on the top flat.

A discharge affects only the particular dominant tenement or tenements in respect of which it was granted, and common interest continues to be enforceable by other dominant proprietors in the same obligation who have not acceded to the discharge.

1 Land Registration (Scotland) Act 1979 (c 33), s 18(1).
2 See para 374 below.
3 Conveyancing and Feudal Reform (Scotland) Act 1970 (c 35), s 1(2). The definition is applied by the Land Registration (Scotland) Act 1979, s 18(2).

4 See para 426 below.
5 Ie provided such minute is registered in terms of the Land Registration (Scotland) Act 1979, s 18(1).

369. Implied consent: acquiescence. It is thought that the rules of implied consent by acquiescence which have developed for real burdens[1] apply also to common interest. Acquiescence is likely to be of assistance only where the obligation breached is a restriction (an obligation not to do something), as opposed to a positive obligation to do something such as to maintain a tenement roof.

1 See paras 427 ff below.

370. Negative prescription. An obligation founded in common interest is extinguished if for a period of twenty years there is neither a 'relevant claim' by the dominant proprietor nor a 'relevant acknowledgement' by the servient proprietor[1]. A 'relevant claim' means a claim for implement or part implement of the obligation made in any court proceedings or arbitration[2]. A 'relevant acknowledgement' means, in the case of a positive obligation, performance of the obligation[3] and, in the case of a restriction, complying with the restriction[4]; but with the alternative, in both cases, of an unequivocal written admission by the servient proprietor to the dominant proprietor clearly acknowledging the subsistence of the obligation[5]. Prescription extinguishes only the particular obligation which has not been enforced and has no effect on other obligations which may also arise out of common interest.

1 Prescription and Limitation (Scotland) Act 1973 (c 52), s 7 (amended by the Prescription and Limitation (Scotland) Act 1984 (c 45), ss 5(3), 6(1), Sch 1, para 2, and the Consumer Protection Act 1987 (c 43), s 6(6), Sch 1, Pt II, para 8).
2 Prescription and Limitation (Scotland) Act 1973, s 9(1), (4) (amended by the Prescription and Limitation (Scotland) Act 1984, Sch 1, para 3(a); the Companies Consolidation (Consequential Provisions) Act 1985 (c 9), s 30, Sch 2; the Bankruptcy (Scotland) Act 1985 (c 66), s 75(1), Sch 7, para 11; the Prescription (Scotland) Act 1987 (c 36), s 1(1), (2)).
3 Prescription and Limitation (Scotland) Act 1973, s 10(1)(a) (amended by the Prescription and Limitation (Scotland) Act 1984, Sch 1, para 4).
4 Prescription and Limitation (Scotland) Act 1973, s 10(4).
5 Ibid, s 10(1)(b) (as amended: see note 3 above).

371. Dominant and servient tenements coming into single ownership. Where the dominant and servient tenements come into single ownership, common interest ceases to be enforceable on the principle of confusion. However, if the tenements are later separated it is thought that common interest either revives or is created of new, because it is the very act of dividing a thing into several ownership which brings about the creation of common interest.

372. Physical changes affecting either tenement. For as long as physical changes make an obligation impossible or impractical to perform, performance cannot be required, although the burden is not extinguished and may become enforceable once again in the event of the changes being reversed[1]. In the law of the tenement it is settled that the common interest obligations of support and shelter apply only for so long as the tenement remains as a going concern, after which they fall into abeyance unless or until the tenement is rebuilt[2].

1 For the more developed rule for real burdens, see para 434 below.
2 See para 235 above.

373. Mutuality principle. There can be no enforcement of a common interest obligation if the party seeking to enforce it is himself in breach of a common interest obligation in a question with the party against whom enforcement is sought[1]. This is the mutuality principle. Its effect is not to extinguish the obligation but to render it unenforceabale for the period of the dominant proprietor's own default.

1 See para 435 below.

374. Variation and discharge by the Lands Tribunal. As a 'land obligation' within the relevant legislation[1], it appears that common interest may be varied or discharged by the Lands Tribunal[2], on application by the servient proprietor[3]; and while no application appears yet to have been made in respect of common interest so that the Tribunal has made no express acknowledgment of jurisdiction, there seems no reason to doubt that the jurisdiction exists.

A Lands Tribunal order takes effect on registration of an extract of the order in the Register of Sasines or Land Register[4], and binds all dominant proprietors. The Tribunal may exercise its power only where it is satisfied in all the circumstances that:

(1) by reason of changes in the character of the servient tenement or the neighbourhood thereof or other circumstances which the Tribunal may deem material, the obligation is or has become unreasonable or inappropriate; or

(2) the obligation is unduly burdensome compared with any benefit resulting or which would result from its performance; or

(3) the existence of the obligation impedes some reasonable use of the servient tenement[5].

The servient proprietor may be ordered to pay compensation[6], and the Lands Tribunal is empowered to impose such substitute obligations as appear to it reasonable as a result of the variation or discharge and as may be accepted by the servient proprietor[7].

1 See para 368 above.
2 As to the Lands Tribunal for Scotland generally, see CONVEYANCING, vol 6, paras 512, 513; COURTS AND COMPETENCY, vol 6, paras 1139–1154.
3 Conveyancing and Feudal Reform (Scotland) Act 1970 (c 35), ss 1, 2. See further J M Halliday *Conveyancing Law and Practice in Scotland* vol II (1986) pp 284–300; W M Gordon *Scottish Land Law* (1989) ch 25.
4 Conveyancing and Feudal Reform (Scotland) Act 1970, s 2(4) (amended by the Land Tenure Reform (Scotland) Act 1974 (c 38), s 19).
5 Conveyancing and Feudal Reform (Scotland) Act 1970, s 1(3). However, this third ground may not be available if the Tribunal considers that, due to exceptional circumstances relating to amenity or otherwise, money would not be an adequate compensation for any loss which a dominant proprietor would suffer from the variation or discharge: s 1(4).
6 Ibid, s 1(4).
7 Ibid, s 1(5).

8. REAL BURDENS

(1) INTRODUCTION

375. Terminology. At one time the term 'real burden' (sometimes 'real lien' or 'onus reale') was used in Scots law to denote a special type of heritable security which could be created by reservation in dispositions and in other deeds of conveyance[1]. In the early nineteenth century, however, the position was greatly complicated by the introduction on a large scale of a second type of obligation which quickly assumed both the rules of constitution, and before long the actual name, of the pre-existing heritable security[2]. This new real burden was not a heritable security at all. Indeed its closest analogue was servitude. Its purpose was to impose conditions on the use of the land being conveyed, whether in the interests of the superior or of a neighbour or sometimes of both; and its introduction was associated with the rapid urbanisation which accompanied the Industrial Revolution. In the early years of its development the new real burden was frequently confused with the old, and qualities belonging to the one type of obligation were often attributed to the other. To a considerable extent the problem was one of terminology, for if two obligations share the same name, confusion is unavoidable. New names, therefore, were required and by around 1860 the courts had supplied them. The old heritable security became known, slightly inaccurately[3], as a ' pecuniary real burden', and the new obligation which imposed conditions on the use of the land was called an 'inherent condition of the right'[4] or, more simply, a 'condition of the right'[5]. However, the re-naming was not successful, or at least not outside Parliament House. Conveyancers, resistant to change in this as in other matters, continued to use 'real burden' to refer to both types of obligation. More recent attempts to re-name the condition as to use as a 'real condition' have not been any more successful in practice[6].

Today the risk of confusion seems slight. Real burdens in the sense of heritable security have long since disappeared from active conveyancing practice and there seems no good reason for refusing to follow the terminology favoured by the solicitors' profession[7]. Accordingly, in this title[8], 'real burden' is used to denote the condition as to use which first became prominent in the early nineteenth century, and 'pecuniary real burden' to denote the obsolete heritable security; and, as discussed above[9], 'real condition' is used as a generic term for real burdens, servitudes, rights of common interest and for all other rights which run with the land.

1 See further para 383 below.
2 Real burdens in this second sense, although known in a rudimentary way long before 1820, were little used until about that time. The early history is described in detail in paras 376 ff below.
3 Inaccurately because, strictly, a real burden in this sense is not confined to securing obligations to pay money.
4 *Stewart v Duke of Montrose* (1860) 22 D 755 at 803, per Lord Deas.
5 *McNeill v Mackenzie* (1870) 8 M 520 at 525, per Lord Justice-Clerk Moncreiff; *Leslie v Wyllie* (1870) 43 SJ 95 at 96, OH, per Lord Gifford; *Corbett v Robertson* (1872) 10 M 329 at 334, per Lord Deas; *Perth Magistrates v Earl of Kinnoull* (1872) 10 M 874 at 888, per Lord President Inglis. As these cases show, it did not matter whether the condition was in a feu disposition or in an ordinary disposition.
6 See eg J M Halliday *Conveyancing Law and Practice in Scotland* vol II (1986) para 19-16 and W M Gordon *Scottish Land Law* (1989) pp 711 ff.
7 See *Anderson v Dickie* 1915 SC (HL) 79 at 89, 1915 1 SLT 393 at 399, per Lord Dunedin.
8 But cf CONVEYANCING, vol 6, para 496, where 'real condition' is used.
9 See paras 344 ff above.

(2) ORIGINS AND DEVELOPMENT

376. Origins. A feudal grant of 1459 contained an obligation to maintain certain causeways[1]. Another of 1569 prohibited the use of the land for secular purposes[2]. These were probably the exceptions. In general there is little evidence that real burdens in the modern sense were much used before the eighteenth century[3]. Thus Erskine[4], in his detailed account of the clauses in a feu charter, makes no mention of real burdens and indeed real burdens are not mentioned by any institutional writer before Bell[5]. It is true that from the earliest times[6] feudal grants contained obligations, enforceable against successive vassals by successive superiors, such as feuduty, feudal casualties, personal services and the like, but these were feudal prestations arising out of the personal relationship of superior and vassal and not attempts to regulate the future use of the land feued for the protection of some proprietorial interest held by the superior or a neighbour.

Even if the origins of real burdens can be traced to earlier times, there seems little doubt that their development in a form recognisable to the modern law is attributable to the rapid urbanisation which began in the last decades of the eighteenth century. A symbolic starting date, if one is required, would be 1767, the year in which James Craig's plan for the Edinburgh New Town was adopted by the Town Council. From this time onwards, the building of private houses, in Edinburgh and elsewhere, proceeded on a scale far greater than had ever been seen before. Naturally the expansion was not constant. It was interrupted, not long after it had started, by the war against France. Later it was to follow the highs and lows of the trade cycle. Nevertheless the overall trend was not in doubt.

Today a new housing development will usually involve a single firm of builders. The builders buy the land, build the houses, and then sell them individually. Georgian and Victorian builders worked on a much smaller scale. The typical pattern, to be repeated again and again throughout Scotland, was the following. The original owner of the land prepared a feuing plan showing the projected lines of streets and marking the individual plots on which houses were to be built. Sometimes building lines were also shown. The plots were then sold individually, usually by roup. Often each plot was bought by a different person. Finally the houses themselves were built. Since each house might be erected by a different builder, some means had to be found of maintaining an acceptable standard of workmanship and an appropriate level of uniformity at a time when there was no public law regime of planning control[7]. The real burden solved this problem and at the same time allowed control over the future use and development of the land.

1 *Perth Magistrates v Earl of Kinnoull* (1872) 10 M 874. The burden began: 'And also the said Robert sall uphauld for ewir for passage for man and hors the calsay streikand fra the charter hous yet to the burne of Craigie sufficientlie as effeiris, with stane and sand...'.
2 *Johnston v Canongate Magistrates* 30 May 1804 FC, (1804) Mor 15112.
3 Certainly there is little evidence in the law reports. It appears that some late medieval Crown charters contained obligations which in the modern law might be regarded as real burdens. See R Nicholson 'Feudal Developments in Late Medieval Scotland' 1973 JR 1. It should be borne in mind, however, that in so far as they related to fortalices, obligations were in effect grants of the right to build, because fortalices were at that time considered to be legal separate tenements. See para 210 above.
4 Erskine *Institute* II,3,19 ff.
5 Bell *Principles* s 868.
6 For early forms of feudal writs, see P Gouldesbrough *Formulary of Old Scots Legal Documents* (Stair Soc vol 36, 1985). See also paras 63 ff above.
7 However, a measure of control was provided by the Dean of Guild Courts.

377. The Edinburgh New Town cases. The building of the Edinburgh New Town was the earliest substantial programme of urban development in the period under consideration. Its importance to the early law is difficult to exaggerate. Of course other developments, and in other cities, also made a significant contribution to the law. Indeed, the most important case of all, *Corpn of Tailors of Aberdeen v Coutts*[1], which was decided in 1840, concerned Bon-Accord Square in Aberdeen. Another important case involved the Blythswood Estate in Glasgow[2]. But the majority of the early cases on real burdens and related matters concern the Edinburgh New Town and the experience of feuing on such a large scale and over so many years was to have a profound and lasting effect on the law and practice of real burdens.

1 *Corpn of Tailors of Aberdeen v Coutts* (1840) 1 Robin 296, HL.
2 *Campbell v Dunn* (1823) 2 S 341 (NE 299), IH, (1825) 1 W & S 690, HL (remitted back to the Court of Session for the opinions of the full court, reported at (1828) 6 S 679).

378. Feuing by plan: the period 1767–1818. Craig's celebrated plan for the Edinburgh New Town was adopted by the Town Council in July 1767 and the first three plots were sold, all to the same person, on August 3[1]. By the end of 1767 seventeen other plots had been sold. Building work started with St Andrew Square and moved west along Princes Street, George Street and, more slowly, along Queen Street. By the early 1790s Hanover Street and Frederick Street had been reached and were all but completed. The first feu was sold in Charlotte Square in 1792 although building work was then held up by the outbreak of the War against France. Heriot Row and the streets immediately surrounding it were built in the first twenty years of the new century and the Moray Feu (the Drumsheugh Estate) including Moray Place and Ainslie Place, followed in the 1820s. By 1830 much of the building of the New Town had been completed.

The early grants in feu were all made on land owned by the Town Council and it was not until the later period that private landowners also came to be involved. At first, and indeed for many years afterwards, the charters which were granted contained little in the way of building conditions[2]. Some in fact contained no conditions at all[3], while in most charters the only condition to be found was an 'express burden' that the feuar and his successors

'shall in all time coming maintain and uphold upon their own expenses the arches of the . . . cellarage and communication with the common sewers and also the said pavement covering the said cellars and communication'[4].

Occasionally charters were more ambitious. The feus of St Andrew Square and, much later, of Charlotte Square also, provided that the shared garden in the middle

'be used allernarly for the pleasure, health, or other accommodation of the feuars or their families, but in no way to be converted into a common thoroughfare, or used to any other different purpose whatever'[5].

and made further provision for its joint maintenance. A feu in George Street to the President and Fellows of the Royal College of Physicians granted in February 1777 contained an obligation to lay out the building in terms of a plan signed by the parties, an attested copy of which was delivered as relative to the charter[6]. But on the whole, no attempt was made to regulate either the type of building to be built, or its future use. This is not surprising, for in the eighteenth century real burdens were in their infancy. When they were used at all, they were used sparingly[7] and, it almost seems, speculatively, for the question of enforceability had not yet been properly resolved[8].

In the absence of real burdens, the Town Council was able to control the initial construction work as a matter of ordinary contract[9], while, in a question with successors of the original feuars, control was left to rest on the plan on which the original feuing had proceeded. A number of different feuing plans were in operation for the New Town. Craig's famous plan, which has already been mentioned, applied only to the 'first' New Town, from St Andrew Square in the east to Charlotte Square in the west[10]. A detailed plan for Charlotte Square itself, including building elevations, was prepared by Robert Adam in 1791, and there were a number of further plans, most notably the plan of 1802 by Sibbald and Reid for the area around Heriot Row[11] and Gillespie Graham's plan of 1822 for the Moray Feu. These plans were often referred to in the original feudal grants[12], but there was no attempt to use them as the basis for real burdens.

What was the status of these plans? In 1772, only five years after the feuing of the New Town first began, this question was tested in the House of Lords in the case of *Deas v Edinburgh Magistrates*[13]. The issue, an important one for the future of the city, was whether building was permitted on the south side of Princes Street. Craig's plan showed building on the north side of the street only and a number of feus on that side were taken in reliance on the plan. When, therefore, in 1769 and 1770, the Council proposed to feu some of the ground to the south of the street, fourteen feuars on the north side, including David Hume the philosopher, applied for a bill of suspension and interdict against the Council. The Council sought to meet the argument of reliance by pointing to an Act of Council of 29 July 1767 in which the possibility of building on the south side of Princes Street was expressly contemplated. This did not impress the House of Lords. Lord Mansfield, in a powerful, even intemperate, speech, explained the position of the feuars thus:

> 'After some time, the plaintiffs were surprised by the appearance of buildings upon the ground, which they always supposed destined to the health and beauty of the place; and in place of terraces and walks upon the North Loch they find a new street amaking in its way, as a peculiar favourite of the corporation, under the name of Canal Street. These gentlemen immediately bring the complaint before the corporation; they appeal to the *plan* [that is, Craig's plan], and pray to be informed how such an infringement could ever be imagined, far less carried into execution; — or how the town could allow themselves to act against the good faith of the public and express terms of their sale. Now, my Lords, what answer did the corporation make to all this; — "Plan!" say they, "Why, gentlemen, you have egregiously deceived yourselves, that is not the plan at all". "No!" say the plaintiffs, "Where is it then?" "Here", replied the corporation, "in an act of our Council of such a date". "Did you never see that before gentlemen?" "No, indeed", rejoined the feuars, "we never did". "Impossible", continue the magistrates; "You are men of business, your receipts for the money bear the date of this act; and it is in vain to say you could so far neglect, or impose upon yourselves. Why, you are to have no canal, no walk, no terrace, no pleasure ground. Here is Canal Street! there is a coach house! there a butcher's shop! there a tallow-chandler!!" Can your Lordships approve the conduct of this corporation on the contemptible idea upon which this conduct has been endeavoured to be justified? '[14].

The answer to Lord Mansfield's question was not in doubt, but the House of Lords' decision was concerned only with interim arrangements and when the merits of the case came to be considered by the Court of Session it found for the Council. However, the threat of a further appeal persuaded the Council to agree to arbitration and by a decree-arbitral of 19 March 1776 an appropriate compromise was pronounced[15].

The legal basis of the view taken by the House of Lords in *Deas* is elusive. As Lord Eldon LC was to observe in the later case of *Gordon v Marjoribanks*, Lord Mansfield's speech 'is addressed a great deal too much to the taste and honour of parties, instead of dwelling upon their contracts, and following the steps of that correct judicial path within which a Judge is by his duty confined'[16]. The report of the *Deas* case in Dow includes in its summary of the arguments put forward by the feuars the word 'servitude', but it seems more likely that, the dispute being between the original parties to the feudal grant, the case was decided on contract[17]. Be that as it may, however, the decision came to be taken in a very wide sense as authority for the proposition that the mere exhibition of a feuing plan by a superior is sufficient to make both parties, and their successors, bound by its terms. In the words of Lord Meadowbank in the later case of *Young v Dewar*:

> 'I apprehend it to be clear, that though there is not one word of restraint in the charter, yet, if it is a feu of a piece of ground within a liberty or district, which is perfectly understood by the public in general, as not to be used in a certain way, it is just as effectual as if it had been described *ad longum* in the charter. It would be a very long and tedious task to describe the rules which regulate this matter in every particular burgh; but I have not the least conception, that in any case where streets are feued according to a plan, the feuar is entitled to overlook that plan'[18].

Young was one of a number of cases in which a feuar was successfully prevented by his neighbour from carrying out building operations which were contrary to the feuing plan — in the case of *Young*, Craig's plan of 1767[19]. Interestingly, none involve enforcement by the superior. The legal basis of these decisions is not entirely clear. Sometimes there is the suggestion that the exhibition of the plan gives rise to a servitude *non aedificandi*[20] but in *Young* the model seems more that of an implied real burden ('just as effectual as if it had been described *ad longum* in the charter') being enforced by a co-feuar.

1 The standard work on the feuing of the New Town is A J Youngson's masterly *The Making of Classical Edinburgh* (1966).
2 The complete Chartularies of Town Council grants are held in the Edinburgh City Archives. The details of individual grants also appear from a number of reported cases. See *Edinburgh Magistrates v Brown* (1833) 11 S 255 (George Street); *Gordon v Marjoribanks* (1818) 6 Dow 87, HL (St Andrew Square); *Heriot's Hospital Governors v Cockburn* (1826) 2 W & S 293, HL (India Street); *Edinburgh Magistrates v Macfarlane* (1857) 20 D 156 (Dundas Street); *Croall v Edinburgh Magistrates* (1870) 9 M 323 (Charlotte Square); *Liddall v Duncan* (1898) 25 R 1119, 6 SLT 77 (Dundas Street).
3 Eg Charter in favour of David Auchterlonie and David Mitchell (Rose Street), April 1788 (Edinburgh City Archives: *Chartulary* (Extended Royalty) vol 5, folio 62).
4 Eg Charter in favour of John Watson and others, February 1773 (Edinburgh City Archives: *Chartulary* vol 1, folio 46); Charter in favour of James Cowan (George Street), October 1776 (Edinburgh City Archives: *Chartulary* vol 1, folio 186); Charter in favour of Robert Burn (Princes Street), November 1787 (Edinburgh City Archives: *Chartulary* vol 5, folio 17). See also *Croall v Edinburgh Magistrates* (1870) 9 M 323 (Charlotte Square).
5 Eg Charter in favour of James Stirling (St Andrew Square), September 1773 (Edinburgh City Archives: *Chartulary* vol 1, folio 58). See also *Gordon v Marjoribanks* (1818) 6 Dow 87, HL (St Andrew Square), and *Croall v Edinburgh Magistrates* (1870) 9 M 323 (Charlotte Square).
6 Charter, February 1777 (Edinburgh City Archives: *Chartulary* vol 1, folio 212). Despite, or perhaps because of, these precautions, the building did not satisfy the Royal College of Physicians and it stood for only sixty years. See *Youngson* p 95.
7 The reported case law gives some indication of the scale of use in the eighteenth century. See *Nicolson v Melvill* (1708) Mor 14516 (High Street, Edinburgh: obligation to maintain a roof contained, unusually, in a disposition); *Garden v Earl of Aboyne* (1734) Mor 10275 (prohibition against cutting trees, described in the report as 'this remarkable restriction'); *Heriot's Hospital Governors v Ferguson* (1773) Mor 12817, affd (1774) 3 Pat 674, HL (Edinburgh, land to east of New Town: prohibition against digging for coal); *Andrew Lauder* 16 June 1815 FC (Newington, Edinburgh: prohibition of breweries and other nuisances); *Browns v Burns* (1823) 2 S 298 (NE 261) (George Square, Edinburgh: prohibition of use for trade).
8 The issue of enforceability was not properly resolved until the decision of the House of Lords in *Corpn of Tailors of Aberdeen v Coutts* (1840) 1 Robin 296, HL. See paras 380, 384, below.
9 *Youngson* pp 80–82. The Dean of Guild jurisdiction must have been a further source of control.
10 It is reproduced in *Youngson* at p 72.
11 On this plan, see *Heriot's Hospital Governors v Cockburn* (1826) 2 W & S 293, HL; *Edinburgh Magistrates v Macfarlane* (1857) 20 D 156; *Liddall v Duncan* (1898) 25 R 1119, 6 SLT 77.
12 The early charters granted by the Town Council invariably included the following narrative: 'Considering that by Act of Council bearing date 29 July 1767 the Plan for feuing out the ground within the Extended Royalty of the said City was settled and the terms and conditions upon which the same was to be feued is thereby fixed and ascertained and that in terms of the said Plan and Proposals exhibited upon our part . . .'.
13 *Deas v Edinburgh Magistrates* (1772) 2 Pat 259, HL. For the background to this case, see *Youngson* pp 86–91. An interesting discussion of this, and subsequent cases, is contained in *Alexander v Stobo* (1871) 9 M 599 at 612 ff, per Lord Deas.
14 *Deas v Edinburgh Magistrates* (1772) 2 Pat 259 at 262, 263, HL.
15 See *Youngson* p 90: 'Thus was saved, in spite of the Town Council, the most important asset and the true singularity of Edinburgh; the physical separation and the visible conjunction of the Old Town and the New'. Those buildings which were built were demolished in the late nineteenth century. Further building was prohibited by a private Act of Parliament of 1816. For later developments, see *MacGregor v North British Rly Co* (1893) 20 R 300.
16 *Gordon v Marjoribanks* (1818) 6 Dow 87 at 112, HL.
17 Since the Council had already feued the offending plots and were now only superiors it is difficult to see how the case could have been decided on servitude. Another possible interpretation of the decision is that it turns on the Council's obligations in public law.
18 *Young v Dewar* 17 Nov 1814 FC.
19 Others are *Dirom v Butterworth* (1812) (reported as a footnote to the report of *Young v Dewar* 17 Nov 1814 FC) and *Schulze v Campbell* 29 Nov 1815 FC. *Dirom* concerned a minor deviation from Adam's

plan for Charlotte Square, which was characterised by Lord Meadowbank, the Lord Ordinary, following a site visit, as a 'disgusting deformity'.
20 When the whole issue was reviewed by the House of Lords in *Gordon v Marjoribanks* (1818) 6 Dow 87, HL, it was treated as a case of servitude.

379. A plan put into words: the New Town after 1818. By the time that *Young v Dewar*[1] was decided, in November 1814, the rule laid down in *Deas*[2] was under serious challenge[3]. Only six months earlier, in *Heriot's Hospital Governors v Gibson*[4], the House of Lords had doubted *Deas* and argued that the decision, proceeding as it did on an interim order, was not a binding precedent. The Lord Chancellor, Lord Eldon, commented:

'He could easily conceive that deference to his opinion [the opinion of Lord Mansfield in *Deas*] had put an end to farther proceedings in that case, the Corporation having been perhaps almost frightened out of their senses by his speech; but still this was no judgment upon the question of right . . .'[5].

In *Young v Dewar* the Court of Session came to Lord Mansfield's defence, Lord Meadowbank observing tartly that:

'I have the greatest respect for the decisions of the House of Lords; but my respect is not confined to its recent decisions . . .'[6].

But the House of Lords was not now to be stopped. In 1818, forty-six years after the decision in *Deas*, the House was given a second opportunity to decide a case involving Craig's plan and this time it came to a different conclusion. The case was *Gordon v Marjoribanks*[7]. Here the defenders, who operated the New Club, then located in St Andrew Square, sought to build a kitchen, a billiard room and baths in the back garden of their feu. This was opposed by their immediate neighbour as contrary to Craig's plan of 1767. It was held, however, that no obligation had been created by the mere exhibition of the plan. The court did not go so far as to say that a servitude could never be created in this way. The position might be different where the plan had been signed and then mentioned in the charter[8]. But mere exhibition was not enough[9].

The decision in *Gordon* seems to have led to a major change in feuing practice, for no longer could plans be relied upon as a means of controlling future development. By the time the decision was pronounced the Town Council had little land left unfeued in the New Town, but such charters as were now granted contained a veritable profusion of conditions. Here, for example, is part of a charter granted in December 1821 of a plot in London Street:

'But declaring that the houses to be built in London Street shall be according to an elevation made by Thomas Brown, Superintendent of Public Works, and similar to those already built; Declaring . . . that none of the said buildings shall exceed fifty feet in depth over walls . . . and shall have double roofs, and the height of the roofs shall not exceed one third of their span or one sixth part of the depth of the buildings. That the sunk areas in front of said buildings shall have good and substantial iron railings, such sunk areas and foot pavements thereof, being respectively of the same breadth as delineated on said ground plan. That there shall be no storm windows nor any raised breaks in imitation of French roofs . . . And the masonry plain and ornamental shall be similar in every respect to the houses already built in the said street [and so on]'[10].

The pattern was the same in the Moray Feu, one of the main developments in the New Town in the 1820s, where the feu contracts granted by the Earl of Moray contained detailed real burdens concerning the erection of buildings and their use and maintenance[11]. Similar burdens and conditions also appear in the contemporaneous development of Bon-Accord Square and surrounding streets in Aberdeen[12], and of the Blythswood estate in the centre of Glasgow[13]. No doubt there were other examples[14]. Of course, as has been seen, the use of real burdens was not in itself new.

But what was new was the extent of the use, the attempt to provide through real burdens a detailed programme for the development and use of the property feued. There was indeed a sense in which real burdens had become a feuing plan put into words[15].

1 *Young v Dewar* 17 Nov 1814 FC.
2 *Deas v Edinburgh Magistrates* (1772) 2 Pat 259, HL.
3 In *Young v Dewar* 17 Nov 1814 FC Lord Bannatyne observed: 'I consider this as one of the most important cases that was ever before us. The rights of the whole New Town of Edinburgh depend on it. If every man is entitled to build as he likes, what would be the situation of the city?'. Not everyone supported such uniformity of building. According to Lord Deas in *Alexander v Stobo* (1871) 9 M 599 at 613, the result of the ultimate collapse of the rule in *Deas* was the construction of 'a series of lofty, varied, and palatial buildings . . . in George Street and Princes Street [which] replaced the miles of low, dull, monotonous uniformity which these streets previously presented'.
4 *Heriot's Hospital Governors v Gibson* (1814) 2 Dow 301, HL.
5 (1814) 2 Dow 301 at 311, HL. Both of Lord Eldon's points were vigorously disputed in *Young v Dewar* 17 Nov 1814 FC. Lord Mansfield's speech in *Deas v Edinburgh Magistrates* (1772) 2 Pat 259, HL was unquestionably hostile to the Town Council, which he accused (at 265) of being no better than a 'burgh committee' intent only on profit. But in *Young* Lord Meadowbank insisted that 'Lord Mansfield was not only the greatest lawyer of his age, and a great nobleman, — he was a perfect gentleman, and was utterly incapable of availing himself of his exalted situation, of the terror of his name, in order to frighten any set of men into an abandonment of their rights'.
6 *Young v Dewar* 17 Nov 1814 FC.
7 *Gordon v Marjoribanks* (1818) 6 Dow 87, HL.
8 This happened in *Dirom v Butterworth* (reported as a footnote to the report of *Young v Dewar* 17 Nov 1814 FC) which the House of Lords in *Gordon* seems to have regarded as correctly decided: *Gordon v Marjoribanks* (1818) 6 Dow 87 at 110, 111, HL. In the later case of *Stewart v Burk* 9 Dec 1820 FC, where the feuing plan was also referred to in the feu charter, the Second Division observed that *Gordon* 'was not an authority which must needs rule this question'. See also *Henderson v Nimmo* (1840) 2 D 869, a decision perhaps best explained by the fact that the question arose between the original parties to the feu disposition. It is unlikely that the modern law would accept that negative servitudes can be constituted by bare reference to a plan; and of course there can be no question that a document not reproduced in the Register can create real burdens. See *Croall v Edinburgh Magistrates* (1870) 9 M 323 and para 388 below.
9 Once again the court distanced itself from the approach adopted by Lord Mansfield in *Deas*. Thus Lord Eldon LC in *Gordon v Marjoribanks* (1818) 6 Dow 87 at 106, 107, HL, said: 'Let it not be supposed that I disregard the taste and the beauty of the city of Edinburgh. Far from it; I saw it once when it was less beautiful and elegant than it is now; although it was even then a very striking and beautiful object. But I say, as I said on a former occasion [that is, in *Heriot's Hospital Governors v Gibson* (1814) 2 Dow 301, HL], that whatever may be due to the taste and beauty of the city of Edinburgh, we are not here to support them at the expense of the legal rights of the parties, nor to carry our respect and regard for taste and beauty so far as to establish a contract where there is no such thing', and again (at 115): 'This is the opinion which I offer to your Lordships. I do not profess to have much taste; but if I had, I should not think myself at liberty to indulge it at the expense of doing that which is consistent neither with law nor the contracts of parties'.
10 Charter in favour of Archibald Haig, December 1821 (Edinburgh City Archives: *Chartulary* (Extended Royalty) vol 22, folio 24). See eg Charter in favour of Miss Frances Oswald (Drummond Place), January 1823 (Edinburgh City Archives: *Chartulary* vol 22, folio 152). The articles of roup are also incorporated by reference, a practice which the later law was to brand as ineffectual: see para 388 below. There is no mention of the term 'real burden'.
11 See *Main v Lord Doune* 1972 SLT (Lands Trib) 14. The feu contracts were preceded by detailed articles of roup: see A J Youngson *The Making of Classical Edinburgh* (1966) pp 217–223, where the articles are quoted in part.
12 See *Corpn of Tailors of Aberdeen v Coutts* (1837) 2 Sh & Macl 609 at 620 ff, HL (further proceedings (1840) 1 Robin 296, HL) where the disposition is given in full.
13 *Campbell v Dunn* (1823) 2 S 341 (NE 299), IH, (1825) 1 W & S 690, HL (remitted back to the Court of Session for the opinions of the full court, reported at (1828) 6 S 679); *Campbell v Clydesdale Banking Co* (1868) 6 M 943.
14 Thus *Porteous v Grieve* (1839) 1 D 561 discloses a similar development in the 1820s in Edinburgh's Portobello.
15 Of course real burdens could achieve much more detailed regulation than a feuing plan, particularly in respect of use and maintenance.

380. Juristic basis of real burdens. From about 1820 onwards, real burdens began to be used regularly and extensively in conveyances of land, and earlier doubts as to their enforceability, such as they were, were rapidly stilled in a series of decisions[1]. But two important questions remained unanswered. First, what precisely were the rules for the valid constitution of real burdens? Secondly, what was their juristic basis? The answer to the first question depended upon the answer to the second, because if real burdens were, for example, a type of servitude, then the applicable rules of constitution were to be found in the law of servitudes.

In the 1820s and 1830s three pre-existing types of obligation were available as possible prototypes for the new real burden. These were: (1) servitudes, (2) feudal conditions, and (3) pecuniary real burdens[2].

1 *Heriot's Hospital Governors v Ferguson* (1773) Mor 12817, affd (1774) 3 Pat 674, HL; *Pollock v Turnbull* (1827) 5 S 195 (NE 181); *Campbell v Dunn* (1823) 2 S 341 (NE 299), IH, (1825) 1 W & S 690, HL (remitted back to the Court of Session for the opinion of the full court reported at (1828) 6 S 679); *Porteous v Grieve* (1839) 1 D 561.
2 As to servitudes, feudal conditions and pecuniary real burdens, being possible prototypes, see paras 381–383 below.

381. Servitudes. Servitudes[1] were received into Scots law from Roman law and were well established several centuries before the first emergence of real burdens[2]. In the early years of the real burden, and indeed not just in the early years, servitudes and real burdens were often confused[3], and 'servitude' was sometimes used as a generic term to include servitudes proper, real burdens and common interest. The points of resemblance are obvious. Servitudes and real burdens both run with the land. Both restrict the use to which land can be put. Both, in short, are examples of real conditions. Moreover, negative servitudes can equally happily be constituted as real burdens, and where, in the modern law, an obligation fails as a real burden it is often argued that it succeeds as a servitude[4]. Nonetheless the two are fundamentally different, for three reasons. First, in a servitude there cannot usually be a positive obligation on the servient proprietor, such as an obligation to maintain a building. Secondly, servitudes are restricted to certain known types, so that an obligation is valid if and only if it can be brought within one of those types[5]. Finally, and most importantly of all, servitudes require a neighbouring piece of land to act as a dominant tenement, a condition which is not fulfilled by real burdens where they occur in grants in feu. Thus if A feus to B imposing real burdens, which are then enforceable by A and his successors as proprietors of the superiority interest against B and his successors as proprietor of the *dominium utile*, A's reserved superiority is not a dominant tenement in the sense recognised by the law of servitudes[6].

1 For servitudes, see paras 439 ff below.
2 'Servitude' is a separate title in Morison's Dictionary of Decisions and forty-six cases are listed. The earliest is *Knockdolian v Tenants of Parthick* (1583) Mor 14540.
3 Thus in 1781 Edinburgh Town Council feued a New Town plot subject to a 'servitude' of not erecting a building. But in the absence of a dominant tenement of the kind recognised in the law of servitudes, this seems more accurately classified as a real burden. See *Edinburgh Magistrates v Brown* (1833) 11 S 255.
4 Eg *Campbell's Trustees v Glasgow Corpn* (1902) 4 F 752, 10 SLT 9; *Braid Hills Hotel Co Ltd v Manuels* 1909 SC 120, 16 SLT 523.
5 These first two points also led to the development of common interest a century earlier. See paras 354 ff above. Both are brought out in *Nicolson v Melvill* (1708) Mor 14516. Here builders refurbished a tenement in the High Street in Edinburgh and sold off the individual flats, inserting in each disposition an obligation to maintain the roof. In a question between successors it was held, by a narrow majority, that the obligation was not a servitude. 'If this were once allowed, then other unheard of servitudes might be introduced, such as that you shall bear a share of the expenses of the floors and glass windows of your neighbouring tenements, seeing you are benefited thereby': (1708) Mor 14516 at 14516, 14517. To modern eyes the obligation looks like a real burden, but the report suggests that its terms were not repeated in the instrument of sasine following the disposition, with the result that it would not have appeared in the Register of Sasines.

6 See para 443 below. However, as will be argued later (para 408 below), the right of the superior to enforce real burdens is in some senses anomalous, and certainly of the three prototypes of real burdens it is the servitude which in the modern law seems the most important.

382. Feudal conditions. If the servitude model fails to account for real burdens occurring in grants in feu, the feudal conditions model fails to account for the other case of real burdens, namely those occurring in ordinary dispositions. Unless, therefore, real burdens in feudal grants are regarded as different in kind from real burdens in dispositions, this model falls to be rejected. But there are also other, important reasons for its rejection.

It was of the very essence of the feudal relationship that the vassal came under certain obligations in relation to his superior[1]. These were the *reddendo* paid by the vassal in return for the use of the feu. Some obligations, such as the obligation to pay a stipulated amount in feuduty, had to be set out expressly in the charter while others, such as obligations in relation to casualties, were implied. There were also reciprocal obligations on the superior[2]. Almost all of the standard feudal prestations have now been discontinued by statute: personal services in 1715[3], prohibitions on alienation in 1746[4], prohibitions on subinfeudation in 1874[5], casualties in 1914[6], and feuduty in 1974[7], although in the 1820s this process was still at an early stage. More importantly for present purposes, the standard prestations could be supplemented by additional obligations[8]. Hume records a case in which the vassal was taken bound to drive his cattle off the lands when the superior should come to hunt[9]. In another case the obligation was for the maintenance of a boat for the superior's use together with six rowers and a steersman[10]. Other obligations sometimes found were that the vassal should bring his malt to the superior's brewery to be made into ale or have his ironwork manufactured at the superior's smithy[11]. In *Campbell v Dunn*[12], lengthy consideration was given to an obligation, later declared void by statute[13], that all dispositions of the subjects feued be prepared by the superior's law agents. The court was divided, a majority of the consulted judges accepting the validity of the obligation and Lord Balgray asserting that '[a] superior may put into the dispositive clause whatever conditions . . . he chooses, and, if these are not contra bonos mores, they are effectual against the whole world'[14]. But four judges dissented, arguing that 'We cannot see how it can be made real upon the lands, more than if it were stipulated that the vassal should always come to Glasgow by a particular coach, or employ a tailor, butcher, baker, or doctor, to be named by the superior'[15].

There can be no doubt that the modern real burden owes a considerable debt to such feudal conditions[16], for it was a short step from the standard feudal obligations to new obligations regulating the use of the land. During the eighteenth century that step was beginning to be taken[17]. Yet feudal conditions fail as a model in two important respects. In the first place, feudal conditions (other than the obligation to pay feuduty itself[18]) were not enforceable by direct personal action[19]. The idea of the superior-vassal relationship as an ordinary contract, giving rise to contractual remedies and renewed periodically by the investiture of successive vassals, seems to have been largely a Victorian invention[20]. If a superior in 1820 wished to enforce a feudal condition, two methods alone were available to him. One was to refuse entry to the next vassal until the condition was fulfilled[21]. The other, available only where irritant and resolutive clauses were included in the original grant, was to irritate the feu[22]. More direct enforcement was impossible.

The other reason why feudal conditions fail as a model is that they are feudal not just in form but also in content. The conditions are the *reddendo* for the feu. They enure to the personal benefit of the superior. Often they have little or nothing to do with the land itself and resolve into the payment of money[23]. Real burdens are quite different. Their whole purpose is to regulate the use to which the land is put. Beyond the fact that they sometimes appear in a feu grant there is nothing feudal about them at all[24].

1 For feudalism generally, see paras 41 ff above.
2 Today these have shrunk to the obligation, implied by the Land Registration (Scotland) Act 1979 (c 33), s 16(3)(b), to relieve the vassal of overfeuduties. For earlier obligations on superiors, see *M'Culloch v Laurie* (1835) 13 S 1029; *Stewart v Duke of Montrose* (1860) 22 D 755, affd (1863) 1 M (HL) 25; *Stewart v M'Callum* (1868) 6 M 382, affd (1870) 8 M (HL) 1.
3 Highlands Services Act 1715 (c 54), ss 10–14 (repealed) effective from 1 August 1717.
4 Tenures Abolition Act 1746 (c 50), s 10 (amended by the Statute Law Revision Act 1867 (c 59)) effective from 25 March 1748. Section 12 of the 1746 Act (repealed) allowed entry by resignation, but a superior could not be compelled to grant entry by confirmation until the Transference of Lands (Scotland) Act 1847 (c 48), s 6 (repealed). The Tenures Abolition Act 1746, s 10, does not apply to clauses of pre-emption: *Matheson v Tinney* 1989 SLT 535, OH.
5 Conveyancing (Scotland) Act 1874 (c 94), s 22. This applied to future deeds only. A blanket annulling of prohibitions on subinfeudation was introduced by the Conveyancing Amendment (Scotland) Act 1938 (c 24), s 8.
6 Feudal Casualties (Scotland) Act 1914 (c 48).
7 Land Tenure Reform (Scotland) Act 1974 (c 38), s 1. This does not affect existing feuduties although provision is made in the Act for their redemption: ss 4–6.
8 Ie the so-called *accidentalia feudi*. See Craig *Jus Feudale* 1,9,28, and Erskine *Institute* II,3,11.
9 Hume *Lectures* vol IV (Stair Soc vol 17 (1955), ed G C H Paton) p 200. See also *Hemming v Duke of Athole* (1883) 11 R 93 (reservation of deer).
10 *Duke of Argyle v Creditors of Tarbert* (1762) Mor 14495.
11 *Corpn of Tailors of Aberdeen v Coutts* (1840) 1 Robin 296 at 317, per Lord Corehouse. Lord Corehouse adds: 'These conditions have fallen into disuse, but they have never been declared illegal by statute. The Court, however, at present refuses to enforce them, as being inconsistent with public policy'.
12 *Campbell v Dunn* (1823) 2 S 341 (NE 299), (1825) 1 W & S 690. The case was remitted back to the Court of Session for the opinions of the full court, reported at (1828) 6 S 679, but the case was then settled, according to Lord Corehouse in *Corpn of Tailors of Aberdeen v Coutts* (1840) 1 Robin 296 at 319, because '. . . the superior discovered that the condition was exceedingly injurious to himself, and of no advantage to any one but his agent'.
13 Conveyancing (Scotland) Act 1874, s 22.
14 *Campbell v Dunn* (1825) 1 W & S 690 at 693. A similar position was adopted by Lord President Hope (at 697): 'There is nothing illegal in this condition. It may be ruinous on the one hand, and it may have been foolish on the other, to agree to it. But they agreed to this condition'.
15 *Campbell v Dunn* (1828) 6 S 679 at 689, per Lord Alloway, Lord Cringletie, Lord Mackenzie and Lord Eldin.
16 This point is often emphasised, probably more strongly than it deserves. See eg *Stewart v Duke of Montrose* (1860) 22 D 755.
17 See para 378 above.
18 For the personal action to recover feuduty, see Stair *Institutions* II,4,7; Erskine II,5,2; Hume vol IV, p 193; Bell *Principles* s 700. The case usually cited for the personal action is *Bishop of Galloway v His Vassals* (1632) Mor 4186 and it is not clear whether there is earlier authority. The basis of the personal action is not clear.
19 The early editions of Bell's *Principles* provide important evidence about the state of the law in the years between 1820 and 1840, when the watershed decision in *Corpn of Tailors of Aberdeen v Coutts* (1840) 1 Robin 296, HL, was handed down. Thus in the second edition of *Principles*, published in 1830, Bell gives the following account of the enforceability of feudal conditions (s 861): 'Conditions introduced into the feudal grant may be enforced in two several ways, and to different effects; — by insertion as a condition of the bargain, or grant, to accompany it in all its transmissions, and be published in the record; or by the addition of a clause irritant. And the rules on this subject are, — 1. That lawful conditions for maintaining valuable interests on the part of the superior, when bargained for, and inserted in the vassal's investiture, and published in the Record of Sasines, entitle the superior to refuse an entry either to an heir or a singular successor unless the condition be complied with. 2. That if the condition be farther enforced by an irritant and resolutive clause, it will give the superior not only the passive right of refusing an entry, but an active title to challenge and interrupt the disponee's right'.
20 This is not of course to deny that the superior-vassal relationship contained elements of reciprocal obligation, but if the obligation was founded on contract (which seems uncertain) it did not allow of the usual contractual remedies in enforcement. A possible alternative view of the law might be to say that conditions not *inter naturalia* of the feu (eg, obligations to use the superior's agent as opposed to obligations to pay feuduty) were not treated as part of the feudal contract and so were not enforceable by personal action.
    One of the reasons for hesitation in the use of the contractual model may have been that feu charters (but not feu contracts) were unilateral in form, and it was not until the early nineteenth

century that the doctrine of obligation by acceptance of delivery was clearly established. See *Marquis of Abercorn v Marnoch's Trustee* 26 June 1817 FC, and *Hunter v Boog* (1834) 13 S 205. A version of the contract model can be found earlier than the nineteenth century: see *Wallace v Ferguson* (1739) Mor 4195, and indeed feu farm tenure was commonly regarded as a type of *emphyteusis*. But it was not until the middle Victorian period that the contract model was fully developed and widely discussed. See further para 393 below.

21 Thus the majority in *Campbell v Dunn* (1828) 6 S 679 at 682 (obligation to use superior's agent), which favoured the burden's enforceability, saw the only remedy of the superior as being to refuse entry until the condition was complied with.

22 It is because of the difficulties of enforcement that irritant and resolutive clauses were considered so important in the early history of entails. In *Corpn of Tailors of Aberdeen v Coutts* (1840) 1 Robin 296, HL, where the obligations were in a disposition so that refusal of entry was not available, it was to be argued, in the end unsuccessfully, that a real burden could not be effectual in the absence of such clauses.

23 Thus they can be assigned separately from the superiority (*Stair* II,4,10), which is not possible for real burdens.

24 Except that some real burdens, eg the obligation to build and maintain a house, can be justified as providing security for the superior's claim to feuduty. See eg *Clark v City of Glasgow Life Assurance and Reversionary Co* (1850) 12 D 1047 at 1050, OH (affd (1850) 12 D 1047, IH, revsd (1854) 1 Macq 668, HL).

383. Pecuniary real burdens.

A pecuniary real burden is a type of heritable security, probably still competent[1], but in practice now long since obsolete[2]. In 1820, however, it was at the height of its popularity[3]. Of the three possible prototypes for the modern real burden, the pecuniary real burden is much the least convincing, yet it has had an unexpected and enduring influence on the development of its namesake[4].

The pecuniary real burden is a heritable security created by reservation in a conveyance of land. The creditor's title is constituted by the infeftment of the debtor on the conveyance and there is no separate infeftment of the creditor. The real burden was used as a means of securing obligations by the grantee of a conveyance which were owed either to the granter or to some third party, and in practice it was particularly common in conveyances within families. A contract of ground annual is a special example of a pecuniary real burden, the obligation to pay ground annual being secured by reservation in the original grant[5].

The only point of resemblance between the pecuniary real burden and the modern real burden is that both appear in conveyances of land. Otherwise they are quite different. A real burden in the modern sense is a perpetual personal obligation, undertaken by the owner for the time being of the servient property in favour of the owner for the time being of the dominant property. A pecuniary real burden is not an obligation at all but rather is a means of securing an obligation otherwise existing; and the obligation which it secures (invariably an obligation to pay money) is usually temporary, personal[6] and wholly unconnected with the land itself. Moreover, while, as a real right, the pecuniary real burden affects the land until the obligation which it secures is satisfied, the obligation itself is personal to the original debtor and does not run with the land. In this respect the pecuniary real burden is no different from other heritable securities such as a standard security. Thus if A dispones to B, reserving a real burden for the sum of £5,000, and B then dispones to C, personal liability for payment of the debt remains with B and does not transmit to C. But of course C's land remains as security for the debt and in the event of default A has the option of proceeding against the land. The pecuniary real burden, however, does not confer a power of sale and the creditor's real remedies are confined to poinding of the ground and real adjudication. Like other heritable securities, but unlike the modern real burden[7], the pecuniary real burden is assignable[8].

1 Conveyancing and Feudal Reform (Scotland) Act 1970 (c 35), s 9(3), which abolished the bond and disposition in security and the *ex facie* absolute disposition, appears to have left the real burden

untouched. This is because the definition of 'heritable security' in s 9(8)(a) as a right constituted by disposition in security appears to exclude those securities, like the real burden, which are constituted by reservation. The continuing existence of pecuniary real burdens is presupposed by the Housing (Scotland) Act 1987 (c 26), s 72(7). For a fuller analysis, see K G C Reid 'What is a Real Burden?' (1984) 29 JLSS 9 at 12.

2 *Wells v New House Purchasers Ltd* 1964 SLT (Sh Ct) 2 at 4, per Sheriff-Substitute A G Walker. However, there is a statutory implied real burden in respect of unpaid redemption monies on the compulsory redemption of feuduty: Land Tenure Reform (Scotland) Act 1974 (c 38), s 5(5).

3 There are numerous reported cases on pecuniary real burdens in the eighteenth and early nineteenth centuries. For a detailed contemporary account of the law, see Erskine *Institute* II,3,49 ff.

4 Ie including the fact that it is its namesake. See para 384 below.

5 In later practice this was supplemented by an express re-grant in security. New ground annuals are now disallowed and provision is made for the redemption of existing ground annuals. See the Land Tenure Reform (Scotland) Act 1974, ss 2, 4–6.

6 The obligation to pay feuduty, which is itself secured by an implied real burden, is an exception in this respect.

7 The modern real burden cannot be separated from the dominant tenement to which it is attached: see para 397 below.

8 Conveyancing (Scotland) Act 1874 (c 94), s 30 (amended by the Succession (Scotland) Act 1964 (c 41), s 34(2), Sch 3).

384. Tailors of Aberdeen v Coutts. The early history of the real burden is dominated by three decisions of the House of Lords. The first two of these, *Deas v Edinburgh Magistrates* (1772)[1] and *Gordon v Marjoribanks* (1818)[2], respectively allowed and then disallowed the device of taking successors bound by the exhibition of a feuing plan. The third, *Corpn of Tailors of Aberdeen v Coutts* (1840)[3], adjudicated on the validity of real burdens, which had emerged in the years after *Gordon v Marjoribanks* as the principal device for regulating the use of land in a question with successors. The importance of *Tailors of Aberdeen* can scarcely be overstated[4]. It was the first case to give detailed consideration to the new device of the real burden. It was also the first decision of the House of Lords on the subject. Until *Tailors of Aberdeen* the enforceability of real burdens was, at least to some degree, a matter of speculation. Much was at stake, as the pursuers in the case were not slow to point out:

'The effect of them [the conditions under consideration] was to secure the proper execution of that plan of building and of laying out the subjects, which the appellants were entitled originally to regulate, and at all times to enforce. Upon the observance of them the elegance, the commodiousness, the value, and the permanence of the feus materially depended. And if it is to be maintained that there is no means in the law of Scotland by which proprietors, disposing of building ground, can fix a plan upon which the buildings and streets are to proceed, beyond the mere personal obligation of the first contractor or purchaser, this would be a limitation upon the legal interests of parties never hitherto contemplated in law, and which, in practice, would be accompanied with the most injurious results... According to the respondent's argument it is impossible to enforce any fixed plan as to a street or square beyond the first feuar, and according to his doctrine it is not by their legal effect, but it is by mere accident, or ignorance, or favour, that the plans laid down for the more regular parts of Aberdeen, Edinburgh, and Glasgow are observed for a single year'[5].

The decision in *Tailors of Aberdeen* not only confirmed that real burdens were enforceable but prescribed detailed rules of constitution and enforcement which continue to form the basis of the law today.

The facts of *Tailors of Aberdeen* arose out of the building of Bon-Accord Square in Aberdeen in the 1820s. In 1825 the Tailors of Aberdeen (one of the old merchant corporations) granted a disposition of part of the proposed square to a George Nicol. An ordinary disposition was used because the land was burgage and could not be feued[6]. In terms of the disposition Nicol came under a number of obligations including the obligation to build houses, to erect a railing, to lay the pavement, to pay two thirds of the cost of forming and enclosing the area in the middle of the square, and to refrain from carrying on any business which might constitute a nuisance[7]. Nicol subsequently became insolvent[8] and the land was conveyed by his trustee to Coutts, the defender in the case[9]. A question then arose between Coutts and the Tailors as to whether the obligations undertaken by Nicol in his original disposition could be enforced against Coutts[10], and in 1829 the Tailors raised a personal action against Coutts seeking enforcement of the principal obligations. It was to be a long litigation. In 1837, the case finally having reached the House of Lords, the Lords ordered that it be remitted back to the Court of Session to consider and state to the House its opinion on four specific questions. This was to be the most important part of the case. The leading opinion in the Court of Session, given by Lord Corehouse[11] and concurred in, subject to minor qualification, by the other members of the Court, is an exhaustive analysis of the law which has never been superseded. Ultimately the case returned to the House of Lords, which in 1840 accepted the views of the Court of Session and declared most of the obligations to be enforceable against Coutts[12].

In *Tailors of Aberdeen* the court was mainly concerned with questions of what had to be done in order to create a valid real burden. With two exceptions, the obligations in Nicol's disposition had not been fenced by an irritancy clause, and it was argued strongly by Coutts, on an analogy with the rules for entails[13], that this omission was fatal to their enforceability against successors[14]. Lord Corehouse rejected this argument, and in rejecting it provided for the first time a set of rules for the constitution of real burdens. These rules are considered later[15]. For present purposes the important point to note is that they were borrowed, substantially unaltered, from the already well-established rules which had developed for the pecuniary real burden[16].

What was the relationship between the real burden, as acknowledged and developed in *Tailors of Aberdeen,* and the three prototypes discussed earlier? The issue was clearly focused in the argument put for the pursuers:

> 'It is inappropriate to talk of these stipulations as being [pecuniary] real burdens. The question is not whether the appellants can be ranked preferably for them in a competition with creditors, or whether they can adjudge or poind the ground for implement of such conditions; neither are they to be considered with reference to mere feudal peculiarities. They are to be viewed as inherent and standing conditions in a grant of lands, which form between the parties a permanent and a transmissible mutual contract'[17].

On this aspect of the case Lord Corehouse's opinion is less satisfactory. The argument of the pursuers, that the real burden is a fourth category distinct from its three prototypes, was not discussed. Instead the modern real burden was seen as part of a large and undifferentiated category of obligation which included the pecuniary real burden, the feudal condition and the servitude; indeed, as has been seen, it was the pecuniary real burden which was treated as the principal model, at least in respect of rules of constitution[18]. This approach is the more surprising when it is recalled that the form of action was a direct personal action against Coutts, for a personal action was available neither for pecuniary real burdens[19] nor, at least traditionally, for feudal conditions[20]. While it was true that servitudes were enforceable by personal action, the obligations in Nicol's disposition were positive in nature and so could not be servitudes[21]. Consequently, the result, if not the reasoning, of *Tailors of Aberdeen,* implied clearly the emergence of a new kind of obligation, distinct from any of its prototypes; but it was to be several decades before this fact was widely and adequately acknowledged.

1 *Deas v Edinburgh Magistrates* (1772) 2 Pat 259, HL. See para 378 above.
2 *Gordon v Marjoribanks* (1818) 6 Dow 87, HL. See para 379 above.
3 *Corpn of Tailors of Aberdeen v Coutts* (1837) 2 Sh & Macl 609, HL (further proceedings (1840) 1 Robin 296, HL).

4 The parallels between this decision and the only slightly later decision of the House of Lords in *Tulk v Moxhay* (1848) 2 Ph 774, 41 ER 1143, HL are striking, for just as *Corpn of Tailors of Aberdeen v Coutts* established the modern law of real burdens in Scotland, so *Tulk v Moxhay* established the modern law of restrictive covenants in England and Wales. On *Tulk* see further A W B Simpson *A History of the Land Law* (2nd edn, 1986) pp 257 ff.

5 *Corpn of Tailors of Aberdeen v Coutts* (1837) 2 Sh & Macl 609 at 646, HL.

6 In fact this was the second attempt. Earlier, in April 1824, the Tailors had granted Nicol a feu charter, which was withdrawn and replaced by the disposition when it was discovered that the land was burgage. This was to prove a source of continuing confusion, both in the case itself and subsequently. Thus on several occasions the House of Lords (but not the Court of Session: see *Corpn of Tailors of Aberdeen v Coutts* (1840) 1 Robin 296 at 306) refers to Nicol's deed as a feu charter.

7 For the deed in full, see *Corpn of Tailors of Aberdeen v Coutts* (1837) 2 Sh & Macl 609 at 620 ff, HL.

8 The fate of builders throughout the ages.

9 Coutts was an advocate in Aberdeen who had previously been joint clerk to the Tailors and under whose professional supervision the original disposition to Nicol was prepared. That disposition failed to include a clause, contained in the articles of roup, requiring that the burdens be repeated in subsequent conveyances and indeed they were not repeated in the disposition granted to Coutts. Claiming that Coutts was now benefiting from his own professional omission, the Tailors had an alternative case against him in fraud, but this was later abandoned. These unjustified 'attacks made upon his character' were eventually taken into account by the House of Lords in the award of expenses: see *Corpn of Tailors of Aberdeen v Coutts* (1840) 1 Robin 296 at 343, HL.

10 The immediate *casus belli* was that Coutts, during nightfall and without permission, cut a channel through the street from his houses to the common sewer which had been provided by the Tailors.

11 *Corpn of Tailors of Aberdeen v Coutts* (1840) 1 Robin 296 at 305 ff. ·

12 Ie most but not all. The reason why certain obligations were said not to be enforceable was that they failed to meet the new rules of constitution prescribed by Lord Corehouse.

13 Originally irritant and resolutive clauses were used in entails in the hope, in the event misplaced, that this would prevent a defaulting heir from conferring a good title on a purchaser buying in breach of the entail. When entails came to be regulated by the Entail Act 1685 (c 26) irritant and resolutive clauses became a prerequisite of valid constitution.

14 This was a question of enforcement as well as of constitution because in the law as then understood it was unclear that a condition in a *disposition* could be enforced against successors by any other method. It was only as a result of the actual decision in *Tailors of Aberdeen* that it came to be accepted that a direct personal action was possible.

15 See paras 386 ff below.

16 See K G C Reid 'What is a Real Burden?' (1984) 29 JLSS 9 at 11. All the authorities referred to by Lord Corehouse in his exposition of the rules of constitution (*Corpn of Tailors of Aberdeen v Coutts* (1840) 1 Robin 296 at 306–308) are authorities concerning pecuniary real burdens. Why Lord Corehouse chose to borrow the rules for pecuniary real burdens is not known.

17 *Corpn of Tailors of Aberdeen v Coutts* (1837) 2 Sh & Macl 609 at 646, 647, HL. For an earlier version of this kind of argument see *Campbell v Dunn* (1828) 6 S 679 at 682, per Lord Justice-Clerk Boyle and Lord Pitmilly, Lord Meadowbank and Lord Medwyn and again (at 689) per Lord Alloway, Lord Cringletie, Lord Mackenzie and Lord Eldin.

18 This was also the approach of Lord Brougham in the House of Lords: see *Corpn of Tailors of Aberdeen v Coutts* (1837) 2 Sh & Macl 609 at 662 ff, HL.

19 See para 383 above. This fundamental point may have been less clearly focused in the 1830s than it is today, for the pecuniary real burden was often used within families where a new owner would have incurred personal liability as a universal successor. It is also worth noting that it was not until 1853 that it was decided that the personal obligation in a ground annual does not run with the land (*Millar v Small* (1853) 1 Macq 345, HL) the First Division having earlier decided the contrary (*Peddie v Gibson* (1846) 8 D 560).

20 See para 382 above. Of course since the deed in *Tailors of Aberdeen* was an ordinary disposition, the conditions could not have been feudal conditions in any case.

21 See para 381 above.

385. The emergence of real burdens as a separate category. It has been seen that there were three possible prototypes for the modern real burden, namely servitudes, feuing conditions, and pecuniary real burdens. *Corpn of Tailors of Aberdeen v Coutts*[1] made clear that a real burden was not a servitude[2], but nor, equally, was it a feudal condition, if only because there was in that case no relationship of superior and vassal between the pursuers and the defender[3]. The position with respect to pecuniary real burdens was, however, less certain. No proper distinction is made in Lord Corehouse's opinion between pecuniary real burdens and real burdens in the modern sense[4]. The same name[5] and, with minor qualifications[6], the same rules of constitution are applied to both. This was to prove both advantageous and also disadvantageous in the future development of the law. The advantage of Lord Corehouse's approach was that it provided the new obligation with ready-made rules of constitution and also with a name. The disadvantage was that it led to a persistent confusion between the two types of real burden, a confusion all the more remarkable when it is considered how dissimilar the two are in nature.

Evidence of confusion between the two senses of real burden was present in *Clark v City of Glasgow Life Assurance and Reversionary Co* (1850)[7], the first case of significance to be decided after *Tailors of Aberdeen*. *Clark* concerned the enforcement of real burdens in the modern sense of conditions governing the use of the land, but the distinction between the two senses of real burden was vigorously disputed by the defenders who pleaded:

'... the argument of the pursuers was directed not so much to establish that the obligations sought to be enforced were a [pecuniary] real burden or condition, as to maintain that, though purely personal, it [*sic*] was an essential condition of the feu-contract, and binding upon the defenders as singular successors. The notion implied in this proposition, of an essential condition of the feu, binding as such upon singular successors, yet distinct from a real condition or burden, was an entire novelty in law'[8].

The pursuers in *Clark* were successful, and over the next few years the distinction neglected in *Tailors of Aberdeen* and complained of in *Clark* gradually came to be established. As recently as 1964, however, defenders in an action to enforce real burdens (in the modern sense) felt able to argue that the only remedies available to the pursuer were poinding of the ground and real adjudication, the two real remedies available under the old pecuniary real burden[9]. But by 1964 it was far too late for arguments of this kind. In a series of judgments a hundred years earlier the real burden had emerged finally and conclusively from the shadow of the pecuniary real burden[10]. This clarification is particularly associated with Lord Deas and it is appropriate to end this section on origins and development of real burdens with an extract from his leading opinion in the case of *Marquis of Tweeddale's Trustees v Earl of Haddington*:

'Now, there is no doubt a sense in which all burdens which directly affect the land, or, to use the English phraseology, "run with the land" are real burdens. For instance an inherent condition of the right [that is, a real burden in the modern sense[11]] is often called a real burden even in the deed by which it is constituted, in order to mark its immediate connection with the land; but that sort of real burden is totally different in respect of the rights and remedies it confers from the real burden of a specific debt or sum of money, which last is usually what our writers mean by a real burden when treating of our different forms of heritable security ... it [the pecuniary real burden] imports no personal obligation, and can only be made effectual against the lands themselves by the roundabout and expensive process of adjudication or poinding of the ground ... On the other hand, an inherent condition of the right has the advantage of being enforceable by personal action against the proprietor or proprietors for the time being at the instance of whosoever has an interest to enforce it, whether named in the deed or not'[12].

1 *Corpn of Tailors of Aberdeen v Coutts* (1840) 1 Robin 296.
2 It was accepted by Lord Corehouse that the rules of constitution were different: see (1840) 1 Robin 296 at 309, 310.
3 The land was held burgage, so that the conveyance was a disposition and not a feu disposition. The relationship between feudal conditions and real burdens remains problematic. Commentators have often seen real burdens as a type of feudal condition; but since real burdens are the broader category, if there is a direct relationship between the two (which seems open to doubt) it can only be that feudal conditions of this kind are a type of real burden. Feudal conditions may, however, fall within

the decision in *Corpn of Tailors of Aberdeen v Coutts* (1840) 1 Robin 296, HL, at least to the extent of allowing direct enforcement by personal action, which was previously not permitted. See also para 393 below.

4 But see the observation of Lord Deas in *Marquis of Tweeddale's Trustees v Earl of Haddington* (1880) 7 R 620 at 635: 'On analysing the passages now quoted it will be observed that although the object of the opinion was not to define the difference between a real burden for a capital sum of debt as contrasted with an inherent condition of the right [ie a modern real burden] that difference is throughout distinctly recognised'. This view is open to question. The distinction is, however, made in the opinion of Lord Medwyn: see *Corpn of Tailors of Aberdeen v Coutts* (1840) 1 Robin 296 at 332, 333.

5 The famous passage in which Lord Corehouse sets out the rules of constitution begins with the words: 'To constitute a real burden or condition, either in feudal or burgage rights, which is effectual against singular successors . . .': see *Corpn of Tailors of Aberdeen v Coutts* (1840) 1 Robin 296 at 306.

6 Lord Corehouse appears to suggest that a lesser degree of specification is required for (modern) real burdens when he says: 'If the condition is one usually attaching to the lands in a feudal or burgage holding, — in particular if it has a *tractus futuri temporis,* or is of a continuous nature, which cannot be performed and so extinguished by one act of the disponee or his heir, words less clear and specific will suffice to create it than when the burden appears to be of a personal nature [that is, personal to the original disponee only]; for example, the payment of a sum of money once for all in terms of a family settlement': (1840) 1 Robin 296 at 308, and again when he says (at 310, 311) 'But there is another class of cases, as already mentioned, where the words must be much more precise and specific to make the obligation binding on singular successors. Thus, where the disponee is burdened with the payment of a sum of money, whether it be reserved to the superior himself or made payable to a third party, if the amount of the sum is not exactly specified in the investiture, it is unavailing, for the law of Scotland does not admit any indefinite burden attaching to lands'. These passages contain the seeds of the modern doctrine that real burdens are restricted as to content. See para 391 below.

7 *Clark v City of Glasgow Life Assurance and Reversionary Co* (1850) 12 D 1047, revsd (1854) 1 Macq 668, HL.

8 *Clark v City of Glasgow Life Assurance and Reversionary Co* (1850) 12 D 1047 at 1052, OH (affd 12 D 1047, IH). The arguments for the pursuers also show signs of confusion.

9 *Wells v New House Purchasers Ltd* 1964 SLT (Sh Ct) 2. The judgment of Sheriff-Substitute A G Walker is carefully argued and repays study.

10 See *Edinburgh Magistrates v Begg* (1883) 11 R 352, and the cases cited in note 12 below. For later restatements, see *Campbell's Trustees v Glasgow Corpn* (1902) 4 F 752 at 758, 10 SLT 9 at 10, per Lord Kinnear (with which may be compared the same judge's remarks in *Falconar Stewart v Wilkie* (1892) 19 R 630 at 641); *Maguire v Burges* 1909 SC 1283 at 1290, 1291, 1909 2 SLT 219 at 222, per Lord President Dunedin. See also *Arbroath Magistrates v Dickson* (1872) 10 M 630 where, however, an obligation to pay 'feuduty' in a burgage disposition seems to have been regarded as personally binding on all successive proprietors.

11 See para 375 above.

12 *Marquis of Tweeddale's Trustees v Earl of Haddington* (1880) 7 R 620 at 630–634. For earlier analyses by the same judge, which, however, do not bring out the difference in remedies, see *Stewart v Duke of Montrose* (1860) 22 D 755 at 803 and *Corbett v Robertson* (1872) 10 M 329 at 334.

(3) RULES OF CONSTITUTION

386. Introduction. The rules of constitution of real burdens were first set out in the judgment of Lord Corehouse in *Corpn of Tailors of Aberdeen v Coutts*[1] and, to a considerable extent, they were borrowed from rules which had already evolved for pecuniary real burdens. These original rules have since been considerably developed and expanded by many reported decisions, and in their expanded form may be said to consist of five principal elements:

(1) There must be a dominant and a servient tenement. A real burden is an obligation imposed on the owner of the servient tenement for the benefit of the owner of the dominant tenement;

(2) The burden must be contained in full either in a conveyance of the servient tenement or in a statutory deed of conditions;

(3) The burden must be registered in the Register of Sasines or the Land Register;

(4) There are additional requirements as to the form in which the burden must be written; and

(5) There are additional requirements as to the content of the burden.

1 *Corpn of Tailors of Aberdeen v Coutts* (1840) 1 Robin 296.

387. Rule 1: a dominant and a servient tenement. Real burdens, like obligations of common interest and servitudes, are a type of real condition[1]. Real conditions are discussed elsewhere in this title[2], but briefly they may be defined as obligations relating to one piece of property, known as the servient property or servient tenement, imposed for the benefit of another piece of property, known as the dominant property or dominant tenement. A real condition is enforceable against the owner for the time being of the servient tenement (the 'servient proprietor')[3], and the right to enforce lies with the owner for the time being of the dominant tenement (the 'dominant proprietor'). The right, and also the correlative obligation, both run with the land and not with the person so that, at least as a general rule, ownership of the dominant and servient tenements is the determinant of, respectively, right and obligation.

Real burdens are created either in a conveyance of the servient tenement or in a statutory deed of conditions made with reference to the servient tenement. Usually, therefore, there is no difficulty in identifying the servient tenement. The identity of the dominant tenement is determined by the type of conveyance used or, in the case of burdens in a deed of conditions, by the type of conveyance granted along with the deed of conditions[4]. Thus where the conveyance is a grant in feu (whether a feu disposition, feu charter or feu contract) the dominant tenement is the reserved superiority of the granter, with the result that the burden is enforceable by the superior for the time being, and against the vassal for the time being, of the same property. But where the conveyance is an ordinary disposition, so that in feudal terms there is substitution and not subinfeudation, no interest in the land conveyed remains in the granter and there is often no other interest in land capable of acting as a dominant tenement. For this reason real burdens are not usually possible in ordinary dispositions[5]. The difficulty is solved, however, if either the disponer owns neighbouring land, or if he nominates such land as a dominant tenement notwithstanding that it is owned by a third party. Thus if A dispones Whitemains to B but retains ownership of Blackmains, being adjoining land, Blackmains can act as a dominant tenement for any real burdens imposed on Whitemains. The burdens are then enforceable by the owner for the time being of Blackmains against the owner for the time being of Whitemains. In a well-drawn disposition the right conferred on Blackmains will be clearly expressed[6], but even where not so expressed there is probably an implied right to enforce arising from the mere fact of the disponer having reserved adjoining land[7].

Without both a dominant and a servient tenement there can be no real burden. But it is competent, and indeed not uncommon, for there to be more than one such tenement. This occurs if the original conveyance creating the burden confers enforcement rights not merely on the property reserved by the granter but on other, neighbouring property. It also occurs if the original dominant or servient tenements are later subdivided and come into separate ownership.

1 Many of the issues raised in this para are discussed more fully at paras 397 ff below.
2 See paras 344 ff above.
3 But some real conditions, notably servitudes, are *in rem* and hence are enforceable against 'the world': see para 347 above. For the equivalent rule for real burdens, see para 413 below.
4 Occasionally there is no accompanying conveyance, in which case the dominant tenement must be specified in the deed of conditions.
5 *Corbett v Robertson* (1872) 10 M 329 at 335, per Lord Ardmillan. Of course the obligation is enforceable as a matter of contract in a question between the original parties. The rule is the same in

English law, where a restrictive covenant must be attached to a dominant tenement. In *Scott v Howard* (1880) 7 R 997, affd (1881) 8 R (HL) 59, where there was no dominant tenement (but the burden was held to fail on other grounds), it is suggested (in this writer's view, improbably) that where the obligation is repeated in subsequent dispositions of the property, the original disponer might be entitled to enforce the obligation on the (contractual) principle of *jus quaesitum tertio*. See (1880) 7 R 997 at 1012, 1013, per Lord Ormidale, and (1881) 8 R (HL) 59 at 65, per Lord Watson.
6 *Braid Hills Hotel Co Ltd v Manuels* 1909 SC 120, 16 SLT 523.
7 *J A Mactaggart & Co v Harrower* (1906) 8 F 1101, 14 SLT 277. See further para 403 below.

388. Rule 2: conveyance or deed of conditions. Until 1979 real burdens could be created only in a conveyance of the servient property. In practice this was sometimes an inconvenient rule. It meant that, while a seller of land could impose real burdens on a purchaser, the proprietor of Plot A was unable to create a real burden in favour of his neighbour, the proprietor of Plot B. There was no equivalent for real burdens of a simple deed of servitude. A difficulty of a different kind was that the purchaser of a house or other small unit in a proposed large development could have no guarantee that the real burdens to which his own property was being made subject would be imposed *mutatis mutandis* on the remaining units in the development. The best that could be done was to take the personal obligation of the developer, which might or might not be honoured when the remaining units came to be conveyed[1].

The Land Registration (Scotland) Act 1979[2] solved these, and other, difficulties by making provision for the use of deeds of conditions. Deeds of conditions were not invented in 1979. They had been competent since 1874[3] as a method of setting out in a separate deed the real burdens under which land was intended to be conveyed and they were widely used by developers in order to save the labour of reciting the burdens in the conveyance of each individual unit[4]. But a deed of conditions was effective only if, and to the extent that, it was incorporated into a subsequent conveyance of the proposed servient tenement. In substance it was no more than a statutory method of incorporating extraneous material into conveyances. Under the 1979 Act a deed of conditions is now effective on its own account, except where the deed itself states otherwise[5]. Incorporation into a conveyance is not required. The actual effect of such a deed will, however, depend upon the circumstances in which it is used. Therefore, if the proprietor of Plot A grants a deed of conditions in favour of the proprietor of Plot B, the real burdens come into operation as soon as the deed is registered (unless the deed stipulates otherwise). The same is true of a deed of conditions granted by the proprietors within a tenement where each proprietor is to have reciprocal rights of enforcement. However, if a developer grants a deed of conditions over land which he owns and is in the process of developing, there is a servient tenement but no dominant tenement, and the deed has no effect until the conveyance of individual units, with reciprocal rights of enforcement[6], brings into existence a series of dominant (and servient) tenements.

The modern law, therefore, is that real burdens may be created either in conveyances or in deeds of conditions. They cannot be created in a deed of any other kind[7]. Neither of the permitted deeds has a statutory form. Since registration is required[8], the deed is in practice always made self-evidencing by being executed under section 3 of the Requirements of Writing (Scotland) Act 1995. Except in some cases involving bodies corporate[9], section 3 requires attestation by a witness. The granter must be infeft or, in the case of dispositions only, uninfeft but able to deduce title through appropriate midcouples[10]. In dispositions and other conveyances the convention is to place burdens at the end of the dispositive clause and, while there appears to be no positive requirement to adhere to this convention, the fact that an obligation is placed elsewhere in the deed will be taken as an indication, although not as a conclusive indication, that it was not intended to be real[11]. Deeds of conditions are usually unilateral in form, granted and executed, as the statute directs[12], by the proprietor or proprietors of the servient tenement, but a deed in the form of a bilateral contract has also been accepted as a valid exercise of the statutory facility[13].

The conveyance or, as the case may be, the deed of conditions must relate to the servient tenement. This means that, unlike the rule for servitudes[14], a real burden cannot competently be created in a conveyance of the dominant tenement[15]. The reason is fair notice to third parties: a burden contained in a deed relating to other land would not be discoverable by a purchaser of the servient tenement in the course of examination of title. Furthermore, and for the same reason, the full terms of the burden must appear from the four corners of the deed itself[16]. In *Corpn of Tailors of Aberdeen v Coutts* it was said that:

> 'They [the cases] prove incontestably the necessity of making whatever obligation is to be cast upon the purchaser apparent on the face of the title, and that not merely by giving him a general notice that there is such a burden, but by specifying its exact nature and amount; not merely calling his attention to it, and sending him to seek for it in a known and accessible repository, or even referring to it as revealed in the same repository, but of disclosing it fully upon the face of the title itself...'[17].

In application of this rule, real burdens cannot be created in one deed by the importation by reference of terms set out in another[18], and this is so even where the imported deed has itself been registered in the Register of Sasines or Land Register[19]. Nor is it permissible 'to go to the other titles which have been granted by the same disponer in order, so to speak, to form a glossary of the disponer's words'[20]. Only the principal deed (the conveyance or, as the case may be, the deed of conditions) may be consulted. In one well-known case a burden was said to be fatally flawed by its reference to a statute, the terms of which were not given in the deed[21]. A further aspect of this rule is that evidence extrinsic to the deed is not admissible to supplement the terms of provisions purporting to create real burdens, in effect a heightened form of the usual rule against extrinsic evidence in the interpretation of written documents. But extrinsic evidence is not excluded in absolutely all circumstances, for, as has been pointed out judicially[22], it will always be necessary to go beyond a deed in order to apply its terms to the external facts. The restriction in the deed must be matched up with the facts as they appear on the ground, even although the actual terms of the restriction can only be found from the deed itself[23].

1 Sometimes it was not honoured: see eg *Leith School Board v Rattray's Trustees* 1918 SC 94, 1917 2 SLT 247. In *Maguire v Burges* 1909 SC 1283, 1909 2 SLT 219, the real burdens were duly included in a subsequent feu but were utterly contradicted by other burdens which accompanied them.
2 Land Registration (Scotland) Act 1979 (c 33), s 17.
3 Conveyancing (Scotland) Act 1874 (c 94), s 32.
4 Traditionally they were used much more in the Glasgow area than elsewhere in Scotland.
5 Land Registration (Scotland) Act 1979, s 17.
6 Ie assuming provision is made for such rights, which may or may not be the case. Property reserved by the developer can also act as a dominant tenement.
7 So eg a minute of waiver cannot be used for the creation of new real burdens. See the Land Registration (Scotland) Act 1979, s 18.
8 If a deed is to be registered it must be executed under s 3, or set up by a court under s 4, of the Requirements of Writing (Scotland) Act 1995 (c 7): see s 6.
9 Ibid, s 7(7), Sch 2.
10 Conveyancing (Scotland) Act 1924 (c 27), s 3. In the case of Land Register titles a formal clause of deduction of title is no longer required: Land Registration (Scotland) Act 1979, s 15(3).
11 *Kemp v Largs Magistrates* 1939 SC (HL) 6, 1939 SLT 228. The condition was in the tenendas clause. This was not the only reason why the burden failed and Lord Macmillan was careful to say (1939 SC (HL) 6 at 16, 1939 SLT 228 at 233) that the various reasons were 'cumulatively sufficient' for the ultimate result. Before 1858 the position was different. As Lord Macmillan points out (1939 SC (HL) 6 at 14, 1939 SLT 228 at 232) under reference to Duff's *Treatise on the Deeds and Forms used in the Constitution, Transmission, and Extinction of Feudal Rights* (1838) p 81, the tenendas clause was not repeated in the instrument of sasine, so that, until direct registration of conveyances was introduced in 1858, an obligation contained only in the tenendas clause would not enter the Register of Sasines

and could not be real. This may still be the rule for pecuniary real burdens, at least where the burden is contained in a (non registrable) general conveyance: see *Cowie v Muirden* (1893) 20 R (HL) 81 at 87, per Lord Shand; *Scott v Scott's Trustees* (1898) 6 SLT 119, OH.

12 Conveyancing (Scotland) Act 1874, s 32.

13 *Gorrie and Banks Ltd v Burgh of Musselburgh* 1973 SC 33, 1974 SLT 157. A further unusual feature of this case is that the burdens were intended to be enforceable, not by the granter of the deed of conditions, but by the other party to the deed, who was the granter's superior.

14 See *Balfour v Kinsey* 1987 SLT 144, OH.

15 Eg *Jolly's Executrix v Viscount Stonehaven* 1958 SC 635, 1959 SLT 97. But cf *Wilson's Trustees v Brown's Executors* (1907) 15 SLT 747, OH.

16 The phrase 'four corners of [the deed]' is Lord Guthrie's: see *Anderson v Dickie* 1914 SC 706 at 717, 1914 1 SLT 484 at 489 (affd 1915 SC (HL) 79, 1915 1 SLT 393); *Scottish Temperance Life Assurance Co v Law Union and Rock Insurance Co* 1917 SC 175 at 185, 1917 1 SLT 4 at 7.

17 *Corpn of Tailors of Aberdeen v Coutts* (1837) 2 Sh & Macl 609 at 663, HL, per Lord Brougham (further proceedings (1840) 1 Robin 296, HL).

18 The rule is otherwise where the real burden has already been properly created in the other deed and its terms are being imported for some other purpose, eg to qualify the dispositive clause in order to limit the granter's obligation of warrandice. See the Conveyancing (Scotland) Act 1874, s 32, and para 396 below.

19 *Campbell's Trustees v Glasgow Corpn* (1902) 4 F 752, 10 SLT 9. A statutory exception is found in the Conveyancing (Scotland) Act 1874, s 32, which relates to burdens set out in a deed of conditions; but this is of little importance in modern practice because, unless it stipulates to the contrary, a deed of conditions is now directly effective on registration and does not depend on incorporation into a subsequent conveyance. See the Land Registration (Scotland) Act 1979, s 17.

20 *Bainbridge v Campbell* 1912 SC 92 at 96, 1911 2 SLT 373 at 375, per Lord President Dunedin. See also *Dunedin Property Management Services Ltd v Glamis Property Co Ltd* 1993 GWD 31-2006.

21 *Aberdeen Varieties Ltd v James F Donald (Aberdeen Cinemas Ltd)* 1939 SC 788, 1940 SLT 58, revsd 1940 SC (HL) 52, 1940 SLT 374. The burden read: the subjects '. . . shall not be used in all time coming for the performance of pantomime, melodrama or comic opera or any stage play which requires to be submitted to the Lord Chamberlain under the Act for regulating Theatres Sixth and Seventh Victoria Chapter Sixty-eight'. See also *Liddall v Duncan* (1898) 25 R 1119, 6 SLT 77. Thus the burdens, sometimes encountered in practice, which make reference to the need to obtain planning permission in terms of the Town and Country Planning (Scotland) Act 1972 (c 52) are, it seems, invalid on this principle.

22 *McLean v Marwhirn Developments Ltd* 1976 SLT (Notes) 47; *Lothian Regional Council v Rennie* 1991 SCLR 709, 1991 SLT 465.

23 *Anderson v Dickie* 1915 SC (HL) 79 at 86, 1915 1 SLT 393 at 397, per Lord Kinnear.

389. Rule 3: registration. The burden must be registered, either in the Register of Sasines or, in appropriate cases[1], in the Land Register[2]. To this rule there is only one exception, now obsolete, which operated in questions between superiors and vassals prior to the introduction of implied feudal entry in 1874[3].

For Sasine titles registration may be either of the original deed in which the burden is created, or alternatively of some later deed which owes its validity to the original deed: a notice of title, for example, or a second conveyance deducing title through the first. In the second case the burdens are transcribed in full from the original conveyance to the notice of title (or as the case may be)[4]. It is not sufficient to register some other deed which happens to contain details of the burdens[5]. Up until 1858 ordinary conveyances were not registrable and burdens required to be transcribed into an instrument of sasine which could then be registered. Today conveyances are registered directly[6].

The same general rules apply to the Land Register but the procedure is different. In the Land Register the original conveyance or deed of conditions always accompanies the application for registration even where there has been a supervening deed, such as a second conveyance[7], which itself requires to be registered[8]. The Keeper then enters the terms of the burden, or a summary thereof, in the burdens section[9] of the title sheet of the servient tenement[10]. In practice the burden is usually entered in full, but where a summary is used there is a statutory presumption that it is a correct statement of the burden[11].

Until registration a real burden is ineffective except at a contractual level, and for this reason conveyances sometimes take the grantee bound to register within a limited period, such as six months, transfer usually being prohibited until registration has taken place[12]. But while a burden is ineffectual until registration, the mere fact of registration (even registration in the Land Register) does not perfect a burden which fails to comply with the other rules of constitution[13]. No indemnity is payable by the Keeper of the Land Register for a burden which proves to be unenforceable[14].

1 For the appropriate cases, see the Land Registration (Scotland) Act 1979 (c 33), s 2.
2 *Corpn of Tailors of Aberdeen v Coutts* (1840) 1 Robin 296 at 306, 307, per Lord Corehouse: the burden 'must be inserted in the sasine which follows on the conveyance, and of consequence appear upon the record'. This proposition has been reasserted on numerous occasions. See eg *Croall v Edinburgh Magistrates* (1870) 9 M 323 and *Liddall v Duncan* (1898) 25 R 1119, 6 SLT 77. For Land Register titles it is expressly provided that a proprietor is affected only by burdens which appear on the Register: see the Land Registration (Scotland) Act 1979, s 3(1)(a).
3 See further para 393 below.
4 See eg *Peter Walker & Son (Edinburgh) Ltd v Church of Scotland General Trustees* 1967 SLT 297 (notarial instrument).
5 *Campbell's Trustees v Glasgow Corpn* (1902) 4 F 752, 10 SLT 9.
6 Titles to Land Consolidation (Scotland) Act 1868 (c 101), s 15. See para 91 above.
7 There are no notices of title in registration of title: Land Registration (Scotland) Act 1979, s 3(6).
8 For this reason there is no need to repeat the terms of the burdens in the second conveyance. Usually, however, the original deed will be referred to for burdens: see the Land Registration (Scotland) Act 1979, s 15(2).
9 Land Registration (Scotland) Rules 1980, SI 1980/1413, r 7(1)(a).
10 Land Registration (Scotland) Act 1979, ss 5(1), 6(1)(e), (2). It may also appear in the title sheet of the dominant tenement.
11 Ibid, s 6(2).
12 A typical provision is 'to AB and his executors and assignees whomsoever but excluding assignees before infeftment and declaring that these presents shall not be a warrant for infeftment more than six months after the date hereof'. It may be a question whether the exclusion of 'assignees' would be sufficient to prevent a grantee from using the facility introduced by the Conveyancing (Scotland) Act 1924 (c 27), s 3, of disponing the land under deduction of title.
13 For the Land Register, the Land Registration (Scotland) Act 1979, s 3(1)(b), is subject to the general proviso 'insofar as the right or obligation is capable, under any enactment or rule of law, of . . . being made real'.
14 Land Registration (Scotland) Act 1979, s 12(3)(g).

390. Rule 4: form. Form is regulated in two different ways. First, there are a number of rules of draftsmanship. Thus real burdens must be precisely drawn; there must be adequate identification of the servient and of the dominant tenements[1]; the clause must plainly impose an obligation and not merely express a wish[2]; and the nature and extent of the obligation or restriction sought to be imposed must be clearly defined[3]. Failure to meet these standards, where it does not actually render the burden unenforceable, may result in an interpretation of the words much narrower than intended by their draftsman[4], for real burdens are read *contra proferentem* and, as has been seen[5], extrinsic evidence is not generally admissible. In interpreting a burden one is concerned, not with the (subjective) intention of the original parties to the deed, but with whether, in a legal sense, that intention has been properly realised[6].

Secondly, the law requires clear indication from the deed itself that the obligation as so drafted is to run with the lands. 'Words must be used in the conveyance which clearly express or plainly imply that the subject itself is affected, and not the grantee and his heirs alone'[7] although '. . . it is not essential that any *voces signatae* or technical form of words should be employed'[7]. In practice a well-drawn deed will declare[8] that the obligation is a real burden, that it is to bind not only the grantee but his successors as well[9], and that it is to be repeated in all future transmissions of the subjects[10], and, while each deed must be a matter of individual construction so that generalisations are hazardous[11], it is thought that the presence of any one of these three declarations is usually sufficient by itself to indicate that the burden is real[12]. An irritancy clause is also a favourable indicator[13]. To some extent the requirements depend upon the type of deed and also upon the type of obligation. Thus clearer words are needed in ordinary dispositions, which do not as a rule create real burdens, than in feu dispositions, which do; and very little indeed is required in deeds of conditions, which are statutory creations whose only purpose is to create real burdens. So far as type of obligation is concerned, the rule is that:

> '... if the obligation is to be performed, and so extinguished, by a single act, the presumption is that the granter of the feu-right meant to impose it on the grantee and his heirs exclusively, and not to extend it against singular successors; the case being the reverse of those where the obligation has a continuance and is, comparatively, of little use unless it remains attached to the subject'[14].

But this is a presumption only[15], and obligations to perform single acts, such as building a house or fencing a garden, are frequently imposed and have frequently been enforced against successors[16].

1 See further paras 397 ff (dominant tenement), 410 (servient tenement), below.
2 *Kemp v Largs Magistrates* 1939 SC (HL) 6, 1939 SLT 228.
3 See eg *Anderson v Dickie* 1915 SC (HL) 79, 1915 1 SLT 393. These rules do not appear in *Corpn of Tailors of Aberdeen v Coutts* (1840) 1 Robin 296 itself and do not seem to have been developed until the last twenty years of the nineteenth century. See further paras 415 ff below.
4 See para 419 below.
5 See para 388 above.
6 See *Arbroath Magistrates v Dickson* (1872) 10 M 630 at 635, per Lord President Inglis where he says: 'We are not to construe a deed of conveyance of this kind as we construe a will, for the purpose of arriving by all means, and even by something like conjectural means, at what the intention of the testator is'. See also *Anderson v Dickie* 1915 SC (HL) 79 at 90, 1915 1 SLT 393 at 399, per Lord Dunedin; *Peter Walker & Son (Edinburgh) Ltd v Church of Scotland General Trustees* 1967 SLT 297.
7 *Corpn of Tailors of Aberdeen v Coutts* (1840) 1 Robin 296 at 306, 307, per Lord Corehouse.
8 The three declarations which follow appear in Lord Corehouse's opinion in *Corpn of Tailors of Aberdeen v Coutts* (1840) 1 Robin 296 at 307: '... a declaration that the obligation is real, that it is a *debitum fundi*, that it shall be inserted in all the future infeftments, or that it shall attach to singular successors'. Lord Corehouse's fourth declaration, that the obligation is a *debitum fundi*, is applicable to pecuniary real burdens only and is an indication of the persistent confusion in *Tailors of Aberdeen* between the two senses of real burden.
9 Ie his successors as proprietor of the servient tenement, as opposed to his personal representatives and those entitled to succeed to his estate on death. These are 'singular' as opposed to 'universal' successors: see para 598 below. In practice burdens are often declared binding on a named grantee and 'his foresaids', which refers back to the words of the destination at the start of the dispositive clause; but since the standard 'ordinary' destination is 'to A and his executors and *assignees* whomsoever' this practice is vulnerable to the criticism that disponees are excluded. See G L Gretton 'Heirs, Executors and Assignees' (1984) 29 JLSS 103 and the cases there cited.
10 *Nicholson v Glasgow Asylum for the Blind* 1911 SC 391, 1911 1 SLT 37; *Lees v North East Fife District Council* 1987 SLT 769.
11 *Peter Walker & Son (Edinburgh) Ltd v Church of Scotland General Trustees* 1967 SLT 297 at 300, per Lord Justice-Clerk Grant. In that case the obligation in dispute was declared binding on a named grantee and not, like other obligations in the deed, on the grantee and his foresaids, and this was considered fatal to the argument that the obligation was real.
12 *Matheson v Tinney* 1989 SLT 535, OH, appears to be an example.
13 *Corpn of Tailors of Aberdeen v Coutts* (1840) 1 Robin 296 at 316, 317, per Lord Corehouse.
14 (1840) 1 Robin 296 at 311, per Lord Corehouse, and earlier (at 308): 'If the condition is one usually attaching to the lands in a feudal or burgage holding — in particular if it has a *tractus futuri temporis*, or is of a continuous nature, which cannot be performed and so extinguished by one act of the disponee or his heir, words less clear and specific will suffice to create it than when the burden appears to be of a personal nature ...'.
15 For examples of the presumption in operation, see *Edinburgh Magistrates v Begg* (1883) 11 R 352, and *Jolly's Executrix v Viscount Stonehaven* 1958 SC 635, 1959 SLT 97.
16 An example is the obligation, in *Tailors of Aberdeeen* itself, to erect houses within a certain time, which was characterised by Lord Corehouse ((1840) 1 Robin 296 at 322, 323) as 'a condition

extremely common in feu-rights, granted for the purpose of building; its validity was never doubted, and it is daily enforced'.

391. Rule 5: content. A real burden is restricted as to content[1]. Like other real conditions, such as servitude and common interest, it must regulate the servient tenement for the benefit of the dominant tenement[2]. That is why real conditions have the privilege of running with the lands. An obligation which does not fulfil this fundamental rule as to content cannot be a real burden or indeed a real condition of any other kind.

The rule just stated has two aspects. First, a real burden must 'relate to the use or employment of the [servient] land, or of buildings erected upon it'[3]. It must not be a merely personal obligation upon the grantee which is unrelated to the land itself[4]. This applies to all real burdens, including those created in grants of feu[5]. Secondly, the regulation of the servient tenement must confer some palpable benefit on the dominant tenement, and not merely on the particular person who happens to be its proprietor[6]. In short, a real burden must be praedial, not only at the servient end but at the dominant end as well. It may be doubted whether some of the burdens commonly found in modern deeds of conditions (for example, conditions relating to the composition and conduct of residents' associations and conditions purporting to confer rights and obligations on factors) are in conformity with this rule. So far as the dominant tenement is concerned, the rule requiring praedial benefit is in effect the same as the more familiar rule that the dominant proprietor must have a praedial (or patrimonial) interest to enforce and is considered further in that context[7].

In addition, there are two further restrictions on content, one in respect of character and the other in respect of extent. The restriction in respect of character is that the obligation must neither be illegal nor contrary to public policy[8]. Illegality speaks for itself. Public policy is potentially of greater significance, although there seems to be no reported decision in which a real burden has failed solely upon this ground. In *Corpn of Tailors of Aberdeen v Coutts* it is suggested that an obligation is contrary to public policy where either it impedes commerce or where it creates a monopoly[9], but this is stated too broadly, for it seems beyond doubt that an obligation such as is commonly found in the titles of dwelling houses prohibiting their use for trade is unobjectionable and enforceable[10]. Perhaps the most which can be said is that a restriction as to use for trade may be challengeable in cases where the subjects are in their nature particularly suitable for the trade in question, although in practice if such restrictions fail, they are more likely to do so on the ground that there is no praedial interest in the dominant tenement[11]. Whether there are other categories of breach of public policy is unclear.

There is also a restriction as to extent. In order to be real, is has repeatedly been said, the obligation must be a natural incident of the grant in which it is contained[12]. 'You cannot make a man proprietor and yet prohibit him from exercising the rights of proprietorship'[13]. 'The general rule is, that conditions or limitations in a property title which are repugnant to the common legal notion of property and proprietary rights, shall be deemed invalid'[14]. The scope of this important rule may be tested by classifying the content of real burdens as falling into three distinct groups, namely:

(1) obligations on the servient proprietor to do something;
(2) restrictions, which is to say, obligations on the servient proprietor not to do something; and
(3) obligations to allow the dominant proprietor to make some use of the servient property.

Of these three types the second (restrictions) is the least likely to be considered 'repugnant to the common legal notion of property'; and this is so whether the restriction is expressed negatively (certain use or uses prohibited, such as the sale of alcohol[15] or the keeping of pets or the use of the subjects for trade) or positively (only one stipulated use permitted, such as use as a dwelling house for one family only[16]). But while the servient proprietor may competently be restricted as to the use which he makes of his subjects, he may not as a general rule be restricted as to the performance of juristic acts:

> 'I think that to insert in a proprietary title — a feu-charter conferring a right of property in fee-simple — a prohibition against letting . . . would be bad from repugnancy, just as a prohibition against selling[17] would be bad from repugnancy . . . There are certain restrictions which may be imposed. These are generally of a well-known character, and illustrated by well-known decisions, but a restriction against alienation, or a restriction against letting — that is, alienating for a term — would, I think, as at present advised, be bad from repugnancy'[18].

There may, however, be a difference between absolute restrictions and qualified restrictions[19], and certainly rights of pre-emption are accepted as enforceable[20].

The position may be different for burdens of the other two types. A type (1) burden (obligation to do something) is potentially a great deal more onerous than a type (2) burden (obligation not to do something). There is an obvious difference between, say, an obligation not to sell alcohol (which is perfectly lawful) and an obligation that alcohol must be sold (which almost certainly is not). In *Burnett v Great North of Scotland Railway Co*[21] ground was feued to the defenders, a railway company, subject to the burden of building a railway station thereon 'at which all passenger trains shall regularly stop'. In a question with a successor of the original superior the House of Lords, reversing the Court of Session[22], held that the obligation to halt passenger trains at the station was binding on the feuar. How this burden could be complied with by a future feuar who did not happen to operate a railway company was not explored, and for this and for other reasons the decision seems questionable. Most type (1) burdens are less colourful. Typical are obligations to build a house or a fence or to maintain the common parts of a tenement and there can be no doubt as to their enforceability.

Where type (3) burdens (obligation to allow use of the servient tenement) are encountered at all in conveyancing practice, they are usually (positive) servitudes and not real burdens. It has been said that there is no reason in principle why a real burden may not include an obligation to suffer or endure an act on the part of the dominant proprietor[23]; but, apart from the case in which these remarks appeared, there seems to be no reported decision in which a type (3) obligation has been enforced as a real burden, while the following have been held not to be enforceable, although whether on the basis of repugnancy to ownership or on some other ground is not always clear: an exclusive right of shooting on the servient tenement[24]; a right to free places at a theatre[25]; a right to use part of a building 'at such times and for such purposes as may be deemed necessary'[26]; and a reserved power to erect buildings on part of the ground disponed[27].

1 Unlike a 'pecuniary' real burden, which can secure an obligation of almost any kind. Thus Lord Deas in *Stewart v Duke of Montrose* (1860) 22 D 755 at 803: 'Almost any obligation of a definite nature, however collateral, — however extrinsic, — however naturally unconnected with the particular estate, — and however temporary the purpose to be served by it, — for instance, money owing, or a legacy bequeathed, may be created a pecuniary real burden . . .'.
2 See para 348 above and para 444 below.
3 *Earl of Zetland v Hislop* (1882) 9 R (HL) 40 at 43, per Lord Selborne LC. A real burden must have 'immediate connection with the estate': *Stewart v Duke of Montrose* (1860) 22 D 755 at 803, 804, per Lord Deas, and repeated in *Marquis of Tweeddale's Trustees v Earl of Haddington* (1880) 7 R 620 at 633, per Lord Deas.
4 Thus an obligation to enter into a personal bond is not a real burden. See *Corpn of Tailors of Aberdeen v Coutts* (1840) 1 Robin 296, and *Aberdeen Magistrates v Wyllie* (1870) 43 SJ 95, OH.
5 *Earl of Zetland v Hislop* (1881) 8 R 675 at 681, 682, per Lord Young (revsd (1882) 9 R (HL) 40).
6 Eg *Aberdeen Varieties Ltd v James F Donald (Aberdeen Cinemas) Ltd* 1939 SC 788, 1940 SLT 58, revsd 1940 SC (HL) 52, 1940 SLT 374.
7 See paras 407, 408, below.
8 *Corpn of Tailors of Aberdeen v Coutts* (1840) 1 Robin 296 at 307, per Lord Corehouse.

9 *Corpn of Tailors of Aberdeen v Coutts* (1840) 1 Robin 296 at 307, and again at 317–319, per Lord Corehouse. The suggestion is made (at 319) that the majority view in *Campbell v Dunn* (1825) 1 W & S 690, HL (remitted back to the Court of Session for the opinion of the full court, reported at (1828) 6 S 679), in support of the validity of a condition that all subsequent dispositions be prepared by the superior's law agent, is unsound as creating a monopoly.

10 See the discussion in *Co-operative Wholesale Society v Ushers Brewery* 1975 SLT (Lands Trib) 9.

11 See para 407 below.

12 *Stewart v Duke of Montrose* (1860) 22 D 755 at 804, per Lord Deas; *Marquis of Tweeddale's Trustees v Earl of Haddington* (1880) 7 R 620 and 633, per Lord Deas; *Edinburgh Magistrates v Begg* (1883) 11 R 352 at 354, OH, per Lord M'Laren, and (affd) (1883) 11 R 352 at 356, IH, per Lord President Inglis; *Macrae v Mackenzie's Trustee* (1891) 19 R 138 at 149, per Lord M'Laren; *Secretary of State for Scotland v Portkil Estates* 1957 SC 1 at 15, 1957 SLT 209 at 216, per Lord Mackintosh. Although not so acknowledged, this phrase seems to derive from Stair *Institutions* II,3,57: 'Provisions also inconsistent with the nature of the right, are ineffectual, as if it were provided that the vassal should not owe fidelity to his superior, or that the right should be valid by the charter without seasin . . .'.

13 *Moir's Trustees v M'Ewan* (1880) 7 R 1141 at 1145, per Lord Young. As will be seen from notes 14, 15, below this whole doctrine is particularly associated with Lord Young.

14 *Earl of Zetland v Hislop* (1881) 8 R 675 at 681, per Lord Young (revsd (1882) 9 R (HL) 40).

15 In *Earl of Zetland v Hislop* (1881) 8 R 675, Lord Young argued strongly that a prohibition on the sale of 'malt or spirituous liquors' was repugnant to a right of property, but this view was rejected by the House of Lords. See *Earl of Zetland v Hislop* (1882) 9 R (HL) 40.

16 *Colquhoun's Curator Bonis v Glen's Trustee* 1920 SC 737, 1920 2 SLT 197.

17 Prohibitions on alienation and on subinfeudation were declared unenforceable by, respectively, the Tenures Abolition Act 1746 (c 50), s 10 (amended by the Statute Law Revision Act 1867 (c 59)) and the Conveyancing (Scotland) Act 1874 (c 94), s 22.

18 *Moir's Trustees v M'Ewan* (1880) 7 R 1141 at 1145, per Lord Young. So on this principle a real burden cannot prevent *pro indiviso* proprietors from pursuing division and sale: *Grant v Heriot's Trust* (1906) 8 F 647 at 658, per Lord President Dunedin.

19 Stair II,3,58.

20 *Matheson v Tinney* 1989 SLT 535, OH. For clauses of pre-emption, see CONVEYANCING, vol 6, para 520.

21 *Burnett v Great North of Scotland Rly Co* (1885) 12 R (HL) 25.

22 *Burnett v Great North of Scotland Rly Co* (1883) 11 R 375 (revsd (1885) 12 R (HL) 25).

23 *B & C Group Management v Haren* (4 December 1992, unreported), OH.

24 *Beckett v Bisset* 1921 2 SLT 33, OH. However, in *Harper v Flaws* 1940 SLT 150, OH, the Lord Ordinary seemed favourably disposed, without having to decide the point, to a real burden of trout fishing. *Beckett* was not cited. See also the discussion in *Patrick v Napier* (1867) 5 M 683.

25 *Scott v Howard* (1881) 8 R (HL) 59.

26 *Kirkintilloch Kirk-Session v Kirkintilloch School Board* 1911 SC 1127, 1911 2 SLT 146.

27 *Scottish Temperance Life Assurance Co v Law Union and Rock Insurance Co* 1917 SC 175, 1917 1 SLT 4. It has been suggested that the courts are reluctant to accept as real burdens 'any obligations which depart very far from servitude rights'. See W M Gordon *Scottish Land Law* (1989) p 741. But while this may possibly be true of type (3) burdens, it seems not to be true of other burdens. Indeed one of the principal reasons for the development of real burdens as a separate category was the rule of the law of servitudes which does not allow the servient proprietor to be placed under positive (ie type (1)) obligations. See para 381 above.

392. Failure to comply with rules of constitution. The rules of constitution are mandatory and a condition not complying in full will fail as a real burden. A failed real burden is incapable of rescue. It makes no difference, for example, that the condition is referred to in subsequent conveyances of the land[1]. Nor does it matter that successive proprietors know of the condition and so are in bad faith as to its terms[2]. If a burden is not real in the first place, it necessarily follows that successors are unaffected.

However, while a failed real burden cannot affect successors it often binds the original parties to the deed in which it is contained[3]. For a conveyance, although unilateral in form[4], is itself a type of contract. By accepting delivery of the deed the grantee is considered to have accepted its terms and is bound by them[5] except where, unusually, they also fail by the rules of the law of contract.

1 *Leslie v Wyllie* (1870) 43 SJ 95, OH. See further para 396 below.
2 *Morier v Brownlie and Watson* (1895) 23 R 67, 3 SLT 135; *Beckett v Bisset* 1921 2 SLT 33, OH. Bad faith is irrelevant here, as it usually is in property law.
3 *Kirkintilloch Kirk-Session v Kirkintilloch School Board* 1911 SC 1127, 1911 2 SLT 146.
4 Ie except in the case of feu contracts, which are bilateral. Today feu contracts are almost unknown.
5 *Marquis of Abercorn v Marnoch's Trustee* 26 June 1817 FC; *Hunter v Boog* (1834) 13 S 205 at 208, per Lord President Hope and eight other concurring judges; *Scottish Co-operative Wholesale Society Ltd v Finnie* 1937 SC 835 at 843, 1938 SLT 78 at 81, per Lord Mackay; *Watters v Motherwell District Council* 1991 SLT (Lands Trib) 2.

393. Inherent conditions of the feu and the perpetual feudal contract. The importance of the traditional feudal conditions as a model for real burdens has already been examined[1], and it was perhaps to be expected that, after real burdens emerged as a separate category of right in the early nineteenth century, attempts should then be made to redefine them in feudal terms. From this act of redefinition arose the view (still sometimes found even today but of particular prominence at the end of the nineteenth century) that the right of a superior to enforce conditions of title against his vassal is founded both on 'tenure' and also on 'contract'[2]. The precise nature of the distinction between 'tenure' and 'contract' was and remains unclear[3], but the essential point appears to be the following[4].

Suppose that A grants to B a feu disposition in which certain conditions are imposed. From the moment that delivery of the conveyance is accepted B is bound by the conditions. Registration is not required. The reason why B is bound is that a feu disposition is not only a conveyance but a contract also and by accepting the deed B is taken to have accepted its contractual terms[5]. Once B registers the feu disposition, however, and provided the rules of constitution described earlier have been properly complied with, the conditions become real burdens on the *dominium utile*. At this point the conditions are effective twice over, first by virtue of contract and now by virtue of 'tenure'. Conditions which are effective by contract are often called 'inherent conditions of the feu'[6] or, perhaps surprisingly, 'conditions of tenure'. Conditions which are effective by tenure are, at least in the terminology adopted in this title, real burdens.

The distinction between contract and tenure is not confined to questions between the original parties, or at least was not so confined prior to the introduction of implied feudal entry in 1874. Thus suppose that in the example already given B, having taken infeftment, now comes to dispone the land to C. Until 1874 the usual procedure[7] was for B's disposition to be *a me vel de me* so that C took immediate (base) infeftment as the vassal of B, the defeasible mid-superior. Thereafter C could take feudal entry with A, signified by the grant of a charter of confirmation, at which point B's interest would disappear and C would hold directly of A. On taking base infeftment as the vassal of B, C became liable, as a matter of 'tenure', for any conditions which had been constituted real burdens in the original feudal grant from A to B[8]. But on taking public entry C received a charter of confirmation and so entered into direct contractual relations with A[9]. This is the perpetual feudal contract, the investiture renewed personally by each successive vassal with each successive superior, which came to dominate judicial accounts of this area of law in the closing years of the nineteenth century and beyond. Thus Lord President Dunedin:

> '... there is absolutely no difference between the position of the first vassal and any subsequent vassal who is entered ... as regards their contractual relation to the superior ... Accordingly, one will find all through the cases that it is always recognised that every successive vassal is in the relation of personal contract to the superior for the time being over and above his relation depending purely on tenure'[10].

In practice, the conditions contained in the charter of confirmation (the inherent conditions of the feu) were usually the same as those contained and feudalised in the original feu disposition (the real burdens): hence the view that the vassal was bound twice, once by tenure and then again by contract. It will be observed that in the case of successors of the original vassal, liability by tenure preceded liability by contract and that if public entry was not taken there was no liability by contract at all.

Of the two bases of liability, liability by tenure was and is by far the more important. The primary reason why conditions bind successors is because they are real burdens and not because they are inherent conditions of the feu. The contractual basis of liability was always of restricted scope and of limited use. It was confined to conditions in feudal grants and so could not explain why conditions created in ordinary dispositions could also bind successors; and even within feudal grants it was unable to explain the enforcement rights of co-feuars, or the liability of subfeuars, or the enforcement rights of a superior acquiring title after his vassal had already entered[11]. Why, then, was the contractual model persevered with and given so much prominence? Partly, it may be suggested, this was because of the rise of contract law, and the accompanying decline of property law, which began about the middle of the nineteenth century. Partly too there may have been a wish to emphasise continuity with the old feudal law[12], accompanied, in some cases, by a desire to display learning in that law[13]. By the mid-nineteenth century the feudal system had been abandoned by all other countries in Europe, and Scotland stood alone as an exponent of medieval land law, a fact which was not generally regarded as being to its disadvantage. But there were two further reasons of substance. One was that since the feudal contract was bilateral, it could be used, as real burdens could not, to explain obligations which had been imposed on the superior. This subject is considered further below[14]. The other reason, of more immediate concern here, is that as compared with real burdens, inherent conditions of the feu were governed by different, and more lenient, rules of constitution. A condition which failed as a real burden might nevertheless succeed as an inherent condition[15].

The rules of constitution of real burdens have already been considered[16]. For a condition to succeed as an inherent condition of the feu, it was necessary only that it appear in the charter of confirmation. It need not even appear in full, for unlike the rule for real burdens it could be incorporated by reference[17]. Since the charter of confirmation was not itself registered, it followed that inherent conditions might not appear in the Register of Sasines at all[18]. In practice the charter of confirmation usually repeated the conditions contained in the original grant and it seems that a superior could refuse entry to a vassal who would not accept a charter in such terms[19]. There were further differences too arising from the fact that the governing law was the law of contract and not the law of real conditions. In particular this avoided both the rule as to content, which for real burdens requires that the condition regulate the servient tenement for the benefit of a dominant tenement[20], and also the rule that the superior must have an interest to enforce[21]. These are important and substantial differences. Nonetheless there appears to be only one reported decision in which a condition which failed as a real burden was then enforced as an inherent condition[22].

The dictum by Lord Dunedin quoted earlier[23] was handed down in a case decided in 1909 and it is a remarkable fact that the majority of the dicta which emphasised the contractual nature of the superior-vassal relationship were pronounced after 1874, when the introduction of implied feudal entry unsettled the very basis of the doctrine[24]. For in 1874 charters of confirmation ceased to be competent and direct entry taken from the superior disappeared. By section 4(2) of the Conveyancing (Scotland) Act 1874 (c 94), on registration of a disposition the grantee is impliedly entered with the superior 'as if such superior had granted a writ of confirmation according to the existing law and practice'. The actual contract is replaced by a deemed contract. It is true that section 4(2) further provides that 'such implied entry shall not be held to confer or confirm any rights more extensive than those contained in the original charter'[25], so giving rise to the argument that a

condition which appeared in the original charter but which fails as a real burden
might nonetheless be treated as included in the deemed writ of confirmation to the
effect of binding the grantee[26]. However, it is thought that this argument would
probably not now succeed[27], for although the doctrine of the perpetual contract
remains on the lips of judges even today the reported decisions since 1874 suggest
that in substance the doctrine has long since disappeared[28]. If this is so, then the
doctrine is now devoid of practical significance.

1 See para 382 above.
2 Eg 'privity both of contract and estate': *Morier v Brownlie and Watson* (1895) 23 R 67 at 71, OH, per
   Lord Low (affd (1895) 23 R 67, 3 SLT 135, IH).
3 Cf the views of Lord Curriehill and Lord Deas in *Hyslop v Shaw* (1863) 1 M 535.
4 See W M Gloag *The Law of Contract* (2nd edn, 1929) pp 228, 229.
5 See para 392 above.
6 This is the terminology favoured by some recent writers. See J M Halliday *Conveyancing Law and
   Practice in Scotland* vol II (1986) para 19-14 and W M Gordon *Scottish Land Law* (1989) para 22–34. In
   fact 'inherent condition' where it is used in the case law, at it often was in the nineteenth century, is a
   synonym for 'real burden' in the sense used in this part of the PROPERTY title. See para 375 above.
7 See further paras 99 ff above.
8 This is because he was a subvassal of A and so one of the proprietors of the servient tenement. See
   para 414 below.
9 Unless and until he did so, B remained A's vassal and hence liable to A in contract in respect of real
   burdens and feuduty. See *Hyslop v Shaw* (1863) 1 M 535.
10 *Maguire v Burges* 1909 SC 1283 at 1288, 1289, 1909 2 SLT 219 at 221.
11 In none of these cases is there a direct contractual link between the creditor and the debtor in the
   obligation. Thus a vassal has not entered with the new superior and there is no mechanism for him
   to do so; a subfeuar is in contractual relations with the mid-superior but not with the over-superior;
   and the right of a co-feuar depends on his ownership of adjacent land and so is praedial rather than
   contractual. (On this last point, see further para 402 below.) These shortcomings are acknowledged
   by Lord President Dunedin in *Maguire v Burges* 1909 SC 1283 at 1289 ff, 1909 2 SLT 219 at 222.
12 This was because the inherent condition was seen as a new form of the old feudal condition which
   was itself an important source for the modern real burden. See para 382 above.
13 In *Maguire v Burges* 1909 SC 1283 at 1288, 1909 2 SLT 219 at 221, Lord President Dunedin
   complained that 'I am . . . driven to this observation that, in these modern days, when everybody is
   accustomed to abbreviated titles, the more elementary a proposition is as regards the feudal system
   the more likely it is to be overlooked'. Learning in the feudal law was particularly associated with
   Lord Dunedin and with his contemporary judges such as Lord Kinnear. In *Kemp v Largs Magistrates*
   1939 SC (HL) 6 at 12, 13, 1939 SLT 228 at 231, Lord Macmillian was to describe Lord Kinnear as 'an
   acknowledged master of the law of Scottish feudal conveyancing' and Lord Dunedin as one 'to
   whom this branch of the law was equally familiar'. Today these claims appear overstated. The
   bowdlerised feudalism of the late nineteenth and early twentieth centuries was far removed from
   historical feudalism, and the 'mastery' of those such as Lord Dunedin was impressive only by
   comparison with judges of later generations who were too young to have had direct experience of
   conveyancing prior to the reform of 1874. See also para 51 above.
14 See para 394 below.
15 Thus it has been said that '[t]he later professors and writers on conveyancing have been unanimous
   in stating that, *inter superiorem et vassalem*, the question may more suitably and appropriately be asked
   in the form as to whether it is a condition of the tenure. Some at least of the criteria . . . as stated by
   Lord Corehouse in [Corpn of] *Tailors of Aberdeen* [(1840) 1 Robin 296], were rendered necessary
   because he was dealing with the matter as one of the constitution of a real burden by a deed of
   disposition, so that the successors were strangers': *Kemp v Largs Magistrates* 1938 SC 652 at 674, 1938
   SLT 560 at 571, per Lord Mackay (affd 1939 SC (HL) 6, 1939 SLT 228).
16 See paras 386 ff above.
17 *Edinburgh Magistrates v Macfarlane* (1857) 20 D 156.
18 *Stewart v Duke of Montrose* (1860) 22 D 755 at 803, 804, per Lord Deas; *Robertson v North British Rly
   Co* (1874) 1 R 1213. In *Robertson* Lord President Inglis dissented and the decision was subsequently
   doubted by Lord Watson in *Hislop v MacRitchie's Trustees* (1881) 8 R (HL) 95 at 104. Both the
   dissension and the doubt show the reluctance of the courts to invest the contractual analysis with
   any real substance, a point considered further in the text to notes 24 ff below.
19 *Robertson v North British Rly Co* (1874) 1 R 1213.
20 *Campbell v Dunn* (1823) 2 S 341 (NE 299), (1825) 1 W & S 690 (remitted back to the Court of Session
   for the opinion of the full court reported at (1828) 6 S 679). All that was required was that the
   inherent condition be not *contra bonos mores*. See para 382 above for a discussion of this decision. But

see also the attempt by Lord Deas in *Stewart v Duke of Montrose* (1860) 22 D 755 at 803, 804, to apply to inherent conditions the same rules as apply to real burdens, a further indication that in practice the contractual analysis was largely without substance. Careful attention needs to be paid to the terminology employed by Lord Deas in this important passage. 'Inherent condition of the right' is used, as it was often used at this period (see para 375 above), to mean (modern) real burdens and also, in this case, inherent conditions of the feu. The passage has sometimes been taken as distinguishing (modern) real burdens from inherent conditions of the feu, with stricter rules as to content being applied to the latter as the price of their otherwise lenient rules of constitution. See *Halliday* vol II, para 19-14 and *Gordon* para 22–34. But in fact Lord Deas' distinction is between (pecuniary) real burdens on the one hand and (modern) real burdens (including inherent conditions) on the other. The restrictions as to content, that the conditions must have 'the qualities of permanency, immediate connection with the estate, natural relation to the objects of the grant, and so on', are simply the familiar restrictions which apply to all (modern) real burdens, and indeed to all real conditions. See para 391 above.

21 *Maguire v Burges* 1909 SC 1283, 1909 2 SLT 219.
22 *Edinburgh Magistrates v Macfarlane* (1857) 20 D 156. One reason why the contractual route was not employed more may have been the rule, which seems to have existed at least until 1840, that in enforcing a breach of a feudal condition the superior could not use ordinary contractual remedies, so that the only remedies were irritancy and the refusal of feudal entry. See para 382 above. No mention is found of this rule in the contractual analysis of feuing conditions favoured by courts in the late nineteenth century, but whether it disappeared, and if so when, is not clear.
23 See text to note 10 above.
24 See eg *Hislop v MacRitchie's Trustees* (1881) 8 R (HL) 95 at 102, per Lord Watson; *Macrae v Mackenzie's Trustees* (1891) 19 R 138 at 145, per Lord Kinnear; *Marshall v Callander and Trossachs Hydropathic Co Ltd* (1895) 22 R 954 at 957, OH, per Lord Kyllachy, (1895) 22 R 954, 3 SLT 94, IH (affd (1896) 23 R (HL) 55); *Howard de Walden Estates Ltd v Bowmaker Ltd* 1965 SC 163 at 182, 1965 SLT 254 at 264, per Lord President Clyde.
25 See Erskine *Institutes* II,3,20: '... all clauses in the original charter are, in the judgment of law, implied in charters by progress, if there be no express alteration'.
26 In fact this argument, even if accepted, would save very few real burdens. The doctrine was at its most important before direct registration of conveyances was introduced in 1858, at a time when a condition would sometimes appear in the charter but not in the sasine. Today the charter is almost always registered with the result that the condition is registered also. Indeed for Land Register titles registration is now a precondition of the validity of the burden: Land Registration (Scotland) Act 1979 (c 33), s 3(1). Nonetheless it is possible to think of cases, at least in Sasine conveyancing, where a condition might not appear on the Register: eg A grants a feu disposition to B imposing burdens, B does not register but grants a disposition to C deducing title through the feu disposition but without repeating the burdens, and C then registers the disposition.
27 *Gloag* p 229 concludes that it is not the law 'that each successive vassal, on entering with the superior, incurs all the liabilities imposed on the original vassal'. Even Professor W M Gordon, a more enthusiastic exponent of the contractual theory, concedes that 'there is some doubt as to whether the logic of this is entirely accepted by the courts': *Gordon* p 714.
28 There has been no case since 1874 in which the perpetual contract theory has actually been applied, and the indications in the case law are not encouraging. Thus it has been accepted that, at least from the point of view of interest to enforce, successors are not in the same position as the original superior and vassal. See *Waddell v Campbell* (1898) 25 R 456, 5 SLT 285, and *Gammell's Trustees v The Land Commission* 1970 SLT 254 at 260, OH, per Lord Fraser (successor requires interest to enforce, original superior does not). In *Liddall v Duncan* (1898) 25 R 1119, 6 SLT 77, the Second Division refused to follow *Edinburgh Magistrates v Macfarlane* (1857) 20 D 156 in upholding the validity of conditions which had not been recorded in full although the circumstances were almost identical save that in the earlier case the charter of confirmation was actual and not merely 'deemed' under the 1874 Act. But it should be noted that in *Liddall* the conditions were not actually contained in the original feudal grant and a court has yet to consider the validity of conditions contained in the original grant but not recorded in the Register of Sasines.

394. Obligations burdening the superior.

In addition to real burdens on the vassal, a feu disposition or other grant in feu may also contain obligations which are intended to burden the superior. In principle these too are enforceable in perpetuity, so that a successor of the original superior may have continuing liabilities to a successor of the original vassal. However, liability is confined strictly to the superiority of the particular land feued and none attaches to adjoining land *dominium* of which[1] may happen to be held by the granter at the time when the feu was granted. This is so even where it is expressly declared that adjoining land is to be bound[2]. Thus if A feus plot 1 to B imposing real burdens and taking himself bound to impose similar burdens on plot 2, which he also owns, the obligation to impose the burdens on plot 2 is in A as the superior of plot 1. But if A then dispones plot 2 to C, while disponing the superiority of plot 1 to D, the obligation owed to B passes to D notwithstanding the fact that he is not in a position to perform it. Neither A nor C have any liability[3]; and if, when C comes to feu plot 2 the real burdens are not duly imposed, D is liable to his vassal, B, in damages[4].

The example just given, of an obligation on a superior to impose burdens on other land owned by him, was very common in practice until 1979, since when developers have been able to burden the whole of their land in advance by means of a statutory deed of conditions[5]. The only other examples of obligations on commonly found are the obligations, once express but now implied by statute, to make the title deeds and searches available to the vassal and to relieve him of public burdens and over-feuduties[6], and also, where minerals are reserved, an obligation to pay compensation for subsidence[7]. Other obligations are of course possible, and indeed it seems that there are no restrictions as to content beyond the usual restriction about public policy. Any obligation must be expressed on the face of the deed[8], and it must be clear from its terms that it is intended to run with the superiority. An ordinary obligation of warrandice is considered personal to the granter and so does not run with the superiority[9].

However, while it is a settled rule that obligations can run with the superiority, the legal basis of the rule is uncertain. Plainly the obligations are not real burdens[10]. A real burden requires to be in a conveyance of the servient tenement[11] and must regulate the use of that property for the benefit of the dominant tenement[12]. By contrast, obligations on a superior are contained in a conveyance of the dominant tenement (the *dominium utile*) and are not subject to any restrictions as to content. Indeed, the fact that they are not contained in a conveyance of the servient tenement presents considerable difficulties for purchasers of the superiority who may be unable to discover from normal examination of title the burdens to which they are to be subject[13].

The explanation usually offered for obligations on superiors is that they are 'inherent conditions of the feu' and so part of the perpetual feudal contract between successive superiors and successive vassals. Thus viewed they are the counterpart of the obligations customarily imposed upon the vassal:

> 'The investiture created by this feu-contract was completed by infeftment, and that investiture is sustained by a feudal tenure as abiding as itself. The obligation of relief [which was imposed on the superior] is an intrinsic and essential part of the mutual stipulations in the feu-contract. It qualifies and defines the estate conveyed and retained. The rights and obligations of the superior and vassal under that feudal investiture are co-relative and counterpart . . . The foundation and the measure of the relative rights and obligations of the parties must be sought in the original charter, which is the title constituting the tenure, and to that title both parties must recur'[14].

This analysis, which is taken from the thirteen judge decision of *Stewart v Duke of Montrose* (1860)[15], is fully consonant with nineteenth-century feudal theory. Whether it continues to hold good today will depend upon whether the idea of renewed feudal investiture survived the introduction of implied entry in 1874, a subject which has already been considered[16]. The whole issue has some theoretical interest but is of no importance for modern conveyancing practice.

1 Ie whether *dominium utile* or *dominium directum*.
2 This is because the obligation cannot be a real burden since it is not contained in a conveyance of the servient tenement (the adjoining land) and nor does it fall within the special rule for obligations on superiors which is the subject of the present paragraph. See *Morier v Brownlie and Watson* (1895) 23 R

67, 3 SLT 135. *Meldrum v Kelvinside Estate Trustees* (1893) 20 R 853, 1 SLT 89, which might seem to suggest a different rule, was a case between the original parties to the feu contract.

3 *Jolly's Executrix v Viscount Stonehaven* 1958 SC 635, 1959 SLT 97 (liability of A); *Morier v Brownlie and Watson* (1895) 23 R 67, 3 SLT 135 (liability of C). See also *Assets Co Ltd v Lamb and Gibson* (1896) 23 R 569, 3 SLT 299.

4 *Leith School Board v Rattray's Trustees* 1918 SC 94, 1917 2 SLT 247.

5 See para 388 above.

6 Land Registration (Scotland) Act 1979 (c 33), s 16(2), (3)(b).

7 See paras 264 ff above.

8 *Duncan v Church of Scotland General Trustees* 1941 SC 145, 1941 SLT 133. Under the old law, however, certain obligations were implied arising out of the feudal role of the superior, eg the obligation to receive and enter the new vassal. See *Stewart v Duke of Montrose* (1860) 22 D 755 at 800, per Lord Deas.

9 'The ordinary clause of warrandice ... as it applies only to defects antecedently to the grant, naturally attaches only to the granter and his heirs': *Stewart v Duke of Montrose* (1860) 22 D 755 at 803, per Lord Deas.

10 But see *Duncan v Church of Scotland General Trustees* 1941 SC 145, 1941 SLT 133.

11 See para 388 above.

12 See para 391 above.

13 'A purchaser from the superior, in order to be safe, must look at the superior's own title, to ascertain his obligations to the Crown; and at the feu-rights granted by him (which, in a transfer of the superiority, are always excepted from the warrandice), to ascertain his obligations to his vassals. He cannot trust to find the superior's obligations in the vassal's sasine, which may feudalise and perfect certain burdens on the *dominium utile*, but not on the *dominium directum*. Conditions which, from their nature, are inherent in the grant, must be looked for in the grant itself': *Stewart v Duke of Montrose* (1860) 22 D 755 at 804, per Lord Deas.

14 (1860) 22 D 755 at 782, per Lord Wood and Lord Ardmillan.

15 *Stewart v Duke of Montrose* (1860) 22 D 755. The court was divided in this case and there were powerful counter-arguments. Thus Lord Justice-Clerk Inglis, Lord Benholme and Lord Neaves said (at 777): '... the position of the superior in a feu right is wholly different from that of the vassal ... The superior's title does not flow from the vassal, or depend on any act or deed of his ... But it is a subversion altogether of the feudal relation to suppose that a superior as such, or a singular successor in the superiority, is not merely to lose the *dominium utile* given to the feuar, and to content himself with certain restricted payments, prestations, and casualties from the feu, but that he in his turn shall be liable to make payments to the vassal far exceeding, it may be, the whole value of the reserved right of superiority. This is to make him a debtor and not a superior ... It is to throw upon him a personal obligation, which is neither a condition of his title, nor a [real] burden on his estate, nor is in any competent way connected with that estate'.

16 See para 393 above. But even if implied entry brings the new vassal into direct contractual relations with an existing superior, it is difficult to see how this would then affect a new superior. The problem is not new. Thus *Stewart v Duke of Montrose* (1860) 22 D 755 at 777, per Lord Justice-Clerk Inglis, Lord Benholme and Lord Neaves: 'A singular successor in the superiority does not connect himself directly with the vassal, but holds the lands themselves on titles independent of and anterior to the vassal's rights'.

395. Constitution by the Lands Tribunal. In the course of varying or discharging an existing real burden the Lands Tribunal is empowered to add or substitute such provision or provisions as appear to be reasonable as the result of the variation or discharge[1]. A substituted provision is in effect a new real burden and is enforceable in the same manner as the obligation which it replaces[2]. The provision is contained in the order made by the Tribunal and is effective on registration of an extract of the order in the Register of Sasines or Land Register[3].

Substitute provisions must be directly related to the variation or discharge originally sought and in practice are used as a means of controlling the new situation created by the relaxation of the original restriction[4]. Thus in one case, which may be regarded as typical, the Tribunal agreed to discharge a real burden which prevented the subjects from being used as a licensed hotel, but under the substitution of provisions requiring double glazing and an extractor fan[5]. It is an open question whether the new provisions must comply with the rules of real burdens in relation to form and content, and in particular with the rule that a burden must confer praedial benefit on an identified dominant tenement[6]. Substitute provisions can be rejected by the applicant[7], but naturally an applicant will often accept such provisions if the alternative is that his application for variation or discharge will be refused.

1 Conveyancing and Feudal Reform (Scotland) Act 1970 (c 35), s 1(5).
2 Ibid, s 1(6).
3 Ibid, s 2(4) (amended by the Land Tenure Reform (Scotland) Act 1974 (c 38), s 19).
4 *Strathclyde Regional Council v Mactaggart and Mickel Ltd* 1984 SLT (Lands Trib) 33.
5 *Leney v Craig* 1982 SLT (Lands Trib) 9.
6 As to the rules in relation to form and content, see respectively paras 390, 391, above.
7 Conveyancing and Feudal Reform (Scotland) Act 1970, s 1(5).

396. Repetition of real burdens in subsequent conveyances. Not only do real burdens appear in the conveyance or deed of conditions originally constitutive of the right, but as a general rule they are repeated in all subsequent conveyances of the servient property. In Sasine titles this is done by listing in the dispositive clause the names of the deed or deeds in which the burdens first appeared, introduced by words such as 'but always with and under, so far as still valid, subsisting and applicable, the real burdens, conditions and others specified in . . .'; and a listing in this form is, by statute, the equivalent of a full transcription of the individual burdens[1]. With Land Register titles incorporation by reference is even further refined: the title sheet already contains a full transcription of the burdens[2] and this is deemed to be incorporated into all subsequent conveyances without further mention[3].

The repetition of real burdens is a matter of practice rather than a matter of law. Repetition has no effect on the validity of the burdens, nor does it interrupt negative prescription[4]. So if a burden is validly constituted in the first place, it will continue to affect the servient tenement whether or not it appears in subsequent conveyances of that tenement; and conversely, if a burden is not validly constituted, the fact that it does appear will not repair its initial invalidity[5]. It has been argued that a failed real burden might be valid, at least as a matter of contract, in a question between the parties to any deed in which it was repeated[6], but the better view is that mere repetition does not confer on the granter of the deed any rights of enforcement with respect to the burden and that this is made plain by the use of the words 'so far as still valid, subsisting and applicable' which introduce the burden[7].

There are, however, three grounds on which the practice of repetition of burdens may be supported. First, repetition provides a purchaser with a convenient list of the burdens affecting the property. Indeed, in Sasine titles it is the only list available and is usually accepted as accurate and exhaustive if only because of the difficulty of establishing otherwise. Secondly, the effect of listing the burdens in the dispositive clause is to exclude them from the obligation of warrandice. A burden which is not listed and which is found to reduce the value of the property allows a claim in warrandice against the granter of the deed[8]. Finally, it is often provided in the original deed constituting burdens that the burdens are to be repeated in all future transmissions of the servient tenement on pain of nullity[9]. Repetition avoids the irritancy, although even where burdens are omitted there are now statutory methods of repairing the error[10].

1 Titles to Land Consolidation (Scotland) Act 1868 (c 101), s 10, Sch D; Conveyancing (Scotland) Act 1874 (c 94), s 32, Sch H. In *Williamson and Hubbard v Harrison* 1970 SLT 346, Lord President Clyde attached special significance to the words 'so far as still subsisting and applicable', but in practice this is a more or less universal qualification of the statutory style.
2 Land Registration (Scotland) Act 1979 (c 33), s 6(1)(e).
3 Ibid, s 15(2).
4 Repetition is not a 'relevant acknowledgement' by the debtor in the burden within the Prescription and Limitation (Scotland) Act 1973 (c 52), s 10(1)(b) (amended by the Prescription and Limitation (Scotland) Act 1984 (c 45), s 6(1), Sch 1, para 4) because, even if it otherwise satisfies that provision

(which is open to doubt) it is not made to the creditor in the burden. For prescription in relation to real burdens, see further para 431 below.

5 In the most famous case of all, *Corpn of Tailors of Aberdeen v Coutts* (1840) 1 Robin 296, HL, the burdens in the original disposition had not been repeated in the disposition granted in favour of Coutts, the defender. See also *Leslie v Wyllie* (1870) 43 SJ 95, OH, and A J McDonald 'The Enforcement of Title Conditions by Neighbouring Proprietors' in D J Cusine (ed) *A Scots Conveyancing Miscellany: Essays in Honour of Professor J M Halliday* (1987) p 17.

6 Or, again, that it might be valid in a question with the original party imposing the burden, on the principle of *jus quaesitum tertio*. See *Scott v Howard* (1880) 7 R 997 at 1012, 1013, per Lord Ormidale; (affd) (1881) 8 R (HL) 59 at 65, per Lord Watson.

7 *Anderson v Dickie* 1915 SC (HL) 79, 1915 1 SLT 393.

8 *Welsh v Russell* (1894) 21 R 769, 1 SLT 594, which concerned a servitude but the principle is the same. See para 705 below.

9 This is a common provision in practice. As well as encouraging repetition, it is useful as an indication that the burdens are intended to run with the land (para 390 above) and it may also help an inference that co-grantees are to have enforcement rights (para 401 below).

10 For present omissions a deed of acknowledgement of omitted conditions may be registered, while past omissions are cured if the burdens are listed in the current conveyance. See Conveyancing (Scotland) Act 1924 (c 27), s 9(3), (4).

(4) DOMINANT TENEMENT: THE RIGHT TO ENFORCE

397. Introduction. In order to enforce a real burden a person must be able to show both title and interest.

A person has title to enforce a real burden if, and only if, he is proprietor of an interest in land which is a dominant tenement in relation to the burden in question[1]. In real burdens, as in other real conditions such as servitudes, rights to enforce are attached to and run with a dominant tenement without the need for special assignation[2], and indeed they cannot competently be assigned or reserved separately from the dominant tenement[3]. So if A is the proprietor of a dominant tenement, the right to enforce is in him, but if he then dispones that tenement to B, the right passes with the tenement from A to B. The transferee (B) must be infeft before the right to enforce passes, for otherwise both parties would be simultaneously in right in virtue of the same dominant tenement[4]. It is not unusual for there to be more than one dominant tenement in relation to the same burden, for example where a burden is enforceable by co-feuars as well as by a superior.

The deed creating a real burden should specify the dominant tenement or tenements, but even where, as often happens, it fails to do so, a dominant tenement will usually be implied, this being an unexpected exception to the usual rule that real burdens must be set out in full with nothing left to implication[5]. The complex rules relating to implied dominant tenements are described below[6], but in summary the position depends upon whether the original grant is a grant in feu or an ordinary disposition[7]. Where land is feued it is implied that the dominant tenements are, in the first place, the reserved superiority, and, in the second place and provided that certain conditions are satisfied, the feus of all co-feuars holding of the same superior. Where, however, land is disponed the dominant tenements are any other land reserved by the disponer (if there is such land), and also, provided certain conditions are met, the land of all co-disponees acquiring from the same disponer.

In addition to title a dominant proprietor must also show interest, and just as title to enforce is praedial[8], so too is interest to enforce. Hence it must be shown that enforcement of the real burden confers benefit on the dominant tenement itself and not merely on the person who happens to be its proprietor for the time being[9].

1 See para 387 above.
2 *Braid Hills Hotel Co Ltd v Manuels* 1909 SC 120, 16 SLT 523.

3 *Bannerman's Trustees v Howard and Wyndham* (1902) 10 SLT 2 at 3, per Lord Moncreiff; *J A Mactaggart & Co v Harrower* (1906) 8 F 1101 at 1106, 14 SLT 277 at 280, Dean of Guild Court (affd (1906) 8 F 1101, 14 SLT 277).
4 *Gammell's Trustees v The Land Commission* 1970 SLT 254, OH.
5 See para 390 above.
6 See paras 398 ff below.
7 With deeds of conditions, the position depends on the deed used by the granter in the subsequent division of the estate.
8 Ie based upon the ownership of land.
9 See further paras 407, 408, below.

398. Implied rights: the superior. Where real burdens are imposed in a feu disposition or other grant in feu, it is implied that they are to be enforceable by the granter of the deed and by his successors as superior. Notwithstanding the doubts expressed in one case[1], there is no requirement that the burdens be traditional feudal incidents, which indeed, usually they are not. The dominant tenement, therefore, is the superiority[2]. If, as often happens, the superior also owns land adjacent to the land he has just feued, there may be an argument, by analogy with the rule for ordinary dispositions[3], that this land too ought to be an implied dominant tenement. In practice, and particularly in modern times, burdens are often more for the benefit of the adjoining land than for the benefit of the superiority. This precise question seems never to have been properly canvassed in a reported case; but since the issue does not become live until superiority and adjoining land come to be in different ownership, and since the very process of separating one from the other may have the effect of making the grantee of the adjoining land a co-feuar and so eligible for enforcement rights under a different principle[4], it may be that the problem is not often encountered in practice. A case in which the issue was raised, albeit obliquely, was *Stevenson v Steel Co of Scotland Ltd*[5]. Here, land having been feued subject to real burdens, the adjoining land, which also belonged to the superior, was later separated from the superiority of the feued land by ordinary disposition[6]. The question arose as to whether the real burdens in the original feudal grant could be enforced by the new owner of the adjoining land. In the event, the burden founded on was held to be unenforceable on other grounds, but it was indicated by Lord Watson that the answer might otherwise have been in the affirmative. Probably the case does not much advance the argument. The real burden, which was an obligation to form two streets, was already prestable at the time of the disposition of the adjoining land, and, presumably for this reason[7], was considered to have been impliedly assigned by that deed[8]. No consideration was given to the more interesting question of whether the adjoining land could be considered as a second dominant tenement, carrying rights of enforcement independent of assignation.

1 *Burnett v Great North of Scotland Rly Co* (1883) 11 R 375 at 385, 386, per Lord Young (revsd (1885) 12 R (HL) 25).
2 This means the immediate superiority. So if B, who holds of A, subfeus to C imposing burdens, the burdens are enforceable by B but not by A. See, however, the remarks to the contrary, made in the different context of feuduty, in *Marquis of Tweeddale's Trustees v Earl of Haddington* (1880) 7 R 620 at 636, per Lord Deas.
3 As to this rule, see para 403 below.
4 Ie provided (1) that the adjoining land is feued and not disponed and (2) that the feuar is made subject to similar or at least equivalent burdens. See further para 400 below.
5 *Stevenson v Steel Co of Scotland Ltd* (1899) 1 F (HL) 91.
6 One result of the use of a disposition, as opposed to a grant in feu, was to remove the argument that the grantee was a co-feuar of the grantee of the original conveyance.
7 Obligations not yet prestable or which are continuous in nature cannot be assigned separately from the dominant tenement which supports them. See para 345, note 2, and para 397, above.
8 Lord Watson founds, not perhaps very appropriately, on Stair *Institutions* III,2,1, and on Erskine *Institute* II,7,2, which deal with the rule *majori minus inest*. A more secure basis for the decision would seem to have been the assignation of writs clause. The effect of an assignation is of course for the

superior to be divested and the disponee invested in his place, whereas if the adjoining land were to be treated as an additional dominant tenement in its own right, both superior and disponee would have concurrent rights of enforcement. See *Hislop v MacRitchie's Trustees* (1881) 8 R (HL) 95 at 103, per Lord Watson.

399. Implied rights: co-feuars.

Parties holding from the same superior or over-superior and subject to identical or comparable real burdens may have an implied right to enforce these burdens among themselves[1]. This is in addition to, and not in substitution for, the implied right of the superior[2]. Shared real burdens indicate or may indicate the existence of a common feuing plan on the part of the common superior, and this is said to create a mutuality of interest among the co-feuars sufficient to support reciprocal rights of enforcement *inter se*[3]. To put the same point more simply, where an estate held of the same superior but by different feuars is subject to common burdens, conceived for the benefit of the estate as a whole, there is obvious sense in allowing reciprocal enforcement, for a co-feuar has an immediate and direct interest in seeing that his neighbour observes the common conditions. The superior, by contrast, does not and indeed in the arthritic feudalism of today may not feel disposed to enforce burdens at all.

Four conditions must be satisfied for rights of enforcement to be implied in this way. First, as has already been said, the co-feuars must hold[4] from the same superior or, as the case may be, from the same over-superior[5]. Secondly, the grant or grants from the superior must impose, both on the party seeking to enforce the burden (the dominant co-feuar) and on the party against whom enforcement is sought (the servient co-feuar) real burdens which are either substantially identical or at least in some sense equivalent. The burdens constitute the 'common plan'[6] under which the 'estate' as a whole is being feued, 'estate' in this sense being any area of ground, however small[7], which is owned by a single person and then subfeued. Thirdly, the prospective servient co-feuar must have notice in his own title of the common feuing plan and hence of the possibility of reciprocal rights of enforcement[8]. This is to comply with the rule that real burdens must appear in full in the title of the servient proprietor[9]. Finally, there must be nothing in the title of the servient co-feuar which is inconsistent with the idea of enforcement rights in co-feuars. So where a title confers an express and exclusive right in the superior to waive all or any of the burdens, any inference which otherwise might have existed as to enforcement rights of co-feuars is displaced in respect of that burden or burdens[10].

From the point of view of conveyancing practice, there are two different ways in which co-feuars can become subject to a common feuing plan. The first is where a landowner makes successive grants in feu of neighbouring plots of land, all subject to the same (or equivalent) real burdens. The other is where a landowner makes a single grant in feu, subject to real burdens, and the land granted is later subdivided by the feuar with the result that each part of the subdivided feu is subject to the original burdens. Both methods were recognised by Lord Watson in an influential passage from the leading case of *Hislop v MacRitchie's Trustees*:

'... (1) where the superior feus out his land in separate lots for the erection of houses, in streets or squares, upon a uniform plan; or (2) where the superior feus out a considerable area with a view to its being subdivided and built upon, without prescribing any definite plan, but imposing certain general restrictions which the feuar is taken bound to insert in all sub-feus or dispositions to be granted by him'[11].

Each requires further and separate consideration[12].

1 The leading modern analysis of this subject is A J McDonald 'The Enforcement of Title Conditions by Neighbouring Proprietors' in D J Cusine (ed) *A Scots Conveyancing Miscellany: Essays in Honour of*

Professor J M Halliday (1987) pp 9–32. For an earlier account, see W M Gloag *The Law of Contract* (2nd edn, 1929) pp 243–247.

2 As to the implied right of the superior, see para 398 above.

3 'No single feuar can, in my opinion, be subjected in liability to his co-feuars, unless it appears from the titles under which he holds his feu that such similarity of conditions and mutuality of interest among the feuars either had been or was meant to be established': *Hislop v MacRitchie's Trustees* (1881) 8 R (HL) 95 at 102, per Lord Watson.

4 Ie hold or, in some cases, have held, for it is no objection to the exercise of a right of enforcement that the servient co-feuar has consolidated his feu. See *Murray's Trustees v St Margaret's Convent Trustees* (1906) 8 F 1109, 14 SLT 307 (affd 1907 SC (HL) 8, 15 SLT 2) and *Brookfield Developments Ltd v Keeper of the Registers of Scotland* 1989 SCLR 435, 1989 SLT (Lands Trib) 105.

5 This condition is satisfied even where the common author is superior to one feuar but over-superior to another: *Smith v Taylor* 1972 SLT (Lands Trib) 34.

6 There is, of course, no necessary relationship between a 'common plan' in the sense used here and a map attached to the deed and showing the location of the estate.

7 In *Hislop v MacRitchie's Trustees* (1881) 8 R (HL) 95 at 103, Lord Watson refers at one point to a superior feuing out 'a considerable area', and in another early case, *Miller v Carmichael* (1888) 15 R 991, a group of four houses was said to be too small. But the modern law is different: see A J McDonald in *A Scots Conveyancing Miscellany: Essays in Honour of Professor J M Halliday* pp 26, 27.

8 *Hislop v MacRitchie's Trustees* (1881) 8 R (HL) 95.

9 See para 388 above.

10 *Thomson v Alley and Maclellan* (1883) 10 R 433; *Walker and Dick v Park* (1888) 15 R 477; *Turner v Hamilton* (1890) 17 R 494. The rule is different where enforcement rights to co-feuars have been expressly granted: *Lawrence v Scott* 1965 SC 403, 1965 SLT 390.

11 *Hislop v MacRitchie's Trustees* (1881) 8 R (HL) 95 at 103.

12 See respectively paras 400, 401, below.

400. Successive grants. A general account of the conditions for implying reciprocal rights of enforcement has already been given[1]. In the case of successive grants by a superior, the co-feuar seeking enforcement (the dominant co-feuar) must be able to show that the burdens in his own grant are substantially similar to those in the grant made to the prospective servient co-feuar[2], or that, if they are not substantially similar (for example, because the two properties are different in character) that his own burdens are the equivalent under a common feuing plan of the different burdens in the servient title[3]. As Lord President Clyde observed:

'I am not prepared to hold that restrictions must be absolutely identical in order to make them mutually enforceable. It may well be that conformity to a general plan ... for street buildings, by which the character of corner tenements may vary from the character of those forming the general line, and so on, may be made mutually enforceable as between the feuars or disponees of corner tenements and of front-line tenements ... Indeed I see no reason, as at present advised, why a vassal or disponee should not be asked, and (if he agrees) should not be bound, to subject his land to a restriction upon condition that other vassals or disponees subject their lands to a different restriction enforceable by him'[4].

It is undecided whether all, or at least most, of the burdens in the title must pass this test of similarity or equivalence, or whether it is sufficient that the actual burdens sought to be enforced do so.

Similarity or equivalence are not by themselves sufficient to found reciprocal rights of enforcement: the servient co-feuar must also have proper notice of the fact of similarity or equivalence within his own title[5]. This means notice within the original grant from the common superior, although in one case it was said, somewhat incoherently, that if the original grant contains 'the foundation' of notice, it is then competent to refer to other titles, including it appears the titles of the dominant co-feuar, in order to find further 'indications of evidence'[6]. The distinction between 'foundation' of evidence and further 'indications' is not clear and does not seem to have been applied in any other case.

Two methods of giving notice to the servient co-feuar are recognised and there may possibly be others[7]. The strongest case is where the original grant in favour of the servient co-feuar contains an obligation by the superior to include identical or equivalent burdens in subsequent grants of the same estate[8], for 'There could be no reason for putting the superior under such an obligation, unless the vassal was to enforce the conditions agreed to be inserted'[9]. It appears not to matter for this purpose that the co-feuar now seeking to enforce the burden received his feu first, so that the obligation on the superior in the servient co-feuar's grant cannot have referred to him[10]. The modern practice of using deeds of conditions[11], which since 1979 have been effective immediately upon registration[12], means that obligations on superiors to insert common burdens are rarely found today; but it is suggested that, at least since 1979[13], the existence of a registered deed of conditions is of itself sufficient notice to a feuar of a common scheme of real burdens in respect of all those affected by the deed, and hence of mutual rights of enforcement[14].

The other recognised method of giving notice is for reference to be made in the servient co-feuar's grant to a common feuing plan[15]. 'Plan' is not used here in the sense of map[16], although in many cases a map will, of course, exist. What is required, rather, is an indication from the superior that the individual feu is part of a larger and uniform development, that the uniformity will be policed by real burdens such as the ones in the grantee's title, and therefore, by implication, that the burdens will be enforceable by co-feuars *inter se*. There is some uncertainty as to how specific the reference to a common plan need be. Clearly, it is sufficient if the grant discloses the existence of a formal written plan and indicates that common conditions are to be in every feu, as is the case in some parts of the Edinburgh New Town[17]. Equally clearly it is insufficient if a written plan is referred to only for the purpose of identifying the property[18]. Somewhere between these two cases is *Johnston v The Walker Trustees* where the grant provided:

> 'that as the tenement built on the said area has been erected in strict conformity to the plan and elevation adopted for [Coates Crescent and Manor Place] . . . it shall not be in the power of the said [George John Murray] or his foresaids to convert the said dwelling-house or others hereby disponed into a shop or shops . . .'[19].

It was held by the First Division, not without hesitation[20], that the burden could be enforced by a co-feuar.

Rights of enforcement are not always reciprocal. The fact that co-feuar A can enforce a burden against co-feuar B does not mean that co-feuar B can enforce the equivalent burden against co-feuar A. Whether he can do so will depend on there being notice of the common feuing plan in A's title, and where there is no notice there is no right of enforcement in B[21].

---

1 See para 399 above.

2 Thus '. . . it is essential that the conditions to be enforced . . . shall in cases be similar, if not identical . . .': *Hislop v MacRitchie's Trustees* (1881) 8 R (HL) 95 at 101, per Lord Watson. For a case where they were not similar, with the result that no right to enforce arose, see *Stevenson v Steel Co of Scotland Ltd* (1899) 1 F (HL) 91.

3 *Botanic Gardens Picture House Ltd v Adamson* 1924 SC 549, 1924 SLT 418; *Lees v North East Fife District Council* 1987 SLT 769 (a case of single grant followed by subdivision).

4 *Botanic Gardens Picture House Ltd v Adamson* 1924 SC 549 at 563, 1924 SLT 418 at 425.

5 This requirement was introduced by *Hislop v MacRitchie's Trustees* (1881) 8 R (HL) 95. For the earlier law, see W M Gloag *The Law of Contract* (2nd edn, 1929) p 243 and the cases there cited.

6 *Nicholson v Glasgow Asylum for the Blind* 1911 SC 391, 1911 1 SLT 37.

7 In *Nicholson v Glasgow Asylum for the Blind* 1911 SC 391, 1 SLT 37, some weight is attached, under reference to remarks by Lord Watson in *Hislop v MacRitchie's Trustees* (1881) 8 R (HL) 95 at 103, to a declaration that the burdens are to be inserted in all subsequent conveyances of the servient tenement. But the passage from Lord Watson relied upon is concerned, not with the present situation where successive grants are made by a superior, but with the situation where there is a single grant followed later by subdivision. See para 401, note 5, below.

8 Eg *M'Gibbon v Rankin* (1871) 9 M 423.

9 *Johnston v The Walker Trustees* (1897) 24 R 1061 at 1075, per Lord M'Laren.

10 *Nicholson v Glasgow Asylum for the Blind* 1911 SC 391, 1911 1 SLT 37.

11 See para 388 above.
12 Land Registration (Scotland) Act 1979 (c 33), s 17.
13 Except where ibid, s 17, is expressly disapplied in the deed.
14 *Wells v New House Purchasers Ltd* 1964 SLT (Sh Ct) 2 (a pre-1979 example). There are obvious similarities between this situation, of a deed of conditions which binds the entire estate, and the situation described in para 401 below of a single grant in feu which also binds the entire estate; and if enforcement rights are implied in the latter situation, as they are, they ought also to be implied in the former.
15 *Hislop v MacRitchie's Trustees* (1881) 8 R (HL) 95 at 98, per Lord Selborne LC.
16 *Botanic Gardens Picture House Ltd v Adamson* 1924 SC 549 at 563, 1924 SLT 418 at 425, per Lord President Clyde.
17 *Main v Lord Doune* 1972 SLT (Lands Trib) 14.
18 *Murray's Trustees v St Margaret's Convent Trustees* (1906) 8 F 1109, 14 SLT 307 (affd 1907 SC (HL) 8, 15 SLT 2).
19 *Johnston v The Walker Trustees* (1897) 24 R 1061.
20 Thus Lord Kyllachy said in *Johnston v The Walker Trustees* (1897) 24 R 1061 at 1068, OH (affd (1897) 24 R 1061, IH): 'Now although the point is narrow and difficult, and I am far from confident that I am right in the view which I have come to take . . .'. The main obstacle was the fact that the feuing plan was not made obligatory on the superiors. In the event various other aspects of the deed were regarded as fortifying the court's conclusion, eg the fact that there were burdens in relation to such items of common use as a pleasure ground and sewers, and an inference which could be drawn that the superiors could not lawfully alter the plan in relation to the dominant co-feuar.
21 *Bannerman's Trustees v Howard and Wyndham* (1902) 10 SLT 2.

401. Single grant followed by subdivision. The general conditions for implying enforcement rights have already been considered[1]. In the case of successive grants by a superior, it was seen that the main difficulty lies in demonstrating appropriate notice of a common feuing plan in the title of the servient co-feuar[2]. This is not a difficulty in the case where a single grant in feu is followed later by subdivision; for where a superior feus a plot of ground, and the plot is then subdivided by the feuar, whether by disposition or by further grants in feu, the original feudal grant is part of the title of each of the ultimate feuars, and provided that the original grant itself discloses a common feuing plan, there can be no question of absence of notice to a servient co-feuar[3].

This invites consideration of the anterior question, of what must a grant in feu contain in order to demonstrate a feuing plan such as is enforceable by co-feuars. The requirements are modest. There must of course be real burdens, and the burdens must apply to the whole feu. It is, however, no objection that different burdens apply to different parts of the feu, so long as the observance of one set of burdens can be regarded as a reasonable equivalent of the right to enforce another set of burdens[4]. It is usually considered helpful if the original feuar is enjoined to repeat the burdens in all subsequent conveyances[5], although this point seems more directed at the initial validity of the burdens than at the establishment of co-feuars' rights[6]. Finally, and negatively, there must be nothing in the grant to indicate that the superior alone has the right to enforce. Thus the reservation by the superior of an express right to waive performance excludes co-feuars' rights in relation to the burden or burdens affected by the waiver[7]. The position is the same in regard to express prohibitions on subdivision, for if there is to be no subdivision there are to be no co-feuars and enforcement rights are necessarily in the superior alone. The fact that subdivision has actually taken place can make no difference because the existence of co-feuars' rights stands or falls on the terms of the original feudal grant[8]; and presumably this is so even where the prohibition on subdivision is later discharged by the superior or by the Lands Tribunal[9]. On the same basis, there may be an argument that a feu of a single house, where subdivision, though not actually prohibited, is clearly not intended by the superior may be incapable of sustaining co-feuars' rights in the event of subdivision actually occurring.

It is thought that co-feuars' rights arise as soon as the first plot of ground is broken off from the original feu. So if A feus to B imposing real burdens, and B then dispones part of the feu to C, retaining the rest for the time being, the result is that B can enforce the burdens against C, C can enforce against B, and A as superior can enforce against both B and C.

1　See para 399 above.
2　See para 400 above.
3　'[A] sub-feuar or disponee acquiring a building lot, subject to a particular condition, with notice in his titles that the common author, whether his immediate or over-superior, has imposed that condition upon the whole area of which his lot formed a part, must be taken as consenting that the condition shall be for mutual behoof of all the feuars or disponees within the area, and that all who have interest shall have a title to enforce it': *Hislop v MacRitchie's Trustees* (1881) 8 R (HL) 95 at 104, per Lord Watson. See further eg *Low v Scottish Amicable Building Society* 1940 SLT 295, OH.
4　*Lees v North East Fife District Council* 1987 SLT 769. Conveyancers will smile at the weight placed by Lord Justice-Clerk Ross on the fact that no attempt was made in the disposition to the servient co-feuar to indicate that only certain of the burdens in the original grant applied to the subjects.
5　This arises from a casual remark by Lord Watson in *Hislop v MacRitchie's Trustees* (1881) 8 R (HL) 95 at 103 in describing the category of single grant followed by subdivision: '... where the superior feus out a considerable area with a view to its being subdivided and built upon, without prescribing any definite plan, but imposing certain general restrictions which the feuar is taken bound to insert in all sub-feus or dispositions to be granted by him'. For an example, see *Lees v North East Fife District Council* 1987 SLT 769. It is possible that Lord Watson's reference to inserting burdens refers to the doctrine expressed in some of the earlier cases that a subfeuar is not otherwise liable to an over-superior. See para 414 below.
6　See para 390 above. See further the comments in A J McDonald 'The Enforcement of Title Conditions by Neighbouring Proprietors' in D J Cusine (ed) *A Scots Conveyancing Miscellany: Essays in Honour of Professor J M Halliday* (1987) p 17.
7　*Turner v Hamilton* (1890) 17 R 494.
8　*Girls School Co Ltd v Buchanan* 1958 SLT (Notes) 2.
9　*Williamson and Hubbard v Harrison* 1970 SLT 346.

402. Juridical basis of co-feuars' rights. Lord Watson explained in *Hislop v MacRitchie's Trustees* that:

> 'The right of the [co-]feuar, though arising *ex contractu*, is of the nature of a proper servitude, his feu being the dominant tenement'[1].

'Servitude' is in fact a common attribution for co-feuars' rights in the older case law[2], and it must be understood as meaning, not servitude *stricto sensu*, but servitude as a generic term for what in this title is described as a 'real condition'[3]. Lord Watson's point is a simple one but of considerable importance. Thus suppose that A feus to B imposing real burdens and that C, D and E are co-feuars, also holding from A, with enforcement rights against B. So far as the burdens in B's title are concerned, there is one servient tenement (the *dominium utile* of B) but four distinct dominant tenements, namely the superiority of A and the separate *dominium utile* interests held by C, D and E. The right of the co-feuars, no less than the right of the superior, is praedial and not personal. Co-feuar C can enforce the real burdens against B only for as long as he remains co-feuar. If he dispones his feu to F, F is co-feuar in his place and succeeds to his right of enforcement.

An alternative analysis which is frequently found is to classify co-feuars' rights as an example of *jus quaesitum tertio*[4]. It is submitted, however, that this analysis is both inadequate as an explanation and also that it has the potential to mislead. The analysis is inadequate because it fails to explain all the cases in which co-feuars' rights arise[5]. It is potentially misleading because the very term *jus quaesitum tertio* hints at a connection with the law of contract which in truth barely exists. The model often presented is of a perpetual feudal contract between superior and vassal with the co-feuar as a *tertius*, but in the modern law the perpetual feudal contract is a shadowy, if not actually an illusory, concept, and the liability of a vassal to his superior is primarily a matter of property law[6].

1 *Hislop v MacRitchie's Trustees* (1881) 8 R (HL) 95 at 102.
2 *Alexander v Stobo* (1871) 9 M 599 at 612, per Lord Deas; *Robertson v North British Rly Co* (1874) 1 R 1213 at 1218, per Lord Ardmillan; *Earl of Zetland v Hislop* (1881) 8 R 675 at 680, per Lord Young (revsd (1882) 9 R (HL) 40).
3 For real conditions, see paras 344 ff above.
4 Naturally this is particularly attractive to contract lawyers. See W M Gloag *The Law of Contract* (2nd edn, 1929) pp 243 ff. The history of trusts provides an interesting parallel here, because at one time the right of a beneficiary was also attributed to *jus quaesitum tertio*. See W A Wilson and A G M Duncan *Trusts, Trustees and Executors* (1975) pp 12–14.
5 Thus suppose that A feus to B and B then subfeus to C, and further suppose that D (who holds directly from A) is a co-feuar with enforcement rights against C. C has no contractual relationship with A. He is not the 'second party' to a perpetual feudal contract, and from the point of view of enforcement rights, D's relationship to C is indistinguishable from A's relationship to C. The problems are even more difficult when the *jus quaesitum* model is applied to burdens created in ordinary dispositions (for which see para 404 below).
6 See para 393 above. Of course in the case of real burdens created in dispositions there is not even a pretence of a perpetual contract.

403. Implied rights: the disponer.

Enforcement of a real burden presupposes the existence of an interest in land which is capable of acting as a dominant tenement[1]. For a superior that function is fulfilled by the reserved superiority[2], but in the case of an ordinary disposition nothing is usually reserved to the disponer. In the absence of a dominant tenement, there are no enforcement rights[3], except that a disponer can always enforce the terms of a disposition against the original disponee as a matter of simple contract[4].

The position is, or may be, different where the disponer also owns land adjacent to the land which he is now disponing. Thus suppose that A subdivides a piece of ground. Plot 1 is disponed to B. Plot 2 is retained by A but later disponed to C. The disposition of plot 1 contains real burdens which are plainly for the benefit of plot 2. Who can enforce these burdens? A is able to enforce the burdens against B as a matter of contract, and this is so even after he has disposed of the property[5]. But what of C? The burdens are for the benefit of plot 2, which C now owns. Sometimes, of course, it is expressly provided in the original disposition of plot 1 that the burdens are to be enforceable by A and by his successors as proprietors of plot 2. The matter is then beyond doubt: plot 2 is the dominant tenement in the burden and C, as its current owner, has the right to enforce the burdens against the proprietor of the servient tenement, plot 1[6]. But what if, as more often happens, the disposition is silent, so that there is nothing to indicate that the disponer owns adjoining land, still less that that land is to be the dominant tenement in the burdens? Is the mere fact that the disponer owns such land sufficient for it to act as dominant tenement, as it were by implication? This important question was considered twice within twenty years by the Inner House of the Court of Session but to opposite effect. There are no other reported decisions.

The first case was *J A Mactaggart & Co v Harrower*[7] decided by the Second Division in 1906 as an appeal from the Dean of Guild Court in Glasgow. The Division did little more than approve the 'very clear and able exposition' of the Dean of Guild (King)[8] and the substance of the decision is to be found in the Dean of Guild's judgment. It is indeed exceptionally clear and able and repays examination. The question before the court in *Mactaggart* was whether a right to enforce lay in C, the successor of the original disponer as owner of land adjacent to the land originally disponed. The main argument against such a right was that the original disposition was silent on the matter. That, the Dean of Guild conceded, was a difficulty but one which could be overcome by analogy with the law of servitudes:

'A well drawn conveyance—particularly a conveyance which does not bring about any feudal relationship between granter and grantee—would undoubtedly, after imposing the restriction, set forth or indicate the creditor area [that is, the dominant tenement]. But whether the law of real burden makes that a necessity is another matter. The law of Scotland, it is true, does not admit an indefinite burden upon land. But, so far as the

Dean has found, that statement has hitherto been used only when the burdened area was in question, and the indefiniteness of the creditor area has not been the subject of judicial decision. Taking the matter on principle, the Dean does not think that the want of an express specification of the creditor area makes a real burden, otherwise well imposed, invalid. A real burden of the kind in question is praedial in its character; it is for the benefit of some lands or the owners thereof, as owners, and not as individuals; and, considering the nature of the grant under which the burden in question was imposed, it must be taken to have been imposed for the benefit of the lands remaining in the person of those who imposed it, or at all events, of so much of these remaining lands as might be injuriously affected by operations or buildings on the ground restricted. That would, the Dean takes it, be the position as regards the dominant tenement under the law of servitude proper, and he thinks the same rule holds in the case of real burden'[9].

The opposite view was taken in *Botanic Gardens Picture House Ltd v Adamson*[10], decided by the First Division in 1924. Remarkably, there is no evidence from the report that *Mactaggart* was cited to the court in the later case, and the argument that the land reserved by the disponer might form an implied dominant tenement seems not to have been presented[11]. Instead the court viewed the facts as a simple case of co-disponees' rights. C, like B, was a co-disponee of A, the original granter. C's right to enforce the restrictions in B's title depended on whether he could bring himself within the rules in *Hislop v MacRitchie's Trustees*[12]. He could not do so and accordingly his right of action failed. In fact the rules in *Hislop* had already been considered and dismissed as irrelevant in *Mactaggart*:

'The objectors here [that is, C] do not need to found or rely on a case of mutuality and community of rights and obligations. This is not a case of restrictions being imposed upon a feuar by a superior, and being pleaded by another feuar not a party to the deed imposing the restrictions . . . [T]he present question arises as to a real burden imposed for the benefit of the estate retained or reserved by the party imposing it, and the parties seeking to enforce it are now in right of the reserved estate . . . They are not *tertii*. They are in reality the continuation of the *persona* at whose instance and for the benefit of whose reserved estate the burden was imposed'[13].

In *Mactaggart* there was an express assignation in the disposition of the dominant tenement, granted by A to C, of the enforcement rights against B, whereas in *Botanic Gardens* there was none. Strictly therefore the cases are not on all fours[14], but since it is settled that rights to enforce real burdens pass with the dominant tenement without assignation and indeed that assignation away from the dominant tenement is ineffectual[15], the difference is not material and the two cases seem irreconcilable. Of the two *Mactaggart* is probably to be preferred for not only is it the better argued but it was also decided first. The decision in *Botanic Gardens*, reached without reference to *Mactaggart*, was *per incuriam*[16]. While, however, the rule in *Mactaggart* works satisfactorily in cases of simple subdivision[17], it is less well adapted to developments on a larger scale where its interaction with the established rules on co-disponees' rights leads to complexity and incoherence[18].

1 See para 397 above.
2 See para 398 above.
3 Ie other than rights which may be held by co-disponees, for which, see para 404 below. In the typical case of a disposition there is neither land reserved to the disponer nor are there co-disponees, so that there can be no real burdens.
4 See para 392 above.
5 *Scottish Co-operative Wholesale Society Ltd v Finnie* 1937 SC 835, 1938 SLT 78, expressly disapproving remarks in *J A Mactaggart & Co v Harrower* (1906) 8 F 1101, 14 SLT 277.
6 *Braid Hills Hotel Co Ltd v Manuels* 1909 SC 120, 16 SLT 523; *Aberdeen Varieties Ltd v James F Donald (Aberdeen Cinemas) Ltd* 1939 SC 788, 1940 SLT 58 (revsd 1940 SC (HL) 52, 1940 SLT 374.
7 *J A Mactaggart & Co v Harrower* (1906) 8 F 1101, 14 SLT 277.
8 (1906) 8 F 1101 at 1108, 14 SLT 277 at 280, per Lord Kyllachy (with whom the other judges concurred). Nonetheless Lord Kyllachy does not seem to have fully understood the Dean of Guild's reasoning, attributing the decision to an assignation of the disponer's original contractual right.

9 (1906) 8 F 1101 at 1104, 14 SLT 277 at 279, Dean of Guild Court (affd (1906) 8 F 1101, 14 SLT 277).
10 *Botanic Gardens Picture House Ltd v Adamson* 1924 SC 549, 1924 SLT 418.
11 It may be that the court was misled by *Braid Hills Hotel Co Ltd v Manuels* 1909 SC 120, 16 SLT 523, which, by treating the express reservation of enforcement rights to a disponer and his successors as a case of co-disponees' rights, laid a false trail.
12 *Hislop v MacRitchie's Trustees* (1881) 8 R (HL) 95.
13 *J A Mactaggart & Co v Harrower* (1906) 8 F 1101 at 1105, 1106, 14 SLT 277 at 279, Dean of Guild Court (affd (1906) 8 F 1101, 14 SLT 277).
14 Another small difference is that in *Botanic Gardens* the plots of ground, although held on separate titles, were originally disponed to the same person and only later came into separate ownership. But this was expressly stated by Lord President Clyde not to affect the result of the case: see *Botanic Gardens Picture House Ltd v Adamson* 1924 SC 549 at 564, 1924 SLT 418 at 425.
15 See para 397 above. Even if required, an assignation would probably be implied. See *Stevenson v Steel Co of Scotland Ltd* (1899) 1 F (HL) 91, and *Braid Hills Hotel Co Ltd v Manuels* 1909 SC 120, 16 SLT 523.
16 However, certain remarks by Lord Cullen in the most recent reported case, *Lees v North East Fife District Council* 1987 SLT 769 at 772, OH (affd 1987 SLT 769, IH), may be read as supporting the conclusion reached in *Botanic Gardens*.
17 Indeed it is probably indispensable. For example, if A dispones part of his back garden to B for construction of a house and includes in the disposition a number of detailed provisions in relation to the house and its future use, it would be unfortunate if the burdens could not be enforced by A's successor in the principal house. A's successor would not be within the rule in *Hislop v MacRitchie's Trustees* (1881) 8 R (HL) 95 because he has no equivalent burdens in his own title.
18 See para 404 below.

404. Implied rights: co-disponees.

In principle co-disponees are governed by the same rules as co-feuars[1]. These rules were discussed earlier[2]. As with co-feuars, it is possible to identify two distinct cases in which enforcement rights arise. One is where there is a single disposition of an area of land which is later subdivided, so creating a body of co-disponees holding from a common author. The burdens in the original disposition are then enforceable *inter se*[3]. Except where the original disponer reserves to himself an area of ground which is capable of acting as a dominant tenement[4], the real burdens remain latent and unenforceable until subdivision ultimately takes place[5]. For this reason, but not only for this reason[6], it is difficult to accept the view often expressed[7] that co-disponees' rights are an example of *jus quaesitum tertio*.

The other case is where a disponer comes to make successive grants of adjoining areas of land subject to the same or equivalent real burdens. So far as the rights of co-disponees' are concerned, the law is the same as in the corresponding situation for co-feuars, which is to say that enforcement rights arise only if the particular disposition sought to be enforced contains either an obligation to impose similar or equivalent burdens in subsequent grants or alternatively clear evidence of a common plan for the whole development[8]. But the position is complicated by the decision in *J A Mactaggart & Co v Harrower*[9], which provides that land reserved by a disponer is an implied dominant tenement in any real burdens created by the disposition. An example explains the difficulty.

Suppose that a builder completes a building containing eight flats, and further suppose that, as happened on innumerable occasions in the years between about 1870 and 1914, he comes to dispone the individual flats subject to real burdens providing for maintenance of certain common parts of the building such as the roof. Unless the dispositions confer express rights of enforcement (which was and remains rare) the enforcement rights held by each flat will depend upon the order in which they happened to be first sold off. Thus when the first flat comes to be disponed, the remaining seven flats, as the land at the time reserved by the disponer, form dominant tenements in the real burden. This is the rule in *Mactaggart*. Thus in a question with the proprietor of the first flat, the proprietors of any other flat have automatic rights of enforcement. The position is different for the second and subsequent flats. When the second flat is disponed the six flats then remaining with the disponer are dominant tenements as before, but the first flat is no longer owned by the common disponer and so cannot benefit from the rule in *Mactaggart*. Any enforcement rights must be founded on the different and much stricter rules relating to co-disponees' rights set out in *Hislop v MacRitchie's Trustees*[10] and subsequent cases. As the flats are successively sold off, so enforcement rights deteriorate in quality, and by the time the final flat comes to be disponed, the rule in *Mactaggart* ceases to apply at all and enforcement rights in relation to that flat depend solely on the rules for co-disponees[11].

The effect of the interaction of these two separate sets of rules may be summarised in this way. In a development of the kind described, the right of the proprietor of any one piece of land to enforce common burdens against any other piece of land will depend on the chronology of the original grants. Where the potential dominant tenement was disponed after the potential servient tenement there is an automatic right of enforcement (provided of course that interest can be shown[12]) in virtue of the rule in *Mactaggart*; but conversely, where the potential dominant tenement was disponed prior to or simultaneously[13] with the servient tenement, there is no automatic right of enforcement and the dominant proprietor must satisfy the rules in *Hislop v MacRitchie's Trustees*[14], which often he will be unable to do[15]. That such a difference should result merely from an accident of chronology seems difficult to justify[16].

1 *Braid Hills Hotel Co Ltd v Manuels* 1909 SC 120, 16 SLT 523.
2 See paras 399–402 above.
3 *Lees v North East Fife District Council* 1987 SLT 769.
4 This happened in *Lees v North East Fife District Council* 1987 SLT 769.
5 In effect they are like burdens in a deed of conditions after registration but prior to subdivision. See para 388 above.
6 For other reasons, see para 402 above.
7 Eg *Nicholson v Glasgow Asylum for the Blind* 1911 SC 391, 1911 1 SLT 37.
8 See para 400 above.
9 *J A Mactaggart & Co v Harrower* (1906) 8 F 1101, 14 SLT 277. The status of this decision may, however, be open to question: see para 403 above.
10 *Hislop v MacRitchie's Trustees* (1881) 8 R (HL) 95.
11 *Bannerman's Trustees v Howard and Wyndham* (1902) 10 SLT 2. The difference between the situation in *Bannerman's Trustees* and the situation in *Mactaggart* is explained fully by the Dean of Guild (King) in the latter case: see *J A Mactaggart & Co v Harrower* (1906) 8 F 1101 at 1106, 14 SLT 277 at 279, Dean of Guild Court (affd (1906) 8 F 1101, 14 SLT 277).
12 For interest to enforce, see para 407 below.
13 This was the case in *Nicholson v Glasgow Asylum for the Blind* 1911 SC 391, 1911 1 SLT 37.
14 *Hislop v MacRitchie's Trustees* (1881) 8 R (HL) 95.
15 But in the particular example given there will be an argument, depending on the precise wording employed, that an obligation to contribute to the maintainance of a roof in a tenement building evidences a common plan and hence reciprocal rights of enforcement. The position is stronger still if a deed of conditions is used: see para 400 above.
16 In practice this problem has hitherto been overlooked or ignored.

405. Express rights. A well-drawn deed will put enforcement rights beyond doubt by making these the subject of express provision. In most cases an enforcement clause does no more than express the rule which would otherwise have been implied by law. Therefore, in a grant in feu it will often be provided that the burdens are enforceable by the superior and his successors as superior, while in a disposition the burdens will be declared enforceable by the disponer and his successors as proprietors of an area of reserved land[1]. The real utility of express clauses is in relation to co-feuars and co-disponees who must otherwise rely on the complex and sometimes uncertain rules set out in *Hislop v MacRitchie's Trustees*[2] and subsequent cases[3]. Naturally, express clauses are not confined to restating the implied rules, and rights to enforce can competently be conferred on any party who owns an interest in land which is sufficiently proximate[4] to act as a dominant tenement[5].

1 *Braid Hills Hotel Co Ltd v Manuels* 1909 SC 120, 16 SLT 523; *Aberdeen Varieties Ltd v James F Donald (Aberdeen Cinemas) Ltd* 1939 SC 788, 1940 SLT 58 (revsd 1940 SC (HL) 52, 1940 SLT 374).
2 *Hislop v MacRitchie's Trustees* (1881) 8 R (HL) 95.
3 For an example of an express clause, see *Lawrence v Scott* 1965 SC 403, 1965 SLT 390.
4 If it is not sufficiently close there will be no interest to enforce. See para 407 below.
5 For an example, see *Gorrie and Banks Ltd v Burgh of Musselburgh* 1973 SC 33, 1974 SLT 157.

406. Rights of tenants and other non-owners. Only the person who is proprietor of the appropriate dominant tenement has the right to enforce a real burden[1]. Probably he must be infeft. Thus there is no right to enforce in tenants[2], in heritable creditors[3] or in other parties whose rights in the property are less than that of ownership.

1 That is the rule too for servitudes. See para 481 below.
2 *Eagle Lodge Ltd v Keir and Cawder Estates Ltd* 1964 SC 30, 1964 SLT 13.
3 *Smith v Taylor* 1972 SLT (Lands Trib) 34.

407. Interest to enforce. This paragraph contains a general discussion of the question of interest to enforce. Certain specialities which apply in the case of superiors only are considered in the immediately following paragraph[1].

Real burdens, it has been said, are:

'. . . restraints upon one tenement for the benefit of some other tenement which stand to each other in some relation of neighbourhood, and they are allowed by the law as being conducive to the full use and enjoyment of the dominant property'[2].

A real burden must be 'for the benefit of some other tenement'; or, as the rule is often expressed, the burden must confer patrimonial (praedial) benefit. This is both a rule of enforcement and also a rule of constitution. It is a rule of enforcement because a party seeking compliance with a burden requires not only title to enforce (ownership of a dominant tenement[3]) but also interest, which is to say that the burden must confer benefit on the dominant tenement which he owns[4]. It is a rule of constitution because a condition which does not confer patrimonial benefit is not a real burden in the first place[5]. It may sometimes happen that, owing to changes in circumstances, a condition which confers patrimonial benefit at the time when it is first imposed later ceases to do so, and in that case the burden is automatically extinguished. The effect of change in circumstances is considered more fully below in the context of extinction of burdens[6].

If, as the law requires, real burdens consist of 'restraints upon one tenement'[7] then such restraints will almost inevitably confer at least some 'benefit on some other tenement', typically one or more of the neighbouring pieces of land. Thus an obligation not to build may protect the light or prospect of a neighbour[8], while an obligation to build in conformity with a given plan will protect the uniformity of a particular development and confer aesthetic benefit on all the proprietors within the development[9]. An obligation not to make a specified use of the property will usually reduce noise or otherwise contribute to overall amenity, and an obligation in the title of a tenement flat to contribute to the cost of maintaining common parts benefits the other flats within the building. There are many other possible examples. The benefit must, however, be patrimonial and not personal: it must touch the property as distinct from the person who happens to be its proprietor. In practice, of course, many burdens confer benefit of both kinds, and it is no objection to an interest to enforce, otherwise unexceptionable, that there is incidental personal benefit. But where the benefit is personal only and has no bearing on the property (an example is an obligation to pay a fixed sum of money) then there is no interest to enforce, at least as a real burden[10].

There is some uncertainty concerning the status of commercial benefit. In *Aberdeen Varieties Ltd v James F Donald (Aberdeen Cinemas Ltd)*[11] a theatre was disponed subject to a burden that it should not be used for putting on plays of a certain kind. The dominant tenement was expressed as being a second theatre half a mile away. The only benefit conferred was of a commercial nature, the restraint on a rival having the effect of increasing the profits of the dominant tenement, and it was held that there was no interest to enforce. However, the main reason for the decision appears to have been the distance between the two tenements and in a later case a commercial interest was accepted in circumstances where dominant and servient tenements were immediately adjacent[12]. It may be argued in favour of admitting commercial benefit that, if domestic use may legitimately be protected, for example by preventing certain activities on the servient tenement which might lead to noise and disturbance, there can be no reason why there should not be equivalent protection for commercial use, subject of course to the overriding principle that a burden must not be contrary to public policy[13]. Restrictions of both kinds are 'conducive to the full use and enjoyment of the dominant property'. The counter-argument is that, while burdens protective of domestic use will normally be of benefit to the dominant tenement regardless of its future ownership, the same cannot be said of burdens protective of commercial use, which are of benefit only to proprietors engaged in commerce. The law remains in doubt.

The interest of a superior to enforce a real burden is presumed[14] as is the interest of a disponer in a question with the original disponee[15], although in both cases the presumption can be rebutted. In all other cases it is for the party seeking to enforce a burden to aver and prove interest[16]. In practice the difference is smaller than might at first appear. Usually interest to enforce is obvious. Indeed the very fact that a party is incurring the expense of enforcement is itself strongly suggestive of an interest. Where dominant and servient tenements are close together, and where the burden regulates the servient tenement in some way, it is difficult to say that there is not at least some patrimonial interest; and 'some' interest is sufficient to sustain an action[17]. There is no need to show that non-observance of the burden will reduce the value of the pursuer's property[18], although naturally it is helpful if it will; and although the point seems open to doubt, it was said in one case that even if reduction in value can be proved, this is not conclusive as to interest to enforce[19]. Where a burden (and hence the possible benefit) is utterly trivial in nature, there is no interest to enforce:

> 'Of course I do not mean to include extreme and absurd cases — such, for instance, as if the feu contained regulations as to painting the outside of the houses, and one directed the house to be painted sea green, while all the rest had become dark blue, I do not mean to say that the superior could insist on the sea green'[20].

Where interest to enforce is lacking it is usually because the physical distance between the tenements is too great. On this matter it is difficult to lay down precise rules. Much depends on the burdens in question. It is in the nature of some restrictions to benefit only immediate neighbours. Others are of benefit to those in the same street, and others still to those within the same building development, which may comprise a number of different streets. In *Aberdeen Varieties*[21], the only reported case in which distance determined the decision, a distance of half a mile was held to be too much. Similar problems arise in the law of servitudes, where the rule is no more certain[22]. The issue is of particular importance in modern housing estates where a large area may be governed by the same deed of conditions supported by reciprocal enforcement rights, but where there are obvious difficulties in a houseowner at one end of the estate demonstrating interest in a question with a houseowner at the other end.

1 See para 408 below.
2 *Aberdeen Varieties Ltd v James F Donald (Aberdeen Cinemas Ltd)* 1939 SC 788 at 800, 1940 SLT 58 at 63, per Lord Justice-Clerk Aitchison (revsd 1940 SC (HL) 52, 1940 SLT 374).
3 See paras 397 ff above.
4 *Corpn of Tailors of Aberdeen v Coutts* (1840) 1 Robin 296 at 307, per Lord Corehouse.

5 Thus it is included amongst the rules of constitution in *Corpn of Tailors of Aberdeen v Coutts* (1840) 1 Robin 296 at 307. For an example, see *Aberdeen Varieties Ltd v James F Donald (Aberdeen Cinemas) Ltd* 1939 SC 788, 1940 SLT 58, revsd 1940 SC (HL) 52, 1940 SLT 374. See further para 391 above.

6 See para 430 below.

7 See para 391 above.

8 Examples which have been given of interest to enforce are 'the protection of the amenity or comfortable enjoyment of other lands' and the protection of 'light, or air, or support, or amenity': *Aberdeen Varieties Ltd v James F Donald (Aberdeen Cinemas) Ltd* 1939 SC 788 at 796, 801, 1940 SLT 58 at 61, 64, per Lord Wark and Lord Justice-Clerk Aitchison (revsd 1940 SC (HL) 52, 1940 SLT 374).

9 *Stewart v Bunten* (1878) 5 R 1108.

10 So an obligation to pay a sum of money cannot be made a real burden (in the sense meant here), but even as a failed real burden the obligation would remain enforceable as a contractual term in a question between the original parties.

11 *Aberdeen Varieties Ltd v James F Donald (Aberdeen Cinemas Ltd)* 1939 SC 788, 1940 SLT 58 (revsd 1940 SC (HL) 52, 1940 SLT 374).

12 *Co-operative Wholesale Society v Ushers Brewery* 1975 SLT (Lands Trib) 9. But cf *Phillips v Lavery* 1962 SLT (Sh Ct) 57.

13 As to public policy, see para 391 above. In *Aberdeen Varieties Ltd v James F Donald (Aberdeen Cinemas) Ltd* 1940 SC (HL) 52, 1940 SLT 374, as was observed by Lord Thankerton in the House of Lords (at 56, 375), there was some confusion as to whether the condition under consideration was lawful but with no interest to enforce or simply an unlawful restraint of trade.

14 See para 408 below. Interest to enforce servitudes is also presumed: see para 481 below.

15 *Scottish Co-operative Wholesale Society Ltd v Finnie* 1937 SC 835, 1938 SLT 78. Oddly, since both are based on contracts, the equivalent rule for grants in feu is said to be that no interest is required at all: *Waddell v Campbell* (1898) 25 R 456, 5 SLT 285.

16 *Aberdeen Varieties Ltd v James F Donald (Aberdeen Cinemas Ltd)* 1940 SC (HL) 52, 1940 SLT 374.

17 But *Maguire v Burges* 1909 SC 1283, 1909 2 SLT 219, can be read as supporting a stricter rule. Here a co-feuar seeking to prevent his neighbour from building a church rather than residential buildings was said to have no interest to enforce. Lord President Dunedin (at 1291, 223) expressed the robust view that 'he has not a shadow of interest. The only thing that he has ever said is that he is a physician, and that if part of the ground is occupied as a church instead of dwellinghouses he will get less practice. That is really so ridiculous as to be quite elusory ... A church is not a thing which would deteriorate the neighbourhood'. In fact the averments made on behalf of the co-feuar were 'that a church occupying ground designed by the titles for tenements and dwellinghouses would injuriously affect his interests as a medical practitioner and neighbouring proprietor'; and since the first is personal only and the second is fatally vague, it may be that the true explanation of the decision is failure to aver relevant interest. See W M Gloag *The Law of Contract* (2nd edn, 1929) p 256. Certainly it is difficult to see why a neighbour should not have an interest to prevent the building of a church.

18 *Stewart v Bunten* (1878) 5 R 1108 at 1115, per Lord Gifford.

19 *Aberdeen Varieties Ltd v James F Donald (Aberdeen Cinemas) Ltd* 1939 SC 788, 1940 SLT 58 (revsd 1940 SC (HL) 52, 1940 SLT 374). There is indeed an argument that the fact that non-observance would lead to a reduction in value meant that, for a burden of the type considered in this case, the distance of half a mile between the tenements was not after all too great.

20 *Edinburgh Magistrates v Macfarlane* (1857) 20 D 156 at 171, per Lord Justice-Clerk Hope. An alternative analysis is to say that, as a rule of content, trivial restrictions are incapable of being made real burdens. See *Waddell v Campbell* (1898) 25 R 456 at 458, OH, per Lord Pearson (affd (1898) 25 R 456, 5 SLT 285, IH), a case which itself might be thought to involve a burden too trivial to enforce had the question not been between the original parties to the grant.

21 *Aberdeen Varieties Ltd v James F Donald (Aberdeen Cinemas) Ltd* 1939 SC 788, 1940 SLT 58 (revsd 1940 SC (HL) 52, 1940 SLT 374).

22 See para 481 below.

408. Interest of superiors. In principle, and subject to two important qualifications discussed below, the law as to interest to enforce is the same for superiors as for other dominant proprietors such as disponers or co-feuars; but in practice the real and substantial interest to enforce a burden will often lie with co-feuars and interest is only attributed to the superior, as is usually the case, by the application of a certain amount of ingenuity.

It was generally assumed during the nineteenth century that for superiors, as for other dominant proprietors, interest to enforce must be patrimonial, which is to say that it must be founded upon the ownership of land[1]. This indeed was the basis of the decision of the House of Lords in *Earl of Zetland v Hislop*[2], the leading case in this whole area. More recently, however, the rule has come under challenge. In *Menzies v Caledonian Canal Comrs*[3], decided in 1900, superiors asserted their right to enforce a real burden prohibiting the vassal from having on his feu a public-house or inn for the sale of exciseable or other liquors. Nearby the superiors operated, but apparently did not own[4], a canal on which a number of workmen were employed and they were anxious in the interests of public safety that alcohol should not be readily available. In the event there was ample patrimonial interest to enforce the burden, but Lord President Balfour indicated[5] that he would have been prepared to recognise as a valid interest the public safety concerns of the superiors even although they could not be said to be patrimonial. The Lord President's remarks were *obiter*, but even if they are accepted as authoritative they could be regarded as a special exception in the interests of public safety. However, a number of later cases contain *dicta* to the effect that the interest to enforce of a superior may be personal as well as patrimonial although in none of these cases was this the basis of decision[6]. It is thought that these *dicta* are incorrect, not only because they are inconsistent with older authority but because the rule suggested seems incoherent. For as Lord Kincairney, the Lord Ordinary, pointed out in the *Caledonian Canal* case[7] a superior will always have a personal interest to enforce at least in the sense that the vassal may be willing to pay for a minute of waiver[8]; and consequently a rule admitting personal interest collapses into a rule that interest to enforce is always and under all circumstances conclusively present[9].

So far as interest to enforce is concerned there are two important differences between the position of superiors and the position of other dominant proprietors such as disponers and co-feuars. The first concerns the land from which patrimonial interest may be drawn. For other dominant proprietors the rule is that title and interest must coincide, so that the land which is benefited by the real burden must also be the dominant tenement in that burden. However, in the case of superiors, interest may be uncoupled from title, an unexpected and a surprising rule[10]. It is sufficient, therefore, if the burden benefits any land which the superior happens to own in the vicinity of the servient tenement[11], and there is no requirement that the dominant tenement itself (which is to say, the superiority) should also benefit. For example in *Earl of Zetland v Hislop*[12], where a burden affecting on the land on which Grangemouth was ultimately built prohibited the sale of alcohol, Lord Selborne, the Lord Chancellor, compiled a meticulous list of the different interests in land belonging to the superior which could be said to benefit from the restriction[13]. First there was the superiority itself 'by virtue of which in certain contingencies the *dominium utile* in the premises feued might revert to him, which interest alone would be enough to justify him in seeking to maintain unimpaired the value of the houses erected on all such premises'. Then there were a number of houses in the centre of Grangemouth which were rented out. Next there were 140 acres of building ground, as yet unfeued. Finally there was the superior's own mansion house which was within half a mile of town. At the time when the action was raised there were in Grangemouth two hotels, seven dram-shops, four grocers' shops and a restaurant, all selling alcohol to a population of around five thousand; but while it was generally accepted that the real motive behind enforcement was the promotion of temperance and social reform, it was plain that there was ample patrimonial interest to sustain the action.

While a superior must not act merely oppressively or capriciously[14], it has been said that the degree of interest required of the superior is not high:

'When it is said that the superior must have an interest, I apprehend that it is not intended that he must be able to prove that the maintenance of the restriction will be beneficial to him. He cannot be bound to do more than shew that is may possibly be beneficial, and that it is not obviously useless. If he can state a legal interest, it must be for him to judge whether in any particular case he will benefit by enforcing it'[15].

Nevertheless there will be circumstances where even this undemanding standard cannot be attained, and this is particularly likely to occur where the only interest retained by the superior is the bare superiority. For not all real burdens are of benefit to a superiority. On this subject it is often said that there is patrimonial benefit to the superiority from the maintenance of the value of the *dominium utile*, either because there is always the contingent possibility, however remote in practice, that it will one day revert to the superior[16], or because (a poor argument today) the *dominium utile* is security for payment of feuduty[17]. If this is correct, then it follows that a superior always has patrimonial interest in respect of burdens designed to maintain value; but conversely a bare superiority may confer no interest in respect of other burdens. A parallel distinction was drawn, in one case, between restrictions on building and restrictions on use and it was suggested that a breach of the latter, ephemeral as it was bound to be, might not be enforceable by a superior holding on a bare superiority[18]. The suggestion remains untested[19].

There is also a second difference between the position of superiors and the position of other dominant proprietors. In *Earl of Zetland v Hislop* it was said by Lord Watson, in a famous passage, that:

'*Prima facie*, the vassal in consenting to be bound by the restriction concedes the interest of the superior; and, it therefore appears to me, that the *onus* is upon the vassal who is pleading a release from his contract to allege and prove that, owing to some change of circumstances, any legitimate interest which the superior may originally have had in maintaining the restriction has ceased to exist'[20].

This passage must be approached with caution. The main proposition advanced, that with superiors, unlike other dominant proprietors, interest to enforce is presumed, is of course beyond dispute[21]. But, as was pointed out in a later case[22], the reference to proof of change of circumstances suggests an irrebuttable presumption that there was an interest to enforce at the time when the burden was first created. It is clear from *Corpn of Tailors of Aberdeen v Coutts*[23] that there is no such irrebuttable presumption; and while in practice a vassal will usually argue loss of interest to enforce through change of circumstances[24], there is also available the argument that there was no interest to enforce in the first place and hence no need to show change of circumstances[25].

In a question between the original superior and the original vassal no interest to enforce is required[26], although Gloag suggests that the rule might be different after some years had elapsed[27].

1 The only case in which this proposition was denied appears to be *Edinburgh Magistrates v Macfarlane* (1857) 20 D 156. This is also the only reported case ever to have applied the theory of the perpetual feudal contract (see para 393 above) and patrimonial interest was not required because successive superiors and vassals were considered to be in precisely the same position as the original parties to the grant.
2 *Earl of Zetland v Hislop* (1882) 9 R (HL) 40.
3 *Menzies v Caledonian Canal Comrs* (1900) 2 F 953, 8 SLT 87.
4 If they had owned the canal their interest to protect its safe running would have been patrimonial.
5 *Menzies v Caledonian Canal Comrs* (1900) 2 F 953 at 962, 8 SLT 87 at 88.
6 *J & F Forrest v George Watson's Hospital Governors* (1905) 8 F 341 at 348, 12 SLT 818 at 819, OH, per Lord Dundas (affd (1905) 8 F 341, 13 SLT 590, IH); *Scottish Co-operative Wholesale Society Ltd v Finnie* 1937 SC 835 at 848, 1938 SLT 78 at 85, per Lord Wark; *Macdonald v Douglas* 1963 SC 374 at 390, 1963 SLT 191 at 199, per Lord Justice-Clerk Grant; *Howard de Walden Estates Ltd v Bowmaker Ltd* 1965 SC 163 at 181, 1965 SLT 254 at 264, per Lord President Clyde.
7 *Menzies v Caledonian Canal Comrs* (1900) 2 F 953 at 955, OH (affd (1900) 2 F 953, 8 SLT 87, IH).
8 There is, however, an element of circularity here. The possibility of receiving a waiver payment is used as evidence that the burden is enforceable, but waiver payments are due only if the burden is in fact enforceable.

9   Such a rule would make it irrelevant to show loss of interest by change of circumstances (see para 430 below), for a superior could never lose at least this interest.

10   Unless it can be argued that the adjoining land is also an implied dominant tenement. See para 398 above.

11   This is the case whether his interest therein is *dominium utile* or, it appears, *dominium directum*. On the latter, see *J & F Forrest v George Watson's Hospital Governors* (1905) 8 F 341, 13 SLT 590.

12   *Earl of Zetland v Hislop* (1881) 8 R 675, revsd (1882) 9 R (HL) 40. See also *Porteous v Grieve* (1839) 1 D 561, and *Naismith v Cairnduff* (1876) 3 R 863.

13   *Earl of Zetland v Hislop* (1882) 9 R (HL) 40 at 45.

14   *Menzies v Caledonian Canal Comrs* (1900) 2 F 953 at 960, OH, per Lord Kincairney (affd (1900) 2 F 953, 8 SLT 87, IH); *Macdonald v Douglas* 1963 SC 374 at 390, 1963 SLT 191 at 199, per Lord Justice-Clerk Grant; *Howard de Walden Estates Ltd v Bowmaker Ltd* 1965 SC 163, 1965 SLT 254. But while this rule has been stated, it has never been applied.

15   *Menzies v Caledonian Canal Comrs* (1900) 2 F 953 at 958, OH, per Lord Kincairney (affd (1900) 2 F 953, 8 SLT 87, IH). See also further remarks by Lord Kincairney at 960. The rule appears to be much the same for other dominant proprietors.

16   Eg *Earl of Zetland v Hislop* (1882) 9 R (HL) 40.

17   Eg *Naismith v Cairnduff* (1876) 3 R 863.

18   *Menzies v Caledonian Canal Comrs* (1900) 2 F 953 at 959, OH, per Lord Kincairney (affd (1900) 2 F 953, 8 SLT 87, IH).

19   It is rare in reported decisions for reliance to be placed only on the bare superiority. *Howard de Walden Estates Ltd v Bowmaker Ltd* 1965 SC 163, 1965 SLT 254 is an example, but while an interest to sue was held to exist in respect of a restriction on use, the burdens in the defenders' title also included a restriction on building. In any event, the possible significance of the difference does not appear to have been canvassed in argument.

20   *Earl of Zetland v Hislop* (1882) 9 R (HL) 40 at 47.

21   The rule was not a new one. See *Campbell v Clydesdale Banking Co* (1868) 6 M 943 at 950, per Lord Neaves.

22   *Menzies v Caledonian Canal Comrs* (1900) 2 F 953 at 957, 958, OH, per Lord Kincairney (affd (1900) 2 F 953, 8 SLT 87, IH).

23   *Corpn of Tailors of Aberdeen v Coutts* (1840) 1 Robin 296 at 307, per Lord Corehouse: as a rule of constitution '[t]he superior or the party in whose favour it is conceived, must have an interest to enforce it'.

24   Invariably this argument will be without success: see para 430 below.

25   In many cases this may turn out to be the stronger argument.

26   *Waddell v Campbell* (1898) 25 R 456, 5 SLT 285.

27   W M Gloag *The Law of Contract* (2nd edn, 1929) p 249.

409. Division of the dominant tenement. A dominant tenement in a real burden is either a *dominium utile* of land or it is a superiority. A superiority is not, or at least not in the usual case, capable of subdivision[1]. But a *dominium utile* may be subdivided, either physically or feudally, the distinction being that in physical subdivision the land is split up into two or more separate parts by disposition, while in feudal subdivision the land is subfeued so that in place of the original *dominium utile* there is now a new *dominium utile* and a reserved superiority.

The effect of division on enforcement rights is not entirely clear[2]. The only discussion of physical division in a reported case appears to be the following from the Dean of Guild (King) in *J A Mactaggart & Co v Harrower*:

'The point was not taken, but the Dean sees it could be argued that restrictions in favour of a reserved estate belonging to one person become much more burdensome when the reserved estate is split up and comes to be held by several persons — that by conveying the reserved estate, otherwise than as a whole, the burden has been increased. But the Dean does not think that this argument is conclusive in any case, and, particularly so, in a case like the present, where everything pointed to the development of the estate, and the splitting of it up into lots'[3].

If this is correct, as it may be, it is at odds with the equivalent rule for servitudes where subdivision of the dominant tenement will often offend the principle that the burden on the servient tenement is not to be increased[4]. So far as feudal division is concerned, it has been held by the Lands Tribunal that the new *dominium utile* is to be regarded as a dominant tenement[5], and it may be that the same is also true of the reserved superiority.

For subdivision of both kinds the matter may often come to be settled by reference to interest to enforce. Thus it is difficult to see how interest attaches to a reserved superiority, and in the case of physical subdivision some of the now separate parts may be too distant from the servient tenement for interest to be established.

1 Further feudal subdivision is of course impossible, and physical subdivision is normally possible only with the consent of the vassal: Erskine *Institute* II,3,12; Hume *Lectures* vol IV (Stair Soc vol 17, 1955 ed G C H Paton) p 201.
2 See also para 345 above.
3 *J A Mactaggart & Co v Harrower* (1906) 8 F 1101 at 1106, 14 SLT 277 at 279, 280, Dean of Guild Court (affd (1906) 8 F 1101, 14 SLT 277).
4 See para 465 below. This principle is of particular relevance to obligations allowing the dominant proprietor to make some use of the servient tenement (ie positive servitudes), but it is not clear that obligations of this kind can be real burdens: see para 391 above.
5 *Smith v Taylor* 1972 SLT (Lands Trib) 34.

(5) SERVIENT TENEMENT: LIABILITY IN THE OBLIGATION

410. Identification of the servient tenement. The servient tenement in a real burden must be adequately identified and it appears that the requirements here are stricter than in the case of a dominant tenement[1]. In practice, however, identification seldom gives rise to difficulties. In most cases the servient tenement is simply all of the land conveyed by the deed in which the burdens are first created, and in the absence of express stipulation to the contrary this is probably implied. Provided, therefore, that a description is sufficiently clear to convey the property at all[2] it is also sufficient to identify the servient tenement.

Sometimes a particular burden or set of burdens is intended to affect part only of the subjects conveyed, and here a more exacting standard of description is required, in line with the generally strict rules of draftsmanship which apply to real burdens[3]. The leading case is the decision of the House of Lords in *Anderson v Dickie* where the clause in dispute read:

'. . . it shall not be lawful to the said Joseph Colen Wakefield or his foresaids to sell or feu any part of the ground occupied as the lawn between the ground feued by me to William Miller, merchant in Glasgow, and the present mansion-house of Eastwood Park . . .'[4].

The deed was granted in 1864 and no doubt at that time the description was clear enough. The difficulty was to know, many years later, the exact site of the lawn at the time of the original deed. The description was held to be insufficient. Future purchasers of land, it was said, 'cannot be sent . . . to seek for a real burden in sources so remote from the title as the memory of gardeners and foresters'[5]. The description, therefore, must be good, not just for the time when the deed was first granted, but for the future as well.

1 *J A Mactaggart & Co v Harrower* (1906) 8 F 1101 at 1104, 14 SLT 277 at 279, Dean of Guild Court (affd (1906) 8 F 1101, 14 SLT 277). For identification of the dominant tenement, see paras 397 ff above.

2 For description of property, see CONVEYANCING, vol 6, para 482 ff.
3 See para 390 above.
4 *Anderson v Dickie* 1915 SC (HL) 79, 1915 1 SLT 393. See also *Scottish Temperance Life Assurance Co v Law Union and Rock Insurance Co* 1917 SC 175, 1917 1 SLT 4.
5 *Anderson v Dickie* 1915 SC (HL) 79 at 86, 1915 SLT 393 at 397, per Lord Kinnear.

411. *Pro indiviso* shares as servient tenements. In view of the generally unsatisfactory nature of the rules of common property[1], *pro indiviso* owners may wish to make their own rules in a form which will bind successors. This is only possible by the use of real burdens, typically involving the use of a deed of conditions. There may, however, be difficulties in identifying suitable dominant and servient tenements. Where, as often happens, common property is held in conjunction with other property which is owned separately by individual *pro indiviso* owners (as in the case of tenement buildings), the properties in separate ownership are available as dominant and servient tenements to support burdens on the areas owned in common[2]. But where there is no other property in several ownership the question arises as to whether the *pro indiviso* shares may themselves be used as dominant and servient tenements[3]. If that were possible, each share would be both a servient tenement (making its owner bound to obey the rules) and also a dominant tenement (allowing its owner to enforce the rules against his fellow owners). This possibility appears never to have been considered by the courts[4], but it seems unobjectionable on technical grounds of property law and there is much to be said for it on grounds of policy[5].

1 For the rules of common property, see paras 23 ff above.
2 Eg *Grant v Heriot's Trust* (1906) 8 F 647, 13 SLT 986; *Fearnan Partnership v Grindlay* 1990 SLT 704, affd 1992 SLT 460, HL (servitude).
3 Arguably this situation also arises where there was at one time both common property and neighbouring property owned individually by the *pro indiviso* proprietors, but the common property has come to be separated from the neighbouring property. In this case it could be said that the burdens relate only to the common property and, following the separation, attach exclusively thereto. See further para 414 below.
4 However, in *Wilson's Trustees v Brown's Executors* (1907) 15 SLT 747, OH, where the burden failed on other grounds, the fact that the servient tenement was a *pro indiviso* share was not said to be an objection.
5 For the equivalent rule in relation to common interest, see para 232 above.

412. Liability of servient proprietor. Liability for implementation of real burdens rests with the proprietor of the servient tenement for the time being. It might therefore be expected that infeftment is the test of liability, in the same way as infeftment in the dominant tenement determines the location of the right to enforce[1]. But the rules which have evolved are very much more complex than this simple principle. Two main questions are addressed by these rules, which apply except where the original conveyance clearly indicates otherwise[2]. First, at what point in the transfer process does a transferee assume liability for the real burdens? Secondly (for the answer is not the same) at what point does the transferor cease to be liable?

The answer to the first question is not in doubt. A transferee becomes liable on acceptance of delivery of the disposition[3]. He is then an 'uninfeft proprietor'. Neither infeftment nor, it is thought, possession[4] are required. A right under missives is, however, insufficient[5]. In the case of judicial transfers, liability follows the judicial conveyance so that an executor is liable on confirmation and a trustee in sequestration on obtaining the act and warrant. If a transferee is actually infeft, the reason why he is liable is that he is the owner of the servient tenement. If he is uninfeft (and so not owner) the reason for his liability is unclear, although it has been suggested that in accepting delivery of the disposition he must be taken to have adopted all the obligations which burden the right[6].

The answer to the second question, namely, at what point does the transferor cease to be liable, is more difficult. It seems clear that the earliest time that liability may be lost is on the infeftment of the transferee, for until infeftment the transferor remains owner of the servient tenement[7]. It follows, therefore, that there will always be a period of concurrent liability, beginning with delivery of the disposition and ending with infeftment; and if the transferee fails to procure himself infeft, as sometimes happens[8], concurrent liability remains with the transferor indefinitely. But not even infeftment may be sufficient to displace liability, for in two circumstances some liability remains with the transferor notwithstanding divestiture of ownership.

The first of these is where the transferor omits to send a statutory notice of change of ownership to his immediate superior. Notices of change of ownership are the means by which superiors are informed of a change of vassal, following the introduction of implied feudal entry in 1874. Unless and until a notice is sent, the former vassal remains liable for all obligations owed to the superior, although not of course for obligations owed to others such as an over-superior or a co-feuar[9]. The new vassal is also liable. In modern practice notices of change of ownership are almost never sent, but the rule remains.

The other circumstance in which the transferor remains liable despite the infeftment of his transferee is in relation to positive obligations which were already prestable prior to the transfer. The rule here was settled in *Marshall v Callander and Trossachs Hydropathic Co Ltd*[10] where the defenders, having failed to rebuild a building destroyed by fire, as required by their titles, sought to avoid liability by transferring the property to a company without any assets. The attempt was unsuccessful, the court holding that both transferor and transferee were liable. Although not so presented, the decision appears to have been influenced by the apparent injustice of the defenders' actions[11]. Some aspects of the rule remain uncertain. Thus it is not clear when precisely an obligation becomes prestable. Presumably an obligation to act within a time limit is considered to become prestable only when the time limit expires[12], but often there is no time limit. Does a general obligation to maintain a tenement roof become prestable when the first slate falls off, or when the disrepair becomes more serious, or only when a demand for maintenance is made by one of the dominant proprietors[13]? It has been held that where, in implement of an obligation to maintain, work has actually been carried out and payment is due, the obligation to pay for the work is personal to the transferor and does not pass to successors at all[14]. There is also doubt about the date at which the risk of continuing liability is removed. Must the obligation become prestable before delivery of the disposition, or is it sufficient if it arises after delivery but before registration? No guidance is to be found from *Marshall* where the obligation arose before both registration and delivery[15].

Where liability is held concurrently by transferor and transferee it is joint and several, but there is no guidance in the authorities as to the respective liabilities of the parties *inter se*[16]. In some cases this matter is expressly provided for in missives of sale.

---

1 See para 397 above.
2 Thus the precise wording of the deed creating the burdens is not usually of significance. See eg *Macrae v Mackenzie's Trustee* (1891) 19 R 138. But for a case where it was, see *Dundee Police Comrs v Straton* (1884) 11 R 586.
3 *Hyslop v Shaw* (1863) 1 M 535 at 575 ff, per Lord Curriehill.
4 Lord Kyllachy refers to the need for possession in *Marshall v Callander and Trossachs Hydropathic Co Ltd* (1895) 22 R 954, OH ((1895) 22 R 954, 3 SLT 94, IH, affd (1896) 23 R (HL) 55) but not in the later case of *Rankine v Logie Den Land Co Ltd* (1902) 4 F 1074, 9 SLT 474, OH (affd (1902) 4 F 1074, 10 SLT 278, IH).
5 *Wells v New House Purchasers Ltd* 1964 SLT (Sh Ct) 2. For the liability of a possessor without title, see para 413 below.

6   *Marshall v Callander and Trossachs Hydropathic Co Ltd* (1895) 22 R 954 at 964, OH, per Lord Kyllachy ((1895) 22 R 954, 3 SLT 94, IH, affd (1896) 23 R (HL) 55). The same argument is sometimes used in relation to the liability of subfeuars: see para 414 below.

7   *Hyslop v Shaw* (1863) 1 M 535.

8   As Lord President M'Neill pointed out in *Hyslop v Shaw* (1863) 1 M 535 at 566 this is a matter over which the transferor has no control: he cannot force the transferee to register.

9   Conveyancing (Scotland) Act 1874 (c 94), s 4(2).

10   *Marshall v Callander and Trossachs Hydropathic Co Ltd* (1895) 22 R 954, 3 SLT 94, affd (1896) 23 R (HL) 55, followed in *Rankine v Logie Den Land Co Ltd* (1902) 4 F 1074, 10 SLT 278.

11   Certainly there was nothing in the law as it then stood which pointed to the conclusion reached by the court. In particular the reliance placed on *Hyslop v Shaw* (1863) 1 M 535 seems misplaced since in that case the defender remained infeft in the feu, a crucial difference.

12   Occasionally it may become prestable even before this. Thus if the obligation is to build a house within two years, and a house takes six months to build, it might be said that the obligation becomes prestable after eighteen months.

13   In *Marshall v Callander and Trossachs Hydropathic Co Ltd* (1895) 22 R 954, 3 SLT 94, affd (1896) 23 R (HL) 55, a court action had been raised by the superior.

14   *David Watson Property Management v Woolwich Equitable Building Society* 1992 SCLR 357, 1992 SLT 430, HL.

15   This was also the case in *Rankine v Logie Den Land Co Ltd* (1902) 4 F 1074, 10 SLT 278.

16   In cases of failure to send a notice of change of ownership, liability is probably 100 per cent with the transferee. See the Conveyancing (Scotland) Act 1874, s 4(2), where that rule is expressly provided for in the case of feuduty.

413. Liability of tenants and other non-owners. Unlike a servitude, a real burden is not a real right in the strict sense of the term[1]. The right is *in personam* and not *in rem* and the person against whom it may be enforced is the proprietor for the time being of the servient tenement. Thus Lord Kinnear:

'. . . I should certainly think it very difficult to suppose that a superior imposing an obligation to build houses upon his land should look to anyone for the performance of that obligation, excepting to the owner of the land for the time being . . . [T]hese are obligations or conditions of the grant binding upon the vassal who for the time being holds the land in terms of the grant, and upon nobody else'[2].

Those with lesser interests in the servient tenement, such as tenants, liferenters, or possessors without a title[3], are in general free from liability. A different rule applies in the case of feuduties, where a distinctive basis of liability has developed[4].

The rule that only the servient proprietor has liability must be taken subject to two qualifications. First, it is provided by statute that a creditor under a standard security who is in lawful possession of the security subjects is liable for all the obligations of the proprietor which relate to their management and maintenance[5], including obligations taking the form of real burdens[6]. The second qualification is less clearly established. Where a real burden imposes a restriction, as opposed to an obligation to perform positive acts, and where the servient tenement has been leased, it seems that the burden may be enforced not only against the servient proprietor but against his tenant also. In one case interdict was granted against both landlord and tenant[7], while in another case, in which the burden was ultimately held not to have been breached, the form of action was once again an interdict against landlord and tenant[8]. In neither case, however, was the form of action discussed, and a later case, in which the issue did not arise for decision, approached the subject with caution:

'If a superior desires to take action in connexion with a breach of condition, it is the vassal, and no one else, who is under obligation to him and, whether the breach is committed by the hand of the vassal, or by the hand of a lessee, it is the vassal against whom the superior must proceed, although he may, no doubt, also convene the lessee. From the point of view of the superior, the lessee is merely the vassal's agent'[9].

It is thought that these authorities are sufficient to support the statement that a real burden, provided that it is negative in nature, may be enforced directly against a tenant[10], at least where the action is also raised against his landlord[11]. Certainly this is a highly convenient result, especially where the lease is a long one; and it is not unreasonable in itself that a tenant should take the property subject to some at least of the burdens in his landlord's title, especially where these burdens are set out in a public register. It remains to be seen what legal principle can be found to justify a tenant's liability[12].

1 See paras 344 ff above.
2 *Macrae v Mackenzie's Trustee* (1891) 19 R 138 at 145, 146. See also *Property Law: Abolition of the Feudal System* (Scot Law Com Discussion Paper no. 93 (1991)) para 3.106.
3 *Wells v New House Purchasers Ltd* 1964 SLT (Sh Ct) 2.
4 Tenants are liable to the extent of their rents, and possessors intromitting with the fruits (if there are fruits) to the extent of those fruits. See Bell *Principles* s 700 and W M Gordon *Scottish Land Law* (1989) para 22–07. The first functions like an accelerated form of arrestment, while the second may be a special rule of the law of possession. Both may be due to the fact that feuduty, unlike real burdens, is heritably secured on the feu: see *Hyslop v Shaw* (1863) 1 M 535 at 575, per Lord Curriehill.
5 Conveyancing and Feudal Reform (Scotland) Act 1970 (c 35), s 20(5)(b). Surprisingly, if the possession is unlawful the creditor appears to escape liability.
6 *David Watson Property Management v Woolwich Equitable Building Society* 1992 SCLR 357, 1992 SLT 430, HL. In the event the obligation founded upon was held to be personal to the debtor, with the result that no liability was assigned to the heritable creditor. See also *Patterson v Robertson* 1912 2 SLT 494, OH (creditor in an *ex facie* absolute disposition who was not in possession held not to be liable in respect of a positive real burden).
7 *Colquhoun's Curator Bonis v Glen's Trustee* 1920 SC 737, 1920 2 SLT 197.
8 *Mathieson v Allan's Trustees* 1914 SC 464, 1914 1 SLT 308.
9 *Eagle Lodge Ltd v Keir and Cawder Estates Ltd* 1964 SC 30 at 45, 1964 SLT 13 at 19, per Lord Sorn. But Lord Guthrie (at 47, 20) may possibly be read as saying that an action against the tenant alone is competent.
10 Whether it may also be enforced against other non-owners, and, if so, which, is an open question.
11 See further the discussion in para 347 above.
12 Similar problems arise in explaining the liability of subfeuars following the feudal division of the original servient tenement, for which see para 414 below. In the case of tenants, however, there is an obvious difficulty in explaining why, as a matter of principle, there should be liability for negative real burdens but not for positive real burdens.

414. Division of the servient tenement. The original servient tenement in a real burden may come to be divided, by disposition, into two or more parts. If the burden in question affected the whole property, then necessarily it will continue to affect each separated part of the former whole. Conversely, if the burden was confined to a defined and smaller area then only the part or parts within that area will be subject to the burden and the remaining parts will be free. It may not always be easy to decide into which category a particular burden falls. Thus an obligation to maintain a house, imposed in a disposition of the house and its garden, might be assumed to burden the whole subjects of grant; but if part of the garden then comes to be sold separately there is a strong argument that it is free from the burden. Where separate parts of a former single tenement are burdened by a positive obligation, for example an obligation of maintenance, liability is presumably joint and several, but difficult and unresolved questions arise as to rights of relief and liability *inter se*.

A servient tenement may also be subject to feudal division, often in practice accompanied by physical division. So if A conveys land to B, whether by grant in feu or by ordinary disposition, and real burdens are imposed in the conveyance, and B then subfeus to C, the original servient tenement (the *dominium utile* of B) has been divided into a new *dominium utile* held by C and a reserved superiority held by B. Since C is in possession of the land he is best placed to comply with the burdens and various theories have been advanced in order to justify his liability. Thus it has been said that C is liable to A provided that the burdens are made conditions of his own grant from B[1], or again that in accepting the grant from B, C must be deemed to have adopted the burdens in B's title[2]. But whatever the theoretical basis of the doctrine the modern view is that C and his successors are subject to the burdens[3]; and since B and his successors also remain subject to the burdens[4] there are then two servient tenements, namely the new *dominium utile* and the reserved superiority[5].

1 *Clark v City of Glasgow Life Assurance and Reversionary Co* (1850) 12 D 1047, revsd (1854) 1 Macq 668, HL; *Hyslop v Shaw* (1863) 1 M 535 at 551, per Lord Justice-Clerk Inglis, Lord Cowan, Lord Benholme, Lord Neaves and Lord Mackenzie.
2 *Hyslop v Shaw* (1863) 1 M 535 at 558, per Lord Ormidale.
3 This is presupposed in the modern law of rights of co-feuars and co-disponees, for which see paras 399 ff above. See also *Marquis of Tweeddale's Trustees v Earl of Haddington* (1880) 7 R 620 and *Marshall v Callander and Trossachs Hydropathic Co Ltd* (1895) 22 R 954, 3 SLT 94 (affd (1896) 23 R (HL) 55).
4 *Hyslop v Shaw* (1863) 1 M 535.
5 It is thought, however, that B cannot enforce the burdens against C.

(6) INTERPRETATION

415. General principles. In *Heriot's Hospital Governors v Ferguson*[1], one of the early leading cases on real burdens, the principles of interpretation were vigorously debated. For the pursuers, who were seeking to enforce the burden, it was argued that:

'no person is bound to part with it [property], by his voluntary act, but upon such conditions as he judges proper ... Such being the nature of feu-grants, it follows of consequence, that they ought to be strictly interpreted against the grantee, and favourably constructed for the granter, so that he may be held to have granted away no more than he has clearly expressed'[2].

In reply the defenders argued that, whatever might have been the appropriate canon of interpretation at the time when feudalism was still in full vigour, a new age and new circumstances demanded a new rule:

'The rights of the superior have been, by degrees, greatly abridged, partly by statute, and partly by usage. The favour of the law clearly is for the beneficial use of those rights, which are naturally consequent on the power of disposal in the vassal. It is a matter of public and manifest expediency, that all restraints upon property should be strictly interpreted, and that no limitation should ever be implied, whether in questions with the superiors or others'[2].

It was the argument of the defender which prevailed, both in *Heriot's Hospital* itself and in subsequent case law. But while the *Heriot's Hospital* case, and others like it, established that the dominant proprietor should not be favoured, it was for many years unclear how far the balance ought to be tilted in favour of the servient proprietor. It could be, and was, argued that feudal contracts should be interpreted in the same way as commercial contracts, words being given their natural meaning without favour to either side. Thus Lord President Inglis, in a case decided in 1877:

'I think that though restrictions on property are not to receive a loose or wide interpretation as against the proprietor, still they are to receive a fair and not a malignant interpretation as against the superior'[3].

But by the time this dictum was pronounced, the view which it expressed was already under challenge from those who sought to interpret real burdens against the dominant proprietor and in favour of the servient proprietor, and before the end of the nineteenth century this latter view had come to prevail[4]. It remains the law today. Thus there is said to be a presumption that land is free from perpetual restrictions. A granter is presumed not to derogate from his grant. A real burden must therefore be expressed with great clarity and precision. The courts will decline to enforce a condition which is not immediately intelligible, while an ambiguous condition will receive the interpretation most favourable to the servient proprietor. The implications of these rules are considered more fully below[5].

There is a certain amount of danger in the approach now adopted by the courts, for the drafting of a restrictive condition can always be improved, at least with the benefit of hindsight, and if a court is so minded there are few conditions which will escape its censure. In the last third of the nineteenth century the Second Division, and in particular Lord Young[6], came close to adopting the 'malignant interpretation' complained of by Lord President Inglis in the dictum quoted earlier[7], and, although not at first universally accepted[8], this hostile approach was carried forward with renewed zeal by Lord Kinnear and other members of the First Division into the twentieth century. Perhaps this shift in judicial attitudes was not altogether surprising. By the end of the nineteenth century, real burdens had been in common use for eighty years or more, and no doubt many restrictions had become elderly and inappropriate. If a real burden could not readily be extinguished by any other method there was obvious merit in extinction by judicial interpretation. Since 1970, however, the existence of the special Lands Tribunal jurisdiction has made the variation or extinction of burdens very much easier[9], and indeed the possibility of a Lands Tribunal application now acts as a strong incentive for dominant proprietors to grant voluntary minutes of waiver. No doubt burdens should continue to be interpreted against the dominant proprietor, but there may now be room for a more relaxed approach than at one time seemed desirable[10].

There are two circumstances in which the rule of interpretation just described may not apply. One is where burdens are enforceable by co-feuars and co-disponees *inter se* without being enforceable by a superior or other outside party. Here the burdens (in practice, often contained in a deed of conditions) provide a model set of rules for the mutual benefit of everyone and there seems no reason why they should not be interpreted in an even-handed way[11]. The other circumstance where the usual rule does not apply is in a question between the original parties to a grant, so that the condition is being enforced, not as a real burden but simply as an ordinary contractual term[12].

1 *Heriot's Hospital Governors v Ferguson* (1773) Mor 12817, affd (1774) 3 Pat 674, HL.
2 (1773) Mor 12817 at 12818.
3 *Ewing v Campbells* (1877) 5 R 230 at 233. See also *Porteous v Grieve* (1839) 1 D 561; *Buchanan v Marr* (1883) 10 R 936 at 939, per Lord Craighill; *Burnett v Great North of Scotland Rly Co* (1885) 12 R (HL) 25.
4 See eg *Frame v Cameron* (1864) 3 M 290 at 292, 294, per Lord Curriehill and Lord Deas; *The Walker Trustees v Haldane* (1902) 4 F 594 at 596, 9 SLT 350 at 350, OH, per Lord Low (affd (1902) 4 F 594, 9 SLT 453, IH); *Anderson v Dickie* 1915 SC (HL) 79 at 89, 1915 1 SLT 393 at 399, per Lord Dunedin. In *Shand v Brand* (1907) 14 SLT 704, OH, however, both views are adopted without any suggestion of mutual inconsistency.
5 See also paras 388, 390, above.
6 Lord Young frequently complained about the inadequate draftsmanship of conveyancers, eg *Burnett v Great North of Scotland Rly Co* (1883) 11 R 375 at 387 (revsd (1885) 12 R (HL) 25): 'It is excessively bad conveyancing'.
7 Eg *Moir's Trustees v M'Ewan* (1880) 7 R 1141; *Buchanan v Marr* (1883) 10 R 936; *Miller v Carmichael* (1888) 15 R 991.
8 Thus the Second Division's general approach was the subject of a rebuke by the House of Lords in *Burnett v Great North of Scotland Rly Co* (1885) 12 R (HL) 25. It made no difference.
9 Conveyancing and Feudal Reform (Scotland) Act 1970 (c 35), s 1. On this subject, see further CONVEYANCING, vol 6, paras 511 ff.
10 In a recent case, *Lothian Regional Council v Rennie* 1991 SCLR 709, 1991 SLT 465, the court was divided, with one judge (Lord McCluskey) adopting a benign approach which would have pleased Lord President Inglis a century earlier. Another benign decision is *Church of Scotland General Trustees v Phin* 1987 SCLR 240, Sh Ct. One possible approach is for real burdens now to be interpreted in the same manner as servitudes: against the dominant tenement of course but accompanied by a certain amount of flexibility. For the interpretation of servitudes, see para 450 below.

11 A more formal justification might be that, since no rights of enforcement are reserved by the granter of the original deed, this is not a case for the application of the principle that a granter does not derogate from his grant. This general issue was raised in argument, inconclusively, in *Arnold v Davidson Trust Ltd* 1987 SCLR 213 at 217, Sh Ct.

12 *Porteous v Grieve* (1839) I D 561.

416. Subsidiary rules. The overriding principle of interpretation is a presumption for freedom so that, in cases of doubt, burdens are read against the dominant proprietor and in favour of the servient proprietor; and in support of this principle a number of subsidiary rules have developed, which are given below. It cannot, however, be pretended that these rules are applied in a mechanical and predictable manner. Much depends on the burden in question, and on the strictness with which the court chooses to read it. Moreover, to some extent the rules overlap with one another, so that the court may be able to select one rule in preference to another. For example, a simple obligation to maintain a fence, without any indication of the standard to which the maintenance should be carried out, may be treated as insufficiently precise, in which case it will fail[1], or perhaps as ambiguous, in which case the lowest possible standard of maintenance will be adopted[2], or again as capable of including an implied standard, for example that the fence must be stockproof, which was the result actually reached in a reported case[3].

It is suggested that in applying the general principle that burdens are to be interpreted against the dominant proprietor, the courts are guided by six subsidiary rules, namely[4]:

(1) Additional words cannot be implied.
(2) The nature and extent of the obligation or restriction sought to be imposed must be clearly defined if the burden is not to be void from uncertainty.
(3) Ambiguous expressions are read *contra proferentem*, against the dominant proprietor.
(4) Interpretation may be aided by consideration of the object with which the burden was imposed.
(5) Burdens relating to buildings will be read as restricting either the structure of the building or its use, but not both unless both are clearly stipulated for.
(6) Where a burden requires the consent of the superior or other dominant proprietor, it is implied that that consent must not be unreasonably withheld.

1 See para 418 below (rule 2).
2 See para 419 below (rule 3).
3 *Church of Scotland General Trustees v Phin* 1987 SCLR 240, Sh Ct. See further para 417 below.
4 Useful tables classifying the interpretation of burdens by subject matter will be found in J M Halliday *Conveyancing Law and Practice in Scotland* vol II (1986) pp 263–266 and in W M Gordon *Scottish Land Law* (1989) pp 719–723.

417. Rule 1: words cannot be implied. In interpreting a real burden a court confines its attention to the words actually before it, and will not usually admit evidence extrinsic to the deed[1]. Nor will it be willing to imply words, for 'no fetters are to be raised by implication'[2]. This at least is the general rule although it is not always adhered to by the courts. Thus, in support of the general rule, it is settled that an obligation to do X does not import a prohibition on doing anything other than X. So an obligation to erect buildings of a certain type does not import a prohibition on the erection, in addition, of other buildings of a different type[3]. But while, consistently with the general rule, an obligation to build does not include an obligation thereafter to maintain[4], an obligation to build buildings of a certain kind has been held to include a prohibition on altering the buildings so as to take them out of the permitted class[5], and an obligation to maintain has been held to include an obligation to re-build where the subjects were later destroyed by fire[6].

Similar issues, and similar inconsistencies, arise where some positive obligation has been imposed but there is then a dispute as to the standard at which it is to be performed[7]. Thus in one case, where land feued for the construction of a reservoir was placed under an obligation to supply water to a number of neighbouring buildings, the court was unwilling to imply that such water must be fit for drinking purposes[8]. In a more recent case a dispute arose in relation to an obligation to maintain a mutual fence. The servient proprietor argued that a bare obligation to maintain could impose no higher standard than the condition of the fence at the time when the obligation was first created; but it was held that where, as in this case, one of the areas bordering the fence was used for agricultural purposes, there must be implied an obligation to keep the fence stockproof[9].

1 See para 388 above.
2 *Corpn of Tailors of Aberdeen v Coutts* (1837) 2 Sh & Macl 609 at 667, HL, per Lord Brougham.
3 *Ross v Cuthbertson* (1854) 16 D 732; *Buchanan v Marr* (1883) 10 R 936; *Cowan v Edinburgh Magistrates* (1887) 14 R 682; *Fleming v Ure* (1896) 4 SLT 26; *Carswell v Goldie* 1967 SLT 339.
4 *Peter Walker & Son (Edinburgh) Ltd v Church of Scotland General Trustees* 1967 SLT 297. Nor does an obligation to maintain a church include an obligation actually to use it: *Fraser v Church of Scotland General Trustees* 1986 SC 279, 1986 SLT 692.
5 This is taken for granted in eg *Cochran v Paterson* (1882) 9 R 634 and *Thom v Chalmers* (1886) 13 R 1026. But in *Johnston v MacRitchie* (1893) 20 R 539 at 544–549, opposing views are expressed by Lord Justice-Clerk Macdonald and by Lord Young.
6 *Clark v City of Glasgow Life Assurance and Reversionary Co* (1854) 1 Macq 668, HL.
7 Another possible approach to cases such as this is to treat the obligation as unenforceable for lack of certainty. See para 418 below (rule 2). Much will depend on the drafting of the principal obligation. In practice, however, courts are slow to find an obligation completely unenforceable.
8 *Anstruther's Trustees v Burgh of Pittenweem* 1943 SLT 160, OH.
9 *Church of Scotland General Trustees v Phin* 1987 SCLR 240, Sh Ct. See further the discussion at para 416 above.

418. Rule 2: requirement of precision. The nature and extent of the obligation or restriction sought to be imposed must be clearly defined, for the servient proprietor must know beyond doubt the burdens which affect his land. A burden which fails to meet this standard of draftsmanship is unenforceable. But in applying this rule it must be borne in mind that language is inherently imprecise and that absolute certainty of meaning, however desirable, is also unattainable. In a modern case an obligation to maintain the supply of water in a mill lade sufficient to cleanse and drain it to the reasonable satisfaction of the dominant proprietor was held to fail on the basis that the words 'reasonable satisfaction' did not import a sufficiently precise standard of performance[1]. Nonetheless as a general rule courts are reluctant to strike burdens down under this head.

An exhaustive citation of the reported cases on precision is not possible here, but the most important decisions, classified by subject matter, are given below.
(1) *Style of building.* It is sufficient if the style of a building to be erected by the servient proprietor is described by reference to other pre-existing buildings, for example '. . . not of a class inferior to the houses sometime ago built by . . .'[2]. If no such reference is made, the words of description must be chosen with care, and both 'conventional dwellinghouse'[3] and 'building of an unseemly description'[4] have been found to be too vague.
(2) *Time limit for construction.* An obligation to perform a single act, such as to erect a house, is unenforceable if it is not accompanied by a time limit within which the act must be completed[5]; and even where there is a time limit, such an obligation is presumed not to run with the land in the absence of clear language to the contrary[6].
(3) *Nuisance clauses.* Clauses prohibiting nuisances under reference to 'the usual grotesque enumeration of noxious and offensive businesses and trades'[7] are often found in titles, but although such clauses have frequently been the subject

of litigation for other reasons, only once have they been challenged on the ground of lack of precision. In that case[8] the clause prohibited the carrying on of:

'... any soap work candle work tan work slaughter house cattle mart skin work dye work oil work lime work distillery brewery or other manufacture or chemical process of any kind nor to deposit nauseous materials thereon nor to lay any nuisance or obstructions on the roads or streets adjoining said ground nor to do any other act which may injure the amenity of the place and neighbourhood for private residences'.

The challenge was unsuccessful, the sheriff commenting that, although a restriction must be clearly expressed, it may competently be expressed 'in words descriptive of general principle rather than of the minutiae of detail'[9].

(4) *Obligation of maintenance.* A maintenance obligation may be expressed either as a direct obligation to maintain, or indirectly, as an obligation to contribute to the cost of maintenance. The two formulations may have different results in law. Thus there is no doubt as to the enforceability of a direct obligation to maintain. The fact that the obligation will not generally indicate a standard of performance does not seem to matter[10], and at least in the usual case the obligation will be measured by the condition of the property at the time when it was first imposed[11]. An obligation to maintain includes an obligation to rebuild[12].

A direct obligation to maintain is inappropriate in cases where the property to be maintained is not part of the servient tenement[13], but some doubt surrounds the validity of an obligation in the alternative form of requiring a contribution to the cost of maintenance[14]. In *Corpn of Tailors of Aberdeen v Coutts*[15] one of the burdens sought to be enforced was the obligation 'to pay me and my foresaids a proportion of two third parts of the expense of forming and enclosing the area in the middle of the said square'. No burden caused greater difficulty for the court. Lord Corehouse's opinion was that the obligation was not enforceable:

'That is not a real burden, for it is an obligation to pay an indefinite sum of money, which cannot be imposed by the law of Scotland[16]. On this point it may be proper to explain, that an obligation *ad factum praestandum* may be enforced, and is so every day, though indirectly and practically it may resolve into payment of an indefinite sum ... But these obligations are unquestionably real burdens, because the fact to be performed is in itself specific'[17]

This view was not supported by the majority of the consulted judges in the Court of Session, who argued that there was no sustainable distinction between an obligation to maintain and an obligation to meet the cost of maintenance, and that there was nothing lacking in precision in requiring payment for an act which was itself precisely specified[18]. The House of Lords, however, supported the minority in the court below and held the burden to be unenforceable. Two reasons for this decision are given by Lord Brougham. In the first place, there was no clear indication that the obligation was intended to run with the land, a matter of particular importance in relation to an obligation to perform a single act[19]:

'Here the conveyance does not declare it [the obligation] a real burden; there is nothing to show (in the words of the learned judges) "that the subject itself is meant to be affected", and it is not one of the necessary or natural burdens of such rights'[20].

In the second place, the obligation required the payment of an indefinite sum of money:

'It is not "*ad factum praestandum*", at least not directly or immediately, but only to pay a proportion of the expense occasioned by a certain fact, if done. It is an obligation to bear an unascertained expense, that is, an unascertained sum of money, which it is on all hands agreed cannot be imposed'[20].

This is an unfortunate decision, and one with potentially serious consequences for the large number of modern titles which contain burdens in this form. The ruling may not, however, apply to all such burdens as Lord Brougham proceeded to explain:

'In a matter confessedly of some nicety, and on which I have great doubts, it seems the safe course to consider this obligation as it directly and apparently is, — an obligation to pay an indefinite sum, unconnected with the *naturalia* of the right. The obligation to pay the expense or any proportion of the expense of repairing, immediately connected with the subject granted, would clearly stand in a different predicament'[20].

It may be taken from this passage that a burden is not to fail merely on the ground that it does not specify the sum due. There was, after all, a second ground of decision in the House of Lords, namely that there were no clear words indicating that the burden was to run with the land; and it is submitted that even a burden involving an indefinite sum of money will succeed if its status as a real burden is made manifest. This appears to be the underlying sense of Lord Brougham's requirement that, in order to 'stand in a different predicament', an obligation must be 'immediately connected with the subject granted'[21]. The small number of more recent cases to have touched upon this subject are consistent with this analysis, although the law cannot be said to be entirely free from doubt[22].

1 *Lothian Regional Council v Rennie* 1991 SCLR 709, 1991 SLT 465 (Lord McCluskey dissenting).
2 *Morrison v M'Lay* (1874) 1 R 1117. See also *Middleton v Leslie* (1894) 21 R 781, 2 SLT 42 ('similar in style and quality to and not exceeding in height the houses already erected ...').
3 *Lawson v Hay* 1989 GWD 24-1049, Sh Ct.
4 *Murray's Trustees v St Margaret's Convent Trustees* (1906) 8 F 1109, 14 SLT 307, affd 1907 SC (HL) 8, 15 SLT 2.
5 *Gammell's Trustees v The Land Commission* 1970 SLT 254, OH, distinguishing *Anderson v Valentine* 1957 SLT 57, OH. The law is incorrectly stated in J M Halliday *Conveyancing Law and Practice in Scotland* vol II (1986) para 19-30.
6 See para 390 above.
7 *Porter v Campbell's Trustees* 1923 SC (HL) 94 at 99, 1923 SLT 619 at 621, per Lord Shaw of Dunfermline.
8 *Mannofield Residents Property Co Ltd v Thomson* 1983 SLT (Sh Ct) 71. The absence of punctuation is typical of many real burdens.
9 1983 SLT (Sh Ct) 71 at 72. See also *Meriton Ltd v Winning* 1993 SCLR 913, 1995 SLT 76, OH.
10 However, it may be that if a standard is actually prescribed, the standard must be adequately specified otherwise the burden will fail. See *Lothian Regional Council v Rennie* 1991 SCLR 709, 1991 SLT 465.
11 But see *Church of Scotland General Trustees v Phin* 1987 SCLR 240, Sh Ct.
12 *Clark v City of Glasgow Life Assurance and Reversionary Co* (1854) 1 Macq 668, HL.
13 The reason for this is that A has no right to enter and carry out repairs to property belonging to B. See *Duncan Smith and MacLaren v Heatly* 1952 JC 61, 1952 SLT 254.
14 See eg *Halliday* vol II, para 19-27.
15 *Corpn of Tailors of Aberdeen v Coutts* (1840) 1 Robin 296.
16 Here there may be evidence of confusion between the two senses of real burden. See K G C Reid 'What is a Real Burden?' (1984) 29 JLSS 9 at 11.
17 *Corpn of Tailors of Aberdeen v Coutts* (1840) 1 Robin 296 at 323, 324.
18 See especially (1840) 1 Robin 296 at 332, 333, per Lord Medwyn.
19 For obligations to perform single acts, see para 390 above.
20 *Corpn of Tailors of Aberdeen v Coutts* (1840) 1 Robin 296 at 340, HL.
21 Lord Brougham may have had in mind the earlier remarks by Lord Corehouse in the Court of Session ((1840) 1 Robin 296 at 308) that 'If the condition is one usually attaching to the lands in a feudal or burgage holding, — in particular if it has a *tractus futuri temporis*, or is of a continuous nature,

which cannot be performed and so extinguished by one act of the disponee or his heir, words less clear and specific will suffice to create it than when the burden appears to be of a personal nature; for example, the payment of a sum of money once for all in terms of a family settlement'. In fact, Lord Brougham's requirement that the obligation be 'immediately connected with the subject granted' is one of the indispensable requirements for any real burden: see para 391 above.

22 In *Edinburgh Magistrates v Begg* (1883) 11 R 352 an obligation to pay for the cost of a single act (completing a roadway) failed, the court emphasising that it was not a natural burden connected with a property of this description. Conversely, in *Wells v New House Purchasers Ltd* 1964 SLT (Sh Ct) 2 an obligation to pay for the cost of maintaining the common parts of a tenement was enforced. See also *Tennant v Napier Smith's Trustees* (1888) 15 R 671. The authorities are reviewed by the House of Lords in *David Watson Property Management v Woolwich Equitable Building Society* 1992 SCLR 357, 1992 SLT 430, HL, but without any definite conclusion being reached on this point.

419. Rule 3: ambiguous expressions are read *contra proferentem*. It is some-times said that the effect of ambiguity is to make a burden unenforceable[1]. Strictly, however, this is incorrect. Rather, the rule for real burdens, as for contractual provisions in general[2], is that ambiguous expressions are read, *contra proferentem*, against the person who seeks to rely on them, who in almost every case involving real burdens will be the dominant proprietor[3]. The dividing line between ambi-guity on the one hand and uncertainty on the other (rule 2 above) is not easily drawn, and a condition which is capable of more than one interpretation will sometimes fail on grounds of uncertainty[4]. In practice the result may come to depend upon whether the burden is a positive obligation (an obligation to do something) or a restriction (an obligation not to do something). If the burden is an obligation to do something, the nature of the thing to be done must be adequately specified otherwise it cannot be done at all. An ambiguity (the existence of two or more possible meanings for the act to be performed) will often be treated as creating a fatal degree of uncertainty[5]. With restrictions, however, the need for absolute certainty is less strong and it is usually sufficient if the core idea of the prohibited activity is reasonably clear. In enforcing a restriction, therefore, a court is much more likely to say that the particular activity complained of does not fall within the clause than that the whole clause is void[6]. An example frequently encountered in practice is a restriction of use to use as a 'private dwelling house'. Here the core idea is clear enough — if the house is used by a family to live in the restriction is complied with — but at the periphery there is ample scope for debate. Is the restriction complied with if the house is used for giving music lessons, or for legal consul-tations? Or what is the position if it is used to accommodate, not a family, but twenty five orphan girls? The latter, it has been held, is not in breach of the restriction[7], and nor is the former provided that the business use is ancillary to residential use[8]. It has never been suggested that the restriction as a whole might be void from uncertainty.

The *contra proferentem* rule may be applied only in genuine cases of ambiguity. It is a misuse of the principle to search adequately drafted burdens for imaginary ambiguities which can then be interpreted to the advantage of the servient pro-prietor[9]. Nor is it the case that the least restrictive interpretation will always be adopted, for if one interpretation is markedly more plausible than the other or others then it will be chosen even if it is not the most restrictive[10].

1 *Hunter v Fox* 1964 SC (HL) 95 at 99, 1964 SLT 201 at 202, per Lord Reid.
2 W W McBryde *The Law of Contract in Scotland* (1987) pp 430, 431.
3 Eg *Cochran v Paterson* (1882) 9 R 634 at 638, per Lord Craighill.
4 Thus Lord Kinnear said in *Middleton v Leslie* (1894) 21 R 781 at 786, that ambiguities are interpreted *contra proferentem* and then later, in *Anderson v Dickie* 1915 SC (HL) 79 at 83, 1915 1 SLT 393 at 395, and with equal conviction, that 'if the language admits of two different interpretations there is no valid real burden'.
5 Eg *Lothian Regional Council v Rennie* 1991 SCLR 709, 1991 SLT 465. For failure by uncertainty, see para 418 above.

6 Eg *The Walker Trustees v Haldane* (1902) 4 F 594, 9 SLT 453.
7 *Brown v Crum Ewing's Trustees* 1918 1 SLT 340, OH.
8 *Colquhoun's Curator Bonis v Glen's Trustee* 1920 SC 737, 1920 2 SLT 197; *Low v Scottish Amicable Building Society* 1940 SLT 295, OH.
9 *Frame v Cameron* (1864) 3 M 290 at 294, per Lord Deas; *Cochran v Paterson* (1882) 9 R 634 at 638, per Lord Craighill.
10 Another way of expressing this proposition is to say that where there are two interpretations, one probable and the other improbable, there is no real ambiguity.

420. Rule 4: objects rule. The object in imposing a particular burden is sometimes expressed in the deed itself or is obvious in some other way. It has been said, for example, that an obligation to construct buildings to a certain value, which was a very common provision in Victorian titles, exists for the purpose of securing the superior's claim to feuduty[1]. Where a particular object is expressed or is otherwise apparent it may be used by the courts as an interpretative aid and, while not usually 'conclusive of the matter'[2], it may be a useful means of choosing between rival interpretations[3]. Thus it has been held both that a general prohibition on building includes a prohibition on building underground and, in a later decision, that it does not include such a prohibition, on the basis that in one case the burden was designed only to preserve light, and so was not breached by an underground building, while in the other case it had wider objects[4]. As the example just given shows, the objects rule may be applied even where this favours a less restrictive interpretation[5].

Where a purpose is expressed it does not usually form part of the operative burden and so cannot be enforced in its own right[6].

1 *Wyllie v Dunnett* (1899) 1 F 982.
2 *Ben Challum Ltd v Buchanan* 1955 SC 348 at 358, 1955 SLT 294 at 302, per Lord Russell.
3 But in *Johnston v Canongate Magistrates* 30 May 1804 FC, (1804) Mor 15112 the objects rule was used to modify a restriction of use which was itself unambiguous. However, the restriction had been imposed in 1569 and the circumstances were otherwise unusual.
4 *Edinburgh Magistrates v Paton and Ritchie* (1858) 20 D 731; *Gray v Malloch* (1872) S J 445 (noted briefly at 10 M 774).
5 *Scot v Cairns* (1830) 9 S 246; *Inglis v Boswall* (1849) 6 Bell App 427, HL. But cf *Graham v Shiels* (1901) 8 SLT 368, OH.
6 *Graham v Shiels* (1901) 8 SLT 368, OH. However, cf *Russell v Cowpar* (1882) 9 R 660.

421. Rule 5: structure and use are different. The suggestion that in the interpretation of real burdens structure and use ought to be distinguished seems first to have been made by the Lord Chancellor (Lord Cottenham) in *Inglis v Boswall*[1], a case decided in 1849. In *Inglis* the titles prohibited the erection of any buildings other than stables and coach-houses, but while stables were duly erected they later came to be used as a painter's shop. There was said to be no breach of the condition. The building retained the structure of stables, as was required, and there was nothing in the condition limiting the use to which that structure could be put. For a time this distinction was resisted by the Court of Session[2], but long before the end of the nineteenth century it was well established[3]. Its effect is that a burden will be read as restricting either structure or, as the case may be, use, but not both, unless there is clearly stipulation for both. In practice the difficulty often lies in deciding whether the condition under consideration is truly directed at structure or at use[4].

In an important series of cases decided at the end of the nineteenth century, the distinction between structure and use came to be applied by the Second Division in a novel and, it may be said, in a malign way[5]. The essential facts of all the cases were the same. In terms of his titles the servient proprietor was permitted to erect only a 'self-contained'[6] dwelling house. He then sought to alter the structure in such a way that the houses were converted into flats, work which typically involved the provision of an additional staircase. It was held that the burden went to structure only whereas, it was said, the real objection of the dominant proprietor now seeking enforcement was to the proposed use as flatted dwelling houses. That a certain amount of structural work had been carried out was of course conceded, but so long as the altered building remained capable of use as a self-contained house then its original structure remained intact and the burden was not breached[7].

1 *Inglis v Boswall* (1849) 6 Bell App 427, HL.
2 *Ewing v Campbells* (1877) 5 R 230. Lord Shand, who dissented, had already supported the *Inglis* analysis in *Fraser v Downie* (1877) 4 R 942.
3 Eg *Middleton v Leslie* (1894) 21 R 781, 2 SLT 42. The change can be traced to as far back as *M'Ewan v Shaw Stewart* (1880) 7 R 682.
4 *Mathieson v Allan's Trustees* 1914 SC 464, 1914 1 SLT 308; *Fettes Trust v Anderson* 1947 SN 167, OH; *Fraser v Church of Scotland General Trustees* 1986 SC 279, 1986 SLT 692.
5 *Moir's Trustees v M'Ewan* (1880) 7 R 1141; *Buchanan v Marr* (1883) 10 R 936; *Miller v Carmichael* (1888) 15 R 991. Lord Rutherfurd Clark, however, was a consistent dissentient. An attempt was made to challenge this whole line of authority in *Porter v Campbell's Trustees* 1923 SC (HL) 94, 1923 SLT 619, but by then it was far too late.
6 In one case a 'detached' dwelling house was permitted.
7 These decisions take the distinction between structure and use to extreme lengths. Previous cases had decided that a requirement of structure X was not a prohibition on use Y. These cases decide that a requirement of structure X is not a prohibition on structure Y provided that structure Y can plausibly be used for use X.

422. Rule 6: the consent of the dominant proprietor not to be unreasonably withheld. Titles often require that the consent of a superior or other dominant proprietor be obtained before a particular use is made of the property, but there is surprisingly little authority on the question of how this discretion is to be exercised. In *Ewing v Campbells* Lord Shand said of a provision requiring the prior approval of plans by the superior that it

'... must be construed reasonably, not as giving a power which could be exercised capriciously to prevent the proprietor having the fair use of the ground, but which could be used to prevent him from erecting any house of an unsightly nature, or even, it may be, of an architectural design obviously unsuitable to the ground or its neighbourhood'[1].

However, these remarks were obiter and in the course of a dissenting judgment. The issue was raised sharply in a later case where, the superior having refused to give his consent without payment of £1000, an attempt was made to dispense with the consent on the basis that the refusal was unreasonable and not in honest exercise of the superior's rights under the feu disposition. The case, however, failed on the preliminary question of title to sue and no view was expressed on the merits of the action[2].

1 *Ewing v Campbells* (1877) 5 R 230 at 236. See also *Wyllie v Dunnett* (1899) 1 F 982 at 984.
2 *Eagle Lodge Ltd v Keir and Cawder Estates Ltd* 1964 SC 30, 1964 SLT 13.

(7) ENFORCEMENT

423. Remedies. The question of title and interest to sue has already been discussed[1]. Apart from irritancy, which requires separate consideration[2], the principal remedies available to a dominant proprietor are interdict[3], implement[4] and, in appropriate cases, damages, accompanied sometimes by a preliminary declarator. In addition, where the breach founded upon consists of unlawful construction, it is competent to conclude for the removal of the buildings and other erections[5]. However, by analogy with the rule for encroachment[6], there may be discretion in the court to withhold this remedy if the loss to the defender would far exceed any possible benefit to the pursuer. If the pursuer allowed building works to proceed without intimating his objection he may also be vulnerable to a plea of personal bar. Where implement is sought in respect of an obligation *ad factum praestandum* it is for the pursuer to indicate the time limit within which the obligation should now be completed[7], and there will usually be an alternative conclusion for damages[8]. In one case it was provided in the original feu contract that a vassal in breach should pay double feuduty for the duration of his default[9], and this seems unobjectionable, subject to the usual rules about penalty clauses[10]. Unlike the old pecuniary burden[11], obligations imposed by the modern real burden are not secured on the servient tenement, with the result that the real diligences of poinding of the ground and real adjudication are not available[12].

There is concurrent jurisdiction in the sheriff court[13] and the Court of Session.

1 See paras 397 ff above.
2 See para 424 below.
3 Eg *Howard de Walden Estates Ltd v Bowmaker Ltd* 1965 SC 163, 1965 SLT 254.
4 Eg *Marshall v Callander and Trossachs Hydropathic Co Ltd* (1895) 22 R 954, 3 SLT 94 (affd (1896) 23 R (HL) 55).
5 *Alexander v Stobo* (1871) 9 M 599; *Naismith v Cairnduff* (1876) 3 R 863.
6 See para 178 above. It appears that the rule may not be confined to cases of encroachment: see *Stockton Park (Leisure) Ltd v Border Oats Ltd* 1991 SLT 333, OH.
7 *Middleton v Leslie* (1892) 19 R 801. The principle is that the defender must know what it is that he has to do: see *Lothian Regional Council v Rennie* 1991 SCLR 709 at 713, 1991 SLT 465 at 471, per Lord Sutherland. The pursuer's time limit stands in place of the time limit, now expired, the existence of which is a precondition of the enforceability of an obligation *ad factum praestandum*. See para 418 above.
8 Eg *Rankine v Logie Den Land Co Ltd* (1902) 4 F 1074, 10 SLT 278.
9 *Dalrymple v Herdman* (1878) 5 R 847. See also *Corpn of Tailors of Aberdeen v Coutts* (1840) 1 Robin 296 at 315, per Lord Corehouse (penalty of £100 for failure to build houses).
10 For the rules about penalty clauses, see OBLIGATIONS.
11 See para 383 above.
12 See *Wells v New House Purchasers Ltd* 1964 SLT (Sh Ct) 2, where it had been argued that real diligence was the only remedy for a (modern) real burden. Real diligence is now virtually obsolete, and is of little use in practice except in relation to monetary burdens.
13 Sheriff Courts (Scotland) Act 1907 (c 51), s 5(4).

424. Irritancy. 'A clause irritant is that which expresses a condition or event, on the existence of which the charter, contract, or other deed, to which it is annexed, is voided'[1]. There is a legal (implied) irritancy for non-payment of feuduty for five years[2], but in the case of real burdens a right of irritancy exists only where expressly provided for in the original deed creating the burdens. An irritancy clause[3] is not mandatory, whatever was once thought to be the law[4], but the presence of the clause is taken as an indication that the obligations referred to are to be real[5], and it confers on the dominant proprietor a valuable additional[6] remedy.

Irritancy clauses are commonly found only in grants of feu, and there is disagreement as to whether they are also competent in ordinary dispositions[7]. The disposition in *Corpn of Tailors of Aberdeen v Coutts*[8] contained an irritancy clause which was assumed by the court to be perfectly enforceable. But in a later case, where the court was considering the terms under which a disposition was to be granted, Lord President Inglis commented:

'The defender's [disponer's] contention is that the pursuer's [disponee's] obligation shall be fortified by irritant and resolutive clauses, but I have heard no explanation, and do not understand how these are to be carried into effect after the pursuer's entry with the superior. Is it to be said that, after the purchaser's entry, the seller could thrust him out, and substitute himself in his room? I think that consideration is of itself sufficient to show the absurdity of this proposal . . .'[9].

This is not the real difficulty, however, for if A dispones to B subject to an irritancy clause, and B defaults on his obligations, the irritancy annuls the right of B and so necessarily reinvests A. That is what happened in *Duncanson v Giffen*[10] where the irritancy was enforced against a disponee, subject only to a right to purge. In cases of this kind irritancy operates like a reduction or like the equivalent irritancy in a grant in feu. The position is different where successors are involved. Thus if B complies with his obligations to A but then dispones to C, who does not, it is unclear whether the irritancy can affect C as well, for there is no grant which can be irritated. C's grant (his disposition) is from B and not from A. Even if it were possible for A to irritate the disposition from B to C, there is the further difficulty of showing how the property is then to revert to A[11]. Nonetheless it is stated by Lord Corehouse in *Corpn of Tailors of Aberdeen v Coutts*[12] that the property will indeed revert to the original disponer. However, in the absence of authority bearing directly on the question, the law must be considered as in doubt[13]. In practice irritancy clauses are rare in dispositions except in relation to the obligation to repeat the real burdens in future transmissions of the property[14].

Although it is frequently provided in an irritancy clause that default in the performance of real burdens is to make the grant '*ipso facto* null and void', it has been settled since at least the time of Stair[15] that recourse to the courts is required and that the title of a defaulting party is voidable merely and not void[16]. The appropriate action is one for declarator of irritancy, accompanied if necessary by conclusions to remove the servient proprietor. Decree will not be granted if the defender is no longer in default, either because he is now complying with the burden[17], or because the burden itself has come to be extinguished, for example by order of the Lands Tribunal[18] or as a result of prescription. The effect of decree, in an action by a superior, is for the estate of the vassal to be extinguished, so that the *dominium directum* becomes a *dominium utile* once more. In *Cassels v Lamb*[19] it was decided by a bare majority of the whole court that if the vassal has since subfeued, so that his estate is a mid-superiority only, the subfeus and all subsidiary rights such as rights in security are extinguished also[20]. No compensation is due by the superior, either for the return of the feu or for improvements, but subvassals will have a remedy against the mid-superior in warrandice. By contrast, in irritancy by a disponer, if such is competent, it is thought that those holding subsidiary real rights will be protected on the basis that the title of the granter, although voidable[21], had not been avoided at the time when the grant was made. Where the default affects part of the servient tenement only, it may be expressed[22], or it may be possible to imply[23], that irritancy is to affect that part alone. The fact that, usually, default by a servient proprietor is continuous in nature prevents the right to irritate from being lost by prescription, whether positive or negative[24], and even substantial delay on the part of the dominant proprietor does not prevent the eventual raising of an action[25] although it may evidence acquiescence in the default[26].

The underlying purpose of an irritancy clause is to stimulate performance of the burdens rather than to confer a windfall profit on the dominant proprietor[27], and for this reason the court will usually continue the action to give the servient proprietor time to 'purge' the irritancy by remedying his default[28]. But there is no absolute right to purge: in *Precision Relays Ltd v Beaton* it was emphasised that 'unless the irritancy is capable of instant purgation as by the payment of money, the question of whether or not to allow purgation is a matter for the Court's discretion'[29]. In common with the other cases on purgation *Precision Relays* concerned an obligation *ad factum praestandum*, but there seems no reason to suppose that the same principles do not apply where the burden takes the form of a restriction. In the exercise of its discretion the court is more concerned with the probability of future compliance[30] than with the fact that the defender has no reasonable excuse for his past default[31]. A judicial undertaking may be required of the defender, and if he then fails without reasonable excuse to comply with the time limit set by the court the declarator of irritancy will usually be granted[32].

1 Erskine *Institute* II,5,25.
2 Feuduty Act 1597 (c 17) (amended by the Land Tenure Reform (Scotland) Act 1974 (c 38), s 15, whereby the original period of two years was increased to five).
3 An irritancy clause is more strictly termed clauses irritant and resolutive. The distinction is only of significance in entails. Thus if an heir of entail in possession dispones the land in breach of the entail, the clauses (1) extinguish the right of the disponee and (2) carry the land from the defaulting heir to the next heir succeeding under the entail. The former is achieved by the irritant clause and the latter by the resolutive clause.
4 *Corpn of Tailors of Aberdeen v Coutts* (1840) 1 Robin 296.
5 See para 390 above.
6 An irritancy clause does not affect the right to use other remedies: *Macrae v Mackenzie's Trustee* (1891) 19 R 138.
7 The doubt only applies in respect of real burdens. For entails, irritant and resolutive clauses are mandatory under the Entail Act 1685 (c 26). At common law they were ineffective to prevent alienations, the irritancy not being part of the title of the alienee. See Stair *Institutions* (ed G Brodie, 1826) p 264. For entails generally, see W M Gordon *Scottish Land Law* (1989) ch 18.
8 *Corpn of Tailors of Aberdeen v Coutts* (1840) 1 Robin 296.
9 *Corbett v Robertson* (1872) 10 M 329 at 334. See further, much more recently, the remarks of Sheriff substitute A G Walker in *Wells v New House Purchasers Ltd* 1964 SLT (Sh Ct) 2 at 6.
10 *Duncanson v Giffen* (1878) 15 SLR 356, OH. However, the point was not argued.
11 There may possibly be an argument that, on the model of entails (for which see note 3 above), this is achieved by the resolutive clause.
12 *Corpn of Tailors of Aberdeen v Coutts* (1840) 1 Robin 296 at 328: 'An irritancy cannot be declared against a singular successor without giving back the subject to some person. In feu rights the subject reverts to the superior or his heirs. In burgage holdings [which are constituted by disposition] it reverts not to the superior, who is sovereign, but to the granter of the burgage disposition. In strict entails, when an irritancy is declared the contravener is struck out of the destination, and the fee descends to the heirs of his body, if the forfeiture is not directed against them, and if so, to the next heir in the destination after the contravener'.
13 Cf eg *Gordon* para 23–16 (irritancy available) with *Property Law: Abolition of the Feudal System* (Scot Law Com Discussion Paper no. 93 (1991)) pp 71–73 (irritancy not available). See also para 85 above.
14 For this obligation, see para 396 above.
15 Stair *Institutions* IV,18,3; Erskine *Institute* II,5,25; Bell *Principles* s 701; *Corpn of Tailors of Aberdeen v Coutts* (1840) 1 Robin 296 at 323, HL. The early writers refer to 'penal' clauses of irritancy, for which see W W McBryde *The Law of Contract in Scotland* (1987) para 20–146.
16 *Duncanson v Giffen* (1878) 15 SLR 356 at 358, OH, per Lord Curriehill.
17 *Forsyth and Johnston v Kennedy* (1708) Mor 7255.
18 *Fraser v Church of Scotland General Trustees* 1986 SC 279, 1986 SLT 692.
19 *Cassels v Lamb* (1885) 12 R 722, approved three months later in *Sandeman v Scottish Property Investment Co* (1885) 12 R (HL) 67.
20 It was said that the position would be different if the subfeus were confirmed by the (over-)superior. The various points at issue were vigorously disputed by judges on both sides of the debate. The final decision was reached by an intriguing mixture of hard feudal law and the practical need, as it was perceived, to give the superior adequate security for his feuduty. See also para 85 above.
21 If the default had not then occurred the title would be good beyond reproach.
22 *Cassels v Lamb* (1885) 12 R 722 at 771, per Lord M'Laren.
23 *Welsh v Jack* (1882) 10 R 113. But cf *Marquis of Linlithgow v Paterson* (1903) 11 SLT 486, OH, where the defenders were not so fortunate.
24 However, the obligation might itself prescribe: see para 431 below.
25 *Napier v Spiers' Trustees* (1831) 9 S 655.
26 *Ardgowan Estates Ltd v Lawson* 1948 SLT 186, OH.
27 *Cassels v Lamb* (1885) 12 R 722 at 777, per Lord Kinnear.
28 *Duncanson v Giffen* (1878) 15 SLR 356, OH; *Anderson v Valentine* 1957 SLT 57, OH.
29 *Precision Relays Ltd v Beaton* 1980 SC 220 at 224, 1980 SLT 206 at 209, OH, per Lord Ross.
30 In *Precision Relays Ltd v Beaton* 1980 SC 220 at 224, 1980 SLT 206 at 209, OH, Lord Ross refers to the possibility of the servient proprietor being 'a man of straw with no financial resources available'.
31 *Duncanson v Giffen* (1878) 15 SLR 356 at 358, OH, per Lord Curriehill.
32 (1878) 15 SLR 356, OH.

425. Defences. The principal defences to an action brought in enforcement of a real burden are that the pursuer has no title to sue[1], that he has no interest to sue[2], that he has acquiesced in the breach[3], that the burden has not been properly constituted in the first place[4], and that on a proper interpretation of the burden there has been no breach by the defender[5].

1 See paras 397 ff above.
2 Ie whether because he never had interest (paras 407, 408 above) or because that interest has now been lost (para 430 below).
3 See paras 427–429 below.
4 See paras 386 ff above.
5 See paras 415 ff above.

(8) EXTINCTION

426. Express consent. A dominant proprietor may agree to discharge a real burden, either in whole or in part. Usually a sum of money is expected in exchange[1] although the introduction in 1970 of the Lands Tribunal jurisdiction for variation and discharge of burdens has tended to keep the amount requested within reasonable bounds[2]. As an agreement relating to heritable property, the discharge must be in formal writing, although an informal consent which can be evidenced by writ or oath[3] may be set up by *rei interventus* or homologation[4]. There is no prescribed form of discharge, but in normal conveyancing practice it is effected by a short unilateral deed known as a minute of waiver[5]. Registration of the deed in the Register of Sasines or Land Register has, by statute[6], the effect of binding successors both of the dominant and of the servient proprietors: although the Act does not expressly say so, it may be doubted whether successors are bound in the absence of registration[7]. A minute of waiver or other deed of discharge may also be used for the purpose of varying existing burdens[8] but not to impose new burdens[9].

For superiors, but not for other dominant proprietors, a charter of novodamus is provided by the feudal law as an alternative to a minute of waiver[10]. A charter of novodamus is a re-grant of the original feu but under different conditions. In order to bind successors the charter must be registered. Unlike minutes of waiver, charters of novodamus can impose new burdens, but except where this facility is required they are little used today.

Consent is personal to the dominant proprietor granting it, and to his successors in that dominant tenement. The rights of other dominant proprietors, where there are such proprietors, are unaffected except insofar as they too give their consent. Thus a minute of waiver by a superior does not bind co-feuars or co-disponees[11], and equally a minute of waiver by a co-feuar binds neither other co-feuars[12] nor the superior[13]. In practice, the existence of a large number of co-feuars or co-disponees is an effective bar to proceeding by minute of waiver and the servient proprietor will usually have recourse to the Lands Tribunal.

1 Eg *Howard de Walden Estates Ltd v Bowmaker Ltd* 1965 SC 163, 1965 SLT 254.
2 See para 438 below. While compensation may be payable for a discharge ordered by the Lands Tribunal, it is not available to cover sums that might have been payable under a future minute of waiver. See eg *Keith v Texaco Ltd* 1977 SLT (Lands Trib) 16.
3 *Scot v Cairns* (1830) 9 S 246.
4 *Simpson v Mason and M'Rae* (1884) 21 SLR 413 (servitude).
5 For a typical style of minute of waiver, see J M Halliday *Conveyancing Law and Practice in Scotland* vol II (1986) para 17-106.
6 Land Registration (Scotland) Act 1979 (c 33), s 18. The provision is retrospective.
7 But there is a possible counter-argument, by analogy with the position for implied consent discussed in para 427 below.

8 Variation is expressly contemplated by the Land Registration (Scotland) Act 1979, s 18.
9 See para 388 above.
10 See also para 95 above. For a style of charter of novodamus, see *Halliday* vol II, para 17-105.
11 *Dalrymple v Herdman* (1878) 5 R 847. Cf *Campbell v Bremner* (1897) 24 R 1142, criticised in A J McDonald 'The Enforcement of Title Conditions by Neighbouring Proprietors' in D J Cusine (ed) *A Scots Conveyancing Miscellany: Essays in Honour of Professor J M Halliday* (1987) p 21.
12 *Arnold v Davidson Trust Ltd* 1987 SCLR 213, Sh Ct.
13 *Campbell v Clydesdale Banking Co* (1868) 6 M 943.

427. Implied consent: acquiescence. Express consent requires that the dominant proprietor do something, typically execute and deliver a minute of waiver. But in certain circumstances absence of action may also be taken for consent[1]. If a servient proprietor is allowed to default on an obligation without protest or intervention, the dominant proprietor may be regarded as having acquiesced in the default and hence as having given his implied consent. Two conditions must be satisfied before acquiescence in the sense meant here can be established. First, the dominant proprietor must know of the default. There can be no implied consent to the unknown[2]. Knowledge by an agent, such as an estate factor, is the equivalent for this purpose of knowledge by the principal[3]. The second condition is that the servient proprietor must have acted in reliance on the implied consent and to his prejudice, so that if the obligation were now to be enforced against him he would be in a less favourable position than if the obligation had been enforced at the time of first default[4]. In the absence of such prejudice, mere delay in enforcing a right does not amount to acquiescence[5]. The paradigm case of acquiescence is where building works are carried out in breach of a burden but without interference from the dominant proprietor. It is then too late to object. The building has already been erected and the servient proprietor cannot, in equity, be prevented from making use of it[6]. The requirement of reliance and prejudice probably confines acquiescence to those real burdens which take the form of restrictions; because an owner who defaults on a positive obligation (an obligation to erect a house, for example, or an obligation to pay for the cost of roof repairs) is not prejudiced but positively benefited if the dominant proprietor is slow to require compliance[7].

The effect of acquiescence is that the dominant proprietor is deemed to have consented to the contravention[8], and although the issue has never been properly focused[9], it is taken for granted in a number of cases that such consent affects the successors of both parties[10]. Hence acquiescence is pleadable by a successor of the defaulting servient proprietor against a successor of the acquiescing dominant proprietor[11], implied consent following the rule for express consent rather than the usual rule for acquiescence, which is that personal bar is personal to the party whose actings are founded upon[12].

Consent to a contravention does not, or at least may not, effect a complete discharge of the obligation contravened. Whether it does so or not depends on the nature both of the obligation and of the act of contravention. Thus, if the burden is a direct prohibition of activity X, and the dominant proprietor acquiesces in that precise activity, then, necessarily, the burden is extinguished, at least in a question with the acquiescing proprietor[13]. But if the burden takes the form of a more general prohibition, for example a prohibition on building, the fact that there is acquiescence in the erection of a structure of type Y does not imply acquiescence in the future erection of a structure of type Z, and the prohibition remains in force, except in relation to structures of the precise kind acquiesced in. So in *Stewart v Bunten*[14], where implied consent was established in relation to a storm window in the roof, the consent was held not to extend to the act now proposed by the servient proprietor, namely the building of a whole additional storey. The rule was set out by Lord Gifford as follows:

'... it would be very dangerous to lay down a rule that a party holding a restriction against his neighbour building in a certain way or to a certain height cannot relax that restriction in the least degree without abandoning it altogether — cannot even tolerate small storm windows which are almost entirely concealed by the front parapet without by such tolerance enabling his neighbour to build to what height he pleases. This would not be a reasonable doctrine, and it is not supported by any of the cases. The real principle seems to be that acquiescence goes no further than the things acquiesced in, or things *ejusdem generis* . . .'[15].

Implied consent affects only the party who is deemed to give the consent and the rights of other dominant proprietors, if there are such, remain unimpaired, but in practice facts which are sufficient to set up acquiescence in a question with one dominant proprietor are often sufficient to infer acquiescence against others[16].

These are the general principles. Where acquiescence is pled in practice it usually involves one of two situations. The first is where the contravention of the burden has already taken place and the question is whether the burden can still be enforced against the proprietor in breach. The second is where the contravention is in contemplation only and the servient proprietor wishes to establish in advance that he is no longer subject to the burden. Substantially different issues are raised by these two situations and they require separate treatment[17].

1 For the distinction between acquiescence and waiver, see W W McBryde *The Law of Contract in Scotland* (1987) para 23–06.
2 *M'Gibbon v Rankin* (1871) 9 M 423.
3 *Ben Challum Ltd v Buchanan* 1955 SC 348, 1955 SLT 294. But for an earlier and more restrictive formulation, see *Campbell v Clydesdale Banking Co* (1868) 6 M 943 at 948, per Lord Cowan.
4 *Howard de Walden Estates Ltd v Bowmaker Ltd* 1965 SC 163 at 171, 1965 SLT 254 at 259, OH, per Lord Kissen (1965 SC 163, 1965 SLT 254, IH).
5 *McBryde* para 23–20.
6 See para 428 below.
7 *Rankine v Logie Den Land Co Ltd* (1902) 4 F 1074, 10 SLT 278.
8 Eg 'that implied consent which acquiescence involves': *Ben Challum Ltd v Buchanan* 1955 SC 348 at 356, 1955 SLT 294 at 300, per Lord President Clyde.
9 See J M Halliday 'Acquiescence, Singular Successors and the Baby Linnet' 1977 JR 89 at 94: 'What is extraordinary is that, in a field so much fought over, there is an almost total absence of judicial analysis of the reasons which justify the application of a principle of personal bar to a superior or co-feuar on the basis of the actings of another person altogether, his predecessor in title, from whom he has simply derived a property right'.
10 See the cases on common building plans cited at para 429 below.
11 *Ben Challum Ltd v Buchanan* 1955 SC 348, 1955 SLT 294.
12 For the application of that rule in the law of encroachment, see para 176 above.
13 But other dominant proprietors, if there are such, are unaffected: see text to note 16 below.
14 *Stewart v Bunten* (1878) 5 R 1108.
15 (1878) 5 R 1108 at 1115, 1116. See also *Johnston v The Walker Trustees* (1897) 24 R 1061, 5 SLT 86; *Ben Challum Ltd v Buchanan* 1955 SC 348, 1955 SLT 294. The law is incorrectly stated in *Johnston v MacRitchie* (1893) 20 R 539, per Lord Justice-Clerk Macdonald and Lord Trayner.
16 At least this will usually be the case in respect of a completed contravention (para 428 below) unless one of the dominant proprietors did not know of it until after completion. But the position may often be different for prospective contraventions: see *Mactaggart & Co v Roemmele* 1907 SC 1318, 15 SLT 319 discussed in para 429 below.
17 See paras 428, 429, below.

428. Completed contravention.

428. Completed contravention. This is the simple case of acquiescence. Where an act of contravention has been completed[1] without objection, the dominant proprietor or proprietors may be barred from enforcing the terms of the real burden contravened[2]. To some extent, however, this depends upon the nature of the contravention. In *Johnston v The Walker Trustees*[3] a burden requiring use as a dwelling house had been breached for a number of years but without major changes being made to the building. The absence of such changes was said to be fatal to a plea of acquiescence:

'It may be true that structures erected, or structural alterations made in breach of building restrictions, in the knowledge of, and without objection by, those having right to object, cannot after completion be pulled down. But the mere use of a dwelling-house in a manner contrary to the title, however long permitted in the past, cannot, as it seems to me, have any efficacy as to the future'[4].

And again:

'The case would have been different if the defenders [the dominant proprietors] had stood by and allowed Mr Aitken [the servient proprietor] to incur considerable expense in the conversion of his premises into a shop. In that case I think it is clear that they would have been barred from objecting to his occupying it as a shop . . .'[5].

The underlying reason for this distinction, between default by construction and default by use, is the need to show prejudice[6]. A person who has incurred 'considerable expenditure' in reliance on non-enforcement would suffer prejudice if the restriction were now to be enforced. A person who has incurred little or no expenditure would not. To some extent it appears that expenditure is measured by reference to the means of the servient proprietor. In *Ben Challum Ltd v Buchanan*, the leading modern case, where the installation of five petrol pumps by the proprietor of a general store in Tyndrum was said to be a sufficient expenditure to prevent their later removal at the instance of the superior, Lord President Clyde said:

'. . . what really clinches the matter . . . is that the erections in question were no trivial matter, particularly for feuars of this small area of ground in a remote district'[7].

In terms of the general law of personal bar, the expenditure must be incurred in reliance on the implied consent of the person who is barred[8], but it is uncertain how far this doctrine is taken in relation to real burdens. Certainly there is no suggestion in the reported cases that the servient proprietor should have reasonable grounds for supposing that enforcement will not be attempted, and the truth is that he will usually have no means of knowing the position until building work actually begins. Of course, proper inquiries could be made in advance, but to many this may seem like an invitation to retribution. The position may be different where the dominant proprietor indicates his opposition before building work actually starts. It has been held in the sheriff court that initial opposition falling short of legal proceedings does not prevent acquiescence[9], but it is difficult to see how in such a case there is either implied consent or indeed reliance.

In addition to prejudice to the servient proprietor there must also be knowledge on the part of the dominant proprietor[10]. In the words quoted earlier from *Johnston v The Walker Trustees* he must have 'stood by' and allowed the expenditure to take place. The expenditure must not, however, precede the knowledge. Gloag[11] suggests that actual knowledge may not be necessary provided that the dominant proprietor had 'full means of knowledge', by which is presumably meant that the building work was obvious and was of reasonable duration, and it may be that without this extended meaning it would nowadays often be difficult to impute any knowledge to a superior.

1 For a case where it was partially completed only, see *Campbell v Clydesdale Banking Co* (1868) 6 M 943.
2 There is a broadly comparable rule for servitudes: see para 474 below.
3 *Johnston v The Walker Trustees* (1897) 24 R 1061, 5 SLT 86.
4 (1897) 24 R 1061 at 1070, OH, per Lord Kyllachy (affd (1897) 24 R 1061, 5 SLT 86, IH).
5 (1897) 24 R 1061 at 1074, 5 SLT 86 at 87, per Lord Adam. This passage was quoted with approval in *Ben Challum Ltd v Buchanan* 1955 SC 348 at 356, 1955 SLT 294 at 300, 301, per Lord President Clyde.
6 See para 427 above.
7 *Ben Challum Ltd v Buchanan* 1955 SC 348 at 356, 1955 SLT 294 at 301.
8 W W McBryde *The Law of Contract in Scotland* (1987) paras 23–09, 23–20. There is a difference here between acquiescence (inaction) and waiver (action). See also PERSONAL BAR .
9 *Gray v MacLeod* 1979 SLT (Sh Ct) 17. Although the case also involved real burdens, the discussion about acquiescence seems to have been in the context of servitudes.

10 See para 427 above. For a case where there was no knowledge, see *M'Gibbon v Rankin* (1871) 9 M 423.
11 W M Gloag *The Law of Contract* (2nd edn, 1929) p 253, quoted with approval in *Ben Challum Ltd v Buchanan* 1955 SC 348 at 355, 356, 1955 SLT 294 at 300, per Lord President Clyde.

429. Prospective contravention. There can, of course, be no acquiescence in respect of an act of contravention which has yet to take place. Nonetheless acquiescence is not wholly irrelevant even here; for where separate properties are held subject to the same burdens[1] and enforceable by the same person according to a common plan, and where that person then discharges, whether expressly or, much more commonly in practice, as a result of acquiescence[2] the burdens in respect of some of these properties, he is then unable to enforce the same burdens against the remaining properties. It is not that the dominant proprietor has acquiesced in the prospective contravention, for clearly he has not, but by acquiescing in or otherwise consenting to past contraventions by other proprietors he is disabled from preventing future contraventions from whatever source they may come. The rule is expressed by Lord Kyllachy thus:

'. . . wherever in a feuing area some building restriction imposed for the general benefit has been generally contravened, and the contravention is past challenge, the restriction so placed in abeyance can no longer be enforced in individual cases either by the superior or co-feuars'[3].

Why this should be so is not clear. Sometimes the rule is explained as an example of loss of interest to enforce, either because the past contraventions have made the restriction pointless, or because, where burdens support a common plan, a superior may be said to have no interest to enforce beyond the plan itself, with the result that once the plan is breached there is no interest remaining[4]. Neither explanation seems reconcilable with the rule that only the most notional interest is required for a dominant proprietor, and especially for a superior[5]. A more plausible explanation is loss of title to enforce. From the point of view of the dominant proprietor this is often presented as an implied 'abandonment' of the common restriction through acquiescence in past contraventions[6]. From the point of view of the servient tenement it is a question of fairness. For where restrictions are part of a common plan, the servient proprietor accepts the restrictions only 'on the footing that'[7] they are to be enforced against his neighbours also. The dominant proprietor is not free to enforce the restriction in some cases but not in others. That is 'against the faith of the contract'[8] and indeed the analogy is with the principle of mutuality in the law of contract: for if one party to the real burden fails to perform then the other party is released from his obligation. Thus Lord Neaves said:

'The Court will have in view the nature and object of the stipulation. Its nature here is, that it is not an individual and independent restraint upon the holder of this feu, but a complete and comprehensive provision . . . Now, if the superior has so acted that the other houses of the compartment are liberated from the condition, he cannot enforce the stipulation in its integrity, and ought not to be allowed to enforce it inequitably against one house only, while the others are free'[9].

Two conditions must be satisfied before a burden can be extinguished in this way. First, it must be shown that the burden is part of a common plan affecting two or more properties. From the earliest cases a clear distinction is drawn between grants made as part of a common plan, and what may be described as 'stand-alone' grants where the burdens on one property bear no direct relation to the burdens on any other property, even although both properties may share a common author[10]. A stand-alone grant is viewed in isolation, and the fact that a neighbour or neighbours are treated differently is not considered relevant, even where the treatment is at the hands of a common superior[11]. But with grants made as part of a common plan, the discharge of burdens on one part of the estate may have a direct effect on their enforceability on another part. The existence of separate rights to enforce in co-feuars or co-disponees is a useful, although not an infallible, guide to the presence of a common plan[12]. Moreover, a stand-alone grant can sometimes be converted into a grant subject to a common plan, as where the single feu originally granted is subdivided with the result that each separate co-feuar has reciprocal rights of enforcement in respect of the original burdens[13].

The second condition is that the burden in question has ceased to be enforceable against a number of other proprietors in the same estate, either because it has been expressly discharged in whole or in part or because it has been so 'generally contravened'[14] that acquiescence has operated. The burden, or relevant part thereof, must be the same in all cases: the fact that a burden has been generally discharged to the effect of allowing a building of type X will not avail a proprietor who now proposes to erect a building of type Y[15].

The main uncertainty in the law concerns the number of individual discharges required before a complete discharge comes into effect. So if an estate governed by a common plan comprises twenty different properties, is a burden extinguished for the estate as a whole if it has been discharged in respect of five of the properties? Or are ten discharges required, or fifteen? No simple arithmetical formula exists to determine the answer, and it appears that the position will depend at least to some extent on the size of the estate, on the location of the properties in respect of which discharges have been given in relation to the property currently under consideration, and on whether the person seeking to enforce the burden is a superior or a neighbour. In several reported cases, including the early leading case of *Campbell v Clydesdale Banking Co*[16], a large majority of properties had been the subject of discharges, whether express or implied, so that, as was said, 'It is not the street which it was at the date of these feu-contracts'[17]. Clearly this is more than the law actually requires. Conversely some remarks by Lord Dunedin in a later case appear to suggest that even a single discharge is sufficient to extinguish the burden for the whole estate[18], but this is certainly not the law. Between these two positions there is a substantial area of uncertainty which is illustrated by the cases of *Ewing v Campbells*[19] and *Calder v Merchant Co of Edinburgh*[20]. In *Ewing*, where the 'estate' consisted of two feus only, a twenty-year waiver granted in respect of a burden on one of the feus was held to be insufficient to infer a discharge of the same burden on the estate as a whole. Lord Shand dissented. To Lord President Inglis' comment[21] that the present facts were far from the 'continuous and systematic departure from the conditions of the feu' seen in cases such as *Campbell v Clydesdale Banking Co*, Lord Shand replied that this was only a small estate and one in which 'the conditions have been waived with reference to about one-half of the whole'[22]. Perhaps the real reason for the decision was the fact that the original discharge was only for twenty years[23], and certainly in every other respect the case is difficult to reconcile with the later decision by the same Division in *Calder v Merchant Co of Edinburgh*, where the single act of the superior in expressly discharging the burdens affecting one third of the estate was held to extinguish the burdens over the remainder[24].

Discharge of a burden is more easily established in a question with a superior than in a question with a neighbour. In *Mactaggart & Co v Roemmele*[25], where a prohibition on the erection of tenements had been contravened in a number of different parts of the estate but not in the immediate vicinity of the objectors, who were co-feuars, it was held that failure to object to earlier but more distant contraventions did not imply a discharge of a right to enforce the prohibition against a neighbouring property. The policy reasons for this rule are clear:

'... it would be a very inconvenient, not to say inequitable, rule that a feuar who becomes aware of some infraction of building conditions by a feuar from the same superior, but at such a distance from himself that the infraction causes no inconvenience to him, must either apply for an interdict or be taken to have waived his right to enforce the condition in a question with conterminous feuars or disponees'[26].

The point is not that a co-feuar has no interest to enforce more distant contraventions, although in some cases that might be so, but rather that, unlike a superior whose interest is the same throughout the estate, a co-feuar has a much greater level of interest in his own immediate neighbourhood than in the rest of the estate. Consequently, the fact that he is content to see a prohibition discharged at a distance does not infer that he discharges the same prohibition in a question with the house next door[27]. In practice this rule is an important limitation on the implied discharge of restrictions, for in most cases where there is a common plan there are also enforcement rights in co-feuars and co-disponees, and it is of little help to a proprietor that a restriction is discharged in a question with the superior if it can still be enforced by his neighbour. It appears, however, that where there has been a general abandonment of a restriction in different parts of an estate, a co-feuar or co-disponee will lose his title to enforce even if there have been no actual contraventions in his immediate vicinity[28].

1 The same rule applies where separate properties are held subject to at least equivalent burdens.
2 Ie on the rules considered in para 428 above.
3 *Johnston v The Walker Trustees* (1897) 24 R 1061 at 1069, OH, per Lord Kyllachy (affd (1897) 24 R 1061, 5 SLT 86, IH).
4 '[T]his restriction had not in my view any personal object or interest of the superior, but was stipulated for in order to the benefit of his feuars, to the utility of their possession of the subjects, and to the ornament of the street in which their buildings were situated': *Campbell v Clydesdale Banking Co* (1868) 6 M 943 at 947, per Lord Cowan. See more generally J M Halliday 'Acquiescence, Singular Successors and the Baby Linnet' 1977 JR 89 at 96.
5 See paras 407, 408, above. In practice it seems almost impossible to show that interest to enforce has been lost: see para 430 below.
6 Eg *Calder v Merchant Co of Edinburgh* (1886) 13 R 623 at 629, per Lord Adam; *Johnston v The Walker Trustees* (1897) 24 R 1061 at 1073, 5 SLT 86 at 87, per Lord Adam. An alternative method of expressing the same thing is to say that the dominant proprietor and his successors are now personally barred from enforcing the burden: see eg *Howard de Walden Estates Ltd v Bowmaker Ltd* 1965 SC 163 at 182, 1965 SLT 254 at 264, per Lord President Clyde. Somewhat awkwardly, this is personal bar induced by past acquiescence.
7 *Calder v Merchant Co of Edinburgh* (1886) 13 R 623 at 633, per Lord Shand.
8 *Ewing v Campbells* (1877) 5 R 230 at 240, per Lord Shand.
9 *Campbell v Clydesdale Banking Co* (1868) 6 M 943 at 950. See also the comments of Lord Watson about *Campbell* in *Earl of Zetland v Hislop* (1882) 9 R (HL) 40 at 51 where he said: 'Any other decision would, in my opinion, have been unjust and contrary to the good faith of the contract, because, in consequence of the inaction of the superior himself, the object which the contracting parties contemplated in creating the prohibition could no longer be attained by enforcing it against each or all of the feuars by whom it had not been violated'.
10 *Campbell v Clydesdale Banking Co* (1868) 6 M 943 (common plan); *Earl of Zetland v Hislop* (1882) 9 R (HL) 40 (no plan); *Cheyne v Taylor* (1899) 7 SLT 276, OH (no plan); *Marquis of Linlithgow v Paterson* (1903) 11 SLT 486, OH (no plan); *Robertson's Trustees v Bruce* (1905) 7 F 580, 12 SLT 803 (common plan); *Howard de Walden Estates Ltd v Bowmaker Ltd* 1965 SC 163, 1965 SLT 254 (no plan). But in the last case Lord President Clyde does not seem absolutely to exclude the application of the rule under consideration to stand-alone grants, although it is difficult to see how this could be realised in practice.
11 *Marquis of Linlithgow v Paterson* (1903) 11 SLT 486, OH.
12 For such rights to enforce, see paras 399 ff above. It is not an infallible guide because the existence of a common plan is not a sufficient condition for the creation of implied enforcement rights (see eg *Currie's Trustee v Chisholme's Trustees* (1896) 3 SLT 303), nor is it a necessary condition for the creation of express enforcement rights.
13 See eg *Calder v Merchant Co of Edinburgh* (1886) 13 R 623.
14 *Johnston v The Walker Trustees* (1897) 24 R 1061 at 1069, OH, per Lord Kyllachy (affd (1897) 24 R 1061, 5 SLT 86, IH).
15 *Stewart v Bunten* (1878) 5 R 1108; *Johnston v The Walker Trustees* (1897) 24 R 1061, 5 SLT 86; *Macdonald v Douglas* 1963 SC 374, 1963 SLT 191.
16 *Campbell v Clydesdale Banking Co* (1868) 6 M 943.

17 (1868) 6 M 943 at 948, per Lord Cowan. See also *Fraser v Downie* (1877) 4 R 942; *Robertson's Trustees v Bruce* (1905) 7 F 580, 12 SLT 803.

18 *Mactaggart & Co v Roemmele* 1907 SC 1318 at 1323, 15 SLT 319 at 322.

19 *Ewing v Campbells* (1877) 5 R 230.

20 *Calder v Merchant Co of Edinburgh* (1886) 13 R 623.

21 *Ewing v Campbells* (1877) 5 R 230 at 235.

22 (1877) 5 R 230 at 241. Cf *Currie's Trustee v Chisholme's Trustees* (1896) 3 SLT 303, another 50 per cent case but where a different result was reached.

23 Further, the pursuer may have spoiled his argument by insisting that all the burdens (and not just the one discharged) had been extinguished: see *Ewing v Campbells* (1877) 5 R 230 at 235, per Lord President Inglis.

24 Cf the decision in *Calder v Merchant Co of Edinburgh* (1886) 13 R 623 with the decision in *North British Rly Co v Clark* 1913 1 SLT 207, OH, on very similar facts except that the burdens discharged were not the same as the burdens on the rest of the estate.

25 *Mactaggart & Co v Roemmele* 1907 SC 1318, 15 SLT 319. See also *Liddall v Duncan* (1898) 25 R 1119 at 1131, per Lord Moncreiff.

26 *Mactaggart v Roemmele* 1907 SC 1318 at 1325, 15 SLT 319 at 323, per Lord M'Laren.

27 A similar situation may occur if the superiority itself is divided up so that the same estate becomes held of a number of different superiors: see *Currie's Trustee v Chisholme's Trustees* (1896) 3 SLT 303.

28 *Fraser v Downie* (1877) 4 R 942; *Mactaggart & Co v Roemmele* 1907 SC 1318 at 1325, 15 SLT 319 at 323, per Lord M'Laren. The view of Lord President Dunedin in the latter case seems to have been different: see 1907 SC 1318 at 1323, 1324, 15 SLT 319 at 322.

430. Loss of interest to enforce. While the interest of a superior is presumed, the interest of co-feuars and co-disponees must first be established, usually by showing that the dominant tenement is sufficiently close to the servient tenement for the restriction to be of benefit[1]. However, once established or presumed, it is very difficult to show that interest to enforce has been lost and there are no reported cases in which the plea has met with success[2]. Interest to enforce is lost only where, owing to changes in circumstances, a burden has become pointless and hence unworthy of enforcement. In *Howard de Walden Estates Ltd v Bowmaker Ltd*[3], which was a case between superior and vassal, it was held that interest to enforce a burden restricting use to use as a dwelling house would be lost only if the original residential character of the neighbourhood had completely disappeared. It was not sufficient to show that the neighbourhood was no longer wholly residential[4]. Even this, it appears, might not be sufficient if the dominant proprietor owns property in the immediate vicinity of the servient tenement, for a restriction which seems pointless in the context of a neighbourhood as a whole will often continue to confer direct benefit on a person who is an immediate neighbour[5]. In arguing that the character of a neighbourhood has changed it is not necessary to show that the changes were consented to by the person now trying to enforce the burden, who in any case may have had no title to prevent such changes[6]; and indeed where there has been consent, whether express or implied, title to sue will usually be lost on the principles considered above[7] long before there can be any serious question of loss of interest to sue.

1 See paras 407, 408, above.

2 See, however, *Fraser v Church of Scotland General Trustees* 1986 SC 279 at 288, 1986 SLT 692 at 696, per Lord Justice-Clerk Ross (fact that burden now discharged by the Lands Tribunal a 'change of circumstances' sufficient to exclude interest to enforce in respect of a past breach).

3 *Howard de Walden Estates Ltd v Bowmaker Ltd* 1965 SC 163, 1965 SLT 254.

4 See also *Earl of Zetland v Hislop* (1882) 9 R (HL) 40; *Macdonald v Douglas* 1963 SC 374, 1963 SLT 191.

5 Thus it will generally be harder to show loss of interest to enforce in a question with a co-feuar or co-disponee than in a question with a superior. See *Macdonald v Douglas* 1963 SC 374, 1963 SLT 191. But a superior may also own adjacent land and, if so, will also be entitled to the benefit of the rule: *Wingate's Trustees v Oswald* (1903) 10 SLT 517, OH; *Howard de Walden Estates Ltd v Bowmaker Ltd* 1965 SC 163 at 191, 1965 SLT 254 at 269, per Lord Guthrie.

6 This is because the rule depends not on personal bar but on the proposition that the restriction has become pointless. However, the contrary view has sometimes been expressed: see *Wingate's Trustees v Oswald* (1903) 10 SLT 517, OH; *Howard de Walden Estates Ltd v Bowmaker Ltd* 1965 SC 163

at 184, 1965 SLT 254 at 266, per Lord President Clyde (founding on a passage by Lord Watson in *Earl of Zetland v Hislop* (1882) 9 R (HL) 40 at 51 which does not appear to support the Lord President's view).
7 See para 429 above.

431. Negative prescription. While it is clear that real burdens are, at least as a general rule, subject to negative prescription, doubt has sometimes been expressed in relation to burdens constituted by a grant in feu[1]. The doubt seems unfounded. It appears to derive from the special status in relation to prescription of feuduty and feudal casualties:

> 'A vassal cannot prescribe an immunity from the feu-duties, services, and casualties of superiority, due to his overlord, though he should not have made payment of them for forty[2] years; and consequently the superior's right to these cannot be lost by his silence, or neglecting to exact them; for the right of feu-duties, and of feudal casualties, being inherent in, and essential to, the superiority itself, or *dominium directum*, is accounted a right of lands, which does not suffer the negative prescription . . .'[3].

The question therefore is whether, like feuduty, real burdens are 'inherent in, and essential to, the superiority itself' so as to be considered an integral part of that estate in land and hence imprescriptible[4], or whether, like servitudes[5], they are a mere burden on the *dominium utile* and so capable of being extinguished by prescription[6]. The answer seems not to be in doubt. Far from being among the essentials of a feudal grant[7] real burdens are, strictly, not feudal at all[8] and are obviously closer in nature to servitudes than to feuduty and other feudal *reddendo*.

Real burdens prescribe under section 7 of the Prescription and Limitation (Scotland) Act 1973 and not under section 8[9]. The relevant period is twenty years, and where for that period there has been neither a 'relevant claim' by the dominant proprietor nor a 'relevant acknowledgment' by the servient proprietor the burden is extinguished[10]. 'Relevant claim' means a claim for implement or part implement of the obligation made in any court proceedings or arbitration[11]. 'Relevant acknowledgment' means, in the case of a positive obligation, performance of the obligation[12] and, in the case of a restriction, complying with the restriction[13], but with the alternative, in both cases, of an unequivocal written admission by the servient proprietor to the dominant proprietor clearly acknowledging the subsistence of the obligation[14]. The fact that a real burden is referred to in the current title of the servient proprietor is not a relevant acknowledgement in the sense of the Act and does not interrupt prescription[15]. Nor is prescription interrupted by a change in ownership of either the dominant or the servient tenement. Except in a case where liability is joint and several, for which special provision is made in the Act[16], it is thought that a burden which affects more than one tenement, whether dominant or servient, is to be treated as a separate burden in respect of each such tenement. Therefore, if by subdivision a restriction originally affecting one area of land comes to affect two, non-compliance for twenty years leading to extinction by prescription on the first area will not, it is thought, extinguish the burden in relation to the second[17].

1 See eg W M Gordon *Scottish Land Law* (1989) para 22–82.
2 The period is now twenty years: Prescription and Limitation (Scotland) Act 1973 (c 52), s 7(1).
3 Erskine *Institute* III,7,12. See also Stair *Institutions* II,12,16.
4 Prescription and Limitation (Scotland) Act 1973, Sch 3, para (a). The suggestion in *Gordon* para 22–82 that real burdens in feudal grants might be imprescriptible as *res merae facultatis* fails to explain why the same should not also be true of real burdens in dispositions.
5 Including servitudes in a grant in feu reserved in favour of the superior: M Napier *Commentaries on the Law of Prescription in Scotland* (1854) p 583. See also *Brown v Carron Co* 1909 SC 452, 1909 1 SLT 8.
6 *Napier* p 591: '[T]he one is regarded as a mere burden upon the right of property, while the other is considered to be property reserved *pro tanto* . . . The purpose of negative prescription is to relieve from the burden of a debt or obligation, not to transfer the rights of property from the *verus dominus* to the *non dominus*'.

7 For these, see Craig *Jus Feudale* 1,9,28 and *Erskine* II,3,11.
8 See para 382 above.
9 This is because there are no real burdens which confer rights without at the same time imposing correlative obligations. See also para 9, note 1, above.
10 The Prescription and Limitation (Scotland) Act 1973 provides for the extinction both of the obligation on the servient proprietor (s 7(1)) and of the correlative right held by the dominant proprietor (s 15(2)).
11 Prescription and Limitation (Scotland) Act 1973, s 9(1), (4) (amended by the Prescription and Limitation (Scotland) Act 1984, s 6(1), Sch 1, para 3(a); the Companies Consolidation (Consequential Provisions) Act 1985 (c 9), s 30, Sch 2; the Bankruptcy (Scotland) Act 1985 (c 66), s 75(1), Sch 7, para 11; the Prescription (Scotland) Act 1987 (c 36), s 1(1), (2)).
12 Prescription and Limitation (Scotland) Act 1973, s 10(1)(a) (amended by the Prescription and Limitation (Scotland) Act 1984, Sch 1, para 4).
13 Prescription and Limitation (Scotland) Act 1973, s 10(4).
14 Ibid, s 10(1)(b) (as amended: see note 12 above).
15 *Graham v Douglas* (1735) Mor 10745 (servitude). See also *Napier* pp 582, 583, 590, correcting Bell *Principles* s 609.
16 Prescription and Limitation (Scotland) Act 1973, s 10(2) (as amended: see note 12 above).
17 The same would be true if there was more than one dominant proprietor. So the fact that a burden had prescribed in a question with a superior would not necessarily mean that it had prescribed in a question with a co-feuar.

432. Consolidation and irritancy. Where there is consolidation or irritancy of a feu[1], the *dominium utile* is reabsorbed[2] into the immediate superiority and ceases to exist as a separate interest in land[3]. The effect on real burdens attaching to the former *dominium utile* is not entirely clear. An initial distinction may be made between burdens created in the original grant of the feu which has now come to be extinguished, and burdens created subsequent to that grant, by ordinary disposition. Burdens in the original grant are automatically extinguished by consolidation or irritancy, at least in a question between superior and vassal, and the position is the same whether the burden was laid on the vassal or, as sometimes happens, on the superior[4]. But neither consolidation[5] nor, probably, irritancy[6], affects the rights of co-feuars or other dominant proprietors in the burden, if there are such, with the result that the burden may not be fully extinguished[7].

Burdens created by subsequent disposition raise different considerations. Thus suppose that A dispones Whitemains to B imposing real burdens for the benefit of Blackmains, being adjoining land retained by A. If the immediate superior of the servient tenement (Whitemains) later irritates the feu the real burdens in favour of Blackmains are probably extinguished, on the basis that a superior is not to be prejudiced by posterior rights granted by his vassal[8]. The position may possibly be different if there is consolidation and not irritancy. In the converse situation of consolidation affecting the dominant tenement (Blackmains), it has been suggested that the right to enforce the burdens survives and can be exercised by the owner of the consolidated feu[9]. The equivalent rule for irritancy is uncertain.

1 See further paras 85, 98, 424, above.
2 This is the expression favoured by the Land Registration (Scotland) Act 1979 (c 33), s 2(4).
3 Cf *Park's Curator Bonis v Black* (1870) 8 M 671 at 675, per Lord President Inglis, with *Earl of Zetland v Glover Incorpn of Perth* (1870) 8 M (HL) 144 at 151, 154, per Lord Hatherley LC and Lord Westbury.
4 For obligations on the superior, see para 394 above.
5 *Stevenson v Steel Co of Scotland Ltd* (1899) 1 F (HL) 91 at 93, per Lord Watson; *Murray's Trustees v St Margaret's Convent Trustees* (1906) 8 F 1109 at 1117, 14 SLT 307, at 312, per Lord Kinnear (affd 1907 SC (HL) 8, 15 SLT 2). But cf *Calder v Merchant Co of Edinburgh* (1886) 13 R 623, criticised by A J McDonald in '*The Enforcement of Title Conditions by Neighbouring Proprietors*' in D J Cusine (ed) *A Scots Conveyancing Miscellany: Essays in Honour of Professor J M Halliday* (1987) p 21.
6 *Dalrymple v Herdman* (1878) 5 R 847 at 857, per Lord Shand.
7 *Brookfield Developments Ltd v Keeper of the Registers of Scotland* 1989 SCLR 435, 1989 SLT (Lands Trib) 105.
8 See para 424 above.
9 W M Gloag *The Law of Contract* (2nd edn, 1929) p 727.

433. Dominant and servient tenement coming into single ownership. Where the superiority and the *dominium utile* of land come to be owned by the same person, without consolidation taking place, or, more generally, where the dominant and servient tenements in a real burden come into single ownership, the burden ceases to be enforceable on the principle of confusion[1], although third party rights are presumably unaffected. Whether confusion extinguishes the burden, or whether the burden is merely suspended and revives in the event of the tenements resuming separate ownership[2], is unclear, reflecting the lack of certainty in this area of law as a whole[3].

1 *Ross v Beck* 1991 GWD 26–1517, Sh Ct.
2 This was suggested in *Botanic Gardens Picture House Ltd v Adamson* 1924 SC 549 at 564, 1924 SLT 418 at 425, per Lord President Clyde. See also *Motherwell v Manwell* (1903) 5 F 619, (1903) 10 SLT 768.
3 W W McBryde *The Law of Contract in Scotland* (1987) para 23–30. The same uncertainties occur with servitudes: see paras 453, 476, below, and W M Gordon *Scottish Land Law* (1989) pp 790, 791.

434. Physical changes affecting either tenement. Physical changes may make compliance with a burden impractical, or even impossible. Sometimes such changes will result in the burden being extinguished on one of the grounds already considered, for example by negative prescription or by loss of interest to enforce[1]. However, whether extinction would occur otherwise, by physical change alone, is less certain. In *Perth Magistrates v Earl of Kinnoull*[2] the court declined to enforce an obligation of 1459 to maintain certain roads 'for passage for man and hors' due to changes in circumstances, in particular to a very large increase in traffic and the fact that the roads themselves were now considerably longer. But the burden was said not to be extinguished and the court suggested that it be commuted into an equivalent monetary payment[3].

1 See paras 430, 431, above.
2 *Perth Magistrates v Earl of Kinnoull* (1872) 10 M 874.
3 For the equivalent rule for servitudes, see para 475 below.

435. Mutuality principle. If in a grant in feu imposing real burdens on the vassal there are also counter-obligations on the superior, neither party can enforce the terms of the grant against the other for as long as he is in breach of his own obligations[1]. This is the mutuality principle, familiar from the law of contract but not confined to that law. Similarly where, as often happens with co-feuars and co-disponees, neighbouring proprietors are subject to reciprocal real burdens, coupled with reciprocal rights of enforcement, a proprietor who is himself in default cannot enforce the burdens against his neighbour[2]. The effect of the mutuality principle is not to extinguish burdens but to render them unenforceable for the period of the dominant proprietor's default. Nevertheless, where there is no possibility of the default ever being remedied the burdens may be treated as extinguished[3].

1 *Stevenson v Steel Co of Scotland Ltd* (1899) 1 F (HL) 91.
2 *Mactaggart & Co v Roemmele* 1907 SC 1318 at 1324, 15 SLT 319 at 322, per Lord President Dunedin.
3 *Stevenson v Steel Co of Scotland Ltd* (1899) 1 F (HL) 91.

436. Compulsory purchase. It is often said that in land acquired by compulsory purchase there is automatic severance of the feudal relationship with the superior and hence automatic extinction of all real burdens consequent on that relationship, except perhaps in a question with co-feuars[1]. But this view of the law is not established beyond dispute, for the statutory provision on which it is founded[2] seems not to address the question of feudal severance, and judicial opinion is not unanimously favourable[3]. In the absence, therefore, of a reported decision turning directly on the question[4], the law may be regarded as in doubt.

In the case of non-feudal real conditions, such as real burdens in dispositions and ordinary servitudes, it has been judicially stated that

'... when land is so taken by a railway company [by compulsory purchase] it is taken absolutely, with a resulting extinction of all servitudes ...'[5].

No authority was cited for this view, and there appears to be none. In fact it is difficult to see why compulsory purchase should have this effect, and the existence of statutory provisions for extinction in particular cases[6] suggests that by the general law such burdens are preserved[7].

1 *Elgin Magistrates v Highland Rly Co* (1884) 11 R 950; *Inverness Magistrates v Highland Rly Co* (1893) 20 R 551; *Inverness Magistrates v Highland Rly Co* 1909 SC 943, 1909 1 SLT 407; *Fraser v Caledonian Rly Co* 1911 SC 145, 1910 2 SLT 367; *Duke of Argyll v London, Midland and Scottish Rly Co* 1931 SC 309, 1931 SLT 362. See also COMPULSORY ACQUISITION, vol 5, para 85.

2 Ie the Lands Clauses Consolidation (Scotland) Act 1845 (c 19), s 80. The 1845 Act applies to acquisitions proceeding by schedule conveyance, but s 80 was extended to acquisitions by general vesting declaration by the Town and Country Planning (Scotland) Act 1972 (c 52), s 278, Sch 24, para 37.

3 Unfavourable opinions are found in: *Inverness Magistrates v Highland Rly Co* (1893) 20 R 551 at 560–562, per Lord M'Laren; *Heriot's Trust v Caledonian Rly Co* 1914 SC 601 at 614 ff, 1914 1 SLT 391 at 396 ff, per Lord Skerrington (Lord President Strathclyde concurring), and (affd) 1915 SC (HL) 52 at 64 ff, 1915 1 SLT 347 at 354 ff, per Lord Dunedin; *Campbell's Trustees v London and North-Eastern Rly Co* 1930 SC 182 at 194, 1930 SLT 128 at 134, per Lord President Clyde.

4 *Heriot's Trust v Caledonian Rly Co* 1914 SC 601 at 609, 1914 1 SLT 391 at 393, per Lord Skerrington (affd 1915 SC (HL) 52, 1915 1 SLT 347).

5 *Oban Town Council v Callander and Oban Rly Co* (1892) 19 R 912 at 914, per Lord President Robertson.

6 Eg Town and Country Planning (Scotland) Act 1972, s 117 (amended by the Telecommunications Act 1984 (c 12), s 109(1), Sch 4, para 54(4)). See *Largs Hydropathic Ltd v Largs Town Council* 1967 SC 1, 1967 SLT 23.

7 But a different view is taken in para 479 below. See also COMPULSORY ACQUISITION, vol 5, paras 86, 87.

437. Failure to appear on the Land Register. The proprietor of an interest in land registered in the Land Register holds 'subject only to the effect of any matter entered in the title sheet of that interest'[1]. Real burdens are entered in the burdens section of the title sheet[2]. It follows that if for any reason an existing burden fails to appear on the title sheet of an interest in land, the burden is automatically extinguished, subject, however, to the possibility that it may later be entered on the Register as a result of rectification[3]. In practice there are two main reasons why a burden might fail to appear on the Register. One is where, on first registration of an interest in land, an existing real burden, which was duly recorded in the Register of Sasines, is omitted from the title sheet, whether by accident or because the Keeper takes the view that it has ceased to be enforceable[4]. The other is where the proprietor of a registered interest in land satisfies the Keeper, or on appeal the Lands Tribunal[5], that a burden listed in the title sheet is no longer enforceable, with the result that it is removed by rectification[6].

1 Land Registration (Scotland) Act 1979 (c 33), s 3(1)(a).

2 Land Registration (Scotland) Rules 1980, SI 1980/1413, r 7.

3 Land Registration (Scotland) Act 1979, s 9 (amended by the Matrimonial Homes (Family Protection) (Scotland) Act 1981 (c 59), s 6(4)(b), and the Law Reform (Miscellaneous Provisions) (Scotland) Act 1985 (c 73), s 59(1), Sch 2, para 21).

4 This is because the Keeper is directed to enter only 'subsisting real burdens': see the Land Registration (Scotland) Act 1979, s 6(1)(e).

5 Ibid, s 25.

6 *Brookfield Developments Ltd v Keeper of the Registers of Scotland* 1989 SCLR 435, 1989 SLT (Lands Trib) 105. Of course if the burden really is unenforceable, then it is extinguished whether rectification takes place or not. The mere fact that a burden appears on the Land Register is no guarantee as to its validity: see para 389 above.

438. Variation and discharge by the Lands Tribunal. Since 1970 the Lands Tribunal for Scotland has been empowered, on application by a servient proprietor, to grant an order varying or discharging real burdens and other real conditions[1]. The order takes effect on registration of an extract in the Register of Sasines or Land Register and is binding on all persons having interest[2]. The Tribunal may exercise its power only where it is satisfied in all the circumstances:

(1) that by reason of changes in the character of the servient tenement or the neighbourhood thereof or other circumstances which the Tribunal may deem material, the obligation is or has become unreasonable or inappropriate; or

(2) that the obligation is unduly burdensome compared with any benefit resulting or which would result from its performance; or

(3) that the existence of the obligation impedes some reasonable use of the servient tenement[3].

In exchange for an order granting variation or discharge, the servient proprietor may be directed to pay to one or more dominant proprietors either a sum to compensate for any substantial loss or disadvantage resulting from the order or a sum to make up for any effect which the real burden produced, at the time when it was first imposed, in reducing the consideration paid for the servient tenement[4]. There is also power to impose such substitute real burdens as appear to the Lands Tribunal to be reasonable as a result of the variation or discharge of the original burden and as may be accepted by the servient proprietor[5].

A large number of applications for variation or discharge have been made since the jurisdiction was first introduced in 1970, and the voluminous case law is surveyed elsewhere[6].

1 Conveyancing and Feudal Reform (Scotland) Act 1970 (c 35), ss 1, 2 (amended by the Land Tenure Reform (Scotland) Act 1974 (c 38), s 19). The power relates to 'land obligations' which are defined to mean, in effect, real conditions: Conveyancing and Feudal Reform (Scotland) Act 1970, s 1(2).
2 Conveyancing and Feudal Reform (Scotland) Act 1970, s 2(4) (as so amended).
3 Ibid, s 1(3). But the third ground is not available if the Lands Tribunal considers that, due to exceptional circumstances relating to amenity or otherwise, money would not be an adequate compensation for any loss which a dominant proprietor would suffer from the variation or discharge: see s 1(4).
4 Ibid, s 1(4).
5 Ibid, s 1(5). See further para 395 above.
6 See CONVEYANCING, vol 6, paras 511 ff. See also J M Halliday *Conveyancing Law and Practice in Scotland* vol II (1986) pp 284–300; W M Gordon *Scottish Land Law* (1989) ch 25.

9. SERVITUDES

(1) NATURE AND ORIGIN OF SERVITUDES

439. Praedial and personal servitudes distinguished. In practice the term 'servitude' is applied only to certain uses and restraints affecting heritable property: these are more specifically described as praedial servitudes. Formerly servitudes were regarded as being in two categories, praedial and personal. Under that classification, the only personal servitude is liferent, and the modern view is to treat the rights of liferent and fee as forming two separate and co-existent estates limited in their nature and creating mutual restraints on each other. The liferenter is no longer regarded as a mere burdener but as an interim proprietor of the subjects liferented[1]. Liferent and fee will not be considered further in this title[2].

1 W J Dobie *Manual of the Law of Liferent and Fee in Scotland* (1949) p 1. See also Erskine *Principles* II,9,4, Bell *Principles* s 1037, and J Rankine *The Law of Land-ownership in Scotland* (4th edn, 1909) pp 719, 720.
2 See LIFERENT AND FEE, vol 13, paras 1061 ff.

440. Meaning of 'praedial servitude'. As in so many other subjects, the basic rules applying to praedial servitudes in Scots law are derived from the Roman law; this is reflected in the terms by which most of the long-established servitudes are known. It has been said that 'the English law of easements and the nearly corresponding institution of servitudes in Scots law were formulated with constant assistance from the Roman law'[1]. From that basis the law has developed in the main through the decisions of the courts. The subject has, however, received extensive consideration in the works of the Institutional writers. The treatment in Bell's *Principles*[2] is generally regarded as most accurately indicating the scope and nature of the praedial servitude in Scots law[3]. Bell describes the praedial servitude as:

'a burden on land or houses . . . whereby the owner of the burdened or "servient" tenement . . . must submit to certain uses to be exercised by the owner of the other or "dominant" tenement; or must suffer restraint in his own use and occupation of the property'[4].

Bell goes on to explain that as servitudes properly constituted are effective against singular successors in the servient tenement and available to singular successors in the dominant tenement even if not followed by infeftment, they have had to be limited to such uses or restraints as are well established and defined, leaving others as mere personal agreements[4]. That statement of the law forms a suitable basis for the examination in more detail of the various features common to praedial servitudes.

1 See J Mackintosh *Roman Law in Modern Practice* (1934) p 141. The term 'easement' as used in English law is somewhat narrower than 'servitude' as used in both Scottish and English systems. 'Easement' does not include servitudes which involve taking substances from the servient tenement. In England these are classified as profits *à prendre*, but that category includes rights not attaching to any particular property as a dominant tenement: see 14 *Halsbury's Laws of England* (4th edn) para 3.
2 Bell *Principles* ss 979 ff.
3 Some writers have tended to give the concept a wider scope than Bell. In this respect Bell's view appears preferable to that of Stair *Institutions* II,6 and 7, and Erskine *Principles* II,9,1.
4 Bell s 979.

(2) ESSENTIAL CHARACTERISTICS OF THE PRAEDIAL SERVITUDE

441. Positive or negative in form. A servitude is either positive or negative. A positive servitude entitles the proprietor of the dominant tenement to exercise some right or privilege affecting the servient tenement not otherwise available to him, such as a right of way or passage or a right to draw water. On the other hand, a negative servitude precludes the servient owner from exercising some right inherent in his ownership of his property as, for example, where he is restricted as to the buildings he can erect. The maxim *servitus in faciendo consistere nequit* epitomises the important general rule that not even a positive servitude can involve a positive obligation on the part of the servient owner. The rule is exemplified by the decision in an early case that an obligation on the proprietor of a lower flat in a tenement to share the responsibility for the maintenance of the roof, which by law rests solely on the proprietor of the top flat, could not be constituted as a servitude[1]. Such an obligation, if it is not to be merely personal to a particular owner but to affect his singular successors, will require to be constituted in the appropriate manner as a real burden or condition affecting his property[2].

1 *Nicolson v Melvill* (1708) Mor 14516. As to the suggestion that the servitude *oneris ferendi* forms an exception to this rule, see para 484 below.
2 See *Allan v MacLachlan* (1900) 7 SLT 427, and *M'Laren v British Railways Board* 1971 SC 182. See CONVEYANCING, vol 6, paras 496 ff.

442. Natural rights of property distinguishable. Servitudes have to be distinguished from natural rights inherent in the ownership of land and operating by force of law. Examples of such natural rights are (1) the right of a landowner, within certain limits, to draw water from a stream bounding or passing through his land; and (2) the right of a landowner to have surface water, not in a defined channel, drain on to lower ground belonging to another person.

Sometimes such natural rights are described or referred to as servitudes, with which they have certain features in common[1]. But servitudes, in their strict and proper sense, confer rights not implied by law and accordingly have to be constituted with the consent or agreement of the servient owner or by some means which the law recognises as an acceptable equivalent to such consent or agreement[2].

1 See W M Gordon *Scottish Land Law* (1989) para 24-02, and *Logan v Wang* (UK) Ltd 1991 SLT 580, OH. See also para 355 above.
2 On the question whether the creation of a positive servitude by prescription should be regarded as based on the implied agreement or consent of the servient owner, see para 459 below.

443. Operative as between heritable properties in separate ownership. Servitudes are rights which affect one heritable property, the servient tenement, for the benefit of another heritable property, the dominant tenement; accordingly there must, for the existence of the servitude right, be two tenements separately owned[1]. This requirement may, however, be met by ownership by the same party but in different capacities, for example as trustee in one case and beneficiary in the other[2]. In general, however, the maxim *nemo res sua servit* applies. Thus a party cannot create a servitude over his own land to become effective when he disposes of part of it[3].

While it is clear that the servient tenement must be represented by property in land, certain questions have arisen as to what may constitute a dominant tenement. It appears that salmon fishings may in themselves constitute a dominant tenement in respect of such access rights as are required over adjoining land for the exercise of the fishing rights[4].

There is authority to the effect that a superiority does not qualify, but this ruling, applying as it did to a case of a superior creating a servitude over the land he was feuing, was based on the ground that the superior had himself an interest in this land rather than on the incorporeal nature of the superiority right[5].

There are cases in which rights of dominant proprietor have been held effectively vested in bodies such as the magistrates of a town or burgh collectively for the benefit of the inhabitants[6]. Again, in certain cases the inhabitants of a particular town or village or a group of co-feuars have been regarded as together holding the interest of dominant proprietors and as such entitled, as a group or through a representative, to assert a servitude right[7]. A distinction, however, is required to be drawn between, on the one hand, cases in which a category of persons such as householders within a town are claiming rights of the nature of servitudes over private property and, on the other hand, cases where the inhabitants of a town or burgh are claiming rights over ground held by the town or burgh for public use[8]. Certain privileges such as golfing facilities[9] not within the category of recognised servitudes and not governed by the rules applicable to servitudes have been successfully claimed on the latter basis[10].

1 *Baird v Fortune* (1861) 4 Macq 127, HL. As explained in para 449 below, separate tenancies are not sufficient for this purpose. A servitude is a type of real condition in the sense used in this title: see paras 344 ff above.
2 See *Grierson v Sandsting and Aithsting School Board* (1882) 9 R 437, where the different capacities in which the board held the respective properties were recognised in this way.
3 See *Hamilton v Elder* 1968 SLT (Sh Ct) 53, distinguishing the circumstances apparently envisaged in certain remarks of Lord Watson in *North British Rly Co v Park Yard Co Ltd* (1898) 25 R (HL) 47 at 52.

A different position applies in the case of real burdens or conditions which a proprietor may create by a conveyance in his own favour.

4　*Berry v Wilson* (1841) 4 D 139; *Lord Advocate v Sharp* (1878) 6 R 108; *Middletweed Ltd v Murray* 1989 SLT 11, OH.

5　*Hemming v Duke of Athole* (1883) 11 R 93 at 98, per Lord Craighill.

6　See *Murray v Peebles Magistrates* 8 Dec 1808 FC, and *Macdonald v Inverness Magistrates* 1918 SC 141 at 150, 1918 1 SLT 51 at 55, per Lord Johnston.

7　*Smith v Denny and Dunipace Police Comrs* (1888) 7 R (HL) 28; *Maitland v Lees* (1899) 6 SLT 296, OH. See also *Sharp v Duke of Hamilton* (1829) 7 S 679, where the question was raised but not decided whether the inhabitants of a burgh of barony were entitled to pursue a declarator of servitude. They in fact succeeded in the capacity of feuars.

8　See *Dyce v Hay* (1849) 11 D 1266 at 1272, per Lord Justice-Clerk Hope, and the same case reported on appeal, *Dyce v Hay* (1852) 1 Macq 305, HL, where particular reference is made to subjects such as village greens and playgrounds.

9　See *Kelly v Burntisland Magistrates* (1812) noted in *Home v Young* (1846) 9 D 286 at 293n.

10　See *Sanderson v Lees and Brown* (1859) 21 D 1011; sequel (1859) 22 D 24, where the burgh magistrates were held not entitled to resist an interdict against the use of part of the common ground for a farming development by pleading that it would leave sufficient ground for the exercise by the inhabitants of their privileges, which plea might have succeeded in the case of a servitude right (see para 469 below). Cf *Earlsferry Magistrates v Malcolm* (1829) 7 S 755.

444. Benefit to heritable property forming the dominant tenement. The rights represented by a servitude must constitute a benefit to the dominant tenement as a heritable subject or estate. Certain personal privileges or facilities commonly enjoyed in connection with landownership are not regarded as meeting this requirement. It has been decided that there cannot be attached to a person's land as praedial servitudes rights such as angling in a stream on another's ground[1] or shooting or hunting over another's ground[2]. Similarly, facilities for skating or curling on another's property cannot be constituted servitudes[3]. When a servitude takes the form of a right to obtain substances such as seaware or peat from the servient property, the right must be exercised to meet only the requirements of the owners or occupiers of the dominant property, and not for purposes such as sale or disposal[4]. As applied to negative servitudes, the principle means that a restriction, for instance on the erection of buildings on one property, which, by reason of their respective situations, is of no benefit to another property, cannot be constituted a servitude in favour of that other property[5].

1　*Patrick v Napier* (1867) 5 M 683, followed in *Harper v Flaws* 1940 SLT 150 at 151, OH, concerning the right of rod fishing in an inland loch. In *Murray v Peddie* (1880) 7 R 804, it was, however, held that a right of angling granted in a Crown charter, if not a right of servitude, was still a right capable of feudalisation.

2　*Hemming v Duke of Athole* (1883) 11 R 93. In *Marquis of Huntly v Nicol* (1896) 23 R 610, 3 SLT 297, the court, although bound in terms of a decision of the House of Lords which was *res judicata* to recognise as a permanent heritable right a privilege of fowling and shooting over the land of the pursuer's neighbour, was of opinion that the facilities should be regarded as a personal privilege and not as a servitude: see Lord M'Laren at 616 and at 298.

3　*Harvey v Lindsay* (1853) 15 D 768.

4　*M'Taggart v M'Douall* (1867) 5 M 534 at 547, per Lord Benholme.

5　*Alexander v Stobo* (1871) 9 M 599 at 612, per Lord Deas. See also paras 391, 407, above (real burdens).

445. Burden on heritable property forming the servient tenement. As Bell has stated, a servitude represents a burden on land or houses[1]: it is therefore distinguishable from any form of proprietary interest or right of exclusive possession — even temporary — such as that of a tenant. There is no servitude known in law as a servitude of the exclusive use of a common subject[2]. While the existence of a servitude, if of a sufficiently burdensome nature, will constitute a breach of the warrandice given by a seller of heritable property to his purchaser, it does not represent eviction from the property entitling the purchaser to have the transaction cancelled but justifies only indemnification for the loss sustained[3]. As a general rule, servitudes are not regarded as within the category of lands and heritages which are rateable subjects for the purposes of regional or district rates, although a question of rating may arise where the dominant proprietors have required to install substantial works to exercise their rights[4]. The acquisition for payment of a servitude restricting building on an adjoining property was not regarded as a change of circumstances increasing the letting value of the dominant tenement for rating purposes although it was indicated that the resultant increase in capital value could be relevant on a revaluation[5]. Servitudes constituted by deeds entering the property register are interests in land which could be the subject of a standard security[6]. In practice, however, as a servitude requires to be attached to a dominant tenement, it will not by itself be made the subject of such a security; but as a right, perhaps of considerable value, it can be embodied in a security over the dominant tenement[7].

When a party is seeking to assert rights outwith the apparent bounds of his own property, there may sometimes be difficulty in determining from the relevant documents or the particular circumstances whether a servitude or some form of proprietary interest has been constituted. In one case, the interest of a property owner in an area described in the title deeds as 'mean property for the preservation of light' was held to be a servitude right and not a right of common property[8]. On the other hand, a conveyance with certain land of the sheilings and grass of particular subjects was construed as carrying the full right of property in the ground thus described[9]. A similar interpretation was put on a right to the waterside grass as given to feuars in a street adjoining a river[10].

The limitations of the rights applying where only a servitude is established are demonstrated in cases where the dominant proprietor is entitled to obtain water or substances such as peat from the servient tenement. Since the servitude confers no proprietary interest, the water or substance in question remains at the disposal of the servient proprietor so far as not required for the proper purposes of the dominant tenement[11].

The distinction between servitude rights and rights of a proprietary nature, is, however, important not only where the alternative to a servitude right is sole ownership but also where that alternative is some form of common right, which in practice may be particularly difficult to distinguish from a servitude right[12]. A common interest and not a servitude right was held to have been created where urban feuars were required by their title deeds to leave a lane or passage of a certain width behind their feus for the use of themselves and neighbouring feuars, each feuar being bound to make up the part of the passage within his own feu[13]. The facts that the passage ran partly within the feuar's property and that the scheme involved a positive obligation on those whose property was affected were regarded as inconsistent with the existence of a servitude right. A proprietary right held in common involves a veto on any action affecting its subjects being taken without the consent of each interested party. By contrast, the holder of a servitude right can prevent only such actions by the proprietor of the servient tenement as can be shown to be prejudicial to the exercise of the servitude right. In this respect the position of the dominant proprietor in a servitude resembles that of a party having a common interest as contrasted with a right of common property in a heritable subject. The holders of a common interest, however, have the right to insist that the subject of it be adequately maintained by the proprietor of that subject, who thus comes under a positive obligation which could not affect a servient owner. Again, it would appear that there are situations in which the existence of a common interest in another person's property gives the holder certain restrictive rights which he might not have if his interest were restricted to a servitude. In the case last mentioned[13], the existence of a common interest meant that the feuars on either side of the passage were prevented from bridging over the passage, an operation which, as not prejudicing the exercise of his right of passage, would probably not have been open to objection by the holder of a servitude right[14].

1 Bell *Principles* s 979.
2 *Leck v Chalmers* (1859) 21 D 408. Cf *Robertson's Trustees v Bruce* (1905) 7 F 580, 12 SLT 803.
3 *Welsh v Russell* (1894) 21 R 769, 1 SLT 594. See further paras 705, 712, below.
4 See S B Armour *Valuation for Rating* (5th edn, 1985 by J J Clyde and J A D Hope) para 14.05.
5 *Sharp v Haddington Assessor* 1923 SC 703, 1923 SLT 287.
6 Conveyancing and Feudal Reform (Scotland) Act 1970 (c 35), s 9(8)(b): see RIGHTS IN SECURITY, vol 20, para 150.
7 See J M Halliday *The Conveyancing and Feudal Reform (Scotland) Act 1970* (2nd edn, 1977) para 6.06.
8 *Baird v Ross* (1836) 14 S 528.
9 *Beaumont v Lord Glenlyon* (1843) 5 D 1337. Cf *Hilson v Scott* (1895) 23 R 241, 3 SLT 189, concerning a mill lade.
10 *Wright v Logan* (1829) 8 S 247, affd *sub nom Logan v Wright* (1831) 5 W & S 242, HL. See also *Johnston, Beveridge and Gibb v Duke of Hamilton* (1768) Mor 2481, and *William Baird & Co v Kilsyth Feuars* (1878) 6 R 116, in which various decisions on the matter are reviewed by Lord Mure at 128.
11 See *Earl of Morton v Covingtree* (1760) Mor 13528, and *Agnew v Lord Advocate* (1873) 11 M 309, both being cases concerning the right to take seaweed, and *Crichton v Turnbull* 1946 SC 52, 1946 SLT 156, concerning a water right. *Per contra*, see *Lord Blantyre v Dunn* (1848) 10 D 509, and *Mackenzie v Woddrop* (1854) 16 D 381, illustrating the larger rights in watercourses enjoyed by parties having a right of common property or even a common interest.
12 See J Rankine *The Law of Land-ownership in Scotland* (4th edn, 1909) pp 601, 602, dealing with a problem of distinguishing between a servitude right of pasturage and the form of right (now virtually obsolete) known as 'commonty'.
13 *Mackenzie v Carrick* (1869) 7 M 419.
14 Similar rulings were given in *Bennett v Playfair* (1877) 4 R 321 and *Shiel v Young* (1895) 3 SLT 171, OH, where emphasis was placed on the right of light as an incidental to the right of open passage. On these cases, see para 362 above.

446. Running with the land without transmission.

Servitudes run with the land representing the respective tenements, affecting all successors in ownership and not requiring any form of transmission[1]. The adjectives 'heritable' and 'irredeemable' are commonly used in deeds constituting servitudes, reflecting the essentially permanent nature of the servitude and distinguishing it from rights or restrictions personal to the proprietors for the time being, as contracting parties[2]. In this respect the servitude resembles a real burden or condition duly constituted, although unlike such a burden or condition its effectiveness does not necessarily depend on its appearance in a property register[3]. Perpetual endurance, however, is not essential for the validity of a servitude. A servitude may be created for a certain purpose and become inoperative when that purpose is fulfilled or ceases to exist[4]. Again, it may be created for the duration of a liferent[5], and while it is perhaps unusual in practice, there would seem to be no reason why it should not be constituted expressly on the basis of endurance for a certain time or until the happening of some event.

1 *Braid Hills Hotel Co Ltd v Manuels* 1909 SC 120, 16 SLT 523. While the division of the servient tenement leaves the servitude unaffected, more difficult questions arise where the dominant tenement is divided: see paras 465, 476, below.
2 See para 450 below.
3 See para 451 below.
4 See *Winans v Lord Tweedmouth* (1888) 15 R 540 at 568, per Lord Mure.
5 W J Dobie *Manual of the Law of Liferent and Fee in Scotland* (1949) p 74.

447. Restricted generally to certain uses or restraints.

The category of servitudes is basically restricted to certain recognised uses or restraints, but has never been regarded as finally closed[1]. As servitudes may exist without appearing on the property registers, it is necessary for the benefit of parties acquiring interest in the servient tenements that the scope and incidence of the servitudes should thus be restricted and that if any use or restraint outwith the established instances are to be recognised, these should conform to the essential characteristics of the established servitudes. Stair's opinion that there may be as many servitudes as there are ways of burdening property[2] goes beyond the bounds within which the law has in fact developed. Some at least of the uses or restraints which Stair envisaged could not be effectively constituted servitudes, although they might fall within the wider category of real burdens or conditions requiring entry in the property registers.

The existence of an element of flexibility in the scope of the category of servitudes has, however, been emphasised more than once in judicial dicta. It has been said that where new inventions come into use they may have the benefit of servitudes, since the law will accommodate its practical operation to the varying circumstances of mankind[3]. In fact, the additions to the long-established forms of servitude, as mainly derived from Roman law, have been confined to positive servitudes[4], and even these have been few in number[5]. To some extent this may be explained on the ground that existing forms of servitude have proved adaptable to changing conditions[6]. Another factor, however, is undoubtedly the proliferation of statutory conditions which, for the purposes of industrial and other developments, particularly in the field of public undertakings, have created rights fulfilling the same functions as servitudes, but which do not necessarily conform to the requirements of servitudes as recognised at common law[7].

1 *Harvey v Lindsay* (1853) 15 D 768 at 775, per Lord Ivory.
2 Stair *Institutions* II,7,5, referred to in *Murray v Peebles Magistrates* 8 Dec 1808 FC.
3 *Dyce v Hay* (1852) 1 Macq 305 at 312, HL, per Lord St Leonards. Cf *Harvey v Lindsay* (1853) 15 D 768, and *Patrick v Napier* (1867) 5 M 683 at 709, per Lord Ardmillan.
4 The possession or use of positive servitudes, as contrasted with negative servitudes, may be evident to parties such as prospective purchasers of servient tenements.
5 For examples, see para 491 below.
6 See *Crawford v Lumsden* 1951 SLT 64, OH, concerning motor vehicles on cart roads, reversed on the facts *Crawford v Lumsden* 1951 SLT (Notes) 62.
7 See para 493 below.

(3) CREATION OF SERVITUDES

(a) Introduction

448. Ways in which servitudes can originate. Apart from statutory provisions such as those connected with the compulsory acquisition of land[1] and the very rare case of judicial decree[2], there may be said to be four ways in which servitudes can originate:
(1) in writing by express grant or reservation[3];
(2) by grant or reservation inferred or implied[4];
(3) by possession or use for the period of positive prescription[5]; and
(4) by acquiescence inferring the agreement of the servient owner[6].
While positive servitudes can originate in any of these ways, the accepted view has been that negative servitudes can be constituted only by express provision in writing[7].

1 See para 463 below.
2 See *Edinburgh School Board v Simpson* (1906) 13 SLT 910, concerning a servitude created by decree of the Court of Session. In an action for division of common property the decree might create appropriate servitude rights in respect of the separate units.
3 See paras 450, 451, below.
4 See paras 452 ff below.
5 See paras 458–461 below.
6 See para 462 below.

7 *Dundas v Blair* (1886) 13 R 759 at 762, per Lord President Inglis, referring to Erskine *Institute* II,9,35, and Bell *Principles* s 994, followed in *Inglis v Clark* (1901) 4 F 288, 9 SLT 328. See, however, para 456 below.

449. Questions of right, title and capacity as affecting the creation of servitudes. Before the various ways in which servitudes may be created are examined in detail, certain matters of right, title and capacity should be noticed. Although applying particularly to the creation of servitudes by express written provision, these issues can arise whatever form the creation of a servitude may take.

It has been seen that in terms of the maxim *nemo res sua servit*, the conception of a servitude involves the existence of two properties or tenements in separate ownership[1]. It follows that servitude rights cannot be created by or in favour of parties holding only tenancy rights or as between tenants of the same landlord, even where they hold on long lease[2]. A proprietor of land cannot create a servitude over subjects which he owns in favour of subjects which he has let[3]. Rights created under such conditions will usually be personal to the original parties: they may in certain circumstances be enforced on a possessory basis, but not as servitudes[4]. *Pro indiviso* owners cannot by themselves create servitudes affecting their own shares of the common property[5]. It is doubtful if a servitude can be created when the servient owner is not infeft in his property[6], but accretion has been held to operate on his subsequent infeftment[7]. While normally a grantee of a servitude should be infeft in the dominant property, it has been held that a servitude right of way granted in favour of a party who was expected to acquire the dominant tenement became effective when he did so, provided such use took place as would constitute reasonable notice to prospective singular successors in the servient tenement[8].

The grant of a servitude right has been held not to be an ordinary act of administration within the powers impliedly vested in an agent such as an estate factor[9]. The creation of servitudes is not among the powers listed as statutorily conferred on gratuitous trustees[10]: however, on the basis of the greater including the lesser[11], the power to grant a servitude can be regarded as encompassed in the general power of disposal of land represented by the trustees' power of sale[12]. A grant of servitude by a liferenter is valid, but can subsist only for the duration of the liferent[13]. When land has been acquired compulsorily for certain purposes, this precludes the creation of any servitude rights the exercise of which could be prejudicial to these purposes[14].

While the point may tend to be disregarded in modern practice, there is authority for the view that the superior of land held on feudal tenure must consent to the creation of a servitude affecting that land if it is to be valid in any question with him and his successors: it has been held that a superior is entitled to object to any such encroachment of the feu even if the vassal has agreed to it[15]. The superior's rights in this matter are, however, unlikely to become a live issue except in two particular circumstances. If the servitude, as operated or used, conflicts with feuing conditions, those conditions will prevail. Again, if the superior recovers the land by a process of irritancy he would be entitled to treat as nullified any servitude rights emanating from the vassal. In any proceedings directed to establishing the existence of a servitude right, the superior of the servient tenement, at least if known, should *ob majorem cautelam* be called as a defender[16]. While it appears that a servitude may be granted by the reversionary owner of property subject to a security constituted by *ex facie* absolute disposition[17], the consent of any heritable creditors to the creation of servitude rights over the servient tenement must be taken if these are to be effective in questions with the heritable creditors and their successors. Again, there may be circumstances in which it is necessary, or at least advisable, that the consent of tenants be obtained when a servitude right is being created over a property which is let. This will be so if there is any possibility of the servitude right conflicting with the tenants' rights under their tenancy contracts[18].

1 See para 443 above.
2 *M'Tavish's Trustees v Anderson* (1900) 8 SLT 80, OH; *Metcalfe v Purdon* (1902) 4 F 507, 9 SLT 413; *Safeway Food Stores Ltd v Wellington Motor Co (Ayr) Ltd* 1976 SLT 53, OH. See also J Rankine *The Law of Land-ownership in Scotland* (4th edn, 1909) p 415.
3 *Duncan v Scott* (1876) 3 R (HL) 69. In the earlier case of *Dinwiddie v Corrie* (1821) 1 S 164 (NE 156), a grant of peat cutting rights to the tenants of a barony was construed as not being personal to the tenants for the time being and so not extinguished on the expiry of their leases.
4 *M'Donald v Dempster* (1871) 10 M 94.
5 *Grant v Heriot's Trust* (1906) 8 F 647 at 661, 662, 13 SLT 986 at 993, 994, per Lord President Dunedin, followed in *WVS Office Premises Ltd v Currie* 1969 SC 170, 1969 SLT 254, and in *Fearnan Partnership v Grindlay* 1990 SLT 704, affd 1992 SLT 460, HL. See further para 28 above.
6 *Sivright v Wilson* (1828) 7 S 210 at 213, per Lord President Hope. See J M Halliday *Conveyancing Law and Practice in Scotland*, vol II (1986) para 20-05, and J Burns *Conveyancing Practice* (4th edn, 1957 by F MacRitchie) p 425. *Per contra*, see J Rankine *The Law of Land-ownership in Scotland* (4th edn, 1909) p 427, and W M Gordon *Scottish Land Law* (1989) paras 24-31, 24-45. The statutory provisions for deeds being granted by uninfeft persons (the Conveyancing (Scotland) Act 1924 (c 27), s 3) do not cover servitude rights, being confined, except in the case of standard securities, to deeds transmitting but not creating rights.
7 *Stephen v Brown's Trustees* 1922 SC 136, 1922 SLT 112. Lord Hunter dissented, but the majority ruling followed that in *Glassford's Executors v Scott* (1850) 12 D 893, where a heritable bond was held validated by accretion: see *Stephen v Brown's Trustees* 1922 SC 136 at 145, 1922 SLT 112 at 114. In *Halliday*, para 20-05, it is indicated that for accretion to operate the grant of servitude must carry absolute warrandice. While that may be the rule where there is a conveyance of property, there could be difficulty in applying it to certain grants of servitude rights. As to warrandice in grants of servitudes, see para 450 below.
8 *North British Rly Co v Park Yard Co Ltd* (1898) 25 R (HL) 47, 6 SLT 82, distinguished in *Hamilton v Elder* 1968 SLT (Sh Ct) 53.
9 *Macgregor v Balfour* (1899) 2 F 345, 7 SLT 273.
10 See the Trusts (Scotland) Act 1921 (c 58), s 4(1) (as amended), and TRUSTS, vol 24, para 202.
11 This was applied in *Bowman Ballantine* (1883) 10 R 1061, a case of an heir of entail, interpreting the Entail (Scotland) Act 1882 (c 53), s 19, as authorising the grant of a servitude.
12 Trusts (Scotland) Act 1921, s 4(1)(a).
13 W J Dobie *Manual of the Law of Liferent and Fee in Scotland* (1949) p 74. A different position arises if the liferenter is a fiduciary fiar: *Dobie* p 45.
14 *Ayr Harbour Trustees v Oswald* (1883) 10 R (HL) 85; *Ellice's Trustees v Caledonian Canal Comrs* (1904) 6 F 325, 11 SLT 620. Cf *Edinburgh Magistrates v North British Rly Co* (1904) 6 F 620, 12 SLT 20, a case concerning a public right of way.
15 See *Marquis of Breadalbane v Campbell* (1851) 13 D 647, where the running of prescription which the superior could have interrupted was held to make a servitude right effective against him. Cf *Dalmorton Tenants v Earl Cassillis* (1666) Mor 5005 (a thirlage case), and see *Rankine* p 376.
16 *Lean v Hunter* 1950 SLT (Notes) 31, OH.
17 *Union Heritable Securities Co Ltd v Mathie* (1886) 13 R 670.
18 *Burns* p 428.

(b) Creation by Written Provision

450. Authentication, form and construction. Relating as it does to heritable property, the writing constituting a servitude must be probative of the granter: however, an improbative document or even a verbal agreement may be rendered effective by actings constituting *rei interventus* or by acquiescence[1]. An agreement or undertaking to grant a servitude does not *per se* constitute the servitude[2]. While servitudes will normally be constituted by *inter vivos* deeds, it appears that a *mortis causa* deed could also be effective for the purpose[3], although there is no reported case where this has happened[4].

Broadly speaking, the forms in which servitudes are created by express written provision may be said to fall into three categories:

(1) a deed other than a conveyance of the land affected, variously described as an agreement, a bond or a grant of servitude[5];

(2) a conveyance of land with provisions constituting, for the land conveyed, a servitude right over other land retained by the granter[6]; and

(3) a conveyance of land reserving to the granter a servitude right over that land in favour of the land retained by him[7].

The question of consideration for the grant will arise when a servitude is constituted otherwise than in a conveyance of land[8]. The consideration, if any, could be a single payment or a periodical payment made by the owner of the dominant tenement. The right to such a periodical payment will run with the ownership of the servient tenement[9].

Significant in relation to the drafting and construction of deeds constituting servitudes is a presumption of freedom from restrictions on the inherent rights of landowners. Accordingly, *in dubio* the construction which involves least burden or restriction on the servient tenement will be adopted[10]. Where the servitude is constituted by reservation, the general presumption against derogation from a grant will also apply. The intention to create a permanent right or restriction of the nature of a servitude as opposed to an arrangement merely personal to the parties involved must be evident[11]. It is not, however, essential that the word 'servitude' or any particular terminology should be used[12]. A reasonable measure of specification with precision as regards the nature, effect and scope of the right or restriction is always required[13], but defective drafting, so long as not obscuring the meaning of a provision or creating ambiguity, will be disregarded in deciding whether or not a servitude has been constituted[14].

The requirements for the constitution of a servitude have been distinguished from those applying to the constitution of a real burden[15]. In *McLean v Marwhirn Developments Ltd*, the court considered that:

> 'it has never been held that the exceptionally strict tests of the sufficiency of a real burden proper apply to the description of a known servitude contained in an express grant'[16].

Accordingly, the grant in a disposition to the pursuer's predecessor of the right 'to use for . . . drainage . . . all existing . . . pipes, connections, drains, sewers . . . in and under' the defender's land was held to constitute a servitude involving the use of the facilities existing at the time of the grant. While a deed constituting a servitude should contain data sufficient to identify the respective tenements, descriptions, particular or by reference, which meet the requirements for registration for publication are not essential[17]. Deficiencies of drafting affecting the identification of the tenements — or either of them — can, like other deficiencies in deeds constituting servitudes, be made good by extrinsic evidence[18].

A question may be said to arise as to the warrandice or warranty which is implied or should be expressed in a grant of servitude. Warrandice as an incident of a contract of transfer of the property is strictly speaking inapplicable to a grant of servitude although grants of positive servitudes are sometimes expressed as conveyances of the right[19]. In any event, the statutory interpretation of a clause of warrandice as appearing in a conveyance of heritable property[20] will not apply. However, at least where there is consideration for the grant of servitude, it would be appropriate that the granter should in some way warrant his right and title to create the servitude[21], whether or not such warranty would be implied[22].

1 See W M Gloag *The Law of Contract* (2nd edn, 1929) p 163, founding on *Kincaid v Stirling* (1750) Mor 8403 (a case of verbal consent), and D M Walker *Principles of Scottish Private Law* (4th edn, 1989) vol 3, p 197, referring to *Stirling v Haldane* (1829) 8 S 131, and *Macgregor v Balfour* (1899) 2 F 345, 7 SLT 273. As authorities for the particular proposition, these cases seem inconclusive as in none of them was a servitude right held to have been constituted in this way. In *Safeway Food Stores Ltd v Wellington Motor Co (Ayr) Ltd* 1976 SLT 53, OH, Lord Maxwell at 56 cast doubts on the proposition as it appeared in the 1st edition of Walker's work (1970) at p 1326. However, as to the constitution of servitudes by acquiescence with agreement based solely on implication, see para 462 below.
2 *Safeway Food Stores Ltd v Wellington Motor Co (Ayr) Ltd* 1976 SLT 53, OH.

3 J Rankine *The Law of Land-ownership in Scotland* (4th edn, 1909) p 425.

4 See, however, *Campbell v Halkett* (1890) 27 SLR 1000, where a claim that a will by the owner of two estates, bequeathing them to different beneficiaries, resulted in an implied grant of servitude failed on other grounds.

5 For examples, see 8 *Encyclopaedia of Scottish Legal Styles* pp 377–383. While the word 'dispone' is commonly used in deeds creating positive servitudes, this does not constitute the deed a conveyance of heritable property, although for stamp duty purposes it is so treated (see note 8 below).

6 8 *Encyclopaedia of Scottish Legal Styles* pp 56–58; J Burns *Conveyancing Practice* (4th edn, 1957 by F MacRitchie) p 430.

7 *Burns* p 431.

8 In the case of a deed in category (1) constituting a positive servitude, 'Conveyance on Sale' stamp duty will be payable on the lump sum or on the aggregate of the periodical payments falling due within twenty years of the execution of the deed. A stamp clause in the usual form should be included where exemption from duty or a restricted rate of duty can be claimed. If there is no pecuniary consideration, no stamp duty will be due. As from 26 March 1985, the question of *ad valorem* duty on the value of a voluntary grant does not arise: see the Finance Act 1985 (c 54), s 82. While a deed creating a positive servitude is regarded for stamp duty purposes as a conveyance, a deed creating a negative servitude is not so regarded and does not attract stamp duty even where there is a consideration passing. See J M Halliday *Conveyancing Law and Practice in Scotland*, vol II (1986) para 20-11.

9 *Stewart v Steuart* (1877) 4 R 981. Although the servitude in this case was constituted in a feu charter, the right to the periodical payments ran with the ownership of the servient tenement and not with the superiority: see the opinion of Lord President Inglis at p 984.

10 Examples of the application of this rule can be found in *Craig v Gould* (1861) 24 D 20; *Banks & Co v Walker* (1874) 1 R 981; *Russell v Cowpar* (1882) 9 R 660; *Clark & Sons v Perth School Board* (1898) 25 R 919; and *Cronin v Sutherland* (1899) 2 F 217.

11 *Cowan v Stewart* (1872) 10 M 735.

12 *Ferguson v Tennant* 1978 SC (HL) 19 at 63, 1978 SLT 165 at 178, per Lord Fraser of Tullybelton. In practice the use of the term 'servitude' is not always confined to servitudes in the strict and proper sense of the term, but can be found applied to rights or restrictions coming within the wider category of burdens or conditions on land.

13 See *Murray's Trustees v St Margaret's Convent Trustees* (1906) 8 F 1109, 14 SLT 307, affd 1907 SC (HL) 8, 15 SLT 2, in which a prohibition of buildings 'of an unseemly description' was held too vague to constitute a servitude.

14 *Hunter v Fox* 1964 SC (HL) 95, 1964 SLT 201.

15 Ie as laid down in cases such as *Anderson v Dickie* 1914 SC 706, 1913 2 SLT 198. See further paras 390, 415 ff, above.

16 *McLean v Marwhirn Developments Ltd* 1976 SLT (Notes) 47 at 49. Cf *Lean v Hunter* 1950 SLT (Notes) 31, OH.

17 *Ferguson v Tennant* 1978 SC (HL) 19 at 66, 67, 1978 SLT 165 at 180, per Lord Fraser of Tullybelton. But in practice these requirements should be observed if it is intended that the deed enter the property registers.

18 *Robson v Chalmers Property Investment Co Ltd* 1965 SLT 381, OH. Cf *Houldsworth v Gordon Cumming* 1910 SC (HL) 49, 1910 2 SLT 136.

19 See *Dumfries and Maxwelltown Water-Works Comrs v M'Culloch* (1874) 1 R 975, where a clause of absolute warrandice appeared in a conveyance of a servitude right to draw water from a loch. See also note 5 above and note 22 below. As to warrandice generally, see paras 701 ff below.

20 Titles to Land Consolidation (Scotland) Act 1868 (c 101), s 8: see CONVEYANCING, vol 6, para 543.

21 See 8 *Encyclopaedia of Scottish Legal Styles* pp 380, 381, where in the form of a grant of a water right the granter binds himself and his successors to warrant the servitude right to the grantee at all hands. In vol 8, pp 378, 379, the grant of a servitude *non altius tollendi* contains a clause of absolute warrandice, but this may relate to the conveyance of the servient tenement which is included in compliance with the requirement of simultaneous infeftment applicable to the creation of a real burden or condition. No warrandice provisions appear in the forms of grant of servitude contained in *Burns* pp 430, 431, or in the form contained in *Halliday* vol II, para 20-11.

22 In *Dumfries and Maxwelltown Water-Works Comrs v M'Culloch* (1874) 1 R 975 at 978, Lord Benholme proceeds on the basis of an implication of warrandice safeguarding the water supply against pollution by actings of the servient proprietor. It is not clear, however, that he is founding on the warrandice clause in the deed, which on general principles would be restricted to matters of right and title. If pollution by future action only were to be covered, simple warrandice would be sufficient for the purpose.

451. Significance of possession and/or registration for publication. A servitude constituted by grant or reservation in a conveyance of the dominant or servient tenement will appear in the property register in which the deed is registered. Where a servitude is constituted in a deed not forming a conveyance, it is appropriate, though not essential, that the deed should sufficiently identify the respective tenements to enable it to appear in the registers in respect of either or both of the subjects affected[1]. Whether the servitude right originates in express written provision or is created by any of the other means discussed below, its appearance in the register is not necessary for its effectiveness either as between the parties to its creation or in questions with their successors, universal or singular[2]. Unlike a real burden, the validity of a servitude does not rest upon recording but on its being well known to the law[3]. In the case of a positive servitude, however, if the writ containing it does not appear on the register, the effectiveness of the servitude in questions with singular successors will be dependent on its having been followed by such use or quasi-possession as is consistent with the terms of the right[4]. On the other hand, although there can be no demonstrable use or possession of a negative servitude, that servitude, if duly constituted by express written provision clearly indicative of a praedial servitude as opposed to a merely personal right, is effective in questions with singular successors whether or not it appears on the property register[5].

Where a servitude does not appear on the register, the knowledge of its existence by, for example, an intending purchaser of the servient tenement depends on observation of circumstances indicating the possible or likely existence of one or more of the recognised servitudes[6]. In the case of positive servitudes, but not in that of negative servitudes, use or exercise disclosing their existence may be evident. The position as regards negative servitudes has been described as an anomaly of the law which should not be extended[7].

Thus, with both positive and negative servitudes, the titles and searches relating to the servient tenement may contain nothing which will alert parties concerned to the fact that there is such a burden or restriction on the property[8]. Again, the continued effectiveness of the servitude which has appeared on the property register is not dependent, as is the case of a real burden or condition, on its having been repeated or referred to in subsequent transmissions of the property[9]. Hence an examination of the prescriptive progress of title may not disclose the existence of a servitude which has appeared in the property register at some earlier date.

The authorities referred to in relation to this issue were, of course, concerned with the recording of deeds for publication in the Register of Sasines. While registration of title in the Land Register of Scotland is discussed in detail elsewhere in this encyclopaedia[10], it is appropriate to refer here to certain features of this system as it affects rights such as servitudes. For the purposes of registration of title, servitudes are classified as overriding interests in relation to the servient tenement[11]. Thus a servitude may subsist although not disclosed in the title sheet or the land certificate relating to that tenement. The Keeper of the Land Register is, however, empowered and, in certain cases, bound to take note of the existence of a servitude in making up the title sheet, but any matter so noted is excluded from the guarantee given in respect of the content of the register[12]. The right of the dominant owner in a servitude is, by contrast, an interest in land[13] which, if brought to his notice, the Keeper will register as a pertinent in the title sheet of the dominant tenement[14]. But because of the possibility that the servitude may be extinguished by non-use, the Keeper's indemnity is limited in the case of servitudes so noted to a guarantee as to the validity of the constitution of the right and does not warrant that the right continues in existence[15]. Thus, under the system of registration of title, the position is similar to that existing under the system of recording of deeds, namely that appearance in the Land Register of Scotland in respect of either or both tenements is not a *sine qua non* of the existence and effectiveness of a servitude right. While registration in the Land Register is to supersede recording in the General Register of Sasines, this is without prejudice to the creation of real rights and obligations by other means such as prescription in the case of servitudes[16]. But because the system of registration of title makes some provision for the appearance of servitudes in the Land Register, in time servitudes such as those arising from prescription or implication may be disclosed in the register where this was not possible in the Register of Sasines as a result of the absence of any appropriate documentation.

1 See J Burns *Conveyancing Practice* (4th edn, 1957 by F MacRitchie) p 428.
2 *Turnbull v Blaneme* (1622) Mor 14499; *Pennymuir* (1632) Mor 14502; *Garden v Earl of Aboyne* (1734) Mor 14517; *Gray v Ferguson* (1792) Mor 14513, cited in *Sivright v Wilson* (1828) 7 S 210 at 212; *Tailors of Aberdeen v Coutts* (1840) 1 Robin 296 at 309, 310, HL (contrasting the position as regards real burdens or conditions); *North British Rly Co v Park Yard Co Ltd* (1898) 25 R (HL) 47 at 52, 6 SLT 82 at 83 per Lord Watson.
3 *McLean v Marwhim Developments Ltd* 1976 SLT (Notes) 47.
4 See the cases of *Turnbull, Garden* and *Gray* (cited in note 2 above), exemplifying the creation of a servitude by unrecorded deeds on which possession or use has followed. For an exceptional situation, see *Greig v Brown* (1829) 7 S 274, where a right of access for one tenement over another was held effectual without registration or possession, both tenements being held on unrecorded titles from the same author, but the title of the dominant tenement being the earlier in date.
5 *Cowan v Stewart* (1872) 10 M 735; *Banks & Co v Walker* (1874) 1 R 981. However, see the observations of Lord Kinnear in *Campbell's Trustees v Glasgow Corpn* (1902) 4 F 752 at 757, 758, casting some doubt on this proposition as applied to a servitude *non aedificandi*.
6 As to the problems thus arising in practice, see *Burns* p 427, and J M Halliday *Conveyancing Law and Practice in Scotland*, vol II (1986) para 20-22.
7 *Sivright v Wilson* (1828) 7 S 210 at 213, per Lord Gillies.
8 See *Balfour v Kinsey* 1987 SLT 144, OH, applying this rule in the case of a right of access. Lord Sutherland's opinion refers to Bell *Principles* s 922; J Craigie *The Scottish Law of Conveyancing —Heritable Rights* (3rd edn, 1899) p 285; and *Burns* p 425. The passage in *Bell*, referring as it does to the sasine being qualified, might perhaps be read as meaning the sasine of the servient tenement.
9 *Clelland v Mackenzie* (1739) Mor 14506; *Boswell v Inglis* (1848) 10 D 888, affd sub nom *Inglis v Boswall* (1849) 6 Bell App 427, HL; *Cooper and M'Leod v Edinburgh Improvement Trustees* (1876) 3 R 1106; *M'Gavin v W A M'Intyre & Co* (1874) 1 R 1016 at 1023, 1024, per Lord Neaves.
10 See CONVEYANCING, INCLUDING REGISTRATION OF TITLE, vol 6, paras 705 ff. See also *Halliday*, vol II, paras 20-12(2), 20-34, 20-35, where the relevant statutory provisions as applying in practice are dealt with in some detail.
11 Land Registration (Scotland) Act 1979 (c 33), s 28(1) ('overriding interest' (d)).
12 Ibid, s 6(4).
13 Ibid, s 28(1) ('interest in land').
14 See ibid, s 2(4).
15 See ibid, ss 6(4), 12(3)(l). See also *Scheme for the Introduction and Operation of Registration of Title to Land in Scotland* (the Henry Report) (Cmnd 4137) (1969) para 40, and J M Halliday *The Land Registration (Scotland) Act 1979* (1979) 33/12.
16 Land Registration (Scotland) Act 1979, s 3(2).

(c) Creation by Inference or Implication

452. Implication from provisions not expressly creating servitudes. The creation of servitudes by inference or implication as opposed to express grant or reservation represents a departure from the basic presumption against encroachment on the inherent rights of property owners. It is, however, an exception of considerable importance involving a substantial body of case law.

It is necessary to distinguish between cases where the existence of a servitude right is sought to be supported on the basis of documents containing something other than the express or specific provisions for the creation of such a right and, on the other hand, cases where the claim is based mainly, if not solely, on facts and circumstances such as those existing on the division of a property. There are a number of reported instances of documentation held ineffective to create, by inference, a negative servitude which normally requires express written provision[1]. The existence of a positive servitude, however, may in some circumstances be inferred from the terms of documents not expressly providing for it. Thus a right of access to property may, if consistent with the circumstances and the actings of the parties, be inferred as existing by means of a path, road or lane forming the boundary of the property as described in the title deeds[2].

1 *Morris v M'Kean* (1830) 8 S 564; *Free St Mark's Church Trustees v Taylor's Trustees* (1869) 7 M 415; *King v Barnetson* (1896) 24 R 81, 4 SLT 127.
2 See *Argyllshire Comrs of Supply v Campbell* (1885) 12 R 1255; *Louttit's Trustees v Highland Rly Co* (1892) 19 R 791; *Boyd v Hamilton* 1907 SC 912, 15 SLT 57.

453. Implied grant of positive servitude on severance of property.

Where the implication of a servitude arises from facts and circumstances rather than from the terms of any documents, the law relating to implied grants was stated by Lord Campbell in the leading case of *Ewart v Cochrane* as follows:

> 'when two properties are possessed by the same owner, and there has been a severence made of part from the other, anything which was used, and was necessary for the comfortable enjoyment of that part of the property which is granted, shall be considered to follow from the grant, if there are the usual words in the conveyance. I do not know whether the usual words are essentially necessary; but where there are the usual words I cannot doubt that that is the law'[1].

As this passage makes clear, it is essential that the right thus claimed should be necessary for the comfortable enjoyment of the property acquired. In the particular case, the owner of a tanyard with an adjoining house and garden had constructed a drain for the tanyard to a cesspool in the garden. When he later sold the tanyard, retaining the house and garden, the purchaser of the tanyard was held entitled to retain the drain in its position since this was necessary for his comfortable enjoyment of the premises. The 'usual words' referred to in the passage would appear to be the words 'as presently possessed' or words to that effect[2]. Whether or not such words appear, the right which is held to be implied in the grant or conveyance of part of a property the rest of which is retained by the granter must, as well as being necessary for the reasonable enjoyment of the subject of the grant, have been exercised by the granter up until the time of severance[3]. In only one reported case[4] has a facility not in existence or use at the date of the conveyance been held to be created by implication as a servitude, and this has been regarded as a special case decided entirely upon its peculiar circumstances[5].

While the passage above from *Ewart v Cochrane* indicates that a variety of rights could arise by implication on the division of a property, it is established that to be created in this way the rights must be among the recognised servitudes[6]. A number of reported cases have been concerned with rights of access. Where a party sells a part of his property to which there has been access through the part he is retaining, a grant of such access is implied[7]. While the disponee of part of the disponer's property will in any event not be left with a subject which is landlocked and deprived of any access, there is also what has been described as an almost irresistible presumption that the land is sold with such access as then existed[8]. Where, however, the disponee claims some other means of access, the onus lies on the disponee to demonstrate, from the terms of the title which he obtained, that it was not the intention of the parties that he should be restricted to the existing means of access[9]. Thus the fact that the property sold had a roadway as one of its boundaries did not entitle the purchaser to access by means of that roadway in addition to or in place of the means of access previously in use[10].

Where a right such as that of access is expressly provided in respect of part of a property which is sold, the right to another — or additional — means of access which happens to have been in use prior to the sale will not be implied[11]. The claim to such a right can be refuted not only on the principle *expressio unius est exclusio alterius*, but probably also on the ground that the additional facilities are unnecessary for the convenient and comfortable enjoyment of the subjects[12]. Again, if a proprietor buys land to form an addition to his existing property, the presumption is that he is to obtain access through his own property and does not, by implication, acquire the right to such means of access over the seller's property as has previously been in use[13].

A strong case for the implied grant of a servitude such as a right of access arises where the part of the property which is being sold has at some time in the past been separately owned or at least separately occupied, with its owner or occupier enjoying certain facilities over the other part of the property[14]. It might be thought that on the principle of *res sua nemini servit*, the effect of the properties coming into single ownership would be to extinguish *confusione* any servitude rights in favour of one property or the other: however, the view has been taken that when two properties under separate titles are united, servitudes are not always extinguished *confusione* to the extent of making it necessary for them to be constituted *de novo* when the subjects previously forming the dominant tenement are subsequently separately alienated[15]. For a servitude right of access to arise by implication on the redivision of what was originally two separate properties, it is not sufficient that the owner or occupier of the properties when they were united used the access for his own convenience, the presumption being against the implication of a servitude if the facility was not used when the properties were originally in separate ownership[16]. In practice, when a sale has the effect of dividing a property into units of which it formerly comprised, express provision is desirable, depending on whether it is the intention of the parties that rights existing before the properties became a single unit should revive[17].

1   *Ewart v Cochrane* (1861) 4 Macq 117 at 122, HL. Cf the opinion of Lord Justice-Clerk Moncreiff in *M'Laren v City of Glasgow Union Rly Co* (1878) 5 R 1042 at 1047, 1048, that on the basis of contract every land sale implies all incidental rights necessary for the reasonable enjoyment of the subjects sold, the presumption being strong in the case of rights of constant necessity such as light, water and drainage and again in the case of rights of access, and the implication being irresistible if no reasonable man would have bought the property without the right in question.
2   See the opinion of Lord Kinnear in *Shearer v Peddie* (1899) 1 F 1201 at 1208, 7 SLT 137 at 139; but in *Alexander v Butchart* (1875) 3 R 156 the use of similar words was held insufficient to entitle the purchasers to a right which was not among the recognised servitudes and not reasonably necessary for the enjoyment of the property.
3   *Ewart v Cochrane* (1861) 4 Macq 117, HL; *Shearer v Peddie* (1899) 1 F 1201, 7 SLT 137.
4   *Union Heritable Securities Co Ltd v Mathie* (1886) 13 R 670, a case of implied reservation.
5   *Cullens v Cambusbarron Co-operative Society* (1895) 23 R 209 at 213, per Lord Low (Ordinary).
6   *Alexander v Butchart* (1875) 3 R 156.
7   *Walton Bros v Glasgow Magistrates* (1876) 3 R 1130, following *Ewart v Cochrane* (1861) 4 Macq 117, HL.
8   *M'Laren v City of Glasgow Union Rly Co* (1878) 5 R 1042 at 1047, 1048, per Lord Justice-Clerk Moncreiff.
9   *Louttit's Trustees v Highland Rly Co* (1892) 19 R 791 at 799, per Lord M'Laren.
10   *Louttit's Trustees v Highland Rly Co* (1892) 19 R 791.
11   *Fraser v Cox* 1938 SC 506, 1938 SLT 374.
12   See *McEachen v Lister* 1976 SLT (Sh Ct) 38.
13   *Cullens v Cambusbarron Co-operative Society* (1895) 23 R 209, 3 SLT 168.
14   *M'Laren v City of Glasgow Union Rly Co* (1878) 5 R 1042 at 1047, 1048, per Lord Justice-Clerk Moncreiff; *Gow's Trustees v Mealls* (1875) 2 R 729 at 736, per Lord Neaves.
15   *Walton Bros v Glasgow Magistrates* (1876) 3 R 1130 at 1133, per Lord President Inglis. For an earlier authority, see *Carnegie v MacTier* (1844) 6 D 1381 at 1407, 1408, per Lord Medway.
16   *Gow's Trustees v Mealls* (1875) 2 R 729 at 736, per Lord Neaves.
17   See J Burns *Conveyancing Practice* (4th edn, 1957 by F MacRitchie) pp 430, 431, exemplifying forms of clauses for various contingencies.

454. Implied reservation of positive servitude on severance of property. Where a landowner disposes of part of his property and he or his successor claims that in relation to the part unsold a servitude right has been reserved by implication over the property sold, the principle that a person is presumed not to derogate from his own grant will apply to fortify the presumption against encroachment on the purchaser's rights of ownership. As has been seen, there may be an implied grant to a purchaser of part of a property of a positive servitude representing some existing facilities necessary for the reasonable and comfortable enjoyment of the subjects purchased and without which he would not have made the purchase. The creation of a servitude by reservation to a seller, however, will not be implied unless the servitude is absolutely essential for the occupation and use of the property retained. Accordingly, the cases in which such a reservation has been established are not numerous, the view being generally taken that if a seller intends to retain such a right for himself, he should stipulate such a right in clear and definite terms[1]. Thus a superior who had feued parts of his property without expressly reserving any rights of access was held not to have retained the right to create servitude rights over the subjects already feued for the benefit of feus which he subsequently granted[2].

The position will, however, be different if the right claimed to be reserved by implication is essential for the continued occupation and use of the retained subjects in any form. As mentioned below, there may be other grounds on which subjects may be prevented from being completely landlocked[3], but, this exceptional situation apart, it appears that a case may be made for the reservation by implication of a servitude right when it is the only practicable means of access to part of a divided property[4]; on a similar basis, reservation of other servitude rights may also be implied. Thus the proprietor of a mill who, without making any reservation, disposed of land through which ran part of the mill lade was held to have reserved, by implication, a servitude right of aqueduct along with the requisite right of access to the mill lade as a necessary adjunct of the mill property which he was retaining[5]. On the other hand, in an English case sometimes referred to in Scotland, a right of support as between a dock and an adjoining wharf was held not to have been reserved by implication as an easement of necessity on the sale of the wharf as a separate subject[6]. Again, in a Scottish case, it was held that there was no implied reservation in respect of a water supply, the pipe for which, unknown to the purchaser, ran under the property he had acquired[7]: somewhat surprisingly, the argument that a supply of water to a house should be regarded as a necessity was rejected and the absence of knowledge on the part of the purchaser was considered to exclude the element of agreement or intention regarded, in certain English cases[8], as justifying the implication of a reservation.

In any case of this kind the crucial question is what is to be regarded as constituting necessity. Is it to be confined to cases in which, without the right or facility claimed, the subjects retained could not be used for any purpose whatever, perhaps by reason of being cut off from access to any public place? If so, this would exclude the situation in which the servitude right claimed is required merely to enable the retained property to be used, as envisaged, for some particular purpose.

In respect of both implied reservation or implied grant, there is English authority which accepts the basic rule that, to be effective, a derogation from a grant should be in express terms[9], but which appears to admit the possibility of implied reservation in circumstances not amounting to absolute necessity irrespective of intended use. In the words of Lord Parker of Waddington,

'The law readily implies a grant or reservation of such easement as may be necessary to give effect to the common intention of the parties to a grant of real property with reference to the manner or purposes in and for which the land granted or some land retained by the grantor is to be used. But it is essential for this purpose that the subjects of the grant or the land retained by the grantor should be used in some definite and particular manner. It is not enough that the subjects of the grant or the land retained should be intended to be used in a manner which may or may not involve this definite and particular use'[10].

While the matter has not been enunciated precisely in this way in any reported case in Scotland, there are Scottish cases in which the decisions may be said to proceed on the basis of a specific intended use of the subjects for which the servitude right is claimed[11].

1 *Wheeldon v Burrows* (1879) 12 Ch D 31 at 49, CA, per Lord Thesiger, as referred to and followed in *Shearer v Peddie* (1899) 1 F 1201, 7 SLT 137.
2 *Shearer v Peddie* (1899) 1 F 1201, 7 SLT 137.
3 See para 457 below.
4 *Union Heritable Securities Co Ltd v Mathie* (1886) 13 R 670, a case which is exceptional in that the particular access claimed had not been in use prior to the division of the property.
5 *Fergusson v Campbell* 1913 1 SLT 241, OH.
6 *Union Lighterage Co v London Graving Dock Co* [1902] 2 Ch 557, CA.
7 *Murray v Medley* 1973 SLT (Sh Ct) 75. Cf *Harper v Stuart* (1907) 15 SLT 550.
8 Eg *Pwllbach Colliery Co Ltd v Woodman* [1915] AC 634, HL.
9 *Wheeldon v Burrows* (1879) 12 Ch D 31, CA.
10 *Pwllbach Colliery Co Ltd v Woodman* [1915] AC 634 at 646, 647, HL. Cf *Wong v Beaumont Property Trust Ltd* [1965] 1 QB 173, [1964] 2 All ER 119, CA, applying the principle in a case concerning English leasehold property.
11 *Union Heritable Securities Co Ltd v Mathie* (1886) 13 R 670; *Fergusson v Campbell* 1913 1 SLT 241, OH. In *Murray v Medley* 1973 SLT (Sh Ct) 75, the sheriff regarded the absence of knowledge of the facility claimed as precluding an argument on these lines.

455. Implication of positive servitude where single property disposed of in parts. Bell suggests that the principle whereby the creation of a servitude can be implied on the division of a property applies not only where the proprietor disposes of part of the property while retaining the remainder, but also where severance occurs by simultaneous conveyances of the whole property to different parties[1]. In this situation, rights such as servitudes operative as between the different parts of the property may be required, at least, for the convenient enjoyment of the separate units. In Scotland, judicial authority on this particular situation is lacking, but in England there is some authority that the following approach should be taken:

'The doctrine that upon a severance of the quasi-dominant and quasi-servient tenements continuous and apparent accommodations become easements applies to cases where the severance is effected by a simultaneous disposition of both tenements, as well as to cases where the common owner disposes of the quasi-dominant tenement and retains the quasi-servient tenement'[2].

On this basis, rights of way or access have been held to come into existence as easements or servitudes where a property, formerly let to different tenants, was sold by auction in lots corresponding to the tenancies[3]. In such cases, the implication may be said to be the equivalent of express provisions which should have been made as part of the scheme disposing of the property as lots at one and the same time. Its application on this limited basis would not be inconsistent with the decision in a Scottish case that a landowner feuing his land over an extended period could not claim to have reserved by implication the right to impose on earlier feuars servitudes required in the interests of subsequent feuars[4].

1 Bell *Principles* s 992.
2 14 *Halsbury's Laws of England* (4th edn) vol 14, para 68, citing a series of cases including *Nicholls v Nicholls* (1899) 81 LT 811.
3 *Hansford v Jago* [1921] 1 Ch 322, the decision in which was approved in *Wheeldon v Burrows* (1879) 12 Ch D 31, CA, and would seem to accord with the views expressed by Lord Parker in *Pwllbach Colliery Co Ltd v Woodman* [1915] AC 634, HL. See also *Cory v Davies* [1923] 2 Ch 95.
4 *Shearer v Peddie* (1899) 1 F 1201, 7 SLT 137. A ruling on the lines of the English decisions might, however, have been given in *Campbell v Halkett* (1890) 27 SLR 1000, which involved the division of

a testator's heritable property as between beneficiaries, had there not been available another, although less convenient, means of access which was sufficient to exclude the implication of servitude right in favour of the property bequeathed to one beneficiary over the property bequeathed to another.

456. Inapplicability of implication to grant of negative servitudes. Consistent with the rule that negative servitudes require to be constituted by express written provision, the Scottish cases on implication of servitude rights are only concerned with positive servitudes[1]. In England, however, it appears that negative servitudes such as those protecting light or air may be created by implication on the division of a property where the need for their existence is clearly evident[2]. A Scottish case in which, on the division of a property, a servitude of light and air was held to have been constituted by implication[3] has not been followed in later cases[4]: it has been indicated that such an implication can be justified only as an application of common interest under the law of tenement[5]. It also appears that there is no case in which a negative servitude, having been eliminated *confusione* as a result of the single ownership of the dominant and servient tenements, has been held to revive by implication on the subsequent separation of the two tenements[6].

In one case, however, there is a dissenting judgment strongly maintaining the possibility of the implication of a negative servitude[7], and there are dicta in other cases not inconsistent with that view[8]. While modern developments in such matters as planning and building control may be said to have reduced the likelihood of such situations arising, it is thought that it should not be impossible for the common law to resolve by implication a situation such as that necessitating the protection of light or air, where no statutory remedy is available.

1 The view that negative servitudes cannot be created by implication finds support in K G C Reid 'The Law of the Tenement' (1983) 28 JLSS 472 at 474, and also in J M Halliday *Conveyancing Law and Practice in Scotland*, vol II (1986) para 20-04.
2 See *Wheeldon v Burrows* (1879) 12 Ch D 31, CA, and the authorities cited in 14 *Halsbury's Laws of England* (4th edn) paras 68, 69.
3 *Heron v Gray* (1880) 8 R 155. See also *Boswell v Edinburgh Magistrates* (1881) 8 R 986.
4 *Inglis v Clark* (1901) 4 F 288, 9 SLT 328; *Metcalfe v Purdon* (1902) 4 F 507, 9 SLT 413. See also J Rankine *The Law of Land-ownership in Scotland* (4th edn, 1909) pp 426, 439, 440.
5 See *Calder v Merchant Co of Edinburgh* (1886) 13 R 623; *Metcalfe v Purdon* (1902) 4 F 507, 9 SLT 413; and *Birrell v Lumley* (1905) 12 SLT 719, OH. These cases demonstrate that common interest cannot afford the protection to amenity or prospect which could be secured by a servitude duly constituted.
6 *Union Bank of Scotland v Daily Record (Glasgow)* (1902) 10 SLT 71 at 73, 74, OH, per Lord Low.
7 *Inglis v Clark* (1901) 4 F 288 at 294, 295, per Lord Moncreiff.
8 See the opinions of Lord Anderson in *Ross v Cuthbertson* (1854) 16 D 732 at 734, and Lord Justice-Clerk Moncreiff in *M'Laren v City of Glasgow Union Rly Co* (1878) 5 R 1042 at 1047.

457. Exceptional position of access as right inherent in landownership. The question arises whether the implication of a servitude from facts and circumstances can occur only on the division of a property which has been in single ownership. This was the situation in most, if not all, the reported cases. In a number of these, the matter at issue was the right of access. It has been held that a proprietor has no right of access to his property over his neighbour's land simply *ex propinquitate* or because of the lack of any other convenient means of access[1]; but there are dicta indicating that a right of access might arise if the property was completely landlocked[2]. There is support for this view in Stair, who states that in such circumstances the right of access prevails over the right of property, being a right arising not out of any contract but out of natural obligation[3]. Even if it applies only to the question of access, the matter is of practical importance, first because there may be great difficulty in ascertaining from title deeds or otherwise whether or not certain properties have ever been in single ownership; and secondly because it could meet the situation where the only existing and available access to the property is destroyed or rendered permanently unusable by some occurrence such as an act of God.

1 *Menzies v Marquis of Breadalbane* (1901) 4 F 59. See the opinion of Lord Traynor at 61. However, absolute necessity was not proved, as access was possible by fording a river.
2 Eg *M'Laren v City of Glasgow Union Rly Co* (1878) 5 R 1042 at 1047, per Lord Justice-Clerk Moncreiff; *Rome v Hope Johnstone* (1884) 11 R 653 at 858, per Lord Justice-Clerk Moncreiff.
3 Stair *Institutions* II,7,10.

(d) Creation by Operation of Prescription

458. Prescription applicable only to positive servitudes. Only positive servitudes can be affected by the operation of the positive prescription, since the essential elements of possession, actual and apparent, cannot apply in relation to negative servitudes[1]. This is so whether prescription is being invoked (1) to make good some defect in the creation of a servitude based on express grant or reservation, or (2) to bring into operation a servitude for which there is no antecedent writ or document.

1 Bell *Principles* s 994; J Rankine *The Law of Land-ownership in Scotland* (4th edn, 1909) p 426; *Dundas v Blair* (1886) 13 R 759; *Inglis v Clark* (1901) 4 F 288 at 294, 295, per Lord Moncreiff; *Anderson v Robertson* 1958 SC 367 at 372, per Lord Justice-Clerk Thomson. There would appear to be some doubt about whether the servitude *oneris ferendi* (see para 484 below) should be classified as a positive or as a negative servitude, but in the English case of *Dalton v Angus* (1881) 6 App Cas 740 at 831, HL, Lord Watson appeared to regard it as a positive servitude in applying to it the English equivalent of positive prescription.

459. The statutory provisions on prescription. The modern statute law on prescription, as amended and re-enacted in the Prescription and Limitation (Scotland) Act 1973[1], as subsequently amended, reflects the recommendations of the Scottish Law Commission[2]. For the purposes of positive prescription, servitudes are excluded from the general category of interests in land[3] and are treated separately along with public rights of way[4]. The provisions of the Act relating to prescription came into force on 25 July 1976[5], but are retrospective to the extent that a prescriptive period may be held to have commenced but not to have run completely prior to that date[6].

The operative provisions of the Act as affecting servitudes[7] deal first with a case of a servitude constituted by deed[8]. If the servitude has been possessed for a continuous period of twenty years openly, peaceably and without judicial interruption[9] and the possession was founded on and followed the execution of a deed which is sufficient in respect of its terms (whether expressly or by implication) to constitute the servitude, then as from the expiration of the prescriptive period the validity of the servitude as so constituted is exempt from challenge, except on the ground that the deed is *ex facie* invalid or was forged[10]. Thus, while as a general rule the creation of a servitude is not readily inferred, provided the intention to create a servitude is clear, prescriptive possession may make good a defect such as a lack of specification in respect of its extent and effect. As under the pre-1976 law[11], the deed founded upon does not require to appear in the property registers: as prescription is stated to follow upon the *execution* of the deed[12], the date of execution is the terminus *a quo* even if there has been recording or registration of the deed.

Dealing with the case where there is no constitutive document, the Act provides that if a positive servitude over land has been possessed for a continuous period of twenty years openly, peaceably and without judicial interruption, the existence of the servitude as so possessed will thereafter be exempt from challenge[13]. While the matter may now be largely academic, in the past some difference of opinion existed as to the rationale of prescription in relation to the constitution of a servitude not otherwise evidenced. On one view, the servitude was not constituted by prescription but the exercise of the right was evidence that the right existed. The creation of a servitude in this way was variously attributed to implied grant[14], presumed consent[15] or presumed grant[16]. But such questions disappear if the view expressed by Lord Watson with reference to prescription in the case of public rights of way is applicable to servitudes, namely that the constitution of the right does not depend on any legal fiction but on the fact of user as a matter of right continuously and without interruption for the full prescriptive period[17].

1 As to prescription generally, see PRESCRIPTION AND LIMITATION.
2 *Reform of the Law relating to Prescription and Limitation of Actions* (Scot Law Com no. 15) (1970). See particularly paras 12, 19, concerning positive prescription and servitudes and public rights of way.
3 Prescription and Limitation (Scotland) Act 1973 (c 52), s 15(1) ('interest in land').
4 See ibid, s 3.
5 Ie three years after the passing of the Act: ibid, s 25(2).
6 Ibid, s 14(1)(a).
7 See ibid, s 3(1), (2).
8 'Deed' includes judicial decree: ibid, s 5(1). In special circumstances such as those of a process of division and sale a servitude right could be created by decree: see para 448 above.
9 For the meaning of 'judicial interruption', see ibid, s 4(1), and para 460 below.
10 Ibid, s 3(1).
11 See *North British Rly Co v Park Yard Co Ltd* (1898) 25 R (HL) 47 at 52, 6 SLT 82 at 83, per Lord Watson.
12 Prescription and Limitation (Scotland) Act 1973, s 3(1)(b).
13 Ibid, s 3(2).
14 *Macnab v Munro Ferguson* (1890) 17 R 397 at 402, per Lord Young.
15 Erskine *Institute* II,9,3.
16 J Rankine *The Law of Land-ownership in Scotland* (4th edn, 1909) p 427.
17 *Mann v Brodie* (1885) 12 R (HL) 52 at 57.

460. The requirement of possession or user. In both cases of the application of prescription, it is a requirement that possession must be continuous[1]. The difficulty of proving continuity of possession should be considerably lessened as a result of the reduction in the period of prescription from forty to twenty years[1]. Virtually all the reported cases arose when the longer period was in force and demonstrate a tendency on the part of the courts to relax, to some extent, the normal requirements of proof in relation to possession. Thus, where there had been adequate proof of user over a period just short of the prescriptive period, something less than conclusive proof in respect of the earliest part of the prescriptive period might be accepted[2]. Such an approach, however, has not been regarded as acceptable where the inadequacy of evidence of possession or use affects a substantial part of the period of prescription[3], but it has been held that a change in the mode of exercising the right during the period of prescription does not break the continuity of possession[4].

Prior to the Prescription and Limitation (Scotland) Act 1973 taking effect, the continuity of use required for prescription to operate could be broken either extra-judicially or judicially. Extra-judicial interruption took the form of natural interruption by adverse possession or civil interruption by notarial protest. Judicial interruption occurs when a servient proprietor institutes proceedings challenging the possession in question. The only form of interruption now operative is judicial[5]. As defined for this purpose, 'judicial interruption' involves a person who has a proper interest to do so[6] challenging the possession in appropriate proceedings[7]. The date of interruption is the date on which the claim is made[8], except in the case of arbitration, where, if the claim is stated in a preliminary notice[9], the date of service of that notice is the date of interruption[10]. Despite the demise of extra-judicial interruption, it must not be assumed that actions which formerly constituted natural interruption by adverse possession are now of no significance: adverse possession may, for example, lead to a perceptible break in the continuity of use or possession or give rise to a question whether the possession has, in fact, been peaceable[11]. While continuity of use is expressed as a legal requirement[12], it is not applied strictly and literally where the situation is such that the facility represented by the servitude right is one which would normally be used intermittently or at intervals[13].

Following the previous law, the Act requires that the possession founded upon be open and peaceable[14], a requirement traditionally embodied in the maxim *nec vi nec clam nec precario*. As well as being exercised without violence such as threatening behaviour or forced entry, the requisite possession or use must take place with the full knowledge of the quasi-servient owner and not stealthily, as by night. Possession or use must be as of right and not attributable to the consent or tolerance of the quasi-servient owner[15]: where, however, there has been long continued uninterrupted possession or use it is presumed to have been as of right[16]. It has been said that the acts of possession must be overt, in the sense that they must in themselves be of such character or be done in such circumstances as to indicate unequivocally to the proprietor of the servient tenement the fact that a right is asserted, and the nature of the right[17]. In one case where the drawing of water from a well was ascribed to tolerance and not to the exercise of a right it was observed that the assent of the quasi-servient proprietor could be attributed to the ordinary dictates of humanity rather than to considerations of neighbourliness, as might apply in the case of a road or path[18].

The Act makes clear that, like physical possession, civil possession on the part of the quasi-dominant owner is effective[19]. Thus anyone who is in possession of the quasi-dominant tenement may exercise or possess the servitude on the proprietor's behalf[20], but civil possession does not include use of facilities, such as an access, by occupants of neighbouring property[21].

Infeftment in the quasi-dominant tenement is no longer essential[22]. Since a servitude is an incorporeal right, the fact that the quasi-dominant proprietor has a bounding title — even without a clause of parts and pertinents — does not preclude his acquisition of a servitude by prescription[23].

It has been said obiter that:

> 'There ... ought to be a practical distinction recognised between the prescriptive possession which establishes a new and adverse right in the possessor, and the prescriptive possession which the law admits, for the purposes of construing and explaining, in a question with its author, the limits of an antecedent grant or conveyance. In the first case the rule obtains *tantum prescriptum quantum possessum*. In the second, ... a much more liberal effect has been given to partial acts of possession as evidencing proprietary possession of the whole, in cases where the subject of controversy has been in itself a distinct and definite tenement'[24].

This passage was approved in a case concerning a servitude for drainage[25]. In the particular circumstances, the rule *tantum prescriptum quantum possessum* was applied with the result that the prescriptive right to use a channel through the servient tenement for the disposal of waste water could not be extended to cover the disposal of sewage, solid or liquid: a fireclay drain installed by the dominant proprietor in compliance with sanitary requirements was thus an encroachment on the servient property which he could be required to remove[26]. On the other hand, where use over the prescriptive period has established as a servitude right a general facility such as a route for carts or vehicles, the scope of that right will not be restricted by reference to the purposes for which in the past the facility has been used unless it can be demonstrated from the character of the dominant tenement or the nature of the right that the servitude existed for a special or limited purpose[27]. The conception of a prescriptive servitude of way limited to agricultural or market garden purposes has been rejected as foreign to Scots law[28]. Again, it is not necessary that the full use of the servitude as claimed should have been made throughout the prescriptive period; actions consistent with the general nature of the right claimed may be sufficient for the purpose[29].

As an example of the operation of positive prescription, in construing and explaining the terms of a document on which a claim to a servitude is based, there may be mentioned a case decided in the eighteenth century in which the tolerance of a specific number of windows on the walls of a tenement was held to have been extended by long continued user to permit of a greater number than that specified in the document[30].

The provisions of the 1973 Act for the acquisition of servitudes and rights of way by the operation of positive prescription are made without prejudice to its provisions for the extinction of obligations by the long negative prescription[31].

1 Prescription and Limitation (Scotland) Act 1973 (c 52), s 3(1), (2).
2 *Harvie v Rodgers* (1828) 3 W & S 251, HL; *M'Gregor v Crieff Co-operative Society* 1915 SC (HL) 93, 1915 1 SLT 401.
3 *Carstairs v Spence* 1924 SC 380 at 389, per Lord President Clyde.
4 *Harper v Stuart* (1907) 15 SLT 550.
5 Prescription and Limitation (Scotland) Act 1973, s 3(1)(a), (2).
6 Ie an interest, normally of a proprietary nature, in the quasi-servient tenement.
7 Prescription and Limitation (Scotland) Act 1973, s 4(1). 'Appropriate proceedings' means (1) any proceedings in a court of competent jurisdiction in Scotland or elsewhere, except proceedings in the Court of Session by summons not subsequently called, or (2) any arbitration in Scotland, or (3) any arbitration elsewhere the award in which is enforceable in Scotland: s 4(2)(a)–(c).
8 Ibid, s 4(3)(b).
9 For the meaning of 'preliminary notice', see ibid, s 4(4).
10 Ibid, s 4(3)(a).
11 See D M Walker *The Law of Prescription and Limitation of Actions in Scotland* (3rd edn, 1981) p 38, referring to such cases of extra-judicial interruption as *Stevenson v Donaldson* 1935 SC 551, 1935 SLT 444. Cf the observations of Sheriff Younger in *Strathclyde (Hyndland) Housing Society Ltd v Cowie* 1983 SLT (Sh Ct) 61, a case concerning the application of the provisions of the Prescription and Limitation (Scotland) Act 1973 to a public right of way.
12 Ibid, s 3(1), (2).
13 See *Carstairs v Spence* 1924 SC 380 at 394, per Lord Blackburn, and *Scotland v Wallace* 1964 SLT (Sh Ct) 9.
14 Prescription and Limitation (Scotland) Act 1973, s 3(1)(a), (2).
15 *M'Inroy v Duke of Athole* (1891) 18 R (HL) 46. See also *Middletweed Ltd v Murray* 1989 SLT 11, OH.
16 *Grierson v Sandsting and Aithsting School Board* (1882) 9 R 437.
17 *M'Inroy v Duke of Athole* (1891) 18 R (HL) 46 at 48, per Lord Watson.
18 *Macnab v Munro Ferguson* (1890) 17 R 397 at 400, per Lord Justice-Clerk Macdonald.
19 Prescription and Limitation (Scotland) Act 1973, s 15(1) ('possession').
20 *Drummond v Milligan* (1890) 17 R 316.
21 *Earl of Morton v Stuart* (1813) 5 Pat 720, HL.
22 Prescription and Limitation (Scotland) Act 1973, s 3(4).
23 *Beaumont v Lord Glenlyon* (1843) 5 D 1337; *M'Donald v Dempster* (1871) 10 M 94 at 98, per Lord Neaves; *Troup v Aberdeen Heritable Securities and Investment Co Ltd* 1916 SC 918 at 929, 1916 2 SLT 136 at 143, per Lord Guthrie.
24 *Lord Advocate v Wemyss* (1899) 2 F (HL) 1 at 9, 7 SLT 172 at 175, per Lord Watson.
25 *Kerr v Brown* 1939 SC 140 at 147, per Lord Justice-Clerk Aitchison.
26 Other examples of the application of the rule include *Scouller v Robertson* (1829) 7 S 344 at 347, per Lord Pitmilly, and *J White & Sons v J and M White* (1905) 8 F (HL) 41 at 47, per Lord Watson.
27 *Carstairs v Spence* 1924 SC 380 at 386, per Lord President Clyde, referring to the early case of *Porteous v Allan* (1773) Mor 14512, where there was held to have been established by prescription a servitude restricted to the passage of sheep to and from a certain market.
28 See *Carstairs v Spence* 1924 SC 380 at 388, per Lord President Clyde. Cf *Swan v Buist* (1834) 12 S 316, and *Malcolm v Lloyd* (1886) 13 R 512.
29 *Carstairs v Spence* 1924 SC 380 at 394, per Lord Blackburn. See also the opinion of Lord President Clyde at 387.
30 *Forbes v Wilson* (1724) Mor 14505.
31 Prescription and Limitation (Scotland) Act 1973, s 3(5), referring to s 7.

461. Possessory rights arising from possession or use for less than the prescriptive period. The establishment of a servitude by prescription requires possession or exercise over the statutory prescriptive period[1]. On a common law basis, however, possession or exercise of the facilities involved in a positive servitude for some lesser period may entitle a party to what is known as a possessory right or remedy. This may enable him to retain, for the time being, the use of the facilities, but without prejudice to the right of the servient owner to rid himself of the burden on his property by an action of reduction or other competent process[2]. It has been considered an established rule that a party who has enjoyed peaceable possession of a right for as long as seven years is entitled to protection against summary inversion of the state of possession[3]. To justify such a possessory judgment, however, the claimant must have some form of title to the servitude right[4], although that title need not appear on the property register[5]. It can take the form of a bounding title which makes no reference to the servitude right claimed and has no clause of parts and pertinents[6].

1 See para 459 above.
2 *Maxwell v Maxwell* (1636) Mor 10639, a case of thirlage (for which see para 492 below) dealt with as a form of servitude. As to the seven-year possessory judgment generally, see para 146 above.
3 *Liston v Galloway* (1835) 14 S 97 at 99, per Lord Balgray. Cf *Drummond v Milligan* (1890) 17 R 316.
4 *Carson, Warren & Co v Miller* (1863) 1 M 604 at 611, per Lord Justice-Clerk Inglis, contrasting the position with that of servitudes unevidenced except by prescriptive possession.
5 See *Knox v Brand* (1827) 5 S 714 (NE 666), where the seven-year period was held to run from the date of the deed and not from that of a sasine following upon it.
6 *Liston v Galloway* (1835) 14 S 97, apparently overruling in this matter the earlier decision in *Saunders v Reid and Hunter* (1830) 8 S 505.

(e) Creation by Acquiescence

462. Acquiescence as a source of servitude rights. It has been seen that positive servitudes can originate from grant or reservation, express or implied, or from prescriptive possession. There remains the question whether, like certain other rights, positive servitudes can emerge on a basis of personal bar and at the same time be effective in questions with singular successors.

Reference has been made earlier to the possible effect of *rei interventus* or acquiescence in rendering a verbal agreement or improbative document effective to constitute a servitude[1]. The concern here, however, is with the situation where there is no express agreement in any form and the claim to the servitude is based solely on the actings of the parties which have not continued for sufficiently long to establish a prescriptive right to the servitude or, perhaps, even to justify a possessory judgment in favour of the quasi-dominant proprietor. As affecting servitudes, direct authority on this matter is lacking; however, applying principles recognised in other areas (where there has been neither a previous contract nor judicial proceedings), it seems clear that there must be something more than mere acquiescence before a claim to a servitude will succeed; in other words, there must be something capable of being construed as implied consent or permission followed by acts in the nature of *rei interventus*. It has been argued:

'Where great cost is incurred by operations carried on under the eye of one having a right to stop them; or where, under the eye and with the knowledge of him who has the adverse right, something is allowed to be done which manifestly cannot be undone, the law will presume an agreement or conventional permission as a fair ground of right'[2].

Thus, though the claim was rejected on other grounds in the case where those words of Bell were cited, it has been accepted that a servitude may under certain circumstances be established by acquiescence inferring a grant and creating a bar against its exercise being challenged by the party acquiescing and even, in some cases, by his singular successors[3].

Thus, for example, if it were proved that a landowner was aware that, in reliance on his assent, a pipe was being laid through his land for the benefit of a neighbouring property, he, and perhaps his singular successors, would be barred from objecting to the pipe remaining in that position and thus constituting, in effect, a servitude right[4]. In principle, acquiescence as a form of personal bar would leave singular successors unaffected[5], but a right of a permanent nature such as a servitude may be held to have been created when its exercise, as assented to by the servient owner, has involved substantial expenditure on the part of the dominant owner and the situation thus created is obvious to potential singular successors such as prospective purchasers of the servient tenement[6].

1 See para 450 above.
2 *Cowan v Lord Kinnaird* (1865) 4 M 236 at 243, 244, per Lord Justice-Clerk Inglis, citing Bell *Principles* s 946. Cf *Stirling v Haldane* (1829) 8 S 131, a case concerning the diversion of a watercourse.
3 *Macgregor v Balfour* (1899) 2 F 345 at 351, 352, 7 SLT 273 at 274, per Lord President Balfour. Cf *Bicket v Morris* (1866) 4 M (HL) 44 at 49, per Lord Chelmsford.
4 *Robson v Chalmers Property Investment Co Ltd* 1965 SLT 381, OH.
5 See *Brown v Baty* 1957 SC 351, 1957 SLT 336, OH.
6 *Bicket v Morris* (1866) 4 M (HL) 44; *Macgregor v Balfour* (1899) 2 F 345, 7 SLT 273; *More v Boyle* 1967 SLT (Sh Ct) 38.

(f) Creation under Statutory Authority

463. Statute as a source of servitude rights. Servitudes may come into existence by virtue of statutory provisions or by the exercise of statutory powers, particularly in connection with the compulsory acquisition of land[1]. However, it has been held in England that, in the absence of express provision, an acquiring authority cannot compel the grant of ancillary rights such as servitudes which did not previously exist over land other than that which it is acquiring[2]. The effect of a particular statutory provision may be to create by implication a servitude right as recognised at common law, but in many cases the rights created by statutory provisions, although similar in effect to servitudes, do not constitute servitudes in the strict and proper sense of the term[3].

1 As to compulsory acquisition, see generally COMPULSORY ACQUISITION AND COMPENSATION, vol 5, paras 1 ff.
2 *Sovmots Investments Ltd v Secretary of State for the Environment* [1979] AC 144, [1977] 2 All ER 385, HL. Lord Keith, at 184 and at 402, indicated that in Scotland the particular problem before the court, involving as it did a tenement property, would have been resolved by an application of the law of tenement. Cf *Re Metropolitan District Rly Co and Cosh* (1880) 13 Ch D 607, CA.
3 See *Central Regional Council v Ferns* 1979 SC 136, 1980 SLT 126, OH, where the Water (Scotland) Act 1946 (c 42), s 26 (now the Water (Scotland) Act 1980 (c 45), s 23: see WATER SUPPLY, vol 25, para 520) (power to lay mains etc), was held to have created by implication a servitude of aqueduct with consequent restrictions on the servient owner. As to rights of statutory origin similar to but not constituting servitudes, see para 493 below.

(4) RIGHTS AND DUTIES OF DOMINANT AND SERVIENT PROPRIETORS

(a) The Dominant Proprietor

464. Exercise of servitude rights. It is generally accepted that the dominant proprietor must exercise his servitude rights *civiliter*, that is, so as to cause the minimum of disturbance or inconvenience to the owners or occupiers of the servient tenement. He is not entitled to encroach on their exercise except in so far as necessary for the due exercise of the servitude right[1]. Thus it has been held that a right of access attaching by implication to the ownership of salmon fishings was restricted to non-vehicular use, being the form of use adequate for the beneficial enjoyment of the fishing right and at the same time least prejudicial to the interests of the servient proprietor[2]. The right of the dominant proprietor may be exercised by parties such as tenants or feuars in occupation of the dominant tenement or parts thereof, so long as this does not materially increase the burden on the servient tenement[3]. However, the servitude right must always be exercised solely for the benefit of the dominant tenement and may not be diverted or extended to benefit other properties or to achieve other purposes: it is inconsistent with the nature of a servitude that the dominant proprietor should have power to communicate its benefit to any third party[4]. Thus the extent of the servitude right to take turf for fuel or similar purposes is regulated by the proper and ordinary uses of the dominant tenement[5]. Rights of access granted in respect of one property cannot be used for the purpose of reaching some other property which the dominant proprietor happens to own[6]. There are, however, English decisions to the effect that the exercise of a servitude right for the benefit of the dominant tenement is not open to objection because it incidentally benefits other land belonging to the dominant proprietor or to some third party[7]. Again, it has been held in the House of Lords that a public or major road to which access is obtainable by the exercise of a servitude right should not be regarded as a contiguous tenement separate from the dominant tenement and generating additional and excessive traffic over the servient tenement[8]. In practice, it may be difficult to substantiate a challenge to the exercise of a servitude right, such as a right of access, solely on the ground that it is being used partly for purposes unconnected with the dominant tenement[9]. In such circumstances, however, the servient proprietor may be able to demonstrate an increase in the burden on his property to a level not contemplated in the right as constituted.

That ground of objection is, of course, always available to the servient proprietor should the circumstances justify it, and is likely to be invoked when there is some development such as a change of use affecting the dominant tenement. On this basis, it was held that a right of access to ground situated behind a house and garage could not be utilised for the purposes of a housing scheme subsequently erected on that ground[10]. Similarly, in an English case, it was held that a party who had reserved the right of access to a field on his farm over railway property was not entitled to have the right exercised for the purposes of a caravan park established on the field: however, the court indicated that to justify such an objection by a servient owner the increase of user must be such as to create a different or additional burden from that originally existing[11]. Again, the Scottish courts have refused to allow a servitude which involved receiving and carrying off waste water from a tenement to be extended to deal with the additional water resulting from the dominant proprietor erecting a distillery on his property[12].

The right to extract from a river water for a mill was held to be restricted to the quantity of water which the dominant proprietor had extracted during the prescriptive period over which the servitude right had been established. The concept of a mill as a growing concern with expanding requirements was said to have no place in the discussion with other riparian proprietors about a servitude constituted by use[13]. On the other hand, the conversion of a lint mill to a forge, which did not materially affect the demand for water, was held not to be objectionable in relation to a servitude right of aqueduct granted for the mill, the reference to the lint mill having been made for purposes of description and not as defining or limiting the purpose of the right[14]. But in a case decided in the eighteenth century, the dominant owner in a servitude of dam and aqueduct constituted by prescription was permitted to retain in use enlargements of the dam on the servient tenement[15]. These enlargements had been made to provide him with the quantity of water he required for draining his colliery. However, the process of enlargement had continued over a period of some forty years before it was challenged.

Accordingly, while the general rule remains that a dominant owner cannot enlarge his use or exercise of a servitude right so as to increase the burden on the servient tenement except in so far as such change may be necessary to make the servitude effective to the extent originally created[16], where a servitude has been constituted by prescription, it may be extended beyond its former usage to cover such use or development of use as may fairly be held to be involved in the possession proved[17].

A case for enlargement may arise by reason of irreversible physical changes for which neither party is responsible, such as the alteration of the course of a river or stream. Where the ground under a dam erected in exercise of a servitude right had been carried away by flood water, the dominant proprietor was held entitled to extend the dam to reach the new level of the ground[18]. But where a dominant proprietor, without making any averment of physical changes, proposed to deepen a drain of unspecified depth as installed in terms of a servitude right, on the plea that it did not effectively drain his property, he was refused permission to do so[19].

In determining the scope of servitude rights and the purposes for which they may be exercised, a distinction falls to be drawn between servitudes constituted in writing on the one hand and servitudes arising from prescriptive use on the other. While in the latter case the nature and extent of possession will always be significant, it has for long been established[20] and has recently been emphasised in the House of Lords that where the claim to a servitude right is based on writing its scope and availability must be determined, primarily at least, on the terms of that writing and without reference to such possession or use as has taken place[21].

1 *Rattray v Tayport Patent Slip Co* (1868) 5 SLR 219 at 220, per Lord Ardmillan; *Agnew v Lord Advocate* (1873) 11 M 309 at 333, per Lord Neaves; *Donaldson v Earl of Strathmore* (1877) 14 SLR 587.
2 *Middletweed Ltd v Murray* 1989 SLT 11, OH.
3 *Murdoch v Carstairs* (1823) 2 S 159 (NE 145); *Carstairs v Brown* (1829) 7 S 607. See also *Watson v Sinclair* 1966 SLT (Sh Ct) 77. Such parties cannot exercise the right concurrently with the dominant proprietor.
4 *Murray v Peebles Magistrates* 8 Dec 1808 FC. See also *Lord Blantyre v Dumbarton Water-Works Comrs* (1888) 15 R (HL) 56 at 64, per Lord Watson.
5 *Brown v Kinloch* (1775) Mor 14542. See also *Carstairs v Brown* (1829) 7 S 607, and *Watson v Sinclair* 1966 SLT (Sh Ct) 77.
6 *Stewart v Caithness* (1788) Hume 731; *Scott v Bogle* 6 July 1809 FC; *Anstruther v Caird* (1861) 24 D 149; *Irvine Knitters Ltd v North Ayrshire Co-operative Society Ltd* 1978 SC 109, 1978 SLT 105. Cf *Harris v Flower* (1904) 74 LJ Ch 127, CA. See also *Farquharson v Byres* (1866) 1 SLR 268, HL, where the principle adopted in these cases was accepted although a different result was arrived at on the basis of the terms of a decree arbitral.
7 *Simpson v Godmanchester Corpn* [1897] AC 696, HL. Cf *Williams v James* (1867) LR 2 CP 577.
8 *Alvis v Harrison* 1991 SLT 64, HL.
9 See *Irvine Knitters Ltd v North Ayrshire Co-operative Society Ltd* 1978 SC 109, 1978 SLT 105.
10 See *Keith v Texaco Ltd* 1977 SLT (Lands Trib) 16, founding on Bell *Principles* ss 986, 988.
11 *British Railways Board v Glass* [1965] Ch 538 at 567, 568, [1964] 3 All ER 418 at 432, CA, per Davies LJ.
12 *Scouller v Robertson* (1829) 7 S 344.
13 *J White & Sons v J and M White* (1905) 8 F (HL) 41 at 47, 13 SLT 655 at 657, per Lord Robertson.
14 *Hay v Robertson* (1845) 17 SJ 186.
15 *Dalrymple v Bruce* (1741) Elchies 'Servitude' 2.
16 Bell *Principles* s 988.
17 Erskine *Institute* II,9,4; J Rankine *The Law of Land-ownership in Scotland* (4th edn, 1909) pp 50, 51.
18 *Laird of Gairlton v Laird of Stevenson* (1677) Mor 14536.
19 *Dunbar Magistrates v Sawers* (1829) 7 S 672. See also *M'Culloch v Dumfries and Maxwelltown Water-Works Comrs* (1863) 1 M 334, where in special circumstances the quantity of water drawn under a servitude right was allowed to be increased on payment of compensation.
20 See *Gibb v Bruce* (1837) 16 S 169.
21 *Alvis v Harrison* 1991 SLT 64, HL.

465. The effect of division of the dominant tenement. A question on which clear authority seems to be lacking is whether, and to what extent, a dominant tenement may be split up and disposed of in parts with the servitude right remaining available to all or some of those parts. Where the proprietor of a moss had feued part of his land, giving the vassal a servitude right to cut peat for fuel for himself and for sale, it was held that the vassal could not communicate this right to tenants or sub-feuars of the land to which the privilege attached[1]. However, the court indicated that a less restrictive ruling might be appropriate in relation to other servitude rights whose nature suggested that the benefit should be shared[2]. Once again, the extent to which the change or development increases the burden on the servient tenement would seem to be the determining factor. In practice the matter is likely to arise in the context of servitude rights of access. The division of the dominant tenement in a development such as a housing scheme will clearly increase the burden on the servient tenement beyond what its owner can be required to accept unless it can be said that such a development was within the contemplation of the parties when the servitude right was created[3]. On the other hand, the division of a single residential property into two or perhaps three parts might, in certain circumstances at least, not be regarded as materially increasing the burden represented by a servitude right of access over another property[4].

1   *Carstairs v Brown* (1829) 7 S 607.
2   *Carstairs v Brown* (1829) 7 S 607 at 610, per Lord Pitmilly, referring to shooting or walking.
3   *Keith v Texaco Ltd* 1977 SLT (Lands Trib) 16; *Alba Homes Ltd v Duell* 1993 SLT (Sh Ct) 49. See also para 475 below.
4   See para 475 below. For the comparable rule in the case of real burdens, see para 409 above.

466. Responsibility for maintenance etc. The owner of the dominant tenement must take any action necessary to maintain in operation the facilities derived from a positive servitude; the owner of the servient tenement is under no obligation to do so. For this purpose, the dominant owner is entitled to access to the servient tenement, but he is responsible for any damage that may be caused by his operations thereon[1]. In the case of a servitude right of access by means of a road, the dominant proprietor has been held entitled to carry out the repairs necessary for its use by any permissible form of traffic[2]. But he is not entitled, without the consent of the servient proprietor, to change the levels of or otherwise alter the nature of the access roadway to the prejudice of the servient tenement[3]. When plant, apparatus or other *opus manufactum* has been installed, as in a servitude of aqueduct, there is an obligation on the dominant proprietor to maintain the installation so that damage to the servient tenement or any other property caused, for instance, by flooding or overflowing of water, does not occur[4]. While such an obligation is sometimes made an express condition of the servitude as constituted in writing, it is in any event a condition which must be complied with by the dominant owner so long as he exercises the servitude right[5]. In the absence of express stipulation, however, a dominant owner cannot be compelled to take steps to remedy defects which affect the exercise of the servitude right but do not damage or endanger property: should a servient owner wish such defects remedied, he must take the necessary action himself[6]. In some cases the necessary action will be located on the dominant as opposed to the servient tenement: when carrying out such work on his own property, the dominant proprietor must ensure that his operations do not materially increase the burden affecting the servient tenement[7].

While as a general rule a dominant owner will be free to discontinue or renounce a servitude right at any time, he is obliged, in the absence of express provision to the contrary, to restore the *status quo* on the servient tenement as existing when the servitude was created and remove any installations made for the purposes of the servitude right[8].

1 *Preston's Trustees v Preston* (1860) 22 D 366. Cf *Laird of Gairlton v Laird of Stevenson* (1677) Mor 14536.
2 *Smith v Saxton* 1928 SN 59, OH.
3 See *Stevenson v Biggart* (1867) 3 SLR 184, where the rights of the dominant proprietor in a servitude right of access are considered in some detail. The decision in the case is cited with approval in *Alvis v Harrison* 1991 SLT 64, HL, where the holder of a servitude right of access was held entitled to carry out certain constructional work on the access way.
4 *Parsons of Dundee v Inglish* (1687) Mor 14521; *Gray v Maxwell* (1762) Mor 12800; *Scottish Highland Distillery Co v Reid* (1877) 4 R 1118.
5 See *Tennant v Napier Smith's Trustees* (1888) 15 R 671, confirming that a singular successor exercising the servitude right would come under such an obligation. Cf W M Gloag *The Law of Contract* (2nd edn, 1929) p 232.
6 *Carlile v Douglas* (1731) Mor 14524.
7 *Young v Cuddie* (1831) 9 S 500, which concerned the rebuilding of a tenement as affecting a servitude *oneris ferendi* (see para 484 below).
8 *Bridges v Lord Saltoun* (1873) 11 M 588; *Macdonald v Inverness Magistrates* 1918 SC 141, 1918 1 SLT 51.

467. Dominant owners with a common servient tenement. Similar questions to those arising between dominant and servient proprietors may arise between parties who as dominant proprietors hold servitude rights over the same servient tenement. Such parties are regarded as sharing a common interest in the servient tenement. Accordingly, none may take any action in relation to the servient tenement which would prejudice the enjoyment of the rights of the other dominant proprietors. In practice, if not in principle, this places a greater measure of restraint on dominant proprietors than the existence of a servitude right places on the servient proprietor in his use and enjoyment of his property[1].

1 *Bennett v Playfair* (1877) 4 R 321; *Taylor's Trustees v M'Gavigan* (1896) 23 R 945 at 952 per Lord President Robertson, and at 954 per Lord M'Laren. See also para 362 above.

(b) The Servient Proprietor

468. Freedom from positive obligations. Because of the passive nature of a servitude right, in a question with the dominant owner the owner of the servient tenement has no responsibility for maintaining the land which is subject to the servitude nor any installations on it. Before he would have any maintenance obligations there would have to be express provision to that effect; and before such an obligation could affect singular successors it would have to be constituted as a real burden or condition[1].

1 *Allan v MacLachlan* (1900) 7 SLT 427.

469. Retention of rights of ownership. In general, the servient owner is free to exercise fully his rights of ownership, except in so far as these require to be restricted for the purposes of the servitude right[1]. Thus the servient owner may make changes or carry out operations on his property, provided they are not prejudicial to the exercise of the servitude right; the onus rests on the dominant proprietor to show that the actions of the servient owner constitute an infringement of the servitude right[2]. For example, in a servitude of feal and divot[3], the servient owner was held entitled to restrict the area over which the servitude could be exercised to such part of the muir as would be sufficient for the purposes of the dominant proprietor[4]. Again, in the case of a servitude for the watering of cattle, the servient owner was permitted to cover the watercourse leaving only sufficient open for a reasonable exercise of the servitude right[5].

The effect on servitude rights of changes made by the servient owner on his own property arises particularly in the context of rights of way or passage. In one case, the substitution of a more circuitous route for the existing one was sanctioned by the court subject to the route adopted being adjusted to meet the mutual convenience of the parties[6]. Such diversions or alterations may be permissible when the servitude is established by possession or results from implication or, while expressly constituted, is in fairly general or indefinite terms. On the other hand, a servitude expressly constituted in precise form represents a contract between the respective parties which requires to be implemented in accordance with its terms. Thus, the court declined to sanction the diversion of an access route which, according to the constituting deed, was to be by way of a certain passage, precisely described: the dominant proprietor was held entitled to insist on compliance with the terms of the grant, irrespective of considerations of convenience[7]. Again, when the titles of a house provided for access by means of a certain close which from time immemorial had been of certain dimensions, the house owner was held entitled to object to structural alterations to adjoining buildings reducing the width of the close, the court drawing a distinction between a right of passage over some vacant ground and a right of access by means of a specific passage[8].

1 *Earl of Morton v Covingtree* (1760) Mor 13528; *Craig v Gould* (1861) 24 D 20.
2 *Crichton v Turnbull* 1946 SC 52, 1946 SLT 156, where it was held that this onus had not been discharged.
3 As to feal and divot, see para 489 below.
4 *Watson v Dunkennan Feuars* (1667) Mor 14529. Cf *Leslie v Cumming* (1793) Mor 14542, where it was held that the extent of the servitude is regulated by the proper and ordinary uses of the dominant tenement.
5 *Beveridge v Marshall* 18 Nov 1808 FC.
6 *Macdonald v Farquharson* (1833) 6 SJ 100. See also *Bruce v Wardlaw* (1748) Mor 14525 and *Ross v Ross* (1751) Mor 14531. The matter is further discussed in the context of the servitude of way or passage in para 487 below.
7 *Moyes v M'Diarmid* (1900) 2 F 918, 7 SLT 378. Cf *Hill v Maclaren* (1879) 6 R 1363. *Per contra*, see *Thomson's Trustees v Findlay* (1898) 25 R 407, 5 SLT 268, referred to in *Moyes v M'Diarmid* as a case decided on its own particular facts.
8 *Grigor v Maclean* (1896) 24 R 86 at 89, per Lord Justice-Clerk Macdonald.

(5) RESTRICTION, SUSPENSION AND EXTINCTION OF SERVITUDE RIGHTS

(a) Express Writing

470. Discharge of servitudes. An express provision for the limitation or termination of the exercise of a servitude right must be in probative writing[1]. While not essential, it is desirable that the relative deed should be in a form suitable to enter the property register for each tenement, particularly if the constitution of the servitude right appears on the register[2]. While the deed should be granted by a person infeft in the dominant tenement, accretion would apparently operate to validate the grant by an uninfeft proprietor on his subsequently completing his title[3]. Where heritable securities affect the dominant tenement, the consent of the creditors should be taken. It has been suggested that the consent of any tenants of the dominant tenement should be obtained[4], but presumably this will apply only if the restriction or extinction of the servitude right would affect the tenant's interest[5].

1 Styles of deed customarily adopted will be found in 8 *Encyclopaedia of Scottish Legal Styles* pp 384–386, J Burns *Conveyancing Practice* (4th edn, 1957 by F MacRitchie) p 432, and J M Halliday *Conveyancing Law and Practice in Scotland* vol II (1986) para 20-33, but there is no settled or required

form of documentation in this matter. A discharge of a positive servitude for payment of a consideration attracts conveyance on sale stamp duty on the consideration if not within the exemption limits, but not so a discharge of a negative servitude.

2 As to the practice in this matter, particularly where registration of title is operative, see *Halliday* vol II, para 20-34.

3 As is the position with a grant of servitude: see para 449 above.

4 *Burns* p 432.

5 Clearly a tenant, even if holding under a long lease or having statutory security of tenure, could not, without his landlord's consent, discharge or renounce a servitude right: see *Macdonald v Macdonald* (1960) 48 SLCR 22.

(b) Operation of Negative Prescription

471. Negative prescription as affecting positive and negative servitudes respectively. Whether positive or negative, a servitude may be extinguished by the operation of negative prescription. In the case of a positive servitude, this arises where the dominant proprietor has failed throughout the prescriptive period to possess the servitude by exercising his rights under it[1]. In the case of a negative servitude, the enjoyment of which involves no physical possession, it is extinguished when the servient proprietors have continued to disregard the restrictions imposed for the prescriptive period[2].

1 *Graham v Douglas* (1735) Mor 10745. See also *Walker's Executrix v Carr* 1973 SLT (Sh Ct) 77.

2 *Wilkie v Scot* (1688) Mor 11189, a case of building in contravention of a servitude *non altius tollendi*.

472. The statutory provisions. The extinction of servitudes by negative prescription is now regulated by the Prescription and Limitation (Scotland) Act 1973[1]. As in the case of positive prescription, the Act reduces the period of prescription from forty to twenty years[2]. For the purpose of the relevant provisions, the duty of the servient proprietor to permit the exercise of the rights involved in a positive servitude, or to comply with the restrictions imposed by a negative servitude, is regarded as an obligation co-relative to the right belonging to the dominant proprietor[3]. Sections 6 and 7 of the Act deal with the extinction of obligations by prescription. While servitudes are excluded from the application of the five-year prescription under section 6[4], they are subject to the long negative or twenty-years prescription in terms of section 7[5]. As applicable to servitudes, its effect is that if, after the date when the servitude right became enforceable, it has subsisted for a continuous period of twenty years unexercised or unenforced and has not been relevantly claimed or acknowledged, then the servitude right is extinguished as from the expiration of that period[6].

In the case of a positive servitude, the period will run from the last date on which the dominant proprietor exercised his rights or from the date when the servitude became operative if these rights have never been exercised. In the case of a negative servitude, the period will run from the date on which the servient proprietor first committed a breach of the restrictions imposed[7]. A relevant claim is one made by or on behalf of the dominant proprietor in appropriate proceedings[8] for implement of the servient proprietors' obligations[9]. A relevant acknowledgment may take the form of an unequivocal written admission by or on behalf of the servient proprietor clearly acknowledging that the servitude right subsists[10]. Alternatively, the acknowledgment may be implied from the actings of the servient proprietor which, in the case of a positive servitude, would involve permitting the exercise by the dominant proprietor of his rights, and in the case of a negative servitude complying with or ceasing to disregard the restrictions it imposes[11]. Contracting out of the statutory provisions for negative prescription is not permissible[12], and the prescription will operate despite the disclosure of the servitude in the titles of the dominant tenement and/or the servient tenement[13].

1 The notes on this topic which follow refer to provisions of the Prescription and Limitation (Scotland) Act 1973 (c 52), reflecting the recommendations in *Reform of the Law relating to Prescription and Limitation of Actions* (Scot Law Com no. 15) (1970).
2 Prescription and Limitation (Scotland) Act 1973, s 7(1). Allowance for minority or other legal disability is excluded: s 14(1)(b).
3 See ibid, ss 10(4), 15(2).
4 See ibid, s 6(2), Sch 1, para 2(a).
5 Ibid, s 7(1). In D M Walker *Principles of Scottish Private Law* (4th edn) vol 3 (1989), pp 204, 354, in D M Walker *The Law of Prescription and Limitation of Actions in Scotland* (3rd edn, 1981) p 68, and in J M Halliday *Conveyancing Law and Practice in Scotland* vol II (1986) para 20-29, the view is taken that the Prescription and Limitation (Scotland) Act 1973, s 8, contains the provisions of the Act applicable to the negative prescription of servitudes. That view would, however, appear to be inconsistent with the reference in Sch 1, para 2(e), to 'an obligation to recognise a servitude', and again with s 3(5), declaring the provisions of s 3 (which concern the positive prescription of servitudes and public rights of way) to be without prejudice to the operation of s 7. While the same prescriptive period applies under ss 7 and 8, the application of s 8 would have the result that the provisions of s 10 concerning the acknowledgment of obligations or rights would not apply to servitudes.
6 Ibid, s 7(1). As to relevant claims and acknowledgments, see below.
7 As to the precise computation of the period in particular circumstances, see ibid, s 14.
8 For the meaning of 'appropriate proceedings', see ibid, s 4(2), and para 460, note 7, above. That definition is applied by s 9(4).
9 Ibid, s 9(1). Section 9(3) deals with the case, perhaps unlikely to arise in relation to a servitude, where the claim is made in arbitration proceedings.
10 Ibid, s 10(1)(b).
11 Ibid, s 10(1)(a), (4).
12 Ibid, s 13.
13 *Graham v Douglas* (1735) Mor 10745.

473. Exclusion of servitudes from category of *res merae facultatis*. Some

doubt appears to have existed as to whether a servitude can, in any circumstances, constitute *res merae facultatis* unaffected by negative prescription[1]. The right to open a door on to a common stair in a tenement has been treated as being in that position, but this was stated not to be a servitude[2]. On the other hand, in a case where it was regarded as implied that a right of access expressly granted was not to be exercised until some future date when occasion arose, the right, although of the nature of a servitude, was held to be in effect *res merae facultatis*[3]. As a general rule, however, the negative prescription applies to servitudes distinguishing them in this respect from rights of a proprietary nature. Thus, while a right of pasturage which a superior reserved to himself in feuing his land was regarded as a reservation of property *pro tanto* and so not subject to extinction by non-use, a similar right constituted in favour of a third party would have been regarded as an accessory to — as opposed to a part of — that party's property, and as a servitude would have been subject to negative prescription[4]. With the period of negative prescription reduced to twenty years, it may be advisable to have the grant of a servitude, of which immediate or early use is not contemplated, made on the basis that the dominant proprietor's rights will not be exercisable until some future date, event or development[5].

1 See the Prescription and Limitation (Scotland) Act 1973 (c 52), Sch 3, referred to in s 7(2).
2 *Gellatly v Arrol* (1863) 1 M 592 at 600 per Lord Cowan, and at 602 per Lord Neaves.
3 *Smith v Stewart* (1884) 11 R 921.
4 *Graham v Douglas* (1735) Mor 10745. See also *Brown v Carron Co* 1909 SC 452, 1909 1 SLT 8, where it was held that thirlage (as to which see para 492 below), regarded for this purpose as a quasi-servitude, was extinguished by the operation of negative prescription.

5 *Smith v Stewart* (1884) 11 R 921. However, an arrangement as flexible as existed there may not often be acceptable in practice.

(c) Implication from Actings of Parties

474. Actings which may affect servitude rights. There is authority to the effect that servitude rights which depend not on any deed or instrument, but were established by possession or use, may be extinguished by non-use for a period less than that of the negative prescription. However, the cases generally founded on for this proposition were decided before the period of negative prescription was reduced from forty to twenty years, and proceed on a period of disuse of upwards of twenty years[1]. It does not therefore necessarily follow that the same ruling would apply to periods such as ten or fifteen years, even if the evidence of intention to abandon were reasonably clear.

The cases to which reference has been made are instances of prolonged failure by a dominant proprietor to exercise his rights under a positive servitude. The extinction or restriction of servitude rights — positive or negative — may, however, result from the actings of servient proprietors, or someone representing or deriving right from them, which have been acquiesced in by the dominant proprietor. Thus a servitude *non aedificandi* which constitutes a restriction on building on the servient tenement may be regarded as extinguished when substantial expense is incurred in the erection of buildings in contravention of its terms with the knowledge and assent, at least implied, of the dominant proprietor[2]. Further, a singular successor in the dominant tenement who is aware when acquiring the property of the existence of such buildings will not be entitled to insist on their removal to comply with the servitude right[2]. In such cases, however, the position may be different if the party acting in contravention of the servitude right was aware of its existence and should have appreciated the effect of his actings on the interests of the dominant proprietor[3]. In some cases the acquiescence will not involve the complete extinction of the servitude right but will bring about some restriction or other change in its effect. In one case where the erection of a building with the knowledge and consent of the dominant proprietor had narrowed the passage in respect of which there was an express servitude right of access, the servitude right was held to have been reduced from a cart track to a footpath[4]. In another case it was held that acquiescence in the erection of a building which obstructed a right of passage was conditional on the provision of a substituted passage from the use of which the dominant proprietor could not be excluded[5]. It is, however, not always essential, in order to keep a servitude in force in accordance with the terms in which it has been created, that it should be constantly exercised to its full extent. A right of pasturage was held not be have been restricted and reduced because it was not being exercised during certain months of the year when the dominant proprietor had other facilities available[6].

1 *Hill v Ramsay* (1810) 5 Pat 299, HL; *Douglas v Hozier* (1878) 16 SLR 14, OH; *Rutherglen Magistrates v Bainbridge* (1886) 13 R 745 at 748, per Lord Young. *Per contra*, see the early case of *Beaton v Ogilvie* (1670) Mor 10912, where actings in contravention of the servitude right were held not to extinguish the right as their duration fell short of the forty-years period of negative prescription then in force.
2 *Muirhead v Glasgow Highland Society* (1864) 2 M 420. See also paras 427, 428, above (real burdens).
3 *Tennant's Trustees v Dennistoun* (1894) 2 SLT 78.
4 *Millar v Christie* 1960 SC 1, 1961 SLT 154. Cf *Stewart v Bunten* (1878) 5 R 1108, a case concerning a building restriction in the form of a real burden, to which Lord President Clyde refers in *Millar v Christie* 1960 SC 1 at 6, 7, 1961 SLT 154 at 157.
5 *Davidson v Thomson* (1890) 17 R 287.
6 *Monro v Mackenzie* (1760) Mor 14533.

(d) Change of Circumstances

475. Physical changes affecting either tenement. Physical changes in either the dominant or the servient tenement may affect the subsistence of servitude rights. While a permanent change in the physical condition of the servient tenement could, if great enough, extinguish the servitude, a temporary change, such as the growth of heather on a moor, would not do so[1]. Clearly, the complete destruction of either tenement must put an end to a servitude right. For this purpose, the destruction of buildings in existence when the servitude was created will in some cases be sufficient. Thus a right of access to a theatre was held to have terminated when the theatre was destroyed by fire: it was not therefore available for the benefit of any building which might be erected to replace the theatre[2]. Less fundamental changes can have the same effect where the servitude right has been constituted for some special purpose. The opinion has been expressed that a servitude right of way to a mill for the purpose of conveying grain would come to an end if the mill ceased to be used for this purpose[3]. A right of access over an adjacent farm, conferred by title deeds on feuars to enable them to maintain a boundary wall, was held to have become inoperative when the extension of a building made such maintenance unnecessary: moreover it would remain inoperative so long as the extension existed[4]. In a case concerning the scope of a servitude right of access as established by prescription, it was said that it was open to the proprietor of the servient tenement to demonstrate, either from the character of the dominant tenement or from the nature of the right as evidenced by prescriptive user, that the servitude existed for a special and limited purpose other than that of ordinary ish and entry, and would be extinguished on the disappearance of that purpose[5]. However, in relation to servitudes such as rights of access, such a limitation or purpose will not be inferred but must be established either from the terms of the document constituting the servitude right or from the nature of its use if it depends on prescription[6]. A servitude right established by implication on the basis of necessity or the convenient enjoyment of the dominant tenement will be extinguished on the creation or emergence of other comparable facilities available to the dominant proprietor. While the division of the servient tenement into parts has no effect on a servitude right[7], the effect of the division of the dominant tenement[8] is a matter on which there is a lack of definite authority. The effect of such a division may differ according to the nature of the servitude right involved; but it would appear that in the absence of any material increase in the burden on the servient tenement there is no reason why a servitude should not be transmissible, either to a number of part successors or to one part successor to the exclusion of others. The particular nature of the right may tie it to a certain part of the original dominant tenement, for example where a right of way is of use to only one of the divided parts or a servitude restricting building has no relevance to certain parts. Again, there may be circumstances in which the absence of any subsisting interest on the part of the dominant proprietor renders a servitude right inoperative. It would appear, however, that so long as the right confers a benefit on some part or parts of the dominant tenement, it can be transmitted so as to be exercisable in respect of such part or parts.

1 *Ferguson v Tennant* 1978 SC (HL) 19 at 69, 1978 SLT 165 at 181, per Lord Fraser of Tullybelton. See also para 434 above (real burdens).
2 *Scott v Howard* (1880) 7 R 997, affd (1881) 8 R (HL) 59.
3 *Winans v Lord Tweedmouth* (1888) 15 R 540 at 568, per Lord Mure.
4 *Gray v MacLeod* 1979 SLT (Sh Ct) 17.
5 *Carstairs v Spence* 1924 SC 380 at 393, per Lord Skerrington, referring to the early case of *Porteous v Allan* (1773) Mor 14512, which concerned a drove road for sheep.
6 *Carstairs v Spence* 1924 SC 380 at 388, per Lord Clyde.
7 *Grierson v Sandsting and Aithsting School Board* (1882) 9 R 437.

8 This has already been referred to in relation to the rights of dominant proprietors: see para 465 above.

476. Dominant and servient tenements coming into single ownership. A change of circumstances which inevitably affects a servitude right is when the dominant and servient tenements come into single ownership. Here the maxim *nemo res sua servit*[1] operates to extinguish the right *confusione*, except where the respective subjects are owned in different capacities, for example trustee and beneficial owner or, in former times, heir of entail and proprietor in fee simple. In these exceptional cases the operation of the servitude will merely be suspended pending some further change of ownership[2].

The question whether, when extinction *confusione* has taken place, a subsequent separation of the two tenements results in servitudes, formerly operative, coming into existence again without requiring to be constituted *de novo* has already been discussed in connection with the creation of servitudes by implication[3]..

1 See para 443 above.
2 *Donaldson's Trustees v Forbes* (1839) 1 D 449. See also *Union Bank of Scotland v Daily Record (Glasgow)* (1902) 10 SLT 71, OH, where it was indicated that revival without reconstitution had not been applied to negative servitudes.
3 See para 453 above.

(e) Statutory Provisions or Powers

(A) THE LANDS TRIBUNAL FOR SCOTLAND

477. Jurisdiction and powers of the Lands Tribunal for Scotland. Servitudes are rights enforceable by proprietors of land against the proprietors of other land: they therefore fall within the category of 'land obligation' as defined in the Conveyancing and Feudal Reform (Scotland) Act 1970[1]. The provisions of this Act apply whether the servitude is constituted in writing, is recorded or unrecorded, or is created by other means such as prescription[2]. Accordingly, any servitude is subject to variation or discharge by the Lands Tribunal for Scotland on the application of the servient owner as the 'burdened proprietor'[3] on the ground:
(1) that by reason of changes in the character of the land which the servitude affects or of the neighbourhood or other material circumstances it has become unreasonable or inappropriate; or
(2) that it is unduly burdensome compared with the benefits it confers; or
(3) that its existence is impeding some reasonable use of the land[4].
The dominant owner, as 'benefited proprietor'[5], receives notice of the application and is entitled to oppose it[6]. In the case of a servitude created by a written document, an application to the tribunal may not be made until two years have elapsed since the execution of the document[7].

The tribunal's decision is subject to review by the Court of Session on a point of law[8]. In the event of its varying or discharging a servitude, the tribunal is empowered to award monetary compensation to the dominant proprietor for any substantial loss or disadvantage thus caused to him or to compensate him for any effect which, at the time it was created, the servitude had in reducing the consideration paid for the servient tenement[9]. The tribunal may refuse to discharge or vary a servitude if it considers that, as a result of exceptional circumstances related to amenity or otherwise, money would not be adequate compensation for any resulting loss or disadvantage[10]. The tribunal also has power to add or substitute provisions — not being awards of money otherwise than as compensation — if this appears reasonable and is acceptable to the applicant: the tribunal may make the acceptance of such provisions a condition of the exercise of its power to vary or discharge the servitude[11]. Except in these circumstances, the tribunal has no power to create new conditions affecting either of the parties to the application or any other landowner[12]. The orders of the tribunal when recorded for publication are binding on all persons having interests[13]. Orders of the tribunal affecting servitude rights should be recorded in the General Register of Sasines or registered in the Land Register for Scotland as the case may be, whether or not the servitude rights affected appear on either register.

 1 Conveyancing and Feudal Reform (Scotland) Act 1970 (c 35), s 1(2).
 2 For the meaning of 'interest in land', see ibid, s 2(6).
 3 Ibid, s 2(6) ('burdened proprietor'). As to the constitution, functions and jurisdiction of the Lands Tribunal for Scotland, see COURTS AND COMPETENCY, vol 6, paras 1139 ff. As to its jurisdiction in relation to land obligations, see vol 6, para 1142.
 4 Conveyancing and Feudal Reform (Scotland) Act 1970, s 1(3)(a)–(c).
 5 Ibid, s 2(6) ('benefited proprietor').
 6 Ibid, s 2(1), (2).
 7 Ibid, s 2(5).
 8 Tribunals and Inquiries Act 1992 (c 53), s 11(1), (7)(a), (b), Sch 1, para 54.
 9 Conveyancing and Feudal Reform (Scotland) Act 1970, s 1(4). See also para 478, note 5, below.
10 Ibid, s 1(4).
11 Ibid, s 1(5).
12 See *Murrayfield Ice Rink Ltd v Scottish Rugby Union* 1973 SLT 99 at 106, 107, per Lord Justice-Clerk Grant.
13 Conveyancing and Feudal Reform (Scotland) Act 1970, s 2(4) (amended by the Land Tenure Reform (Scotland) Act 1974 (c 38), s 19).

478. Tribunal decisions concerning servitudes. Most of the cases coming before the Lands Tribunal for Scotland under the provisions relating to servitudes[1] have concerned feuing or building provisions in the form of real burdens or conditions. These are discussed elsewhere[2]. As yet there have been few instances of the tribunal's jurisdiction being invoked in respect of servitudes.

In one case a servitude right of access and egress was reserved by the National Coal Board when disponing to building contractors the property subsequently acquired by the applicant, and retaining adjacent land[3]. The National Coal Board subsequently sold the adjacent land to a local doctor for the purposes of a surgery, and the doctor had formed thereon an access for pedestrian and vehicular traffic. As a result, only limited use was being made of the servitude right of access. In these circumstances the tribunal considered that by reason of changes in the character of the neighbourhood, the servitude right had become unreasonable and inappropriate. Claims for compensation by the doctor and the building contractor were rejected by the tribunal; in the doctor's case, because he had suffered no loss by being deprived of such legitimate use of the servitude right as was being made, and in the contractor's case, because there was no evidence that the existence of the servitude right had affected the price paid for the land[5].

In another case, an application for the discharge of a servitude right of access which could have been impeded by the erection of an ash bin shelter was refused by the tribunal on the ground that, while the erection of the ash bin shelter represented a reasonable use of the property, it could be so sited as to leave the access right unaffected[6].

In the most recently reported case the tribunal was asked to discharge a servitude right of access over ground belonging to two adjoining owners, and a right of use as a play area of ground belonging to one of the owners[7]. The tribunal granted the application in respect of the play area which was unused and undeveloped, but refused it in respect of the access right, which was conceived in the interests of a substantial number of people, some of whom were in fact using it. The applicants' intention being simply to enclose the ground with their adjoining property, no reasonable use was being prevented by the existence of the access, and the tribunal rejected as affecting matters outwith its jurisdiction the applicants' argument based on considerations of safety at the junction of the access with a major road.

1 See para 477 above.
2 See CONVEYANCING, vol 6, paras 511 ff.
3 *Devlin v Conn* 1972 SLT (Lands Trib) 11.
4 See the Conveyancing and Feudal Reform (Scotland) Act 1970 (c 35), s 1(3)(a), and head (1) in para 477 above.
5 The tribunal doubted whether an award could have been made when the original seller was no longer owner of the dominant tenement.
6 *Orsi v McCallum* 1980 SLT (Lands Trib) 2.
7 *Spafford v Brydon* 1991 SLT (Lands Trib) 49.

(B) OTHER STATUTORY PROVISIONS OR POWERS

479. Instances of statutory provisions affecting servitudes. Provisions in either public or private Acts may have the effect of extinguishing servitude rights or restricting their operation[1]. Only a brief reference to this matter can be made in this title.

In the absence of any saving provisions in the relevant statutes, where land is acquired compulsorily its acquisition results in the extinction of all servitude rights[2], at least in so far as their continued existence could conflict with the statutory purposes of the acquisition[3]. Various statutes make express provision for the extinction of such rights or enable them to be overridden by parties such as public authorities holding special powers[4]. In all cases of compulsory acquisition, and also in cases where bodies having compulsory powers acquire land by agreement[5], the proprietor of the dominant tenement will be entitled as holder of a servitude right to claim compensation for any loss he can be shown to have sustained[6], the amount of such compensation, as payable by the acquirers, being determined, failing agreement, by the Lands Tribunal for Scotland[7]. It has been held that an acquiring authority is not entitled to reduce its liability for compensation by accepting restrictions on the use of the land acquired, for the benefit of the former owner's adjoining property[8].

1 Certain of these provisions are discussed in detail under titles in this encyclopaedia such as COMPULSORY ACQUISITION AND COMPENSATION, vol 5, paras 86, 87, 115.
2 *Oban Town-Council v Callander and Oban Rly Co* (1892) 19 R 912; *MacGregor v North British Rly Co* (1893) 20 R 300; *Largs Hydropathic Ltd v Largs Town Council* 1967 SC 1, 1967 SLT 23. See also *Great Western Rly Co v Swindon and Cheltenham Extension Rly Co* (1884) 9 App Cas 787, HL.
3 See J Burns *Conveyancing Practice* (4th edn, 1957 by F MacRitchie) p 427, referring by analogy to *Edinburgh Magistrates v North British Rly Co* (1904) 6 F 620, 12 SLT 20, cited in para 449, note 14, above.
4 See eg the New Towns (Scotland) Act 1968 (c 16), s 19, the Town and Country Planning (Scotland) Act 1972 (c 52), ss 108, 117, and the Housing (Scotland) Act 1987 (c 26), s 95(2), Sch 8, para 9(4).
5 See *Burns* p 427, referring to *Kirby v Harrogate School Board* [1896] 1 Ch 437, CA.
6 See *Edinburgh School Board v Simpson* (1906) 13 SLT 910, where the result was arrived at by equating the servitude right to a right to land for the purposes of the statutory provisions in question.
7 Ie in terms of the relevant provisions of the Land Compensation (Scotland) Act 1973 (c 56).
8 *Ayr Harbour Trustees v Oswald* (1883) 10 R (HL) 85.

(6) JUDICIAL PROCEEDINGS

480. Jurisdiction. Actions concerning servitude rights are competent either in the Court of Session or in the sheriff court of the sheriffdom in which the land affected is situated[1]. There are now no courts or tribunals which correspond to the former Dean of Guild Courts[2], where, in the past, matters relating to servitudes arose not infrequently. Authorities concerned with planning and building control will, however, occasionally find it necessary to take cognisance of the existence and effect of servitude rights; so also will the Lands Tribunal for Scotland even where its statutory jurisdiction[3] is not being invoked in respect of the servitude right as a land obligation[4].

1 Sheriff Courts (Scotland) Act 1907 (c 51), s 5(4). See also W J Dobie *Law and Practice of the Sheriff Courts in Scotland* (1949) p 73, indicating that actions concerning servitudes will normally fall under s 6(a) or s 6(e) of the 1907 Act, but suggesting that the sheriff has jurisdiction irrespective of the Act if the land is within his sheriffdom.
2 The jurisdiction of the Dean of Guild Courts was superseded with the abolition of those courts on 16 May 1975 by the Local Government (Scotland) Act 1973 (c 65), s 227.
3 See para 477 above.
4 *Keith v Texaco Ltd* 1977 SLT (Lands Trib) 16.

481. Title to sue and interest. Normally, the pursuer in an action maintaining the existence of a servitude right will be the proprietor infeft in the dominant tenement with the proprietor infeft in the servient tenement as defender. These roles are reversed when the existence or extent of the servitude right is being challenged. Part owners of the respective tenements will be entitled to sue or defend proceedings concerning servitude rights, but tenants, even under long leases, are not in that position, although they may be involved in certain proceedings of a possessory nature[1]. As a result of the rule that a servitude right must benefit the dominant tenement and its owners and occupiers, it might be assumed that, if the existence of a servitude is admitted or established, the question of interest to enforce it should not arise. Theoretically, however, anyone asserting a servitude right must have an interest to do so. As was said in a case concerning a servitude restriction on building,

> 'if the owner of the dominant tenement had no interest to enforce it, the Court would not be disposed to sustain it, if nimiously sought to be enforced *in æmulationem vicini*'[2].

However, it is clear that the onus of proving lack of interest on the part of a dominant proprietor who seeks to enforce a servitude right, such as a restriction on building, rests on the servient proprietor taking that plea[3]. Although a negative servitude may be expressed in terms for the general benefit of a certain estate, nevertheless there may be a question whether a particular house or property within the protected area is so situated as to derive any advantage from the restriction involved[4]. Rights within the category of known servitudes may be constituted in title deeds in terms of which the dominant proprietors may have the option of enforcing them as servitude rights or as conditions of title in virtue of a *jus quaesitum tertio*[5]. The advantage of the former course will be that, initially at least, the defender will have the onus of disproving the pursuer's interest to enforce the right whereas the *tertius* seeking to enforce a condition of title must always prove his interest to do so. Again, provided it is clear that the pursuer is in the position of proprietor of the dominant tenement, the question of title to sue will not arise as it may do where a neighbouring owner seeks to enforce conditions of title. For these advantages to accrue, the right sought to be enforced must, of course, be within the category recognised as servitudes as opposed to the wider category of rights or restrictions which may form conditions of title[6].

1 See *M'Donald v Dempster* (1871) 10 M 94, and *Stobbs v Caven* (1873) 11 M 530 (a case of thirlage).
2 *Gould v M'Corquodale* (1869) 8 M 165 at 170, per Lord President Inglis.
3 *Royal Exchange Buildings, Glasgow, Proprietors v Cotton* 1912 SC 1151 at 1161, 1912 2 SLT 199 at 204, per Lord Johnston, and at 1163 and at 205, per Lord Mackenzie (as referred to with approval by Lord Fraser of Tullybelton in *Ferguson v Tennant* 1978 SC (HL) 19 at 69, 1978 SLT 165 at 181).
4 *Royal Exchange Buildings, Glasgow, Proprietors v Cotton* 1912 SC 1151 at 1160, 1912 2 SLT 199 at 203, per Lord Kinnear.

5 See *Johnston v MacRitchie* (1893) 20 R 539, where Lord Young, in a dissenting judgment, treated building restrictions evidenced by a building plan as negative servitudes upon each feu in favour of the other feuars in the scheme. As to *jus quaesitum tertio*, see further paras 399 ff above.

6 See *M'Gibbon v Rankin* (1871) 9 M 423 at 433, per Lord Deas, and *Braid Hills Hotel Co Ltd v Manuel* 1909 SC 120 at 126, 16 SLT 523 at 526, per Lord President Dunedin.

482. Procedure and forms of action. To establish the existence of a servitude and/or enforce the rights of the dominant proprietor thereunder, the appropriate process will normally be an action of declarator with conclusions, as the circumstances may require, for interdict, removal of obstructions and, in some cases, damages[1]. Where it is sought to prevent some trespass or encroachment on private property made on the pretext of a servitude right, the quasi-servient owner should raise an action of declarator of immunity, with other conclusions as circumstances may require[2]. A declarator will also be appropriate where the existence of a servitude right is admitted but its extent or effect is disputed[3]. In certain circumstances, however, a process of suspension and interdict without declaratory conclusions may be adopted to assert a servitude right[4] or to challenge its existence[5].

In the past, questions of servitudes were often made the subject of jury trials which in purely factual disputes were regarded as having certain advantages such as finality[6]. In modern practice, however, servitude cases are normally sent for proof before a judge alone[7].

As has been seen, servitude rights may be the subject of possessory judgments giving no absolute right but an authority to exercise certain rights *pro tem*[8]. Historically such judgments were the outcome of special forms of action which are now obsolete, the process now usual in such circumstances being an action of interdict or suspension and interdict[9].

1 See 8 *Encyclopaedia of Scottish Legal Styles* p 59, exemplifying a Court of Session action for declarator of a servitude right of way. A similar action raised in the sheriff court is exemplified at p 60. See also the forms in W J Dobie *Styles for Use in the Sheriff Courts in Scotland* (1951) pp 453, 509, 510, exemplifying cases of servitudes based on implied grant, actings of parties and prescriptions. Declarators of negative servitudes are exemplified in the *Encyclopaedia* at vol 8, p 387, and in *Dobie* at pp 84, 508 ff.

2 See 8 *Encyclopaedia* p 409, and *Dobie* pp 119, 237, 512.

3 See *Dobie* pp 513, 514.

4 See *Union Heritable Securities Co Ltd v Mathie* (1886) 13 R 670, and *MacGregor v North British Rly Co* (1893) 20 R 300.

5 See *Smith v Denny and Dunipace Police Comrs* (1888) 7 R (HL) 28, *Smith v Stewart* (1884) 11 R 921, and *Maitland v Lees* (1899) 6 SLT 296, OH.

6 See *Malcolm v Lloyd* (1885) 12 R 843 at 848, per Lord President Inglis. The report contains an example of issues as adjusted for jury trial. See also 8 *Encyclopaedia* p 61.

7 J A Maclaren *Court of Session Practice* (1916) pp 547, 548.

8 See para 461 above.

9 *Maclaren* p 639. See eg *Knox v Brand* (1827) 5 S 714 (NE 666) (bill of suspension), and *Liston v Galloway* (1835) 14 S 97 (interdict).

(7) PARTICULAR SERVITUDES

(a) Classification by Subjects affected

483. Urban and rural servitudes. The classification of servitudes as urban, on the one hand, and rural, on the other, may be said to be misleading rather than informative. Nevertheless, it has generally been adhered to in textbooks. The classification does not, as might have been thought, refer to the nature of the district or locality of the subjects affected but depends solely on whether or not the servitude relates to buildings or other structures upon land. If so, it is termed an urban servitude. Otherwise, it will be classified as a rural servitude. Urban servitudes may be said to fall into three categories involving respectively the support of buildings, facilities for disposal of water affecting buildings and the protection of light and prospect for buildings. Rural servitudes, all of which are positive, include rights of way or passage, rights of pasturing stock, the right to take substances from the servient tenement for fuel and other purposes and certain rights concerned with water.

(b) Urban Servitudes

484. Support of buildings. For the support of buildings there are the servitudes known as *tigni immittendi* and *oneris ferendi*. The former entitles the dominant owner to insert and retain a beam in a wall on a neighbouring property belonging to the servient owner. The servitude *oneris ferendi* involves the right of the dominant proprietor to have his building superimposed upon and supported by the building or structure of the servient owner. In practice, servitudes involving rights of support are as likely to arise from use permitted to continue long enough for prescription to operate[1] as to be the subject of express grant or reservation[2]. Whether servitudes in these categories should be regarded as positive or negative servitudes is, however, a question on which opinions have differed. The effect of the servitudes is such that they may be said to involve both a right exercisable by the dominant proprietor and a restriction on the servient proprietor. Their classification as positive servitudes is, however, consistent with the fact that they may be created otherwise than by express grant or reservation and accords with the views expressed by Lord Watson in the leading English case of *Dalton v Angus*[3]. Whatever view may be taken on this point, difficult questions can arise as to the rights and obligations of the respective parties under these servitudes. In the case of the servitude *tigni immittendi*, it is clear that there is no obligation on the servient owner to maintain his building in such a condition as to permit the continued exercise of the servitude right. While such an obligation could be created in conjunction with an express grant of the servitude, it would not bind singular successors unless constituted and kept up in the title deeds of the servient tenement as a real condition or burden.

More doubtful is the position in respect of the servitude *oneris ferendi*, which on one view represents an exception to the basic rule embodied in the maxim *servitus in faciendo consistere nequit*[4]. Where, as often happens, the claim for support arises within a tenement, the matter may be dealt with under the principles of common interest as applying in the law of tenement[5]. There are, however, instances of the servitude *oneris ferendi* not affecting tenement buildings, as where a gable is erected on a neighbour's wall[6]. In such cases, there is authority that the servitude in itself cannot impose any obligation of maintenance or otherwise. Thus where, under statutory powers, part of a street had been carried over private property by means of an embankment, arched viaduct and bridge, when the condition of the arches of the bridge became dangerous the court rejected a claim that, on the principle of the maxim *inaedificandum solo cedit solo*, the owner of the ground was responsible for their repair[7]. It was held that the only burden imposed on these owners as a result of the exercise of statutory powers was in the nature of a servitude *oneris ferendi* and therefore involved no obligation of upkeep. As with certain other servitudes, however, it is clear that the dominant proprietor may demand facilities to carry out repairs on the servient tenement for his own benefit[8], and it seems possible that he may recover from the servient owner *in quantum lucratus* for any benefit thus conferred on the latter.

These two servitudes involve support derived from other buildings in contact with the building comprising the dominant tenement. There may, however, be a right of support of the nature of a servitude with the servient tenement not being buildings but the land itself. While the right of support implied by law between contiguous areas of land in separate ownership does not extend to buildings erected on the respective areas[9], a right of support from an area of land to buildings or other structures on an adjoining area may be constituted in the same way as any other servitude right. Such a servitude right may be impliedly created when a landowner disposes of part of his property for a purpose known to involve the erection of buildings or other structures requiring support from the adjoining land[10]. This form of right has, however, been described as a positive servitude *habendi* similar to the servitude *oneris ferendi* discussed above[11].

1 See *Murray v Brownhill* (1715) Mor 14521.
2 A right of support created by express grant is exemplified in 8 *Encyclopaedia of Scottish Legal Styles* pp 377, 378.
3 *Dalton v Angus* (1881) 6 App Cas 740 at 831, HL, per Lord Watson.
4 J Rankine *The Law of Land-ownership in Scotland* (4th edn, 1909) p 416. See also *Murray v Brownhill* (1715) Mor 14521.
5 See para 233 above. This was the position adopted by certain of the institutional writers: see Stair *Institutions* II,7,6; Bankton *Institute* II,7,9; and Erskine *Institute* II,9,11. See also *Rankine* pp 659–662, and *Thomson v St Cuthbert's Co-operative Association Ltd* 1958 SC 380, 1959 SLT 54, where, by implication at least, the court appeared to have proceeded on this basis in dealing with the duties of mutual support affecting proprietors within a tenement building.
6 *Troup v Aberdeen Heritable Securities and Investment Co Ltd* 1916 SC 918 at 928, 1916 2 SLT 136 at 142, per Lord Salvesen, rejecting an argument that the only example of the servitude is in flatted tenements.
7 *Robertson v Scottish Union and National Insurance Co* 1943 SC 427 at 439, 1944 SLT 202 at 206, per Lord Justice-Clerk Cooper.
8 *Stair* II,7,6.
9 However, a different view is expressed in para 260 above.
10 *Caledonian Rly Co v Sprot* (1856) 2 Macq 449, HL. Cf *Bald v Alloa Colliery Co* (1854) 16 D 870, a case concerning mineral workings. See paras 257, 269, above.
11 *Rankine* p 496. For a detailed examination of the matter of support as arising particularly in connection with the working of minerals which may be owned separately from the surface, see pp 495–510. See also paras 252 ff above.

485. Disposal of water from buildings. The servitude which provides for the disposal of water gathering on buildings is known as 'eavesdrop' or 'stillicide'[1]. While the proprietor of land is obliged by law to accept water draining naturally on to his ground from a neighbour's ground, a servitude right in the form of stillicide or eavesdrop is required if water from buildings erected on one property is to be permitted to drop on ground outwith the proprietor's boundary. The servitude is more likely to originate from implication or use extending over the prescriptive period than from express grant or reservation. In so far as it exists in urban areas, it has been attributed to general custom rather than any written rule of law[2]. Cases concerning the assertion or negativing of the right sometimes involve questions of the boundary line between two properties, there being, of course, no doubt that the owner of a building or other structure is entitled to have water from it drop on to his own land[3]. It has been said that where the boundary between two properties is indeterminate, the exercise of a right of eavesdrop over a long period may point to a right of property as opposed to a mere servitude right for the party who exercises the facility[4]. However, the existence of a right of eavesdrop for the benefit of a neighbour will not restrict a landowner's right to build on his own property except in so far as it can be shown that buildings would obstruct or prejudice the operation of the servitude right[5].

1 An agreement for eavesdrop is exemplified in 8 *Encyclopaedia of Scottish Legal Styles* p 383.
2 *Garriochs v Kennedy* (1769) Mor 13178.
3 *Jack v Lyall* (1835) 1 Sh & Macl 77, HL.

4 *Mathieson v Gibson* (1874) 12 SLR 134.
5 *Scouller v Pollock* (1832) 10 S 241.

486. Prohibition of restriction on building development.

In the absence of servitude rights or other restrictions, at common law there is nothing to prevent a landowner occupying the whole of his property with buildings or other structures of unlimited size and height[1]. While a rule of the law of tenement prevents a lower proprietor obstructing the light or air of a proprietor above him, the upper proprietor has no implied right of prospect to prevent his view being obstructed[2].

The negative servitudes which protect light and prospect are commonly referred to by their Latin names *non aedificandi, altius non tollendi* and *luminibus non officiendi*. They tend to be treated as variants of the same right[3]. There is, however, a significant difference between the right of prospect, represented at its highest by the servitude *non aedificandi* which prohibits building on the servient tenement or on some part of it, and the servitude *luminibus non officiendi,* which places no limitation on buildings on the servient tenement so long as they do not obstruct or cut off the light for buildings on the dominant tenement. The servitude *non altius tollendi* may, according to circumstances, be directed to protecting light and prospect and/or air. Consistent with the rule that servitude rights are to be strictly construed and not extended beyond their scope as clearly envisaged, a right to the protection of light will not be treated as creating a right of prospect which would involve an absolute prohibition of building on the servient tenement[4]. Again, where the height of buildings is restricted to a certain level, the court will not extend this restriction on the ground that it is in the circumstances ineffective to achieve its intended purpose[5].

Questions have arisen as to what constitutes the erection of buildings in contravention of a servitude *non aedificandi.* For example, a shed with a flat roof which rested on cast iron pillars not fixed to the ground was held in the particular circumstances to be a building[6]. In marginal cases, however, the decision may turn on the purpose of the restriction as expressed in the deed or inferred from the circumstances. A servitude which the seller of property granted over the property he was retaining to provide light and air for the property sold was held not to preclude the formation of an underground passage within a vacant space[7]. On the other hand, the construction of cellars underground was held to contravene a prohibition in a feu charter of the erection of any buildings whatsoever on a certain part of the feu[8]. It appeared that the intention of the prohibition was to protect the structure of a church on adjoining ground from risks to which it would be exposed by buildings, whether above or underneath the surface.

In the same context as the servitudes restricting building operations, the institutional writers refer to a servitude which prevents the formation within buildings on the servient tenement of windows or other apertures, the presence of which would prejudice the privacy of a neighbouring property[9]. Despite a lack of reported cases, it has been suggested that this is a true servitude although the dominant proprietor could have achieved the same result by surrounding his property with a wall of adequate height[10].

1 *Dundas v Blair* (1886) 13 R 759 at 761, 762, per Lord President Inglis.
2 *Birrell v Lumley* (1905) 12 SLT 719, OH.
3 For exemplification of the creation of a servitude of this type, see J M Halliday *Conveyancing Law and Practice in Scotland,* vol II (1986) para 20-29, and 8 *Encyclopaedia of Scottish Legal Styles* pp 378, 379, 382, 383.
4 *Ogilvie v Donaldson* (1678) Mor 14534; *Russell v Cowpar* (1882) 9 R 660. The distinction drawn in *Taylor's Trustees v M'Gavigan* (1896) 23 R 945 at 953, per Lord Adam, between the wording under consideration there and that involved in the *Russell* case may seem questionable, but in *Taylor's Trustees* the court was dealing with an issue between dominant proprietors with servitude rights over the same subjects: see para 467 above.

5 *Craig v Gould* (1861) 24 D 20. Other cases illustrating the restricted application of this form of servitude are *Ross v Cuthbertson* (1854) 16 D 732; *Banks & Co v Walker* (1874) 1 R 981; and *Clark & Sons v Perth School Board* (1898) 25 R 919.
6 *Edinburgh Magistrates v Brown* (1833) 11 S 255.
7 *Gray v Malloch* (1872) 10 M 774.
8 *Edinburgh Magistrates v Paton and Ritchie* (1858) 20 D 731.
9 Stair *Institutions* II,6,9; Erskine *Institute* II,9,10; Bell *Principles* ss 1005–1007.
10 J Rankine *The Law of Land-ownership in Scotland* (4th edn, 1909) p 461.

(c) Rural Servitudes

487. Passage or way. The most important of the rural servitudes is the servitude variously referred to as a right of access, a right of passage or a right of way. The last of these terms is more often applied to the distinguishable concept of the public right of way[1].

The servitude right takes a number of different forms according to the facilities enjoyed by the dominant proprietor. Roman law recognised three forms of servitude under this head, namely *iter,* the right of horse or foot passage; *actus,* a right for carriages drawn or cattle driven by men; and *via,* which comprises the first two rights but extends also to carriages drawn by horses or other animals[2]. According to Erskine, the analogous servitudes in Scotland are foot road, horse road and cart or carriage road[3]. From these basic concepts, the law has developed through decisions of the courts. It has, for instance, been held that the provision of a road or way for carrying peats from a moss fell into the category of a cart road[4]. Again, it has been held that a covered passage is not the same as an open way, with the result that building over a road or pathway which is the subject of a servitude right can be prohibited[5]. In its most restricted form, the servitude may be limited to use by pedestrians. At the other extreme, what were originally cart or carriage roads now commonly extend to all forms of vehicular traffic. As a general rule this will cover motors and other mechanically propelled vehicles[6], but that interpretation will not apply to a servitude right in terms inapplicable to such traffic if constituted since machines such as motors came into common use[7]. The intermediate form of right covering use by horses as well as pedestrians includes the drove roads[8], for long a feature of rural areas. As in Roman law, the rule applies whereby, in the absence of evidence to the contrary, the greater form of right will be presumed to include the facilities comprised in the lesser forms[9].

There is authority for the view that a drove road or similar right of passage may include stances where animals may be pastured, the right then being referred to as a right of passage and pasturage[10]. This prompts the question whether, under modern conditions, the demand for parking facilities for vehicles could be met by an extension of the servitude of way or passage or would fall to be regarded as a new form of right which might or might not qualify as a servitude. In a case decided before motor vehicles were invented, the claim to use, for the loading and unloading of carts, certain ground adjoining the area covered by a servitude right of passage was unsuccessful[11], but more recently the courts have appeared willing at least to contemplate the possibility of a servitude of parking[12]. On the other hand, it is established that the servitude of way cannot be extended to include a right to take land for the formation of a roadway, that right not being in itself among the servitudes which the law recognises[13].

As with other servitudes, the servitude of passage may have its scope restricted by reason of its having been constituted for a particular purpose, for example the taking of sheep from a farm to a certain market or the provision of access to a particular mill[14]. Thus a right of passage provided for the conveyance of fuel or manure was held not available for the transport of the contents of an ash pit[15]. The disappearance of the particular purpose for which the servitude right of way or passage was provided, for example, in the cases instanced, the discontinuance of the market or mill, would terminate the servitude right or at least suspend its operation[16]. Such limitations of the right of passage by reference to its purpose, however, will not be readily inferred. If they are to apply they must be evidenced, as the case may be, by the terms of the document by which the right is constituted or by the circumstances in which the right has been implied or, if it is based on prescription, by some special features of its use such as its terminus being at a market or mill[17].

The document constituting a servitude right of passage should, of course, define with reasonable precision its direction and extent[18], but where the right depends on prescription these features may be indisputably established in the course of use[19]. In any case, however, where there is doubt or dispute on these matters the court, provided that the existence of a right of passage is clear or admitted, will settle the terms of the right so far as in dispute[20].

Rights of passage were involved in certain cases referred to earlier concerning the question whether a servitude right or a proprietary right had been created[21]. In one case, the fact that those having the right in terms of their titles to use a certain passage were expressly given that right along with others and required to share the maintenance of the passage was held to indicate rights of common property[22]. It was pointed out that the word 'passage' may signify an actual passage in which there is a proprietary right or a right of passage over some ground by virtue of a servitude right of way. The practical result of such a distinction is that operations such as building above a passage or erecting gates thereon may be permissible by a servient owner as not prejudicing the exercise of a servitude right but will not be allowed without the consent of all concerned where there are a number of proprietary interests in the passageway[23].

As with other servitude rights, the use and enjoyment by the servient owner of his property is not to be restricted further than is necessary for the exercise of the right of passage. Questions have arisen as to the extent to which obstructions such as gates may be placed in the passageway. Stiles or swing gates as commonly used for the protection or segregation of livestock have been held permissible[24]. A locked gate or doorway obstructing the passage is, however, objectionable, even if a key is provided for the use of the dominant proprietor. A defect in the lock may render it impossible to open the gate or door and, in any event, it is not practicable to have keys available for all persons other than the dominant proprietor himself who may be entitled to use the passage[25]. Again, it has been held that where there is a right of passage through unfenced ground the servient proprietor is not entitled to have dangerous animals such as bulls grazing on the ground[26].

Another question arising in this context is the extent to which the servient proprietor is entitled unilaterally to alter the line or course of the passage or to reduce its width. A broad distinction exists between, on the one hand, a right of passage or access over some area of ground not more precisely specified and, on the other hand, a right of passage with the route specifically prescribed by means of a plan or otherwise[27]. In the former case, the servient owner has a limited right to make alterations, such as a change of route, but he will be well advised before doing so to seek the agreement of the dominant proprietor and, failing such agreement, to refer the matter to the court[28]. There are early cases reported in which the substitution of an alternative route was permitted on the court being satisfied that the exercise of the servitude right would not be materially prejudiced[29]. Where there were two routes connecting a mill, a peat moss, a church and a market, the more direct one being through a corn field which the proprietor proposed to close, the court remitted to an engineer to see that the more circuitous route was altered to suit the convenience of the parties concerned before declaring it to be the only route available in future[30]. On the other hand, it was held that a superior was not entitled to replace by another passage the passage shown on a deed plan of a feu, it being indicated that the court could not authorise the alteration of a servitude right of way constituted in such definite terms[31]. By contrast, the court upheld the action of a superior in diverting the means of access provided for in a feu contract where the diversion did not in any way inconvenience the vassal whose objection appeared to be motivated by a desire to prevent building on the superior's adjoining ground[32]. Even, however, where the right of access or passageway of which alteration is sought is not constituted in writing but has been established by the operation of prescription, the courts have declined to sanction the alteration of a route the precise position and direction of which have been demonstrated by consistency of use[33].

1 See paras 495 ff below. As confirmed in *Smith v Saxton* 1927 SN 98, a servitude right of access and a public right of way can co-exist over the same road or path.
2 See *Malcolm v Lloyd* (1886) 13 R 512, and *Carstairs v Spence* 1924 SC 380.
3 Erskine *Institute* II,9,12.
4 *Dingwall v Farquharson* (1797) 3 Pat 564, HL.
5 *Bennett v Playfair* (1877) 4 R 321. However, this case involved an element of common interest with several parties holding servitude rights over the same passageway.
6 *Smith v Saxton* 1928 SN 59, OH.
7 *Crawford v Lumsden* 1951 SLT (Notes) 62. Cf *Walker's Executrix v Carr* 1973 SLT (Sh Ct) 77.
8 See *Swan v Buist* (1834) 12 S 316.
9 *Malcolm v Lloyd* (1886) 13 R 512.
10 *Reid v Haldane's Trustees* (1891) 18 R 744 at 750, per Lord Justice-Clerk Macdonald, a case in which the decision was that a right of property and not of servitude had been constituted.
11 *Baird v Ross* (1836) 14 S 528.
12 See *Murrayfield Ice Rink Ltd v Scottish Rugby Union* 1973 SLT 99, an appeal from the Lands Tribunal for Scotland to the Inner House. See also *Devlin v Conn* 1972 SLT (Lands Trib) 11, where the tribunal, although basing its decision on other grounds, appeared to have been of opinion that the off-loading of petrol tankers on a vehicle access could have been permissible.
13 *Campbell's Trustees v Glasgow Corpn* (1902) 4 F 752, 10 SLT 9.
14 *Porteous v Allan* (1773) Mor 14512.
15 *Cronin v Sutherland* (1899) 2 F 217.
16 *Winans v Lord Tweedmouth* (1888) 15 R 540.
17 *Carstairs v Spence* 1924 SC 380 at 388, per Lord Clyde.
18 This was the case in *Moyes v M'Diarmid* (1900) 2 F 918, 7 SLT 378. For a form of deed creating the servitude, see J M Halliday *Conveyancing Law and Practice in Scotland*, vol II (1986) para 20-11.
19 Eg *Grigor v Maclean* (1896) 24 R 86, 4 SLT 129.
20 *Cooper and M'Leod v Edinburgh Improvement Trustees* (1876) 3 R 1106.
21 See para 445 above.
22 *Mackenzie v Carrick* (1869) 7 M 419.
23 *Mackenzie v Carrick* (1869) 7 M 419 at 420, per Lord Justice-Clerk Patton. Cf *Bennett v Playfair* (1877) 4 R 321, and *Shiel v Young* (1895) 3 SLT 171, OH.
24 *Wood v Robertson* 9 March 1809 FC. Cf *Sutherland v Thomson* (1876) 3 R 485, a case of a public right of way where, however, the rules as applying to private servitudes are referred to at 495, 496, by Lord Gifford and at 488, 489, by Lord Neaves. See also *Stevenson v Donaldson* 1935 SC 551, 1935 SLT 444, where temporary obstructions placed across an access right of way for the protection of tenants was held not to constitute an extra-judicial interruption of prescription in terms of the law then in force (see para 459 above). And see *Drury v McGarvie* 1993 SLT 987.
25 See *Borthwick v Strang* 1799 Hume 513, decided as a case of servitude but with the alternative of common property considered; and *Oliver v Robertson* (1869) 8 M 137.
26 *Lanarkshire Water Board v Gilchrist* 1973 SLT (Sh Ct) 58.
27 *Grigor v Maclean* (1896) 24 R 86 at 89, per Lord Justice-Clerk Macdonald.
28 *Bain v Smith* (1871) 8 SLR 539 at 540, per Lord President Inglis and Lord Deas.
29 *Bruce v Wardlaw* (1748) Mor 14525; *Ross v Ross* (1751) Mor 14531.
30 *Macdonald v Farquharson* (1833) 6 SJ 100.
31 *Hill v Maclaren* (1879) 6 R 1363 at 1366, per Lord Justice-Clerk Moncreiff; *Moyes v M'Diarmid* (1900) 2 F 918, 7 SLT 378.
32 *Thomson's Trustees v Findlay* (1898) 25 R 407 at 410, 5 SLT 268 at 268, per Lord Traynor, distinguishing the case from *Hill v Maclaren* (1879) 6 R 1363.
33 *Grigor v Maclean* (1896) 24 R 86. Cf *Ferrier v Walker* (1832) 10 S 317, where a possessory judgment in the form of an interdict prevented encroachment on a passageway of long standing.

488. Pasturage. The servitude of pasturage entitles one or more proprietors to have the use for their animals of pasture land on the property of another person. It has been held not to include the right of killing game on the servient tenement[1]. The right to exercise the servitude is sometimes restricted to certain seasons or parts of the year on the basis that at other times the animals will be accommodated on the property of the dominant owners[2]. While such an arrangement has been common, there are also many instances in which the pasturage right extends over the whole year or at least for as long as there is grass available to be consumed by the animals[3]. Where the servitude originates in an express grant or reservation, the number and nature of the animals to be pastured may be specified. In one case a grazing right restricted to one cow was regarded as effectively constituted as a servitude right[4]. In the absence of such specification, or in cases where the right has arisen by prescription, the use of the pastoral facilities must, on the principle of benefit to the dominant tenement, be restricted to animals proper to that tenement[5]. This may involve what is known as the *utilitas* test originally devised to allocate grazing as between several dominant proprietors but applicable also where there is only one such proprietor involved, its function being to limit the amount of grazing to what is reasonably useful to the dominant tenement. In cases where the period or season of grazing is restricted on the basis that the stock will be wintered on the dominant tenement, the carrying capacity of that tenement will normally determine the maximum numbers of stock that can be grazed on the servient tenement[6]. Applying these rules, it may be said that a provision for the grazing of animals of a kind or numbers out of keeping with the nature and requirements of the dominant tenement would not qualify as a servitude of pasturage. In one early case, it was held that the nature of a burgh of barony made it an unsuitable title for the prescriptive acquisition of a servitude of pasturage, the extent of which could not well be measured by the requirements of the dominant tenement[7].

Clearly, it would be inconsistent with these rules for the grass of a servient tenement, instead of being consumed by stock belonging to the dominant proprietor, to be cut and used or disposed of by the dominant proprietor for other purposes[8]. But the dominant proprietor in this servitude is not required to exhaust the pasture available on his own ground before resorting to pasture on the servient tenement, the principle of *utilitas praedii dominantis* and not that of *necessitas praedii dominantis* applying[9]. In accordance with the general rule that a servient proprietor may use his property in any way not prejudicial to the exercise of a servitude right affecting it, normal tilling operations or tree planting may continue, and the grazing of the servient proprietor's animals is permissible provided it leaves adequate grazing for those of the dominant proprietor[10]. On the other hand, operations such as peat cutting, particularly if conducted on a commercial scale, may be open to objection as prejudicial to the exercise of pasturage rights. Thus, the operations of a company with which the servient owner of certain mosses had contracted for the extraction of peat in large quantities were interdicted at the instance of the dominant proprietor and restricted to a section of the mosses so as not to prejudice his rights[11].

1 *Forbes v Anderson* 1 Feb 1809 FC.
2 See *Lord Breadalbane v Menzies of Culdares* (1741) 5 Brown's Supp 710.
3 See *Lord Breadalbane v Menzies of Culdares* (1741) 5 Brown's Supp 710; *Menzies of Culdares v Lord Breadalbane* (1741) 5 Brown's Supp 724; *Monro v Mackenzie* (1760) Mor 14533; *Ferguson v Tennant* 1978 SC (HL) 19 at 68, 1978 SLT 165 at 181, per Lord Fraser of Tullybelton.
4 See *Feaman Partnership v Grindlay* 1988 SLT 817, OH, revsd on other grounds 1990 SLT 704, 1992 SLT 460, HL.
5 Erskine *Institute* II,9,14; *Cuninghame v Dunlop* (1838) 16 S 1080 at 1084, per Lord Gillies; *Beaumont v Lord Glenlyon* (1843) 5 D 1337; *Ferguson v Tennant* 1978 SC (HL) 19 at 65, 66, 1978 SLT 165 at 179, per Lord Fraser of Tullybelton.
6 See *Fraser v Secretary of State for Scotland* 1959 SLT (Notes) 36.

7 *Dunse Feuars v Hay* (1732) Mor 1824. In the same case it was decided that infeftment in a house with or without a yard was sufficient title for the prescription of the servitude.
8 *Cuninghame v Dunlop* (1836) 15 S 295 at 298, per Lord Gifford.
9 *Lord Breadalbane v Menzies of Culdares* (1741) 5 Brown's Supp 710.
10 *Fraser v Secretary of State for Scotland* 1959 SLT (Notes) 36.
11 *Ferguson v Tennant* 1978 SC (HL) 19, 1978 SLT 165.

489. Fuel, feal and divot. The terms 'fuel', 'feal' and 'divot' are generally applied to the positive servitudes which entitle the dominant proprietor to take certain substances from the servient tenement for use on or in connection with the dominant tenement. The servitude of fuel entitles him to obtain material such as peat, to the extent necessary to meet the requirements of those in occupation on the dominant tenement[1]. While it is clear this servitude right covers the extraction of peat[2], it is doubtful if it could be validly constituted for the extraction of mineral substances such as coal[3]. The servitudes of feal and divot entitle the dominant proprietor to take turf for use on the dominant tenement[4]. On the principle of minimising the burden on the servient tenement, each of these rights may be restricted to such part of the servient tenement as provides sufficient material for the requirements of the dominant tenement[5]. The extent to which these rights may be extended to parties such as feuars or sub-feuars of the dominant proprietor is doubtful. As a general rule they will not be permitted to be used to obtain materials for manufacturing purposes or sale[6]. In a case where the right of cutting peat was given to feuars, the deeds were construed as permitting this right to be made available to tenants occupying the feus[7]; but in another case the holder of such a right was not permitted to exercise the right concurrently with his tenants nor could he communicate it to a plurality of tenants or feuars to an extent materially increasing the burden on the servient tenement[8]. Certain rights ancillary to and necessary for the exercise of these servitude rights have been held to be constituted by implication along with the particular servitude right. A right of access or passage extending to vehicles such as carts has been held to originate in this way[9]. Again, grazing facilities for horses used for the transport of peat or turf from the servient tenement to the dominant tenement may have to be provided on the servient tenement, as will facilities for the laying out of turf to dry on ground adjoining the area from which it is being taken[10]. The rights of feal and divot may themselves originate as ancillary to another servitude right such as that of aqueduct[11].

1 *Leslie v Cumming* (1793) Mor 14542.
2 Stair *Institutions* II,7,13; Bell *Principles* s 1014.
3 *Harvie v Stewart* (1870) 9 M 129 at 137, per Lord Deas, and at 148 per Lord Ardmillan.
4 Erskine *Institute* II,9,17; Bell s 1014.
5 *Watson v Dunkennan Feuars* (1667) Mor 14529; *Brown v Kinloch* (1775) Mor 14542; *Leslie v Cumming* (1793) Mor 14542.
6 *Carstairs v Brown* (1829) 7 S 607.
7 *Watson v Sinclair* 1966 SLT (Sh Ct) 77.
8 See *Murdoch v Carstairs* (1823) 2 S 159 (NE 145).
9 *Ross v Ross* (1751) Mor 14531.
10 Stair II,7,13; Erskine II,9,17.
11 *Prestoun v Erskine* (1714) Mor 10919.

490. Rights in relation to water on land. The servitudes known by the Roman law terms of *aquaehaustus* and *aquaeductus* provide respectively for the supply and conveyance of water. *Aquaehaustus* constitutes the right to take water for the purposes of the dominant tenement from a loch, stream or other watercourse on the servient tenement. In the past, the purpose of this servitude was usually to provide a means of watering cattle or other animals belonging to occupiers of the dominant tenement, but it can have other uses. Whatever its purpose, the servitude confers no exclusive or proprietary right to the source of the water on which it depends. For primary purposes, such as domestic use, the servient owner is free to draw on the supply so long as sufficient is left for the purposes for which the dominant proprietor is entitled to use the water[1]. A servient owner was held entitled, by the introduction of covers, to restrict the means of access to a stream from which cattle were watered, on leaving the watercourse sufficiently open to allow reasonable use of the facility[2].

On principle, the servient proprietor is under no obligation for the maintenance of the supply of water, either as regards quantity or quality. It is for the dominant proprietor, in agreement with the servient proprietor or failing such agreement with the authority of the court, to take any action necessary to protect his interests in these respects and he must make good any damage thus caused to the servient tenement[3]. For his part, however, the servient owner must do nothing which could possibly pollute the water and so render it unfit for the purposes for which the dominant proprietor is entitled to use it[4]. The established cases of *aquaehaustus* involve the water being drawn from a natural source on the servient tenement. It is therefore doubtful whether a servitude right can be established for the drawing of water from an artificial source which has been created by the proprietor for his own purposes. There is authority to the effect that use for the prescriptive period would not be effective to establish such a right as a servitude[5].

The servitude of *aquaeductus* (sometimes referred to as 'aqueduct') entitles the dominant proprietor to lead water through the servient tenement by installing and maintaining piping[6]. Not infrequently it will include the right, by means such as a weir or dam, to discharge on to the servient tenement water which would not otherwise reach it[7]. Whatever its precise form and terms, the servitude will involve installations (sometimes referred to as *opus manufactum*) on the servient tenement to divert the water from its natural course[8]. In principle, the dominant proprietor is responsible for the provision of these installations and for their maintenance in such condition that they do not cause damage to the servient tenement or any other property[9]; for these purposes, he will be entitled as necessary to access to the servient tenement[10]. The servient owner may take such action as may be necessary to remedy conditions such as stagnation or choking of waterways for which the dominant proprietor has not been responsible[11], but must do so without adversely affecting the exercise of the servitude right[12]. It appears that installations of the kind commonly used in connection with this servitude may be regarded as remaining the property of the dominant proprietor whether or not the manner of their attachment would otherwise have resulted in their becoming part of the heritable property comprising the servient tenement. In the absence of stipulation or agreement to the contrary, the dominant proprietor, when exercising his right to terminate or renounce the servitude, will be obliged to remove such installations, making good any resulting damage and generally restoring the *status quo* on the servient tenement as it existed when the servitude originated[13].

1 *Donaldson v Earl of Strathmore* (1877) 14 SLR 587. See further paras 287, 288, above.
2 *Beveridge v Marshall* 18 Nov 1808 FC, where the court was called upon to resolve a dispute about the extent to which the stream should be left open.
3 *Preston's Trustees v Preston* (1860) 22 D 366.
4 *Dumfries and Maxwelltown Water-Works Comrs v M'Culloch* (1874) 1 R 975.
5 See *Strachan v Aberdeen Magistrates* (1905) 12 SLT 725, OH. See also *Harper v Stuart* (1907) 15 SLT 550, in which the court distinguished *Smith v Denny and Dunipace Police Comrs* (1888) 7 R (HL) 28, where the source of water providing the servitude right of *aquaehaustus* for the inhabitants of a village was a natural one.
6 This is exemplified in 8 *Encyclopaedia of Scottish Legal Styles* pp 379–381.
7 J Rankine *The Law of Land-ownership in Scotland* (4th edn, 1909) p 573. In such cases the right may be described as a servitude of dam and aqueduct.
8 *Scottish Highland Distillery Co v Reid* (1877) 4 R 1118 at 1122, per Lord Gifford.
9 *Parsons of Dundee v Inglish* (1687) Mor 14521; *Gray v Maxwell* (1762) Mor 12800; *Scottish Highland Distillery Co v Reid* (1877) 4 R 1118.

10 *Middleton v Town of Aberdeen* (1705) 5 Brown's Supp 904; *Pringle v Duke of Roxburgh* (1767) 2 Pat 134, HL; *Weir v Glenny* (1834) 7 W & S 244, HL.
11 *Carlile v Douglas* (1731) Mor 14524; *Gray v Maxwell* (1762) Mor 12800.
12 *Tennant's Trustees v Dennistoun* (1894) 2 SLT 78. See also *Central Regional Council v Ferns* 1979 SC 136, 1980 SLT 126, OH, concerning a right of aqueduct originating in a statutory provision.
13 *Bridges v Lord Saltoun* (1873) 11 M 588; *Macdonald v Inverness Magistrates* 1918 SC 141, 1918 1 SLT 51.

(d) Other Rights recognised as Servitudes

491. Miscellaneous instances. As has been explained earlier, while the category or class of servitudes is not closed, the additions made to it over the years have not been numerous[1]. There are, however, certain rights which, although not within any of the basic forms as derived mainly from Roman law, have long been recognised as positive servitudes[2]. One of these entitles the dominant proprietor to take seaware or seaweed from the shore pertaining to the servient tenement for use in the occupation of the dominant tenement[3]. Like the servitudes of fuel, feal and divot[4], this right is restricted to the quantity or supply of the material required for domestic purposes. It does not warrant the abstraction of materials for disposal or sale in the form of kelp or otherwise[5]. Another example is the right of bleaching and drying clothes which belong to the occupants of the dominant tenement on ground comprising the servient tenement[6].

Servitudes have also been recognised whereby the dominant proprietor may abstract from the servient tenement sand and/or gravel[7] or quarry slate or stone[8], but in each case only for the purposes of the dominant tenement and not for disposal to other parties by means of sale or otherwise[8].

Under the head of water rights, there has been recognised a servitude right to discharge waste water from the dominant tenement on to the servient tenement[9].

There have been suggestions that rights such as that of the inhabitants of a town or burgh to take part in recreations such as golf over certain areas of ground could be regarded as a form of servitude, but that view is not generally accepted[10].

In another context the question has been raised whether a right of parking vehicles may be regarded either as a permissible extension of the servitude of passage or way, or as a servitude in its own right[11]. The rights conventionally reserved to the owners of minerals, enabling them for the purpose of working the minerals to enter upon or lower the surface of the ground, are sometimes regarded as servitudes with the minerals as the dominant tenement and the surface owner's property as the servient tenement[12]. In practice, such rights will be constituted in a deed recorded for publication, but recording is not essential to constitute them servitudes; in any event they do not require to be mentioned or referred to in subsequent deeds to protect them against extinction by the operation of positive prescription on a title in which they were not disclosed[13]. If, however, as not infrequently happens, they remain unexercised for twenty years or more, their extinction will result from the operation of the long negative prescription[14].

1 See para 447 above.
2 For reasons already explained, negative servitudes are restricted to established forms of right: see para 447, text and note 4, above.
3 *Earl of Morton v Covingtree* (1760) Mor 13528. See also para 318 above.
4 See para 489 above.
5 *M'Taggart v M'Douall* (1867) 5 M 534 at 547, per Lord Balfour; *Agnew v Lord Advocate* (1873) 11 M 309 at 333, per Lord Neaves.
6 *Sinclair v Dysart Magistrates* (1779) Mor 14519, affd *sub nom St Clair v Dysart Magistrates* (1780) 2 Pat 554, HL, a case in which the magistrates were regarded as dominant proprietors representing collectively the inhabitants of Dysart. See, however, *Home v Young* (1846) 9 D 286, where Lord President Boyle suggested at 296 that a right to use certain ground for bleaching purposes being operative within the burgh for which it was claimed should be regarded as a right of use or easement rather than as a servitude.

7 *Duke of Hamilton v Aikman* (1832) 6 W & S 64, HL.
8 *Murray v Peebles Magistrates* 8 Dec 1808 FC.
9 *Kerr v Brown* 1939 SC 140, where it was held that the right did not extend to the discharge of sewage waste. A servitude of drainage for domestic purposes is exemplified in 8 *Encyclopaedia of Scottish Legal Styles* pp 381, 382.
10 In *Cleghorn v Dempster* 17 May 1805 FC, a reservation in a feu by a town enabling its inhabitants to play golf on the area feued was held effective but was not described as a servitude. In certain other cases, rights of this kind regarded as of the nature of *spatiendi* were rejected as servitudes: see para 444 above.
11 See para 487 above.
12 See *Smith Sligo v James Dunlop & Co* (1885) 12 R 907.
13 *M'Gavin v W A M'Intyre & Co* (1874) 1 R 1016 at 1023, 1024, per Lord Neaves.
14 See paras 471, 472, above.

(8) RIGHTS RESEMBLING BUT NOT CONSTITUTING SERVITUDES

492. Common law instances. There are certain instances of rights recognised at common law which, while not regarded as servitudes, are, like servitudes, effective in questions with singular successors even although they are not constituted as real burdens or conditions. While sporting rights in general are excluded from the category of servitudes, on the ground that they do not confer on the dominant tenement and its occupants the type of benefit which is characteristic of a praedial servitude, there are cases in which rights of this nature have been accorded a permanent effect similar to that of a servitude right. Thus, on the basis of an earlier ruling which was regarded as *res judicata*, the court held that a right of fowling over another person's property, although not a servitude, was a franchise conferred as a heritable right forming an appendage to the holder's property and so constituting a real right as opposed to a personal privilege. This right could also be exercised through others such as tenants and servants[1]. In an earlier case, a similar ruling had been given in relation to a right of fishing exercised by a party within the bounds of fishings which another party held from the Crown[2].

A matter on which views have differed is whether the ancient institution or custom of thirlage, the restriction of land and its inhabitants to particular mills for the grinding of corn, constituted a servitude. Thirlage, which usually originated in the provisions of charters or other feudal grants of land, is now virtually obsolete. Statutory provisions for the commutation into money of the rights which thirlage gave the superiors as mill owners have been in force since 1799[3], and thirlage clauses have now disappeared from feudal grants. Although in essence a trade restraint or monopoly, thirlage has not infrequently been classified as a form of servitude; moreover, thirlage cases have been decided and reported as cases of servitudes[4]. However, on the basis of the maxim *servitus in faciendo consistere nequit*, Rankine, although noting the existence of certain judicial dicta in its favour[5], emphatically rejects the classification as a servitude of thirlage; instead he describes it as a relict of an old form of feudal service[6].

By far the most important of the common law rights which have similarities with servitudes is the public right of way, which has much in common with the servitude of passage. The public right of way and the features which distinguish it from the servitude right are discussed at some length below[7].

1 *Marquis of Huntly v Nicol* (1896) 23 R 610, 3 SLT 297.
2 *Murray v Peddie* (1880) 7 R 804.
3 The Thirlage Act 1799 (c 55) entitled either party to require commutation.
4 Examples of cases in which thirlage was treated as a servitude include *Maxwell v Maxwell* (1636) Mor 10639; *Blair v Rigg's Creditors* (1686) Mor 14505; *Harris v Dundee Magistrates* (1863) 1 M 833; *Stobbs v Caven* (1873) 11 M 530; and *Forbes' Trustees v Davidson* (1892) 19 R 1022.
5 *Harris v Dundee Magistrates* (1863) 1 M 833 at 842, per Lord Curriehill. However, at 844 Lord Deas rejects the servitude approach, which is adopted in *Brown v Carron Co* 1909 SC 452, 1909 1 SLT 8, a

case which, although decided before J Rankine *The Law of Land-ownership in Scotland* (4th edn, 1909) was published, may not have been reported when that work went to press.
  6 *Rankine* p 416. See also pp 457, 458. Bell *Principles* s 1017 supports this view.
  7 See paras 495 ff below.

493. Rights of statutory origin. Modern legislation has created numerous rights which in their effects on private land are very similar to servitudes[1]. Public undertakings such as those concerned with electricity, water supply and telecommunications have statutory powers to obtain rights over privately-owned property similar in effect to the praedial servitude of the common law. In some cases, the terms of the relevant statutory provisions may be such that a servitude right in the accepted sense, with resultant consequences, can be said to have been created[2]. In many cases, however, the right which is created by statute is outwith the category of servitude by reason of the absence of an identifiable heritable property forming the dominant tenement. The term 'wayleave' is frequently applied to arrangements between bodies conducting public undertakings on the one hand and owners or occupiers of land on the other, enabling cables, wire or pipes — sometimes forming permanent installations — to be carried through, over or under private property[3]. The word 'wayleave' is not a defined *nomen juris* in Scots or English law, in which system it appears to have originated. It has been described as a right of way over or through land for such purposes as the carriage of minerals from a mine or quarry or for the laying of electric cables[4] or, in more general terms, as a permission to pass over heritable property for a particular purpose subsidiary to the other uses of the property[5]. Doubts as to its precise meaning have, however, been indicated in at least one Scottish case[6]. The use of the term appears to have originated in connection with the working of coal or other minerals, but it is also found in connection with railway developments proceeding under statutory powers[7]. It has, however, become the standard term for such non-proprietary rights over land as are required by public bodies and authorities in the exercise of their functions. At common law, the absence of an identifiable dominant tenement must exclude such rights from the category of servitudes. Prima facie this will result in their acquisition from a landowner not being effective in questions with his singular successors unless the rights can be constituted real burdens or conditions in the appropriate manner. But the fact that a servitude cannot in the circumstances be created may not make it impossible to create some other species of heritable right which would be good against the successor of the original proprietor. In any event, such difficulties will not in practice be a matter of serious concern to the holders of statutory rights. They will either be in the position of having the rights declared perpetual by statute or retaining powers which they could invoke in the event of any challenge to the rights by parties such as singular successors in the land affected. Certain statutory provisions relating to public undertakings confer powers to exercise rights of this kind without recourse to compulsory acquisition procedure[8]. Again, an authority acquiring land in exercise of compulsory powers may be empowered to acquire rights similar to servitudes over other land[9].

Whether or not the statutory provisions in question describe the rights to which they give rise as servitudes or easements, the existence and effectiveness of these rights will depend on statutory warrant and not on conformity with any common law requirements. A private servitude right will not as a rule be regarded as coming within the category of land and heritages rateable by local authorities. But installations such as pipelines for public undertakings passing through private ground have been held to render the undertakers liable to rating in that although they have no title to the *solum*, they have exclusive possession of the ground so far as occupied by their installations[10]. In practice, there are many cases in which arrangements such as those embodied in wayleaves are negotiated and constituted without resort to statutory powers and in forms which at common law would not constitute them servitudes or real conditions. Such arrangements are common when permanence or indefinite duration is not envisaged and the payment the owner or occupier of the land receives is on a periodical as opposed to a lump sum basis. The existence of statutory powers which can at any time be invoked will, however, be sufficient security to the undertakers for the continuance of the facilities so long as required by them.

1 For more detailed treatment of these rights, see titles in this encyclopaedia concerned with the particular fields of legislation in which they arise.
2 See *Central Regional Council v Ferns* 1979 SC 136, 1980 SLT 126, OH, in which the Water (Scotland) Act 1946 (c 42), s 26 (now the Water (Scotland) Act 1980 (c 45), s 23), was held to have created, by implication, a servitude right of aqueduct.
3 Such corporations cannot be regarded as representing the inhabitants or residents of a particular area as do entities such as royal burghs, which have in some cases of servitude rights been treated as dominant proprietors.
4 Earl Jowitt *Dictionary of English Law* (2nd edn, 1977 by J Burke).
5 D M Walker *Principles of Scottish Private Law* vol 3 (4th edn, 1989) p 329. Cf *Independent Television Authority v Lanarkshire Assessor* 1968 SC 249 at 258, 1968 SLT 393 at 398, LVAC, per Lord Fraser.
6 *Independent Television Authority v Lanarkshire Assessor* 1968 SC 249 at 258, 1968 SLT 393 at 398, LVAC, per Lord Fraser, at 259 and at 399 per Lord Avonside, and at 263 and at 401 per Lord Thomson.
7 See 4 *Encyclopaedia of Scottish Legal Styles* p 260, providing a form of disposition of wayleave for a railway tunnel which, though conveying a perpetual right of wayleave to the company heritably and irredeemably, makes clear that no right of property is created and no right of use of or access to the surface is given.
8 See eg the Sewerage (Scotland) Act 1968 (c 47), s 3, and the Water (Scotland) Act 1980, s 23.
9 However, this requires express statutory provision: see *Sovmots Investments Ltd v Secretary of State for the Environment* [1979] AC 144, [1977] 2 All ER 385, HL.
10 See S B Armour *Valuation for Rating* (5th edn, 1985 by J J Clyde and J A D Hope) paras 8.09, 8.11, 14.05, and the cases there cited, including in particular *Hay v Edinburgh Water Co* (1850) 12 D 1240, and *Strathblane Heritors v Glasgow Corpn* (1899) 1 F 523, sub nom *M'Ewan v Glasgow Corpn* (1899) 6 SLT 312; affd sub nom *Glasgow Corpn v M'Ewan* (1899) 2 F (HL) 25. There would seem to be no reason in principle why the same ruling should not apply to a private installation connected with a servitude right such as aqueduct, but all the reported cases on the matter appear to have concerned public bodies.

10. PUBLIC RIGHTS OVER LAND AND WATER

(1) INTRODUCTION

494. General. Members of the public at large have certain rights in respect of the sea, rivers and other waters, and also in respect of the foreshore and other adjacent land. The public rights include the right of navigation, the right of fishing for white fish and shellfish, and the right of recreation[1]. In addition, there may also be public rights of way over any piece of (dry) land, provided that the rules of constitution for such rights have been satisfied[2].

Although similar in function, the two kinds of public rights are juridically distinct. Thus, for the most part the public rights of navigation and other like rights come into being automatically, by operation of law, but public rights of way depend upon user for the prescriptive period of twenty years. Further, public rights of way are held directly by the public whereas, at least in theory, the public rights in water are held by the Crown for behoof of the public. Both kinds of right are, however, real rights, directly enforceable by members of the public against the owners of the land or water in question and against any third party interfering with their exercise[3].

1 See further paras 514 ff below.
2 See further paras 495 ff below.
3 See para 5, head (7), above, and paras 512, 515, below.

(2) PUBLIC RIGHTS OF WAY

(a) Nature and Characteristics of Public Rights of Way

495. Public rights of way distinguishable from servitudes of way or passage and from public highways or streets. In common with the servitude of passage or way, as opposed to the public street or highway, the public right of way is a right of passage over private land, the *solum* of which remains the property of the landowner. It is, however, distinguishable from the servitude right:

(1) in existing for the benefit of members of the public generally and not merely for use in connection with some other property forming a dominant tenement[1]; and

(2) in requiring to form a route or connection between public places, as contrasted with a servitude right, which gives access to and from some private property[2].

A public right of way is distinguishable from a public street or highway maintainable at the public expense which requires at all times to be kept free of obstruction in any form. Like the servient owner in a servitude right of passage, the landowner whose property is traversed by a public right of way is under no obligation for the maintenance of the route or way and is free to carry out operations on his own property such as the erection of gates, stiles or fences so long as these are not prejudicial to the exercise of the public right[3].

1 *Sutherland v Thomson* (1876) 3 R 485 (see the opinion of Lord Gifford at 496, suggesting that the dominant tenement of a public right of way is the whole kingdom). Cf *M'Robert v Reid* 1914 SC 633 at 639, 640, 1914 1 SLT 434 at 439, 440, per Lord President Strathclyde.
2 In *Thomson v Murdoch* (1862) 24 D 975 at 982 Lord Deas refers to various differences between private servitudes and public rights of way. See also *Ayr Burgh Council v British Transport Commission* 1955 SLT 219 at 224.
3 *Sutherland v Thomson* (1876) 3 R 485; *Lord Donington v Mair* (1894) 21 R 829; *Reilly v Greenfield Coal and Brick Co Ltd* 1909 SC 1328 at 1338, 1909 2 SLT 171 at 175, per Lord President Dunedin. See also para 508 below.

496. Public places as termini of rights of way. As has been seen, a public right of way must connect public places[1], but what constitutes a public place for this purpose can be a question of some difficulty. A churchyard has been held to qualify[2], but doubts have been expressed in the case of a market place open only on certain days of the week[3]. It has been held that a sub-post office located in private property is not a public place, the public having no right to resort to it without the owner's consent[4]. A small town or village identified by its name can constitute a public place for this purpose, but it depends on a degree of public resort for recreation or other purposes whether any part of the seashore should be so regarded[5]. In one case a small natural harbour used primarily by fishermen, but also to some extent by other members of the public, was held to be a public place, the question being left open whether its use by fishermen alone would have justified that conclusion[6]. In this matter, a distinction has been drawn between land above the high water mark and ground forming part of the foreshore[7]. In the former case, for a *locus* to constitute a public place, there must be evidence of specific dedication in some form to public use or of long continued use effecting such dedication. In the case of the foreshore, however, which belongs to the Crown subject to the public right of access, a limited degree of exercise of this right in the form of occupation or resort will be sufficient to make the particular *locus* a public place. The significance of the distinction is exemplified in a case where it was held that a quite exiguous practice of resort by fishing boats and pleasure boats to a natural creek or harbour was sufficient to constitute the area of foreshore which it occupied a public place[8], whereas, by an earlier decision in the same litigation, a more general practice of resort to a rock forming a local landmark but not on the foreshore, was held not to have that effect[9]. Where it is established that a particular *locus* has at some time constituted a public place, it will not readily lose that character even if the extent of its use by the public has materially diminished[10].

1 See para 495 above.
2 *Smith v Saxton* 1927 SN 98.
3 *Ayr Burgh Council v British Transport Commission* 1955 SLT 219 at 222, per Lord Carmont.
4 *Love-Lee v Cameron of Lochiel* 1991 SCLR 61, Sh Ct.
5 *Darrie v Home Drummond* (1865) 3 M 496; *Richardson v Cromarty Petroleum Co Ltd* 1982 SLT 237, OH.
6 *Scott v Home Drummond* (1867) 5 M 771.
7 See *Marquis of Bute v M'Kirdy and M'Millan* 1937 SC 93 at 131, 1937 SLT 241 at 258, per Lord Moncreiff.
8 *Duncan v Lees* (1871) 9 M 855.
9 *Duncan v Lees* (1870) 9 M 274.
10 *Duncan v Lees* (1871) 9 M 855 at 857, per Lord Deas; *Marquis of Bute v M'Kirdy and M'Millan* 1937 SC 93, 1937 SLT 241.

497. Right of way constituting route between termini. The requirement that a public right of way must form a route between its termini means that it must follow some definable course and cannot confer the privilege of strolling or wandering indefinitely over private land[1]. This, however, does not imply that there must always be a visible track[2]. The nature of the terrain traversed, for example some part of a foreshore, could make such a requirement impossible to satisfy. Doubts or disputes as to the course or direction of a right of way the existence of which is admitted or established can be resolved by the court[3]. While the route must be one used by members of the public proceeding from end to end, this does not preclude its use as a means of access to properties situated at some intermediate point on the route[4]. In a case concerning elevated walkways in a shopping development it has been held that there is no objection in principle to a public right of way comprising in whole or in part the line of an artificial structure[5]. On the other hand, it has been held that the public right of navigation in a non-tidal but navigable river, as established by use from time immemorial, is not a public right of way: it does not require to form a route between public places and it is not, like a servitude or public right of way, extinguished by non-use[6].

1 *Mackintosh v Moir* (1871) 9 M 574 at 575, per Lord President Inglis (referring particularly to the case of a right of way over unenclosed ground), and at 579 per Lord Ardmillan.
2 *Rhins District Committee of Wigtownshire County Council v Cuninghame* 1917 2 SLT 169 at 171, OH, per Lord Sands. Cf J Rankine *The Law of Land-ownership in Scotland* (4th edn, 1909) pp 332, 333.
3 *Mackintosh v Moir* (1872) 10 M 517. This is usually by remit to a man of skill, on whose report the court's decision will be based.
4 *M'Robert v Reid* 1914 SC 633, 1914 I SLT 434. See, however, a dissenting opinion of Lord Johnson at 642 and at 442 that there must be a praedial servitude independently constituted in some appropriate manner for the route to be used as an access to private property situated between its public termini.
5 *Cumbernauld and Kilsyth District Council v Dollar Land (Cumbernauld) Ltd* 1993 SLT 1318, HL.
6 *Wills' Trustees v Cairngorm Canoeing and Sailing School Ltd* 1976 SC (HL) 30, 1976 SLT 162. See para 523 below.

(b) Creation of Public Rights of Way

(A) CREATION BY EXPRESS WRITTEN PROVISION

498. Grant or dedication of right of way. A public right of way may be created by express grant or dedication as evidenced by a document in appropriate terms signed by the landowner. In practice, creation in this way is rare. Since it creates a right over heritable property, the document should be probative, but it does not require to enter the Sasine Register or the Land Register of Scotland. Where registration of title is in operation, the document, although creating an overriding interest as opposed to an interest in land, on coming to the notice of the Keeper may, under optional provisions, be entered on the Land Register in respect of the property affected[1]. There appears to be no authority for saying that as in the case of a positive servitude the grant or dedication of a public right of way must for permanent effectiveness be followed by possession if not appearing in a property register. It seems likely, however, that such grant and dedication having been made to provide a facility desired by the public, use by the public will ensue.

1 Land Registration (Scotland) Act 1979 (c 33), s 6(4), read with s 28(1) ('overriding interest' (g)).

(B) CREATION BY USER DURING PRESCRIPTIVE PERIOD

499. Positive prescription as applying to public rights of way. The great majority of public rights of way originate from public user continuing for at least the period of positive prescription. In the past, there appears to have been some doubt whether the statutory provisions regulating positive prescription applied to public rights of way[1]. The question has been raised whether the creation of a public right of way by user should be regarded as based on a presumption of grant or assent on the part of the landowner. It is consistent with such a view that, as in the case of servitudes, the right cannot come into existence by user if express grant by the owner of the land for the time being would not have been within his power[2]. Likewise, when land has been acquired compulsorily and is held under statutory provisions, while the possibility of a right of way coming into existence by use is not *ipso facto* excluded, no such right could be created if it conflicts in any way with the statutory purposes for which the land is held[3]. For most purposes, however, the question of the basis on which user operates to create a public right of way may now be regarded as academic. As was said in one case:

> 'The question is not whether the existence of a right of way has been acquired by forty years user but whether the existence of a way has been proved by evidence of forty years user. The origin of the right the law is content to leave in obscurity'[4].

1 *Davidson v Earl of Fife* (1863) 1 M 874 at 884, per Lord President Inglis, indicating that prescription in this context meant merely the presumption which arose from immemorial possession, for which forty years' possession was in general a sufficient equivalent.
2 See *Kinross-shire County Council v Archibald* (1899) 7 SLT 305 at 306, OH, per Lord Kilcairney.
3 *Edinburgh Magistrates v North British Rly Co* (1904) 6 F 620 at 633, invoking the *ultra vires* principle.
4 *Rhins District Committee of Wigtownshire County Council v Cuninghame* 1917 2 SLT 169 at 170, OH, per Lord Sands. Cf *Mann v Brodie* (1885) 12 R (HL) 52 at 57, per Lord Watson. *Per contra*, see *Napier's Trustees v Morrison* (1851) 13 D 1404 at 1405, per Lord Justice-Clerk Hope.

500. The statutory provisions as to prescription. The establishment of public rights of way by user is now regulated by the Prescription and Limitation (Scotland) Act 1973, which provides that if a public right of way over land[1] has been possessed by the public for a continuous period of twenty years openly, peaceably and without judicial interruption[2], then, as from the expiration of that period, the existence of the right as so possessed is to be exempt from challenge[3]. As in the case of servitudes, the Act reduces the required period of possession or user to twenty years[4] and restricts interruptions to those in judicial form[5], and excludes allowances for disability such as minority[6].

1 'Land' includes heritable property of any description: Prescription and Limitation (Scotland) Act 1973 (c 52), s 15(1).
2 'Judicial interruption' is defined in ibid, s 4: see para 460 above.
3 Ibid, s 3(3). In a case decided with the Act in force, the judge rejected, without hesitation, an argument that the terms of this provision presupposed the existence of a public right of way before it could be said that the public had possession. That would have the result that the provisions of the Act would not operate unless continuous use for at least forty years had been proved: *Richardson v Cromarty Petroleum Co Ltd* 1982 SLT 237, OH.
4 This period may have commenced but not completely run before the Act came into force on 25 July 1976: see the Prescription and Limitation (Scotland) Act 1973, s 14(1)(a), read with s 25(2)(b).
5 Ibid, s 3(3).
6 Ibid, s 14(1)(b).

501. The requirements of possession or user. Subject to the changes which have been mentioned above, the Prescription and Limitation (Scotland) Act 1973 may be said to have left in force the previously existing law. It has been held that the period in respect of which possession is established need not immediately precede the taking of an action to assert or establish the right of way[1]. Thus it will be sufficient to prove public use during any period of twenty years terminating within the last twenty years[2]. When the forty-year period was applicable, it was held that a case could succeed despite a certain lack of evidence of exercise of the right during the early part of the period, the inference being that there had been exercise similar to that evidenced for the later part of the period[3]. Presumably this discretionary concession will still be applied in appropriate circumstances, although the prospects of justifying its application would appear to be lessened by the reduction of the period of user required to twenty years. As in the past, however, it will continue to be the rule that when one route has, with consent or at least without objection, been substituted for another, the period of public use of the respective routes may be aggregated for the purposes of prescription[4]. Again, in deciding what volume or extent of use is required in particular circumstances to create a public right of way, the court will have regard to the nature of the district, urban or rural, populous or otherwise[5]. In using the words 'openly' and 'peaceably', the 1973 Act is in effect adopting the existing law requiring that possession should be as of right and not attributable to tolerance. Accordingly, the prescriptive period will not run in the face of indications of opposition by a landowner, short of judicial interruption[6]. While the basic rules in this matter may appear relatively clear and simple, their application in particular circumstances can create difficulties for those seeking to establish the existence of a public right of way[7]. The situation in this respect is exemplified by two cases decided since the passing of the 1973 Act. In one of these, the pursuer failed because there were several ways of reaching the area of foreshore which as a public place was claimed to be a terminus, and there was held to be insufficient evidence of the use of a particular tract or route[8]. In the other case, the action failed because of insufficient evidence of the end-to-end use of a mews lane from which various private properties at intermediate points could be reached[9]. Consistently with the nature of a public right of way as already explained, the use founded on must be for the purpose of reaching one point from the other. It cannot consist of strolling about within some part of a landowner's property[10]. If the termini in question are connected by a public road or highway not materially less direct, an alternative route in the form of a public right of way would be unlikely to be established by user. Use of a road or track by parties in consequence of some private or personal right is of no significance in creating a public right of way, and the use by members of the public of a road or track which the landowner has formed for his own purposes will tend to be attributed to tolerance[11]. In any case, where a right of way is claimed to have been created over a route already in existence, the use founded on must accord with the nature of the route. There could not be a right of way in a form of footpath established by user over a road constructed for carriage and vehicular traffic or vice versa[12].

Since there is no document which could be recorded, public rights of way established by use are not disclosed in the Sasine Register. Under registration of title, the interest of members of the public in a right of way constitutes, like a servitude, an overriding interest in the property traversed and does not require to enter the Land Register of Scotland[13]. Since there is no dominant tenement to which the right pertains, it does not constitute an interest in land for the purposes of registration. It is possible, however, that as a result of proceedings to establish it or in some other way the existence of a right of way could come to the notice of the Keeper of the Registers of Scotland and so be registered in respect of the subjects traversed under the optional provisions of the land registration legislation[14].

1 *Davidson v Earl of Fife* (1863) 1 M 874 at 886, per Lord Justice-Clerk Inglis.
2 See *Harvie v Rodgers* (1828) 3 W & S 251, HL, a case concerning a servitude right of way, and *Mercer v Reid* (1840) 2 D 520, as establishing the rule under the law then in force.
3 *Harvie v Rodgers* (1828) 3 W & S 251, HL; *Young v Cuthbertson* (1854) 1 Macq 455, HL; *Elgin Magistrates v Robertson* (1862) 24 D 301.
4 *Hozier v Hawthorne* (1884) 11 R 766; *Kinloch's Trustees v Young* 1911 SC (HL) 1, 1910 1 SLT 2.
5 *Macpherson v Scottish Rights of Way and Recreation Society Ltd* (1888) 15 R (HL) 68 at 71, per Lord Watson.
6 Leading cases exemplifying the application of these rules are *Mann v Brodie* (1885) 12 R (HL) 52, and *Scottish Rights of Way and Recreation Preservation Society Ltd v Macpherson* (1887) 14 R 875; affd *sub nom Macpherson v Scottish Rights of Way and Recreation Society Ltd* (1888) 15 R (HL) 68. See also *Cumbernauld and Kilsyth District Council v Dollar Land (Cumbernauld) Ltd* 1993 SLT 1318, HL.
7 The publication of the Scottish Rights of Way Society Ltd *Rights of Way — Guide to the Law of Scotland* (1991) contains an informative treatment of the subject as a whole, particularly useful being an appendix summarising the essential questions relating to the establishment of a public right of way.
8 *Richardson v Cromarty Petroleum Co Ltd* 1982 SLT 237, OH.
9 *Strathclyde (Hyndland) Housing Society Ltd v Cowie* 1983 SLT (Sh Ct) 61, in which the sheriff's opinion contains an extensive citation and review of the relevant authorities.
10 *Jenkins v Murray* (1866) 4 M 1046.
11 *Napier's Trustees v Morrison* (1851) 13 D 1404. See also *Wallace v Dundee Police Comrs* (1875) 2 R 565 at 578, per Lord Deas, and *Brodie v Mann* (1884) 11 R 925 at 930 per Lord M'Laren, and at 933 per Lord Mure.
12 *Napier's Trustees v Morrison* (1851) 13 D 1404.
13 See the Land Registration (Scotland) Act 1979 (c 33), s 28(1) ('overriding interest' (g)).
14 Ibid, s 6(4).

(C) CREATION UNDER STATUTORY AUTHORITY

502. Local government legislation. Rights of way may be created by the exercise of certain powers conferred by local government legislation on islands councils, district councils and general planning authorities[1]. These are empowered to make certain developments on land in their ownership or, with the agreement of parties interested, on private land with the object of enabling members of the public to enjoy the countryside[2]. These developments include the provision of footpaths leading to such amenities as public areas and viewpoint stances established by the authorities in exercise of their powers[3] and can involve the creation of public rights of access for pedestrians on such terms as may be prescribed or, in the case of land in private ownership, agreed with any interested party[4].

1 See the Local Government and Planning (Scotland) Act 1982 (c 43), s 9(1), Sch 1, Pt I. The general planning authorities are the Highland, Borders and Dumfries and Galloway Regional Councils and the islands councils: see the Local Government (Scotland) Act 1973 (c 65), s 172(4).
2 Local Government (Development and Finance) (Scotland) Act 1964 (c 67), s 2(1) (amended by the Countryside (Scotland) Act 1967 (c 86), s 2(1)). See also the Local Government (Development and Finance) (Scotland) Act 1964, s 3, and the Countryside (Scotland) Act 1967, s 2(2A), (2B) (added by the Local Government and Planning (Scotland) Act 1982, s 9(2), Sch 1, Pt II, para 20).
3 Local Government (Development and Finance) (Scotland) Act 1964, s 2(2); Countryside (Scotland) Act 1967, ss 52(2A), (3), 67(7)(c), 73(1).
4 Local Government (Development and Finance) (Scotland) Act 1964, s 3; Countryside (Scotland) Act 1967, ss 52(2A), (3).

503. The Countryside Acts. The main statutory source of public rights of way is now represented by the Countryside (Scotland) Acts 1967 and 1981. In terms thereof general and district planning authorities[1] may enter into a public path creation agreement with any landowner who has the necessary power for the creation by that person of a public path across land in the area of the authority[2]. The agreement specifies the terms as to payment or otherwise and includes, if so agreed, any conditions affecting any public right of way over the path[3]. In this and other relevant provisions of the Act 'public path' means a way which is a footpath or a bridleway or a combination of those[4]. When it is satisfied of the need for a public path, having taken into account the interest of the general public as well as those of the persons interested in the land to be affected and who will be entitled to be compensated, but it is also satisfied that it is impracticable to proceed by way of a public path creation agreement, the authority is empowered to proceed by way of a public path creation order creating a right of way by public path conditionally or unconditionally[5]. Provision is made for publication of the intention to make the order and for adverse representations[6]. If there is opposition to the order but not otherwise, it requires to be confirmed by the Secretary of State before becoming effective[7]. The form prescribed for such orders includes the provision of a map defining the land affected[8]. Provision is made for compensation to be paid for depreciation in the value of land or for disturbance resulting from the operation of the order[9].

Every public path creation agreement and public path creation order requires to contain a description of the land affected[10], and it is the duty of the authority to have the agreement or order recorded in the Register of Sasines or registered in the Land Register of Scotland in an area in which registration of title is operative[11]. Such recording or registration makes the agreement or order enforceable at the authority's instance against successors of the present proprietor[12], but it is not enforceable against a third party who in good faith and for value has acquired rights, whether with a complete title or not, prior to the recording or registration of the agreement or order or anyone deriving right from such a third party[13].

The Secretary of State will not make or confirm a public path creation order or certain other orders relating to public paths involving rights of way over land where there is on the land apparatus belonging to or used by statutory undertakers without their consent, although this consent is not to be unreasonably withheld[14].

It should be noted that the provisions of the Countryside (Scotland) Act 1967 for the creation of long distance routes[15] may result in the creation of public rights of way. On the other hand, the provisions of that Act for public access to the open country[16] which do not constitute routes between definable termini are not productive of public rights of way in the accepted sense[17].

1 See the Local Government and Planning (Scotland) Act 1982 (c 43), s 9(1), Sch 1, Pt I. As to general planning authorities, see para 502, note 1, above. District planning authorities are district councils within the region of a regional planning authority (other than Highland, Borders and Dumfries and Galloway): see the Local Government (Scotland) Act 1973 (c 65), s 172(4).

2 Countryside (Scotland) Act 1967 (c 86), s 30(1) (amended by the Local Government (Scotland) Act 1973 (c 65), s 172(2), and the Local Government and Planning (Scotland) Act 1982, s 9(1), (2), Sch 1, Pt I, Sch 1, Pt II, para 10): see LOCAL GOVERNMENT, vol 14, para 674.
3 Countryside (Scotland) Act 1967, s 30(2).
4 Ibid, s 30(3).
5 Ibid, s 31(1), (2) (amended by the Local Government (Scotland) Act 1973, s 172(2), and the Local Government and Planning (Scotland) Act 1982, ss 9(1), (2), 66(1), Sch 1, Pt I, Sch 1, Pt II, para 11, Sch 3, para 8).
6 Countryside (Scotland) Act 1967, Sch 3 (amended by the Local Government and Planning (Scotland) Act 1982, s 66(1), (2), Sch 3, para 11, Sch 4, Pt I).
7 Countryside (Scotland) Act 1967, s 31(4), and Sch 3 (as so amended). Section 35A (added by the Countryside (Scotland) Act 1981 (c 44), s 5), removed the necessity for confirmation by the Secretary of State in respect of unopposed orders, while leaving in force the provisions for their publication and for their being challenged on certain grounds in the Court of Session. For the procedure in relation to these and certain other orders under the Countryside (Scotland) Act 1967, see Sch 3 (as amended: see note 6 above).
8 Ibid, s 31(3).
9 Ibid, s 37(1), (2), (4).
10 Ibid, s 38(4). The description may be a particular one or a description by reference in terms of the conveyancing legislation.
11 Ibid, s 38(5); Land Registration (Scotland) Act 1979 (c 33), s 29(2).
12 Countryside (Scotland) Act 1967, s 38(5).
13 Ibid, s 38(5) proviso.
14 Ibid, s 38(6).
15 See ibid, ss 39–42, and LOCAL GOVERNMENT, vol 14, para 675.
16 See ibid, Pt II (ss 10–29), and LOCAL GOVERNMENT, vol 14, para 673.
17 For the purposes of any enactment or rule of law as to the circumstances in which a right of way or servitude may be constituted, the use of land by the public or by any person at any time while it is comprised in an access agreement or order is to be disregarded: ibid, s 16(3).

504. Town and country planning legislation. Under the legislation for town and country planning, facilities of the nature of rights of way may come into existence where the Secretary of State exercises his power to stop up or divert a road to enable some development to be carried out[1]. In such cases, provision may be made for the creation of another route which may take the form of a right of way. The planning authority is empowered to create alternative footpaths or bridleways and improve such facilities as exist when it issues orders stopping up or diverting footpaths or bridleways to enable certain developments to be carried out[2]. An order by the planning authority, if opposed, does not take effect until confirmed by the Secretary of State[3]. The Secretary of State may, on the application of the appropriate local authority[4], order the conversion of a road into a footpath or bridleway or other track extinguishing or at least restricting any right to the use of the route by vehicles[5].

1 Town and Country Planning (Scotland) Act 1972 (c 52), s 198(1) (amended by the Local Government, Planning and Land Act 1980 (c 65), s 179, Sch 32, para 19(4), and the Roads (Scotland) Act 1984 (c 54), s 156(1), Sch 9, para 70(8)): see ROADS, vol 20, para 654.
2 Town and Country Planning (Scotland) Act 1972, s 199 (amended by the Local Government (Scotland) Act 1973 (c 65), s 172(2)): see ROADS, vol 20, para 654.
3 Town and Country Planning (Scotland) Act 1972, s 206 (amended by the Local Government (Miscellaneous Provisions) (Scotland) Act 1981 (c 23), s 40, Sch 3, para 17, and the Roads (Scotland) Act 1984, s 156(1), (3), Sch 9, para 70(15), Sch 11). For the procedure, see the Town and Country Planning (Scotland) Act 1972, Sch 18 (amended by the Local Government (Scotland) Act 1973, s 184, Sch 23, para 34, the Local Government (Miscellaneous Provisions) (Scotland) Act 1981, Sch 3, para 23, and the Roads (Scotland) Act 1984, Sch 9, para 70(22)).
4 Ie the regional, islands or district council: Town and Country Planning (Scotland) Act 1972, s 201(9) (amended by the Local Government (Scotland) Act 1973, Sch 23, para 27).
5 Town and Country Planning (Scotland) Act 1972, s 201(1), (2) (amended by the Local Government (Miscellaneous Provisions) (Scotland) Act 1981, s 25, Sch 2, para 27, and the Roads (Scotland) Act 1984, Sch 9, para 70(10)).

(c) Rights and Duties arising from the Existence of a Public Right of Way

505. Availability for different types of traffic. Where a public right of way is constituted by grant or dedication, the relevant document may be expected to indicate the scope of the right with any conditions or restrictions such as limitations on the type of traffic for which the right is to be available. In the much more common case of public right of way established by prescriptive possession, the scope and conditions of the right[1] will be determined by the nature of the use founded on as establishing it. Thus if the existence of the right is based on pedestrian use, it will not be available for vehicular traffic[2]. Where, however, the user establishing the right has been that of vehicular traffic of the kind then common, the right will become available for vehicular traffic of types subsequently introduced, always provided that the nature of the track or route is such that it can accommodate such traffic without requiring alteration or sustaining damage. It appears that for this purpose no distinction is drawn between mechanically propelled traffic such as motor vehicles and other forms of wheeled traffic, so that a right of way originally established and exercised for horsedrawn vehicles would be available for use by motor vehicles[3].

1 *Macfarlane v Morrison* (1865) 4 M 257.
2 See *Cuthbertson v Young* (1851) 14 D 300 at 306, per Lord Medwin, and *Jenkins v Murray* (1866) 4 M 1046, per Lord President McNeil, exemplifying the different forms that the use of a right of way may take by reference to the different categories of persons using it.
3 *Forbes v Forbes* (1829) 7 S 441; *Mackenzie v Bankes* (1868) 6 M 936. See also *Smith v Saxton* 1927 SN 98 and *Smith v Saxton* 1928 SN 59, OH, a servitude case in which there was contemplated the possibility of a public right of way affecting the same route.

506. Establishment and maintenance of the way. The line or track of the right of way may or may not have been laid out by the landowner; in any event, like the servient owner in the private servitude right, he is under no obligation to maintain or repair the track or to take any action necessary to keep it usable[1]. Because the planning authority has a duty under statute to assert, protect and keep free from obstruction or encroachment any public right of way wholly or partly within its area, the authority is empowered, without prejudice to the liability resting on any other authority or person, to repair and maintain any such public right of way not being a road or footway[2]. The planning authority is also empowered to authorise the erection and maintenance by private persons of guide posts and direction notices on any public right of way other than a public road[3].

1 *Rodgers v Harvie* (1829) 7 S 287; sequel (1830) 8 S 611.
2 Countryside (Scotland) Act 1967 (c 86), s 46(1), (2) (amended by the Local Government (Scotland) Act 1973 (c 65), s 172(2), the Countryside (Scotland) Act 1981 (c 44), s 7(a), and the Roads (Scotland) Act 1984 (c 54), s 156(1), Sch 9, para 60(2)).
3 Countryside (Scotland) Act 1967, s 46(3). 'Public road' is defined in s 47 (amended by the Roads (Scotland) Act 1984, Sch 9, para 60(6)(b)) by reference to the definition in s 151 of the 1984 Act, namely a road which a roads authority has a duty to maintain.

507. Occupier's liability in respect of the land traversed. The question has arisen for judicial determination of the extent of the liability as occupier of a landowner whose property is traversed by a public right of way[1]. Although the landowner is under no duty to maintain the public right of way in a usable condition, it was held that he had a duty to persons resorting to his land in use of the public right of way, to take such care as is reasonable in the circumstances[2]. In the particular circumstances of the case this was held not to involve posting notices or erecting handrails to ensure the safety of pedestrians on a towpath walk. In a case decided before the Occupier's Liability (Scotland) Act 1960, it was indicated that since users of a public right of way were on the ground as of right, they were neither trespassers, licensees nor invitees[3]. It has since been pointed out that there is no material or common interest connecting the proprietor to such users which would bring them into the category of invitees[4]. It is, however, clear that the landowner must not do anything which would create a danger for members of the public using a right of way, such as allowing dangerous animals like bulls to graze on a field through which the way passes[5]. In this matter the common law has been supplemented by a statutory provision which, without detracting from or limiting such civil rights as may exist, makes it an offence to have a bull of more than ten months old belonging to any of the recognised dairy breeds, or to another breed if not with cows or heifers, in a field containing a public right of way[6].

1 As to this liability, see the Occupier's Liability (Scotland) Act 1960 (c 30), particularly s 2.
2 *Johnstone v Sweeney* 1985 SLT (Sh Ct) 2.
3 *Plank v Stirling Magistrates* 1956 SC 92 at 119, 120, 1956 SLT 83 at 93, per Lord Mackintosh.
4 *Johnstone v Sweeney* 1985 SLT (Sh Ct) 2.
5 See A T Glegg *The Law of Reparation in Scotland* (4th edn, 1955 by J L Duncan) p 359. Cf *Lanarkshire Water Board v Gilchrist* 1973 SLT (Sh Ct) 58, a case concerning a servitude right of way.
6 Countryside (Scotland) Act 1967 (c 86), s 44(1).

508. Rights of ownership as affected by the right of way. Like the servient owner in the case of a private right of way, the landowner whose property is affected by a public right of way is entitled to exercise his rights of ownership in any way not prejudicial to the public's use of the right of way. His position in this respect has been strengthened, if not actually extended, by statutory provisions which apply when agricultural land is traversed by a public right of way and enable the way as well as the land to be ploughed in the interests of good husbandry, subject to notification being given to the planning authority and reinstatement of the surface of the way taking place as soon as possible[1]. At common law the owner of land traversed by a public right of way, like the servient proprietor affected by a private right of way, may erect gates, stiles or similar obstructions in or across the route where these can be shown to be necessary in the interests of his estate and are not materially prejudicial to the public's exercise of the right of way[2]. While a stile or swing gate will normally be permissible, a locked gate is in a different position because of the difficulty of making arrangements for the availability of the key[3]. In this matter of obstructions, the common law has been supplemented by a statutory provision enabling the owner, tenant or occupier of land which is in use or is being brought into use for agriculture or forestry and which is subject to a public right of way to apply to a planning authority for permission to erect stiles, gates or other obstructions preventing the ingress or egress of animals[4]. Sanction may be given on such conditions as may be imposed for the maintenance of the right of way and for its being used without undue inconvenience to the public[5].

1 Countryside (Scotland) Act 1967 (c 86), s 43(1)–(3). However, the right may be excluded by the terms of a public path creation agreement, a public path creation order or a public path diversion order: s 43(1) proviso.
2 *Sutherland v Thomson* (1876) 3 R 485, followed in *Orr Ewing & Co v Colquhoun's Trustees* (1877) 4 R (HL) 116, a case concerning obstructions affecting a public right of navigation in a non-tidal river. See also *Midlothian District Council v McKenzie* 1985 SLT 36, OH, where it was held that a fence restricting the width of a public right of way is allowable if justified in the interest of the landowner's estate and if it does not prevent the passage of the traffic entitled to use the route.
3 See *Lord Donington v Mair* (1894) 21 R 829, where locked gates were permitted, but only so far as required to exclude traffic not entitled to use the right of way.

4 Countryside (Scotland) Act 1967, s 45(1), (3) (amended by the Countryside (Scotland) Act 1981 (c 44), s 15, Sch 2).
5 Countryside (Scotland) Act 1967, s 45(1).

509. Alteration or diversion of the route. The question has sometimes arisen as to how far the route or course of a public right of way, as established by user, may be subsequently altered. While there would seem to be no objection to alteration or diversion taking place as a result of members of the public, with the consent of the landowner, using a different route over his property[1], it is clear that the landowner may not on his own initiative divert the course of an established public right of way[2]. Statutory provision has, however, been made for the diversion of public paths where the owner, tenant or occupier of the land they cross satisfies the planning authority that for securing the efficient use of the land traversed or other land held with it, or providing a shorter or more convenient path, the line of the path should be diverted on to other land of the owner or of another owner, tenant or occupier: in these circumstances the authority may by a public path diversion order create a new path, subject to such conditions as may be considered appropriate, and extinguish wholly or partially the right of way over the existing path[3].

1 See *Cadell v Stevenson* (1900) 8 SLT 8, OH.
2 *Hozier v Hawthorne* (1884) 11 R 766. See also J Rankine *The Law of Land-ownership in Scotland* (4th edn, 1909) p 349, and *Kinloch's Trustees v Young* 1911 SC (HL) 1, 1910 1 SLT 2.
3 Countryside (Scotland) Act 1967 (c 86), s 35 (amended by the Local Government (Scotland) Act 1973 (c 65), s 172(2), and the Local Government and Planning (Scotland) Act 1982 (c 43), ss 9(2), 66(1), Sch 1, Pt II, para 15(b), Sch 3, para 10(a), (b)). As to procedure, see para 503, note 7, above.

(d) Extinction of Public Rights of Way

510. Non-user. Like servitude rights of way, public rights of way, whether established by grant or dedication or by prescriptive user, will be extinguished by non-use during the twenty-year period of negative prescription[1]. The running of prescription will be interrupted by a claim in the form of appropriate proceedings for the assertion of the right raised by any person entitled to do so[2], or by some occurrence establishing relevant acknowledgment of the existence of the right[3]. A period of non-use shorter than that of the long negative prescription may suffice to extinguish the right of way if the landowner openly and without challenge has carried on operations making the use of the way impossible[4]. Non-user will not have the effect of extinguishing rights of way which exist as a result of public path creation orders[5], since these are an exercise of statutory powers by a public authority. Public path creation agreements[5] will normally have a specified duration but otherwise would appear to be prescriptible.

1 Prescription and Limitation (Scotland) Act 1973 (c 52), s 7. For a discussion of the application to servitudes of ss 7–9, see para 472 above. These provisions would appear to operate in respect of public rights of way in the same way as they do in the case of positive servitudes, members of the public being in the position of dominant proprietors and the owners of the land affected in that of servient proprietors. For reasons indicated in para 472, note 5, above, it is considered that the negative prescription of public rights of way, like that of servitudes, is regulated by s 7 and not by s 8.
2 Ibid, s 9(1), in which (by s 9(4)), the definition of 'appropriate proceedings' in s 4(2) (see para 460, note 7, above) is applied.
3 Ibid, s 10.
4 See J Rankine *The Law of Land-ownership in Scotland* (4th edn, 1909) p 337.
5 As to these orders and agreements, see para 503 above.

511. Statutory provisions or the exercise of statutory powers. Like servitude rights of way, public rights of way may be extinguished on the compulsory acquisition of the land they traverse. Where there subsists over any part of land acquired compulsorily a public right of way, not being a right enjoyable by vehicular traffic, the Secretary of State, if satisfied of the existence or availability of a suitable alternative right of way or of its not being required, may order extinction of the existing right of way[1]. In the case of a public path, general and district planning authorities are empowered when they consider it expedient to have it closed by public path extinction order[2]. Whether statutory power authorising the closing of roads includes power to close public rights of way depends on the construction to be put upon the term 'road' as used in the particular Act[3]. It would appear that the definition of 'road' in the consolidation Act currently in force[4] means that the power of a roads authority to close up roads by order[5] applies to public rights of way except those resulting from public path agreements[6] or being footpaths forming part of long distance routes under the countryside legislation[7]. Again, under town and country planning legislation, when any land has been acquired or appropriated for planning purposes and is for the time being held by a local authority for such purposes, the Secretary of State may by order extinguish any public right of way over the land if he is satisfied that an alternative right of way will be provided or that the provision of an alternative right of way is not required[8]. Similar orders may be made by local authorities[9], subject to confirmation by the Secretary of State if they are opposed[10]. Public rights of way not being rights enforceable by members of the public as owning an interest in land to which a title can be recorded are excluded from the category of land obligations which may be varied or discharged by the Lands Tribunal for Scotland[11].

1 Acquisition of Land (Authorisation Procedure) (Scotland) Act 1947 (c 42), s 3(1) (amended by the Statute Law (Repeals) Act 1973 (c 39), Sch 1, Pt IX). The Acquisition of Land (Authorisation Procedure) (Scotland) Act 1947, s 3(2), (3), make provision for notification of the order proposed and for a public local inquiry in the event of there being objections.
2 Countryside (Scotland) Act 1967 (c 86), s 34 (amended by the Local Government and Planning (Scotland) Act 1982 (c 43), ss 9(1), (2), 66(1), (2), Sch 1, Pt I, Sch 1, Pt II, para 14, Sch 3, para 9, Sch 4, Pt I). As to the procedure, see para 503, note 7, above.
3 *Pollock v Thomson* (1858) 21 D 173; *Murray v Arbuthnot* (1870) 9 M 198; *Lord Blantyre v Dickson* (1885) 13 R 116. See also J Rankine *The Law of Land-ownership in Scotland* (4th edn, 1909) p 349, referring to *Murray v Arbuthnot* (1870) 9 M 198, and *Hope Vere v Young* (1887) 14 R 425.
4 Roads (Scotland) Act 1984 (c 54), s 151(1) (amended by the New Roads and Street Works Act 1991 (c 22), s 168(1), Sch 8, para 94(b)) ('any way (other than a waterway) over which there is a public right of passage (by whatever means, and whether subject to a toll or not) . . .'). The significance of this provision and related provisions in the 1984 Act as affecting servitude rights of access and right of way generally is examined at length in A J Black 'Access, Rights of Way and the Roads (Scotland) Act 1984' (1990) 35 JLSS 57.
5 Roads (Scotland) Act 1984, s 68: see ROADS, vol 20, para 652.
6 See the Countryside (Scotland) Act 1967, s 30(1) (amended by the Local Government (Scotland) Act 1973 (c 65), s 172(2), and the Local Government and Planning (Scotland) Act 1982, s 9(1), (2), Sch 1, Pt I, Sch 1, Pt II, para 10): see LOCAL GOVERNMENT, vol 14, para 674. See also para 503 above.
7 See para 503 above.
8 Town and Country Planning (Scotland) Act 1972 (c 52), s 203(1)(a).
9 Ibid, s 203(1)(b) (amended by the Local Government (Miscellaneous Provisions) (Scotland) Act 1981 (c 23), ss 25, 41, Sch 2, para 28, Sch 4).
10 Town and Country Planning (Scotland) Act 1972, s 206 (amended by the Local Government (Miscellaneous Provisions) (Scotland) Act 1981, s 40, Sch 3, para 17, and the Roads (Scotland) Act 1984, s 156(1), (3), Sch 9, para 70(15), Sch 11).
11 J M Halliday *The Conveyancing and Feudal Reform (Scotland) Act 1970* (2nd edn, 1977), para 2.05. The Conveyancing and Feudal Reform (Scotland) Act 1970 (c 35), s 2(6) ('interest in land') refers.

(e) Judicial Proceedings

512. Title to sue and related matters. Proceedings for the establishment of a public right of way may be brought by any member of the public even although not residing locally or having any particular interest. The right to sue is regarded as commensurate with the right to use the way or route[1]. As a result, there exists the possibility of proceedings being raised frivolously or without justification or sometimes by indigent persons unable to meet such expenses as may be awarded against them. Persons in that position may sometimes be put forward to litigate by parties who, being the true *domini litis*, seek to avoid personal liability or expenses. Such a situation may be met by the court ordering the pursuer to find caution for expenses[2] or, alternatively, requiring some party or parties to be sisted as pursuers before the action proceeds[3]. Where, however, an action for declarator of a public right of way is raised by a number of persons, the death of one or more of these persons *pendente lite* does not necessitate the sisting of their representatives. The right for which declarator is sought by more than one person is not a joint one which the pursuers can only maintain together but an individual right which each member of the public can by himself assert[4]. Application of the same principles entitles companies or associations, formed for the preservation of public rights of way, to institute proceedings just as their members as individuals could do[5].

Proceedings at the instance of parties interested in land which may be affected by a public right of way may be defended by any party who could sue for establishment of the right of way or claim to assert that right[6].

Local authorities have for long had statutory powers entitling them to involve themselves in proceedings concerning public rights of way in their areas[7]. The provisions formerly operative have now been replaced by provisions making it the duty of planning authorities to assert, keep open and free from obstruction or encroachment public rights of way wholly or partly within their areas, for which purposes they are entitled to take such steps as they may deem expedient, including instituting or defending procedings[8].

1 *Torrie v Duke of Athole* (1849) 12 D 328; affd *sub nom Duke of Atholl v Torrie* (1852) 1 Macq 65, HL.
2 *Jenkins v Robertson* (1869) 7 M 739. *Per contra*, see *Potter v Hamilton* (1870) 8 M 1064, where the court by a majority refused to order caution, but in a dissenting judgment Lord Justice-Clerk Moncreiff at 1069, 1070, indicated that certain persons should have been sisted as parties.
3 *Robertson v Duke of Atholl* (1905) 13 SLT 215, OH, where the course suggested in the dissenting judgment referred to in note 2 above was adopted.
4 *Hay v Earl of Morton* (1861) 24 D 116.
5 *Macfie v Scottish Rights of Way and Recreation Society Ltd* (1884) 11 R 1094, where the society's application to be sisted as defender in an action of declarator was granted. In *Scottish Rights of Way and Recreation Preservation Society Ltd v Macpherson* (1886) 14 R 7, the society, as pursuer, was allowed to proceed to proof without its title to sue being questioned.
6 *Macfie v Scottish Rights of Way and Recreation Society Ltd* (1884) 11 R 1094.
7 See the Local Government (Scotland) Act 1894 (c 58), ss 24(1)(c), (e), 42, and the Local Government (Scotland) Act 1929 (c 25), ss 1(2)(a), 2(1) (all repealed). Examples of the exercise of such powers under the legislation then in force are to be found in *Alston v Ross* (1895) 23 R 273, 3 SLT 213; *Norrie v Kirriemuir Magistrates* 1945 SC 302, 1945 SLT 263; and *Alexander v Picken* 1945 SN 66, 1946 SLT 91.
8 Countryside (Scotland) Act 1967 (c 86), s 46(1) (amended by the Local Government (Scotland) Act 1973, s 172(2)).

513. Jurisdiction, forms of procedure and effect of judgment. Proceedings relating to a public right of way may be raised in the Court of Session or in the sheriff court within whose area the property is located[1]. Such proceedings will usually take the form of an action of declarator confirming or negativing the right, but when the existence of the right is not in dispute interdict against obstruction or encroachment may be sought without other conclusions or craves.

Where the existence of a right of way is admitted, the jurisdiction of the court may be invoked to define the course or track which is to be followed[2].

In the past, actions in the Court of Session concerning public rights of way have been sent for trial by jury[3] unless the parties have agreed otherwise or special cause has been shown[4]. The reports, however, do not contain any very recent instances of jury trials in relation to public rights of way, but various decisions in the nineteenth century exemplified the circumstances in which special cause for proof instead of jury trial could be established. An action concluding alternatively for a private servitude right or a public right of way was regarded as too complex for trial by jury[5], and the same view was taken where declarator of a right of way by four different routes and affecting land of two proprietors was involved: the possibility that the minds of local persons available to be called as jurors had been prejudiced by media coverage in the matter was also taken into account[6]. In another case, the fact that there had been certain correspondence in the press and a report made by the pursuers as a society to its members resulted in proof instead of jury trial being ordered[7], but special cause for that course was held not to have been shown where the press coverage involved was in a paper having a limited circulation and had for the most part appeared before the issue had been raised in court proceedings[8]. The difficulty of distinguishing the types of traffic using the right of way in question was held not sufficient to render the case unsuitable to be sent for trial by jury in accordance with what was described as the usual practice[9].

Provided the proceedings concerning the existence or non-existence of a public right of way are duly raised and decided otherwise than by way of a compromise embodied in the court's ruling, the judgment in what is regarded as an *actio populanis*, whether given in a court of first instance or on appeal, is, in effect, *res judicata* against anyone subsequently raising the issue and at least bars any person from having the matter reopened[10].

1 Sheriff Courts (Scotland) Act 1907 (c 51), s 5(4). The sheriff has full jurisdiction in the matter, and not merely power of possessory judgment as was at one time the case: see *M'Robert v Reid* 1914 SC 633 at 647, 1914 1 SLT 434 at 445, per Lord Skerrington.
2 For exemplification of forms of writ, see 8 *Encyclopaedia of Scottish Legal Styles* pp 51–56, and W J Dobie *Styles for Use in the Sheriff Courts in Scotland* (1951) p 343.
3 For an example of an issue, see 8 *Encyclopaedia of Scottish Legal Styles* p 61.
4 J A Maclaren *Court of Session Practice* (1916) p 548. In the sheriff court, proof and not jury trial is the normal course: see W J Dobie *Law and Practice of the Sheriff Courts in Scotland* (1948) p 339.
5 *Macfie v Stewart* (1872) 10 M 408.
6 *Blair v Macfie* (1884) 11 R 515.
7 *Scottish Rights of Way and Recreation Preservation Society Ltd v Macpherson* (1886) 14 R 7.
8 *Hope v Gemmell* (1898) 25 R 678, 5 SLT 344.
9 *Robertson v Duke of Atholl* (1905) 8 F 150, 13 SLT 577.
10 *Jenkins v Robertson* (1867) 5 M (HL) 27; *Potter v Hamilton* (1870) 8 M 1064; *Macfie v Scottish Rights of Way and Recreation Society Ltd* (1884) 11 R 1094. Where an action for declarator of a public right of way is successfully defended, the decree, which will in effect be *res judicata*, should be a decree of absolvitor: see *Strathclyde (Hyndland) Housing Society Ltd v Cowie* 1983 SLT (Sh Ct) 61. See also *Greig v Kirkcaldy Magistrates* (1851) 13 D 975 at 981, per Lord Cunninghame, indicating that if the decision in such an *actio populanis* is not technically *res judicata*, it should be regarded as equivalent to a precedent directly in point.

(3) PUBLIC RIGHTS OVER WATERS AND ADJACENT DRY LAND

(a) Nature of Public Rights

514. Regalia majora. Members of the public at large have certain rights in respect of the sea within territorial waters[1], and in respect of rivers, lochs and the foreshore. Prominent among these are the right of navigation[2] and the right to fish for white fish and shellfish[3]; but there are also a number of other rights[4]. While, however, these rights are exerciseable by the public, in strict law they are not held by the public but by the Crown for the public's behoof. The Crown is trustee; the public is the beneficiary. The Crown's trusteeship is inalienable and consequently numbered among the *regalia majora*[5]. The interposition of a trust between the right on the one hand and its exercise on the other is cumbersome, and is disregarded in practice so that, unlike true trust rights, the right of the public is treated as *in rem* and directly enforceable against anyone who challenges it[6]. It has been said that the Crown's position as trustee 'is anomolous, and appears to have no modern analogue on dry land'[7]. It is especially anomolous in relation to those public rights which require to be established by public user[8].

The trust doctrine seems to have developed, almost by accident, as a result of the major redefinition of Crown property rights which took place in the middle years of the nineteenth century. Until that time, Scots law followed Roman law in treating the sea and the foreshore as *res publicae*[9]. To satisfy feudal theory, ownership was technically in the Crown, but that ownership was in trust only, for the satisfaction of various public rights. Thus Erskine wrote:

> 'If our kings have that right of sovereignty in the narrow seas, which is affirmed by all our writers, and consequently in the shore as an accessory of the sea, it must differ much in its effects from private property, which may be disposed of or sold at the owner's pleasure; for the king holds both the sea and its shore as a trustee for the public'[10].

In the second half of the nineteenth century this doctrine was discarded, and the Crown was said to own sea and foreshore, not merely in trust, but beneficially, in full *dominium*. The property was *inter regalia minora* and not, as it had been before, *inter regalia majora*. It could be alienated by the Crown to private individuals[11]. The public rights, of course, remained, and the simplest course might have been to treat them as a public limitation on Crown or, as the case may be, on private ownership of the sea and foreshore, on the model of public rights of way. Instead, however, the idea of a trust, discarded now from ownership itself, came to be attached to the limitation on ownership[12]. Thus in the modern law the sea and foreshore belong fully and beneficially to the Crown or its disponees. But that beneficial ownership is limited by certain public rights also held by the Crown in its capacity as trustee for the public. In many cases, therefore, sea and foreshore are at one and the same time *inter regalia minora* (owned beneficially by the Crown) and *inter regalia majora* (subject to rights held by the Crown on behalf of the public)[13].

1 The territorial sea extends for 12 nautical miles in terms of the Territorial Sea Act 1987 (c 49), s 1(1). For public rights in the high seas beyond the territorial sea, see FISHERIES, vol 11, paras 65 ff, and SEA AND CONTINENTAL SHELF.
2 See para 520 below.
3 See para 521 below.
4 See para 526 below.
5 For regalian rights generally, see W M Gordon *Scottish Land Law* (1989), pp 862–864.
6 See para 515 below.
7 *Burnet v Barclay* 1955 JC 34 at 39, 1955 SLT 282 at 284, per Lord Justice-Clerk Thomson.
8 See para 516 below.
9 Erskine *Institute* II,1,6, and II,6,17; Hume *Lectures* vol IV (Stair Soc vol 17, 1955 ed G C H Paton) pp 238, 239; Bell *Principles* s 638.
10 *Erskine* II,1,6.
11 See paras 310, 311, 314, above.
12 For an early example of this doctrine, see *Paterson v Marquis of Ailsa* (1846) 8 D 752 at 770, per Lord Moncreiff.
13 An example is *Crown Estate Comrs v Fairlie Yacht Slip Ltd* 1979 SC 156.

515. Enforcement. With one exception, the public rights in water and adjacent land prevail over any merely private rights, including private rights conferred by the

Crown[1]. So far as private rights are concerned, what is prohibited is any material interference with the exercise of the public rights[2]. However:

'Mere inconvenience or nuisance is not enough to satisfy the test of material interference. It must amount to something more although not necessarily a hazard or danger'[3].

The exception is that 'the [public] right of white fishing must be so used as not to interfere with or injure the [private] right of salmon fishing'[4]. This may be explained partly by the fact that the right of white fishing was at one time also thought to be private[5] and partly by the favour customarily shown by the law to salmon fishings[6]. In a competition between the two principal public rights, namely the rights of navigation and of white fishing, the former prevails[7]. Where one of the public rights is under threat, it may be asserted and enforced either by individual members of the public in an *actio popularis*[8] or by the Crown as trustee of the public right[9]. In the leading case on enforcement, *Colquhoun's Trustees v Orr Ewing & Co*, a bridge had been built across the River Leven, a navigable but non-tidal river, in such a way that two of its piers rested on the *alveus*. The pursuer, a member of the public, sought removal of the piers, but his claim, successful in the First Division[10], foundered in the House of Lords on the basis that the threat to the public right of navigation was contingent rather than present[11]. In some circumstances the enforcement of public rights is prevented by statute[12].

1 *Colquhoun's Trustees v Orr Ewing & Co* (1877) 4 R 344; revsd *sub nom Orr Ewing & Co v Colquhoun's Trustees* (1877) 4 R (HL) 116. In *Grant v Duke of Gordon* (1781) Mor 12820, affd (1782) 2 Pat 582, HL, the court resolved a conflict between the public right of navigation and the private right of salmon fishing by regulating the exercise of each on the basis that the 'rights were not incompatible, if not emulously used'. But this approach is unlikely to find favour with a modern court: see *Wills' Trustees v Cairngorm Canoeing and Sailing School Ltd* 1976 SC (HL) 30 at 57, per Lord Maxwell.
2 *Crown Estate Comrs v Fairlie Yacht Slip Ltd* 1979 SC 156 at 178, per Lord President Emslie. See also *Colquhoun v Paton* (1853) 16 D 206; *Colquhoun v Paton* (1859) 21 D 996; and *Earl of Stair v Austin* (1880) 8 R 183.
3 *Walford v David* 1989 SLT 876 at 878, OH, per Lord Cowie. The court would not be drawn on a fuller definition. See also *Walford v Crown Estate Comrs* 1988 SCLR 113, 1988 SLT 377, OH.
4 *Gilbertson v Mackenzie* (1878) 5 R 610 at 621, per Lord Justice-Clerk Moncreiff. See also *Duke of Buccleuch v Smith* 1911 SC 409, 1911 1 SLT 59, and *Earl of Mansfield v Parker* 1914 SC 997, 1914 2 SLT 171.
5 See para 521 below.
6 For salmon fishings, see paras 320 ff above.
7 Bell *Principles* ss 645, 646.
8 *Colquhoun's Trustees v Orr Ewing & Co* (1877) 4 R 344; revsd *sub nom Orr Ewing & Co v Colquhoun's Trustees* (1877) 4 R (HL) 116; *Gilbertson v Mackenzie* (1878) 5 R 610; *Walford v David* 1989 SLT 876, OH. The rule is the same for public rights of way, where the law is more developed. See para 512 above.
9 *Crown Estate Comrs v Fairlie Yacht Slip Ltd* 1979 SC 156 at 178, per Lord President Emslie.
10 *Colquhoun's Trustees v Orr Ewing & Co* (1877) 4 R 344.
11 *Orr Ewing & Co v Colquhoun's Trustees* (1877) 4 R (HL) 116.
12 For an example, see the Offshore Petroleum Development (Scotland) Act 1975 (c 8), s 5(3). See also *Burnet v Barclay* 1955 JC 34, 1955 SLT 282.

516. 'Tacit' rights and 'acquired' rights. Most public rights over water and adjacent ground arise automatically, by operation of law. They do not have to be specially acquired. Such rights may be termed 'tacit'. However, certain public rights, of which the most important is the right of navigation in non-tidal waters[1], are not tacit but fall to be acquired by repeated public user over a number of years. Such rights may be termed 'acquired'.

Acquired rights defy ready categorisation. At first sight they seem to be examples of rights created by positive prescription, on the model of public rights of way, but this model falls to be rejected, for two reasons. In the first place, public rights over water are not provided for in the Prescription and Limitation (Scotland) Act 1973, the only public rights which may be acquired under that Act being public rights of way[2]. No doubt it is for this reason that forty years' possession is required to establish a right in respect of water, and not the shorter period of twenty years introduced by the 1973 Act. The 1973 Act repeals all previous Acts on prescription[3], and, since positive prescription seems not to have existed at common law[4], there appears to be no source for a rule of prescription in relation to public rights over water. The second reason for rejecting a model based on prescription is that, although acquired public rights over water depend on user for creation, they do not depend on user to measure extent once created. The cardinal maxim of positive prescription, *tantum praescriptum quantum possessum*, does not apply[5]. It seems therefore that public rights over water cannot be classified as rights created by prescription, and that they must be regarded as customary rights *sui generis*, anomalous in nature but of considerable importance in practice.

1 See para 523 below.
2 Prescription and Limitation (Scotland) Act 1973 (c 52), s 3(3).
3 Ibid, s 16(2), Sch 5, Pt I.
4 M Napier *Commentaries on the Law of Prescription in Scotland* (1839) pp 35, 36.
5 See para 523 below.

517. Extinction of public rights. Physical impossibility, for example the effect of the silting up of a river, results in the extinction of public rights. But apart from this single case it is difficult to see how public rights can be extinguished. It has been said that negative prescription does not apply[1], and public rights do not fall within the jurisdiction of the Lands Tribunal for Scotland in respect of the variation and discharge of land obligations[2].

1 *Wills' Trustees v Cairngorm Canoeing and Sailing School Ltd* 1976 SC (HL) 30 at 126, 1976 SLT 162 at 192, per Lord Wilberforce. But this can be so only if public rights fall within the list of imprescriptible rights given in the Prescription and Limitation (Scotland) Act 1973 (c 52), Sch 3, and it has yet to be shown that this is the case. If Sch 3 does not apply, then public rights prescribe after twenty years under s 8.
2 Public rights are not 'land obligations' within the Conveyancing and Feudal Reform (Scotland) Act 1970 (c 35), s 1(2), because they are enforceable by the public at large and not by the proprietor of a dominant tenement.

(b) Tidal Waters

518. Crown ownership subject to public rights. The *alveus* (bed) of the sea and other tidal waters is owned by the Crown[1], but subject to the public rights of navigation and of fishing. Both public rights are tacit[2]. To these rights, both well vouched for by authority, it might be thought that a third, a right of swimming for recreation, should be added to satisfy reasonable public expectations.

1 See further paras 309 ff above. In theory, however, the Crown can transfer ownership of the seabed to subject proprietors.
2 Ie arise automatically by operation of law: see para 516 above.

519. Right of navigation. There is a public right of navigation in all tidal waters provided only that the waters are 'navigable'. Tidal waters are 'navigable' if in their normal state they are physically capable of being navigated. For this purpose account may be taken of seasonal spates but not of exceptional floods[1]. The meaning of 'navigation' must be taken reasonably:

'the fact that some stretch of water is navigable or passable by some acrobatic tour de force does not establish a public right of passage'[2].

But, on the other hand, it is sufficient to establish the public right if a river is navigable downstream only[3]. The right is primarily one of passage and is not a right to sail over every square metre of the sea, and no objection can be taken to a private use, for example for the purposes of fish farming, which does not substantially interfere with passage[4].

1   *Wills' Trustees v Cairngorm Canoeing and Sailing School Ltd* 1976 SC (HL) 30 at 165, 1976 SLT 162 at 214, per Lord Fraser.
2   *Wills' Trustees v Cairngorm Canoeing and Sailing School Ltd* 1976 SC (HL) 30 at 124, 1976 SLT 162 at 191, per Lord Wilberforce.
3   *Grant v Duke of Gordon* (1781) Mor 12820, affd (1782) 2 Pat 582, HL; Hume *Lectures* vol IV (Stair Soc vol 17, 1955 ed G C H Paton) pp 243, 244; Bell *Principles* s 648.
4   *Crown Estate Comrs v Fairlie Yacht Slip Ltd* 1979 SC 156 at 178, per Lord President Emslie; *Walford v David* 1989 SLT 876, OH.

520. Meaning of 'navigation'. The public right of navigation permits 'any operation that could reasonably be described as navigation, by any vessel that could be reasonably described as a boat'[1]. Historically, the right was one of passage from one place to another, but it may now be taken to include repeated passage over the same stretch of water, whether for recreation, as in canoeing or dinghy sailing, or for fishing[2]. Navigation must be taken in a reasonable sense. It does not, for example, include 'every kind of user which physical prowess or exorbitant technology may make possible'[3]. Nor does it include propelling a boat by wading on the *alveus*[4].

In addition to a right of passage, navigation includes rights ancillary to passage but reasonably necessary for its proper exercise[5]. Some ancillary rights are exerciseable on the water itself, for example dropping anchor or tying up to fixed moorings while in the course of a continuing voyage[6]. Others are exerciseable on the foreshore[7], on the banks of rivers[8], or in ports and harbours[9]. An exhaustive list of ancillary rights cannot be made. In the leading modern case, *Crown Estate Commissioners v Fairlie Yacht Slip Ltd*[10], the First Division held, after a careful review of the authorities, that the laying of fixed moorings on the seabed is not a right ancillary to navigation[11]. The contrast here is with the case of temporary moorings, or with the temporary use, in the course of a voyage, of fixed moorings which have been put in place with the consent of the Crown.

District and islands councils are empowered to make byelaws in regulation of navigation in rivers, lochs, and the sea within 1,000 metres of the foreshore[12], and statute may sometimes be the source of other restrictions, for example in relation to pilotage[13].

1   *Wills' Trustees v Cairngorm Canoeing and Sailing School Ltd* 1976 SC (HL) 30 at 169, 1976 SLT 162 at 216, per Lord Fraser.
2   *Burton's Trustees v Scottish Sports Council* 1983 SLT 418; *Scammell v Scottish Sports Council* 1983 SLT 462, OH.
3   *Wills' Trustees v Cairngorm Canoeing and Sailing School Ltd* 1976 SC (HL) 30 at 124, 1976 SLT 162 at 191, per Lord Wilberforce.
4   *Scammell v Scottish Sports Council* 1983 SLT 462, OH. The question whether it includes a boat which is out of control and drifting with the wind was raised but not decided in *Walford v David* 1989 SLT 876 at 879, OH.
5   *Crown Estate Comrs v Fairlie Yacht Slip Ltd* 1979 SC 156 at 175, per Lord President Emslie.
6   Anchorage at the termination of a voyage is not navigation: see *Crown Estate Comrs v Fairlie Yacht Slip Ltd* 1979 SC 156 at 162 per Lord Dunpark, and at 181, 182 per Lord Cameron. See also *Campbell's Trustees v Sweeney* 1911 SC 1319, 1911 2 SLT 194, and *Leith-Buchanan v Hogg* 1931 SC 204, 1931 SLT 164.
7   See para 525 below.
8   See para 528 below.
9   See paras 334–336 above, and para 529 below.
10   *Crown Estate Comrs v Fairlie Yacht Slip Ltd* 1979 SC 156.

11 Nor is the depositing of dredgings: see *Lord Advocate v Clyde Navigation Trustees* (1891) 19 R 174.
12 See the Civic Government (Scotland) Act 1982 (c 45), s 121, and LOCAL GOVERNMENT, vol 14, para 278.
13 See WATER AND WATER RIGHTS, vol 25, para 307.

521. Right to take white fish and shellfish. By 'white fish' is meant all floating fish other than salmon[1]. 'Shellfish', so far as the public right is concerned, means all shellfish, including, probably, lobsters[2], except for mussels and oysters which, like salmon, are *inter regalia minora*[3].

The institutional writers disagreed as to the existence of a public right to fish for white fish (including shellfish); but they were unanimous that, whatever residual rights the public might have, an exclusive right of white fishing could be conferred on a private individual by Crown grant[4]. While, however, this unanimous view was an accurate reflection of contemporary Crown practice — for rights of white fishing were granted in just the same way as rights of salmon fishing[5] — it stood in direct opposition to express statutory provision. In terms of the Fisheries Act 1705[6] and the Fisheries (Scotland) Act 1756[7], express rights of fishings were conferred on the general public. Thus, by the Act of 1705, in a passage which is still in force:

> 'Her Majesty with advice and consent of the Estates of Parliament Authorizes and Impowers all her good subjects of this Kingdom to take . . . herring and white fish in all sundry and seas channells bays firths lochs rivers etc of this her Majesties ancient Kingdom and Islands thereto belonging wheresoever herring or white fish are or may be taken'.

It was not, however, until the second half of the nineteenth century that the view associated with the institutional writers was finally displaced and the modern law established[8]. Under that law all grants to private individuals of fishing for white fish are treated as ineffectual. Instead, white fish and shellfish within tidal waters are available for the general public. In relation to white fishing the public right is conferred by the Fisheries Act of 1705, but it seems clear that the right exists also at common law[9]. Whatever may have been the position at one time[10], it now appears to be settled that the right to fish exists regardless of whether the waters are navigable[11]. If, however, waters are not navigable, there is no public right of navigation and the fishing must presumably be accomplished without the use of a boat.

1 For salmon, see paras 320 ff above.
2 The issue was raised, but not decided, in *Duke of Portland v Gray* (1832) 11 S 14. In reading this case, it should be borne in mind that it was decided at a time when grants of white fishing were treated as valid. See also W M Gordon *Scottish Land Law* (1989), para 8-31.
3 See paras 331 ff above.
4 Stair *Institutions* II,3,69 and 76; Erskine *Institute* II,6,6; Hume *Lectures* vol IV (Stair Soc vol 17, 1955 ed G C H Paton) p 258; Bell *Principles* s 646.
5 *Duke of Portland v Gray* (1832) 11 S 14 at 16, 17, per Lord Corehouse.
6 The Fisheries Act 1705 (c 48) was repealed in part by the Statute Law Revision (Scotland) Act 1906 (c 38), Schedule.
7 The Fisheries (Scotland) Act 1756 (c 23) was repealed by the Inshore Fishing (Scotland) Act 1984 (c 26), s 10, Sch 2.
8 *Hall v Whillis* (1852) 14 D 324 at 328, per Lord Justice-Clerk Hope; *M'Douall v Lord Advocate* (1875) 2 R (HL) 49 at 55, per Lord Cairns LC; *Parker v Lord Advocate* (1902) 4 F 698, 9 SLT 499, affd (1904) 6 F (HL) 37, 12 SLT 33. But traces of the earlier view remained: see eg *Gilbertson v Mackenzie* (1878) 5 R 610 at 615, per Lord Ormidale. See also para 333 above.
9 *Bowie v Marquis of Ailsa* (1887) 14 R 649. As to sea fisheries generally, see FISHERIES, vol 11, paras 65 ff.
10 Until 1877 waters which were not navigable were considered to be in private ownership, which would exclude a public right of fishing. Since 1877, however, the boundary between Crown and private ownership has been determined by whether the water is tidal or non-tidal, and navigability is no longer relevant. See further para 275 above.
11 *Bowie v Marquis of Ailsa* (1887) 14 R 649.

(c) Non-tidal Waters

522. Private ownership subject to the public right of navigation. Non-tidal waters are in private ownership[1]. Public rights in non-tidal waters are correspondingly less extensive than in tidal waters. Thus there is no public right of fishing there[2], and often there is no public right of navigation[3].

1 See para 275 above.
2 *Fergusson v Shireff* (1844) 6 D 1363; *Grant v Henry* (1894) 21 R 358, 1 SLT 448. See further para 280 above.
3 See para 523 below.

523. Right of navigation. The meaning of 'navigation' has already been considered[1]. The right of the public to navigate non-tidal rivers and lochs subsists only where the rivers and lochs are 'navigable'. It has been seen that tidal waters are treated as 'navigable' in law if they are *de facto* capable of being navigated[2]. Consequently, the public right of navigation in tidal waters is tacit, that is to say, it arises automatically provided only that the factual test of navigability is satisfied[3]. For a long time the rule for non-tidal waters was less clear. On one view of the law, no distinction was to be made between tidal and non-tidal waters, and in both cases physical navigability sufficed. But there was also a competing view which argued that the right of navigation was not tacit but must be positively acquired. Physical navigability, on this view, was a necessary but not a sufficient requirement, and in addition there must have been public use. The firmest expression of this second view appeared in the opinions given by Lord President Inglis and Lord Deas in *Colquhoun's Trustees v Orr Ewing & Co*[4], where the public right of navigation was said to be analogous to public rights of way. Authorities could, however, be found for both views[5], and the law remained uncertain[6] until the leading case of *Wills' Trustees v Cairngorm Canoeing and Sailing School Ltd*[7] in 1976.

In *Wills' Trustees* the defenders, a sailing school, were in the habit of canoeing down a section of the River Spey. The pursuers, who owned the river and also the salmon fishings at the material point, complained that the canoeing caused injury to the fishings. Interdict was accordingly sought, and the case turned on whether the river could be said to be 'navigable' and so available for the public right of navigation which the defenders claimed to be exercising. Both views of the law described earlier were canvassed. At first instance, and again in the Inner House, it was held that physical navigability was sufficient and that the public right of navigation was tacit[8]. In the House of Lords, however, the opposite conclusion was reached. Although the analogy with public rights of way suggested in *Colquhoun's Trustees* was not accepted, the court nevertheless held that navigation could not exist without user for time immemorial. The equivocal state of the authorities allowed the House of Lords to give due weight to policy objectives. Thus Lord Fraser:

'In all the Scottish cases that were brought to our attention where a public right of navigation was involved, the river had evidently been used for navigation (or at least for floating), for many years and there was no question of setting up a new right. That is what is to be expected in a country like Scotland which has been inhabited and relatively settled for centuries. It seems most unlikely that any river in Scotland which is capable of providing a useful channel of communication or transport would not have been used by now ... If the fact of navigability alone was decisive, without proof of actual use, the result might be intolerable for riparian heritors. It would mean that a new right of navigation might emerge suddenly, and might seriously interfere with existing rights of a riparian proprietor. And it might be open to any person to insist on attempting to navigate any river, however small, by asserting that it was capable of being navigated. I am aware of no authority which compels or encourages me to hold that the law of Scotland leads to such inconvenient results. In my opinion therefore it is not now possible, as a matter of law, for a public right of navigation, hitherto unsuspected, to be successfully asserted in a non-tidal river that has not been used for some form of navigation from time immemorial'[9].

Lord Fraser then elaborated on the nature of the user required:

'The expression "time immemorial", when used in relation to the acquisition of rights of way on land by prescription has until recently been treated as equivalent to forty years ... but the prescriptive period for establishing a public right of way on land has now been reduced to twenty years — Prescription and Limitation (Scotland) Act 1973, s 3(3). That Act is concerned with *inter alia* the establishment by positive prescription of positive servitudes and public rights of way over land but it does not, in my opinion, apply to the period of use required to prove navigability of a river. In the latter context I think "time immemorial" must retain its customary meaning of forty years, though it is possible that proof of actual use for less than forty years might suffice if there was proof that the river had long been regarded as a public channel of communication by public opinion in the neighbourhood, what was called in Roman law *existimatio circumcolentium* ... The use which is required for proof of navigability must, in my opinion, be regular habitual use, not necessarily throughout the year, but at least for a sufficient part of normal years to make the river of substantial practical value as a public channel of communication or transportation'[10].

Once a stretch of water is established as navigable, the public may use it for navigation right up to its full physical extent. The measure of the public right is thus physical capacity and not past user[11].

1 See para 520 above. 'Navigation' has the same meaning in non-tidal waters as in tidal waters: *Crown Estate Comrs v Fairlie Yacht Slip Ltd* 1979 SC 156 at 173, per Lord President Emslie.
2 See para 519 above.
3 For the difference between tacit and acquired rights, see para 516 above.
4 *Colquhoun's Trustees v Orr Ewing & Co* (1877) 4 R 344; revsd *sub nom Orr Ewing & Co v Colquhoun's Trustees* (1877) 4 R (HL) 116.
5 Until 1877 the only suggestion that public user was required for navigation in rivers was in Hume *Lectures* vol IV (Stair Soc vol 17, 1955 ed G C H Paton) p 243. After 1877 the authorities were more equivocal. For non-tidal lochs, see *Macdonnell v Caledonian Canal Comrs* (1830) 8 S 881.
6 'I doubt if it has ever been settled whether the public character of the non-tidal part of a navigable river depends (1) on the fact of navigability, or (2) on prescriptive possession by the public. What makes the difficulty is that actual use for navigation is probably the best evidence of the fact of navigability': *Leith-Buchanan v Hogg* 1931 SC 204 at 211, 1931 SLT 164 at 167, per Lord President Clyde.
7 *Wills' Trustees v Cairngorm Canoeing and Sailing School Ltd* 1976 SC (HL) 30, 1976 SLT 162.
8 On the basis of *Grant v Duke of Gordon* (1781) Mor 12820, affd (1782) 2 Pat 582, HL, the First Division decided that there was a class intermediate between non-navigable and fully navigable rivers. But this novel view was rejected by the House of Lords.
9 *Wills' Trustees v Cairngorm Canoeing and Sailing School Ltd* 1976 SC (HL) 30 at 165, 1976 SLT 162 at 213, 214.
10 1976 SC (HL) 30 at 165, 1976 SLT 162 at 214.
11 1976 SC (HL) 30 at 169, 1976 SLT 162 at 216, per Lord Fraser.

(d) Foreshore

524. Crown or private ownership subject to public rights. Some parts of the foreshore around Scotland belong to private individuals while other parts remain in Crown ownership[1]. Regardless of ownership, however, the foreshore, so long at least as it remains foreshore[2], is subject to a number of public rights[3], and the proprietor must exercise his ownership in such a way that the public rights are not prejudiced. It is an open question whether there is prejudice in circumstances where the rights, though freely exerciseable over most of the foreshore, are wholly excluded from a particular part[4].

The public rights over the foreshore fall into two categories. In the first place there are the tacit rights[5] of navigation and fishing, the existence of which is not controversial[6]; and in the second place there are certain further rights, the nature and scope of which are less certain[7].

The public rights are exerciseable only on the foreshore itself and carry with them no separate rights of access to the foreshore. Of course the foreshore can always be approached from the sea, in exercise of the public right of navigation; but, in practice, unless it can also be reached by a public road or by a public right of way, the opportunities for exercise of the various rights are likely to be sparse.

District and islands councils are empowered to preserve the amenity of the seashore through byelaws and the executing of works[8]; but in the exercise of their powers they are directed to 'have regard to the need to protect and maintain any public rights under the guardianship of the Crown'[9].

1 See paras 313 ff above.
2 *Smith v Lerwick Harbour Trustees* (1903) 5 F 680 at 689, per Lord President Kinross.
3 Lord Young's view in *Hope v Bennewith* (1904) 6 F 1004 at 1013, 12 SLT 243 at 247, that all subsidiary public rights disappear when the foreshore is conveyed to a private individual, is not correct. It is probably a survivor of the now discredited view that certain public rights may be transferred exclusively to private individuals.
4 Cf *Colquhoun v Paton* (1853) 16 D 206 and *Colquhoun v Paton* (1859) 21 D 996 with *Earl of Stair v Austin* (1880) 8 R 183. See also *Walford v David* 1989 SLT 876, OH (rights in respect of the sea).
5 For the difference between tacit rights and acquired rights, see para 516 above.
6 See para 525 below.
7 See para 526 below.
8 See the Civic Government (Scotland) Act 1982 (c 45), ss 121, 122, and LOCAL GOVERNMENT, vol 14, paras 278, 686. 'Seashore' is defined in s 123(1) as including the land between low water mark and high water mark of ordinary spring tides.
9 Ibid, ss 121(11), 122(3).

525. Rights of navigation and white fishing. There is a public right of navigation[1] and of fishing for white fish and shellfish[2] in and from the foreshore. The right includes the right to perform activities necessarily ancillary to navigation and fishing, and these are of particular importance in the case of the foreshore. According to Stair the ancillary activities include:

> '. . . casting anchors, disloading of goods, taking in of ballast, or water rising in fountains there, drying of nets, erecting of tents, and the like'[3].

In one case doubt was expressed as to the existence and extent of the suggested right to take sand for ballast[4]; and in a second case the court considered, but did not decide, whether affixing iron bolts to rocks could be regarded as ancillary to the public right of fishing[5]. These two cases aside, however, Stair's dictum has remained undisturbed either by judicial decision or by judicial comment.

The common law rights are supplemented by statute. Thus in terms of the Fisheries Act 1705 certain specified rights ancillary to fishing may be exercised on the shore and on forelands[6], while it is an offence under the Coast Protection Act 1949 to use the foreshore without Department of Trade and Industry approval in a manner which obstructs or endangers navigation[7].

1 As to the public right of navigation, see para 520 above.
2 As to the public right of white fishing, see para 521 above.
3 Stair *Institutions* II,1,5.
4 *Carswell v Nith Navigation Comrs* (1878) 6 R 60.
5 *Nicol v Blaikie* (1859) 22 D 335.

6 The Fisheries Act 1705 (c 48) was repealed in part by the Statute Law Revision (Scotland) Act 1906 (c 38), Schedule. A foreland is a rocky promontory jutting out into the sea beyond the ordinary line of the shore but forming part of the shore.

7 Coast Protection Act 1949 (c 74), ss 34(1), 36(1) (s 34(1) being amended by the Merchant Shipping Act 1988 (c 12), s 36(2)). It is, however, possible to read these provisions of the 1949 Act as meaning that actions on the foreshore otherwise illegal as contrary to the public rights become legal provided Department of Trade and Industry approval has been granted.

526. Other public rights. In Scotland, unlike in England and Wales[1], public rights over the foreshore go further than the rights of navigation and fishing already mentioned. Little else, however, is certain. There is disagreement both as to the nature and as to the extent of such additional rights. The disagreement about nature concerns whether the rights are tacit[2], as is the case with navigation and fishing, or whether they fall to be acquired by user for forty years. This disagreement is of some importance. If the rights are tacit, they exist throughout the coastline of Scotland. If, however, they do not exist automatically but have to be acquired, their presence is precarious and depends on evidence of prolonged public use. The point has never arisen directly for decision, and dicta may be found in support of both views, but the modern judicial tendency is towards the view that the rights are tacit[3].

So far as extent is concerned, Lord Kinloch inquired in *Nicol v Blaikie*:

'Has not the public . . . right to use the shores for the purpose of recreation, in walking or riding? May they not have a pic-nic on the beach, if not riotous, or use it for bathing, if decorous?'[4].

Lord Kinloch's questions cannot be satisfactorily answered even today. That there is a public right of recreation[5], and that the public right includes the right to discharge shotguns[6], may be taken as settled. But it is easier to say what the right of recreation does not include than what it does include. Thus it has been held that it does not include the right to gather sea-ware[7], to erect tents or huts[8], or to sell refreshments[9].

In addition to the public right of recreation, there is also a public right of passage along and through the foreshore[10].

1 For the English law, see 49 *Halsbury's Laws of England* (4th edn) paras 301 ff.
2 A 'tacit' right is one which arises automatically, by operation of law: see para 516 above.
3 *Marquis of Bute v M'Kirdy and M'Millan* 1937 SC 93, 1937 SLT 241; *Burnet v Barclay* 1955 JC 34, 1955 SLT 282. Earlier cases suggested otherwise: see *Officers of State v Smith* (1846) 8 D 711 at 721, per Lord Moncreiff, and *Keiller v Dundee Magistrates* (1886) 14 R 191 at 201, per Lord M'Laren.
4 *Nicol v Blaikie* (1859) 22 D 335 at 340.
5 *Officers of State v Smith* (1846) 8 D 711, affd sub nom *Smith v Officers of State* (1849) 6 Bell App 487, HL; *Nicol v Blaikie* (1859) 22 D 335; *Keiller v Dundee Magistrates* (1886) 14 R 191; *Marquis of Bute v M'Kirdy and M'Millan* 1937 SC 93, 1937 SLT 241.
6 *Hope v Bennewith* (1904) 6 F 1004, 12 SLT 243; *Burnet v Barclay* 1955 JC 34, 1955 SLT 282; *McLeod v McLeod* 1982 SCCR 130.
7 *Paterson v Marquis of Ailsa* (1846) 8 D 752; *Lord Saltoun v Park* (1857) 20 D 89. The right to wreck and ware is a servitude and must be separately acquired: see para 318 above.
8 Temporary erection in the exercise of navigation or white fishing may be permitted: *Mather v Alexander* (1925) 41 Sh Ct Rep 177, affd 1926 SC 139.
9 *Marquess of Ailsa v Monteforte* 1937 SC 805, 1937 SLT 614.
10 *Officers of State v Smith* (1846) 8 D 711, affd sub nom *Smith v Officers of State* (1849) 6 Bell App 487, HL; *Marquis of Bute v M'Kirdy and M'Millan* 1937 SC 93, 1937 SLT 241.

(e) Dry Land beyond the Foreshore

527. Use of uncultivated land for herring fisheries. The White Herring Fisheries Act 1771 provides that all persons employed in herring fisheries may use 'any waste or uncultivated land' up to 100 yards from the high-water mark:

'for landing their nets, casks, and other materials, utensils, and stores, and for erecting tents, huts and stages, and for the landing, pickling, curing, and reloading their fish, and in drying their nets'[1].

The meaning of 'waste or uncultivated land' has been judicially considered on several occasions[2].

1 The White Herring Fisheries Act 1771 (c 31) was repealed in part by the Sea Fisheries Act 1868 (c 45), s 71. As to the 1771 Act generally, see FISHERIES, vol 11, para 120.
2 *Scott v Gray* (1887) 15 R 27; *Campbeltown Shipbuilding Co v Robertson* (1898) 25 R 922, 6 SLT 38. See also *M'Callum v Patrick* (1868) 7 M 163.

528. Use of river banks. The public right of navigation carries with it certain ancillary rights over the banks of navigable waters which may be exercised for as long as the voyage is still in progress[1]. As with other public rights, it makes no difference that the banks are in private ownership[2]. There is very little authority on this whole area, and the only extended treatment is that given by Hume in his *Lectures*:

'[Banks] are only as far public, as respects the public uses of the stream — in the mooring of vessels for instance — the unloading of goods — the taking of ballast — the erecting of wharfs and the like. In all other articles of profit, they continue *sub dominio* of the adjacent heritors... Or rather it would be more accurate to say, that there is no partition of the right of property between the public and the individual heritors — that there is a right of servitude only laid upon the private property, in favour of the stream, that the public interest therein may be fully and conveniently enjoyed... Nay, even as to the extent of the burthen towards the uses of navigation and the like, this cannot be carried all lengths, but must be measured and circumscribed by custom — by the state of immemorial usage and possession in that quarter; and as referable to the natural state of the particular river and its banks. The public, for instance, without the aid of Statutes, could not claim right at once to construct and establish a towing path, for the tracking of vessels along the banks of a public river, if either the banks were not naturally susceptible of such a thing, or if that mode of conducting navigation had never been practised there'[3].

As will be seen from this passage, the right to use the banks for navigation is not tacit but falls to be acquired by forty years' user[4].

1 Stair *Institutions* II,1,5; Bankton *Institute* I,3,4; Erskine *Institute* II,1,5; *Scammell v Scottish Sports Council* 1983 SLT 462, OH. Mooring or beaching between voyages is not part of the public right of navigation: *Campbell's Trustees v Sweeney* 1911 SC 1319, 1911 2 SLT 194; *Leith-Buchanan v Hogg* 1931 SC 204, 1931 SLT 164.
2 However, for the contrary view, see *Crown Estate Comrs v Fairlie Yacht Slip Ltd* 1979 SC 156 at 173, per Lord President Emslie.
3 Hume *Lectures* vol IV (Stair Soc vol 17, 1955 ed G C H Paton) pp 244, 245.
4 The leading example is *Carron Co v Ogilvie* (1806) 5 Pat 61, HL.

(f) Port and Ferry

529. Right to use ports and ferries. Where a port or ferry is provided as a result of a Crown grant, the public has the right both to use the facilities provided, in return for payment, and to insist that they are maintained to a reasonable standard[1].

1 See para 335 above.

11. CORPOREAL MOVEABLE PROPERTY

(1) INTRODUCTION

530. Preliminary. Bell remarked that:

'Moveables were of little consideration under our early law . . . Moveables unaffected by any of the rules of the feudal law, remained under the rules of a jurisprudence immediately derived from the Civilians; in many of its doctrines modified, and in some respects improved, by the Canonists'[1].

The influence of Roman law and, more particularly, of Roman legal terminology on the Scots law of corporeal moveable property is clear; in this respect, Scots law is little different from other systems which have been exposed to that influence. At the same time, it must be noted that Scots law, even in its Roman garb, is not necessarily identical to the law as found in Justinian's *Corpus Iuris Civilis*. As Bell's reference to the Canonists indicates, the influence of Roman law is combined with other influences and even where Roman law itself is concerned, account must be taken not only of the texts of the *Corpus Iuris Civilis* but of the interpretation of these texts by later scholars[2].

One other important influence to which Bell does not advert specifically is that of the ideas on Natural law which were current in the seventeenth and eighteenth centuries. These ideas are particularly important because it was in these centuries that shape was given to Scots law by the institutional writers and it is clear that the ideas on Natural law then current formed a significant element in their thinking. This appears not only from express reference to leading Natural lawyers, such as Grotius, but from the whole tenor of their works. The law of moveable property (along with the law of obligations) has been particularly exposed to external influence because of the relative lack of native material to which Bell rightly refers for his own day. In some areas, indeed, little has been added since Bell and institutional authority is therefore still of prime importance.

1 Bell *Principles* s 1283.
2 As to the influence of Roman law on Scots law generally, see SOURCES OF LAW (GENERAL AND HISTORICAL), vol 22, paras 548 ff.

(2) OWNERSHIP

531. Definition of 'ownership'. Erskine says of ownership that:

'. . . the sovereign or primary real right is that of property; which is the right of using and disposing of a subject as our own, except in so far as we are restrained by law or paction'[1].

Further, he observes that ownership gives the right to exclude others, to charge or burden the thing owned with inferior real rights in favour of others and to pledge the thing in security. Bell gives a similar definition:

'Ownership in moveables is a right of exclusive and absolute use and enjoyment, with uncontrolled powers of disposal, provided no use be made of the subject and no alienation attempted, which, for purposes of public policy, convenience, or justice, are, by the general disposition of the common law, or by special enactments of the Legislature, forbidden; or from which, by obligation or contract, the owner has bound himself to abstain'[2].

Stair refers to the owner's rights of alienation and disposal[3], meaning by the latter apparently the power to grant inferior rights such as rights of liferent or rights in security. All of these definitions or descriptions concentrate on the owner's powers but in view of the extent to which any enumeration of an owner's rights must be qualified it is probably more satisfactory to consider ownership of corporeal moveables as the relationship between the owner and the thing of which ownership is claimed.

As a basically civilian system Scots law recognises ownership as the highest or ultimate right in corporeal moveable property[4]. The law assumes that ownership of things which are owned is vested in some person legal or natural (or in a group of persons where ownership is held jointly or in common). *Res nullius* apart, in theory at least, there is always someone who is 'the owner' and only one such person who, in principle, can claim the property from anyone else. In that sense Scots law regards ownership as an absolute right. It does not admit that there may be several possible owners some of whom may have better rights than others, as do legal systems which recognise ownership as a relative right. It does not work — as English law apparently does — with a concept of ownership which includes the better right to possession[5]. However, Scots law does not work out the principle that there is only one owner at any one time with the same rigour as does Roman law from which its concept of ownership is derived. In Roman law a very clear distinction was drawn between ownership and possession and a very clear separation was made between an action claiming ownership and an action claiming possession[6]. In an action claiming ownership in Roman law, even bona fide possession did not per se allow the defender to retain the thing against an owner who established his title. Conversely, ownership as such was no answer to a claim based on possession. In Scots law, the distinction between the remedies of owner and possessor is blurred. As Stair puts it:

> '... we make not use of the name or nature of Vindication ... We have shown before (*Lib* 1, *Tit* Restitution [I, 7]) that there is a real obligation upon possessors, not having a title sufficient to defend their possession, to restore or re-deliver, not only to the proprietor, but to the lawful possessor, which is also consonant to that common principle of the Roman law *suum cuique* [to each his own]'[7].

While in Scots law the owner is, in principle, entitled to recover his property from any other holder, his claim to it is not based as firmly on his ownership as it is in Roman law. His claim is rather that the present possessor is not entitled to withhold the property from him because of the circumstances in which he acquired it. His action is therefore a petitory action for delivery based on the fact that the possessor has no title to withhold the property in question, rather than a claim for delivery based on his ownership, although there may also be a declaratory conclusion that the pursuer is owner of the property claimed. In so far as the owner does base himself on ownership, he is also able to rely on a presumption of ownership arising from previous possession of the thing, as discussed more fully below.

To sum up, the owner of a corporeal moveable who claims ownership to it, can in theory at least, establish title in the sense of 'the' title to it, and in principle, he is able to claim his property from anyone who has no title to withhold it. When a question of title to a corporeal moveable arises it may therefore be important to establish the basis of the title which is claimed as being either an original title to what was not previously owned or a derivative title from the previous owner. In practice, however, the owner who tries to reclaim his property does not need to trace his title back to some original grant. Instead, he is able to rely on a presumption of ownership arising from his previous possession of the thing. In Scots law — as in some other systems — there is a strong presumption that the possessor of a corporeal moveable is its owner. Accordingly, where an action for delivery is brought, it will be enough to show that the pursuer was possessor and that he gave up or lost possession in a way consistent with retention of his title to the property, for example, that he lent it to someone who has lost it or parted with it wrongfully, or that it was lost by himself (but not abandoned), or that it was taken from him wrongfully[8]. The mere fact that an owner has voluntarily parted with natural possession does not prevent him from asserting the ownership of the thing which he retains as he also retains civil possession. If, however, he parts with natural possession in circumstances which would allow third parties to assume that the person in natural possession is entitled to dispose of the property then he is personally barred from asserting his title if that person does dispose of it wrongfully. Thus, at common law in Scotland, a mercantile factor can give to third parties a title which is good against the true owner because the factor has implied authority to dispose of the property he holds and third parties are therefore allowed by the law to assume that a factor has powers of disposal unless they are warned of a limitation on his authority[9]. On the other hand, a hirer or borrower has no such apparent authority and so if such a person parts with the thing the owner can reclaim it[10].

1 Erskine *Institute* II,1,1.
2 Bell *Principles* s 1284.
3 Stair *Institutions* II,1,28.
4 See generally paras 3 ff above.
5 English law does use the concept of ownership (see eg 35 *Halsbury's Laws of England* (4th edn) paras 1127 ff) but distinguishes 'absolute property' where there are no competing rights to possession and 'qualified property' where there are competing rights as in the case of a bailment, such as loan. Again the bailee was formerly said to have a 'special property' in the thing (35 *Halsbury* para 1115). But the English law of corporeal personal property is much concerned with possession and the right to possession. Possession, including the owner's possession and right thereto, is protected by delictual remedies (45 *Halsbury's Law of England* (4th edn) paras 1416 ff) namely, conversion (45 *Halsbury* paras 1422 ff) and trespass to goods (45 *Halsbury* paras 1491 ff). The tort of detinue which formerly also lay to protect proprietary interests was abolished by the Torts (Interference with Goods) Act 1977 (c 32), s 2(1).
6 The action claiming ownership was typically the *vindicatio rei* (vindication of a thing); the classical possessory remedies were the possessory interdicts which in later law became possessory actions.
7 *Stair* IV,3,45. See further paras 158 ff above.
8 *Stair* II,1,42; IV,45,17; VIII; *Erskine* II,1,24; Bell *Commentaries* I,269; Bell *Principles* s 1313. See further para 150 above.
9 *Pochin & Co v Robinows and Marjoribanks* (1869) 7 M 622 at 638, per Lord Kinloch. See paras 670, 671, below.
10 *Lamonby v Foulds Ltd* 1928 SC 89, 1928 SLT 42. See para 680 below.

532. Reputed ownership. What is meant by 'possession' in questions of ownership and possession of corporeal moveables is discussed more fully above[1]. However, it is appropriate to note at this point the doctrine of 'reputed ownership'. Because Scots law attaches importance to possession as raising a presumption of ownership, it was at one time readily held that a person who was in natural possession of another person's property with the consent of that person, such as a seller who had delivered goods but retained them temporarily for the buyer's convenience, might be reputed owner of the property which he apparently held as owner, with the result that the property was open to the diligence of his creditors[2]. This followed from the reliance placed on possession. It was also one counterpart of the rule that the creation of security over corporeal moveables required some apparent change of the state of possession so that it would be clear to other creditors of the granter of the security right that a security existed. The doctrine has come to be restricted in scope because it is now more readily recognised that it is quite normal to separate ownership and the actual holding of property, so that, for example, the mere existence of a hire-purchase transaction does not allow creditors of the hire-purchaser to claim the property although he may be apparently in full control of it; the true owner must have acted so as to mislead potential creditors[3].

The courts have not applied the logic of this view to permit the arrangement of finance from a finance company by selling to the finance company property already owned by the debtor and hiring the property back, without physical delivery and redelivery of the property. The objection taken has been that a purported sale in these circumstances would not transfer the property to the finance company because the Sale of Goods Act 1979 (like its predecessor of 1893) provides that the provisions of the Act allowing transfer of property by agreement do not apply where the object of a transaction is to create a right in security[4]. A delivery of possession followed by redelivery is therefore, it seems, required where a sale linked with a security transaction is involved and the security transaction should then be effective[5]. However, the view that the transaction cannot be carried out simply by agreement between the party seeking and the party granting security overlooks the form of delivery known in Roman law as *constitutum possessorium* (possessory declaration or agreement) in which property is regarded as transferred in virtue of an agreement with the transferee that the transferor will hold the property on some subordinate title from the transferee, such as liferent or hire; where there is such an arrangement, it is unnecessary for the thing to be handed over and taken back again by the transferor. There are few cases in which such a transaction has been upheld in Scots law but the institution has been recognised[6]. It could, therefore, quite appropriately be applied to a bona fide transaction the object of which was to raise finance by a transfer to a finance company followed by hire from the company. Today no commercial creditor could seriously maintain that he believed that all the property in the hands of his potential debtor actually belonged to him. Moreover, there is no practical difference between a hire-purchase transaction arranged at the time of purchase and one arranged thereafter. A transaction which is intended to create an unfair preference can always be set aside. Accordingly, it seems to go too far to regard any arrangement of the nature of *constitutum possessorium* in this context as automatically invalid in Scots law, wise as it may be to scrutinise such arrangements closely.

1 See paras 114 ff above.
2 For a full discussion, see Bell *Commentaries* I, 269 ff. The doctrine was always based in principle on the fraud, collusion or carelessness of the true owner. The passing of the Mercantile Law Amendment Act (Scotland) 1856 (c 60), s 1 of which allowed the buyer of goods left in the possession of the seller to claim the goods in preference to creditors of the seller in case of his bankruptcy, and a clearer recognition of the fact that there are many legitimate occasions for the separation of ownership and possession combined to reduce the importance of the doctrine of reputed ownership. The reduction in its importance is noted by Lord Justice-Clerk Moncreiff in *Robertsons v M'Intyre* (1882) 9 R 772 at 778.
3 *Marston v Kerr's Trustee* (1879) 6 R 898; *Duncanson v Jefferis' Trustee* (1881) 8 R 563; *George Hopkinson Ltd v Napier & Son* 1953 SC 139, 1953 SLT 99.
4 Sale of Goods Act 1979 (c 54), s 62(4) (formerly the Sale of Goods Act 1893 (c 71), s 61(4)). See *Scottish Transit Trust Ltd v Scottish Land Cultivators Ltd* 1955 SC 254, 1955 SLT 417; *G and C Finance Corpn Ltd v Brown* 1961 SLT 408; *Ladbroke Leasing (South West) Ltd v Reekie Plant Ltd* 1983 SLT 155, OH. See also para 637 below.
5 *M'Bain v Wallace & Co* (1881) 8 R(HL) 106. See also G L Gretton 'Security over Moveables without Loss of Possession' 1978 SLT (News) 107. Some form of constructive or symbolical transfer may suffice. See *Scottish Transit Trust Ltd v Scottish Land Cultivators Ltd* 1955 SC 254 at 268, 1955 SLT 417 at 423, per Lord Carmont; *Ladbroke Leasing (South West) Ltd v Reekie Plant Ltd* 1983 SLT 155 at 158, OH, per Lord Grieve.
6 See para 623 below.

533. Content of the right of ownership. It is not profitable to attempt to enumerate the rights of an owner — it is simpler to say that he has any right to deal with property of which he is not deprived by law or by his own contract. But it may be noted here that the main positive rights of an owner are a right to use the property, a right to grant subordinate rights in it and a right to alienate the property *inter vivos* or *mortis causa*. In principle, the right of use is unlimited but restraints may be imposed by the civil or the criminal law. Thus a particular use may be interdicted if it causes a nuisance to a neighbour, for example, playing the bagpipes at 2 am in a quiet residential area. If damage is caused by a particular use, damages may be payable under the law of reparation. If a particular use amounts to a criminal offence the appropriate sanctions may be imposed at common law or under statute, and the sanctions may include forfeiture of the property used in committing the offence. If regulation of a particular activity is thought to be necessary in the public interest a system of licensing may be introduced. Use without a licence or in breach of a licence will probably involve criminal penalties but there may be other sanctions such as a prohibition of holding a licence in the future. It would be impossible to pursue all these topics in detail in the present context.

534. Grant of subordinate rights. The grant of subordinate rights involves two possibilities: (1) the grant of a contractual or other personal right to use the thing, and (2) the grant of a subordinate real right in the thing.

(1) *Grant of a contractual or other personal right to use the thing.* Where a contractual right is given, as where something is hired out or lent, the owner clearly retains his title and he clearly retains civil possession. But it is not clear how far possessory rights pass to the contractual holder as there is some uncertainty over the cases in which Scots law regards the holder of a contractual right as possessor of the thing and therefore as having a right to recover the thing from third parties. The point is discussed more fully above[1]. The holder of a contractual right may, therefore, have merely a personal right to retain the thing against the granter to him, in accordance with his contract. From the point of view of the owner, however, even the grant of a contractual right is a way of making use of the thing, and potentially profitable use in the case of hire. The owner is also certainly at least civil possessor while the thing is in the hands of the person who has been allowed the use of it, and so will retain some possessory rights, even if he does not have the sole possessory rights in the thing.

(2) *Grant of a subordinate real right in the thing.* The subordinate real rights which may be granted are liferent and security rights. These are discussed in detail in other titles[2] but it may be noted that the grantees do have possession or, in the case of hypothecs, a right to possession which is good against third parties. Scots common law, however, has been reluctant to recognise security rights in corporeal moveables where there is no actual transfer of possession to the security holder giving warning of the existence of the security right. In general, a security right has to take the form of a pledge and not a hypothec or similar arrangement giving security without immediate transfer of possession[3]. Hire-purchase was and is used as an evasion of the common law principle and retention of title can achieve the effect of security without possession[4]. The floating charge which expressly permits security without transfer of possession is a relatively recent statutory creation. In any case, it is only available to incorporated companies and to industrial and provident societies[5].

1 See paras 125–128 above.
2 See LIFERENT AND FEE, vol 13, and RIGHTS IN SECURITY, vol 20. For a list of real rights, see para 5 above.
3 There were limited exceptions such as bonds of bottomry and *respondentia* (see vol 20, paras 6, 26, 27, 281) and the legal hypothecs of the landlord for rent (see LANDLORD AND TENANT, vol 13, paras 513 ff) and of the superior for feuduty (see para 69 above).
4 *Armour v Thyssen Edelstahlwerke AG* 1991 SCLR 139, 1990 SLT 891, HL. Retention of title is discussed more fully in para 638 below, and RIGHTS IN SECURITY, vol 20, paras 29 ff.
5 Floating charges were introduced by the Companies (Floating Charges) (Scotland) Act 1961 (c 46). The current provisions are in the Companies Act 1985 (c 6), Pt XVIII (ss 462–487) (see further COMPANIES, vol 4, paras 651 ff). There are other more particular statutory hypothecs or charges contained in legislation such as the Merchant Shipping Act 1894 (c 60) and the Agricultural Credits (Scotland) Act 1929 (c 13): see vol 20, para 28.

535. Alienation. In principle, an owner may alienate his corporeal moveable property by *inter vivos* act or by act *mortis causa*, assuming that he has the requisite capacity[1]. Succession to corporeal moveables may be regulated by a destination but it does not appear to be possible unilaterally to impose a destination which will prevent the holder from disposing of them once possession of them has been taken[2]. A contract binding a person to make a will disposing of his property in a particular way is a valid contract[3] but must be proved by writ or oath of the party alleged to be bound because it is regarded as an innominate or unusual contract[4]. It would only have effect as a contract between the parties to the agreement: it does not impose a restraint on third parties even if they had knowledge of the contract. As a general rule, restraints on alienation of corporeal moveables are effective only as a matter of contract and do not affect third parties[5]. In the case of a trust, which affects the title of the trustees and imposes limitations on their dealings with the trust property, third parties who knew that they were dealing with trustees formerly could not acquire title if the trustees acted in breach of trust. But third parties dealing with trustees now have statutory protection against a claim for recovery of the trust property or its value from them on the ground that the act of the trustees was in conflict with the terms or purposes of the trust. This protection applies even although the third parties know of the existence of the trust and might not at common law obtain a good title[6]. Third parties taking in good faith and for value without knowledge of the trust have always obtained good title. As the new protection covers only acts done under the statutory powers given to trustees, it will not normally cover gratuitous transactions.

  1 See para 599 below; FAMILY LAW, vol 10, paras 1049 ff; OBLIGATIONS. See also the Age of Legal Capacity (Scotland) Act 1991 (c 50).
  2 See *Dyer v Carruthers* (1874) 1 R 943; *Cochrane's Executrix v Cochrane* 1947 SC 134, 1947 SLT 69; WILLS AND SUCCESSION, vol 25, para 737.
  3 *Paterson v Paterson* (1893) 20 R 484.
  4 *Smith v Oliver* 1911 SC 103, 1910 2 SLT 304.
  5 W M Gloag *The Law of Contract* (2nd edn, 1929) pp 266–269. See also para 353 above.
  6 See the Trusts (Scotland) Act 1961 (c 57), s 2(1), and TRUSTS, TRUSTEES AND JUDICIAL FACTORS, vol 24, paras 49–52, 202. See also para 691 below.

(3) MULTIPLE OWNERSHIP

536. Joint and common ownership. Scots law recognises the possibility that ownership may be held simultaneously by two or more parties. It makes a distinction also between two types of sharing of ownership, which may be described respectively as joint ownership and common ownership[1]. Unfortunately while the concepts are clear the terminology is not always used as accurately as would be desirable. Joint ownership implies that, although the ownership of the property in question is shared so long as the parties are joint owners, the joint owners do not have separate rights in their share of the property which they can deal with as their own; they cannot dispose of their share or burden it and if they leave the relationship their share simply accresces to the remaining owners[2]. Typical examples are ownership by joint trustees or ownership of club property by members of a club (which is not a proprietary club of which members simply have the use). This type of shared holding arises from the relationship of the parties and the rights and duties of the joint owners will be determined by the rules of that relationship. These are discussed elsewhere in this work[3].

    Common ownership describes a form of shared ownership in which the common owners have separate shares in the ownership which they can, within limits, dispose of independently of the other common owners[4]. In a relationship of common ownership, when one owner leaves, in principle, he takes his share with him, either physically by claiming its separation or otherwise by claiming its value. Common owners cannot be compelled to remain in the relationship if they wish to leave it and when they wish to leave they can insist on division of the common property or sale of the common property and division of the proceeds of sale[5]. Although the action known as an action of division and sale relates to heritable property the same principles would apply to a dispute over corporeal moveables owned in common.

1 See generally paras 17 ff above.
2 *Banff Magistrates v Ruthin Castle Ltd* 1944 SC 36 at 68, 1944 SLT 373 at 387, 388, per Lord Justice-Clerk Cooper approving the statement of the law in W M Gloag and R C Henderson *Introduction to the Law of Scotland* (3rd edn, 1939) pp 489, 490 (9th edn, 1987 by A B Wilkinson and W A Wilson, pp 689, 690).
3 See paras 34–36 above; TRUSTS, TRUSTEES AND JUDICIAL FACTORS, vol 24, paras 170 ff; ASSOCIATIONS AND CLUBS, vol 2, paras 810 ff.
4 Their shares may be described as *pro indiviso* (undivided) shares in that there is no physical division of the property during the common ownership, but the term *pro indiviso* is sometimes used to refer to joint ownership as described in the text above, eg in *Cargill v Muir* (1837) 15 S 408.
5 *Brock v Hamilton* (1852) 19 D 701 reported in a note to *Anderson v Anderson* (1857) 19 D 700. The case related to heritable property.

537. Management of property in multiple ownership. Most of the authorities on joint and common property relate to heritable property but they exemplify principles which apply equally well to corporeal moveables and in terms of management there are features common to both joint and common property. Thus in principle and in the absence of special agreement all joint and common owners are entitled to a share in the management of the property of which ownership is shared and decisions on management must be unanimous. The maxim applied is *melior est conditio prohibentis* (the objector has the stronger position). Thus in principle any owner can object to proposed new uses of the thing and to changes in it. He can even object to improvements, although he cannot object to necessary repairs; in the case of repairs the need for preservation of the property overrides the right of objection[1]. In the case of joint property, however, the rules of management will commonly be determined by the rules governing the relationship which gave rise to it.

Where common ownership is concerned, if the owners cannot agree and there is no provision for settlement of disagreements, the remedy is to break up the community of ownership by division or by sale, allowing the objecting owners to buy out the others or the others to buy them out, or allowing a division of the price if division of the property is not suitable. In the case of joint ownership, the rights of the respective joint owners are determined by the contract or other relationship which holds them together. Specific rules of law relating to management and disposal of the property contained, for example, in the law of trusts may therefore be relevant. Problems of disagreement over management cannot normally be resolved by division of the property among the joint owners or by sale, although dissolution of the relationship may be a possible course of action. If the relationship is dissolved this may involve the realisation of the property in question following the dissolution. These matters cannot be pursued in the general context of the law of corporeal moveable property and are dealt with elsewhere in this work[2].

1 See Bell *Principles* s 1075; *Deans v Woolfson* 1922 SC 221, 1922 SLT 165. And see more generally paras 23 ff above.
2 See ASSOCIATIONS AND CLUBS, vol 2, paras 803 ff; TRUSTS, TRUSTEES AND JUDICIAL FACTORS, vol 24, paras 170 ff.

(4) OWNERSHIP IN TRUST

538. Ownership without beneficial interest. Ownership in trust needs only brief mention as trusts are dealt with in detail elsewhere in this work[1]. Where ownership is held in trust the trustees are owners of the property but they hold that ownership not for their own benefit but for the benefit of the beneficiaries of the trust. Conversely, the beneficiaries are not owners of the trust property but they can insist that the trustees use and dispose of the property in terms of the trust (or as permitted by the law of trusts) and account to them for their management[2]. So far as third parties are concerned, the trustees are on the face of it owners of the property but they are limited owners and it is a principle of trust that if a trustee parts improperly with trust property the beneficiaries may 'follow' the property, so long as it is traceable, into the hands of anyone who has taken it in bad faith or gratuitously or with notice of the existence of the trust[3]. To put it another way, only a third party who has taken in good faith and for value and without notice of the trust is safe from a claim by a beneficiary unless, of course, he can rely on some rule granting him special protection[4]. In the case of corporeal moveables there is normally less chance of the existence of the trust being apparent, in the absence of documentary evidence of title.

In recent years attempts have been made to provide security to sellers of raw materials and partly finished products and to wholesalers and other merchants by the device of retention of title clauses in the sale contract: these are very often combined with clauses which attempt to set up trust ownership of the goods supplied to the purchaser or of the proceeds of such goods. The object is to allow a claim that the supplier is the owner or beneficial owner of the goods in case the person supplied goes bankrupt and thus to allow the supplier to reclaim the goods out of the bankrupt estate. The courts were understandably reluctant to give effect to such devices, which could be self-defeating if widely used and create great uncertainty over title to moveables, but, as already noted, the House of Lords has accepted the validity of widely-drafted clauses of retention of title[5]. The use of trusts remains a matter of discussion[6].

1 See TRUSTS, TRUSTEES AND JUDICIAL FACTORS, vol 24, paras 1 ff.
2 Bell *Commentaries* I,36; *Inland Revenue v Clark's Trustees* 1939 SC 11, 1939 SLT 2; *Parker v Lord Advocate* 1960 SC (HL) 29. See also vol 24, para 49.
3 *Taylor v Forbes* (1830) 4 W & S 444, HL; *Bertram Gardner & Co's Trustee v King's and Lord Treasurer's Remembrancer* 1920 SC 555, 1920 2 SLT 141. See also vol 24, paras 50–52.
4 Thus the Trusts (Scotland) Act 1961 (c 57), s 2(1), protects parties who are dealing with trustees purporting to exercise the powers given by the Trusts (Scotland) Act 1921 (c 58), s4(1)(a)–(ee), against any claim that the act of the trustees was at variance with the terms or purposes of the trust. See para 691 below.
5 See para 534 above.
6 See RIGHTS IN SECURITY, vol 20, paras 29 ff, and para 691, note 6, below.

(5) ORIGINAL ACQUISITION OF OWNERSHIP OF CORPOREAL MOVEABLE PROPERTY

(a) Introduction

539. Original and derivative acquisition. In Scots law ownership of corporeal moveable property can be acquired by a new title or by a title derived from the title of the previous owner. Where there is a new title the case is referred to as 'original acquisition' of ownership. This should be contrasted with 'derivative acquisition' which refers to cases where ownership is acquired by a title which depends on the title of a previous holder from whom ownership has been acquired[1]. The 'original' acquirer has a new or original title to the thing in question either because it had no previous owner or because any previous owner has lost his ownership or loses it by the act which gives rise to the new owner's title. Thus, where a corporeal moveable has never had an owner, it may be acquired by taking it, that is by the mode of acquisition which is generally known by the Roman term *occupatio* (occupation or seizure) or its English equivalent, occupancy. Where one thing is made into another the new thing may be acquired by a mode of acquisition which carries a name derived from Roman law, *specificatio*, or specification, that is, the making of a new *species* or thing. In the former case, the title of the owner is necessarily original because there is no owner from whom he could derive title; in the latter case, the making is regarded as the source of the new owner's title, at least, in those cases where he does acquire title[2]. His title is not derived from the title of the previous owner of the thing which has been given a new form and so again the case is treated as one of original acquisition. This is not a matter of logical necessity; it is simply a description of how the case is treated in Scots law, which in this respect follows Roman law. Positive prescription gives rise to ownership by possession for the relevant period and again the title is an original one. Finally property may be acquired by accession when an accessory is added to a principal thing and the ownership of the accessory is absorbed into the ownership of the principal thing.

In all these cases a new individual ownership results. However, there are two cases in which a union of things belonging to different owners results neither in the making of a new thing with acquisition of ownership by specification nor the absorption of one thing by another with acquisition of ownership by accession. These cases are commixtion (*commixtio*) of solids and confusion (*confusio*) of liquids and, where there is any change of ownership, the union results in the creation of common ownership of the things which have been united.

Occupatio, specificatio and prescription are dealt with in this section on acquisition, along with other related questions. The treatment of *commixtio* and *confusio* follows on the treatment of *specificatio* as there may be a question in a particular case into what category a union falls. Accession is dealt with separately below[3]. Derivative acquisition is dealt with under the heading of transfer of ownership below[4].

1 Bell *Principles* s 1286.
2 The precise circumstances in which he does so are considered at paras 559 ff below.
3 See paras 570 ff below. It may be noted here that the institutional writers treat specification as an aspect of accession but this arrangement is open to criticism. See para 588 below.
4 See paras 597 ff below.

(b) *Occupatio* or Occupancy

540. Definition and scope. As a general rule in Roman law, anything which was capable of private ownership and which was not already owned could be acquired by *occupatio*, that is, by taking possession of it; *quod nullius est fit occupantis* (what belongs to no-one becomes the property of the taker)[1]. *Occupatio* applied both to things which had never had an owner, such as shells on the seashore, and things which had ceased to have an owner, for example, because they had been abandoned. The only exception to this rule was *thesaurus* or treasure, to which special rules applied[2]. In Scots law, the term *occupatio* is also used. However, in Scots law *occupatio* or occupancy as a mode of acquisition applies only to things which have never had an owner[3]. Where things were once owned but no longer have an owner, the general rule is that they belong to the Crown: *nullius est fit domini regis* (what belongs to no-one becomes the property of the lord king)[4]. Thus if a question arises over the ownership of things which have once been appropriated but have now no traceable owner, the Crown will have title unless some special rule applies.

1 Justinian *Institutes* II,1,12; *Digest* 41,1,1,3 and 5.
2 See Justinian *Institutes* II,1,39; *Digest* 41,1,31,1; 63 preamble; W W Buckland *Textbook of Roman Law* (3rd edn, 1963 by P Stein) pp 218 ff.
3 Stair *Institutions* I,7,3; II,1,5 and 33; Erskine *Institute* II,1,10; Bell *Principles* ss 1287–1288.
4 *Stair* II,1,5; III,3,27: *Erskine* II,1,12; *Bell* s 1291.

541. Appropriation. Where occupancy is possible the first question which arises is what amounts to an appropriation sufficient to give owneship. Essentially the question is one of taking possession or gaining control of the thing[1]. Bell says that:

'The act of appropriation is effectual to vest the property only when complete. But it is held complete while fairly proceeding towards full accomplishment'[2].

Bell deduces from this that wounding an animal to death or so that it cannot escape gives ownership as does having it 'in pursuit, and not beyond reach'[2]. Referring to Stair, he says that anyone coming in and taking the animal does not deprive the pursuer who is 'deemed the lawful occupant'[3].

The view stated by Bell was regarded as 'the general law of occupancy' in *Sutter v Aberdeen Arctic Co*[4]. However, the court also held that the matter might be determined by local customary rules and in fact the issue in that case was determined by the customs of whalers in the northern seas[5]. Apart from whale-fishing cases there is no direct authority on the matter of what constitutes taking in Scots law, other than Bell and Stair, but there is indirect authority in the case of taking of animals classed as game. The fact that close pursuit of wild animals gives or may give ownership does not mean that such a pursuit of animals classed as game may not amount to a trespass in pursuit of game, which constitutes a criminal offence under the game laws. But entry on land to retrieve dead or moribund game or game apparently dead is not a trespass in pursuit of game, which implies that the animal has already been taken[6].

A second question which arises is whether the taking must be lawful if it is to give rise to ownership. On this point the institutional writers are unanimous; any taker acquires ownership of what had no previous owner, almost as a matter of logical necessity[7]. Hence it is irrelevant, as it was in Roman law, that the taker is a trespasser on private land or indeed that the owner of the land has a specific right to take the things in question, such as salmon in a salmon fishery; in these cases the right is in general a right to take and not a right to what is taken[8]. It is also irrelevant that the taking is in breach of legislation such as the game laws, aimed at preserving things which at common law are *res nullius*[9].

1 The point was disputed in Roman law, in particular in relation to the capture of wild animals. One view was that ownership went to the person in close pursuit of the animal even if the animal was killed by someone else; the view approved in the *Corpus Iuris Civilis*, however, is that actual capture is necessary to give ownership, on the principle that the animal must be taken and close pursuit does not guarantee capture. Justinian *Institutes* II,1,13; *Digest* 41,1,5,1.
2 Bell *Principles* s 1289.
3 Ie Stair *Institutions* II,1,33. Stair in fact propounds the more subtle rule that where one party is in pursuit 'with a probability to reach his prey' and another interferes and makes the actual capture the person making the capture is owner but must restore the property to the person whom he has unjustly deprived of it.
4 *Sutter v Aberdeen Arctic Co* (1861) 23 D 465 especially at 475, 476, per Lord President M'Neill (revsd (1862) 4 Macq 355, HL).
5 According to these customs a whale harpooned, or one once harpooned and still caught in the harpoon line, was a 'fast fish' and belonged to the striker even if others helped to catch it with further harpoons; if it broke free from the harpoon it was a 'loose fish' and could be caught by anyone. See *Addison v Row* (1794) 3 Pat 334, HL; *Hutchison v Dundee Whale Fishing Co* (1830) 5 Murr 164. Other customs applied in other seas so that several strikers might share the whale.
6 *Donald v Boddam* (1828) Syme 303; *Lord Macdonald v Maclean* (1879) 6 R (J) 14, 4 Coup 205; *Nicoll v Strachan* (1913) SC (J) 18, 1912 2 SLT 383. Removal of a deer carcase by a person having no legal

right to take or kill deer and without permission of a person having such a right is an offence under the Deer (Scotland) Act 1959 (c 40), s 22(2) (added by the Deer (Amendment) (Scotland) Act 1982 (c 19), s 6(c)). See GAME, vol 11, para 938.

7 Stair II,1,33; Erskine *Institute* II,1,10; *Bell* s 1286. Erskine in fact refers to 'the necessity of law'.

8 See FISHERIES, vol 11, para 3, and paras 320 ff above. For game, see para 545 below and GAME, vol 11, para 803.

9 So far at least, none of the relevant legislative provisions (for details of which see FISHERIES and GAME in vol 11) specifically deprive the person who contravenes them of the right to what he has taken. Rather the legislation assumes that ownership has been acquired by providing for forfeiture of the thing acquired as a possible penalty (along with other penalties). Thus, the fact that the taking may amount to a criminal offence does not appear to prevent acquisition, although it is arguable that this is not so and that provisions for forfeiture need imply no more than that the taker can be deprived of any right which he may have. Undoubtedly he would have possession, as even a *mala fide* taker, including a thief, obtains possession of what he takes.

542. Things which can be acquired. On the question what precisely can be acquired by occupancy in Scots law, the institutional writers, clearly influenced by the Roman texts, refer to such things as shells, pearls, gems, pebbles or precious stones on the sea-shore[1] as well as animals *ferae naturae* (wild by nature). The term animals *ferae naturae* refers to all creatures, beasts, birds or fish, which are not normally kept as tame or domesticated animals, with the exception that 'royal fish' are not open to occupancy[2]. While other creatures *ferae naturae* are roaming freely they can be acquired. However, the fact that they have been acquired does not mean that ownership is retained until, say, the animal is abandoned; as in Roman law, in principle ownership is retained only so long as control is kept[3]. 'Control', on the other hand, does not mean that the animals must be closely caged. It is enough that they are confined within a particular area such as a deer park or pond and so the animals in a wild-life park or a 'natural' zoo would still be owned while confined. Animals which roam but return to a specific place are also owned so long as they keep returning. The examples of pigeons and bees, cited by the institutional writers, are taken from Roman law[4], but presumably any wild animal which had been so tamed that it would return would still be owned[5] (although for the purpose of liability for damages caused it would be classed as animal likely to cause injury or damage[6]). Finally, even if a wild animal escapes or a 'tamed' animal which has the habit of returning gives up this habit, as do bees when swarming, the animal is still owned so long as the owner pursues it and has a reasonable chance of recovering it. In this case, there is no doubt that actual capture is unnecessary to retain ownership[7]. The intervention of a third party would be theft if the act were done *mala fide*[8]. Once a wild animal escapes it is again open to occupancy, as in Roman law[9]. This is a practical rule and it conflicts with the principle that property which was once owned and thereafter lost goes to the Crown.

1 Given that the shore belongs to the Crown, unless it has been alienated to a subject, it is not clear why pebbles should not be regarded as belonging to the Crown or its alienee but presumably they are regarded as not forming part of the shore. Erskine *Institute* II,1,10, refers specifically to pebbles 'cast on the shore'. There would therefore seem room for dispute over any pebbles the value of which made the cost of litigation worth while.

2 See Stair *Institutions* I,7,3; II,1,5 and 33; *Erskine* II,1,10; Bell *Principles* ss 1287, 1288. As to 'royal fish', see para 543 below.

3 See the authorities referred to in note 2 above and *Bell* s 1290. As to escape, see below.

4 Justinian *Institute* II,1,14 and 15; *Digest* 41,1,9,2–5; ht 44.

5 Stair II,1,33; *Erskine* II,1,10; *Bell* s 1290. Bell includes animals 'marked for private property, as deer and swans with collars'.

6 Animals (Scotland) Act 1987 (c 9), s 1(1), (3); Dangerous Wild Animals Act 1976 (c 38), s 7(4), Schedule (substituted by the Dangerous Wild Animals Act 1976 (Modification) Order 1984, SI 1984/1111).

7 *Erskine* II,1,10; *Bell* s 1290. For the Roman law authorities, see note 4 above.

8 Stair II,1,33; *Bell* s 1290.

9 *Valentine v Kennedy* 1985 SCCR 89. But both the learned sheriff and the writer of the note on the case seem somewhat to confuse controlled animals *ferae naturae*, such as fish, and domesticated

animals, such as sheep. It may be, however, that the courts will be prepared specifically to decide that farmed fish are domesticated animals and not animals *ferae naturae*. If farmed fish are not domesticated, as the sheriff apparently thought, because he doubted whether fish could be tamed (1985 SCCR 89 at 91) they would not belong to the Crown after their escape: see the text to, and the authorities in, note 8 above.

It is specifically made an offence by the Theft Act 1607 (c 6) to break dovecots and to steal bees and 'fisches in propir stankis and loches': see *Pollok v M'Cabe* 1910 SC (J) 23, 1910 I SLT 83.

Under the Sea Fisheries (Shellfish) Act 1967 (c 83), s 7(2), shellfish in a several fishery granted under s 1 of the Act and oysters in private beds sufficiently marked out or sufficiently known as such, are the absolute property of the grantees or owners of the beds and are deemed to be in their actual possession. Under s 7(3) all shellfish or oysters removed from the fishery or bed are the absolute property of the grantees of the fishery or bed and the absolute right to possession is deemed to be in them unless the shellfish or oysters are sold in market overt (in England only, presumably) or disposed of by or under the authority of the grantees or owner.

543. Royal fish. The one exception to the rule that wild creatures can be acquired by occupancy is 'royal fish'[1]. The right to take them is *inter regalia minora* (among the lesser royal rights) as are salmon fishings, but in this case, unlike salmon fishings, not only does the Crown (or its grantee) have the right to take the fish but it has the right to the fish themselves, if it chooses to exercise it. The Crown apparently does not exercise its right[2], which may be exercised at the discretion of the Crown Estate Commissioners, but as it is a right of property and so a *res merae facultatis*, it is not lost by prescription[3] and so it could be re-asserted if the Crown chose to do so. It would be possible to acquire the right from the Crown by grant or prescription but it does not seem that many such rights have been acquired or that any are asserted[4]. Smaller stranded whales which do not qualify as 'royal fish' belong to their captors, as do all whales caught in the open sea or even in Scottish territorial waters if the Crown's claim is limited to stranded whales[5]. A custom in Shetland whereby a landlord could claim a share of small 'caaing whales' caught by his tenants was declared to be not just or reasonable and denied the force of law[6].

1 It is sometimes said that the term 'royal fish' covers whales, sturgeon and other 'great fish' such as grampuses, dolphins and porpoises either caught in the territorial seas, or stranded — see C Stewart *The Law of Scotland related to Rights of Fishing* (2nd edn 1892, by J C Shairp) pp 57, 58; J Ferguson *Law of Water and Water Rights in Scotland* (1907) pp 28–30; J H Tait *A Treatise of the Law of Scotland as applied to the Game Laws and Trout and Salmon Fishing revised and with a new section on Sea Fishery Law* (2nd edn, 1928 by J O Taylor) pp 264, 338 — but it appears that this statement is based on purely English authority, namely, Hale's *De Jure Maris* (printed in F Hargrave *Legal Tracts* (1787)). The only Scottish authority on the question allows the Crown to claim whales which are too large to be drawn to land by a wain pulled by six oxen and apparently allows a claim only to stranded whales. See Stair *Institutions* II,1,5 (where he is rather vague) and II,1,33 (apparently allowing acquisition of whales in the open seas); Erskine *Institute* II,1,10 (referring to the *Leges Forestarum* para 17 — on which see the edition of the *Leges* by J M Gilbert in *Hunting and Hunting Reserves in Medieval Scotland* (1979) p 298); Balfour *Practicks* (Stair Soc vol 22, 1963 ed P G B McNeill) p 555, c viii; *Fragmenta quaedam veterum legum et consuetudinum Scotiae undique collecta*, c 1, *De inventione ceti* (APS i, App V, 384 (red pagination 748)).

2 See the textbooks referred to in note 1 above; *Bruce v Smith* (1890) 17 R 1000.

3 Prescription and Limitation (Scotland) Act 1973 (c 52), s 8, Sch 3; PRESCRIPTION AND LIMI-TATION.

4 See the textbooks referred to in note 1 above.

5 The textbooks referred to in note 1 above suggest that large whales caught in Scottish territorial waters belong to the Crown but this doctrine seems to be derived from Hale's statement of the position in English law (in *De Jure Maris*). As to the legislation on whale-fishing, see FISHERIES, vol 11, paras 226 ff.

6 *Bruce v Smith* (1890) 17 R 100 — despite *Stove v Colvin* (1831) 9 S 633 and *Scott v Reid* (11 July 1838, unreported) where the custom was applied. See the critical discussion of *Bruce* by W D H Sellar in SOURCES OF LAW (FORMAL), vol 22, paras 386–388.

544. Game and game legislation. Certain wild animals and birds are classed as 'game' and protected by legislation but there is no precise definition of the term 'game' in Scots law; most of the relevant statutes avoid the problem by listing the particular animals or birds which are affected by their provisions. One suggested definition of game is animals or birds killed for sport and dealt in as food[1]. In a case where the relevant statutory definition included the general term 'game', as well as a list of specific kinds of game, it was held that capercailzie were game because they were among the animals or birds killed for sport and dealt in as food[2]. This double criterion excludes foxes which are hunted for sport but are not eaten[3] and rabbits which are used for food but unlike hares are caught rather than hunted for sport[4]. But to add to the difficulty of attaining a precise definition, rabbits are referred to as 'ground game' in the Ground Game Act 1880[5]. Most of the legislation known as the Game Acts in fact deals with game birds and hares and there is separate legislation on deer and on salmon and trout.

Early legislation restricted the right of hunting to substantial landholders. Moreover, certain rights of hunting or fishing were by common law or statute reserved to the Crown as *regalia minora*[6]. Of these, only the right to salmon fishing has survived as a separate right.

The general purpose of all the game legislation, both the Game Acts and the other special legislation, is the protection of the animals in question so that they can be pursued for sport. This protection takes various forms, but typically it consists of the introduction of close times for taking the animals (the close times usually covering the breeding season); restrictions on the methods which may lawfully be used to take them; penalising trespass in pursuit of them; and controlling their sale[7]. The game legislation imposes criminal sanctions for breaches of its protection provisions. These sanctions may include forfeiture of animals unlawfully taken, but such forfeiture does require express provision[8].

1 J H Tait *A Treatise on the Law of Scotland as applied to the Game Laws and Trout and Salmon Fishing* revised and with a new section on Sea Fishery Law (2nd edn, 1928 by J O Taylor) p 1. A F Irvine *Treatise on the Game Laws of Scotland* (3rd edn, 1883) pp 1, 2, makes the criteria of 'game' their value as articles of food or the pleasure afforded by their pursuit but restricts game in a legal sense to 'those creatures which the enactments of positive law have distinguished from others by the imposition of certain restrictions as to their capture'. See GAME, vol 11, para 802.
2 *Colquhoun's Trustees v Lee* (1957) SLT (Sh Ct) 50, (1957) 73 Sh Ct Rep 165.
3 There is no right to pursue foxes for sport on the lands of others (*Marquis of Tweedale v Dalrymple* (1778) Mor 4992) but it may be possible to enter land to destroy foxes which are causing damage eg to sheep, on payment of damage caused (*Colquhoun v Buchanan* (1785) Mor 4997).
4 *Moncrieff v Arnott* (1828) 6 S 530.
5 Rabbits are also included in the statutory definitions of game in the Night Poaching Acts of 1828 (c 69) and 1844 (c 29), and in the provisions of the Game (Scotland) Act 1832 (c 68) (dealing with day trespass) and the Poaching Prevention Act 1862 (c 114) (concerning the criminal law on poaching).
6 Thus the Act of 1621 (c 31) formally repealed by the Statute Law Revision (Scotland) Act 1964 (c 80) but already in desuetude, imposed a penalty on persons hunting or hawking who did not have 'a pleughe [that is a ploughgate, extending to approximately 104 Scots acres] of land in heritage'. The Crown could at one time declare land to be 'forest' thus bringing it within the special forest laws and restricting the right to hunt deer and other 'greater game' such as wild boar and wild goats. It could then alienate that right to a subject. However, the Crown ceased to make such grants in the later seventeenth century because forest rights could be exercised oppressively. The forest laws have fallen into desuetude even so far as the Crown itself is concerned. In any case, a right of forest was interpreted in *Duke of Athole v Macinroy* (1862) 24 D 673 as giving no right to the animals themselves, but as carrying only a right to hunt them in the forest. In other words, the Crown's claim was seen as a claim to control hunting and not as a claim to the 'greater game' as such. They were not 'royal animals' as whales were 'royal fish'.
  Stair does take the royal right to deer as inferring that only those with a right of forest could lawfully kill deer; others were confined to chasing deer from their lands and ultimately back to some forest: *Institutions* II,3,68. However, he does not say that deer unlawfully killed belong to the Crown and the idea that deer were royal beasts was rejected in *Duke of Athole v Macinroy*. Treating the Crown right to deer as a right to dispose of the privilege of hunting them would be in conformity with the rule in salmon fishings. Salmon fishings are *inter regalia minora* and commonly have been granted to subjects. But the right to salmon fishings is a right separate from any right in the lands

beside which the fishings may lie. It is also a right to catch salmon not a right to any salmon which are caught.

Stair states that 'swans are particularly reserved to the king' and that the privilege to kill swans must be specifically granted even in a barony title but he gives no indication of his authority: II,3,60. It is clear that the Crown has a right to swans in England but apart from Stair's opinion there appears to be no other evidence in the authorities that the privilege exists or has been claimed in Scotland.

The Crown took an interest in other fowl, especially those pursued by hawks, such as herons, and the Scottish Parliament legislated for their protection: but it does not seem that the birds (and animals) to be protected were claimed as Crown property. The motives seem to have been more the preservation of birds and animals for the 'manly exercise' of hawking and hunting. See eg the Acts of 1493 c 19 (APS ii, 235); 1567 c 17 (APS iii, 26); 1600 c 34 (APS iv, 236); 1685 c 24 (APS viii, 475b). See also GAME, vol 11, para 800.

7 For details, see vol 11, paras 800 ff; W M Gordon *Scottish Land Law* (1989) ch 9.
8 *Simpson v Fraser* 1948 JC 1. General powers of forfeiture are contained in the Criminal Procedure (Scotland) Act 1975 (c 21), s 223 (solemn procedure), and s 436 (summary procedure) (substituted by the Criminal Justice (Scotland) Act 1980 (c 62), s 83(2), Sch 7, para 71). See PROCEDURE, vol 17, para 807.

545. Property in game.

So far as property rights are concerned, the question whether or not a wild animal is game is not very important. It is true that only the owner of land is entitled to hunt game on the land; even a tenant has no such right[1] unless it is given by his lease or by legislation[2]. But game animals are not owned simply because they are on the land or because their existence on land makes hunting or shooting rights over the land valuable. The value of the game on his land may lead a landowner to exercise with rigour his right to exclude those who enter without his authority and so may reduce the opportunities for others to take game but game itself is not owned and so may be acquired even by a poacher unless the particular animals concerned are so confined that they are in the possession of the person claiming them[3]. It is then the confinement of the animals which matters and not their qualification as game. However, game taken in contravention of the game legislation may be forfeited as a penalty.

1 *Welwood v Husband* (1874) 1 R 507.
2 See eg the Ground Game Act 1880 (c 47) which allows the taking of hares and rabbits.
3 See para 542 above.

546. Conservation of wildlife.

The game legislation is specifically concerned with animals which are hunted for sport. Although some of these animals are also commercially exploited and the commercial interest or the commercial exploitation of the sporting interest may now be a dominant factor in the operation of the legislation, the historical ground for the legislation was in the first place preservation for sport. In more modern times a wider interest in protection of wildlife has developed, starting with the protection of birds. The result of this interest in conservation has been the passing of extensive legislation for this purpose[1].

Also relevant in this connection are the international measures against traffic in endangered species of wildlife. These are given effect in the United Kingdom by legislation[2].

1 See in particular the Wildlife and Countryside Act 1981 (c 69) which consolidates most of the existing legislation as well as introducing new provisions and which is supplemented by legislation on individual species such as seals and badgers. It would be out of place to consider this Act and the other relevant legislation in detail in the present context but it may be said that the legislation makes provision for protection of the animals with which it deals similar to that in the game legislation. Like that legislation it operates by imposing criminal sanctions which may include forfeiture. See further ANIMALS, vol 2, paras 273 ff, and GAME, vol 11, paras 878–886.
2 See the Endangered Species (Import and Export) Act 1976 (c 72). The Act provides that its schedules may be modified by subordinate legislation and they have been revised to take account of the Washington Convention on International Trade in Endangered Species of Wild Fauna and Flora (CITES). See further vol 2, paras 206, 215–217, 228.

(c) Lost and Abandoned Property

547. Definitions. Lost property may be defined as property the ownership of which is temporarily uncertain; abandoned property as property which has once been owned but the ownership of which has been given up by its owner. However, where lost property is not claimed, it may become abandoned. Moreover, when property is found with no apparent owner it may not be clear immediately whether ownership has been abandoned and so lost property and abandoned property must be considered together. Once it is clear that ownership has been abandoned, at common law the question of title is simple because the Crown acquires ownership under the general principle that ownerless property goes to the Crown (*quod nullius est fit domini regis*)[1]. Until the position is clear, there is a question of interim custody and disposal of the property, which was settled by the older law in various ways[2]. The position is now mainly regulated by statute but the common law on possession and *negotiorum gestio* may still be relevant.

1 See para 540 above.
2 The older law distinguished between waif (or waith) goods in general and waif or waith goods in the sense of strays, meaning strayed cattle or other farm animals. At common law, the finder if honest would hold the property as *negotiorum gestor* for the true owner if he chose to take custody of it; if dishonest he would be a *mala fide* possessor and a thief. As *negotiorum gestor*, the honest finder would be obliged to look after it with reasonable care and would be entitled to reimbursement from the owner of his reasonable and proper expenses, but there was an old statutory provision in the case of strayed cattled that the finder should give public notice of the finding and if the owner did not appear within a year and a day the cattle were escheated to the Crown or its donatory of escheats. There might also be local provisions to similar effect by acts of local courts. Again, if cattle (horses, nolt, sheep, swine or goats) strayed on to private land, the Winter Herding Act 1686 (c 21) allowed the owner of the land to impound the cattle until payment of any damage done, a half merk penalty per beast and the expenses of the keep of the cattle while impounded, but the 1686 Act was primarily concerned with damage done by the straying beasts and has been repealed and replaced by the provisions of the Animals (Scotland) Act 1987 (c 9). See ANIMALS, vol 2, para 167. The Burgh Police (Scotland) Act 1892 (c 55), ss 386, 387, which allowed police to impound cattle at large, were repealed by the Local Government (Scotland) Act 1973 (c 65), s 229(1).
     There was also more modern provision, both general and special, in the case of lost property other than stray cattle. In the case of burghs, the general provisions were contained in the Burgh Police (Scotland) Act 1892 or local legislation; elsewhere the Lost Property (Scotland) Act 1965 (c 27) (now repealed) applied. Special legislation applied and still applies to stray dogs, lost property in public transport, abandoned vehicles and property left behind by a secure tenant of public sector housing who abandons his tenancy: see paras 548–552 below.

548. Care of lost and abandoned property. Dealing with lost or abandoned property is now mainly regulated by the Civic Government (Scotland) Act 1982[1] which largely supersedes previous legislation. The finder[2] of such property must take reasonable care of the property and he must without unreasonable delay deliver it or report the fact that he has taken possession of it to a constable or any other person specified in the statutory provisions[3]. Any report must describe the property and indicate where it was found[4]. An owner or occupier of land or premises who takes possession of property or receives a report about its finding must in turn deliver the property or report that he has taken possession of it to a constable or to any of the other specified persons[5]. A person with apparent authority to act on behalf of any of the specified persons must similarly deliver the property or make a report to a constable or to any of the others so specified[6]. When a report is made to a constable, the chief constable may require the person holding the property to deliver it to such person at such time as he may direct[7]. Failure to comply with any provisions of the relevant section without reasonable excuse is a summary offence[8]. The provisions therefore assume that when property which seems to be lost or abandoned is found it should be returned to the owner or the person entitled to possession of it, for example, a pledgee, or to the apparent representative of either of these; or that it should be handed over or reported either to the occupier of the land or premises on which it is found or to his apparent representative, such as a lost property department in a store; or to the police, who may require that it be handed over to the police or to any one else. It seems to be assumed that a finder who reports to the owner or occupier of premises or to an apparent representative will hand the property over so that it can be delivered or reported as required of them. It would also seem necessary to the scheme that if the property is not handed over a record should be made of the finder who is in possession of it so that an owner or person entitled to possession who is making enquiry about lost property can trace it.

Neither the finder of lost or abandoned property nor the employer of a finder nor the owner or occupier of land or premises on which the property is found has any right to claim ownership of it by reason only of the finding, although a right may be acquired under the procedure for disposal of the property found[9]. The legislation is binding on the Crown[10] and the Crown's rights in lost or abandoned property are capable of being extinguished by a disposal in terms of the relevant Act[11] but the Crown's rights are affected only by such a disposal[12]. A chief constable must therefore consider any possible claims by the Crown before proceeding to disposal as he is required to 'take reasonable steps to ascertain the identity of the owner or person having right to the possession of the property and to notify him where it can be collected'[13].

1 See the Civic Government (Scotland) Act 1982 (c 45), Pt VI (ss 67–79). The provisions of this Act are based on but do not in every detail follow the recommendations of a report by the Scottish Law Commission, ie the *Report on Lost and Abandoned Property* (Scot Law Com no. 57 (1980)). Had these recommendations been followed the provisions on lost property would not have been inserted in the 1982 Act, in which they do not most naturally belong, and they would have been comprehensive. As it is, there are exceptions from the general provisions, namely (1) property found in public transport or premises used by public transport, (2) abandoned motor vehicles, (3) stray dogs, and (4) property left behind by a secure tenant of public sector housing who has abandoned his tenancy. In each case there is alternative provision and these exceptions are dealt with at para 552 below.
2 Ie any person taking possession of any property without the authority of the owner in circumstances which make it reasonable to infer that the property has been lost or abandoned: Civic Government (Scotland) Act 1982, s 67(1). The Act has been held not to apply to property taken into the possession of the police with a view to criminal proceedings: *Fleming v Chief Constable of Strathclyde* 1987 SCLR 303, Sh Ct.
3 The persons specified in the Civic Government (Scotland) Act 1982, s 67(3), are (1) the owner, (2) the person having right to possession of the property, (3) the owner or occupier of the land or premises on which the property was found, or (4) any person apparently having the authority to act on behalf of any of these persons.
4 Ibid, s 67(1).
5 Ibid, s 67(4)(a): the persons specified are those listed in s 67(3) (see note 3 above).
6 Ibid, s 67(4)(b).
7 Ibid, s 67(5). The 'chief constable' means the chief constable for the police area in which the property is found, including a constable acting under his direction for the purposes of Pt VI of the Act: s 79.
8 Ibid, s 67(6).
9 For powers of disposal, see ibid, ss 71, 74, and para 549 below.
10 Ibid, s 78(1).
11 Ibid, s 78(2).
12 Ibid, s 78(3).
13 Ibid, s 68(3). This subsection would require communication with the Queen's and Lord Treasurer's Remembrancer and also with the local receiver of wrecks in the case of treasure or wreck. See paras 553, 554 ff, below.

549. Disposal of lost and abandoned property. Having set out the basic obligations of the finder, the Civic Government (Scotland) Act 1982 goes on to deal with disposal of the property by the chief constable, who is responsible for property delivered or reported to or found by a constable[1]. The property must normally be kept for a minimum period of two months from the date on which it was delivered or reported to a constable[2], but if in the chief constable's opinion it cannot be safely or conveniently kept for this period it may be disposed of sooner in such manner as he thinks fit[3]. While it is held by the chief constable appropriate arrangements must be made for its care and custody[4] and it is made clear that it may be appropriate to leave a living creature in the care of the finder at his request[5]. Reasonable steps must also be taken to ascertain the identity of the owner or person with a right to possession of the property and to notify him where it can be collected[6].

While the property is in the possession of the chief constable or anyone holding it by arrangement with him it can be claimed by the owner or the person entitled to possession of it[7]. If the chief constable is satisfied that the claimant is entitled to have the property he can have it delivered to the claimant on such conditions as he thinks fit. These may include payment of reasonable charges (including expenses) and a reward[8]. The chief constable may determine the reward having regard to the whole circumstances, including the nature and value of the property, the ability of the claimant to pay and the actings of the finder[9]. Any decision of the chief constable may be appealed to the sheriff[10].

If the property has neither been successfully claimed[11] nor already disposed of[12], after two months the chief constable may dispose of it[13]. There are four possibilities:

(1) having regard to the whole circumstances, including the nature and value of the property and the actings of the finder the chief constable may offer it to the finder[14];

(2) if the chief constable thinks it inappropriate to offer the property to the finder he may sell it[15];

(3) if an offer is inappropriate and a sale is impracticable the chief constable may dispose of it or make arrangements for its disposal otherwise as he thinks fit[16];

(4) in the special case where a living creature other than a stray dog or livestock[17] has been in the care and custody of the person who found it by an arrangement with the chief constable[18] and no claimant has appeared within two months, the creature becomes the property of the person who has looked after it[19].

1 Civic Government (Scotland) Act 1982 (c 45), s 68(1).

2 Ibid, s 68(4).

3 Ibid, s 68(5).

4 Ibid, s 68(2).

5 Ibid, s 74.

6 Ibid, s 68(3).

7 Ibid, s 69(1). The section does not appear to allow for adjudication of competing claims: *Fleming v Chief Constable of Strathclyde* 1987 SCLR 303, Sh Ct.

8 Civic Government (Scotland) Act 1982, s 69(2). The reward is determined under s 70. Nothing in s 69 affects any right to or interest in the property arising otherwise than by virtue of the section: s 69(3). The action taken by the chief constable under s 69 does not therefore affect the rights of the true owner or a security holder if the claimant is not in fact entitled to the property.

9 Ibid, s 70(2)(a)–(c).

10 See ibid, s 76.

11 Ie under ibid, s 69.

12 Ie under ibid, s 68(5).

13 Ie under ibid, s 68(4).

14 Ibid, ss 68(4), 70(1)(b). The chief constable may give part of the property to the finder: s 70(1)(b).

15 Ibid, s 68(4). But in terms of s 70(1)(b) he may apparently pay the finder such sum as he determines under s 70(2) as a reward. No guidance is given on when it may be inappropriate to offer it to the finder, but an example might be a packet of drugs which it would be an offence to possess.

16 Ibid, s 68(4). Again there would be the possibility of a reward to the finder under s 70.

17 'Livestock' means cattle, horses, asses, mules, hinnies, sheep, pigs, goats and poultry, deer not in the wild state and while in captivity, pheasants, partridges and grouse; and 'poultry' means the domestic varieties of fowls, turkeys, geese, ducks, guinea-fowls, pigeons and quails: ibid, s 129(5) (applied by s 74).

18 Ie under ibid, s 68(2).

19 Ibid, s 74.

550. Title to lost and abandoned property under the Act. As noted above[1] finding of itself does not under the Civic Government (Scotland) Act 1982 give title to the property found. In principle, the rights of the owner of lost property and the Crown's rights in abandoned property are preserved. But where property is given to the finder or is otherwise disposed of in terms of the Act, a person taking it in good faith is, in principle, given title[2]. However, if the property has not been acquired for value, the previous owner may 'recover possession of the property as owner' within a year[3]. He makes his claim 'as owner' and would be met, it would seem by any defence open to a bona fide possessor against the true owner. If the property has been disposed of for value, the acquirer gets a title which is not open to challenge but where the net proceeds of sale exceed £100[4] the previous owner can claim compensation from the chief constable[5]. This compensation is limited to the amount of the net proceeds of sale[6] and the claim must be made within a year of the disposal[7]. The chief constable must keep a record of property disposed of by him for a period of one year from the date of disposal[8].

1 See para 548 above.
2 Civic Government (Scotland) Act 1982 (c 45), s 71(1).
3 Ibid, s 71(2). Presumably on the principle of *negotiorum gestio* he would require to pay any expenses properly incurred by the taker in good faith although the statute does not say so expressly.
4 Ibid, s 72(3). The sum of £100 may be increased by statutory instrument made by the Secretary of State. The statutory instrument is subject to annulment by resolution of either House of Parliament.
5 Ibid, s 72(1).
6 See ibid, s 72(3). The 'net proceeds of sale' means the sum received on disposal after deduction of (1) any expenses incurred in connection with the disposal, (2) any amount paid as a reward under s 70, and (3) any reasonable charges (including any reasonable expenses incurred by him or on his behalf) as determined by the chief constable: s 72(4).
7 Ibid, s 72(2).
8 Ibid, s 68(6). Under s 77 any sums accruing to the chief constable as a result of the operation of the Act are payable to the police authority, which is responsible for providing the funds to operate it.

551. Appeals. Decisions of the chief constable affecting (1) the owner or person having right to possession of any property in the possession of the chief constable[1], (2) a finder or claimant[2], and (3) a previous owner[3], may be appealed to the sheriff[4]. If the sheriff upholds the appeal he may remit the case with the reasons for his decision to the chief constable for reconsideration, or reverse or alter the chief constable's decision[5].

1 Ie under the Civic Government (Scotland) Act 1982 (c 45), s 69.
2 Ie referred to in ibid, s 70.
3 Ie claiming under ibid, s 72.
4 Ibid, s 76(1), (2). The appeal is by summary application to be lodged with the sheriff clerk within twenty-one days of the decision (s 76(3)) but the time may be extended on good cause shown (s 76(4)).
5 Ibid, s 76(5)(a), (b). Cf *Caithness v Bowman* 1987 SCLR 642, Sh Ct.

552. Exceptional cases. Four special cases which form exceptions to the general scheme of the Civic Government (Scotland) Act 1982 are set out in the Act itself[1] which does not apply to:
(1) property found on premises belonging to or used by an undertaking which provides a transport service for the public, that is, such premises as omnibus stations, ports, airports or other similar places, or to property found on any vehicle, vessel or aircraft used by such an undertaking, if there is other statutory provision for such lost or abandoned property[2];
(2) property found on the premises of or used by the British Railways Board or on any vehicle, train or vessel used by it[3];
(3) abandoned motor vehicles, on which there are various statutory provisions, the application of which depends on the circumstances of the abandonment[4];

(4) stray dogs, so far as these are dealt with under the Dogs Act 1906 as amended[5].
In addition, special provision is made:
(5) for the disposal of property left behind by a secure tenant of public sector
housing who has abandoned his tenancy[6].

1 Civic Government (Scotland) Act 1982 (c 45), s 67(2).
2 There is such provision in the case of public service vehicles and premises referred to in the Airports
Act 1986 (c 31). In respect of vehicles, see the Public Service Vehicles (Lost Property) Regulations
1978, SI 1978/1684 (amended by SI 1981/1623) made under authority now contained in the Public
Passenger Vehicles Act 1981 (c 14), s 60. In respect of airports designated by or managed by the
Secretary of State, the airport operator may make bye-laws dealing with 'property not in proper
custody' found within the airport or in aircraft within the airport: Airports Act 1986, s 63(1)(j).
Bye-laws made or having effect under earlier corresponding legislation (ie the Airports Authority
Act 1975 (c 78), s 16 (repealed), and the Civil Aviation Act 1982 (c 16), ss 32, 33, 58 (repealed)),
subject to certain conditions, have effect as if they were bye-laws made under the power in the 1986
Act: Airports Act 1986, s 83(4), Sch 5, para 11(2). See the British Airports Authority (Lost Property)
Regulations 1972, SI 1972/1027. See further AVIATION AND AIR TRANSPORT, vol 2, para 933.
3 See the Standard Terms and Conditions of Carriage of Passengers and their Luggage, as published
by the British Railways Board from time to time.
4 The main provisions are:
(1) the Refuse Disposal (Amenity) Act 1978 (c 3), s 3 (amended by the Local Government Planning
and Land Act 1980 (c 65), s 1(3), Sch 3, para 14; and the Roads (Scotland) Act 1984 (c 54), s 156(1),
Sch 9, para 78) which imposes a duty on district and islands councils to remove motor vehicles
abandoned without lawful authority on any land in the open air or on any other land forming part of
a road. The Refuse Disposal (Amenity) Act 1978, ss 4, 5, deal with disposal of vehicles, charges and
recovery of expenses. See also the Removal and Disposal of Vehicles Regulations 1986, SI 1986/
183, and ROADS, vol 20, para 691. The Secretary of State may by order direct that the provisions of
the Refuse Disposal (Amenity) Act 1978 or regulations in force under any of its provisions in their
application to designated airports are to have effect subject to modifications: Airports Act 1986, s 66.
As to abandoned vehicles at designated airports, see further AVIATION AND AIR TRANSPORT, vol 2,
para 937. On the regulations, see *Fraser v Glasgow Corpn* 1972 SC 162, 1972 SLT 177.
(2) the Road Traffic Regulation Act 1984 (c 27), s 99(1)(c) (amended by the Roads (Scotland) Act
1984 (c 54), Sch 9, para 93) which allows the removal of vehicles which have been permitted to
remain at rest on a road, or on any land in the open air, in such a position or in such condition or in
such circumstances as to appear to a relevant authority to have been abandoned without lawful
authority. Exercise of the power of removal is governed by the Removal and Disposal of Vehicles
Regulations 1986, and ss 100–103 of the Road Traffic Regulation Act 1984 make additional
provision for disposal of vehicles and for charges and the recovery of expenses. (The relevant
provisions are not restricted to abandoned vehicles.)
5 Dogs Act 1906 (c 32), ss 3, 4 (as amended): see ANIMALS, vol 2, para 105.
6 The Housing (Scotland) Act 1987 (c 26), ss 49, 50, allows the housing authority to recover
possession of an abandoned tenancy. For the procedure governing the disposal of a tenant's
property, see the Secure Tenancies (Abandoned Property) (Scotland) Order 1982, SI 1982/981. As
to abandonment of a secure tenancy, see further HOUSING, vol 11, para 1948.

(d) Treasure

553. Definition. In their definitions of treasure the institutional writers[1] are
clearly influenced by the definition of its equivalent in Roman law, *thesaurus*, which
meant, broadly speaking, hidden valuables the ownership of which could no longer
be traced[2]. The definitions of the institutional writers reflect the uncertainties
which are already to be found in the Roman definition; but while the meaning of
thesaurus was of some consequence in Roman law, in which the destination of
property might depend on whether it was *thesaurus* or was simply ownerless
property open to *occupatio,* the precise meaning of treasure in Scots law is not, as the
law stands, of vital importance. In principle, all ownerless property belongs to the
Crown if it has once been owned. Thus, where title to the property is concerned, it
does not matter whether or not it is classed as treasure unless it should be claimed by
a donatory from the Crown of the right to treasure. In fact, it does not appear that

any grants of the right to treasure have survived if they were ever made. The definition, therefore, really matters only so far as notification of the finding is concerned. Treasure found should be reported to the Queen's and Lord Treasurer's Remembrancer[3] either by the finder, who otherwise risks prosecution for theft, or by the chief constable to whom it is delivered in terms of the Civic Government (Scotland) Act 1982 and who is required to notify the owner of lost or abandoned property where the owner can reasonably be identified[4].

The precise nature of the Crown's right to treasure in Scots law came under close examination in the case of the 'St Ninian's Isle Treasure'[5]. This case concerned a hoard of objects, mostly of silver, found in the Shetland Islands by an archaeological expedition from the University of Aberdeen. The main point at issue in that case was whether the Crown could claim the hoard, given that it was found in udal land. It was argued that the *regalia*, of which the right to treasure is one, are feudal rights and that on the analogy of salmon fishings, which in the Orkneys and Shetlands are not *inter regalia* where the land is udal[6], treasure likewise could not be claimed by the Crown when the treasure was found in udal land. The decision was that the Crown's right is based on its sovereignty and not on its ultimate feudal superiority and that treasure is simply a particular form of ownerless property claimable by the Crown on the principle *quod nullius est fit domini regis*. It was also held that treasure is not *pars soli* claimable by the owner of the land[7] as part of the land[8] and that, although treasure is described by the institutional writers as 'hidden valuables', it is not necessary to show that the treasure was in fact hidden by its former owner; hidden implies merely that it has had to be found. Finally, it was held that although treasure in Scots law does not mean merely articles of gold and silver, as in England[9], but any valuables or precious things, the hoard found, which included a porpoise bone of no great intrinsic value, was to be treated as all one 'treasure'. Not all the views expressed are entirely convincing but, as already remarked, it does not seem that the matter is likely to be tested further in the courts as, in the absence of a claim by a donatory of the Crown, the only real issue is whether the property is ownerless or not.

The Crown is advised on disposal of treasure by the Treasure Trove Advisory Panel which may, for example, suggest where it should be housed and displayed. The panel also determines the value of any treasure found. Normally a reward is paid to the finder[10].

1 Stair *Institutions* II,1,5; II,3,60 ('. . . money hid in the ground, the owner whereof is not known' referring to Justinian *Code* 10,15,1, and *Digest* 41,1,31,1); III,3,27; Erskine *Institute* II,1,12 (a class of 'moveable subjects which are presumed to have once had a proprietor, who is now unknown').

2 *Digest* 41,1,31,1 (Paul) '. . . *vetus quaedam depositio pecuniae cuius non exstat memoria, ut iam dominium non habeat'* (some ancient deposit of money (property) of which there is no record (memory) so that it is no longer owned); *Code* 10,15,1 (*Codex Theodosianus* 10,18,2) referring to *mobilia* (moveables) and *monilia* (jewels, valuables) respectively.

3 The office of the Queen's and Lord Treasurer's Remembrancer (Q and LTR) is now held by the Crown Agent although it remains a separate office and some functions originally performed by the Q and LTR have been transferred to others. See THE CROWN.

4 Civic Government (Scotland) Act 1982 (c 45), s 68(3) (see para 549 above).

5 *Lord Advocate v Aberdeen University and Budge* 1963 SC 533, 1963 SLT 361.

6 *Lord Advocate v Balfour* 1907 SC 1360, 15 SLT 7, OH: see UDAL LAW, vol 24, para 315.

7 Whether he could claim to be possessor is a separate question on which English authority such as *Elwes v Brigg Gas Co* (1886) 33 Ch D 562 and *South Staffordshire Water Co v Sharman* [1896] 2 QB 44 is not helpful because the English courts are not addressing the same question as Scottish courts are or ought to be addressing. See para 124 above.

8 'Land' probably includes a building for this purpose: *Cleghorn and Bryce v Baird* (1696) Mor 13522.

9 8 *Halsbury's Laws of England* (4th edn) paras 1513–1515.

10 Information kindly supplied by the Queen's and Lord Treasurer's Remembrancer.

(e) Wreck

554. Common law. Wreck, in the sense of wrecked ships and property which is on a wrecked ship or has come from a shipwreck or which appears to have come from a shipwreck because it is floating in or cast up from the sea[1], like treasure, forms a special category of property which may be claimable by the Crown as ownerless or abandoned property. In early Scots law according to an Act attributed to Alexander II[2] wrecked goods were confiscated by the Crown if no living creature were found on board the wreck or if the owner of a wrecked vessel on which a living creature was found failed to establish his claim within a year and a day. A later Act[3] laid down the principle that wrecks of foreign ships were to be claimed only if the nation to which the ship belonged applied the rule of confiscation; if restitution were allowed by the relevant foreign law, restitution was to be made to the owner. But Stair[4], while referring to the older statutes, prefers to treat wreck as ownerless property, rationalising the Act of Alexander II as a provision for the case in which ownership could be traced through the living creature which survived. In *Monteir v Agnew*[5] it was held that this Act was in desuetude and that the owner of wreck could claim it at any time, not only within a year and a day, so long as he could instruct his property. Wreck therefore can be claimed by the Crown only if its ownership cannot be established. The Crown's right, however, is one of the *regalia minora* and it can be alienated to a subject, as it commonly was when rights of admiralty were granted.

1 The older Scottish cases *Hamilton v Cochran* (1622) Mor 16791 and *Jacobson v Earl of Crawford* (1674) Mor 16792 deal only with the remains of ships or with goods cast up from a shipwreck but a wider definition is applied in nineteenth century cases, *Customs and Excise Comrs v Lord Dundas* 2 Dec 1812, FC, and *Lord Advocate v Hebden* (1868) 6 M 489, corresponding roughly with the definition in the Merchant Shipping Act 1894 (c 60): see para 555, note 1, below. See more generally para 213 above.
2 Act of Alexander II (c 25) in Skene's editions of the *Regiam Majestatem* and *Auld Lawes*. See also Stair *Institutions* III,3,27, and Erskine *Institute* II,1,13.
3 Act of 1429 c 124 (APS c 15).
4 *Stair* III,3,27. See also on wreck II,1,3 and 5.
5 *Monteir v Agnew* (1725) Mor 16796. See also Bankton *Institute* I,8,6.

555. Wreck under the Merchant Shipping Acts. Administrative provisions for dealing with wreck are set out in the Merchant Shipping Act 1995[1]. 'Wreck' for the purposes of the Act covers not only wrecked ships themselves and goods from a shipwreck but also all goods found floating in the sea or washed up from it, so long as no one can show ownership of them. The definition uses terms taken from English law, 'jetsam, flotsam, lagan and derelict' but corresponds roughly with the definition applied in nineteenth-century Scottish cases.

British statutes dating from Queen Anne gave custody of wrecks and stranded vessels to officers of customs and excise, partly to secure them against plunder and partly to prevent evasion of customs duties payable on the cargo. Then, in 1854, provision was made for the appointment of 'receivers of wreck' who might or might not be customs officers. This scheme is taken over in the current provisions. The general superintendence of matters relating to wreck is given to the Secretary of State for Trade[2] who appoints receivers of wreck, normally customs officers, coastguards, or officers of the inland revenue. The duty of receivers is to take command of operations when notified of a vessel wrecked, stranded or in distress, with a view to preserving the vessel, the lives of persons belonging to it and the cargo and apparel[3]. The receiver also takes charge of any wreck; and any person finding or taking possession of wreck within the United Kingdom or bringing wreck into the United Kingdom must, if he is owner of it, give notice to the receiver or, if he is not owner, deliver it up to the receiver[4]. Similarly, any cargo or other articles from a vessel wrecked, stranded or in distress must be delivered to the receiver, who can use force to obtain it if delivery is refused; even the owner is liable to a fine for secreting, keeping possession of or refusing to deliver up such articles[5].

The receiver of wreck must give notice of wreck of which he takes possession to the nearest custom house within forty-eight hours and if its value exceeds £5,000 must also give notice to Lloyds[6]. The owner of wreck may claim it from the receiver within a year on payment of salvage, fees and expenses[7], but the receiver has power to sell any wreck in his custody if its value is under £5,000, or if it is so damaged or so perishable that it cannot with advantage be kept or if its value is insufficient to pay for warehousing. The proceeds of sale, less expenses, are held as if the wreck had remained unsold[8].

  1   See the Merchant Shipping Act 1995 (c 21), Pt IX, Ch II (ss 231–260). 'Wreck' is defined as jetsam, flotsam, lagan, and derelict found in or on the shores of the sea or any tidal water: s 255(1). On derelict, see *Pierce v Bemis* [1986] QB 384, [1986] 1 All ER 1011.
  2   Merchant Shipping Act 1995, s 248 (formerly the Board of Trade).
  3   Ibid, ss 231, 232. In his absence a series of other officers or other persons may act: s 231. For special powers to call for assistance and pass over adjoining lands, see ss 233, 234, and for communal liability if there is riotous plunder or damage, see s 235. The person making the report has all the powers of a Department of Trade inspector: s 259(1).
  4   Ibid, s 236.
  5   Ibid, s 237.
  6   Ibid, s 238.
  7   Ibid, s 239.
  8   Ibid, s 240. As to unsold wreck, see para 556 below.

556. Title to wreck under the Acts. Unclaimed wreck falls to the Crown or its donatories[1]. Donatories of the right to wreck must deliver to the receiver a statement of their title and are then entitled to be given notice of any wreck of which the receiver has taken possession[2]. If no claim to the wreck held by a receiver is established within a year, the wreck is delivered to any donatory entitled to receive it (after payment of expenses etc) or it is sold and the proceeds are paid to the Crown[3]. Delivery to a donatory or payment over to the Crown discharges the receiver of liability but his discharge is without prejudice to any question raised by third parties regarding right or title to the wreck or title to the soil of the place where the wreck was found[4].

  1   Merchant Shipping Act 1995 (c 21), s 241.
  2   Ibid, s 242.
  3   Ibid, s 243.
  4   Ibid, s 244.

557. Wreck from aircraft and hovercraft. The provisions of the Merchant Shipping Act 1995 (c 21)[1], are applied to wreck from aircraft[2] and hovercraft[3] but a donatory of the Crown cannot claim wreck from aircraft[4] or hovercraft[5].

  1   See paras 555, 556, above.
  2   Civil Aviation Act 1982 (c 16), s 87; Aircraft (Wreck and Salvage) Order 1938, SR & O 1938/136, art 2, as applied by the Civil Aviation Act 1982, s 87(4). See further AVIATION AND AIR TRANS-PORT, vol 2, para 1065.
  3   Hovercraft (Application of Enactments) Order 1972, SI 1972/971, art 8(1)(a) (amended by SI 1995/1299).
  4   Aircraft (Wreck and Salvage) Order 1938, art 2(b).
  5   Hovercraft (Application of Enactments) Order 1972, art 8.

(f) *Occupatio* in International Law

558. *Occupatio*. *Occupatio* is a ground of acquisition not only in the municipal law of Scotland but also in public international law. Although now relatively rarely applicable because most territory has been claimed, it has considerable historic importance and may be relevant to disputes over title to territory. It was used as a basis of a claim to jurisdiction over the island of Rockall by Great Britain when it became apparent that the bed of the sea around Rockall might contain oil-bearing strata[1]. The principle is the same as in municipal law, and acquisition depends on effective occupation in the name of the country claiming to acquire[2].

1 *Ob majorem cautelam* the island of Rockall was incorporated in Scotland by the Island of Rockall Act 1972 (c 2). See also D L Gardner 'Legal Storm Clouds over Rockall' 1976 SLT (News) 257 and J J Rankin 'Life on Rockall' 1985 SLT (News) 321.
2 See further PUBLIC INTERNATIONAL LAW, vol 19, para 667.

(g) *Specificatio* or Specification

559. Definition. *Specificatio* is the name, of medieval origin, given to the acquisition of property by making a new *species,* a new kind of thing, out of material belonging to another person but not by arrangement with that person. There is, of course, no problem of title where a person makes something out of his own material. There is a different problem when there is an arrangement because in that case title will depend on the arrangement or on interpretation of the arrangement which has been made[1].

Specificatio comes into play where a new thing has been created in circumstances where the parties — the maker of the thing and the owner of the material — have made no arrangement either because the maker has acted dishonestly or because the maker has acted in error. The major questions which arise are when there is a new thing, who is owner of the new thing and what compensation, if any, is given to the party who has lost the materials or the time and effort which have gone into the making of the new thing which he does not own.

1 See *Wylie and Lochhead v Mitchell* (1870) 8 M 552; D L Carey Miller 'Logical Consistency in Property' 1990 SLT (News) 197 at 198, 199.

560. *Specificatio* in Roman law. The problems arising from the making of a new thing out of materials belonging to someone else were discussed in Roman law. Bell in his *Commentaries* sums up the final position reached in the law of Justinian in a very unflattering way as:

> 'the famous controversy of the Proculeiani and Sabiniani concerning specification, which, after a course of perplexed and subtile reasoning, turning on imaginary and vain distinctions, was by Tribonian and the other lawyers appointed by Justinian to digest the Roman jurisprudence, decided according to a rule as distant perhaps from plain sense, or any useful purpose, as the opinions which it professed to reconcile' [1].

Certainly in Roman law, where the question when there is a new thing is dealt with by examples, such as the making of wine from grapes, three views on the question of ownership of the new thing were maintained, namely:
(1) the Sabinians' view that ownership went to the owner of the materials;
(2) the Proculians' view that ownership went to the maker of the new thing; and
(3) the others' view, apparently already held in classical law, that ownership went to the maker if the materials could not be reduced to their former state but otherwise it remained with the owner of the materials.

This last view is the *media sententia* (middle view) favoured by Justinian[2]. It also appears that it was immaterial in Roman law whether the maker was in good or bad faith. His good or bad faith only affected the remedies available to recover the thing or the value of the materials or workmanship. The owner of the materials if he had lost ownership but was in possession, could resist a claim by the new owner to the thing if he was not offered the value of his materials. At least in Justinian's law, a claim for compensation against the maker was probably given to the party who had lost his ownership and was not in possession if the maker had acted in good faith, although there is little evidence and there has been much discussion[3]. *Specificatio* in bad faith entailed liability for theft, whether ownership was acquired or not and this meant liability both to a penalty and for compensation for the value of the materials, failing their return.

1 Bell *Commentaries* I,295. Bell departs from this somewhat jaundiced view in *Principles* s 1298: see para 561 below.
2 See Justinian *Institutes* II,1,25; *Digest* 41,1,7,7 (Gaius), 41,1,24 (Paul). It may be that a problem of ownership arose only if no materials were contributed by the maker in that if he contributed materials as well as work he was always owner of his creation. This rule is stated in *Institutes* II,1,25. See J A C Thomas 'Form and Substance in Roman Law' 1966 Current Legal Problems 145 at 152.
3 See W W Buckland *Textbook of Roman Law* (3rd edn, 1963 by P Stein) pp 217, 218.

561. Specificatio in the institutional writers. Questions of *specificatio* have not often come before the Scottish courts and a good deal of the discussion of the law in the institutional writers has been based on the Roman texts. As the Roman solutions have not been regarded as authoritative, Scots law has not· followed Roman law completely even where that appears to have been settled. Stair, indeed, says that there is no clear rule in Scots law. He suggests that 'without injustice' any of various solutions, including the Roman ones, could be followed by the positive law 'reparation being always made to the party who loses his interest', unless the work was performed *animo donandi* (with intention of making a gift)[1]. Erskine says that where the new thing can be reduced to the materials of which it is made, it is regarded as still belonging to the owner of the materials: but if it cannot, there is no room for this *'fictio iuris'* and it belongs to the maker[2].

Bell in his *Principles*[3] states that Scots law follows the *media sententia* so far as ownership is concerned: this means that ownership is given to the maker if the thing made cannot be restored to its original raw materials. But he also states that Scots law allows the owner of the materials a claim for the equivalent materials or their price if the thing cannot be restored to its constituent materials and allows the workman a claim for indemnity *in quantum lucratus* (to the extent of his enrichment) against the owner of the new thing if restoration is possible. Again, departing from Roman law, he requires that the making be in good faith if ownership is to be acquired.

1 Stair *Institutions* II,1,41. His discussion draws heavily on Grotius *De Jure Belli ac Pacis* 2,8,19.
2 Erskine *Institute* II,1,16, referring to Justinian *Institutes* II,1,25. From what Erskine says in II,1,15, it would appear that he would allow acquisition by the maker in bad faith. He does not deal with compensation but, by implication from the rules on accession he would give a claim for recompense in case of good faith: see *Erskine* III,1,11, on the bona fide builder on land owned by another.
3 Bell *Principles* s 1298.

562. Case law. There have been only two cases in the Court of Session dealing directly with specification, that is *International Banking Corporation v Ferguson Shaw & Sons*[1] and *McDonald v Provan (of Scotland Street) Ltd*[2]. These accept the views stated by Bell[3]. In the former case, oil had been used in good faith to make margarine and it was held that while the margarine belonged to the maker, the value of the oil must be paid to the former owner. In the latter case, a motor car had been made from the parts of two other cars, one of which had been stolen, and it was argued the new car belonged to the maker. It was held that the car could be reduced to its parts so that the making was not a specification resulting in a change of ownership. But it was observed that ownership could not have been acquired in any case because the new thing had been made in bad faith. In taking this latter view, the case departs from what seems to have been the Roman rule and the rule which applies in acquisition by accession but nevertheless follows Bell. The argument used was that it would not be equitable to allow the maker in bad faith to claim the thing but the result is to allow the owner of the materials to claim the thing even from a bona fide purchaser from the maker because the maker can give no title to stolen property. Perhaps the bona fide purchaser would be allowed to claim in respect of the work done by the maker in that he would have given value for it, although he would in theory have recourse against the seller on warrandice in the sale if he had to yield the thing up to the owner of the materials. The logic of the Roman rule was that it was a new thing of which there would be a new ownership even if that thing was made in bad faith. The owner of the materials was left to his remedies against the maker in bad faith based on the theft which the maker had committed. The owner of the materials in Scots law has two bites at the cherry as he could claim reparation from the maker in bad faith if he were unable to recover the thing[4].

Specification was also discussed in *Wylie and Lochhead v Mitchell*[5] but was inapplicable in the circumstances because there was a contract between the parties. It also arose in relation to the question of the effect of a change of form of materials supplied in relation to a retention of title clause relating to the materials in *Armour v Thyssen Edelstahlwerke AG*[6], but again it was not strictly relevant because the clause in question dealt expressly with the possibility of processing and other operations. However, in the Outer House, Lord Mayfield expressed the view that there had been specification where stainless steel strip coils had been cut into shapes and there was evidence that the stainless steel could not be recovered in its original composition; there was thus a new thing over which, in his view, there was no security. On appeal, the judges of the Second Division expressed opinions *obiter* to the opposite effect, but taking a somewhat different view of the evidence as interpreted by Lord Mayfield[7].

1 *International Banking Corpn v Ferguson Shaw & Sons* 1910 SC 182, 1909 2 SLT 377, followed in *M'Laren Sons & Co Ltd v Mann, Byars & Co Ltd* (1935) 51 Sh Ct Rep 57, where stolen cloth had, in good faith, been made up into garments.
2 *McDonald v Provan (of Scotland Street) Ltd* 1960 SLT 231, OH.
3 An attempt to apply the doctrine of specification by analogy in the case of a sale covered by the Hire Purchase Act 1964 (c 53), s 27(3) (which protects a private individual who buys in good faith a motor vehicle which is subject to a hire-purchase agreement and so makes the vehicle irrecoverable from him by the true owner) was rejected in *North-West Securities Ltd v Barrhead Coachworks Ltd* 1976 SC 68, 1976 SLT 99, OH, disapproving *F C Finance Ltd v Langtry Investment Co Ltd* 1973 SLT (Sh Ct) 11. As to the Hire Purchase Act 1964, ss 27–29, see further para 683 below, and CONSUMER CREDIT, vol 5, para 801, note 3. *Oliver and Boyd v Marr Typefounding Co Ltd* (1901) 9 SLT 170, OH, was a case which is the converse of specification, in that cast type which had been stolen was reduced to its original metal by the bona fide possessor. He was held liable for the full value of the type which he was now unable to restore. On Erskine's view of specification (see para 561, note 2, above) return of the metal to the owner of the type would have been return of what he owned.
4 See also the discussion in D L Carey Miller *Corporeal Moveables in Scots Law* (1991) para 4.04.
5 *Wylie and Lochhead v Mitchell* (1870) 8 M 552.
6 *Armour v Thyssen Edelstahlwerke AG* 1986 SLT 94 (proof before answer allowed by Lord Cowie); 1986 SLT 452, OH (before Lord Mayfield).
7 *Armour v Thyssen Edelstahlwerke AG* 1989 SCLR 26, 1989 SLT 182 (revsd 1991 SCLR 139, 1990 SLT 891, HL).

563. Proposals of the Scottish Law Commission. The Scottish Law Commission has expressed dissatisfaction with the present rules on specification both in respect of the attribution of ownership and in respect of the remedies available to the party who loses ownership[1]. The Commission put forward for comment alternative proposals, one linking specification with adjunction and commixtion and the other dealing with these cases separately but both giving greater scope to common ownership and to intervention by the court to provide an equitable solution to the problems of attribution of ownership and of compensation[2]. The proposals would apply only where the producer of a new thing from another's materials was not already protected by the rules on bona fide onerous acquisition of another's property. Alternatives were also suggested to protect the onerous bona fide acquirer of a new thing where the thing had been disposed of without the consent of all interested parties[3]. No action has yet been taken on the proposals.

1 *Corporeal Moveables: Mixing, Union and Creation* (Scot Law Com Consultative Memorandum no. 28) (1976) paras 11–23.
2 Ibid, para 33, alternatives A and B.
3 Ibid, paras 35–38.

(h) Commixtion and Confusion

564. General. Not every union of things belonging to different owners will result in specification (or accession). There will not necessarily be a new and different thing nor will one thing necessarily be regarded as the principal thing to which the other accedes. In Roman law, where there was such a union, a distinction was drawn between the result of the mixing of solids, such as heaps of corn, or of separate entities, such as the sheep in a flock, and the mixing of liquids. The former is usually referred to as *commixtio* or commixtion and the latter as *confusio* or confusion although the terminology of the sources does not make such a clear distinction. In the case of commixtion there was no change of ownership unless the mixture was made by agreement (when it became common property): the owners of the things contributing to the mixture could vindicate what they owned of the mixture, for example, individual sheep in a flock, or a share of the mixture, for example, ten sackfuls of a heap of corn. In the case of confusion the mixture was owned in common by the owners of the liquids contributing to it[1]. A procedural issue was involved concerning the appropriate action which the owners might bring to assert their claims, a vindication or an action for division of common property.

Commixtion and confusion are dealt with by the institutional writers on the basis of the Roman texts[2] but the Roman law is not followed exactly. The view taken is that common ownership results from both commixtion and confusion if the mixture cannot be separated into its components or if the mixture has been made by consent. If the elements of the mixture are separable, as in the case of a flock of sheep which are marked or otherwise recognisable, there is no change of ownership and so the respective owners can claim their own property. Where there is common ownership but no agreement on how the mixture is to be shared the ownership is shared in proportion to the quantity or, where components of different value are involved, the value of the respective contributions[3].

Where the mixing results in a new thing then the rules of specification discussed above are applied[4]. Similarly, if one of the things is regarded as the principal thing the rules of accession will be relevant[5].

1 See Justinian *Institutes* II,1,27 and 28; *Digest* 6,1,3–5; *Digest* 41,1,7,8; 9.
2 Stair *Institutions* II,1,36 and 37; Erskine *Institute* II,1,17; Bankton *Institute* II,1,14–16; Bell *Principles* s 1298(2). Commixtion was seen as relevant by the Court of Session in *Tyzack and Branfoot Steamship Co Ltd v Frank Stewart Sandeman & Sons* 1913 SC 19, 1912 2 SLT 159, but not by the House of Lords in reversing their decision, 1913 SC (HL) 84, 1913 2 SLT 158, although Lord Moulton (1913 SC (HL) 84 at 94, 1913 2 SLT 158 at 162, 163) made some remarks obiter or *per incuriam* on the English law applicable to commixtion.
3 *Stair* II,1,36 and 37; *Erskine* II,1,17; *Bell* s 1298(2).

4 See paras 559 ff above.
5 For accession, see paras 570 ff below.

(6) PRESCRIPTION

565. Introduction. Prescription is scarcely necessary as a basis of acquisition of ownership of corporeal moveables in Scots law because, at least as a general rule, possession in itself presumes ownership[1]. Indeed, whether prescription is recognised at all in this context is somewhat doubtful. There is certainly no clear statutory basis for positive prescription as in the case of heritable property[2], although there is some authority for a forty-year prescription[3] based on analogy with the forty-year prescription which formerly applied in heritable property[4].

1 See para 130 above.
2 No provision for positive prescription in moveables is made in the Prescription and Limitation (Scotland) Act 1973 (c 52) and there was no previous specific statutory provision.
3 See the old cases of *Aberscherder Parishioners v Parish of Gemrie* (1633) Mor 10972 and *Ramsay v Wilson* (1666) Mor 9113, the latter especially in Stair's report at 9115; Stair *Institutions* II,12,9–13; IV,40,20; Forbes *Institutes* 3,5,1; Bankton *Institute* II,12,1; Hume *Lectures* vol III (Stair Soc vol 15, 1952 ed G C H Paton) p 228. But while the *Aberscherder* case is indexed in Morison's Dictionary of Decisions under positive prescription the report suggests that the decision was based on negative prescription of the lender's right to recover property lent (in that case a kirk bell). See further the Appendix to *Corporeal Moveables: Usucapion or Acquisitive Prescription* (Scot Law Com Consultative Memorandum no. 30) (1976); D L Carey Miller 'Moveables: Do We Need Acquisitive Prescription?' 1989 SLT (News) 285; and D L Carey Miller *Corporeal Moveables in Scots Law* (1991) ch 7.
4 See now the Prescription and Limitation (Scotland) Act 1973 (c 52), ss 1–5, and para 674 below. In general the period is now ten years.

566. Positive prescription. Assuming that there is such a positive prescription it does not allow a trustee to acquire title to property held on trust against the beneficiaries; trust property cannot be acquired by a trustee by prescription[1]. By analogy, property placed on deposit could never be acquired by the depositee (who would not in any case have the necessary possession[2]) but obligations to repay money deposited are subject to the five-year negative prescription[3] and the right to recover property placed on deposit is not included as one of the statutory imprescriptible rights[4]. The effect may be that the owner loses his right to recover from the depositee after twenty years[5], in the absence of a relevant claim or acknowledgment, but he does not in theory lose his ownership[6]. The depositee on the other hand would not acquire ownership but he could dispose of the property after prescription had run without committing theft.

Property *extra commercium* cannot be acquired by prescription because it is incapable of being owned by private persons[7]. The right to recover stolen property from the thief or any person privy to the theft is imprescriptible[8] and stolen property can be recovered from a bona fide holder until prescription runs in his favour as it apparently does, so far as positive prescription is recognised[9].

The Scottish Law Commission has proposed that the law on positive prescription as applied to corporeal moveables should be reformed but has not proceeded beyond consultation at present[10]. The Commission's suggestion is that there should be a short five-year prescription based on apparent title and good faith and a longer ten-year prescription based simply on open peaceful possession adverse to the owner. The ten-year prescription would not give title to a thief or, possibly, to persons aware that the property had been stolen but bad faith in the sense of awareness of lack of title would not prevent acquisition. Possession originally acquired on a limited title would not found prescription unless there was a change of circumstances making clear that the possession was now being held against the owner, such as a challenge to the owner's right by the possessor or, perhaps some action by the owner which led the possessor to believe that the owner was relinquishing his right.

1 *Bertram Gardner & Co's Trustee v King's and Lord Treasurer's Remembrancer* 1920 SC 555, 1920 2 SLT 141; Prescription and Limitation (Scotland) Act 1973 (c 52), ss 7(2), 8(2), Sch 3(e). For the meaning of 'trustee', see s 15(1). As to trust property received by a third party not in good faith, see Sch 3(f).
2 See paras 123, 125, above.
3 Prescription and Limitation (Scotland) Act 1973, s 6, Sch 1, Sch 2, para 2. The prescription runs from the specified date for repayment or from the date of a written demand. See PRESCRIPTION AND LIMITATION.
4 Ibid, Sch 3.
5 Ibid, s 7(2), Sch 3.
6 Ie unless he loses ownership under ibid, s 8. See para 567 below.
7 *Edinburgh Presbytery v Edinburgh University* (1890) 28 SLR 567; Prescription and Limitation (Scotland) Act 1973, s 8(2), Sch 3(d).
8 Prescription and Limitation (Scotland) Act 1973, s 8(2), Sch 3(g).
9 Stair *Institutions* II,12,10, has been referred to as authority for the proposition that, as in Roman law, in Scots law theft creates a *vitium reale* or *labes realis* (a real vice or defect) which cannot be cured by prescription at all; but in the passage in question Stair is referring to Roman law. Erskine *Institute* III,7,14, points out that Scots law does not follow the Roman law rules on *usucapio* (acquisitive prescription — the term was applied particularly to moveables in later law) and that in Roman law itself by the so-called *longissimi temporis praescriptio* (very long term prescription) even possession begun in bad faith ripened into ownership after forty years. Theft is, of course, a *vitium reale* in the sense that stolen property is not acquired by a taker in good faith for value. See para 618 below.
10 *Corporeal Moveables: Usucapion or Acquisitive Prescription* (Scot Law Com Consultative Memorandum no. 30) (1976) paras 9, 10–14. See also D L Carey Miller, 'Moveables: Do We Need Acquisitive Prescription?' 1989 SLT (News) 285.

567. Negative prescription. Negative prescription cannot give a positive title to corporeal moveables but it may cut off claims to recover them from the present possessor. Arguably, however, ownership of corporeal moveables is lost by the negative prescription of twenty years under the Prescription and Limitation (Scotland) Act 1973[1]. It is not specifically declared to be imprescriptible as is the right of ownership of land[2]. Moreover, the case of *Aberscherder Parishioners v Parish of Gemrie*[3] can be interpreted as accepting that there was (or indeed still is) a forty-year negative prescription of the right to assert one's ownership at common law. The argument that ownership is lost by prescription assumes that ownership of corporeal moveables is not covered by the provision of the 1973 Act that *res merae facultatis* are imprescriptible[4]. If negative prescription applies, but the forty-year positive prescription which may apply at common law[5] has not yet run, the possessor will not in fact be owner but he will be able to rely on the presumption of ownership arising from his possession to recover the thing from third parties. In theory at least, the true owner would also be able to recover from a third party until a title was acquired against him by positive prescription or at least until his right of recovery was lost by negative prescription if it is so lost.

1 Prescription and Limitation (Scotland) Act 1973 (c 52), s 8. See also para 675 below.
2 Ibid, Sch 3(a).
3 *Aberscherder Parishioners v Parish of Gemrie* (1633) Mor 10972.
4 Prescription and Limitation (Scotland) Act 1973, Sch 3(c).
5 See para 565 above.

(7) EXTINCTION OF PROPERTY

568. Destruction or abandonment. Ownership of corporeal moveables may be lost by the physical destruction of the moveables themselves (including their conversion into a new thing[1]). It may also be lost by abandonment, the abandoned property being acquired by the Crown[2]. The mere loss of property in the sense of mislaying it does not deprive the owner of title although it does deprive him of possession if the thing is lost in circumstances where there is no control over its possible location[3]. If, however, the owner discards a thing deliberately, ownership is lost. The question is when it has been discarded deliberately and this is a matter of proof of intention. The intention may be clear as where something is thrown into a public litter-bin but there are circumstances in which the precise intention may be uncertain, or in which there may be room for argument when the intention has been carried out. Thus, property may be lost and apparently abandoned but the owner may not have given up hope of retrieving it, as where a golf ball disappears into rough and is not found within the five minutes of search permitted by the rules of golf before the ball is deemed to be lost[4]. The player may play on, but still hope to find the ball later. Again, property washed off a ship in a storm or discarded to lighten it may not be given up for good; the provision made for a claim to wreck by the owner implicitly accepts this[5]. Where a person puts property in his own dust-bin it probably cannot be regarded as abandoned until the dust-bin is emptied[6]. Indeed, the better concept in such a situation may be that the property is transferred to the refuse disposal authority or its contractor rather than that it is abandoned and picked up by the authority or contractor as abandoned (with the implied leave of the Crown). The same theory would justify the common practice among golfers of treating lost balls as open to acquisition by other golfers using the course[7]. One thing which is clear in Scots law is that the dishonest taking of property which has been abandoned is theft because the property belongs to the Crown, as discussed above; it is unnecessary to locate possession in anyone, as is or was the case in English law[8]. The statutory provisions on disposal of lost or abandoned property have been considered already[9].

1 Ie specification (see paras 559 ff above). As to extinction, see generally para 9 above.
2 See para 547 above.
3 See para 122 above.
4 For its facts (the taking of lost golf balls by a trespasser), see the English case of *Hibbert v M'Kiernan* [1948] 2 KB 142, [1948] 1 All ER 860.
5 See paras 555, 556, above.
6 Cf *Williams v Phillips* (1957) 41 Cr App Rep 5.
7 Cf the Roman *traditio incertae personae*, delivery to an indefinite person, but one of a defined group such as election supporters (Justinian *Institutes* II,1,46) used to justify acquisition of abandoned property by the taker in II,1,47.
8 Conviction in a case such as *Hibbert v M'Kiernan* [1948] 2 KB 142, [1948] 1 All ER 860, should create no problem: see *Mackenzie v Maclean* 1981 SLT (Sh Ct) 40. Under English law abandoned property cannot be stolen (Theft Act 1968 (c 60), ss 4(4), 5; 11(1) *Halsbury's Laws of England* (4th edn, reissue 1990) para 548) but property is not readily held to be totally abandoned.
9 See paras 548, 549, above.

569. Loss of rights by prescription. Apart from abandonment or physical destruction of property, rights in property may be lost by prescription either in the sense that the right is lost by negative prescription or in the sense that someone else acquires it by positive prescription. Whether ownership is one of these rights is a matter of some uncertainty in the present law. Positive prescription as a possible mode of acquisition of corporeal moveables has been considered above[1]. Whether ownership can be lost by negative prescription has also been considered[2] along with the proposals of the Scottish Law Commission on both matters. The presumption of ownership of corporeal moveables arising from their possession means that in practice ownership may effectively be lost once possession has been acquired by someone else in good faith. As already noted[3] stolen property is always recoverable from the thief thereof or from any person privy to the theft but while theft is a *vitium reale* in the sense that ownership of stolen property is not acquired immediately by a taker in good faith, even if the taker acquires for value[4], it appears that in Scots law theft does not prevent the acquisition of ownership by positive prescription so far as positive prescription is recognised[5].

1 See para 566 above.
2 See para 567 above.
3 See para 566 above.
4 See para 618 below.
5 See para 566, note 9, above.

12. ACCESSION

(1) GENERAL PRINCIPLES

570. Definition. Accession (*accessio*) occurs whenever two pieces of property become joined together in such a way that one (known as the 'accessory') is considered to have become subsumed in the other (known as the 'principal'). The rule is *accessorium principale sequitur*: the accessory follows the principal. So it is accession if a new gear box is fitted to a car, or a central heating system into a house, and the accessory (the gear box or, as the case may be, the heating system) becomes part of the principal (the car or the house). Only corporeal property can be subject to accession. The modern law is drawn from Roman law and, except in the area of accession by moveables to land, there have been very few reported cases.

If accession is classified according to the type of property involved, three categories appear, namely (1) accession by moveables to land[1], (2) accession by moveables to moveables[2], and (3) accession by land to land[3]. Accession may also be by 'fruits', by which the offspring of animals or the produce of land are treated as part of the parent or, as the case may be, of the land which nurtured them[4]. Accession by fruits involves fundamentally different considerations from the normal case of accession and its treatment is postponed until later[5]. The remarks in this introductory section are confined to the standard cases of accession.

1 See paras 578 ff below.
2 See paras 588 ff below.
3 See paras 592 ff below.
4 The distinction between accession by fruits and standard accession is more or less the same as the traditional distinction between natural accession and industrial accession, for which see Erskine *Institute* II,1,15, and Bell *Principles* ss 1297, 1298. But natural accession includes alluvion and so is wider than accession by fruits.
5 See paras 595 ff below.

571. Physical attachment, functional subordination and permanency. All cases of accession[1] involve three distinct elements. In the first place, there must be two (or more) pieces of corporeal property which have become joined together in some way. Secondly, one of the pieces (the accessory) must be subordinate in function to the other (the principal). Thirdly, the attachment must be permanent or quasi-permanent in nature. If all three elements are present in a sufficient degree, then accession takes place[2]. If one element is absent there is usually no accession.

What qualifies as present 'in a sufficient degree' is a difficult issue and, at least to some extent, depends on the category of property under consideration. So far as the first element, physical attachment, is concerned, it is certainly not necessary that the constituent bodies be actually incapable of separation. Indeed, in the case of accession by moveables to land, it is sometimes sufficient for the accessory to be attached by no more than its own weight[3]. Functional subordination, the second element, is more elusive and more resistant to analysis. The essential idea is that the accessory must operate, at least in some sense, for the benefit of the principal. In the example given earlier, the gear box engages the engine of the car and the central heating system heats the house. But functional subordination is not inconsistent with the accessory continuing to operate for its own benefit and maintaining a separate identity of its own. The final element, permanence or quasi-permanence, operates mainly in a negative sense and prevents the operation of accession in cases where the attachment is of a very short duration. The law is complicated by the fact that accession operates through a combination of the three elements. While all three must normally be present, it is not necessary that each be present at full strength, and insufficiency on the part of one may sometimes be compensated for by, at it were, oversufficiency on the part of the others.

The three elements required for accession give some indication of the policy considerations underlying the law. These are that property which cannot easily be separated should not forcibly be broken up[4], and that an accessory which serves a particular principal and which might be of little or no use elsewhere should be left where it is. Rather than destroying the conjoined property, it is better to preserve it by awarding ownership to the owner of the principal and, in appropriate circumstances, by making monetary compensation to the owner of the accessory[5].

1 Ie other than accession by fruits, for which see paras 595 ff below.
2 With corporeal moveables the result is not accession in absolutely every case. Thus (1) where a new species is formed, distinct from either or any of the constituent parts, the result is specification (for which see paras 559–563 above); and (2) where moveables are mixed or fused rather than joined, the result is commixtion and confusion (for which see para 564 above).
3 See para 580 below. There may be greater emphasis on actual physical attachment in the case of accession by moveables to moveables, although there is so little case law that it is difficult to state the rules with any confidence. See further para 589 below.
4 Erskine *Institute* II,1,15.
5 For monetary compensation, see para 577 below.

572. Rejection of subjective factors. Accession operates mechanically and without regard to the circumstances which gave rise to it. So long as the three elements of attachment, subordination and permanency are sufficiently present, accession is the automatic result. So it is irrelevant that the accessory and the principal were formerly owned by different people, or even that the accessory was stolen by the owner of the principal[1]. There is no requirement that the person carrying out the act of accession was in good faith[2]. Nor does the consent of the parties matter[3]. Consent by the owner or owners of the principal and the accessory can no more bring about accession where the essential elements are lacking than absence of that consent can prevent accession where they are present[4]. Still less can the parties contract out of the rules of accession[5]. In short, the approach of the law is objective, and this accords with the general tendency of the law of property to trade justice in particular cases in the interests of certainty in all cases. What matters is that there should be a single clear rule; and in the case of accession the rule adopted has the obvious advantage that third parties coming to deal with the property will not be prejudiced because they did not know, and could not reasonably have discovered, subjective factors which, under a different rule, might have been of significance[6].

1 Stair *Institutions* II,1,38,39.
2 *Stair* II,1,38,39; Erskine *Institute* II,1,15. But questions of faith may affect rights to compensation: see para 577 below.
3 This is because accession is a form of original acquisition and does not depend on the will of the owner of the accessory: see para 574 below.
4 Thus *Dixon v Fisher* (1843) 5 D 775 at 793, per Lord Cockburn: 'In considering this subject, I entirely disregard the view said to have been formed upon it by the deceased himself. His opinion of the law is clearly immaterial; for no man can make his property real or personal merely by thinking it so. And I do not conceive this to be a question which depends even upon his intention . . .'. But consent can deal with the consequences of accession. Thus A and B may agree to unite two pieces of

property on the basis that the resulting new thing should belong to them both. Of course, accession will then take place notwithstanding, with the result that the new thing belongs to the owner of the principal; but the effect of the agreement, where accompanied by the appropriate form of transfer (registration or delivery), is to reallocate ownership to both A and B.

5 *Shetland Islands Council v BP Petroleum Development Ltd* 1990 SLT 82 at 94, OH, per Lord Cullen.
6 Eg *Scottish Discount Co Ltd v Blin* 1985 SC 216 at 242, 1986 SLT 123 at 133, per Lord Cameron.

573. Importance of chronology. Accession may be affected by chronology. Thus suppose that A installs a system of storage heating into a house belonging to B. In such a case it is settled law that the heating system accedes to the house even although individual heaters are readily separated[1]. Because it is installed in a single act, the system is treated as a *unum quid* (a single thing). Either the whole system has acceded or none of it has, and the law is that the whole system accedes. But the result might have been different if the chronology was different. Thus suppose that, instead of installing the whole system, A installs the wiring only; and further suppose that ten years elapse before the heaters themselves are installed. There are then two acts and not one. The first act, the installation of the wiring, is clearly an act inducing accession. But the position of the second act is less clear. In the original version of the example the potential accessory was the entire heating system. In the revised example only the heaters remain as possible accessories, for the wiring acceded ten years' before. The question therefore is no longer the same; and since the storage heaters are attached by nothing more substantial than a cable it is arguable that the answer is also no longer the same[2].

The role of chronology must not, however, be exaggerated. It is far from being the case that everything which is installed in the course of a single act will be viewed as a *unum quid*. For this, more is required than the coincidence of timing. The separate elements will not be regarded as a single system unless they are also closely related[3]. Perhaps the most that can be said is that in doubtful cases the fact of a single act, as opposed to a series of acts separated by intervals of time, will help promote a finding of accession.

1 *Fife Assessor v Hodgson* 1966 SC 30, 1966 SLT 79, LVAC.
2 There is a different situation again where, the whole system having been installed at once, a replacement heater comes to be added. If the old heater acceded (as it did), then so, it is thought, must the new one.
3 The line is not easy to draw. Thus it is thought that a washing machine does not form a single system with its plumbing. The plumbing accedes and the machine does not. See also *Dowall v Miln* (1874) 1 R 1180 (machines in the same factory treated separately); *Scottish Discount Co Ltd v Blin* 1985 SC 216, 1986 SLT 123 (industrial shears treated separately from their concrete foundations and their shelter).

574. The three effects of accession. Accession may be said to have three separate effects. In the first place, the accessory becomes part of the principal. It is considered, in law if not in fact, to have lost its identity as a separate item of property. Accordingly, if the principal is sold, or if subsidiary rights are created in respect of it, the accessory is affected in precisely the same way as the principal of which it now forms a part.

Secondly, where the accessory is moveable and the principal is heritable, accession has the effect of making the accessory heritable[1].

Thirdly, accession extinguishes the existing title to the accessory. As part of the principal, the accessory now belongs to the owner of the principal[2]. Where therefore principal and accessory were, at the time when accession took place, owned by different people, there is original acquisition[3] of the accessory by the owner of the principal. If the principal was owned by more than one person, the result is common ownership of the accessory[4]. If the principal was feudal land, the accessory is feudalised in turn and is owned, for their respective interests, by the vassal and by all the superiors in that land[5]. The owner or owners of the principal may be obliged to pay compensation to the owner of the accessory[6].

There is a sense in which these three separate effects are really just one single effect, for the result of accession is that the accessory becomes part of the principal, and from that proposition everything else follows.

The three effects of accession stem from the fact that principal and accessory are conjoined. What is the position where, as may happen, they subsequently come to be separated? The answer is that the first effect (accessory subsumed in principal) and the second effect (moveable becomes heritable) are reversed, but that the third effect (ownership passes to owner of principal) is not. On separation, the accessory regains its former status as a separate item of property, and in the case of accession to land it becomes moveable once more. But it remains in the ownership of the owner of the principal[7]. A thief does not become the owner of lead merely by stripping it from the roof of a building, and nor does a tenant become the owner of fixtures originally attached by him merely by the act of disattachment[8]. Title does not revert to the former owner or other person carrying out the separation without some further act of original or derivative acquisition.

1 Erskine *Institute* II,2,2,4.
2 Stair *Institutions* II,1,34; Erskine II,1,14; Bell *Principles* ss 1297, 1298.
3 Ie original acquisition as opposed to derivative acquisition. The difference is that, while derivative acquisition is acquisition by transfer from an existing owner, original acquisition is acquisition without reference to the previous ownership of another person. See further para 539 above.
4 *Bell* s 1076.
5 See para 587 below.
6 See para 577 below.
7 However, in *Scottish Discount Co Ltd v Blin* 1985 SC 216 at 226, OH, Lord Murray the Lord Ordinary expressed the view that title reverts to the former owner. *Stair* II,1,38, suggests that the former title revives in the case of property which was stolen.
8 But where the separation is in exercise of a right of severance, ownership passes to the tenant (whether he is the original tenant who installed the fixtures or a successor of that person). See para 586 below.

575. Relevance of type of parties in dispute. The fact that accession has three separate effects[1] has sometimes prompted the view that there are three (or even more) separate sets of rules for accession. On this view, the question of whether accession has taken place depends upon which of the three effects is being considered and on the type of parties who are in dispute. Usually questions between a seller and buyer of the principal concern the first effect (accessory subsumed in principal), questions between beneficiaries succeeding to an estate concern the second effect (moveable accessory becomes heritable), and those between landlord and tenant the third effect (ownership of accessory passes to owner of principal), and the applicable rules are said not to be the same.

The distinction is really between the third effect and the other two. The third effect results in original acquisition by the owner of the principal at the expense of the owner of the accessory, of which the case of landlord and tenant (where a tenant attaches articles to a building belonging to his landlord) is a prominent, although not of course the only, example. Since the law has a natural reluctance to deprive a person of property without his consent, the argument arises that in such a case accession should not readily be conceded. But with the other two effects the policy considerations are different. A buyer or other person acquiring rights over an object will expect to obtain all the parts properly associated with that object. There seems no reason to restrict accession here. The same is true of the second effect, which was important mainly in the rules of intestate succession in force prior to the passing of the Succession (Scotland) Act 1964 in terms of which heritable property fell to the heir-at-law and the moveable property passed, through the mediation of an executor, to the other close relatives[2]. On this view of the law, the question of whether, for example, a machine accedes to the floor of a factory is decided differently depending on the nature of the parties who happen to be in dispute. If the factory was tenanted, and the dispute arises between landlord and tenant, there will usually, on this view, be no accession. The tenant is not to be deprived of his property. But if the factory was not tenanted, so that both principal and accessory belong to the same person, accession is much more likely to be found, and if the factory is subsequently sold or if its owner dies, the machine will be considered as part of the factory[3].

The view just described was accepted in Scots law until the decision of the House of Lords in *Brand's Trustees v Brand's Trustees* in 1876[4]. *Brand's Trustees* concerned machinery attached to the land by a tenant holding under a nineteen-year lease. In the Second Division it was said that, in the absence of other strong indicators to the contrary, the existence of the lease — the fact, in other words, that a question of original acquisition arose — prevented accession from taking place. In the House of Lords this approach was rejected. The fact that the land was tenanted was considered to be irrelevant, and accession was said to have occurred.

Brand's Trustees established the idea of a unitary law of accession. In determining whether accession has taken place the same rules are to be applied in all cases, and no attention is paid to the identity of the parties who happen to be in dispute. The modern law is objective and not subjective[5]. Nonetheless, the influence of *Brand's Trustees* has not been sufficient to eliminate all traces of the former law, a version of which has reappeared in some modern cases[6].

1 See para 574 above.
2 As to intestate succession to moveable estate prior to the Succession (Scotland) Act 1964 (c 41), see WILLS AND SUCCESSION, vol 25, para 682.
3 But while this view of the law produces inconsistent results in relation to similar sets of facts, it is thought that it at least produces consistent results in relation to any one piece of property. So if an article is attached by a tenant, then it is not regarded as a fixture, even if the actual dispute happens to involve a buyer and seller or, as in the case of *Brand's Trustees v Brand's Trustees* (1874) 2 R 258, revsd (1876) 3 R (HL) 16, an heir and executor.
4 *Brand's Trustees v Brand's Trustees* (1876) 3 R (HL) 16. On this case see K G C Reid 'The Lord Chancellor's Fixtures' (1983) 28 JLSS 49.
5 See para 572 above.
6 Most notably in *Christie v Smith's Executrix* 1949 SC 572, 1950 SLT 31, and *Scottish Discount Co Ltd v Blin* 1985 SC 216, 1986 SLT 123. This revival has been criticised: see *Corporeal Moveables: Some Problems of Classification* (Scot Law Com Consultative Memorandum no. 26) (1976) paras 24, 25. See further para 583 below.

576. 'Accessories' which have not acceded. The idea that different rules must be applied as between different parties is not wholly unknown even in the modern law, but this is not a direct consequence of the law of accession. An example explains why. Suppose that A carries out work on a car belonging to B. He installs a new engine. He adds new tyres. He puts a new spare wheel in the boot. From the point of view of accession, only the first act is of relevance. The engine accedes to the car and becomes the property of B. The other acts do not, probably, induce accession[1]. Suppose, however, that the example is changed and that the acts were carried out by B on his own car, and further suppose that B now comes to sell the car to C. From the point of view of the law of accession nothing has changed, for since the decision in *Brand's Trustees v Brand's Trustees*[2] the fact that principal and accessory were in separate ownership in the first case but not in the second is of no significance. In both cases only the engine accedes. Yet when C comes to collect the car he will expect more than just the new engine. Neither the tyres nor the spare wheel have acceded, but there is little doubt that C is entitled to both. The reason for this lies in the law of contract and not in the law of property. In buying a car C is entitled to the car itself and to everything which has acceded to it. But, depending on the terms, express or implied, of his contract, he may also have a wider entitlement, and there seems little doubt that in the sale of a car the tyres and spare wheel are impliedly included[3].

The rule just identified for the law of sale applies equally to donation, security, and indeed to all other rights which may be created in respect of property. The rule is important in the case of vehicles and of machinery generally where there may be a number of loose parts which have not, strictly, acceded. Elsewhere it is probably unimportant. In particular, in the absence of express stipulation a purchaser of land is entitled to no more than what has acceded to the land[4], and for this reason missives of sale usually contain a detailed enumeration of any moveable items that are to be included in the sale.

In principle, the rule applies to gifts made on death as much as to lifetime gifts, but since it depends on the intention of the parties it can have no application to cases of intestate succession. Yet even here a similar result is achieved, albeit by a different route. Intestate succession, even in the modern law, requires a decision on which part of the estate of the deceased is heritable and which part moveable; and the rule is that a moveable item which is so completely designed for the benefit of another article, itself heritable, that it has no utility in isolation, is considered to be constructively heritable for the purposes of succession. Examples falling into this class, known as 'constructive fixtures', include the keys of a house and the moveable parts of a machine otherwise heritable[5].

1 *J L Cohen Motors v Alberts* (1985) 2 SA 427. This is arguably because the new tyres and the new spare wheel can be separated without material damage to the principal: see para 589 below.
2 *Brand's Trustees v Brand's Trustees* (1876) 3 R (HL) 16. See para 575 above.
3 One result of a unitary approach to the law is that, in order to protect the position of owners of accessories, courts may be more reluctant to acknowledge that accession has taken place; and, if that is so, the role of contract for cases such as sale becomes more important.
4 Eg *Christie v Smith's Executrix* 1949 SC 572, 1950 SLT 31. But where a machine has acceded to the land, moveable parts of that machine will be impliedly included.
5 *Fisher v Dixon* (1843) 5 D 775 at 801, per Lord Cockburn. See also para 15 above. The idea of constructive accession is sometimes used in a wider sense as an alternative method of explaining why a purchaser receives parts which have not acceded. See eg D L Carey Miller *Corporeal Moveables in Scots Law* (1991) para 3.22. Another possible way of analysing at least some of the situations described here is by reference to the idea of a *unum quid* (see para 573 above): on this view, the whole machine, including its moveable parts, may be treated as a *unum quid*, so that the accession of the machine carries with it the accession of its moveable parts.

577. Compensation. If principal and accessory belonged to different people, the owner of the accessory loses his property to the owner of the principal. But he may have a right to compensation for his loss. Accession can occur either naturally ('natural' accession) or through human intervention ('industrial' or 'artificial' accession)[1]. Whether compensation is due in the case of natural accession[2] has never been decided and is perhaps of little importance in practice. In the case of industrial accession, much the more common of the two, entitlement to compensation depends upon which party performed the act of accession. Here there are three possibilities:

(1) Where the act of accession was instructed or performed by the owner of the principal, the owner of the accessory is entitled to repayment of its value. Good faith is not a defence, although bad faith may allow a claim in reparation and so a larger amount of compensation[3].

(2) Where, as happens much more frequently, the act of accession was performed or instructed by the owner of the accessory, there is in general no entitlement to compensation. However, if the owner of the accessory acted in the reasonable but mistaken belief, either that the principal was his, or at least that he had some right to it which was other than merely transient, then he has a claim to the extent that the owner of the principal has been enriched[4]. So if A takes a twenty-year lease of land from B and proceeds to build a house, he has no claim against B in respect of the house. He is considered to have carried out the expenditure for his own convenience during the currency of the lease[5]. But if

C, in the genuine but mistaken belief that he has a twenty-year lease, builds a house on land belonging to D and is ejected after five years, compensation is payable to the extent of D's enrichment. The former owner of the accessory is entitled to retain possession of the principal until his claim for compensation has been satisfied[6]. There is no claim for compensation where the value of the principal has actually declined, as, for example, by the addition of modern work to a valuable antique, and indeed the workman might attract liability in delict.

(3) Finally, where the act of accession was performed or instructed by some third party, the owner of the accessory has two possible claims. The third party is liable for the value of the accessory if he acted in bad faith[7], and perhaps even if he acted in good faith[8]; and there is at least an argument that the owner of the principal is liable to the extent of his enrichment. Presumably recovery under one head would prevent recovery under the other.

The right to compensation is founded on unjustified enrichment and as a personal right, its value depends on the solvency of the obligant. No claim for compensation can be made against a person coming subsequently to own the principal[9].

1 Erskine *Institute* II,1,15; Bell *Principles* ss 1297, 1298.
2 As where A sows with B's seeds, or where C's female animal is impregnated by D's male animal.
3 Stair *Institutions* II,1,38 and 39; Bankton *Institute* I,9,43; II,1,17. In Roman law bad faith allowed the former owner of the accessory to proceed for theft, with the result that he could recover the value of the accessory by a personal action for compensation, the *condictio furti*, and at least twice its value by a penal action.
4 *Stair* I,8,6; II,1,39 and 40; *Bankton* I,8,15; *Erskine* III,1,11; *Bell* s 538. But, despite Stair, good faith is a prerequisite for a claim: *Barbour v Halliday* (1840) 2 D 1279; *Buchanan v Stewart* (1874) 2 R 78; *Duke of Hamilton v Johnston* (1877) 14 SLR 298. In Roman law *quantum* was measured by loss and not by enrichment.
5 *Stair* II,1,40; *Erskine* III,1,11; *Wallace v Braid* (1900) 2 F 754.
6 See para 173 above. This was also the rule in Roman law.
7 *Stair* I,7,2; *Erskine* III,1,10.
8 *Oliver and Boyd v Marr Typefounding Co Ltd* (1901) 9 SLT 170, OH; *International Banking Corpn v Ferguson Shaw & Sons* 1910 SC 182, 1909 2 SLT 377. But cf *North-West Securities Ltd v Barrhead Coachworks Ltd* 1976 SC 68, 1976 SLT 99, OH.
9 *Beattie v Lord Napier* (1831) 9 S 639.

(2) MOVEABLES TO LAND: FIXTURES

578. Introduction. Corporeal moveable property which is attached to corporeal heritable property (that is, land) may become part of that property by accession. If this happens, the moveable property is the accessory and the heritable property the principal, for land cannot accede to moveable property. Often accession involves direct physical contact between the accessory and the land[1], but accession may also occur by attachment to some other object, such as a building, which has itself become part of the land by accession[2]. So it is accession to build a house on land, but it is also accession to install new wiring in the house. In the second case the wiring accedes to the house and hence to the land itself[3].

Articles of moveable property which accede to a building are often referred to as 'fixtures' and the term can be used as convenient shorthand for all cases of moveable accession to land. 'Fixtures' are usually contrasted with 'fittings'. 'Fittings' are moveable articles such as carpets and furniture which, although present in a building, have not acceded to it. However, the terminology is not always faithfully observed, and conveyancers have a particular liking for the phrase 'heritable fixtures and fittings'[4].

The subject of fixtures is one of the most frequently litigated in the law of property. Many of the older cases are about succession law. Until 1964, the disposal of property on intestacy depended upon whether it was moveable or heritable and the issue was sometimes keenly disputed. Today the question is only of minor significance in succession law, but it remains of importance elsewhere. So in the purchase of land a purchaser is entitled to the buildings and other fixtures — for they are part of the land — but not to the fittings[5]. If a seller wishes to retain certain fixtures or, conversely, if a buyer wishes to acquire certain fittings, these must be separately contracted for. Similarly, when a right in security is granted over land, the security affects the fixtures but not the fittings[6]. In the law of landlord and tenant all fixtures attached by a tenant become the property of the landlord, subject to a limited right of severance[7].

The decision of the House of Lords in 1876 in the case of *Brand's Trustees v Brand's Trustees*[8] marked the adoption of a unitary law of accession in Scotland, replacing the previous rule that where accessory and principal were separately owned a finding of accession would not normally be made[9]. For this reason cases decided prior to 1876 require to be treated with considerable caution. One result of the decision in *Brand's Trustees* was to bring Scots law into line with English law, and the law in the two jurisdictions, if not identical, is at least now very similar. English case law is therefore available to supplement the Scottish decisions, a rare occurrence in the law of property[10]. A third source of law is the valuation cases, that is to say, cases concerned with the valuation of land for the purposes of (non-domestic) rates. Rates are exigible only from 'lands and heritages', an expression which has an extensive statutory definition[11]. It has been frequently asserted, and probably as frequently denied, that the question of whether plant or machinery or other structures are 'lands and heritages' for the purposes of rating is the same as the question of whether, under the general law of fixtures, a moveable item has acceded to the land[12]. In practice, valuation cases tend to cite mainly other valuation cases while non-valuation cases cite non-valuation cases, and although there is a great deal of common ground, the case law has developed in the form of two parallel lines, running in the same direction but never properly converging[13].

1 There is, at least in theory, a distinction between things originally moveable which accede to the land, and things which are part of the land (*pars soli*) and so were never moveable. Things that are part of the land in this sense include soil, stones and minerals.
2 Erskine *Institute* II,1,16.
3 But where a building has been divided into separate tenements, accession does not operate across the boundaries of the individual separate tenement and there is no accession to the land itself. See para 585 below.
4 'Fittings' in the strict sense cannot be 'heritable'. Nonetheless it remains standard conveyancing practice to include in a disposition a conveyance of the 'fixtures and fittings'. Of this practice it has been observed that 'a sound conveyancer in framing a disposition . . . will not think it necessary to insert a futile conveyance of the moveables which would carry nothing': see *Jamieson v Welsh* (1900) 3 F 176 at 182, per Lord Kinnear.
5 Eg *Christie v Smith's Executrix* 1949 SC 572, 1950 SLT 31.
6 Eg *Scottish Discount Co Ltd v Blin* 1985 SC 216, 1986 SLT 123.
7 *Brand's Trustees v Brand's Trustees* (1876) 3 R (HL) 16. For rights of severance, see para 586 below.
8 *Brand's Trustees v Brand's Trustees* (1876) 3 R (HL) 16.
9 This former law was sometimes expressed, not quite accurately, as making a distinction between questions involving landlord and tenant and questions involving heir and executor. In the former case accessory and principal were originally separately owned, whereas in the latter case they were both owned by the same person. See further para 575 above.
10 Perhaps caution is needed here also. There is a large body of English case law, sufficient, it sometimes seems, to vouch any proposition however contradictory to any other proposition. The writer is unenthusiastic about the use of English authority.
11 Lands Valuation (Scotland) Act 1854 (c 91), s 42 (amended by the Sporting Lands Rating (Scotland) Act 1886 (c 15), s 4): 'lands and heritages' include all lands, houses, shootings and deer forests, fishings, woods, copses and underwood from which revenue is actually derived, ferries, piers, harbours, quays, wharfs, docks, canals, railways, mines, minerals, quarries, coalworks, waterworks, limeworks, brickworks, ironworks, gasworks, factories, and all buildings and pertinents thereof, and all machinery fixed or attached to any lands or heritages. In practice, attention has usually

focused on the final part of the definition ('all machinery fixed or attached to any lands or heritages'). A number of special rules for machinery are contained in the proviso to the Lands Valuation (Scotland) Act 1854, s 42 (added by the Lands Valuation (Scotland) Amendment Act 1902 (c 25), s 1; amended by the Valuation (Plant and Machinery) (Scotland) Order 1983, SI 1983/120, art 3), for which see VALUATION FOR RATING, vol 24, para 700.

12 Cf *Christie v Smith's Executrix* 1949 SC 572 at 579, 586, 1950 SLT 31 at 33, 36, per Lord Justice-Clerk Thomson and Lord Jamieson, with *Scottish Discount Co Ltd v Blin* 1985 SC 216 at 235, 1986 SLT 123 at 129, per Lord President Emslie. Writers on valuation for rating have usually adopted the view that the rules are the same: see VALUATION FOR RATING, vol 24, paras 440, 441, and S B Armour *Valuation for Rating* (5th edn 1985, by J J Clyde and J A D Hope) para 7-04; and it is probably the case that valuation cases have used non-valuation cases with greater enthusiasm than the other way about. See also J A Copeland 'Fixture in and out of Valuation' (1967) 12 JLSS 54.

13 Except, presumably, at infinity, a point which the law of property has not yet reached. Valuation cases often seem to proceed on an antique version of the law of fixtures, making free use of cases which are now of doubtful authority as decided prior to *Brand's Trustees v Brand's Trustees* (1876) 3 R (HL) 16 (see eg *Lothian Region Assessor v Blue Circle Industries plc* 1986 SLT 537, LVAC), and emphasising that the rules to be applied are those between heir and executor (see eg VALUATION FOR RATING, vol 24, para 441), a proposition which denies the unitary nature of the modern law.

579. The three conditions for accession. The factors necessary in order for accession to take place may be, and indeed have been[1], analysed in a number of different ways, but there is broad agreement both as to their nature and as to their relative importance[2]. In terms of the analysis adopted in the present title, three conditions require to be met before accession can be said to have taken place[3]. First, there must be some physical connection, and normally attachment, between principal and accessory[4]. Secondly, the accessory must be subordinate in function to the principal[5]. Finally, the attachment must be permanent, or at least more than merely temporary[6]. All three are found in Erskine's succinct definition of heritable accession:

'Things by their own nature moveable, might become immoveable by their being fixed or united to an immoveable subject for its perpetual use'[7].

Usually all three conditions must be satisfied, at least to some degree, before accession can take place[8], but functional subordination is discounted in the case of large pieces of machinery and other very substantial structures. Furthermore, a court may sometimes take other factors into account although these cannot be regarded as preconditions for the operation of accession[9].

1 Thus W M Gloag lists seven separate factors: 7 *Encyclopaedia of the Laws of Scotland* (ed Lord Dunedin and J Wark, 1929) para 362. W M Gordon *Scottish Land Law* (1989) para 5-05, groups the various factors under three main headings (fact of annexation, purpose of annexation, and custom of district). D L Carey Miller *Corporeal Moveables in Scots Law* (1991) para 3.12, also has three main headings (physical circumstances, role factors and annexer's intention) although they are not the same as Gordon's.

2 The only important difference relates to the role of subjective intention, which Gordon is willing to admit as a relevant factor (see *Gordon* para 5-03) but which Gloag would not admit (7 *Encyclopaedia of the Laws of Scotland* paras 362, 364). Carey Miller adopts a position intermediate between the two (*Carey Miller* para 3.15). The present writer agrees with Gloag: see para 583 below.

3 The same conditions apply also to other cases of accession: see para 571 above.

4 See para 580 below.

5 See para 581 below.

6 See para 582 below.

7 Erskine *Institute* II,2,2. See also *Erskine* II,2,4; Bankton *Institute* I,13,17.

8 The view expressed in *Cliffplant Ltd v Kinnaird* 1981 SC 9, 1982 SLT 2, that only the first condition, physical attachment, is required for accession to take place was overruled by a court of seven judges in *Scottish Discount Co Ltd v Blin* 1985 SC 216, 1986 SLT 123.

9 See para 584 below.

580. Condition (1): physical attachment. In the early law, physical attachment was not always insisted upon. In the seventeenth century, Stewart was able to answer Dirleton that horses and other moveable objects necessary to work a horse mill, and buckets and chains used in a coal work, were heritable and fell to the heir[1]. With the limited exception of constructive fixtures[2], however, this is no longer the law. The modern rule is that moveable property can accede to land (or to another object which has itself acceded to land) only where there is physical union between accessory and principal. Usually actual attachment is required, although in the case of very heavy objects it is sufficient if they rest on their own weight[3]. But while minimal attachment is sufficient, at least where other factors are also present, the greater the degree of attachment, the more likely an article is to be considered a fixture. For much the same kind of reasons, a heavy object is more likely to accede than a light one[4]. Substantial attachment and substantial weight are also strong evidence of permanency, one of the other preconditions of accession[5].

In one case physical attachment is decisive[6]. Where an article is fixed in such a way that it cannot be separated without serious injury either to itself or to the principal, the article is regarded as having acceded[7], for the policy of the law is to preserve property and not to destroy it[8]. However, this does not include articles which are capable of later reassembly. So wallpaper pasted on to a wall is a fixture on the basis of physical attachment alone, while a substantial machine which can only be separated in parts is not, provided it is capable of later reassembly[9].

1   Lord Dirleton's *Some Doubts and Questions in the Law* (1698) and Stewart's *Answers* 'Executry', 'Mill' (see Sir James Stewart *Dirleton's Doubts and Questions in the Law of Scotland Resolved and Answered* (2nd edn, 1762)). This statement was probably influenced by the principle of heritable by destination (see para 15 above) which was sometimes applied in questions between heirs and executors.
2   For constructive fixtures, see para 576 above.
3   *Christie v Smith's Executrix* 1949 SC 572, 1950 SLT 31.
4   *Scottish Discount Co Ltd v Blin* 1985 SC 216, 1986 SLT 123; *TSB Scotland plc v James Mills (Montrose) Ltd (in receivership)* 1991 GWD 39-2406, OH.
5   See para 582 below.
6   The three-condition analysis given in para 579 above is preserved by saying that in cases of extreme physical attachment, the other conditions are also usually present. Thus Lord Justice-Clerk Thomson in *Christie v Smith's Executrix* 1949 SC 572 at 578, 1950 SLT 31 at 33: 'No doubt the element of annexation to the soil is of importance, and on occasion it may be conclusive, as the annexation may be of such a character as to imply the presence of the other main elements pointing to the structure's being heritable.'
7   Bell *Commentaries* I,787; *Dowall v Miln* (1874) 1 R 1180 at 1182, per Lord Justice-Clerk Moncreiff.
8   See para 571 above.
9   But it may of course be a fixture once other factors come to be considered; and the fact that it can only be separated in parts is an indication of permanency: see para 582 below.

581. Condition (2): functional subordination. The second condition of accession is that the accessory is in some sense subordinate in function to the principal. The fixture must serve the land or the building to which it is attached. This condition is often expressed in the form of a question: is the article attached for the improvement of the land or building, or is it attached for the better enjoyment of the article itself? Only if the article is attached for the improvement of the land or building is the condition of functional subordination satisfied. It is for this reason that storage heaters and central heating systems accede to the house in which they are placed[1], while pictures and tapestries do not[2]. For while central heating acts for the benefit of the house, it may be argued that the house acts for the benefit of the pictures by providing a space for them to be hung. On this view, the crucial difference between the two types of object is that only the second has value for its own sake, in this case aesthetic value. Accordingly, the picture preserves its separate identity while the central heating system merges with the identity of the house.

Aesthetic value is not, in fact, an absolute barrier to accession, at least if there is also irrevocable physical attachment. It has never been doubted, for example, that a fresco accedes to the wall on which it is painted[3]. But even judged by reference to functional subordination, a work of art might be considered as so integrated into the aesthetic design of a particular room as to have acceded to it. Something of this kind of reasoning was employed in the leading case of *Cochrane v Stevenson*[4], which concerned three substantial oil paintings. Two were clearly moveable, but the third, although painted on canvas and not directly on to the wall, was hung in such a way that it took the place of a piece of panelling. Its removal would make a break in the panelling by exposing a bare wall. In these circumstances it was argued that the picture was an integral part of the overall design of the room, and one judge[5] was sufficiently persuaded to hold the picture as moveable only because he felt that all three pictures should be treated in the same way.

A difficulty with a formula which attempts to oppose 'improvement of the land' with 'better enjoyment of the article' is that many instances of attachment will satisfy both criteria. Even in the case of a picture it can be said that the attachment is both for the better enjoyment of the house (a house with pictures being better than one without) and for the better enjoyment of the picture itself. In such a case it becomes necessary to evaluate which of the two receives the greater benefit from the attachment.

Unlike the other two conditions for accession, which are mandatory in all cases, the condition of functional subordination is excused in the case of buildings, large items of machinery, and other substantial structures[6]. Houses, on the whole, are erected for the better enjoyment of the house rather than for the better enjoyment of the land[7], but in such cases the degree of attachment and sheer bulk are considered sufficient to bring about accession even in the absence of functional subordination. However, some cases of machinery, most notably mining machinery, may also satisfy the condition of functional subordination[8].

1 *Fife Assessor v Hodgson* 1966 SC 30, 1966 SLT 79, LVAC.
2 *Cochrane v Stevenson* (1891) 18 R 1208; *Leigh v Taylor* [1902] AC 157, HL.
3 Erskine *Institute* II,1,16.
4 *Cochrane v Stevenson* (1891) 18 R 1208. This issue has arisen in a number of English cases, eg *D'Eyncourt v Gregory* (1866) LR 3 Eq 382.
5 *Cochrane v Stevenson* (1891) 18 R 1208 at 1216, per Lord M'Laren.
6 This exception is confined to the law of fixtures. Functional subordination remains essential in other cases of accession: see para 571 above.
7 But see *Christie v Smith's Executrix* 1949 SC 572, 1950 SLT 31, where one of the reasons for the finding that a summerhouse was heritable was that it filled what would otherwise have been a gap between the garden wall and the end of the farmhouse.
8 *Dowall v Miln* (1874) 1 R 1180 at 1184, 1185, per Lord Neaves; *Fisher v Dixon* (1843) 5 D 775, affd 4 Bell App 286, HL; *Brand's Trustees v Brand's Trustees* (1876) 3 R (HL) 16.

582. Condition (3): permanence. Accession requires a degree of permanence, and an object which is fixed only for a short period is not regarded as having lost its identity to the principal. As T B Smith points out, there is an obvious difference between seats screwed into the floor of a cinema by its owner and seats similarly fixed to the floor of a hall for a night's boxing[1]. But while the temporary nature of an attachment will prevent accession, there is now no requirement that the union be truly permanent. The law was altered by the decision of the House of Lords in *Brand's Trustees v Brand's Trustees*[2]. Until that decision the fact that an attachment was made by a temporary occupier of land, such as a tenant or liferenter, was usually sufficient to prevent a finding of accession[3]. In *Brand's Trustees* the rule of English law was applied in which the test of permanency is satisfied wherever a tenant or other possessor on a limited title attaches an article for the duration of his lease or other right. Where, however, the occupation of land is of very short duration, the law remains as before and there is no accession.

Evidence of permanence is a more difficult matter. As with the other preconditions for accession, the principle is that the evidence ought to be 'patent for all to see'[4] so that a third party coming to the land with no knowledge of the background circumstances is able to form an accurate view as to whether accession has taken place[5]. But in the case of permanence, at least, this ideal may not always be attainable[6]. Clearly, the best evidence of permanence is the fact that a thing has indeed been attached for a substantial period of time, but questions of accession frequently arise in relation to attachments made relatively recently and for cases such as this other factors must also be considered.

Four factors have been treated by the courts as being of relevance. First, there is the question of whether the degree of attachment employed is greater than is strictly necessary to secure the article. Often the reason why objects are attached to land or to buildings is because that is the only way in which they can be used. Pictures require to be hung, fitted carpets to be tacked down, machinery to be stabilised, and so on. The mere fact of this kind of attachment does not give rise to accession. But where the degree of attachment employed is markedly greater than is necessary to secure the object, an inference of permanence, and hence of accession, arises[7].

Secondly, there is the issue of mutual special adaptation. If the principal has been specially adapted to fit the potential accessory or the accessory to fit the principal, this argues for accession. Wall cupboards specially designed for a particular kitchen are fixtures; ordinary cupboards may not be. The issue is of particular importance for industrial machinery, where mutual adaptation may sometimes produce a finding of accession despite the fact that the actual attachment is slight and that there is no functional subordination. Certainly this was the result in the leading case of *Howie's Trustees v M'Lay*[8] where lace looms rested on their own weight and were tied by iron stays to the roof framing but where there had been some modest adaptation of the building to the looms. It greatly assists a finding of accession if it can be said that 'if the machinery were removed, the buildings in their present condition would be useless'[9]. In practice, the question of accession may often turn upon whether special foundations have been prepared for the machine. Foundations themselves are of course heritable, and the view taken by the courts is that if a machine is attached to foundations, and if these foundations are specially adapted for the machine in question and could not be used for other machines, then accession has occurred[10].

A third factor sometimes used for measuring permanency is whether the article is of a kind which is usually left, or alternatively usually taken, when a building changes occupancy[11]. Domestic articles, such as washing machines and carpets, are often taken by the outgoing occupier, although presumably this is an area where changing social habits may in the end produce changes in the law[12]. Substantial industrial plant and machinery, however, are often left, the factory being sold or leased as a going concern. Thus Lord M'Laren:

> 'the presumption of attachment to the inheritance is stronger in the case of machinery used for industrial purposes than in the case of articles of domestic utility or ornament, which are usually carried by the owner from one residence to another'[13].

Finally, there is the question of installation and removal time. Where, as happened in one reported decision[14], a machine takes three months to install and almost as long to remove, the conclusion that it is a permanent part of the heritage is almost irresistible.

1 T B Smith *A Short Commentary on the Law of Scotland* (1962) p 504. See also *Holland v Hodgson* (1872) LR 7 CP 328 at 335, per Blackburn J:
2 *Brand's Trustees v Brand's Trustees* (1876) 3 R (HL) 16.
3 Bell *Commentaries* I,787; *Syme v Harvey* (1861) 24 D 202; *Duke of Buccleuch v Tod's Trustees* (1871) 9 M 1014.
4 *Hobson v Gorringe* [1897] 1 Ch 182 at 193, per Smith LJ, adopted in *Christie v Smith's Executrix* 1949 SC 572 at 587, 1950 SLT 31 at 37, per Lord Jamieson.
5 See para 572 above.
6 But while latent evidence may be admissible in certain circumstances, purely subjective evidence is not. Thus while it is permissible to show, as was shown in *Scottish Discount Co Ltd v Blin* 1985 SC

216, 1986 SLT 123, that a particular machine is of a type which is usually installed 'for life', it is not permissible to show that the person carrying out the attachment did or did not intend a permanent attachment.

7 *Leigh v Taylor* [1902] AC 157, HL.
8 *Howie's Trustees v M'Lay* (1902) 5 F 214, 10 SLT 475. See also *McDonald's Nurseries v Fifeshire Assessor* 1956 SLT 270, LVAC. These decisions may be compared with *Dowall v Miln* (1874) 1 R 1180 where spinning machines attached to the floor were held to be moveable in circumstances where there had been no special adaptation of the building.
9 *Luke v Smith* (1894) 1 SLT 545 at 546, OH, per Lord Wellwood.
10 *Scottish Discount Co Ltd v Blin* 1985 SC 216, 1986 SLT 123; *TSB Scotland plc v James Mills (Montrose) Ltd (in receivership)* 1991 GWD 39-2406, OH. The issue has also arisen in a number of valuation cases.
11 Stair *Institutions* II,1,2: 'things immoveable are . . . things fixed to the earth, not to be removed therefrom, as trees, houses, etc, which though they may possibly moved, yet it is not their use so to be'.
12 Eg fitted carpets are now often left in place following a change in occupancy whereas at one time (when such carpets were themselves relatively uncommon) they were often taken. The point may have been reached, or may soon be reached, where fitted carpets are regarded as heritable.
13 *Howie's Trustees v M'Lay* (1902) 5 F 214 at 220, 10 SLT 475 at 478, per Lord M'Laren.
14 *TSB Scotland plc v James Mills (Montrose) Ltd (in receivership)* 1991 GWD 39-2406, OH. See also *Scottish Discount Co Ltd v Blin* 1985 SC 216, 1986 SLT 123.

583. The role of intention. The question of whether any regard can be paid to the intention of 'the annexer' (that is, the person by whom or at whose instructions the act of annexation was carried out) has often been debated and has a long history in Scots law[1]. Those who argue that intention has a role to play usually explain that intention is to be viewed objectively. The concern, it is insisted, is not with the actual intention of the particular annexer but with what, from the relevant facts and circumstances, a reasonable annexer must be deemed to have intended. Of course, if this assurance is taken at face value, the use of the word 'intention' becomes redundant. For if all that may competently be considered is the objective evidence, and in particular the physical relationship of potential accessory to potential principal, then no real question of intention arises. It is, after all, a simple matter to re-phrase the three conditions for accession already mentioned in such a way that they appear to involve questions of intention[2], but if the evidence which may then be consulted remains the same in both cases, the difference is one of presentation and not one of substance[3]. It appears, however, that the assurance cannot be taken entirely at face value and that, at least in some circumstances, subjective evidence may be admissible.

In considering the role of subjective intention in the law of heritable accession, it is necessary to distinguish between, on the one hand the actual intention of particular annexers and, on the other hand, the deemed intention of all annexers of a particular class. Up until the decision of the House of Lords in 1876 in the case of *Brand's Trustees v Brand's Trustees*[4] evidence of both was regarded as relevant[5]. The effect of *Brand's Trustees* was to exclude consideration of either, and this remains the law today, at least as far as actual intention is concerned. Evidence of what the annexer said or wrote as indicating whether or not he wished to achieve accession is unquestionably inadmissible in the modern law[6]. The position about deemed intention has, however, now become unclear as a result of the decision in *Scottish Discount Co Ltd v Blin*[7]. The facts of *Scottish Discount* can be viewed as the facts of *Brand's Trustees* in inversion. In *Brand's Trustees* the annexer owned the potential accessory but not the potential principal, of which he was only the tenant. In *Scottish Discount* the annexer owned the principal but not the accessory, which was in the process of being acquired under a contract of hire purchase. Where principal and accessory belong to different parties, accession brings about a change of ownership in the accessory. Usually this consequence is unintended[8]. Accordingly, it was argued in the two cases that annexers belonging to the class of tenants (*Brand's Trustees*) and of hirers (*Scottish Discount*) must have a deemed intention not to effect accession. In *Brand's Trustees* this argument was rejected by the House of Lords, on the basis that only objective factors were relevant. In *Scottish Discount*, however, the argument was accorded cautious acceptance by the First Division, although in circumstances in which it was not necessary to give it effect. The fact that *Brand's Trustees* was opposed to this approach does not appear to have been brought to the attention of the court in *Scottish Discount*. It is suggested that on this matter a future court would be bound to follow *Brand's Trustees*. Acceptance of the reasoning in *Scottish Discount* would signal the abandonment of the unitary approach to accession established in 1876 and a return to the older view that stricter rules are to be applied whenever a change of ownership in the accessory is in issue[9].

1 Modern writers continue to disagree: see para 579, note 2, above.
2 This is particularly easy in the case of the second and third conditions, which indeed are often presented as being about 'the purpose of annexation'. See eg W M Gordon *Scottish Land Law* (1989) paras 5-12 ff. Thus 'did the annexer attach the accessory for the better enjoyment of the principal or for the better enjoyment of the accessory?', and 'did the annexer intend to effect a permanent improvement on the land?'.
3 The point is persuasively argued by D L Carey Miller *Corporeal Moveables in Scots Law* (1991) para 3.15.
4 *Brand's Trustees v Brand's Trustees* (1876) 3 R (HL) 16.
5 *Syme v Harvey* (1861) 24 D 202; *Dowall v Miln* (1874) 1 R 1180 at 1182, per Lord Justice-Clerk Moncreiff.
6 *Scottish Discount Co Ltd v Blin* 1985 SC 216, 1986 SLT 123; *Shetland Islands Council v BP Petroleum Development Ltd* 1989 SCLR 48, 1990 SLT 82, OH.
7 *Scottish Discount Co Ltd v Blin* 1985 SC 216, 1986 SLT 123.
8 Which, of course, is why accession is classified as an example of original acquisition of ownership.
9 See para 575 above. There was, of course, much to be said for the older view of the law. See K G C Reid 'The Lord Chancellor's Fixtures' (1983) 28 JLSS 49. Under the modern unitary law the owner of the accessory more readily loses his ownership, and is then left with, at best, a right of severance (see para 586 below) or a personal claim for monetary compensation (see para 577 above) and in many cases with no rights or claims at all.

584. Other factors. It has been seen that three conditions must normally be satisfied before accession can take place. But accession does not always follow even where all three are present. Of course, if an object is firmly and permanently attached to heritable property in such a way that its separate identity has been lost, there can be no doubt as to the result. But often matters are a great deal less clear than this, and it has been justly observed that with fixtures 'the difficulty is not the formulation but the application of the law'[1]. In these circumstances a court may occasionally have regard to other factors which, although not necessary for a finding of accession, are nonetheless regarded as helpful towards such a finding.

Even if it were useful to do so, which may be open to question[2], a complete list of such factors cannot be attempted here. But two may be mentioned. First, it has been suggested that in appropriate cases a court might have regard to local custom[3]. Secondly, a court may sometimes seek to argue by analogy under reference to well-recognised examples of accession rather than to proceed laboriously through the numerous individual criteria mentioned above. The question then becomes whether the object under consideration sufficiently resembles some other thing which is universally acknowledged as a fixture. This method of reasoning has found particular favour in valuation cases, where the usual analogue is buildings. Thus in a number of cases considerable ingenuity has been expended in arguing whether particular examples of mobile home belong to the *genus* dwelling house (in which case they accede) or to the *genus* camp (in which case they do not)[4].

1 *Berkley v Poulett* [1977] EG Dig 754 at 761, per Scarman LJ.
2 It is not to be supposed that decisions as to accession are always (or perhaps even often) made by drawing up lists of favourable indicators and unfavourable indicators and then by weighing the one against the other. In practice, decisions are sometimes impressionistic in nature. It may seem

perfectly obvious to a court that a particular object is, or is not, a fixture; and in such a case a recitation of the various conditions and factors operating in favour of or against accession may be an *ex post facto* rationalisation of a view which was in fact arrived at in a different way.

3 W M Gordon *Scottish Land Law* (1989) para 5-15. See also *Campbell v McCowan* 1945 SLT (Sh Ct) 3.
4 *Oman v Ritchie* 1941 SLT (Sh Ct) 13; *Renfrewshire Assessor v Mitchell* 1965 SC 271, 1966 SLT 53, LVAC; *Dunbarton Assessor v L K McKenzie & Partners* 1968 SLT 82, LVAC; *Glasgow Assessor v RNVR Club (Scotland)* 1974 SLT 291, LVAC ; *Redgates Caravan Parks Ltd v Ayrshire Assessor* 1973 SLT 52, LVAC.

585. No accession across separate tenements. 'Separate tenement' is the name given to heritable property owned separately from the *solum* of the ground[1]. Common examples are mineral estates, and the individual flatted units within a block of flats. For the purposes of the law of accession, separate tenements are treated as distinct from the estate from which they are withdrawn. This means that while accession operates normally within a given separate tenement, it cannot operate across its boundaries. So a flat situated on the second floor of a block of flats does not accede to the *solum* but is owned separately[2]; and if the owner adds parquet tiles to his floor, the tiles accede to the flat but not to the flat underneath.

1 As to separate tenements, see paras 207 ff above.
2 At common law the *solum* goes with the ground floor flat and not with the upper flats. See para 228 above. But even if the common law is altered, this is usually to the effect of making the *solum* common property, with the result that the upper flats (which are in individual ownership) continue to be held separately from the ownership of the *solum*.

586. Right of severance. If the accessory and the principal belonged to different parties, accession confers ownership of the accessory on the owner of the principal. When this occurs, the former owner of the accessory has two possible claims in respect of his loss. In the first place, he may have a right to monetary compensation, usually against the owner of the principal. This right has already been considered[1]. In the second place, and alternatively, he may have a right to sever the accessory from the principal. The effect of severance, where it is lawfully exercised, is to reinvest ownership in the person holding the right[2]. Unlawful severance, however, does not reinvest ownership, which remains in the owner of the principal[3].

A right of severance may arise either by operation of law or by agreement. The main case of a right arising by law is the right of a tenant to remove such fixtures as he attached for the purposes of his trade[4]. On attachment the fixtures become the property of the landlord, as the owner of the principal, but the tenant has a right of severance[5] which may be exercised at any time during the currency of the lease[6] or within a short period of its termination[7]. It is thought that this right may be exercised, not merely against the original landlord, but also against a successor of that landlord or his heritable creditor or, although this is less certain, against his trustee in sequestration[8]. There is a parallel, but statutory, rule in relation to agricultural fixtures[9]. In English law the right of a tenant is not confined to trade fixtures but includes domestic and ornamental fixtures provided that they can be removed without damage either to themselves or to the heritage[10]. Whether the same rule applies in Scotland has never been decided[11]. Naturally, the right of severance need be invoked only where accession has actually taken place. Objects used during the lease but which have not acceded remain the property of the tenant and may be removed at will. It is probably the law that a liferenter has the same, or at least equivalent, rights of severance to those held by a tenant[12]. Other temporary possessors appear to have no rights of severance, although a bona fide possessor has a claim in recompense in respect of improvements[13].

A right of severance may also arise by agreement, although this is uncommon in practice. An agreement confers a personal right only and so is not enforceable against a successor of the owner of the combined principal and accessory, at least if he is in good faith[14]; and in a question with the trustee in sequestration of the obligant it resolves into an unsecured claim for damages[15].

A person who, at the time of the attachment, owned both the accessory and the principal is always free to sever the former from the latter, unless he has contracted not to do so[16]. But, in common with other rights in relation to severance, this freedom to sever takes no account of the fact that land is held on feudal tenure and that accession confers proprietorial rights on superiors. This subject is explored further in the immediately following paragraph.

1 See para 577 above.
2 Whether this is original or derivative aquisition is difficult to say. The argument in favour of the latter is that the existence of a right to sever signifies consent to the acquisition on the part of the owner of the principal.
3 See para 574 above.
4 *Brand's Trustees v Brand's Trustees* (1876) 3 R (HL) 16; *Ferguson v Paul* (1885) 12 R 1222. Fixtures which can be removed are sometimes referred to as 'tenant's fixtures', as opposed to 'landlord's fixtures' which cannot be removed. But both are the property of the landlord for as long as they are affixed.
5 *Brand's Trustees v Brand's Trustees* (1876) 3 R (HL) 16 changed the law. Until that case the fact that the annexer was a tenant or other temporary occupier was usually sufficient to prevent accession. As a result of *Brand's Trustees* the fact of temporary occupation ceased to be relevant for the purposes of accession but conferred instead a right of severance. See para 575 above. Thus until 1876 trade articles attached by a tenant did not usually accede. After 1876 they acceded but could be severed by the tenant.
6 *David Boswell Ltd v William Cook Engineering Ltd* 1989 SLT (Sh Ct) 61.
7 *Cliffplant Ltd v Kinnaird* 1981 SC 9 at 17, 18, 1982 SLT 2 at 6, per Lord Stewart.
8 One possible way of analysing the law is to say that the right of severance is an implied term of the contract of lease. The doubt about the trustee in sequestration is that if a landlord's obligations under a lease are correctly classified as real conditions *in personam* (see para 351 above), a claim against his trustee will sound only in damages.
9 Agricultural Holdings (Scotland) Act 1991 (c 55), s 18. This is wider than the equivalent common law right for trade fixtures and it includes, eg, the right to remove buildings. Section 18 provides that fixtures which may be removed remain the property of the tenant, ie in effect that they are not fixtures at all. See also AGRICULTURE, vol 1, para 779.
10 27 *Halsbury's Laws of England* (4th edn) para 149.
11 However, since the whole doctrine of severance is an English one, imported into Scotland by *Brand's Trustees*, there may be an argument that Scotland is assumed to have imported all aspects of the doctrine.
12 W M Gordon *Scottish Land Law* (1989) para 5-24.
13 See para 173 above.
14 Where he is in bad faith the rule against 'offside goals' appears to apply. See paras 695 ff below.
15 It is thought that the suggestion to the contrary by *Gordon* paras 5-36 and 5-37 is not correct. Gordon founds on the principle of latent trusts, but an ordinary contractual agreement is not a trust. See para 694 below.
16 A contract for the sale of land may often include an implied obligation not to sever certain fixtures which are to be left for the purchaser. A standard security may possibly include an implied obligation not to sever fixtures (see *Howie's Trustees v M'Lay* (1902) 5 F 214, 10 SLT 475), although if pushed too far this principle would prevent a debtor from changing wallpaper without the consent of his heritable creditor.

587. Accession and feudalism. Bell noted that:

'A double system of jurisprudence, in relation to the subjects of property, has . . . arisen in Scotland, as in most European nations; — the one regulating Land and its accessories according to the spirit and arrangements of the feudal system; the other regulating the rights to Moveables according to the principles of Roman jurisprudence which prevailed before the establishment of feus'[1].

The difficulties of accommodating within a single legal system two radically different traditions of property law is an interesting and important question which cannot be explored further here[2]. For present purposes it is sufficient to notice one example of these difficulties. The law of accession is Roman in origin and takes no account of the fact that land is held on feudal tenure. So when an article accedes to the land, it is generally taken that it becomes the absolute property of the 'owner' of the land, by which is meant the proprietor of the *dominium utile*. The law of accession then takes for granted that the 'owner' is entitled to use the accessory in any manner he wishes. He can sever it; he can allow others, such as a tenant, to sever it; he can sell it; and so on. But this view overlooks the interests of superiors and oversuperiors. If an article accedes to feudal land, then necessarily it becomes feudal in turn and so subject to the rights of superiors. If the vassal has *dominium* in fixtures, so too have the superiors. The logical consequence of this argument is that a vassal is unable to sever and dispose of a fixture without the consent of the superiors, whose property it also is. It can hardly be doubted that this is not actually the law, and that superiors have no continuing rights in respect of fixtures which have been severed, but why this should be the case has never been explained.

1 Bell *Principles* s 636.
2 For the difficulties of reconciling the Roman idea of undivided *dominium* with the feudal idea of separate estates of *dominium*, see paras 49 ff above.

(3) MOVEABLES TO MOVEABLES

588. Introduction. The principle of acquisition by accession also applies where one moveable is united inseparably with another moveable. Accession is treated by the institutional writers as a method of acquisition which may include specification[1] or industrial or artificial accession[2]. There are undoubtedly links between accession and specification and some cases can be construed as either. For example, Erskine[3] suggests that the Roman rule that canvas accedes to a painting made on it[4] can be explained on the basis that the painting is a new thing acquired by the painter. However, different principles appear to be involved because where there is acquisition by accession an existing ownership is extended by an addition to the object of that ownership. The greater then absorbs the less. But where there is acquistion by specification, it is a question of attributing ownership of a new thing. Specification has, therefore, been treated separately above[5].

Solids and liquids may also be mixed (as opposed to united), and the mixing may then give rise to questions of ownership of the resulting mixture involving the doctrines of commixtion and confusion. The legal issues which arise in this situation are considered separately[6].

1 Stair *Institutions* II,1,41, deals with it at the end of a series of clear cases of accession in II,1,34 ff.
2 Erskine *Institute* II,1,14 ff; Bankton *Institute* II,1,12 and 13; Bell *Principles* ss 1296, 1298.
3 *Erskine* II,1,15.
4 Justinian *Institute* II,1,34, settling an earlier controversy.
5 See paras 559 ff above.
6 See para 564 above.

589. The need for an indissoluble union. In the case of artificial accession between moveables the general rule is clear. The Latin maxim *accessorium principale sequitur*, the accessory follows the principal thing, applies and the owner of the principal thing acquires ownership of an accessory which has been inseparably joined to it[1]. This rule applies regardless of the intention of the parties involved and regardless of the good faith or otherwise of the party making the union[2]. Intention and good or bad faith are relevant only to possible compensation for the party losing ownership[3].

Ownership in the accessory passes to the owner of the principal thing only if there has been an indissoluble union. As Bell[4] puts it, accession applies where there 'can be no separation'. This appears to mean no separation without material damage to principal or accessory[5]. It is partly a question of technology, as in Roman law, where soldering was not regarded as a permanent union while welding was[6]. It is important to remember that the fact that a thing is made functionally part of another, as where a part is built into a machine, need not necessarily deprive the owner of the part of his ownership even if it is clear that that part is an accessory to the machine seen as a whole thing[7]. The issue where accession is concerned is generally whether it has been made an inseparable accessory. So it can quite logically be held that a part is an accessory but that there has been no accession in the sense of acquisition of ownership.

In Roman law, where there was a separable union the owner of the principal thing could nevertheless claim it along with the accessory from a third party, although the owner of the accessory could normally sue to have his property separated out[8]. It would be sensible to apply the same rule in Scots law; commonly the same result would follow from the fact that the action for recovery would be based on previous possession rather than on ultimate title[9].

1 Stair *Institutions* II,1,34; Erskine *Institute* II,1,14; Bankton *Institute* II,1,12 ff; Bell *Principles* s 1298.
2 See para 572 above. See also D L Carey Miller 'Does Confusio need to Confuse?' 1988 SLT (News) 270, contrasting Scots and English approaches to the question, and D L Carey Miller *Corporeal Moveables in Scots Law* (1991) paras 3.01, 3.21.
3 See para 577 above.
4 *Bell* s 1298.
5 See *Wylie and Lochhead v Mitchell* (1870) 8 M 552 especially at 557, per Lord President Inglis; *Zahnrad Fabrik Passau GmbH v Terex Ltd* 1986 SLT 84, OH.
6 *Digest* 6,1,23,5.
7 Cf the facts of *Zahnrad Fabrik Passau GmbH v Terex Ltd* 1986 SLT 84, OH.
8 *Digest* 6,1,23,5,7. There was a rule prohibiting demolition of buildings which might prevent immediate recovery of building materials.
9 See paras 148 ff above.

590. Identification of principal and accessory. A question which does not arise in the case of accession of moveables to heritable property is, which of the things joined together is to be regarded as the principal thing? Sometimes the answer will be obvious, as in the example of an arm welded on to a statue. In other cases it will not. Bell gives the following guidance on which is the principal:

'The rules by which this is to be ascertained are: That of two substances, one of which can exist separately, the other not, the former is the principal: that where both can exist separately, the principal is that which the other is taken to adorn or complete: that in the absence of these indications, bulk prevails; next value'[1].

It is not clear that bulk should precede value in the hierarchy if a strict hierarchy is intended. Stair, dealing with the question under the heading of contexture[2], refers to examples from Roman law, the weaving of valuable materials into existing cloth and the addition of a valuable gem to a ring, in which the materials and gem are regarded as acceding to the cloth and ring respectively, while a gem set in gold carries the gold setting. He explains the principle as being the design of what has been made and observes that in case of doubt the more valuable thing will be regarded as principal. The question is one of 'equity and utility'. Both he and Erskine[3] support the view that a canvas or board would accede to a painting on it, following the opinion favoured by Justinian for Roman law, and they extend it to writing on paper or other writing material, contrary to the rule in Roman law[4] which Stair says is 'every where in desuetude'. As noted above[5], Erskine is inclined to regard these cases as cases of specification. The view that paper accedes to the material on which it is written appears to be followed, although not expressly, in *Rollo v Thomson*[6] but the issue of copyright of sketches made by a draughtsman in the course of his employment was also involved in that case. The issues of ownership of the material on which ideas are expressed and ownership of copyright in the expression of the ideas are separate[7].

1 Bell *Principles* s 1298.
2 Stair *Institutions* II,1,39.
3 Stair II,1,39; Erskine *Institute* II,1,15. See also Bankton *Institute* II,1,18. Stair is less positive on painting saying that positive law might resolve the question either way without injustice. He also distinguishes painting on a canvas or the like from painting something such as a wall or shrine for adornment.
4 Justinian *Institute* II,1,33.
5 See para 588 above.
6 *Rollo v Thomson* (1857) 19 D 994.
7 See D L Carey Miller *Corporeal Moveables in Scots Law* (1991) p 61. On the question of copyright, see paras 931 ff below.

591. Reform of the law. In a consultative memorandum (which also dealt with specification) the Scottish Law Commission made critical comment on the present rules of accession as being ill adapted to modern circumstances[1]. In its alternative A[2], accession is linked with specification and the basic principle is that there should be common ownership with the court having power to make equitable adjustment of the parties' rights. In alternative B[2], adjunction and commixtion are treated separately. The rule suggested is common ownership in proportion to value or acquisition by the owner of the principal thing where a principal thing can be distinguished or one thing is of substantially greater value, with adjustment of claims for loss on the basis of unjustified enrichment or liability for fault. Protection for third parties acquiring in good faith from a party without title is also discussed[3] but the proposals made have not proceeded beyond consultation.

1 *Corporeal Moveables: Mixing Union and Creation* (Scot Law Com Consultative Memorandum no. 28) (1976). As to the Commission's proposals in respect of specification, see para 563 above.
2 *Corporeal Moveables: Mixing Union and Creation* para 33.
3 Ibid, paras 35–38.

(4) LAND TO LAND: ALLUVION

592. Introduction. The boundaries between those parts of the earth's surface covered by water and those parts which are dry are in a state of constant, although gradual, flux. Where the area of dry land increases, whether by the imperceptible addition of soil washed towards it by the water's action, or by the gradual retreat of the water, the additional part accedes to the existing dry land. Conversely, where the area of land under water increases, the additional part accedes to the land already under water. In both cases the accession is called alluvion[1]. For alluvion to operate two conditions must be satisfied. In the first place, the addition must not be merely temporary. Ordinary seasonal fluctuations in the level of water do not result in alluvion. In the second place, the addition must be gradual or at least imperceptible. Sudden violent alterations involving the detachment and redeposit of a distinct body of land or a sudden change in the position of a channel are not alluvion but avulsion[2]. Avulsion has no property consequences: the land added does not accede but persists as a separate feudal tenement, its ownership unaffected by the physical alteration. The different consequences attending alluvion and avulsion arise from the very nature of accession. Accession generally requires that the accessory is either physically, or at any rate functionally, inseparable from principal[3]. With alluvion the requirement of inseparability is satisfied; with avulsion it is not or may not be. Erskine explains the rule in this way:

'. . . what is added to a field by an imperceptible accretion cannot be distinguished from the ground itself to which it was joined, in order to its being restored to the former proprietor; and it may perhaps have been brought from another place than the adjacent ground; whereas one can easily distinguish in the sudden alterations occasioned by a flood of water what ground formerly belonged to each proprietor'[4].

1 Stair *Institutions* II,1,35; Bankton *Institute* II,1,10; Erskine *Institute* II,1,14; Hume *Lectures* vol IV (Stair Soc vol 17, 1955 ed G C H Paton) pp 225, 226. Bell *Principles* ss 642, 643, 935, 936.
2 *Stirling v Bartlett* 1992 SCLR 994, OH.
3 See para 571 above.
4 *Erskine* II,1,14.

593. Reclamation by human act. In its paradigm form, alluvion requires that the addition of land to land should arise naturally, without human agency. In practice, however, the boundary between wet and dry land is often altered by a deliberate human act, as in the case of a barrier constructed against the sea. It might be thought that the reclamation of land in this way is avulsion and not alluvion, but it is now settled that alluvion operates, and that the reclaimed land accedes to the immediately adjacent dry land[1]. It makes no difference to the result whether the reclamation was deliberate or accidental[2], whether it was carried out by the owner of the principal or by some other party[3], or indeed whether the act of reclamation was one which the party was entitled to make[4].

1 *Smart v Dundee Magistrates* (1796) 3 Pat 606, HL; *Campbell v Brown* 18 Nov 1813 FC. But see *Stirling v Bartlett* 1992 SCLR 994, OH.
2 In English law deliberate reclamation excludes alluvion: see 49 *Halsbury's Laws of England* (4th edn) paras 297, 298.
3 *Smith v Lerwick Harbour Trustees* (1903) 5 F 680, 10 SLT 742. But see *Todd v Clyde Trustees* (1840) 2 D 357 at 363, per Lord Jeffrey (affd (1841) 2 Robin 333, HL).
4 Eg the barrier may be built on land belonging to someone else. But in such a case the person whose land is encroached upon may be entitled to have the barrier removed: see paras 178, 179, above.

594. Five examples of alluvion. Five main examples of alluvion may be identified:
(1) *Transmission of soil from one bank to another.* 'The insensible addition which grounds lying on the banks of a river receive by what the water washes gradually from other grounds . . . accrues by natural accession to the owner of the land which receives the addition'[1].
(2) *Formation of islands.* Where an island is formed in the middle of a river or loch by the gradual accumulation of soil, the island accedes to the *alveus*[2]. The accessory (the island) then becomes the property of the owner of the principal (the *alveus*). Usually the owner of the *alveus* is a private individual in the case of non-tidal waters, and the Crown in the case of tidal waters[3].
(3) *Retreat of tidal waters.* When tidal waters retreat, whether naturally or as a result of human act, the land which is reclaimed accedes to the adjacent dry land. In a passage which has been approved in a number of subsequent cases, Lord Glenlee explained the law thus:

'. . . when a landholder is bounded by the sea, it is true he has a bounding charter. But it is a boundary moveable and fluctuating, *sua natura*; and when the sea recedes, he must be entitled still to preserve it as his boundary . . . [W]hen the sea goes back, the shore advances, and the proprietor is entitled to follow the water to the point to which it may naturally retire, or be artificially embanked'[4].

The effect of the retreat of tidal waters is that part of the former foreshore is now dry land, and that part of the former sea or river bed is or may now be foreshore. From this it appears to follow that, where dry land and adjacent foreshore were in separate ownership, the reclaimed dry land belongs to the owner of the dry land and the reclaimed foreshore belongs to the owner of the foreshore. The owner of the foreshore thus both gains land and also loses land[5].

(4) *Retreat of non-tidal waters.* When non-tidal waters retreat, so that the river or loch alters its course, the land reclaimed accedes to the immediately adjacent bank. This process is sometimes referred to as *alvei mutatio*[6].

(5) *Advance of waters.* When waters advance, the land newly made *alveus* accedes to the existing *alveus*. In *alvei mutatio* there is advance as well as the retreat of waters: the proprietor of one bank gains land from the water while the proprietor of the opposite bank loses land to the water[7].

1 Erskine *Institute* II,1,14.
2 J Rankine *The Law of Land-ownership in Scotland* (4th edn, 1909) pp 114, 115.
3 See para 275 above.
4 *Campbell v Brown* 18 Nov 1813 FC at 447. This passage was cited with approval in *Kerr v Dickson* (1840) 3 D 154 at 163, per Lord Medwyn, and in *Young v North British Rly Co* (1887) 14 R (HL) 53 at 53, per Lord Watson. *Blyth's Trustees v Shaw Stewart* (1883) 11 R 99 is a straightforward example of this rule in operation. Accession was held not to have taken place in *Todd v Clyde Trustees* (1840) 2 D 357, affd (1841) 2 Robin 333, HL, but the case is probably best regarded as confined to its own, unusual, facts.
5 This was the subject of express decision in *Lockhart v North Berwick Magistrates* (1902) 5 F 136, 10 SLT 382, and it is also the law in England. See also *Secretary of State for Scotland v Coombs* 1991 GWD 30-2404, OH. However, obiter suggestions that only the foreshore proprietor benefits from the retreat of tidal waters can be found in *Montrose Magistrates v Commercial Bank of Scotland Ltd* (1886) 13 R 947 and in *Smith v Lerwick Harbour Trustees* (1903) 5 F 680 at 691, 10 SLT 742 at 747, per Lord Kinnear.
6 Rankine pp 113, 114. Bell, however, disputes that accession takes place: see Bell *Principles* s 936. Gordon suggests that accession may not take place if the change of course is so sudden as to amount to avulsion: see W M Gordon *Scottish Land Law* (1989) para 4-23.
7 *Marquis of Tweeddale v Kerr* (1822) 1 S 397 (NE 373); *Stirling v Bartlett* 1992 SCLR 994, OH.

(5) ACCESSION BY FRUITS

595. Meaning of fruits. Accession by fruits is like other cases of accession in respect that it depends on the fact of physical union between principal and accessory, but it is also unlike other cases in respect that the accessory is produced wholly or partly by the principal and may have had no prior existence.

There are three main examples of accession by fruits:[1]

(1) The young of animals, while still *in utero*, are part of, and accede to, their mothers[2].

(2) All natural products of the animal or plant kingdoms, such as the milk of cows or apples on a tree, are, until separation, accessories of the animals or plants from which they derive.

(3) Trees, plants and other crops accede to the soil in which they grow upon taking root and drawing nourishment[3]. But industrial growing crops do not accede[4] and remain separate items of moveable property for all purposes including sale[5], succession and diligence[6]. Industrial growing crops are crops requiring annual seed and labour. So a tenant who plants barley retains ownership of the crop; a tenant who plants grass or trees loses ownership to his landlord[7]. It is thought that a crop qualifies as industrial where it is in fact re-seeded every year even if it is capable of being perennial, so that wild potatoes probably accede whereas cultivated potatoes do not[8]. The view is sometimes expressed[9] that plants grown commercially in a nursery do not accede even where they are not, strictly, industrial growing crops, but this view seems open to question and the issue has never been the subject of express decision[10].

1 Stair *Institutions* II,1,34; Bankton *Institute* II,1,10; Erskine *Institute* II,1,14; Bell *Principles* s 1297. There may also be fruits without accession, ie incorporeal fruits such as the rent of land or interest payable on money. See para 168 above. Accession is confined to corporeal property: para 570 above.

2 *Lamb v Grant* (1874) 11 SLR 672.

3 *Erskine* II,1,15.

4 *Stair* II,1,2 and 34; *Bankton* II,1,10; *Erskine* II,2,4; II,6,11; Bell *Commentaries* II,2; Bell *Principles* s 1473. This was not the Roman law and some uncertainty has surrounded its status in Scots law. Thus the Roman rule was followed in *Chalmers' Trustee v Dick's Trustee* 1909 SC 761, 1909 1 SLT 324. *Chalmers' Trustee* was subsequently doubted in *McKinley v Hutchison's Trustees* 1935 SLT 62 and it seems clear that the law is as stated in the text. Its normal justification is that industrial fruits are insufficiently permanent for accession to operate.

5 Sale of industrial growing crops is therefore regulated by the Sale of Goods Act 1979 (c 54): see eg *Kennedy's Trustee v Hamilton and Manson* (1897) 25 R 252. The definition of 'goods' in s 61(1) of the Sale of Goods Act 1979 also includes ordinary (ie heritable) crops 'attached to or forming part of the land which are agreed to be severed before sale or under the contract of sale'. On this last point, see *Morison v A and D F Lockhart* 1912 SC 1017, 1912 2 SLT 189; *Munro v Balnagowan Estates Co Ltd Liquidator* 1949 SC 49, 1949 SLT 85; J J Gow 'When are Trees "Timber"?' 1962 SLT (News) 13.

6 See DILIGENCE, vol 8, para 229.

7 *Paul v Cuthbertson* (1840) 2 D 1286 (trees).

8 *Marquis of Tweeddale v Somner* 19 Nov 1816 FC (hay); *McKinley v Hutchison's Trustees* 1935 SLT 62 (cultivated potatoes). But presumably purely subjective factors are disregarded, so that idiosyncratic methods of cultivation, such as the annual uprooting and re-rooting of trees, cannot alter the status of the plant.

9 Eg D L Carey Miller *Corporeal Moveables in Scots Law* (1991) para 3.06.

10 In *Gordon v Gordon* (1806) Hume 188 the court 'inclined to distinguish between the case of a nursery garden kept for sale, whereof the produce is moveable, as destined to be disposed of in the market, and the case of a nursery intended for the service of an estate of lands, of which it is part'. But this is an example of the principle of destination, which is effective only as to questions of succession: see *Bell* s 1475, and para 15 above. In a later case, *Begbie v Boyd* (1837) 16 S 232, the question of whether nursery plants were heritable or moveable was left open, although Lord Corehouse (at 236) inclined to the view that they were heritable.

596. Effect of severance. Accession depends on the fact of physical connection. Consequently, when that connection is at an end — when crops are harvested or young are born — accession is at an end also. Usually severance has no consequences for ownership of the accessory, a proposition which follows from first principles of the law of accession[1]. So, at least as a general rule, harvested fruits continue to belong to the owner of the principal which produced them. But the result may be different where the principal was possessed, and the fruits harvested, by a person other than the owner. Where the possession by a non-owner was as of right, entitlement to fruits will depend on the nature and terms of the right on which possession proceeded. A liferenter, for example, is always entitled to the fruits[2]. A lessee is entitled to some fruits but not, it appears, to others:

> 'In a lease of lands, the use which the lessee acquires in the subject let is not understood to comprise every right, which was before competent to the landlord, but is limited to those yearly fruits which either naturally, or by the lessee's industry, spring up from the surface. He is not, therefore, entitled to any of the woods or growing timber above ground, nor to the minerals, coal, limestone etc, underneath the surface, the use of the which consumes the subject, except in so far as the proprietor has given him right by a special clause in the tack'[3].

Other cases of lawful possession are more doubtful[4]. Where possession of the principal was without right, there is in general no entitlement to fruits unless the possessor was in good faith, when special rules apply[4]. The legal basis of the acquisition of fruits depends on the lawfulness of the possession. In the case of lawful possession, acquisition results from the consent of the owner of the principal, harvesting is the equivalent of delivery, and the title is derivative. In the case of bona fide but unlawful possession, there is no consent and the title is original.

Industrial growing crops do not accede and may be removed by a non-owning possessor where his possession of the land was either lawful or unlawful but in good faith[5].

1 See para 574 above.
2 See LIFERENT AND FEE, vol 13, para 1634.
3 Erskine *Institute* II,6,22. See also *Morkel v Malan* 1933 CPD 370; *Tucker v Farm and General Investment Trust Ltd* [1966] 2 QB 421, [1966] 2 All ER 508, CA.
4 See para 171 above.
5 See para 595, note 4, above.

13. TRANSFER OF OWNERSHIP

(1) INTRODUCTION

597. Derivative acquisition. By derivative acquisition of ownership is meant acquisition by transfer from the existing owner. Owner A transfers title to new owner B, with the result that B is invested and A divested. Derivative acquisition is contrasted with original acquisition, which is acquisition without reference to the previous ownership of another person, either because there was no previous owner or because the law extinguishes the title of the previous owner and confers a new title on the acquirer[1]. The principal cases of original acquisition are occupancy (*occupatio*)[2], accession (*accessio*)[3], specification (*specificatio*)[4], commixtion (*commixtio*) and confusion (*confusio*)[5], positive prescription[6], and registration of title[7].

Transfer of ownership is either voluntary or it is involuntary. The distinction is that, while consent to the transfer by the transferee is required in both cases, in the case of voluntary transfer the consent of the transferor is also required. In voluntary transfer the transferor agrees to the transfer; in involuntary transfer he does not. Voluntary transfer is the normal case of transfer[8]. Examples of involuntary transfer include transfer on death, transfer on bankruptcy and transfer by compulsory purchase[9].

1 See para 539 above. The latter type of original acquisition is to be distinguished from involuntary derivative acquisition. In involuntary derivative acquisition the law takes the title from A and confers it on B. In original acquisition the law extinguishes the title of A and confers a new title upon B. Positive prescription is the main example.
2 See paras 540 ff above.
3 See paras 570 ff above.
4 See paras 559 ff above.
5 See para 564 above.
6 See paras 674, 675, below.
7 See para 673 below.
8 For voluntary transfer, see paras 619 ff below.
9 For involuntary transfer, see paras 663 ff below.

598. Singular and universal successors. In the transfer of land a distinction is sometimes made between singular successors and universal successors. Thus Erskine wrote:

'A vassal may transfer his right, either upon his death to heirs . . . or while he is yet alive, to those who acquire by gift, purchase, adjudication, or other particular title. He who thus transmits a feudal right in his lifetime is called *the disponer* or *author*; and he who acquires it *the singular successor*, because he succeeds to that subject by a singular title — in opposition to an heir who succeeds to the whole estate of the deceased by the title of universal representation'[1].

The distinction depends upon the rule of succession in force until 1964 by which the heir-at-law succeeded to the entire heritable property of the deceased[2], a rule which until 1868[3] could not be avoided even by a will to contrary effect[4]. By succeeding to all of the deceased's heritage, the heir was indeed a 'universal successor', whereas purchasers or donees acquiring only a particular piece of heritage were regarded as 'singular successors'. A universal successor inherited obligations as well as rights and so might come under certain liabilities which would not affect a singular successor. Strictly, the distinction has no counterpart in modern law, which no longer provides for a universal legatee of heritage in the event of intestacy[5], but the term 'singular successor' continues to be used by conveyancers as indicating acquisition by purchase or gift as opposed to acquisition by succession. The companion term 'universal successor' has largely disappeared although there may be an argument that its true modern equivalent is an executor or trustee in sequestration or other party who succeeds to the whole rights and obligations of someone else.

1　Erskine *Institute* II,7,1. See also Bell *Principles* s 783. The concepts of singular and universal succession are derived from Roman law.
2　See WILLS AND SUCCESSION, vol 25, para 676.
3　The Titles to Land Consolidation (Scotland) Act 1868 (c 101), s 20 (as originally enacted) provided that succession to lands could be settled by testamentary deed: see WILLS AND SUCCESSION, vol 25, para 1037.
4　But there were other ways round the rule: see para 55 above.
5　See WILLS AND SUCCESSION, vol 25, paras 688 ff.

599. Capacity. A successful transfer requires legal capacity both of the transferor and also of the transferee. Except in the case of mental incapacity, natural persons aged sixteen and over have full capacity to transfer property of all kinds[1]; but a person under the age of twenty-one years may make application to the court to set aside a transaction which he entered into while he was over the age of sixteen but under the age of eighteen and which was a 'prejudicial transaction' within the meaning of the Age of Legal Capacity (Scotland) Act 1991[2]. Natural persons under the age of sixteen years have no active capacity and any transfer must be carried out by a guardian on their behalf[3].

The rule for juristic persons is more complicated. So far as transfer of ownership is concerned, both partnerships[4] and companies incorporated under the Companies Acts[5] have capacity equivalent to that of adult natural persons, but since they can only act through agents, such as partners[6] and directors[7], the position is complicated in practice by considerations of actual and ostensible authority. Special statutory protection exists for parties dealing in good faith with companies[8]. In the case of corporations other than companies incorporated under the Companies Acts, capacity is limited by considerations of *vires*.

Trusts are not juristic persons, trust property being owned not by the trust but by trustees. While the purposes of the trust may restrict the powers of the trustees, this restriction is a matter of obligation and not of capacity, so that a conveyance by trustees receives effect even where it is in breach of trust[9].

Capacity is required not only of the transferor but also of the transferee at least in the passive sense that he must be capable of owning the property being transferred. As a general rule all persons, whether natural or juristic, are capable of owning property, but in the case of persons under sixteen consent to the transfer of the property, and also consent for entering into any preliminary contract, must be given by a guardian[10]. It is usually said that partnerships cannot own land or other feudalised real rights such as proper liferents, and the practice is to take title in the name of trustees, typically some or all of the individual partners, for behoof of the partnership[11].

1　Age of Legal Capacity (Scotland) Act 1991 (c 50), s 1(1)(b). Although bankruptcy does not go to capacity, it is nonetheless an exception to the rule that a person aged sixteen or over is able to transfer property freely. See the Bankruptcy (Scotland) Act 1985 (c 66), s 32(8).
2　Age of Legal Capacity (Scotland) Act 1991, s 3(1). A 'prejudicial transaction' is defined in s 3(2) as 'a transaction which (a) an adult, exercising reasonable prudence, would not have entered into in the circumstances of the applicant at the time of entering into the transaction, and (b) has caused or is

likely to cause substantial prejudice to the applicant'. A number of cases in which an application is not available are set out in s 3(3), including a transaction in the course of the applicant's trade, business or profession.

3 Ibid, ss 1(1)(a), 2(5). For guardians, see s 5.
4 See further G L Gretton 'Who Owns Partnership Property?' 1987 JR 163.
5 See the Companies Act 1985 (c 6), s 35(1) (substituted by the Companies Act 1989 (c 40), s 108(1)), which in effect abolishes the *ultra vires* rule. See further COMPANIES, vol 4, para 326.
6 Partnership Act 1890 (c 39), s 5.
7 Companies (Table A to F) Regulations 1985, SI 1985/805, Schedule, Table A, reg 70.
8 Companies Act 1985, ss 35A, 35B (added by the Companies Act 1989, s 108(1)).
9 Stair *Institutions* I,13,7; Hume *Lectures* vol IV (Stair Soc vol 17, 1955 ed G C H Paton) p 315; *Redfearn v Somervail* (1813) 1 Dow 50, 5 Pat 707, HL. The contrary view expressed in *Kidd v Paton's Trustees* 1912 2 SLT 363, OH, is incorrect. See further para 691 below.
10 Thus title may be taken in the name of a person under sixteen: see the Age of Legal Capacity (Scotland) Act 1991, s 1(3)(e). See also *Report on the Legal Capacity and Responsibility of Minors and Pupils* (Scot Law Com no. 110 (1987)) para 3.23. But the consent of the transferee which is required for the transfer of ownership (see para 613 below) can only be given by a guardian.
11 J M Halliday *Conveyancing Law and Practice* vol 1 (1985) para 2–127. But see also S C Styles 'Why Can't Partnerships Own Heritage?' (1989) 34 JLSS 414 and G L Gretton 'Problems in Partnership Conveyancing' (1991) 36 JLSS 232.

600. Inalienable property. Certain things are considered incapable of ownership, such as air or running water[1], while certain other things, although capable of initial acquisition, cannot thereafter be alienated. At one time feudal land was considered to be inalienable. A modern example of inalienable property is a right such as a lease or other contract in respect of which the doctrine of *delectus personae* applies[2].

There is a distinction between property which is truly inalienable and property otherwise alienable but which the owner has taken himself bound not to alienate. An example of the latter is property subject to a right of pre-emption. In the first case a purported alienation will be wholly void, while in the second case ownership will pass notwithstanding the prohibition although the title so conferred may then be voidable at the instance of the creditor in the prohibition[3].

1 Erskine *Institute* II,1,5.
2 For *delectus personae*, see OBLIGATIONS.
3 Ie if the transferee is in bad faith or does not give value for the transfer. See para 698 below.

601. Void and voidable titles. A person either owns a thing or he does not own a thing; from which proposition it follows that a person holding an ostensible title to a thing either has a good, 'subsistent' title to that thing or he has no title at all. There is no intermediate category of title which is subsistent in some respects but not in others. A 'void' title is, quite simply, no title at all. So if A dispones to B land which he does not own, and if B registers the disposition in the Register of Sasines, B has an ostensible title to the land but one which is void[1]. The land does not belong to B. But if the land had in fact belonged to A, ownership would have passed to B on registration and B would have acquired a title which was absolutely good, or in other words, a subsistent title[2].

There is also a third possibility. Instead of being either absolutely good or absolutely bad (void), a title may also be 'voidable'. A voidable title is a subsistent title — like an absolutely good title — but it is a subsistent title subject to the possibility of future challenge. So if A dispones land which he owns to B, but the disposition is subject to challenge, for example as a gratuitous alienation in defraud of A's creditors[3], the existence of the right to challenge does not prevent B from becoming owner on registration, for the land belonged to A and the transfer process has been properly carried out. But while B's title is subsistent it is also voidable, which is to say that it is capable of being reduced: the real right of ownership is unqualified but the party who holds it, B, incurs personal liability in a question with

The Law of Property in Scotland

the party holding the right to reduce. It frequently happens in practice that voidable titles are not reduced at all, and for as long as there is no reduction B remains owner in precisely the same sense as one whose title is absolutely good. Thus if B dispones to C, C will acquire a valid title in turn[4]. But if while the land continues to be held by B a reduction is led, then, assuming the reduction to be catholic in effect[5], the land will revert to the person from whom it was most recently acquired, in the example given, A.

1 The rule is *nemo dat quod non habet*: see paras 669 ff below.
2 What is being asserted here is that B owns the thing beyond challenge. But of course that is not to say that his ownership is free from adverse real rights (eg rights in security) and real conditions (eg real burdens).
3 See the Bankruptcy (Scotland) Act 1985 (c 66), s 34.
4 See eg the Sale of Goods Act 1979 (c 54), s 23, which is declaratory of the common law. For the effect of bad faith in the sub-purchaser, see para 692 below.
5 Catholic as opposed to *ad hunc effectum* (ie effective as between the parties to the action only). An example of the latter is a reduction founded on an inhibition: see G L Gretton *The Law of Inhibition and Adjudication* (1987) p 94. The question of when reductions are catholic and when only *ad hunc effectum* is an important and difficult question which cannot be considered here.

602. Transfer as a public act. Different methods of transfer are required for property of different kinds. Broadly speaking, Scots law recognises three methods: for corporeal moveable property, for land, and again for incorporeal property. A common feature of all three is publicity. Real rights cannot usually be conferred by private act, known only to the immediate parties. At the very least, as with incorporeal property, intimation to some third party is needed; and the doctrine finds its fullest expression in the case of land where there must be registration in a public register. Publicity is required for various reasons. Partly it is to promote certainty and, in cases of challenge, to facilitate proof. Partly it is to alert third parties with a legitimate interest in the property of the transferor that a change in its status has or may have taken place. Partly too it is because public knowledge of ownership is conceived as a good in itself.

603. Instantaneous effect of transfer. Scots law, following Roman law, is 'unititular', which is to say that in respect of any one thing at any one time, only one title of ownership is capable of recognition[1]. That single title can, of course, be shared, as for example when two people own a thing as common property; but where competing titles are asserted to the same thing, only one of the competing parties is owner. One necessary result of this rule is that the transfer of ownership, when it occurs, is always instantaneous in effect. There is, in other words, a single moment of transfer, and in Scots law that moment is when the final solemnities required by the law have been fully complied with. So if property is being transferred from A to B, there can never be a stage where ownership is partly with A and partly with B; and since ownership is a real right, ownership cannot be with B in a question between transferor and transferee but with A in a question with third parties[2]. Either A is the owner, or B is; and the rule is that A remains owner until the final act of transfer has been performed when ownership passes at once to B. Up until the moment of transfer, A remains full owner with power to burden the property or to transfer it to someone else, although to do either is usually to break his contract with B; and the property also remains vulnerable to A's creditors. But once the moment of transfer arrives B becomes owner in turn and A's rights in the property are extinguished immediately and absolutely.

1   Erskine *Institute* II,1,1. See further para 6 above and T Honore *Making Law Bind* (1987) pp 186, 187.
2   There is no 'personal' right of ownership. See para 3 above. See also K G C Reid 'Unintimated Assignations' 1989 SLT (News) 267 at 269.

604. Adverse real rights and real conditions. Properly conducted, the transfer process confers on the transferee a subsistent title to the property. The transferee becomes owner in place of the transferor. But it may not confer an unencumbered title, for often, and especially in the case of land, a title is subject to subordinate real rights and real conditions. Thus land may be leased. A building society may hold a right in security over it. There may be servitudes and real burdens in respect of which the land is the servient tenement. Such rights and conditions, unless previously discharged, continue to affect the property in the hands of the transferee, a proposition which follows from the very nature of real rights and real conditions[1]. Whether, and if so to what extent, a transferee has a claim against the transferor in respect of such incumbrances depends on the warrandice provisions of his grant and on the terms of any contract between the parties[2].

Only real rights and real conditions run with the property. Personal rights prestable against the transferor do not, and, at least as a general rule[3], are of no concern to the transferee even where he knows of their existence[4]. So if A sells to B who re-sells to C, the fact that A is unpaid by B cannot affect C: B's obligation to A is contractual and hence personal to B.

1   For real rights, see paras 3 ff above, and for real conditions, see paras 344 ff above.
2   For warrandice, see paras 701 ff below.
3   But see paras 690, 693, below.
4   Bell *Commentaries* I,307; Hume *Lectures* vol IV (Stair Soc vol 17, 1955 ed G C H Paton) pp 311 ff; *Wallace v Simmers* 1960 SC 255, 1961 SLT 34.

605. Grants of subordinate real rights. In this section we are concerned with the transfer of an existing real right, namely ownership of property; and since incorporeal property itself consists of rights, both personal and real, we are also concerned, indirectly, with the transfer of lesser rights[1]. What we are not concerned with is the creation of new rights: with the exception of servitude[2], the grant of subordinate real rights, such as lease and security, is beyond the scope of the present title[3]. It may, however, be useful to bear in mind that many of the general rules which apply to the transfer of ownership apply also to the granting of subordinate real rights.

1   Thus to transfer ownership of a lease is also to transfer the lease itself. See further para 16 above.
2   For servitudes, see paras 439 ff above.
3   But see LANDLORD AND TENANT, vol 13, LIFERENT AND FEE, vol 13, and RIGHTS IN SECURITY, vol 20.

(2) CONTRACT AND CONVEYANCE

(a) General

606. Introduction. In common with other Civilian systems, Scots law makes a clear distinction in the transfer of ownership between, on the one hand, the conveyance and, on the other hand, the contract which in many cases precedes the conveyance. Only in the sale of goods, where the law has been anglicised by statute, is the distinction not fully observed, although even here transfer of ownership requires an act of intention which, at least in principle, is separate from the contract of sale[1].

The conveyance is the act of transfer itself, or in other words the process or series of processes which in law is required to carry ownership from transferor to transferee. The contract is an agreement to grant a conveyance and has of itself no effect on the location of *dominium*. The rule is *traditionibus non nudis pactis dominia rerum transferuntur*: ownership is transferred by delivery (or other conveyance) and not by bare contract[2]. On conclusion of the contract each party has a personal, contractual right against the other, and it is only on completion of the conveyance that ownership passes and the transferee has his real right[3]. Stair's analysis is masterly:

> 'There may be three acts of the will about the disposal of rights; a resolution to dispone, a paction, contract or obligation to dispone, and a present will or consent that that which is the disponer's be the acquirer's. Resolution terminates with the resolver, and may be dissolved by a contrary resolution, and so transmits no right; paction does only constitute or transmit a personal right or obligation, whereby the person obliged may be compelled to transmit the real right. It must needs then be the present dispositive will of the owner, which conveyeth the right to any other . . .'[4].

1 Sale of Goods Act 1979 (c 54), s 17(1): ownership is transferred 'at such time as the parties to the contract intend it to be transferred'. But while this intention is separate from the intention required for the conclusion of the contract, in practice the distinction is blurred by s 18 and in particular by rule 1 of that section which provides that in certain circumstances ownership passes when the contract is made.
2 Stair *Institutions* III,2,5; Erskine *Institute* II,1,18.
3 See eg *Gibson v Hunter Home Designs Ltd* 1976 SC 23, 1976 SLT 94.
4 *Stair* III,2,3.

607. Voidable contracts and voidable titles. There is a parallel distinction, not always scrupulously observed, between a voidable contract and a voidable title[1]. In property law a voidable contract signifies that the *causa* of transfer — the personal right inducing transfer — is reducible, whereas a voidable title signifies the reducibility of the conveyance and of the real right created thereby. There is no exact correspondence between a voidable contract and a voidable title. Often if a contract is voidable then so is the title following thereon[2], but a title may also be voidable for reasons unconnected with the contract[3] and a voidable contract may sometimes lead to an unimpeachable title. If a contract is actually void, the transferee's title is usually voidable[4] and will itself be void if directly affected by the same infirmity as affects the contract[5].

Where both contract and conveyance are voidable, either or both may be reduced; but if only the contract is reduced, ownership remains undisturbed in the hands of the transferee, a point which is sometimes overlooked[6].

Reductions, other than reductions *ope exceptionis*, are within the privative jurisdiction of the Court of Session. Where the title of the defender rests on a written deed of transfer, such as a disposition or assignation, the reduction should be directed at that deed. In certain circumstances partial reduction is competent[7]. It seems that reduction is not available in the case of corporeal moveables, because there is no written deed of transfer to reduce, and the equivalent remedy is an action for reconveyance by redelivery of the goods[8]. By statute[9] reduction of a disposition or other deed relating to land is not pleadable[10] against a third party acquirer taking without notice, but registration of the extract decree in the Register of Sasines is sufficient notice for this purpose. In the case of Land Register titles the defender remains owner even after decree unless or until his name is removed from the Register, and it has been held that the pursuer must use the rectification procedure and is unable to register the extract decree directly[11]. If the defender is in possession, rectification is often not available — but in that case indemnity can usually be recovered from the Keeper[12]. It has been said that the court has an equitable power to refuse reduction where the disbenefit to the defender is greatly in excess of any benefit to the pursuer and where some other arrangement can be made by way of compensation[13].

1 For voidable titles, see para 601 above.
2 Eg a sale induced by fraud.
3 Eg where the so-called rule against 'offside goals' applies. See paras 695 ff below.
4 The acceptance of the abstract theory of *justa causa traditionis* prevents the title from being automatically void. See paras 608 ff below.
5 Eg where one of the parties lacks the requisite legal capacity.
6 T B Smith 'Error and Transfer of Title' (1967) 12 JLSS 206.
7 *McLeod v Cedar Holdings Ltd* 1989 SLT 620.
8 *A W Gamage Ltd v Charlesworth's Trustee* 1910 SC 257, 1910 1 SLT 11.
9 Conveyancing (Scotland) Act 1924 (c 27), s 46(1) (renumbered by the Law Reform (Miscellaneous Provisions) (Scotland) Act 1985 (c 73), s 59(1), Sch 2, para 7). This provision has no effect on void titles, since *nemo dat quod non habet*: see G L Gretton 'Reductions of Heritable Titles' 1986 SLT (News) 125.
10 The wording of the Conveyancing (Scotland) Act 1924, s 46(1), is awkward. Is it intended that the reduction should be pleadable against subsequent acquirers with notice? The statutory protection is fully effective only if it operates *in rem*.
11 *Short's Trustee v Keeper of the Registers of Scotland* 1996 SLT 166, HL.
12 Rectification is available against a proprietor in possession only in the limited circumstances set out in s 9(3)(a) of the Land Registration (Scotland) Act 1979 (c 33). Indemnity is payable under s 12 of the Act. For a fuller discussion, see K G C Reid 'Void and Voidable Deeds and the Land Register' (1996) 1 SLPQ 265.
13 *Stockton Park (Leisure) Ltd v Border Oats Ltd* 1991 SLT 333, OH.

(b) Failure of the Contract

608. Justa causa traditionis. The effect on a conveyance of failure of the contract depends on the relationship which exists between the two. Traditional accounts of the transfer process, such as that given by Bell, tend to emphasise the importance, and hence perhaps the interdependence, of both elements. The contract is referred to as the *titulus* or *causa transferendi* (the title or basis for the transfer) and the conveyance as the *modus transferendi* (the method of transfer):

> 'Lawyers distinguish, in transference, the *titulus transferendi dominii* and the *modus transferendi dominii*; the former being the conventional will to convey; the latter, the overt act by which the real right is transferred'[1].

Writing a few years' later than Bell, Savigny[2] offered a new and, in European terms, influential analysis of transfer. Savigny saw the conveyance not as one part of a composite act but as a separate act in itself, a 'real contract' (*Realvertrag*) in the sense not of a contract constituted by delivery of a thing, which is the normal meaning of 'real contract' in Roman law and Civilian systems, but in the sense of a contract relating to transfer of a thing or *res*. This 'contract' was distinct from any contract such as sale which might, but need not, precede the conveyance. In other words, the conveyance was distinct from the *causa* of the older analysis. It does not appear that Scots law accepts Savigny's analysis, at least in its developed form, although it found sufficient favour in Germany to be adopted into the Civil Code at the end of the nineteenth century[3].

In a transfer the contract (or *causa*) may fail in a number of different ways. Thus *consensus in idem* may never have been reached, or the contract may not comply with certain formalities of constitution, such as the requirement of writing in the case of contracts relating to land, or again it may be a *pactum illicitum*. What is the effect of a failed contract on the conveyance which follows? The answer depends upon how the transfer process as a whole is perceived. An analysis which lays stress on the *causa* will tend to say that a transfer without a *causa* is not effective, whereas one which views the conveyance as a legal act which is at least partially independent of the *causa* will tend to the opposite conclusion. Two possible answers therefore emerge, in Scotland as in other Civilian systems. The first, known in modern times as the causal basis of transfer, insists on the need for *justa causa traditionis* (proper cause of conveyance). If the contract is invalid there is no *justa causa* and hence no transfer of ownership notwithstanding that the conveyance itself is otherwise unobjectionable. The other answer, known as the abstract basis of transfer, views the conveyance 'abstractly', in isolation from the *causa*. Provided only that the conveyance is valid ownership passes to the transferee, although the title acquired will usually be voidable.

It is uncertain whether Roman law adhered to the 'abstract' or to the 'causal' basis of transfer. The Roman texts raise the question of what happens when one party thinks that delivery of goods is made on the basis of gift and the other that it is made on the basis of a loan for consumption (*mutuum*)[4]. It seems probable that for Justinian's law the result was that property did pass in such a case but there has been great controversy over whether this solution also represents the classical law and also over how precisely one interprets the law of Justinian. It would be unprofitable to pursue this controversy in detail as the state of the texts makes it unlikely that scholarly opinion will ever agree on what Roman law was or was meant to be. The position is modern Scots law is scarcely less obscure, and to this we now turn.

1 Bell *Principles* s 1299. See also Bell *Commentaries* I,177, and Erskine *Institute* II,1,18. Bell (*Principles*) refers to Voet *Comm ad Pandectas* 41,1,35.

2 F C von Savigny *System des heutigen römischen Rechts* (1840–49) vol 4, pp 158 ff; *Obligationenrecht* (1851–53) vol 2, pp 256 ff.

3 BGB, s 929 (moveable property). The BGB (*Bürgerliches Gesetzbuch*) is the German Civil Code. For a general discussion of the theory of abstraction in German law, see K Zweigert and H Kötz *Introduction to Comparative Law* (1st edn 1977, trans T Weir) pp 177 ff.

4 See *Digest* 12,1,18; 41,1,36. There is an enormous literature on the the question of the role of *causa* in the Roman law of *traditio* and on the conflict between these two texts. See the ample references in the discussion by P van Warmelo 'Justa Causa Traditionis' in *Studi in onore di C Sanfilippo* I (1982) p 615. See also most recently R Evans-Jones and G D MacCormack '*Iusta causa traditionis*' and W M Gordon 'The Importance of the *justa causa* of *traditio*' both in P Birks (ed) *New Perspectives in the Roman Law of Property: Essays for Barry Nicholas* (1989) pp 99, 123.

609. Corporeal moveables. Bell[1] echoing Erskine[2] defines delivery as 'the delivery of possession by the owner with the design of transferring the property to the receiver' but he does not make clear how far the 'design of transferring the property' is affected by the *causa*. What he says could be understood as meaning that the existence of a *causa* is merely evidence of the design or intention, in which case the validity of the *causa* would not necessarily be in issue, although he does seem to contemplate reference to a single *causa*. Where parties differed on the *causa*, therefore, the delivery might not be effective as a means of transferring ownership. Erskine[3] speaks of 'the intention or consent of the former owner to transfer it [the object being transferred] upon some just or proper title of alienation, as sale, gift, exchange etc', laying stress on the intention of the transferor. It may be legitimate to deduce from this that he would have accepted that ownership was transferred where the transferor intended to transfer ownership and the transferee intended to receive it, even if the transferee thought of a different but equally just or proper title. Neither Erskine nor Bell, however, expressly discusses the problems which might arise in the case of difference of opinion over the *causa* or of dispute about its validity. A possible reason for the absence of discussion both here and also in the reported decisions is the traditional emphasis in Scots law on possession as the badge of ownership[4] which directs attention to the question of whether possession has been legitimately acquired from the former owner. An owner who has parted with ownership, or even thinks that he has parted with it, is not in a strong position to claim that ownership has not passed. If he claims that there is some defect in the *causa* he should have recourse to any claim he may have under the law of obligations.

There are in fact two practical problems involved in the question whether delivery of moveables is causal or abstract. The first is whether the owner (or former owner) can recover the thing from the purported transferee; the second is whether the purported transferee can give a good title to third parties. So far as the parties themselves are concerned it may not be very important whether the transferor recovers the thing itself or its value in cases where there is some defect which either prevents the purported transfer from taking effect or, at least, gives rise to a possible challenge. It will be important only if the interests of creditors of the transferor are involved or the specific thing is of peculiar interest or value to one of the parties. In so far as the action is directed to the recovery of the thing, the remedy will be an action for delivery and this action may be based either on ownership or on an obligation to restore ownership. Where, however, third parties are involved it is essential to decide whether ownership has passed or not because in general only an owner can give title. At this point the emphasis of Scots law on possession as giving rise to a presumption of ownership becomes relevant. Once the transferee is in possession he is presumed to be owner and anyone taking from him will have the benefit of the same presumption. It would seem that only if the purported transferee's taking could be characterised as theft would the original transferor be able to follow the property into the hands of a bona fide acquirer from the transferee. In accordance with its principles, therefore, Scots law should favour an abstract system of transfer. This has been the conclusion of other modern commentators[5], and it brings moveables into line with the established rule for corporeal heritable property[6]. The position of moveables transferred under the Sale of Goods Act 1979 (c 54) is considered separately below[7].

So far as particular *causae* of delivery are concerned the potential *causae* are loan for consumption (the Roman *mutuum*), gift, barter, sale, *ex facie* absolute transfer in security and transfer in trust, expressly or otherwise. In all these cases transfer of ownership is intended when a corporeal moveable is delivered in order to constitute the legal relationship, carry out the transaction or perform the obligation in question.

1 Bell *Principles* s 1300. He refers to Stair *Institutions* II,1,11, Erskine *Institute* II,1,19, and M P Brown *The Law of Sale* (1821) p 390.
2 *Erskine* II,1,18.
3 *Erskine* II,1,18, a passage which is not confined to corporeal moveables.
4 See para 130 above.
5 T B Smith *A Short Commentary on the Law of Scotland* (1962) pp 539, 540; D L Carey Miller *Corporeal Moveables in Scots Law* (1991) pp 106–114. See also *Corporeal Moveables — Passing of Risk and of Ownership* (Scot Law Com Consultative Memorandum no. 25) (1976) paras 12–17 (with which T B Smith was closely associated).
6 See para 611 below.
7 See para 610 below.

610. Corporeal moveables under the Sale of Goods Act 1979. The Sale of Goods Act 1979 preserves, albeit precariously, the distinction of the common law between contract and conveyance. It is not the case that ownership passes simply as a result of the conclusion of the contract, as is sometimes suggested, because section 17 of the Act expressly requires of the parties some further and separate act of intention. But it may be conceded that the distinction is then somewhat blurred by the rules of deemed intention contained in section 18 and in particular by rule 1 of that section which provides in certain circumstances for the transfer of ownership on conclusion of the contract. While, however, conveyance and contract are distinguished in the 1979 Act their fate is inextricably connected, for the 1979 Act only applies where there is a contract of sale[1]. If there is no contract or the contract is void, then there can be no conveyance under the Act. In effect, therefore, the Act contains within it the causal theory of transfer. But while the absence of a valid contract of sale necessarily bars transfer under the Act it may not be a complete bar to transfer[2], for the invalid contract may have been followed by a form of conveyance which is valid at common law, that is to say, by delivery of the goods accompanied by mutual intention to transfer ownership; and if it is correct that the abstract theory governs transfers at common law then there can be no reason to deny effect to such a transaction. A valid conveyance has followed on an invalid contract, with the result that ownership passes to the 'buyer'[3].

1　Sale of Goods Act 1979 (c 54), s 1(1).
2　*Corporeal Moveables — Passing of Risk and of Ownership* (Scot Law Com Consultative Memorandum no. 25) (1976) para 15.
3　*Morrisson v Robertson* 1908 SC 332, 15 SLT 697, and *MacLeod v Kerr* 1965 SC 253, 1965 SLT 358, although not inconsistent in result with the argument just presented, appear to proceed on the basis that transfer of ownership of goods depends upon whether or not the *contract* is void. If it it void then (as in *Morrisson*) ownership does not pass; if it is good or (as in *MacLeod*) voidable but not avoided, ownership does pass. This is to ignore the property law aspects of transfer. What matters is not the validity of the contract but the validity of the conveyance. A good conveyance will save a bad contract. See further T B Smith 'Error and Transfer of Title' (1967) 12 JLSS 206.

611. Land. In the transfer of land, according to Stair[1], 'we do not follow that subtility of annulling deeds, because they are *sine causa*', a robust rejection of the causal theory of *justa causa* which has never been challenged. In view of the fact that the conveyance of land requires a written deed and hence a new act of consent manifestly separate from the *causa*, this rejection is not perhaps surprising, and it has never been suggested that a registered disposition might fail on account of infirmities affecting the missives of sale. Indeed the acceptance of the abstract theory seems clearly acknowledged in the prior communings rule, by which a delivered disposition supersedes the missives[2], and in the statutory rule that registration in the Land Register passes ownership[3].

1　Stair *Institutions* II,3,14. The passage continues: '. . . and therefore narratives expressing the cause of the disposition, are never inquired into, because, though there were no cause, the disposition is good . . . And though charters be granted relative to prior obligements, yet they are good, without necessity to prove these'.
2　For the prior communings rule, see CONVEYANCING, vol 6, para 566.
3　Land Registration (Scotland) Act 1979 (c 33), s 3(1)(a). This rule does not require even a valid conveyance, let alone a valid preliminary contract. See para 673 below.

612. Incorporeal property. The abstract basis of transfer applies to corporeal property, as has been seen above, and in the absence of authority one way or another there seems no reason for supposing that the rule for incorporeal property is different. If this is correct, the validity of an assignation is unimpaired by the failure of the preliminary contract to assign.

(c) Intention as part of the Conveyance

613. Consent of transferor and transferee. As a general rule, two things are required for the transfer of ownership, namely (1) some positive act, the nature of which varies with the type of property, for example delivery (for moveables) or the granting and registration of a disposition (for land)[1], accompanied by (2) the intention of both parties, the intention of the transferor to be divested and the intention of the transferee to be invested[2]. Intention to transfer is separate from and in addition to the consent required for any preliminary contract such as a contract of sale. If the positive act — the delivery, the disposition or as the case may be — is not accompanied by the requisite intention, no transfer of ownership can take place, for property cannot be expropriated without the consent of the owner. Indeed for Stair[3] and Erskine[4] intention was the paramount requirement of transfer, the requirement of the natural law, with the positive act being added only 'for utility's sake . . . that thereby the will of the owner may sensibly touch the thing disponed, and thereby be more manifest and sure'[5].

There are exceptions. In transfers under the Sale of Goods Act 1979 there is no need for a positive act, the mutual intention of the parties being sufficient for the passing of ownership[6]. Conversely, the law recognises a number of cases of 'involuntary' transfer where no consent is required of the 'transferor'. Transfer on death, transfer on bankruptcy, and compulsory purchase are the most commonly encountered examples[7]. There appears, however, to be no case which dispenses with the consent of the transferee.

Where the positive act takes the form of executing a formal deed, as is the case in transfers of land and of incorporeal property, the deed contains words of *de praesenti* conveyance such as 'dispone' and 'assign' which are usually conclusive of the transferor's consent to the transaction[8]. The consent of the transferee is indicated by acceptance of delivery of the deed[9]. There is no general requirement of writing in the transfer of corporeal moveables[10] and here the intention of the parties must usually be inferred from the surrounding facts and circumstances, in particular from the *causa* of transfer, which is to say, the contract on which the transfer proceeds[11]. So if A contracts to exchange goods with B and delivery follows, it may be assumed from the existence of the contract that delivery was accompanied by the requisite intention. It should be emphasised, however, that the conveyance does not stand or, fall with the validity of the *causa*, and that Scots law follows the abstract, and not the causal, theory of transfer[12].

1 See further paras 619 ff below (corporeal moveables) and 640 ff below (land).
2 See eg Erskine *Institute* II,1,18. The need for consent by the transferee is emphasised in Stair *Institutions* III,2,4. The requirement of mutual consent is sometimes analysed as a real contract (*Realvertrag*), for which see para 608 above.
3 *Stair* III,2,3–5.
4 *Erskine* II,1,18.
5 *Stair* III,2,5.
6 Sale of Goods Act 1979 (c 54), s 17. Delivery is not required.
7 For involuntary transfer, see paras 663 ff below.
8 *Royal Bank of Scotland plc v Purvis* 1990 SLT 262, OH. For exceptions to this rule, see para 614 below.
9 See eg *Hunter v Boog* (1834) 13 S 205.
10 However, in a small number of cases writing is required by statute, eg the sale of ships, for which see the Merchant Shipping Act 1894 (c 60), ss 24, 26, and the Merchant Shipping Act 1988 (c 12), ss 19, 20.
11 Thus the Sale of Goods Act 1979, s 17(2).
12 See paras 608 ff above.

614. Vices of consent and real vices. Where a transaction is accompanied by error or fraud or force and fear, difficult questions may arise as to whether consent to the transfer has truly been given. The answer depends upon whether the error or other vice is a 'real vice' (*vitium reale* or *labes realis*) or merely a 'vice of consent', the distinction being that a real vice absolutely prevents the giving of consent. Where there is a real vice and hence no consent there can, of course, be no transfer. Conversely, where there is consent, albeit wrongfully induced, ownership passes but the title of the transferee is voidable at the instance of the transferor[1]. A vice of consent, therefore, makes a title voidable whereas a real vice makes it void[2].

The difficulty lies in classifying the different vices[3]. It appears that usually error, fraud, and force and fear are vices of consent only and so do not prevent the passing of ownership[4]. But where a party signs a written deed of transfer in the mistaken belief that he is signing some other document entirely, whether that belief is induced[5] or, probably, even where it is uninduced[6], the error constitutes a real vice and ownership does not pass[7]. This is an exception. In the normal case a signature on a written deed of transfer is very strong evidence as to consent[8], and real vices, where they are found at all, are found mainly with corporeal moveables which do not require writing for their transfer.

1 Assuming, of course, that the error or other vice affected the transferor and not the transferee. A right to reduction may be lost, eg by waiver or acquiescence or impossibility of *restitutio in integrum*.
2 For the distinction between void and voidable titles, see para 601 above.
3 Unilateral error is usually regarded neither as a vice of consent nor as a real vice, that is to say, it is not recognised as affecting consent at all, except in the case of gratuitous transactions. On another view all error affects consent but a party is barred from relying on his own error except in gratuitous transactions.
4 See paras 615 ff below.
5 *Royal Bank of Scotland plc v Purvis* 1990 SLT 262 at 265, OH, per Lord McCluskey.
6 *Ellis v Lochgelly Iron and Coal Co Ltd* 1909 SC 1278 at 1282, 1909 2 SLT 224 at 226, per Lord President Dunedin.
7 It is different where, as in *Royal Bank of Scotland v Purvis* 1990 SLT 262, OH, the party is mistaken not about the deed but about its content. See also *Boyd v Shaw* 1927 SC 414, 1927 SLT 398.
8 But while this excludes real vices it does not exclude vices of consent. The fact that ownership passes does not mean that the transferee's title cannot be reduced. So eg a disposition of land induced by fraud is voidable.

615. Force and fear. A transfer of property brought about by force and fear is often said to be void and is certainly open to reduction as affected by a vice of consent[1], but the better view may be that only robbery creates a real vice[2]. The threats or force need not be applied by the transferee in order to allow reduction[3].

1 Stair *Institutions* I,9,8; Erskine *Institute* III,1,16; Hume *Lectures* vol III (Stair Soc vol 15, 1952 ed G C H Paton) p 238, and vol IV (Stair Soc vol 17, 1955 ed G C H Paton) p 321; Bell *Commentaries* I,299. For fuller discussion including discussion of the meaning of 'force and fear', see OBLIGATIONS.
2 Clearly stated by *Stair* IV,40,21 and 28. See also Bankton *Institute* I,10,59, and *Corporeal Moveables— Protection of the Onerous Bona Fide Acquirer of Another's Property* (Scot Law Com Consultative Memorandum no. 27) (1976) para 18.
3 *Nisbet v Stewart* (1708) Mor 16512.

616. Fraud. Fraud is a vice of consent and not a real vice. Thus a transfer brought about by fraud passes ownership but can be reduced as against the transferee, and reduction is available irrespective of whether the fraud induces an error which would in itself give ground for reduction. The fraud must, however, have induced the transfer. The fraud can be pleaded only against the person using it and if the property has been passed to a third party before the transfer is set aside it cannot be recovered[1] except where the third party has notice[2]. The transferor is left to claim damages. False but not fraudulent misrepresentations will also allow reduction of a transfer[3] but they do not ground an action for damages unless there has been negligence[4].

1 This is of course the usual rule for voidable titles. See *MacLeod v Kerr* 1965 SC 253, 1965 SLT 358.
2 Stair *Institutions* IV,40,21; Sale of Goods Act 1979 (c 54), s 23. See further para 692 below.
3 *Mair v Rio Grande Rubber Estates Ltd* 1913 SC (HL) 74 at 82, 1913 2 SLT 166 at 170, per Lord Shaw.
4 Law Reform (Miscellaneous Provisions) (Scotland) Act 1985 (c 73), s 10.

617. Error. In the transfer of property, error may qualify as a vice of consent or, more rarely, as a real vice. A third possibility, at least where the error is unilateral and uninduced, is that there may be no impairment of consent so that the title conferred on the transferee is unimpeachable. Roman law recognised five categories of error, namely (1) error *in persona* (error as to person), (2) error *in corpore* (error as to the object transferred), (3) error *in pretio* (error as to consideration payable), (4) error *in causa* or *negotio* (error as to *causa*), and (5) error *in dominio* (error as to ownership), but in none of these is there much authority in Scots law.
(1) *Error in persona.* It is possible to conceive of error either on the part of the transferee with regard to the transferor or on the part of the transferor with

regard to the transferee. The classic case is *Morrisson v Robertson*[1] where the transferor believed that he was delivering two cows to the agent for a transferee whom he knew; in fact the 'agent' had no authority and so there was no transfer either to him or to the supposed transferee. The transferor was allowed to recover the property from a bona fide third party, implying that error *in persona* is a real vice and that the purported transfer was void[2]. There was in fact no transferee who could take. But the transferee was also dishonest and his conduct would seem to amount to theft[3], itself a real vice sufficient to prevent the transfer of ownership[4]. An error regarding the qualities of a person, such as his creditworthiness, would not affect the transfer.

(2) *Error in corpore.* An error regarding the subject matter of the transfer would also avoid the transfer if it affected the identity of the thing transferred. If, for example, goods were delivered to the wrong household by a delivery-man, the householder to whom they were delivered would not obtain ownership of them. If the error merely related to the qualities of the thing, ownership would still pass, as in the case of error relating to the qualities of a person, but the transfer might be reduced and damages would be payable in appropriate circumstances.

(3) *Error in causa and in negotio.* Error regarding the transaction or *negotium* entered into would prevent ownership passing if either the transferor or the transferee was not contemplating a transfer of ownership, but it is not clear that each must have the same transaction in contemplation; it is also not clear, although probable, that by 'transaction' is to be understood the delivery itself and not any underlying *causa*[5]. However, the *causa* supposed to underlie the delivery would also be relevant as an error involving a *causa* which would not justify a transfer of ownership would mean that the delivery was not intended as a transfer of ownership.

(4) *Error in pretio.* It would not seem that an error regarding the consideration for a transaction would necessarily prevent the passing of ownership so long as there was the intention to pass ownership. There might of course be a contractual, quasi-contractual or delictual remedy for the party prejudiced. Certainly ownership would pass if delivery is abstract, as has been argued[5], because the intention to transfer would be clear and the error regarding the consideration would affect the motive only.

(5) *Error in dominio.* In Roman law there are cases which are described as *error in dominio*, where a person transfers property which turns out to be his own, believing that it belonged to someone else. A typical example is transfer by an agent of property which he thinks belongs to his principal. The texts are not entirely consistent but the effect seems to be that, on the one hand, ownership does not pass, but, on the other, the transferor may not be able to reclaim the thing because he is liable in warrandice to the transferee if he does so[6]. In Scots law the question would depend on whether the transferor was personally barred from reclaiming his property. If, for example, it was apparent that the transferor was not intending to transfer his own property, because he purported to transfer as agent, he should be able to recover.

1 *Morrison v Robertson* 1908 SC 332, 15 SLT 697.

2 See also *Lombard North Central Ltd v Lord Advocate* 1983 SLT 361, OH, discussed in K G C Reid 'Unintimated Assignations' 1989 SLT (News) 267 at 270.

3 *Corporeal Moveables — Protection of the Onerous Bona Fide Acquirer of Another's Property* (Scot Law Com Consultative Memorandum no. 27) (1976) para 19; T B Smith *Property Problems in Sale* (1978) pp 170–172.

4 See para 618 below.

5 See para 609 above.

6 See *Digest* 41,1,35; 18,1,15,2; 17,1,49; and W W Buckland *Textbook of Roman Law* (3rd edn 1963 by P Stein) pp 228, 229, and p 229, note 2.

618. Theft. Theft is a real vice and stolen property is not acquired even by a bona fide taker for value. Scots law does not, like English law, recognise purchase in market overt as giving a good title, unless English law is the proper law of the acquisition[1].

1 *Todd v Armour* (1882) 9 R 901; Sale of Goods Act 1979 (c 54), s 22(2).

(3) CORPOREAL MOVEABLES

(a) Transfer at Common Law

619. Forms of delivery as a mode of transfer. Where delivery is required for transfer of ownership of corporeal moveables, as it is by common law and so still in all cases other than sale, it may be referred to as the *modus transferendi*, or method of transfer, following the institutional writers, who in turn adopt Civilian terminology. The delivery may take various forms. The simplest case is actual delivery where a thing is handed over from one person to another. There is then delivery in a literal sense. But delivery may equally take the form of allowing the transferee to have control of the thing as owner. There are many examples in the authorities of situations in which a transaction other than simple handing over is held to amount to a delivery for the purpose of transferring ownership. Such a transaction may be referred to as a fictitious or constructive delivery. For convenience, the examples may be fitted into categories borrowed from Roman law — namely delivery *longa manu* (by a long hand), symbolical delivery, delivery *brevi manu* (short hand), and *constitutum possessorium* (possessory agreement or declaration) — because Roman law, as understood by the Civilian writers, clearly influenced the treatment of this topic by the institutional writers. However, it should be emphasised that these categories are used for convenience. The essential question for Scots law is whether the thing in question can reasonably be regarded as having passed from one person to another. As will appear, in deciding this question the Scottish courts have laid some stress, perhaps excessive stress, on whether third parties are liable to be misled by assuming ownership from a particular state of actual or apparent possession. They have been particularly reluctant to recognise as a delivery a transaction which leaves the former owner still in possession or a transaction which is seen as an attempt to create security over a corporeal moveable without transfer of possession.

620. Delivery *longa manu*. Roman law recognised various cases in which a transferee acquired property by delivery without actually taking hold of the object transferred[1]. For example, the contents of a warehouse could be transferred by handing over the keys of the warehouse, at least if the keys were handed over beside the warehouse[2]. Such cases may be referred to as delivery *longa manu*, literally with a long or extended hand. The cases in the Roman texts appear to be cases in which the transferor is in personal possession of the thing to be transferred but physical delivery is difficult or impossible, as where a heap of logs or a heavy stone column is in question, or cases in which the transferee does not immediately lay hands on the thing, as where money is laid down in front of him or goods are delivered to his house[3]. Whatever the Roman view of them, they are cases which can be explained as cases in which the transferee obtains control of the thing and this is the interpretation put on them by the institutional writers in Scots law[4]. The cases offer a number of examples[5]. Two points may be noted: (1) that delivery will not easily be held to have taken place if the thing in question is left in the hands of the transferor unless there is some arrangement which explains why the thing is still in his hands, for example, a separate contract of hire[6]; in other words, it is generally held that the transferee must have control, but (2) in deciding whether a delivery has taken place the courts do have regard to the circumstances of the alleged delivery and may more readily accept a delivery where the interests of creditors or others who have given value are not involved, for example, where there is a gift to one member of a family and no question of insolvency[7].

The Scottish courts, however, following mercantile practice, have also developed another form of delivery *longa manu* where the thing to be transferred is not in the hands of the transferor but is in the hands of a third party, such as a warehousekeeper, who is holding the thing subject to the instructions of the transferor. In such a case, delivery can be made by giving instructions to the holder to hold on behalf of the transferee. Once the instructions are accepted the general rule of the law is that the delivery is complete[8] although there is a real or apparent exception where sale of goods is involved. In English law, such a delivery is described as delivery by attornment but in English law the custodier must acknowledge to the acquirer that he holds for him[9]. This is the regime of the Sale of Goods Act 1979 where no document of title is involved[10]. However, in the normal case where this type of delivery is in question there will be a document of title and so the provisions of the Act are less important than appears. It is unfortunate that the English rule is stated as the general provision.

In theory, there is no reason why delivery of property physically held by someone else should not be effected by giving instructions to a servant of the transferor who has actual custody of the thing but the Scottish courts insist that the holder should be independent of the transferor, presumably in order to reduce the risk of fraudulent entries in the transferor's stockbooks[11]. For a delivery to be effective not only must the instructions be received by the custodier[12] but the thing or things to be transferred must be identified in the custodier's hands as now being the property of the transferee[13]. A delivery of so many bags of flour, for example, would not be effective if the bags belonging to the transferee could not be distinguished from any others.

1 For details, see W M Gordon *Studies in the Transfer of Property by Traditio* (1970) ch III.
2 Justinian *Institutes* II,1,45: *Digest* 41,1,9,6; 18,1,74; *Gordon* pp 56 ff, 80 ff.
3 See *Digest* 41,2,1,21; 41,2,51 (columns and logs); 46,3,79 (things laid down — this text uses the phrase *quodammodo manu longa tradita* — in a sense, delivered by a long (or extended) hand); 41,2,18,2 (delivery to a house).
4 See Stair *Institutions* II,1,11; Erskine *Institute* II,1,19; Bell *Principles* s 1302.
5 See eg *Macdougall v Whitelaw* (1840) 2 D 500; *Moore v Gledden* (1869) 7 M 1016 (a case of pledge); *Thomson v Scoular* (1882) 9 R 430.
6 See eg *Boak v Megget* (1844) 6 D 662; *Anderson v Buchanan* (1848) 11 D 270; *Orr's Trustee v Tullis* (1870) 8 M 936; *Robertsons v M'Intyre* (1882) 9 R 772. Contrast *Sim v Grant* (1862) 24 D 1033 where the seller continued to use the thing as his own. *M'Bain v Wallace & Co* (1881) 8 R 360, affd (1881) 8 R (HL) 106 (like other cases) is complicated by the fact that the House of Lords preferred to rest its judgment on the Mercantile Law Amendment Act (Scotland) 1856 (c 60), s 1 (repealed). In *Scott v Scott's Trustee* (1889) 16 R 504, 26 SLR 362, the decision also turned on that Act.
7 See the facts of *Morris v Riddick* (1867) 5 M 1036 and *Hutchieson's Executrix v Shearer* 1909 SC 15, 16 SLT 404.
8 *Connal & Co v Loder* (1868) 6 M 1095; *Black v Incorporation of Bakers of Glasgow* (1867) 6 M 136; *Inglis v Robertson and Baxter* (1898) 25 R (HL) 70.
9 41 *Halsbury's Laws of England* (4th edn) para 764.
10 The Sale of Goods Act 1979 (c 54), s 29(4), provides in relation to delivery of goods in the possession of a third person when they are sold that there is no delivery by seller to buyer unless and until the third person acknowledges to the buyer that he holds the goods on his behalf, which is declaratory of English common law — see text and note 9 above. But the section also states that 'nothing in this section affects the operation of the issue or transfer of any document of title to goods'. It would appear therefore that in Scots law in a sale of goods for which the seller has no document of title (which by virtue of s 61(1) has the same meaning as in the Factors Acts) acknowledgment by the possessor to the buyer is needed under this sub-section but where there is a document of title intimation to the custodier suffices, in terms of the saving clause. Normally in commercial transactions there will be a document of title.

11 *Anderson v M'Call* (1866) 4 M 765; *Pochin & Co v Robinows and Marjoribanks* (1869) 7 M 622; *Dobell, Beckett & Co v Neilson* (1904) 7 F 281, 12 SLT 543.
12 *Tod and Co v Rattray* 1 Feb 1809 FC; *Auld v Hall and Co* 12 June 1811 FC.
13 *Hayman & Son v M'Lintock* 1907 SC 936; *Price and Pierce Ltd v Bank of Scotland* 1910 SC 1095. See also para 627 below and *Bulk Goods: Section 16 of the Sale of Goods Act 1979 and Section 1 of the Bills of Lading Act 1855* (Scot Law Com Discussion Paper no. 83) (1989).

621. Symbolical delivery. It is doubtful whether Roman law recognised symbolical delivery in the sense of delivery of a symbol of the thing being transferred in place of the thing itself, although there are cases which can be so construed[1]. In spite of references to symbolical delivery in the institutional writers[2] it is clear that Scots law recognises only two[3] actual cases, namely, delivery of a bill of lading which represents delivery of the goods specified in it[4] and delivery of a bill of exchange which can be seen as a symbolical transfer of money[5]. Bills of exchange are dealt with elsewhere and need not be considered further in this context[6].

If a bill of lading is made out to bearer, delivery alone is sufficient: but if it is made out to a specified person it must also be indorsed by the party in whose favour it is made out. Normally the bill of lading will refer to specific goods identified in it but it has been said that a bill of lading may serve to transfer non-specific goods such as part of a bulk cargo or a number of identical sacks of flour although this is questionable[7]. While delivery of a bill of lading may transfer ownership of the goods which it represents it is not entirely clear whether the bill can be used to transfer possession only, so as to constitute a right of pledge although it seems the better view that it can do so[8]. As the bill represents the goods a pledge ought to be possible and it is certainly possible in a case to which the Factors Acts apply[9].

A bill of lading is a document of title in the fullest sense in that it both evidences title to the goods specified in it and represents those goods. In the case of documents of title[10] other than bills of lading, such as warehouse receipts, or delivery orders, it is held that the document is no more than evidence of title and authority to obtain possession of the goods specified in it. Transfer of the document therefore gives a good *jus ad rem* in the sense of a right to claim the goods from the holder but it does not normally[11] give a real right in the goods effective against third parties unless the transfer has been intimated to the holder of the goods, so that he and third parties are aware of the fact of transfer of the document and of the right in the goods, and the goods transferred are identifiable in his hands[12].

Transfer of a document of title of this sort is effected either by delivery if the document is to bearer or by indorsation and delivery if it is made out to a specified person. It has been held that in all cases the normal effect of transfer of the document and intimation is to give ownership of the goods referred to in the document to the transferee, even if the purpose is to create a more limited security right: however the decision is open to question[13]. The transferee on the view criticised would become *ex facie* absolute owner and not merely a pledgee with a right of possession.

To the rules described above as normal there is or may be a statutory exception in cases where the Factors Acts apply, namely, where a disposition is made by a mercantile agent who in the customary course of his business as such agent has authority to sell goods or consign goods for the purpose of sale or to buy goods or to raise money on the security of goods[14]. In these Acts 'document of title' is defined as including 'any bill of lading, dock warrant, warehouse keeper's certificate, and warrant or order for the delivery of goods, and any other document used in the ordinary course of business as proof of the possession or control of goods, or authorising or purporting to authorise, either by endorsement or by delivery, the possessor of the document to transfer or receive goods thereby represented'[15]: it is further provided that 'a pledge of the documents of title to goods shall be deemed to be a pledge of the goods'[16]. This provision seems to allow pledge as opposed to *ex facie* absolute transfer and to allow the documents to represent the goods in this instance but it does not allow an *ex facie* absolute transfer, or indeed an absolute transfer, by transfer of the documents alone. In the case of a bill of lading, however, such a transfer is possible at common law, and where the Acts apply this provision removes any doubt about the competency of a pledge of a bill of lading[17].

1 Eg delivery of keys of a warehouse and in Justinian *Code* 8,53(54),1, delivery of documents of title to slaves.
2 See eg Stair *Institutions* II,1,15; Erskine *Institute* II,1,19.
3 Apart from the special case of documents of title dealt with by a mercantile agent in terms of the Factors Acts: see text and note 14 below.
4 *Bogle v Dunmore & Co* (1787) Mor 14216.
5 Bills of Exchange Act 1882 (c 61), ss 2, 31.
6 See COMMERCIAL PAPER, vol 4, paras 137 ff.
7 *Hayman & Son v M'Lintock* 1907 SC 936 at 952, per Lord M'Laren. But see also J P Benjamin *Sale of Goods* (4th edn, 1992) para 18-133 and *Peter Cremer v Brinkers' Groustoffen BV* [1980] 2 Lloyd's Rep 605.
8 See *Hayman & Son v M'Lintock* 1907 SC 936. But the contrary view was taken in the Court of Session in *North-Western Bank Ltd v Poynter, Son and Macdonalds* (1894) 21 R 513 (see especially at 524, per Lord Trayner) and assumed in the House of Lords (revsd (1894) 22 R (HL) 1, [1895] AC 62). *Hayman* is inconsistent with the decision of the House of Lords in *Sewell v Burdick* (1894) LR 10 App Cas 74: see A Rodger 'Pledge of Bills of Lading in Scots Law' 1971 JR 193; *Bulk Goods: Section 16 of the Sale of Goods Act 1979 and Section 1 of the Bills of Lading Act 1855* (Scot Law Com Discussion Paper no. 83) (1989) para 3.2.2, note 2; and G L Gretton 'Pledge, Bills of Lading, Trusts and Property Law' 1990 JR 23 at 27 ff.
9 See later in this para.
10 There is no definition of document of title. It appears to mean any document which at least provides evidence that the holder is entitled to claim the property specified in it. The Factors Act 1889 (c 45), s 1(4), lists various documents which are classed as documents of title for the purpose of the Act but does not define the term. A vehicle registration document is not a document of title because it merely identifies the 'keeper': *Joblin v Watkins and Roseveare (Motors) Ltd* [1949] 1 All ER 47; *Central Newbury Car Auctions Ltd v Unity Finance Ltd* [1957] 1 QB 371, [1956] 3 All ER 905, CA.
11 The exception under the Factors Acts, dealt with below, has been noted. In theory at least, a document of title can attain the same status as a bill of lading by mercantile custom: see *Bovill v Dixon* (1854) 16 D 619, revsd (1856) 3 Macq 1, HL; *Merchant Banking Co v Phoenix Bessemer Steel Co* (1877) 5 Ch D 205. It may be given the same effect by statute: for the English law position, see 41 *Halsbury's Laws of England* (4th edn) para 757.
12 See para 620 above.
13 *Hamilton v Western Bank of Scotland* (1856) 19 D 152. See, however, the critical discussion by A F Rodger and G L Gretton in the articles cited in note 8 above.
14 Factors Act 1889 (applied to Scotland by the Factors (Scotland) Act 1890 (c 40), s 1(1)).
15 Factors Act 1889, s 1(4).
16 Ibid, s 3.
17 See text and note 8 above.

622. Delivery brevi manu. Delivery *brevi manu* (literally shorthand delivery) occurs when the transferee already has possession or is in possession of the moveables to be transferred, as a borrower for example, and the transferor agrees that he may have them as his own. Although it gave rise to some discussion in Roman law it is clear that it was recognised[1] and there is no doubt about its recognition in Scots law[2]. Given that possession gives rise to a presumption of ownership, delivery *brevi manu* is unproblematical as it brings about the union of possession and ownership which the presumption treats as normal. Erskine[2] indeed questions whether this form of delivery can be described as fictitious because the transferee has control over the thing delivered but it can be argued that the fiction consists in an assumed return to the transferor to terminate the existing legal relationship and a re-delivery on a new basis.

1 See Justinian *Institute* II,1,44. See also W M Gordon *Studies in the Transfer of Property by Traditio* (1970) ch II.
2 Erskine *Institute* II,1,19.

623. *Constitutum possessorium*. The name *constitutum possessorium*, possessory agreement or declaration, is not found in the Roman texts[1]. However, it was recognised in Roman law that in certain circumstances a delivery had taken place although the transferor remained in possession after the delivery so that there was no visible transfer of the thing from transferor to transferee. The examples in the texts are cases where the transferor remains in possession as tenant or usufructuary under a lease or usufruct granted by the transferee[2]. Such an arrangement with a specific basis for retention or *causa detentionis* may be described as a *constitutum possessorium*, an arrangement that possession, and hence ownership, has passed. But in the medieval period it came to be accepted that a simple declaration (or *constitutum*) by the transferor that he now held possession on behalf of the transferee without any specific subordinate title was enough to constitute delivery[3]. This position was achieved by what may be regarded as a somewhat forced interpretation of the texts and it is clear that a *constitutum possessorium* in this sense is virtually a transfer by agreement. It therefore negates whatever virtue there may be in requiring delivery as a mode of transfer of property. In particular it allows the former owner to give up his ownership without any indication that he has done so and may mislead third parties into supposing that he is still owner. It may also allow the creation of concealed security rights if the transfer is only *ex facie* absolute or if possession is transferred with a view to constituting a right of pledge. Even the more restricted form in which the transferor retains a subordinate title opens up such possibilities, which may be regarded as dangerous in that appearances are created which do not correspond with reality.

Given the importance which Scots law attaches to the presumption of ownership arising from possession of corporeal moveables, it is not surprising to find that Scots law has had some difficulty in accommodating *constitutum possessorium* even in the sense of an arrangement that the transferor will hold in future on a limited title derived from the transferee[4]. It has been recognised, albeit with some hesitation on the part of the courts, where the transferor takes a new subordinate title at the time of the transferee's acquisition[5]. The courts have not apparently seen its application to cases where a transferee has acquired the property, say, by sale and then seeks to enter into a sale and leaseback or hire-purchase arrangement with a view to raising immediate capital[6]. There appears to be no good reason why such an arrangement should not be effective if it is a genuine transaction and not an attempt to defeat the claims of unsecured creditors and it is thought that the authorities should be reconsidered[7]. There is no practical or legal difference between an initial hire-purchase transaction which is acceptable and a hire-purchase transaction arranged to raise money by use of assets already owned, although the latter may require close scrutiny if the debtor becomes bankrupt soon after the arrangement.

As in the case of delivery *longa manu* the precise circumstances of the alleged delivery will always be important and it may again be easier to recognise a *constitutum possessorium* as a good delivery if there is no question of insolvency or onerous third parties are not involved[8].

---

1 The term is derived from *Digest* 41,2,17,1, but seems first to have been used by Tiraquellus in the sixteenth century in his *Tractatus de iure constituti possessorii*.

2 See *Digest* 6,1,77; *Code* 8,53(54), 28 and 35,5.

3 See W M Gordon *Studies in the Transfer of Property by Traditio* (1970) chs VI, VII.

4 See *Gordon* pp 218–222.

5 *Eadie v Young* (1815) Hume 705; *Orr's Trustee v Tullis* (1870) 8 M 936; *Milligan v Ross* 1994 SCLR 430, OH. See also in this connection cases involving the Mercantile Law Amendment Act, Scotland 1856 (c 60), s 1 (repealed), which provided that specific goods in a deliverable state sold but still left in the possession of the seller were not affected by diligence by the seller's creditors and did not pass to his trustee in bankruptcy eg *M'Bain v Wallace & Co* (1881) 8 R (HL) 106; *Scott v Scott's Trustee* (1889) 16 R 504, 26 SLR 362. For a discussion of the issues, see D L Carey Miller *Corporeal Moveables in Scots Law* (1991) paras 8.23–8.25, 11.10, 11.11, 12.05, 12.06.

6 *Scottish Transit Trust Ltd v Scottish Land Cultivators Ltd* 1955 SC 254, 1955 SLT 417; *G and C Finance Corpn Ltd v Brown* 1961 SLT 408; *Ladbroke Leasing (South West) Ltd v Reekie Plant Ltd* 1983 SLT 155, OH.
7 See para 532 above and para 637 below.
8 See *Thompson v Aktien Gesellschaft für Glasindustrie* 1917 2 SLT 266, OH.

(b) The Sale of Goods Act 1979

624. Introduction. This Encyclopaedia's founding General Editor, the late Professor Sir Thomas Smith, criticised the whole application of the Sale of Goods Act 1893 (c 71)[1] to Scotland and has trenchantly argued its fundamental inconsistency with Scots common law principles[2]. This he argued creates serious practical as well as conceptual problems. The purpose of this present contribution is to give an account of the relevant provisions of the Sale of Goods Act 1979 as they apply in Scotland so as to complement Sir Thomas Smith's radical critique of the present law.

1 Now consolidated in the Sale of Goods Act 1979 (c 54).
2 T B Smith *Property Problems in Sale* (1978); *Corporeal Moveables — Passing of Risk and Ownership* (Scot Law Com Consultative Memorandum no. 25) (1976). See also J J Gow *The Mercantile and Industrial Law of Scotland* (1964) ch 2, especially at pp 73, 75, 76.

625. The purpose of a sale transaction. The key to the problem of sale is the concept that it is a contractual arrangement with consequences in property law. Sale involves both contract and conveyance. It has been well expressed judicially in England that 'the whole object of a sale is to transfer property from one person to another'[1]. This is the foundation of the scheme of the Sale of Goods Act 1979. The contract binds the seller to divest himself of his proprietary interests in the goods and to transfer these to the buyer who is bound to accept them. Essentially the seller is contracting to pass title to the goods. Thus one of the vital contractual provisions of the Act, which cannot be excluded, relates to the implied warranties on title, freedom from encumbrance and quiet possession[2]. That provision is the link between the two aspects of sale. Indeed, the statutory definition of the contract of sale of goods includes provisions relating to the transfer of property. A contract of sale can be either *a sale* by which the property is to be transferred or *an agreement to sell* by which the property is transferred at a later date[3]. The latter is purely a contractual arrangement until the appropriate time. The former as stated above is both contract and conveyance[4]. Sir Thomas Smith has argued for the proposition that the conveyance aspect should be limited to real rights as between the seller and the buyer[5]. Presumably, other issues of real right would be determined by common law rules. The more accepted view which is taken in this contribution has not made this distinction and has assumed that real or property rights in general are transferred in a contract of sale, not only as between the parties but as against the world[6]. This view assumes that 'property' as used in section 2 of the Act means *dominium* in Scotland and that this is equivalent to 'general property' as section 61 of the Act defines 'property'. The view has been expressed in the House of Lords that '*dominium*' is being transferred under a contract of sale of goods[7]. This it is submitted, gives high judicial authority to the view taken by the present writer. However regrettable to some Scots lawyers it may be, it appears therefore that the Act has in the normal case replaced the common law of sale of moveables by an assimilation to English law.

1 *Rowland v Divall* [1923] 2 KB 500 at 506, 507, CA, per Atkin LJ.
2 Sale of Goods Act 1979 (c 54), s 12. See para 715 below, and SALE AND EXCHANGE, vol 20, para 821.
3 Ibid, s 2(1).
4 Ibid, s 2(4)–(6).
5 See T B Smith 'Property Problems in Sale: Three Footnotes' 1987 SLT (News) 241.
6 W M Gloag and R C Henderson *Introduction to the Law of Scotland* (9th edn, 1987 by A B Wilkinson and W A Wilson) pp 98, 200, 201; D M Walker *Principles of Scottish Private Law* (4th edn, 1989) vol 3, pp 433, 435. There is somewhat more emphasis on the possible distinctions between seller and buyer and questions involving third parties in the wording used by E A Marshall *Scots Mercantile Law* (2nd edn, 1992) pp 183, 184, 212, 213. The distinction made by Sir Thomas Smith is not, however, developed by that author in detail. Strictly, of course, it is contradictory to say that a real right, such as ownership, can be transferred only as between the parties: see para 603 above.
7 *Armour v Thyssen Edelstahlwerke AG* 1991 SCLR 139 at 144, 1990 SLT 891 at 896, HL, per Lord Jauncey of Tullichettle (a Scottish Lord of Appeal in Ordinary).

626. Transfer of property — general. Following Roman law the common law position in Scotland was that property passed on delivery of the goods. Only then was a real right in the goods acquired by the buyer[1]. It is worthy of note that one leading commentator on the English law of sale of goods has expressed a preference for the Civilian approach to the passing of property based on delivery over that of the Sale of Goods Act 1979[2]. Under the Act, property in specific or ascertained goods passes when the parties intend it to pass[3]. Thus delivery and passing of title can be separated. The Act makes this clear by including 'a bargain and sale' as well as a 'sale and delivery' in the definition of sale[4]. Each are equally sales. If property is not to be transferred until a later date or until a condition is fulfilled, then the arrangement is not sale but agreement to sell[5]. The point at which property passes is of crucial importance in the insolvency of the seller or the buyer and in regard to the validity of diligence involving the goods[6]. Risk in the goods also normally follows property[7].

1 A clear expression of this is to be found in Bell *Commentaries* I,177. Delivery did not always have to be literal provided, it appears, that there was possession by or on behalf of the buyer: *Orr's Trustee v Tullis* (1870) 8 M 936. See further paras 619 ff above.
2 P Atiyah *Sale of Goods* (8th edn, 1990) p 286. This passage represents a modification of his former view.
3 Sale of Goods Act 1979 (c 54), s 17. No property can be transferred unless or until the goods are ascertained (s 16). As will be seen (para 628 below) delivery may play some role in ascertaining the parties' intention.
4 Ibid, s 61.
5 Ibid, s 2(5), (6). See eg *Dampskibsaktieselskapet Aurdal v Compania de Navigacion La Estrella, The SS Elorrio* 1916 SC 882, 1916 2 SLT 154. In this case a contract relating to a ship was held to be an agreement to sell and not a sale, as the transfer of the property was to be carried out by execution of a bill of sale (see 888, 158, per Lord Justice-Clerk Scott Dickson). So far as conditions are concerned, it appears that a suspensive condition relating to property transfer normally renders the contract one of 'agreement to sell'. However, even a contract properly considered 'a sale' can be conditional (Sale of Goods Act 1979, s 2(3)) but in this case the relevant condition will be resolutive in character. Thus in *Gavin's Trustee v Fraser* 1920 SC 674, 1920 2 SLT 221, the arrangement was held to be sale even although there was a condition that the seller could repurchase his plant at a specified price and within a specified period.
6 However, the Sale of Goods Act 1979, s 41, confers a lien on an unpaid seller in possession which gives him a preference over other creditors of the buyer. See further SALE AND EXCHANGE, vol 20, paras 870, 873.
7 Ibid, s 20. See further para 639 below, and SALE AND EXCHANGE, vol 20, para 846.

627. Ascertainment of the goods. Generally, it is a prerequisite of the passing of property that the goods be ascertained[1]. No property can pass unless or until this has been done[2]. This rule is now subject to an important exception discussed below, relating to unascertained goods which form part of an identifiable bulk[3]. It must be stressed that ascertainment, when it is still required, does not automatically lead to the passing of property. Under the Sale of Goods Act 1979 that depends on the intention of the parties[4]. However, unless the exception applies, their intention cannot come into effect until goods are first of all ascertained. Unascertained goods are goods which cannot be specifically and particularly identified at the time of contract and can only be referred to by description[5]. Three categories of goods are included, namely:

(1) generic goods, that is, goods of a certain kind referred to by quantity without any further identification;
(2) most cases of future goods[5]; and
(3) unidentified parts of a larger quantity of bulk goods of which the source is ascertained[6].

The ascertainment rule posed particular problems for traders in commodities. These are well illustrated in *Hayman & Son v M'Lintock*[7]. Following a report of the Law Commissions[8], there has been legislative reform in this area. Provisions added to the Sale of Goods Act 1979[9] provide that in the case of the sale of a specified quantity of unascertained goods from an identified bulk[10], property in an undivided share[11] of the bulk passes to the buyer when he pays the price in whole or in part. Thereupon he becomes an owner in common of the bulk, with no need for ascertainment. The right of ownership thus conferred prevails in the event of the seller's insolvency over claims by the seller's creditors as the goods no longer form part of the assets of the seller. The provision is subject to any contrary agreement by the parties[12]. Parties may also specifically choose a later date for the passing of property in the undivided share of the bulk and the creation of common ownership[12]. There are supplementary provisions modifying the usual consequences of co-ownership when the provisions in respect of bulk goods apply. All co-owners are deemed to have consented to (a) any delivery out of the bulk to any other co-owner of the goods due to that co-owner by his contract of sale and (b) all dealings, including disposal, by the other co-owners with the goods within their shares[13]. The contractual arrangements between buyers for adjustments between themselves and indeed all contractual rights of buyers are not affected[14]. These provisions on sales out of bulk largely apply in practice to commercial sales and in particular to trading in commodities. However, they are not so restricted by the terms of the statutory text. Thus they could conceivably apply to certain consumer transactions also, for example certain purchases of wine. Ascertainment means the individualisation or particular identification of the goods. This will involve a physical separation of the goods from any larger bulk in which they are contained, for example, by severing, weighing or measuring[15]. It has been held in England that, in the case of bulk goods coming from an ascertained source, ascertainment can take place by exhaustion[16]. It has also been held in England that ascertainment of bulk goods is sufficiently done when all the goods destined for one buyer are ascertained together, that is, it is not necessary for further and more particular ascertainment of the goods by earmarking of them to particular consignments arising from separate contracts between the seller and the same buyer to take place[17]. Issues of ascertainment and appropriation are intimately linked in practice. As explained, ascertainment rests on a mandatory provision of the Act. It is a *sine qua non* of the passing of property but not itself part of that process. Appropriation forms part of the establishment of intention regarding passing of property under rule 5 of section 18 of the Act but can be overcome by evidence of a contrary intention. The same set of acts can raise both questions and the same act can easily be held both to be ascertainment and appropriation. Explicit statutory provision now recognises appropriation by means of exhaustion of an identifiable bulk when the goods in question are in a deliverable state[18].

1 The matter of ascertainment of goods is fully documented with copious citation of the English authorities in J P Benjamin *Sale of Goods* (4th edn, 1992) paras 5-058–5-063.
2 Sale of Goods Act 1979 (c 54), s 16.

3 Ibid, s 20A (added by the Sale of Goods (Amendment) Act 1995 (c 28), s 1(3)) gives details of the exception described. The 1995 Act applies to contracts of sale made after 19 September 1995: see the 1995 Act, s 3(2). Section 16 of the 1979 Act is subject to s 20A: see s 16 (amended by the 1995 Act, s 1(1)).
4 Sale of Goods Act 1979, ss 17, 18. Section 16 does not depend on the intention of parties. It is a mandatory provision: *The Elafi* [1982] 1 All ER 208 at 212. Section 16 of the 1979 Act is subject to s 20A: see s 16 (as so amended).
5 The Sale of Goods Act 1979 itself does not define either 'ascertained' or 'unascertained' goods. J J Gow in *The Mercantile and Industrial Law of Scotland* (1964) p 123 describes ascertained goods very well as 'goods individualised and identifiable as *the* goods under contract'. In *Re Wait* [1927] 1 Ch 606, CA, a case relating to a bulk cargo of wheat, ascertainment was taken to mean identification of the goods at a date later than the contract date. If identification has taken place at or before the contract date then the goods are specific goods.
6 'Future goods' mean goods to be manufactured or acquired by the sellers after the making of the contract of sale: Sale of Goods Act 1979, s 61. It is thought that in most cases they are also unascertained goods. Rule 5 of section 18 seems to distinguish between future goods and unascertained goods although it applies to both of them. For rule 5, see para 635 below.
7 *Hayman & Son v M'Lintock* 1907 SC 936, 15 SLT 63. In this case two separate consignments of sacks of flour out of a much larger number of sacks held for the seller in store were sold. The consignments were not marked or separated from the rest of the sacks in the store and were thus held to be unascertained. Consequently, property in them could not pass to the buyers even though the store-keeper had received intimation of the sale and had acknowledged to the buyers that he held on their orders. Such a result could be seen as penalising purchasers of bulk goods, prejudicing them against the seller's creditors and thus defeating legitimate, commercial expectations. This appears to be the only reported Scottish case on the point. It has been applied and followed in England.
8 *Bulk Goods — Section 16 of the Sale of Goods Act 1979 and Section 1 of the Bills of Lading Act 1855* (Scot Law Com Discussion Paper no. 83) (1989) p 2.
9 Sale of Goods Act 1979, s 20A (as added: see note 3 above).
10 See ibid, s 61(1) ('bulk') (added by the Sale of Goods (Amendment) Act 1995, s 2). Identification should take place by contract or a subsequent agreement: Sale of Goods Act 1979, s 20A(1)(a) (as added: see note 3 above).
11 The share is the proportion of the goods to the bulk as a whole: Sale of Goods Act 1979, s 20A(3), (4) (as added: see note 3 above).
12 Ibid, s 20A(2) (as so added).
13 Ibid, s 20B(1) (as so added). Thus each co-owner can deal with his own share without any need for specific consent from the rest. Persons, eg liquidators, acting on the basis of the deemed consents are protected against court action: s 20B(2) (as so added). However, no obligation is imposed on a buyer from the bulk to compensate any other buyer from the same bulk for any shortfall in the goods received by that buyer: s 20B(3)(a) (as so added).
14 Ibid, s 20B(3)(b), (c) (as so added).
15 Eg in *Hayman & Son v M'Lintock* 1907 SC 936, 15 SLT 63, no steps were taken to separate the sacks in any way from the others in the store or to mark or identify them as distinct consignments. This rule applies even to bulk shipments on c i f terms: *The Julia* [1949] AC 293, [1949] 1 All ER 269, HL.
16 Thus in *Wait and James v Midland Bank* (1926) 31 Com Cas 172 the seller gave the buyer delivery orders of 850 quarters of wheat out of 1250 stored in bulk. When the seller disposed of 400 quarters, it was held that the 850 had become ascertained. This principle does not appear to apply to purely generic goods as distinct from bulk goods sold from an identified source: *Re London Wine Co (Shippers) Ltd* (1975) 126 NLJ 1977, which related to a specified quantity of bottles of a certain vintage of wine where no specified larger bulk or shipment was mentioned.
17 *The Elafi* [1982] 1 All ER 208 (which also applies the exhaustion approach discussed in note 10 above).
18 See the Sale of Goods Act 1979, s 18, rule 5(3), (4) (added by the Sale of Goods (Amendment) Act 1995, s 1(2)).

628. Passing of property — intention. Subject to ascertainment, if required[1], or if it has always been clear which goods are the particular and individual subjects of the contract of sale[2], the Sale of Goods Act 1979 fixes the time of the passing of property as being when the parties intend it to pass[3]. There is a special rule for the passing of property in the sale of unascertained goods from an identifiable bulk. Subject to that exception, intention is the test both in regard to ascertained and unascertained goods[4]. As mentioned above[5] this contribution assumes that the passing of property entails the transfer of *dominium,* a real right valid against third parties. However, whether one takes this view or the alternative that it passes property rights only between the parties, it is important to note that the passing of property relates to questions of title (and the consequential issue of risk under section 20 of the Act). It does not affect contractual or statutory rights under the Act, including rights relating to rejection of the goods because of disconformity to contract. It has been held that passing of property is not itself acceptance precluding rejection on that ground[6].

The distinction between a timing of the passing of property based on delivery or equivalent in possession and a timing based on intention, is the key to the difference of approach between the Act and Scots common law. It is, however, possible to exaggerate the practical difference between the Scots common law and the approach of the Act. One eminent English judge has stated that very little evidence is needed to yield the inference that the parties intention is that property only passes on delivery or payment[7]. Timing can be crucial in questions of bankruptcy or insolvency, diligence or the passing of risk, hence the importance of this provision. The Act provides that intention is to be gleaned from the terms of the contract, the conduct of parties and the circumstances of the case[8]. This is further elaborated by a set of five so called rules[9] for ascertaining the parties' intention regarding the time of the passing of property, in the absence of proof of an intention different from their effect, for example by contractual terms or circumstances[10]. It is important to note that it has been held that a contract *subsequent* to the passing of property under the rules will not prevent them from having their due effect. The relevant contract or other circumstances must exist at or prior to the passing of property[11]. These rules are subsidiary to the principle as stated in section 17 which emphasises the parties' intention[12].

Obviously the best course is for the contract to make express and specific provision on when the passing of property is to take place. That will represent the definitive statement of the parties' intention[13]. This issue has arisen sharply in regard to reservation of title clauses. For some time there was considerable academic and judicial discussion in Scotland about the validity of so called *Romalpa* clauses[14] where title was reserved until all sums owing to the seller were paid[15]. The validity of such clauses in Scotland was accepted and affirmed by the House of Lords in *Armour v Thyssen Edelstahlwerke AG*[16]. One of the grounds of decision in that case was that such clauses were an example of the application of section 17 of the Act. The parties were agreeing to postpone the passing of property until all relevant debts were paid although physical possession had passed to the buyer[17]. Emphasis was placed on the clear expression of intention to that effect stated in the contract which the House of Lords stated should be implemented[18]. Such clauses were also held valid in the light of the provisions of section 19 of the Act (Reservation of Title)[19] and also held not subject to attack under section 62(4) (sales purporting to create rights in security)[20].

1   See para 627 above.
2   For a description of 'ascertained goods', see para 627 above. 'Specific goods' mean goods identified and agreed on when the contract is made: Sale of Goods Act 1979 (c 54), s 61(1). Ascertained goods (not defined in the Act) are goods identified at a date later than the date of contract. Section 17 refers to specific or ascertained goods.
3   Ibid, s 17. For intention in the passing of property generally, see D L Carey Miller *Corporeal Moveables in Scots Law* (1991) pp 142–167. For a full discussion of the English cases regarding ascertained and unascertained goods, see also J P Benjamin *Sale of Goods* (4th edn, 1992) paras 5-016–5-057, 5-065–5-101.
4   *Ginzberg v Barrow Haematite Steel Co* [1966] 1 Lloyd's Rep 343 at 352. For the exception, see para 627 above.
5   See para 625 above.
6   *Nelson v William Chalmers & Co Ltd* 1913 SC 441, 1913 1 SLT 190.
7   *R V Ward Ltd v Bignall* [1967] 1 QB 534 at 545, [1967] 2 All ER 449 at 453, CA, per Diplock LJ.

8 Sale of Goods Act 1979, s 17(2). It has been judicially stated that parties are free to decide the issue of property passing themselves by 'any intelligible expression of intention': *McEntire v Crossley Bros Ltd* [1895] AC 457 at 467, HL, per Lord Watson.

9 Sale of Goods Act 1979, s 18.

10 In that event that ibid, s 18, does not come into effect at all. See eg *Sir James Laing & Sons Ltd v Barclay Curle & Co Ltd* 1908 SC (HL) 1 at 2, 15 SLT 644 at 645, per Lord Robertson; *Woodburn v Andrew Motherwell Ltd* 1917 SC 533 at 538, 1917 1 SLT 345 at 347, per Lord President Strathclyde. See also *Re Anchor Line (Henderson Bros) Ltd* [1937] Ch 1, where it was held that an intention contrary to the rules of s 18 could and should be gleaned from a construction of the contract as a whole.

11 *Dennant v Skinner* [1948] 2 KB 164, [1948] 2 All ER 29.

12 See *R V Ward Ltd v Bignall* [1967] 1 QB 534 at 545, [1967] 2 All ER 449 at 453, CA, per Diplock LJ; *Lacis v Cashmarts* [1969] 2 QB 400 at 407, per Lord Parker LCJ.

13 See eg *Nelson v William Chalmers & Co Ltd* 1913 SC 441, 1913 1 SLT 190; *McLaren's Trustee v Argylls Ltd* 1915 2 SLT 241. The importance of a specific provision is underlined by a judicial comment that the parties' intention is 'seldom or never capable of proof': *Smyth & Co v Bailey & Co* [1940] 3 All ER 60 at 67, HL, per Lord Wright.

14 This description derives from the case of *Aluminium Industrie Vaasen BV v Romalpa Aluminium Ltd* [1976] 2 All ER 552, [1976] 1 WLR 676, CA, where such clauses were first judicially considered in England.

15 See paras 637, 638, below. See also RIGHTS IN SECURITY, vol 20, para 842.

16 *Armour v Thyssen Edelstahlwerke AG* 1991 SCLR 139, 1990 SLT 891, HL.

17 1991 SCLR 139 at 143, 144, 1990 SLT 891 at 894, 896, HL, per Lord Keith of Kinkel and Lord Jauncey of Tullichettle.

18 1991 SCLR 139 at 143, 1990 SLT 891 at 894, HL, per Lord Keith of Kinkel.

19 See para 638 below.

20 See para 637 below.

629. Absence of express provision. In the absence of express provision on when the passing of property is to take place, the matter will be determined at large from the evidence by the courts, guided by the rules of section 18 of the Sale of Goods Act 1979 if appropriate, with special and primary reference to the terms of the written contract (if any)[1]. Thus in *Sir James Laing & Sons Ltd v Barclay Curle & Co Ltd*[2] it was emphasised in the House of Lords that the issue is first of all one of the construction of the contract. There it was held that where a ship was being paid for in instalments during its construction, but under the contract a trial trip was required before delivery and final acceptance would take place, property had not passed in the absence of such a trip. The contract as a whole showed an intention to link passing of property to the final handing over of the completed ship by the builders[2]. It has been held that in a c i f contract the endorsement of the bill of lading transferred the property in the goods, as being an expression of intention[3]. In a case relating to a sale of ricks of hay it was held that property passed when, under the contract, the purchaser had the hay placed at his disposal for packing and baling even although it was still stored in the seller's premises. This was on the ground that the baling was inconsistent with ownership remaining with the seller and consistent with ownership by the buyer[4]. When the timber of standing trees is being sold, severance of the trees from the ground will, in the absence of contrary specific contractual provision, pass the property rather than the removal of the timber. The severance itself transfers the trees into timber[5].

One matter which has arisen in the English authorities is the inference to be drawn from specific contractual provision on the passing of risk when there is silence on the passing of property in the same contract. In some cases it has been stressed that, as risk follows property under the general law of sale a strong presumption arises that parties intend property to follow their expressed intention on risk[6]. On the other hand, in at least one case the opposite inference has been drawn. There the view was taken that a specific provision on risk is a pointer to an intention to separate the passing of risk and property in that had the parties intended that property should pass, risk would automatically have passed with it[7]. There is thus no absolute rule. It is submitted that the matter has to be decided by a construction of the clause on risk in the light of the contract as a whole and any relevant surrounding circumstances[8]. This discussion underlines the importance of a specific clause on the passing of property being inserted in a contract of sale to avoid any dispute on the point.

1 Although probably not with exclusive reference to the written contractual terms, despite the parole evidence rule. See *Peebles & Co v Kerr Ltd* (1902) 9 SLT 372, OH, where evidence of a supplementary oral agreement and its alleged implementation by the fixing of a plate declaring that property was retained by the seller was admitted. The disregard of the strict effect of the parole evidence rule is supported by the wide terms of the Sale of Goods Act 1979 (c 54), s 17(2).

2 *Sir James Laing & Sons Ltd v Barclay Curle & Co Ltd* 1908 SC (HL) 1, 15 SLT 644. See also the earlier case *Reid v McBeth and Gray* (1904) 6 F (HL) 25, 11 SLT 783.

3 *Pommer and Thomsen v Mowat* (1906) 14 SLT 373, OH.

4 *Woodburn v Andrew Motherwell Ltd* 1917 SC 533, 1917 1 SLT 345.

5 *Munro v Balnagown Estates Co Ltd Liquidator* 1949 SC 49, 1949 SLT 85.

6 *The Parchim* [1918] AC 157 at 168, PC; *Carlos Federspiel & Co SA v Charles Twigg & Co Ltd* [1957] 1 Lloyd's Rep 240 at 255.

7 *Re Anchor Line (Henderson Bros) Ltd* [1937] Ch 1 at 11.

8 [1937] Ch 1.

630. The section 18 rules. The rules laid down in section 18 of the Sale of Goods Act 1979[1] will often apply in the absence of any written contract of sale or at least of any clauses in such a contract from which inferences contrary to their effect could be drawn[2]. However, it would be perilous to draw the conclusion that they will always and automatically apply in the absence of a relevant written term. The crucial test is intention. The rules are always subject to intention[3], provided it is not expressed subsequently to the passing of property[4]. Thus a contrary intention will overcome the effects of the rules, even if it is one which is held to emerge from facts and circumstances. One important example is that it has been held in England that in a sale in a supermarket or a cash and carry, property only passes on payment of the price. This result was stated to be in accord with commercial realities. As it was also held to represent the intention of the parties, it overcame the effect of one of the rules[5]. It appears that in consumer sales a cash payment secures the passing of property even if the seller retains possession[6]. The general issue is that the Act entrusts the passing of property to the autonomy of parties. They are free to express this intention implicitly, provided they do so clearly and intelligibly[7]. Thus in a case not directly falling within the rules, it was held that retention of shipping documents indicated an intention to retain property in the goods they represented, although possession of them had been lost[8]. On the other hand, intention may not be expressed at all clearly from facts and circumstances. At least one eminent English judge has expressed pessimism on intention being easily ascertained[9]. Although the cases mentioned above regarding cash sales[10] show a somewhat greater readiness to infer intention, the difficulty of establishing intention is what led to the rules in the first place. They thus represent the parties' presumed intention in important sets of circumstances. Although not all-embracing in their scope (in that they do not cover every possible situation) and subject to contrary intention as described above, they are of considerable significance especially when there is no specific express contractual provision on the passing of property.

1 See the Sale of Goods Act 1979 (c 54), s 18, and paras 631–635 below.

2 See the authorities cited in para 628, note 10, above.

3 See the authorities cited in para 628, note 12, above.

4 See *Dennant v Skinner* [1948] 2 KB 164, [1948] 2 All ER 29.

5 *Lacis v Cashmarts* [1969] 2 QB 400; *Davis v Leighton* [1978] Crim LR 575. It should be noted that these cases arose out of the English statutory law of theft which differs from Scots law on that subject.

6 *Watts v Seymour* [1967] 2 QB 647, [1967] 1 All ER 1044.

7 See the dictum of Lord Watson in *McEntire v Crossley Bros Ltd* [1895] AC 457 at 467, HL (para 628, note 8, above).

8 *Cheetham & Co Ltd v Thornham Spinning Co Ltd* [1964] 2 Lloyds Rep 17.
9 See the dictum of Lord Wright in *Smyth & Co v Bailey & Co* [1940] 3 All ER 60 at 67, HL (para 628, note 13, above).
10 See the cases cited in notes 5 and 6 above.

631. Rule 1. Rule 1 provides that in the case of an unconditional contract for the sale of specific goods in a deliverable state, property passes when the contract is made irrespective of the postponement of either payment or delivery or both[1]. Two interesting issues have arisen in English academic discussion of this rule. The first relates to the meaning of 'unconditional'. The view is taken that this means 'unconditional' only in the sense of having no conditions relevant to the issue of passing of property rather than having no conditions at all[2]. It is argued that to press the latter approach too far would be to exclude the application of the rule to most, if not all, contracts of sale. It is submitted that the more restrictive interpretation argued for by the English textbooks is correct and should be accepted in Scotland. The issue does not appear to be addressed directly in any reported case. It has also been suggested by an academic commentator on the Sale of Goods Act 1979 that it is permissible for a contract to have resolutive conditions attached and the phrase 'unconditional' refers only to the absence of suspensive conditions[3]. Thus it is submitted that 'unconditional' must be read as meaning 'not subject to any suspensive condition on the passing of property'. The most detailed treatment on the Scots law of sale appears to support this submission[4]. In any event, as argued earlier[5], a suspensive condition on the passing of property renders the contract one of agreement to sell. In contrast, a resolutive condition on this matter can attach to a contract which is truly sale, albeit conditional[6]. This it is submitted, is consistent with the view taken on the meaning of the word 'unconditional'.

The second question relates to the phrase 'in a deliverable state'. This is defined in the Act[7]. The question arises whether defects in the goods, for example rendering them unmerchantable, take them out of the effect of rule 1 or whether 'in a deliverable state' merely means that nothing further has to be done to them by the seller before the buyer must take delivery. The English textbooks take the latter view strongly[8]. This appears to be supported by such case law as there is[9] and it is submitted that the more narrow approach is correct and should be followed in Scotland. It is analogous to the distinction taken in the Scottish cases between property passing and acceptance of the goods[10]. Thus it is probably the case that defects in the goods do not hinder the property passing. Under rule 1, at an auction sale property passes at the drop of the auctioneer's hammer, that is, at the time the contract is formed[11]. If it appears from the evidence that under the contract certain work had to be done to the item of property before the buyer became obliged to accept it, rule 1 does not apply and the matter is covered by rule 2[12].

In consumer sales for cash, the English courts have generally held that rule 1 is inapplicable and that property passes on payment[13]. There is no Scottish authority on this point. In addition, it has been accepted in England (albeit not directly in the context of the passing of property) that a sale where the buyer uses a credit or charge card is essentially a cash sale[14]. The logic of that decision is that on such sales property passes on the completion of the credit card transaction between the purchaser and the seller.

1 Sale of Goods Act 1979 (c 54), s 18, r 1. See *Kennedy's Trustee v Hamilton and Manson* (1897) 25 R 252. For the meaning of 'specific goods', see para 628, note 2, above.
2 R Goode *Commercial Law* (1985) pp 180–182; J P Benjamin *Sale of Goods* (4th edn, 1992) para 282. See also P Atiyah *Sale of Goods* (8th edn, 1990) pp 288–290.
3 *Goode* p 181.
4 J J Gow *The Mercantile and Industrial Law of Scotland* (1964) p 126. It would appear that in the penultimate sentence of his discussion of rule 1 at p 126, the vital word '*not*' has been omitted. (The word 'not' is included in a comment earlier in the discussion albeit there the discussion is more focused on English Law). It should be noted that much of Gow's discussion is dominated by a

difference between English law and Scots law which has disappeared. The Sale of Goods Act 1893 (c 71), s 11(1), contained a provision which was not applicable to Scotland and which was repealed in respect of England and Wales by the Misrepresentation Act 1967 (c 7), s 4. The provision in the 1893 Act led to many of the difficulties in this area in England because of the interaction of the rules on the right of rejection and the passing of property. It had clear implications for the question of 'deliverable state' discussed at para 633 below.

5　See para 626 above.

6　See para 626, note 5, above.

7　Goods are in a deliverable state when they are in such a state that the buyer would under the contract be bound to take delivery of them: Sale of Goods Act 1979 (c 54), s 61(5).

8　*Atiyah* pp 291, 292; *Goode* pp 182, 183; *Benjamin* paras 5-023, 5-024.

9　*Underwood v Burgh Castle Syndicate* [1922] 1 KB 343, CA.

10　*Nelson v William Chalmers & Co Ltd* 1913 SC 441, 1913 1 SLT 190.

11　*Shankland & Co v Robinson & Co* 1920 SC (HL) 103 at 107, 1920 2 SLT 96 at 98, per Viscount Finlay; *Dennant v Skinner* [1948] 2 KB 164, [1948] 2 All ER 29.

12　*Brown Bros v Carron Co* (1898) 6 SLT 231, OH; *Underwood v Burgh Castle Syndicate* [1922] 1 KB 343, CA.

13　On this point, see the cases cited at para 630, notes 5, 6, above.

14　*Re Charge Card Services Ltd* [1988] 3 All ER 702 especially at 710, 711, per Sir Nicolas Browne-Wilkinson V-C.

632. Rule 2. Rule 2 provides that where in the sale of specific goods the seller is bound to do something to the goods to make them deliverable, the property does not pass until the thing is done and the buyer has notice that it has been done[1]. This has been applied in Scotland to the fitting of plugs and a pipe to a crane[2], the lifting and pitting of a crop of growing potatoes[3], and the completion of the construction of a yacht[4]. The classic English case related to the severing of a piece of machinery from a building to which it was affixed[5].

1　Sale of Goods Act 1979 (c 54), s 18, r 2.

2　*Brown Bros v Carron Co* (1898) 6 SLT 231, OH.

3　*Cockburn's Trustee v Bowe & Sons* 1910 2 SLT 17, OH. This case distinguished between pitting the potatoes and carting them to the station. Carting relates to delivery. Pitting relates to putting them in a deliverable state. Property passed when the potatoes had been pitted. In *Paton's Trustees v Finlayson* 1923 SC 872, 1923 SLT 593, a similar decision was taken but it was held that although property had passed to the buyer he had not gained possession. Thus s 43 of the Sale of Goods Act 1893 (c 71) applied, giving the seller a lien.

4　*Lombard North Central Ltd v Lord Advocate* 1983 SLT 361, OH.

5　*Underwood v Burgh Castle Syndicate* [1922] 1 KB 343, CA.

633. Rule 3. Rule 3 provides that in the case of the sale of specific goods in a deliverable state where the seller is bound to weigh, measure or test or do any other act for the purpose of ascertaining price, property does not pass until the relevant act is done and the buyer has notice of it being done[1]. This rule only applies where the seller is bound contractually to weigh or otherwise deal with the goods[2]. Like all the rules it gives way before a contrary intention and even if its terms are fulfilled in a certain situation, it is irrelevant that this is so if the parties have shown a differing intention regarding the passing of property[3].

It is worthy of note that rules 2 and 3 are expressed negatively whereas rule 1 is expressed positively. Rules 2 and 3 thus express minimum provisions for the passing of property which may not in all circumstances be sufficient criteria. Ultimately the question depends on the parties' intention.

1　Sale of Goods Act 1979 (c 54), s 18, r 3. For the meaning of 'specific goods', see para 628, note 2, above, and for the meaning of 'in a deliverable state', see para 631, text and note 8, above.

2 See *Kennedy's Trustee v Hamilton and Manson* (1897) 25 R 252 (where there was no proof of any contractual provision on weighing); *Nanka-Bruce v Commonwealth Trust Ltd* [1926] AC 77, PC (where weighing under the contract was to be done by third parties, not the seller).

3 *Woodburn v Andrew Motherwell Ltd* 1917 SC 533, 1917 1 SLT 345.

634. Rule 4. Rule 4 deals with the delivery of goods on approval, sale or return, or similar terms. It provides that the property in such goods passes to the buyer:

(1) when he signifies his approval or acceptance or does any other act adopting the transaction; or

(2) where he refuses the goods without giving notice of rejection after the expiration of the time fixed for their return, or the expiration of a reasonable time[1].

Although at least one Scottish case distinguishes sales on approval from those on sale or return[2], for the purposes of rule 4 this distinction does not appear to be necessary as both and indeed all similar arrangements are covered by it. Usually these arrangements arise between wholesalers and retailers to enable the former to increase market share and the latter to hold adequate stocks. The retailer is bound to return the goods if unsold by him after a specified or reasonable time and the wholesaler is bound to receive them again in these circumstances[3]. It is noticeable that rule 4 does not refer to a contract of sale and it has been suggested in at least one English academic commentary that the arrangement of sale or return is not a contract of sale at all but technically is only an offer to sell. The qualification is made that, in practice, it is a consensual arrangement[4]. According to this view, the passing of property on sale and return is secured only by the wording and operation of rule 4. In Scotland, however, a sale or return arrangement has been judicially considered a contract of sale, albeit subject to a suspensive condition[5]. Nonetheless, it is a highly special arrangement in that in another Scottish case a situation was categorised in terms as being only a sale subject to a suspensive condition rather than a sale or return contract[6]. Whatever the legal analysis adopted, unless, as described below, the relationship between the parties is considered to be one of agency, rule 4 is so drafted as to cover the situation.

In the absence of the matters mentioned in rule 4 operating, it has been held that the property remains with the seller in a sale or return arrangement. Thus goods covered by such an arrangement did not pass to the buyer's trustee on his bankruptcy[7]. Also in accordance with the usual position parties can expressly deal with the issue of the passing of property and override rule 4 by showing a contrary intention. In one case the documentation expressly fixed the passing of property at the payment of the price by the retailer or at least his being debited with it by the wholesaler and this was given effect by the court[8]. The effect of the rule, where it is not so excluded, is to pass property firstly when the buyer signifies his approval or acceptance to the seller, that is makes a commitment to purchase the goods or otherwise adopts the transaction, for example by pledging the goods to a third party[9]. Alternatively, if he does not signify approval or acceptance but retains the goods without giving notice of rejection, property passes on the expiry of any time fixed for their return or if there is no fixed time on the expiry of a reasonable time. What a reasonable time is, is a question of fact[10].

The above discussion must be read subject to the possibility that the relationship between the parties may be held to be truly one of agency rather than sale or return. That decision depends on the terms of the written agreement, if any, and the totality of the arrangement between them. Thus in *Michelin Tyre Co Ltd v Macfarlane (Glasgow) Ltd*[11] the majority in the House of Lords took the view that the contracts between a tyre manufacturer and their retail stockists were truly sale and return and not agency. If the relationship is held to be agency, quite different results in regard to the pledging and indeed the sale of the goods to third parties can arise. This is because of the implied authority in respect of these operations conferred on a mercantile agent by the common law and the Factors Acts. The authority thus granted prevails over a contractual provision reserving property to the wholesaler which, it has been held, only has effect under the regime of rule 4[12]. It is obviously in the interests of suppliers to secure that their contracts with stockists are not considered to be agency contracts in the strict legal sense.

1 Sale of Goods Act 1979 (c 54), s 18, r 4.
2 *Brown v Marr Barclay & Co* (1880) 7 R 427.
3 *Brown v Marr Barclay & Co* (1880) 7 R 427 at 433. See the discussion in R Goode *Commercial Law* (1985) pp 188, 189.
4 The sending of wholly unsolicited goods is an entirely different situation. See the Unsolicited Goods and Services Act 1971 (c 30).
5 *Ross v Plano Manufacturing Co* (1903) 11 SLT 7 at 9.
6 *Bell Rannie & Co v White's Trustee* (1885) 22 SLR 597, OH.
7 *Ross v Plano Manufacturing Co* (1903) 11 SLT 7 following the pre-1893 case *Macdonald v Westren* (1888) 15 R 988.
8 *Weiner v Gill* [1906] 2 KB 574, CA. In this English case the arrangement of sale and return appears to be treated as a contractual one.
9 *Kirkham v Attenborough* [1897] 1 QB 201, CA; *London Jewellers v Attenborough* [1934] 2 KB 206, CA.
10 *Poole v Smith's Car Sales (Balham) Ltd* [1962] 2 All ER 482, [1962] 1 WLR 744, CA.
11 *Michelin Tyre Co Ltd v Macfarlane (Glasgow) Ltd* 1917 2 SLT 205, HL.
12 *Weiner v Harris* [1910] 1 KB 285, CA, distinguishing *Weiner v Gill* [1906] 2 KB 574, CA. For a discussion of the Factors Acts, see para 671 below.

635. Rule 5. Rule 5 is one of the most complex of the rules but it is also perhaps the most important in commercial transactions[1]. It applies to a contract for the sale of unascertained[2] or future[3] goods by description[4]. When goods of the contractual description and in a deliverable state are unconditionally appropriated to the contract, either by the seller or the buyer (in either case with the other's assent) property in the goods then passes to the buyer. The assent may be expressed or implied and may be given before or after appropriation is made. Where delivery in pursuance of the contract is made by the seller to the buyer or to a carrier or custodier for transmission to the buyer, that is taken as unconditional appropriation unless the seller reserves the right of disposal. (This is really a special example of appropriation.) It has been argued in one academic commentary in England that 'deliverable state' in rule 5 has a different and wider meaning than in rules 1 and 2 and refers to the actual condition of the goods. According to this view, the state of the goods must be such that the buyer would not be entitled to reject them or at least that they are accepted by him as being in a deliverable state[5]. With respect, very little argumentation is provided for this assertion and it seems prima facie peculiar that the same phrase should receive such a different interpretation in the same set of statutory rules found in one section of an Act. In the one reported case on the definition of 'deliverable state' for the purpose of rule 5 (admittedly not raising the above precise question), the same statutory definition was applied as in a case under rules 1 and 2[6]. The result was that a carpet was held not to be in a deliverable state until laid by a fitter. Property had not passed when it had merely been left at the buyer's premises as a large bale. The key question is clearly appropriation and this in practice is usually intermixed with and indistinguishable from ascertainment[7]. Essentially it means the earmarking of the goods so that they and no other goods are the subjects of the sale[8]. Usually this will be the last act performed by the seller[9], often involving some kind of delivery (actual or constructive), to the buyer[10]. Thus in one of the leading cases on the matter, to prepare cycles for shipment was not appropriation when they were being shipped on an f o b contract. Appropriation would have required sending the goods to the port and having them shipped. These were further and decisive acts which the buyer was obliged to perform[11]. Thus mere selection by the seller of the goods which were to be the contract goods and shipped as such was not sufficient as being short of unconditional appropriation. If no shipping is involved, it may be held that designation of the goods in storage is appropriation. Designation to be effective appropriation cannot merely be in the mind of the party involved. The goods, it appears, must be distinguishable by marking, or in records or at least by being clearly set apart in the store[12]. In another case, appropriation was held to have clearly taken place when a delivery note was accepted on behalf of the seller by a warehouseman and goods already deposited and standing ready for loading were identified as the subjects of the contract[13]. Similarly, it was considered that property in a lorry load of coal only passed when the weight was ascertained and the statutory weight ticket was issued and accepted by the buyer, rather than on loading[14]. (This case was also partially based on the need for assent to appropriation.) On the other hand, it has also been held in England that filling a tank with petrol immediately passes the property in the petrol to the buyer as being an appropriation with the consent of both parties[15]. It appears that in a sale where the goods are to be transported by post, posting is appropriation on the basis that it is delivery to the postal authorities who are agents for the buyer[16]. In the case of sales from an identifiable bulk, appropriation can taken place by exhaustion[17].

Assent to appropriation is required by rule 5 but this can fairly easily be inferred in most cases, for example by the whole nature of the contract[18] or by a lapse of a reasonable time after notice of appropriation is given[19]. Assent is thus rarely a problem.

Like all the other rules, rule 5 will always have to give way to proof of contrary intention. Thus in one case property was held to pass on the transfer of shipping documents under a c i f contract (as is the usual case in such contracts), as being the parties' intention rather than on appropriation[20].

1 Sale of Goods Act 1979 (c 54), s 18, r 5.
2 As to 'unascertained goods', see para 627 above.
3 For the meaning of 'future goods', see para 627, note 5, above.
4 As to 'sale by description', see the Sale of Goods Act 1979, s 13. See also SALE AND EXCHANGE, vol 20, para 822.
5 R Goode *Commercial Law* (1985) p 185.
6 *Philip Head & Sons Ltd v Showfronts Ltd* [1970] 1 Lloyd's Rep 140.
7 In *Wardar's Co Ltd v Norwood & Sons Ltd* [1968] 2 QB 663, [1968] 2 All ER 602, CA, Harman LJ decided on ascertainment (671, 604) and Salmon LJ decided on appropriation (673, 605). See also *The Elafi* [1982] 1 All ER at 215, per Mustill J.
8 *Healy v Howlett & Sons* [1917] 1 KB 337; *Carlos Federspiel & Co SA v Charles Twigg & Co Ltd* [1957] 1 Lloyd's Rep 240. In *Re Blyth Shipbuilding and Dry Docks Co Ltd* [1926] Ch 494 at 518, CA, it was stated that appropriation is a term of art with a definite meaning but this is hard to sustain on the authorities as a whole.
9 *Carlos Federspiel & Co SA v Charles Twigg & Co Ltd* [1957] 1 Lloyd's Rep 240 at 255. This was another ground of decision in *Philip Head & Sons Ltd v Showfronts Ltd* [1970] 1 Lloyd's Rep 140.
10 *Carlos Federspiel & Co SA v Charles Twigg & Co Ltd* [1957] 1 Lloyd's Rep 240 — another interesting example of the greater congruence of Scots law and the Sale of Goods Act 1979 than might at first sight appear. Delivery appears a key factor in deciding appropriation and thus the intention of the parties.
11 *Carlos Federspiel & Co SA v Charles Twigg & Co Ltd* [1957] 1 Lloyd's Rep 240.
12 *Donaghey's Rope and Twine v Wright, Stephenson & Co* (1906) 25 NZLR 641. This case represents perhaps the minimum required for appropriation.
13 *Wardar's Co Ltd v Norwood & Sons Ltd* [1968] 2 QB 663, [1968] 2 All ER 602, CA.
14 *National Coal Board v Gamble* [1959] 1 QB 11, [1958] 3 All ER 203.
15 *Edwards v Ddin* [1976] 3 All ER 705, [1976] 1 WLR 942 (raising issues of the English law of theft).
16 *Badische Anilin und Soda Fabrik v Basle Chemical Works* [1898] AC 200, HL. (This case also involves specialities of patent law.)
17 This rule is now statutory: Sale of Goods Act 1979, s 18, rule 5(3), (4) (added by the Sale of Goods (Amendment) Act 1995 (c 28), s 1(2)). See also *Wait and James v Midland Bank* (1926) 31 Com Cas 172; *The Elafi* [1982] 1 All ER 208.
18 *Widenmeyer v Burn Stewart & Co Ltd* 1967 SC 85 at 101, 1967 SLT 129 at 134, per Lord President Clyde. This was a case of barter decided by Scots common law. In *National Coal Board v Gamble* [1959] 1 QB 11, [1958] 3 All ER 203, express consent was held to be present.
19 *Pignataro v Gilroy* [1919] 1 KB 459.
20 *The Elafi* [1982] 1 All ER 208. See also *Pommer and Thomsen v Mowat* (1906) 14 SLT 373, OH.

636. Summary. The combined effect of sections 16 and 18 of the Sale of Goods Act 1979 (c 54) in regard to unascertained goods is that ascertainment is a *necessary* condition for the passing of property. Passing of property itself will usually take place on the definitive and unconditional appropriation of the goods. The act held to be ascertainment can be now designated as appropriation which is a *sufficient* condition to pass property, assuming it has been assented to, and unless a contrary intention is shown.

In summary the law on the passing of property under the Act is that the test is the intention of the parties. That may be expressed explicitly by contract or implicitly by inference from other contractual terms. It may also be held to arise from facts and circumstances and in that situation particular but not necessarily conclusive regard is paid to the detailed provisions of the rules laid down in the Act as being parties' presumed intentions.

637. Sales intended to operate in security. One effect of the introduction of the Sale of Goods Act regime that property passes when intended to pass by the parties[1] was to create a clear distinction between what was necessary to pass *dominium* on the one hand and a real right in security on the other[2]. The latter requires delivery to the lender by the borrower to be legally effective in Scots law[3]. This rule can often be commercially inconvenient as sometimes the only security which can be offered for an advance is moveable property which forms a necessary part of the working plant of a business[4]. In that situation it is often impossible to comply with the common law on rights in security. One possible way to deal with this problem would be to set up arrangements using sale as a legal device which would give effective security to lenders without the difficulties to borrowers caused by the requirement of delivery to or possession by lenders. That, however, is struck at by the Sale of Goods Act 1979[5] which seeks to prevent circumvention of the common law on rights in security. It does so by providing that its provisions about contracts of sale do not apply to a transaction in the form of a contract of sale which is intended to operate by way of pledge or other security. If a transaction is thus categorised, it cannot take effect if the requirements of the law of pledge are not observed. In particular, property will not pass under such a contract as if it were an ordinary contract of sale. Thus if possession is not transferred, no valid security right will be created, nor will any property pass[6].

The key is thus the categorisation of the transaction. The courts have to decide whether it is truly a genuine sale or a pledge or security. This has to be decided on the basis of all the facts and circumstances. The aim is to find out the reality of the matter whatever the form of the contract and even any declaration of the parties[7]. In deciding this the parole evidence rule is set aside and the formal contract of purported sale can be contradicted by evidence of contrary intention[8]. The provision applies whenever parties use the form of a sale[9]. It has the effect of taking the transaction out of the Sale of Goods Act regime if the common intention of parties is considered to be to produce the legal relationships of security holder and reversioner[10]. In the leading case of *Scottish Transit Trust v Scottish Land Cultivators*[11] it was held that the choice between pure sale and security is to be made on the basis of all the relevant circumstances of a particular transaction[12]. The aim is to identify the substance of the transaction and in particular the true intention of the parties. If it is clear from the evidence that their purpose was to raise finance on the one hand or provide security on the other, then the purported sale will be ineffective[13].

It should be mentioned that in *Armour v Thyssen* the House of Lords held that an 'all sums reservation of title clause' was not struck at by these provisions as it was part of a genuine contract of sale[14].

1 Sale of Goods Act 1979 (c 54), ss 17, 18. See paras 630–636 above.
2 On sales intended to operate in security, see generally D L Carey Miller *Corporeal Moveables in Scots Law* (1991) pp 241–244, 281–284.

3 *Clark v West Calder Oil Co* (1882) 9 R 1017.
4 *Scottish Transit Trust Ltd v Scottish Land Cultivators Ltd* 1955 SC 254 at 261, 262, 1955 SLT 417 at 420, per Lord Russell.
5 Sale of Goods Act 1979, s 62(4).
6 *Jones & Co's Trustee v Allan* (1902) 4 F 374; *Bisset's Trustee v Mathieson* (1903) 5 F 591; *Hepburn v Law* 1914 SC 918, 1914 1 SLT 228.
7 *Robertson v Hall's Trustee* (1896) 24 R 120 at 134, per Lord Moncreiff.
8 (1896) 24 R 120 at 134, per Lord Moncreiff.
9 *Gavin's Trustee v Fraser* 1920 SC 674 at 686, 1920 2 SLT 221 at 228, per Lord President Clyde.
10 1920 SC 674 at 686, 687, 1920 2 SLT 221 at 228, per Lord President Clyde.
11 *Scottish Transit Trust Ltd v Scottish Land Cultivators Ltd* 1955 SC 254, 1955 SLT 417.
12 1955 SC 254 at 263, 1955 SLT 417 at 421, per Lord Russell. See also *Newbigging v Ritchie's Trustee* 1930 SC 273, 1930 SLT 333.
13 *G and C Finance Corpn Ltd v Brown* 1961 SLT 408; *Ladbroke Leasing (South West) Ltd v Reekie Plant Ltd* 1983 SLT 155, OH.
14 *Armour v Thyssen Edelstahlwerke AG* 1991 SCLR 139 at 143, 1990 SLT 891 at 895, HL, per Lord Keith of Kinkel. See para 638 below.

638. Reservation of title. The Sale of Goods Act 1979 allows the seller to reserve contractually the right of disposal of the goods until certain conditions are fulfilled and provides that property in the goods does not pass until fulfilment of these conditions even if the goods have been delivered to the buyer[1]. It applies to specific goods and also to goods subsequently appropriated to the contract. In one sense, this is a specific example of the separation of property and delivery under the Act. It also represents a specific instance of leaving the passing of property to the autonomy of the parties.

The obvious situation where this statutory provision could be invoked is where title is reserved until the price is paid. It is clear that even at common law a contractual clause with this effect was valid[2]. There is thus no doubt that a reservation of title clause in these terms is valid in Scotland standing both the terms of the Act and the common law decisions[3]. This view is also supported by the subsequent case law discussed below. Much more sophisticated clauses have now been developed. These are usually described as 'all sums' clauses or 'Romalpa' clauses. The latter title is derived from the leading English case in which they were first judicially recognised[4]. Such clauses essentially provide that title remains with the seller until all sums owed to him by the buyer are paid, not merely the actual price of the contract goods. There may be further variations, for example, the creation of a trust over the goods in favour of the seller[5], the assertion of rights over new goods created from the subject of sale or under sub-contracts entered into by the buyer.

The advent of such clauses led to considerable litigation in Scotland on the subject of retention of title. The Court of Session generally evinced a hostile attitude to 'all sums' clauses. So-called simple reservation of title clauses were accepted as valid[6]. In sharp contrast wider clauses were regarded as ineffectual[7], largely on the ground that they purported to create security rights without possession[8]. This was stated to be contrary to common law principle in Scotland. However in *Armour v Thyssen Edelstahlwerke AG*[9] the House of Lords accepted and indeed asserted the validity of 'all sums' clauses in Scots law. As mentioned above, this was partially on the ground of the right of parties to regulate the passing of property by a contractual expression of intention[10]. Their Lordships also held that the statutory provision saved such a clause and that the clause was a legitimate reservation of title[11]. They also held that such clauses were not in any proper sense attempts to create rights in security[12] nor were they struck at by the provisions in the Act dealing with sales intended to operate in security[13]. Essentially, contrary to the approach of the Court of Session, the House of Lords treated 'all sums' clauses as being no different in principle from simple reservation of title clauses and consequently as equally effective. Their validity in Scots law is thus no longer in any doubt. It should be emphasised, however, that in *Armour* the additional provisions referred to above were not in issue but rather a pure all sums clause. Questions may thus still arise on certain terms in reservation of title clauses and it would be rash to assume that all such terms are valid, especially those purporting to create trusts[14].

The Act also deals with situations which can arise in international trade[15]. It appears that the statutory provisions refer to practices which evolved when communications were difficult and protracted and before bankers' confirmed credits had been developed[16]. The practices were designed to give protection against default or insolvency by the buyer abroad. That protection is now usually given by bankers' commercial credits. Firstly, when goods are shipped and by a bill of lading are deliverable to the order of the seller or his agent, the seller is prima facie deemed to have reserved the right of disposal[17]. The effect of this device is that the seller's agent controls disposal of the goods and the bill of lading will not normally be transferred unless against payment[18]. This is thus an example of reservation of title by action by the seller. The same applies to the second situation which is provided for. Where the seller of goods draws on the buyer for the price and transmits the bill of exchange and the bill of lading to the buyer together to secure acceptance of payment of the bill of exchange, the buyer is bound to return the bill of lading if he does not honour the bill of exchange, and if he wrongfully retains the bill of lading, the property in the goods does not pass to him[19]. In some situations covered by this provision the buyer may still have a power of disposal sufficient to give good title to an innocent third party[20].

1 Sale of Goods Act 1979 (c 54), s 19(1). See generally D L Carey Miller *Corporeal Moveables in Scots Law* (1991) pp 275–298. See also RIGHTS IN SECURITY, vol 20, paras 29–33.

2 *Cowan v Spence* (1824) 3 S 42 (NE 28) appears to be the classic case.

3 Such a clause was accepted as valid without any particular comment by the House of Lords in *Michelin Tyre Co Ltd v Macfarlane (Glasgow) Ltd* 1917 2 SLT 205, HL.

4 *Aluminium Industrie Vaasen BV v Romalpa Aluminium Ltd* [1976] 2 All ER 552, [1976] 1 WLR 676, CA.

5 The difficulties in effectively creating a trust in these circumstances under Scots law are well illustrated by *Clark Taylor & Co Ltd v Quality Site Development (Edinburgh) Ltd* 1981 SC 111, 1981 SLT 308, where it was held that the purported trust had not been validly constituted.

6 *Archivent Sales and Development Ltd v Strathclyde Regional Council* 1985 SLT 154, OH. (This case also raises issues under the Sale of Goods Act 1979, s 25, discussed at para 682 below). See also *Zahnrad Fabrik Passau GmbH v Terex Ltd* 1986 SLT 84 at 88, OH.

7 This is well illustrated by *Glen v Gilbey Vintners Ltd* 1986 SLT 553, OH, where a contract contained one provision with a reservation of title until the price was paid and also an 'all sums' clause. These provisions were held to be separable and the former was considered valid while the latter was not.

8 *Emerald Stainless Steel Ltd v South Side Distribution Ltd* 1983 SLT 162, OH; *Deutz Engines Ltd v Terex Ltd* 1984 SLT 273, OH. See also the opinions in the Outer House and the Inner House in *Armour v Thyssen Edelstanhlwerke AG* 1986 SLT 452, OH; 1989 SCLR 26, 1989 SLT 182 (revsd 1991 SCLR 139, 1990 SLT 891, HL). These cases led to academic debate: see the authorities cited in vol 20, para 842, note 7.

9 *Armour v Thyssen Edelstahlwerke AG* 1991 SCLR 139, 1990 SLT 891, HL.

10 See para 628 above.

11 *Armour v Thyssen Edelstahlwerke AG* 1991 SCLR 139 at 143, 1990 SLT 891 at 895, HL, per Lord Keith of Kinkel.

12 1991 SCLR 139 at 143, 144, 1990 SLT 891 at 895, HL, per Lord Keith of Kinkel and Lord Jauncey of Tullichettle.

13 See para 637 below.

14 In *Armour v Thyssen Edelstahlwerke AG* 1991 SCLR 139, 1990 SLT 891, HL, there is no discussion of the issues on the creation of a trust mentioned in note 5 above, and *Clark Taylor & Co Ltd v Quality Site Development (Edinburgh) Ltd* 1981 SC 111, 1981 SLT 308, is not overruled. See also *Tay Valley Joinery Ltd v CF Financial Services Ltd* 1987 SLT 207. There is a full discussion of reservation of title clauses including drafting hints in W W McBryde *The Law of Contract in Scotland* (1987) pp 289–296. This account must now be read in the light of *Armour* and the above discussion of the current law. For a critical discussion of *Armour*, see A Clark 'All Sums Retention of Title' 1991 SLT (News) 155.

15 These provisions have not been covered in detail. There do not appear to be any Scottish authorities on them and they interact with the law on eg c i f contracts and f o b contracts, bills of lading, and bills of exchange. For an interesting discussion, see R Goode *Commercial Law* (1985) pp 190–192, 587–589, 592, 593. For a full account of the law with detailed citation of English authorities, see J P Benjamin *Sale of Goods* (4th edn, 1992) paras 5-105–5-112.
16 J J Gow *The Mercantile and Industrial Law of Scotland* (1964) p 134.
17 Sale of Goods Act 1979, s 19(2).
18 Ultimately everything turns on the intention of the parties and the presumption of ibid, s 19(2) can be overcome.
19 Ibid, s 19(3).
20 This can arise under ibid, s 25. See para 682 below. See also *Cahn v Pocketts Bristol Channel Steam Packet Co* [1899] 1 QB 643, CA.

639. The passing of risk. Risk is not defined in the Sale of Goods Act 1979. Essentially the passing of risk is a matter of who bears the loss resulting from the accidental damage to, deterioration or destruction of the goods[1]. At common law in Scotland, apparently following Roman law, risk passed to the buyer on the conclusion of the contract of sale and was thus separated from property which passed on delivery[2]. The Inner House has had occasion to comment on the common law in this matter. In one case it was held that on a contract of barter, risk passed on completion of a perfected contract[3]. Similarly, it has been held that risk passes on the completion of missives for the sale of heritable property[4]. In both situations the pre-1893 law of sale of moveables was referred to by analogy. In contrast, under the Sale of Goods Act 1979 risk prima facie follows property. Indeed, many of the disputes on the passing of property which have found their way into the reported cases have arisen because what was really at stake between the parties was the passing of risk. The Latin maxim which expresses the current rule is *res perit suo domino*, risk falls on the owner. The Act provides that goods remain at the seller's risk until the transfer of property to the buyer. On the transfer of property, the goods are on the buyer's risk whether there has been delivery or not (subject to contrary agreement)[5]. The consequence of goods being at the buyer's risk is that he must pay the price even although he did not have possession, if the goods are lost, destroyed or damaged.

It follows from the linking of the passing of property and risk that risk cannot generally pass in the case of unascertained goods. This is a result of the peremptory provision making ascertainment a necessary precondition of the passing of property[6]. This affects so-called quasi-specific goods (that is, goods supplied from an ascertained bulk) as well as goods supplied from a bulk which is itself unascertained[7]. Interestingly, the same result was reached by a different route at common law in Scotland[8]. However, in one important case in England an interesting approach was taken. There a quantity of white spirit was sold out of a larger bulk in a particular storage tank. There was deterioration before severance from the bulk but after the buyers had accepted a delivery warrant from the sellers entitling them to obtain immediate delivery of the goods from the storage company. The Court of Appeal held that the risk had passed to the buyers irrespective of the position on the property[9]. The basis of this decision appears to be the question of who had the right of control over the goods in bulk[10]. Although not spelled out in the judgments, it appears that the court was accepting that on the facts there was an implied contract removing the effect of section 20 of the Act. One leading academic commentator has stated that this case has general application wherever the seller gives constructive delivery of quasi-specific goods and thereby passes control to the buyer, provided by doing so he meets his delivery obligations under the contract[11]. The question of risk in quasi-specific goods can of course always be dealt with by express contract. Any alteration of the law on the passing of property in bulk goods will, standing section 20, affect the passing of risk in such goods also[12].

Risk does not follow property where the position is regulated by contrary agreement[13]. This can be express agreement specifically stating the terms of the parties' contract. If parties state their agreement on passing of property, that will almost certainly determine the risk as well. If they state an agreement on risk but not on property that will determine risk and may also affect property[14]. They may also in terms determine and specify the passing both of risk and of property and consequently separate them[15]. It appears that a term affecting the passing of risk need not use that exact terminology provided that its effect as construed by the court is to apportion risk between the parties[15]. The passing of property and risk can be separated by implicit agreement[16] or by a reasonable and notorious custom of trade[17]. In the classic forms of export sales the position appears to be as follows. In an f o b contract, property and risk only pass on loading[18]. In a c i f contract property prima facie passes to the buyer on payment against the document but risk generally passes as from the time of shipment[19].

Risk under section 20 of the Act can also be shifted from its link with property in two situations of fault[20]. Firstly, where there has been delayed delivery the goods are at the risk of the party at fault for such delay as regards any loss which might not have occurred but for the fault[21]. Secondly, the breach by either party of duties of care and custody leads to liability on the party in breach[22]. In both cases only that part of the risk is shifted which relates to the relevant fault.

In what appears to be the only reported British case on section 20(2) a delay in delivery was held to be due to the fault of the buyer (his breach of contract) and the risk of the putrefaction of a quantity of apple juice thus fell on him[23]. It appears from that case that goods need not necessarily be ascertained for the sub-section to apply, provided they are goods assembled by the seller to fulfil his contract[24]. It was also held that the sub-section does not go so far as to place the onus on the party at fault to show that the loss did not occur. The party alleging loss must establish in all the circumstances that it can be attributed to the failure to accept (or to give) delivery[25]. It should be noted that this sub-section applies not to the passing of property but to delivery, that is the passing of possession.

In contrast to section 20(2) which creates a definite statutory rule, section 20(3) merely preserves the common law of care and custody[26] with its appropriate liabilities for a custodier when either seller or buyer acts as such in respect of goods in which he has no property rights. This effectively displaces the rules on risk. The law applicable is the normal common law. Thus in one case, the sellers of a pony had custody of it for a few days. During that time the pony was injured. The sellers were held liable as gratuitous bailees in England even if property had passed to the buyer. As such they had to show that they had taken the care of a reasonably prudent owner in respect of his own property[27]. It appears that the duties of a gratuitous custodian at common law in Scotland are virtally identical[28]. In a Scottish case, a boat was purchased but after property had passed to the buyer it remained in the seller's possession. During that time he sailed it without the buyer's permission. It was held that he did so at his own risk and in breach of his duty as custodier. He was thus liable for damage sustained on the trip[29]

For a full picture of the practical impact of the law commercially, brief mention should be made of three related areas[30]. Firstly, a party with the risk possesses an insurable interest in the goods whether or not he has the property in them[31]. Secondly, the interaction between the rules on risk with those of frustration of contract especially as the latter are set out in the Sale of Goods Act 1979 should be noted[32]. Thirdly there are specific rules in the Act on risk in relation to transit. These are contained in the provisions on delivery[33].

1 A more formal definition is provided in J J Gow *The Mercantile and Industrial Law of Scotland* (1964) p 136.

2 *Hansen v Craig and Rose* (1859) 21 D 432. This common law rule only applied to specific goods. It did not apply if the goods were unascertained: *Anderson and Crompton v Walls & Co* (1870) 9 M 122.
3 *Widenmeyer v Burn Stewart & Co Ltd* 1967 SC 85, 1967 SLT 129.
4 *Sloans Dairies Ltd v Glasgow Corpn* 1977 SC 223, 1979 SLT 17.
5 Sale of Goods Act 1979 (c 54), s 20.
6 See para 627 above.
7 See eg *Healy v Howlett & Sons* [1917] 1 KB 337.
8 *Anderson and Crompton v Walls & Co* (1870) 9 M 122.
9 *Sterns v Vickers* [1923] 1 KB 78, CA.
10 [1923] 1 KB 78 at 83, CA, per Strutton L]. In *Comptoir d'Achat v Luis de Ridder* [1949] 1 All ER 269 at 273, HL, Lord Porter alludes to *Sterns v Vickers* [1923] 1 KB 78, CA, in wide terms as if the case was based on the buyer's interest in an undivided part of a bulk of goods. It appears that the decision has a narrower basis which is recognised more clearly by Lord Normand in *Comptoir d'Achat* at 281, where he alludes to situations where the buyer has an immediate right to delivery of part of the bulk under a delivery warrant.
11 R Goode *Commercial Law* (1985) pp 201, 202. J P Benjamin *Sale of Goods* (4th edn, 1992) paras 6-004, 6-005, takes a more cautious line describing *Sterns v Vickers* [1923] 1 KB 78, CA, as depending on its special facts.
12 See para 627 above.
13 Sale of Goods Act 1979, s 20(1).
14 *Re Anchor Line (Henderson Bros) Ltd* [1937] Ch 1, [1937] 2 All ER 823.
15 *Horn v Minister of Food* [1948] 2 All ER 1036.
16 *Sterns v Vickers* [1923] 1 KB 78, CA.
17 *Bevington and Morris v Dale & Co Ltd* (1902) 7 Com Cas 112.
18 *Cunningham v Munro* (1922) 28 Comm Cas 42; *Goode* pp 587–589.
19 *Goode* pp 587–589. In *Pommer and Thomsen v Mowat* (1906) 14 SLT 373, OH (a c i f case) it is stated that the risk of extraordinary unusual deterioration remains on the seller if the buyer cannot inspect until arrival, even although property passed earlier on transfer of the documents. However, the case is really more concerned with the buyer's right of rejection of the goods.
20 'Fault' means wrongful act or default: Sale of Goods Act 1979, s 61(4).
21 Ibid, s 20(2).
22 Ibid, s 20(3).
23 *Demby Hamilton & Co Ltd v Barden* [1949] 1 All ER 435.
24 [1949] 1 All ER 435 at 437, per Sellars J.
25 [1949] 1 All ER 435 at 437, per Sellars J. It is arguable that the exact wording of the Sale of Goods Act 1979, s 20(2), could be read as placing an onus on the party at fault.
26 In England bailment. For an account of the common law, see W M Gloag and R C Henderson *Introduction to the Law of Scotland* (9th edn, 1987 by A B Wilkinson and W A Wilson) para 28.12. See also DEPOSIT, vol 8, para 13.
27 *Wiehe v Dennis Bros* (1913) 29 TLR 250.
28 *Copland v Brogan* 1916 SC 277, 1916 1 SLT 13: Bell *Principles* s 212.
29 *Knight v Wilson* 1949 SLT (Sh Ct) 26.
30 See the helpful integrated discussion in *Goode* pp 193–217.
31 *Anderson v Morice* (1876) 1 App Cas 713 at 724, HL. See INSURANCE, vol 13, para 850.
32 Sale of Goods Act 1979, ss 6, 7. See SALE AND EXCHANGE, vol 20, para 845.
33 Ibid, ss 31, 32. See vol 20, paras 846, 861.

(4) CORPOREAL HERITABLE PROPERTY

640. Introduction. Almost all land in Scotland is held on feudal tenure, so that by the transfer of ownership (*dominium*) of land is meant the transfer either of the *dominium utile* (the interest of the vassal) or of the *dominium directum* (the interest of the superior)[1]. Subject to minor qualifications the same rules apply in both cases. In feudal terms transfer denotes substitution, as distinct from subinfeudation, the transferee taking the place in the feudal chain vacated by the transferor.

Just as at common law delivery (*traditio*) was required for the transfer of corporeal moveables[2], so in feudal law delivery was required also for the transfer of land[3]; and since actual delivery was obviously impossible, a number of symbols, mandatory in use, were developed, for example earth and stone for land, hasp and staple for houses within burghs, and for the separate tenements[4] of salmon fishings and mills, respectively net and coble and clap and happer. The formal ceremony of delivery, which took place on the land itself, was known as the giving of sasine and was recorded in a notarial deed called an instrument of sasine which, after 1617, required to be registered in the Register of Sasines. When feudalism was in full vigour, and indeed for a long time thereafter, the transfer of land was a process of considerable complexity, so much so that, as the pages of Morison's Dictionary amply testify, parties embarking on transfer had not always completed all the formalities even after the lapse of many years. The modern law was introduced in a series of statutes passed between 1845 and 1874 and, at least as compared to the system which it replaced, is simple and coherent. Under the modern law the transfer of ownership requires the execution and delivery by the transferor to the transferee of a written deed of conveyance, known as a disposition, followed by the registration of the disposition in the Register of Sasines or Land Register[5]. In the case of sale, transfer is preceded by a contract between the parties, usually taking the form of missives of sale, so that there are three identifiable stages in the transfer process, namely (1) conclusion of missives, (2) execution and delivery of the disposition, and (3) registration of the disposition. These are considered more fully below. Ownership remains with the transferor until completion of registration, the third and final stage, when it passes to the transferee.

A number of features of the pre-1845 method of transfer remain competent even today although they have long ceased to be used[6]. More importantly, the current method of transfer is defined entirely by reference to the old law, so that registration of the disposition is the equivalent both of feudal entry with the superior by charter of confirmation[7] and of registration of an instrument of sasine[8], and the deemed registration of the instrument of sasine is itself the equivalent of the giving of sasine by symbolical delivery[9].

1 For feudalism, see paras 41 ff above.
2 See paras 619 ff above.
3 In fact the requirement of delivery is probably pre-feudal. In the Romanised feudalism character-istic of Scotland it was seen as the equivalent of the Roman law *traditio*: see Erskine *Institute* II,1,19.
4 For separate tenements, see paras 207 ff above.
5 Strictly, what is registered in the Land Register is not the disposition but the title which the disposition evidences, but the usage 'registration of the disposition' is convenient and is used in this work.
6 Titles to Land Consolidation (Scotland) Act 1868 (c 101), s 163. But charters by progress other than novodamus were abolished by the Conveyancing (Scotland) Act 1874 (c 94), s 4(1) (amended by the Succession (Scotland) Act 1964 (c 41), 34(2), Sch 3). On 22 August 1979, the ceremony of symbolical delivery was conducted in respect of a grant of land by the North of Scotland Hydro Board to Banff and Buchan District Council. See (1979) 24 JLSS 461.
7 Conveyancing (Scotland) Act 1874, s 4(2).
8 Titles to Land Consolidation (Scotland) Act 1868, s 15.
9 Infeftment Act 1845 (c 35), s 1.

641. Stage (1): missives of sale. The first stage in the transfer of land by sale is the conclusion of a contract between buyer and seller, in most cases in the form of an exchange of letters between the parties or their solicitors known as 'missives of sale'[1]. The individual letters must be subscribed by or on behalf of the sender[2], and in practice the signature is often witnessed. Usually the first letter in a set of missives is the offer to purchase[3]. At one time an extremely brief document, in recent years this has greatly increased in length as solicitors have sought to protect their clients against a growing number of hazards, real or imaginary. Probably offers to purchase have doubled in length in the past ten years alone, with solicitors quick to adopt new clauses coined by their competitors[4]. The process shows no sign of slowing down. In 1991, in an attempt to control the growth of offers and to hasten the conclusion of missives, the Law Society of Scotland produced a set of standard missive clauses, twenty eight in all, with the intention that they be incorporated into offers to purchase houses[5], but in practice they were little used and the experiment has now been abandoned[6]. Among the clauses usually found in offers to purchase are those requiring: redemption of feuduty; evidence that the roads and sewers are maintained by the local authority; that any statutory notices issued by the local authority prior to the date of entry will be the responsibility of the seller; that there are no unusual or unduly onerous real conditions; evidence that planning permission and building consent have been obtained for alterations; that liability for maintenance of parts common to the subjects of sale and other subjects is equitably shared; that risk will not pass until the date of entry; that there will be produced satisfactory evidence of title; that there are no subsisting occupancy rights under the Matrimonial Homes (Family Protection) (Scotland) Act 1981 (c 59); that the central heating system is in good working order; that the remedy of the *actio quanti minoris* will be available to the buyer; and that the missives of sale will remain in force for two years beyond delivery of the disposition. In the case of offers to purchase commercial property, the clauses are slightly different but no less numerous.

Occasionally land is sold by auction (roup) in which case a standard-form contract, known as articles of roup, is prepared in advance and signed in probative form by the seller. At the conclusion of the auction the successful bidder accedes to the contract, the terms of which are not usually negotiable, by signing a minute of enactment and preference which is attached to the articles[7].

In general, contracts for the sale of land prescribe after twenty years[8], but many of their provisions may cease to be enforceable within a few weeks, following delivery[9] of the disposition, because of the rule of the law of evidence that the contract is superseded by the disposition[10]. In practice attempts are usually made to avoid this rule by use of a non-supersession clause, which is to say, a clause providing that the contract shall remain in force for a specified period notwithstanding the delivery of the disposition. On the termination of this period the whole contract then ceases to be enforceable[11]. It remains an open question whether a non-supersession clause requires to be repeated in the disposition itself[12], but recent case law has in any event cast doubt on the effectiveness of such clauses[13]. In the absence of an effective non-supersession clause only those provisions of the contract which are 'collateral' to the transfer of land survive delivery of the disposition, but the meaning of 'collateral' in this context is uncertain and not all the decisions on the subject can be reconciled[14].

1　For a fuller discussion of missives of sale, see CONVEYANCING, vol 6, paras 552 ff, and G L Gretton and K G C Reid *Conveyancing* (1993) chs 2, 3.
2　Requirements of Writing (Scotland) Act 1995 (c 7), ss 1(2)(a)(i), 2.
3　Occasionally the first letter comes from the seller in the form of an offer to sell.
4　The observation of Walter Ross in connection with the *tenendas* clause in charters is brought to mind. He observed that 'The moment a new term was invented by any body, and known, the ordinary list became enriched by it; in so much, indeed, that in many charters we find repetitions of the same thing, under different words; which proves that conveyancers were more attentive to the practice of each other, than to the sense of what they themselves were doing': W Ross *Lectures on the History and Practice of the Law of Conveyancing and Legal Diligence* (2nd edn, 1822) II, p 165.
5　The clauses were incorporated into a Deed of Declaration made by the Law Society of Scotland on 31 July 1991 and registered in the Books of Council and Session on 9 August 1991.
6　See (1995) 40 JLSS 326.
7　See further CONVEYANCING, vol 6, paras 577, 578.
8　The quinquennial prescription is excluded by the Prescription and Limitation (Scotland) Act 1973 (c 52), s 6, Sch 1, para 2(e) in the case of obligations relating to land. But while the principal obligations of missives, such as the obligation to deliver a disposition, fall within para 2(e), it is not clear that certain collateral obligations will do so. See *Barratt Scotland Ltd v Keith* 1993 SCLR 120, 1994 SLT 1343; *Stewart's Executors v Stewart* 1993 SLT 440, OH (revsd, on a different point, 1993 SCLR 641, 1994 SLT 466); *Wright v Frame* 1992 GWD 8-447, Sh Ct. In such cases the five-year prescription will apply.
9　But see Lord Watson's erroneous adoption of the English law doctrine, that a deed becomes effective on execution, in the formulation of the prior communings rule which is most frequently

quoted — 'According to the law of Scotland, the execution of a formal conveyance, even when it expressly bears to be in implement of a previous contract, supersedes that contract *in toto*, and the conveyance thenceforth becomes the sole measure of the rights and liabilities of the contracting parties': *Lee v Alexander* (1883) 10 R (HL) 91 at 96.

10 On the background to this rule see K G C Reid 'Prior Communings and Conveyancing Practice' (1981) 26 JLSS 414. See also CONVEYANCING, vol 6, para 566. For an examination of the recent case law, see *Gretton and Reid* ch 19. It is sometimes said, on the authority of *Young v M'Kellar Ltd* 1909 SC 1340, 1909 2 SLT 196, that the rule does not apply to articles of roup.

11 Even those parts which, but for the non-supersession clause, would survive as 'collateral' obligations: see *Pena v Ray* 1987 SLT 609, OH; *Strathclyde University (Properties) Ltd v Fleeting Organisation Ltd* 1992 GWD 14-822, Sh Ct; *Ferguson v McIntyre* 1993 SLT 1269, OH.

12 Cf *Finlayson v McRobb* 1987 SLT (Sh Ct) 150 and *Wood v Edwards* 1988 SLT (Sh Ct) 17 with *Fetherston v McDonald (No 2)* 1988 SLT (Sh Ct) 39 and *Jamieson v Stewart* 1989 SLT (Sh Ct) 13. For an example of such a clause, see the disposition set out in para 642 below.

13 *Greaves v Abercromby* 1989 SCLR 11, Sh Ct; *Porch v MacLeod* 1992 SLT 661, OH; *Parker v O'Brien* 1992 SLT (Sh Ct) 31. But cf *Glazik v Iyer* 1996 SCLR 270, Sh Ct.

14 The meaning of 'collateral' is considered in the following cases: *Winston v Patrick* 1980 SC 246, 1981 SLT 41; *Central Govan Housing Association Ltd v R Maguire Cook & Co* 1988 SLT 386, OH; *Jones v Heenan* 1988 SLT (Sh Ct) 53; *Jamieson v Stewart* 1989 SLT (Sh Ct) 13; *Greaves v Abercromby* 1989 SCLR 11, Sh Ct; *Taylor v McLeod* 1989 SCLR 531, 1990 SLT 194, OH; *Bourton v Claydon* 1990 SLT (Sh Ct) 7; *Porch v MacLeod* 1992 SLT 661, OH; *Parker v O'Brien* 1992 SLT (Sh Ct) 31; *King v Gebbie* 1993 SLT 512, OH; *Meek v Bell* 1993 GWD 20-1238, OH; *Rae v Middleton* 1995 SLT (Sh Ct) 60; *Callander v Midlothian District Council* 1996 GWD 23-1340, OH. On the whole, recent cases appear to be moving away from the restrictive approach of the Second Division in *Winston v Patrick*, and it may now be the law that any obligation which is capable of running in the future is collateral for the purposes of the prior communings rule.

642. Stage (2): execution and delivery of a disposition. Although a number of its clauses are the subject of statutory regulation, there is no statutory form of disposition[1]. The following is a typical disposition of a *dominium utile*[2]:

I, ADAM JAMES BENSON, residing at Forty four Madras Road, Aberdeen, heritable proprietor of the subjects hereinafter disponed, IN CONSIDERATION of the price of two hundred thousand pounds (£200,000) paid to me by Hamish Ranald Johnston and Clare Janet Baxter or Johnston, residing at Thirty two Fairlie Drive, Dundee, of which sum I hereby acknowledge receipt, HAVE SOLD and DO HEREBY DISPONE to the said Hamish Ranald Johnston and Clare Janet Baxter or Johnston equally between them ALL and WHOLE that detached dwellinghouse and garden ground known as Number Forty four Madras Road, Aberdeen, being the subjects in the County of Aberdeen described in Feu Contract between Andrew Dalrymple Balfour and the Trustees for the firm of Morrison and Smith dated fourteenth and eighteenth and recorded in the Division of the General Register of Sasines for the County of Aberdeen twenty fourth all February Nineteen hundred and two: TOGETHER WITH (One) the garage and other outbuildings erected thereon, (Two) the fittings and fixtures, (Three) the parts and pertinents, and (Four) my whole right, title and interest, present and future: BUT ALWAYS WITH AND UNDER, so far as valid, subsisting and applicable, the real burdens and conditions specified in (First) the said Feu Contract between Andrew Dalrymple Balfour and the Trustees for the firm of Morrison and Smith dated and recorded as aforesaid, and (Second) Feu Disposition by William Henry Smith in favour of Robert William Alexander dated fourth and recorded in the said Division of the General Register of Sasines tenth both October Nineteen hundred and six: WITH ENTRY and actual occupation as at First February Nineteen hundred and ninety six; And I grant warrandice; And the missives of sale which I have concluded with the said Hamish Ranald Johnston and Clare Janet Baxter or Johnston and which are constituted by letters dated third, fourth, sixth and ninth January Nineteen hundred and ninety six will form a continuing and enforceable contract notwithstanding the delivery of these presents except insofar as fully implemented thereby, but the said missives shall cease to be enforceable after a period of two years from the date of entry hereunder except insofar as they are founded on in any court proceedings which have commenced within the said period: IN WITNESS WHEREOF these presents are subscribed at Aberdeen on Twenty ninth January Nineteen hundred and ninety six in the presence of Fiona Allison Macdonald, Ninety four Bon-Accord Square, Aberdeen.

[*signature of transferor and witness*]

REGISTER on behalf of the within named Hamish Ranald Johnston and Clare Janet Baxter or Johnston in the Register of the County of Aberdeen.

[*signature of transferees' solicitors*]

Solicitors, Aberdeen
Agents

This is the form used for land registered in the Register of Sasines. For land which has been registered in the Land Register under the system of registration of title the disposition is shorter and simpler[3]. Dispositions require to be executed in accordance with section 3 of the Requirements of Writing (Scotland) Act 1995[4], which in most cases means that a witness is needed[5].

A disposition serves a number of different functions. Primarily, of course, it is a conveyance of the land described in the deed, the words 'do hereby dispone' indicating and at the same time giving effect to the granter's intention to transfer[6]. But in virtue of clauses which were formerly expressed but since 1979 have been implied by statute[7], a disposition is also an assignation of certain ancillary rights held by the transferor, namely the writs and, where the land is tenanted, the rents also. The meaning of the implied assignation of writs[8] is obscure. It places the transferor under certain obligations as to the title deeds, including the obligation to deliver all titles relating exclusively to the land conveyed[9]; and it also assigns to the transferee some, although not all, of the contractual rights conferred by the granters of previous deeds forming part of the title[10]. In the days of antique conveyancing this second aspect of the clause was of considerable importance, but today it is probably confined to an assignation of prior grants of warrandice[11] and if the parties wish to transfer other contractual rights, an express assignation is required, for which a statutory form is given in the Conveyancing (Scotland) Act 1874[12]. Under registration of title the first aspect of the assignation of writs clause (the obligation to deliver title deeds) ceases to have effect once the disposition is registered in the Land Register[13], presumably on the basis that successful registration removes the need to rely on prior titles[14], but the second aspect (the assignation of warrandice) is apparently unaffected[15].

As well as operating as a conveyance of the land, and of the writs and rents, a disposition also contains a number of clauses which are purely contractual in effect[16]. Thus, as can be seen from the style above, the transferor obliges himself to give vacant possession on a specified date, he guarantees the title to the land and also to the writs and rents through his grant of warrandice[17], and he undertakes to relieve the transferee of all feuduties, ground annuals, annuities and public, parochial and local burdens exigible prior to the date of entry[18]. The non-supersession clause, which provides that the missives of sale shall remain in force for a specified period, is also contractual in effect.

The contractual provisions in the disposition become effective as soon as delivery of the disposition is accepted by the transferee[19], which in the case of sale is usually at 'settlement' (completion) of the transaction on the date of entry, at which time the disposition is exchanged for the purchase price. But the part of the deed which conveys the land does not take effect until the disposition is registered in the

Register of Sasines or Land Register, while the assignations of writs and rents require the further step of intimation to the debtor in the obligation[20].

1 For more detailed consideration of some of the issues discussed here, see CONVEYANCING, vol 6, paras 579 ff, and G L Gretton and K G C Reid *Conveyancing* (1993) ch 9.
2 A disposition of the *dominium directum* is identical save that, for Sasine titles, feu rights are excluded from the grant of warrandice. As with the *dominium utile* what is conveyed is the land itself although, as Stair observed (*Institutions* II,4,1), 'sometimes, through the ignorance of writers, infeftments bear expressly to be "of superiority" '.
3 See *Registration of Title Practice Book* (1981) para G.3.22.
4 Or set up under s 4 of the Requirements of Writing (Scotland) Act 1995 (c 7). By s 6 a disposition cannot be registered unless it falls within s 3 or s 4.
5 But there are special rules for companies and other bodies corporate in ibid, s 7(7), Sch 2.
6 For the requirement of intention to transfer, see paras 613, 614, above. It is provided in the Conveyancing (Scotland) Act 1874 (c 94), s 27, that the word 'dispone' is not necessary in a disposition provided that the deed contains some 'other word or words importing conveyance or transference, or present intention to convey'; but in practice 'dispone' is always used.
7 Land Registration (Scotland) Act 1979 (c 33), s 16.
8 Ibid, s 16(1).
9 This of course is a contractual obligation and not an assignation.
10 The relevant words in the Land Registration (Scotland) Act 1979, s 16(1), are 'import an assignation to the grantee of the title deeds and searches and all deeds not duly recorded'.
11 *Stair* II,3,46. See para 712 below.
12 Conveyancing (Scotland) Act 1874, s 50, Sch M. In practice express assignations are almost unknown.
13 Land Registration (Scotland) Act 1979, s 3(5).
14 For this reason ibid, s 3(5), does not apply where indemnity has been excluded. But since under s 9 of the Act the Keeper can rectify the Register even where indemnity has not been excluded, the provision is in some respects a surprising one.
15 This is because ibid, s 3(5), refers not to 'assignations' but only to 'obligations to assign'. The assignation of warrandice is a present assignation.
16 Hence the prior communings rule, by which a later contract (the disposition) supersedes an earlier one (the missives of sale).
17 For the meaning of the words 'I grant warrandice', see the Titles to Land Consolidation (Scotland) Act 1868 (c 101), s 8. For warrandice generally, see paras 701 ff below.
18 Ie the 'obligation of relief' clause, formerly express but now implied by the Land Registration (Scotland) Act 1979, s 16(3)(b).
19 Eg *Hunter v Boog* (1834) 13 S 205.
20 Unless there is prior intimation by some other method, intimation is effected by registration of the disposition in the Register of Sasines or Land Register. See para 656 below.

643. Stage (3): registration of the disposition. The final stage in the transfer of ownership is registration of the disposition[1]. In areas which are operational for registration of title, that is the Counties of Renfrew[2], Dumbarton[3], Lanark[4], Barony and Regality of Glasgow[5], Clackmannan[6], Stirling, West Lothian, Fife, Aberdeen and Kincardine[7], registration is in the Land Register provided either that the land conveyed is already registered there[8] or, if it is not, that the disposition is granted for valuable consideration or in consideration of marriage[9]. Otherwise, and notwithstanding that the area is operational for registration of title, registration is in the Register of Sasines[10]. For land situated in other parts of Scotland registration in all cases is in the Register of Sasines. Any stamp duty due on the transaction must be paid prior to registration[11]. A fee, payable in advance, is charged for both Registers[12]. At the Register itself the disposition is copied and returned, and in the case of the Land Register the transferee is issued with an official copy of the title sheet known as a land certificate[13].

Dispositions presented for registration in the Register of Sasines must contain a warrant of registration signed by or on behalf of the transferee[14], and the warrant is regarded as a successor of the instrument of sasine which was in use prior to 1858[15].

There is no reason to suppose that a warrant of registration is not also required for registration in the Land Register, but the requirement is waived in practice[16] and in its place a statutory application form is completed by the transferee or his agent[17].

The effect of registration, assuming the disposition itself to be valid, is to confer ownership on the transferee[18]. Accordingly, at the precise moment of registration, transferor and transferee are respectively divested of and invested in the land. In feudal terms registration amounts to entry with the superior and the transferee is infeft as his vassal[19].

1 In the Land Register what is registered, strictly, is not the disposition itself but the transferee's title to the *dominium utile* or *dominium directum*. But the usage 'registration of the disposition' is convenient.
2 Land Registration (Scotland) Act 1979 (Commencement No 1) Order 1980, SI 1980/1412.
3 Land Registration (Scotland) Act 1979 (Commencement No 2) Order 1982, SI 1982/520.
4 Land Registration (Scotland) Act 1979 (Commencement No 3) Order 1983, SI 1983/745.
5 Land Registration (Scotland) Act 1979 (Commencement No 4) Order 1985, SI 1985/501.
6 Land Registration (Scotland) Act 1979 (Commencement No 5) Order 1992, SI 1992/815.
7 Land Registration (Scotland) Act 1979 (Commencement) Orders: (No 6) 1992, SI 1992/2060; (No 7) 1993, SI 1993/922; (No 8) 1994, SI 1994/2588 and (No 9) 1995, SI 1995/2547. The projected timetable for future operational areas is set out at 1996 SLT (News) 220.
8 Land Registration (Scotland) Act 1979 (c 33), s 2(4)(a).
9 Ibid, s 2(1)(a)(ii), (iii).
10 Ie unless the Keeper accepts an application under ibid, s 2(1)(b), for voluntary registration in the Land Register.
11 See the Stamp Act 1891 (c 39), s 17, which makes it a criminal offence for an official to register an unstamped deed. For stamp duty on dispositions, see CONVEYANCING, vol 6, para 447.
12 Land Registers (Scotland) Act 1995 (c 14), s 1. For the fees, see the Fees in the Registers of Scotland Order 1995, SI 1995/1945.
13 See further CONVEYANCING, vol 6, paras 452, 453 (Register of Sasines) and paras 701 ff (Land Register).
14 Titles to Land Consolidation (Scotland) Act 1868 (c 101), s 141. There is a statutory form of warrant of registration in the Conveyancing (Scotland) Act 1924 (c 27), Sch F.
15 Titles to Land Consolidation (Scotland) Act 1868, s 15.
16 *Registration of Title Practice Book* (1981) para A.1.06(iv). Whether, in view of the clear terms of the legislation, this waiver is wise may be open to question: see K G C Reid 'A Non Domino Conveyances and the Land Register' 1991 JR 79 at 89 ff.
17 There are three forms (forms 1–3) for use in different situations. See the Land Registration (Scotland) Rules 1980, SI 1980/1413, r 9, Sch A (amended by SI 1988/1143).
18 Registration Act 1617 (c 16), as interpreted by *Young v Leith* (1847) 9 D 932 (Register of Sasines); Land Registration (Scotland) Act 1979, s 3(1)(a), (4)(a) (Land Register).
19 Conveyancing (Scotland) Act 1874 (c 94), s 4(2); Land Registration (Scotland) Act 1979, s 3(4)(b).

644. Evaluation of the three stages of transfer. The effect of the first and of the last stages in the transfer process may easily be described. On completion of the first stage (missives) the transferee has a personal, contractual right against the transferor to acquire ownership against payment of the price; and on completion of the final stage (registration) he acquires the real right of ownership. But the effect of the intermediate stage (delivery of the disposition) has sometimes been disputed. In conveyancing practice this is the moment at which the price is paid; and unless a preferential right is acquired in exchange, the transferee is at risk of the transferor becoming insolvent in the short period before the disposition can be registered[1]. Hence it has sometimes been argued that on delivery of the disposition the transferee acquires a 'personal' or 'inchoate' right of ownership which, for reasons never fully explained, will give the transferee a preference in the transferor's insolvency[2]. This argument is contrary both to principle[3] and to long-settled authority[4]. Nonetheless it has been kept alive in recent years by some unguarded obiter dicta[5], and the whole issue was recently revived and re-argued in the landmark case of *Sharp v Thomson*[6].

The weaknesses of an argument of this kind are readily exposed. Once it is accepted that ownership does not pass until registration, any kind of prior investiture or divestiture of the parties seems to be excluded[7]. For as the First Division recognised in *Sharp v Thomson*[8], the law of property in Scotland is unititular in character: there is only one title of ownership in any one thing at any one time. So if transferor A is owner, then, necessarily, transferee B is not. There is no point in the transaction when ownership is shared by both parties. Prior to registration, B's rights is *in personam* only; for he does not have a real right, and all rights which are not real are personal[9].

A feudal analysis leads to the same conclusion. In feudal law delivery *(traditio)* of land by the giving of sasine is required before *dominium* is transferred, and in the modern law the statutory equivalent of delivery of land is registration of the disposition[10]. The rule is *nulla sasina nulla terra*[11]; and until the registration there is no sasine and hence no divestiture.

In *Sharp v Thomson* the First Division upheld the view that until registration a transferee has a personal right and not a property right. An appeal was due to be heard by the House of Lords in November 1996, but it seems unlikely that the House will disturb the fundamental and long-settled principle reaffirmed by the Division and it may be that the appellants' arguments will largely turn on other matters.

The question remains, however, as to the precise effect of delivery of the disposition. Gloag and Irvine note that:

> 'Beyond the general statement that it constitutes a *jus ad rem* and not a *jus in re* and yet is more than a mere *jus actionis* it would be difficult to define it'[12].

Nonetheless an attempt at a definition must be made. It has been seen that a disposition contains a number of obligations of a contractual nature and one effect of delivery is to bring these obligations into operation. Moreover, in a practical sense the holder of a delivered disposition is in a much stronger position than one who holds merely under missives, for he has the means of becoming owner simply by registering the deed, and alternatively, and by statutory concession, he can dispone the land or grant a standard security over it provided that he deduces title[13]. But since the transferor remains owner the transferor can also grant those deeds and indeed other deeds, such as feu dispositions and leases, for which deduction of title is not available. Erskine summarised the position of the holder of a delivered disposition in these words:

> 'A charter or disposition which is not yet followed by seisin, creates in the disponee a right barely personal. It lays the granter, and his heirs, under an obligation to divest themselves agreeably to the tenor of the grant. But it has not the effect of transferring to the acquirer the feudal right of the lands'[14].

At the time when Erskine was writing, the giving of sasine involved a future act on the part of the transferor, and the disposition conferred on the transferee a right to obtain performance of that act. In the modern law there is deemed sasine by registration and so no future act by the transferor is required. Apart, therefore, from the purely contractual obligations referred to earlier, no further right against the transferor is conferred by delivery of the disposition; and nor, since the transferee's right is personal and not real, can there be a right in the land itself[15]. Rather, what is conferred by the disposition is, in Hohfeldian terms, a 'power'[16], which is to say a right neither against a person nor in a thing but simply a right for the transferee to procure himself infeft by registration of the deed.

It is sometimes said that on registration the personal right conferred by missives and the disposition is 'converted' into a real right[17], but this too is misleading. For the real right of ownership obtained on registration is not an improved version of an earlier personal right but rather is a different right entirely; and indeed, subject to the rule against prior communings, the unimplemented personal rights conferred by missives and the disposition continue to be enforceable by the transferee after acquiring ownership in precisely the same manner as before the disposition was registered.

1 In practice conveyancers have long been familiar with this risk and take steps to avoid it. See further
   K G C Reid 'Sharp v Thomson: Property Law Preserved' (1995) 1 SLPQ 53 at 56, 57.
2 I Doran 'Ownership on Registration' 1985 SLT (News) 165; R Rennie 'Dead on Delivery' 1994
   SLT (News) 183. A different but related argument is to say that the transferor holds the property on a
   constructive trust for the transferee. This second argument was rejected both in *Gibson v Hunter
   Home Designs Ltd* 1976 SC 23, 1976 SLT 94, and in *Sharp v Thomson* 1995 SCLR 683, 1995 SLT 837.
3 K G C Reid 'Ownership on Delivery' 1982 SLT (News) 149; K G C Reid 'Ownership on
   Registration' 1985 SLT (News) 280; G L Gretton 'Sharp Cases Make Good Law' 1994 SLT (News)
   313; K G C Reid '*Sharp v Thomson*: A Civilian Perspective' 1995 SLT (News) 75; N R Whitty
   '*Sharp v Thomson*: Identifying the Mischief' 1995 SLT (News) 79.
4 *Mitchell v Ferguson* (1781) Mor 10296, (1781) 3 Ross LC 120; *Young v Leith* (1844) 6 D 370; (1847) 9 D
   932, affd (1848) 2 Ross LC 103, HL.
5 Especially the remarks by Lord President Emslie in *Gibson v Hunter Home Designs Ltd* 1976 SC 23 at
   27, 1976 SLT 94 at 96. In *Sharp v Thomson* 1995 SCLR 683 at 699, 1995 SLT 837 at 848, Lord
   President Hope described these remarks as 'not, with great respect, entirely accurate'.
6 *Sharp v Thomson* 1994 SLT 1068, OH, affd 1995 SCLR 683, 1995 SLT 837.
7 *Young v Leith* (1847) 9 D 932 at 945, per Lord Fullerton. If indeed there was divestiture, even to some
   small extent, it would disturb the settled rule that a transferor can grant a second, competing
   disposition which, if registered first, defeats the earlier disposition. An example is the 'race to the
   register' between a transferee and the trustee in sequestration of the transferor, for which see
   para 648 below.
8 *Sharp v Thomson* 1995 SCLR 683 at 698, 1995 SLT 837 at 847, per Lord President Hope, following
   para 603 above.
9 'Scots law does not recognise a right which lies between the personal right on the one hand and the
   real right on the other': *Sharp v Thomson* 1995 SCLR 683 at 697, 1995 SLT 837 at 847, per Lord
   President Hope.
10 Infeftment Act 1845 (c 35), s 1; Titles to Land Consolidation (Scotland) Act 1868 (c 101), s 15.
11 Stair *Institutions* II,3,16.
12 W M Gloag and J M Irvine *Law of Rights in Security* (1897) p 33.
13 Conveyancing (Scotland) Act 1924 (c 27), s 3; Conveyancing and Feudal Reform (Scotland) Act
   1970 (c 35), s 12. For deduction of title, see para 645 below.
14 Erskine *Institute* II,3,48.
15 Because only a real right is a *jus in re*. See para 3 above.
16 See GENERAL LEGAL CONCEPTS, vol 11, especially paras 1083, 1087.
17 See eg CONVEYANCING, vol 6, para 452.

645. Uninfeft proprietors and deduction of title. In a strict sense there can be
no such thing as an 'uninfeft proprietor' of land, for infeftment signifies the
acquisition of a feudalised real right, and one who is uninfeft and has no real right
cannot be a 'proprietor'. But although loose, the expression is undeniably convenient and is widely used. In normal usage an 'uninfeft proprietor' is one whose
title to land is a delivered disposition or other conveyance which has not been
registered in the Register of Sasines or Land Register. In the analysis used above[1],
the transferee has reached the second but not yet the final stage in the transfer of
land. A person in this position is, in a loose sense, a 'proprietor' because he is the
grantee of a conveyance; and he is 'uninfeft' because registration, and hence
infeftment, has not taken place.

   The position of uninfeft proprietors in relation to land registered in the Land
Register is considered below. So far as land registered in the Register of Sasines is
concerned, uninfeft proprietors fall into two distinct classes, namely those holding
on a conveyance ('general conveyance'[2]) which cannot competently be registered
and those holding on a conveyance ('special conveyance') which can be, but which
has not been, so registered. A properly drawn disposition is always a special
conveyance in the sense meant here, the main examples of general conveyances
being conveyances by court decree, for example the confirmation of executors
awarded on death or the act and warrant in favour of a trustee in sequestration[3].
Assuming a conveyance to be registrable, it is usually registered within a few days of
its delivery, and so for ordinary dispositions the stage of uninfeft proprietor is simply
part of the process of becoming an infeft proprietor. If a conveyance is not
registrable it is possible to register in its place a special statutory deed called a notice

of title which 'deduces' the transferee's title through the unregistrable conveyance and procures the grantee infeft[4].

Instead of completing title by registration, whether of the conveyance itself or of a notice of title proceeding on the conveyance, an uninfeft proprietor is able to transfer the land provided that in the disposition he deduces his title through the conveyance in the manner required by statute[5]. Such a disposition is directly registrable by the grantee. But while one who is uninfeft and so admittedly does not own land is thus enabled to confer ownership of that land on someone else this is not, as might at first appear, an exception to the rule *nemo dat quod non habet* (no one can give that which he does not have)[6]. This is because even before the facility of deducing title was introduced by statute in 1924, an uninfeft proprietor was, on general principles of property law, free to assign such right in relation to the land as he had[7], namely the right (power) to become infeft[8], and the deduction of title procedure introduced in 1924 is merely a statutory shortcut for achieving the same end.

Registration of title offers a further refinement of the system introduced in 1924. Thus for land already registered in the Land Register all conveyances, including 'general' conveyances, are now directly registrable[9], while in a disposition of such land by an uninfeft proprietor there is no need to deduce title although the grantee must produce the unregistered conveyance or other link in title ('midcouple') in support of his own application for registration[10].

1 See para 644 above.
2 *Studd v Cook* (1883) 10 R (HL) 53 at 59, per Lord Watson.
3 For further discussion of these examples of involuntary transfer, see para 664 below.
4 Conveyancing (Scotland) Act 1924 (c 27), s 4(1), Sch B, Form 1. The notice of title supersedes an earlier deed, the notarial instrument, although notarial instruments remain competent. The notarial instrument was itself first introduced in 1858 as part of the conveyancing reforms of that year which included the replacement of the instrument of sasine by direct registration of conveyances. Since direct registration was not suitable for all conveyances, it was necessary to have some device for indirect registration. The instrument of sasine had been such a device and the notarial instrument was to some extent conceived as a replacement for the instrument of sasine. The current provisions on notarial instruments are contained in the Titles to Land Consolidation (Scotland) Act 1868 (c 101), especially ss 19, 23.
5 Conveyancing (Scotland) Act 1924, s 3, Sch A, Form 1. For a fuller discussion, see CONVEYANCING, vol 6, para 589, and G L Gretton and K G C Reid *Conveyancing* (1993) ch 22.
6 For the rule *nemo dat quod non habet* and the exceptions to it, see paras 669 ff below.
7 The deed was sometimes known as a disposition and assignation. Between 1858 and 1970 a special statutory facility existed whereby an uninfeft proprietor holding on a registrable conveyance could grant an assignation which was itself directly registrable: see the Titles to Land Consolidation (Scotland) Act 1868, s 22, and the Conveyancing (Scotland) Act 1924, s 7. This facility, latterly almost unused, was abolished by the Conveyancing and Feudal Reform (Scotland) Act 1970 (c 35), s 48, Sch 11, Pt II.
8 See para 644 above.
9 Land Registration (Scotland) Act 1979 (c 33), s 3(6).
10 Ibid, s 15(3).

646. Allodial land. Allodial (non-feudal) land is discussed elsewhere in this title[1]. The most important category of allodial land, udal land in Orkney and Shetland, was historically quite distinct from feudal land although there has been considerable assimilation of feudal ideas in the modern period[2]. The transfer of udal land requires neither registration nor indeed writing[3], although the modern practice is to have both and both will be mandatory once Orkney and Shetland become operational areas for the purposes of registration of title[4]. It is thought that other examples of allodial land, such as kirkyards, are in modern law transferred in the same way as feudal land.

1 See para 47 above.
2 See UDAL LAW, vol 24, para 307.
3 Stair *Institutions* II,3,11; Erskine *Institute* II,3,18.
4 Land Registration (Scotland) Act 1979 (c 33), s 3(3).

647. The estate transferred. The rights which attach to landownership are considered elsewhere in this title[1], but in summary an owner of land owns *a coelo usque ad centrum*, which is to say that he owns the surface of the land together with the airspace above, the soil underneath and any buildings or other things which have become part of the surface by accession[2], subject to 'separate tenements' such as minerals which may be in separate ownership[3]. He may also own certain 'pertinents' beyond his own boundaries[4]. Where the estate owned is not land proper but a separate tenement in that land, the transfer process is the same, that is to say, by registered disposition, and this is so even where the tenement is itself incorporeal, for example a right to fish for salmón[5].

A transferee takes the land subject to real rights and real conditions, but he is not affected by ordinary personal rights prestable against his author[6].

A disposition transfers heritable property only[7]. Any moveable property which is part of the same transaction[8] must be transferred according to the rules for property of that kind.

1 See paras 196 ff above.
2 For accession, see paras 570 ff above.
3 For separate tenements, see paras 207 ff above.
4 See paras 199 ff above.
5 This is therefore an exception to the usual rule that incorporeal property is transferred by assignation.
6 See para 604 above. In practice, however, a transferor will usually arrange to discharge any heritable securities affecting the land.
7 See eg *Jamieson v Welsh* (1900) 3 F 176, 8 SLT 298.
8 Whether it is part of the same transaction will depend on the terms, express or implied, of the contract (of sale). In the sale of houses and other buildings, disputes sometimes arise as to whether certain items are heritable by accession (ie 'fixtures'), and if they are not, whether they are nonetheless included in the sale. See eg *Christie v Smith's Executrix* 1949 SC 572, 1950 SLT 31, and para 576 above.

648. Death or insolvency of the transferor. The effect of the death or insolvency[1] of the transferor depends upon the stage of the transfer process at which the event occurs. Three stages of transfer were identified earlier[2], namely (1) conclusion of missives, (2) delivery of the disposition, and (3) registration of the disposition, and these are now considered in reverse order.

If the disposition has actually been registered, ownership is in the transferee and his title is unaffected by the death or insolvency of the transferor, for with the act of registration the transferor has ceased to have any further connection with the property, subject to the rules about gratuitous alienations and unfair preferences[3]. In practical terms the only effect on the transferee will be in respect of any personal claims, such as claims under missives, which may remain outstanding against the transferor.

If the disposition has been delivered but not yet registered the position is more complex. Where a person dies or is sequestrated there is a judicial conveyance to the executor, or trustee in sequestration, as the case may be, of the land formerly owned by the dead or insolvent person. This is effected by, respectively, the confirmation of the executor[4] and the act and warrant in favour of the trustee[5]. But while there is a conveyance, there is no automatic infeftment, and the usual rule applies that infeftment requires registration. Further, since a judicial conveyance is a 'general' conveyance what falls to be registered, in the case of the Register of Sasines, is not the conveyance itself but a notice of title deducing title through the conveyance[6]. The result is a 'race to the Register', for there are two competing unregistered conveyances to the same property, namely the original disposition in favour of the transferee and the judicial conveyance in favour of the trustee in sequestration (or as the case may be, the executor). The first person to register will become owner, to the effect of making the second conveyance *a non domino* and thus ineffective to pass ownership[7]. Bad faith in the sense of knowledge of the competing title has no effect on the title acquired by the first to register[8]. Thus if the original transferee registers first he will become owner on an unchallengeable title; but if he registers second he will obtain no title at all and will be left with a claim for breach of contract which, if the transferor is insolvent, will resolve into a ranking on his estate. In practice one of the competitors may decline to enter the race, and this is almost always the case with executors who, except where the estate is actually insolvent, are bound to implement missives of sale in full and have nothing to gain from completing title in their own name[9].

A race to the Register may also arise if the transferor is a company because, although there is no vesting of property in a liquidator, a statutory facility exists for the liquidator to complete title to heritable property by notice of title[10].

Finally, if the transaction has not progressed beyond the conclusion of missives, the executor or trustee in sequestration[11] or liquidator is bound by the contract and must either honour it or face a claim for breach. Until such time as the contract is honoured, however, ownership remains with the transferor or his judicial transferee. Sometimes the disposition has already been executed but this does not improve the transferee's position except where this was followed by delivery[12]. In *Gibson v Hunter Home Designs Ltd,* where the seller went into insolvent liquidation after concluding missives, the buyer was left with an unsecured claim for the return of the purchase price which, imprudently, had been paid in advance[13]. In normal conveyancing practice the purchase price is paid only against delivery of the disposition, with the result that the risk to a purchaser of the seller's insolvency is restricted to the period between delivery and registration.

Further aspects of competition of title are considered later[14].

1 For diligence against the transferor, see G L Gretton *The Law of Inhibition and Adjudication* (1987) pp 149–151 and the same author's 'Delivery of Deeds and the Race to the Register' (1984) 29 JLSS 400.
2 See para 640 above.
3 The land is not the property of the transferor and so cannot vest in his executor or trustee in sequestration.
4 Succession (Scotland) Act 1964 (c 41), s 14(1).
5 Bankruptcy (Scotland) Act 1985 (c 66), s 31(1).
6 See para 645 above.
7 G L Gretton 'Delivery of Deeds and the Race to the Register' (1984) 29 JLSS 400; W W McBryde *Bankruptcy* (1989) p 104.
8 Bad faith only affects the title if it triggers the rule against 'offside goals'. That rule cannot apply to the original transferee, because he was the first person to obtain a personal right in relation to the property, and it does not apply at all in the case of judicial transferees such as trustees in sequestration. See further paras 690, 694, below.
9 In practice the executor will confirm to the sale proceeds rather than to the land sold. For succession purposes, once the contract of sale has been concluded the land is regarded as having been constructively converted into moveable property, which appears to be just another way of saying that the executor is bound to continue with the sale and that the land is not available for distribution to beneficiaries. See further para 14, head (3), above.
10 Titles to Land Consolidation (Scotland) Act 1868 (c 101), s 25. A liquidator may also apply to the court for an order under s 145 of the Insolvency Act 1986 (c 45). On s 25 of the 1868 Act, see G L Gretton 'The Title of a Liquidator' (1984) 29 JLSS 357; A J McDonald 'Bankruptcy, Liquidation and Receivership and the Race to the Register' (1985) 30 JLSS 20; G L Gretton and K G C Reid 'Insolvency and Title: a Reply' (1985) 30 JLSS 109. In place of the notarial instrument specified in s 25 of the 1868 Act there may now be used a notice of title: see the Conveyancing (Scotland) Act 1924 (c 27), s 4. In practice liquidators rarely complete title in their own name.
11 Bankruptcy (Scotland) Act 1985, s 42(1).
12 *Stamfield's Creditors v Scot's Children* (1696) 4 Brown's Supp 344.

13   *Gibson v Hunter Home Designs Ltd* 1976 SC 23, 1976 SLT 94. The court rejected the argument that a constructive trust had been established on the model of English law, with the seller holding the property in trust for the purchaser.

14   See paras 684 ff below.

649. Death or insolvency of the transferee.

As with the transferor, so with the transferee, death or insolvency has no effect upon the transaction unless it occurs during the period after the conclusion of missives and before the registration of the disposition. Once missives have been concluded an executor or trustee in sequestration or a liquidator coming to administer the estate of the transferee must either proceed with the transaction or face a claim for breach of contract by the transferor. An executor will usually proceed with the transaction, but if the contract is not obviously to the benefit of the estate a trustee in sequestration or liquidator will often refuse to adopt it, being content to accept an unsecured claim for damages[1]. Where an executor proceeds with the transaction the disposition is usually taken in his own name as executor[2]. If the disposition had already been granted and delivered before the date of the grantee's death, it cannot now be registered[3], but in this situation a confirmed executor succeeds the deceased as uninfeft proprietor and is able to make up title in his own name[4]. In the case of insolvency a disposition may be taken either in the name of the insolvent person or company or in the name of the trustee in sequestration, and the practice is for trustees in sequestration to take title in their own name but for liquidators to take title in the name of the company. If the disposition was delivered but not registered prior to the insolvency it may be registered now although a trustee in sequestration, already an uninfeft proprietor on his own account, may prefer to complete title in his own name[5].

1   Bankruptcy (Scotland) Act 1985 (c 66), s 42. For liquidators, see J B St Clair and J E Drummond Young *The Law of Corporate Insolvency in Scotland* (2nd edn, 1992) pp 25, 26, and the authorities there cited. In general an action of specific implement against a trustee in sequestration or liquidator is not competent.

2   Alternatively it may be taken directly in the name of a beneficiary or subpurchaser, with the executor signing as a consenter.

3   Titles to Land Consolidation (Scotland) Act 1868 (c 101), s 142 (amended by the Public Registers and Records (Scotland) Act 1950 (c 11), s 1(2), Schedule; the Conveyancing and Feudal Reform (Scotland) Act 1970 (c 35), s 52(3), Sch 11, Pt III; and the Land Registration (Scotland) Act 1979 (c 33), s 29(4), Sch 4).

4   The links in title are (1) the unregistered disposition in favour of the deceased and (2) the confirmation.

5   Ie by notice of title the links being (1) the unregistered disposition and (2) the act and warrant. See the Bankruptcy (Scotland) Act 1985, s 31(3). Even if title is completed in the name of the insolvent transferee, the land is *acquirenda* so that the trustee in sequestration remains an uninfeft proprietor (s 32(6)) with the option of completing title in his own name at a later date.

650. Subinfeudation.

In feudal terms the transfer of ownership is classified as 'substitution'[1], the transferee taking the place in the feudal chain vacated by the transferor. This may be contrasted with subinfeudation[2], where the granter remains in the feudal chain and extends it by taking the grantee as his vassal. But while the formal differences between substitution and subinfeudation remain, the gradual dismantling of the feudal system in recent years and in particular the abolition of new feuduties[3] has meant that, from a functional point of view, they are now barely distinct. Overwhelmingly, substitution is the normal method of transferring land, but where a transferor wishes to impose real burdens there are certain attractions in proceeding by subinfeudation, in particular the availability of continuing rights of enforcement[4]. Since 1858 subinfeudation has been a relatively simple procedure, requiring the execution and registration of a feu disposition or other conveyance *de me*. A full discussion of the conveyancing aspects of subinfeudation is given elsewhere in this work[5].

1 Ie the conveyance is *a me de superiore meo*.
2 Where the conveyance is *de me et successoribus meis*.
3 Land Tenure Reform (Scotland) Act 1974 (c 38), s 1(1). For a detailed account of feudalism, see paras 41 ff above.
4 See paras 397, 398, above.
5 See CONVEYANCING, vol 6, paras 473 ff.

651. The passing of risk. Risk concerns liability for accidental damage to or destruction of the subjects of sale in the interval between the conclusion of the contract and the transfer of ownership[1]. Where a contract has been concluded, any damage occurring prior to the conclusion of the contract is not covered by risk and, except where the contract provides otherwise, must be borne by the buyer[2].

In the sale of heritable property risk passes from the seller to the buyer when the contract of sale is concluded, except where the contract contains a suspensive condition in which case risk does not pass until the condition is purified[3]. This rule may be altered by agreement and in the usual case the contract of sale will delay the passing of risk until the date of entry. It has been suggested by the Scottish Law Commission that this standard practice should now be enacted as the normal rule so that, except where the contrary was agreed, risk would remain with the seller until entry[4].

The passing of risk does not relieve a seller remaining in control of the property of a duty to take reasonable care of it, and if he fails in this duty he is liable in damages to the buyer[5].

1 On risk generally, see A D M Forte 'Must a Purchaser Buy Charred Remains?' (1984) 19 Irish Jurist 1.
2 If the contract is silent, the buyer is taken to have agreed to buy the property in the state in which it stood as at the date of the contract.
3 *Sloans Dairies Ltd v Glasgow Corpn* 1977 SC 223, 1979 SLT 17.
4 *Report on the Passing of Risk in Contracts for the Sale of Heritable Property* (Scot Law Com no. 127 (1990)).
5 *Meehan v Silver* 1972 (Sh Ct) 70. But cf *Chapman's Trustees v Anglo Scottish Group Services Ltd* 1980 SLT (Sh Ct) 27.

(5) INCORPOREAL PROPERTY

652. Property incapable of transfer. Incorporeal property consists of rights, and rights may either be personal, such as a right in contract or in delict, or real, such as a right in security or in lease.

In principle all personal rights are capable of transfer[1]. Real rights are also capable of transfer except that real conditions, such as servitudes, cannot be separated from the dominant tenement to which they are attached and pass automatically with that tenement as a pertinent thereof[2]. Where a contract confers a number of separate rights, the rights may be transferred separately and to different people. A right is not, however, transferable if it involves *delectus personae*[3] or if, as commonly happens in the case of leases, assignation is expressly prohibited, or again if and to the extent that the right is alimentary in nature[4]. Statute may also prohibit transfer, as for example in the case of certain social security benefits[5]. In all the cases mentioned a purported transfer would be void[6].

A special rule applies in respect of the real right of ownership *(dominium)*[7]. Unlike other real rights, ownership is not itself regarded as capable of being owned. So if A owns a car the property *(res)* is the car and not the ownership of the car, and the appropriate rules of transfer are those for corporeal moveable property and not those for incorporeal property. Thus the right of ownership is not incorporeal property, and indeed is not, strictly, property at all.

Difficult questions arise concerning the assignation of future rights, such as a *spes successionis* or rights to payment under contracts which have yet to be entered into. It appears that while some future rights may be transferred, others may not, and the reported cases give little indication of underlying principle. To some extent, of course, the issue turns on the practical question of whether there is in existence a debtor to whom intimation can be made[8].

1 Erskine *Institute* III,5,2: '[T]he general rule is, that whoever is in the right of any subject, though it should not bear to assignees, may at pleasure convey it to another, except where he is barred either by the nature of the subject or by immemorial custom'. So in *Libertas-Kommerz GmbH* 1978 SLT 222, OH, it was held that floating charges may be assigned although not expressly so authorised by statute.
2 See paras 201, 345, above.
3 See OBLIGATIONS.
4 W W McBryde *The Law of Contract in Scotland* (1987) para 17-29.
5 Social Security Act 1975 (c 14), s 87.
6 *W and A Geddes Ltd v Stewart* 1991 GWD 13-752, OH.
7 See para 16 above.
8 For a full review of the law, see G L Gretton 'The Assignation of Contingent Rights' 1993 JR 23.

653. The three stages of transfer. In most cases incorporeal property is transferred by the execution and delivery of a written deed, known as an assignation, followed in the case of personal rights by intimation to the debtor in the right and in the case of real rights by registration of the assignation or by possession. If the transfer is for consideration the assignation is usually preceded by a contract of sale. In many cases, therefore, there are three identifiable stages in the transfer process, namely (1) contract of sale, (2) assignation, and (3) intimation (personal rights) or registration or possession (real rights)[1]. It is only at the last of the three stages that the transfer itself occurs and unless or until that stage is completed the transferor is wholly undivested. In assignations the transferor is usually referred to as the 'cedent' and the transferee as the 'assignee', while the verb of transfer is to 'assign'.

The rules of transfer just given apply to most but not to all kinds of incorporeal property. Negotiable instruments, for example, are transferred, in the case of bearer instruments by delivery and in the case of order instruments by indorsement and delivery[2]. No deed of assignation is required. Special statutory rules are also provided in a number of other cases, including shares in a company[3], copyright[4], designs[5] and patents[6]. The separate tenements in land, such as the right to fish for salmon and the right to gather mussels and oysters, are treated in the same way as land itself and are transferred by disposition registered in the Register of Sasines or Land Register[7]. The right of an uninfeft proprietor of land is usually transferred by disposition supported by deduction of title although assignation is also competent[8].

1 See CONVEYANCING, vol 6, paras 591 ff, and RIGHTS IN SECURITY, vol 20, paras 43 ff (assignations in security).
2 Bills of Exchange Act 1882 (c 61), s 31. See also COMMERCIAL PAPER, vol 4, paras 140 ff.
3 See COMPANIES, vol 4, paras 372 ff.
4 See paras 1006 ff below.
5 See paras 1197 ff below.
6 See paras 878 ff below.
7 See paras 207 ff and 319 ff above.
8 See para 645 above. At common law the bond and disposition in security was transferred by disposition (also known as disposition and assignation) followed by sasine. Statute now provides for assignation, as it does for the standard security. For bonds and dispositions in security, see the Titles to Land Consolidation (Scotland) Act 1868 (c 101), s 124, Sch (GG) (amended by the Succession (Scotland) Act 1964 (c 41), s 34(2), Sch 3); and the Conveyancing (Scotland) Act 1924 (c 27), s 28, Sch K, Form 1. For standard securities, see the Conveyancing and Feudal Reform (Scotland) Act 1970 (c 35), s 14, Sch 4, Forms A, B.

654. Stage (1): contract of sale. The first stage in the transfer of incorporeal property is often the conclusion of a contract of sale. The contract may be oral or in writing. Its terms will depend upon the nature of the right being assigned, and the great variety of possible rights makes generalisations unhelpful. The prior communings rule applies, so that on delivery of the assignation the contract is superseded and cannot be founded upon, but this rule is subject to a number of exceptions[1]. Sometimes the contract incorporates the assignation, and there is no proper separation of contract and conveyance.

1 See para 641 above.

655. Stage (2): execution and delivery of an assignation. In general, writing is required for the assignation of incorporeal heritable property[1] but not for the assignation of incorporeal moveables[2]. The universal practice, however, is for assignations to be in writing executed under the Requirements of Writing (Scotland) Act 1995.

As to form, 'an assignation doth necessarily require the clear expressing of the cedent, assignee, and thing assigned' coupled with 'terms that may express the transmission of the right assigned from cedent to the assignee'[3]. The law does not insist on the word 'assign' or on other formal words of transfer provided that, as was said in a recent case, there are '[other] words which may be construed as effecting an immediate transfer'[4]. The issue of 'other words' arises particularly where no formal assignation has been granted and it is argued that a contract to assign should be read as including a *de praesenti* assignation[5]. It has been held in the Outer House that words effecting a transfer need not be express but may be implied into a deed but this decision seems open to question[6].

In some cases a statutory form of assignation exists, sometimes mandatory but more often permissive. Examples of mandatory forms are the assignation of life assurance policies[7], standard securities[8] and registered leases[9]. In other cases parties are free to use whatever form they choose. The Transmission of Moveable Property (Scotland) Act 1862, which contains a number of provisions regulating the transfer of incorporeal property, provides a suggested form of assignation[10] and in practice this is often used, even in the assignation of heritable rights. An assignation in the form provided by the 1862 Act is in the following terms[11]:

> I, FIONA ALISON MACMILLAN, residing at Twenty three Bracton Drive, Glasgow, IN CONSIDERATION of the sum of Fifteen Thousand Pounds (£15,000) paid to me by ROBERT ANDREW SANDERSON, residing at Eighty Fenners Lane, Alloa, of which sum I hereby acknowledge receipt, DO HEREBY ASSIGN to the said Robert Andrew Sanderson the Personal Bond for Seventeen Thousand Pounds (£17,000) granted in my favour by Alan Seymour Smith, residing at Two hundred and two Troon Terrace, Ayr, which Bond is dated Fourteenth December Nineteen hundred and ninety two: IN WITNESS WHEREOF these presents are subscribed at Glasgow on Nineteenth February Nineteen hundred and ninety six in the presence of Elizabeth Anne Smith, Four Woodend Terrace, Glasgow.

In addition to operating as a conveyance, an assignation may, like a disposition of land[12], contain clauses which are purely contractual in effect. A common example is a clause of warrandice, but warrandice is implied even where no clause is expressed[13].

Like other unilateral deeds an assignation is not binding on the cedent until it is delivered to the assignee[14].

1 Registration of Leases (Scotland) Act 1857 (c 26), s 3(1), Sch A (s 3(1) renumbered by the Law Reform (Miscellaneous Provisions) (Scotland) Act 1985 (c 73), s 3); Conveyancing and Feudal Reform (Scotland) Act 1970 (c 35), s 14, Sch 4, Form A, B; Requirements of Writing (Scotland) Act 1995 (c 7), s 1(2)(b).

2 Requirements of Writing (Scotland) Act 1995, s 11(3)(a).
3 Stair *Institutions* III,1,4.
4 *Gallemos Ltd v Barratt Falkirk Ltd* 1990 SLT 98 at 100, per Lord Dunpark. The wording ('reserve the right to contra') was held not to satisfy this test. For earlier authorities, see in particular *Carter v M'Intosh* (1862) 24 D 925 and *Brownlee v Robb* 1907 SC 1302, 15 SLT 261. Bell (*Principles* s 1461), however, seems to require actual words of transference.
5 See eg *Bank of Scotland v Liquidators of Hutchison Main & Co Ltd* 1914 SC (HL) 1, 1914 SLT 111.
6 *Lombard North Central Ltd v Lord Advocate* 1983 SLT 361.
7 Policies of Assurance Act 1867 (c 144), s 5, Schedule.
8 Conveyancing and Feudal Reform (Scotland) Act 1970, s 14, Sch 4, Forms A, B.
9 Registration of Leases (Scotland) Act 1857 (c 26), s 3(1), Sch A (as so renumbered: see note 1 above).
10 Transmission of Moveable Property (Scotland) Act 1862 (c 85), s 1, Schs A, B.
11 For further styles of assignation, see J M Halliday *Conveyancing Law and Practice* vol I (1985) ch 7.
12 For dispositions of land, see para 642 above.
13 For warrandice, see paras 717 ff below.
14 Erskine *Institute* III,5,3. But see *Smith v Place D'Or 101 Ltd* 1988 SLT (Sh Ct) 5, which seems best explained on the basis that the assignation was bilateral, thus removing the requirement of delivery.

656. Stage (3): for personal rights, intimation. A personal right is a right against a person, so that the right in the creditor is matched by a correlative obligation in the debtor. In the transfer of personal rights the final obligatory stage in the transaction is intimation of the assignation to the debtor. Intimation is almost always carried out by the assignee but it seems that intimation by the cedent is also sufficient[1]. Until intimation there is no transfer of the right and no divestiture of the cedent; and intimation performs the additional function of notifying the debtor that performance is due to the assignee and not to the cedent. These two functions of intimation (transfer and notification) are quite distinct[2], so that where there is more than one debtor, intimation to any one completes the transfer, but intimation to all is necessary to prevent performance being tendered to the cedent[3].

The Transmission of Moveable Property (Scotland) Act 1862 provides for two methods of intimation[4]. The more usual method is to send by post a certified copy of the assignation. Alternatively a certified copy may be formally delivered by a notary public[5]. In both cases intimation is complete at the moment when the debtor receives a copy, and it is sufficient evidence of such receipt if the debtor issues a written acknowledgment or, in the case of notarial intimation, if the notary issues a certificate in the prescribed form[6]. Other evidence of receipt is also admissible where necessary. Special rules for intimation in the case of life assurance policies are provided by the Policies of Assurance Act 1867[7].

The methods of intimation prescribed by the 1862 Act are without prejudice to other possible methods[8]. But while intimation may be effected in a number of other ways, the law insists on a degree of formality and certainty consistent with the fact that intimation brings about the actual transfer of ownership. In particular mere knowledge privately acquired by the debtor is not considered sufficient intimation[9]. Of the various alternative methods of intimation which have been recognised, the following are of particular importance[10].

(1) *Acknowledged letter.* A written communication which falls short of the requirements of the 1862 Act may nonetheless constitute intimation. An informal letter suffices, but while the letter or other communication need not disclose the details of the assignation, it must make clear that the right has been transferred and that the assignee is asserting his claim against the debtor[11]. Where part only of a right has been assigned, the communication must specify clearly which part[12]. The communication must be acknowledged by the debtor in order to demonstrate that, despite its informality, he understands and accepts its terms, and intimation does not take effect until acknowledgment is made[13]. It is uncertain whether the acknowledgment requires to be in writing[14].

(2) *Performance.* Performance or part performance by the debtor for the benefit of the assignee is considered the equivalent of intimation[15].

(3) *Court action or diligence.* A court action[16] or diligence[17] by the assignee against the debtor and expressly founded on the assignation is treated as sufficient intimation.

(4) *Registration.* Usually registration of the assignation in a public register is not treated as intimation[18]. But where an assignation is contained in a deed the registration of which, in the Register of Sasines or Land Register, is declared by statute the equivalent of the giving of sasine under the old law[19], such registration is regarded as intimation[20]. The rule owes its existence to the fact that the giving of sasine was an act of which general members of the public, including the debtor, might reasonably be expected to have been aware, and, rather improbably, the rule survived the introduction of deemed sasine in 1858. The only deeds in contemporary use producing a deemed sasine on registration are dispositions and feu dispositions[21], and the practical significance of the rule is confined to the assignations of rents and writs contained in these deeds.

1 *A v B* (1540) Mor 843; *Wyllie's Trustees v Boyd* (1891) 18 R 1121 at 1126, per Lord Kincairney; *Libertas-Kommerz GmbH* 1978 SLT 222 at 227, OH, per Lord Kincraig. Cf the rules for the transfer of land (see para 643 above) where the disposition must be presented for registration by the transferee.

2 Stair *Institutions* III,1,6; Erskine *Institute* III,5,3.

3 *Stair* III,1,10; *Erskine* III,5,5.

4 Transmission of Moveable Property (Scotland) Act 1862 (c 85), s 2. In practice these are also used for heritable rights.

5 This replaced an earlier and more ornate method of notarial intimation which, although still competent, is now obsolete.

6 For the prescribed form, see the Transmission of Moveable Property (Scotland) Act 1862, Sch C.

7 The Policies of Assurance Act 1867 (c 144), s 3, requires a 'written notice of the date and purport' of the assignation sent to a principal place of business of the insurance company.

8 Transmission of Moveable Property (Scotland) Act 1862, s 3.

9 *Erskine* III,5,5; Bell *Commentaries* II,17.

10 For other methods of intimation, see W W McBryde *The Law of Contract in Scotland* (1987) pp 402, 403.

11 *Libertas Kommerz GmbH* 1978 SLT 222 at 226, OH, per Lord Kincraig.

12 *Gallemos Ltd v Barratt Falkirk Ltd* 1990 SLT 98.

13 *Wallace v Davies* (1853) 15 D 688; *Donaldson v Findlay, Bannatyne & Co* (1855) 17 D 1053 at 1069, 1070, per Lord Justice-Clerk Hope.

14 *Erskine* III,5,4, and *Bell* II,17, rather suggest that writing is not required.

15 *Bell* II,17.

16 *Carter v McIntosh* (1862) 24 D 925.

17 *Erskine* III,5,4.

18 *Tod's Trustees v Wilson* (1869) 7 M 1100.

19 Titles to Land Consolidation (Scotland) Act 1868 (c 101), s 15. McBryde's statement (in *The Law of Contract in Scotland* p 403) that registration in the Land Register is not deemed intimation, appears to overlook s 29(2) of the Land Registration (Scotland) Act 1979 (c 33) which applies s 15 of the 1868 Act to the Land Register.

20 *Paul v Boyd's Trustees* (1835) 13 S 818; *Edmond v Aberdeen Magistrates* (1855) 18 D 47, affd (1858) 3 Macq 116, HL.

21 As the cases in note 20 above show, the bond and disposition in security also produced a deemed sasine: see the Titles to Land Consolidation (Scotland) Act 1868, s 118 (substituted by the Titles to Land Consolidation (Scotland) Amendment Act 1869 (c 116), s 6; amended by the Statute Law Revision Act 1893 (c 14)). This provision does not apply to standard securities: see the Conveyancing and Feudal Reform (Scotland) Act 1970 (c 35), s 32, Sch 8.

657. Stage (3): for real rights, registration or possession. There can be no intimation in the assignation of real rights because there is no person to whom intimation can be made, a real right being a right in a thing (*res*) and not a right against a person. For real rights the final stage in transfer is some public act in relation to the thing in which the right is held, in practice either taking possession of the thing or registration of the assignation in the Register of Sasines or Land Register. The choice depends on the method by which the right being assigned was originally made real. So if a right requires possession for its constitution, for example a pledge of goods or a short lease of land[1], it requires possession equally for its assignation and until the assignee takes possession of the goods or, as the case may be, the land, there is no transfer and the cedent is undivested[2]. Similarly in the case of rights requiring registration for their constitution, such as standard securities or long leases[3], transfer is completed only by registration of the assignation in the Register of Sasines or Land Register[4].

In practice real rights are usually accompanied by 'back-to-back' personal rights. So standard securities secure debts, leases contain a number of personal rights enforceable against the landlord, and so on. Usually an assignation of the real right will carry the personal rights also[5], so that only a single assignation is required, but on the principles already mentioned the transfer of the personal rights is not completed without intimation to the debtor in the obligation. The practical consequence is that in the assignation of a standard security or of a registered lease there must be both registration and also intimation[6].

1 A short lease is a lease for twenty years or less. A long lease is one for more than twenty years. See the Registration of Leases (Scotland) Act 1857 (c 26), s 1 (amended by the Statute Law Revision Act 1892 (c 19), the Burgh Registers (Scotland) Act 1926 (c 50), s 4, and the Land Tenure Reform (Scotland) Act 1974 (c 38), s 18, Sch 6, para 1).

2 *Clark v West Calder Oil Co* (1882) 9 R 1017. In the case of leases it is only in modern times that the requirement of possession has become fixed: see J Rankine *The Law of Leases in Scotland* (3rd edn, 1916) p 182 ('A controversy has raged for a long period . . . ').

3 In areas not yet operational for the purposes of registration of title, long leases can still be constituted by possession, in which case possession is required for their assignation. For the areas which are currently operational, see para 643 above.

4 Conveyancing and Feudal Reform (Scotland) Act 1970 (c 35), s 14(1); Registration of Leases (Scotland) Act 1857, s 3(1) (renumbered by the Law Reform (Miscellaneous Provisions) (Scotland) Act 1985 (c 73), s 3). For registered leases registration is defined as being the equivalent of possession (Registration of Leases (Scotland) Act 1857, s 16(1)), and until 1974 an assignee's right was as well completed by possession as by registration. This is no longer so, and while it continues to be the case for Sasine titles that an assignee may complete his right by possession, since 1 September 1974 his right as so completed is defeated by a competing assignation which has been followed by registration. See the Registration of Leases (Scotland) Act 1857, s 16(2) (added by the Land Tenure Reform (Scotland) Act 1974 (c 38), s 18, Sch 6, para 3). For Land Register titles registration is mandatory in all cases and possession confers no right on the assignee: Land Registration (Scotland) Act 1979 (c 33), s 3(3).

5 With assignations of standard securities this occurs in virtue of the implied clause of assignation of writs (Conveyancing and Feudal Reform (Scotland) Act 1970, s 14(2)), with the consequence that in Form B securities (ie Sch 2, Form B), where the personal bond is not part of the 'writs', a separate express assignation may be required. See J M Halliday *Conveyancing Law and Practice* vol III (1987) para 40-14.

6 G C H Paton and J G S Cameron *The Law of Landlord and Tenant in Scotland* (1967) p 160; Halliday vol III, p 457 and note 36.

658. Evaluation of the three stages of transfer. The three stages identified in the transfer of incorporeal property follow closely the equivalent stages in the transfer of land[1]. Thus on the conclusion of the contract of sale each party becomes personally bound to proceed with the transaction; on delivery of the executed assignation, usually against payment of the price, each party has fulfilled his principal obligation in terms of that contract; and on intimation, or the equivalent in the transfer of real rights, ownership passes from the cedent to the assignee.

The importance of intimation or its equivalent requires emphasis. In some countries, for example the Federal Republic of Germany, the purpose of intimation is merely to ensure that the debtor pays the correct creditor and ownership passes even where intimation has not occurred[2]. Stair speculates that this may once also have been the law of Scotland[3], but however that may be the modern law is otherwise. That law is expressed succinctly by Bankton:

'The assignation is not completed by executing and delivering it to the assignee, but it must likewise be intimated to the debtor, till which is done, the cedent is not understood in our law to be denuded'[4].

An assignee holding on a delivered but unintimated assignation is in much the same position as a disponee of land holding on a delivered but unregistered disposition. In both cases ownership remains with the transferor, although the transferee has it within his power to become owner; and in both cases the deed of transfer operates at a contractual level, binding the transferor not to derogate from his grant, guaranteeing the title, and so forth[5]. Indeed in cases where there is no separate contract of sale the delivery of the assignation is the first occasion on which the cedent enters into binding obligations in relation to the assignee.

1 For which see para 644 above.
2 BGB ss 398, 407. As to the BGB, see para 608, note 3, above.
3 Stair *Institutions* III, 1, 6: 'The assignation itself is not a complete valid right, till it be orderly intimated to the debtor, which, though at first, (it is like) hath been only used to put the debtor *in mala fide*, to pay to the cedent, or any other assignee; yet now it is a solemnity requisite to assignations . . .'.
4 Bankton *Institute* III, 1, 6. A recent restatement is given in *Gallemos Ltd v Barratt Falkirk Ltd* 1990 SLT 98 at 101, per Lord Dunpark: 'Intimation of an assignation to a debtor is the equivalent of delivery of a corporeal moveable and is necessary to complete the title of the assignee'.
5 See further K G C Reid 'Unintimated Assignations' 1989 SLT (News) 267.

659. Death or insolvency. The effect of the death or insolvency of the cedent in the course of transfer will depend upon the stage which the transaction has reached. Thus:
(1) If the transfer has been completed, by intimation of the assignation or its equivalent, the assignee owns the property and is unaffected by the subsequent death or insolvency of his author, subject always to the rules about gratuitous alienations and unfair preferences.
(2) If the assignation has been delivered but not intimated, the assignation is defeated and the assignee is left with a contractual claim which, in the case of insolvency, will resolve into an unsecured ranking on the cedent's estate. The reason for this is that both death[1] and sequestration[2] result in a completed judicial conveyance of the cedent's incorporeal property in favour of, respectively, the executor and the trustee in sequestration, thus rendering the original assignation *a non domino* and ineffectual to transfer ownership. The position may, however, be different in a question with the liquidator of a company[3]. A different rule also applies in those cases where registration is required in order to complete the assignation for here the statutory title of the executor or trustee in sequestration is also incomplete and there is a 'race to the register' with the original assignee, the first party to register taking the right to the exclusion of the other party[4].
Arrestment also defeats an unintimated assignation[5].
(3) If the transaction has progressed no further than a concluded contract, the executor, trustee in sequestration or, as the case may be, the liquidator can either adopt the contract or concede a claim in damages[6].
Where it is the assignee who dies or becomes insolvent, the result is the same as in the case of the death or insolvency of a transferee of land and is discussed further in that context[7].
Further aspects of competition of title are dealt with below[8].

1 Succession (Scotland) Act 1964 (c 41), s 14(1). The judicial conveyance is the confirmation of executors. It is uncertain what the position is if the assignee intimates after the death of the cedent but before the confirmation of his executor, but unless the estate is insolvent this is of little practical importance.
2 Bankruptcy (Scotland) Act 1985 (c 66), s 31(4). The act and warrant is a deemed intimated assignation in favour of the trustee.

3 There is no automatic vesting in a liquidator and, as Professor W A Wilson has pointed out, there is no direct equivalent in the Insolvency Act 1986 (c 45) to the former provisions of the Companies Acts that winding up is the equivalent of an arrestment in execution and decree of furthcoming: W A Wilson *The Scottish Law of Debt* (2nd edn, 1991) para 25.7. It may therefore be doubted whether a liquidator has any special priority, so that the outcome of a competition with an assignee would depend on whether intimation occurred before the liquidator could obtain a vesting order under s 145 of the Insolvency Act 1986.

4 This is similar to the race to the Register in the case of land, for which see para 648 above.

5 Stair *Institutions* III,1,44; Erskine *Institute* III,6,19. See DILIGENCE AND ENFORCEMENT OF JUDGMENTS, vol 8, para 262.

6 *Bank of Scotland v Liquidators of Hutchison Main & Co Ltd* 1914 SC (HL) 1, 1914 1 SLT 111.

7 See para 649 above.

8 See paras 684 ff below.

660. The rule *assignatus utitur jure auctoris*. The assignation of personal rights is subject to the rule *assignatus utitur jure auctoris* (the assignee exercises the right of his author)[1]. Sometimes this rule is treated as part of the rule *nemo dat quod non habet* (no one can give what he does not have)[2] but in fact the two are quite distinct. The *nemo dat* rule is concerned with the transferor's title to the property being transferred and provides that absence or qualification of title in the person of the transferor will result in a corresponding absence or qualification of title in the person of the transferee. The rule applies to property of every kind, and as applied to incorporeal property means that if the cedent does not own the right being assigned then he cannot confer ownership on the assignee[3].

The *assignatus utitur* rule has no general application in property law but is confined to the transfer by assignation of personal rights. Within the field of incorporeal property it does not apply to the transfer of real rights[4] and nor does it apply to negotiable instruments, which are transferred by negotiation and not by assignation[5]. Bell distinguishes between conditions which are incorporated within a right (conditions *in corpore juris*) and conditions which are extraneous to it (conditions *extra corpus juris*)[6], and using this distinction it may be said that whereas the *nemo dat* rule is concerned with extrinsic conditions, the rule *assignatus utitur jure auctoris* is concerned with intrinsic conditions. The *nemo dat* rule governs the relationship of the cedent to the right being assigned whereas the *assignatus utitur* rule governs the relationship of the cedent, within the right itself, to the debtor in the correlative obligation. Thus suppose that A assigns to B the benefit of a contract entered into with C. The *assignatus utitur* rule focuses on the relationship between A and C; and it provides that when assignee B comes ultimately to enforce the right against debtor C, any defence or claim which C could have pled against cedent A is available equally against assignee B. The principle is that the position of the debtor is not worsened by assignation and nor is the position of the holder of the right improved. The assignee exercises precisely the right of his cedent.

The *assignatus utitur* rule is concerned with the utilisation by the debtor against the assignee of claims which first arose against the cedent. For this purpose three types of claim against the cedent may be distinguished, namely (1) claims by the debtor prestable under the right being assigned, (2) claims by the debtor outwith the right being assigned but prestable under the same contract, and (3) claims by the debtor prestable under a different contract. In principle the *assignatus utitur* rule applies in all three cases. In *Scottish Widows' Fund v Buist*[7], the leading case in this whole area, a policy of assurance over the life of the cedent was voidable at the instance of the insurers on account of certain mis-statements in the proposal form. It was held that since the policy was voidable in a question with the cedent it remained voidable in a question with the assignee. The initial defect could not be cured by the assignation, and it did not affect the issue that the assignee paid value and was in good faith[8].

Scottish Widows' Fund is an example of a type (1) claim. An example of a type (2) claim is where C contracts to pay A a sum of money in return for work to be carried out; A assigns to B, not the whole contract, but the right to receive the money; and A then fails to carry out the work. Since A could not have claimed the money from C so neither can B[9]. For type (3) claims any right of compensation (set-off) pleadable by the debtor against the cedent at the time of intimation of an assignation will continue to be pleadable by the debtor against the assignee[10]. Post-intimation rights of compensation are excluded. This final example of the rule may owe something to the origin of assignation as a form of mandate in which the assignee was viewed simply as agent for the cedent[11].

1 Stair *Institutions* III,1,20; Erskine *Institute* III,5,10; Bell *Principles* s 1468.
2 For this rule, see paras 669 ff below.
3 Conversely if, as in *Redfearn v Somervail* (1813) 1 Dow 50, 5 Pat 707, HL, he does own it (albeit in trust), ownership will pass. *Redfearn* is sometimes misclassified as falling within the *assignatus* rule, a point made by Lord President Inglis in *Scottish Widows' Fund v Buist* (1876) 3 R 1078 at 1082.
4 Bankton *Institute* III,1,8. This is because there is no debtor in a real right.
5 Bills of Exchange Act 1882 (c 61), s 38(2). See COMMERCIAL PAPER, vol 4, para 149.
6 Bell *Commentaries* I,302–04.
7 *Scottish Widows' Fund v Buist* (1876) 3 R 1078.
8 Among the other propositions vouched for by this case is the proposition that in property law good faith is usually irrelevant.
9 See W W McBryde *The Law of Contract in Scotland* (1987) paras 17-86, 17-87.
10 Erskine III,4,14; Bell *Commentaries* II,131. An example is *Shiells v Ferguson* (1876) 4 R 250.
11 Thus 'Recollecting the principles upon which assignations were originally admitted as procuratories *in rem suam*, it will not appear wonderful that persons acquiring by assignation the right to debts and other *jura incorporalia* should be considered as coming precisely into the place of the cedent, and as liable, of course, to all the personal exceptions pleadable against him': Bell *Commentaries* I,303, note 5.

661. Retrocession. A retrocession is an assignation of a previously assigned right from the original assignee back to the original cedent[1]. The verb of transfer is 'retrocess'. A retrocession is a type of assignation and is governed by the same rules as other assignations. The most common use of retrocessions in practice is in the discharge of assignations in security, especially in relation to life assurance policies.

1 Erskine *Institute* III,5,1.

662. Assignation of obligations. Assignation is usually of rights and it is unclear whether obligations can be assigned also[1]. It is thought that a bare obligation cannot be assigned, so that if A owes C £10,000, A cannot escape liability by assigning the obligation to B, a person (or company) of straw[2]. This rule, which seems an obvious one, may if necessary be justified by reference to *delectus personae*. The position is probably different where what is being assigned includes rights as well as obligations, for contracts typically involve both and if the rule is that contracts may be assigned, it seems to follow that obligations may be assigned also[3]. A well-known example is *Cole v Handasyde & Co*[4] in which the assignee, having duly performed the obligation due under the contract, was held entitled to exercise the linked right and recover the stipulated price from the other contracting party. Whether any liability then remains with the cedent, for example in respect of defective performance by the assignee, is an open question[5]. In the law of landlord and tenant it is settled that, following the assignation of a lease, the liability of the cedent is restricted to rent and other obligations attributable to the period prior to the assignation[6].

1 W M Gloag *The Law of Contract* (2nd edn, 1929) pp 416, 417; W W McBryde *The Law of Contract in Scotland* (1987) p 382.
2 Presumably the position would be different if the assignation occurred before the loan was advanced, so that the loan was made to assignee B and not the cedent A. This would be a case where the contract being assigned included a right as well as an obligation.

3 There will of course be marginal cases in which the extent of the obligations greatly exceeds the value of the rights and such cases may possibly be ruled by *delectus personae*.
4 *Cole v Handasyde & Co* 1910 SC 68, 1909 2 SLT 358. See also *Asphaltic Limestone Concrete Co Ltd v Glasgow Corpn* 1907 SC 463, 14 SLT 706.
5 Gloag's view is that liability does remain, at least in the usual case. See *Gloag* p 416.
6 *Skene v Greenhill* (1825) 4 S 25 (NE 26); *Lord Elphinstone v Monkland Iron and Coal Co Ltd* (1886) 13 R (HL) 98 at 102, per Lord Watson; *Burns v Martin* (1887) 14 R (HL) 20 at 24. But the lease may provide otherwise.

(6) INVOLUNTARY TRANSFER

663. Introduction. The transfer of ownership is involuntary if it occurs without the active consent of the 'transferor'. A's title passes to B, but without A's participation. That B receives A's title and not a good statutory title requires emphasis. For as in other cases of derivative acquisition, the transaction is subject to the rule *nemo dat quod non habet*[1] and to the rules governing competition of title[2], so that if A does not own the property in the first place, the 'transfer' is ineffectual. In this way involuntary transfer is distinguished from certain cases of original acquisition, for example acquisition by positive prescription, because in original acquisition the title of the existing owner, if there is one, is extinguished and a new title conferred on the acquirer[3].

Naturally, involuntary transfer is the exception and not the rule, for it is a cardinal principle that a person is not to be deprived of property without his consent[4]. Most transfers are, and are required to be, voluntary, and if the transferor refuses his consent ownership remains with him[5]. Nonetheless, in certain limited circumstances involuntary transfer is permitted. The most important are given below, but they include where the 'transferor' is dead or insolvent or where he refuses to pay a debt due or where, in the public interest, property is expropriated by a government department or other public body. For each case the law prescribes a detailed procedure to take the place of the usual consensual act of transfer, and safeguards are included for the protection of the transferor.

1 See paras 669 ff below.
2 See paras 684 ff below.
3 For the distinction between original and derivative acquisition, see para 597 above.
4 Stair *Institutions* II,1,34: '*Quod meum est, sine me alienum fieri nequit*'. Tony Honore lists, 'right to security' as one of his standard incidents of ownership: see *Making Law Bind* (1987) p 171.
5 See eg *Armour v Thyssen Edelstahlwerke AG* 1991 SCLR 139, 1990 SLT 891, HL.

664. Judicial conveyance. In certain circumstances the court is empowered to effect the transfer of property. There is, however, a difference between a power to effect a transfer and a power to order a transfer, for in the first case there is a judicial conveyance while in the second case there is merely an order that a conveyance should take place in the future. Strictly, only the first is an involuntary transfer, although with the second the consent of the transferor is given under the stimulus of a court order. Examples of the second category include the power of a court to order transfer in implement of a contract of sale, and property transfer orders made in the course of an action for divorce[1].

Where a power of the first category, to effect transfer, is invoked successfully the actual transfer occurs at the time when the relevant court interlocutor is pronounced, except that in the case of land the further step of registration, in the Register of Sasines or Land Register, is also required[2]. Among the examples of judicial conveyance are the following:

(1) *Act and warrant of trustee in sequestration.* On sequestration the act and warrant issued by the court on confirmation of the appointment of the permanent

trustee has the effect of conveying to the trustee the whole estate of the debtor other than trust property and such property as is exempted from poinding[3]. The conveyance is backdated to the date of sequestration[4].

(2) *Vesting of company property in liquidator.* The winding up of a company does not of itself have the effect of transferring the property of the company to a liquidator. But the court may on the application of the liquidator direct that all or any part of the property of the company is to vest in the liquidator[5].

(3) *Adjudication.* An obligation to convey heritable property can be enforced by raising an action of adjudication in implement. The decree of the court is then a judicial conveyance which may be registered directly in the Register of Sasines or Land Register. Adjudication may also be used by a creditor as a general diligence on the heritable property of his debtor, but in such a case decree confers no more than a judicial heritable security until ten years has elapsed when, by an action of declarator of expiry of the legal, the security title may be converted into ownership. Neither type of adjudication is common[6].

(4) *Confirmation of executors.* Until the passing of the Succession (Scotland) Act 1964 confirmation of executors was available only in respect of moveable property. Under the 1964 Act confirmation now has the effect of vesting in the executor, or, if there is more than one, in the executors as joint property, the whole estate of the deceased falling to be administered under the law of Scotland[7]. The vesting is not retrospective. If the deceased left a trust disposition and settlement containing an express conveyance of his estate to executors or trustees, this forms an alternative, and consensual[8], route of title for his personal representatives, although the normal practice is still to obtain confirmation[9].

(5) *Judicial factor.* It appears that the interlocutor appointing a judicial factor has the effect of conveying to him all the moveable property of the ward[10]. But except in the case of a factor appointed on a pre-existing trust estate[11], there is no automatic conveyance of heritable property although warrant may be specially sought from the court either in the original petition for appointment or in a note by the factor[12].

(6) *Trustee appointed by the court.* Whereas with the appointment of a judicial factor there is an automatic conveyance of the moveable property but not of the heritable property, with the appointment of a trustee by the court[13] there is an automatic conveyance of the heritable property[14] but not of the moveable property[15]. A warrant may, however, be sought in respect of the moveable property[16].

(7) *Forfeiture as a criminal penalty.* In certain criminal offences, for example offences involving poaching, the court has power to order the forfeiture of property belonging to the person convicted of the offence[17]. There are extensive and complex provisions in Part I of the Criminal Justice (Scotland) Act 1987 empowering the High Court to make a confiscation order in respect of the realisable property of a person convicted of certain specified drug-related offences[18]. A procedure exists for the realisation of such property by administrators appointed by the Court of Session on the application of the Lord Advocate[19].

(8) *Reduction.* It appears that reduction may either be catholic, affecting all parties, or *ad hunc effectum*, affecting only the parties to the action. Usually the effect of reduction is catholic[20]. Where a conveyance, such as a disposition or assignation, is reduced and the reduction is catholic, the result is to undo the original effect of the deed so that the transferee is divested and the transferor reinvested[21]. In the case of dispositions and other deeds relating to land the extract decree should be registered in the Register of Sasines or Land Register, and an unregistered reduction is not pleadable against a third party acquirer who takes without notice[22].

1 Family Law (Scotland) Act 1985 (c 37), s 8(1)(aa) (added by the Law Reform (Miscellaneous Provisions) (Scotland) Act 1990 (c 40), s 74(1), Sch 8, para 34). If the defender refuses to execute a conveyance of the property, the court has power to order execution by the clerk of court and such execution is sufficient to convey the property. This procedure is barely distinguishable from a judicial conveyance. See eg *Mackay v Campbell* 1966 SC 237, 1966 SLT 329, affd 1967 SC (HL) 53, 1967 SLT 337; *Boag* 1967 SC 322, 1967 SLT 275. For the procedure in the sheriff court, see the Sheriff Courts (Scotland) Act 1907 (c 51), s 5A (added by the Law Reform (Miscellaneous Provisions) (Scotland) Act 1985 (c 73), s 17).

2 In the Register of Sasines the interlocutor cannot be recorded directly but may be used as a midcouple for the purposes of deducing title. If the transferee wishes to complete title he must record a notice of title. In the Land Register, title is completed by submitting the interlocutor to the Keeper: see the Land Registration (Scotland) Act 1979 (c 33), s 3(6).

3 Bankruptcy (Scotland) Act 1985 (c 66), ss 31, 33 (s 31 amended by the Housing Act 1988 (c 50), s 118(1), (2); and the Social Security Act 1989 (c 24), s 22(7), (8), Sch 4, Pt IV, para 23). By s 31(4) of the Bankruptcy (Scotland) Act 1985 the trustee is excused taking possession of corporeal moveable property or intimating to the debtor in the case of incorporeal moveable property. The list of property exempted from poinding is given in the Debtors (Scotland) Act 1987 (c 18), s 16. See also BANKRUPTCY, vol 2, paras 1381 ff.

4 Bankruptcy (Scotland) Act 1985, s 31(1).

5 Insolvency Act 1986 (c 45), s 145(1). But while there is no express judicial conveyance, a liquidator may nonetheless complete title to land in accordance with the Titles to Land Consolidation (Scotland) Act 1868 (c 101), s 25 (amended by the Statute Law Revision Act 1893 (c 14)).

6 See DILIGENCE, vol 8, paras 189 ff.

7 Succession (Scotland) Act 1964 (c 41), s 14(1). See WILLS AND SUCCESSION, vol 25, paras 1059 ff. So far as moveable property is concerned, McLaren's opinion was that confirmation conferred an immediate real right: see J McLaren *The Law of Wills and Succession as administered in Scotland* (3rd edn, 1894) II, para 1602. With heritable property registration is required in order to complete the transfer.

8 Which is to say, an example not of involuntary but of voluntary transfer. No delivery is required, the trust disposition and settlement taking effect automatically on death.

9 See 'Opinion on Completion of Title' by the Professors of Conveyancing (1965) 10 JLSS 153.

10 Judicial Factors (Scotland) Act 1889 (c 39), s 13. See TRUSTS, TRUSTEES AND JUDICIAL FACTORS, vol 24, para 244. In some cases, eg shares, further steps are required to complete title. Doubt has been expressed about the effect of such a conveyance where there is a living ward: see N M L Walker *Judicial Factors* (1974), p 85.

11 Conveyancing Amendment (Scotland) Act 1938 (c 24), s 1.

12 *Walker* pp 83–85.

13 Ie under the Trusts (Scotland) Act 1921 (c 58), s 22 (amended by the Law Reform (Miscellaneous Provisions) (Scotland) Act 1980 (c 55), s 13).

14 Or, more strictly, the trustee is able to complete title by registration using the act and warrant as a midcouple: Conveyancing Amendment (Scotland) Act 1938, s 1.

15 See TRUSTS, TRUSTEES AND JUDICIAL FACTORS, vol 24, para 161.

16 *Boazman* 1938 SN 103, 1938 SLT 582, OH.

17 Eg Salmon and Freshwater Fisheries (Protection) (Scotland) Act 1951 (c 26), s 1 (amended by the Freshwater and Salmon Fisheries (Scotland) Act 1976 (c 22), Sch 2, and the Salmon Act 1986 (c 62), Sch 4, para 7); Deer (Scotland) Act 1959 (c 40), s 22 (amended by the Deer Amendment (Scotland) Act 1982 (c 19), ss 6(c), (d), 14, Sch 1). The animal poached belongs to the poacher by occupation.

18 Criminal Justice (Scotland) Act 1987 (c 41), s 1(1). Part I of the Act comprises ss 1–47.

19 Ibid, s 13(1). On confiscation orders, see further MEDICINES, POISONS AND DRUGS, vol 14, paras 1255–1257.

20 The leading example of a reduction *ad hunc effectum* is a reduction on the grounds of inhibition. See DILIGENCE, vol 8, para 168.

21 Stair's expression is 'reducing and annulling any pretended right': *Institutions* IV,20,2.

22 Conveyancing (Scotland) Act 1924 (c 27), s 46 (renumbered and amended by the Law Reform (Miscellaneous Provisions) (Scotland) Act 1985 (c 73), ss 23, 59, Sch 2, para 7). In the case of the Land Register, an extract decree may be given effect to only by rectification: *Short's Trustee v Keeper of the Registers of Scotland* 1996 SLT 166, HL. See further para 607 above.

665. Transfer by Act of Parliament.

Property is sometimes conveyed directly by Act of Parliament or delegated legislation. A well-known example is the provision, consequent on the reorganisation of local government in 1975, that 'property vested in any existing local authority shall be transferred to and vest in such new local authority as shall, as from 16th May 1975, have the duty of discharging the function or functions for which the said property was wholly or mainly used. . .'[1].

A number of other examples appear on the statute book[2].

1 Local Authorities (Property etc) (Scotland) Order 1975, SI 1975/659, art 4(a)(i). For heritable property the further step of registration in the Sasine or Land Register is required.
2 Eg the National Health Service (Scotland) Act 1972 (c 58), s 27(2) (transfer from local health authorities and education authorities to the Secretary of State); the Roads (Scotland) Act 1984 (c 54), s 112 (vesting of trunk roads in the Secretary of State), and s 115 (vesting of *solum* of stopped up roads in frontagers).

666. Compulsory purchase of land. General statutory powers authorising the compulsory purchase of land are held by a number of public bodies, for example, local authorities and government departments[1]. Where these powers are exercised, land can be acquired without the consent of the existing owner, but compensation must be paid[2]. The process of compulsory purchase falls into two distinct stages. There is, first, the application of general powers of acquisition to a particular area of land for a particular project, usually effected by the making of a compulsory purchase order[3]. Secondly, there is the transfer process itself, which may be carried out either by a statutory conveyance executed by the owner of the land[4] or by a general vesting declaration executed by the acquiring authority[5]. Both require registration in the Register of Sasines or Land Register in order to make the acquiring authority owner[6]. It is only when the general vesting declaration procedure is used that the transfer is truly involuntary.

It is sometimes said, contrary to the usual rule for involuntary transfer[7], that a title acquired by general vesting declaration is free from any defects existing in the hands of the 'transferor'[8]. On this view general vesting declarations form an exception to the rule *nemo dat quod non habet*, so that if land belonging to A is actually acquired from B, and compensation is paid to B, then the acquiring authority becomes owner notwithstanding the absence of title in B. But it may be doubted whether this view is correct, for it is provided in the legislation that a general vesting declaration has the same effect as if the acquiring authority had expeded a notarial instrument in terms of the Lands Clauses Consolidation (Scotland) Act 1845[9]; and the effect of such a notarial instrument, as provided in the 1845 Act, is that 'all the estate and interest in such lands of the parties for whose use and in respect whereof such purchase money or compensation shall have been deposited shall vest absolutely' in the acquiring authority[10]. If the party being compensated has no title, then it would appear to follow that no title is gained by the acquiring authority[11].

1 Eg the Local Government (Scotland) Act 1973 (c 65), s 71.
2 For a detailed account of compulsory purchase and compensation, see COMPULSORY ACQUISITION, vol 5, and J Rowan-Robinson *Compulsory Purchase and Compensation: the law in Scotland* (1990).
3 Acquisition of Land (Authorisation Procedure) (Scotland) Act 1947 (c 42), Sch 1.
4 See the Lands Clauses Consolidation (Scotland) Act 1845 (c 19), s 80, Sch A. The provisions of the 1845 Act are applied to compulsory purchases regulated by the Acquisition of Land (Authorisation Procedure) (Scotland) Act 1947 by s 1(3) and Sch 2 of the 1947 Act.
5 Town and Country Planning (Scotland) Act 1972 (c 52), s 278, Sch 24. For the prescribed form of general vesting declaration, see the Compulsory Purchase of Land (Scotland) Regulations 1976, SI 1976/820, Sch 1, Form 7.
6 Lands Clauses Consolidation (Scotland) Act 1845, s 80 (statutory conveyance); Town and Country Planning (Scotland) Act 1972, Sch 24, para 37 (general vesting declaration).
7 See para 663 above.
8 See eg COMPULSORY ACQUISITION, vol 5, para 90.
9 Town and Country Planning (Scotland) Act 1972, Sch 24, para 7.

10 Lands Clauses Consolidation (Scotland) Act 1845, s 76. By s 75 the land is to be purchased from 'the owner'.
11 Although it may be that lesser defects are cured by ibid, s 76.

667. Sale by creditor. Usually a secured creditor has a power of sale in the event of default by the debtor although sometimes the power can be exercised only by permission of the court[1]. An unsecured creditor, by contrast, has no nexus over particular assets of his debtor unless or until he does diligence against them. Only some diligences, however, most notably poinding, confer a power of sale, with the permission of the court[2]. Where a power of sale exists and is exercised, there is conferred on the purchaser the title of the original debtor, and, since no consent has been given[3], the transfer is classified as involuntary.

1 For powers of sale by creditors, see RIGHTS IN SECURITY, vol 20, para 14 (pledge) and paras 202 ff (standard securities).
2 See DILIGENCE, vol 8, para 234.
3 Ie at least not by the debtor. An alternative analysis of the transaction would be as a voluntary, consensual transfer by the creditor, but in that case it breaches the rule *nemo dat quod non habet*. See para 672 below. A third possible analysis, at least in the case of a sale by secured creditors, is to treat the creditor as an agent of the debtor. There would then be a consensual transfer by an agent of the owner.

668. Personal bar in the sale of goods. Various statutory provisions in the Sale of Goods Act 1979[1] and elsewhere[2] have the effect of allowing a seller of goods who does not own them to transmit to the purchaser the title of some third party who does or at any rate may do. The result is an involuntary transfer from the third party to the purchaser[3]. These statutory provisions are a development of the law of personal bar and are considered further in the context of the rule *nemo dat quod non habet*[4].

1 Sale of Goods Act 1979 (c 54), ss 21, 24, 25.
2 Factors Act 1889 (c 45), ss 8, 9 (extended to Scotland by the Factors (Scotland) Act 1890 (c 40), and amended by the Consumer Credit Act 1974 (c 39), s 192(3), Sch 4, para 2); Hire Purchase Act 1964 (c 53), s 27 (substituted by the Consumer Credit Act 1974, Sch 4, para 22).
3 In a sense there are two transferors here, namely (1) the non-owning seller who consents to the transfer and (2) the third party from whom title is then taken.
4 See paras 672 ff below.

(7) THE RULE *NEMO DAT QUOD NON HABET*

(a) General

669. The rule itself. Derivative acquisition presupposes a good title in the transferor. If the transferor does not own the property in question, no title can be conferred on the transferee. This is the rule *nemo dat quod non habet*: no one can give that which he does not have[1]. So if A draws up and executes a disposition of Edinburgh Castle in favour of B and B registers the disposition in the Register of Sasines, the whole procedure is pointless unless A happens to own the Castle in the first place[2]. By itself mere observance of the solemnities of transfer achieves nothing. Moreover, good faith on the part of the transferee is irrelevant, as it usually is in property law[3]. B may buy from A in circumstances which cast no suspicion whatsoever on A's title; but if A does not own the property, no ownership is conferred upon B. For in this situation there are two innocent parties one of whom must suffer loss, and in general the policy of the law is that the loss should fall on the transferee and not on the true owner. The latter is therefore free to vindicate his property[4].

The rule *nemo dat quod non habet* applies to transfers of property of all kinds, whether heritable or moveable, corporeal[5] or incorporeal, and it applies also to the creation of subordinate real rights, such as lease and security. The cause of absence of title is unimportant and the same proprietary consequences follow where the transferor has borrowed that which he is now attempting to sell as where he has stolen it, theft having no special status in the law of property, except in relation to an aspect of negative prescription[6].

A small number of exceptions are recognised to the *nemo dat* rule, some requiring good faith of the transferee and some not[7].

Related to the *nemo dat* rule is a second rule that if the transferor does indeed own the property at the time of the transfer[8], then, provided that the transfer process itself is properly carried out, ownership is conferred on the transferee[9]. It makes no difference for this purpose whether the title of the transferor is subsistent and absolutely good or subsistent but voidable, for a voidable title subsists until it is reduced[10]. However, the fact that a title is subsistent does not mean that it is unencumbered[11]. Often, and especially in the case of land, a title is subject to subordinate real rights and real conditions which, unless previously discharged, will continue to affect the property in the hands of the transferee. Conversely, a transferee is not in general[12] affected by contractual and other purely personal rights which were prestable against his author.

1 Erskine *Institute* III,1,10; III,3,8; Hume *Lectures* vol III (Stair Soc vol 15, 1952 ed G C H Paton) pp 231–233; M P Brown *A Treatise on the Law of Sale* (1821) pp 417–421. The phrase *nemo dat quod non habet* is not actually used in any institutional work and may have passed into Scottish legal vocabulary from English law, where it is widely used. The phrase found in the *Digest* 50,17,54, is *nemo plus juris ad alienum transferre potest, quam ipse haberet*.

2 There is, however, always the possibility that the absence of title might be cured in the future either by positive prescription (see para 674 below) or by accretion (see para 677 below).

3 *Wright v Butchart* (1662) Mor 9112; *Henderson v Gibson* 17 June 1806 FC; *Stobie v Smith* 1921 SC 894, 1921 2 SLT 189.

4 Many other countries show greater favour to the transferee. See *Corporeal Moveables: Protection of the Onerous bona fide Acquirer of Another's Property* (Scot Law Com Consultative Memorandum no. 27) (1976) pp 1–15.

5 The suggestion by Bell in his *Commentaries* I,304–307 (but not in his *Principles*) that a bona fide purchaser of corporeal moveables acquires a good title regardless of the state of title in the seller is unfounded. It may be an attempt to introduce a form of the English law rule of market overt. For the common law, see M P Brown *A Treatise on the Law of Sale* (1821) pp 418–426 (where Bell's views are attacked) and *Erskine* III,1,10. For the statutory position, see the Sale of Goods Act 1979 (c 54), s 21(1): '. . . where goods are sold by a person who is not their owner, and who does not sell them under the authority or with the consent of the owner, the buyer acquires no better title to the goods than the seller had . . .'. See also the discussion in D L Carey Miller *Corporeal Moveables in Scots Law* (1991) pp 197–200.

6 A right to recover stolen property from the person by whom it was stolen or from any person privy to the stealing thereof is imprescriptible: Prescription and Limitation (Scotland) Act 1973 (c 52), Sch 3(g). Theft is one of the real vices, to the effect of preventing ownership passing to the thief: see para 618 above.

7 For the exceptions, see paras 672 ff below.

8 Or even, by the doctrine of accretion, owns the property after the time of the transfer: see paras 677 ff below.

9 The Conveyancing and Feudal Reform (Scotland) Act 1970 (c 35), s 9(3), may be an exception to this rule insofar as it renders ineffective dispositions granted *ex facie* absolutely but truly in security.

10 For voidable titles, see paras 601, 607, above, and 692 below.

11 See para 604 above.

12 But see para 690 below.

670. Transfer by agent of the transferor.

While the transferor must own the property which is being transferred, there is no requirement that he conduct the transfer process personally. For this purpose a suitably authorised agent is perfectly sufficient. Thus in the commercial world agents often buy and sell goods on behalf of their principals, while dispositions of land executed under a power of attorney are encountered quite frequently in practice and are unquestionably valid. Under modern legislation a deed is validly executed by a company if it is signed by a person authorised to do so[1]. Nor is the use of agents of recent origin, for in the unreformed system of land transfer in operation prior to 1845 it was normal for sasine to be given by a 'bailie' of the transferor to the 'bailie' of the transferee.

Acts by agents suffer the important limitation that they are effective only insofar as authorised by the principal, whether that authorisation is given expressly or by implication. The acts must be within the agent's actual authority. Purported transfers which are not authorised are void[2] even, it is thought, where they lie within an agent's apparent (ostensible) authority although in that case the principal is personally barred from challenging the title of the transferee[3]. The requirement of authority creates difficulties in practice, for it is not always possible to know whether an agent truly has authority to give title, and even if a power of attorney or other authorisation is produced there remains the danger that the authority thereby conferred has since been withdrawn. A power of attorney granted on or after 1 January 1991 does not lapse merely because of the supervening mental incapacity of the principal[4].

1 Requirements of Writing (Scotland) Act 1995 (c 7), s 7(7), Sch 2, para 3(1). However, in order to be self-evidencing, a second signatory is required: see s 3 (as modified by Sch 2, para 3(5)).
2 But there may be subsequent ratification by the principal. This is really a form of accretion and is discussed in para 679 below in that context.
3 In general, personal bar does not confer ownership on the transferee but merely prevents the true owner from asserting his title, a view which seems to be taken for granted by the Sale of Goods Act 1979 (c 54), s 21(2)(a). But it is possible that personal bar within the terms of s 21(1) does have the effect of conferring ownership. See para 680 below.
4 Law Reform (Miscellaneous Provisions) (Scotland) Act 1990 (c 40), s 71.

671. Mercantile agents under the Factors Acts. Contrary to the rule given above[1], a mercantile agent within the Factors Acts can confer a good title in respect of the sale of goods notwithstanding that he is acting beyond his actual authority[2]. This is provided for by section 2(1) of the Factors Act 1889:

> 'Where a mercantile agent is, with the consent of the owner, in possession of goods or of the documents of title to goods, any sale, pledge, or other disposition of the goods, made by him when acting in the ordinary course of business of a mercantile agent, shall, subject to the provisions of this Act, be as valid as if he were expressly authorised by the owner of the goods to make the same; provided that the person taking under the disposition acts in good faith, and has not at the time of the disposition notice that the person making the disposition has not authority to make the same'[3].

A number of requirements must be met in order to satisfy the terms of this provision in relation to the sale of goods, namely:

(1) *The seller was a mercantile agent.* 'Mercantile agent' means 'a mercantile agent having in the customary course of his business as such agent authority either to sell goods, or to consign goods for the purposes of sale, or to buy goods, or to raise money on the security of goods'[4]. Despite the title of the Factors Act 1889, an agent need not show that he is a factor, that is to say, someone who has usual or customary authority to sell or buy goods in his own name. Generally, a mercantile agent is a professional agent whose business activity is the purchase and sale of goods on behalf of others. However, in England it has also been held that when goods are entrusted to someone in a particular business situation to be dealt with as they would be by a mercantile agent then the person who receives the goods may thus be constituted a mercantile agent[5]. In other words, these authorities suggest that a mercantile agent can be someone who acts for a single principal in a single transaction.

(2) *The mercantile agent was entrusted with possession.* Possession includes civil possession[6] and possession of documents of title[7]. Thus an agent who has goods

deposited in a warehouse which is holding them on his behalf still has possession of the goods for the purpose of the Factors Act. The agent must be holding with the owner's consent, but this is presumed from possession of the goods unless the contrary is shown[8]. It has been held that he must hold the particular goods in the capacity of a mercantile agent and not in some other capacity, even although his business is generally within the definition of mercantile agency. The owner must also consent to the agent's possession being in that capacity[9]. Thus if a car owner places his vehicle with a car dealer for repair he is not generally entrusting it to him as a mercantile agent with the apparent authority to sell the car. There are English authorities in which it has been held that consent of the owner obtained by a fraud on him is still valid consent for the purposes of the agent's possession under the Factors Acts at least unless and until the consent is rescinded[10]. This point has not arisen for decision in Scotland but it is submitted that the view expressed in these cases almost certainly represents Scots law as well. There are analogous Scottish decisions[11] and the view taken in the above English cases is accepted as correct by Scottish textbook writers[12]. The result would be different if the conduct of the mercantile agent amounted to theft. The House of Lords has held in an English case that if the agent's possession derives from a thief or a person deriving title from a thief he cannot give good title under the Factors Acts[13]. Their Lordships did not directly address the situation where the owner is the victim of theft by the mercantile agent himself but it would appear that the same result would follow.

(3) *The seller sold the goods acting in the ordinary course of business of a mercantile agent.* This means that the seller acted in the way a duly authorised agent would have acted as respects time, place, manner, presentation of the goods and so on[14]. This requirement should not, however, be read too strictly, for example in the light of customs of particular trades[15].

(4) *The buyer acted in good faith and without notice that the agent lacked actual authority to sell the goods.* The onus of establishing good faith rests on the buyer. Usually this will involve him showing that he believed that the selling agent was either the owner of the goods himself or had actual authority to sell[16]. The ordinariness or otherwise of the transaction is an important factor in deciding issues of good faith[17].

(5) *The transaction was for value*[18].

There is no requirement that the buyer acquire possession. Where section 2 of the 1889 Act applies the transaction is as valid as if expressly authorised by the owner. The provision appears to confer on the mercantile agent a combination of actual and apparent authority. Thus in a question with a buyer the authority is deemed to be actual and a good title is conferred; but in a question with the principal the authority is apparent only and there may be liability for exceeding the actual authority[19].

1 See para 670 above.
2 Therefore this is an exception to the rule *nemo dat quod non habet*.
3 Factors Act 1889 (c 45), s 2(1). See also the Sale of Goods Act 1979 (c 54), s 21(2)(a). The Factors Act 1889 was extended to Scotland by the Factors (Scotland) Act 1890 (c 40). For a history of the law, see J J Gow *The Mercantile and Industrial Law of Scotland* (1964) pp 101–109. In *Vickers v Hertz* (1871) 9 M (HL) 65 it had been held that the Factors Acts applied to Scotland.
4 Factors Act 1889, s 1(1). The definition is repeated in the Sale of Goods Act 1979, s 26.
5 *Weiner v Harris* [1910] 1 KB 285, CA; *Lowther v Harris* [1927] 1 KB 393.
6 Factors Act 1889, s 1(2). For civil possession, see para 121 above.
7 For the meaning of 'documents of title', see ibid, s 1(4), where the expression is defined very widely.
8 Factors Act 1889, s 2(4). Note also s 2(2), (3), which relate to the termination of consent by the owner only being effective against a third party who has notice of it and to possession of documents of title arising from possession of goods with the owner's consent.
9 *Staffs Motor Guarantee Ltd v British Wagon Co Ltd* [1934] 2 KB 305; *Astley Industrial Trust Ltd v Miller* [1968] 2 All ER 36.

10 *Lowther v Harris* [1927] 1 KB 393; *Pearson v Rose and Young Ltd* [1951] 1 KB 275, [1950] 2 All ER
     1027, CA.
11 *Vickers v Hertz* (1871) 9 M (HL) 65; *MacLeod v Kerr* 1965 SC 253, 1965 SLT 358.
12 *Gow* p 109. See also D M Walker *Principles of Scottish Private Law* (4th edn, vol 3, 1989) p 426 who
     takes a more cautious view.
13 *National Employers Mutual General Insurance Association Ltd v Jones* [1988] 2 All ER 425 at 427, HL.
14 *Pearson v Rose and Young Ltd* [1951] 1 KB 275, [1950] 2 All ER 1027, CA; *Stadium Finance Ltd v
     Robbins* [1962] 2 QB 664, [1962] 2 All ER 633, CA.
15 *Oppenheimer v Attenborough & Son* [1908] 1 KB 221, CA.
16 *Heap v Motorists Advisory Agency Ltd* [1923] 1 KB 577.
17 *Oppenheimer v Attenborough & Son* [1908] 1 KB 221, CA.
18 Factors Act 1889, s 5; Factors (Scotland) Act 1890, s 1(2). The Factors Act 1889, s 5, defines the
     consideration which is possible under the Factors Acts.
19 Factors Act 1889, s 12(1).

672. Exceptions to the *nemo dat* rule. Naturally most transfers of property are
carried out by owners, while in the small minority of transfers which are *a non
domino* (by a non-owner) the rule is usually *nemo dat quod non habet*. In the first case,
the transferee obtains ownership while in the second case he does not. But the rule
nemo dat quod non habet does not always apply to transfers *a non domino*. In a small
number of cases — in a minority of a minority of all cases of transfer — the transferee
receives ownership notwithstanding the absence of title in his author. Three such
exceptions to the *nemo dat* rule are recognised:

(1) *Original acquisition*[1]. In original acquisition of ownership the law confers a new
     and good title on the acquirer; and, except in those few cases where the
     property was previously unowned[2], this has the necessary consequence of
     extinguishing the title of the former owner[3]. Usually original and derivative
     acquisition are distinct and arise out of different circumstances, but there is also a
     certain degree of overlap so that a transferee who is going through the form of
     derivative acquisition may find, if the transfer was *a non domino*, that he acquires
     title nonetheless but by original acquisition. The two leading examples of
     original acquisition carrying title where compliance with the rules of derivative
     acquisition would not are positive prescription and registration of title in the
     Land Register.

(2) *Accretion*. A transfer which was *a non domino* at the time it was made is perfected,
     and ownership conferred on the transferee, if the transferor subsequently
     acquires ownership and hence a title to grant.

(3) *Involuntary transfer*. In a small number of cases property which belongs to A may
     nonetheless be successfully transferred by B to C. These cases may be character-
     ised, with equal accuracy, either as cases of involuntary transfer[4] or as cases of
     voluntary transfer *a non domino*. Thus, from the point of view of A, the original
     owner of the property, there has been an involuntary transfer to C, whereas
     from the point of view of B, who neither owns the property nor has the
     authority of the person who does, there is a successful transfer in breach of the
     rule *nemo dat quod non habet*. The main examples occur in the sale of goods
     where, in certain circumstances, ownership may be acquired by a buyer from a
     non-owning seller[5]. In such cases the law requires reliance by the buyer on the
     apparent ownership of the seller, usually as evidenced by his possession of the
     goods, and on one view the rule can be regarded as a development of the law of
     personal bar[6].

Of the three cases just mentioned, only the third, strictly, is an exception to the rule
nemo dat because only here does the transferor, by an act of intention, give that
which he does not have[7]. By contrast, in the first case (original acquisition) there
may be no 'giving' at all, the rule operating to confer title regardless of whether the
non-owning transferor truly intended to transfer ownership[8], while in the second
case (accretion) the transferor does come to own the property in the end so that the
transfer is not *a non domino*. In the first case, therefore, the transferor does not 'give'

while in the second case the transferor 'has', and only in the third case does he give that which he does not have. But all three cases have in common that the performing of at least the outward trappings of the transfer process by a non-owning transferor results in the acquisition of ownership by the transferee, and, despite their differences, they are conveniently grouped together.

One further difference deserves attention. It is only in the first case (original acquisition) that the title conferred on the transferee is assuredly good. In the other two cases the acquisition is derivative and not original and is itself governed by the *nemo dat* rule. Thus any deficiency affecting the supervening title acquired by the transferor (in the case of accretion) or the title of the party from whom it is taken (in the case of acquisition by involuntary transfer) will affect the title in the hands of the transferee[9].

The three cases are considered in turn below.

1 For original acquisition, see paras 539 and 597 above.
2 Ie as when *occupatio* applies.
3 This is because Scots law does not recognise two competing titles to the same piece of property. If A is owner, then it necessarily follows that B, his competitor, is not. See para 603 above.
4 But of course most cases of involuntary transfer, like most cases of original acquisition, do not arise out of ostensible acts of voluntary transfer. See paras 663 ff above.
5 Another possible example is sale by a creditor of his debtor's property: see para 667 above.
6 J J Gow *The Mercantile and Industrial Law of Scotland* (1964) p 113; D L Carey Miller *Corporeal Moveables in Scots Law* (1991) p 211. They are, however, a development of the law in two senses. First, unlike common law personal bar, statutory bar has proprietary consequences. With the possible exception of the Sale of Goods Act 1979 (c 54), s 21(1), the effect of statutory bar is to take the title from the person who is barred and confer it on the person pleading reliance. Secondly, statutory bar admits the doctrine in circumstances where no common law plea would arise.
7 So if there is no intention to pass ownership, or if the goods are sold subject to retention of title, the Sale of Goods Act 1979, s 17, is not satisfied and ownership cannot pass. As to the Sale of Goods Act 1979, s 17, see para 628 above.
8 Eg the only requirement for positive prescription as applied to land is that there be a deed of conveyance which is not *ex facie* invalid or forged. See the Prescription and Limitation (Scotland) Act 1973 (c 52), s 1(1A) (added by the Land Registration (Scotland) Act 1979 (c 33), s 10). It is no bar to prescription that the transferor knew that he had no title and intended nothing by his grant.
9 *National Employers Insurance v Jones* [1988] 2 All ER 425.

(b) Original Acquisition

673. Registration in the Land Register. Registration in the Land Register confers on the applicant a good statutory title[1]. The rule for the Register of Sasines is otherwise. Thus if A grants a disposition to B of land in an area operational for the purposes of registration of title, and if the land actually belongs to C, the effect of B's registration in the Land Register is that C ceases to be owner and B becomes owner in his place. Good faith is not required. The same rule applies to subordinate real rights such as leases and standard securities.

At first sight this seems a startling result, and in a sense so it is. Nonetheless its effect in everyday practice is limited by three other factors. First, most deeds are not granted by non-owners. Secondly, the Keeper of the Register is not bound to accept deeds granted *a non domino*[2] although in practice he will usually do so subject to the exclusion of the state indemnity[3]. Exclusion of indemnity has no effect on the quality of title conferred by registration, but it both helps the applicant, by allowing positive prescription to run[4], and at the same time hinders him, by making possible rectification of the Register[5]. Thirdly, the *nemo dat* rule continues to operate at a certain level even on registered titles with the consequence that B's registration is treated as an 'inaccuracy' on the Register and so, in principle at least, capable of rectification at the instance of C[6]. The effect of rectification would be to delete B's name from the proprietorship section of the title sheet and replace it with C's name, with the result that ownership reverts to C. Where, however, the registered proprietor (B) is in possession of the land, whether natural or civil[7], rectification is only possible on certain limited grounds of which the most important is that the title is subject to an exclusion of indemnity[8]. In practice, of course, C may not know about B's registration and the Keeper is enjoined not to tell him[9]. The right to rectify is lost by the long negative prescription of twenty years[10], if it has not been lost earlier by the running of positive prescription in favour of the proprietor in possession[11].

In summary, where registration proceeds on an *a non domino* deed the title conferred on the applicant is subsistent but voidable[12] by the process of rectification already described. Once the right to rectify has been lost, whether by positive or by negative prescription, the title ceases to be voidable and becomes absolutely good.

1 Land Registration (Scotland) Act 1979 (c 33), s 3(1)(a). See K G C Reid 'A Non Domino Conveyances and the Land Register' 1991 JR 79.
2 Land Registration (Scotland) Act 1979, s 4(1).
3 *Registration of Title Practice Book* (1981) para H.1.08.
4 Prescription and Limitation (Scotland) Act 1973 (c 52), s 1 (amended by the Land Registration (Scotland) Act 1979, s 10).
5 Land Registration (Scotland) Act 1979, s 9(3)(a)(iv).
6 See K G C Reid 'New Titles for Old' (1984) 29 JLSS 171 at 172, 173.
7 In the Keeper's view 'possession' includes civil possession: see (1984) 29 JLSS 171 at 176. There is no definition of 'possession' in the Land Registration (Scotland) Act 1979.
8 Land Registration (Scotland) Act 1979, s 9(3). As to rectification, see further CONVEYANCING, vol 6, paras 750 ff.
9 Land Registration (Scotland) Rules 1980, SI 1980/1413, r 21(2).
10 Prescription and Limitation (Scotland) Act 1973, s 7.
11 For positive prescription, see para 674 below.
12 See para 601 above.

674. Positive prescription: heritable property. Ownership of land, both *dominium utile* and *dominium directum*, may be acquired by positive prescription[1]. So too may the subordinate real rights in land, that is to say standard security, lease and proper liferent[2]. So far as Sasine titles are concerned two requirements must be satisfied in order for prescription to run. First there must be registered in the Register of Sasines a deed, usually referred to as a 'foundation writ', which is sufficient in respect of its terms to constitute a title to the land. Secondly, the registration of the foundation writ must be followed by ten years' possession, either by the grantee of the foundation writ or by the grantee and his successors[3]. The possession must be continuous, open, peaceable and without judicial interruption and must be 'founded' on and attributable to the foundation writ[4]. Possession includes civil possession[5]. The standard foundation writ for the acquisition of ownership is a disposition, although certain other deeds may also be used, for example a feu disposition or a notice of title. The deed must describe the property in a manner that may be construed as including the land possessed, although it is not necessary that this is its only or natural construction[6]. There is no requirement that the foundation writ actually be valid, provided that the fact of invalidity is not clearly apparent from the face of the deed and provided also that it is not forged[7]. So a disposition *a non domino* is a valid foundation writ for the purposes of prescription. Further, there is no requirement that the possessor be in good faith in the sense of believing in the validity of the foundation writ.

The effect of prescription is to confer in relation to the land possessed the right which the foundation writ bears to carry. So where the foundation writ is a disposition the effect of possession is to confer ownership of the land possessed. Thus if A conveys to B land which belongs to C, registration of B's disposition in the Register of Sasines does nothing to disturb C's ownership, for *nemo dat quod non habet*; but if B then proceeds to possess the land, at the end of ten years C's title will be extinguished and ownership conferred on B. Original acquisition, by means of positive prescription, cures the defective title arising out of the derivative acquisition from A.

The title conferred by prescription is not only subsistent but, in the words of the Prescription and Limitation (Scotland) Act 1973[8], 'exempt from challenge', which is to say that it is not voidable; but this immunity from reduction is confined to grounds of challenge which existed prior to the start of the ten years' possession.

Thus far only Sasine titles have been considered. Positive prescription cannot run on Land Register titles except in the highly unusual circumstances of state indemnity having been excluded[9]. When this has been done the requirements of prescription are similar to those for Sasine titles — a title sheet relating to the land in question followed by ten years' possession — but the effects are slightly different. Thus to return to the example given earlier of A conveying to B land which belongs to C, the effect of B registering his title in the Land Register is to confer on him immediate ownership — land registration itself being a form of original acquisition — but subject to the possibility of future rectification by C. B's title is thus immediately subsistent, but voidable[10]. If indemnity has been excluded and if B is in possession, so that prescription runs, the effect is that at the end of ten years B's title is 'exempt from challenge' and hence no longer vulnerable to rectification.

The distinction made by the legislation between Land Register titles with exclusion of indemnity, when prescription can run, and titles without exclusion of indemnity, when it cannot, is not entirely satisfactory. Usually it is sought to be justified on the basis that only the former are vulnerable to rectification and so in need of the protection of positive prescription[11]. But while it is true that rectification will occur most commonly where indemnity has been excluded, it is not the law that rectification cannot occur in other cases[12] and for these cases the right to rectify will continue until extinguished by the long negative prescription of twenty years.

1 The governing legislation is the Prescription and Limitation (Scotland) Act 1973 (c 52), ss 1–5 (amended by the Land Registration (Scotland) Act 1979 (c 33), s 10). On the general subject of prescription, see further PRESCRIPTION AND LIMITATION; D M Walker *The Law of Prescription and Limitation of Actions in Scotland* (4th edn, 1990). The only full scholarly treatment is M Napier's dated but masterly *Commentaries on the Law of Prescription in Scotland* (1839 and 1854).

2 The Prescription and Limitation (Scotland) Act 1973, s 1(2), applies to 'any interest in land the title to which can competently be recorded [in the Register of Sasines] or which is registrable in the Land Register of Scotland'. 'Interest in land' is the term favoured by parliamentary draftsmen for real rights in land. Different rules of prescription are provided for servitudes and public rights of way: see s 3.

3 Ibid, s 1(1). A 'successor' is one who derives his title from the grantee of the foundation writ — in practice usually a disponee of that person.

4 For an example of possession which was not so founded, see *Houstoun v Barr* 1911 SC 134, 1910 2 SLT 286. As to the meaning of 'judicial interruption', see the Prescription and Limitation (Scotland) Act 1973 (c 52), s 4.

5 Prescription and Limitation (Scotland) Act 1973, s 15(1).

6 *Auld v Hay* (1880) 7 R 663 at 668, per Lord Justice-Clerk Moncreiff: 'The terms of the grant may be ambiguous, or indefinite, or general, so that it may remain doubtful whether the particular subject is or is not conveyed, or, if conveyed, what is the extent of it. But if the instrument be conceived in terms consistent with and susceptible of a construction which would embrace such a conveyance, that is enough, and forty [now ten] years' possession following on it will constitute the right to the extent possessed'. See also *Suttie v Baird* 1992 SLT 133.

7 The foundation writ must not be invalid *ex facie* or forged: Prescription and Limitation (Scotland) Act 1973, s 1(A)(a) (added by the Land Registration (Scotland) Act 1979 (c 33), s 10). For a case involving a deed which was invalid *ex facie*, see *Cooper Scott v Gill Scott* 1924 SC 309, 1924 SLT 204.

8 Prescription and Limitation (Scotland) Act 1973, s 1(1).

9 Ibid, s 1(1)(b). For exclusion of indemnity, see the Land Registration (Scotland) Act 1979, s 12(2).

10 See para 673 above.

11 *Registration of Title Practice Book* (1981) para C.63.

12 Ie where the Register is 'inaccurate' and either (1) the registered proprietor is not in possession or (2) the Land Registration (Scotland) Act 1979, s 9(3)(a)(i), (ii) or (iii), applies.

675. Positive prescription: moveable property. The Prescription and Limitation (Scotland) Act 1973 makes no provision for positive prescription in relation to moveable property, and while it is sometimes argued that in the case of corporeal moveables there is a forty years' prescription at common law, the evidence is inconclusive and the question remains an open one[1]. If prescription does exist it is unclear, length of possession apart, what its constituent rules may be.

In terms of the 1973 Act ownership of corporeal moveables prescribes negatively after twenty years[2], except that the right of an owner to recover from a thief or from a person privy to the theft is imprescriptible[3]. So if A sells to B a ring belonging to C, C will lose his ownership after twenty years, assuming that the terms of the 1973 Act are satisfied. But unless the existence of positive prescription is recognised the ring does not thereby become the property of B. Instead it is *res nullius* and thus, it is thought, the property of the Crown[4]. In practice, however, there is little prospect of B's title being challenged.

There is no positive prescription in relation to incorporeal moveable property.

1 See para 565 above; D L Carey Miller *Corporeal Moveables in Scots Law* (1991) pp 95–98.
2 Prescription and Limitation (Scotland) Act 1973 (c 52), s 8. See para 567 above.
3 Ibid, Sch 3(g).
4 See paras 540, 547, above.

676. Other cases. A bona fide acquirer for value ('holder in due course') of a negotiable instrument receives a good title notwithstanding the absence of title in his author[1]. So too does a bona fide acquirer of lost and abandoned property from the police[2]. These are statutory examples of original acquisition. A purchaser of bricks from a non-owner who then uses them to build a house on his land will acquire the bricks by accession, while an equivalent purchaser of raw materials manufacturing them into a new species will acquire the materials by specification. There is no requirement of good faith in accession although the position for specification is less clear[3]. In both cases there is liability to the former owner for the value of the materials[4]. Relatively speaking, however, these are unusual examples, and the facts giving rise to the common law cases of original acquisition, such as occupancy, accession and specification, do not often involve derivative acquisitions *a non domino*.

1 Bills of Exchange Act 1882 (c 61), s 38(2). For the meaning of holder in due course', see s 29.
2 Civic Government (Scotland) Act 1982 (c 45), s 71. See para 550 above. It may, of course, be questioned whether a purchaser of lost and abandoned property from the police can ever be in good faith.
3 For the possible requirement of good faith in specification, see paras 561, 562, above, and D L Carey Miller *Corporeal Moveables in Scots Law* (1991) pp 68–70.
4 Stair *Institutions* II,1,38 and 39; *International Banking Corpn v Ferguson Shaw & Sons* 1910 SC 182, 1909 2 SLT 377.

(c) Accretion

677. Heritable property. Where, subsequent to a conveyance of land *a non domino*, the transferor acquires ownership of the land conveyed, the doctrine of accretion operates to perfect the original conveyance and carry ownership from the transferor to the transferee. No new conveyance is necessary[1]. As Bell expresses it[2], accretion is 'the law doing what the granter is bound to do', and the basis of the doctrine is that, since a granter who includes in his original conveyance either a grant of absolute warrandice[3] or an obligation to convey his whole right, title and interest present and future to the property[4] would be bound in the circumstances described to grant a second conveyance, the need for a second deed is dispensed with and a transfer is effected by operation of law.

Accretion works by a legal fiction. The transferor is deemed to have owned the property at the time of the original grant. Accordingly, that transfer is retrospectively validated. From the moment the property is acquired by the transferor it passes, in virtue of the earlier act of transfer, to the transferee. It will be seen that accretion is an exception to the rule *nemo dat quod non habet* only in a technical sense. It is an exception because it gives effect to an act of transfer by a non-owner; but since the doctrine only operates on the subsequent acquisition of title by the transferor the essentials of the rule are preserved.

Historically, accretion developed as a rule of land law, probably in response to the complexity of the unreformed system of land transfer. Until the reforms of the mid-nineteenth century[5] failure to complete title in the interval between first acquisition and subsequent disposal was a frequent occurrence and accretion became a useful protection for purchasers. Indeed the doctrine may at one time have been confined to this situation of right to land not completed by infeftment[6], but it is now settled that it applies even where there is no right to the property whatsoever at the time when the conveyance is granted[7]. Accretion applies in the transfer of heritable property, both corporeal and incorporeal, and also in the creation of subordinate real rights in land, for example leases and standard securities[8]. It applies both to Sasine and to Land Register titles, although in the second case its effect is not to confer title[9] but to prevent a possible future rectification of the Register.

In its application to the transfer of land the rules of accretion are now largely settled. Absence of title at the time of the original grant is cured by the subsequent acquisition of title by the granter, provided that the original disposition contained either a grant of absolute warrandice or a conveyance of the granter's whole right, title and interest, future as well as present. In practice dispositions usually contain both. Accretion requires that the granter become infeft. Supervening sequestration prevents accretion, regardless of whether title then comes to be acquired by the granter or by his trustee in sequestration[10]. The position may be different where the granter has died and title comes to be acquired by his executor[11]. Since accretion depends on a grant of absolute warrandice or an equivalent obligation to convey future title, parties to deeds who do not grant warrandice, notably consenters, are not subject to the doctrine and may assert a subsequent title against the grantee[12]. Much the same rules apply where accretion is pled in support of a grant of subordinate real rights, such as leases and standard securities.

It has been seen that accretion back-dates acquisition of title to the date of the original grant. But this legal fiction operates for two purposes only. One is to validate the original grant, so removing the need for a fresh one. The other is to determine ranking as between competing grantees. So if A, a non-owner, dispones the same piece of land successively to B, C and D, all of whom register their dispositions in the Register of Sasines, A's subsequent acquisition of ownership is regarded as validating each grant in turn. But, *fictione juris*, the validation is retrospective and not current. If it was current, each grantee would have an equal claim to the property. Since, however, it is retrospective, each disposition being deemed retrospectively to have been properly granted, the new owner is whichever of B, C or D had been first to register[13].

The fiction of retrospective ownership has no application outside the two situations just described. Thus suppose that in year one A grants B a disposition of land which belongs to C, and that in year eight C dispones the land to A, and further suppose that the title is a Sasine title[14]. At the moment when A registers his disposition from C, B becomes owner because, for the purposes of the validity of the A–B disposition A is deemed to have become owner in year one. But in all other respects the law recognises that A became owner only in year eight. So if in year three C had granted a standard security to D, D's security right would be unchallengeable and would continue to burden the property even in the hands of B[15].

1　See generally Stair *Institutions* III,2,1 and 2; Bankton *Institute* III,2,16–18; Erskine *Institute* II,7,3 and 4; Bell *Commentaries* I,737 and 738; Bell *Principles* ss 881, 882.
2　Bell *Principles* s 881.
3　Stair III,2,2; Bankton III,2,18; Erskine II,7,3. For warrandice, see paras 701 ff.
4　Stair III,2,2; Bankton III,2,16; Erskine II,7,3.
5　There have been no reported cases on accretion in the last 100 years. This may be contrasted with the twenty-four cases given in Morison's Dictionary under the heading '*Jus superveniens auctoris accrescit successori*'.
6　Bell *Principles* s 882(2).
7　*Swans v Western Bank* (1866) 4 M 663.
8　*Neilson v Murray* (1738) Mor 7773 (heritable security); *Neilson v Menzies* (1671) Mor 7768 (lease).
9　Title already being conferred by the Land Registration (Scotland) Act 1979 (c 33), s 3(1)(a). See para 673 above.
10　Bankruptcy (Scotland) Act 1985 (c 66), s 31(3). The law prior to 1985 was uncertain: see 1 *Encyclopaedia of the Laws of Scotland* (ed Lord Dunedin and J Wark, 1926) para 112.
11　This is because an executor is *eadem persona cum defuncto*. *Keith v Grant* (1792) Mor 2933, 7767, denied accretion in the case of an heir but the decision appears to be confined to heritable rights completed by infeftment and so would not apply eg to leases and standard securities. See also Lord Dirleton *Some Doubts and Questions in the Law* (1698) p 248. There is the further point that an executor may not be in the same position as an heir.
12　Bankton III,2,17; Erskine II,7,4; *Forbes v Innes* (1668) Mor 7759; *Stuart v Hutchison* (1681) Mor 7762.
13　Bankton III,2,16; *Neilson v Murray* (1738) Mor 7773; *Paterson v Kelly* (1742) Mor 7775.
14　If the title was a Land Register title the result would be different, for B would become owner in year one and would remain owner unless C rectified the Register against him. Consequently D's standard security would be *a non domino* and hence ineffective.
15　*Munro v Brodie* (1844) 6 D 1249. It is thought that the mid-impediment (the standard security) does not prevent accretion but renders the accresced title subject to the security. This question did not arise in *Munro* because the mid-impediment exhausted the subjects.

678. Moveable property. There are no reported cases or other authorities touching on the application of accretion to moveable property. But since accretion is based on warrandice, and since warrandice occurs in the transfer of moveable property in much the same way as in the transfer of heritable, it might be thought that accretion should apply here also[1]. There is the further point that although accretion developed in the context of land law it has been said not to be a rule of feudal law[2]. The position, however, remains uncertain.

1　W A Wilson 'Romalpa and Trust' 1983 SLT (News) 106 at 108; P S Atiyah *The Sale of Goods* (8th edn, 1990) p 357. The question appears not to be discussed in D L Carey Miller *Corporeal Moveables in Scots Law* (1991).
2　*Swans v Western Bank* (1866) 4 M 663 at 669, per Lord Ardmillan.

679. Ratification by principal of transfer by agent. In the context of the transfer of ownership, the ratification by a principal of the unauthorised act of his agent appears to be a species of accretion. So if A purports to transfer property belonging to B, and there is subsequent ratification by B, the transfer is, it seems, effective at the moment of ratification. As with other cases of accretion, ratification produces the legal fiction that A had title to transfer (as agent) at the time of the original conveyance, with the result that no new conveyance is required. A must have purported to act as agent at the time of the transfer[1], and there is an argument that in the case of land, ratification requires to be in formal writing. There is probably no requirement that the conveyance contain a grant of absolute warrandice or a conveyance of the granter's future interest[2]. An example of the doctrine is the charter of confirmation used in land transfers prior to 1874: in granting the charter the superior ratified, with retrospective effect, the sasine given earlier by the transferor[3].

1 See AGENCY AND MANDATE, vol 1, para 625.
2 This is because there is no question of the agent ever acquiring or retaining ownership in his own name. The only possibilities are (1) that ownership remains with the principal and (2) that ownership passes to the transferee.
3 Confirmation was regarded as an example of accretion in *Swans v Western Bank* (1866) 4 M 663 at 668, per Lord Curriehill.

(d) Involuntary Transfer: Personal Bar in the Sale of Goods

680. Owner by his conduct precluded from denying seller's authority to sell. The enactment of the general rule *nemo dat quod non habet* is qualified to exclude the application of *nemo dat* where the owner of the goods is precluded by his conduct from denying the seller's authority to sell[1]. It appears that this provision is intended to codify the English law on estoppel which seems to operate to grant a title to an innocent third party when the owner has by his conduct allowed the transaction with the third party to take place. This is based on equity and justice. The Scottish concept of personal bar, though broadly analogous to estoppel, would not go so far in its effect (as it is primarily a rule of evidence rather than substantive law). This divergence between the underlying common law in England and Scotland creates difficulties in the operation of the provision in Scotland and also emphasises the need for care in handling the English authorities in this area. There does not appear to be any reported Scottish decision on the effect of this provision. It has, however, been argued that where an owner has voluntarily surrendered control of the goods and has thus facilitated the dishonest disposal of them, the Scottish courts should so construe this provision that an onerous and bona fide acquirer would receive a good title[2]. An alternative formulation would be that the provision will operate wherever the true owner has made any representation or holding out of apparent ownership or right to sell on the part of the person selling the goods[3]. It is submitted that the meaning and purpose of the provision are given effect to by either of these suggestions. Presumably in Scotland the actual conferring of title would be by statutory authority.

On the other hand, it has been submitted that the situation must be such that the third party was not only misled by his relying on the owner's actions but was entitled thus to rely. Thus if an element entitling reliance is absent, the section will not apply[4]. It could be argued in reply that this is to import more of the common law on personal bar into the statutory provision than is warranted. In any event there will be few cases where this fine point of distinction will arise. It should be noted that the Court of Appeal has held that the provision does not come into effect at all unless the purported relationship between the seller and the third party is one of sale rather than merely agreement to sell[5], a technical decision.

1 Sale of Goods Act 1979 (c 54), s 21(1): '... where goods are sold by a person who is not their owner, and who does not sell them under the authority or with the consent of the owner, the buyer acquires no better title to the goods than the seller had, *unless the owner of the goods is by his conduct precluded from denying the seller's authority to sell*' (emphasis added). See D L Carey Miller *Corporeal Moveables in Scots Law* (1991) pp 208–211. Cf para 671 above. As to the general rule *nemo dat quod non habet*, see paras 669 ff above.
2 See *Corporeal Moveables—Protection of the Onerous bona fide Acquirer of Another's Property* (Scot Law Com Consultative Memorandum no. 27) (1976) paras 27, 28.
3 This was stated to be the effect of the provision by Devlin J in *Eastern Distributors Ltd v Goldring* [1957] 2 QB 600 at 610, [1957] 2 All ER 525 at 532, CA. In *Central Newbury Car Auctions Ltd v Unity*

Finance Ltd [1957] 1 QB 371, [1956] 3 All ER 905, CA, the plaintiff largely failed because it was considered that passing over the registration book did not amount to a representation on freedom to deal with the car as the registration book was not a document of title.

4 J J Gow *The Mercantile and Industrial Law of Scotland* (1964) pp 116, 117.

5 *Shaw v Metropolitan Police Comr* [1987] 3 All ER 405, [1987] 1 WLR 1332, CA.

681. Seller in possession. The Factors Act 1889 introduced a provision for sales by sellers in possession[1]. This provision was reproduced in the Sale of Goods Acts 1893 and 1979[2] but the provision in the 1889 Act was never repealed. Thus, confusingly, there are parallel statutory enactments for no apparent reason. In a system where property passed on delivery, the issue with which these provisions are concerned would not arise. Where a person has sold goods[3] and continues or is in possession of them or documents of title to them, delivery by him or his mercantile agent[4] of the goods or documents under any sale or any agreement to sell[5] to any person who receives in good faith and without notice of the previous sale, has the same effect as if the transferor had the express authority of the owner of the goods for the transfer.

The legislative technique used is a fiction of agency with a consequential statutory power to contract and to sell. The seller is deemed to be the agent of the first purchaser and as such can give as good title as the former has to a second purchaser. He will remain liable to the first purchaser. It has been held by the House of Lords in England that the statutory expression 'the owner' in the 1979 Act refers to the original purchaser and not the true owner if different[6]. This seems correct given that the basic principle of the law remains *nemo dat* but a different opinion has been expressed as to the law of Scotland, (albeit prior to the above decision)[7].

To obtain the statutory title the second purchaser must show:

(1) The seller continued or was in possession of the goods or documents of title to them. It has been held that this possession need not be with the first buyer's consent and all that is required is physical possession in whatever legal capacity[8]. This differs from the position where the sale is by a mercantile agent[9] or by a buyer in possession[10]. The possession may be by an agent for the seller[11]. It has been judicially stated that there has to be a continuity in the possession[12].

(2) He has received a delivery of transfer of the goods from the seller or the seller's mercantile agent[13]. There appears that there has to be actual delivery or the transfer of the documents of title[14]. That requirement does not apply to dispositions by a mercantile agent in possession of goods with the consent of the owner.

(3) He has received the goods or the documents of title to them in good faith and without notice of the previous sale. He must still be acting in good faith at that point. It appears that the notice required must be actual notice[15]. There is no statutory requirement that the disposition be for value unlike one by a mercantile agent in possession of goods[16]. The question of value will thus be relevant only as a factor in assessing good faith unless the courts construe 'disposition' as necessarily requiring onerous consideration.

1 Factors Act 1889 (c 45), s 8. (The Act was extended to Scotland by the Factors (Scotland) Act 1890 (c 40)). See D L Carey Miller *Corporeal Moveables in Scots Law* (1991) pp 211–214.

2 Sale of Goods Act 1893 (c 71), s 25(1) (repealed); Sale of Goods Act 1979 (c 54), s 24. This paragraph refers only to sale. The statutory text also includes a reference to pledge or other disposition of the goods.

3 If the relationship between the seller and the first purchaser is one of agreement to sell, then the provision does not come into effect. There the seller will still have property in the goods and he can give a good title to a second purchaser. If he resells, he will be liable for breach of his agreement to sell to the first purchaser. The second purchaser will not, however, have to show lack of notice of that agreement to sell to retain his title to the goods.

4 For the meaning of 'mercantile agent', see the Factors Act 1889, s 1(1), and the Sale of Goods Act 1979, s 26.

5 The phrase 'agreement to sell' appears in the Factors Act 1889, s 8, but not in the Sale of Goods Act 1979, s 24. Thus the Factors Act provision covers a contractual angle as well as the property one. Also if the disposition between the seller and second purchaser is a sale, title will pass under the present provisions presuming they are fulfilled. If the disposition is an agreement to sell between these parties it has contractual effect under the Factors Act 1889, s 8. Thereafter passing of property takes place in accordance with the agreement of the parties or under the Sale of Goods Act 1979, s 18. (For the s 18 rules, see paras 630 ff above.) The second purchaser is, however, still preferred over the first in that situation.

6 *National Employers Mutual General Insurance Association Ltd v Jones* [1988] 2 All ER 425, HL.

7 In *Corporeal Moveables—Protection of the Onerous bona fide Acquirer of Another's Property* (Scot Law Com Consultative Memorandum no. 27) (1976) para 30, the view is taken that 'owner' in Scotland may mean full and true owner and that the effect of the statutory provisions is that a bona fide acquirer would take an unchallengeable title.

8 *Pacific Motor Auctions Pty Ltd v Motor Credits (Hire Finance) Ltd* [1965] AC 867, [1965] 2 All ER 105, PC; *Worcester Works Finance Ltd v Cooden Engineering Co Ltd* [1972] 1 QB 210, [1971] 3 All ER 708, CA.

9 Factors Act 1889, s 2. See para 671 above.

10 Ibid, s 9; Sale of Goods Act 1979, s 25. See para 682 below.

11 *City Fur Manufacturing Co Ltd v Fureenbond (Brokers) London Ltd* [1937] 1 All ER 799.

12 *Worcester Works Finance Ltd v Cooden Engineering Co Ltd* [1972] 1 QB 210 at 217, 218, [1971] 3 All ER 708 at 712, CA, per Lord Denning MR.

13 It appears that a transfer by an agent must be by a mercantile agent as defined in the statute (see note 4 above). However, this may no longer always be the case: see *Four Point Garage v Carter* [1985] 3 All ER 12.

14 *Nicholson v Harper* [1895] 2 Ch 415.

15 *Worcester Works Finance Ltd v Cooden Engineering Co Ltd* [1972] 1 QB 210 at 218, [1971] 3 All ER 708 at 712, CA, per Lord Denning MR.

16 Factors Act 1889, s 5; Factors (Scotland) Act 1890, s 1(2).

682. Buyer in possession. Once again special provision for a good title to be given by a buyer in possession was introduced by the Factors Act 1889[1] and also made in the Sale of Goods Acts 1893 and 1979[2]. Like the enactments relating to the seller in possession, this provision thus rests anomalously on two parallel statutory provisions. There are some differences both in the form and substance of the provisions. Where a person who has bought or agreed to buy goods obtains with the seller's consent possession of the goods or documents of title to them, the delivery or transfer by him or his mercantile agent[3] of the goods or documents of title to them under any sale or any agreement for sale[4] to a person receiving the goods or the documents in good faith and without notice of any lien or other right of the original seller is to have the same effect as the delivery or transfer by a mercantile agent in possession of the goods with the owner's consent. The technique of deeming an agency is used once again, but is carried further in that the effect of the conditions of the provision being fulfilled is that the sale of the second purchaser is equated to one by a mercantile agent with statutory apparent authority[5]. This is a fairly artificial legislative approach. There appears to be no good reason why the situations of seller and buyer are not dealt with in the same manner.

The situation covered by these provisions is where a buyer has possession and appears to be the owner[6] of the goods yet does not have property in them, for example, because of the operation of a valid retention of title clause[7]. It has been stated by an academic commentator that the statutory provisions have been strictly construed so that it is difficult for the third party to obtain good title under them[8].

To obtain the statutory title, the second purchaser or acquirer must show[9]:

(1) *The disposition was by a buyer or a person who has agreed to buy.* The double reference covers not only those who do not have property in the goods but also those who do. The question arises as to the need for reliance on the provision in that case. It has been suggested that possibly this covers buyers under a voidable title who resell after their title has been avoided. Purchasers from them cannot rely on the provisions dealing with voidable titles but may be able to rely upon the protection for sales by a buyer in possession, if all relevant conditions are

fulfilled[10]. The statutory provisions exclude buyers under a conditional sale agreement if it is one covered by the Consumer Credit Act 1974[11]. Purchasers under hire purchase are also outwith these provisions[12]. It has also been held that someone who was acting as an agent and not contracting for his own personal interest in the original transaction with the first seller is not covered by the provision and cannot pass good title to a purchaser from him[13].

(2) *The person making the disposition was in possession of the goods*[14] *and had such possession with the consent of the seller.* Thus, unlike the provisions relating to a seller in possession consent to possession by the other party to the first transaction has to be shown. It appears that this consent can be valid even if induced by fraud[15]. If consent is withdrawn, title can still be passed unless and until a third party has notice of withdrawal[16].

(3) *The goods (or any documents of title to them) were delivered or transferred to him*[17]. The provisions state that this delivery has to be by the buyer in possession or his mercantile agent. It would appear from this that delivery or transfer by an agent who does not come into the statutory definition of a mercantile agent is not enough. However, in one English case it was held that there could be delivery to the second purchaser even by the original seller acting as agent for the buyer and presumably by any other agent. It was conceded that the seller was not acting as a *mercantile* agent for the buyer in the circumstances[18]. It is submitted that this decision is doubtful on this point. Admittedly the original seller was acting at the direct request of the buyer. The delivery or transfer of the goods must involve an actual or constructive change of possession[19].

(4) *He received the goods or documents to title in good faith*[20] *and without notice of any lien or other right of the original seller, for example, under a retention of title clause in the original contract of sale*[21].

(5) *The buyer in his re-selling was acting in a way that would have been in the ordinary course of business of a mercantile agent had he been a mercantile agent.* The Court of Appeal has held that this is the effect of the deeming of mercantile agency included in the provision[22]. Effectively this incorporates the requirements of a sale by a mercantile agent in possession into the provision on sale by a buyer in possession and adds them to the requirements laid down for that situation both when the buyer in possession is and is not himself a mercantile agent. The alternative view would be to regard the relevant words as merely providing that the sale would take effect as if by a mercantile agent in possession and that thus title would simply pass to the third party. There is high judicial opinion in Scotland which infers this alternative view[23]. A more recent Outer House decision appears to follow and apply the view of the Court of Appeal but perhaps not wholly consistently[24]. There may be some small doubt as to how the Scottish Courts would deal with this question if squarely faced with it especially where a buyer in possession was clearly not himself a mercantile agent.

(6) *The disposition was for value.* This is not explicitly stated in the statutes but it appears that whatever view is taken on the issue raised above the deeming of mercantile agency implies that the transaction be for valuable consideration[25]. This is different from the position regarding a seller in possession.

The title conferred by the operation of this provision will be good against the seller but not necessarily against the true owner if different. In *National Employers Mutual General Assurance Ltd v Jones* the House of Lords held that 'the owner' whose mercantile agent the buyer is deemed to be is in fact the seller and that someone deriving title from a thief, even if actually a mercantile agent, cannot confer a good title against the true owner[26].

1 Factors Act 1889 (c 45), s 9 (amended by the Consumer Credit Act 1974 (c 39), s 192, Sch 4, Pt I, para 2). (The Factors Act 1889 was extended to Scotland by the Factors (Scotland) Act 1890 (c 40).) See D L Carey Miller *Corporeal Moveables in Scots Law* (1991) pp 214–217.

2 Sale of Goods Act 1893 (c 71), s 25(2) (repealed); Sale of Goods Act 1979 (c 54), s 25. This paragraph refers only to sale. The language of the Act includes references to pledge and other dispositions of the goods.
3 For the meaning of 'mercantile agent', see the Factors Act 1889, s 1(1), and the Sale of Goods Act 1979, s 26.
4 The phrase 'agreement to sell' appears in the Factors Act 1889, s 9, but not in the Sale of Goods Act 1979, s 25.
5 The exact effect of this deeming is discussed in head (5) in the text. For sales by a mercantile agent in possession of goods, see para 671 above.
6 In *Thomas Graham & Sons Ltd v Glenrothes Development Corpn* 1968 SLT 2 at 8, Lord President Clyde refers to the buyer in possession as an 'apparent owner'.
7 *Archivent Sales and Development Ltd v Strathclyde Regional Council* 1985 SLT 154, OH; *Four Point Garage v Carter* [1985] 3 All ER 12.
8 R Goode *Commercial Law* (1985) p 411.
9 See *Thomas Graham & Sons Ltd v Glenrothes Development Corpn* 1968 SLT 2 at 8, 9, per Lord President Clyde, and 9, 10, per Lord Migdale.
10 *Goode* p 411. For sales under voidable titles (Sale of Goods Act 1979, s 23), see paras 601, 692, below.
11 Factors Act 1889, s 9 (as amended: see note 1 above); Sale of Goods Act 1979, s 25(2).
12 *Helby v Matthews* [1895] AC 471, HL.
13 *Shaw v Metropolitan Police Comr* [1987] 3 All ER 405, [1987] 1 WLR 1332, CA.
14 This is presumed to be the case, as under the Factors Act 1889, s 8, and the Sale of Goods Act 1979, s 24. Possession by an agent will suffice. Even the seller can be the buyer's agent. See *Four Point Garage v Carter* [1985] 3 All ER 12.
15 *Du Jardin v Beadman Brothers Ltd* [1952] 2 QB 712, [1952] 2 All ER 160. See also the discussion of the same point under the Factors Act 1889, s 2, in para 671 above.
16 *Cahn v Pocketts Bristol Channel Steam Packet Co* [1899] 1 QB 643, CA.
17 Whether there had been delivery or not was a major point of dispute in both *Thomas Graham & Sons Ltd v Glenrothes Development Corpn* 1968 SLT 2 and *Archivent Sales and Development Ltd v Strathclyde Regional Council* 1985 SLT 154, OH.
18 *Four Point Garage v Carter* [1985] 3 All ER 12.
19 *Ladbroke Leasing (South West) Ltd v Reekie Plant Ltd* 1983 SLT 155, OH.
20 *Wilkes v Livingstone* 1955 SLT (Notes) 19, OH; *Newtons of Wembley Ltd v Williams* [1965] 1 QB 560, [1964] 3 All ER 532, CA.
21 *Archivent Sales and Development Ltd v Strathclyde Regional Council* 1985 SLT 154, OH.
22 *Newtons of Wembley Ltd v Williams* [1965] 1 QB 560, [1964] 3 All ER 532, CA. See especially the judgment of Pearson LJ at 578–580, 538–540.
23 In *Thomas Graham & Sons Ltd v Glenrothes Development Corpn* 1968 SLT 2 at 9, Lord President Clyde, referring to the deeming provision, states that 'this just means that he will have the ostensible authority of a mercantile agent to pass the property in the goods'. *Newtons of Wembley Ltd v Williams* [1965] 1 QB 560, [1964] 3 All ER 532, CA, does not appear to have been cited to the First Division in *Thomas Graham*.
24 In *Archivent Sales and Development Ltd v Strathclyde Regional Council* 1985 SLT 154 at 157, OH, Lord Mayfield refers to and applies *Newtons of Wembley Ltd v Williams* [1965] 1 QB 560, [1964] 3 All ER 532, CA, but at 156 he states that the result of the statutory provisions applying is that the disposition 'will have the same effect as if the person making the delivery or transfer was a mercantile agent in respect of the goods with the consent of the owner'. It appears from a careful reading of Lord Mayfield's judgment that he may have been assuming that the contractors were actually mercantile agents rather than deemed to be such. However, he makes no direct finding to that effect. He certainly and rightly considered them to be agents. Likewise in *Wilkes v Livingston* 1955 SLT (Notes) 19, OH, it appears at least highly arguable that the defenders were actually within the definition of mercantile agents as well as being buyers in possession.
25 *Thomas Graham & Sons Ltd v Glenrothes Development Corpn* 1968 SLT 2 at 9, per Lord President Clyde (referring to the Factors Acts in general), and 9, 10, per Lord Migdale. Logically this insistence on consideration fits better with the approach to the matter found in *Newtons of Wembley Ltd v Williams* [1965] 1 QB 560, [1964] 3 All ER 532, CA.
26 *National Employers Mutual General Insurance Association Ltd v Jones* [1988] 2 All ER 425, HL.

683. Motor vehicles subject to hire purchase. A special statutory exception to the *nemo dat quod non habet* principle is enacted by the Hire Purchase Act 1964[1]. Essentially this provides that when the hirer of a motor vehicle under a hire purchase agreement or the buyer under a conditional sale agreement disposes of the vehicle to a private purchaser purchasing in good faith and without notice of the relevant agreement the disposition has the same effect as if the hirer or the buyer under conditional sale had been vested with title at the date of the disposition[2]. In other words, a private purchaser receives a good title in these circumstances, even although the hirer or buyer has acted in breach of his agreement with the provider of credit. He also receives a good title if it is an intermediate 'trade or finance purchaser'[3] who dispones the vehicle to him provided the above statutory conditions are met[4].

A private purchaser is defined as someone who does not carry on business as a trade or finance customer[5]. The key to the application of this definition is the status of the purchaser not the capacity in which he purchases or the purpose for which he purchases. Thus it has been held that a person who had a part time motor sales business purchasing a car for his own private use did not benefit from the legislative protection[6]. On the other hand, someone who purchases for business use but who does not come into the restrictive definition of 'trade or finance purchaser' will receive a good title. The policy rationale for the distinction between the two classes of purchaser is the assumption that trade and finance purchasers will have access to ready means to checking whether a vehicle is subject to hire-purchase or conditional sale whereas private purchasers will not[7].

As well as general good faith, the private purchaser must not have notice of the agreement covering the vehicle and preventing the hirer or buyer from disposing. It has been held that this only refers to knowledge of the relevant agreement. Knowledge of other agreements where all instalments have been paid is immaterial[8].

In *North West Securities Ltd v Barrhead Coachworks Ltd*[9] the position of the deprived original owner when a private purchaser had obtained good title after a purchase from the intermediate trade or finance purchaser was considered. It was held that he had no proprietary remedy at all against the intermediate dealer. His only claim was in restitution and this is limited in the case of a bona fide intermediate dealer to the extent that he is enriched[10]. The position in England appears to be different and a claim in conversion is open[11].

---

1 See the Hire Purchase Act 1964 (c 53), ss 27–29 (substituted by the Consumer Credit Act 1974 (c 39), s 192(3)(a), Sch 4, para 22, and amended by the Sale of Goods Act 1979 (c 54), s 63(1)(a), Sch 2, para 4). See also D L Carey Miller *Corporeal Moveables in Scots Law* (1991) pp 217–219; R Goode *Commercial Law* (1985) p 414–420.

2 Hire Purchase Act 1964, s 27(2) (as so substituted).

3 'Trade or finance purchaser' means a person who carries on a business consisting wholly or partially in the purchase of vehicles for sale or the provision of finance by the purchase of vehicles for the purpose of hire purchase or conditional sale: ibid, s 29(2) (as so substituted).

4 Ibid, s 27(3) (as so substituted).

5 Ibid, s 29(2) (as so substituted).

6 *Stevenson v Beverley Bentinck Ltd* [1976] 2 All ER 606, CA.

7 *Stevenson v Beverley Bentinck Ltd* [1976] 2 All ER 606 at 608, CA, per Lord Denning MR; *North-West Securities Ltd v Barrhead Coachworks Ltd* 1976 SC 68 at 70, 1976 SLT 99 at 100, OH, per Lord M'Donald.

8 *Barker v Bell* [1971] 2 All ER 867, CA. In this case the private purchaser was falsely informed that all instalments had been paid and he honestly believed that misinformation. He was held to have obtained a good title. Note that the requirements of good faith and lack of notice are cumulative.

9 *North-West Securities Ltd v Barrhead Coachwords Ltd* 1976 SC 68, 1976 SLT 99, OH. The Hire Purchase Act 1964, s 27(6) (as substituted: see note 1 above), preserves the possible liability of a trade purchaser to the original owner. This leaves open the question of what the liability in Scotland is.

10 *North-West Securities Ltd v Barrhead Coachworks Ltd* 1976 SC 68 at 70, 1976 SLT 99 at 100, OH. Claims based on *specificatio* and on natural equity were rejected. The use of *specificatio* in this context is supported by *F C Finance Ltd v Langtry Investment Co Ltd* 1973 SLT (Sh Ct) 11 but this case was disapproved in *North-West Securities Ltd*.

11 In *Moorgate Mercantile Co Ltd v Twitchings* [1976] 2 All ER 641, [1976] 3 WLR 66, HL, possible defences to such a claim based on estoppel by negligence or misrepresentation were rejected.

(8) COMPETING TITLES

(a) Competing Real Rights

684. Rule of first completion. Competition of title can occur for many different reasons. For example a seller, having sold property once, may in fraud sell the same property twice, or property which is in the course of being transferred may be attached by a creditor of the transferor, or again a transferor's title may be voidable and so vulnerable to reduction. Except in the case of titles to land registered in the Land Register, for which a special rule applies[1], the applicable rule in competitions of title is the rule of first completion, the party who is first to complete his right being the party who prevails. *Prior tempore potior jure* (prior in date, preferable in right) states the law accurately. It will be seen that the rule follows from first principles of property law[2]. So if A dispones land to B and then fraudulently dispones the same land to C, the new owner is whichever of B and C is first to register in the Register of Sasines. The relevant date is the date of registration and not the date on which the dispositions were granted or on which missives of sale were concluded. Deeds registered on the same day rank equally regardless of the actual time of registration[3]. The reason why ownership passes to the disponee who is first to register is that both parties to that disposition intended the transfer of ownership and the full formalities of transfer have been duly complied with. And the reason why ownership cannot then pass to the disponee who is second to register is that ownership having already passed to the first disponee, the disponer no longer has title to grant with the result that the disposition is *a non domino*. The second disponee is left with a personal claim against the fraudulent disponer, in practice usually a contractual claim in warrandice.

The same rule applies to moveable property. So in the case of incorporeal moveable property competition of title is regulated by priority of intimation of assignation[4], while for corporeal moveables the successful party is the one who first completes the entire transfer process whether by delivery of the goods or, in the case of transfers regulated by the Sale of Goods Act 1979, by compliance with the requirements of that Act[5]. Finally, the same rule also regulates competing grants of subordinate real rights such as leases. Rights in security raise some special issues and are considered separately[6].

1 See para 685 below.
2 In the case of Sasine titles to land this rule is given statutory form in the Real Rights Act 1693 (c 22).
3 Titles to Land (Consolidation) (Scotland) Act 1868 (c 101), s 142 (amended by the Statute Law Revision Act 1893 (c 14); the Public Registers and Records (Scotland) Act 1950 (c 11), s 1(2), Schedule; the Conveyancing and Feudal Reform (Scotland) Act 1970 (c 35), s 52(3), Sch 11, pt III; and the Land Registration (Scotland) Act 1979 (c 33), s 29(1), (4), Sch 2, para 2, Sch 4); Land Registers (Scotland) Act 1868 (c 64), s 6 (amended by the Public Registers and Records (Scotland) Act 1948 (c 57), s 3; the Land Registration (Scotland) Act 1979, s 29(1), (4), Sch 2, para 1, Sch 4). The amendments made by the Land Registration (Scotland) Act 1979 were brought into force on 6 April 1981 by the Land Registration (Scotland) 1979 (Commencement No 1) Order 1980, SI 1980/1412. They are not retrospective. Their effect is to bring the Sasine Register into line with the Land Register, for which see s 7(2) of the 1979 Act. The previous rule for the Sasine Register was that account was taken of the time within a particular day that registration took place, so that a deed registered at 10 a m prevailed over a deed registered at 11 a m. One consequence of the post-1981 rule appears to be that if two competing dispositions are registered on the same day, each disponee will receive a one half *pro indiviso* share of the property.
4 Stair *Institutions* III,1,6: '... if there be diverse assignations, the first intimation is preferable, though of the last assignation ...'. See also Erskine *Institute* III,5,3.
5 But in some cases of transfer under the Sale of Goods Act 1979 (c 54) the second party to complete may, contrary to the general rule, gain a good title by virtue of s 24 or s 25 of the Act. See paras 681, 682, above.
6 See para 686 below.

685. Land Register titles: rule of last completion. In Land Register titles the normal rule is inverted and the party who is last to register prevails, although in some circumstances his success may turn out only to be temporary. Thus suppose that A dispones to B and then fraudulently dispones the same land to C, and further suppose that the order of registration is, first C and then B. On registration of C's title C will become owner. In this respect there is no difference between the Register of Sasines and the Land Register. But despite the fact that C's registration renders B's disposition *a non domino*[1], B will nonetheless become owner on the subsequent registration of his own title, assuming that his application is accepted by the Keeper[2]; and if B becomes owner then it necessarily follows that C ceases to be owner. The reason for this result is that land registration is a form of original acquisition, registration conferring on each successive disponee a good statutory title[3], and since B is the last to register he becomes the current holder of the statutory title.

But while at one level the Land Register operates the novel rule of last completion, at another level it continues to adhere to the usual rule of property law which would give good title to the first to complete. This is because the question of whether the Land Register is 'inaccurate' and so capable of rectification within section 9 of the Land Registration (Scotland) Act 1979 is regulated by the general law of property[4]. So in the example given above, B is owner but (since he was the second to register) the Register is inaccurate and C can seek rectification to the effect of substituting his name for the name of B in the proprietorship section of the title sheet. Ownership would then revert to C[5]. Rectification is not always achievable in practice because of the special protection given by the Act to a proprietor in possession[6], but in the absence of rectification C may have a claim for indemnity against the Keeper[7].

1 Ie because ownership has passed from A, the granter of both dispositions, to C.
2 As usually it will be: see *Registration of Title Practice Book* (1981) para H.108. The Keeper is however empowered to refuse an *a non domino* application by the Land Registration (Scotland) Act 1979 (c 33), s 4(1).
3 Land Registration (Scotland) Act 1979, s 3(1)(a). See para 673 above. See also K G C Reid 'A Non Domino Conveyances and the Land Register' 1991 JR 79.
4 See K G C Reid 'New Titles for Old' (1984) 29 JLSS 171 at 172, 173.
5 An alternative way of achieving the same result would appear to be for C in turn to register a fresh *a non domino* disposition, thus obtaining the benefit of the rule of last completion.
6 Land Registration (Scotland) Act 1979, s 9(3) (amended by the Law Reform (Miscellaneous Provisions) (Scotland) Act 1985 (c 73), s 59(1), Sch 2, para 21).
7 Land Registration (Scotland) Act 1979, s 12(1)(b).

686. Competing rights in security. Slightly different issues are raised by competing rights in security. Subject to the special status of Land Register titles, it has been seen that if an owner conveys the same property twice, the party completing the transfer process second cannot acquire a title, for the fundamental reason that his conveyance is by then *a non domino*. The position for double grants of lease is the same as for double grants of ownership. But where a debtor grants two securities over the same property, and the right is completed by both creditors, it cannot be said that one security is valid and that the other is not. On the contrary, both securities are valid, for the fact that an owner has granted one security does not of itself prevent him from granting a second[1]. The real question which arises, therefore, is not which security is valid but which security ranks first, and the answer to this question does not depend upon any fundamental principle of property law. The general rule for all rights in security is the rule *prior tempore potior jure* already referred to[2], so that the security completed first ranks first. This rule applies to heritable securities as much as to moveable securities, to Land Register titles[3] as much as to Sasine titles, and to floating charges as much as to fixed securities[4]. But unlike the position for other real rights, the rule as it applies to rights in security can be contracted out of, so that creditors are free to make their own agreement, known usually as ranking agreements[5]. In the commercial world ranking agreements are commonplace.

1 The first security may, however, contain a prohibition on the granting of any further securities and in that event it seems that a further security would be voidable if the creditor knew of the prohibition. See para 697 below.
2 See para 684 above.
3 Land Registration (Scotland) Act 1979 (c 33), s 7. The sidenote in the Act is 'ranking'.
4 A floating charge does not become real until it attaches ('crystallises'). Thus it is that floating charges rank behind fixed securities, although floating charges rank *inter se* by date of registration. See the Companies Act 1985 (c 6), s 464(4).
5 See eg the Conveyancing and Feudal Reform (Scotland) Act 1970 (c 35), s 13(3)(b), and the Companies Act 1985, s 464(1)(b) (prospectively amended by the Companies Act 1989 (c 40), s 140(2), (3)).

687. A transferee is affected by subordinate real rights. Often when different real rights are claimed over the same property the rights are capable of co-existence, so that in a competition of rights the interests of all or both parties may turn out to be satisfied in full. Ownership, for example, can and often does co-exist with subordinate real rights such as lease and security, and if property is affected by subordinate real rights these rights continue to affect the property in the hands of a transferee[1]. But this statement must be taken subject to the rule of first completion expressed above, so that 'rights' derived from the transferor and completed after the right of the transferee are invalid as granted *a non domino* and do not affect the property[2].

1 See para 604 above.
2 But the rule for Land Register titles is different: see para 685 above.

(b) Personal Rights in competition with Real Rights

688. A grantee is not bound by the personal obligations of his author. It is a fundamental rule of the law of property that, on acquiring the real right of ownership in the course of voluntary transfer[1], a transferee has no concern with any personal rights[2] which may be prestable against his author[3]. The rule arises out of the very nature of real and personal rights, for while a transferee has a right in a thing (the property being transferred), a holder of a personal right has no more than a right against a person and the person against whom the right is held is the transferor and not the transferee. In general it makes no difference to the rule just stated that the transferee knows of the existence of the personal right. As has been observed:

'If the personal obligation did not affect the lands, then knowledge on the part of the purchasers that such an obligation had been granted appears to be of no moment. Assuming that they knew of the obligation, they knew also that it did not affect the lands'[4].

But to this statement that knowledge does not matter there is an important exception which is considered below[5].

At one time the position of holders of incorporeal property was thought to be different, for it was argued that the rule *assignatus utitur jure auctoris* made an assignee liable for all the obligations of his cedent in relation to the right being assigned[6]. The modern law, established by the House of Lords in 1813 in the leading case of *Redfearn v Somervail*[7], is otherwise. The effect of *Redfearn* was and is to restrict the rule *assignatus utitur* to obligations intrinsic to the right being assigned, that is to say to obligations owed by the cedent to the debtor in the right; and obligations owed by the debtor to other parties (extrinsic obligations) do not now transmit[8]. Intrinsic obligations in the sense defined here are unique to incorporeal property, and with respect to extrinsic obligations the position of incorporeal property is now assimilated to that of corporeal property.

1 Ie voluntary on the part of the transferor. In those cases of involuntary transfer where the whole property of the debtor vests in someone else, eg in an executor or a trustee in sequestration, the personal rights transmit also, although if the estate is insolvent the right resolves into an unsecured claim for damages.

2 Ie other than real conditions such as real burdens and rights of common interest which, although personal in nature, transmit against successive owners of the servient tenement. See paras 344 ff above.

3 Erskine *Institute* II,3,48; Hume *Lectures* vol IV (Stair Soc vol 17, 1955 ed G C H Paton) pp 311–318; Bell *Commentaries* I,307 and 308.

4 *Morier v Brownlie and Watson* (1895) 23 R 67 at 74, OH, per Lord Low (affd (1895) 23 R 67, IH). In this there is an echo of a much earlier dictum by Lord Kilkerran in *Stirling v Johnson* (1756) 5 Brown's Supp 323. See also *Bell* I,307; *Hume* vol IV, pp 311 ff; *Wallace v Simmers* 1960 SC 255, 1961 SLT 34 (where Lord Low's dictum is quoted with approval).

' 5 See para 690 below.

6 Stair *Institutions* IV,40,21; *Erskine* III,5,10. Bell (I,302, note 5), writing shortly after the decision in *Redfearn v Somervail* (1813) 1 Dow 50, 5 Pat 707, HL, commented on this older doctrine as follows: 'Recollecting the principles upon which assignations were originally admitted as procuratories *in rem suam*, it will not appear wonderful that persons acquiring by assignation the right to debts and other *jura incorporalia* should be considered as coming precisely into the place of the cedent, and as liable, of course, to all the personal exceptions pleadable against him. In that way arose the maxim, '*Assignatus utitur jure auctoris*', which has so often been misunderstood, and held to imply a responsibility like that of an heir. But this doctrine, in so far as it has been considered applicable to any other exceptions than those competent to the debtor in defence against the claim, should not be held good in the present day, when the whole aspect of the law relative to assignation is altered; and when, instead of being a mere procurator of the original creditor, the assignee is considered as a proper purchaser, holding . . . the full *jus obligationis* transferred by intimation, as [corporeal] property is by delivery'.

7 *Redfearn v Somervail* 22 Nov 1805 FC, (1805) Mor 'Personal and Real' App No 3, revsd (1813) 1 Dow 50, (1813) 5 Pat 707, HL. For an enlightening account of the arguments in the case, see *Bell* I,303, note 1.

8 For the distinction between intrinsic and extrinsic obligations, and for the *assignatus utitur* rule generally, see para 660 above.

689. A granter's power to grant is unimpaired by personal obligation. It sometimes happen that a person who proposes to make a grant of ownership or other real right has previously undertaken to a third party not to make this precise grant. An undertaking of this kind may be made expressly, as for example in the case of a right of pre-emption or of standard condition 6 of the standard conditions governing standard securities which prohibits the granting of a lease[1]; but more often it arises by implication, usually in the context of a positive obligation to transfer the property to someone else. Mere obligation, however, cannot impair an owner's power to grant. So if in respect of the same piece of land A concludes missives to sell to B, and contracts to grant a standard security to C and a lease to D, yet for as long as no real right is actually conferred on these various parties A remains unfettered owner and can grant an unfettered title to someone else entirely. Hume expresses the position thus:

'[T]he powers and privileges of alienation, disposal incumbrance and so forth . . . cannot be extinguished by any transaction, or covenant, of what form soever, which leaves that condition of real connection subsisting, undissolved as before. Tis true the owner . . . may have come under engagements as to the disposal of his property, and he is blameable, and shall be liable in damages, if he infringe or forget them. But still, though under promise, he is owner and possessor, undivested of his real power and natural command of the thing; and if he shall use and apply that power, by sale and delivery to another, the ordinary effect of a transference of the property must ensue'[2].

The disappointed parties have a personal claim against the granter for breach of contract; and if they had acted more promptly they might have prevented the grant by interdict. But on the principle that a grantee is not bound by the obligations of his author[3], no claim lies against the successful grantee. His title is secure. To this last statement, however, there is an important exception which is considered in the following paragraph.

1 Conveyancing and Feudal Reform (Scotland) Act 1970 (c 35), s 11(2), Sch 3, condition 6.
2 Hume *Lectures* vol IV (Stair Soc vol 17, 1952 ed G C H Paton) p 313.
3 See para 688 above.

690. The rule against 'offside goals'. Notwithstanding the general rule that a grantee is not concerned with the personal obligations of his author, where an owner makes a grant, whether of ownership or of some other real right, in breach of an obligation not to do so, the grantee is affected by the obligation if he knew of it or if the grant was made without consideration. The paradigm case is a double sale. Thus in the leading case of *Rodger (Builders) Ltd v Fawdry*[1] the owner of land concluded missives for its sale. At the contractual date of entry the buyer failed to pay and, after two weeks, the seller issued a three-day ultimatum. Payment still not having been made, the seller resold to a second party, who, although aware of the prior missives, accepted the seller's assurance that they were no longer in force. The original buyer, now in funds, wished to proceed with the purchase and sought reduction of the registered disposition granted to the second party and implement of his missives of sale. He was successful. The court held that, punctual payment of the price not being of the essence of a contract of sale, the seller had not validly rescinded the original contract. Resale was a breach of an implied term of this contract and the second party, by failing to make his own independent inquiries into the circumstances surrounding that contract, was in bad faith. As Lord Justice-Clerk Thomson explained in an arresting metaphor:

'The appellants [the second party] assumed that their title would be safe once the goal of the Register House was reached. But in this branch of the law, as in football, offside goals are disallowed'[2].

A full analysis of this important rule against 'offside goals' is given later[3].

1 *Rodger (Builders) Ltd v Fawdry* 1950 SC 483, 1950 SLT 345.
2 1950 SC 483 at 501, 1950 SLT 345 at 353.
3 See paras 695 ff below.

691. Grant in breach of trust. Trust property is owned by the trustees and not by the beneficiaries, but the beneficiaries have a personal right against the trustees to ensure the proper performance of the terms of the trust. These terms are set out, in the first place in the deed of trust itself and in the second place and so far as not at variance with the deed of trust, in section 4 of the Trusts (Scotland) Act 1921. The powers conferred on trustees by section 4 include the power (1) to sell the trust estate, heritable as well as moveable, (2) to grant feus of the heritable estate, (3) to grant leases of any duration, and (4) to borrow money on the security of the trust estate or any part thereof, heritable as well as moveable[1]. Where, therefore, section 4 applies in full, trustees are empowered to sell the trust property and can confer an unchallengeable title on the purchaser. But even where the power to sell in section 4 is disapplied because a sale would be at variance with the terms of the trust, a trustee is still able to confer a valid title. This is because, although in breach of obligation (breach of trust), the conveyance is not in excess of capacity[2]. The trustee really does own the property and limitations founded on obligation do not prevent him from conferring ownership on a purchaser[3]. The law is concisely stated by Stair:

'[T]he property of the thing intrusted, be it land or moveables, is in the person of the intrusted, else it is not a proper trust: so if it be transmitted to singular successors, acquiring *bona fide*, they are secure, and the trustee is only liable personally upon the trust . . .'[4].

Stair's reference to the need for bona fides is an acknowledgement that at common law the rule against 'offside goals' applied, so that a grantee taking either without consideration or in the knowledge that the grant was in breach of trust received a subsistent title but one which was voidable at the instance of the beneficiaries[5]. This is still the law in respect of grants without consideration, but where trustees make any of the grants referred to in section 4 of the 1921 Act, including a disposition on sale, a lease, a standard security and a floating charge[6], it is provided by section 2 of the Trusts (Scotland) Act 1961 that the validity of the transaction and of any title acquired by the second party under the transaction is not to be challengeable by the second party[7] or by any other person on the ground that the act in question is at variance with the terms or purposes of the trust. The effect of section 2 of the 1961 Act is that where, in breach of trust, trustees make any of the grants stipulated in section 4 of the 1921 Act, the title conferred on the grantee is unimpeachable regardless of questions of good faith, and the beneficiaries are left with a personal claim against the trustees for breach of trust.

1 Trusts (Scotland) Act 1921 (c 58), s 4(1)(a)−(d).
2 For capacity of trustees, see para 599 above.
3 See para 689 above.
4 Stair *Institutions* I,13,7. See also Hume *Lectures* vol IV (Stair Soc vol 17, 1952 ed G C H Paton) p 315. The contrary view expressed in *Kidd v Paton's Trustees* 1912 2 SLT 363, OH, is incorrect.
5 See *Redfearn v Somervail* (1813) 1 Dow 50, 5 Pat 707, HL, where the assignee's good faith prevented the rule from applying.
6 A common use of trusts in recent years has been as a surrogate right in security, with the debtor as trustee and the creditor as beneficiary. See eg *Clark Taylor & Co Ltd v Quality Site Development (Edinburgh) Ltd* 1981 SC 111, 1981 SLT 308. But since the right of a beneficiary/creditor under such a trust does not prevail against a standard security or a floating charge, it seems of limited value. See K G C Reid 'Trusts and Floating Charges' 1987 SLT (News) 113 at 115. More recently, W A Wilson has questioned whether for this purpose floating charges fall to be treated in the same way as other rights in security: see *The Scottish Law of Debt* (2nd edn, 1991) p 120.
7 The reference to 'second party' discloses the genesis of the Trusts (Scotland) Act 1961 (c 57), s 2, as a means of preventing purchasers and other grantees from questioning the power of the trustees to make the grant.

692. Grant by one holding on a voidable title. A title is voidable[1] where consent to the transfer has been induced by fraud, by error or by force and fear, or where the rule against 'offside goals' applies[2]. A title may also be voidable by virtue of statute, for example as a gratuitous alienation by one who is insolvent[3] or as a gift to defeat a claim for aliment or financial provision on divorce[4]. Numerous other examples of voidable titles exist, both at common law and by statute.

Voidability does not of itself impair validity, so that a person holding on a voidable title is the owner of the property, and remains owner unless or until his title is avoided. A voidable title, after all, is a subsistent title. The usual method of avoiding a voidable title is by reduction, but in the case of corporeal moveables, where no written title exists, the equivalent remedy is an action for reconveyance by delivery of the property[5]. If a title is voidable then so usually is any contract on which it proceeded, but reduction of the contract does not have the effect of reducing the title, a point often overlooked in the context of sale of goods[6]. In practice voidable titles are rarely avoided.

For as long as he remains owner, a person holding on a voidable title can alienate the property or grant subordinate real rights in respect of it. That follows from the very nature of ownership, any limitation in his right being a limitation in obligation only[7]. But where the grant is made without consideration or where the grantee is in bad faith, the title so conferred is itself voidable. In effect this is an application of the rule against 'offside goals', for a right of reduction is a personal right against the holder of the voidable title and its correlative obligation includes, it is thought, an implied obligation that the property should not be alienated or burdened. Thus a grantee taking the property either gratuitously or in the knowledge of the antecedent personal right of reduction is subject to that personal right, with the consequence that his title is voidable in turn. Only a bona fide acquirer for value will receive an unimpeachable title[8].

If a voidable title is avoided, by reduction or equivalent action, ownership reverts to the party leading the reduction[9] and any subsequent grant by the former holder is then void as *a non domino*.

1 For the meaning of 'voidable title', see para 601 above.
2 For a discussion of these 'vices of consent', see paras 614 ff above.
3 Bankruptcy (Scotland) Act 1985 (c 66), s 34.
4 Family Law (Scotland) Act 1985 (c 37), s 18.
5 *A W Gamage Ltd v Charlesworth's Trustee* 1910 SC 257, 1910 1 SLT 11. See further para 607 above.
6 It is overlooked in *Morrisson v Robertson* 1908 SC 332, 15 SLT 697, and *MacLeod v Kerr* 1965 SC 253, 1965 SLT 358. See T B Smith 'Error and Transfer of Title' (1967) 12 JLSS 206. Doubtless the mistake arises from the manner in which in the Sale of Goods Act 1979 (c 54) conveyance is compressed into contract, although it is noteworthy that s 23 of that Act talks of voidable title and not of voidable contract.
7 See para 689 above.
8 Stair *Institutions* IV,40,21; Erskine *Institute* III,5,10; Hume *Lectures* vol III (Stair Soc vol 15, 1952 ed G C H Paton) pp 236–238; M P Brown *A Treatise on the Law of Sale* (1821) pp 416, 417. The principle has often been illustrated in the reported cases: see eg *Price and Pierce Ltd v Bank of Scotland* 1910 SC 1095, 1910 2 SLT 126, affd 1912 SC (HL) 19, 1911 2 SLT 469; *MacLeod v Kerr* 1965 SC 253, 1965 SLT 358. The rule is restated in various contexts by a number of statutes, eg the Sale of Goods Act 1979, s 23; the Bankruptcy (Scotland) Act 1985, s 34(4); and the Family Law (Scotland) Act 1985, s 18(3).
9 Ie assuming that it is catholic in effect. See para 664 above.

693. Personal rights and secured creditors. A secured creditor, like a transferee, takes free from the personal obligations of his author[1], for a right in security is a real right, and real rights prevail over personal rights. But, as with transferees, this statement is subject to the rule against 'offside goals' so that a creditor who takes his right in the knowledge that the granter was legally bound not to grant it, whether expressly or by implication, receives a title which is voidable at the instance of the holder of the antecedent personal right. *Trade Development Bank v Crittall Windows Ltd*[2] is the leading modern authority. Here missives were concluded for the sale of land. Subsequently, and before implementing the missives, the owner granted a standard security which was duly registered. The creditor knew of the existence of the missives. It was held that the standard security was voidable at the instance of the purchaser, apparently[3] on the basis that a contract for the sale of land contains an implied prohibition on the subsequent grant of securities and that a heritable creditor who knows of this prohibition is bound by it.

If, as a general rule, a secured creditor is not affected by personal obligations of his debtor which precede his own real right then, *a fortiori*, he is unaffected by subsequent personal obligations. Thus in the exercise of a power of sale arising under a security it is thought that a creditor could not be called upon to honour a contract of sale in respect of the same property entered into by his debtor subsequent to the original security but instead would be free to sell to some other party at a better price[4].

1 Eg *Redfearn v Somervail* (1813) 1 Dow 50, 1 Pat 707, HL (assignee in security not affected by *jus crediti* under a trust enforceable against his debtor).
2 *Trade Development Bank v Crittall Windows Ltd* 1983 SLT 510.
3 But the reasons are not fully articulated. See para 697 below.
4 *Morier v Brownlie and Watson* (1895) 23 R 67 at 72, OH, per Lord Low (affd (1895) 23 R 67, IH). The contract, of course, remains enforceable against the debtor. See the Insolvency Act 1986 (c 45),

s 57(4). In England a receiver has been required to honour a contract of sale previously entered into by the company (see *Freevale Ltd v Metrostore Holdings Ltd* [1984] Ch 199, [1984] 1 All ER 495), but this case may depend on the speciality of English constructive trusts or on the fact that, unlike a secured creditor, a receiver is agent of the company.

694. Personal rights and unsecured creditors. The question of whether, and if so to what extent, unsecured creditors are affected by the personal obligations of the debtor in relation to property which is attached by diligence or mercantile sequestration has a long and a complicated history. It is frequently stated that a creditor takes the property *tantum et tale*, as it stood in the debtor, but this phrase evades rather than confronts the difficulties. At one time the law may have been that, by contrast to a purchaser or a secured creditor, an unsecured creditor was affected by most or even by all of the personal obligations of his debtor in relation to the property being attached[1]. But if this was ever the law it began to change in the last years of the eighteenth century, particularly during the Lord Presidency of Ilay Campbell[2]. Thus in *Wylie v Duncan*[3], the most important case of this period and one in which Lord President Campbell presided, it was held that an adjudger took heritable property free of a *pactum de retrovendendo* (obligation to reconvey) entered into by his debtor[4]. Despite this decision, however, the law continued to be in doubt[5], especially in relation to incorporeal property where the rule *assignatus utitur jure auctoris* was thought to weaken the position of creditors[6]. In the modern law, however, no distinction is made between corporeal and incorporeal property[7].

The modern rule is that a creditor — or trustee in sequestration or liquidator — is not in general affected by the personal obligations of his debtor in relation to the property being attached[8]. Thus Lord Kinnear in *Colquhoun's Trustee v Campbell's Trustees*:

> 'The rule relied on is that the trustee [in sequestration] takes the ... estate of the bankrupt subject to the conditions which affect the constitution of the real right in his person, but free from personal liabilities or engagements which would have bound the bankrupt himself if he had been solvent. That is a correct statement of the law, but the decision in *The Heritable Reversionary Company v Miller*[9] shews that it is subject to the qualification that the estate must honestly belong to the bankrupt, and that the creditors cannot enlarge the estate for distribution by adopting a fraud on the part of the bankrupt, or doing something which would have been a fraud if it had been done by him when solvent'[10].

Like a purchaser or a secured creditor, therefore, an unsecured creditor is affected by real rights but not by personal rights[11]. In one respect his position is better than that of a secured creditor (or purchaser) and in another respect it is worse. His position is better than that of a secured creditor because he is not subject to the rule against 'offside goals', which is confined to grants made voluntarily and contrary to an earlier obligation of the granter[12]. But his position is worse because, as Lord Kinnear notes in the passage quoted earlier, he is affected both by trusts and by fraud.

So far as fraud is concerned, a title of the debtor which is voidable as having been fraudulently acquired remains voidable in the hands of an attaching creditor[13]. The real right of the creditor is thus subject to the personal right of reduction, contrary to the usual rule. Whether the exception for fraud is wider than this single rule is a matter of conjecture[14].

The exception for trusts is more complex. It was settled at the latest by the decision of the House of Lords in *Paul v Jeffrey*[15] in 1835 that a creditor cannot attach property which is held by the debtor in trust. At first it seemed that this rule might be confined to patent trusts, particularly in the case of land where a creditor was relying on the state of the title as disclosed by the Register of Sasines[16], but in *Heritable Reversionary Co Ltd v Millar*[17] it was held by the House of Lords that latent trusts fall under the same rule. So far as trustees in sequestration are concerned, the rule that trust property is exempt from creditors is now statutory[18]. The policy considerations in favour of the rule are obvious, for while trust property is and ought to be attachable for the debts of the trust, it is unjust that it should also be attachable for the private debts of individual trustees. But the courts struggled to find a justification in the law of property. The difficulty was and is that the right of a beneficiary under a trust is a personal right only, and in principle personal rights do not prevail against creditors. In *Heritable Reversionary Co Ltd* itself Lord Watson justified the victory of the beneficiary by advancing the notion, contrary to Stair[19], that in a trust ownership is not in the trustee but in the beneficiary:

> 'As between them [that is, the trustee and the beneficiary] there can, in my opinion, be no doubt that according to the law of Scotland[20] the one, though possessed of the legal title, and being the apparent owner, is in reality a bare trustee; and that the other, to whom the whole beneficial interest belongs, is the true owner'[21].

The modern law has not followed this approach. Ownership, it is accepted, is in the trustee[22] but the trustee is regarded as having a double persona, as trustee and also as an individual. Property owned as an individual cannot be attached in respect of debts incurred as a trustee; and conversely property owned as a trustee cannot be attached in respect of debts incurred as an individual. In this theory of double persona there is a tacit recognition that in practice trusts operate much like separate legal persons. The fact that trust property is exempt from the personal creditors of the trustee has in recent years attracted the attention of commercial lawyers and led to the use of trusts as surrogate rights in security whereby a debtor creates a 'trust' over his property in favour of his creditor[23]. It has also encouraged the view that a constructive trust should be recognised if, at the time of the attachment, the debtor is already under a contractual obligation to grant a real right to a third party, but this view has not found favour in the courts[24].

Finally, mention should be made of a difference between, on the one hand, creditors carrying out diligence and, on the other hand, trustees in sequestration and liquidators. Trustees and liquidators represent all creditors and must distribute the assets of the insolvent debtor amongst them according to the rules of bankruptcy. Their duty extends to unsecured creditors, that is to say to holders of personal rights, as well as to secured creditors who hold real rights. In a sense, therefore, trustees and liquidators are affected by personal rights, at least to the extent of giving an unsecured ranking on the insolvent estate. But on insolvency there is a separation of the debtor's property from the debtor's unsecured obligations, and a trustee or liquidator takes, and may dispose of, the former without regard to the latter.

1 Erskine *Institute* II,12,36 (although see also II,3,48); *Livingston and Shaw v The Creditors of Grange* (1664) Mor 10200; *Thomson v Douglas Heron & Co* (1786) Mor 10229.
2 Hume *Lectures* vol IV (Stair Soc vol 17, 1955 ed G C H Paton) pp 473, 474.
3 *Wylie v Duncan* (1803) 3 Ross LC 134.
4 See also *Mitchell v Ferguson* (1781) Mor 10296, (1781) 3 Ross LC 120 (adjudger prevails over purchaser holding on an unrecorded disposition).
5 Bell *Commentaries* I,300 ff.
6 *Dingwall v McCombie* (1822) 1 S 463 (NE 431); *Gordon v Cheyne* 5 Feb 1824 FC.
7 See eg *Bank of Scotland v Liquidators of Hutchison Main & Co Ltd* 1914 SC (HL) 1, 1914 1 SLT 111 (liquidator takes incorporeal property free of personal obligation to grant an assignation in security).
8 *Bank of Scotland v Liquidators of Hutchison Main & Co Ltd* 1914 SC (HL) 1, 1914 1 SLT 111; *Gibson v Hunter Home Designs Ltd* 1976 SC 23, 1976 SLT 94. 'If one have lent money on the promise of the borrower that an heritable security shall be granted, or that goods shall be delivered to him in pledge, and the borrower fail before the pledge be given, or sasine taken on the heritable bond; still the lender is but a personal creditor, entitled to no preference, though the bankrupt, had he continued solvent, must have implemented the engagements he had undertaken, and action would have lain *ad factum praestandum*': Bell I,308.
9 *Heritable Reversionary Co Ltd v Millar* (1892) 19 R (HL) 43.
10 *Colquhoun's Trustee v Campbell's Trustees* (1902) 4 F 739 at 743, 744.
11 Sometimes there is a 'race' between a grantee and a creditor to complete their respective real rights. The winner takes free of the uncompleted right of the other party. See paras 648, 659, above.

12 Stair *Institutions* I, 14, 5 and 6; *Bell* I, 308; *Mitchell v Ferguson* (1781) Mor 10296, (1781) 3 Ross LC 120. Stair suggests that the exemption might extend to heritable creditors obtaining a security in satisfaction of a prior debt.

13 *Bell* I, 309 and 310; *Mansfield v Walker's Trustees* (1835) 1 Sh & Macl 203, HL; *A W Gamage Ltd v Charlesworth's Trustee* 1910 SC 257, 1910 1 SLT 11.

14 *Molleson v Challis* (1873) 11 M 510; *Clydesdale Bank v Paul* (1877) 4 R 626 at 629, per Lord Shand; *Graeme's Trustee v Giersberg* (1888) 15 R 691; *Dunn's Trustee v Hardy* (1896) 23 R 621.

15 *Paul v Jeffrey* (1835) 1 Sh & Macl 767, HL. See also *Fleeming v Howden* (1868) 6 M (HL) 113.

16 *Wylie v Duncan* (1803) 3 Ross LC 124; *Watson v Duncan* (1879) 6 R 1247 at 1252, per Lord Deas.

17 *Heritable Reversionary Co Ltd v Millar* (1892) 19 R (HL) 43.

18 Bankruptcy (Scotland) Act 1985 (c 66), s 33(1)(b).

19 *Stair* I, 13, 7.

20 'According to the law of Scotland' was a favourite expression of Lord Watson's especially where, as here, he was applying the law of England.

21 *Heritable Reversionary Co Ltd v Millar* (1892) 19 R (HL) 43 at 46, 47. But if the trustee did not own the property how then could he convey it, as undoubtedly he could? Lord Watson's answer (at 47) was that the beneficiary was personally barred from challenging such a conveyance: '. . . the validity of a right acquired in such circumstances by a *bona fide* disponee for value does not rest upon the recognition of any power in the trustee which he can lawfully exercise, because breach of trust duty and wilful fraud can never in themselves be lawful, but upon the well-known principle that a true owner who chooses to conceal his right from the public, and to clothe his trustees with all the *indicia* of ownership, is thereby barred from challenging rights acquired by innocent third parties for onerous considerations under contract with his fraudulent trustee'.

22 TRUSTS, TRUSTEES AND JUDICIAL FACTORS, vol 24, paras 12, 49. See also W A Wilson and A G M Duncan *Trusts, Trustees and Executors* (1975) pp 14–16.

23 *Export Credits Guarantee Department v Turner* 1979 SC 286, 1981 SLT 286; *Clark Taylor & Co Ltd v Quality Site Development (Edinburgh) Ltd* 1981 SC 111, 1981 SLT 308; *Tay Valley Joinery Ltd v CF Financial Services Ltd* 1987 SLT 207; *Balfour Beatty Ltd v Britannia Life Ltd* 1995 GWD 5-228, OH. See also G L Gretton 'Using Trusts as Commercial Securities' (1988) 33 JLSS 53.

24 *Bank of Scotland v Liquidators of Hutchison, Main & Co Ltd* 1914 SC (HL) 1, 1914 1 SLT 111; *Gibson v Hunter Home Designs Ltd* 1976 SC 23, 1976 SLT 94; *Sharp v Thomson* 1995 SCLR 683, 1995 SLT 837.

(c) The Rule against 'Offside Goals'

695. Introduction. Mention has already been made of the rule against 'offside goals'[1]. In summary the rule is that a real right granted in breach of a pre-existing contract or other obligation is voidable at the instance of the creditor in that obligation if the grantee knew of the obligation or if the grant was not for value. In the metaphor employed by Lord Justice-Clerk Thomson in *Rodger (Builders) Ltd v Fawdry*[2], the 'goal' (the real right of the grantee) is 'offside' (voidable at the instance of the creditor in the obligation). This is an exception to the usual rule that a purchaser or other grantee takes property free from the personal obligations of his author[3].

The rule against offside goals is of some antiquity in Scots law and was already well established by the time of Stair[4]. The paradigm example of its operation is in cases of double sale. Thus Lord Kinloch in *Morrison v Somerville*:

'[It has] been long firmly settled in the law of Scotland, that, wherever an individual becomes bound to sell to one party, and another, in the knowledge of that obligation, takes a second right, this second right is ineffectual and reducible in a question with the first purchaser. The principle is an obvious and equitable one. In granting a second right, the seller is guilty of fraud on the first purchaser. Against the seller himself the transaction would be clearly reducible. But, in taking the second right in the knowledge of the first, the second disponee becomes an accomplice in the fraud, and the transaction is reducible against both alike. The principle is equally applicable in regard to moveables as to heritage, and has been applied in both cases indiscriminately'[5].

In his final sentence Lord Kinloch indicates that the rule applies to property of all kinds, whether heritable or moveable, corporeal or incorporeal, and it is thought that the position has not been altered in the case of corporeal moveables by the passing of the Sale of Goods Acts 1893 and 1979[6]. The reported cases are, however, exclusively concerned with heritable property.

From its origins as an equitable solution to the problem created by double grants of the same right, the offside goals rule has gradually been extended both in scope and in importance. Indeed the process of enlargement has not yet finished, the 1980s in particular seeing significant developments of the rule in the three *Trade Development Bank* cases[7]. Legal analysis has not always managed to keep pace with these changes, and if the law itself may now be stated with reasonable confidence, there is less confidence about the reasons for the law and the principles underlying it. The early authorities usually attributed the offside goals rule to fraud. The granter had defrauded some third party and the grantee, through his knowledge of the fraud, had become a participant with the result that the fraud was pleadable against him[8]. The dictum by Lord Kinloch quoted earlier is an example of this view. Sometimes too the offside goals rule was seen, not perhaps very convincingly, as a development of the law of personal bar[9]. Later authorities, however, are more reticent, and the major changes effected by the *Trade Development Bank* cases have been introduced almost without explanation. Any attempt to identify a principle capable of explaining all the different manifestations of the rule is to some degree hazardous, but it is thought that the original analysis based on 'fraud' remains correct, provided that 'fraud' is not confined to its narrow modern meaning[10]. In current legal language the principle is expressed more accurately by saying that what is required is the breach by the granter of an antecedent obligation which was binding upon him. Thus the situation envisaged is that a granter undertakes, expressly or by implication, that he will not make a particular grant; nonetheless he makes the grant; and the grantee, either knowing of the obligation or failing to take for value, is affected by it. It is thought that this analysis is sufficient to explain all the examples of the offside goals rule which are currently recognised, and that it is likely to control and determine the future development of the rule.

In order for the rule against offside goals to operate it appears that all of the following must be shown, namely:

(1) that there was an antecedent contract or other obligation affecting the granter[11];
(2) that the grant was in breach of a term, express or implied, of that obligation[12]; and
(3) either that the grantee knew of the antecedent obligation prior to the completion of his own right or that the grant was not for value[13].

1 See para 690 above.
2 *Rodger (Builders) Ltd v Fawdry* 1950 SC 483 at 501, 1950 SLT 345 at 353.
3 See paras 688, 689, above.
4 Stair *Institutions* I,14,5; Hume *Lectures* vol IV (Stair Soc vol 17, 1955 ed G C H Paton) pp 318, 319. The earliest case listed in Morison's Dictionary under the heading 'Private Knowledge of a Prior Right' was decided in 1582 (*Stirling v White and Drummond* (1582) Mor 1689).
5 *Morrison v Somerville* (1860) 22D 1082 at 1089, OH, per Lord Kinloch (affd (1860) 22D 1082, IH).
6 By the Sale of Goods Act 1979 (c 54), s 62(2) (derived from the Sale of Goods Act 1893 (c 71), s 61(1)(repealed)) the rules of the common law are preserved except in so far as inconsistent with the Act. No inconsistency has been detected. The rule against offside goals, however, is not mentioned in D L Carey Miller *Corporeal Moveables in Scots Law* (1991), the standard modern text.
7 Ie *Trade Development Bank v Warriner and Mason (Scotland) Ltd* 1980 SC 74, 1980 SLT 223; *Trade Development Bank v David W Haig (Bellshill) Ltd* 1983 SLT 510; and *Trade Development Bank v Crittall Windows Ltd* 1983 SLT 510.
8 See eg Stair I,14,5: 'But certain knowledge, by intimation, citation, or the like, inducing *malam fidem*, whereby any prior disposition or assignation made to another party is certainly known . . . such rights acquired, not being of necessity to satisfy prior engagements, are reducible *ex capite fraudis*, and the acquirer is partaker of the fraud of his author, who thereby becomes a granter of double rights . . .'.
9 See eg *Petrie v Forsyth* (1874) 2 R 214 at 223, per Lord Gifford. See also J Rankine *The Law of Personal Bar in Scotland* (1921) p 39.

10 T B Smith *A Short Commentary on the Law of Scotland* (1962) pp 838, 839: 'Before the rigid
construction of the term "fraud" to conform to the English tort of deceit, "fraud" was used in
Scotland, so far as contract was concerned, as a general term to imply lack of bona fides, and
comprised a variety of situations in which one party had taken unfair advantage of the other'. See
also *Rodger (Builders) Ltd v Fawdry* 1950 SC 483 at 499, 1950 SLT 345 at 353, per Lord Jamieson: '[It
was argued] that, in order to have the missives reduced, it must be shown that Mr Bell [the grantee]
acted fraudulently and that he was, in consequence, barred from insisting on his contract. But fraud
in the sense of moral delinquency does not enter into the matter'.
11 See para 696 below.
12 See paras 697, 698, below.
13 See para 699 below.

696. Antecedent contract or other obligation. The granter must be subject to
a pre-existing obligation not to make the grant[1]. The source of the obligation is
unimportant, and common examples include contract, disposition or other conveyance[2], and trust. The obligation must precede any right, personal or real, in the
grantee. Thus if A contracts to sell land to B and then, in breach of the first contract,
contracts to sell the same land to C, and if A then conveys the land to B (in breach of
his contract with C), the offside goals rule cannot apply in favour of C because B's
contractual right preceded the contractual right in C.

1 If there is no obligation the offside goals rule cannot apply: *Moncrieff v Lawrie* (1896) 23 R 577, 3 SLT
298; *Imperial Hotel (Aberdeen) Ltd v Vaux Breweries Ltd* 1978 SC 86, 1978 SLT 113, OH. The result is
the same if an obligation which once existed has been extinguished, eg by negative prescription or
by the rescinding of a contract. *MacRae v MacDonald* 1980 SC 337, 1981 SLT 13, in which there was
no enforceable obligation, appears to have been wrongly decided.
2 Stair *Institutions* I,14,5 ('prior disposition and assignation'). For a case involving standard securities,
see para 697 below.

697. Double grants and breach of warrandice. The paradigm case for the
application of the offside goals rule was, and remains, the case of the double grant.
Thus if A contracts to grant a real right to B and A then contracts to grant a real right
in the same property to C, then, regardless of whether the real rights are the same or
are different, the proposed grant to C is almost always in breach of the warrandice,
express or implied, in A's original contract with B[1]. Consequently if A then
proceeds to implement the grant to C and C completes his right in the knowledge of
the breach of warrandice, the offside goals rule applies and C's title is voidable at the
instance of B. It makes no difference to the result that A also implements the grant to
B, which depending on the nature of C's right he may still be able to do[2]. Nor does it
matter if B's real right is actually completed first provided that C's real right is also
effectually completed[3]. In practice, of course, the right granted to one party often
excludes the right contracted to be granted to the other[4]; but even if both rights can
stand together the test is not which party completes his right first but whether the
real right granted to C is in breach of the original contract between A and B.

The offside goals rule also applies where the warrandice claim of the first party (B)
arises under a delivered deed such as a disposition or a standard security, provided
only that the deed was delivered prior to the conferring of any rights, real or
personal, in the second party (C)[5]. In practice there will often be both a contract and
then later a delivered deed, and both will contain grants of warrandice, and in such a
case the first party (B) is protected if the contract precedes any right in the second
party (C) notwithstanding the fact that the deed may have been delivered after such
a right is created.

A double grant means a double grant of real rights[6]. In *Wallace v Simmers*[7] the
owner of a farm had granted a contractual licence to a relative to occupy a cottage
on the estate. Later the farm was sold. Although the purchaser knew of the licence
he was held not to be affected by it. The licence, it was said, was not a personal right
to a real right (a *jus ad rem*) but a personal right *simpliciter*. 'Any other result would be

surprising indeed for it would convert what was and has never been anything but a mere personal right into something real and enforceable against singular successors'[8]. The basis of the decision appears to be that, unlike a *jus ad rem*, an ordinary personal right contains no grant of warrandice, either express or implied. Consequently when a subsequent real right comes to be granted there is no breach of the antecedent personal right and hence no scope for the rule against offside goals[9].

Double grants of real rights may be classified into two different groups. In the first group there are those rights which are incompatible with each other in the sense that the completion of the right in the second party (C) has the consequence that no grant can now be made to the first party (B). This always occurs where the right conferred on the second party is ownership because if the second party becomes owner, any grant subsequently made to the first party fails as *a non domino*. The standard example of this situation is where the same property is sold twice, the first conveyance to be granted removing the effectiveness of any subsequent conveyance, and it has been held on a number of occasions that the offside goals rule applies here[10]. It is thought that the rule applies also where there is a contract to grant a subordinate real right, such as a right in security, followed by a conveyance of the property to someone else, for once again the granting of the conveyance prevents the implementation of the prior contract[11]. The offside goals rule has been held not to apply where there is an antecedent obligation to grant a lease followed by a conveyance to someone else preventing its implementation[12], but this is inconsistent with the general framework of the law and it is suggested that the decisions ought to be reconsidered[13]. Finally, another case of incompatible rights is a double grant of a lease in the same property, and this may be contrasted with double grants of a right in security or a servitude, which fall into the second group discussed below.

In the second group of double real rights the rights are compatible, by which is meant that the completion of one of the rights does not of itself prevent the completion of the other. The two real rights may therefore stand together. For a long time it was unclear whether the offside goals rule applied at all to compatible rights and the issue did not finally arise for decision until *Trade Development Bank v Crittall Windows Ltd* in 1983[14]. The facts were that the owner of heritable property[15], having concluded a contract for its sale, granted a standard security to a bank. The security was recorded in the Register of Sasines before the sale could be completed, but the bank knew of the sale and so was in bad faith. There was no incompatibility of rights because the sale could still go ahead notwithstanding the grant of the standard security, but it was held that the offside goals rule applied nonetheless and that the security was voidable at the instance of the purchaser. The reasons for reaching this decision are not fully articulated by the court, but since the contract of sale contained an obligation of warrandice[16], and since the subsequent grant of the security was in breach of that obligation, it is thought that the decision is entirely consistent with earlier cases on the rule. On a more practical level the decision is justified by the fact that the purchaser would have been severely prejudiced if the property which he had purchased unburdened had then turned out to be burdened by a security[17].

The decision in *Crittall Windows* reaffirms, if only by implication, the primacy of the requirement that the grant which is being challenged must breach an antecedent obligation, and this requirement seems the key to the future development of the law. Consider, for example, the case of a standard security. A standard security contains a warranty that there are no prior securities[18]. It also contains, as one of the standard conditions implied by law, a prohibition against the leasing of the property[19]. It may also contain a number of other prohibitions, for example against alienation or against the granting of a further security. If therefore, as often happens, a debtor grants standard securities to two creditors, and if the second creditor registers first with the result that his security is ranked first, there is a breach of the warrandice contained in the first security such that, if the second creditor is in bad faith, his security is reducible[20] by the first creditor[21]. If, however, the order of registration had been reversed, the second creditor would have no remedy against the first because the granting of the first security preceded, and hence was not in breach of, the rights conferred on him by his own security[22]; but the first creditor would have still a remedy against him if, as sometimes happens, the first security contained a blanket prohibition on all other securities, posterior as well as prior[23]. In *Trade Development Bank v Warriner and Mason (Scotland) Ltd*[24] a debtor who had granted a standard security proceeded to lease the property in breach of one of the standard conditions implied into the security. Since the tenant had notice of the standard conditions, it was held that his lease was voidable at the instance of the heritable creditor[25]. The test in all these cases is whether the grant was in breach of a pre-existing obligation; and if there was such an obligation and if the obligation was known to the grantee, the offside goals rule applies and the grant is reducible.

1 Usually warrandice guarantees a good title and one free from adverse real rights. See further paras 701 ff. Of course the implementation of the grant to B will also usually be in breach of the later grant of warrandice to C. But the offside goals rule does not apply because, by the time warrandice came to be granted to C, the grant to B was one which A was already bound to make. See Stair *Institutions* I,14,5 ('being of necessity to satisfy prior engagements').
2 *Trade Development Bank v Crittall Windows Ltd* 1983 SLT 510 (B's right ownership, C's right a standard security).
3 *Trade Development Bank v Warriner and Mason (Scotland) Ltd* 1980 SC 74, 1980 SLT 223 (B's standard security was completed before C's sublease).
4 As where both parties are to be granted ownership of the same thing.
5 Warrandice becomes effective as soon as the deed is delivered: see para 642 above. Usually the same warrandice is implied, and expressed, in both the preliminary contract and in the deed following on from the contract. The rule that warrandice in dispositions of land is not incurred without eviction does not apply to cases of double grant: see *Burnet v Johnston* (1666) Mor 16586; *Smith v Ross* (1672) Mor 16596; Bankton *Institute* II,3,124; Erskine *Institute* II,3,30; Bell *Principles* s 895.
6 Or possibly a double grant of real conditions. Thus if A contracts to grant a deed of conditions (containing real burdens) to B, and if A then dispones to C without implementing the obligation, it is thought that the offside goals rule might apply if C was in bad faith.
7 *Wallace v Simmers* 1960 SC 255, 1961 SLT 34.
8 1960 SC 255 at 259, 260, 1961 SLT 34 at 37, per Lord President Clyde.
9 See *Birkbeck v Ross* (1865) 4 M 272 and *Mann v Houston* 1957 SLT 89.
10 *Lang v Dixon* 29 June 1813 FC; *Morrison v Somerville* (1860) 22 D 1082; *Petrie v Forsyth* (1874) 2 R 214; *Rodger (Builders) Ltd v Fawdry* 1950 SC 483, 1950 SLT 345.
11 This result has been held to occur where the prior contract is an obligation to subfeu. See *Stodart v Dalzell* (1876) 4 R 236 and *Ceres School Board v M'Farlane* (1895) 23 R 279, 3 SLT 198.
12 *Jacobs v Anderson* (1898) 6 SLT 234, OH. See also *Millar v M'Robbie* 1949 SC 1, 1949 SLT 2.
13 Indeed the reasoning in *Wallace v Simmers* 1960 SC 255, 1961 SLT 34, almost presupposes that the decisions are wrongly decided. In South Africa, where a rule very similar to the offside goals rule is recognised, no distinction is made between obligations to grant leases and obligations to grant other real rights. See H S Silberberg and J Schoeman *The Law of Property* (2nd edn, 1988) p 69. It is thought that the rule in Scotland ought to be the same.
14 *Trade Development Bank v Crittall Windows Ltd* 1983 SLT 510.
15 In fact a long lease rather than *dominium utile*.
16 It provided for 'a valid marketable and recordable assignation'.
17 The court seemed particularly influenced by this point: see *Trade Development Bank v Crittall Windows Ltd* 1983 SLT 510 at 517, per Lord President Emslie.
18 Conveyancing and Feudal Reform (Scotland) Act 1970 (c 35), s 10(2).
19 Ibid, s 11(2), Sch 3, condition 6.
20 It may be that the reduction would only be *ad hunc effectum*, ie effective only to the extent of reversing the ranking as between the two securities.
21 More or less this situation arose in *Leslie v McIndoe's Trustees* (1824) 3 S 48 (NE 31) where the offside goals rule was not applied. See also *Henderson v Campbell* (1821) 1 S 103 (NE 104). But *Leslie* was disapproved, although not formally overruled, by *Trade Development Bank v Crittall Windows Ltd* 1983 SLT 510 and it seems clear that the offside goals rule would now apply. See *Scotlife Home Loans (No 2) Ltd v W & A S Bruce* (17 June 1994, unreported), Dunfermline Sh Ct, but cf *Scotlife Home*

Loans (No 2) Ltd v Muir 1994 SCLR 791, Sh Ct. It has been argued that where at the time the second security is granted the subjects are sufficient to repay both debts, the second security should not be regarded as in fraud of the first: see *Blackwood v The Other Creditors of Sir George Hamilton* (1749) Mor 4898; *Morrison v Somerville* (1860) 22 D 1082 at 1089, OH, per Lord Kinloch (affd (1860) 22 D 1082, IH). But it is thought that this argument cannot survive the decisions in the *Trade Development Bank* cases. (For the *Trade Development Bank* cases, see para 695, note 7, above).

22 There would, however, be a remedy in warrandice against the debtor.

23 This follows from the decision in *Trade Development Bank v Warriner and Mason (Scotland) Ltd* 1980 SC 74, 1980 SLT 223.

24 1980 SC 74, 1980 SLT 223.

25 This decision was later followed in *Trade Development Bank v David W Haig (Bellshill) Ltd* 1983 SLT 510.

698. Breach of antecedent obligation: other cases. The rule against offside goals is not confined to the case of double grants but applies more generally wherever a grant is made in the face of an obligation prohibiting its making. Thus the rule has been recognised as applying in the following cases:

(1) *Rights of pre-emption and options to purchase.* A right of pre-emption confers a right to buy back property at the time when the current owner comes to sell[1]. It has been held that if the current owner sells without regard to the right of pre-emption, the title of the purchaser is voidable at the instance of the creditor in the right[2]. The purchaser must, of course, be in bad faith but it is sufficient for this purpose if the right of pre-emption appears from the Register of Sasines or Land Register[3]. It may be taken that the rule is the same in the case of options to purchase[4].

(2) *Trust rights.* A grant by trustees made in breach of trust is reducible by the beneficiaries subject to the usual requirement of bad faith or of not taking for value[5]. This is the common law rule. But absolute protection is given by statute to grantees for value in respect of certain classes of grant, including ownership, security and lease[6]. The subject is considered more fully elsewhere[7].

(3) *Rights of reduction.* A grantee taking from a person holding on a voidable title will himself receive a title which is voidable if either he knew of the voidability or if he does not take for value[8]. This rule is well established on its own account, and it can be regarded as part of the rule against offside goals if a grant by one holding on a voidable title is treated as being in breach of the antecedent right of reduction.

(4) *Other cases.* All the cases in which the offside goals rule has been recognised have in common that the person entitled to found on the rule either already has a real right in the property in question[9] or, alternatively and more usually, is the creditor in an obligation to confer such a right[10]. The primary use of the rule, therefore, is to regulate competitions of property rights. Whether the rule may also have a wider application is unclear. Thus suppose that an owner of property enters into a contractual obligation that he will not make a particular grant and suppose that he then makes the prohibited grant. The contract confers no rights on the other party beyond the bare right to enforce the prohibition. In particular that party has no real right in the property, actual or prospective. Nonetheless it is conceivable that the prohibition would be enforceable against a grantee who took in bad faith. Against that conclusion is the view expressed in *Wallace v Simmers*[11] that the benefit of the offside goals rule is restricted to those holding a personal right to a real right, but this statement must be taken in the context of the type of case in which it was made[12] and it is not clear that it advances a proposition which is valid for all other cases[13].

1 For rights of pre-emption in relation to land, see CONVEYANCING, vol 6, para 520.

2 *Matheson v Tinney* 1989 SLT 535, OH; *Roebuck v Edmunds* 1992 SCLR 74, 1992 SLT 1055, OH. The same rule applies in respect of *pacta de retrovendendo: King v Douglas* (1636) Durie 820; *Workman v*

The Law of Property in Scotland

Crawford (1672) Mor 10208. The earlier law may have been different: see *Stirling v Johnson* (1756) 5 Brown's Supp 323 and Erskine *Institute* II,3,13.
3 See para 699 below.
4 *Davidson v Zani* 1992 SCLR 1001, Sh Ct. Cf *Bisset v Aberdeen Magistrates* (1898) 1 F 87 where the option, which was contained in a lease, was granted in favour of a predecessor of the pursuer as tenant, and where the issue was analysed as being whether the option was a real condition binding on the defenders as successors of the original landlord. See para 351 above.
5 *Redfearn v Somervail* (1813) 1 Dow 50, 5 Pat 707, HL.
6 Trusts (Scotland) Act 1961 (c 57), s 2.
7 See para 691 above.
8 See further para 692 above.
9 The real right may indeed exist not just at the time of seeking the remedy but at the time when the disputed grant was made. See *Trade Development Bank v Warriner and Mason (Scotland) Ltd* 1980 SC 74, 1980 SLT 223.
10 This is true, not just in the typical case of double grants, but also in the case of a right of reduction (which is a right to acquire ownership). It is also true of trust rights if the beneficiary has a specific entitlement to the property in question, but not presumably in other cases of trusts.
11 *Wallace v Simmers* 1960 SC 255 at 259, 1961 SLT 34 at 37, per Lord President Clyde. This statement has been adopted in later cases, eg *Trade Development Bank v Crittall Windows Ltd* 1983 SLT 510 at 517, per Lord President Emslie.
12 Ie a potential case of double grants of real rights.
13 It is not, for instance, valid for cases like *Trade Development Bank v Warriner and Mason (Scotland) Ltd* 1980 SC 74, 1980 SLT 223, where a real right (in that case a standard security) already exists.

699. Bad faith or absence of value. The final requirement of the rule against offside goals is that the grantee take in bad faith or without giving value for his grant. But while it follows from this that a grantee who takes in good faith and for value will thus gain a title which is unimpeachable, this should not be taken as an example of an equitable exception in favour of bona fide acquirers; for since *ex hypothesi* the granter owns the property in the first place, the initial result of a grant must always be to confer upon the grantee a subsistent title[1], and it is only if he is in bad faith or does not give value that that title, initially good, falls to be reduced by the creditor in the antecedent personal obligation. The effect of the rule, therefore, is not to reward good faith — for since the acquirer already has a good title he requires no reward — but rather to punish bad faith by depriving the acquirer of that title which he already has.

So far as bad faith is concerned, Stair required of the grantee 'certain knowledge, by intimation, citation, or the like, inducing *malam fidem,* whereby any prior disposition or assignation made to another party is certainly known'[2]. It is thought that this is still the law, and that a grantee is in bad faith only where he has clear knowledge, at least in general terms, of the antecedent prohibition of the grant[3]. In the case of heritable property, however, a grantee is deemed to know the contents of relevant deeds or entries in the Sasine or Land Register[4]. Once a party knows of an antecedent prohibition, he is not entitled to assume without enquiry that it is no longer in force nor is he entitled to rely on the assurances of the granter[5]. Bad faith is relevant only if it existed at or before the time when the grantee completed his real right, and knowledge gained after this date has no effect on the title which has been acquired[6].

It appears that a failure to take for value has the same effect as taking in bad faith[7]. This applies most obviously to cases of pure donation, but it may perhaps also apply where, despite the payment of some consideration, the grant is taken at a material under-value.

1 Bell *Commentaries* I,308: '[A]lthough the seller be liable to punishment, the right of the second purchaser, if first completed, is effectual. The property was complete in the seller; and it is only a dishonest use of that property with which he is chargeable'. See para 689 above.
2 Stair *Institutions* I,14,5.
3 *Petrie v Forsyth* (1874) 2 R 214.
4 *Trade Development Bank v Warriner and Mason (Scotland) Ltd* 1980 SC 74, 1980 SLT 49.

5 *Lang v Dixon* 29 June 1813 FC; *Rodger (Builders) Ltd v Fawdry* 1950 SC 483, 1950 SLT 345; *Trade Development Bank v Warriner and Mason (Scotland) Ltd* 1980 SC 74, 1980 SLT 223.
6 *Stair* IV,40,21: 'supervenient knowledge will not prejudge them'.
7 Hume *Lectures* vol IV (Stair Soc vol 17, 1955 ed G C H Paton) pp 317, 318.

700. Remedies. The remedy usually pursued by the creditor in the antecedent obligation is reduction of the prohibited grant. So in the case of a double sale, for example, reduction of the unlawful conveyance will reinvest the granter and enable him to fulfil the antecedent contract of sale[1]. Sometimes a more useful and appropriate remedy than reduction is to have the grantee declared bound by some or all of the terms of the antecedent obligation[2]. This will be so in the case of double sales if the original granter has become insolvent, for here reduction would only confer a windfall on the granter's creditors and the interests of the first purchaser are much better served by taking a conveyance directly from the second purchaser[3]. Similarly, where an antecedent obligation to grant a subordinate real right has been defeated by a conveyance of the property to another party, it is a much simpler resolution of the dispute to have the purchaser grant the subordinate right directly than to reduce the purchaser's conveyance. Finally, it should be noted that the offside goals rule can also be pled as a defence to an attempted enforcement of the prohibited grant against the creditor in the antecedent obligation[4].

1 Eg *Petrie v Forsyth* (1874) 2 R 214; *Rodger (Builders) Ltd v Fawdry* 1950 SC 483, 1950 SLT 345. In *Rodger (Builders) Ltd* reduction was granted not only of the prohibited disposition but also of the contract of sale on which it had proceeded; but it is difficult to see what interest the first purchaser has in a contract of sale to which he is not a party or indeed how his position is improved by its reduction.
2 *Davidson v Zani* 1992 SCLR 1001, Sh Ct. See also the observation of Lord Gifford in *Stodart v Dalzell* (1876) 4 R 236 at 243, that 'there is enough to make Stodart [the grantee] liable in the obligations of his author, so far as relates to the subject in question'.
3 This raises, but does not solve, the problem of whether the price should be paid to the granter (now insolvent) or to the second purchaser.
4 *Lang v Dixon* 29 June 1813 FC; *Stodart v Dalzell* (1876) 4 R 236; *Trade Development Bank v Crittall Windows Ltd* 1983 SLT 510.

(9) GUARANTEE OF TITLE: WARRANDICE

(a) General

701. Introduction. Usually a transferor will warrant (guarantee) the title being transferred. This guarantee, which is often known as 'warrandice', is implied first into the contract of sale or other contract entered into between the parties; and where, as with land and incorporeal property, the contract is then followed by a written conveyance, warrandice is implied into the conveyance also and takes effect when the conveyance is delivered. But while warrandice is thus implied in the transfer of property[1], it is usual for an express grant of warrandice to be made even although in most cases this does no more than repeat the terms of the implied obligation.

Whether it appears in a contract or in a conveyance warrandice is a personal, contractual obligation on the granter and does not import real liability. Of course, like any other personal obligation, performance of warrandice can be secured by the grant of a standard security or other appropriate security over property being retained by the transferor, and until its abolition in 1924 this was sometimes done in the transfer of land by the grant of 'real warrandice'[2]. Securing the performance of warrandice is unknown in modern practice.

The content of the guarantee of title given by a transferor depends upon the type of property being transferred. Thus it will be necessary to consider separately (1) corporeal heritable property[3], (2) corporeal moveable property[4], and (3) incorporeal property[5].

1 Warrandice is also implied in the creation of subordinate real rights such as leases and rights in security.
2 Real warrandice was implied into contracts of excambion. The Conveyancing (Scotland) Act 1924 (c 27), s 14(1), now provides that '[f]rom and after the commencement of this Act [1 January 1925], it shall not be competent to dispone lands in real warrandice of a conveyance of other lands, and such real warrandice shall not arise ex lege from any contract or agreement entered into after the commencement of this Act'.
3 See paras 702–714 below.
4 See paras 715, 716, below.
5 See paras 717–719 below.

(b) Corporeal Heritable Property

(A) CONTENT OF WARRANDICE

702. The law in summary. In the transfer of land warrandice is implied both in the missives of sale and in the disposition also, although in the case of missives the seller's obligation is more usually described as an obligation to deliver a good and marketable title. In practice express grants of warrandice are normal in both cases and sometimes the express grant departs from the guarantee which would have been given by implication. So far as the implied grant is concerned, there is no difference between warrandice in missives and warrandice in the disposition save that in the case of the disposition judicial eviction is sometimes required before a claim can be made.

In a sale the implied obligation of warrandice may be said to comprise four separate warranties namely:
(1) that the transferor has a title to the property being transferred which is absolutely good[1];
(2) that the property is not affected by any subordinate real rights[2];
(3) that the property is not affected by any real conditions which are unusual, material and unknown to the transferee[3]; and
(4) that the transferor will do nothing in the future to prejudice the title of the transferee[4].

It will be seen that the first three warranties are guarantees of the state of the title as at a particular date. In the case of missives of sale the relevant date is the contractual date of entry. In the case of the disposition it is the date on which the disposition is delivered. Usually these two dates coincide, although if settlement of the transaction is delayed for some reason the date of delivery of the disposition may be later than the contractual date of entry[5]. The fourth and final warranty is not confined to a fixed date but offers a guarantee in respect of the transferor's own acts which extends into the future.

1 See para 703 below.
2 See para 704 below.
3 See para 705 below.
4 See para 706 below.
5 Sometimes, however, the parties renegotiate the date of entry, in which case the two dates will coincide even where settlement has been delayed. It is unclear whether a variation in the contractual date of entry requires formal writing: cf *Imry Property Holdings Ltd v Glasgow Young Men's Christian Association* 1979 SLT 261, OH, with *Jayner Ltd v Allander Holdings Ltd* 1990 GWD 30–1717, OH.

703. The first warranty: absolutely good title. The transferor warrants that as at the relevant date he owns (or, if the relevant date has not yet arrived, will own as at that date[1]) the property and so is (or will be) in a position to confer ownership on the transferee. He further warrants that his title is absolutely good and not voidable[2], and in the case of Land Register titles this probably includes a further warranty that the title is not subject to an exclusion of indemnity[3].

The transferor's title must be to the whole property being transferred, the extent of his obligation being measured by the manner in which the property is described in missives or, as the case may be, in the disposition. Thus where property is described merely as a flat ('that second floor flatted dwelling house') there is no obligation to convey the *solum* on which the building is erected, although in practice an express obligation to that effect is often added; but where the property is described as comprising actual land ('that area or plot of land lying to the east of the High Street, Dunkeld together with the dwelling house erected thereon') the obligation is to convey the whole land *a coelo usque ad centrum* (from the heavens to the centre of the earth) subject only to the legal separate tenements such as salmon fishings[4]. There have been a number of cases in which a purchaser was held able to rescind missives of sale where the minerals[5] were reserved to the superior on the basis that the seller did not then own *a coelo usque ad centrum*[6] and the modern practice is to avoid this particular difficulty by making clear in the description in both missives and the disposition that the minerals are not or may not be included in the sale[7].

1 In the case of missives there is a time gap between conclusion of the contract and date of entry, which is the relevant date for the purposes of the warranty. So a seller is not in breach of warrandice merely because he does not own the property at the date of conclusion of missives.
2 For the distinction between absolutely good and voidable titles, see para 601 above.
3 That is not, of course, the same as a warranty that the transferee's own title will be registered without exclusion of indemnity, although it is standard practice to include such a warranty in missives. See *Registration of Title Practice Book* (1981) paras G.2.08, G.3.05.
4 For separate tenements, see paras 207 ff.
5 Minerals are conventional and not legal separate tenements and are included in a sale unless expressly reserved.
6 *Whyte v Lee* (1879) 6 R 699; *Crofts v Stewart's Trustees* 1927 SC (HL) 65, 1927 SLT 362; *Mossend Theatre Co Ltd v Livingstone* 1930 SC 90, 1930 SLT 108; *Campbell v M'Cutcheon* 1963 SC 505, 1963 SLT 290. It is suggested in some of these cases that prior knowledge of the reservation of minerals will preclude a claim. Whether this is based on personal bar (as Burns suggests in 13 *Encyclopaedia of the Laws of Scotland* (ed Lord Dunedin and J Wark 1932) para 405), on construction of the missives, or on an attempt to assimilate minerals to real conditions (for which see para 705 below) is not clear; but it is thought that there is no general doctrine that prior knowledge of the transferor's absence of title prevents a claim in warrandice.
7 For missives this is effected by a provision that the minerals are included in the purchase price only in so far as the seller has right thereto. Although this provision is for the benefit of the seller it is usually found in the offer to purchase. In dispositions the deed reserving the minerals is referred to for burdens in the dispositive clause and hence incorporated by reference into the description of the property being conveyed.

704. The second warranty: no subordinate real rights. The transferor warrants that as at the relevant date the property is not (or will not be) subject to subordinate real rights, other than leases[1]. It is thought that this warranty extends to occupancy rights under the Matrimonial Homes (Family Protection) (Scotland) Act 1981 which, although not real rights in the strict sense, are capable of allowing continued occupation of a house by a non-entitled spouse of the transferor or earlier owner even after ownership has passed to the transferee[2]. Often property which is being sold is burdened by a standard security which the seller is unable to have discharged until after he has received the purchase price at settlement of the transaction. Until the discharge is registered there is a technical breach of warrandice, but the practice is to overlook this although the purchaser will often insist on delivery of the executed discharge at settlement so that he may effect registration himself.

Leases are treated in a different way from other real rights. In the early law owner occupation was relatively unusual, most conveyancing was of large estates, and the existence of leases was normal and accepted. No claim appears to have been possible under warrandice[3]. In the only modern case, *Lothian and Border Farmers Ltd v M'Cutcheon*[4], the Lord Ordinary followed the old authorities and refused a claim in warrandice in respect of a lease over a dwelling house. But this decision has been questioned and may not represent the current law[5]. In his *Lectures* Hume suggested that warrandice is incurred 'by a very long tack, at a low rent, or bestowing high and singular powers'[6]. Conversely, if the lease is on favourable terms from the point of view of the landlord, and if the property is of a kind which is usually bought for renting, it seems clear that no claim will arise[7], for leases are distinguished from other subordinate real rights by the fact that they may bring benefit to the owner of the land. The difficult case is the one raised by *Lothian and Border Farmers,* namely a lease in terms not in themselves unreasonable over property of a type which is usually bought for owner occupation; and it is thought that, despite the view reached by the court in that case, a claim in warrandice might now succeed. In practice conveyancers usually circumvent the uncertainty in the law by making express provision for 'entry and actual occupation' (or 'vacant possession') of the property which is being bought[8].

1 M P Brown *A Treatise on the Law of Sale* (1821) p 259; Hume *Lectures* vol IV (Stair Soc vol 17, 1955 ed G C H Paton) p 150; Bell *Principles* s 895; *Dewar v Aitken* (1780) Mor 16637 (right in security).
2 Matrimonial Homes (Family Protection) (Scotland) Act 1981 (c 59), s 6 (amended by the Law Reform (Miscellaneous Provisions) (Scotland) Act 1985 (c 73), s 13(6), and the Law Reform (Miscellaneous Provisions) (Scotland) Act 1990 (c 40), s 74(1), (2), Sch 8, para 31, Sch 9). In practice this is usually dealt with by express provision in missives of sale.
3 *Simpson v Zoung* (1563) Mor 16565; *Lady Pitferran* (1629) Mor 16577.
4 *Lothian and Border Farmers Ltd v M'Cutcheon* 1952 SLT 450, OH.
5 J M Halliday *Conveyancing Law and Practice in Scotland* vol I (1985) para 4-38(6).
6 *Hume* vol IV,149.
7 Thus many leases are not actionable in warrandice — hence the warrandice as to rents imported by the Titles to Land Consolidation (Scotland) Act 1868 (c 101), s 8 (amended by the Statute Law Revision Act 1893 (c 14)). This is the answer to the reliance placed on that section by the Lord Ordinary in *Lothian and Border Farmers Ltd v M'Cutcheon* 1952 SLT 450, OH.
8 Provision is made both in the missives of sale and also in the disposition. For the meaning of the expression 'entry and actual occupation', see *Stuart v Lort-Phillips* 1977 SC 244 and *Scottish Flavour Ltd v Watson* 1982 SLT 78, OH.

705. The third warranty: no unusual real conditions. For a long time there was doubt as to whether the existence of real conditions, such as servitudes and real burdens, came within the obligation of warrandice at all. A number of cases can be found in Morison's Dictionary in which particular claims were rejected, without, however, entirely closing the door to the idea that a more suitable claim might ultimately succeed[1]. Juristic opinion was also divided, Bankton and Bell rejecting outright the idea of a claim[2], but Stair and Erskine accepting that a claim might be possible if the condition in question was not merely 'moderate' or 'light'[3]. The first reported case in which a claim was allowed for a real condition was not until 1835[4], but since then a number of cases have followed and the doctrine is now well established[5].

The modern law is as follows. The transferor warrants that as at the relevant date the property is not (or will not be) subject to any real condition which satisfies each of the following three requirements, namely:
(1) that the condition was unknown to the transferee at the time when the grant of warrandice was made;
(2) that the condition is unusual either generally or in relation to the type and location of the property in question; and
(3) that the condition results in a material diminution in the value of the property[6].

Unless all three requirements are satisfied a claim in warrandice will fail[7].

With respect to requirement (1), the relevant date for knowledge in the transferee is the date when the grant of warrandice is made[8], which is the date of conclusion of missives or, as the case may be, the date of delivery of the disposition, and the onus of demonstrating such knowledge rests on the transferor[9]. Thus if a transferee learns of a particular condition prior to conclusion of missives, he has no claim in warrandice at all; if he learns of it after the conclusion of missives but prior to delivery of the disposition he cannot claim on the warrandice in the disposition but he has a good claim in respect of the warrandice in the missives; and finally if he learns of it only after the delivery of the disposition he can claim either under the disposition or, provided that the missives have not been superseded, under the missives. In practice a transferor will usually seek to confer knowledge on the transferee as early as possible, for example by sending the title deeds before missives are concluded, and by listing the deeds containing real burdens and servitudes in missives and in the dispositive clause of the disposition[10]. There may, however, be servitudes which are not constituted in any written deed. Moreover, so far as warrandice in the missives is concerned, it is possible that the express provision which is commonly found ('there are no unusual or unduly onerous burdens') can be read as departing from the implied warrandice to the extent of abandoning the requirement of absence of knowledge[11].

Requirement (2), that the condition be unusual either generally or in relation to the type and location of the property, is of some antiquity. Thus it was decided as early as a case of 1549 that feudal casualties do not give rise to a claim in warrandice

> 'because ward, releif, and non-entres pertenis to the superiour be the commoun law of this realme, fra the quhilk na man is exemit, and sould be knawin to all our soverane Lordis lieges'[12].

If the transferee is taken by surprise this is due to his 'negligence and inexcusabill ignorance', a phrase which draws attention to the underlying basis of the requirement as a form of constructive knowledge[13]. A transferee is deemed to know of and to expect real conditions of a standard type. The rule is a practical one because without it

> 'it would generally be impossible to make an effective sale of a house in town without a very minute and ponderous written contract specifying all restrictions and conditions, however usual, that applied to it. If a man simply buys a house he must be taken to buy it as the seller has it, on a good title, of course, but subject to such restrictions as may exist if of an ordinary character, and such as the buyer may reasonably be supposed to have contemplated as at least not improbable'[14].

The test is not an easy one to apply[15]. In the leading modern case, *Armia Ltd v Daejan Developments Ltd*[16], it was held that a servitude right of access which included a ten-foot frontage to the street was 'unusual' in the context of a property in Kirkcaldy High Street, and it may be that, at least in urban properties, servitudes are more likely than real burdens to be deemed actionable in warrandice[17].

1   *Sandilands v Earl of Haddington* (1672) Mor 16599; *Paton v Gordon* (1682) Mor 14170; *Gordonston and Nicolson v Paton* (1682) Mor 16606. *Falconer v The Earl Marshall* (1614) Mor 16571, an apparent exception, seems to have turned on the speciality that the holding was blench.

2   Bankton *Institute* II,3,125; Bell *Principles* s 895.

3   Stair *Institutions* I,14,7; Erskine *Institute* II,3,31.

4   *Urquhart v Halden* (1835) 13 S 844.

5   *Louttit's Trustees v Highland Rly Co* (1892) 19 R 791; *Welsh v Russell* (1894) 21 R 769, 1 SLT 594; *Smith v Soeder* (1895) 23 R 60, 3 SLT 135; *M'Connell v Chassells* (1903) 10 SLT 790, OH; *Armia Ltd v Daejan Developments Ltd* 1979 SC (HL) 56, 1979 SLT 147; *Morris v Ritchie* 1991 GWD 12–712, 1992 GWD 33-1950, OH.

6   *Welsh v Russell* (1894) 21 R 769, 1 SLT 594; *M'Connell v Chassells* (1903) 10 SLT 790, OH; *Armia Ltd v Daejan Developments Ltd* 1978 SC 152, 1977 SLT (Notes) 9, 49, revsd 1979 SC (HL) 56, 1979 SLT 147; *Morris v Ritchie* 1992 GWD 33-1950, OH.

7 See, however, *Umar v Murtaza* 1983 SLT (Sh Ct) 79 where the sheriff principal overlooked requirement (2).

8 It is not the date to which the warrandice actually relates which in the case of missives will usually be later. See para 702 above.

9 *M'Connell v Chassells* (1903) 10 SLT 790 at 793, OH, per Lord Kincairney.

10 The transferor warrants only the property as described in the missives or, as the case may be, the disposition. By listing the burdens there the transferor is in effect preventing a claim in warrandice.

11 In practice the seller often avoids the difficulty, if indeed it is a difficulty, by deleting the provision from the purchaser's offer and sending the title deeds to him with a stipulation that he must satisfy himself as to their terms within a stipulated (and short) period.

12 *Drummond v Steuart* (1549) Mor 16565. See also *Buntin v Murray* (1686) Mor 16608 and *Brownlie v Miller* (1878) 5 R 1076.

13 This raises the question as to whether other forms of constructive knowledge might also be relevant, eg the fact that real burdens are set out in a public register. On this point see K G C Reid 'Warrandice in the Sale of Land' in D J Cusine (ed) *A Scots Conveyancing Miscellany: Essays in Honour of Professor J M Halliday* (1987) p 160.

14 *Whyte v Lee* (1879) 6 R 699 at 701, per Lord Young.

15 The court was sharply divided in both *Whyte v Lee* (1879) 6 R 699 and *Smith v Soeder* (1895) 23 R 60, 3 SLT 135.

16 *Armia Ltd v Daejan Developments Ltd* 1979 SC (HL) 56, 1979 SLT 147.

17 This is particularly so in respect of servitudes of access, although even here it cannot be said that there will always be a breach of warrandice. See *Morris v Ritchie* 1991 GWD 12–712, 1992 GWD 33-1950, OH.

706. The fourth warranty: no future acts prejudicial to the title. Finally, the transferor warrants that he will not by future act cause prejudice to the title conferred on the transferee. Unlike the other warranties, this warranty is not tied to a particular date; but nor is it an absolute guarantee, for what is warranted is not the absence of future defects but rather the absence of such future defects as may be brought about by the transferor.

Although the warranty runs from the date of conclusion of missives, when it is first granted, into the indefinite future, it ceases to be of much importance in practice after registration of the disposition. For the usual way in which the warranty is breached is by making a second grant in relation to the same property, for example a second disposition[1] or a standard security[2], and the power to make such a grant disappears on registration of the original disposition[3]. Even after registration, however, breaches may occasionally occur, one possible case being where the transferor remains in possession so that at the end of ten years the land is reacquired by positive prescription[4].

1 *Smith v Ross* (1672) Mor 16596; *Rodger (Builders) Ltd v Fawdry* 1950 SC 483, 1950 SLT 345.

2 *Trade Development Bank v Crittall Windows Ltd* 1983 SLT 510.

3 Any subsequent grant would be ineffectual as *a non domino*, unless cured by positive prescription. Formally speaking this is not so in the case of Land Register titles, but in practice the Keeper will exclude indemnity and the ultimate effectiveness of the grantee's title will also depend upon prescription.

4 *Wallace v University Court of St Andrews* (1904) 6 F 1093, 12 SLT 240; *Love-Lee v Cameron of Lochiel* 1991 SCLR 61, Sh Ct.

707. The need for eviction. In Scots law, as in Roman law[1], eviction in the context of warrandice means judicial eviction[2]. 'Eviction is the loss of a thing, in whole or in part, by the establishment of a right in another preferable to the seller'[3]. What is required is that the true owner[4] of the property successfully assert his title against the transferee. The judicial proceedings must be initiated by the true owner, or at least be in response to some positive act of that person, such as the taking of possession of the disputed property[5]. It is not possible for a transferee to evict himself, for example by raising an action of declarator of non-ownership, and if the true owner does not choose to assert his title there is no eviction[6]. A transferee will usually defend any action which is raised against him, although he is not bound to do so[7], and if he is successful in his defence no claim lies against the transferor for expenses[8]. If he is unsuccessful and decree is pronounced against him the conditions for eviction are satisfied. Similarly, if the action is settled without decree being pronounced there is still eviction provided that the terms are favourable to the pursuer and that there was no stateable defence[9]. It is thought that the requirement of judicial eviction is satisfied by the exercise by the Keeper of his quasi-judicial powers to rectify the Land Register[10].

It is important to emphasise that there is no necessary connection between, on the one hand, judicial eviction and, on the other hand, physical ejection, although the second is often an eventual consequence of the first. A transferee against whom decree has been pronounced is no less evicted because he remains, for the time being at least, in physical possession of the property[11].

The circumstances under which eviction is required in warrandice have sometimes been the subject of misunderstanding[12]. Contrary to what is often stated[13], the general rule is that eviction is not required, so that in most cases a claim in warrandice may be made immediately and without regard to whether the alleged defect in title has been judicially founded on by the person entitled to do so. The rule that eviction is not required applies without qualification to warrandice in missives of sale. It also applies in many cases of warrandice in dispositions; but it does not apply to the first of the four component warranties identified earlier, that is to say, to the warranty of absolutely good title. Here the mere fact that the transferor's title was bad at the time of transfer, with the result that the transferee's title is bad also, does not give rise to a claim in warrandice under the disposition. There must also be eviction of the transferee, and in the absence of eviction there is no remedy[14]. In effect the warranty is reduced to a warranty against eviction. Even in this case, however, the law does not insist on eviction where the absence of title was caused by a second inconsistent deed by the transferor, such as a disposition to a third party[15], or, perhaps, where the defect is admitted by him[16]. No eviction is required in respect of the other component warranties of warrandice in dispositions[17].

1 W W Buckland *Textbook of Roman Law* (3rd edn, 1963 by P Stein) p 490.
2 Stair *Institutions* II,3,46; M P Brown *A Treatise on the Law of Sale* (1821) p 240.
3 Bell *Principles* s 121. Bell also extends his definition to include 'the emerging of an unquestionable burden on the subject purchased', which is not eviction in the strict sense.
4 Or, in the case of a voidable title, the person entitled to lead the reduction.
5 As envisaged by Lord Neaves in *Leith Heritages Co (Ltd) v Edinburgh and Leith Glass Co* (1876) 3 R 789 at 796.
6 *Palmer v Beck* 1993 SLT 485, OH.
7 Bell s 895. But if he does not defend he must intimate the action to the transferor.
8 *Stephen v Lord Advocate* (1878) 6 R 282.
9 *Watson v Swift & Co's Judicial Factor* 1986 SLT 217. See also Stair II,3,46: 'Yea, warrandice will take effect where there is an unquestionable ground of distress, though the fiar transacted voluntarily to prevent the distress'.
10 Land Registration (Scotland) Act 1979 (c 33), s 9.
11 The similarity of the two words seems positively to invite confusion between them. In *Watson v Swift's Judicial Factor* 1986 SLT 217 the reporter refers throughout the rubric to 'ejection' when, as the opinion of the court clearly discloses, he means 'eviction'.
12 K G C Reid 'Warrandice in the Sale of Land' in D J Cusine (ed) *A Scots Conveyancing Miscellany: Essays in Honour of Professor J M Halliday* (1987) 152 especially at 154–159.
13 See eg J M Halliday *Conveyancing Law and Practice in Scotland* vol I (1985) para 4-44. Statements such as this are generally made only with reference to the warrandice in the disposition.
14 Erskine *Institute* II,3,25. See *Cobham v Minter* 1986 SLT 336, OH; *Palmer v Beck* 1993 SLT 485, OH; and *Clark v Lindale Homes Ltd* 1994 SCLR 301, 1994 SLT 1053.
15 *Burnet v Johnston* (1666) Mor 16586; *Smith v Ross* (1672) Mor 16596; Bankton *Institute* II,3,124; Erskine II,3,30; Bell s 895. Stair II,3,46 would extend the principle to any defect 'which will undoubtedly infer a distress' even though not caused by the transferor's act, but this goes beyond the cases relied on.
16 Bell *Principles* ss 121, 895.

17 In order to maintain the view that warrandice in dispositions requires eviction, it is sometimes said that for the other component warranties there must be 'partial eviction'. See eg *Urquhart v Halden* (1835) 13 S 844; *Welsh v Russell* (1894) 21 R 769, 1 SLT 594. But since partial eviction means no more than that the defect complained of exists, and since it requires neither judicial proceedings nor any other act on the part of the person entitled to found on the defect, it will be seen that partial eviction means no eviction.

708. Warrandice in missives of sale.

There is implied into missives of sale full or absolute warrandice comprising the four constituent warranties described above[1]. No eviction is required before a claim can be made:

'[I]n a sale of land the buyer has an absolute right to a good title . . . and unless he shall have unequivocally discharged this right, he is not bound . . . to wait till his right is challenged. It is a sufficient ground of exception to the title if it be liable to challenge'[2].

In order to demonstrate that the title is good and that the obligation of warrandice has been complied with the seller must, in the words of Hume[3], furnish the buyer 'with a sufficient progress of titles to the subject — such a progress (for aught that can be seen) as shall maintain his right against all pretenders'. This means for Sasine titles a good prescriptive progress of title and a clear search in the Sasine and Personal Registers, and for titles registered in the Land Register a land certificate without exclusion of indemnity. The seller's obligation is, however, restricted to prima facie validity. Evidence of absolute validity is not, and could not be, required[4].

In practice warrandice is almost always granted expressly. Typically the seller is taken bound to deliver or exhibit a good and marketable title with clear searches, and it is further provided that there are no conditions of title of an unusual or unduly onerous nature. But while these standard clauses do not appear to vary the warrandice already implied by law[5], it is always open to the parties to effect such variation whether by adding to the burden on the seller or by reducing it. The traditional clause in articles of roup that the buyer is to take *tantum et tale* is an example of the latter[6]. An example of the former is the clause litigated in the leading case of *Armia Ltd v Daejan Developments Ltd*[7] which provided that '[t]here is nothing in the titles of the said subjects which will prevent demolition and redevelopment'.

1 Stair *Institutions* I,14.7. On warrandice in missives, see generally G L Gretton and K G C Reid *Conveyancing* (1993) ch 5. For the four constituent warranties, see paras 703–706 above.
2 Bell *Principles* s 890. See *Nairn v Scrymgeour* (1676) Mor 14169; *Robertson v Rutherford* (1841) 4 D 121; *Dunlop v Crawford* (1850) 12 D 518; *Whyte v Lee* (1879) 6 R 699; *Crofts v Stewart's Trustees* 1927 SC (HL) 65, 1927 SLT 362; *Mossend Theatre Co Ltd v Livingstone* 1930 SC 90, 1930 SLT 108.
3 Hume *Lectures* vol II (Stair Soc vol 13, 1949 ed G C H Paton) p 38.
4 Thus the buyer cannot object to a writ in the prescriptive progress on the basis of some imaginary or speculative latent defect. All writs have the potential to suffer from latent defects. See *Sibbald's Heirs v Harris* 1947 SC 601, 1948 SLT 40.
5 Unless it can be argued that the reference to 'unusual or unduly onerous' conditions of title excludes the third requirement which would otherwise be implied in the case of real conditions, namely that the condition must be unknown to the buyer as at the date of conclusion of missives. See para 705 above. It is also possible that the implied warrandice may not follow the rule, evolved for express warrandice in cases such as *Dryburgh v Gordon* (1896) 24 R 1, 4 SLT 113, which requires a clear search even where the burden disclosed is demonstrably ineffectual.
6 For the meaning of this clause, see J M Halliday *Conveyancing Law and Practice in Scotland* vol II (1986) para 15-146. There is no inconsistency in having a *tantum et tale* clause in missives but a clause of absolute warrandice in the subsequent disposition. Indeed the two amount to much the same thing: *Hay v Panton* (1783) Mor 14183; *Carter v Lornie* (1890) 18 R 353.
7 *Armia Ltd v Daejan Developments Ltd* 1979 SC (HL) 56, 1979 SLT 147. See also *Umar v Murtaza* 1983 SLT (Sh Ct) 79.

709. Warrandice in dispositions.

The rules as to the warrandice implied in dispositions are authoritatively set out by the institutional writers[1]. Where a disposition is granted in implement of a sale there is implied full or absolute warrandice comprising the four constituent elements described above[2]. Conversely, where the grant is gratuitous there is implied simple warrandice only. Simple warrandice corresponds to the fourth of the constituent warranties[3] and is an undertaking that the transferor will do nothing in the future to prejudice the title of the transferee. However, a deed granted in implement of an obligation entered into prior to the disposition is not a breach of simple warrandice[4]. Finally, where a grant is made at an under-value it is stated by Erskine[5] that there is implied only fact and deed warrandice, that is to say, warrandice against defects in title[6] caused by the acts, past as well as future, of the transferor.

In normal conveyancing practice an express warrandice clause is invariable. Usually the grant is of absolute warrandice. Thus in older deeds the title conveyed was warranted *contra omnes mortales* or, in the vernacular, 'against all deadly'[7]. In more modern deeds and in current practice the expression used is, 'and I grant warrandice', which since 1847 has carried as a statutory meaning a grant of absolute warrandice[8]. Sometimes less than absolute warrandice is granted, or absolute warrandice is granted but subject to certain exclusions, for example in respect of leases or servitudes[9]. It is competent by express provision to exclude warrandice entirely although in Erskine's view the granter would still remain bound in simple warrandice, against his future facts and deeds, 'for no agreement, let it be ever so explicit, ought to protect against the consequences of fraud or deceit[10]'.

1 Stair *Institutions* II,3,46; Bankton *Institute* II,3,121 and 122; Erskine *Institute* II,3,25; Bell *Principles* s 894. See also CONVEYANCING, vol 6, paras 543 ff.
2 For the four constituent elements, see paras 703–706 above.
3 Ie 'no future acts prejudicial to the title': see para 706 above.
4 *Stair* II,3,46; *Erskine* II,3,25.
5 *Erskine* II,3,25.
6 By which is meant defects falling within the first three constituent warranties (see paras 703–705 above).
7 *Bankton* II,3,121; *Erskine* II,3,26.
8 The current provision is the Titles to Land Consolidation (Scotland) Act 1868 (c 101), s 8 (amended by the Statute Law Revision Act 1893 (c 14)). The statutory wording also deals with the two subsidiary assignations (writs and rents) contained in a disposition, importing absolute warrandice in respect of the former and fact and deed warrandice in respect of the latter. It is unclear why the assignation of rents should attract only fact and deed warrandice, when the warrandice which would have been implied by law is *debitum subesse* which includes a guarantee as to the validity of the leases.
9 J M Halliday *Conveyancing Law and Practice in Scotland* vol I (1985) para 4-39.
10 *Erskine* II,3,27.

(B) ENFORCEMENT

710. Missives or disposition? Warrandice in missives takes effect on the contractual date of entry and can be enforced from that date onwards but not earlier[1]. Warrandice in the disposition takes effect on the delivery of the disposition, which in most cases is also on the contractual date of entry[2]. Since, however, delivery of the disposition has the effect of superseding the missives and preventing them from being founded upon[3], it might be thought that occasion to enforce warrandice in the missives can never arise. Nonetheless there are three situations in which warrandice in missives may be enforced. The first is where settlement is delayed, with the result that the disposition is delivered later than the contractual date of entry. The second is where the transaction does not proceed to settlement at all so that there is no disposition. The final situation is where, notwithstanding the general rule as to supersession, the missives are kept in force beyond delivery of the disposition by means of express contractual stipulation[4]. Since the buyer carries out an examination of the seller's title in the period between conclusion of missives and the date of entry, it is likely that any defect will be discovered at that stage, in which case the buyer is entitled to delay settlement[5] or, in appropriate cases, to withdraw from the transaction. The first two situations are therefore relatively common in cases where recourse to warrandice is necessary. Further, if settlement proceeds, whether on time or after a delay, it is now almost universal practice to attempt to keep missives in force by contractual stipulation, typically for a fixed period such as two years, although such attempts are not always successful[6].

The content of the two warrandices is the same, but the remedies are not[7]; and while eviction is not required in respect of the warrandice in missives it is sometimes required in respect of the warrandice in dispositions[8]. These factors will determine a buyer's choice of warrandice in circumstances where a choice is available.

1 However, the fourth constituent warranty (no future prejudicial acts by transferor: see para 706 above) can presumably be enforced immediately on conclusion of missives.
2 See para 702 above.
3 See para 641 above.
4 This stipulation is usually known as a non-supersession clause. The clause is included in the disposition.
5 *Bowie v Semple's Executors* 1978 SLT (Sh Ct) 9. See generally G L Gretton and K G C Reid *Conveyancing* (1993) ch 4.
6 See eg *Porch v MacLeod* 1992 SLT 661, OH.
7 See paras 711–714 below.
8 See para 707 above.

711. Warrandice in missives of sale. Where the seller is in breach of warrandice in missives of sale the buyer may rescind the contract and claim damages[1]; but if the warrandice is couched in the form of a positive obligation on the seller, such as an obligation to deliver a good and marketable title, and if the defect in title is remediable, the seller must be given a reasonable time to perform the obligation and rescission cannot take place until the expiry of that time[2]. Complete absence of title to the whole or part of the subjects of sale is not considered to be a remediable defect with the result that immediate rescission is possible[3]. For positive obligations an alternative remedy to rescission is an action of implement of the obligation coupled, if desired, with an alternative conclusion for damages[4]. Implement will be refused if the seller cannot reasonably be expected to perform the obligation, as where he has no title to the property:

'[I]t is impossible to entertain the proposition that the seller is bound to purchase the evicted subjects, because the law does not give him the power of compulsory purchase from the true owner, and the law will not require any man to perform specifically something that is not within his power'[5].

In the absence of rescission, damages are not available in respect of the breach of a bare warranty which is not also supported by a positive obligation, for the remedy of damages without rescission is the *actio quanti minoris* of Roman law which has repeatedly been said not to be part of the Scots law of sale[6]. But this rule is subject to exceptions and may be avoided altogether by express stipulation that the *actio quanti minoris* is to be available[7], and the modern practice is to include such a stipulation in missives of sale.

1 *Smith v Soeder* (1895) 23 R 60, 3 SLT 135; *Armia Ltd v Daejan Developments Ltd* 1979 SC (HL) 56, 1979 SLT 147; *Umar v Murtaza* 1983 SLT (Sh Ct) 79; *Morris v Ritchie* 1992 GWD 33-1950, OH. As to quantum, see *M'Connell v Chassells* (1903) 10 SLT 790, OH; *Fielding v Newell* 1987 SLT 530, OH. On breach of missives of sale, see generally G L Gretton and K G C Reid *Conveyancing* (1993) ch 4.
2 *Carter v Lornie* (1890) 18 R 353; *Kinnear v Young* 1936 SLT 574, OH. The normal practice is to give the seller an ultimatum: *Rodger (Builders) Ltd v Fawdry* 1950 SC 483, 1950 SLT 345. But if the seller refuses to remedy the defect the buyer may rescind immediately: *Gilfillan v Cadell & Grant* (1893) 21 R 269.
3 *Campbell v M'Cutcheon* 1963 SC 505, 1963 SLT 290.
4 It is thought that in such a case the conclusion for damages cannot be treated as an *actio quanti minoris*. See *Hoey v Butler* 1975 SC 87, OH; *Taylor v McLeod* 1989 SCLR 531, 1990 SLT 194, OH.

5 *Welsh v Russell* (1894) 21 R 769 at 773, per Lord M'Laren.
6 *Earl Morton v Cunningham's Creditors* (1738) Mor 14175; *McCormick & Co v Rittmeyer & Co* (1869) 7
   M 854; *Finlayson v McRobb* 1987 SLT (Sh Ct) 150; *Fortune v Fraser* 1995 SCLR 121. See K G C Reid
   'The *Actio Quanti Minoris* and Conveyancing Practice' (1988) 33 JLSS 285; R Evans-Jones 'The
   History of the *Actio Quanti Minoris* in Scotland' 1991 JR 190.
7 *McCormick & Co v Rittmeyer & Co* (1869) 7 M 854. It has been held that a non-supersession clause
   must be read as containing an implied stipulation to this effect: *Jamieson v Stewart* 1989 SLT (Sh Ct)
   13; *Tainsh v McLaughlin* 1990 SLT (Sh Ct) 102.

712. Warrandice in dispositions. The only remedy for breach of warrandice in
a disposition is damages, and rescission is not available. This was the result of the
leading case of *Welsh v Russell*[1], a decision not entirely consistent with earlier
authorities[2] but which has generally been accepted as representing the modern law[3].
Where the breach is that the transferor has no title to all or part of the subjects
conveyed, damages are calculated by reference to the current value of the subjects,
without regard to whether that value is greater or smaller than the original price[4].
Where, however, the breach is that the title is burdened by a real right or a real
condition, the normal basis of damages is the resultant diminution in market value[5]
although there may be an argument that in the case of remediable defects damages
ought to be calculated by reference to the cost of having the real right or condition
discharged. It is doubtful whether a claim lies in respect of *solatium*[6].
   If the defect in title belongs to the class of cases for which eviction is required[7], no
action can be raised unless or until eviction has occurred[8]. But where the transferor
denies that he is bound by the warrandice clause[9] or where he is *vergens ad inopiam*[10],
an action may be raised at once although decree cannot be granted until eviction
takes place.
   The clause of assignation of writs which, formerly express, is now implied into all
dispositions of land[11] effects an assignation of such grants of warrandice made in
earlier conveyances of the same land as have not been extinguished by negative
prescription or by some other means[12]. The transferee may therefore have a choice
of defenders. Usually he will elect to sue his immediate author, but he is also free to
sue such earlier owners of the property as have granted warrandice provided that the
defect founded upon was in existence at the time of that grant or was caused by that
granter's own subsequent actions. A person against whom a claim is successfully
made may then himself have a claim in warrandice against his own author[13], but this
will require to be preceded by a retrocession of the relevant warrandice right by the
current transferee[14]. The clause of assignation of writs does not carry grants of
warrandice made in missives of sale, and while these may be expressly assigned[15], in
practice this is almost unknown.

1 *Welsh v Russell* (1894) 21 R 769.
2 Eg *Louttit's Trustees v Highland Rly Co* (1892) 19 R 791.
3 J M Halliday *Conveyancing Law and Practice in Scotland* vol I (1985) para 4-45.
4 Stair *Institutions* II,3,46: In warrandice of lands 'lands of equal value, or the whole worth of what is
   evicted, as it is at the time of the eviction, is inferred; because the buyer had the lands with the hazard
   of becoming better or worse . . . and therefore is not obliged to take the price he gave'. See also
   Erskine *Institute* II,3,30; Bell *Principles* s 895; *Cairns v Howden* (1870) 9 M 284; *Palmer v Beck* 1993 SLT
   485, OH.
5 *Welsh v Russell* (1894) 21 R 769 at 773, per Lord M'Laren.
6 *Palmer v Beck* 1993 SLT 485, OH. Cf *Watson v Swift & Co's Judicial Factor* 1986 SC 55, 1986 SLT 217,
   OH.
7 For the need for eviction, see para 707 above.
8 Eg *Palmer v Beck* 1993 SLT 485, OH.
9 *Lord Melville v Wemyss* (1842) 4 D 385.
10 Bell *Commentaries* I, 690. See *Garden v M'Iver* (1860) 22 D 1190.
11 Land Registration (Scotland) Act 1979 (c 33), s 16(1).
12 Stair II,3,46. Cf Bankton *Institute* II,3,123, and Erskine II,3,31, where, rather implausibly, the
   transmission of past grants of warrandice is explained on the basis that they are an intrinsic right of
   ownership.

13 *Christie v Cameron* (1898) 25 R 824.
14 *Cobham v Minter* 1986 SLT 336, OH. It is thought that the suggestion made in that case, that the pursuer might fail because he was not the party actually evicted, is unsound. See K G C Reid 'Warrandice in the Sale of Land' in D J Cusine (ed) *A Scots Conveyancing Miscellany: Essays in Honour of Professor J M Halliday* (1987) 152 at 169, 170.
15 Conveyancing (Scotland) Act 1874 (c 94), s 50, Sch M.

713. Warrandice in registration of title. There is no difference in the application of warrandice as between Land Register and Sasine titles. But for Land Register titles there may be an alternative remedy against the Keeper on the basis of the state indemnity imported by registration of title[1]. It is thought that cases where both remedies are available will not occur often[2], but if, as is probable, the transferee then elects to pursue his remedy against the Keeper rather than his remedy against the transferor, the Keeper is subrogated to his rights and is entitled to an assignation of the claim in warrandice[3].

1 Land Registration (Scotland) Act 1979 (c 33), s 12 (amended by the Matrimonial and Family Proceedings Act 1984 (c 42), s 46(1), Sch 1, para 28; the Family Law (Scotland) Act 1985 (c 37), s 28(1), Sch 1, para 10; the Bankruptcy (Scotland) Act 1985 (c 66), s 75(1), Sch 7, para 15; and the Law Reform (Miscellaneous Provisions) (Scotland) Act 1985 (c 73), ss 23, 59, Sch 2, para 22).
2 For a detailed analysis of the possible situations, see *Registration of Title Practice Book* (1981) ch H.3.
3 Land Registration (Scotland) Act 1979, s 13(2), (3).

714. Extinction. Warrandice in missives is extinguished by delivery of the disposition or, if the life of missives is extended for a further period by agreement, by the expiry of that further period[1]. Warrandice in dispositions is extinguished by the long negative prescription of twenty years[2]. The prescriptive period begins on the date on which the obligation first becomes enforceable[3], which is either the date that the disposition is delivered or, for those defects for which eviction is required, the date of eviction[4]. In certain cases the transferee's title may be fortified by positive prescription after only ten years in which case the claim in warrandice ceases to be necessary[5].

1 *Pena v Ray* 1987 SLT 609, OH.
2 Prescription and Limitation (Scotland) Act 1973 (c 52), s 7.
3 Ibid, ss 7(1), 11(1), (4) (amended by the Prescription and Limitation (Scotland) Act 1984 (c 45), s 6(2), Sch 2).
4 This corresponds, respectively, to the second and third, and to the first, of the constituent warranties (see paras 704, 705, and 703 above). Prescription will not begin to run on the fourth constituent warranty (no future acts: see para 706 above) until the future act objected to is actually performed.
5 Prescription and Limitation (Scotland) Act 1973, s 1. Positive prescription cannot apply in respect of the second and third constituent warranties.

(c) Corporeal Moveable Property

715. Sale. There is no written conveyance in the transfer of goods (corporeal moveables) with the result that warrandice is confined to the contract of sale only[1]. The Sale of Goods Act 1979 makes a distinction between ordinary contracts of sale and contracts of sale where there appears from the contract or is to be inferred from its circumstances an intention that the seller should transfer only such title as he or a third person may have[2]. In the first case there is implied into the contract a warranty:
(1) that the seller has (or will have) a right to sell the goods,
(2) that the goods are free, and will remain free until the time when property is to pass, from any right in security or other real right[3] not disclosed or known to the buyer before the contract of sale is made, and
(3) that the buyer will enjoy quiet possession of the goods[4].

In the second case there is implied into the contract a warranty:

(a) that all rights in security and other real rights known to the seller and not known to the buyer have been disclosed to the buyer before the contract is made, and

(b) that the buyer's quiet possession of the goods will not be disturbed by the seller or, if it is intended that the seller should transfer only such title as a third person may have, by that person[5].

In both cases the implied warrandice may be extended in the contract, but it may not be limited or excluded[6].

So far as ordinary contracts of sale are concerned, the most important warranty is the first, that the seller has a right to sell the goods. Adverse real rights (warranty (2)) are rare in the case of goods and usually involve possession, which would prevent the seller from delivering the goods to the buyer[7]. The final warranty, of quiet possession, must, it is thought, be taken as confined to dispossession at the hands of one holding a pre-existing right, for otherwise the seller would be acting as an insurer against future theft[8]; but if that is so then it seems to add little to the other warranties, except perhaps where the seller holds on a voidable title which, the buyer being in bad faith[9], comes subsequently to be avoided[10].

The remedies available for breach of the implied warrandice are rescission and damages, or damages alone[11]. The common law rule which would prevent a claim for damages in the absence of rescission (the *actio quanti minoris*) is excluded by statute[12]. It appears that eviction is not required[13]. Warrandice prescribes after five years[14].

1 See para 701 above.
2 Sale of Goods Act 1979 (c 54), s 12(3).
3 The statutory phrase is 'any charge or encumbrance'.
4 Sale of Goods Act 1979, s 12(1), (2). In Scots law no significance attaches to the distinction between an implied condition and an implied warranty.
5 Ibid, s 12(4), (5).
6 Unfair Contract Terms Act 1977 (c 50), s 20(1)(a) (amended by the Sale of Goods Act 1979, s 63(1), Sch 2, para 21).
7 As he is bound to do: Sale of Goods Act 1979, s 27.
8 P S Atiyah *The Sale of Goods* (8th edn, 1990) pp 93, 94.
9 If the buyer is in bad faith, he is not entitled to the protection of the Sale of Goods Act 1979, s 23.
10 This is because arguably the warranty that the seller has a right to sell the goods is not breached where he holds on a voidable title.
11 Sale of Goods Act 1979, s 15B (added by the Sale and Supply of Goods Act 1994 (c 35), s 5(1)).
12 Sale of Goods Act 1979, s 15B (as so added).
13 At common law the rule was different: see Bell *Principles* s 121.
14 Prescription and Limitation (Scotland) Act 1973 (c 52), s 6.

716. Donation. With corporeal moveables, as with property of other kinds, the warrandice implied in cases of donation is simple warrandice only[1]. Simple warrandice is an undertaking by the donor that he will do nothing in the future which prejudices the right of the donee. It is thought that the warrandice comes into operation at the time when ownership is transferred by delivery[2].

1 Stair *Institutions* II,3,46; Bankton *Institute* I,9,7; Erskine *Institute* III,3,90. See DONATION, vol 8, para 639.
2 Corporeal moveables are transferred by delivery and in most cases of donation there is no contractual document into which warrandice can be implied.

(d) Incorporeal Property

717. Assignation of personal rights. In the assignation of a personal right for value the warrandice which is implied is, as Bell notes, 'that the debt is due, and the title to assign good'[1]. This implied warrandice is usually known as warrandice *debitum subesse*. Traditionally assignations contain an express grant of fact and deed warrandice, but it is often said that fact and deed warrandice is implied even where it is not expressed[2], although whether as a constituent part of the implied warrandice *debitum subesse* or as separate implied warrandice is not clear. An express grant of fact and deed warrandice does not by itself exclude the implied warrandice *debitum subesse*[3] although it is open to the parties to make provision for such an exclusion[4].

The precise content of the fact and deed warrandice and warrandice *debitum subesse* implied in assignations for value is obscure but it includes at least the following constituent warranties, namely (1) that the cedent owns the right being assigned, (2) that the right is a valid right in the sense that the debtor truly owes the obligation to the cedent, and (3) that the cedent has done nothing in the past and will do nothing in the future to prejudice the right of the assignee. Cumulatively these warranties are similar to, or perhaps even identical with, a grant of absolute warrandice[5], although there may be a question as to whether the existence of an adverse real right such as a right in security would be a breach of warrandice *debitum subesse*[6]. In assignations there is no implied warranty as to the solvency of the debtor[7], although such a warranty may be included as an express term.

As with other cases of warrandice, the description of the subjects in the assignation is the measure of the property warranted. So if the debt is said to include a cautionary obligation, the validity of the cautionary obligation is warranted[8]. Similarly, if part of the debt has been repaid, or if the debtor has a right of compensation (set-off) against the cedent which will transmit against the assignee on the principle *assignatus utitur jure auctoris*[9], this must be specified in the assignation or otherwise the cedent is taken to warrant the full amount of the original debt.

Where a personal right is assigned for no consideration, simple warrandice only is implied, to the effect that the cedent will not by future act disturb the right of the assignee[10].

If the assignee fails to receive all or part of the debt assigned, whether because the assignation was *a non domino* or because the debt had previously been discharged or did not exist in the first place, the appropriate remedy is damages. Stair[11] and Bankton[12] state that damages are limited to the amount of the price originally paid, but Erskine[13] is of the view that, at least where an express grant of absolute warrandice is made and perhaps in other cases also, there is no such limitation on the amount which may be claimed. The matter seems not to be the subject of express decision. If, conversely, the assignee does receive the debt assigned but the debt is encumbered, for example by a right in security, it is unclear whether the remedy is damages (the *actio quanti minoris*)[14] or rescission, or indeed whether both remedies are available.

There seems to be no authority touching directly on the question of judicial eviction as applied to assignations, so that whether, and if so to what extent, eviction is required remains a matter of conjecture[15]. It might be thought from the unqualified manner in which the implied warrandice *debitum subesse* is usually described that eviction is not necessary.

Warrandice prescribes after five years[16].

1 Bell *Principles* s 1469.
2 See eg J M Halliday *Conveyancing Law and Practice in Scotland* vol I (1985) para 7-29; W W McBryde *The Law of Contract in Scotland* (1987) para 17-105.
3 *Ferrier v Graham's Trustees* (1828) 6 S 818.
4 But see the comment of Erskine in *Institute* II,3,27, to the effect that simple warrandice is always implied even in the face of an express exclusion clause.
5 Bankton *Institute* III,1,28; Erskine II,3,27; Bell s 1469.
6 J Burns *Conveyancing Practice* (4th edn, 1957 by F MacRitchie) p 688.
7 Stair *Institutions* II,3,46; Erskine II,3,25; Bell s 1469. Stair (at II,3,46) points out that this is simply one aspect of the wider rule in the law of property that warrandice guarantees the title to, but not the quality of, the thing assigned: 'warrandice relates to the point of right, and not to the matter of

fact . . . and therefore will not reach to accidents, the hazard whereof lies always upon the acquirer and the proprietor'.

8 See eg *Reid v Barclay* (1879) 6 R 1007.
9 For the rule *assignatus utitur jure auctoris*, see para 660 above.
10 Stair II,3,46; Bankton I,9,7; Erskine III,3,90. See DONATION, vol 8, para 639.
11 *Stair* II,3,46.
12 *Bankton* II,3,124.
13 *Erskine* II,3,30.
14 An award of damages was the solution reached in *Welsh v Russell* (1894) 21 R 769, 1 SLT 594, for corporeal heritable property. See para 712 above.
15 For judicial eviction, see para 707 above.
16 Prescription and Limitation (Scotland) Act 1973 (c 52), s 6, Sch 1.

718. Assignation of real rights. The statutory style for the assignation of registered leases contains an express grant of absolute warrandice[1]. Where no express grant is made, it has been suggested that the warrandice implied in the assignation of all leases, both registered and unregistered, is absolute warrandice as to the tenant's title to the lease and fact and deed warrandice as to the landlord's power to grant it in the first place[2]. The statutory style for the assignation of standard securities[3] does not include a grant of warrandice but it is thought that absolute warrandice is implied where the assignation is for value[4]. The same rule may apply to assignations of other real rights such as pledge and floating charges but the position seems never to have been judicially determined. Nor has it been determined whether judicial eviction is required before a claim can be made.

Real rights are often tied to ancillary personal rights, so that the assignation carries both rights[5]. In the assignation of the personal right there is an implied warrandice *debitum subesse*[6].

1 Registration of Leases (Scotland) Act 1857 (c 26), ss 3, 20, Sch A (amended by the Conveyancing and Feudal Reform (Scotland) Act 1970 (c 35), s 47, Sch 11, Pt I; and the Law Reform (Miscellaneous Provisions) (Scotland) Act 1985 (c 73), s 3).
2 G C H Paton and J G S Cameron *The Law of Landlord and Tenant in Scotland* (1967) p 158 and the writers there cited; J M Halliday *Conveyancing Law and Practice in Scotland* vol 1 (1985) para 4-36.
3 Conveyancing and Feudal Reform (Scotland) Act 1970, s 14, Sch 4, Forms A, B.
4 *Halliday* vol I, para 4-37: '. . . if granted for consideration, warrandice would be implied of the validity and continued existence of the obligation of the debtor [ie warrandice *debitum subesse* as to the personal obligation of debt] and the sufficiency of the cedent's title to the security [ie absolute warrandice as to the real right in security]'.
5 See para 657 above.
6 See para 717 above.

719–800. Contract of sale. There appears to be no authority on the question of warrandice implied into contracts of sale preceding assignations, but if the case of corporeal heritable property can be regarded as a reliable guide the rule would seem to be that the contract carries the same warrandice as the assignation itself[1].

1 For corporeal heritable property, see paras 702, 708, above.

INDEX

***A coelo usque ad centrum* principle**
generally, 196, 198, 647
law of the tenement, 228
separate tenements, and, 198, 207
Abandoned property, *see* PROPERTY
Access
building repairs, for, doctrine of common
    interest, 359
servitude—
    alteration of diversion, 469
    implied right, on division of property,
        452–456
    landlocked property, 454, 457
Accession
accessorium principale sequitur rule, 570, 589
accessory—
    compensation, payment in respect of by
        owner of principal, 574, 577, 676
    extinction of existing title, 574
    heritable—
        becoming, 574
        definition, 579
    meaning, 570
    moveables to moveables, 590
    owner—
        compensation, right of, 574, 577, 586
        severance, right of, 586
    principal—
        becoming part of, 574
        subsequent separation from, 574,
            574n
alluvion, *see* land to land *below*
annexer, intention of, 583
    actual, 583
    deemed, 583
artificial, 577
building, 578
    tenements, where building divided
        into, 578n, 585
chronology, importance of, 573
commixtion compared, 571n, 588
common property, original acquisition,
    22n
confusion compared, 571n, 588
constructive, 576, 576n
contract, law of, relationship with, 576
corporeal, property must be, 570
crops, 595, 596
death, gifts made on, 576
definition, 570
derivative, 574n

Accession—*contd*
effects—
    accessory becoming part of principal,
        574, 575
    existing title of accessory extinguished,
        574, 575
    heritable nature of accessory, on, 574,
        575
    rules, application of, 575
elements—
    functional subordination, 571, 579
        moveables to land, 579, 581
    permanence or quasi-permanence, 571,
        579
        moveables to land, 579, 581
    physical attachment, 571, 579
        moveables to land, 579, 580
    sufficiently present, must be, 571, 572
elements of—
    permanent attachment, indissoluble
        union, where requirement for, 589
English law compared, 2
feudal law, and, 574, 587
fittings, 578, 578n
fixtures, *see* moveables to land *below*
fruits, by, 570
    crops, 595, 596
    meaning of fruits, 595, 595n
    severance, effect of, 596
functional subordination, element of, 571,
    579
    moveables to land, 579, 581
generally, 1
indissoluble union—
    meaning, 589
    where requirement for, 589
industrial, 577
instruction for performance
    owner of accessory, from, 577
    owner of principal, from, 577
    third party, from, 577
intention, role of 583
intestate succession, questions arising on,
    576
land to land (alluvion)—
    advance of waters, 594
    alvei mutatio, 594
    avulsion compared, 592
    generally, 570, 592
    islands, formation of, 594
    meaning of alluvion, 592

References are to paragraphs

References are to paragraphs

References are to paragraphs

References are to paragraphs

References are to paragraphs

References are to paragraphs

References are to paragraphs

References are to paragraphs

References are to paragraphs

References are to paragraphs

References are to paragraphs

References are to paragraphs

References are to paragraphs

References are to paragraphs

References are to paragraphs

References are to paragraphs

References are to paragraphs

References are to paragraphs

References are to paragraphs

References are to paragraphs

Real burden—*contd*
tenant, liability of, 413
tenant, rights of, 406
time limits, 418
transfer of ownership, and, 604
unassignable nature, 383
unenforceable, burden proving to be, 389
unlawful construction, 423
variation or discharge by Lands Tribunal,
    395, 438
warrandice, obligation of, 705, 705*n*
wording, importance of, 390
Real condition
benefit conferred must be praedial, 348
benefited proprietor, 344*n*
burdened proprietor, 344*n*
characteristics, 344
common interest, *see* COMMON INTEREST
common property, 23, 26
conditions *in personam*, 344, 346, 347
conditions *in rem*, 344, 347
constitution, rules of, 349
content, rules as to, 344, 348
dominant property—
    condition must benefit, 348
    existence presupposed by existence of
        real condition, 349
    more than one, where, 345
    second interest in servient property as,
        349, 351
    separate land as, 349, 350
    servient property need not be contigu-
        ous, 348
    sub-division of, 345, 345*n*
    two or more people owning, 345
dominant proprietor—
    enforcement *in personam* against
        servient proprietor, 346
    meaning, 345
    two or more, where, 345
dominant tenement—
    generally, 344
    lease, in, 351, 352
    right to enforce derived from owner-
        ship of, 344, 345
    standard security, in, 351
    superiority, 351
    use of term, 344*n*
enforcement, right of, 344, 345
floating charges, 353
heritable property, 344, 349
in personam, 344
in rem, 344
invariable pertinent as, 201
land presumed free from perpetual bur-
    dens, 349

Real condition—*contd*
lease, assignation of, 351, 352
meaning, 344, 375
moveable property, 344, 349, 353
property law, as part of, 346
real burden, 344, 381, 387
registration, 349
servient property—
    condition must regulate, 348
    dominant property need not be con-
        tiguous, 348
    dominium utile of land, as, 349
    existence presupposed by existence of
        real condition, 349
    generally, 344
    land, as, 349
    lease, in, 352
    lease, right of, as, 349
    real right over, 344, 347
    second interest in same piece of land,
        349, 351
    separate land as, 349, 350
    servient tenement, use of term, 344*n*
    sublease, right of, as, 349
servient proprietor—
    enforcement *in personam* against, 346
    personal right against, 344, 346
servitude, 344, 381
standard security, in, 351
superiority, in, 351
things, functions of in relation to, 346
third parties, no independent rights of
    enforcement, 345
transfer of ownership, adverse real condi-
    tions, 604
two pieces of property, existence of as
    fundamental feature, 344
who may hold, 344
Real lien
see REAL BURDEN
Real right
air, right to, 5
ancillary personal right, warrandice, 718
assignation, 8
civil possession, title to sue, 141
classification—
    dominium and subordinate rights, 6
    holder of right, by reference to, 7
common interest, right of, 7, 290
competing titles—
    'offside goals', rule against—
        antecedent contract or other obliga-
            tion—
            breach, 698
            generally, 696
            remedies, 700

References are to paragraphs

References are to paragraphs

Real right—*contd*
transfer of ownership—
    adverse real rights, 604
    publicity, requirement for, 602
    subordinate real rights, grant of, 605
    see also TRANSFER OF OWNERSHIP
unsecured creditor, and, 694
which may be held without restriction, 7
Recognition
casualty of, feudal law, 82, 82*n*
Recreation
public rights—
    foreshore, on, 318
    generally, 494
    swimming, 518
Reduction
ad hunc effectum, 664
catholic, 664
judicial conveyance, involuntary transfer
    of ownership by, 664
Regalia
treasure as, 553
Regalian right
alienation, 207
fairs and markets, right to hold, 210
ferry, right of, 210
forestry, 213
generally, 207, 210
heritable jurisdiction, 213
mineral rights, 210
mussels, right to gather, 210
oysters, right to gather, 210
petroleum and natural gas, rights to,
    210
port, right of, 210
salmon fishings, 207, 210
separate tenement by legal implication, as,
    209
wreck (wrak), 213, 213*n*
Regality
feudal law, generally, 54
jurisdiction, 54
Register of Sasines
see GENERAL REGISTER OF SASINES
Relevium
casualty of, feudal law, 79
Relief
casualty of, feudal law, 79, 80
Religion
feudal system, and, 42
Removing
availability of remedy, 153
ejection distinguished, 153
land, recovery of founded on right to pos-
    session, 152, 153
preliminary notice, requirement for, 153

Renunciation
extinction of real right, 9
Res nullius
generally, 531
Resignation
ad remanentiam perpetuam, 97
feudal conveyance, generally, 97, 103
in favorem, 97
Retrocession
transfer of incorporeal property, 661
Right
future time, with tract of, 14
heritable, 13, 14
holder and right, relationship between, 16
incorporeal separate tenements, 10
incorporeal thing, as, 11*n*, 16
jus in personam, *see* personal *below*
jus in re, *see* REAL RIGHT
jus in rem, *see* REAL RIGHT
occupancy, of non-entitled spouse, 10
ownership, and, 16
performance, in, *see* RIGHTS IN PERFOR-
    MANCES
personal—
    ancillary, warrandice, 718
    assignation, 8*n*
        warrandice, 717
    competition with real right, where—
        grant in breach of trust, 691
        grantee not bound by personal oblig-
            ations of author, 688
        granter's power to grant unimpaired
            by personal obligation, 689
        'offside goals', rule against, 690, 693,
            694
        secured creditors, 693
        unsecured creditors, 694
        voidable title, grant by one holding,
            692
delict, contractual right arising under,
    see DELICT
enforcement, 3
feudal tenure, 42
incorporeal property, 11
meaning, 3
negative prescription, 9
possession, 126, 127, 128
    jura ad rem, 128
real right in land, to, 14
secured creditor, and, 693
unsecured creditor, and, 694
real, *see* REAL RIGHT
rights in rights, 16
security, in, *see* RIGHT IN SECURITY
transfer, 16
trust beneficiary, of, 10

References are to paragraphs

References are to paragraphs

Salmon—Salmon fisheries—*contd*
right of salmon fishing—*contd*
exercise of, 326
foreshore, in relation to, 318
free passage of salmon, right to, 327,
330
generally, 319, 320
imprescriptible nature, 326
indefinite boundaries, acquisition
where, 323
inland waters, permitted fishing methods, 326
medium filum, rights across, 327, 329
nature of right, 320
open sea, permitted fishing methods,
326
other fish, right to catch, 326
public right of navigation, and, 515*n*
regalian right, as, 210
restrictions, 326
riparian proprietor's fishing rights, and,
280
salmon farming rights included in, 321
separate tenement, as, 10, 210, 280, 319
trout fishing rights yield to, 326
rod and line, fishing by, 325, 326
Crown right of salmon fishing, 321
stake nets, fishing by, 326
wild salmon, status of, 320
Sasine
ceremony of, 89
clare constat, 108, 109
Crown, of, 48
fealty, oath of, 89
feu charter, 96
feudal law, generally, 89, 99
General Register of, *see* GENERAL REGIS-
TER OF SASINES
investiture, 89
meaning, 89, 93
mortuus sasit vivum, 108
notarial instrument of, 89, 89*n*, 92, 96, 99
nulla sasina nulla terra rule, 644
precepts of, 96, 101, 109
recording, 96, 99
registration, 91
modern law as to, 644
see also GENERAL REGISTER OF SASINES
service, 108, 109
symbols of, 90
title, notice of, 92
Satellite dish
law of the tenement, 238
Sea
artificial barriers against, erection, 318
damage caused by, 318

Sea—*contd*
foreshore, *see* FORESHORE
ownership, udal law, 310
public rights over—
Crown ownership, 514
generally, 5, 7, 494, 514
rock or sand outcrops, 313
swimming, public right of, 518
territorial—
adjacent proprietors, rights of, 312
alienation of subject proprietors, 311
foreshore, *see* FORESHORE
meaning, 309
ownership, 309, 310
wreck, *see* WRECK
Sea-greens
foreshore, not included in, 313
meaning, 313
Seaware and seaweed
servitude right to take, 318, 491
Security
generally, 3
Seisin
see SASINE
Self-help
recovery of possession—
corporeal moveable property, 159
property in place to which the public
have no access, 159, 161
judicial remedies, as alternative to, 151,
156, 160
land, recovery of founded on right to
possession, 152, 156
trespass, against, 182, 184
Separate tenement
see LANDOWNERSHIP
Sequestration
accretion, prevention of, 677
act and warrant of trustee in, judicial conveyance, as, 664
trustee in, personal rights, and, 694
Service
feudal conveyance, 108, 109
Servitude
access, right of—
alteration of diversion, 469
implied, on division of property,
452–456
landlocked property, 454, 457
least interference or inconvenience to
servient proprietor, must cause,
464
obstruction, judicial proceedings, 482
see also RIGHT OF PASSAGE OR WAY
agreement of, 450
agreement or undertaking to grant, 450

References are to paragraphs

References are to paragraphs

References are to paragraphs

References are to paragraphs

Trespass—*contd*
criminal offence, whether, 182
damages in respect of, 182, 185
  straying animals, 190
defences—
  Act of Parliament, intrusion authorised
    by, 181
  consent, 181
  exercise of a right, 181
  judicial warrant, intrusion authorised
    by, 181
  public interest, intrusion in, 181
definition, 180
duty of care in delict, landowner's, 184
fishing, as, 280
future, interdict against, 182, 183
injury as result of, whether, 180
interdict, future trespass, against, 182, 183
land, on, 180
landowner's rights, 195
loch, on, 180
lodging or encamping on private prop-
    erty, 182
person, by, 180
poaching—
  day, 182
  night, 182
possession, defence of, 140, 141*n*
remedies, 182
river, on, 180
self-help against, 182, 184
  straying animals, killing or injuring, 189
thing, by, 180
what qualifies as, 180
wild animal, in pursuit of, 541
Trout
fishing rights, salmon fishing rights, and,
  326
Trust
alienation of trust property, 535
beneficiary, right of—
  nature of right, 10, 14
  personal right against trustees, as, 691
property—
  beneficial interest in, 34
  co-ownership, 18
  joint property, as, 20, 34, 35, 536, 538
    management, rules of, 36, 36*n*
    see also CO-OWNERSHIP
  ownership—
    generally, 39, 691
    passing on death or resignation, 20
    transfer, capacity of trustees, 599
  prescription, no right to acquire by, 566
  title to, 34
  unity of title, 20

Trust—*contd*
property—*contd*
  unsecured creditors, competition of
    title, 694, 694*n*
trustee—
  beneficiaries' personal right against, 691
  court, appointment by, judicial con-
    veyance, 664
  number of trustees reduced to one, 35
  powers of trustees, 449, 691
  resignation or death, 35
  servitude, trustee's power to grant, 449
winding up, 35

Udal law
allodial ownership, as, 47*n*
generally, 44, 47
Orkney—
  allodial land, transfer of ownership, 646
  salmon fishing rights, 321
  seabed, ownership of, 310, 317
Shetland—
  allodial land, transfer of ownership, 646
  salmon fishing rights, 321
  seabed, ownership of, 310, 317
Unincorporated association
members, number of reduced to one, 35
property—
  beneficial interest in, 34
  joint property, as, 20, 34, 34*n*
    characteristics of joint property, 35
    management, rules of, 36, 36*n*
    resignation or death of member, 35
    see also CO-OWNERSHIP
  ownership passing on death or resigna-
    tion, 20
  title to, 34
  unity of title, 20
winding up, 35
see also CLUB
Usufructus
feudal system, and, 43

Vassalage
feudal system, 43, 43*n*
personal, 43, 43*n*
see also FEUDAL LAW
Vehicle
see MOTOR VEHICLE
Violent profits
recovery of possession, in action for, 151
spuilzie, claim arising from, 165
Vitious dispossession
action for, generally, 151, 156
meaning, 161
possession *vi aut clam*, 164

References are to paragraphs

References are to paragraphs

References are to paragraphs